Strategic Marketing Problems

Cases and Comments

Strategic Marketing Problems

Cases and Comments

THIRTEENTH EDITION

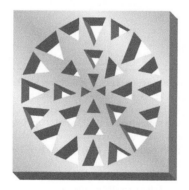

Roger A. Kerin
Southern Methodist University

Robert A. Peterson
University of Texas at Austin

PEARSON

Boston Columbus Indianapolis New York San Francisco Upper Saddle River
Amsterdam Cape Town Dubai London Madrid Milan Munich Paris Montreal Toronto
Delhi Mexico City São Paulo Sydney Hong Kong Seoul Singapore Taipei Tokyo

Editor in Chief: Stephanie Wall
Senior Acquisitions Editor: Erin Gardner
Editorial Project Manager: Kierra Bloom
Editorial Assistant: Jacob Garber
Director of Marketing: Maggie Moylan
Executive Marketing Manager: Anne Fahlgren
Marketing Assistant: Gianna Sandri
Senior Managing Editor: Judy Leale
Production Project Manager: Jacqueline A. Martin
Operations Specialist: Cathleen Petersen
Creative Director: Blair Brown

Senior Art Director: Janet Slowik
Cover Designer: Studio Montage
Senior Media Project Manager, Editorial:
   Denise Vaughn
Full-Service Project Management and
   Composition and Interior Design: S4 Carlisle
   Publishing Services
Printer/Binder: LSC Communications
Cover Printer: LSC Communications
Typeface: 10/12 ITC Garamond Std

Credits and acknowledgments borrowed from other sources and reproduced, with permission, in this textbook appear on the appropriate page within the text.

Many of the designations by manufacturers and sellers to distinguish their products are claimed as trademarks. Where those designations appear in this book, and the publisher was aware of a trademark claim, the designations have been printed in initial caps or all caps.

Library of Congress Cataloging-in-Publication Data
Kerin, Roger A.
   Strategic marketing problems: cases and comments / Roger A. Kerin, Robert A. Peterson. — 13th ed.
     p. cm.
   Includes index.
   ISBN-13: 978-0-13-274725-7
   ISBN-10: 0-13-274725-1
 1. Marketing—Decision making—Case studies.   2. Marketing—Management—Case studies.
 I. Peterson, Robert A. (Robert Allen),   II. Title.
   HF5415.135.K47 2013
   658.8'02—dc23

2012018183

9

PEARSON

ISBN 10:   0-13-274725-1
ISBN 13: 978-0-13-274725-7

To Our Families

Contents

Preface   ix

Chapter 1

**Foundations of Strategic Marketing
Management**   1

    Appendix: A Sample Marketing Plan   19

Chapter 2

**Financial Aspects of Marketing
Management**   35

Chapter 3

**Marketing Decision Making
and Case Analysis**   55

Chapter 4

**Opportunity Analysis, Market
Segmentation, and Market Targeting**   67

    Lancer Gallery   80
    Roger A. Kerin and Robert A. Peterson

    **Fiserv Takes on the E-Billing Market:
How Can We Get Them to Turn Off Paper?**   83
    Kent Grayson and Eric Leiserson

    **Dr Pepper Snapple Group, Inc.: Energy
Beverages**   91
    Roger A. Kerin

    Janmar Coatings, Inc.   105
    Roger A. Kerin

    Breeder's Own Pet Foods, Inc.   113
    Roger A. Kerin

    South Delaware Coors, Inc.   123
    James E. Nelson

Chapter 5

**Product and Service Strategy
and Brand Management**   133

    **Mary Kay India: The Hair Care Product
Line Opportunity**   149
    Roger A. Kerin

    Dr Pepper/Seven Up, Inc.: Squirt Brand   162
    Roger A. Kerin

    **Sanger Automotive Companies:
The Fisker Franchise Decision**   182
    Roger A. Kerin and Charles A. Besio

    **Frito-Lay, Inc.: Sun Chips Multigrain
Snacks**   192
    Roger A. Kerin and Kenneth R. Lukaska

    Dermavescent Laboratories, Inc.   210
    Roger A. Kerin

    Oráteme, Inc.   218
    Robert A. Peterson

    Pate Memorial Hospital   229
    Roger A. Kerin

    Procter & Gamble, Inc.: Scope   240
    *Gordon H. G. McDougall and Franklin
Ramsoomair*

    Frito-Lay Company: Cracker Jack   253
    Roger A. Kerin

Chapter 6

**Integrated Marketing Communication
Strategy and Management**   281

    Haverwood Furniture, Inc. (A)   294
    Roger A. Kerin

    Haverwood Furniture, Inc. (B)   306
    Roger A. Kerin

    Cadbury Beverages, Inc.: Crush Brand   309
    Roger A. Kerin

Astor Lodge & Suites, Inc.   324
Roger A. Kerin

**Drypers Corporation: National Television
Advertising Campaign**   337
Roger A. Kerin

**BBVA Compass: Marketing Resource
Allocation**   347
Sunil Gupta and Joseph Davies-Gavin

Chapter 7

**Marketing Channel and Supply Chain
Strategy and Management**   361

Hawaiian Punch: Go-to-Market Strategy   377
Roger A. Kerin

CUTCO Corporation   390
Robert A. Peterson

Yorktown Technologies   406
*William H. Cunningham, John Sibley
Butler, and Robert A. Peterson*

SaskTel   416
*Marsha Watson
and Elizabeth M. A. Grasby*

Pyramid Door, Inc.   424
Roger A. Kerin

Crafton Industries, Inc.   429
Roger A. Kerin

VF Brands: Global Supply Chain Strategy   437
Gary Pisano and Pamela Adams

Chapter 8

**Pricing Strategy and
Management**   453

**EMI Group, PLC: CD Pricing in the
Recorded Music Industry**   463
Roger A. Kerin

Southwest Airlines   479
Roger A. Kerin

**Hi-Value Supermarkets: Everyday
Low Pricing**   500
Roger A. Kerin

Burroughs Wellcome Company: Retrovir   512
Roger A. Kerin and Angela Bullard

Circle Corporation   524
Robert A Peterson and James Vance

**Augustine Medical, Inc.: The Bair Hugger
Patient Warming System**   534
*Roger A. Kerin, Michael Gilbertson, and
William Rudelius*

**Metabical: Pricing, Packaging, and Demand
Forecasting for a New Weight-Loss Drug**   544
John A. Quelch and Heather Beckham

Chapter 9

**Marketing Strategy Reformulation:
The Control Process**   553

Sonance at a Turning Point   563
Natalie Mizik

Nundies   579
Roger A. Kerin

Coleman Art Museum   594
Roger A. Kerin

Goodyear Tire and Rubber Company   604
Roger A. Kerin

Chapter 10

**Global Marketing Strategy
and Management**   617

**Jolson Automotive Hoist: The
Market-Entry Decision**   626
Gordon H. G. McDougall

Fairchild Water Technologies, Inc.   636
James E. Nelson

Chevrolet Europe   652
Roger A. Kerin and Raj Sethuraman

**Qingdao Haier Ltd: Considering
the Maytag Acquisition**   669
Roger A. Kerin

Appendix:

Preparing a Written Case Analysis   687

Republic National Bank of Dallas   687

**Student Analysis: Republic
National Bank of Dallas: NOW Accounts**   697

**Glossary of Selected Marketing
Terms and Concepts**   703

Subject Index   709

Brand, Company, and Name Index   719

Preface

Decision making in marketing is first and foremost a skill. Like most skills, it possesses tools and terminology. Like all skills, it is best learned through practice. This book is dedicated to the development of decision-making skills in marketing. Textual material introduces concepts, frameworks, and tools useful in framing and solving marketing problems. Case studies describing actual marketing problems provide an opportunity for those concepts, frameworks, and tools to be employed in practice. In every case study, the decision maker must develop a strategy consistent with the relevant underlying factors existing in the situation presented and must consider the implications of that strategy for the organization and its environment.

 ## WHAT'S NEW TO THE THIRTEENTH EDITION

- A new chapter on marketing channel and supply chain strategy and management
- Ten brand-new cases:
  - Fiserv Takes on the E-Billing Market: How Can We Get Them to Turn Off Paper?
  - Mary Kay India: The Hair Care Product Line Opportunity
  - Sanger Automotive Companies: The Fisker Franchise Decision
  - BBVA Compass: Marketing Resource Allocation
  - CUTCO Corporation
  - SaskTel
  - VF Brands: Global Supply Chain Strategy
  - Circle Corporation
  - Metabical: Pricing, Packaging, and Demand Forecasting for a New Weight-Loss Drug
  - Sonance at a Turning Point
- Sixteen revised or updated cases

 ## OVERVIEW OF THE BOOK

The thirteenth edition of *Strategic Marketing Problems: Cases and Comments* seeks a balance between marketing management content and process. The book consists of 10 chapters and 43 cases.

Chapter 1, "Foundations of Strategic Marketing Management," provides an overview of the strategic marketing management process. The principal emphasis is on defining an organization's business, mission, and goals; identifying and framing organizational opportunities; formulating product-market strategies; budgeting; and controlling the marketing effort. Appendix A for Chapter 1 contains a marketing plan for an actual company, Paradise Kitchens, Inc. The plan is annotated to focus attention on substantive elements as well as style and layout elements.

Chapter 2, "Financial Aspects of Marketing Management," reviews basic concepts of managerial accounting and finance that are useful in marketing management. Primary emphasis is placed on concepts such as fixed versus variable cost, relevant versus sunk cost, trade margins, contribution analysis, liquidity, discounted cash flow, customer lifetime value, operating leverage, and pro forma income statements.

Chapter 3, "Marketing Decision Making and Case Analysis," introduces a systematic process for decision making and provides an overview of various aspects of case analysis and written and oral presentations. A sample case and written student analysis are presented in Appendix B at the end of the book. The student analysis illustrates the nature and scope of a written case presentation, including the qualitative and quantitative analyses essential to a good presentation.

Chapter 4, "Opportunity Analysis, Market Segmentation, and Market Targeting," focuses on the identification and evaluation of marketing opportunities. Market segmentation, market targeting, and market potential and profitability issues are considered in some depth.

Chapter 5, "Product and Service Strategy and Brand Management," focuses on the management of the organization's offering. New-offering development, life-cycle management, product or service positioning, branding decisions, brand equity, brand growth strategies, and brand valuation are emphasized.

Chapter 6, "Integrated Marketing Communication Strategy and Management," raises issues in the design, execution, and evaluation of an integrated communication mix program. It also discusses decisions concerned with communications objectives, strategy, budgeting, programming, and effectiveness. Sales management issues are addressed as well.

Chapter 7, "Marketing Channel and Supply Chain Strategy and Management," introduces a variety of considerations affecting marketing channel and supply chain selection and modification. Specific decision areas covered include direct versus indirect distribution, dual and multi-channel distribution, cost–benefit analysis of marketing channel and supply chain choice and management, trade relations, and marketing channel conflict and coordination.

Chapter 8, "Pricing Strategy and Management," highlights concepts and applications in price determination and modification. Emphasis is placed on evaluating demand, cost, and competitive influences when selecting or modifying pricing strategies for products and services. Product-line pricing is also addressed.

Chapter 9, "Marketing Strategy Reformulation: The Control Process," focuses on the appraisal of marketing actions for the purpose of developing reformulation and recovery strategies. Considerations and techniques applicable to strategic and operations control in a marketing context are introduced.

Chapter 10, "Global Marketing Strategy and Management," describes marketing challenges in the global arena. Topics such as deciding to go global, identifying global marketing opportunities, and entering and competing in foreign markets are discussed. Emphasis is placed on crafting a global marketing strategy, including global market segmentation and targeting, standardized versus customized marketing mix options, and global branding and positioning.

The case selection in this edition reflects a broad overview of contemporary marketing problems and applications in a variety of industries and competitive settings and situations. Of the 43 cases included, 30 deal with consumer products and services, and 13 have a business-to-business marketing orientation. Marketing of services is addressed in 7 cases. Sixty percent of the cases are new, revised, or updated for this edition, and many have spreadsheet applications embedded in the case analysis. All text and case material has been classroom-tested.

ACKNOWLEDGMENTS

The efforts of many people are reflected here. First, we thank those institutions and individuals who have kindly granted us permission to include their cases in this edition. The cases contribute significantly to the overall quality of the book, and each individual is prominently acknowledged in the Contents and at the bottom of the page on which the case begins. We specifically wish to thank the Harvard Business School, Northwestern University (Kellogg), Columbia Business School, and the University of Western Ontario (Ivey) for granting permission to reproduce cases authored by their faculty. Second, we wish to thank our numerous collaborators, whose efforts made the difference between good cases and excellent cases. Third, we thank the adopters of the previous twelve editions of the book for their many comments and recommendations for improvements. Their insights and attention to detail are, we hope, reflected here. Finally, we wish to thank the numerous reviewers of this and previous editions for their conscientious and constructive reviews of our material. Naturally, we bear full responsibility for any errors of omission and commission in the final product.

Roger A. Kerin

Robert A. Peterson

Strategic Marketing Problems

Cases and Comments

Chapter 1

Foundations of Strategic Marketing Management

The primary purpose of marketing is to create long-term and mutually beneficial exchange relationships between an entity and the publics (individuals and organizations) with which it interacts. Though this fundamental purpose of marketing is timeless, the manner in which organizations undertake it continues to evolve. No longer do marketing managers function solely to direct day-to-day operations; they must make strategic decisions as well. This elevation of marketing perspectives to a strategic position in organizations has resulted in expanded responsibilities for marketing managers. Increasingly, they find themselves involved in charting the direction of the organization and contributing to decisions that will create and sustain a competitive advantage and affect long-term organizational performance.

The transition of the marketing manager from being only an implementer to being a maker of organization strategy has resulted in (1) the creation of the chief marketing officer (CMO) position in many organizations and (2) the popularity of strategic marketing management as a course of study and practice. Today, almost one-half of *Fortune* 1000 companies have a CMO. Although responsibilities vary across companies, a common expectation is that a CMO will assume a leadership role in defining the mission of the business; analyzing environmental, competitive, and business situations; developing business objectives and goals; and defining customer value propositions and the marketing strategies that deliver on these propositions.

The skill set required of CMOs includes an analytical ability to interpret extensive market and operational information, an intuitive sense of customer and competitor motivations, and creativity in framing strategic marketing initiatives in light of implementation considerations and financial targets and results.[1] *Strategic marketing management* consists of five complex and interrelated processes.

1. Defining the organization's business, mission, and goals
2. Identifying and framing organizational growth opportunities
3. Formulating product-market strategies
4. Budgeting marketing, financial, and production resources
5. Developing reformulation and recovery strategies

The remainder of this chapter discusses each of these processes and their relationships to one another.

DEFINING THE ORGANIZATION'S BUSINESS, MISSION, AND GOALS

The practice of strategic marketing management begins with a clearly stated business definition, mission, and set of goals or objectives. A business definition outlines the scope of a particular organization's operations. Its mission is a written statement of organizational purpose. Goals or objectives specify what an organization intends to achieve. Each plays an important role in describing the character of an organization and what it seeks to accomplish.

Business Definition

Determining what business an organization is in is neither obvious nor easy. In many instances, a single organization may operate several businesses, as is the case with large *Fortune* 500 companies. Defining each of these businesses is a necessary first step in strategic marketing management.

Contemporary strategic marketing perspectives indicate that an organization should define a business by the type of customers it wishes to serve, the particular needs of those customer groups it wishes to satisfy, and the means or technology by which the organization will satisfy these customer needs.[2] By defining a business from a customer or market perspective, an organization is appropriately viewed as a customer-satisfying endeavor, not a product-producing or service-delivery enterprise. Products and services are transient, as is often the technology or means used to produce or deliver them. Basic customer needs and customer groups are more enduring. For example, the means for delivering prerecorded music has undergone significant change over the past 30 years. During this period, the dominant prerecorded music technologies and products evolved from plastic records, to eight-track tapes, to cassettes, to compact discs. Today, digital downloading of music is growing. By comparison, the principal consumer buying segment(s) and needs satisfied have varied little.

Much of the recent corporate restructuring and refocusing has resulted from senior company executives asking the question, "What business are we in?" The experience of *Encyclopaedia Britannica* is a case in point.[3] The venerable publishing company was once known for its comprehensive and authoritative 32-volume, leather-bound book reference series first printed in 1768. In the late 1990s, the company found itself in a precarious competitive environment. CD-ROMs and the Internet had become the study tools of choice for students and were attracting Britannica's core customers. The result? Book sales fell 83 percent between 1990 and 1997. Britannica's senior management was confident that the need for dependable and trustworthy information among curious and intelligent customers remained. However, the technology for satisfying these needs had changed. This realization prompted Britannica to redefine its business. According to a company official: "We're reinventing our business. We're not in the book business. We're in the information business." By early 2006, the company had become a premier information site on the Internet. Britannica's subscription service (eb.com) markets archival information to schools and public and business libraries. Its consumer Web site (britannica.com) is a source of information for over 500,000 subscribers and its search engine provides some 150,000 Web sites selected by expert Britannica staffers for information quality and accuracy. The company began offering its service through Apple's iPhone in 2008 and iPad in 2010 because "People today want information wherever they go," said a company executive.

Business Mission

An organization's business mission complements its business definition. As a written statement, a mission underscores the scope of an organization's operations apparent in its business definition and reflects management's vision of what the organization seeks to do. Although there is no overall definition for all mission statements, most statements describe an organization's purpose with reference to its customers, products or services, markets, philosophy, and technology. Some mission statements are generally stated, such as that for Xerox Corporation:

> Our strategic intent is to help people find better ways to do great work—by constantly leading in document technologies, products and services that improve our customers' work processes and business results.

Others are more specifically written, like that for Hendison Electronics Corporation:

> We serve the discriminating purchasers of home entertainment products who approach their purchase in a deliberate manner with heavy consideration of long-term benefits. We will emphasize home entertainment products with superior performance, style, reliability, and value that require representative display, professional selling, trained service, and brand acceptance—retailed through reputable electronic specialists to those consumers whom the company can most effectively service.

Mission statements also apply to not-for-profit organizations. For instance, the American Red Cross aspires

> to provide for victims of disaster and help people prevent, prepare for, and respond to emergencies.

A carefully crafted mission statement that succinctly conveys organizational purpose can provide numerous benefits to an organization, including focus on its marketing effort. It can (1) crystallize management's vision of the organization's long-term direction and character; (2) provide guidance in identifying, pursuing, and evaluating market and product opportunities; and (3) inspire and challenge employees to do those things that are valued by the organization and its customers. It also provides direction for setting business goals or objectives.

Business Goals

Goals or objectives convert the organization's mission into tangible actions and results that are to be achieved, often within a specific time frame. For example, the 3M Company emphasizes research and development and innovation in its business mission. This view is made tangible in one of the company's goals: 30 percent of 3M's annual revenues must come from company products that are less than four years old.[4]

Goals or objectives divide into three major categories: production, financial, and marketing. Production goals or objectives apply to the use of manufacturing and service capacity and to product and service quality. Financial goals or objectives focus on return on investment, return on sales, profit, cash flow, and shareholder wealth. Marketing goals or objectives emphasize market share, marketing productivity, sales volume, profit, customer satisfaction, customer value creation, and customer lifetime value. When production, financial, and marketing goals or objectives are combined, they represent a composite picture of organizational purpose within a specific time frame; accordingly, they must complement one another.

Goal or objective setting should be problem-centered and future-oriented. Because goals or objectives represent statements of what the organization wishes to achieve in a specific time frame, they implicitly arise from an understanding of the current situation. Therefore, managers need an appraisal of operations or a *situation analysis* to determine reasons for the gap between what was or is expected and what has happened or will happen. If performance has met expectations, the question arises as to future directions. If performance has not met expectations, managers must diagnose the reasons for this difference and enact a remedial program. Chapter 3 provides a discussion on performing a situation analysis.

IDENTIFYING AND FRAMING ORGANIZATIONAL GROWTH OPPORTUNITIES

Once the character and direction of the organization have been outlined in its business definition, mission, and goals or objectives, the practice of strategic marketing management enters an entrepreneurial phase. Using business definition, mission, and goals or objectives as a guide, the search for and evaluation of organizational growth opportunities can begin.

Converting Environmental Opportunities into Organizational Opportunities

Three questions help marketing managers decide whether certain environmental opportunities represent viable organizational growth opportunities:

- What might we do?
- What do we do best?
- What must we do?

Each of these questions assists in identifying and framing organizational growth opportunities. They also highlight major concepts in strategic marketing management.

The *what might we do* question introduces the concept of *environmental opportunity*. Unmet or changing consumer needs, unsatisfied buyer groups, and new means or technology for delivering value to prospective buyers represent sources of environmental opportunities for organizations. In this regard, environmental opportunities are boundless. However, the mere presence of an environmental opportunity does not mean that an organizational growth opportunity exists. Two additional questions must be asked.

The *what do we do best* question introduces the concept of organizational capability, or distinctive competency. *Distinctive competency* describes an organization's unique strengths or qualities, including skills, technologies, or resources that distinguish it from other organizations. In order for any of an organization's strengths or qualities to be considered truly distinctive and a source of competitive advantage, two criteria must be satisfied. First, the strength must be imperfectly imitable by competitors. That is, competitors cannot replicate a skill (such as the direct-selling competency of Avon) easily or without a sizable investment of time, effort, and money. Second, the strength should make a significant contribution to the benefits perceived by customers and, by doing so, provide superior value to them. For example, the ability to engage in technological innovation that is wanted and provides value to customers is a distinctive competency. Consider the Safety Razor Division of the Gillette Company.[5] Its distinctive competencies lie in three areas: (1) shaving technology and development,

(2) high-volume manufacturing of precision metal and plastic products, and (3) marketing of mass-distributed consumer package goods. These competencies were responsible for the Gillette Fusion and Venus razors, which have sustained Gillette's dominance of the men's and women's wet-shaving market.

Finally, the *what must we do* question introduces the concept of success requirements in an industry or market. *Success requirements* (also called "key success factors," or KSFs) are basic tasks that an organization must perform in a market or industry to compete successfully. These requirements are subtle in nature and often overlooked.[6] For example, distribution and inventory control are critical success factors in the cosmetics industry. Firms competing in the personal computer industry recognize that the requirements for success include low-cost production capabilities, access to distribution channels, and continuous innovation.

The linkage among environmental opportunity, distinctive competency, and success requirements will determine whether an organizational opportunity exists. A clearly defined statement of success requirements serves as a device for matching an environmental opportunity with an organization's distinctive competencies. If *what must be done* is inconsistent with *what can be done* to capitalize on an environmental opportunity, an organizational growth opportunity will fail to materialize. Too often, organizations ignore this linkage and pursue seemingly lucrative environmental opportunities that are doomed from the start. ExxonMobil Corporation learned this lesson painfully after investing $500 million in the office products market over a 10-year period only to see the venture fail. After the company abandoned this venture, a former ExxonMobil executive summed up what had been learned: "Don't get involved where you don't have the skills. It's hard enough to make money at what you're good at."[7] By clearly establishing the linkages necessary for success before taking any action, an organization can minimize its risk of failure. An expanded discussion related to identifying marketing opportunities is found in Chapter 4.

SWOT Analysis

SWOT analysis is a formal framework for identifying and framing organizational growth opportunities. SWOT is an acronym for an organization's *S*trengths and *W*eaknesses and external *O*pportunities and *T*hreats. It is an easy-to-use framework for focusing attention on the fact that an organizational growth opportunity results from a good fit between an organization's internal capabilities (apparent in its strengths and weaknesses) and its external environment (reflected in the presence of environmental opportunities and threats). Many organizations also perform a SWOT analysis as part of their goal- or objective-setting process.

Exhibit 1.1 on page 6 displays a SWOT analysis framework depicting representative entries for internal strengths and weaknesses and external opportunities and threats. A strength is something that an organization is good at doing or some characteristic that gives the organization an important capability. Something an organization lacks or does poorly relative to other organizations is a weakness. Opportunities represent external developments or conditions in the environment that have favorable implications for the organization. Threats, on the other hand, pose dangers to the welfare of the organization.

A properly conducted SWOT analysis goes beyond the simple preparation of lists. Attention needs to be placed on evaluating strengths, weaknesses, opportunities, and threats and drawing conclusions about how each might affect the organization. The following questions might be asked once an organization's strengths, weaknesses, opportunities, and threats have been identified:

1. Which internal strengths represent distinctive competencies? Do these strengths compare favorably with what are believed to be market or industry success requirements? Looking at Exhibit 1.1, for example, does "proven innovation skill" strength represent a distinctive competency and a market success requirement?

2. Which internal weaknesses potentially disqualify the organization from pursuing certain opportunities? Look again at Exhibit 1.1, and note that

EXHIBIT 1.1   **Sample SWOT Analysis Framework and Representative Examples**

Selected Internal Factors	*Representative*		*Selected External Factors*	*Representative*	
	Strengths	*Weaknesses*		*Opportunities*	*Threats*
Management	Experienced management talent	Lack of management depth	Economic	Upturn in the business cycle; evidence of growing personal disposable income	Adverse shifts in foreign exchange rates
Marketing	Well thought of by buyers; effective advertising program	Weak distribution network; subpar sales force	Competition	Complacency among domestic competitors	Entry of lower-cost foreign competitors
Manufacturing	Available manufacturing capacity	Higher overall production costs relative to key competitors	Consumer trends	Unfulfilled customer needs on high and low end of product category suggesting a product line expansion possibility	Growing preference for private-label products
R&D	Proven innovation skills	Poor track record in bringing innovations to the marketplace	Technology	Patent protection of complementary technology ending	Newer substitute technologies imminent
Finance	Little debt relative to industry average	Weak cash flow position	Legal/regulatory	Falling trade barriers in attractive foreign markets	Increased U.S. regulation of product-testing procedures and labeling
Offerings	Unique, high-quality products	Too narrow a product line	Industry/market structure	New distribution channels evolving that reach a broader customer population	Low-entry barriers for new competitors

the organization acknowledges that it has a "weak distribution network and a subpar sales force." How might this organizational weakness affect the opportunity described as "new distribution channels evolving that reach a broader customer population"?

3. Does a pattern emerge from the listing of strengths, weaknesses, opportunities, and threats? Inspection of Exhibit 1.1 reveals that low-entry barriers into the market/industry may contribute to the entry of lower-cost foreign competitors. This does not bode well for domestic competitors labeled as "complacent" and the organization's acknowledged high production costs. Similarly, each of the organization's strengths appear to be offset by an equally compelling weakness.

 # FORMULATING PRODUCT-MARKET STRATEGIES

Organizational opportunities frequently emerge from an organization's existing markets or from newly identified markets. Opportunities also arise for existing, improved, or new products and services. Matching products and markets to form product-market strategies is the subject of the next set of decision processes.

Product-market strategies consist of plans for matching an organization's existing or potential offerings with the needs of markets, informing markets that the offerings exist, having offerings available at the right time and place to facilitate exchange, and assigning prices to offerings. In short, a product-market strategy involves selecting specific markets and profitably reaching them through an integrated program called a *marketing mix*.

Exhibit 1.2 classifies product-market strategies according to the match between offerings and markets.[8] The operational implications and requirements of each strategy are briefly described in the following subsections.

Market-Penetration Strategy

A *market-penetration strategy* dictates that an organization seeks to gain greater dominance in a market in which it already has an offering. This strategy involves attempts to increase present buyers' usage or consumption rates of the offering, to attract buyers of competing offerings, or to stimulate product trial among potential customers. The mix of marketing activities might include lower prices for the offerings, expanded distribution to provide wider coverage of an existing market, and heavier promotional efforts extolling the "unique" advantages of an organization's offering over competing offerings. For example, following

EXHIBIT 1.2 **Product-Market Strategies**

		Markets	
		Existing	New
Offerings	Existing	Market penetration	Market development
	New	New offering development	Diversification

the acquisition of Gatorade from Quaker Oats, PepsiCo announced that it expected to increase Gatorade's already dominant share of the sports drink market through broader distribution, new flavors, and more aggressive advertising.[9]

Several organizations have attempted to gain dominance by promoting more frequent and varied usage of their offering. For example, the Florida Orange Growers Association advocates drinking orange juice throughout the day rather than for breakfast only. Airlines stimulate usage through a variety of reduced-fare programs and various family-travel packages designed to reach the primary traveler's spouse and children.

Marketing managers should consider a number of factors before adopting a penetration strategy. First, they must examine market growth. A penetration strategy is usually more effective in a growth market. Attempts to increase market share when volume is stable often result in aggressive retaliatory actions by competitors. Second, they must consider competitive reaction. Procter & Gamble implemented a penetration strategy for its Folgers coffee in selected East Coast cities, only to run head-on into an equally aggressive reaction from Kraft Foods' Maxwell House Division. According to one observer of the competitive situation:

> When Folger's mailed millions of coupons offering consumers 45 cents off on a one-pound can of coffee, Maxwell House countered with newspaper coupons of its own. When Folger's gave retailers 15 percent discounts from the list price . . . , Maxwell House met them head-on. [Maxwell House] let Folger's lead off with a TV blitz . . . . Then [Maxwell House] saturated the airwaves.[10]

The result of this struggle was no change in market share for either firm. Third, marketing managers must consider the capacity of the market to increase usage or consumption rates and the availability of new buyers. Both are particularly relevant when viewed from the perspective of the conversion costs involved in capturing buyers from competitors, stimulating usage, and attracting new users.

Market-Development Strategy

A *market-development strategy* dictates that an organization introduce its existing offerings to markets other than those it is currently serving. Examples include introducing existing products to different geographical areas (including international expansion) or different buying publics. For example, Harley-Davidson engaged in a market-development strategy when it entered Japan, Germany, Italy, and France. Lowe's, the home improvement chain, employed this strategy when it focused attention on attracting women shoppers to its stores.

The mix of marketing activities used must often be varied to reach different markets with differing buying patterns and requirements. Reaching new markets often requires modification of the basic offering, different distribution outlets, or a change in sales effort and advertising.

Like the market-penetration strategy, market development involves a careful consideration of competitor strengths and weaknesses and competitor retaliation potential. Moreover, because the firm seeks new buyers, it must understand their number, motivation, and buying patterns in order to develop marketing activities successfully. Finally, the firm must consider its strengths, in terms of adaptability to new markets, in order to evaluate the potential success of the venture.

Market development in the international arena has grown in importance and usually takes one of four forms: (1) exporting, (2) licensing, (3) joint venture, or (4) direct investment.[11] Each option has advantages and disadvantages. Exporting involves marketing the same offering in another country either directly (through sales offices) or through intermediaries in a foreign country. Because this approach typically requires minimal capital investment and is easy to initiate, it is a popular option for developing foreign markets. Procter & Gamble, for instance, exports its deodorants, soaps, fragrances, shampoos, and other health and beauty products to Eastern Europe and Russia. Licensing is a contractual arrangement whereby one firm (licensee) is given the rights to patents, trademarks, know-how, and other intangible assets by its owner (licensor) in return for a royalty (usually 5 percent of gross sales) or a fee. For example, Cadbury PLC, a London-based multinational firm, has licensed Hershey Foods to sell its candies in the United States for a fee of $300 million. Licensing provides a low-risk, quick, and capital-free entry into a foreign market. However, the licensor usually has no control over production and marketing by the licensee. A joint venture, often called a strategic alliance, involves investment by both a foreign firm and a local company to create a new entity in the host country. The two companies share ownership, control, and profits of the entity. Joint ventures are popular because one company may not have the necessary financial, technical, or managerial resources to enter a market alone. This approach also often ensures against trade barriers being imposed on the foreign firm by the government of the host company. A problem frequently arising from joint ventures is that the partners do not always agree on how the new entity should be run. Direct investment in a manufacturing and/or assembly facility in a foreign market is the most risky option and requires the greatest commitment. However, it brings the firm closer to its customers and may be the most profitable approach for developing foreign markets. For these reasons, direct investment must be evaluated closely in terms of benefits and costs. Direct investment often follows one of the three other approaches to foreign-market entry. For example, Mars, Inc. originally exported its M&Ms, Snickers, and Mars bars to Russia but now operates a $200 million candy factory outside Moscow. Market development efforts in the global arena are expanded on in Chapter 10.

Product-Development Strategy

A *product-development strategy* dictates that the organization create new offerings for existing markets. The approach taken may be to develop totally new offerings (product innovation) to enhance the value to customers of existing offerings (product augmentation), or to broaden the existing line of offerings by adding different sizes, forms, flavors, and so forth (product line extension). Apple's iPod is an example of product innovation. Product augmentation can be achieved in numerous ways. One is to bundle complementary items or services with an existing offering. For example, embedded software, application aids, and training programs for buyers enhance the value of personal computers. Another way is to improve the functional performance of the offering. Digital camera manufacturers have done this by improving photo quality. Many types of product-line extensions are possible. Personal-care companies market deodorants in powder, spray, and gel forms; Gatorade is sold in more than 20 flavors; and Frito-Lay offers its Lay's potato chips in a variety of package sizes.

Companies successful at developing and commercializing new offerings lead their industries in sales growth and profitability. Apple's financial performance is a case in point. A company's likelihood of success is increased if its product-development effort results in offerings that satisfy a clearly understood buyer need. In the toy industry, for instance, these needs translate into products with three qualities: (1) lasting play value, (2) the ability to be shared with other children, and (3) the ability to stimulate a child's imagination.[12] Successful commercialization occurs when the offering can be communicated and delivered to a well-defined buyer group at a price it is willing and able to pay.

Important considerations in planning a product-development strategy concern the market size and volume necessary for the effort to be profitable, the magnitude and timing of competitive response, the impact of the new product on existing offerings, and the capacity (in terms of human and financial investment and technology) of the organization to deliver the offerings to the market(s). More important, successful new offerings must have a significant "point of difference" reflected in superior product or service characteristics that deliver unique and wanted benefits to consumers. Two examples from General Mills illustrate this view.[13] The company introduced Fringos, a sweetened cereal flake about the size of a corn chip. Consumers were supposed to snack on them, but they didn't. The point of difference was not significant enough to get consumers to switch from competing snacks such as popcorn, potato chips, or tortilla chips. On the other hand, General Mills' Big G Milk 'n Cereal Bar, which combines cereal and a milk-based layer, has succeeded because it satisfies convenience-oriented consumers who desire to "eat and go."

The potential for cannibalism must be considered with a product-development strategy. *Cannibalism* occurs when sales of a new product or service come at the expense of sales of existing products or services already marketed by the firm. For example, it is estimated that 75 percent of Gillette's Gillette Fusion razor volume came from the company's other razors and shaving systems. Cannibalism of this degree is common in product-development programs. The issue faced by the manager is whether it detracts from the overall profitability of the organization's total mix of offerings. At Gillette, the cannibalism rate for Fusion is viewed favorably, because its gross profit margin is significantly higher than that of the company's other razors.[14]

Diversification

Diversification involves the development or acquisition of offerings new to the organization and the introduction of those offerings to publics not previously served by the organization. Many firms have adopted this strategy in recent years to take advantage of perceived growth opportunities. Yet diversification is often a high-risk strategy because both the offerings (and often their underlying technology) and the public or market served are new to the organization.

Consider the following examples of failed diversification. Anheuser-Busch recorded 17 years of losses with its Eagle Snacks Division and incurred a $206 million write-off when the division was finally shut down. Gerber Products Company, which holds 83 percent of the U.S. baby-food market, has been mostly unsuccessful in diversifying into child-care centers, toys, furniture, and adult food and beverages. Coca-Cola's many attempts at diversification—acquiring wine companies, a movie studio, and a pasta manufacturer, and producing television game shows—have also proven to be largely unsuccessful. These examples highlight the importance of understanding the link between market success requirements and an organization's distinctive competency. In each of these cases, a bridge was not made between these two concepts and, thus, an organizational opportunity was not realized.[15]

Still, diversifications can be successful. Successful diversifications typically result from an organization's attempt to apply its distinctive competency in reaching new markets with new offerings. By relying on its marketing expertise and extensive distribution system, Procter & Gamble has had success with offerings ranging from cake mixes to disposable diapers to laundry detergents.

Product-Market Strategy Selection

A recurrent issue in strategic marketing management is determining the consistency of product-market strategies with the organization's definition, mission and capabilities, market capacity and behavior, environmental forces, and competitive activities.

Proper analysis of these factors depends on the availability and evaluation of relevant information. Information on markets should include data on size, buying behavior, and requirements. Information on environmental forces such as social, legal, political, demographic, and economic changes is necessary to determine the future viability of the organization's offerings and the markets served. In recent years, for example, organizations competing in the United States have had to alter or adapt their product-market strategies because of political actions (regulation), economic fluctuations (income shifts and changes in disposable personal income), sociodemographic trends (increasing racial and ethnic diversity), attitudes (value consciousness), technological advances (the growth of the Internet), and population shifts (city to suburb and northern to southern United States)—to name just a few of the environmental changes. Competitor activities must be monitored to ascertain their existing or possible strategies and performance in satisfying buyer needs.

In practice, the strategy selection decision is based on an analysis of the costs and benefits of alternative strategies and their probabilities of success. For example, a manager may compare the costs and benefits involved in further penetrating an existing market to those associated with introducing the existing product to a new market. It is important to make a careful analysis of competitive structure; market growth, decline, or shifts; and opportunity costs (potential benefits not obtained). The product or service itself may dictate a strategy change. If the product has been purchased by all of the buyers it is going to attract in an existing market, opportunities for growth beyond replacement purchases are reduced. This situation would indicate a need to search out new buyers (markets) or to develop new products or services for present markets.

The probabilities of success of the various strategies must then be considered. A. T. Kearney, a management consulting firm, has provided rough probability estimates of success for each of the four basic strategies.[16] The probability of a successful diversification is 1 in 20. The probability of successfully introducing an existing product into a new market (market-development strategy) is 1 in 4. There is a 50–50 chance of success for a new product being introduced into an existing market (product-development strategy). Finally, minor modification of an offering directed toward its existing market (market-penetration strategy) has the highest probability of success.

A useful technique for gauging potential outcomes of alternative marketing strategies is to array possible actions, the response to these actions, and the outcomes in the form of a decision tree, so named because of the branching out of responses from action taken. This implies that for any action taken, certain responses can be anticipated, each with its own specific outcomes. Exhibit 1.3 shows a decision tree.

As an example, consider a situation in which a marketing manager must decide between a market-penetration strategy and a market-development strategy.

EXHIBIT 1.3   **Decision-Tree Format**

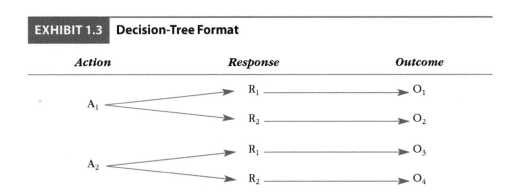

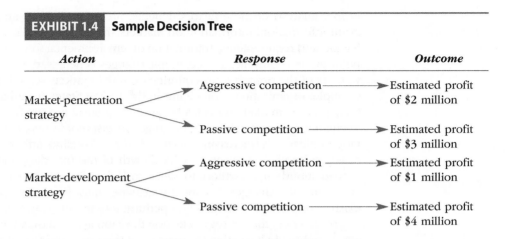

EXHIBIT 1.4   Sample Decision Tree

Action	*Response*	*Outcome*
Market-penetration strategy	Aggressive competition	Estimated profit of $2 million
	Passive competition	Estimated profit of $3 million
Market-development strategy	Aggressive competition	Estimated profit of $1 million
	Passive competition	Estimated profit of $4 million

Suppose the manager recognizes that competitors may react aggressively or passively to either strategy. This situation can be displayed vividly using the decision-tree scheme, as shown in Exhibit 1.4. This representation allows the manager to consider actions, responses, and outcomes simultaneously. The decision tree shows that the highest profit will result if a market-development strategy is enacted and competitors react passively. The manager must resolve the question of competitive reaction because an aggressive response will plunge the profit to $1 million, which is less than either outcome under the market-penetration strategy. The manager must rely on informed judgment to assess subjectively the likelihood of competitive response. Chapter 3 provides a more detailed description of decision analysis and its application.

The Marketing Mix and Customer Value Proposition

Matching offerings and markets requires recognition of the other marketing activities available to the marketing manager. Combined with the offering, these activities form the marketing mix.

A marketing mix typically encompasses activities controllable by the organization. These include the kind of product, service, or idea offered (product strategy), how it is communicated to buyers (communication strategy), the method for distributing the offering to buyers (channel strategy), and the amount buyers will pay for the offering (price strategy). Each of these strategies is described in Chapters 5 through 8. Here it is sufficient to note that each element of the marketing mix plays a complementary role in stimulating a market's (buyers') willingness and ability to buy and creating customer value.

An effective marketing mix also conveys a clear *customer value proposition*—a cluster of benefits that an organization promises customers to satisfy their needs. For example, Walmart's customer value proposition can be summed up as "Everyday low prices for a broad range of goods that are always in stock in convenient locations." Michelin's customer value proposition can be described as "Providing safety-conscious parents greater security in tires at a premium price."[17]

Formulating the Marketing Mix   The appropriate marketing mix for a product or service depends on the success requirements of the market at which it is directed. The "rightness" of the marketing mix depends on the market served. Consider the case of Cover Girl Cosmetics in China. The marketing mix for Cover Girl in China shares only one common element with its marketing mix in other countries—the brand name. All product shades, textures, and colors had to be adjusted to ensure they looked appealing on Chinese skin. Products have been packaged in small containers that resemble pieces of colorful candy, unlike other markets. The advertising and sales effort is localized expressly for the Chinese, and on-site beauty consultants assist buyers in Chinese department stores—not in self-service drug or grocery stores as in Cover Girl's other markets. Cover Girl pricing reflects local competitive conditions. According to Cover Girl's marketing director, "You can't just import cosmetics here. Companies have to understand what beauty means to Chinese women and what they look for, and product offerings, distribution, pricing and communication has to be adjusted accordingly to be right for the market."[18]

Internet-based technologies have created another market setting, called the market*space*. Companies that succeed in the new marketspace deliver customer value through the interactive capabilities of these technologies, which allow for greater flexibility in managing marketing mix elements. For example, online sellers routinely adjust prices to changing environmental conditions, purchase situations, and purchase behaviors of online buyers. Also, interactive two-way Internet-enabled capabilities in marketspace allow a customer to tell a seller exactly what his or her buying interests and requirements are, making possible the transformation of a product or service into a customized solution for the buyer. In addition, the purpose and role of marketing communications and marketing channels in this market setting have changed, as described in Chapters 6 and 7, respectively.

Besides being consistent with the needs of markets served, a marketing mix must be consistent with the organization's capacity, and the individual activities must complement one another. Several questions offer direction in evaluating an organization's marketing mix. First, is the marketing mix internally consistent? Do the individual activities complement one another to communicate a clear customer value proposition? Does the mix fit the organization, the market, and the environment into which it will be introduced? Second, are buyers more sensitive to some marketing mix activities than to others? For example, are they more likely to respond favorably to a decrease in price or an increase in sales promotion? Third, what are the costs of performing marketing mix activities and the costs of attracting and retaining buyers? Do these costs exceed their benefits? Can the organization afford the marketing mix expenditures? Finally, is the marketing mix properly timed? For example, are communications scheduled to coincide with product availability? Is the entire marketing mix timely with respect to the buying cycle of consumers, competitor actions, and prevailing environmental forces?

Implementing the Marketing Mix   Implementation of the marketing mix is as much an art as a science. Successful implementation requires an understanding of markets, environmental forces, organizational capacity, and marketing mix activities with a healthy respect for competitor reactions. An example of an implementation with less than successful results is that of A&P's WEO (Where Economy Originates) program. Prior to implementing the program, A&P had watched its sales volume plateau with shrinking profits, while other grocery retailers continued to increase sales volume and profits. When the WEO program was initiated, it emphasized discount pricing (price strategy) with heavy promotional expenditures (communication strategy). The program increased sales volume by $800 million but produced a profit loss of over $50 million. In the words of one industry observer at the time:

> Its competitors are convinced that A&P's assault with WEO was doomed from the start. Too many of its stores are relics of a bygone era. Many are in poor locations [distribution strategy] . . . . They are just not big enough to support the tremendous volume that is necessary to make a discounting operation profitable [capacity] . . . stores lack shelf space for stocking general merchandise items, such as housewares and children's clothing [product strategy].[19]

The product-market strategy employed by A&P could be classified as a market-penetration strategy. Its implementation, however, could be questioned in terms of internal consistency, costs of the marketing mix activities, and fit with organizational capacity. Moreover, the retail grocery industry was plagued at the time by rising food and energy costs. Both environmental factors had a destructive effect on A&P's strategy success.

BUDGETING MARKETING, FINANCIAL, AND PRODUCTION RESOURCES

The fourth phase in the strategic marketing management process is budgeting. A budget is a formal, quantitative expression of an organization's planning and strategy initiatives expressed in financial terms. A well-prepared budget meshes and balances an organization's financial, production, and marketing resources so that overall organizational goals or objectives are attained.

An organization's master budget consists of two parts: (1) an operating budget and (2) a financial budget. The operating budget focuses on an organization's income statement. Because the operating budget projects future revenues and expenses, it is sometimes referred to as a *pro forma income statement* or profit plan. The financial budget focuses on the effect that the operating budget and other initiatives (such as capital expenditures) will have on the organization's cash position. For example, the master budget for General Motors includes an income statement that details revenues, expenses, and profit for existing Chevrolet models. Its financial budget included the capital expenditures for the all-electric-powered Chevrolet Volt introduced in 2010.[20]

In addition to the operating and financial budget, many organizations prepare supplemental special budgets, such as an advertising and sales budget, and related reports tied to the master budget. For example, a report showing how revenues, costs, and profits change under different marketing decisions and competitive and economic conditions is often prepared. Budgeting is more than an accounting function. It is an essential element of strategic marketing management as well.

A complete description of the budgetary process is beyond the scope of this section. However, Chapter 2, "Financial Aspects of Marketing Management," provides an overview of cost concepts and behavior. It also describes useful analytical tools for dealing with the financial dimensions of strategic marketing management, including cost-volume-profit analysis, discounted cash flow, customer lifetime value analysis, and the preparation of pro forma income statements.

DEVELOPING REFORMULATION AND RECOVERY STRATEGIES

Strategies are rarely timeless. Changing markets, economic conditions, and competitive behavior require periodic, if not sudden, adjustments in marketing strategy.

Marketing audit and control procedures are fundamental to the development of reformulation and recovery strategies. The *marketing audit* is

a comprehensive, systematic, independent, and periodic examination of a company's—or business unit's—marketing environment, objectives, strategies and activities with a view of determining problem areas and opportunities and recommending a plan of action to improve the company's marketing performance.[21]

The audit process directs the manager's attention to both the strategic fit of the organization with its environment and the operational aspects of the marketing program. Strategic aspects of the marketing audit address the synoptic question, "Are we doing the right things?" Operational aspects address an equally synoptic question—"Are we doing things right?"

The distinction between strategic operational perspectives, as well as the implementation of each, is examined in Chapter 9. Suffice it to say here that marketing audit and control procedures underlie the processes of defining the organization's business, mission, and goals or objectives, identifying external opportunities and threats and internal strengths and weaknesses, formulating product-market strategies and marketing mix activities, and budgeting resources.

Developing reformulation and recovery strategies during the planning process serves two important purposes. First, it forces the manager to consider the "what if" questions. For example, "What if an unexpected environmental threat arises that renders a strategy obsolete?" or "What if competitive and market response to a strategy is inconsistent with what was originally expected?" Such questions focus the manager's attention on the sensitivity of results to assumptions made in the strategy-development process. Second, preplanning of reformulation and recovery strategies, or *contingency plans*, leads to a faster reaction time in implementing remedial action. Marshaling and reorienting resources is a time-consuming process itself without additional time lost in planning.

DRAFTING A MARKETING PLAN

A marketing plan embodies the strategic marketing management process. It is a formal, written document that describes the context and scope of an organization's marketing effort to achieve defined goals or objectives within a specific future time period. Marketing plans go by a variety of names depending on their particular focus. For example, there are business marketing plans, product marketing plans, and brand marketing plans. At Frito-Lay, Inc., for instance, a marketing plan is drafted for a particular business (snack chips), for a product class (potato chips, tortilla chips, corn chips), and for specific brands (Lay's potato chips, Doritos tortilla chips, Fritos corn chips). Marketing plans also have a time dimension. Short-run marketing plans typically focus on a one-year period and are called annual marketing plans. Long-run marketing plans often have a three- to five-year planning horizon.

A formal, written marketing plan represents a distillation of and the attention and thought given the five interrelated analytical processes in this chapter. It is the tangible result of an intellectual effort. As a written document, a marketing plan also exhibits certain stylistic elements. Although there is no "generic" marketing plan that applies to all organizations and all situations, marketing plans follow a general format. The appendix at the end of this chapter provides an actual example of a condensed marketing plan for Paradise Kitchens, Inc., a company that produces and markets a unique line of single-serve and microwavable Southwestern/Mexican-style frozen chili products. This example illustrates both the substance and style of a five-year marketing plan.

MARKETING ETHICS AND SOCIAL RESPONSIBILITY

On a final note, it must be emphasized that matters of ethics and social responsibility permeate every aspect of the strategic marketing management process. Indeed, most marketing decisions involve some degree of moral judgment and reflect an organization's orientation toward the publics with which it interacts. Enlightened marketing executives no longer subscribe to the view that if an action is legal, then it is also ethical and socially responsible. These executives are sensitive to the fact that the marketplace is populated by individuals and groups with diverse value systems. Moreover, they recognize that their actions will be judged publicly by others with different values and interests.

Enlightened ethical and socially responsible decisions arise from the ability of marketers to discern the precise issues involved and their willingness to take action even when the outcome may negatively affect their standing in an organization or the company's financial interests. Although the moral foundations on which marketing decisions are made will vary among individuals and organizations, failure to recognize issues and take appropriate action is the least ethical and most socially irresponsible approach.

A positive approach to ethical and socially responsible behavior is illustrated by Anheuser-Busch, which has spent more than $830 million since 1982 to promote responsible drinking of alcoholic beverages through community-based programs and national advertising campaigns. Anheuser-Busch executives acknowledge the potential for alcohol abuse and are willing to forgo business generated by misuse of the company's products. These executives have discerned the issues and have recognized an ethical obligation to present and potential customers. They have also recognized the company's social responsibility to the general public by encouraging safe driving and responsible drinking habits.[22]

NOTES

1. Roger A. Kerin, "Strategic Marketing and the CMO," *Journal of Marketing* (October 2005): 12–14; and David A. Aaker, *Spanning Silos: The New CMO Imperative* (Cambridge, MA: Harvard Business School Press, 2008); and George S. Day and Robert Malcolm, "The CMO and the Future of Marketing, *Marketing Management* (Spring 2012):34–43.

2. Derek E. Abell, *Defining the Business: The Starting Point of Strategic Planning* (Upper Saddle River, NJ: Prentice Hall, 1980); and Roger A. Kerin, Vijay Mahajan, and P. Rajan Varadarajan, *Contemporary Perspectives on Strategic Market Planning* (Boston: Allyn & Bacon, 1990).

3. "End of Era for Britannica," *The Wall Street Journal* (March 14, 2012): B1, B9. "New Britannica Keeps Pace with Change," Encyclopaedia Britannica News Release, March 23, 2005; and "Britannica Reference Work Available for iPhone and iPad," Encyclopaedia Britannica News Release, February 27, 2010.

4. Eric von Hippel, Stephan Thomke, and Mary Sonnack, "Creating Breakthroughs at 3M," *Harvard Business Review* (September–October 1999): 47–56.

5. "Gillette Safety Razor Division," Harvard Business School case #9-574-058.

6. David A. Aaker, *Strategic Market Management*, 9th ed. (New York: John Wiley & Sons, 2010): 58–59.

7. "Exxon's Flop in Field of Office Gear Shows Diversification Perils," *Wall Street Journal* (September 3, 1985): 1ff.

8. This classification is adapted from H. Igor Ansoff, *Corporate Strategy* (New York: McGraw-Hill, 1964): Chapter 6. For an extended discussion on product-market strategies, see Roger A. Kerin, Vijay Mahajan, and P. Rajan Varadarajan, *Contemporary Perspectives on Strategic Market Planning* (Boston: Allyn & Bacon, 1990): Chapter 6.

9. "In Lean Times, Big Companies Make a Grab for Market Share," *Wall Street Journal* (September 5, 2003): A1, A6.

10. H. Menzies, "Why Folger's Is Getting Creamed Back East," *Fortune* (July 17, 1978): 69.

11. Philip R. Cateora, Mary Gilly, and John L. Graham, *International Marketing*, 15th ed. (Burr Ridge, IL: McGraw-Hill/Irwin, 2011): Chapter 11.

12. "Hasbro, Inc.," in Eric N. Berkowitz, Roger A. Kerin, Steven N. Hartley, and William Rudelius, *Marketing*, 5th ed. (Chicago: Richard D. Irwin, 1997): 656–657.

13. Roger A. Kerin, Steven N. Hartley, and William Rudelius, *Marketing*, 10th ed. (Burr Ridge, IL: McGraw-Hill, 2012): 261–262.

14. "Gillette's New Edge," *BusinessWeek* (February 6, 2006): 44.

15. Failed diversification attempts, along with advice on diversification, are detailed in Gordon Walker, *Modern Competitive Strategy*, 4th ed. (Burr Ridge, IL: McGraw-Hill, 2012): Chapter 11.

16. These estimates were reported in "The Breakdown of U.S. Innovation," *BusinessWeek* (February 16, 1976): 56ff.

17. David J. Collis and Michael G. Rukstad, "Can You Say What Your Strategy Is?" *Harvard Business Review* (April 2008): 82–90.

18. "P&G Introduces Cover Girl: U.S. Beauty Brand Gets Local Color," AdAgeChina .com, October 25, 2005.

19. Robert F. Hartley, *Marketing Mistakes*, 5th ed. (New York: John Wiley & Sons, 1992). Items in brackets added for illustrative purposes.

20. "GM Debuts the Chevy Volt," CNNMoney.com, September 16, 2008.

21. Philip Kotler and Kevin Lane Keller, *Marketing Management*, 14th ed. (Upper Saddle River, NJ: Prentice Hall, 2012): 643.

22. "Anheuser Busch Corporate Responsibility," www.beeresponsible.com, downloaded January 4, 2012.

Appendix A

A Sample Marketing Plan

Crafting a marketing plan is hard but satisfying work. When completed, a marketing plan serves as a road map that details the context and scope of marketing activities including, but not limited to, a mission statement, goals and objectives, a situation analysis, growth opportunities, target market(s) and marketing (mix) program, a budget, and an implementation schedule.

As a written document, the plan conveys in words the analysis, ideas, and aspirations of its author pertaining to a business, product, and/or brand marketing effort. How a marketing plan is written communicates not only the substance of the marketing effort but also the professionalism of the author. Writing style will not overcome limitations in substance. However, a poorly written marketing plan can detract from the perceived substance of the plan.

WRITING AND STYLE CONSIDERATIONS

Given the importance of a carefully crafted marketing plan, authors of marketing plans adhere to certain guidelines. The following writing and style guidelines generally apply:

- Use a direct, professional writing style. Use appropriate business and marketing terms without jargon. Present and future tenses with active voice are generally better than past tense and passive voice.

- Be positive and specific. At the same time, avoid superlatives ("terrific," "wonderful"). Specifics are better than glittering generalities. Use numbers for impact, justifying computations and projections with facts or reasonable quantitative assumptions where possible.

- Use bullet points for succinctness and emphasis. As with the list you are reading, bullets enable key points to be highlighted effectively and with great efficiency.

- Use "A-level" (the first level) and "B-level" (the second level) headings under major section headings to help readers make easy transitions from one topic to another. This also forces the writer to organize the plan more carefully. Use these headings liberally, at least once every 200 to 300 words.

This appendix is adapted from Roger A. Kerin, Steven W. Hartley, and William Rudelius, *Marketing*, 10th ed. (Burr Ridge, IL: McGraw-Hill/Irwin, 2011). Used with permission.

- Use visuals where appropriate. Illustrations, graphs, and charts enable large amounts of information to be presented succinctly.
- Shoot for a plan 15 to 35 pages in length, not including financial projections and appendices. An uncomplicated small business may require only 15 pages, while a new business startup may require more than 35 pages.
- Use care in layout, design, and presentation. Laser or ink-jet printers give a more professional look to your report. A bound report with a cover and clear title page adds professionalism.

SAMPLE FIVE-YEAR ANNOTATED MARKETING PLAN FOR PARADISE KITCHENS, INC.

The marketing plan that follows for Paradise Kitchens, Inc. is based on an actual plan developed by the company. To protect proprietary information about the company, a number of details and certain data have been altered, but the basic logic of the plan has been preserved. Various appendices are omitted due to space limitations.

Notes in the margins next to the Paradise Kitchens, Inc. marketing plan fall into two categories:

1. *Substantive notes* elaborate on the rationale or significance of an element in the marketing plan.
2. *Writing style, format,* and *layout notes* explain the editorial or visual rationale for the element.

As you read the marketing plan, you might consider adding your own notes in the margins related to the discussion in the text. For example, you may wish to compare the application of SWOT analysis and reference to "customer value proposition" and "points of difference" in the Paradise Kitchens, Inc. marketing plan with the discussion in Chapter 1. As you read additional chapters in the text, you may return to the marketing plan and insert additional notes pertaining to terminology used and techniques employed.

The Table of Contents provides quick access to the topics in the plan, usually organized by section and subsection headings.

Seen by many experts as the single most important element in the plan, the Executive Summary, with a maximum of two pages, "sells" the document to readers through its clarity and brevity.

The Company Description highlights the recent history and recent successes of the organization.

The Strategic Focus and Plan sets the strategic direction for the entire organization, a direction with which proposed actions of the marketing plan must be consistent. This section is not included in all marketing plans.

The Mission section includes mission statement, which focuses the activities of Paradise Kitchens for the stakeholder groups to be served.

FIVE-YEAR MARKETING PLAN
Paradise Kitchens, Inc.

Table of Contents

1. **Executive Summary**

2. **Company Description**

Paradise Kitchens, Inc. was started by cofounders Randall F. Peters and Leah E. Peters to develop and market Howlin' Coyote Chili, a unique line of single-serve and microwavable Southwestern/Mexican-style frozen chili products. The Howlin' Coyote line of chili was first introduced into the Minneapolis–St. Paul market and expanded to Denver two years later and Phoenix two years after that.

To the Company's knowledge, Howlin' Coyote is the only premium-quality, authentic Southwestern/Mexican-style, frozen chili sold in U.S. grocery stores. Its high quality has gained fast, widespread acceptance in these markets. In fact, same-store sales doubled in the last year for which data are available. The Company believes the Howlin' Coyote brand can be extended to other categories of Southwestern/Mexican food products such as tacos, enchiladas, and burritos.

Paradise Kitchens believes its high-quality, high-price strategy has proven successful. This marketing plan outlines how the Company will extend its geographic coverage from 3 markets to 20 markets by the year 2012.

3. Strategic Focus and Plan

This section covers three aspects of corporate strategy that influence the marketing plan: (1) the mission, (2) goals, and (3) core competence/sustainable competitive advantage of Paradise Kitchens.

MISSION

The mission and vision of Paradise Kitchens are to market lines of high-quality Southwestern/Mexican food products at premium prices that satisfy consumers in this fast-growing food segment while providing challenging career opportunities for employees and above-average returns to stockholders.

The Goals section sets both the financial and nonfinancial targets—where possible in quantitative terms—against which the company's performance will be measured.

GOALS

For the coming five years, Paradise Kitchens seeks to achieve the following goals:

- Nonfinancial goals
  1. To retain its present image as the highest-quality line of Southwestern/Mexican products in the food categories in which it competes.
  2. To enter 17 new metropolitan markets.
  3. To achieve national distribution in two convenience store or supermarket chains by 2008 and five by 2009.
  4. To add a new product line every third year.
  5. To be among the top three chili lines—regardless of packaging (frozen, canned) in one-third of the metro markets in which it competes by 2009 and two-thirds by 2011.

Lists use parallel construction to improve readability—in this case a series of infinitives starting with "To . . ."

- Financial goals
  1. To obtain a real (inflation adjusted) growth in earnings per share of 8 percent per year over time.
  2. To obtain a return on equity of at least 20 percent.
  3. To have a public stock offering by the year 2009.

CORE COMPETENCY AND SUSTAINABLE COMPETITIVE ADVANTAGE

In terms of core competency, Paradise Kitchens seeks to achieve a unique ability (1) to provide distinctive, high-quality chilies and related products using Southwestern/Mexican recipes that appeal to and excite contemporary tastes for these products and (2) to deliver these products to the customer's table using effective manufacturing and distribution systems that maintain the Company's quality standards.

To translate these core competencies into a sustainable competitive advantage, the Company will work closely with key suppliers and distributors to build the relationships and alliances necessary to satisfy the high taste standards of our customers.

4. Situation Analysis

The Situation Analysis is a snapshot to answer the question, "Where are we now?"

This situation analysis starts with a snapshot of the current environment in which Paradise Kitchens finds itself by providing a brief SWOT (strengths, weaknesses, opportunities, threats) analysis. After this overview, the analysis probes ever-finer levels of detail: industry, competitors, company, and consumers.

The SWOT Analysis identifies strengths, weaknesses, opportunities, and threats to provide a solid foundation as a springboard to identify subsequent *actions* in the marketing plan.

Each long table, graph, or photo is given a figure number and title. It then appears as soon as possible after the first reference in the text, accommodating necessary page breaks. This also avoids breaking long tables like this one in the middle. Short tables or graphs that are less than 1½ inches are often inserted in the text without figure numbers because they don't cause serious problems with page breaks.

SWOT Analysis

Figure 1 shows the internal and external factors affecting the market opportunities for Paradise Kitchens. Stated briefly, this SWOT analysis highlights the great strides taken by the Company since its products first appeared on grocers' shelves. In the Company's favor internally are its strengths of an experienced management team and board of directors, excellent acceptance of its lines in the three metropolitan markets in which it competes, and a strong manufacturing and distribution system to serve these limited markets. Favorable external factors (opportunities) include the increasing appeal of Southwestern/Mexican foods, the strength of the upscale market for the Company's products, and food-processing technological breakthroughs that make it easier for smaller food producers to compete.

Figure 1. SWOT Analysis for Paradise Kitchens

Internal Factors	Strengths	Weaknesses
Management	Experienced and entrepreneurial management and board	Small size can restrict options
Offerings	Unique, high-quality, high-price products	Many lower-quality, lower-price competitors
Marketing	Distribution in three markets with excellent acceptance	No national awareness or distribution; restricted shelf space in the freezer section
Personnel	Good work force, though small; little turnover	Big gap if key employee leaves
Finance	Excellent growth in sales revenues	Limited resources may restrict growth opportunities when compared to large competitors
Manufacturing	Sole supplier ensures high quality	Lack economies of scale of large competitors
R&D	Continuing efforts to ensure quality in delivered products	Lack of canning and microwavable food-processing expertise

(Continued)

Figure 1. SWOT Analysis for Paradise Kitchens (*continued*)

External Factors	Opportunities	Threats
Consumer/Social	Upscale market, likely to be stable; Southwestern/Mexican food category is fast-growing segment due to growth in Hispanic American population and desire for spicier foods	Price may limit access to mass markets; consumers value a strong brand name
Competitive	Distinctive name and packaging in its markets	Not patentable; competitors can attempt to duplicate product; others better able to pay slotting fees
Technological	Technical break-throughs enable smaller food produ-cers to achieve many economies available to large competitors	Competitors have gained economies in canning and microwavable food processing
Economic	Consumer income is high; convenience im-portant to U.S. households	Many households "eating out," and bringing prepared take-out into home
Legal/Regulatory	High U.S. Food & Drug Admin. standards eliminate fly-by-night competitors	Mergers among large competitors being approved by government

Among unfavorable factors, the main weakness is the limited size of Paradise Kitchens relative to its competitors in terms of the depth of the management team, available financial resources, and national awareness and distribution of product lines. Threats include the danger that the Company's premium prices may limit access to mass markets and competition from the "eating-out" and "take-out" markets.

INDUSTRY ANALYSIS: TRENDS IN SPICY AND MEXICAN FOODS

Frozen Foods. According to *Grocery Headquarters*, consumers are flocking to the frozen-food section of grocery retailers. The reasons: hectic lifestyles demanding increased convenience and an abundance of new, tastier, and nutritious products. By 2007, total sales of frozen food in grocery retailers, drugstores, and mass merchandisers, such as Target and Costco (excluding Walmart), reached $29 billion. Prepared frozen meals, which are defined as meals or entrees that are frozen and require minimal preparation, accounted for $8.1 billion, or 26 percent of the total frozen-food market.

The Industry Analysis section provides the backdrop for the subsequent, more detailed analysis of competition, the company, and the company's customers. Without an in-depth understanding of the industry, the remaining analysis may be misdirected.

Even though relatively brief, this in-depth treatment of the Spicy Southwestern/Mexican food industry in the United States demonstrates to the plan's readers the company's understanding of the industry in which it competes. It gives readers confidence that the company thoroughly understands its own industry.

As with the Industry Analysis, the Competitor Analysis demonstrates that the company has a realistic understanding of who its major competitors are and what their marketing strategies are. Again, a realistic assessment gives confidence to readers that subsequent marketing actions in the plan rest on a solid foundation.

Sales of Mexican entrees totaled $506 million. Heavy consumers of frozen meals, those who eat five or more meals every two weeks, tend to be kids, teens, and adults 35–44 years old.

Mexican Foods. Currently, Mexican foods such as burritos, enchiladas, and tacos are used in two-thirds of American households. These trends reflect a generally more favorable attitude on the part of all Americans toward spicy foods that include red chili peppers. The growing Hispanic population in the U.S., about 44 million and almost $768 billion in purchasing power in 2007, partly explains the increasing demand for Mexican food. Hispanic purchasing power is projected to be $1.2 billion in 2011.

COMPETITORS IN THE CHILI MARKET

The chili market represents over $500 million in annual sales. On average, consumers buy five to six servings annually. The products fall primarily into two groups: canned chili (75 percent of sales) and dry chili (25 percent of sales).

Bluntly put, the major disadvantage of the segment's dominant product, canned chili, is that it does not taste very good. A taste test described in an issue of *Consumer Reports* magazine ranked 26 canned chili products "poor" to "fair" in overall sensory quality. The study concluded, "Chili doesn't have to be hot to be good. But really good chili, hot or mild, doesn't come out of a can."

Company Analysis

> The Company Analysis provides details of the company's strengths and marketing strategies that will enable it to achieve the mission and goals identified earlier.

Currently, Howlin' Coyote products compete in the chili and Mexican frozen entree segments of the Southwestern/Mexican food market. While the chili obviously competes as a stand-alone product, its exceptional quality means it can complement such dishes as burritos, nachos, and enchiladas and can be readily used as a smothering sauce for pasta, rice, or potatoes. This flexibility of use is relatively rare in the prepared food marketplace. With Howlin' Coyote, Paradise Kitchens is broadening the position of frozen chili in a way that can lead to impressive market share for the new product category.

The Company now uses a single outside producer with which it works closely to maintain the consistently high quality required in its products. The greater volume has increased production efficiencies, resulting in a steady decrease in the cost of goods sold.

The higher-level "A heading" of Customer Analysis has a more dominant typeface and position than the lower-level "B heading" of Customer Characteristics. These headings introduce the reader to the sequence and level of topics covered.

Satisfying customers and providing genuine value to them is why organizations exist in a market economy. This section addresses the question of "Who are the customers for Paradise Kitchens' products?"

CUSTOMER ANALYSIS

In terms of customer analysis, this section describes (1) the characteristics of customers expected to buy Howlin' Coyote products and (2) health and nutrition concerns of Americans today.

Customer Characteristics. Demographically, chili products in general are purchased by consumers representing a broad range of socioeconomic backgrounds. Howlin' Coyote chili is purchased chiefly by consumers who have achieved higher levels of education and whose income is $50,000 and higher. These consumers represent 50 percent of canned and dry mix chili users.

The household buying Howlin' Coyote has one to three people in it. Among married couples, Howlin' Coyote is predominantly bought by households in which both spouses work. While women are a majority of the buyers, single men represent a significant segment.

Because the chili offers a quick way to make a tasty meal, the product's biggest users tend to be those most pressed for time. Howlin' Coyote's premium pricing also means that its purchasers are skewed toward the higher end of the income range. Buyers range in age from 25 to 54 and typically reside in the western United States.

> This section demonstrates the company's insights into a major trend that has a potentially large impact.

Health and Nutrition Concerns. Coverage of food issues in the U.S. media is often erratic and occasionally alarmist. Because Americans are concerned about their diets, studies from organizations of widely varying credibility frequently receive significant attention from the major news organizations. For instance, a study of fat levels of movie popcorn was reported in all the major media. Similarly, studies on the healthfulness of Mexican food have received prominent "play" in print and broadcast reports. The high caloric levels of much Mexican and Southwestern-style food had been widely reported and often exaggerated. Some Mexican frozen-food competitors, such as Don Miguel, Mission Foods, Ruiz Foods, and José Olé, plan to offer or have recently offered more "carb-friendly" and "fat-friendly" products in response to this concern.

Howlin' Coyote is already lower in calories, fat, and sodium than its competitors, and those qualities are not currently being stressed in its promotions. Instead, in the space and time available for promotions, Howlin' Coyote's taste, convenience, and flexibility are stressed.

5. Product-Market Focus

This section describes the five-year marketing and product objectives for Paradise Kitchens and the target markets, points of difference, and positioning of its lines of Howlin' Coyote chilies.

MARKETING AND PRODUCT OBJECTIVES

Howlin' Coyote's marketing intent is to take full advantage of its brand potential while building a base from which other revenue sources can be mined—both in and out of the retail grocery business. These are detailed in four areas below:

> The chances of success for a new product are significantly increased if objectives are set for the product itself and if target market segments are identified for it. This section makes these explicit for Paradise Kitchens. The objectives also serve as the planned targets against which marketing activities are measured in program implementation and control.

- Current markets. Current markets will be grown by expanding brand and flavor distribution at the retail level. In addition, same-store sales will be grown by increasing consumer awareness and repeat purchases, thereby leading to the more efficient broker/warehouse distribution channel.

- New markets. By the end of Year 5, the chili, salsa, burrito, and enchilada business will be expanded to a total of 20 metropolitan areas. This will represent 70 percent of U.S. food store sales.
- Food service. Food service sales will include chili products and smothering sauces. Sales are expected to reach $693,000 by the end of Year 3 and $1.5 million by the end of Year 5.
- New products. Howlin' Coyote's brand presence will be expanded at the retail level through the addition of new products in the frozen-foods section. This will be accomplished through new product concept screening in Year 1 to identify new potential products. These products will be brought to market in Years 2 and 3. Additionally, the brand may be licensed in select categories.

TARGET MARKETS

The primary target market for Howlin' Coyote products is households with one to three people, where often both adults work, with household income typically above $50,000 per year. These households contain more experienced, adventurous consumers of Southwestern/Mexican food and want premium-quality products.

> This section identifies the specific niches or target markets toward which the company's products are directed. When appropriate and when space permits, this section often includes a product-market matrix.

CUSTOMER VALUE PROPOSITION

Howlin' Coyote offers busy households high-quality, "authentic Southwestern/Mexican tasting" chilies that can be prepared easily and quickly at a competitive price.

POINTS OF DIFFERENCE

The "points of difference"—characteristics that make Howlin' Coyote chilies unique relative to competitors—fall into three important areas:

- Unique taste and convenience. No known competitor offers a high-quality, "authentic" frozen chili in a range of flavors. And no existing chili has the same combination of quick preparation and home-style taste.
- Taste trends. The American palate is increasingly intrigued by hot spices, and Howlin' Coyote brands offer more "kick" than most other prepared chilies.
- Premium packaging. Howlin' Coyote's high-value packaging graphics convey the unique, high-quality product contained inside.

> An organization cannot grow by offering only "me-too products." The greatest single factor in a new product's failure is the lack of significant "points of difference" that set it apart from competitors' substitutes. This section makes these points of difference explicit.

Everything that has gone before in the marketing plan sets the stage for the marketing mix actions covered in the marketing program.

This section describes in detail three key elements of the company's product strategy: the product line, its quality and how this is achieved, and its "cutting edge" packaging.

6. Marketing Program

The four marketing mix elements of the Howlin' Coyote chili marketing program are detailed below. Note that "chile" is the vegetable and "chili" is the dish.

PRODUCT STRATEGY

After first summarizing the product line, the approach to product quality and packaging is covered.

Product Line. Howlin' Coyote chili is available in five flavors. The five are Green Chile Chili, Red Chile Chili, Beef and Black Bean Chili, Chicken Chunk Chili, and Mean Bean Chili.

Unique Product Quality. The flavoring systems of the Howlin' Coyote chilies are proprietary. The products' tastiness is due to extra care lavished upon the ingredients during production. The ingredients used are of unusually high quality. Meats are low-fat cuts and are fresh, not frozen, to preserve cell structure and moistness. Chiles are fire-roasted for fresher taste, not the canned variety used by more mainstream products. Tomatoes and vegetables are select quality. No preservatives or artificial flavors are used.

Packaging. Reflecting the "cutting edge" marketing strategy of its producers, Howlin' Coyote bucks conventional wisdom in packaging. It avoids placing predictable photographs of the product on its containers. Instead, Howlin' Coyote's package shows a Southwestern motif that communicates the product's value proposition.

PRICE STRATEGY

Howlin' Coyote chili is, at $3.99 for an 11-ounce package, priced comparably to the other frozen offerings and higher than the canned and dried chili varieties. However, the significant taste advantages it has over canned chilies and the convenience advantages over dried chilies justify this pricing strategy.

PROMOTION STRATEGY

Key promotion programs feature in-store demonstrations, recipes, and cents-off coupons.

In-Store Demonstrations. In-store demonstrations will be conducted to give consumers a chance to try Howlin' Coyote products and learn about their unique qualities. Demos will be conducted regularly in all markets to increase awareness and trial purchases.

Recipes. Because the products' flexibility of use is a key selling point, recipes will be offered to consumers to stimulate use. The recipes will be given at all in-store demonstrations, on the back of packages, and through a mail-in recipe book offer. In addition, recipes will be included in coupons sent by direct mail or freestanding inserts.

Cents-Off Coupons. To generate trial and repeat purchase of Howlin' Coyote products, coupons will be distributed in four ways:

- In Sunday newspaper inserts. Inserts are highly read and will help generate awareness.

This Price Strategy section makes the company's price point very clear, along with its price position relative to potential substitutes. When appropriate and when space permits, this section might contain a break-even analysis.

Elements of the Promotion Strategy are highlighted here with B-headings in terms of the three key promotional activities the company is emphasizing for its product line: in-store demonstrations, recipes featuring its Howlin' Coyote chilies, and cents-off coupons.

> A bulleted list adds many details for the reader, including methods of gaining customer awareness, trial, and repeat purchases as Howlin' Coyote enters new metropolitan areas.

- **In-pack coupons.** Inside each box of Howlin' Coyote chili will be coupons for $1 off two more packages of the chili. These coupons will be included for the first three months the product is shipped to a new market. Doing so encourages repeat purchases by new users.
- **Direct-mail chili coupons.** Those households that fit the Howlin' Coyote demographics described above will be mailed coupons.
- **In-store demonstrations.** Coupons will be passed out at in-store demonstrations to give an additional incentive to purchase.

DISTRIBUTION STRATEGY

> The Distribution Strategy is described here in terms of both (1) the present method and (2) the new one to be used when the increased sales volume makes it feasible.

Howlin' Coyote is distributed in its present markets through a food distributor. The distributor buys the product, warehouses it, and then resells and delivers it to grocery retailers on a store-by-store basis. As sales grow, we will shift to a more efficient system using a broker who sells the products to retail chains and grocery wholesalers.

7. Financial Data and Projections

PAST SALES REVENUES

> All the marketing mix decisions covered in the marketing program have both revenue and expense effects. These are summarized in this section of the marketing plan.

Historically, Howlin' Coyote has had a steady increase in sales revenues since its introduction. In 2003, sales jumped, due largely to new promotion strategies. Sales have continued to rise, but at a less dramatic rate. The trend in sales revenues appears in Figure 2.

Figure 2.   Sales Revenues for Paradise Kitchens, Inc.

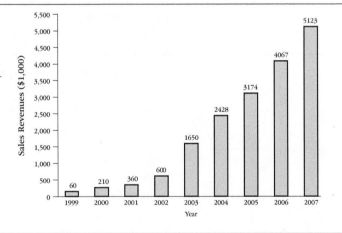

> The graph shows more clearly the dramatic growth of sales revenue than data in a table would do.

FIVE-YEAR PROJECTIONS

Five-year financial projections for Paradise Kitchens appear in Figure 3.

These projections reflect the continuing growth in number of cases sold (with eight packages of Howlin' Coyote chili per case) and increasing production and distribution economies of scale as sales volume increases.

Figure 3. Five-Year Projections: 2007–2012

Financial Element	Units	Actual 2007	Year 1 2008	Year 2 2009	Year 3 2010	Year 4 2011	Year 5 2012
			\[*Projections*\]				
Cases sold	1,000	353	684	889	1,249	1,499	1,799
Net sales	$1,000	5,123	9,913	12,884	18,111	21,733	26,080
Gross profit	$1,000	2,545	4,820	6,527	8,831	10,597	12,717
Selling and general and admin. expenses	$1,000	2,206	3,835	3,621	6,026	7,231	8,678
Operating profit (loss)	$1,000	339	985	2,906	2,805	3,366	4,039

The Five-Year Financial Projections section starts with the forecast of cases sold and the resulting net sales. Gross profit and then operating profit are projected. An actual plan often contains many pages of computer-generated spreadsheet projections, usually shown in an appendix to the plan.

The Implementation Plan shows how the company will turn plans into results. Charts are often used to specify deadlines and assign responsibilities for the many tactical marketing decisions needed to enter a new market.

The essence of Evaluation and Control is comparing actual sales with the targeted values set in the plan and taking appropriate actions. Note that the section briefly describes a contingency plan for alternative actions, depending on how successful the entry into a new market turns out to be.

Various appendices may appear at the end of the plan, depending on the purpose and audience for them. For example, detailed financial spreadsheets often appear in an appendix.

8. Implementation Plan

Introducing Howlin' Coyote chilies to 17 new metropolitan areas is a complex task and requires that creative promotional activities gain consumer awareness and initial trial among the target market households identified earlier. The anticipated rollout schedule to enter these metropolitan markets appears in Figure 4.

Figure 4. Rollout Schedule to Enter New U.S. Markets

Year	New Markets Added	Cumulative Markets	Cumulative Percentage of U.S. Market
Today (2007)	2	5	16
Year 1 (2008)	3	8	21
Year 2 (2009)	4	12	29
Year 3 (2010)	2	14	37
Year 4 (2011)	3	17	45
Year 5 (2012)	3	20	53

The diverse regional tastes in chili will be monitored carefully to assess whether minor modifications may be required in the chili recipes. For example, what is seen as "hot" in Boston may not be seen as "hot" in Dallas. As the rollout to new metropolitan areas continues, Paradise Kitchens will assess manufacturing and distribution trade-offs. This is important in determining whether to start new production with selected high-quality regional contract packers.

9. Evaluation and Control

Monthly sales targets in cases have been set for Howlin' Coyote chili for each metropolitan area. Actual case sales will be compared with these targets and tactical marketing programs modified to reflect the unique sets of factors in each metropolitan area. The speed of the rollout program may increase or decrease, depending on Paradise Kitchens' performance in the successive metropolitan markets it enters.

10. Appendices

Chapter 2

Financial Aspects of Marketing Management

Marketing managers are accountable for the impact of their actions on profit and cash flow. Therefore, they need a working knowledge of basic accounting and finance concepts. This chapter provides an overview of several concepts from accounting and finance that are useful in marketing management: (1) variable and fixed costs, (2) relevant and sunk costs, (3) margins, (4) contribution analysis, (5) liquidity, (6) operating leverage, (7) discounted cash flow, and (8) customer lifetime value analysis. In addition, considerations when preparing pro forma income statements are described.

 ## VARIABLE AND FIXED COSTS

An organization's costs divide into two broad categories: variable costs and fixed costs.

Variable Costs

Variable costs are expenses that are uniform per unit of output within a relevant time period (usually defined as a budget year); yet total variable costs fluctuate in direct proportion to the output volume of units produced. In other words, as volume increases, total variable costs increase.

Variable costs are divided into two categories, one of which is *cost of goods sold*. For a manufacturer or a provider of a service, cost of goods sold covers materials, labor, and factory overhead applied directly to production. For a reseller (wholesaler or retailer), cost of goods sold consists primarily of the cost of merchandise. The second category of variable costs consists of expenses that are not directly tied to production but that nevertheless vary directly with volume. Examples include sales commissions, discounts, and delivery expenses.

Fixed Costs

Fixed costs are expenses that do not fluctuate with output volume within a relevant time period (the budget year) but become progressively smaller per unit of output as volume increases. The decrease in per-unit fixed cost results from the increase in the number of output units over which fixed costs are allocated. Note, however, that no matter how large volume becomes, the absolute size of fixed costs remains unchanged.

Fixed costs divide into two categories: programmed costs and committed costs. *Programmed costs* result from attempts to generate sales volume. *Marketing expenditures* are generally classified as programmed costs. Examples include advertising, sales promotion, and sales salaries. *Committed costs* are those required to maintain the organization. They are usually nonmarketing expenditures such as rent and administrative and clerical salaries.

It is important to understand the concept of fixed cost. Remember that total fixed costs do not change during a budget year, regardless of changes in volume. Once fixed expenditures for a marketing program have been made, they remain the same whether or not the program causes unit volume to change.

Despite the clear-cut classification of costs into variable and fixed categories suggested here, cost classification is not always apparent in actual practice. Many times costs have a fixed and a variable component. For example, selling expenses often have a fixed component (such as salary) and a variable component (such as commissions or bonus) that are not always evident at first glance.

RELEVANT AND SUNK COSTS

Relevant Costs

Relevant costs are expenditures that (1) are expected to occur in the future as a result of some marketing action and (2) differ among marketing alternatives being considered. In short, relevant costs are future expenditures unique to the decision alternatives under consideration.

The concept of relevant cost can best be illustrated by an example. Suppose a manager considers adding a new product to the product mix. Relevant costs include potential expenditures for manufacturing and marketing the product, plus salary costs arising from the time sales personnel give to the new product at the expense of other products. If this additional product does not affect the salary costs of sales personnel, salaries are not a relevant cost.

As a general rule, opportunity costs are also relevant costs. Opportunity costs are the forgone benefits from an alternative not chosen.

Sunk Costs

Sunk costs are the direct opposite of relevant costs. Sunk costs are past expenditures for a given activity and are typically irrelevant in whole or in part to future decisions. In a marketing context, sunk costs include past research and development expenditures (including test marketing) and last year's advertising expense. These expenditures, although real, will neither recur in the future nor influence future expenditures. When marketing managers attempt to incorporate sunk costs into future decisions affecting new expenditures, they often fall prey to the *sunk cost fallacy*—that is, they attempt to recoup spent dollars by spending still more dollars in the future.

MARGINS

Another useful concept for marketing managers is that of *margin*, which refers to the difference between the selling price and the "cost" of a product or service. Margins are expressed on a total volume basis or on an individual unit basis, in dollar terms or as percentages. The three described here are gross, trade, and net profit margins.

Gross Margin

Gross margin, or gross profit, is the difference between total sales revenue and total cost of goods sold, or, on a per-unit basis, the difference between unit selling price and unit cost of goods sold. Gross margin may be expressed in dollar terms or as a percentage.

Total Gross Margin	Dollar Amount	Percentage
Net sales	$100	100%
Cost of goods sold	−40	−40
Gross profit margin	$60	60%
Unit Gross Margin		
Unit sales price	$1.00	100%
Unit cost of goods sold	−0.40	−40
Unit gross profit margin	$0.60	60%

Gross margin analysis is a useful tool because it implicitly includes unit selling prices of products or services, unit costs, and unit volume. A decrease in gross margin is of immediate concern to a marketing manager because such a change has a direct impact on profits, providing that other expenditures remain unchanged. Changes in total gross margin should be examined in depth to determine whether the change was brought about by fluctuations in unit volume, changes in unit price or unit cost of goods sold, or a modification in the sales mix of the firm's products or services.

Trade Margin

Trade margin is the difference between unit sales price and unit cost at each level of a marketing channel (for example, manufacturer → wholesaler → retailer). A trade margin is frequently referred to as a *markup* or *mark-on* by channel members, and it is often expressed as a percentage.

Trade margins are occasionally confusing, since the margin percentage can be computed on the basis of cost or selling price. Consider the following example. Suppose a retailer purchases an item for $10 and sells it at a price of $20—that is, a $10 margin. What is the retailer's margin percentage?

Retailer margin as a percentage of cost is

$$\frac{\$10}{\$10} \times 100 = 100 \text{ percent}$$

Retailer margin as a percentage of selling price is

$$\frac{\$10}{\$20} \times 100 = 50 \text{ percent}$$

Differences in margin percentages show the importance of knowing the base (cost or selling price) on which the margin percentage is determined. *Trade margin percentages are usually determined on the basis of selling price*, but practices do vary among firms and industries.

Trade margins affect the pricing of individual items in two ways. First, suppose a wholesaler purchases an item for $2.00 and seeks to achieve a 30 percent margin on this item based on selling price. What would be the selling price?

$$\$2.00 = 70 \text{ percent of selling price}$$

or

$$\text{Selling price} = \$2.00/0.70 = \$2.86$$

Second, suppose a manufacturer suggests a retail list price of $6.00 on an item for ultimate resale to the consumer. The item will be sold through retailers whose policy is to obtain a 40 percent margin based on selling price. For what price must the manufacturer sell the item to the retailer?

$$\frac{x}{\$6.00} = 40 \text{ percent of selling price}$$

where x is the retailer margin. Solving for x indicates that the retailer must obtain $2.40 for this item. Therefore, the manufacturer must set the price to the retailer at $3.60 ($6.00 − $2.40).

The manufacturer's problem of suggesting a price for ultimate resale to the consumer becomes more complex as the number of intermediaries between the manufacturer and the final consumer increases. This complexity can be illustrated by expanding the above example to include a wholesaler between the manufacturer and retailer. The retailer receives a 40 percent margin on the sales price. If the retailer must receive $2.40 per unit, the wholesaler must sell the item for $3.60 per unit. In order for the wholesaler to receive a 20 percent margin, for what price must the manufacturer sell the unit to the wholesaler?

$$\frac{x}{\$3.60} = 20 \text{ percent wholesaler margin on selling price}$$

where x is the wholesaler margin. Solving for x shows that the wholesaler's margin is $0.72 for this item. Therefore, the manufacturer must set the price to the wholesaler at $2.88.

This example shows that a manager must work backward from the ultimate price to the consumer through the marketing channel to arrive at a product's selling price. Assuming that the manufacturer's cost of goods sold is $2.00, we can calculate the following margins, which incidentally show the manufacturer's gross margin of 30.6 percent.

	Unit Cost of Goods Sold	Unit Selling Price	Gross Margin as a Percentage of Selling Price
Manufacturer	$2.00	$2.88	30.6%
Wholesaler	2.88	3.60	20.0
Retailer	3.60	6.00	40.0
Consumer	6.00		

Net Profit Margin (Before Taxes)

The last margin to be considered is the net profit margin before taxes. This margin is expressed as a dollar figure or a percentage. *Net profit margin* is the remainder after cost of goods sold, other variable costs, and fixed costs have been subtracted from sales revenue. The place of net profit margin in an organization's income statement is illustrated by the following:

	Dollar Amount	Percentage
Net sales	$100,000	100%
Cost of goods sold	−30,000	−30
Gross profit margin	$ 70,000	70%
Selling expenses	−20,000	−20
Fixed expenses	−40,000	−40
Net profit margin	$ 10,000	10%

Net profit margin dollars represent a major source of funding for the organization. As will be shown later, net profit influences the working capital position of the organization; hence, the dollar amount ultimately affects the organization's ability to pay its cost of goods sold plus its selling and administrative expenses. Furthermore, net profit also affects the organization's cash flow position.

 # CONTRIBUTION ANALYSIS

Contribution analysis is an important concept in marketing management. *Contribution* is the difference between total sales revenue and total variable costs, or, on a per-unit basis, the difference between unit selling price and unit variable cost. Contribution analysis is particularly useful in assessing relationships among costs, prices, and volumes of products and services with respect to profit.

Break-Even Analysis

Break-even analysis is one of the simplest applications of contribution analysis. *Break-even analysis* identifies the unit or dollar sales volume at which an organization neither makes a profit nor incurs a loss. Stated in equation form:

$$\text{Total revenue} = \text{total variable costs} + \text{total fixed costs}$$

Because break-even analysis identifies the level of sales volume at which total costs (fixed and variable) and total revenue are equal, it is a valuable tool for evaluating an organization's profit goals and assessing the riskiness of actions.

Break-even analysis requires three pieces of information: (1) an estimate of unit variable costs, (2) an estimate of the total dollar fixed costs to produce and market the product or service unit (note that only relevant costs apply), and (3) the selling price for each product or service unit.

The formula for determining the number of units required to break even is as follows:

$$\text{Unit break-even volume} = \frac{\text{total dollar fixed costs}}{\text{unit selling price} - \text{unit variable costs}}$$

The denominator in this formula (unit selling price minus unit variable costs) is called *contribution per unit*. Contribution per unit is the dollar amount that each unit sold "contributes" to the payment of fixed costs.

Consider the following example. A manufacturer plans to sell a product for $5.00. The unit variable costs are $2.00, and total fixed costs assigned to the product are $30,000. How many units must be sold to break even?

$$\text{Fixed costs} = \$30,000$$
$$\text{Contribution per unit} = \text{unit selling price} - \text{unit variable cost}$$
$$= \$5 - \$2 = \$3$$
$$\text{Unit break-even volume} = \$30,000/\$3 = 10,000 \text{ units}$$

This example shows that for every unit sold at $5.00, $2.00 is used to pay variable costs. The balance of $3.00 "contributes" to fixed costs.

A related question is what the manufacturer's dollar sales volume must be to break even. The manager need only multiply unit break-even volume by the unit selling price to determine the dollar break-even volume: 10,000 units $\times$ $5 = $50,000.

A manager can calculate a dollar break-even point directly without first computing unit break-even volume. First, the *contribution margin* must be determined from the formula:

$$\text{Contribution margin} = \frac{\text{unit selling price} - \text{unit variable cost}}{\text{unit selling price}}$$

Using the figures from our example, we find that the contribution margin is 60 percent:

$$\text{Contribution margin} = \frac{\$5 - \$2}{\$5} = 60 \text{ percent}$$

Then the dollar break-even point is computed as follows:

$$\text{Break-even dollar volume} = \frac{\text{total fixed costs}}{\text{contribution margin}} = \frac{\$30,000}{0.60} = \$50,000$$

In many cases it is useful to develop a graphic representation of a break-even analysis. Exhibit 2.1 provides a visual solution to the problem posed previously. The horizontal line at $30,000 represents fixed costs. The upward-sloping line beginning at $30,000 represents the total cost, which is equal to the sum of fixed plus variable costs. This line has a slope equal to $2.00—each unit increase in volume results in a $2.00 increase in the total cost. The upward-sloping line beginning at zero represents revenue and has a slope of $5.00—each unit increase in sales produces a $5.00 increase in revenue. The distance between the revenue line and the total cost line represents dollars of profit (above the break-even point) or loss (below the break-even point).

EXHIBIT 2.1   **Break-Even Analysis Chart**

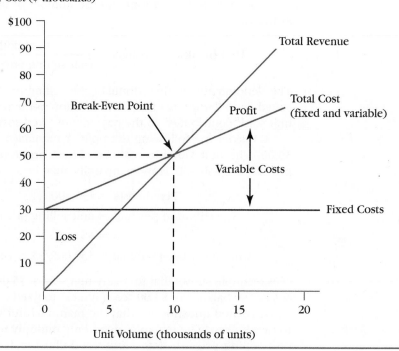

Sensitivity Analysis

Contribution analysis can be applied in a number of different ways, depending on the manager's needs. The following illustrations show how the break-even points in our example can be varied by changing selling price, variable costs, and fixed costs.

1. What would break-even volume be if fixed costs were increased to $40,000 while the selling price and variable costs remained unchanged?

Fixed costs = $40,000

Contribution per unit = $3.00

Unit break-even volume = $40,000/$3.00 = 13,333 units

Dollar break-even volume = $40,000/0.60 = $66,667

Note that the difference between the dollar break-even volume calculated from the contribution margin and the result of simply multiplying unit selling price by unit break-even volume (13,333 $\times$ $5.00 = $66,665) is due to rounding.

2. What would break-even volume be if selling price were dropped from $5.00 to $4.00 while fixed and variable costs remained unchanged?

Fixed costs = $30,000

Contribution per unit = $2.00

Unit break-even volume = $30,000/$2.00 = 15,000 units

Dollar break-even volume = $30,000/0.50 = $60,000

3. Finally, what would break-even volume be if the variable cost per unit were reduced to $1.50, selling price remained at $5.00, and fixed costs were $30,000?

Fixed costs = $30,000

Contribution per unit = $3.50

Unit break-even volume = $30,000/$3.50 = 8,571 units

Dollar break-even volume = $30,000/0.70 = $42,857

Contribution Analysis and Profit Impact

No manager is content to operate at the break-even point in unit or dollar sales volume. Profits are necessary for the continued operation of an organization. A modified break-even analysis is used to incorporate a profit goal.

To modify the break-even formula to incorporate a dollar profit goal, we need only regard the profit goal as an additional fixed cost, as follows:

$$\text{Unit volume to achieve dollar profit goal} = \frac{\text{total dollar fixed costs} + \text{dollar profit goal}}{\text{contribution per unit}}$$

Suppose a firm has fixed costs of $200,000 budgeted for a product or service, the unit selling price is $25.00, and the unit variable costs are $10.00. How many units must be sold to achieve a dollar profit goal of $20,000?

Fixed costs + profit goal = $200,000 + $20,000 = $220,000

Contribution per unit = $25 − $10 = $15

Unit volume to achieve dollar profit goal = $220,000/$15

= 14,667 units

Many firms specify their profit goal as a percentage of sales rather than as a dollar amount ("Our profit goal is a 20 percent profit on sales"). This objective can be incorporated into the break-even formula by subtracting the profit goal from the contribution-per-unit. If the goal is to achieve a 20 percent profit on sales, each dollar of sales must "contribute" $0.20 to profit. In our example, each unit sold for $25.00 must contribute $5.00 to profit (0.20 × $25.00). The break-even formula incorporating a percent profit on sales goal is as follows:

$$\text{Unit volume to achieve profit goal} = \frac{\text{total dollar fixed costs}}{\text{contribution per unit} - \text{unit profit goal}}$$

The unit volume break-even point to achieve a 20 percent profit goal is 20,000 units:

$$\text{Fixed costs} = \$200,000$$
$$\text{Contribution per unit} - \text{unit profit goal} = \$25 - \$10 - \$5 = \$10$$
$$\text{Unit volume to achieve profit goal} = \$200,000/\$10$$
$$= 20,000 \text{ units}$$

Multiple Product Break-Even Analysis

Break-even analysis can be extended to situations that involve multiple products and services. In these situations, a manager will need to determine a sales mix. A *sales mix* is the relative combination of products or services sold by a company.

For example, suppose a company intends to simultaneously introduce a deluxe model and an economy model of a new product. The deluxe model has a unit selling price of $1,000 and a unit variable cost of $500. Therefore, the deluxe model contribution per unit is $500. The economy model has a unit selling price of $500 and a unit variable cost of $300. The contribution per unit for the economy model is $200. Suppose further that the company expects to sell three economy models for every one deluxe model. The expected sales mix is therefore 3 to 1. The introductory marketing program expenditure for the two models is $825,000 and is a fixed cost.

A manager can determine the unit break-even volume given the information provided. First, the weighted average contribution per unit must be calculated based on the sales mix. In this example, the weighted average contribution per unit is $275 ($1,100 ÷ 4 = $275):

Model	Mix	×	Unit Contribution	=	Total Contribution
Economy	3	×	$200	=	$ 600
Deluxe	1	×	$500	=	$ 500
Total	4				$1,100

Next, the break-even formula for a single product can be applied. The total number of deluxe and economy model units needed to be sold to break even is 3,000:

$$\text{Unit break-even volume} = \frac{\$825,000}{\$275} = 3,000 \text{ units}$$

This unit break-even volume consists of 2,250 economy models and 750 deluxe models based on the 3 to 1 sales mix.

Break-even dollar sales can be calculated by multiplying the unit break-even volume (3,000) by the weighted average unit price of $625 [(3 × $500) + (1 × $1,000) ÷ 4]. The dollar break-even volume is 3,000 units × $625 = $1,875,000.

Contribution Analysis and Market Size

An important consideration in contribution analysis is the relationship of break-even unit or dollar volume to market size. Consider the situation in which a manager has conducted a break-even analysis and found the unit volume break-even point to be 50,000 units. This number has meaning only when compared with the potential size of the market segment sought. If the market potential is 100,000 units, the manager's product or service must capture 50 percent of the market sought to break even. An important question to be resolved is whether such a percentage can be achieved. A manager can assess the feasibility of a venture by comparing the break-even volume with market size and market-capture percentage.

Contribution Analysis and Performance Measurement

A second application of contribution analysis lies in performance measurement. For example, a marketing manager may wish to examine the performance of products. Consider an organization with two products, X and Y. A description of each product's financial performance follows:

	Product X (10,000 volume)	*Product Y* (20,000 volume)	*Total* (30,000 volume)
Unit price	$ 10	$ 3	
Sales revenue	100,000	60,000	$160,000
Unit variable cost	4	1.50	
Total variable cost	40,000	30,000	70,000
Unit contribution	6	1.50	
Total contribution	60,000	30,000	90,000
Fixed costs	45,000	10,000	55,000
Net profit	$ 15,000	$20,000	$ 35,000

The net profit figure shows that Product Y is more profitable than Product X. Product X is four times more profitable than Product Y on a unit-contribution basis, however, and generates twice the contribution dollars to overhead. The difference in profitability comes from the allocation of fixed costs to the products. In measuring performance, it is important to consider which products contribute most heavily to the organization's total fixed costs ($55,000 in this example) and then to total profit.

Should a manager look only at net profit, a decision might be made to drop Product X. Product Y would then have to cover total fixed costs, however. If the fixed costs remain at $55,000 and only Product Y is sold, this organization will experience a *net loss* of $25,000, assuming no change in Product Y volume.

Assessment of Cannibalization

A third application of contribution analysis is in the assessment of cannibalization effects. Cannibalization is the process by which one product or service sold by a firm gains a portion of its revenue by diverting sales from another product or service also sold by the firm. For example, sales of Brand X's new gel toothpaste may be at the expense of sales of Brand X's existing opaque white toothpaste. The problem facing a marketing manager is to assess the financial effect of cannibalization.

Consider the following data:

	Existing Opaque White Toothpaste	New Gel Toothpaste
Unit selling price	$1.00	$1.10
Unit variable costs	−0.20	−0.40
Unit contribution	$0.80	$0.70

The gel toothpaste can be sold at a slightly higher price, given its formulation and taste, but the variable costs are also higher. Hence, the gel toothpaste has a lower contribution per unit. Therefore, for every unit of the gel toothpaste sold instead of a unit of the opaque white toothpaste, the firm "loses" $0.10. Suppose further that the company expects to sell 1 million units of the new gel toothpaste in the first year after introduction and that, of that amount, 500,000 units will be diverted from the opaque white toothpaste, of which the company had expected to sell 1 million units. The task of the marketing manager is to determine how the introduction of the new gel toothpaste will affect Brand X's total contribution dollars.

One approach to assessing the financial impact of cannibalization is shown here:

1. Brand X expects to lose $0.10 for each unit diverted from the opaque white toothpaste to the gel toothpaste.

2. Given that 500,000 units will be cannibalized from the opaque white toothpaste, the total contribution *lost* is $50,000 ($0.10 × 500,000 units).

3. However, the new gel toothpaste will sell an additional 500,000 units at a contribution per unit of $0.70, which means that $350,000 ($0.70 × 500,000 units) in additional contribution will be generated.

4. Therefore, the net financial effect is a positive increase in contribution dollars of $300,000 ($350,000 − $50,000).

Another approach to assessing the cannibalization effect is as follows:

1. The opaque white toothpaste alone had been expected to sell 1 million units with a unit contribution of $0.80. Therefore, contribution dollars without the gel would equal $800,000 ($0.80 × 1,000,000 units).

2. The gel toothpaste is expected to sell 1 million units with a unit contribution of $0.70.

3. Given the cannibalism rate of 50 percent (that is, one-half of the gel's volume is diverted from the opaque white toothpaste), the combined contribution can be calculated as follows:

Product	Unit Volume	Unit Contribution	Contribution Dollars
Opaque white toothpaste	500,000	$0.80	$ 400,000
Gel toothpaste:			
Cannibalized volume	500,000	0.70	350,000
Incremental volume	500,000	0.70	350,000
Total	1,500,000		$1,100,000
Less original forecast volume for opaque white toothpaste	1,000,000	0.80	800,000
Total	+500,000		+$ 300,000

Both approaches arrive at the same conclusion: Brand X will benefit by $300,000 from the introduction of the gel toothpaste. The manager should use whichever approach he or she is more comfortable with in an analytic sense.

It should be emphasized, however, that the incremental fixed costs associated with advertising and sales promotion or any additions or changes in manufacturing capacity must be considered to complete the analysis. If the fixed costs approximate or exceed $300,000, the new product should be viewed in a very different light.

LIQUIDITY

Liquidity refers to an organization's ability to meet short-term (usually within a budget year) financial obligations. A key measure of an organization's liquidity position is its working capital. *Working capital* is the dollar value of an organization's *current assets* (such as cash, accounts receivable, prepaid expenses, inventory) *minus* the dollar value of *current liabilities* (such as short-term accounts payable for goods and services, income taxes).

A manager should be aware of the impact of marketing actions on working capital. Marketing expenditures precede sales volume; therefore, cash outlays for marketing efforts reduce current assets. If marketing expenditures cannot be met out of cash, accounts payable are incurred. In either case, working capital is reduced. In a positive vein, a marketing manager's creation of sales volume, with corresponding increases in net profit, contributes to working capital. Since the timing of marketing expenditures and sales volume is often lagged, a marketing manager must be wary of marketing efforts that unnecessarily deplete working capital and must assess the likelihood of potential sales, given a specified expenditure level.

OPERATING LEVERAGE

A financial concept closely akin to break-even analysis is operating leverage. *Operating leverage* refers to the extent to which fixed costs and variable costs are used in the production and marketing of products and services. Firms that have high total fixed costs relative to total variable costs are defined as having high operating leverage. Examples of firms with high operating leverage include airlines and heavy-equipment manufacturers. Firms with low total fixed costs relative to total variable costs are defined as having low operating leverage. Firms typically having low operating leverage include residential contractors and wholesale distributors.

The higher a firm's operating leverage, the faster its total profits will increase once sales exceed break-even volume. By the same token, however, those firms with high operating leverage will incur losses at a faster rate once sales volume falls below the break-even point.

Exhibit 2.2 illustrates the effect of operating leverage on profit. The base case shows two firms that have identical break-even sales volumes. The cost structures

| EXHIBIT 2.2 | Effect of Operating Leverage on Profit |

	Base Case		10% Increase in Sales		10% Decrease in Sales	
	High-Fixed-Cost Firm	High-Variable-Cost Firm	High-Fixed-Cost Firm	High-Variable-Cost Firm	High-Fixed-Cost Firm	High-Variable-Cost Firm
Sales	$100,000	$100,000	$110,000	$110,000	$90,000	$90,000
Variable costs	20,000	80,000	22,000	88,000	18,000	72,000
Fixed costs	80,000	20,000	80,000	20,000	80,000	20,000
Profit	$ 0	$ 0	$ 8,000	$ 2,000	($ 8,000)	($ 2,000)

of the two firms differ, however, with one having high fixed and low variable costs and the other having low fixed and high variable costs. Note that when sales volume is increased 10 percent, the firm with high fixed and low variable costs achieves a much higher profit than the firm with low fixed and high variable costs. When sales volume declines, however, just the opposite is true. That is, the firm with high fixed and low variable costs incurs losses at a faster rate than the firm with high variable and low fixed costs once sales fall below the break-even point.

The message of operating leverage should be clear from this example. Firms with high operating leverage benefit more from sales gains than do firms with low operating leverage. At the same time, firms with high operating leverage are more sensitive to sales-volume declines, because losses will be incurred at a faster rate. Knowledge of a firm's cost structure will, therefore, prove valuable in assessing the gains and losses from changes in sales volume brought about by marketing efforts.

 ## DISCOUNTED CASH FLOW

Another useful concept from finance is discounted cash flow. Discounted cash flow incorporates the theory of the time value of money, or present-value analysis. The idea behind the present value of money is that a dollar received next year is not equivalent to a dollar received today because the use of money has a value reflected by risk, inflation, and opportunity cost. To illustrate, if $500 can be invested today at 10 percent, $550 will be received a year later ($500 + 10% of $500). In other words, $550 to be received next year has a present value of $500 if 10 percent can be earned ($550/1.10 = $500). Following this line of reasoning, the estimated results of an investment (e.g., a business) can be stated as a cash equivalent at the present time (i.e., its present value). *Discounted cash flows* are future cash flows expressed in terms of their present value.

The discounted cash flow technique employs this reasoning by evaluating the present value of a business's *net cash flow* (cash inflows minus cash outflows). A simplified view of cash flow is "cash flow from operations," which is net income plus depreciation charges, because depreciation is a noncash charge against sales to determine net income. The present value of a stream of cash flows is obtained by selecting an interest or discount rate at which these flows are to be valued, or discounted, and the timing of each. The interest or discount rate is often defined by the opportunity *cost of capital*—the cost of earnings opportunities forgone by investing in a business with its attendant risk as opposed to investing in risk-free securities such as U.S. Treasury bills.

A simple application of discounted cash flow analysis illustrates the mechanics involved. Suppose, for example, that a firm is considering investing $105,000 in one of two businesses. The firm has forecast cash flows for each business over the next five years. The discount rate adopted by the firm is 15 percent. Given the discount rate of 15 percent, the cash flow when the investment is made is a negative $105,000 (no cash inflows, only outflows). The first-year cash flow for Business A is discounted by the factor $1/(1 + 0.15)^1$ or $25,000 \times 0.870 = $21,750. The second-year cash flow for Business A is discounted by the factor $1/(1 + 0.15)^2$ or $35,000 \times 0.756 = $26,460, and so forth. Exhibit 2.3 shows the complete analysis for Businesses A and B for the five-year planning horizon.

Three points are of particular interest. First, an important series of numbers is the *cumulative cash flow*. This series shows that the cumulative cash flows from Business B are greater than from Business A. Second, the *payback period* is two years for Business B, as opposed to about three years for Business A. In other words, Business B will recover its investment sooner than will Business A. Finally, the discounted cash flows incorporating the time value of money

EXHIBIT 2.3	Application of Discounted Cash Flow Analysis with a 15 Percent Discount Factor						
		Business A			Business B		
Year	Discount Factor	Cash Flow	Cumulative Cash Flow	Discounted Cash Flow	Cash Flow	Cumulative Cash Flow	Discounted Cash Flow
0	1.000	($105,000)	($105,000)	($105,000)	($105,000)	($105,000)	($105,000)
1	0.870	25,000	(80,000)	21,750	50,000	(55,000)	43,500
2	0.756	35,000	(45,000)	26,460	55,000	0	41,580
3	0.658	50,000	5,000	32,900	60,000	60,000	39,480
4	0.572	70,000	75,000	40,040	65,000	125,000	37,180
5	0.497	90,000	165,000	44,730	70,000	195,000	34,790
Totals				$ 60,880			$ 91,530

are clearly indicated. Business A will produce a higher cash flow in later years than will Business B. However, the present value of these cash flows, when discounted, is less than the value of the cash flows that Business B will produce.

From a decision-making perspective, both businesses produce a positive net present value. This is important given the decision rule when interpreting net present value: An investment should be accepted if the net present value is positive and rejected if it is negative. In which business should the firm invest its capital? Assuming that the firm wishes to create value for its shareholders, the option with the higher net present value (Business B) is preferred.

A valuable characteristic of present-value analysis is that the discount factors and discounted cash are additive. If the projected cash flows from an investment are equal over a specified time period, summing the discount factors for each of the time periods (say three years) and multiplying this figure by the annual cash flow estimate will give the present value.

Suppose, for example, that a firm can expect a constant cash flow of $10 million per year for three years, and the discount rate is 15 percent. The present value of this cash flow can be computed as follows (in millions of dollars):

$$0.870 \times \$10 = \$8.70$$
$$0.756 \times \$10 = \$7.56$$
$$0.658 \times \$10 = \$6.58$$
$$\overline{2.284 \times \$10 = \$22.84}$$

Any basic finance textbook covers discounted cash flow in depth and should be consulted for further study. As a word of caution, the application of discounted cash flow analysis is deceptively simple. Determining appropriate discount rates and projecting future cash flows is not an easy task. Conservative estimates and the use of several "what if" scenarios will ensure that the discounted cash flow technique will highlight investment opportunities that create value for the firm and its shareholders.

 ## CUSTOMER LIFETIME VALUE

Many contemporary marketing managers apply present-value analysis to identify the financial consequences of an organization's long-term customer relationships. They do this by estimating customer lifetime value. *Customer lifetime value* (CLV) is the present value of future cash flows arising from a customer relationship. Recall from the previous discussion on present-value analysis, the present value of any stream of future cash flows is designed to measure the single lump-sum dollar value today of future cash flows. CLV is simply that lump-sum dollar value of a customer relationship. Once known, the estimated CLV sets the upper bound for how much a company would be willing to pay to attract and retain a customer.

A variety of approaches are used to estimate CLV. The approach described here includes the basic variables used and their relationships in arriving at CLV. The CLV calculation requires three pieces of information: (1) the per-period (month or year) cash margin per customer **($M,** defined as sales revenue minus variable costs and other traceable cash expenditures necessary to keep the customer; (2) the retention rate (r), defined as the per-period probability that the customer will be retained, and (3) the interest rate (i) used for discounting future cash flows. A formula for calculating CLV, assuming a constant per-period margin, a constant per-period retention rate, and an infinite time horizon, can be written as follows:

$$\text{Customer lifetime value} = \$M \left[\frac{1}{1+i-r} \right]$$

These simplifying assumptions are made for expository purposes. More complex CLV formulas incorporate changing margins and retention rates per period and limited (5-year or 10-year) time horizons. Their description is beyond the scope of this discussion. However, if per-period margins vary little across periods, per period retention rates are 80 percent or less, and the interest rate for discounting future cash flows is 20 percent or less, the simplifying assumptions result in a CLV estimate that is close to that derived from more complex CLV formulations.

To illustrate the CLV calculation, consider a credit card company. It has a cardmember with an annual margin of $2,000. The typical retention rate for cardmembers is 80 percent. The applicable interest rate to discount future cash flows is 10 percent. Therefore, this cardmember has a CLV of $6,666.67:

$$\text{CLV} = \$2,000 \left[\frac{1}{1+0.10-0.80} \right] = \$6,666.67$$

If the credit card company increases the cardmember retention rate to 90 percent (which represents a 12.5 percent increase), then the CLV would almost double to $10,000.00:

$$\text{CLV} = \$2,000 \left[\frac{1}{1+0.10-0.90} \right] = \$10,000.00$$

This example demonstrates the favorable financial effect of increasing the retention rate, or loyalty, among profitable customers.

Suppose the credit card company observes that cardmember activity grows over time and the margin increases at a constant rate (g) of 6 percent per year. The CLV formula can be modified slightly to include this constant margin growth rate:

$$\begin{array}{l} \text{Customer lifetime} \\ \text{value with constant} = \$M \left[\frac{1}{1+i-r-g} \right] \\ \text{margin growth} \end{array}$$

Therefore, for a cardmember with an initial $2,000 margin that grows at a constant rate of 6 percent per year, an 80 percent retention rate, and a company discount rate of 10 percent, the CLV is $8,333.33:

$$\text{CLV (constant margin growth)} = \$2,000 \left[\frac{1}{1+0.10-0.80-0.60} \right] = \$8,333.33$$

This example illustrates the favorable financial effect of increasing business from a profitable customer.

Marketing efforts play a major role in two of the three determinants of CLV: (1) customer margin, including margin growth, and (2) customer retention. For example, margin results from the price(s) paid for a company's offering(s) as well as the amount purchased. Companies attempt to increase margin by cross-selling related offerings to customers and up-selling; that is, selling customers more expensive offerings. Retention obviously results from customer satisfaction with a company's offerings. In addition, companies often use loyalty programs that reward loyal customers for buying repeatedly and in substantial amounts.

Some companies modify the CLV formula to include the cost of acquiring a customer. In this instance, the acquisition cost (AC) is subtracted to arrive at a net present value CLV as shown below:

$$\text{Customer lifetime value including acquisition cost} = \$M\left[\frac{1}{1+i-r}\right] - AC$$

Even though the CLV calculation is straightforward, its application requires considerable insight into a company's customer relationships. Per-period margin and retention rates can be determined either through analysis of the company's customer database or industry norms. Still, the task is challenging. For example, while the revenue from a customer is relatively easy to identify, tracing acquisition and retention cash expenditures to a specific customer is often difficult.

 # PREPARING A PRO FORMA INCOME STATEMENT

Because marketing managers are accountable for the profit impact of their actions, they must translate their strategies and tactics into pro forma, or projected, income statements. A pro forma income statement displays projected revenues, budgeted expenses, and estimated net profit for an organization, product, or service during a specific planning period, usually a year. Pro forma income statements include a sales forecast and a listing of variable and fixed costs that can be programmed or committed.

Pro forma income statements can be prepared in different ways and reflect varying levels of specificity. Exhibit 2.4 on page 50 shows a typical layout for a pro forma income statement consisting of six major categories or line items:

1. *Sales*—forecasted unit volume times unit selling price.

2. *Cost of goods sold*—costs incurred in buying or producing products and services. Generally speaking, these costs are constant per unit within certain volume ranges and vary with total unit volume.

3. *Gross margin* (sometimes called *gross profit*)—represents the remainder after cost of goods sold has been subtracted from sales.

4. *Marketing expenses*—generally, programmed expenses budgeted to produce sales. Advertising expenses are typically fixed. Sales expenses can be fixed, such as a salesperson's salary, or variable, such as sales commissions. Freight or delivery expenses are typically constant per unit and vary with total unit volume.

5. *General and administrative expenses*—generally, committed fixed costs for the planning period, which cannot be avoided if the organization is to operate. These costs are frequently called overhead.

6. *Net income before (income) taxes* (often called *net profit before taxes*)—the remainder after all costs have been subtracted from sales.

EXHIBIT 2.4	Pro Forma Income Statement for the 12-Month Period Ended December 31, 2012		
Sales			$1,000,000
Cost of goods sold			500,000
Gross margin			$ 500,000
Marketing expenses			
Sales expenses		$170,000	
Advertising expenses		90,000	
Freight or delivery expenses		40,000	300,000
General and administrative expenses			
Administrative salaries		$120,000	
Depreciation on buildings and equipment		20,000	
Interest expense		5,000	
Property taxes and insurance		5,000	
Other administrative expenses		5,000	155,000
Net profit before (income) tax			$ 45,000

A pro forma income statement reflects a marketing manager's expectations (sales) given certain inputs (costs). This means that a manager must think specifically about customer response to strategies and tactics and focus attention on the organization's financial objectives of profitability and growth when preparing a pro forma income statement.

 ## SUMMARY

This chapter provides an overview of basic accounting and financial concepts. A word of caution is necessary, however. Financial analysis of marketing actions is a necessary but insufficient criterion for justifying marketing programs. A careful analysis of other variables impinging on the decision at hand is required. Thus, judgment enters the picture. "Numbers" serve only to complement general marketing analysis skills and are not an end in themselves. In this regard, it is wise to consider some words of Albert Einstein: "Not everything that counts can be counted, and not everything that can be counted counts."

EXERCISES

1. Executives of Studio Recordings, Inc. produced the latest compact disc by the Starshine Sisters Band, titled *Sunshine/Moonshine*. The following cost information pertains to the new CD:

CD package and disc (direct material and labor)	$1.25/CD
Songwriters' royalties	$0.35/CD
Recording artists' royalties	$1.00/CD
Advertising and promotion	$275,000
Studio Recordings, Inc.'s overhead	$250,000
Selling price to CD distributor	$9.00

Calculate the following:

 a. Contribution per CD unit

 b. Break-even volume in CD units and dollars

 c. Net profit if 1 million CDs are sold

 d. Necessary CD unit volume to achieve a $200,000 profit

2. Video Concepts, Inc. (VCI) markets video equipment and film through a variety of retail outlets. Presently, VCI is faced with a decision as to whether it should obtain the distribution rights to an unreleased film titled *Touch of Orange*. If this film is distributed by VCI directly to large retailers, VCI's investment in the project would be $150,000. VCI estimates the total market for the film to be 100,000 units. Other data available are as follows:

Cost of distribution rights for film	$125,000
Label design	5,000
Package design	10,000
Advertising	35,000
Reproduction of copies (per 1,000)	4,000
Manufacture of labels and packaging (per 1,000)	500
Royalties (per 1,000)	500

VCI's suggested retail price for the film is $20 per unit. The retailer's margin is 40 percent.

 a. What is VCI's unit contribution and contribution margin?

 b. What is the break-even point in units? In dollars?

 c. What share of the market would the film have to achieve to earn a 20 percent return on VCI's investment the first year?

3. The group product manager for ointments at American Therapeutic Corporation was reviewing price and promotion alternatives for two products: Rash-Away and Red-Away. Both products were designed to reduce skin irritation, but Red-Away was primarily a cosmetic treatment whereas Rash-Away also included a compound that eliminated the rash.

 The price and promotion alternatives recommended for the two products by their respective brand managers included the possibility of using additional promotion or a price reduction to stimulate sales volume. A volume, price, and cost summary for the two products follows:

	Rash-Away	*Red-Away*
Unit price	$2.00	$1.00
Unit variable costs	1.40	0.25
Unit contribution	$0.60	$0.75
Unit volume	1,000,000 units	1,500,000 units

Both brand managers included a recommendation to either reduce price by 10 percent or invest an incremental $150,000 in advertising.

 a. What absolute increase in unit sales and dollar sales will be necessary to recoup the incremental increase in advertising expenditures for Rash-Away? For Red-Away?

 b. How many additional sales dollars must be produced to cover each $1.00 of incremental advertising for Rash-Away? For Red-Away?

 c. What absolute increase in unit sales and dollar sales will be necessary to maintain the level of total contribution dollars if the price of each product is reduced by 10 percent?

4. After spending $300,000 for research and development, chemists at Diversified Citrus Industries have developed a new breakfast drink. The drink, called Zap, will provide the consumer with twice the amount of vitamin C currently available in breakfast drinks. Zap will be packaged in an 8-ounce can and will be introduced to the breakfast drink market, which is estimated to be equivalent to 21 million 8-ounce cans nationally.

   One major management concern is the lack of funds available for marketing. Accordingly, management has decided to use newspapers (rather than television) to promote Zap in the introductory year and distribute Zap in major metropolitan areas that account for 65 percent of U.S. breakfast drink volume. Newspaper advertising will carry a coupon that will entitle the consumer to receive $0.20 off the price of the first can purchased. The retailer will receive the regular margin and be reimbursed for redeemed coupons by Diversified Citrus Industries. Past experience indicates that for every five cans sold during the introductory year, one coupon will be returned. The cost of the newspaper advertising campaign (excluding coupon returns) will be $250,000. Other fixed overhead costs are expected to be $90,000 per year.

   Management has decided that the suggested retail price to the consumer for the 8-ounce can will be $0.50. The only unit variable costs for the product are $0.18 for materials and $0.06 for labor. The company intends to give retailers a margin of 20 percent off the suggested retail price and wholesalers a margin of 10 percent of the retailers' cost of the item.

   a. At what price will Diversified Citrus Industries be selling its product to wholesalers?

   b. What is the contribution per unit for Zap?

   c. What is the break-even unit volume in the first year?

   d. What is the first-year break-even share of market?

5. Video Concepts, Inc. (VCI) manufactures a line of DVD recorders (DVDs) that are distributed to large retailers. The line consists of three models of DVDs. The following data are available regarding the models:

Model	DVD Selling Price per Unit	Variable Cost per Unit	Demand/Year (units)
Model LX1	$175	$100	2,000
Model LX2	250	125	1,000
Model LX3	300	140	500

   VCI is considering the addition of a fourth model to its line of DVDs. This model would be sold to retailers for $375. The variable cost of this unit is $225. The demand for the new Model LX4 is estimated to be 300 units per year. Sixty percent of these unit sales of the new model is expected to come from other models already being manufactured by VCI (10 percent from Model LX1, 30 percent from Model LX2, and 60 percent from Model LX3). VCI will incur a fixed cost of $20,000 to add the new model to the line. Based on the preceding data, should VCI add the new Model LX4 to its line of VCRs? Why?

6. Max Leonard, vice president of Marketing for Dysk Computer, Inc., must decide whether to introduce a midpriced version of the firm's DC6900 personal computer product line—the DC6900-X. The DC6900-X would sell for $3,900, with unit variable costs of $1,800. Projections made by an independent marketing research firm indicate that the DC6900-X would achieve a sales volume of 500,000 units next year, in its first year

of commercialization. One-half of the first year's volume would come from competitors' personal computers and market growth. However, a consumer research study indicates that 30 percent of the DC6900-X sales volume would come from the higher-priced DC6900-Omega personal computer, which sells for $5,900 (with unit variable costs of $2,200). Another 20 percent of the DC6900-X sales volume would come from the economy-priced DC6900-Alpha personal computer, priced at $2,500 (with unit variable costs of $1,200). The DC6900-Omega unit volume is expected to be 400,000 units next year, and the DC6900-Alpha is expected to achieve a 600,000-unit sales level. The fixed costs of launching the DC6900-X have been forecast to be $2 million during the first year of commercialization. Should Mr. Leonard add the DC6900-X model to the line of personal computers? Why?

7. A sports nutrition company is examining whether a new high-performance sports drink should be added to its product line. A preliminary feasibility analysis indicated that the company would need to invest $17.5 million in a new manufacturing facility to produce and package the product. A financial analysis using sales and cost data supplied by marketing and production personnel indicated that the net cash flow (cash inflows minus cash outflows) would be $6.1 million in the first year of commercialization, $7.4 million in year 2, $7.0 million in year 3, and $5.5 million in year 4.

   Senior company executives were undecided whether to move forward with the development of the new product. They requested that a discounted cash flow analysis be performed using two different discount rates: 20 percent and 15 percent.

   a. Should the company proceed with development of the product if the discount rate is 20 percent? Why?

   b. Does the decision to proceed with development of the product change if the discount rate is 15 percent? Why?

8. Net-4-You is an Internet Service Provider that charges its 1 million customers $19.95 per month for its service. The company's variable costs are $0.50 per customer per month. In addition, the company spends $0.50 per month per customer, or $6 million annually, on a customer loyalty program designed to retain customers. As a result, the company's monthly customer retention rate was 78.8 percent. Net-4-You has a monthly discount rate of 1 percent.

   a. What is the customer lifetime value?

   b. Suppose the company wanted to increase its customers' monthly retention rate and decided to spend an additional $0.20 per month per customer to upgrade its loyalty program benefits. By how much must Net-4-You increase its monthly customer retention rate to avoid reducing customer lifetime value resulting from a lower customer margin?

9. The annual planning process at Century Office Systems, Inc. had been arduous but produced a number of important marketing initiatives for the next year. Most notably, company executives had decided to restructure its product-marketing team into two separate groups: (1) Corporate Office Systems and (2) Home Office Systems. Angela Blake was assigned responsibility for the Home Office Systems group, which would market the company's word-processing hardware and software for home and office-at-home use by individuals. Her marketing plan, which included a sales forecast for next year of $25 million, was the result of a detailed market

analysis and negotiations with individuals both inside and outside the company. Discussions with the sales director indicated that 40 percent of the company sales force would be dedicated to selling products of the Home Office Systems group. Sales representatives would receive a 15 percent commission on sales of home office systems. Under the new organizational structure, the Home Office Systems group would be charged with 40 percent of the budgeted sales force expenditure. The sales director's budget for salaries and fringe benefits of the sales force and noncommission selling costs for both the Corporate and Home Office Systems groups was $7.5 million.

The advertising and promotion budget contained three elements: trade magazine advertising, cooperative newspaper advertising with Century Office Systems, Inc. dealers, and sales promotion materials including product brochures, technical manuals, catalogs, and point-of-purchase displays. Trade magazine ads and sales promotion materials were to be developed by the company's advertising and public relations agency. Production and media placement costs were budgeted at $300,000. Cooperative advertising copy for both newspaper and radio use had budgeted production costs of $100,000. Century Office Systems, Inc.'s cooperative advertising allowance policy stated that the company would allocate 5 percent of company sales to dealers to promote its office systems. Dealers always used their complete cooperative advertising allowances.

Meetings with manufacturing and operations personnel indicated that the direct costs of material and labor and direct factory overhead to produce the Home Office System product line represented 50 percent of sales. The accounting department would assign $600,000 in indirect manufacturing overhead (for example, depreciation, maintenance) to the product line and $300,000 for administrative overhead (clerical, telephone, office space, and so forth). Freight for the product line would average 8 percent of sales.

Blake's staff consisted of two product managers and a marketing assistant. Salaries and fringe benefits for Ms. Blake and her staff were $250,000 per year.

a. Prepare a pro forma income statement for the Home Office Systems group given the information provided.

b. Prepare a pro forma income statement for the Home Office Systems group given annual sales of only $20 million.

c. At what level of dollar sales will the Home Office Systems group break even?

Chapter 3

Marketing Decision Making and Case Analysis

Skill in decision making is a prerequisite to being an effective marketing manager. Indeed, Nobel laureate Herbert Simon viewed managing and decision making as being one and the same.[1] Another management theorist, Peter Drucker, has said that the burden of decision making can be lessened and better decisions can result if a manager recognizes that "decision making is a rational and systematic process and that its organization is a definite sequence of steps, each of them in turn rational and systematic."[2]

One objective of this chapter is to introduce a systematic process for decision making; another is to introduce basic considerations in case analysis. Just as decision making and managing can be viewed as being identical in scope, so the decision-making process and case analysis go hand in hand. For this reason, many companies today use case studies when interviewing an applicant to assess his or her decision-making skills. They have found that the applicant's approach to the case demonstrates strategic thinking, analytical ability and judgment, along with a variety of communication skills, including listening, questioning, and dealing with confrontation.[3]

 ## DECISION-MAKING PROCESS

Although no simple formula exists that can ensure a correct solution to all problems at all times, use of a systematic decision-making process can increase the likelihood of arriving at better solutions.[4] The decision-making process described here is called DECIDE:[5]

Define the problem.

Enumerate the decision factors.

Consider relevant information.

Identify the best alternative.

Develop a plan for implementing the chosen alternative.

Evaluate the decision and the decision process.

A definition and a discussion of the implications of each step follow.

Define the Problem

The philosopher John Dewey observed that "a problem well defined is half solved." What this statement means in a marketing setting is that a well-defined problem outlines the framework within which a solution can be derived. This framework includes the *objectives* of the decision maker, a recognition of *constraints*, and a clearly articulated *success measure*, or goal, for assessing progress toward solving the problem.

Consider the situation faced by El Nacho Foods, a marketer of Mexican foods. The company had positioned its line of Mexican foods as a high-quality brand and used advertising effectively to convey that message. Shortly after the company's introduction of frozen dinners, two of its competitors began cutting the price of their frozen dinner entrees. The firm lost market share and sales as a result of these price reductions; this loss led to reductions in the contribution dollars available for advertising and sales promotion. How might the problem be defined in this situation? One definition of the problem leads to the question: "Should we reduce our price?" A much better definition of the problem leads one to ask: "How can we maintain our quality brand image (objective) and regain our lost market share (success measure), given limited funds for advertising and sales promotion (constraint)?"

The first problem definition asks for a response to an immediate issue facing the company. It does not articulate the broader and more important considerations of competitive positioning. Hence, the problem statement fails to capture the significance of the issue raised. The second definition provides a broader perspective on the immediate issue posed and allows the manager greater latitude in seeking solutions.

In a case study, the analyst is frequently given alternative courses of action to consider. The narrow approach to case analysis is simply to compare these different options. Such an approach often leads to the selection of Alternative A or Alternative B without regard to the significance of the choice in the broader context of the situation facing the company or the decision maker.

Enumerate the Decision Factors

Two sets of decision factors must be enumerated in the decision-making process: (1) *alternative courses of action* and (2) *uncertainties* in the competitive environment. Alternative courses of action are controllable decision factors because the decision maker has complete command of them. Alternatives are typically product-market strategies or changes in the various elements of the organization's marketing mix (described in Chapter 1). Uncertainties, on the other hand, are uncontrollable factors that the manager cannot influence. In a marketing context, they often include actions of competitors, market size, and buyer response to marketing action. Assumptions often have to be made concerning these factors. These assumptions need to be spelled out, particularly if they will influence the evaluation of alternative courses of action.

The experience of Cluett Peabody and Company, the maker of Arrow shirts, illustrates how the combination of an action and uncertainties can spell disaster. Arrow departed from its normal practice of selling classic men's shirts to offer a new line featuring bolder colors, busier patterns, and higher prices (action). The firm soon realized that men's tastes had changed to more conservative styles (environmental uncertainties). The result? The company posted a $4.5 million loss. According to the company president, "We tried to be exciting, and we really didn't look at the market."[6]

Case analysis provides an opportunity to relate alternatives to uncertainties, and these factors *must* be related if decision making is to be effective. No expected outcome, financial or otherwise, of a chosen course of action can realistically be considered apart from the environment into which it is introduced.

Consider Relevant Information

The third step in the decision-making process is the consideration of relevant information. *Relevant information*, like the relevant costs discussed in Chapter 2, consists of information that relates to the alternatives identified by the manager as being likely to affect future events. More specifically, relevant information might include characteristics of the industry, consumers, or competitive environment, characteristics of the organization (such as competitive strengths and position), and characteristics of the alternatives themselves.

Identifying relevant information is difficult both for the marketing manager and for the case analyst. There is frequently an overabundance of facts, figures, and viewpoints available in any decision-making setting. In fact, it has been said that "The truly successful managers and leaders of the [twenty-first] century will . . . be characterized not by how they can access information, but how they can access the most relevant information and differentiate it from the exponentially multiplying masses of nonrelevant information."[7] Determining what matters and what does not is a skill that is best gained through experience. Analyzing many and varied cases is one way to develop this skill.

Two notes of caution are necessary. First, the case analyst must resist the temptation to consider *everything* in a case as "fact." Many cases, including actual marketing situations, contain conflicting data. Part of the task in any case analysis is to exercise judgment in assessing the validity of the data presented. Second, in many instances relevant information must be created. An example of creating relevant information is the blending together of several pieces of data, as in the calculation of a simple break-even point.

It should be clear at this point that even though the consideration of relevant information is the third step in the decision-making process, relevant information will also affect the two previous steps. As the manager or case analyst becomes more deeply involved in considering and evaluating information, the problem definition may be modified or the decision factors may change.

Upon the conclusion of the first three steps, the manager or case analyst has completed a *situation analysis*. The situation analysis should produce an answer to the synoptic question, "Where are we now?" (Specific questions relating to situation analysis are found in Exhibit 3.4 on page 62.)

Identify the Best Alternative

Identifying the best alternative is the fourth step in the decision-making process. The selection of a course of action is not simply a matter of choosing Alternative A over other alternatives but, rather, of evaluating identified alternatives and the uncertainties apparent in the problem setting.

A framework for identifying the best alternative is *decision analysis,* which was introduced in Chapter 1. In its simplest form, decision analysis matches each alternative identified by the manager with the uncertainties existing in the environment and assigns a quantitative value to the outcome associated with each match. Managers implicitly use a decision tree and a payoff table to describe the relationship among alternatives, uncertainties, and potential outcomes. The use of decision analysis and the application of decision trees and payoff tables can be illustrated by referring back to the situation faced by El Nacho Foods.

Suppose that at the conclusion of Step 2 in the DECIDE process (that is, enumerating decision factors), El Nacho executives identified two alternatives: (1) reduce the price on frozen dinners, or (2) maintain the price. They also recognized two uncertainties: (1) Competitors could maintain the lower price, or (2) competitors could reduce the price further. Suppose further that at the

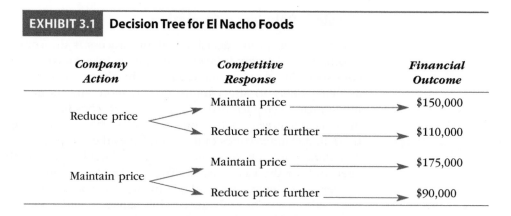

EXHIBIT 3.1   Decision Tree for El Nacho Foods

Company Action	Competitive Response	Financial Outcome
Reduce price	Maintain price	$150,000
	Reduce price further	$110,000
Maintain price	Maintain price	$175,000
	Reduce price further	$90,000

conclusion of Step 3 in the DECIDE process (considering relevant information), El Nacho executives examined the changes in market share and sales volume that would be brought about by the pricing actions. They also calculated the contribution per unit of frozen dinners for each alternative for each competitor response. They performed a contribution analysis because the problem was defined in terms of contribution to advertising and sales promotion in Step 1 of the DECIDE process (defining the problem).

Given two alternatives, two competitive responses, and a calculated contribution per unit for each combination, they identified four unique financial outcomes. These outcomes are displayed in the decision tree shown in Exhibit 3.1.

It is apparent from the decision tree that the largest contribution will be generated if El Nacho maintains its price on frozen dinners *and* competitors maintain their lower price. If El Nacho maintains its price and competitors reduce their prices further, however, the lowest contribution among the four outcomes identified will be generated. The choice of an alternative obviously depends on the likelihood of occurrence of uncertainties in the environment.

A *payoff table* is a useful tool for displaying the alternatives, uncertainties, and outcomes facing a firm. In addition, a payoff table includes another dimension— management's subjective determination of the probability of the occurrence of an uncertainty. Suppose, for example, that El Nacho management believes that competitors are also operating with slim contribution margins and, hence, are most likely to maintain the lower price regardless of El Nacho's action. They believe that there is a 10 percent chance that competitors will reduce the price of frozen dinners even further.[8] Since only two uncertainties have been identified, the subjective probability of competitors' maintaining their price is 90 percent (note that the probabilities assigned to the uncertainties must total 1.0, or 100 percent). Given these probabilities, the payoff table for El Nacho Foods is shown in Exhibit 3.2.

EXHIBIT 3.2   Payoff Table for El Nacho Foods

		Uncertainties	
		Competitors Maintain Price (Probability = 0.9)	*Competitors Reduce Price (Probability = 0.1)*
Alternatives	*Reduce price*	$150,000	$110,000
	Maintain price	$175,000	$90,000

The payoff table allows the manager or case analyst to compute the "expected monetary value" for each alternative. The expected monetary value is calculated by multiplying the outcome for each uncertainty by its probability of occurrence and then totaling across the uncertainties for each alternative. The expected monetary value of an alternative can be viewed as the value that would be obtained if the manager were to choose the same alternative many times under the same conditions.

The expected monetary value of the price-reduction alternative equals the probability that competitors will maintain prices, multiplied by the financial contribution if competitors maintain prices, plus the probability that competitors will further reduce prices, multiplied by the financial contribution if competitors further reduce prices. The calculation is

$$(0.9)(\$150,000) + (0.1)(\$110,000) = \$135,000 + \$11,000 = \$146,000$$

The expected monetary value of maintaining the price is

$$(0.9)(\$175,000) + (0.1)(\$90,000) = \$157,500 + \$9,000 = \$166,500$$

The higher average contribution of \$166,500 for maintaining the price indicates that El Nacho's management should maintain the price. The contribution is higher because competitors are expected to maintain their prices nine times out of ten. Under the same conditions (same outcomes, same probability estimates), El Nacho would achieve an average contribution of \$146,000 if the price-reduction alternative were chosen. A rational management would, therefore, select the price-maintenance alternative.

Familiarity with decision analysis is important for four reasons. First, decision analysis is a fundamental tool for considering "what if" situations. By organizing alternatives, uncertainties, and outcomes in this manner, a manager or case analyst becomes sensitive to the dynamic processes present in a competitive environment. Second, decision analysis forces the case analyst to quantify outcomes associated with specific actions. Third, decision analysis is useful in a variety of settings. For example, Warner-Lambert Canada, Ltd. applied decision analysis when deciding to manufacture and distribute Listerine throat lozenges in Canada; Ford Motor Company used decision analysis in deciding whether to produce its own tires; and Pillsbury used it in determining whether to switch from a box to a bag for a certain grocery product.[9] Fourth, an extension of decision analysis can be used in determining the value of "perfect" information.

Exhibit 3.3 on page 60, shows how the expected monetary value of "perfect" information (EMVPI) can be calculated using the El Nacho Foods example. Simply speaking, EMVPI is the difference between what El Nacho would achieve in contribution dollars if its management knew for certain what competitors would do and the average contribution dollars realized without such information. In other words, if El Nacho knew for certain that competitors would maintain their prices, the "maintain price" alternative would be selected. If El Nacho management knew for certain that competitors would reduce their prices, however, the "reduce price" alternative would be chosen. Assuming El Nacho management faced this decision 10 times and knew what competitor reaction would be each time, El Nacho management would make the appropriate decision each time. The result would be an expected monetary value of \$168,500. The difference of \$2,000 between \$168,500 and \$166,500 (the best alternative without such information) is viewed as the upper limit to pay for "perfect" information. EMVPI is a useful guide for determining how much money should be spent for marketing research information to identify the best alternative or course of action.

EXHIBIT 3.3	Decision Analysis and the Value of Information

Payoff Table Uncertainties

		Competitors Maintain Price (Probability = 0.9)	Competitors Reduce Price (Probability = 0.1)
Alternatives	A_1: Reduce price	$150,000	$110,000
	A_2: Maintain price	$175,000	$90,000

Calculation of Expected Monetary Value (EMV):

$EMV_{A1} = 0.9(\$150,000) + 0.1(\$110,000) = \$146,000$

$EMV_{A2} = 0.9(\$175,000) + 0.1(\$90,000) = \$166,500$

Calculation of Expected Monetary Value of Perfect Information (EMVPI):

$EMV_{certainty} = 0.9(\$175,000) + 0.1(\$110,000) = \$168,500$

$EMVPI = EMV_{certainty} - EMV_{best\ alternative}$

$EMVPI = \$168,500 - \$166,500 = \$2,000$

Develop a Plan for Implementing the Chosen Alternative

The selection of a course of action must be followed by development of a plan for its implementation. Simply deciding what to do will not make it happen. The execution phase is critical, and planning for it forces the case analyst to consider resource allocation and timing questions. For example, if a new product launch is recommended, it is important to consider how managerial, financial, and manufacturing resources will be allocated to this course of action. If a price reduction is recommended, it will be important to monitor whether the reduced prices are reaching the final consumer and not being absorbed by resellers in the marketing channel. Timing is crucial, since a marketing plan takes time to develop and implement.

As a final note, it is important to recognize that strategy formulation and implementation are not necessarily separate sequential processes. Rather, an interactive give-and-take occurs between formulation and implementation until the manager or case analyst realizes that "what might be done can be done," given organizational strengths and market requirements. Another reading of the discussion on the marketing mix in Chapter 1 will highlight these points.

Evaluate the Decision and the Decision Process

The last step in the decision-making process is evaluating the decision made and the decision process itself. With respect to the decision itself, two questions should be asked. First, *Was a decision made?* This seemingly odd question addresses a common shortcoming of case analyses, whereby a case analyst does not make a decision but, rather, "talks about" the situation facing the organization.

The second question is, *Was the decision appropriate, given the situation identified in the case setting?* This question speaks to the issue of insufficient information on the one hand and the failure to consider and interpret information on the other. In many marketing cases, and indeed in some actual business situations, some of the information needed to make a decision is simply not available. When information is incomplete, assumptions must be made. A case analyst is often expected to make assumptions to fill in gaps, but such assumptions should be logically developed and articulated. Merely making assumptions to make the "solution" fit a preconceived notion of the correct answer is a death knell in case analysis and business practice.

The case analyst should constantly monitor how he or she applies the decision-making process. The mere fact that one's decision was right is not a sufficient reason to think that the decision process was appropriate. For example, we have all found ourselves lost while trying to locate a home or business from an address. Eventually we somehow find it but are again at a loss when later asked to direct someone else to the same address. Analogously, the case analyst may arrive at the "correct" solution but be unable to outline (map) the process involved.

After completing a class discussion of a case, a written case assignment, or a group presentation, the case analyst should critically examine his or her performance by answering the following questions:

1. Did I define the problem adequately?

2. Did I identify all pertinent alternatives and uncertainties? Were my assumptions realistic?

3. Did I consider all information relevant to the case?

4. Did I recommend the appropriate course of action? If so, was my logic consistent with the recommendation? If not, were my assumptions different from the assumptions made by others? Did I overlook an important piece of information?

5. Did I consider how my recommendation could be implemented?

Honest answers to these questions will improve the chances of making better decisions in the future.

 ## PREPARING AND PRESENTING A CASE ANALYSIS

How do I prepare and present a case? This question is voiced by virtually every student exposed to the case method for the first time. One of the most difficult tasks in preparing a case for presentation—or, more generally, resolving an actual marketing problem—is structuring your thinking process to address relevant forces confronting the organization in question. The previous discussion of the decision-making process should be of help in this regard. The remainder of this chapter provides some useful hints to assist you in preparing and presenting a marketing case.

Approaching the Case

On your first reading of a marketing case, you should concentrate on becoming acquainted with the situation in which the organization finds itself. This first reading should provide some insights into the problem requiring resolution, as well as background information on the environment and organization.

Then read the case again, paying particular attention to key facts and assumptions. At this point, you should determine the relevance and reliability of the qualitative and quantitative data provided in the context of what you see as the issues or problems facing the organization. Valuable insights often arise from analyzing two or more bits of qualitative and quantitative information concurrently. It is essential that you take extensive notes during the second reading. Working by writing is very important; simply highlighting statements or numbers in the case is not sufficient. Behavioral scientists estimate that the human mind can focus on only seven facts at a time and that our mental ability to link these facts in a meaningful way is limited without assistance.[10] Experienced analysts and managers always work out ideas on paper—whether they are working alone or in a group.

There are three pitfalls you should avoid during the second reading. First, *do not rush to a conclusion.* If you do so, information is likely to be overlooked or possibly distorted to fit a preconceived notion of the answer. Second, *do not "work the numbers"* until you understand their meaning and derivation. Third, *do not confuse supposition with fact.* Many statements are made in a case, such as "Our firm subscribes to the marketing concept." Is this a fact, based on an appraisal of the firm's actions and performance, or a supposition?

Formulating the Case Analysis

The previous remarks should provide some direction in approaching a marketing case. The marketing case analysis worksheet shown in Exhibit 3.4 provides a framework for organizing information. Four analytical categories are shown, with illustrative questions pertaining to each. You will find it useful to consider each analytical category when preparing a case.

Nature of the Industry, Market, and Buyer Behavior   The first analytical category focuses on the organization's environment—the context in which the organization operates. Specific topics of interest include (1) an assessment of the structure, conduct, and performance of the industry and competition, and (2) an understanding of who the buyers are and why, where, when, how, what, and how much they buy.

EXHIBIT 3.4   Marketing Case Analysis Worksheet

Specific Points of Inquiry

Nature of the industry, market, and buyer behavior	1. What is the nature of industry structure, conduct, and performance?
	2. Who are the competitors, and what are their strengths and weaknesses?
	3. How do buyers buy in this industry or market?
	4. Can the market be segmented? How? Can the segments be quantified?
	5. What are the requirements for success in this industry?
The organization	1. What are the organization's mission, objectives, and distinctive competency?
	2. What is its offering to the market? How can its past and present performance be characterized? What is its potential?
	3. What is the situation in which the manager or organization finds itself?
	4. What factors have contributed to the present situation?
A plan of action	1. What actions are available to the organization?
	2. What are the costs and benefits of action in both qualitative and quantitative terms?
	3. Is there a disparity between what the organization wants to do, should do, can do, and must do?
Potential outcomes	1. What will be the buyer, trade, and competitive response to each course of action?
	2. How will each course of action satisfy buyer, trade, and organization requirements?
	3. What is the potential profitability of each course of action?
	4. Will the action enhance or reduce the organization's ability to compete in the future?

The Organization It is important to develop an understanding of the organization's financial, human, and material resources, its strengths and weaknesses, and the reasons for its success or failure. Of particular importance is an understanding of what the organization wishes to do. The "fit" between the organization and its environment represents the first major link drawn in case analysis. This link is the essence of the situation analysis, since it is an interpretation of where the organization currently stands. A SWOT analysis like that described in Chapter 1 might be helpful in organizing your thoughts at this point.

A Plan of Action You should be prepared to identify possible courses of action on the basis of the situation analysis. More often than not, several alternatives are possible, and each should be fully articulated. Each course of action typically has associated costs and revenues. These should be carefully calculated on the basis of realistic estimates of the magnitude of effort expected in their pursuit.

Potential Outcomes Finally, the potential outcomes of all courses of action identified should be evaluated. On the basis of the appraisal of outcomes, one course of action or strategy should be recommended. The evaluation, however, must indicate not only why the recommendation was preferred, but also why other actions were dismissed.

Though it is always useful to consider each of the analytical categories just described, the method in which they are arranged may vary. There is no one way to analyze a case, just as there is no single correct way to attack a marketing problem. Just be sure to cover the bases.

Formulating the Case Analysis in Teams Just as organizations now rely on teams to examine marketing issues, student teams are often assigned a case to analyze. A case analysis by a team will also consider the four analytical categories just discussed. However, a team-based case analysis introduces additional considerations that can affect the quality of a team experience and the analysis itself.

If the instructor asks you to form your own team, take care in choosing team members. Forming teams on the basis of friendships is common but not always wise. Rather, try to create a balanced team where various skills complement one another (financial skills, oral presentation skills, writing skills, and so on). Seek out individuals who are committed and dependable.

The behavior of a team can also affect the quality of marketing decision making and a case analysis.[11] Care should be taken to avoid "groupthink"—the tendency for groups that work together over a period of time to produce poorly reasoned decisions. Groupthink is evident when social pressures and conflict avoidance overtake the desire to rigorously question analyses and alternatives in favor of seeking conformity and consensus. Common outcomes of groupthink are an incomplete survey of issues and alternatives, failure to consider the risks of the group's decision, failure to reappraise initially rejected alternatives, limited recognition and evaluation of case information, and failure to work out contingency plans due to overconfidence in the likelihood of success of a chosen course of action and the correctness of a decision.[12] Alfred Sloan, the legendary chair of General Motors, was acutely aware of groupthink in his executive ranks. He was often heard to say, "I take it we are all in complete agreement on the decision here. Then I propose we postpone further discussion of the matter until our next meeting to give ourselves time to develop disagreement and perhaps gain some understanding of what the decision is all about."[13] Case study teams might do the same to avoid the pitfalls of groupthink.

Communicating the Case Analysis

Three means exist for communicating case analyses: (1) class discussion, (2) oral presentation, and (3) written report.

Class Discussion   Discussing case studies in the classroom setting can be an exciting experience, provided that each student actively prepares for and participates in the discussion. Preparation involves more than simply reading the case prior to the scheduled class period—the case should be carefully analyzed, using the four analytical categories described earlier. Four to five hours of preparation are usually required for each assigned case. The notes developed during the preparation should be brought to class.

Similarly, participation involves more than talking. Other students should be carefully watched and listened to during a class discussion. Attentiveness to the views of others is necessary in order to build on previous comments and analyses. Most class discussions follow a similar format. Class analysis begins with a discussion of the organization and its environment. This discussion is followed first by a discussion of the alternative courses of action and then by a consideration of possible implementation strategies. Knowing where the class is in the discussion is important both for organizing the multitude of ideas and analyses presented and for preparing remarks for the subsequent steps in the class discussion.

Immediately after the class discussion, you should prepare a short summary of the analysis developed in class. This summary, which should include the specific facts, ideas, analyses, and generalizations developed, will be useful in comparing and contrasting case situations.

Oral Presentation   An oral presentation of a case requires a slightly different set of skills. Usually, a group of three to five students conducts a rigorous analysis of a case and presents it to classmates. Role-playing may be featured: Class members may serve as an executive committee witnessing the presentation of a task force or project team.

A polished delivery is very important in oral presentations.[14] Thus, the group should rehearse its presentation, with group members seriously critiquing one another's performance. Oral presentations provide an opportunity to verbalize your analysis and recommendations and visually enhance your remarks with carefully crafted and informative transparencies, electronic slides, or other visual aids. At a minimum, slides or transparencies should cover each of the following areas:

1. An opening slide showing the "title" of the presentation and names of the presenters

2. A slide that outlines the presentation (perhaps with presenters' names by each topic)

3. One or more slides detailing the key problems and strategic issues that management needs to address

4. A series of slides covering your analysis of the company's situation or problem

5. A series of slides containing your recommendations and the supporting arguments and reasoning for each recommendation—one slide for each recommendation and the associated reasoning has a lot of merit

Remember that slides and transparencies help communicate your ideas to the audience. They are not meant to substitute for the oral presentation. Slides and transparencies may be referred to but should *never* be read to the audience. Also keep in mind that too many graphics, images, colors, and transitions may divert the attention of the audience and disrupt the flow of the presentation. Finally, keep in mind that dazzling slides and transparencies will not hide a superficial or flawed case analysis from a perceptive audience.

Written Report   What you need to do to generate a written analysis of a case assignment is similar to what you should do to prepare for class discussion. The only difference is in the submission of the analysis; a written report should be carefully organized, legible (preferably typed), and grammatically correct.

There is no one correct approach to organizing a written case analysis. However, it is usually wise to think about the report as having three major sections: (1) identification of the strategic issues and problems, (2) analysis and evaluation, and (3) recommendations. The first section should contain a focused paragraph that defines the problem and specifies the constraints and options available to the organization. Material in the second section should provide a carefully developed assessment of the industry, market and buyer behavior, the organization, and the alternative courses of action. *Analysis and evaluation should represent the bulk of the written report.* This section should not contain a restatement of case information; it should contain an assessment and interpretation of the facts, qualitative and quantitative data, and management views. The last section should consist of a set of recommendations. These recommendations should be documented with references to the previous section and should be operational given the case situation. By all means, commit to a decision!

A case and a written student analysis of it are presented in the appendix at the end of the book. It is recommended that you carefully study and analyze the case before reading the student analysis.

NOTES

1. Leigh Buchanon and Andrew O' Connell, "A Brief History of Decision Making," *Harvard Business Review* (January 2006): 32–41.

2. "What Executives Should Remember: Classic Advice from Peter Drucker," *Harvard Business Review* (February 2006): 144–152.

3. Melissa Raffoni, "Use Case Interviewing to Improve Your Hiring," *Harvard Management Update* (July 1999): 10.

4. Loren Gary, "Want Better Results? Boost Your Problem-Solving Power," *Harvard Management Update* (October 2004): 1–4.

5. DECIDE acronym copyright © by William Rudelius. Used with permission.

6. "Cluett Peabody & Co. Loses Shirt Trying to Jazz Up the Arrow Man," *Wall Street Journal* (July 28, 1988): 24.

7. Mark David Nevins and Stephen A. Stumpf, "21st-Century Leadership: Redefining Management Education," *Strategy & Business* (Third Quarter, 1999): 41–51.

8. An issue that frequently arises in developing these subjective probabilities is how to select them. One source is past experience, in the form of statistics such as A. T. Kearney's probabilities of success for alternative strategies, presented in Chapter 1. Alternatively, case information can be used to develop probability estimates. At the very least, when two possible uncertainties exist, a subjective probability of 0.5 can be assigned to each. This means that the two uncertainties have an equal chance of occurring. These probabilities can then be revised up or down, depending on case information.

9. These examples and a further reading on decision analysis can be found in Peter C. Bell, *Management Science/Operations Research: A Strategic Perspective* (Cincinnati, OH: South-Western Publishing, 1999): Chapter 3.

10. Sharon Begley, "I Can't Think!" *Newsweek* (March 11, 2011): 28–33.

11. Jared Sandberg, "Some Ideas Are So Bad That Only Team Efforts Can Account for Them," *Wall Street Journal* (September 29, 2004): B1.

12. Max Bazerman, *Judgment in Managerial Decision Making*, 7th ed. (New York: John Wiley & Sons, 2009).

13. This quote appears in David A. Garvin and Michael A. Roberto, "What You Don't Know About Making Decisions," *Harvard Business Review* (September 2001): 108–116.

14. This discussion is based on material in Arthur A. Thompson Jr. and A. J. Strickland, *Strategic Management: Concepts and Cases*, 13th ed. (Burr Ridge, IL: McGraw-Hill/Irwin, 2004): C12–C13.

Chapter 4

Opportunity Analysis, Market Segmentation, and Market Targeting

The development and implementation of marketing strategy are complicated and challenging tasks. At its pinnacle, marketing strategy involves the selection of markets and the development of programs to reach these markets. This process is carried out in a manner that simultaneously benefits both the markets selected (satisfying the needs or wants of buyers) and the organization (typically in dollar-profit terms).

Within this framework, necessary first tasks are opportunity analysis, market segmentation, and market targeting. This chapter describes analytical concepts and tools that marketing managers find useful in performing opportunity analyses, segmenting markets, selecting market targets, and estimating market and sales potential.

 ## OPPORTUNITY ANALYSIS

Opportunity analysis consists of three interrelated activities:

- Opportunity identification
- Opportunity–organization matching
- Opportunity evaluation

Opportunities arise from identifying new types of buyers, uncovering unsatisfied needs of buyers, or creating new ways or means for satisfying buyer needs. Opportunity analysis focuses on finding markets that an organization can profitably serve.

The success of Reebok International, Ltd. illustrates a disciplined approach to *opportunity identification*. In 1981, Reebok had sales of $1.5 million and was known primarily for its high-quality custom running shoes. Consumer interest in running had plateaued, however, and new opportunities had to be identified for the company to grow. Over the next 28 years, Reebok systematically pursued opportunities based on buyer types, buyer needs, and technological innovation as a means of satisfying the needs of buyers. Reebok identified buyer "performance-oriented" needs with a focus on specific athletic activities (such as tennis, basketball, golf, and track and field) and "nonathletic" needs with an emphasis on comfort, fashion, and style for three types of buyers—men, women, and children. Technological innovation, most recently with the launch of Rbk Custom in 2008, a Web-based shoe customization platform, has met the needs of buyers interested in comfort and fit. The result? Reebok broadened its global marketing presence following a merger with adidas in 2006, and now posts global sales of $3.5 billion annually with about half of its sales outside the United States.[1]

Opportunity–organization matching determines whether an identified market opportunity is consistent with the definition of the organization's business, mission statement, and distinctive competencies. This determination usually involves an assessment of the organization's strengths and weaknesses and an identification of the success requirements for operating profitably in a market. A SWOT analysis, like that described in Chapter 1, is often employed to assess the match between identified market opportunities and the organization's strengths and weaknesses.

For some companies, market opportunities that promise sizable sales and profit gains are not pursued because they do not conform to an organization's character. Starbucks is a case in point. The company has built a thriving business serving freshly brewed, specialty gourmet coffee. However, the company refuses to use artificially flavored coffee despite its growth potential. According to company chair Howard Schultz, "A large growth segment in our category is

---

EXHIBIT 4.1   Opportunity Evaluation Matrix: Attractiveness Criteria

Market Niche Criterion	*Competitive Activity*	*Buyer Requirements*	*Demand/ Supply*	*Political, Technological, and Socio-economic Forces*	*Organizational Capabilities*
Buyer type	How many and which firms are competing for this user group?	What affects buyer willingness and ability to buy?	Do different buyer types have different levels of effective demand? How important are adequate sources of supply?	How sensitive are different buyers to these forces?	Can we gain access to buyers through marketing-mix variables? Can we supply these buyers?
Buyer needs	Which firms are satisfying which buyer needs?	Are there buyer needs that are not being satisfied? What are they?	Are buyer needs likely to be long-term? Do we have or can we acquire resources to satisfy buyer needs?	How sensitive are buyer needs to these forces?	Which buyer needs can our organization profitably satisfy?
Means for satisfying buyer needs	What are the strategies being employed to satisfy buyer needs?	Is the technology for satisfying buyer needs changing?	To what extent are the means for satisfying buyer needs affected by supply sources? Is the demand for the means for satisfying buyer needs changing?	How sensitive are the means for satisfying buyer needs to these forces?	Do we have the financial, human, technological, and marketing expertise to satisfy buyer needs?

artificially flavored coffee; it would give us maybe 40 percent incremental volume, but we won't do it." He adds, "It's not in our DNA."[2]

Opportunity evaluation typically has two distinct phases—qualitative and quantitative. The qualitative phase focuses on matching the attractiveness of an opportunity with the potential for uncovering a market niche. Attractiveness is dependent on (1) competitive activity; (2) buyer requirements; (3) market demand and supplier sources; (4) social, political, economic, and technological forces; and (5) organizational capabilities. Each of these factors in turn must be tied to its impact on the types of buyers sought, the needs of buyers, and the means for satisfying these needs. Exhibit 4.1 is an opportunity evaluation matrix containing illustrative questions useful in the qualitative analysis of a market opportunity. The quantitative phase yields estimates of market sales potential and sales forecasts. It also produces budgets for financial, human, marketing, and production resources, which are necessary to assess the profitability of a market opportunity.

 ## WHAT IS A MARKET?

The fact that an opportunity has been identified does not necessarily imply that a market exists for the organization. Although definitions vary, a *market* may be considered to be the prospective buyers (individuals or organizations) willing and able to purchase the existing or potential offering (product or service) of an organization.

This definition of a market has several managerial implications. First, the definition focuses on buyers, not on products or services. People and organizations whose idiosyncrasies dictate whether and how products and services will be sought, acquired, consumed, or used make up markets. Second, by highlighting the buyer's willingness and ability to purchase a product or service, this definition introduces the concept of *effective demand*. Even if buyers are willing to purchase a product or service, exchange cannot occur unless they are able to do so. Likewise, if buyers are able to purchase a product or service but are unwilling to do so, exchange will not occur. These relationships are important to grasp because a marketing strategist must ascertain the extent of effective demand for an offering in order to determine whether a market exists. To a large degree, the extent of effective demand will depend on the marketing mix activities of the organization. Third, use of the term *offering*, rather than *product* or *service*, expands the definition of what organizations provide for buyers. Products and services are not purchased for the sake of purchase; they are purchased for the benefits that buyers expect to derive from them. It is for this reason that the late Charles Revson of Revlon Cosmetics continually reiterated that his company did not sell cosmetics but, rather, hope. This expanded definition of an offering requires strategists to consider benefits provided by a product or service apart from its tangible nature.

Market Structure

Frequently, one hears or reads about the automobile market, the soft drink market, or the health care market. These terms can be misleading because each refers to a composite of multiple minimarkets. Viewing a market as composed of minimarkets allows a marketer to better gauge opportunities. Consider, for example, the "coffee market." Exhibit 4.2 on page 70 shows how the U.S. coffee market might be broken down into multiple markets by a marketing manager for Maxwell House or Folgers. With this breakdown, the manager can more effectively identify who is competing in the caffeinated versus the decaffeinated markets

| EXHIBIT 4.2 | Market Structure for Coffee in the United States |

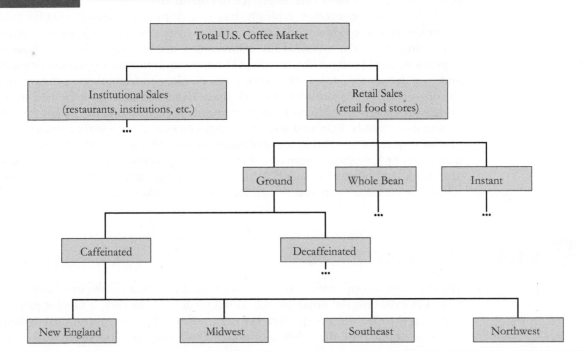

and how they are competing, monitor changes in sales volume for instant versus ground coffee, and appreciate differences between buyer taste preferences and competition in the southwestern and northeastern United States.

Market Share

How a market is defined plays a critical role in determining market share. *Market share* is defined as the sales (in dollars or units) of a company, product, service, or brand divided by the sales of the "market," expressed as a percentage. Consider the market share calculation for Atlantic Blend, a premium caffeinated ground coffee brand sold only in grocery stores and supermarkets in the Mid-Atlantic region of the United States by a coffee roaster in New York state. Atlantic Blend sales are $80 million. Depending on the "market" definition, Atlantic Blend's market share will range from 1 percent to 32 percent, as shown in the following table.

Market Definition	Coffee Dollar Sales	Atlantic Blend Sales	Market Share
Total U.S. coffee market	$8.0 billion	$80 million	1.0%
U.S. retail coffee market	$6.0 billion	$80 million	1.3%
U.S. retail ground coffee market	$4.5 billion	$80 million	1.8%
U.S. retail caffeinated ground coffee market	$3.0 billion	$80 million	2.7%
U.S. retail caffeinated ground coffee market in the Mid-Atlantic region	$230 million	$80 million	32.0%

As a regional (Mid-Atlantic) product and brand, Atlantic Blend is clearly a minor player in the total U.S. coffee market with a 1 percent overall market share. However, Atlantic Blend captures a significant share (32 percent) of the retail caffeinated ground coffee market in the Mid-Atlantic region where it is marketed.

The retail caffeinated ground coffee market in the Mid-Atlantic region of the United States is Atlantic Blend's served market.

A *served market* is the market in which a company, product, service, or brand competes for targeted customers. Marketing managers often look closely at served market share when considering strategic options. For example, if a company has a "high" served market share, a market penetration strategy to gain increased served market share will be more difficult. Market development strategies might be more advisable, such as pursuing sales growth in an adjacent geographic market; that is, Atlantic Blend might enter the New England market. Alternatively, if a company has a "low" served market share, a product development strategy or a market penetration strategy might be perceived as a means to increase market share.

 # MARKET SEGMENTATION

A useful technique for structuring markets is *market segmentation*—the breaking down or building up of potential buyers into groups. These groups are typically termed *market segments*. Each segment is thought of as possessing some sort of homogeneous characteristic relating to its purchasing or consumption behavior, which is ultimately reflected in its responsiveness to marketing programs. Market segmentation grew out of the recognition that, in general, an organization cannot be all things to all people.

Although the legendary Henry Ford is reputed to have said that buyers of his Ford automobiles could have any color they desired as long as it was black, most marketers today agree that such an undifferentiated marketing strategy is no longer appropriate. The idea that an organization can effectively apply one marketing strategy to satisfy all possible buyers is not viable in today's marketing environment.

At the other extreme, unless the organization is highly specialized and sells only to, say, one buyer, it is often not feasible to treat each potential buyer as unique. Thus, as one marketing authority has so aptly written, market segmentation "is a compromise between the ineffectiveness of treating all customers alike and the inefficiency of treating each one differently."[3]

Advances in information technology and flexible manufacturing and service delivery systems have made "segments of one" a reality in some settings. *Mass customization*—tailoring products and services to the tastes and preferences of individual buyers in high volumes and at a relatively low cost—combines the efficiencies of mass production and the effectiveness of designing offerings to a single buyer's unique wants.

Benefits of Market Segmentation

Segmentation offers three principal benefits with regard to the development of marketing strategy.[4] Market segmentation:

1. *Identifies opportunities for new product development.* The analysis of various segments of present and potential buyers can reveal one or more groups whose specific needs are not being well satisfied. These segments represent possible opportunities for new product development. Frito-Lay, Inc. is a case in point. The company identified two attitudinal and lifestyle market segments. "Indulgers" are consumers who know they should limit their fat consumption but cannot and those who simply don't care. This segment represents 47 percent of snack chip consumers who are heavy users of snack chips. The other 53 percent of consumers are "compromisers," who enjoy snacking but restrict their snack chip intake because

of nutritional concerns. Frito-Lay, Inc. decided to invest heavily in the "compromiser" segment. Baked Lay's low-fat potato crisps posted sales of $250 million in their first full year in the market. This success was followed by a line of Ruffles, Doritos, and Tostitos made with a low-fat, calorie-free cooking oil. This line recorded first-year sales of $350 million and was one of the company's most successful food introductions.[5]

2. *Helps in the design of marketing programs that are most effective for reaching homogeneous groups of consumers.* In addition to product development, segmentation permits refinements in the pricing, advertising and promotion, and distribution elements of the marketing mix. For example, Procter & Gamble markets its Crest toothpaste with different advertising and promotion campaigns directed at six different market segments, including children, Hispanics, and senior citizens.

3. *Improves the allocation of marketing resources.* Market segmentation can provide guidance in directing marketing resources. All market segments are not necessarily equal in terms of an organization's ability to serve them effectively and profitably. As with any opportunity assessment, a company's strengths and capabilities relative to each identified segment's needs and competitive situation must be considered. Returning to the athletic shoe "market" discussed earlier, consider how New Balance competes with Nike and adidas, two performance-oriented shoe marketers. Instead of allocating resources to compete directly with Nike and adidas in the "performance" segment, New Balance focuses on the baby boomer (46 to 64 years old) nonathletic segment. It offers comfortable shoes for men and women and spends its marketing resources networking with podiatrists, not athletes.[6]

Bases for Market Segmentation

Two broad types of variables are commonly used for market segmentation. Socioeconomic characteristics of consumers, such as gender, age, occupation, income, family life cycle, education, and geographic location, make up one type. The other type consists of behavioral variables, including benefits sought from products and services, usage behavior, lifestyle, and attitudes. For industrial buyers, socioeconomic characteristics may include company size and location, and industry or customers served. Behavioral variables may include purchasing objectives and practices as well as product and service benefits. The appropriateness of any one or combination of variables in a specific situation will depend on whether or not a variable relates to purchasing, use, or consumption behavior and responsiveness to marketing programs.

The choice of variable(s) to use to segment a market often depends on insights into buyer behavior, provided by creative research. Segmentation of the cell phone market by Nokia illustrates this point. According to the director of America's brand marketing at Nokia, "Different people have different usage needs. Some people want and need all of the latest and most advanced data-related features and functions, while others are happy with basic voice connectivity. Even people with similar usage needs often have differing lifestyles representing various value sets. For example, some people have an active lifestyle in which sports and fitness play an important role, while for others arts, fashion and trends may be very important."[7]

Nokia's research on consumer usage, lifestyles, and individual preferences identified six market segments: "Basic" consumers who need voice connectivity and a low price; "Expression" consumers who want to customize and personalize features; "Active" consumers who desire a rugged product to stand up to an active lifestyle; "Classic" consumers who prefer a more traditional cell phone with some features at a modest price; "Fashion" consumers who want a very small phone as a fashion accessory; and "Premium" consumers who are interested in all the high-end technological and service features.

Requirements for Effective Market Segmentation

Ultimately, market segmentation is a means to an end: to identify and profile distinct groups of buyers who differ in their needs, preferences, and responsiveness to an organization's marketing programs. Effective market segmentation should provide answers to six fundamental buyer-related questions for each market segment:

1. Who are they?
2. What do they want to buy?
3. How do they want to buy?
4. When do they want to buy?
5. Where do they want to buy?
6. Why do they want to buy?

More often than not, the answers to these questions should be expressed in a narrative form documented with quantitative and qualitative research.

From a managerial perspective, effective market segmentation means that each segment identified and profiled satisfies four fundamental requirements.[8] Each market segment should be:

1. *Measurable.* The size and buying power of a market segment can be quantitatively determined.

2. *Differentiable.* A market segment is distinguishable from other segments and responds differently to different marketing programs.

3. *Accessible.* A segment can be effectively reached and served through an economically viable marketing program.

4. *Substantial.* A segment should be large enough in terms of sales volume potential to cover the cost of the organization serving it and return a satisfactory profit.

How are these requirements applied in practice? Consider Harley-Davidson, Inc., the U.S. sales leader in heavyweight motorcycles.[9] Following two years of extensive research studying specific consumer groups, the company concluded that women represented a viable market segment based on these requirements. Women account for about 10 percent of total U.S. motorcycle owners, and the percentage is growing. They seek adventure, freedom, and individuality—just as men do. "What they don't want is a special product, a pink motorcycle, for example, but they do want a product that fits them better," said the company's vice president of marketing.

Harley-Davidson's tailored marketing program for women includes a product that requires less strength to operate a motorcycle and lowered seat heights. The communications program includes advertisements in magazines, such as *Allure, Vanity Fair, Glamour,* and *Self,* and at local dealer events to introduce first-time women riders to the product and the sport of cycling. For Harley-Davidson, the female segment is measurable, differentiable from males, accessible through communications and distribution channels, and substantial enough in terms of sales and profit to warrant attention.

MARKET TARGETING

After a market has been segmented, a marketing manager needs to address three questions:

- Where to compete?
- How to compete?
- When to compete?

Where to Compete?

The manager must first decide *where to compete*. This question focuses on which market segment(s) the company should choose for marketing efforts, or market targeting. *Market targeting* (or target marketing) is the specification of the market segment(s) the organization wishes to pursue.

For example, recognizing that Walmart, Lowe's, and a host of regional competitors were targeting the home-improvement "do-it-yourselfer" segment for home repairs and remodeling, Home Depot decided to pursue the "professional" segment for growth alongside the "do-it-yourselfer" segment. This segment consisted of housing professionals, such as managers of major apartment and condominium complexes and hotel chains, and professional building contractors. Once that was decided, the company modified its merchandise assortment to meet the needs of the "professional" segment and broadened its services, including longer store hours, delivery, commercial credit, truck and equipment rental, and ordering via phone, fax, or the Internet. Today, "professional" customers account for 4 percent of Home Depot customers, but account for about one-third of company sales.[10]

How to Compete?

Next, a manager must decide *how to compete*. This question focuses on how many market segments the organization will pursue and the marketing strategies to employ.

Two frequently used market targeting approaches are *differentiated marketing* and *concentrated marketing*. In a differentiated marketing approach, the organization simultaneously pursues several different market segments, with a unique marketing strategy for each. An example of this type of marketing is the strategy of Nokia following its segmentation research described earlier. Exhibit 4.3 shows Nokia's differentiated marketing strategy in 2005 featuring seven different cell phone models designed for and uniquely marketed to six market segments.[11] Nokia's differentiated marketing approach, along with continued technological advancements, has contributed to its status as one of the world's leading cell phone handset marketers. As a rule, differentiated marketing is expensive to implement. Managing multiple products across multiple market segments increases marketing, inventory, administrative, and advertising and promotion costs as well as product development expenditures.

In a concentrated approach, the organization focuses on a single market segment. An extreme case would be one in which an organization marketed a single product offering to a single market segment. More commonly, an organization will offer one or more product lines to a single segment. For many years, Gerber proclaimed that "babies are our only business" and focused almost exclusively on baby foods. Gerber still offers prepared baby foods, which is its primary business. However, today Gerber offers companion lines of baby skin care and health care products; baby care products such as bottles, pacifiers, playthings, clothing,

EXHIBIT 4.3 Nokia's Differentiated Marketing Strategy

Market Segments

Offering Characteristics	BASIC — First-time users. Teens needing voice connectivity	EXPRESSION — Younger buyers who desire customized and personalized products	ACTIVE — Cool, young active adults desiring to connect with friends; sports enthusiasts	CLASSIC — Travelers with various business needs who prefer functionality	FASHION — Buyers who want to "show off" with a personal sense of style	PREMIUM — World travelers wanting PDA, connectivity, and games
Durable, ease of use, and low price	Series 1000/ Series 2000					
Changeable covers, color displays, downloadable ring tones, and games		Series 3000				
Small size, stylish, durable, user friendly, color displays, and fitness monitor			Series 5000			
Traditional style, Web browser, networking, phone book, calendar, and camera				Series 6000		
MP3 music player, styling, games, camera, color display, and Internet access					Series 7000	
Enhanced user interface, camera, color display, multimedia messaging, and PDA						Series 8000

and accessory items; and insurance policies.[12] Through a concentrated marketing approach, a company gains a strong knowledge of a segment's needs and can achieve a strong market position—Gerber commands an 83 percent market share in prepared baby foods in the United States. Furthermore, concentrated marketing provides operating economics through specialization in manufacturing and marketing. However, concentrated marketing has risks. Specializing in one segment can limit a company's growth prospects, particularly if the segment size declines. Also, competitors might invade the segment.

When to Compete?

Third, the manager must determine *when to compete*. This question relates to timing.[13] Some organizations adopt a "first-to-market" posture, while others take a "wait-and-see" stance concerning the pursuit of market segments. Historically, Matsushita has generally deferred to Sony and other firms to identify market segments to be served. When the market segment potential has been demonstrated,

Matsushita relies on its production and marketing expertise, backed by large investments, to capture a disproportionate share of the market segment.

Timing in market targeting can have a significant effect on sales and profit. For instance, companies that targeted the Hispanic market segment early with a unique offering or marketing program were rewarded in sales and profit. Metropolitan Life Insurance is such a case. The company was among the first insurance companies to recognize this opportunity and is now one of the largest insurers of Hispanic consumers in the United States.

On the other hand, in the early 1970s, marketing executives at Frito-Lay identified a "better for you" benefit segment of snack users who desired healthier snack chips. The company created a multigrain snack chip called Prontos and launched the brand with a supporting marketing program only to post disappointing sales and profit. According to a marketing executive, the "better-for-you segment was too narrow a target market and a multigrain snack chip may have been invented and introduced before its time." Frito-Lay tracked this segment's development over the next decade and launched another multigrain snack chip with the Sun Chips name. Today, the Sun Chips brand produces sales of $100 million annually.

MARKET SALES POTENTIAL AND PROFITABILITY

An essential activity in opportunity evaluation is the determination of market sales potential and profitability. Estimating a market's sales potential for offerings is a difficult task even for a seasoned marketing executive. Markets and offerings can be defined in numerous ways that can lead to different estimates of market size and dollar sales potential. This was illustrated earlier in the description of market structure and resulting market shares in the U.S. coffee industry. For innovative offerings or new markets, marketing analysts must often rely almost entirely on judgment and creativity when estimating market sales potential. Therefore, it is understandable that market sales potential estimates vary greatly for high-definition television (HDTV) and hybrid (gasoline- and battery-powered) automobiles. The underlying technology for both offerings is still evolving as is the physical form. In such dynamic settings, measures for identifying prospective market segments are uncertain.

Estimating Market Sales Potential

Market sales potential is a quantitative approximation of effective demand. Specifically, *market sales potential* is the maximum level of sales that might be available to all organizations serving a defined market in a specific time period given (1) the marketing mix activities and effort of all organizations, and (2) a set of environmental conditions. As this definition indicates, market sales potential is not a fixed amount. Rather, it is a function of a number of factors, some of which are controllable and others not controllable by organizations. For instance, controllable marketing mix activities and marketing-related expenditures of organizations can influence market sales potential. On the other hand, consumer disposable income, government regulations, and other social, economic, and political conditions are not controllable by organizations, but do affect market sales potential. These uncontrollable factors are particularly relevant in estimating market sales potential in developing countries.

Three variables are commonly considered when estimating market sales potential.[14] These include (1) the number of prospective buyers (B) who are willing and able to purchase an offering; (2) the quantity (Q) of an offering purchased by an average buyer in a specific time period, typically one calendar year; and (3) the price (P) of an average unit of the offering. Market sales potential is the product of these three variables:

$$\text{Market sales potential} = B \times Q \times P$$

Though simple, this expression contains the building blocks for developing a more complex formulation through what is called the *chain ratio method*, which involves multiplying a base number by several adjusting factors that are believed to influence market sales potential. An application of this method by Coca-Cola and Pepsi-Cola is shown in the following calculation of cola-flavored carbonated soft drink potential in a South American country:

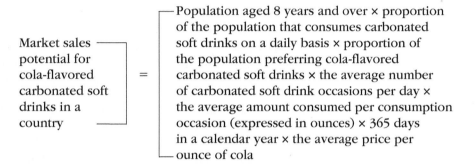

Market sales potential for cola-flavored carbonated soft drinks in a country = Population aged 8 years and over × proportion of the population that consumes carbonated soft drinks on a daily basis × proportion of the population preferring cola-flavored carbonated soft drinks × the average number of carbonated soft drink occasions per day × the average amount consumed per consumption occasion (expressed in ounces) × 365 days in a calendar year × the average price per ounce of cola

The chain ratio method serves three important purposes. First, it yields a quantitative estimate of market sales potential. Second, it highlights factors that are controllable and not controllable by organizations. Clearly, a country's population aged 8 years and older is an uncontrollable factor. However, the other factors are controllable or can be influenced to some degree. For example, organizations can influence the proportion of a population that consumes carbonated soft drinks through primary demand advertising and the cost of cola drinks through pricing. If either of these two factors change, market sales potential changes, other things being equal. Finally, it affords a manager flexibility in estimating market sales potential for different buyer groups and different offerings. For example, by including another factor such as the proportion of the population preferring diet colas, the potential for this offering can be calculated.

Sales and Profit Forecasting

Sales and profit forecasting follow the estimation of market sales potential. A *sales forecast* is the level of sales a single organization expects to achieve based on a chosen marketing strategy and an assumed competitive environment. An organization's forecasted sales are typically some fraction of estimated market sales potential.

Forecasted sales reflect the size of the target market(s) chosen by the organization and the marketing mix chosen for the target market(s). Forecasted sales also reflect the assumed number of competitors and competitive intensity in the chosen target market(s). For example, suppose an organization's target market represents one-fourth of 1 million prospective buyers for a particular offering. The marketing channel chosen for the offering provides access to about three-fourths of these buyers and the communication program (advertising) reaches these same buyers. Suppose further that the average purchase rate is 20 units of an offering per year and the average offering unit price is $10. Using a version of the chain ratio method, forecasted sales might be calculated as follows:

Total estimated prospective buyers	1 million
times	
Target market (25% of total buyers)	× 0.25
times	
Distribution/Communication coverage (75% of target market)	× 0.75
times	
Annual purchase rate (20 units per year)	× 20
times	
Average offering unit price ($10)	× $10
Forecasted sales	$37.5 million

The $37.5 million sales forecast does not consider the number of competitors vying for the same target market nor does it consider competitive intensity. Therefore, this sales forecast should be adjusted downward to reflect these realities.

Forecasting sales, like estimating market sales potential, is not an easy task. Nevertheless, the task is central to opportunity evaluation and must be undertaken. For this reason, sales forecasting is addressed again in Chapter 5 in reference to product and service life cycles.

Finally, a pro forma income statement should be prepared showing forecasted sales, budgeted expenses, and estimated net profit (Chapter 2). When completed, the marketing analyst can review the identified opportunities and decide which can be most profitably pursued given organizational capabilities.

NOTES

1. The Reebok example is based on Roger A. Kerin, Steven Hartley, Eric N. Berkowitz, and William Rudelius, *Marketing*, 8th ed. (Burr Ridge, IL: McGraw-Hill/Irwin, 2006): 231–235; and "Reebok," adidas-group.com, February 2, 2010.

2. Terry Lefton, "Schultz' Caffeinated Crusade," *BRANDWEEK* (July 5, 1999): 20–25.

3. Ben M. Enis, *Marketing Principles: The Management Process*, 2nd ed. (Pacific Palisades, CA: Goodyear, 1977): 241.

4. Orville C. Walker Jr. and John Mullins, *Marketing Strategy: A Decision-Focused Approach*, 7th ed. (Burr Ridge, IL: McGraw-Hill/Irwin, 2011): Chapter 6.

5. "American Marketing Association Edison Award Best New Product," *Marketing News* (January 16, 1999): special supplement.

6. Stephanie Kang, "New Balance Steps Up Marketing Drive," *Wall Street Journal* (March 21, 2008): B3.

7. "Nokia: A Phone for Every Segment," in Roger A. Kerin, Steven Hartley, Eric N. Berkowitz, and William Rudelius (reference cited): 255–257.

8. Philip Kotler and Kevin Lane Keller, *Marketing Management*, 14th ed. (Upper Saddle River, NJ: Prentice Hall, 2011): 262; and Daniel Yankelovich and David Meer, "Rediscovering Market Segmentation," *Harvard Business Review* (February 2006): 122–131.

9. "Hop on the Back, Jack," *Marketing News* (March 15, 2009): 5; and Terry Box, "Biker Chic," *Dallas Morning News* (June 24, 2007): pp. 1D, 6D.

10. "Home Depot Launches New Initiative to Serve Pros," ProSales Online, December 8, 2010.

11. "The Giant in the Palm of Your Hand," *The Economist* (February 12, 2005): 67–69; and "Nokia: A Phone for Every Segment" (reference cited).

12. "Gerber Products Company," Hoover's.com, January 15, 2012.

13. Sources for examples contained in this discussion include Meg Green, "Winning the Hispanic Market," *BEST'S Review* (September 2004); 24–54; and Roger A. Kerin, P. Rajan Varadarajan, and Robert A. Peterson, "First-Mover Advantage: A Synthesis, Conceptual Framework, and Research Propositions," *Journal of Marketing* (October 1992): 33–52.

14. Portions of this discussion are based on Philip Kotler and Kevin Lane Keller, *Marketing Management* (reference cited): Chapter 4.

Case

Lancer Gallery

Lancer Gallery is a limited liability company that sources and sells a wide variety of South American and African artifacts. It is also a major source of southwestern Indian—especially Hopi and Navajo—authentic jewelry and pottery. Although the firm's headquarters is located in Phoenix, Arizona, there are currently branch offices in Los Angeles, Miami, and Boston.

Lancer Gallery originated as a trading post operation near Tucson, Arizona, in the early 1900s. Through a series of judicious decisions, the company established itself as one of the more reputable dealers in authentic southwestern jewelry and pottery. Over the years, Lancer gradually expanded its product line to include pre-Columbian artifacts from Peru and Venezuela (see Exhibit 1) and tribal and burial artifacts from Africa. Through its careful verification of the authenticity of these South American and African artifacts, Lancer developed a national reputation as one of the most respected sources of these types of artifacts.

In 2001, Lancer further expanded its product line to include items that were replicas of authentic artifacts. For example, African fertility gods and masks were made by craftspeople who took great pains to produce these items so that only the truly knowledgeable buyer—a collector—would know that they were replicas. Lancer now has long-term contracts with native craftspeople in Central America, South America, Africa, and the southwestern United States who produce these items. Replicas account for only a small portion of total Lancer sales; the company agreed to enter this business only at the prodding of the firm's clients, who desired an expanded line. The replicas have found most favor among gift buyers and individuals looking for decorative items.

The company's gross sales are about $35 million and have increased at a relatively constant rate of 20 percent per year over the last decade. Myron Rangard, the firm's national sales manager, attributed the sales increase to the popularity of the company's product line and to the expanded distribution of South American and African artifacts:

> For some reason, our South American and certainly our African artifacts have been gaining greater acceptance. Two of our department store customers featured examples of our African line in their Christmas catalogs last year. I personally think consumer tastes are changing from the modern and abstract to the more concrete, like our products.

EXHIBIT 1   African Ceremonial Mask and Pre-Columbian Water Vessel

Lancer distributes its products exclusively through specialty dealers (including selected interior designers and decorators), firm-sponsored showings, and a few exclusive department stores. Often, the company is the sole supplier to its clients. Rangard recently expressed the reasons for this highly limited distribution:

> Our limited distribution has been dictated to us because of the nature of our product line. As acceptance grew, we expanded our distribution to specialty dealers and some exclusive department stores. Previously, we had to push our products through our own showings. Furthermore, we just didn't have the product. These South American artifacts aren't always easy to get and the political situation in Africa is limiting our supply. Our perennial supply problem has become even more critical in recent years for several reasons. Not only must we search harder for new products, but the competition for authentic artifacts has increased tenfold. On top of this, we must now contend with governments not allowing exportation of certain artifacts because of their "national significance."

The problem of supply has forced Lancer to add three new buyers in the last two years. Whereas Lancer identified 5 major competitors a decade ago, there are 11 today. "Our bargaining position has eroded," noted David Olsen, director of procurement. "We have watched our gross margin slip in recent years due to aggressive competitive bidding by others."

"And competition at the retail level has increased also," injected Rangard. "Not only are some of our larger specialty and exclusive department store customers sending out their own buyers to deal directly with some of our Hopi, Navajo, and African sources, but also we are often faced with amateurs or fly-by-night competitors. These people move into a city and dump a bunch of inauthentic junk on the public at exorbitant prices. Such antics give the industry a bad name." Rangard acknowledged that high-quality, authentically made decorative items were also available on the Internet (see, for example, authenticafrica.com and novica.com).

A recent article in *African Collector* magazine supported Rangard's observation.[1] According to the article, which featured African artifacts:

> It's best to buy from a dealer you can trust since a growing number of fakes are turning up on the market. Throughout Africa, artisans in "craft centers" simply churn out copies of authentic items. And sometimes, "traditional" art is created in the absence of any tradition. In Kenya, for example, masks made by the Masai people sell for anywhere from $50 to $200. But the Masai have never carved masks. [According to an authority on African antiquities] "90% of what's coming into the U.S. are replicas or tourist art that's being made to look old."

In recent years, several mass-merchandise department store chains have begun to sell merchandise similar to that offered by Lancer. Even though product quality was often mixed and most items were replicas, occasionally an authentic group of items was found in these stores, according to company sales representatives. Subsequent inquiries by both Rangard and Olsen revealed that two competitors had signed purchase contracts with these outlets. Moreover, the items were typically being sold at retail prices below those charged by the company's dealers.

In early January 2010, Rangard was contacted by a mass-merchandise department store chain concerning the possibility of carrying a complete line of Lancer products and particularly a full assortment of authentic items. The chain was currently selling a competitor's items but wished to add a more exclusive product line. A tentative contract submitted by the chain stated that it would buy at 10 percent below the company's existing prices, and that its initial purchase would be for no less than $750,000. Depending on consumer acceptance, purchases were estimated to be at least $4 million annually. An important clause in the contract dealt with the supply of replicas. Inspection of this clause revealed that Lancer would have to triple its replica production to satisfy the contractual obligation. Soon after Lancer executives began discussing the contract, the company's president, Andrew Smythe, mentioned that accepting the contract could have a dramatic effect on how Lancer defined its business. Smythe added:

> The contract presents us with an opportunity to broaden our firm's position. The upside is that we have the potential to add $4 million in additional sales over and above our annual growth. This is a plus because revenue growth has slowed due to the recession. On the other hand, do we want to commit such a large percent of our business to replicas? Is that the direction that the market is going? What effect will this contract have on our current dealers, and, I might add, our current customers?
>
> I want you both (Rangard and Olsen) to consider this contract in light of your respective functions and the company as a whole. Let's meet in a few days to discuss this matter again.

---

[1] "Alert," *African Collector* (Autumn, 2008), p. 18.

Case

Fiserv Takes on the E-Billing Market

How Can We Get Them to Turn Off Paper?

Kent Grayson and Eric Leiserson

Jon Black looked up from the market research reports on his desk and turned to the window, watching the Chattahoochee River flow by his Atlanta office. It was March 2009, and Black, the senior VP of marketing and product for Fiserv, faced an exciting but potentially difficult challenge. In five days he was supposed to deliver key recommendations to his manager, e-commerce division EVP Lori Adams, about how Fiserv could make strides in electronic bill presentment, or "e-billing." In the coming year, Fiserv was planning to make recommendations to its e-billing partners regarding how to increase e-billing adoption among its consumers, and Black was in charge of deciding what those recommendations should be.

Later that afternoon, Black was meeting with Dr. Michelle Johnston, a Fiserv consumer research scientist, to discuss potential strategies. Black and Johnston were no strangers to developing marketing strategies for online financial services. Under Adams's championship, the pair had recently helped increase consumer adoption of a related product: electronic bill payment. Using strong segmentation, targeting, and positioning—plus key product enhancements based on consumer needs—Black and Johnston helped drive electronic bill payment into the mainstream, which in turn helped establish Fiserv's position as a market leader.

EXHIBIT 1   Relationships Between Fiserv and Its Direct and Indirect Customers

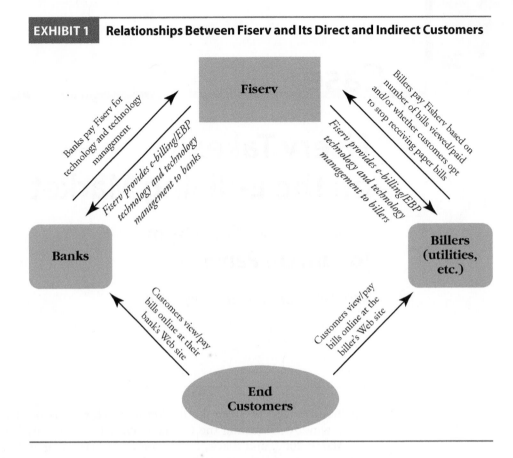

Fiserv, which had acquired CheckFree, the market-leading electronic billing and payment pioneer in 2007, achieved leadership in electronic bill payment by researching and understanding not only billers and financial intermediaries but also end users who paid their bills (see Exhibit 1 for an illustration of Fiserv and its relationships with direct and indirect customers). Electronic bill payment was now gaining wider acceptance, with nearly 70 percent of online households using it as their primary mode of paying bills. But with less than 20 percent of consumers regularly using e-billing technology to view their bills, Black was mulling over the opportunities and challenges he faced at the other end of the adoption curve.

As he considered his options, Black recognized how crucial the e-billing business would likely be for Fiserv. Fiserv's technology already assisted consumers with their "outgoing" interactions—that is, helping them pay bills using electronic bill payment. E-billing focused instead on consumers' "incoming" interactions—helping them receive bills online. If Fiserv played a role in the entire "round trip" of outgoing bills and incoming payments, the company could further its premiere position in the value network of consumers, billers, and financial institutions. E-billing was also a potentially significant revenue stream for Fiserv. Of the 118 million households in the United States in March 2009, 86 million were considered "online" (connected to the Internet), and the average household received 10 bills per month from each of 10 different billers. Moreover, turning off paper was indisputably better for the planet.

But was e-billing a potentially lucrative business for Fiserv? And if so, what was the best strategy to take full advantage of this technology?

FISERV AND ELECTRONIC BILL PAYMENT

Fiserv (NASDAQ: FISV) was formed in July 1984 with the merger of Sunshine State Systems of Tampa and First Data Processing of Milwaukee, regional providers of financial services data processing for small banks and thrifts. Fiserv went public in 1986. By 2009 the *Fortune* 500 company, headquartered in Brookfield, Wisconsin, employed 20,000 people in 230 global locations. The company's 2008 revenues were $4.74 billion, with net income of $537 million. Fiserv competed in several markets: it was the U.S. market leader in core processing services and the largest independent U.S. check processor. It became the leading U.S. Internet banking services provider and leader in bill payment and presentment services when it acquired CheckFree in December 2007.

In 2009 e-billing represented a relatively small revenue stream for Fiserv. A majority of the company's e-commerce division revenues came instead from electronic bill payment. Electronic bill payment was conceived by a former decathlete named Pete Kight while he was managing health clubs in Texas in the late 1970s. At that time, convenient monthly payment methods were not available, so health club consumers were often pressed to pay for an entire year in advance—and each year after. This caused frustration for consumers as well as for the health club salespeople who had to perpetually convince them to renew their memberships.

Having successfully tested an automatic monthly payment arrangement between his health club and a local bank, Kight returned to his hometown of Columbus, Ohio, to launch a company called CheckFree. The company, which he initially ran from his grandmother's basement, provided electronic payment services not just to health clubs but also to any biller and its payee. He was convinced that over time electronic bill payment was more efficient and would win out over paper-based processes. Kight's first customer was a friend who owned an apartment complex. The friend agreed to let Kight use the building's computer at night, and Kight agreed to sign up the friend's tenants to pay their rent electronically.

Building on the technology and knowledge he developed to serve that first customer, Kight led CheckFree through the early days of the Internet and successfully competed against rivals such as IBM, Microsoft, First Data, and Citibank. As the company grew, Kight's management team recognized that encouraging adoption and use of electronic bill payment required not only convincing billers and banks to take part but also successfully marketing the service to end users. The team also realized that banks and billers had many more important priorities than developing strategies for marketing electronic payment services. To maintain leadership among larger rivals, therefore, the company had to understand the marketplace better than anyone else and continually redefine strategies based upon consumer wants and needs.

The company committed itself to understanding consumer behavior in relation to electronic bill payment. Black and Johnston spearheaded many of these activities, and worked with banks in a consultative manner to help them understand market segments, identify which consumers to target, and communicate with targeted consumers. Their efforts helped CheckFree and its partners shift from making key marketing decisions based on managers' intuition or opinions to using a data-based understanding of consumer needs and preferences to drive action.

In August 2007 Fiserv entered into an agreement to acquire CheckFree in an all-cash transaction valued at approximately $4.4 billion.

By 2009 electronic bill payment was gaining wider acceptance, with penetration driven by convenience over traditional payment methods, savings on postage, and improved perceptions of payment security (see Exhibit 2 on page 86 for adoption rates). Electronic bill payment was now so pervasive and advanced that most consumers could use their bank's Web site to pay anyone, including individuals, electronically.

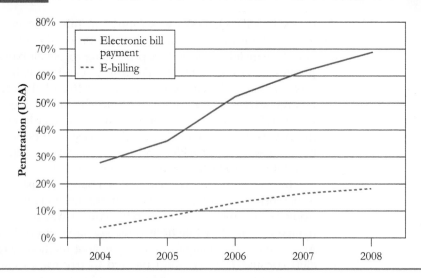

EXHIBIT 2   Consumer Adoption Rates for Electronic Bill Payment and E-Billing

E-BILLING: OPPORTUNITIES AND CHALLENGES

E-bills are electronic versions of paper bills sent to consumers by billers. Billers offering e-billing services included utility companies, cable/satellite TV providers, and financial services firms. E-bills contained the same information as paper bills and offered the same due date. Fiserv developed the technology to allow consumers to receive and view e-bills at a biller's Web site.

Initial feedback from billers reassured Black that they were strongly in favor of converting their consumers from receiving paper bills to receiving e-bills. This enthusiasm was driven in great part by the significant financial savings offered by e-billing. Billers sent monthly bills to consumers. Processing and sending each of these paper bills cost an average of $1.25 per bill, and billers saved up to 45 percent per bill for consumers who no longer received the paper bill. Furthermore, a comparison of sample consumers who received paper bills versus a similar sample of consumers who used e-billing showed that the latter made 10 to 20 percent fewer calls to customer service, thanks mainly to the reduction of payment claims caused by human error in submitting and processing transactions. This created additional annual savings of $2 to $4 per consumer for billers, regardless of whether the e-bill consumer was still receiving paper bills.

Billers also saw e-billing as an opportunity to enhance their environmental practices. One energy company reported that, after converting 130,000 consumers to e-billing, it was able to save 31 tons of paper (the equivalent of 753 trees). Thanks to a reduction in production and delivery costs, e-billing also led to considerable water savings and greenhouse gas reductions.

Billers were also interested in the possibility that e-billing might increase consumer satisfaction. Initial data showed that consumers receiving e-bills were extremely satisfied with the service; this might lead to greater satisfaction with the biller as well as a lower likelihood of defection. Also, because identity thieves often got their information from materials taken from mailboxes and trash receptacles, e-bill consumers enjoyed greater security than consumers who received (and had to dispose of) paper bills.

Recognizing these many benefits, a majority of billers not only offered e-billing to their consumers but also provided it at no charge. Nonetheless, although consumers who tried e-billing expressed high satisfaction with the service, less than 20 percent of online consumers used e-billing as their primary way of viewing bills. Black wondered what was holding up the adoption process.

To better understand consumer perceptions of e-billing, Black asked Johnston to commission several primary consumer research studies. Just as Black and Johnston had used market research to help banks target key segments and effectively position electronic bill payment, they hoped to use research to generate recommendations for billers to convert paper bill–receiving consumers to satisfied end users of e-bills.

 ## E-BILLING MARKET RESEARCH

Online Interviews and Segmentation

Johnston hired a well-known market research firm to study and segment the market for e-billing. As a first step, the firm conducted 1,236 30-minute online interviews with a U.S. sample of e-billing users and potential users. (All respondents had regular Internet access and spent at least one hour online weekly.)

Survey respondents were asked a number of questions about their attitudes and behaviors relating to finances, family life, and professional pursuits. These responses were statistically analyzed, producing six distinct groups with different attitudes and behaviors. These groups are listed and described in Exhibit 3 on page 88.

Focus Groups

Johnston also conducted focus groups with potential consumers who did not use e-billing. Eight groups of 8 individuals (64 total) were given a description of e-billing and asked a series of questions about their willingness to use it. Although focus group participants expressed moderate interest in e-billing overall, they also had several questions, including:

- "Does e-billing automatically pay the bill too?"
- "Who sends the e-bill? The bank or the company I have to pay?"
- "Can I sign up for e-billing through my bank or do I have to ask all the individual companies?"
- "What exactly is the benefit of e-billing?"

Participants also expressed their opinions on e-billing's benefits (e.g., "Getting bills electronically is simpler and quicker than getting them on paper") and drawbacks (e.g., "A paper bill is a physical reminder to pay it; an e-bill doesn't give me that"). One feature that many participants said would help motivate them to use e-billing was "divisibility," or the ability to receive e-bills without being required to stop paper bills.

Concept Test

As a final step, Fiserv conducted a formal concept test of e-billing. The firm contacted 2,000 individuals who were not using e-billing (but who were representative of the overall population of consumers) and encouraged them to try it for two months and then respond to a survey about it. The offer provided a general description of e-billing and allowed consumers to continue receiving paper bills during the trial period. Only 4.5 percent of the sample expressed interest in the offer, though the response rate was close to 8 percent among E-Savvy Planners and

EXHIBIT 3 Consumer Segment Information

	E-Savvy Planners	Maximizers	Self-Improvers	Convenience Seekers	Desperate Avoiders	Paranoid Paper-Pushers
Attitudes	• Will spend $$ on management and time-saving tools • Seek fast, efficient way to manage bills • Prefer electronic bill pay to paper	• View finances as a game to win • Believe they already have a good system to manage bills • Comfortable with new technology	• Very interested in saving time • Do not believe they have a good system for bill management • Minor Internet security concerns	• Dislike clutter • Rarely forget when bills are due • Don't believe better planning leads to better $$ management	• Anxious about unpaid bills • Unsatisfied with their $$ management system • Don't use electronic bill pay	• Avid financial planners • Believe that new technologies waste time
Behaviors	• Early adopters of new technology • Hyperorganized • Regularly check credit report • Most likely to use financial management software	• Often provide financial advice to others • Most likely to check investments online • Have more credit cards than others; pay most off each month	• Sometimes lose bills or forget to pay them • Lack time to balance their checkbooks • Tend to pay bills late when need money for other things	• Keep bill records for a year or more • Don't regularly check their credit reports • Most likely to have no credit cards	• Lose bills and avoid opening them • Forget when bills are due • Unwilling to pay for products that help them save time on $$ management	• Prefer receiving bills by mail and paying by traditional check • Keep a paper schedule of bills and payments • Rarely forget when a bill is due
Demographics	• Avg age: 43 • Avg annual income: $67K • Avg hours online: 14 • College grad or higher: 52%	• Avg age: 43 • Avg annual income: $83K • Avg hours online: 12 • College grad or higher: 75%	• Avg age: 40 • Avg annual income: $60K • Avg hours online: 11 • College grad or higher: 50%	• Avg age: 46 • Avg annual income: $53K • Avg hours online: 12 • College grad or higher: 41%	• Avg age: 40 • Avg annual income: $53K • Avg hours online: 13 • College grad or higher: 47%	• Avg age: 48 • Avg annual income: $63K • Avg hours online: 11 • College grad or higher: 63%
Size	• Percentage of market: 19.7% • Share of bank transactions: 20.6%	• Percentage of market: 24.9% • Share of bank transactions: 27.1%	• Percentage of market: 13.3% • Share of bank transactions: 13.7%	• Percentage of market: 17.5% • Share of bank transactions: 16.9%	• Percentage of market: 15.4% • Share of bank transactions: 12.3%	• Percentage of market: 9.3% • Share of bank transactions: 8.9%

| **EXHIBIT 4** | **Consumer Segments: Attitudes Toward E-Billing** |

Consumers who tried e-billing for two months were asked which features they liked about the service as well as why they might still want to receive a paper bill. The most common responses for each segment are reported below.

	What I Like Most About E-Billing	*Why I Still Want My Paper Bill*
E-Savvy Planners	"It's a lot easier to have all my financial information in one place—on my computer."	No reason: most e-savvy planners were unlikely to see extra value in the paper bill.
Maximizers	"For my daily financial management activities, e-bills make it easier for me to move information between the different programs I use to manage my finances."	"Every detail matters to me when I'm doing financial planning. Paper bills seem to have more complete information."
Self-Improvers	"If all I had was e-billing, it would save me a lot of time opening and handling paper bills."	"I'm always trying to figure out a better way to manage finances. That's easier to do when you can lay out all of your bills on a table."
Convenience Seekers	"I get a lot of bills and statements each month—paper everywhere! If I had e-billing only, it would reduce clutter in my home."	"I know from experience that computer problems can cause a huge waste of time—extremely inconvenient. I need paper backup just in case I experience a breakdown or a disk failure."
Desperate Avoiders	"If I used e-billing only, I know it would really help the environment."	"Getting a paper bill helps remind me that I need to pay."
Paranoid Paper-Pushers	"It's nice to know I have a backup somewhere in case the paper bill gets lost."	"All of my financial planning is in one place in a filing cabinet. It would be too confusing to have most documents there and some on my computer."

Maximizers. When a similar sample was offered $20 in gift cards to try e-billing, 53 percent agreed.

After using e-billing for two months, 73 percent of participants either agreed or strongly agreed with a statement indicating their willingness to adopt e-billing for the long term. Follow-up interviews suggested that the trial period helped ease initial confusion about e-billing and skepticism about its value. For example, one participant noted, "This is a great idea, a great product. But I really needed to use it to understand how great it is."

Consumers were also asked which e-billing features they liked as well as why they might still want a paper bill. Results are reported in Exhibit 4 and are divided by segment.

 # E-BILLING REVENUE MODEL AND CONVERSION COSTS

Fiserv's e-billing revenues came from two potential sources. For consumers who opted to receive an e-bill through Fiserv's biller-direct system but chose to also continue receiving paper bills, the biller paid Fiserv $0.025 each time the consumer viewed the e-bill. For consumers who opted to turn off paper billing in favor of Fiserv's e-billing, the biller paid Fiserv $0.40 per month per consumer regardless of the number of views. Consumers receiving e-bills viewed them an average of once a month, whether or not they had turned off paper billing.

Billers encouraged consumers to adopt e-billing using a combination of direct-mail advertising, e-mail campaigns, billing inserts, and Web-based advertising. These efforts tended to focus on the consumer base as a whole rather than on specific subgroups. Figures from previous campaigns showed that the average cost to convert a consumer directly from all-paper billing to exclusive e-billing was $4.50. The average cost to convert a consumer from all-paper billing to e-bill viewing (while still receiving a paper bill) was $2.00.

Consumers already viewing their bills online (but still receiving paper) were significantly more likely to turn off paper billing than those not receiving e-bills. After consumers used 12 months of e-bill viewing with paper, it cost billers an average of $1.50 per consumer to convince them to turn off paper.

Few data existed about whether consumers receiving e-bills from one biller were more likely to receive e-bills from another. However, a recent survey showed that almost two-thirds of consumers who did not receive paper bills from at least one biller (e-bill only) still received paper bills from at least one other biller.

GETTING THEM TO TURN OFF PAPER

Black and Johnston were encouraged by the market research they had conducted to understand e-billing trends and consumer segments. Although e-billing adoption rates lagged behind those for electronic bill payment, there was strong evidence that consumers saw the value of electronic bill presentment—especially once they tried it. Now Black and Johnston had to develop recommendations based on the market research findings to help billers move their consumers from exclusive paper billing to exclusive e-billing.

Both Black and Johnston recognized that the EVP was expecting strategic recommendations that would convince billers to take specific actions to increase e-billing adoption. This would further establish Fiserv as a provider of user-friendly technologies that billers and banks could employ to make their sites stickier and their consumers more satisfied, in turn making their relationships more profitable and directly improving Fiserv's bottom line. With renewed energy, Black began poring over the research reports to prepare for his strategy session with Johnston.

Case

Dr Pepper Snapple Group, Inc.

Energy Beverages

In early September 2007, Andrew Barker emerged from a lengthy discussion on the energy beverage market in the United States. As a brand manager for Snapple beverages at the Dr Pepper Snapple Group, Inc., he was charged with assessing whether or not a profitable market opportunity existed for a new energy beverage brand to be produced, marketed, and distributed by the company in 2008. Dr Pepper Snapple Group, Inc. was the only major domestic nonalcoholic beverage company in the United States without a significant branded energy drink of its own.

Energy beverages are broadly defined as drinks that provide a consumer with a boost of energy. The central ingredient in most energy beverages is caffeine derived from the guarana bean. Other common ingredients include taurine, ginseng, carnitine, and B vitamins. Energy drinks are considered functional beverages. Other functional beverages include sports drinks, ready-to-drink tea, enhanced fruit drinks, soy beverages, and enhanced water.

The decision to explore a new energy beverage was made by senior company management as part of a corporate business strategy to focus on opportunities in high-growth and high-margin beverage businesses. As part of this strategy, Dr Pepper Snapple Group, Inc. launched the Accelerade RTD brand, a ready-to-drink sports drink, in late May 2007. Barker believed that the decision to introduce the Accelerade RTD brand into a new beverage market for the company (sports drinks) was similar to the situation he faced with recommending whether or not Dr Pepper Snapple Group, Inc. should introduce a new branded product into the energy beverage market.

The cooperation of Dr Pepper Snapple Group, Inc. in the preparation of this case is gratefully acknowledged. This case was prepared by Professor Roger A. Kerin, of the Cox School of Business, Southern Methodist University, as a basis for class discussion and is not designed to illustrate effective or ineffective handling of an administrative situation. Certain case information is disguised and not useful for research purposes. All financial, market, and other information is through 2007, unless otherwise noted. Brand names of Dr Pepper Snapple Group, Inc. are registered trademarks and used with permission. Copyright © 2009 by Roger A. Kerin. No part of this case may be reproduced without written permission of the copyright holder.

DR PEPPER SNAPPLE GROUP, INC.

Dr Pepper Snapple Group, Inc. is a major integrated brand owner, bottler, and distributor of nonalcoholic beverages in the United States, Mexico, and Canada. In 2007, the company posted net sales of $5.748 billion. Eighty-nine percent of company net sales were generated in the United States, 4 percent in Canada, and 7 percent in Mexico and the Caribbean.

Scope of Company Operations

In the United States and Canada, Dr Pepper Snapple Group, Inc. participated primarily in the flavored carbonated soft drink (CSD) market segment. The company's key brands are Dr Pepper, 7UP, Sunkist, A&W, and Canada Dry. The company also sells regional and smaller niche brands. In the CSD market segment, the company is primarily a manufacturer of beverage concentrates and fountain syrups. Beverage concentrates are highly concentrated proprietary flavors used to make syrup or finished beverages. The company manufactures beverage concentrates that are used by its own bottling operations as well as sold to third-party bottling companies. Dr Pepper Snapple Group, Inc. had an 18.8 percent share of the U.S. CSD market segment in 2007 (measured by retail sales), which increased from 18.5 percent in 2006 according to ACNielsen. The company also manufactures fountain syrup that is sold to the foodservice industry directly, through bottlers or through third parties.

In the non-CSD market segment in the United States, Dr Pepper Snapple Group, Inc. participated primarily in the ready-to-drink tea, juice, juice drinks, and mixer categories. The company's key non-CSD brands are Snapple, Mott's, Hawaiian Punch, and Clamato, in addition to regional and smaller niche brands. The company manufactures most of the non-CSDs as ready-to-drink beverages and distributes them through its own distribution network and through third parties or direct to customers' warehouses. In addition to non-CSD beverages, the company manufactures Mott's apple sauce as a finished product. Exhibit 1 displays representative company-owned brands in the United States.

EXHIBIT 1   Representative Dr Pepper Snapple Group, Inc. Beverage Brands

Source: Courtesy of Dr Pepper Snapple Group, Inc.

In Mexico and the Caribbean, Dr Pepper Snapple Group, Inc. participated primarily in the carbonated mineral water, flavored CSD, bottled water, and vegetable juice categories. Its key brands in Mexico include Peñafiel, Squirt, Clamato, and Aguafiel. In Mexico, the company manufactures and sells its own brands through both its own bottling operations and third-party bottlers. In the Caribbean, the company distributes its products solely through third-party distributors and bottlers.

Company Strengths

Dr Pepper Snapple Group, Inc. senior executives have identified seven key strengths that the company brings to the marketplace. Each is summarized below.

Strong Portfolio of Leading, Consumer-Preferred Brands Dr Pepper Snapple Group, Inc. owns a diverse portfolio of well-known CSD and non-CSD brands. Many brands enjoy high levels of consumer awareness, preference, and loyalty rooted in their rich heritage, which drive their market positions. This diverse portfolio provides bottlers, distributors, and retailers with a wide variety of products and provides a foundation for growth and profitability. The company is the number one flavored CSD company in the United States according to ACNielsen. In addition, it is the only major beverage concentrate manufacturer with year-over-year market share growth in the CSD market segment in each of the last four years ended 2007, according to ACNielsen. Its largest brand, Dr Pepper, is the number two flavored CSD in the United States, according to ACNielsen, and the Snapple brand is a leading ready-to-drink tea. Overall, in 2007, more than 75 percent of Dr Pepper Snapple Group, Inc. volume was generated by brands that hold either the first or second position in their category. The strength of these key brands has served as a platform for launching innovations and brand extensions such as Dr Pepper Soda Fountain Classics, Motts for Tots, and Snapple Antioxidant Waters.

Integrated Business Model Dr Pepper Snapple Group, Inc. management believes its brand ownership, bottling, and distribution are more integrated than the U.S. operations of its principal competitors and that this differentiation provides the company with a competitive advantage. The company's integrated business model also provides opportunities for net sales and profit growth through the alignment of the economic interests of its brand ownership and its bottling and distribution businesses.

Strong Customer Relationships Dr Pepper Snapple Group, Inc. brands have long-standing relationships with many of its top customers. Company products are sold to a wide range of customers, from bottlers and distributors to national retailers, large foodservice, and convenience store customers. The company has strong relationships with some of the largest bottlers and distributors, including those affiliated with Coca-Cola and PepsiCo; some of the largest and most important U.S. retailers, including Walmart, Safeway, Kroger, and Target; some of the largest foodservice customers, including McDonald's, Yum! Brands (KFC, Pizza Hut, Taco Bell, Long John Silver's, and A&W All-American Food), and Burger King; and convenience store customers, including 7-Eleven.

Attractive Positioning Within a Large, Growing, and Profitable Market
Dr Pepper Snapple Group, Inc. holds the number three position in each of the United States, Canada, and Mexico beverage markets. Each of these markets is well positioned to benefit from emerging consumer trends such as the need for convenience and the demand for products with health and wellness benefits. In

addition, the company participates in many of the growing categories in the liquid refreshment beverage market, such as ready-to-drink teas. The company does not participate significantly in colas, which have declined in CSD volume share from 70.0 percent in 1991 to 57.4 percent in 2006 in the United States, according to *Beverage Digest*, a major trade publication. Nor does the company participate significantly in the bottled water market segment, which is a highly competitive and generally low-margin market segment. Following its acquisition by Coca-Cola, Energy Brands, Inc. terminated its distribution agreement with the company on August 30, 2007, for Glacéau brand products, including vitamin water, fruit water, and smart water.

Broad Geographic Manufacturing and Distribution Coverage   Dr Pepper Snapple Group, Inc. has 21 manufacturing facilities and approximately 200 distribution centers in the United States, as well as four manufacturing processes. Company warehouses are located at or near bottling plants and geographically dispersed across sales regions to ensure company products are available to meet consumer demand. The company manages transportation of its products using its own fleet of delivery trucks, as well as third-party logistics providers on a selected basis. Following recent bottling acquisitions and manufacturing investment, the company has broad geographic coverage with strategically located manufacturing and distribution capabilities, enabling it to better align its operations with customers, reduce transportation costs, and have greater control over the timing and coordination of new product launches.

Strong Operating Margins and Significant, Stable Cash Flows   The breadth and strength of the Dr Pepper Snapple Group, Inc. product portfolio have enabled the company to generate strong operating margins which, combined with relatively modest capital expenditures, have delivered significant and stable cash flows. These cash flows create stockholder value by enabling the company to consider a variety of alternatives, such as investing in its business, reducing debt, and returning capital to its stockholders.

Experienced Executive Management Team   The Dr Pepper Snapple Group, Inc. executive management team has an average of more than 20 years of experience in the food and beverage industry. The team has broad experience in brand ownership, bottling, and distribution, and enjoys strong relationships both within the industry and with major customers. In addition, the management team has diverse skills that support operating strategies, including driving organic growth through targeted and efficient marketing, reducing operating costs, enhancing distribution efficiencies, aligning manufacturing and bottling and distribution interests, and executing strategic acquisitions.

Company Business Strategy

There are six key elements of the Dr Pepper Snapple Group, Inc. business strategy as described by executive management. Each capitalizes on company strengths.

Build and Enhance Leading Brands   Dr Pepper Snapple Group, Inc. has a well-defined strategy to allocate marketing and sales resources. The company uses an ongoing process of market and consumer analysis to identify key brands that have the greatest potential for profitable sales growth. For example, in 2006 and 2007, the Snapple product portfolio was enhanced by launching brand extensions with functional benefits, such as super premium teas and juice drinks and Snapple Antioxidant Waters. Also, in 2006, 7UP was relaunched with 100 percent natural flavors and no artificial preservatives, thereby differentiating the 7UP brand from other major lemon-lime CSDs. The company intends to invest most heavily in its key brands to drive profitable and sustainable growth by strengthening consumer awareness, developing innovative products and brand extensions to take advantage of evolving consumer trends, improving distribution, and increasing promotional effectiveness.

Focus on Opportunities in High-Growth and High-Margin Categories

Dr Pepper Snapple Group, Inc. is focused on driving growth in its business in profitable and emerging categories. These categories include ready-to-drink teas and functional beverages. For example, the company recently launched Snapple super premium teas and juices, Snapple enhanced waters, and Accelerade RTD, a protein-enhanced sports drink. The company also intends to capitalize on opportunities in these categories through brand extensions, new product launches, and selective acquisitions of brands and distribution rights. Senior management believes the company is well positioned to enter into new distribution agreements for emerging, high-growth third-party brands in new categories that can use its bottling and distribution network. The company can provide these brands with distribution capability and resources to grow. These brands, in turn, can provide the company exposure to growing segments of the market with relatively low risk and capital investment.

Increase Presence in High-Margin Channels and Packages

Dr Pepper Snapple Group, Inc. is focused on improving its product presence in high-margin channels, such as convenience stores, vending machines, and small independent retail outlets, through increased selling activity and significant investments in coolers and other cold drink equipment. The company intends to significantly increase the number of branded coolers and other cold drink equipment over the next few years, which is expected to provide an attractive return on investment. The company also intends to increase demand for high-margin products like single-serve packages for many key brands through increased promotional activity and innovation.

Leverage the Company's Integrated Business Model

The company's integrated brand ownership, bottling, and distribution business model provides opportunities for net sales and profit growth through the alignment of the economic interests of its brand ownership and its bottling and distribution businesses. The company intends to leverage its integrated business model to reduce costs by creating greater geographic manufacturing and distribution coverage and to be more flexible and responsive to the changing needs of large retail customers by coordinating sales, service, distribution, promotions, and product launches.

Strengthen the Company's Route-to-Market Through Acquisitions

The recent acquisition and creation of the Dr Pepper Snapple Bottling Group is part of a longer-term initiative to strengthen the route-to-market for the company's products. Additional acquisitions of regional bottling companies will broaden geographic coverage in regions where the company is currently underrepresented, enhance coordination with large retail customers, more quickly address changing customer demands, accelerate the introduction of new products, improve collaboration around new product innovations, and expand coverage of high-margin channels.

Improve Operating Efficiency

The company's recently announced restructuring will reduce selling, general, and administrative expenses and improve operating efficiency. In addition, the integration of recent acquisitions into the company's bottling group has created the opportunity to improve manufacturing, warehousing, and distribution operations. For example, the company has created multiproduct manufacturing facilities that can provide a sales region with a wide variety of products at reduced transportation and co-packing costs.

THE ENERGY BEVERAGE MARKET IN THE UNITED STATES

Excluding coffee, energy beverages were the fourth largest nonalcoholic beverage category in the United States in 2006 after carbonated soft drinks, sports drinks, and bottled water. However, it was the fastest growing beverage category.

Energy Beverage Sales Growth

As a practical matter, the energy beverage market is defined by major brands, including Red Bull, Monster Energy, Rockstar, and literally hundreds of similarly positioned brands. These brands produced estimated retail dollar sales of $6.2 billion in 2006 according to the market research firm Packaged Facts. Off-premise sales through convenience stores, supermarkets, and mass merchandisers accounted for 71 percent of total retail sales in 2006. On-premise retailers, such as restaurants and nightclubs, accounted for 29 percent of total retail sales. From 2001 to 2006, total energy beverage retail sales grew at an average annual rate of 42.5 percent. In 2006, an estimated 153 million energy beverage cases were sold across all retail channels (one case is equivalent to 36 8-ounce containers, or 288 ounces).

Industry analysts were projecting an average annual growth rate of 10.5 percent from 2007 to 2011. The slower growth rate was attributed to market maturity, increased price and packaging competition, and the entrance of hybrid energy beverages, such as energy water, energy fruit drinks, ready-to-drink energy teas, and energy colas.

Energy beverage sales in 2006 were dwarfed by CSD sales of $72 billion according to *Beverage Digest*. However, CSD sales posted an average year-over-year growth rate of 2.5 percent between 2001 and 2006 and were projected to decline 1 to 2 percent annually through 2011.

The Energy Beverage Consumer

The heavy user of energy beverages consists of males between the ages of 12 and 34 (see Exhibit 2). Average U.S. per capita consumption of energy beverage drinkers increased by 14 percent since 2004, reaching 4.32 8-ounce servings per month in 2006. Energy beverages are most often consumed in the afternoon followed by morning consumption. Most consumers drink energy beverages at home, in the car, and at work/school. The major reasons why consumers drink energy beverages include an energy boost, mental alertness, refreshment, and taste. Energy beverage consumers limit their choice to only 1.4 different brands, on average, which suggests brand loyalty in this market.

Energy Beverage Off-Premise Retail Channels

Convenience stores and supermarkets are the dominant off-premise retail channels for energy beverages. In 2006, convenience stores accounted for 74 percent of off-premise retail dollar sales, down from 81 percent in 2004. Supermarkets recorded 14 percent of off-premise retail sales in 2006, up from 11 percent

EXHIBIT 2 U.S. Population Profile and Energy Beverage Users in 2006

Age				Gender				Race and Ethnicity			
Age Category	% of U.S. Population[1]	% Users[2]	Servings/ Month[3]	Gender Category	% of U.S. Population[1]	% Users[2]	Servings/ Month[3] Category	Race & Ethnic Category	% of U.S. Population[1]	% Users[2]	Servings/ Month[3]
12–17	10%	31%	4.92	F Adult	39%	10%	NA	Hispanic	15%	27%	4.48
18–24	9%	34%	4.93	F Teen	5%	27%	NA	African American	13%	21%	4.69
25–34	14%	22%	4.29	M Adult	34%	17%	NA	Asian	4%	16%	3.49
35–44	15%	25%	4.16	M Teen	6%	34%	NA	Caucasian	66%	12%	4.31
45–54	14%	9%	4.14	F Total	51%	19%	3.87	Others	2%	NA	NA
55+	23%	3%	2.83	M Total	49%	26%	4.60				

Notes: [1] % of U.S. Population is based on U.S. Census estimates for 2006.

[2] % Users represents the percentage of individuals in a specific user category that have consumed an energy beverage in the past year. Therefore, the percent user figures do not total 100 percent. (Source: Mintel/Simmons National Consumer Survey, Fall 2006)

[3] Servings/Month is the average number of 8-ounce servings consumed per month by a specific user category. (Source: Mintel/Simmons National Consumer Survey, Fall 2006)

EXHIBIT 3	Estimated 2006 Dollar Sales and Unit Volume Market Share of U.S. Energy Beverage Competitors

	Estimated Market Share	
Competitor (Major Brands)	Dollar Sales	Unit Case Volume
Red Bull (Red Bull)	43%	30%
Hansen Natural Corporation (Monster Energy)	16	27
Pepsi-Cola (SoBe Adrenaline Rush; AMP Energy)	13	10
Rockstar (Rockstar)	12	17
Coca-Cola (Full Throttle; Tab Energy)	10	10
Others (including private labels)	6	6
	100%	100%

Source: *Mintel Energy Drinks*, March 2007; *Beverage Digest Fact Book*, 2007; and "Energy Drinks Boost U.S. Beverage Market," Beveragedaily.com, March 12, 2007.

in 2004. Industry analysts expected continued sales erosion in the convenience channel in the future. Wal-Mart's share of energy beverage off-premise retail sales increased from 5.4 percent in 2004 to 7.4 percent in 2006.

In general, energy beverage manufacturers with a broad product line and an extensive distribution network have had the greatest success in gaining shelf space in supermarkets and mass merchandisers for their brands. Product turnover is a key consideration among convenience stores. Brands with a limited product line that can demonstrate high turnover are stocked while those with low turnover are discontinued by convenience stores.

Major Energy Beverage Competitors

Five competitors dominate the U.S. energy beverage market: Red Bull North America, Hansen Natural Corporation, Pepsi-Cola, Rockstar, Inc., and Coca-Cola. These companies, and their individual brands, account for 94 percent of dollar sales and unit volume in the United States. Exhibit 3 shows the dollar sales and unit volume market shares for the five competitors.

Red Bull North America   Red Bull North America markets the Red Bull brand in the United States through a network of independent distributors. The company is a subsidiary of Red Bull GMBH headquartered in Austria. The brand was the energy beverage market pioneer when it was introduced to the United States in 1997. It remains the market leader in dollar sales and unit volume. However, its dollar market share has declined in recent years from 82 percent in 2000 to 43 percent in 2006. This decline has been attributed to the entry of new, aggressive competitors, and brands with lower prices. The Red Bull brand was supported by a $39.6 million U.S. media expenditure in 2006 and an estimated $60.9 million media expenditure in 2007.[1]

Hansen Natural Corporation   Hansen Natural Corporation markets a variety of nonalcoholic beverages in the United States. Monster Energy is its most prominent energy drink. The brand was introduced in 2002. Monster Energy sales have benefited from recent distribution agreements. For example, Anheuser-Busch

---

[1] Media expenditure figures for individual brands were reported in company Form 10-K documents and TNS Media Intelligence, AdSpender Online at tns-mi.com.

wholesalers distributed the brand to retailers in different territories in the United States in 2007. Anheuser-Busch also distributes Monster Energy to on-premise retailers including bars, nightclubs, and restaurants in territories selected by Hansen. In early 2007, Hansen announced that PepsiCo Canada would be the exclusive master distributor of Monster Energy throughout Canada. The Monster Energy brand was supported by a $61,100 U.S. media expenditure in 2006 and an estimated $153,800 media expenditure in 2007.

Pepsi-Cola Pepsi-Cola, a division of PepsiCo, markets AMP Energy and SoBe Adrenaline Rush energy beverage brands. AMP Energy was introduced in 2001. SoBe Adrenaline Rush entered the market in 2003. Both brands are marketed through the Pepsi-Cola distribution system in the United States. In addition, Pepsi-Cola markets a wide range of juice-based energy drinks and Mountain Dew MDX, a carbonated energy drink. Neither AMP Energy nor SoBe Adrenaline Rush was supported by significant U.S. media expenditures in 2006.

Rockstar, Inc. Rockstar, Inc. is a producer of alcoholic, juice, cola, and energy drinks. Its Rockstar Energy brand was introduced in 2001. The brand is distributed in the United States and Canada by the Coca-Cola Company, except in the Pacific Northwest and Northern California where Rockstar retains its original distributors. U.S. media expenditures for the Rockstar brand were minimal in 2006. The estimated media expenditure in 2007 was $41,500.

Coca-Cola The Coca-Cola Company markets the Full Throttle and sugar-free Tab Energy brands through its distribution network. Full Throttle was introduced in 2003, Tab Energy in 2006. The company has been acquiring smaller energy beverage brands and pursuing licensing agreements to distribute independent energy brands, such as Rockstar. Full Throttle was supported by $7.3 million in U.S. media expenditures in 2006 and an estimated $492,300 in 2007. The Tab Energy introduction was supported by a $12.6 million U.S. media expenditure in 2006, which resulted in a 2.3 percent dollar market share. The estimated media expenditure in 2007 was $20,500.

Product Proliferation and Price Erosion

The energy beverage market has experienced product proliferation and price erosion in recent years. Product proliferation resulted from line extensions, new packaging and sizes, and market segmentation. Major competitors have extended their product lines and now offer beverages in regular and sugar-free varieties and different flavors. They have introduced multi-packs and increased single-serve package sizes, from the original 8.3-ounce Red Bull package to 16-ounce and 24-ounce packages. (Tab Energy came in a 10.5-ounce package.) Finally, competitors are targeting segments in the energy beverage market. For example, women were the target market for Tab Energy; Coca-Cola is believed to be developing a brand called "Rehab" for people with hangovers; industry analysts expect Rockstar to introduce Rockstar 21, which is premixed with alcohol; and the Full Throttle Demon sub-brand is targeted at young Hispanic men.

Significant price erosion also exists. Energy beverage prices declined 30 percent from 2001 to 2006. Industry analysts attribute this decline to (1) larger package sizes that have a lower price per ounce; (2) the introduction of multi-packs, which offer a lower price per ounce, and (3) increasing availability in supermarkets and mass merchandisers, including Walmart, that operate with lower retail gross margins than convenience stores.

According to ACNielsen, the average retail selling price per case for brands in major off-premise retail channels in late 2007 is shown below.[2]

Brand	All Off-Premise Channels	Supermarkets and Mass Merchandisers Only	Convenience Stores Only
Red Bull	$68.00	$63.00	$70.00
Monster Energy	37.00	32.00	39.00
Rockstar	37.00	32.00	38.00
Full Throttle	36.00	32.00	38.00
AMP Energy	38.00	35.00	39.00
Tab Energy	49.00	45.00	55.00
Channel Average	44.00	40.00	46.00

Red Bull enjoyed a price premium in off-premise retail channels. Other brands were competitively priced with each other.

THE ENERGY BEVERAGE MARKET OPPORTUNITY

Andrew Barker and his team recognized that senior executives at Dr Pepper Snapple Group, Inc. expected that energy beverages presented a profitable market opportunity for the company. Therefore, any proposal to enter the energy beverage market would require a marketing strategy for a branded energy drink, including a first-year sales and profit projection.

Marketing Plan Considerations

The introductory marketing plan for a branded energy drink would require the identification of a target market and marketing mix as well as a recommended budget for the launch.

Target Market   Industry analysts estimated that there were about 43 million energy drink users in the United States, or about 18 percent of the U.S. population 12 years of age or older. Males, between the ages of 12 and 34, were the heaviest users of energy beverages. They were estimated to account for about 70 percent of energy beverage consumption. Energy brands, except for Tab Energy with its focus on female consumers, targeted this population demographic.

Product Line and Brand Positioning   Existing brands typically offer regular and sugar-free varieties. Regular energy beverages have an 80 percent share of the market; sugar-free has 20 percent. Single-serve package sizes range from 8.3 ounces to 24 ounces. The 8.3-ounce size is the most popular due largely to Red Bull, the market leader, which uniquely markets this size. The 16-ounce size, representing about 50 percent of case sales in convenience stores, has posted the fastest growth, increasing 150 percent since 2004. Multi-packs represent a small portion of case sales and typically are marketed through supermarkets and mass merchandisers.

---

[2] The average retail case prices reflect all available package sizes and multi-packs for each brand. All prices are rounded to the nearest dollar. Channel average price is rounded to the nearest dollar and represents a simple column average.

Brand positioning in the energy beverage market typically emphasizes an energy boost, mental alertness, refreshment, and taste. Brand slogans reflect this positioning:

Red Bull:	"Red Bull Gives You Wings"
Monster Energy:	"Unleash the Beast"
Full Throttle:	"Go Full Throttle or Go Home"
Tab Energy:	"Fuel to Be Fabulous"

Rockstar Energy positions itself as the most powerful energy drink with an "edgier" message focusing on "active and exhausting lifestyles—from athletes to rock stars."

Marketing Channel Dr Pepper Snapple Group, Inc. bottlers and distributors deliver to all types of off-premise retailers where energy beverages are sold. However, company bottlers and distributors did not serve all areas of the United States. By early 2008, the company expected to have bottlers and distribution centers in place that would serve 80 percent of the U.S. market for energy beverages. Historically, new energy beverage brands were introduced exclusively to the convenience store channel in single-serve packages because of higher profit margins and then migrated to other channels.

Dr Pepper Snapple Group, Inc. distributed Monster Energy in selected U.S. territories on behalf of Hansen Natural Corporation in 2007.[3] Monster Energy distribution would end effective November 10, 2008.

Manufacturer's Suggested Retail Selling Price and Channel Margins
Single-serve energy beverage drink retail prices have generally settled at roughly $2.00 per single-serve package, regardless of package size. As a consequence, larger single-serve packages are priced lower on a per-ounce basis than smaller packages.

Estimated retail, wholesale, and manufacturer energy beverage margins, on a per-case basis, vary within a fairly tight range.[4] Retailers, such as supermarkets and convenience stores, typically report gross margins in the range of 40 percent (for supermarkets) to 50 percent (for convenience stores), based on the manufacturer's suggested retail price. Wholesalers (distributors and bottlers) typically report a gross margin of 30 to 36 percent of the price sold to retailers. Finally, energy beverage manufacturers typically obtain a gross margin between 60 and 66 percent on sales to wholesalers. Industry sources indicate that the manufacturer's cost of goods sold consisted of a packaging cost (which included cans, trays, shrink wrap, and freight) and a content cost.

Advertising and Promotion Except for Red Bull, brand media advertising in the energy beverage market is modest. Instead, competitors rely on promotional vehicles such as brand Web sites, events, and sponsorships to promote their brands. In 2006, the top five competitors spent an estimated $70 million for measured advertising media.[5] Industry analysts estimated that expenditures for other promotional vehicles were 4 to 6 times higher than media expenditures.

---

[3] Hansen Natural Corporation Form 10-K for the fiscal year ended December 31, 2007, p. 10.

[4] The margin structure estimates are based on interviews with individuals knowledgeable about the industry and are useful for case discussion purposes only.

[5] TNS Media Intelligence, AdSpender Online at tms-mi.com.

For example, Red Bull spends about $300 million annually on sports sponsorships alone.[6]

The Sports Drink Market and the Accelerade RTD Launch

Andrew Barker believed there was a strategic similarity between the launch of Accelerade RTD and the possible introduction of a new energy beverage brand. In both cases, Dr Pepper Snapple Group, Inc. was introducing a new branded product into a new beverage market for the company.

U.S. Sports Drink Market   The U.S. sports drink market posted total retail sales of $7.5 billion in 2006 and a year-over-year growth rate of about 13 percent. Gatorade, marketed by the Pepsi-Cola division of PepsiCo, was the sports drink market pioneer and the perennial market share leader. The brand commanded a market share of 81 percent in 2006 and was supported by $183 million in media expenditures. Powerade, marketed by Coca-Cola, had an 18 percent market share. Gatorade and Powerade offer broad product lines and are competitively priced with each other with Gatorade holding a modest price premium. Each brand was distributed through its company's extensive distribution network that serves convenience stores, supermarkets, mass merchandisers, and a variety of other retailers.

Accelerade   The Accelerade brand was part of an asset purchase agreement by the company whereby Pacific Health Laboratories, Inc., the original brand owner, received an upfront payment, a royalty payment for a period of time, and a royalty-free license to continue selling Accelerade and Endurox in power and gel forms through health and nutrition outlets. Accelerade was already popular with hard-core athletes given its 4:1 ratio of carbohydrate to protein and documented benefits in terms of improved endurance, enhanced rehydration, faster muscle recovery, and less postexercise muscle damage.

Accelerade RTD Brand Launch   Dr Pepper Snapple Group, Inc. introduced the Accelerade RTD, a ready-to-drink sports drink, in late May 2007 to convenience stores, supermarkets, and mass merchandisers through its distribution network. The target market for Accelerade RTD was the 35 million Americans who exercised regularly and were concerned about being competitive.

Accelerade RTD was launched with a 20-ounce single-serve package in four flavors: Citrus Grapefruit, Fruit Punch, Mountain Berry, and Peach Mango. The manufacturer's suggested retail price was $2.79—roughly twice the price of a 20-ounce Gatorade single-serve package. The premium price was attributed to Accelerade RTD's unique point of difference—the first protein-enhanced sports drink. Neither Gatorade nor Powerade had this attribute.

A large marketing budget supported the Accelerade RTD launch, including new-media elements, such as a brand Web site, podcasts, search-engine marketing, and a chat room. The campaign's theme was "Sweat Smarter" to distinguish Accelerade RTD from its rivals by promoting the brand's protein content.[7]

---

[6] Melanie Ho, "For Red Bull, It's Here, There and Everywhere," *The Washington Post* (August 23, 2006), p. E1ff.

[7] Stuart Elliott, "Cadbury Bets on Protein to Promote Its New Sports Drink," *The New York Times*, downloaded June 29, 2007.

Marketing Decisions

Andrew Barker realized that numerous marketing decisions were required in the development and launch of a branded energy drink.

Target Market Selection   He would need to first recommend the target market for the brand. For example, should the target market include all energy drink users or only heavy users? Alternatively, should a select customer group be targeted, as Coca-Cola had done with Tab Energy in 2006?

Product Line and Positioning Choice   Andrew Barker would also need to decide on a product line. Should he introduce the brand in a single-serve package or in a multi-pack? What package size(s) should he choose: 8-ounce, 16-ounce, or 24-ounce? Should he offer both a regular and sugar-free version? How many flavors should be introduced: one or two? He recognized that some trade-offs would be required. For example, he believed that bottlers and distributors and retailers would initially not produce and stock more than two stock-keeping units (SKUs) of a new energy drink brand.[8] Therefore, choosing the appropriate mix of packaging (single-serve, multi-pack), package size(s) (8-, 16-, 24-ounce), versions (regular, sugar-free), and flavors (one, two) was foremost on his mind. Looking forward, Andrew Barker believed that additional SKUs could be introduced.

Brand positioning also required attention. Barker believed that energy brands on the market lacked meaningful differentiation. Energy drink positioning typically focused on providing an energy boost, mental alertness, refreshment, and taste for males 12 to 34. Following discussions with research and development personnel, he wondered whether an opportunity existed to differentiate a new energy brand on the basis of packaging or ingredients. Specifically, manufacturing personnel showed him a 16.9-ounce (0.5 liter) single-serve aluminum bottle shape with a resealable screw cap. The idea of a bottle shape with a resealable screw cap intrigued him. No brand had such packaging. "It would certainly stand out on a store shelf among the cylinder-shaped cans sold by competitors," he said.

An opportunity also existed to differentiate a new brand on the basis of ingredients. Specifically, a new brand could augment the "energy" and "mental alertment" benefits by increasing the amount of caffeine, herbs, and B vitamins per 8-ounce serving.

Alternatively, no brand had positioned itself as an adult energy drink. An adult energy beverage might require a different drink, such as lower carbohydrates in the product formulation. Although adults were less frequent users than teens, such a positioning deserved consideration. Adults, for instance, between the ages of 35 and 54 consumed energy beverages at a rate that was only slightly less than consumers under 24.

Other positioning approaches were also a possibility, including a head-to-head positioning against competitors. Barker knew that his recommendation would require a brand positioning statement that would resonate with energy drink consumers.

---

[8] A stock-keeping unit (SKU) is a specific unit of inventory that is carried as a separate identifiable unit. An 8-ounce can and a 16-ounce can of the same product would be separate SKUs for inventory purposes. Similarly, different flavors for a single brand would each represent a separate SKU. Therefore, two new flavors packaged in two different size packages would be counted as four SKUs for inventory purposes.

Marketing Channel Choice   The Dr Pepper Snapple Group, Inc. bottling and distribution system supplied both off-premise and on-premise retailers. Barker believed that off-premise retailers represented the best choice. However, a decision had to be made about which retailers to serve initially. Should all off-premise retailers be served or should distribution for a new energy drink brand focus on convenience stores only or supermarkets and mass merchandisers only?

Advertising and Promotion   Barker recognized that an introductory media advertising and promotion expenditure necessary to launch a new energy drink brand would be expected as part of his recommendation. "We don't have media advertising funds available to even come close to Red Bull," he said. "At the same time, a new energy brand will require a higher media advertising expenditure than an established brand to create consumer awareness and stimulate brand trial." Expenditures for other promotional vehicles also warranted consideration and funding. He believed that a reasonable "ballpark" expenditure for media advertising and promotion, without specific details, would be sufficient as part of his analysis and recommendation.

Pricing and Profitability

Ultimately, Andrew Barker knew that an analysis of whether or not a market opportunity existed for a new energy brand had to include a manufacturer's suggested retail selling price and a profitability analysis. Retail prices in the energy beverage market had settled in a range around $2.00 per single-serve package, regardless of package size. However, he could recommend a higher or lower price with justification.

The pricing decision, expected unit volume, trade and brand margins, and marketing plan decisions and expenditures would factor into his assessment as to whether or not a profitable market opportunity existed for a new energy beverage brand. A pro forma income statement detailing revenues and costs would reflect his marketing decisions and expectations.

Case

Janmar Coatings, Inc.

In early January 2005, Ronald Burns, president of Janmar Coatings, Inc., slumped back in his chair as his senior management executives filed out of the conference room. "Another meeting and still no resolution," he thought. After two lengthy meetings, the executive group still had not decided where and how to deploy corporate marketing efforts among the various architectural paint coatings markets served by the company in the southwestern United States. He asked his secretary to schedule another meeting for next week.

 ## THE U.S. PAINT COATINGS INDUSTRY

The U.S. paint coatings industry is divided into three broad segments: (1) architectural coatings, (2) original equipment manufacturing (OEM) coatings, and (3) special-purpose coatings. Architectural coatings consist of general-purpose paints, varnishes, and lacquers used on residential, commercial, and institutional structures, sold through wholesalers and retailers, and purchased by do-it-yourself consumers, painting contractors, and professional painters. Architectural coatings are commonly called *shelf goods* and account for 43 percent of total industry dollar sales.

OEM coatings are formulated to industrial buyer specifications and are applied to original equipment during manufacturing. These coatings are used for durable goods such as automobiles, trucks, transportation equipment, appliances, furniture and fixtures, metal containers and building products, and industrial machinery and equipment. OEM coatings represent 35 percent of total industry dollar sales.

Special-purpose coatings are formulated for special applications or environmental conditions, such as extreme temperatures, exposure to chemicals, or corrosive conditions. These coatings are used for automotive and machinery refinishing, industrial construction and maintenance (including factories, equipment, utilities, and railroads), bridges, marine applications (ship and offshore facilities such as oil rigs), highway and traffic markings, aerosol and metallic paints, and roof paints. Special-purpose coatings account for 22 percent of total industry dollar sales.

The U.S. paint coatings industry is generally considered to be a maturing industry. Industry sales in 2004 were estimated to be slightly over $16 billion. Average annual dollar sales growth was forecasted to approximate the general rate of inflation through 2005.

Outlook for Architectural Paint Coatings and Sundries

Industry sources estimated U.S. sales of architectural paint coatings and sundries (brushes, rollers, paint removers and thinners, etc.) to be $12 billion-plus in 2004. Architectural coatings are considered to be a mature market with long-term sales growth projected in the range of 1 to 2 percent per year. Demand for architectural coatings and sundries reflects the level of house redecorating, maintenance, and repair, as well as sales of existing homes, and to a lesser extent new home, commercial, and industrial construction. Industry sources also noted that the demand for architectural coatings and sundries is affected by two other factors. First, the architectural coating segment faced competition from alternative materials, such as aluminum and vinyl siding, interior wall coverings, and wood paneling. Second, paint companies had developed higher-quality products that reduced the amount of paint necessary per application and the frequency of repainting. Counteracting these factors, industry observers foresaw increasing demand for paint sundries due to a trend toward do-it-yourself painting by household consumers.

U.S. paint manufacturers are under growing pressure to reduce emissions of volatile organic compounds (VOCs) from paints and to limit the consumption of solvents. The Environmental Protection Agency (EPA) has adopted a three-step plan for the reduction of VOCs in architectural and industrial maintenance coatings. The first phase of the plan, which took effect in 1996, required a 25 percent reduction in VOC content from the base year of 1990. VOCs were reduced another 35 percent (from the 1990 base year) in 2000 and 45 percent in the third phase in 2003. Compliance with EPA regulations eroded historically low profit margins in the paint industry.

Consolidation and Competition in the Architectural Coatings Segment

Slow sales growth, the necessity for ongoing research and development, and recent compliance with governmental regulations have fueled merger and acquisition activity in the U.S. paint industry. Companies seeking growth and a higher sales base to support increasing costs are making acquisitions. Companies that were unwilling or unable to make capital and research and development (R&D) commitments necessary to remain competitive sold their paint businesses. Industry sources estimate that the number of paint companies is currently 600, or about 40 percent fewer companies than in 1980. The number of paint companies is presently declining at a rate of 2 to 3 percent per year. Merger activity generally involved the purchase of small companies by larger firms to boost their specific market or geographic presence. Still, because of readily available technology and difference in paint formulations associated with regional climatic needs, a small number of regional paint manufacturers, such as Janmar Coatings, have competed successfully against paint manufacturers that distribute their products nationally.

Major producers of paint for the architectural coatings segment include Sherwin-Williams, Benjamin Moore, the Glidden unit of Imperial Chemicals, PPG

Industries, Valspar Corporation, Grow Group, and Pratt & Lambert. These producers account for upward of 60 percent of sales in the architectural coatings segment. They market paint under their own brand names and for retailers under private, controlled, or store brand names. For example, Sherwin-Williams markets the Sherwin-Williams brand and produces paint for Sears.

About 50 percent of architectural coatings are sold under private, controlled, or store brands. Sears, Lowe's, Walmart, and Home Depot are major marketers of these brands. In addition, hardware store groups such as True Value and Ace Hardware market their own paint brands.

Specialty paint stores, lumberyards, and independent hardware stores that sell architectural paint and paint sundries have been able to compete in the paint business despite the presence of mass merchandisers (such as Sears) and home improvement centers (such as Lowe's and Home Depot). Industry sources estimate that specialty paint stores account for about 36 percent of paint and sundry sales; hardware stores and lumberyards account for 14 percent. Furthermore, specialty paint and hardware stores and lumberyards in nonmetropolitan areas have outdistanced mass merchandisers and home improvement centers as sources for paint and paint sundries. This is largely attributable to a lack of home improvement centers and mass-merchandiser distribution in these areas and paint store, hardware, and lumberyard customer relations and service. However, Walmart has been an effective competitor in many nonmetropolitan areas.

Home centers (including wholesale home centers) and mass merchandisers (including membership clubs such as Sam's) represent the two most frequently patronized categories of retailers shopped by do-it-yourself painters for paint and sundry items. Specialty paint stores and lumberyards were the most frequently patronized retail stores by professional painters for paint products and sundry items.

Architectural Coatings Purchase Behavior

Approximately 50 percent of architectural coatings dollar sales are accounted for by do-it-yourselfer painters. Professional painter purchases account for 25 percent of dollar sales. The remainder of architectural coatings dollar sales result from government, export, and contractor sales.

Almost 60 percent of annual architectural coatings sales are for interior paints. Exterior paint represents 38 percent of sales. Lacquers and all other applications make up the balance of sales. Slightly less than one in four households purchase interior house paint in any given year. The percentage of households purchasing exterior house paint is considerably less than that for interior paint. The popularity of do-it-yourself painting, particularly for interior applications, has increased the paint and sundry item product line carried by retail outlets. Paint industry consumer research indicates that the average dollar paint purchase per purchase occasion is about $74.00. The average dollar sundry purchase per purchase occasion is about $12.00.

Research by the Home Improvement Research Institute indicates that do-it-yourself painters first choose a retail outlet for paint and paint sundries, then choose a paint brand. This research also identified four steps in the do-it-yourself decision process for home improvement products, including paint. The results of this research are summarized in Exhibit 1 on page 108.

"Paint has become a commodity," commented Burns. "Do-it-yourself purchasers all too often view paint as paint—a covering—and try to get the best price. But there is a significant number of people who desire service as well in the form

EXHIBIT 1   **Consumer Buying Decision Process for Home Improvement Products**

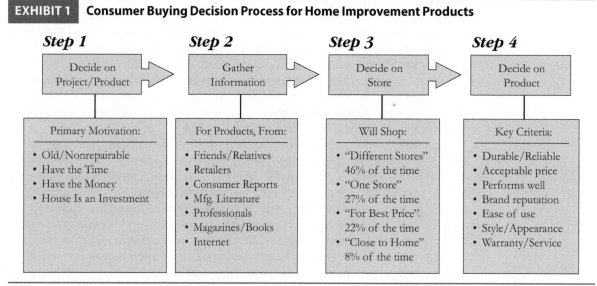

Source: Home Improvement Research Institute. Reprinted from *National Home Center News*, "10 Forces Reshaping the Retail Home Improvement Market,"©1996. Used with permission.

of information about application, color matching, surface preparation, and durability," he added. He conceded that once paint is on the wall, you can't initially tell the difference between premium-priced and competitively priced paint.

"There is a difference between painting contractors and professional painters, however," he continued. "Pot and brush guys [professional painters] do seek out quality products, since their reputation is on the line and maintenance firms don't want to have to paint an office each time a mark appears on a wall. They want paint that is durable, washable, and will cover in a single coat. They also look to retailers who will go the extra mile to give them service. Many request and get credit from stores. They appreciate being able to get to stores early in the morning to pick up paint and supplies. They deal with stores that can mix large quantities of custom colors and expect to work with knowledgeable store employees who can give them what they want. It is not surprising to me that paint stores remain the preferred outlet for paint and sundries for professional painters. Contractors simply want a coating in many instances and strive for the lowest price, particularly on big jobs."

 ## JANMAR COATINGS, INC. SERVICE AREA

Janmar Coatings, Inc. markets its paint and sundry items in over 50 counties in Texas, Oklahoma, New Mexico, and Louisiana from its plant and headquarters in Dallas, Texas. The 11-county Dallas–Fort Worth (DFW) metropolitan area is the major business and financial center in the company's southwestern service area.

Competition at the retail level has accelerated in recent years. Sears and Kmart have multiple outlets in DFW, as do Sherwin- Williams and Home Depot. Competition for retail selling space in paint stores, lumberyards, and hardware stores has also increased. "Our research indicates that 1,000 of these outlets now operate in the 50-county service area, and DFW houses 450 of them," noted Burns. "When you consider that the typical lumberyard or hardware store gets 10 percent of its volume ($65,000) from paint and the typical paint store has annual sales of $400,000 with three brands, you can see that getting and keeping widespread distribution is a key success factor in this industry. Over

EXHIBIT 2	Architectural Paint and Sundry Sales Volume, Excluding Contractor Sales (in Millions of Dollars)		
Year	Total Dollar Sales	DFW Area Sales	Non-DFW Area Sales
2000	$75.7	$50.9	$24.8
2001	76.4	50.8	25.6
2002	77.6	50.5	27.1
2003	78.4	50.7	27.7
2004	80.0	48.0	32.0

1,200 outlets were in operation in the area a decade ago; about 600 were situated in the DFW area."

Competition at the paint manufacturing level has increased as well. The major change in competitive behavior has occurred among paint companies that sell to contractors serving the home construction industry. These companies have aggressively priced their products to capture a higher percentage of the home construction market. "Fortunately, these companies have not pursued the 400 or so professional painting firms in DFW and the 200 professional painters outside the DFW area or the do-it-yourselfer market as yet," said Burns. They have not been able to gain access to retail outlets, but they may buy their way in through free goods, promotional allowances, or whatever means are available to them in the future.

"We believe that mass merchandisers control 50 percent of the do-it-yourselfer paint market in the DFW metropolitan area. Price seems to be the attraction, but we can't quarrel with their quality," noted Burns.

The estimated dollar volume of architectural paint and allied products sold in Janmar's 50-county service area in 2004 was $80 million (excluding contractor sales). DFW was estimated to account for 60 percent of this figure, with the remaining volume being sold in other areas. Do-it-yourself household buyers were believed to account for 70 percent of non–contractor-related volume in DFW and 90 percent of non–contractor-related volume in other areas. A five-year summary of architectural paint and allied product sales in the Janmar service area is shown in Exhibit 2.

JANMAR COATINGS, INC.

Janmar Coatings, Inc. is a privately held corporation that produces and markets architectural paint under the Janmar brand name. In addition to producing a full line of architectural coatings, the company sells paint sundries (brushes, rollers, thinners, etc.) under the Janmar name, even though these items are not manufactured by the company. The company also operates a very large OEM coatings division, which sells its products throughout the U.S. and worldwide.

Company architectural paint and allied products sales volume in 2004 was $12 million, and net profit before taxes was $1,140,000. Dollar sales had increased at an average annual rate of 4 percent per year over the past decade. Paint gallonage, however, had remained stable over the past five years. "We have been very successful in maintaining our margins even with increased research and development, material and labor costs, but I'm afraid we're approaching the threshold on our prices," Burns said. "We are now the highest-priced paint in our service area." In 2004, paint cost-of-goods sold, including freight expenses, was 60 percent of net sales.

Distribution

The company distributes its products through 200 independent paint stores, lumberyards, and hardware outlets. Forty percent of its outlets are located in the 11-county DFW area. The remaining outlets are situated in the other 39 counties in the service area. Janmar sales are distributed evenly between DFW and non-DFW accounts. Exhibit 3 shows the account and sales volume distribution by size of dollar purchase per year.

Retail outlets outside the DFW area with paint and sundry purchases exceeding $50,000 annually carry only the Janmar product line. However, except for 14 outlets in DFW (those with purchases greater than $50,000 annually), which carry the Janmar line exclusively, DFW retailers carry two or three lines, with Janmar's line being premium priced. "Our experience to date shows that in our DFW outlets, the effect of multiple lines has been to cause a decline in gallonage volume. The non-DFW outlets, by comparison, have grown in gallonage volume. When you combine the two, you have stable gallonage volume," remarked Burns.

Promotional Efforts for Architectural Coating Sales

Janmar employs eight sales representatives. They are responsible for monitoring inventories of Janmar paint and sundry items in each retail outlet, as well as for order taking, assisting in store display, and coordinating cooperative advertising programs. A recent survey of Janmar paint dealers indicated that the sales representatives were well liked, helpful, professional, and knowledgeable about paint. Commenting on the survey findings, Burns said, "Our reps are on a first-name basis with their customers. It is common for our reps to discuss business and family over coffee during a sales call, and some of our people even 'mind the store' when the proprietor has to run an errand or two." Sales representatives are paid a salary and a 1 percent commission on sales.

The company spends approximately 3 percent of net sales on advertising and sales promotion efforts. Approximately 55 percent of advertising and sales promotion dollars are allocated to cooperative advertising programs with retail accounts. The cooperative program, whereby Janmar pays a portion of an account's media costs based on the dollar amount of paint purchased from Janmar, applies to newspaper advertising and seasonal catalogs distributed in a retailer's immediate trade area. The remainder of the advertising and sales promotion budget is spent on in-store displays, corporate brand advertising, outdoor signs, regional magazines, premiums, and advertising production costs.

EXHIBIT 3   Account and Sales Volume Percentage Distribution by Dollar Purchase per Year

	Retail Accounts			Dollar Sales Volume		
Dollar Purchase/Year	DFW	Non-DFW	Total	DFW	Non-DFW	Total
$50,000+	7%	10%	17%	28%	28%	56%
$25,000–$50,000	14	20	34	13	13	26
Less than $25,000	19	30	49	9	9	18
Total	40%	60%	100%	50%	50%	100%

PLANNING MEETING

Senior management executives of Janmar Coatings, Inc. assembled again to consider the question of where and how to deploy corporate marketing efforts among the various architectural paint coatings markets served by the company. Burns opened the meeting with a statement that it was absolutely necessary to resolve this question at the meeting in order for the tactical plan to be developed. The peak painting season was soon approaching and decisions had to be made.

Vice President of Advertising: Ron, I still believe that we must direct our efforts toward bolstering our presence in the DFW do-it-yourselfer market. I just received the results of our DFW consumer advertising awareness study. As you can see [Exhibit 4], awareness is related to paint purchase behavior. Industry research on paint purchase behavior indicates that a large number of do-it-yourselfers choose a store before selecting a brand. However, a brand name is also important to consumers because they do think about paint they have seen advertised when choosing a brand. This becomes very important in those stores carrying multiple brands. It seems to me that we need an awareness level of at least 30 percent among do-it-yourselfers to materially affect our sales.

Preliminary talks with our ad agency indicate that an increase of $350,000 in corporate brand advertising beyond what we are now spending, with an emphasis on television, will be necessary to achieve this awareness level. Furthermore, this television coverage will reach non-DFW consumers in some 15 counties as well.

Vice President of Operations: I don't agree. Advertising is not the way to go, and reference to the DFW area alone is too narrow a focus. We have to be competitive in the do-it-yourselfer paint market, period. Our shopper research program indicated that dealers will quickly back off from our brand when the customer appears price-sensitive. We must cut our price by 20 percent

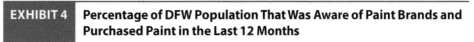

EXHIBIT 4 **Percentage of DFW Population That Was Aware of Paint Brands and Purchased Paint in the Last 12 Months**

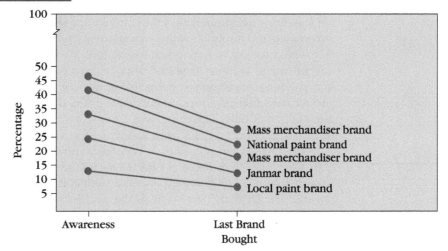

Awareness Question: "What brands come to mind when you think of paint?"

Last Brand Bought: "What paint brand did you purchase the last time you bought paint?"

Note: Sample size was $N = 400$. Percentages are subject to a 5 percent sampling error.

on all paint products to achieve parity with national paint brands. Look here. In today's newspaper, we advertise a price-off special on our exterior paint, and our price is still noticeably higher than a mass merchandiser's everyday price. With both ads on the same page, a customer would have to be an idiot to patronize one of our dealers.

Vice President of Sales: Forget the DFW market. We ought to be putting our effort into non-DFW areas, where half of our sales and most of our dealers exist right now. I hate to admit it, but our sales representatives could be more aggressive. We have added only five new accounts in the last five years; our account penetration in non-DFW areas is only 16 percent. I'm partially at fault, but I'm ready to act. We should add one additional sales representative whose sole responsibility is to develop new retail account leads and presentations or call on professional painters to solicit their business through our dealers. I've figured the direct cost to keep one rep in the field at $60,000 per year, excluding commission.

Vice President of Finance: Everyone is proposing a change in our orientation. Let me be the devil's advocate and favor pursuing our current approach. We now sell to both the homeowner and the professional painter in DFW and non-DFW markets through our dealers. We have been and will continue to be profitable by judiciously guarding our margins and controlling costs. Our contribution margin is 35 percent. Everyone suggests that increasing our costs will somehow result in greater sales volume. Let me remind you, Ron, we have said that it is our policy to recoup noncapital expenditures within a one-year time horizon. If we increase our advertising by an incremental amount of $350,000, then we had better see the incremental sales volume as well. The same goes for additional sales representatives and, I might add, any across-the-board cut in prices.

Mr. Burns: We keep going over the same ground. All of you have valid arguments, but we must prioritize. Let's think about what's best for all of us.

Increased advertising seems reasonable, since national paint firms and mass merchandisers outspend us tenfold in absolute terms. You are right in saying people have to be aware of us before they will buy, or even consider, Janmar. But I am not sure what advertising will do for us given that about 75 percent of the audience is not buying paint. Your reference to DFW as being our major market has been questioned by others. Can't we take that $350,000 of incremental advertising and apply it toward newspapers and catalogs in non-DFW areas?

The price cut is a more drastic action. We might have to do it just to keep our gallonage volume. It would appear from our sales representatives' forecast that gallonage demand for paint in our service area will not increase next year and we can't increase our prices this year. Any increases will have to come out of a competitor's hide. Moreover, since our costs are unlikely to decline, we must recoup gross profit dollars from an increase in volume. Is this possible?

The idea of hiring additional representatives has merit, but what do we do with them? Do they focus on the retail account side or on recruiting the professional painter? Our survey of retail outlets indicated that 70 percent of sales through our DFW dealers went to the professional painter, while 70 percent of our sales through our non-DFW outlets went to do-it-yourselfers. Our contractor sales in DFW and other areas are minimal. We would need a 40 percent price cut to attract contractors, not to mention the increased costs, expertise, and headaches of competitive bidding for large jobs.

Now that I've had my say, let's think about your proposals again. We're not leaving until we agree on a course of action.

Case

Breeder's Own Pet Foods, Inc.

In January 2011, Breeder's Own Pet Foods, Inc. executives looked forward to their meeting with representatives of Marketing Momentum Unlimited, a marketing and advertising consulting firm. The purpose of the meeting was to review the introductory program for the company's entry into the retail branded dog food market in the Boston, Massachusetts, metropolitan market area.

Breeder's Own Pet Foods, Inc. executives viewed the retail dog food market as a growth opportunity for Breeder's Mix, its primary brand, following discussions with food brokers. These brokers had become aware that a product similar to Breeder's Mix was being sold in the freezer section of selected supermarkets in a few large cities in the southwestern and midwestern United States.

THE COMPANY AND THE PRODUCT

Breeder's Own Pet Foods, Inc. is a major producer of dog food for show-dog kennels in the United States. The company has prospered as a supplier of a unique dog food for show dogs called Breeder's Mix. Breeder's Mix was originally formulated by a mink rancher as a means of improving the coats of his minks. After several years of research, he perfected the formula for a specially prepared food and began feeding his preparation to his stock on a regular basis. After a short period of time, he noticed that their coats showed a marked improvement. Shortly thereafter, a nearby kennel owner noticed the improvement and asked to use some of the food to feed his dogs. The dogs' coats improved dramatically, and a business was born.

Breeder's Mix dog food contains federally inspected beef by-products, beef, liver, and chicken. Fresh meat constitutes 85 percent of the product's volume, and the highest-quality fortified cereal accounts for the remaining 15 percent. The ingredients, with no additives or preservatives, are packaged frozen to prevent spoilage of the fresh uncooked meat.

PACKAGING AND DISTRIBUTION MODIFICATIONS

Breeder's Own executives recognized that modifications in the packaging of Breeder's Mix would be necessary to make the transition from the kennel market to the retail dog food market. After some discussion, it was decided that Breeder's Mix would be packaged in a one-pound stand-up pouch with 12 pouches per case. The cost of production, freight, and packaging the meal was $7.87 per case, which represented total variable costs.

The discussions with food brokers indicated that distribution through supermarkets represented a growth opportunity for Breeder's Own Pet Foods, Inc. Frozen dog food is sometimes sold in pet superstores, independent (specialty) pet stores, natural foods grocery stores, and by Internet retailers. A timely entry into supermarkets would preempt competitors from gaining access to valuable space in the frozen-food aisle.

Food brokers would represent Breeder's Mix to supermarkets and would receive a 7 percent commission based on the price to retailers, which had yet to be determined. Supermarkets typically receive a gross margin of 22 percent of their selling price for dog foods.

THE MEETING

Company executives listened attentively to the presentation made by representatives from Marketing Momentum Unlimited. Excerpts from their presentation follow.

During the course of the meeting, Breeder's Own executives raised a number of questions. The questions were primarily designed to clarify certain aspects of the program. One question that was never asked but that plagued Breeder's Own executives was "Will this program establish a foothold in the market for Breeder's Mix?" This direct question implied several subissues:

1. Was the market itself adequately defined and segmented?
2. What was a reasonable estimate of market potential?
3. Could the food brokers get distribution in supermarkets given the sales program?
4. What should be the recommended selling list price to the consumer for Breeder's Mix?
5. Could the company achieve a 15 percent return on sales in its introductory year?

Company executives realized that they had to answer these questions and others before they accepted the proposal. The cost of the proposed plan could be $500,000 to $700,000, exclusive of slotting fees, which company executives considered reasonable, although it would certainly stretch their promotional budget.

PROPOSAL OF MARKETING MOMENTUM UNLIMITED

The following is an excerpted version of the proposal presented to Breeder's Own executives.

The Situation

Our goal is to introduce and promote effectively the sale of Breeder's Mix dog food in the Boston market area in 2011. Breeder's Mix is among the costliest dog foods to prepare and will be available through supermarkets.

Breeder's Mix is a nutritionally balanced frozen dog food. It is of the finest quality and has been used and recommended by professional show-dog owners for years.

Yet, in spite of this history, Breeder's Mix is essentially a new product and is generally unknown to the general public. The fact that Breeder's Mix will be the only dog food located right next to "people food" in the frozen-food section of the supermarket is an advantage that must be capitalized on. The company's history of blue-ribbon winners is another plus. So, in essence, to market Breeder's Mix successfully, we must accomplish two objectives:

- Make the public aware of the Breeder's Mix brand name, what the packaging looks like, and the fact that Breeder's Mix is a high-quality dog food.
- Direct dog owners to shop for dog food in the frozen-food section of supermarkets.

The Environment

Sales of dog food will total about $14 billion in 2011 at manufacturers' prices. Still, fewer than half of the dogs in the United States are regularly fed prepared dog food, which means the dog food industry has yet to tap its full potential.

Four trends indicate that this optimism is well founded. First, the dog food industry has benefited from increasing dog ownership. The U.S. owned-dog population of 78.2 million, spurred on by the owners' desire for companionship or need for protection, is growing steadily and is expected to continue growing. A second important trend is that pet owners continue to invest their animal companions with human qualities and view them as members of the family. For example, research shows that "A person who owns a dog actually identifies with the pet, assigning human characteristics to the dog such as language, thoughts, feelings, and needs." Not surprisingly, 75 percent of dog owners consider themselves "Mom and Dad" to their animal companions and 95 percent pet and hug their dog every day. Therefore, it comes as no surprise that dog owners spend more than $25 billion annually for veterinarian fees; medication for dogs; and dog toys, clothing, accessories, and furniture. A third trend is the growth in premium and superpremium dog foods. These higher-quality, higher-priced dog foods have fueled the growth in dog food sales along with the increase in dog ownership. A fourth trend is the growing emphasis on all-natural, no additives or no preservatives, and vitamin-and-mineral-enriched claims made for new product introductions.

The choice of supermarket distribution focuses on the single largest retail channel for dog food. Supermarkets (and grocery stores) dispense about 36 percent of all dog food sold in the United States, which represents $5 billion in sales at manufacturers' prices. The other 64 percent is sold by mass merchandisers such as Walmart (25%), pet superstores such as PETCO and PetSmart (20%), farm/feed stores (7%), veterinarians (6%), and Internet retailers and independent pet stores (6%). These percentages also apply to the greater Boston market.

Finally, the Boston market is ideal for launching a new dog food. We estimate that the greater Boston area has 1.2 percent of the U.S. population (and 1.2 percent of the dog population since dog and human populations are highly correlated). Also, expenditures for pet products in the Boston market approximate the national average.

The Competition

There are about 50 dog food manufacturers and 350 dog food brands in the United States. However, five companies—Nestlé Purina PetCare (owned by Nestlé SA), Iams (owned by Procter & Gamble, Inc.), Hill's Pet Nutrition (owned by Colgate-Palmolive Company), MasterFoods USA (owned by Mars, Inc.), and Del Monte Foods, Inc.—account for about 75 percent of U.S. dog food sales. Nestlé Purina PetCare, MasterFoods USA, and Del Monte Foods brands are most prominent in the supermarket/grocery store and mass merchandiser channels. Hill's Pet Nutrition is prominent in pet superstores and veterinarian offices. Private label dog food accounted for about 9 percent of total supermarket dog food sales.

Competitor advertising spending and forms of media used will be major considerations in planning the Breeder's Mix's introductory marketing strategy. Total spending for advertising in the dog food industry is about 2 percent of sales. Nestlé Purina PetCare is the leading U.S. dog food advertiser.

The Problems and Opportunities

Introducing a New Dog Food in a New Form This is an opportunity to educate the consumer. Until Breeder's Mix's program breaks, dog foods fall into three categories: dry, canned, and treats. Exhibit 1 shows each category's supermarket share of dog food and brand shares in each category based on our research.

Dry dog foods are usually produced as flakes, small pellets, or large chunks containing about 10 percent moisture and 90 percent solid ingredients. They are chewy, usually well rounded, and priced lower than canned foods. About 95 percent of dog owners feed their dogs dry food during the course of a year. Nestlé's Purina ONE is a brand leader in this category. Its dollar share of the total dog food market is about 4 percent.

Canned dog goods average about 75 percent moisture and 25 percent solid ingredients. They are marketed either as a complete food or as a supplementary food. About one in three dog owners feed their dog canned dog food during the course of a year. Pedigree, marketed by Kars, Inc., is a brand leader in this category. The brand accounts for about 7 percent of total dog food market dollar sales.

Dog treats have a wide variety of ingredients and, while tasty, are not recommended as a complete food. Almost 80 percent of dog owners feed dogs treats. Milk-Bone, marketed by Del Monte, Inc., is the brand leader in this category. The brand captures almost 3 percent of total dog food market sales.

Research on U.S. dog owners indicates that 1 in 10 dog owners buy frozen or refrigerated dog food on a regular basis. Another 15 percent of dog owners say they are interested in buying frozen or refrigerated dog food, but do not currently buy this product. The primary reason was the lack of availability and convenience. Three-fourths of dog owners expressed no interest in buying frozen or refrigerated dog food.

Not surprisingly, it is estimated that frozen or refrigerated dog food accounts for about 1 percent of U.S. dog food dollar volume, or $140 million at manufacturer's prices. Frozen dog food dollar volume increased by 133 percent from 2008 to 2010.

Dry foods, canned foods, and treats are typically marketed in the same area of the supermarket. The consumer must now be taught to shop for dog food in another part of the store—the frozen-food section. Fortunately, some of the work has been done already. A few Boston-area supermarkets carry a frozen dog treat called Frosty Paws Frozen Treats for Dogs, made by Nestlé Purina PetCare. It sells for $4.59 for 13 fluid ounces. This product is often placed near ice cream.

EXHIBIT 1   Major Dog Food Categories and Brands in Supermarkets

Category	Category Dollar Share of Total Dog Food	Category Brands	Category Share
Dry	60%	National brands, such as	68%
		Beneful (Nestlé);	
		Kibbles 'N Bits (Del Monte);	
		Dog Chow (Nestlé);	
		Iams (Iams)	
		Private Label (Store) brands	7
		Other (Regional/Local) brands	25
			100%
Canned (including moist and semi-moist varieties)	20%	National brands, such as	88%
		Alpo (Nestlé);	
		Cesar Select (Masterfoods);	
		Mighty Dog (Nestlé);	
		Pedigree (Masterfoods)	
		Iams (Iams)	
		Private Label (Store) brands	8
		Other (Regional/Local) brands	4
			100%
Treats	20%	National brands, such as	73%
		Milk Bone (Del Monte);	
		Beggin' Strips (Nestlé);	
		Busy Bone (Nestlé)	
		Private Label (Store) brands	12
		Other (Regional/Local) brands	15
			100%

Overcoming Potential Objections to Frozen Dog Food   An objection must be anticipated regarding the requirement for thawing time and freezer space. Therefore, we should state on the container the thawing time, suggestions for quick thawing, how long the food will keep in the refrigerator, plus a gentle reminder to pull that container out of the freezer in the morning. Microwave instructions are a possibility.

Lack of Appeal of Frozen Dog Food   We can quickly turn this problem into an asset in our advertising ("the first dog food made to appeal only to dogs").

Pricing   We have considerable latitude in pricing as shown in Exhibit 2 on page 128. Furthermore, while dog owners in general are price and value sensitive, they are also concerned about the health and welfare of their animal companion. Breeder's Mix's quality suggests a premium price. This view is supported by the food brokers who first recognized the opportunity for Breeder's Mix. They report that Bil Jac, a frozen dog food sold in selected supermarkets in Texas, carried a retail price of $3.59 for a 2-pound package and $6.49 for a 5-pound package.

EXHIBIT 2 **Representative Dog Food Brands, Prices, and Package Sizes in Boston-Area Supermarkets by Product Form**

Dry Foods		Canned Foods		Dog Treats	
Dog Chow	$14.99/17.6 lbs.	Alpo Prime Cuts	$1.50/22 oz.	Milk Bone	$4.49/24 oz.
Purina ONE	$13.49/8 lbs.	Mighty Dog	$ .80/5.5 oz.	Beggin' Strips	$4.00/6 oz.
Iams	$19.45/8 lbs.	Cesar Select	$1.09/3.5 oz.	Pup-Peroni	$4.60/5.6 oz.

We also recommend a price-off coupon be offered to stimulate trial of Breeder's Mix. The dollar amount of the coupon has yet to be determined.

Summary of Opportunities We see Breeder's Mix seizing upon three opportunities:

1. The opportunity to be first to tap the market potential of a complete frozen dog food in Boston supermarkets.

2. The opportunity to capitalize on the growing popularity of organic dog foods. Organic dog food sales grew 64 percent last year. While still a small share of the total dog food market, consumers are willing to pay premium prices for organic dog foods. For example, Newman's Own Organics dog food is sold in a 12.7-ounce can for $2.49.

3. The opportunity to lay the groundwork for a national market roll-out for Breeder's Mix.

Creative Strategies

Positioning Breeder's Mix will be positioned as the finest dog food available at any price and the only thing you will want to feed a dog that is truly a member of the family.

Target Market We believe Breeder's Mix should be targeted at singles and marrieds between the ages of 21 and 54 with a household income greater than $25,000. The reason is that single adults and married couples, with and without children, and roommate households regard their dogs as part of the family. The dog sleeps on the bed and has free run of the house or apartment. Industry research indicates that 79 percent of parents with school-age children buy pet food and supplies, compared with 71 percent of parents with younger or older children, 72 percent of roommate households, and 73 percent of young, childless couples. Income also plays a role in pet spending. Only 48 percent of households with annual incomes of less than $25,000 spend money to keep a pet. However, over 63 percent of households with incomes greater than $50,000 invest in pet food, supplies, and care according to research by the American Veterinary Medical Association. We see little initial opportunity in targeting older households. Only 30 percent of older singles and 41 percent of retired couples spend money on pets.

Concepts Because Breeder's Mix is such a unique product, a variety of concepts can easily be applied, each with adequate justification:

1. The luxurious fur coat

2. The world's finest dog food

3. The guilt concept (shouldn't your dog eat as well as you do?)

4. Now your dog can eat what show champions have been eating for years

All these will be touched on as the campaign progresses.

Creative Directions   Initially, the introduction will focus attention on product identification.

Newspapers will supply a smaller, more retentive audience with facts to justify all claims. The brand name and package will be prominently displayed, and the copy will emphasize the product's quality. Special-interest ads will appear in the society, sports, television, and dining-out sections. This unusual media placement is warranted by the product's unique qualities. Also, placement in these sections will pull a relatively low promotional budget out of the mass of food-section advertising.

Television will provide access to a mass audience. Prime objectives are to register the brand name and the package in the viewer's memory. An imaginative and all-important emotional approach will be taken.

Geographic Directions   The entire campaign has been designed to accommodate product introduction outside the Boston market area. When the product goes national, the television spot will be ready, the introductory ads will be ready, the radio spots will be ready, and the immediate follow-up will be ready.

Sales Packet

The sales packet given to brokers should include, in the most persuasive form possible, the following categories of information:

1. Market potential
2. Suggested manufacturer's list price to consumers and quantity discount schedule
3. Information about Breeder's Mix
4. User endorsements
5. Promotional schedule
6. Order information
7. Reprint of ads
8. Sample shelf strip

The packet should be designed to persuade the supermarket frozen-food buyer to provide freezer space to Breeder's Mix. Two major problems have to be overcome. Because of the organizational modes of supermarket buying departments, we will not be dealing with the regular pet food buyer. Instead, it will be necessary to persuade the frozen-food buyer to stock Breeder's Mix. The other major problem involves the usual higher margin for frozen foods. It will be necessary to persuade the buyer that greater product turnover will compensate for a potentially lower margin for Breeder's Mix.

The task will not be easy. Some 15 percent of new products introduced to supermarkets each year are aimed at the freezer case. Eighty percent of these products fail. It is highly likely Breeder's Own Pet Foods will need to budget about $30,000 for slotting fees paid to supermarkets to buy freezer space.

Creative Strategy by Media

Creative strategies will differ by media. Print media will be utilized to position the product against its competition by comparing it to canned and dry categories. The print campaign will open with an attention-getting ad with a brief product history.

Television will carry the brunt of the attack. The most pressing problem is seen as the difficulty of finding the food in the supermarket, so the TV spot will emphasize location.

In order to give the campaign continuity, each ad will show the package. At the top of each of the ads designed to position the competition, the artwork reproduced on the package will be used.

The myth/fact format in newspapers will be utilized to take advantage of the current publicity dealing with the nutritional value of all-meat dog food and the continued trend toward more natural foods. Exhibit 3 shows a rough artistic rendering for the myth/fact format.

The copy block dealing with Breeder's Mix will turn the problem of Breeder's Mix's being frozen into a product advantage.

Media Plan

Because dog food is heavily advertised, Breeder's Own Pet Foods must follow suit to compete.

EXHIBIT 3   Breeder's Mix Print Advertisement

Learn the facts about dog food.

Myth:
A diet of nothing but dry dog food is healthy for your dog.

Fact:
Dogs are not born vegetarians. Dry dog food contains little if any meat. Dry dog food is inexpensive. Dry dog food is good to chew. Dry dog food must be cooked, which removes nutrition. It must be filled with additives and preservatives to keep it fresh. And because of the low meat content, it must be fortified with various supplements.

Breeder's Mix
It's the perfect marriage of meat and cereal. 85% is federally inspected beef by-products, beef liver, and chicken. The other 15% is the finest cereal made. It promotes and ensures digestion of the meat, plus supplies the vitamins and minerals meat cannot. Breeder's Mix is uncooked because cooking removes nutrition. And it's frozen for freshness. There's no need for additives or preservatives. Find Breeder's Mix in the frozen-food section, right next to people food.

BREEDER'S MIX

Now your dog can eat what show dogs have eaten for years.

General Media Strategy   Advertising objectives are as follows:

1. Create awareness of new brand
2. Obtain distribution through supermarket outlets
3. Motivate trial through coupon redemption
4. Motivate trial through emotional impact of television

Collateral Advertising   Accomplishment of objective 2, getting distribution in supermarkets, is the main purpose of collateral advertising. The sales packet, containing fact sheets, shelf strips, consumer advertising, and testimonial letters, gives the food broker an impressive story to tell to the supermarket buyer. This is recognized as the critical stage of the campaign, for without sufficient distribution, consumer advertising will be delayed.

Newspaper/Magazine   The primary purpose of newspaper advertising is distribution of coupons into the market. This will be accomplished by half-page ads in major Boston newspapers. As a secondary means of distribution, full-page ads will be placed in *Dog Fancy* magazine for distribution throughout most of the Boston market area.

The second phase of coupon distribution will be effected through 30-inch ads in the same newspapers. A final coupon distribution will be made through a 30-inch ad midway through the campaign. Newspaper insertion will be coordinated with TV flights.

Television   The bulk of the budget will be placed in TV production and time. A sizable portion of the time budget will be spent on *The Late Show with David Letterman*. Fixed space will be purchased within the first half-hour of the program. The remainder of the budget will reach daytime and nighttime audiences. Each flight will begin on a Monday, and newspaper advertising will be placed on Thursday of the following week.

Two basic approaches can be used for 30-second TV spots. The first approach capitalizes on the love of pet owners for their dogs. A somewhat frowzy, middle-aged, semigreedy woman is shown enjoying a steak dinner—in contrast to an unappetizing cylinder of canned dog food. The spot ends on a close-up of the product.

A second TV spot will emphasize location of the food in the supermarket. A description of the video and audio characteristics of this spot is as follows:

Video	*Audio*
Supermarket—long establishing shot of small boy with bulge under jacket	Announcer: There are many things to remember about new Breeder's Mix.
Close-up of boy, as puppy pops out of top of jacket	Remember, although it's new to you, champion dogs have eaten it for years.
Manager walks by, boy hides dog, looks relieved	Remember, it contains all the vitamins your dog needs.
Close-up of sign indicating pet foods	Remember, Breeder's Mix is a perfectly balanced diet of meat and enriched cereal.
	Remember, it doesn't come in a can.
Dolly shot of boy looking at competitive brands	
Close-up of boy and dog (sync)	Boy: I don't see it anywhere, Sparky.
Boy walks out of store past frozen-food compartment	Announcer: But most important, remember you find Breeder's Mix in the frozen-food (bark) section, where you shop for other members of your family.
People turn to stare	
Tilt down and zoom in on product	

| | EXHIBIT 4 | **Alternative Advertising and Trade Promotion Expenditure Levels for Breeder's Mix** |

| | *Budget Levels* | |
Item	*$500,000*	*$700,000*
Television[a]	$359,000	$529,000
Newspapers/Magazine[b]	100,500	130,500
Collateral (sales pack)	9,750	9,750
Miscellaneous	5,250	5,250
Agency fees	25,500	25,500
Total	$500,000	$700,000

[a] The difference in television cost is due to the production of a second commercial and larger television schedule.

[b] The difference in newspaper/magazine cost is due to a larger number of insertions in *Dog Fancy* magazine.

Program Budget The budget for the program described can be either $500,000 or $700,000 (Exhibit 4). We see this expense and the $30,000 slotting fee as being the only incremental costs associated with the launch in the Boston market.

We believe that this expenditure is reasonable, since most major established brands are spending $7 to $8 million annually for ongoing nationwide media promotion. For a new product, a higher initial expense is necessary. For instance, about $34 million was spent on television and print advertising to introduce the hugely successful Beneful, a premium dry dog food. A line extension, Alpo Lite, with fewer calories than regular Alpo, was launched with a $10 million national advertising effort.

Case

South Delaware Coors, Inc.

Larry Brownlow was just beginning to realize the problem was more complex than he thought. The problem was giving direction to Manson and Associates regarding which research should be completed by February 20, 2000, to determine market potential of a Coors beer distributorship for a two-county area in southern Delaware. With data from this research, Larry would be able to estimate the feasibility of such an operation before the March 5 application deadline. Larry knew his decision on whether or not to apply for the distributorship was the most important career choice he had ever faced.

 ## LARRY BROWNLOW

Larry was just completing his MBA and, from his standpoint, the Coors announcement of expansion into Delaware could hardly have been better timed. He had long ago decided that the best opportunities and rewards were in smaller, self-owned businesses and not in the jungles of corporate giants. Because of a family tragedy some three years ago, Larry found himself in a position to consider small business opportunities such as the Coors distributorship. Over $500,000 was held in trust for Larry, to be dispersed when he reached age 30. Until then, Larry and his family lived on an annual trust income of about $40,000. It was on this income that Larry decided to leave his sales engineering job and return to graduate school for his MBA.

The decision to complete a graduate program and operate his own business had been easy to make. While he could avoid such challenges, find an "easy" job, and live comfortably using his investment income, Larry knew such a life would not be to his liking. Working with people and the challenge of making it on his own, Larry thought, were far more preferable than enduring a boring job and taking an early retirement.

Larry would be 30 in July, about the time that money would be needed to start the business. In the meantime, he had access to about $15,000 for feasibility research. While there certainly were other places to spend the money, Larry and his wife agreed the distributorship opportunity could not be overlooked.

This case was written by Professor James E. Nelson, University of Colorado at Boulder. It is intended for use as a basis for class discussion rather than to illustrate either effective or ineffective administrative decision making. Some data are disguised. Used with permission.

COORS, INC.

Coors' history dated back to 1873, when Adolph Coors built a small brewery in Golden, Colorado. Since then, the brewery had prospered and become the fourth-largest seller of beer in the country. Coors' operating philosophy could be summed up as "hard work, saving money, devotion to the quality of the product, caring about the environment, and giving people something to believe in." Company operation is consistent with this philosophy. Headquarters and most production facilities are still located in Golden, Colorado, with a new Shenandoah, Virginia, facility aiding in nationwide distribution. Coors is still family operated and controlled. The company had issued its first public stock, $127 million worth of nonvoting shares, in 1975. The issue was enthusiastically received by the financial community despite its being offered during a recession.

Coors' unwillingness to compromise on the high quality of its product is well known both to its suppliers and to its consuming public. Coors beer requires constant refrigeration to maintain this quality, and wholesalers' facilities are closely controlled to ensure proper temperatures are maintained. Wholesalers are also required to install and use aluminum can recycling equipment. Coors was one of the first breweries in the industry to recycle its cans.

Larry was aware of Coors' popularity with many consumers in adjacent states. Most beer consumers considered Coors beer to be a high quality, standard beer, having a light, zesty taste and similar to standard beers from Budweiser or Miller. However, Coors' corporate management was seen by some consumers to hold antiunion beliefs (because of a labor disagreement at the brewery some time ago). A few other consumers perceived the brewery to be somewhat insensitive to minority issues, primarily unemployment and distribution. The result of these attitudes—plus other aspects of consumer behavior—meant that Coors' sales in Delaware would depend greatly on efforts of the two wholesalers planned for the state.

MANSON RESEARCH PROPOSAL

Because of the press of his studies, Larry had contacted Manson and Associates in early January for their assistance. The firm was a Wilmington-based general research supplier that had conducted other feasibility studies in the South Atlantic region. Manson was well known for the quality of its work, particularly with respect to computer modeling. The firm had developed special expertise in modeling such things as population and employment levels for cities, counties, and other units of area for periods of up to 10 years into the future.

Larry had met John Rome, senior research analyst for Manson, and discussed the Coors opportunity and appropriate research extensively in the January meeting. Rome promised a formal research proposal (Exhibit 1 on pages 125 and 126) for the project that Larry now held in his hand. It certainly was extensive, Larry thought, and reflected the professionalism he expected. Now came the hard part—choosing the more relevant research from the proposal—because he certainly couldn't afford to pay for it all. Rome had suggested a meeting for Friday, giving Larry only two more days to decide.

Larry was at first overwhelmed. All the research would certainly be useful. He was sure he needed estimates of sales and costs in a form allowing managerial analysis, but what data in what form? Knowledge of competing operations' experience, retailer support, and consumer acceptance also seemed important for feasibility analysis. For example, what if consumers were excited about Coors and retailers indifferent or the other way around? Finally, several of the studies would provide information that could be useful in later months of operation in the areas of promotion and pricing, for example. The problem now appeared more difficult than before!

| **EXHIBIT 1** | **Manson and Associates Research Proposal** |

January 16, 2000

Mr. Larry Brownlow
1198 West Lamar
Chester, PA 12345

Dear Larry:

It was a pleasure meeting you last week and discussing your business and research interests in Coors wholesaling. From further thought and discussion with my colleagues, the Coors wholesaling opportunity appears even more attractive than when we met.

Appearances can be deceiving, as you know, and I fully agree some formal research is needed before you make an application. Research that we recommend would proceed in two distinct stages and is described below:

Stage One Research, Based on Secondary Data and Manson Computer Models:

Study A: National and Delaware Per Capita Beer Consumption for 1998–2002.
Description: Per capita annual consumption of beer for the total population and population age 21 and over in gallons is provided.
Source: Various publications, Manson computer model
Cost: $1,000

Study B: Population Estimates for 1996–2006 for Two Delaware Counties in Market Area.
Description: Annual estimates of total population and population age 21 and over are provided for the period 1996–2006.
Source: U.S. Bureau of Census, *Sales Management Annual Survey of Buying Power*, Manson computer model
Cost: $1,500

Study C: Coors Market Share Estimates for 2000–2005.
Description: Coors market share for the two-county market area based on total gallons consumed is estimated for each year in the period 2000–2005. This data will be projected from Coors' nationwide experience.
Source: Various publications. Manson computer model
Cost: $2,000

Study D: Estimates Liquor and Beer Licenses for the Market Area, 2000–2005.
Description: Projections of the number of on-premise sale operations and off-premise sale operations is provided.
Source: Delaware Department of Revenue, Manson computer model
Cost: $1,000

Study E: Beer Taxes Paid by Delaware Wholesalers for 1997 and 1998 in Market Area.
Description: Beer taxes paid by each of the six presently operating competing beer wholesalers are provided. This can be converted to gallons sold by applying the state gallonage tax rate ($.06 per gallon).
Source: Delaware Department of Revenue
Cost: $200

Study F: Financial Statement Summary of Wine, Liquor, and Beer Wholesalers for 1999.
Description: Composite balance sheets, income statements, and relevant measures of performance provided for 510 similar wholesaling operations in the United States.
Source: Robert Morris Associates Annual Statement Studies, 2000 ed.
Cost: $49.50

(continued)

EXHIBIT 1   *(Continued)*

Stage Two Research, Based on Primary Data:

Study G: Consumer Study
    Description: Study G involves focus group interviews and a mail question-
    naire to determine consumers' past experience, acceptance, and intention
    to buy Coors beer. Three focus group interviews would be conducted in
    the two counties in the market area. From these data, a questionnaire
    would be developed and sent to 300 adult residents in the market area,
    utilizing direct questions and a semantic differential scale to measure atti-
    tudes toward Coors beer, competing beers, and an ideal beer.
    Source: Manson and Associates
    Cost: $6,000

Study H: Retailer Study
    Description: Group interviews would be conducted with six potential retail-
    ers of Coors beer in one county in the market area to determine their past
    beer sales and experience and their intention to stock and sell Coors. From
    these data, a personal interview questionnaire would be developed and exe-
    cuted at all appropriate retailers in the market area to determine similar data.
    Source: Manson and Associates
    Cost: $4,800

Study I: Survey of Retail and Wholesale Beer Prices
    Description: In-store interviews with a representative sample of 50 retailers
    in the market area to estimate retail and wholesale prices for Budweiser,
    Miller Lite, Miller, Busch, Bud Light, Old Milwaukee, and Michelob.
    Source: Manson and Associates
    Cost: $2,000

Examples of the form of final report tables are attached [Exhibit 2, pages 127–131]. This
should give you a better idea of the data you will receive.

    As you can see, the research is extensive and, I might add, not cheap. However, the
research as outlined will supply you with sufficient information to make an estimate of the
feasibility of a Coors distributorship, the investment for which is substantial.

    I have scheduled 9:00 A.M. next Friday as a time to meet with you to discuss the pro-
posal in more detail. Time is short, but we firmly feel the study can be completed by
February 20, 2000. If you need more information in the meantime, please feel free to call.

Sincerely,

John Rome
Senior Research Analyst

    It would have been nice, Larry thought, to have had some time to perform part
of the suggested research himself. However, there just was too much in the way
of class assignments and other matters to allow him that luxury. Besides, using
Manson and Associates would give him research results from an unbiased source.

INVESTING AND OPERATING DATA

    Larry was not completely in the dark regarding investment and operating data for
the distributorship. In the past two weeks he had visited two beer wholesalers
in his hometown of Chester, Pennsylvania, who handled Anheuser-Busch and

EXHIBIT 2   Examples of Final Research Report Tables

Table A
National and Delaware Resident Annual Beer Consumption Per Capita, 1998–2002 (Gallons)

	U.S. Consumption		Delaware Consumption	
Year	Based on Entire Population	Based on Population over Age 21	Based on Entire Population	Based on Population over Age 21
1998				
1999				
2000				
2001				
2002				

Source: Study A.

Table B
Population Estimates for 1996–2006 for the Two Delaware Counties in Market Area

	Entire Population					
County	1996	1998	2000	2002	2004	2006
Kent						
Sussex						

	Population Age 21 and Over					
County	1996	1998	2000	2002	2004	2006
Kent						
Sussex						

Source: Study B.

Table C
Coors Market Share Estimates for 2000–2005

Year	Market Share (%)
2000	
2001	
2002	
2003	
2004	
2005	

Source: Study C.

(*continued*)

EXHIBIT 2 *(Continued)*

Table D
Liquor and Beer License Estimates for Market Area for 2000–2005

Type of License	2000	2001	2002	2003	2004	2005
All beverages						
Retail beer and wine						
Off-premise beer only						
Veterans beer and liquor						
Fraternal						
Resort beer and liquor						

Source: Study D.

Table E
Delaware Beer Taxes Paid by Beer Wholesalers in the Market Area, 1997 and 1998

Wholesaler	1997 Tax Paid ($)	1998 Tax Paid ($)
A		
B		
C		
D		
E		
F		

Source: Study E.

Note: Delaware beer tax is $0.06 cents per gallon.

Table F
Financial Statement Summary for 510 Wholesalers of Wine, Liquor, and Beer in Fiscal Year 1999

Assets	Percentage
Cash and equivalents	
Accounts and notes receivable, net	
Inventory	
All other current	
Total current	
Fixed assets, net	
Intangibles, net	
All other noncurrent	
Total	100.0

EXHIBIT 2 *(Continued)*

Table F *(Continued)*

Liabilities	Percentage
Notes payable, short-term	
Current maturity long-term debt	
Accounts and notes payable, trade	
Accrued expenses	
All other current	
Total current	
Long-term debt	
All other noncurrent	
Net worth	___
Total liabilities and net worth	100.0
Income Data	
Net sales	100.0
Cost of sales	
Gross profit	
Operating expenses	
Operating profit	
All other expenses, net	
Profit before taxes	
Ratios	
Quick	
Current	
Debt/worth	
Sales/receivables	
Cost sales/inventory	
Percentage profit before taxes, based on total assets	

Interpretation of Statement Studies Figures:
RMA recommends that Statement Studies data be regarded only as general guidelines and not as absolute industry norms. There are several reasons why the data may not be fully representative of a given industry:

1. The financial statements used in the Statement Studies are not selected by any random or statistically reliable method. RMA member banks voluntarily submit the raw data they have available each year, with these being the only constraints: (a) The fiscal year-ends of the companies reported may not be from April 1 through June 29, and (b) their total assets must be less than $100 million.
2. Many companies have varied product lines; however, the Statement Studies categorize them by their primary product Standard Industrial Classification (SIC) number only.
3. Some of our industry samples are rather small in relation to the total number of firms in a given industry. A relatively small sample can increase the chances that some of our composites do not fully represent an industry.
4. There is the chance that an extreme statement can be present in a sample, causing a disproportionate influence on the industry composite. This is particularly true in a relatively small sample.
5. Companies within the same industry may differ in their method of operations, which in turn can directly influence their financial statements. Since they are included in our sample, too, these statements can significantly affect our composite calculations.
6. Other considerations that can result in variations among different companies engaged in the same general line of business are different labor markets, geographical location, different accounting methods, quality of products handled, sources and methods of financing, and terms of sale.

For these reasons, RMA does not recommend that Statement Studies figures be considered as absolute norms for a given industry. Rather, the figures should be used only as general guidelines and in addition to the other methods of financial analysis. RMA makes no claim as to the representativeness of the figures printed in this book.

Source: Study F (Robert Morris Associates, © 2000).

(continued)

EXHIBIT 2 *(Continued)*

Table G
Consumer Questionnaire Results

Consumed Coors in the past:	Yes No		Yes No
Attitudes toward Coors:	%	Usually buy beer at:	%
Strongly like		Liquor stores	
Like		Taverns and bars	
Indifferent/no opinion		Supermarkets	
Dislike		Corner grocery	
Strongly dislike			
Total	100.0	Total	100.0
Weekly beer consumption:	%	Features considered	
Less than 1 can		important when buying beer:	%
1–2 cans		Taste	
3–4 cans		Brand name	
5–6 cans		Price	
7–8 cans		Store location	
9 cans and over		Advertising	
Total	100.0	Carbonation	
Intention to buy Coors:	%	Other	
Certainly will		Total	100.0
Maybe will			
Not sure			
Maybe will not			
Certainly will not			
Total	100.0		

Semantic Differential Scale, Consumers[a]

	Extremely	Very	Somewhat	Somewhat	Very	Extremely	
Masculine	—	—	—	—	—	—	Feminine
Healthful	—	—	—	—	—	—	Unhealthful
Cheap	—	—	—	—	—	—	Expensive
Strong	—	—	—	—	—	—	Weak
Old-fashioned	—	—	—	—	—	—	New
Upper-class	—	—	—	—	—	—	Lower-class
Good taste	—	—	—	—	—	—	Bad taste

[a] Profiles would be provided for Coors, three competing beers, and an ideal beer.

Source: Study G.

EXHIBIT 2 *(Continued)*

Table H
Retailer Questionnaire Results

	Percentage			*Percentage*
Brands of beer carried:	%	Beer sales:		%
Budweiser		Budweiser		
Miller Lite		Miller Lite		
Miller		Miller		
Busch		Busch		
Bud Light		Bud Light		
Old Milwaukee		Old Milwaukee		
Michelob		Michelob		
		Others		
Total	100.0	Total		100.0

Semantic Differential Scale, Retailers[a]

	Extremely	*Very*	*Somewhat*	*Somewhat*	*Very*	*Extremely*	
Masculine	—	—	—	—	—	—	Feminine
Healthful	—	—	—	—	—	—	Unhealthful
Cheap	—	—	—	—	—	—	Expensive
Strong	—	—	—	—	—	—	Weak
Old-fashioned	—	—	—	—	—	—	New
Upper-class	—	—	—	—	—	—	Lower-class
Good taste	—	—	—	—	—	—	Bad taste

Intention to sell Coors:	%
Certainly will	
Maybe will	
Not sure	
Maybe will not	
Certainly will not	
Total	100.0

[a] Profiles would be provided for Coors, three competing beers, and an ideal beer.

Source: Study H.

Table I
Retail and Wholesale Prices for Selected Beers in the Market Area

Beer	*Wholesale[a]* Six-Pack Price (dollars)	*Retail[b]* Six-Pack Price (dollars)
Budweiser		
Miller Lite		
Miller		
Busch		
Bud Light		
Old Milwaukee		
Michelob		

[a] Price that the wholesaler sold to retailers.

[b] Price that the retailer sold to consumers.

Source: Study I.

Miller beer, to get a feel for their operation and marketing experience. It would have been nice to interview a Coors wholesaler, but Coors management had strictly informed all of their distributors to provide no information to prospective applicants.

While no specific financial data were discussed, general information had been provided in a cordial fashion because of the noncompetitive nature of Larry's plans. Based on his conversations, Larry had made the following estimates:

Inventory		
Equipment:		$240,000
Delivery trucks	$150,000	
Forklift	20,000	
Recycling and miscellaneous equipment	20,000	
Office equipment	10,000	
Total equipment		200,000
Warehouse		320,000
Land		40,000
Total investment		$800,000

A local banker had reviewed Larry's financial capabilities and saw no problem in extending a line of credit on the order of $400,000. Other sources also might loan as much as $400,000 to the business.

As a rough estimate of fixed expenses, Larry planned on having four route salespeople, a secretary, and a warehouse manager. Salaries for these people and himself would run about $160,000 annually, plus some form of incentive compensation he had yet to determine. Other fixed or semifixed expenses were estimated as follows:

Equipment depreciation	$35,000
Warehouse depreciation	15,000
Utilities and telephone	12,000
Insurance	10,000
Personal property taxes	10,000
Maintenance and janitorial	5,600
Miscellaneous	2,400
	$90,000

According to the two wholesalers, beer in bottles and cans outsold keg beer by a three-to-one margin. Keg beer prices at the wholesale level were about 45 percent of prices for beer in bottles and cans.

 MEETING

The entire matter deserved much thought. Maybe it was a golden opportunity, maybe not. The only thing certain was that research was needed, Manson and Associates was ready, and Larry needed time to think. Today is Tuesday, Larry thought—only three days until he and John Rome would get together for direction.

Chapter 5

Product and Service Strategy and Brand Management

The fundamental decision in formulating a marketing mix concerns the offering of an organization. Without something to satisfy target market wants and needs, there would be nothing to price, distribute, or communicate. In essence, the ultimate profitability of an organization depends on its product or service offering(s) and the strength of its brand(s). Accordingly, issues in the development of a product, service, and brand strategy are of special interest to all levels of management in an organization.

Three basic offering-related decisions facing the marketing manager concern (1) modifying the offering mix, (2) positioning offerings, and (3) branding offerings. Aspects of each decision are described in this chapter.

In certain ways, offering decisions are extensions of product-market matching strategies described in Chapter 1. Like other marketing-mix decisions, offering decisions must be based on consideration of organization and marketing objectives, organization resources and capabilities, customer needs, and competitive forces.

 ## THE OFFERING PORTFOLIO

The Offering Concept

Before proceeding to a discussion of offering-related decisions, we should define the term *offering*. In an abstract sense, an *offering* consists of the benefits or satisfaction provided to target markets by an organization. More concretely, an offering consists of a tangible product or service (a physical entity) plus related services (such as delivery and setup), brand name(s), warranties or guarantees, packaging, and the like.

Use of the term *offering* rather than *product* or *service* has numerous benefits for strategic marketing management. By focusing on benefits and satisfaction offered, it establishes a conceptual framework. This framework is potentially useful in analyzing competing offerings, identifying the unmet needs and wants of target markets, and developing or designing new products or services. It forces a marketer to go beyond the single tangible entity being marketed and to consider the entire offering, or extended product or service.

In a broader view, an organization's offerings are an extension of its business definition. Offerings illustrate not only the buyer needs served, but also the types of customer groups sought and the means (technology) for satisfying their needs.

The Offering Mix

Seldom do organizations market a solitary offering; rather, they tend to market many product or service offerings. The typical supermarket contains over 40,000 different products; General Electric offers over a quarter million. Banks provide hundreds of services to customers, including computer billing, automatic payroll deposits, checking accounts, and loans of numerous kinds. Similarly, hospitals maintain a complete "inventory" of services ranging from pathology to obstetrics to food services. The totality of an organization's offerings is known as its product or service *offering mix* or *portfolio*. This mix usually consists of distinct offering lines—groups of offerings similar in terms of usage, buyers marketed to, or technical characteristics. Each product or service offering line is composed of individual offers or items.

Offering decisions concern the width, depth, and consistency of the offering portfolio. Marketing managers must continually assess the number of offering lines (the width decision) and the number of individual items in each line (the depth decision). Although these decisions depend, in part, on the competitive situation, as well as organizational resources, they are most often determined by overall marketing strategy. The options are many. At one extreme, an organization can concentrate on one offering; at the other, it can offer complete lines to its customers. In between, it can specialize in high-profit and/or high-volume offerings. Furthermore, managers must consider the extent to which offerings satisfy similar needs, appeal to similar buyer groups, or utilize similar technologies (the consistency decision).

Increasingly, organizations use "bundling" as a means to enhance their offering mix. *Bundling* involves the marketing of two or more product or service items in a single "package" that creates a new offering. For example, McDonald's offers "value meals" that include a sandwich, soft drink, and french fries. Travelocity offers complete vacations, including travel, lodging, and leisure activities. Bundling is based on the idea that consumers value the package more than the individual items. This is due to benefits received from not having to make separate purchases and enhanced satisfaction from one item given the presence of another. Also, bundling often provides a lower total cost to buyers and lower marketing costs to sellers.

MODIFYING THE OFFERING MIX

The first offering-related decision confronting the manager is whether to modify the offering mix. Rarely, if ever, will an organization's offering mix stand the test of changing competitor actions and buyer preferences, or satisfy an organization's desire for growth. Accordingly, the marketing manager must continually monitor target markets and offerings to determine when new offerings should be introduced and existing offerings modified or eliminated.

Additions to the Offering Mix

Additions to the offering mix may take the form of a single offering or of entire lines of offerings. Campbell Soup Company is an example. The company successfully launched a low-sodium line of canned soups in 2007 and notched sales of $101 million.[1]

Whatever the reason for considering new offerings, three questions should direct the evaluation of this action:

- How *consistent* is the new offering with existing offerings?
- Does the organization have the *resources* to introduce and sustain the offering?
- Is there a viable *market* for the offering?

Consistency Demand interrelationships—offering substitutes or complements—must be considered when evaluating the consistency of new offerings with existing offerings. This is necessary to avoid situations in which sales of the new offering may excessively cannibalize those of other offerings. Eastman Kodak did not originally introduce 35 mm cameras, camcorders, and digital cameras for fear of cannibalizing its core products—cameras and film.[2] Consistency also involves considering the degree to which the new offering fits the organization's existing selling and distribution strategies. For example, will the new offering require a different type of sales effort, such as new sales personnel or selling methods? The Metropolitan Life Insurance Company faced such a situation when it added automobile insurance to its line of life and health insurance, since the sales task for auto insurance differs from that for life insurance. Or will the new offering require a different marketing channel to reach the target market sought? Both the cannibalization question and the question of fit with sales and distribution strategies raise a fundamental third question relating to the buyers sought for the new offering. Will the new offering satisfy the target markets currently being served by the existing offering mix? If it will, then the sales and distribution issue may be settled, but the cannibalization question remains. If it will not, then the situation is just the opposite.

Resources Organizational resources also require consideration when adding new offerings. In particular, the financial strength of the organization must be objectively appraised. New offerings often require large initial cash outlays for research, development, and introductory marketing programs. Gillette, for example, spent $200 million in advertising to launch its Gillette Fusion razor shaving system.[3] Other costs of sustaining the new offering before it returns a profit to the organization must also be measured. These costs will be determined, in part, by the speed and magnitude of competitive response to new offerings in the market and by market growth itself. The experience of Royal Crown Company, the original maker of RC Cola, is a case in point. The company pioneered the first can in 1954, the first diet cola in 1962, and the first caffeine-free cola in 1980. All three offerings achieved a respectable market presence only to lose it when Coca-Cola and Pepsi-Cola introduced competitive products.[4]

Market Finally, one must determine whether a market exists for the new offering. Recall from Chapter 4 that buyer willingness and ability to purchase an offering determine whether a market exists. Two questions are important. First, does the new offering have a relative advantage over competitive offerings at a price buyers are willing and able to pay? Second, is there a distinct buyer group or segment for which no present offering is satisfactory? Wyeth Pharmaceuticals seemingly overlooked these questions in the development and marketing of its nasal vaccine, FluMist. This product was approved for marketing to consumers between the ages of 5 and 49 by the U.S. Food and Drug Administration—a seemingly large segment of the U.S. population. However, toddlers (under age 5) and senior citizens are the two age groups most at risk for catching the flu. Furthermore, FluMist cost an average of $46 a dose, more than triple the average cost of a traditional flu shot. The result? FluMist attracted few buyers and sales and profit suffered.[5]

New Offering Development Process

Marketing managers are often faced with new offering decisions. In dealing with the often chaotic process of developing and marketing new offerings, most managers attempt to follow some sort of structured procedure.[6] This procedure typically includes six multifaceted stages: (1) idea generation, (2) idea screening, (3) business analysis, (4) development, (5) market testing, and (6) commercialization.

The Process   New offering ideas are obtained from many sources—employees, suppliers, buyers, and competitors—through formal (marketing research) and informal means. These ideas are screened, both in terms of organizational definition and capability and from the viewpoint of prospective buyers. Ideas deemed incompatible with organizational definition and capability are quickly eliminated. The match between prospective buyers and offering characteristics is assessed through questions such as the following. First, does the offering have a *relative advantage* over existing offerings? Second, is the offering *compatible* with buyers' use or consumption behavior? Third, is the offering *simple* enough for buyers to understand and use? Fourth, can the offering be *tested* by prospective buyers on a limited basis prior to actual purchase? Fifth, are there *immediate benefits* to a buyer from the offering, once it is used or consumed? If the answers to these questions are yes and the offering satisfies a *felt need*, then the idea passes on to the next stage.

At that point, the idea is subjected to a business analysis to assess its financial viability in terms of estimated sales, costs, and profitability. Ideas that pass the business analysis are then developed into prototypes, and various testing procedures are implemented. Marketing-related tests may include product concept or buyer preference tests in a laboratory situation, or field market tests. Ideas that pass through these stages are commercially introduced into the marketplace in the hope that they will become profitable to the organization.

Research on the new offering development process indicated that upward of 3,000 raw ideas are needed to produce a single commercially successful, innovative new product. This research also emphasized that two major factors contribute to the success of new offerings: (1) a fit with market needs, and (2) a fit with organizational strengths and resources.[7]

Business Analysis and Market Testing   Although the stages just outlined are relatively straightforward, two require further elaboration: business analysis and market testing.

Sales analysis and profit analysis are two fundamental aspects of the business analysis stage. Forecasting sales volume for a new offering is a difficult task; nevertheless, preliminary forecasts must be made before further investigation of the offering is warranted. For the most part, profitability analyses are related to investment requirements, break-even procedures, and payback periods. Break-even procedures can be used to determine estimates of the number of units that must be sold to cover fixed and variable costs. An extension of this procedure—and one that is frequently used in evaluating new offerings—is to compute the payback period of the new offering. *Payback period* refers to the number of years required for an organization to recapture its initial offering investment. The shorter the payback period, the sooner an offering will prove profitable. Usually the payback period is computed by dividing the fixed costs of the offering by the estimated incoming cash flows from it. Though widely used, the method is limited in that it does not distinguish among offering investments according to their absolute sizes.

A final method often used is to calculate the common return on investment (ROI). ROI equals the ratio of average annual net earnings (return) divided by average annual investment, discounted to the present time. Like the payback method, the ROI method does not always distinguish among offering alternatives according to their riskiness. Risk must still be subjectively assessed.

Test marketing is a major consideration in the development and testing stage. A test market is a scaled-down implementation of one or more alternative marketing strategies for introducing the new offering. Test markets provide several benefits to managers. First, they generate benchmark data for assessing sales volume when the product is introduced over a wider area. Second, if alternative marketing strategies are tested, the relative impacts of the two programs can be examined under actual market conditions. In a similar vein, test markets allow the manager to assess the incidence of offering trial by potential buyers, repeat-purchasing behavior, and quantities purchased.

A manager should remember, however, that test markets inform competitors of the organization's activities and, thus, may increase the speed and effectiveness of competitive response. Consider Procter & Gamble.[8] Its Olay cosmetics line featuring a skin health benefit was test-marketed for three years, only to be discontinued. Revlon's Almay and Johnson & Johnson's Neutrogena had beat it to the marketplace with the same benefit supported by heavy marketing spending.

Life-Cycle Concept

An important managerial tool related to the development and management of offerings is the concept of the life cycle. A *life cycle* plots sales of an offering (such as a brand of coffee) or a product class (such as all ground coffee brands) over a period of time. Life cycles are typically divided into four stages: (1) introduction, (2) growth, (3) maturity-saturation, and (4) decline. Exhibit 5.1 shows the general form of a product life cycle and the corresponding stages.

The sales curve can be viewed as being the result of offering trial and repeat-purchasing behavior. In other words,

Sales volume = (number of triers × average purchase amount × price) +
(number of repeaters × average purchase amount × price)

Early in the life cycle, management efforts focus on stimulating trial of the offering by advertising, giving out free samples, and obtaining adequate distribution.

EXHIBIT 5.1   **General Form of a Product Life Cycle**

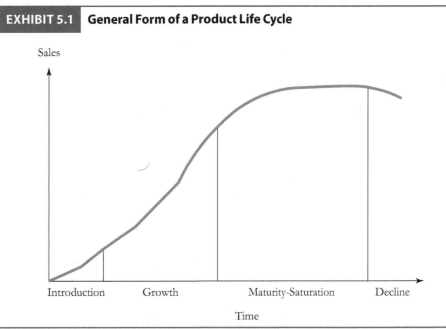

The vast majority of sales volume is due to trial purchases. As the offering moves through its life cycle, an increasing share of volume is attributable to repeat purchases, and management efforts focus on retaining existing buyers of the offering through offering modifications, enhanced brand image, and competitive pricing.

Anticipating and recognizing movement into advanced stages of the life cycle are crucial to managing the various stages. Movement into the maturity-saturation stage is often indicated by (1) an increase in the proportion of buyers who are repeat purchasers (that is, few new buyers or triers exist), (2) an increase in the standardization of production operations and product/service offerings, and (3) an increase in the incidence of aggressive pricing activities by competitors. As the offering enters into and moves through this stage, management efforts typically focus on finding new buyers for the offering, significantly improving the offering, and/or increasing the frequency of usage among current buyers. Ultimately, the decline stage must be addressed. The decision criteria at this stage are outlined in the following discussion on modifying, harvesting, and eliminating offerings.

Services often follow a life cycle similar to the product life cycle described previously. As a service firm approaches maturity, it typically modifies its operations to attract new buyers or increase purchase frequency. Examples include Starbucks with its expanded food menu and barbershops that become hair-stylist operations featuring hair-cutting services for men and women. Often service firms expand their geographical scope by reproducing facilities through franchising and licensing agreements to become multisite operators.

Modifying, Harvesting, and Eliminating Offerings

Modifying offerings is a common practice. Organizations are always on the lookout for new ways to improve the value their offerings provide customers in terms of quality, functions, features, and/or price.

Modification decisions typically focus on trading up or trading down the offering. *Trading up* involves a conscious decision to improve an offering—by adding new features and higher-quality materials or augmenting the offering with attendant services—and raising the price. *Trading down* is the process of reducing the number of features or quality of an offering and lowering the price.

Offering elimination is typically given less attention than new-offering or modification decisions. However, the elimination decision has grown in importance in recent years because of the realization that some offerings may be an unnecessary burden in light of potential opportunities. As an alternative to total elimination, management might consider harvesting the offering when it enters the late-maturity or decline stage of the life cycle.

Harvesting involves reducing the investment in a business entity in the hope of cutting costs and/or improving cash flow. In other words, the decision is not to abandon the offering outright but, rather, to minimize organizational resources allocated to it. Harvesting should be considered when (1) the market for the offering is stable, (2) the offering is not producing good profits, (3) the offering has a small or respectable market share that is becoming increasingly difficult or costly to defend from competitive inroads, and (4) the offering provides benefits to the organization in terms of image or "full-line" capabilities, despite poor future potential.

Elimination means that the offering is dropped from the mix of organizational offerings either outright or through sale to another organization. Generally speaking, if the answer to each of the following questions is "very little" or "none," then an offering is a candidate for elimination.

1. What is the future sales potential of the offering?
2. How much is the offering contributing to offering mix profitability?

3. How much is the offering contributing to the sale of other offerings in the mix?

4. How much could be gained by modifying the offering?

5. What would be the effect on channel members and buyers?

Each of these questions was considered by Ford Motor Company when it made the decision to sell its Jaguar and Land Rover automobile lines to Indian automaker Tata Motors.[9]

 # POSITIONING OFFERINGS

A second major offering-related decision confronting the manager concerns the positioning of offerings. *Positioning* is the act of designing an organization's offering and image so that it occupies a distinct and valued place in the target customer's mind relative to competitive offerings.

Positioning Approaches

There are a variety of positioning approaches available, including positioning by (1) attribute or benefit, (2) use or application, (3) product or brand user, (4) product or service class, (5) competitors, and (6) price and quality.

Positioning an offering by attributes or benefits is the approach most frequently used. Positioning an offering by attributes requires determining which attributes are important to target markets, which attributes are being emphasized by competitors, and how the offering can be fitted into this offering-target market environment. This kind of positioning may be accomplished by designing an offering that contains appropriate attributes or by stressing the appropriate attributes if they already exist in the offering. This latter tactic has been employed by a number of cereal manufacturers that have emphasized the healthy ingredients in their products in response to the growing interest in nutrition among a sizable number of cereal buyers.

In practice, operationalizing the positioning concept requires the development of a matrix relating attributes of the offering to market segments. Using toothpaste as an example, Exhibit 5.2 shows how particular attributes may vary in

EXHIBIT 5.2   Attributes and Marketing Segment Positioning

| Toothpaste Attributes | Market Segments | | | |
	Children	Teens, Young Adults	Family	Adults
Flavor	✓			
Color	✓			
Whiteness of teeth		✓		
Fresh breath		✓		
Decay prevention			✓	
Price			✓	
Plaque prevention				✓
Stain prevention				✓
Principal brands for each segment	Aim, Stripe	Ultra Brite, McCleans	Colgate, Crest	Topol, Rembrandt

Note: A check (✓) indicates principal benefits sought by each market segment.

importance for different market segments.[10] Several benefits accrue from viewing the market for toothpaste in this manner. First, the marketing manager can spot potential opportunities for new offerings and determine if a market niche exists. Second, looking at offering attributes and their importance to market segments permits subjective estimation of the extent to which a new offering might cannibalize existing offerings. If two offerings emphasize the same attributes, then they can be expected to compete with each other for the same market segment. Alternatively, if the offerings have different mixes of attributes, they probably will appeal to different segments. For this reason, Procter & Gamble's introduction of Crest tartar-control-formula toothpaste for adults did not have a major adverse effect on its sales of the existing Crest toothpaste for children. Third, the competitive response to a new offering can be judged more effectively using this framework. By determining which brands serve specific markets, one can evaluate offerings in terms of financial strength and market acceptance.

Organizations can also position their offerings by use or application. Arm & Hammer used this approach to position its baking powder as an odor-destroying agent in refrigerators and a water softener in swimming pools. Public television was originally positioned as a source of educational and cultural programming.

Positioning by user is a third approach. This approach typically associates a product or service with a user group. FedEx positions its delivery service for the busy executive. Certain deodorant brands position themselves for females (Jean Naté by Charles of the Ritz), whereas others focus on males (Brut by Fabergé).

Offerings can be positioned by product or service class as well. For example, margarine brands position themselves against butter. Savings associations position themselves as "banks."

An organization can position itself or its offerings directly against competitors. Avis positions itself against Hertz in the rental car business. For many years, the National Pork Producers Council positioned its product as being like poultry: "Pork: The Other White Meat."

Finally, positioning along a price–quality continuum is also possible. Hewlett-Packard initially priced its line of office personal computers below competitors in an attempt to convey a "value" position among corporate buyers. Hallmark, on the other hand, has pursued a quality positioning stance evidenced by its slogan: "When you care enough to send the very best."

In practice, marketing managers often combine two or more of these approaches when positioning a product, service, or brand. This is evident in the crafting of positioning statements.

Crafting a Positioning Statement

It is now common for marketing managers to prepare a succinct, written positioning statement once the desired positioning has been determined. Marketers write these statements for use internally, and by others, such as advertising agencies engaged in the drafting of a marketing strategy. The statement identifies the target market and needs satisfied, the product (service) class or category in which the organization's offering competes, and the offering's unique attributes or benefits provided. A positioning statement generally takes the following form:

> For (*target market and need*), the (*product, service, brand name*) is a (*product/ service class or category*) that (*statement of unique attributes or benefits provided*).

As an illustration, consider the North American positioning statement for Volvo:

> For upscale American families who desire a carefree driving experience, Volvo is a premium-priced automobile that offers the utmost in safety and dependability.

This statement gives direction to Volvo's overall North American marketing strategy. For example, it focuses Volvo's product development efforts, such as inclusion of side door airbags in its automobiles. It also provides insight for Volvo's marketing communication message. Volvo advertising almost always refers to safety and dependability and these two benefits form the basis for the automaker's "Volvo for life" slogan.

Repositioning

Repositioning is necessary when the initial positioning of a product, service, brand, or organization is no longer competitively sustainable or profitable or when better positioning opportunities arise. However, given the time and cost to establish a new position, repositioning is not advisable without careful study.

Examples of successful repositionings include the efforts behind Johnson & Johnson's St. Joseph Aspirin and Carnival Cruise Lines. Johnson & Johnson repositioned the aspirin from one for babies to an adult "Low Strength Aspirin" to reduce the risk of heart problems or strokes. This repositioning produced a significant boost in sales. Carnival Cruise Lines repositioned itself from a vacation alternative for older people to a "Fun Ship" for younger adults and families. After expanding its service offering to include Las Vegas–style shows, Camp Carnival, and Nautica Spa programs, Carnival became the largest and most successful company in the cruise industry.

Making the Positioning Decision

The challenge facing a manager is deciding which positioning is most appropriate in a given situation. The choice is made easier when the following three questions are considered. First, who are the likely competitors, what positions have they staked out in the marketplace, and how strong are they? Second, what are the preferences of the target consumers sought and how do these consumers perceive the offerings of competitors? Finally, what position, if any, do we already have in the target consumer's mind? Once answered, attention can then be focused on a series of implementation questions:

1. What position do we want to own?
2. What competitors must be outperformed if we are to establish the position?
3. Do we have the marketing resources to occupy and hold the position?

Positioning success depends on a number of factors. First, the position selected must be clearly communicated to and valued by targeted customers. Second, as the development of a position is a lengthy and often expensive process, frequent positioning changes should be avoided. Finally, the position taken in the marketplace should be sustainable and profitable.

 ## BRAND EQUITY AND BRAND MANAGEMENT

Branding offerings is a third responsibility of marketing managers. A brand name is any word, "device" (design, sound, shape, or color), or combination of these that is used to identify an offering and set it apart from competing offerings.

The major managerial implication of branding offerings is that consumer goodwill, derived from buyer satisfaction and favorable associations with a brand, can lead to *brand equity*—the added value a brand name bestows on a product or service beyond the functional benefits provided. This value has two distinct marketing advantages for the brand owner. First, brand equity provides a competitive advantage, such as the Sunkist label that signifies quality citrus fruit and the Gatorade name that defines sports drinks. A second advantage is that consumers are often willing to pay a higher price for a product or service with brand equity. Brand equity, in this instance, is represented by the premium a consumer will pay for one brand over another when the functional benefits provided are identical. Duracell batteries, Coca-Cola, Kleenex facial tissues, Louis Vuitton luggage, Bose audio systems, and Microsoft software all enjoy a price premium arising from brand equity.

Creating and Valuing Brand Equity

Brand equity doesn't just happen. It is carefully crafted and nurtured by marketing programs that forge strong, favorable, and unique consumer associations and experiences with a brand. Brand equity resides in the minds of consumers and results from what they have learned, felt, seen, and heard about a brand over time.

Creating Brand Equity   Marketers recognize that brand equity is not easily or quickly achieved. It arises from a sequential building process consisting of four steps (see Exhibit 5.3).[11]

The first step is to develop positive brand awareness and an association of the brand in consumers' minds with a product class or need to give the brand an identity. Gatorade and Kleenex have done this in the sports drink and facial tissue product classes, respectively.

Next, a marketer must establish a brand's meaning in the minds of consumers. Meaning arises from what a brand stands for and has two dimensions—a functional, performance-related dimension and an abstract, imagery-related dimension. Nike has done this through continuous product development and improvement and its links to peak athletic performance in its integrated marketing communications program.

The third step is to elicit the proper consumer responses to a brand's identity and meaning. Here attention is placed on how consumers think and feel about

EXHIBIT 5.3   Customer-Based Brand Equity Pyramid

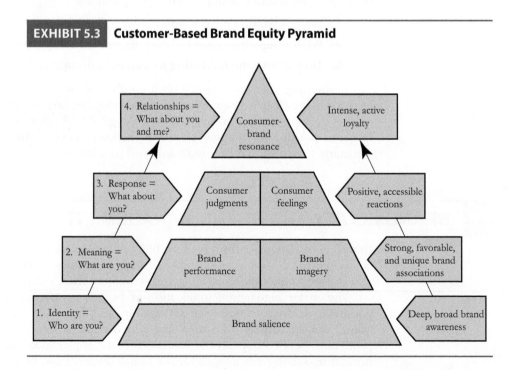

a brand. Thinking focuses on a brand's perceived quality, credibility, and superiority relative to other brands. Feeling relates to the consumer's emotional reaction to a brand. Michelin elicits both responses for its tires. Not only is Michelin thought of as a credible and superior-quality brand, but consumers also acknowledge a warm and secure feeling of safety, comfort, and self-assurance without worry or concern about the brand.

The final, and most difficult, step is to create a consumer-brand resonance evident in an intense, active loyalty relationship between consumers and the brand. A deep psychological bond characterizes consumer-brand resonance and the personal identification consumers have with the brand. Examples of brands that have achieved this status include Harley-Davidson, Apple, and eBay.

Valuing Brand Equity   Brand equity also provides a financial benefit for the brand owner.[12] Successful, established brand names, such as Gillette, Nike, and Gucci, have an economic value because they represent intangible assets. These assets enable their owner to enjoy a competitive advantage, to create earnings and cash flows in excess of the return on its tangible (plant and equipment) assets, and to achieve a high rate of return on investment relative to competitors.

The recognition that brands are assets and have an economic value is apparent in the strategic marketing decision to buy and sell brands. For example, Procter & Gamble bought the Hawaiian Punch brand from Del Monte for $150 million and sold it to Cadbury Schweppes nine years later for $203 million. This example illustrates that brands, unlike tangible assets that depreciate with time and use, appreciate in value when effectively managed. However, brands can lose value when they are not managed properly. The purchase and sale of Snapple brand noncarbonated fruit-flavored drinks and iced tea by Quaker Oats is a case in point. Quaker bought Snapple for $1.7 billion, only to sell it to Triarc Companies three years later for $300 million. The challenge of brand valuation is illustrated in the case study, "Frito-Lay Company: Cracker Jack," at the end of this chapter.

Branding Strategy

Companies can employ different branding strategies. The three most common strategies are multiproduct branding, multibranding, and private branding.

Multiproduct Branding   With *multiproduct branding*, a company uses one name for all its products in a product class. This strategy is sometimes called *family branding* or *corporate branding* when the company's trade name is used. Dell, Gerber, and Sony engage in corporate branding—the company's trade name and brand name are identical. Church & Dwight employs the Arm & Hammer family brand name for all its products featuring baking soda as a primary ingredient. Multiproduct branding is often used when a company wishes to establish dominance in a product or service class, as is the case with Campbell soups and American Express financial offerings.

There are several advantages to multiproduct branding. Capitalizing on brand equity, consumers who have a good experience with one product will transfer this favorable attitude to other company offerings with the same name. This strategy can also result in lower advertising and promotion costs because the same name is used on all products, thus raising the level of overall brand awareness. Increasingly, marketing executives have adopted multiproduct branding as a means to building a global brand identity. A *global brand* is a brand marketed under the same name in multiple countries with similar and centrally coordinated marketing programs. Samsung is a case in point.[13] A decade ago, Samsung marketed consumer electronics under a handful of brand names, including

Wiseview, Tantus, and Yepp, none of which meant much to consumers. The company decided to eliminate these brands and put all of its resources behind the Samsung corporate brand name. A heavy financial investment in innovative product design, development, and quality and a unified global brand message over 10 years has made Samsung one of the world's most visible and valuable brand names in the world.

However, there is a risk with multiproduct branding. Too many uses for one brand name can dilute the meaning of a brand for consumers.

Some companies employ *sub-branding*, which combines a corporate or family brand with a new brand name. The intent is to build on favorable associations consumers have toward the corporate or family brand while differentiating the new offering. For instance, Gatorade, the family brand for sport drinks marketed by PepsiCo, uses sub-branding as evidenced by the introduction of Gatorade G2, Gatorade Bring It, and Gatorade Be Tough, with unique flavors for each. Companies also employ sub-branding to differentiate offerings along a price–quality continuum; that is, by adding higher-end, midlevel, and lower-end offerings. Porsche has done this successfully by introducing the higher-end Porsche Carrera and the lower-end Porsche Boxster. On the other hand, Volkswagen unsuccessfully introduced the higher-end Volkswagen Phaeton and Touareg. Why? As a generalization, higher perceived price–quality brands such as Porsche "stretch" easier along the price–quality continuum than average price–quality brands, and a successful upward brand stretch is more difficult to profitably achieve than a downward brand stretch.

Multibranding Alternately, a company can engage in *multibranding*, which involves giving each product or product line a distinct name. For example, Procter & Gamble assigns individual names to each product (Tide, Cheer, and Era are all laundry detergents sold by Procter & Gamble). Sears assigns one brand name to different product lines (Kenmore home appliances, Craftsman tools, and Diehard car batteries). The use of a single name for a complete product line is akin to family branding.

Multibranding is a useful strategy when each brand is intended for a different market segment or uniquely positioned in the marketplace. Black & Decker markets its line of tools for the household do-it-yourselfer segment with the Black & Decker name. It uses the DeWalt name for its professional tool line. Disney uses the Miramax and Touchstone Picture names for films produced for adult audiences and its Disney name for children's and family films. Marriott International offers 14 hotel and resort brands, each positioned for a particular traveler experience and budget. To illustrate, Marriott Edition hotels and Vacation Clubs offer luxury amenities at a premium price. Marriott and Renaissance hotels offer medium- to high-priced accommodations. Courtyard hotels and Town Place Suites appeal to economy-minded travelers, whereas the Fairfield Inn is for those on a very low travel budget.

Compared with the multiproduct branding strategy, promotional costs tend to be higher with multibranding. The company must generate acceptance among consumers and distributors for each new brand without the benefit of any previous favorable impressions. An advantage of this approach is that each brand is unique to each market segment and there is reduced risk that an individual brand's failure to meet consumer expectations will transfer to the company itself, or other brands. Nevertheless, some large multibrand firms have found that the complexity and expense of implementing this strategy can outweigh the benefits. Unilever recently pruned its brands from some 1,600 to 400 through product deletion and sales to other companies.

Private Branding Private branding (or private labeling) involves a manufacturer supplying a reseller (retailer, wholesaler, distributor) with a product bearing a brand name chosen by the reseller. Rayovac, Paragon Trade Brands, and Ralcorp are major suppliers of private label alkaline batteries, diapers, and grocery products, respectively. Radio Shack, Sears, Walmart, and Kroger are retailers that market their own brand name products supplied by others. Brand name companies also produce private labels. Beauty and fragrance marketer Elizabeth Arden is a case in point. The company sells its Elizabeth Arden brand through department stores and a line of skin care products at Walmart with the "Skinsimple" brand name.

Private branding, as a strategy, should be approached from the perspective of both the supplier and the reseller. From the reseller perspective, the decision is whether or not to carry its own brands. Resellers favor doing this for a number of reasons. By carrying a private brand, a reseller avoids price competition to some extent, since no other reseller carries an identical brand that consumers can use for comparison purposes. Also, any buyer goodwill attributed to an offering accrues to the reseller, and buyer loyalty to the offering is tied to the retailer, not the producer. If a reseller desires a private brand, it must locate a producer willing to manufacture the brand. A marketing manager is then placed in the position of having to decide whether to be the producer.

A potential manufacturer of private brands should consider a number of factors when making this decision. If a producer has excess manufacturing capacity and the variable costs of producing a private brand do not exceed the sale price, the possibility exists for making a contribution to overhead and to utilizing production facilities. Even though a private brand will often compete directly with a producer's brand, the combined sales of the brands and the profit contribution to the producer may be greater than if a competitor obtained the rights to produce the private brand. For these reasons and others, firms such as Del Monte, Whirlpool, and Dial produce private brands of pet foods, home appliances, and bar soap for resellers. However, a danger in producing private brands is the possibility of becoming too reliant on private-brand revenue, only to have it curtailed when a reseller switches suppliers or builds its own production plant. Overreliance on private brands will also affect trade relationships between a producer and reseller. As a generalization, the influence of a producer, in terms of price and channel leadership, is inversely related to the proportion of its output or revenue obtained from a reseller's private brand.

Brand Growth Strategies

An organization has four strategic options for growing its brands (see Exhibit 5.4). The options are dictated by whether a marketing manager wishes to extend existing brands or develop new brands and whether the manager chooses to deploy these brands in product classes presently served or not served by the organization.

EXHIBIT 5.4	**Brand Growth Strategies**

		Product/Service Class Served by the Organization	
		New Product Class	Existing Product Class
	New Brand	New Brand Strategy	Fighting/Flanker Brand Strategy
Brand Name	Existing Brand	Brand Extension Strategy	Line Extension Strategy

Line Extension Strategy The most frequently employed growth strategy is a *line extension strategy*. Line extensions occur when an organization introduces additional offerings with the same brand in a product class that it currently serves. New flavors, forms, colors, different ingredients or features, and package sizes are examples of line extensions. As an example, Campbell Soup Company offers regular Campbell soup, homecooking style, chunky, and "healthy request" varieties, more than 100 soup flavors, and several different package sizes of prepared soups. Line extensions respond to customers' desire for variety. They also can eliminate gaps in a product line that might be filled by competitive offerings, or neutralize competitive inroads. As an example, Ford recently introduced the Fusion, a subbrand, to halt the defection of Ford owners who were buying competitors' midsize cars. According to Ford's car group marketing manager: "Every year, we were losing around 50,000 people from our products to competitors' midsize cars. We were losing Mustang, Focus, and Taurus owners. Fusion is our interceptor."[14]

This strategy also lowers advertising and promotion costs because the same brand is used on all items, thus raising the level of brand awareness. Line extensions do involve risk. There is a likelihood of product cannibalism occurring rather than incremental volume gains as buyers substitute one item for another in the extended product line. Also, proliferation of offerings within a product line can create production and distribution problems and added costs without incremental sales. For example, 8 percent of personal-care and household products sold in the United States account for 84.5 percent of total sales. Such statistics led companies that market these products to prune their product lines in recent years.[15]

Brand Extension Strategy Strong brand equity makes possible a *brand extension strategy*, the practice of using a current brand name to enter a completely different product class. This strategy can reduce the risk associated with introducing an offering in a new market by providing consumers the familiarity of and knowledge about an established brand. For instance, the equity in the Tylenol name as a trusted pain reliever allowed Johnson & Johnson to successfully extend this name to Tylenol Cold & Flu and Tylenol PM, a sleep aid. Equity in the Huggies family brand name allowed Kimberly-Clark to successfully extend its name to a full line of baby and toddler toiletries. Transferring an existing brand name to a new product class requires care.

Research indicates that the perceptual fit of the brand with and the transfer of the core product benefit to the new product class must exist for a brand extension to be successful.[16] This happened with Tylenol and Huggies, and both ventures produced sizable sales volume gains for the brands. However, it did not with Levi business attire, Dunkin' Donuts cereal, Harley-Davidson perfume, and Hooter's Airlines. These efforts failed. Even successful brand extensions involve a risk. Too many uses for a brand name can dilute the meaning of a brand for consumers, as discussed earlier.

A variation on brand extensions is *co-branding*, the pairing of two brand names of two manufacturers on a single product. For example, Hershey Foods has teamed with General Mills to offer a co-branded breakfast cereal called Reese's Peanut Butter Puffs and with Nabisco to provide Chips Ahoy cookies using Hershey's chocolate morsels. Citibank co-brands MasterCard and Visa with American Airlines. Co-branding benefits firms by allowing them to enter new product classes and capitalize on an already established brand name in those product classes.

New Brand Strategy In situations in which an organization concludes that its existing brand name(s) cannot be extended to a new product class, a new brand strategy is appropriate. A *new brand strategy* involves the development of a new brand and often a new offering for a product class that has not been previously served by the organization. Examples of successful new brand strategies include the introduction of Prego spaghetti sauce by Campbell Soup, and Aleve, a non-prescription pain reliever, by Roche Holding, Ltd. In both examples, existing company brand names were not deemed extendable to the new product classes for which they were targeted.

A new brand strategy may be the most challenging to successfully implement and the most costly. The cost to introduce a new brand in some consumer markets ranges from $50 million to $100 million. In many ways, this strategy is akin to diversification, with all the attendant challenges associated with this product-market strategy. The marketing of Eagle brand snacks by Anheuser-Busch described in Chapter 1 is an example of a new brand strategy failure. Launching a new brand (Eagle) in a product class new to the company (salty snacks) meant competing with Frito-Lay, the market leader, and its well-entrenched brands. Without a cost/price or quality advantage, focused distribution, effective advertising, promotion, or sales effort, the Eagle brand never achieved more than a modest market share and operated at a loss for 17 years before Anheuser-Busch scuttled the brand.[17]

Flanker/Fighting Brand Strategy Sometimes new brands are created for a product class already served by the organization when a line extension strategy is deemed inappropriate. These brands expand the product line to tap specific consumer segments not attracted to an organization's existing products/brands or represent defensive moves to counteract competition. As the name suggests, a *flanker brand strategy* involves adding new brands on the high or low end of a product line based on a price–quality continuum. Recall that Marriott did this to attract different traveler segments. In addition to its medium-priced Marriott hotels, it added Marriott Edition hotels to attract the upper end of the traveler market. It added the Fairfield Inn for those with a very low travel budget. Each brand offers a different amenities assortment and a corresponding room rate.

A *fighting brand strategy* involves adding a new brand whose sole purpose is to confront competitive brands in a product class being served by an organization. A fighting brand is typically introduced when (1) an organization has a high relative share of the sales in a product class, (2) its dominant brand(s) is susceptible to having this high share sliced away by aggressive pricing or promotion by competitors, or (3) the organization wishes to preserve its profit margins on its existing brand(s). Mattel launched its Flava brand of hip-hop fashion dolls in response to the popularity of BRATZ brand dolls sold by MGA Entertainment, which were attracting the 8- to 12-year-old girl segment of Barbie brand sales.[18]

Like line extensions, fighting and flanker brand strategies incur the risk of cannibalizing the other brand(s) in a product line. This is particularly likely with lower-priced brands. However, advocates of these brand strategies argue that it is better to engage in *preemptive cannibalism*—the conscious practice of stealing sales from an organization's existing products or brands to keep customers from switching to competitors' offerings—than lose sales volume.[19]

NOTES

1. Emily York, "A Little Less Salt, A Lot More Sales," *Advertising Age* (March 10, 2008): 1, 23.

2. "Mistakes Made on the Road to Innovation," *Bloomberg Businessweek,* www.businessweek.com, downloaded December 2, 2011.

3. Gillette Fusion Case Study (New York: Datamonitor, June 2008).

4. This and other examples appear in Gerard J. Tellis and Peter N. Golder, *Will and Vision: How Latecomers Grow to Dominate Markets* (New York: McGraw-Hill, 2002).

5. "MedImmune: Skies Clearing for FluMist?" Pharmaceutical Business Review Online, February 21, 2007.

6. For an extended treatment of the new product development process, see C. Merle Crawford and Anthony DiBenedetto, *New Products Management*, 10th ed. (Burr Ridge, IL: McGraw-Hill, 2011).

7. "A Survey of Innovation in Industry," *The Economist* (February 20, 1999).

8. "Is Testing the Answer?" *Advertising Age* (July 9, 2001): 23.

9. David Kiley, "Ford Closes Deal with Tata on Jag and Land Rover," Businessweek .com, June 2, 2008.

10. This example is adapted and updated from Russell Haley, "Benefit Segmentation: A Decision-Oriented Research Tool," in Ben Enis, Keith Cox, and Michael Mokwa (eds.), *Marketing Classics*, 8th ed. (Upper Saddle River, NJ: Prentice Hall, 1995): 226–233.

11. Kevin Lane Keller, *Strategic Brand Management: Building, Measuring, and Managing Brand Equity*, 3rd ed. (Upper Saddle River, NJ: Pearson, 2008): Chapter 2.

12. This discussion is based on Roger A. Kerin and Raj Sethuraman, "Exploring the Brand Value Shareholder Value Nexus for Consumer Goods Companies," *Journal of the Academy of Marketing Science* (Winter 1998): 260–273; "P&G Sells to Cadbury Hawaiian Punch Label in $203 Million Accord," *Wall Street Journal* (April 16, 1999): B2; and John Deighton, "How Snapple Got Its Juice Back," *Harvard Business Review* (January 2002): 47–53.

13. "Global Brands," *BusinessWeek* (August 1, 2005): 85–90.

14. "Ribbons Roll Out on Rides," *Dallas Morning News* (September 30, 2005): 8D.

15. Jack Neff, "The End of the Line for Line Extensions," *Advertising Age* (July 7, 2008): 3, 28.

16. Keller, *Strategic Brand Management*.

17. "How Eagle Became Extinct," *BusinessWeek* (March 4, 1996): 68–69.

18. "To Lure Older Girls, Mattel Brings in Hip-Hop Crowd," *Wall Street Journal* (July 18, 2003): A1, A6.

19. For an extended discussion on product cannibalism and preemptive cannibalism, see Roger A. Kerin and Dwight Riskey, "Product Cannibalism," in Sidney Levy (ed.), *Marketing Manager's Handbook* (Chicago: Dartnell, 1994): 880–895.

Case

Mary Kay India: The Hair Care Product Line Opportunity

In late 2010, Sheryl Adkins-Green received a request from a general manager for India to provide a hair care line for women. As vice president, Brand Development, at Mary Kay, Inc., Adkins-Green had among her responsibilities the development of the Mary Kay brand and brand portfolio around the world and global initiatives and products specially formulated for global markets. Approval for a hair care line in India rested solely on her shoulders.

The request for a hair care line came on the heels of a request for a bar soap in India in November 2008. She approved the request. Mary Kay India subsequently introduced a bar soap in October 2010, which was manufactured in India. The bar soap brand, Lotus & Bamboo Indulgent Bath Bar, represented the first time Mary Kay, Inc. approved a customized product for a specific country or regional market. It was still too early to judge the performance of the soap.

Mary Kay, Inc. had introduced a hair care line, first in the 1970s for the United States and then in the 1990s for Europe. Neither initiative met corporate expectations. Adkins-Green's assistant joked, "Maybe the third time will be charmed." Not wishing to rely on fate, Adkins-Green called a meeting of the brand development team to consider the hair care line request.

 ## MARY KAY, INC.

Mary Kay, Inc. is a privately held corporation headquartered in Dallas, Texas. The company is one of the largest direct sellers of skin care and color cosmetics in the world with more than $2.5 billion in wholesale sales in 2009. Mary Kay brand products are sold in more than 35 markets on five continents. The United States, China, Russia, and Mexico are the top four markets served by the company.

Mary Kay Ash founded Mary Kay Cosmetics in 1963 with her life savings of $5,000 and support of her 20-year-old son, Richard Rogers, who currently

The cooperation of Mary Kay, Inc. in the preparation of this case is gratefully acknowledged. This case was prepared by Professor Roger A. Kerin of the Edwin L. Cox School of Business, Southern Methodist University with the assistance of Katherine Henderson, graduate student, as a basis for class discussion and is not designed to illustrate effective or ineffective handling of an administrative situation. Certain company information, including financial data, is disguised and is not useful for research purposes. Copyright © 2011 by Roger A. Kerin. No part of this case may be reproduced without written permission of the copyright holder.

serves as executive chair of Mary Kay, Inc. Mary Kay Ash's founding principles were simple, time-tested, and remain a fundamental company business philosophy. She adopted the Golden Rule as her guiding principle, determining that the best course of action in virtually any situation could be easily discerned by "doing unto others as you would have them do unto you." She also steadfastly believed that life's priorities should be kept in their proper order, which to her meant "God first, family second, and career third." Her work ethic, approach to business, and success resulted in numerous awards and recognitions including, but not limited to, the Horatio Alger American Citizen Award, America's 25 Most Influential Women, and the National Business Hall of Fame.

Today, Mary Kay, Inc. engages in the development, manufacture, and packaging of skin care, makeup, spa and body, and fragrance products for men and women. It offers anti-aging, cleanser, moisturizer, lip and eye care, body care, and sun care products. Overall, the company produces more than 200 premium products in its state-of-the-art manufacturing facilities in Dallas, Texas, and Hangzhou, China.

Direct Selling at Mary Kay, Inc.

The company's approach to direct selling employs the "party plan," whereby independent sales representatives host parties in a customer's home to demonstrate and sell products. A powerful feature of the party plan is that attendees have the opportunity to actually experience products before they make a purchase decision. The company's global independent sales force exceeds 2 million. About 65 percent of the company's independent sales representatives reside outside the United States.

A new Mary Kay independent sales representative purchases a starter kit, which costs about $100 in the United States. The starter kit includes products as well as literature describing the Mary Kay culture, sales techniques, and so forth. Existing representatives subsequently buy Mary Kay products at a 30 to 40 percent discount off the suggested retail selling price, depending on volume purchased. Specific products purchased and inventoried for demonstration and sale are at the sole discretion of the representative.

Growth Opportunities in Asia-Pacific Markets

Asia-Pacific markets represent major growth opportunities for Mary Kay, Inc. Asia-Pacific markets for the company include Australia, China, Hong Kong, India, Korea, Malaysia, New Zealand, the Philippines, Singapore, and Taiwan.

China accounts for the largest sales revenue outside the United States, representing about 25 percent of annual Mary Kay, Inc. worldwide sales. The company entered China in 1995 and currently has some 200,000 independent sales representatives or "beauty consultants" in that country. Part of the success in China has been attributed to the company's message of female empowerment and femininity that resonated in China, a country where young women had few opportunities to start their own businesses. Speaking about the corporate philosophy at Mary Kay, Inc., KK Chua, president, Asia-Pacific, said, "Mary Kay's corporate objective is not only to create a market, selling skin care and cosmetics; it's all about enriching women's lives by helping women reach their full potential, find their inner beauty and discover how truly great they are." This view was echoed by Adkins-Green, who notes that the Mary Kay brand has "transformational and aspirational" associations for consumers and beauty consultants alike.

Mary Kay, Inc. learned that adjustments to its product line and message for women were necessary in some Asia-Pacific markets. In China, for example, the order of one's life priorities—"God first, family second, and career third"—has been modified to, "Faith first, family second, and career third." Also, Chinese women were not heavy users of makeup. Therefore, the featured products include skin cream and anti-aging and whitening creams. As a generalization, whitening products were popular among women in China, India, Korea, and the Philippines where lighter skin is associated with beauty, class, and privilege.

 ## MARY KAY INDIA

Mary Kay, Inc. initiated operations in India in September 2007 with a full marketing launch in early 2008. Senior management believed that India represented a growth opportunity for three reasons. First, the Indian upper and consuming classes were growing and were expected to total over 500 million individuals. Second, the population was overwhelmingly young and optimistic (median age = 26 years old). The youthful population continued to blur the line between luxury and basic items. Third, there was a growing number of working women that had given a boost to sales of cosmetics, body care, skin care, and fragrances in India's urban areas where the great majority of the country's middle-class women reside.

Senior management also believed that the Mary Kay culture was a good fit with the Indian culture and would benefit the company's venture into this market. For example, industry research had shown that continuing modernization of the country had led to changing aspirations, where the need to be good looking, well-groomed, and stylish had taken on newfound importance.

Finally, senior management believed that Mary Kay would need to perform three tasks for the company to be successful in India. Specifically, the company had to build a brand, build a sales force, and build an effective supply chain to service the sales force.

EXHIBIT 1 **Mary Kay India Print Advertisement**

Building a Brand Mary Kay, Inc. executives believed that brand building in India involved media advertising (see Exhibit 1 on page 151), literature describing the Mary Kay culture, the Mary Kay story and image, and educational material for Mary Kay independent sales representatives. In addition, Mary Kay, Inc. arranged to be the cosmetics partner of the Miss India Worldwide Pageant 2008. Mary Kay Miss Beautiful Skin 2008 was crowned at this event.

Brand building also involved the product mix and pricing in India. Four guidelines were followed:

1. Keep the offering simple and skin care focused for the new Indian sales force and for a new operation.
2. Open with accessibly priced basic skin care products in relation to the competition in order to establish Mary Kay product quality and value.
3. Avoid opening with products that would phase out shortly after launch.
4. Address key product categories of skin care, body care, and color-based cosmetics on current market information.

Mary Kay initially introduced 60 products to India. By late 2010, the company offered over 90 products. Representative products, package sizes, and retail prices are shown in Exhibit 2.

Brand pricing focused on offering accessibly priced basic skin care to the average middle-class Indian consumer between the ages of 25 and 54. This

EXHIBIT 2 Representative Mary Kay India Products, Packages, and Retail Prices

Skin Care Category

Product	Package Size	Retail Price Rs/$U.S.
Customized Skin Care Moisturizer	85 grams	Rs. 600/$13.33
3-in-1 Cleanser	113 ml.	Rs. 400/$8.89
MelaCep Whitening System	85 grams	Rs. 1050/$23.33

Makeup Category

Product	Package Size	Retail Price Rs/$U.S.
Mineral Eye Color	1.4 grams	Rs. 199/$4.42
Crème Lipstick	3 grams	Rs. 550/$12.22
Mineral Cheek Color	5 grams	Rs. 425/$9.44

Body Care Category

Product	Package Size	Retail Price Rs/$U.S.
Daytime Body Moisturizer	236 grams	Rs. 1500/$33.33
Shower Gel	6.5 fl. oz.	Rs. 425/$9.44
Body Lotion	236 ml.	Rs. 650/$14.44

Fragrance

Product	Package Size	Retail Price Rs/$U.S.
Eau de Parfum	1.7 fl. oz.	Rs. 2150/$47.78
Eau de Toilette	50 ml.	Rs. 1099/$24.42

Note: Rs. represents *rupees,* the plural form of *rupee,* Indian monetary unit.

strategy, called "mass-tige pricing," resulted in product retail price points that would be above mass-market retail prices, but below retail prices for prestige competitive products. Prices for Hindustan Unilever beauty and personal care products typified mass (market) prices. As a rule, mass-tige pricing resulted in retail price points that were 25 to 30 percent higher than mass-market-priced beauty and personal care products. Following an initial emphasis on offering high-quality, value products, Mary Kay subsequently offered more technologically advanced products that commanded higher price points. For example, the company introduced the Mary Kay MelaCEP Whitening System, consisting of seven products, which was specifically formulated for Asian skin in March 2009. This system was "priced on the lower price end of the prestige category with a great value for money equation," said Hina Nagarajan, a country manager for Mary Kay India.

Building a Sales Force   According to Adkins-Green, "Mary Kay's most powerful marketing vehicle is the direct selling organization," which is a key component of the brand's marketing strategy. New independent sales representatives received two to three days of intensive training and a starter kit that included not only products, but also information pertaining to product demonstrations, sales presentations, professional demeanor, the company's history and culture, and team building. "Culture training is very important to Mary Kay (independent sales representatives) because they are messengers of Mary Kay," said Hina Nagarajan. By late 2010, Mary Kay had 4,000 independent beauty consultants present in some 200 cities out of about 5,100 Indian cities and towns. These cities were located mostly in the northern, western, and northeastern regions of the country. These three regions account for about 75 percent of total branded beauty and personal care product sales in India. Furthermore, urban areas across India accounted for 69 percent of beauty and personal care product sales in 2009.

Creating a Supply Chain   Mary Kay India imported products into India from China, Korea, and the United States. Products were shipped to regional distribution centers in Delhi (northern India) and Mumbai (western India), where Mary Kay Beauty Centers were located. Beauty Centers served as order, pickup, and delivery points for independent sales representatives. Mary Kay beauty consultants purchased products from the company and, in turn, sold them to consumers.

THE BRANDED BEAUTY AND PERSONAL CARE MARKET IN INDIA

The branded beauty and personal care market in India topped U.S. $55.6 billion in 2009, based on manufacturers' prices. This market grew by 57 percent between 2005 and 2009. Industry analysis forecasted 50 percent market growth between 2010 and 2014. The branded beauty and personal care market included the following products: baby care, bath and shower, color cosmetics, deodorants, depilatories, fragrances, hair care, men's grooming products, oral hygiene, skin care, and sun care. Four product categories accounted for 83 percent of total market sales in 2009. They were bath and shower (31.3 percent), hair care (25.2 percent), oral hygiene (15.0 percent), and skin care (11.5 percent).

Major Competitors

Some 50 companies compete in the branded beauty and personal care market in India. Hindustan Unilever accounts for about one-third of market sales. Nine additional companies account for another third of market sales: Colgate-Palmolive (India) Ltd.; Dabur India Ltd.; Godrej Consumer Products Ltd; L'Oréal India Pvt. India; Gillette India Ltd.; Wipro Ltd.; Reckitt Benckiser Ltd.; Procter & Gamble India Ltd.; and CavinKare Pvt. Ltd. All of these companies sell primarily through retail channels (e.g., grocery, drug, department, and mass-merchandise stores) which represent 96.4 percent of market sales in India. Direct sellers, such as Amway India Enterprises, Avon Products, Inc., and Mary Kay India, account for 3.6 percent of beauty and personal care market sales.

The Hair Care Category

The hair care category in India consists of branded and packaged colorants, conditioners, perms and relaxants, shampoos, styling agents, and salon hair care. Total category sales was about U.S. $14.0 billion, based on manufacturers' prices. Conditioners and shampoos alone represented 81 percent of hair care sales in 2009, with conditioners representing 53 percent of sales and shampoos representing 47 percent of sales.

Ten companies, out of some 40 companies in India, captured 77.4 percent of hair care product sales in 2009. Company market shares and shares of their major brands are shown in Exhibit 3. Three of the top five competitors were multinational firms: Hindustan Unilever Ltd., L'Oréal India Pvt Ltd., and Procter Gamble India Ltd. Hindustan Unilever Ltd. is the hair care category market share leader with its Clinic Plus brand. The next largest hair care marketers are Dabur India Ltd. and Marico Ltd.—two domestic firms. Direct seller Amway India Enterprises, with some 80,000 distributors, captures 0.3 percent of the shampoo and conditioner category. Its primary brand is Satinique.

Hair Care Practices and Preferences in India   A recent analysis of the hair care category in India by Euromonitor International, a global market research firm, reported:

> The vast majority of hair care consumers in India are unsophisticated, low-income consumers from rural and semi-urban areas who use traditional hair oils. The at-home use of unbranded and unpackaged herbs and oils such as Henna, Shikakai (Acacia Concinna) and coconut oil for washing, colouring and conditioning hair is very common in India.[1]

Branded and packaged shampoos and conditioners featuring hair oils as ingredients account for nearly 40 percent of hair care sales in India. The market positions of Dabur India Ltd. and Marico Ltd. are due in large part to their dominance in hair oils. Multinational firms have stayed away from hair oils for the most part due to consumers' loyalty to traditional Indian brands and the fact that the use of hair oils is limited to the Indian subcontinent.

Indian consumers, on average, use shampoo infrequently—usually once every 7 to 14 days. Urban middle-class consumers typically shampoo more frequently than rural consumers. Among women, the average usage per shampooing occasion is 6 milliliters (0.20 fluid ounce) which is higher than the usage per occasion in Western countries (4 milliliters). The usage difference is due in large measure

---

[1]*Hair Care-India*, Euromonitor International: Country Sector Briefing (July 2010), p. 2.

EXHIBIT 3	Top-10 Hair Care Company Market Shares and Brand Market Shares in 2009		
Company	*Company Market Share*	*Major Company Brands*	*Brand Market Share*
Hindustan Unilever Ltd.	18.7%	Clinic Plus	9.1%
		Sunsilk	4.7%
		Clear	1.7%
		Clinic All Clear	1.1%
Dabur India Ltd.	13.0%	Dabur	5.7%
		Dabur Vatika	3.9%
Marico Ltd.	9.4%	Parachute	5.1%
		Nihar	2.6%
L'Oréal India Pvt. Ltd.	9.1%	Elvive	3.4%
		L'Oreal Excellence	1.5%
		L'Oreal Professionnel	1.4%
Procter & Gamble India Ltd.	8.6%	Head & Shoulders	4.8%
		Pantene Pro-V	3.7%
CavinKare Pvt. Ltd.	4.7%	Chik	3.2%
		Nyle	0.9%
Godrej Consumer Products Ltd.	4.5%	Godrej	4.2%
Emami Ltd.	4.1%	Himani	4.1%
Hygienic Research Institute Pvt. Ltd.	2.7%	Super Vasmol	2.4%
Bajaj Consumer Care Ltd.	2.6%	Bajaj	2.6%

to the fact that women in India traditionally wear their hair longer than women in Western countries. Ordinary bath soap is often used as a substitute for shampoo.

Nevertheless, sales of branded and packaged shampoos and conditioners has shown consistent growth in India. Industry analysts attribute this growth to three factors. First, the frequency of usage has risen as purchasing power has increased and the emphasis on personal grooming intensifies in urban areas. About 40 percent of households in urban areas use branded shampoos and conditioners. In rural and semiurban areas, a trend toward upgrades from unpackaged herbs and hair oils to packaged goods for washing and conditioning hair is apparent. Even so, only about 10 percent of households in rural and semiurban areas use branded shampoos and conditioners. And third, broadened distribution, lower prices, and mass media efforts by major hair care companies have prompted a switch from bar soap to shampoo for hair washing.

Hair Care Brand and Product Variants Intense competition among hair care companies is apparent with companies segmenting the category on benefit platforms and expanding their brand and product portfolios over the past two years. Three benefit platforms are prominent: (1) cosmetic (shine, health, and strength), (2) anti-dandruff, and (3) damage repair. Cosmetic shampoos account for 50 to 55 percent of shampoo sales, anti-dandruff, 20 to 25 percent of sales, and damage repair, 20 to 25 percent of sales.

Products with specific benefits such as ayurvedic[2] or medicinal ingredients, fragrance, and convenience of usage were introduced. L'Oréal India Pvt. Ltd. launched a new product in January 2010: Garnier Fructis Shampoo + Oil, a 2-in-1 shampoo containing olive, avocado, and shea oil, to specifically appeal to women accustomed to using oil to nourish and condition their hair. Marico Ltd. modernized its packaging by adding a spray nozzle and an electric device for warming its hair oil to make it more convenient for consumers to use the product for regular at-home head and hair massages.

Most of the major shampoo companies offered only two variants of conditioners, one for normal/dry hair and another for oily hair. However, Hindustan Unilever offers a conditioner companion for each of its Dove and Sunsilk shampoo variants.

The range of products has also increased as companies have focused attention on niche local/traditional fragrances and products. For example, CavinKare Pvt. Ltd. has launched shampoo variants containing local/regional fragrances and ingredients. Industry analysts believe that localization of products will increase as companies face increasing competition and try to differentiate their product offerings.

Hair Care Product Packaging and Pricing   Branded and packaged hair care oils, shampoos, and conditioners are sold in sachets and bottles. Sachets are small, closed plastic packets that range in size from 6 to 8 milliliters, with retail prices ranging from 2 to 5 rupees (48.95 Rs. = U.S. $1.00 in 2009). Bottles range in size from 80 to 400 milliliters with retail prices ranging from 27 to 369 rupees. Sixty percent of shampoo and conditioner unit sales in India come from sachets. In addition to making products affordable for lower-income consumers, sachets are used to stimulate trial of new brands and products. Bottles are more popular in urban areas than rural areas and in northern India than in other regions. Exhibit 4 shows representative hair care product packaging and retail pricing in India in late 2010.

THE HAIR CARE PRODUCT OPPORTUNITY

Sheryl Adkins-Green assembled her brand development team in early 2011 to assess the hair care product opportunity in India. She and her team had discussed the opportunity with company product development, manufacturing, sales, and supply chain executives as well as company executives in India prior to the meeting. A consensus view going into the meeting was that hair care represented an opportunity based solely on the size and projected growth of the category. At the same time, executives realized that when and how Mary Kay India pursued the opportunity was crucial to the success of the venture.

When to Launch

Several points of view were raised concerning the timing of a hair care product line launch in India. Some executives believed that it might be too soon to introduce a totally new category for Mary Kay beauty consultants in India. They

---

[2]Ayurveda is a form of traditional medicine practiced in India. It uses mixtures of naturally occurring materials of vegetable, animal, and mineral origin. The medicinal properties of ayurvedic materials and formulations have been used for centuries in Indian culture to cure illness and promote good health. Dabur India Ltd. has aggressively used ayurvedic ingredients.

EXHIBIT 4 Representative Hair Care Product Packaging and Retail Pricing in India (Late 2010)

Company	Brand/Product Variant	Package Size	Retail Price Rs/$U.S.
Amway India	Santinique Advanced	6 ml. sachet	Rs 5/$.11
	Moistening Detangler and Conditioner	250 ml. bottle	Rs 369/$8.20
	Santinique Advanced	6 ml. sachet	Rs 5/$.11
	Dandruff Control Conditioning Shampoo	250 ml. bottle	Rs 369/$8.20
	Santinique Advanced	6 ml. sachet	Rs 5/$.11
	2-in-1 Shampoo and Conditioner	250 ml. bottle	Rs 369/$8.20
Procter & Gamble India	Pantene Pro-V Smooth & Silky	7.5 ml. sachet	Rs 3/$.07
	Pantene Pro-V Volume & Fullness	100 ml. bottle	Rs 51/$1.13
	Pantene Pro-V Long Black	200 ml. bottle	Rs 98/$2.18
	Pantene Pro-V Hair Fall Control		
	Pantene Pro-V Lively Clean		
	Pantene Pro-V Goodness of Coconut Oil		
	Head & Shoulders Smooth & Silky	7.5 ml. sachet	Rs 2/$.04
	Head & Shoulders Refreshing Menthol	90 ml. bottle	Rs 69/$1.53
	Head & Shoulders Clean and Balanced	200 ml. bottle	Rs 167/$3.71
	Head & Shoulders Silky Black	400 ml. bottle	Rs 269/$5.98
	Head & Shoulders Naturally Clean		
	Head & Shoulders Nourishing Aloe Vera		
	Head & Shoulders Anti-Hairfall Conditioner	100 ml. bottle	Rs 50/$1.11
		200 ml. bottle	Rs 99/$2.20
Marico Ltd.	Parachute Advanced Ayurvedic Hair Oil Personal Champi[1]	80 ml. bottle	Rs 27/$1.78
	Parachute Advanced Ayurvedic Hair Oil Hot Champi	170 ml. bottle	Rs 48/$3.78
	Parachute Advanced Ayurvedic Hair Oil Easy Champi	300 ml. sachet packs (50)	Rs 80/$1.78
Hindustan Unilever Ltd.	Sunsilk Thick & Long Shampoo	6 ml. sachet	Rs 3/$.07
	Sunsilk Soft & Smooth Shampoo	100 ml. bottle	Rs 70/$1.56
	Sunsilk Hairfall Solution Shampoo	200 ml. bottle	Rs 105/$2.33
	Sunsilk Damage Repair Shampoo	400 ml. bottle	Rs 179/$3.98
	Sunsilk Blackstone Shampoo		
	Sunsilk Anti-Dandruff Shampoo		

[1]Note: "Champi" is the word for the act of shampooing or messaging the head in India.

(Continued)

EXHIBIT 4   *(Continued)*

Company	*Brand/Product Variant*	*Package Size*	*Retail Price Rs/$U.S.*
	Sunsilk Think & Long Conditioner	100 ml. bottle	Rs 50/$1.11
	Sunsilk soft & Smooth Conditioner	200 ml. bottle	Rs 99/$2.20
	Sunsilk Hairfall Solution Conditioner		
	Sunsilk Damage Repair Conditioner		
	Sunsilk Blackstone Conditioner		
	Sunsilk Anti-Dandruff Conditioner		
	Clinic Plus Clean & Thick Shampoo	7.5 ml. sachet	Rs 2/$.04
	Clinic Plus Natural Shampoo	100 ml. bottle	Rs 46/$1.02
	Clinic Plus Anti-Dandruff Shampoo	200 ml. bottle	Rs 88/$1.96
		400 ml. bottle	Rs 158/$3.51
L'Oréal India	Garnier Fructis Shampoo + Oil 2-1 Normal Hair	7.5 ml. sachet	Rs 3/$.07
		100 ml. bottle	Rs 64/$1.42
		200 ml. bottle	Rs 117/$2.60
	Garnier Fructis Shampoo + Oil 2-1 Dry/Damaged Hair		
	Garnier Fructis Shampoo + Oil 2-1 Long & Strong		
	Garnier Fructis Shampoo + Oil 2-1 Sleek & Shine		
	Garnier Fructis Shampoo + Oil 2-1 Anti-Dandruff		
	L'Oreal Paris 5 Repairing Shampoo	100 ml. bottle	Rs 72/$1.60
		200 ml. bottle	Rs 130/$2.89
		90 ml. bottle	Rs 80/$1.78
	L'Oreal Paris 5 Repairing Conditioner	180 ml. bottle	Rs 150/$3.33

Source: Company websites and comparison shopper observations.

thought that beauty consultants were still learning about the company and existing products, noting that 30 new products were introduced into India in the last two years. A wholly new product category outside of skin and body care and color cosmetics would require considerable training for beauty consultants.

Other executives favored a hair care product launch as early as January 2012. They believed that since the request for hair care products emanated from Mary Kay India executives, their judgment on the matter carried considerable weight. Their request for a bar soap was met and even though it was too early to judge its success. The Lotus & Bamboo Indulgent Bath Bar (see Exhibit 5) had shown initial signs of acceptance in India by beauty consultants and consumers alike. They also noted that a hair care product line offered more alternatives for existing and potential beauty consultants.

Other executives countered that a hair care product line launch was fundamentally different from bar soap. First, bar soap was a single product (stock-keeping unit) and a skin and body care item. Second, they believed shampoos

EXHIBIT 5   **Advertisement for Lotus & Bamboo Indulgent Bath Bar**

Lotus & Bamboo Indulgent Bath Bar ™

Lotus & Bamboo Indulgent Bath Bar is a refreshing body bath bar that gently cleans the skin. The rich moisturization of the Indulgent Bath Bar will leave the skin feeling soft and smooth. Indulge in the enticing clean, crisp scent of Lotus & Bamboo that will provide lingering freshness to the skin.

3X 100gm
Rs. 150

and conditioners were not a product line that could easily be represented and demonstrated by beauty consultants. These executives expressed reservations about a hair care product launch at all, particularly in light of the fact that the hair care line would be marketed only in India. This would be particularly true if the hair care line included hair oils.

How to Launch

Considerable discussion focused on how the marketing of a hair care product line might proceed in India. Different viewpoints were expressed.

Product Line and Packaging Considerations   Some executives believed that a shampoo product and a conditioner might be necessary for each benefit platform (cosmetic, anti-dandruff, and damage repair). Therefore, six stock-keeping units would be needed. If the number of product items was deemed too large, just two conditioner products might be introduced: one for normal/dry hair and another for oily hair. Product development executives were confident that the company could develop these products. A 2-in-1 shampoo and conditioner product was not considered a viable option at the current time.

Packaging also needed attention. Sachets and bottles were both considered, but there was no consensus on whether or not each shampoo and conditioner variant should be packaged only in a sachet for the introduction or in both a sachet and a 100-milliliter bottle. If three shampoo variants, three conditioner variants, and two package sizes for each were introduced, then the hair care line would be composed of 18 stock-keeping units. If three shampoos were introduced with two conditioners, each in two package sizes, then the hair line would have 12 stock-keeping units. "In either case, that would be a lot of inventory for beauty consultants to buy and carry," said a sales support executive.

Other executives believed that a more limited product line should be initially introduced. They said that two, not three shampoo variants should be provided, adding that there was no need to offer a conditioner in a sachet since this practice was not widespread in India.

Product Price and Cost Considerations   Price and cost considerations were also topics for discussion. The mass-tige pricing strategy for skin care and cosmetics had yielded favorable results in India. It was still unclear how this retail pricing strategy would apply to hair care, particularly since a manufacturer and manufacturing cost was yet to be determined. About 87 percent of shampoo and conditioner sales were sold at mass-market prices; 13 percent were sold at prestige or premium prices. Since hair care products were not produced by the company, they would need to be produced by a local, contract manufacturer in India that met Mary Kay's quality standards, ingredient specifications, and quantity requirements. If necessary, the contract manufacturer would need the capability to package these products in sachets and bottles to Mary Kay specifications. Supply chain executives expected that the minimum order quantity per stock-keeping unit for a contract manufacturer would be 100,000 units. Therefore, if three shampoo variants, two conditioner variants, and a single package (sachet) were ordered, a minimum order quantity would be 600,000 units. If a 100-milliliter bottle for shampoos and conditioners was also produced, the minimum order quantity would double.

Although a rough estimate, manufacturing executives thought that the product fill (shampoo; conditioner) and package unit cost for a box of six 6-milliliter sachets delivered to Mary Kay Beauty Centers in Delhi and Mumbai by the local manufacturer could be U.S. $0.60. A local manufacturer's delivered cost per unit for a 100-milliliter bottle could range from U.S. $1.25 to U.S. $1.75. Order processing, product handling, and delivery cost for hair care products would probably range from $0.40 to $0.60 for a 6-sachet box and a 100-milliliter bottle.

Advertising, Promotion, and Sales Considerations   Discussion related to advertising, promotion, and sales support focused on the incremental costs associated with a hair care launch. Mary Kay India used billboards, sponsorships (notably the Miss India Pageant), some print and television advertising, the quarterly *The Look* catalog (see Exhibit 6) and its Web site (www.marykay.co.in) to advertise and promote its products. A rough estimate for the incremental cost necessary to develop and place advertising copy and Web site content and public relations for a hair care line was U.S. $650,000 for the first year of introduction.

Additionally, incremental costs associated with producing sales and product information materials for beauty consultants and providing sales training would be incurred. For example, a training module prepared and delivered by Mary Kay, Inc. personnel would be necessary. The estimated incremental cost associated with developing product information and providing sales training prior to the introduction was U.S. $55,000.

Sheryl Adkins-Green sat alone in the conference room and reviewed her notes after the meeting adjourned. She knew that a product development and a subsequent marketing launch of a hair care line for India could take 18 months once approved. She also knew that a timely "yes–no" reply to the general manager for India was necessary. She e-mailed the brand development team to schedule an all-day meeting for the next week with the subject line: Hair Care Decision For India!

EXHIBIT 6 *The Look:* Mary Kay India Catalog Cover

Case

Dr Pepper/Seven Up, Inc.

Squirt Brand

In mid-summer 2001, Kate Cox, the brand manager at Dr Pepper/Seven Up, Inc. responsible for Squirt, began to draft the brand's annual advertising and promotion plan. Squirt is a caffeine-free, low-sodium carbonated soft drink brand with a distinctive blend of grapefruit juices that gives it a tangy, fresh citrus taste. Squirt is the best-selling carbonated grapefruit soft drink brand in the United States.

Cox believed that market targeting and product positioning might require attention early in Squirt's advertising and promotion plan development. Both topics were highlighted in a June 2001 presentation by the brand's advertising agency, Foote, Cone & Belding, shortly after she assumed responsibility for Squirt. Actions by competitors, notably Coca-Cola and Pepsi-Cola; a recent dip in Squirt case sales volume; and implications of the growing Hispanic community in markets where Squirt was popular were foremost in her mind.

DR PEPPER/SEVEN UP, INC.

Dr Pepper/Seven Up, Inc. is the largest division of Cadbury Schweppes PLC. Cadbury Schweppes PLC is the world's third largest soft drink company and the fourth largest confectionary company, with product sales in almost 200 countries. Headquartered in London, England, Cadbury Schweppes PLC has the distinction of being the world's first soft drink maker and the world's largest non-cola soft drink producer and marketer.

Dr Pepper/Seven Up, Inc. (DPSU) is the largest non-cola soft drink enterprise in North America. The company markets such national brands as Dr Pepper, 7Up, RC Cola, A&W Root Beer, Canada Dry, Squirt, Hawaiian Punch, and

Schweppes, among others. DPSU also owns regional brands including Sundrop and Vernors, among others.

DPSU is the third largest soft drink company in the United States. Its flagship brands—Dr Pepper and 7Up—are consistently ranked among the top-10 soft drink brands in the United States as measured by market share. Its other brands are often the market leader in their specific categories. For example, Canada Dry is the top-selling ginger ale in the United States, Schweppes is the leading tonic water, and Canada Dry seltzers lead the club soda/seltzer category. Squirt is the best-selling grapefruit soft drink, and A&W Root Beer is the leading root beer sold in bottles and cans.

CARBONATED SOFT DRINK INDUSTRY IN THE UNITED STATES

U.S. consumers drink more carbonated soft drinks than tap water. In 2000, Americans consumed 53 gallons of soft drinks per person, compared with about 47 gallons in 1990. Population growth compounded by rising per capita consumption produced an estimated $60.3 billion in carbonated soft drink retail sales in 2000. However, soft drink consumption growth has slowed in recent years.

Industry Structure

There are three major participants in the production and distribution of carbonated soft drinks in the United States.[1] They are concentrate producers, bottlers, and retail outlets. For regular soft drinks, concentrate producers manufacture the basic flavors (for example, lemon-lime and cola) for sale to bottlers, which add a sweetener to carbonated water and package the beverage in bottles and cans, which are then sold to retailers. For diet soft drinks, concentrate producers include an artificial sweetener, such as aspartame, with their flavors. Concentrate producer prices to bottlers differ slightly between regular and diet soft drinks. For example, a concentrate producer's price for regular flavored (non-cola) concentrate is about $1.02 per unit. The diet flavored (non-cola) concentrate price is about $1.18 per unit. A concentrate unit produces the equivalent of one 192-ounce soft drink case (a standard case consists of twenty-four 8-ounce bottles). The Coca-Cola Company, The Pepsi-Cola Company, and Dr Pepper/Seven Up, Inc. are the three major concentrate producers in the United States.

Approximately 500 bottlers in the United States convert flavor concentrate into carbonated soft drinks. Concentrate producers either (1) own or have an equity interest in bottlers or (2) franchise their brands to independent bottlers to produce their products. For example, Coca-Cola Enterprises, Inc. (CCE), with multiple bottler operations, is the largest U.S. bottler of Coca-Cola brand beverage products. CCE accounts for 80 percent of The Coca-Cola Company's soft drink bottle and can volume in North America. Similarly, the Pepsi Bottling Group, Inc., with multiple operations, accounts for 55 percent of Pepsi-Cola brand beverage volume in North America. Independent franchised bottlers are typically granted a right to package and distribute a concentrate producer's branded line of soft drinks in a defined territory and not allowed to market a directly competitive major brand. However, franchised bottlers can represent noncompetitive brands

---

[1]A portion of this discussion is based on "Industry Surveys: Foods & Nonalcoholic Beverages," *Standard & Poor's* (New York: Standard & Poor's, December 6, 2001).

and decline to bottle a concentrate producer's secondary lines. These arrangements mean that a franchised bottler of Coca-Cola cannot sell Pepsi-Cola but can bottle and market Squirt rather than Coca-Cola's Fresca.

The principal retail channels for carbonated soft drinks are supermarkets, convenience stores, vending machines, fountain service, mass merchandisers, and thousands of small retail outlets. Soft drinks are typically sold in bottles and cans, except for fountain service. In fountain service, syrup is sold to a retail outlet (such as McDonald's), which mixes the syrup with carbonated water for immediate consumption by customers. Supermarkets and grocery stores account for about 31 percent of carbonated soft drink industry retail sales.

| EXHIBIT 1 | Top-10 Carbonated Soft Drink Companies and Brands in 2000 |

Top-Ten Soft Drink Companies

Rank	Companies	Market Share %	Share Change[a]	Volume % Change[b]
1	Coca-Cola Co.	44.1	flat	+0.1
2	Pepsi-Cola Co.	31.4	flat	+0.1
3	Dr Pepper/Seven Up (Cadbury Schweppes)	14.7	+0.1	+1.1
4	Cott Corp.	3.3	+0.2	+5.8
5	National Beverage	2.1	flat	+4.2
6	Royal Crown[b]	1.1	−0.1	−1.9
7	Big Red	0.4	flat	+13.4
8	Seagram	0.3	flat	+7.2
9	Monarch Co.	0.1	flat	−35.8
10	Private label/other	2.5	−0.2	−12.2
	Total Industry	100.0		+0.2

Top-Ten Soft Drink Brands

Rank	Brands	Brand Owner	Market Share %	Share Change[a]	Volume % Change[b]
1	Coke Classic	Coca-Cola	20.4	+0.1	+0.5
2	Pepsi-Cola	Pepsi-Cola	13.6	−0.2	−1.0
3	Diet Coke	Coca-Cola	8.7	+0.2	+2.5
4	Mountain Dew	Pepsi-Cola	7.2	+0.1	+1.5
5	Sprite	Coca-Cola	6.6	−0.2	−2.0
6	Dr Pepper	Dr Pepper/Seven Up	6.3	flat	+0.1
7	Diet Pepsi	Pepsi-Cola	5.3	+0.2	+4.0
8	7Up	Dr Pepper/Seven Up	2.0	−0.1	−0.6
9	CF Diet Coke	Coca-Cola	1.7	−0.1	−1.0
10	Barq's Root Beer	Coca-Cola	1.1	flat	+3.0
	Total Top-Ten		72.9		

Notes: [a]Share change and volume change data are based on the difference from 1999.

[b]Royal Crown was purchased by Dr Pepper/Seven Up in the 4th quarter 2000, but treated as a separate company for 2000 data.

Source: "Top-10 U.S. Soft Drink Companies and Brands for 2000," *Beverage Digest* (February 15, 2001). Special Issue. Used with permission.

Competition in the Soft Drink Industry

Three companies command over 90 percent of carbonated soft drink sales in the United States. The Coca-Cola Company leads the industry with a 44.1 percent market share, followed by The Pepsi-Cola Company (31.4 percent), and Dr Pepper/Seven Up, Inc. (14.7 percent). These three companies also market the top-10 brands, measured in market share. Coca-Cola owns 5 of the top-10 brands; Pepsi-Cola owns 3; and Dr Pepper/Seven Up owns 2. These 10 brands account for almost 73 percent of soft drink sales in the United States. Exhibit 1 shows the top-10 carbonated soft drink companies and brands in 2000.

Soft Drink Marketing

Soft drink marketing is characterized by heavy investment in consumer advertising and promotion, selling and trade promotion to and through bottlers to retail outlets, and consumer price discounting. Concentrate producers usually assume responsibility for developing national consumer advertising and promotion programs, product development and planning, and marketing research. Bottlers usually take the lead in developing local trade promotions to retail outlets and local consumer promotions. Bottlers are also responsible for selling and servicing retail accounts, including the placement and maintenance of in-store displays and the restocking of retailer shelves and vending machines with their brands. The different marketing roles assumed by concentrate producers and bottlers are apparent in their comparative income statements. As shown in Exhibit 2, concentrate producers spend about 39 cents of every sales dollar on advertising and promotion. Bottlers spend about 28 cents of every sales dollar on selling and delivery expenses.

Soft Drink Advertising and Promotion   Local advertising and promotion programs are jointly implemented and financed by concentrate producers and bottlers. Concentrate producers and bottlers often split local advertising costs 50–50. For example, if $1 million were spent for local television brand advertising in a bottler's territory, $500,000 would be paid by the brand's local bottler and $500,000 would be paid by the concentrate producer. Bottlers and concentrate

EXHIBIT 2	Comparative Income Statements for the Typical Flavored Concentrate Producer and Soft Drink Bottler in the United States (per standard twenty-four 8-ounce bottle case)	
	Concentrate Producer	*Soft Drink Bottler*
Net sales	100%	100%
Cost of goods sold	−17	−57*
Gross profit	83%	43%
Selling and delivery	2	28
Advertising and promotion**	39	2
General and administrative expense	13	4
Pretax profit	29%	9%

*Packaging represents the major element of a bottler's cost of goods sold.

**Advertising and promotion includes production costs, fees, and media placement expenses.

Source: Industry analysts and case writer estimates.

producers split the cost of local retail-oriented merchandise promotions and consumer promotions 50–50. However, advertising and promotion programs are negotiated, sometimes at the individual bottler level. A bottler may choose, or not choose, to participate in a concentrate producer's advertising or promotion program or negotiate its own financial arrangement.

A variety of merchandising and consumer promotions are used in the soft drink industry. Merchandising promotions include end-of-aisle displays, other types of special freestanding displays, and shelf banners. Concentrate producers will often provide up to 20 cents per case sold to bottlers who implement these merchandising promotions. Consumer promotions include sponsorship of local sports, cultural and entertainment events, plastic cups and napkins with the brand logo, and stylish baseball caps, T-shirts, or sunglasses featuring the brand name. Assorted other promotions are also used, including coupons, on-package promotions, and sweepstakes. Concentrate producers will offer anywhere from 5 cents (for cups, caps, or glasses) to 25 cents (for local event marketing including cups, caps, or glasses) per case sold to bottlers who use these promotions.

Concentrate producers occasionally offer bottlers price promotions in the form of merchandising incentives. These incentives are typically based on case sales and are frequently used to stimulate bottler sales and participation in merchandising activities. These incentives are often in the range of 15 to 25 cents per case depending on the amount of effort requested.

Brand and Flavor Competition   There are more than 900 registered brand names for carbonated soft drinks in the United States. Most of these brands are sold regionally and reflect taste and flavor preferences of consumers in different parts of the Country.

Colas are the dominant flavor in the U.S. carbonated soft drink industry, accounting for about 60 percent of total retail sales in 2000. The dominance of colas has eroded in the past decade from roughly two-thirds of total retail sales in 1990. By comparison, flavored soft drinks have grown in popularity. Flavors such as orange, lemon-lime, cherry, grape, and root beer now represent about one-quarter of carbonated soft drink sales following a 30 percent increase in sales from 1990 to 2000. The changing composition of the U.S. population has been an important factor in the growing popularity of flavored carbonated soft drinks.

Demographics of Soft Drink Consumption   Industry research indicates that the average American consumes 849 eight-ounce servings of carbonated soft drinks annually, or roughly 2.3 servings per day. Nearly all Americans consume at least one soft drink serving in a given year. Most carbonated soft drink volume in the United States is consumed by individuals aged 20 to 49. The prominence of this age group is due mainly to the fact that it is the largest segment of the U.S. population. Consumption of diet soft drinks is more pronounced among consumers over 25 years of age. Teens and young adults generally are heavier consumers of regular soft drinks. Conventional wisdom in the soft drink industry holds that teens and young adults are the primary audience for soft drink marketing, since taste and brand preferences are formed between 12 and 24 years of age.

Per capita consumption of soft drinks is higher among Hispanics and African Americans than other racial and ethnic groups and among teens than adults. Furthermore, the trend favoring flavored carbonated soft drinks has been attributed in part to the changing demographic mix in the United States. Today, about 25 percent of Americans are younger than 18 and one-quarter of the U.S. population is Hispanic and African American. These population groups tend to consume flavored carbonated soft drinks. "The bottom line is that young consumers in recent years have been galvanized by flavor (citrus) brands," notes the editor and publisher of *Beverage Digest*, an industry trade publication.[2] By 2005, Hispanic youth will overtake African Americans to become the largest ethnic youth population, according to U.S. Census 2000 figures. They will account for 17 percent of all youth under age 18, and 45 percent of all minority minors in the United States. By 2010, one minor in five will be Hispanic, amounting to a 22 percent increase in nine years, while during the same period, the number of white youth will experience a decrease of 5 percent.[3]

Major soft drink companies have responded to the growing prominence of Hispanic and African American consumers and teens in different ways. The Coca-Cola Company has elevated Hispanics from its sixth priority to second after teens, according to the senior brand manager for multicutural marketing at Coca-Cola North America.[4] Following this change in priorities, Coca-Cola North America and Coca-Cola Bottling Company of Southern California recently introduced two flavored soft drinks to the Southern California market. In March 2001, Coca-Cola launched Manzana Mía, an apple-flavored soft drink similar to Manzana Lift, a Coca-Cola Company brand sold in Mexico. In addition, Fanta, the Coca-Cola Company's second largest brand that is distributed primarily outside the United States, was introduced to Southern California featuring orange, grape, strawberry, and pineapple flavors. According to a spokesperson at the Coca-Cola Bottling Company of Southern California, "Many Southern Californians know about Manzana Lift and have expressed enthusiasm for having it available here in the United States. They have also told us that they want more fruit-flavored carbonated beverages." Company research specifically indicated that fruit-flavored soft drinks held a special appeal for Hispanics in Southern California. A senior executive at Coca-Cola North America added, "In this case, we evaluated our international beverage portfolio and decided to introduce the Manzana Lift and Fanta beverage concepts in Southern California, adapting their positioning and packaging to meet local consumer preferences."

Marketers of Pepsi-Cola's Mountain Dew also have attended to the growing prominence of Hispanic consumers. Mountain Dew—the fourth largest U.S. soft drink brand and the best-selling flavored (citrus) carbonated beverage—now features advertising that specifically caters to the Hispanic market. According to Mountain Dew's director of marketing, "Ethnic markets are a huge growth opportunity for us and we are investing more in that area." The brand's primary target audience is teens and its base positioning and advertising feature a fun, exhilarating, daring, and adventurous "Dew-x-perience." Twenty- to 39-year-olds make up the brand's secondary market.[5]

Both Coca-Cola and Pepsi-Cola now rank among the top 25 advertisers to the Hispanic community in the United States. It was estimated that Coca-Cola would spend $18.7 million and Pepsi-Cola $16 million in media advertising to the Hispanic market in 2001, or about 2 percent of each company's advertising expenditure.[6]

---

[2]"Flat Colas Anxiously Watch Gen Yers Switch," *Advertising Age* (September 25, 2000), p. 510.

[3]"Targeting Teens," *Hispanic Business* (September 2001), pp. 15–17.

[4]This discussion is based on Hillary Chura, "Identifying a Demographic Sweet Spot," *Advertising Age* (November 12, 2001), p. 16; "New Apple-Flavored Manzana Mía and Popular Fanta Soft Drinks Roll Out in Southern California," the Coca-Cola Company News Release, April 20, 2001; and "Coke Relaunches Fanta, New Drink, Targets Southern California Hispanics," Reuters News Service, April 11, 2001.

[5]"Being True to Dew," *BRANDWEEK* (April 24, 2000), p. 24.

[6]"Top 60 Advertisers in the Hispanic Market, 2001," *Hispanic Business* (December 2001), p. 18.

SQUIRT BRAND HERITAGE AND MARKETING

Squirt has been marketed by Dr Pepper/Seven Up, Inc. since 1995 and by Cadbury Schweppes PLC since 1993. However, the brand's origins are found in the Great Depression of the 1930s.

EXHIBIT 3   **Little Squirt Character**

History of Squirt

The origin of Squirt is traced to Herb Bishop of Phoenix, Arizona, who in 1938 began experimenting with Citrus Club, a then-popular regional noncarbonated beverage. Bishop created a new carbonated soft drink that required less fruit and less sugar to produce. The new drink "seemed to squirt onto the tongue just like squeezing a grapefruit," so Bishop named the drink Squirt. For advertising, Bishop and his partner, Ed Mehren, created a likable character named "Little Squirt" (see Exhibit 3). The appeal of "Little Squirt" was immediate and subsequently broadened Squirt's attraction. Squirt sales grew during World War II because its low sugar content helped bottlers restricted by sugar rationing rules. Squirt established itself as a mixer in the 1950s. By the mid-1970s, Squirt was introduced internationally in Central and South America.

In 1977, Brooks Products, a bottler in Holland, Michigan, purchased Squirt from Bishop. The company reformulated Squirt, updated Squirt's logo, and positioned the brand as a mainstream soft drink. In 1983, taking advantage of new low-calorie soft drink technology, Diet Squirt became the first soft drink in the United States to be sweetened with NutraSweet (aspartame). Squirt joined A&W Brands in 1986, which was subsequently purchased by Cadbury Schweppes PLC in 1993. After the March 1995 acquisition of Dr Pepper/Seven Up Companies, Inc. by Cadbury Schweppes PLC, responsibility for manufacturing, marketing, and distribution of Squirt was assigned to Dr Pepper/Seven Up, Inc. in the United States.

Squirt Marketing

Squirt sales since 1995 have exceeded preacquisition levels due to a broadened bottling and distribution network supported by increased marketing attention and investment. Exhibit 4 shows Squirt case sales volume for the period 1990 through 2000.

Squirt Bottler and Sales Distribution Squirt is bottled and sold by some 250 bottlers in the United States. One-third of these bottlers are independent franchised bottlers or part of the Dr Pepper/Seven Up, Inc. Bottling Group. Two-thirds of Squirt bottlers are affiliated with Coca-Cola Enterprises, Inc. and the Pepsi Bottling Group, Inc. The geographic distribution of these bottlers means that Squirt is available in about 83 percent of U.S. bottler markets that

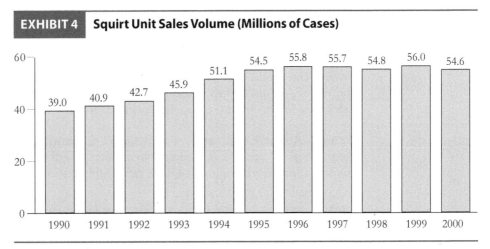

| **EXHIBIT 4** | **Squirt Unit Sales Volume (Millions of Cases)** |

Source: Beverage Digest. Used with permission.

represented about 85 percent of total soft drink volume in the United States. The New York City metropolitan area was the largest market without a Squirt bottler.

Five bottler markets accounted for 50 percent of Squirt case sales volume. These were Los Angeles (30 percent), Chicago (7 percent), Detroit (6 percent), San Diego (4 percent), and Portland, Oregon (3 percent). Another ten bottler markets represented 20 percent of Squirt case volume. ten additional bottler markets accounted for 10 percent of Squirt case volume. The remaining 20 percent of Squirt case volume was divided among other Squirt bottlers. Some 100 bottlers in the western United States accounted for about one-half of Squirt case volume. California alone represented 38 percent of Squirt's case volume in 2000. Squirt bottlers in Southern California were affiliated with Coca-Cola Enterprises, Inc. and in Northern California with the Pepsi Bottling Group, Inc.

Squirt Product Line and Competitive Brands The Squirt product line consists of regular and diet Squirt and regular and diet Ruby Red Squirt—a berry flavor extension introduced in 1993. The diet version of Squirt and Ruby Red Squirt account for about 20 percent of sales. Exhibit 5 displays the Squirt product line.

As a carbonated grapefruit soft drink, Squirt competes directly with Coca-Cola's two carbonated grapefruit soft drink brands—Fresca and Citra. Introduced in the 1960s, Fresca is a caffeine-free, diet soft drink targeted principally at adults (30 years of age and older) and, more recently, used as a mixer.[7] As recently as 1992, Fresca was one of the fastest-growing soft drinks in the United States. Citra was introduced by Coca-Cola in early 1997 as a "sugared" counterpart to Fresca and does not have a diet version. The brand is targeted at teens and young adults and is caffeine free.[8]

In the broader citrus-flavored soft drink category, Squirt also competes with two Coca-Cola brands, Mello Yello and Surge, Pepsi-Cola's Mountain Dew, and Sundrop, marketed by Dr Pepper/Seven Up. All four brands contain caffeine. Except for Surge, all brands are sold in regular and diet versions. Mountain Dew is the largest selling citrus-flavored carbonated soft drink brand in the United States. Industry analysts attribute the brand's popularity to its association with everyday youth culture and connecting with it across alternative sports, hip-hop, and college basketball. Mountain Dew Code Red, a cherry-flavored extension introduced in mid-2001, has leveraged these associations with its tag line: "New Code Red. A cherry rush that'll bring you right back to the streets."[9]

Coca-Cola's Surge brand was introduced in 1997 to attract consumers before they became Mountain Dew drinkers. However, industry analysts speculated in early 2001 that some Coca-Cola's Surge bottlers were discontinuing the brand.[10] Mello Yello, a nationally distributed citrus-flavored brand marketed by Coca-Cola, is most prominent in the southeastern United States. Sun Drop, marketed by Dr Pepper/Seven Up, is a popular regional brand in the southeastern United States. The brand's slogan—"Tastes Good. Nothing Else Matters"—emphasizes the refreshing taste of this beverage. Exhibit 6 on page 172 shows case volume sales data for Squirt and competitive brands for the period 1996–2000.

Squirt Advertising and Promotion Expenditures and Competitor Spending A variety of media have been used to advertise Squirt. These media include freestanding inserts in newspapers, spot television, cable television,

---

[7]"Fresca Enjoys New Bubble of Popularity," *Wall Street Journal* (September 11, 2001), p. A11.

[8]"Citra: Coke Debuts Yet Another Soft Drink in U.S.," *Beverage Digest* (January 22, 1997), p. 38; "Coke Takes Citra National," *Beverage Digest* (February 5, 1999), p. 22.

[9]"Code Red Soft Drink Sales Explode," AdAge.com, downloaded August 27, 2001.

[10]"Coke Shifts Strategy as Surge Fizzles," AdAge.com, downloaded February 12, 2001.

EXHIBIT 5 Squirt Product Line

171

| EXHIBIT 6 | Case Volume Trend for Major Carbonated Grapefruit and Citrus-Flavored Brands in the United States: 1996–2000 |

Company/Brand(s)	Case Volume (millions) by Year				
	1996	1997	1998	1999	2000*
Coca-Cola					
Fresca	28.0	26.2	25.9	25.5	24.1
Citra	NA	NA	21.0	26.2	15.6
Mello Yello	59.0	46.6	42.4	41.6	45.7
Surge	NA	69.0	51.8	26.7	11.8
Pepsi-Cola					
Mountain Dew	605.9	683.2	748.1	793.0	809.8
Regular	535.6	605.2	665.1	705.0	715.6
Diet	70.3	78.0	83.0	88.0	94.2
Dr Pepper/Seven Up					
Sundrop	19.7	20.1	20.4	20.1	20.2
Squirt/Ruby Red	55.8	55.7	54.8	56.0	54.6
Total Case Volume	768.4	900.8	964.4	989.1	981.8

*2000 competitor case volume data represent estimated figures.

Source: *Beverage Digest*. Used with permission.

and spot radio. Squirt also uses retail, consumer, and trade promotions and has a number of cooperative advertising arrangements with individual bottlers. Media advertising expenditures for Squirt are typically less than competitors. However, due to consistent advertising over an extended time period, Squirt enjoys the highest consumer brand awareness among carbonated grapefruit soft drinks in the United States. Squirt expenditures for retail, trade, and consumer promotions and cooperative advertising arrangements often exceed media advertising expenditures. Combined, these expenditures amount to 20 to 25 percent of dollar sales.[11]

Coca-Cola and Pepsi-Cola typically spend more on media advertising and promotion than does Dr Pepper/Seven Up, Inc. for its major carbonated grapefruit and citrus-flavored brands. Mountain Dew is the most heavily advertised brand in this category. As a rule, media advertising expenditures are typically higher, both in dollar terms and as a percent of sales, for new brands. Also, expenditures for retail, trade, and consumer programs often exceed the amount spent for media advertising. Exhibit 7 shows the estimated media advertising spending for major carbonated grapefruit and citrus-flavored brands by concentrate producers in the United States for the period 1996–2000. Planned media expenditures for Squirt in 2001 were the same as 2000.

Squirt Positioning Squirt positioning was addressed soon after Cadbury Schweppes PLC acquired the brand. In 1994, Foote, Cone & Belding recommended, and brand management agreed, that Squirt's unique thirst-quenching attribute should be the dominant positioning dimension upon which to build the brand. Squirt was targeted at adults 18 to 44 years old. Ruby Red Squirt was positioned as a "fruity bold way to refresh your thirst," and targeted at teens and young adults 12 to 24 years old. Advertising for Squirt emphasized the "hip,

---

[11]*Case writer note*: Dr Pepper/Seven Up, Inc. does not disclose promotion expenditure data for its brands. The percent-of-sales figure is provided for case analysis and discussion purposes only.

| EXHIBIT 7 | Estimated Media Advertising Spending for Major Carbonated Grapefruit and Citrus-Flavored Brands in the United States: 1996–2000 |

| | Estimated Media Advertising Expenditures ($000) by Year | | | | |
Company/Brand(s)	1996	1997	1998	1999	2000
Coca-Cola					
Fresca	2,471.5	730.2	672.6	N.S.	N.S.
Citra	NA	1,119.1	6,711.6	10,100.4	98.4
Mello Yello	1,407.8	1,524.2	1,199.7	1,010.6	773.1
Surge	NA	13,611.0	17,846.7	18,967.4	243.8
Pepsi-Cola					
Mountain Dew (Regular & Diet)	28,991.3	33,951.1	40,104.3	37,074.3	50,384.6
Dr Pepper/Seven Up					
Sundrop	10.9	429.6	3.0	391.8	314.1
Squirt Regular/Diet	3,485.1	1,657.6	955.8	601.5	390.0
Squirt Ruby Red	1,807.6	537.2	N.S.	N.S.	N.S.

Key: NA = Not Available: N.S. = No Significant Expenditures

Source: CMR/TNS Media Intelligence U.S. Used with permission.

cool, experiential nature" of the brand with the message: "Beyond the ordinary refreshment—the great citrus taste is incredibly thirst quenching." Ruby Red Squirt advertising emphasized its *bold* taste and extraordinary refreshment with the message: "Its fruity berry and citrus taste is incredibly *exciting*." Advertising featured two television commercials labeled "Mountain Bike" and "Rollerblade" and portrayed Squirt and Ruby Red Squirt in action-oriented biking and skating settings.

In mid-1995, following the acquisition of Dr Pepper/Seven Up by Cadbury Schweppes PLC, Foote, Cone & Belding was asked to revise its creative strategy. The reasoning was that the creative execution was "a bit too intense to fit with the brand." Instead of sport situations that may have suggested Squirt might be an isotonic beverage (a believability issue), Squirt's creative strategy migrated to "everyday, on-the-go experiences." The emphasis on Squirt's thirst-quenching benefit remained but was now portrayed in "spunky, lively, sociable, colorful, and music-driven" advertising vignettes that depicted fun-loving, individualistic young adults. The target market was also narrowed to adults 18 to 34 years old. Advertising copy described Squirt as "Fun relief when you're dry" with the tag line "Squirt Your Thirst." Exhibits 8 and 9 (pages 174 and 175) show television commercials for Squirt and Ruby Red Squirt with this creative execution.

Squirt's positioning and creative execution were revisited in 1999 and again in 2000, following the introduction of Citra by Coca-Cola, but no changes were made. Citra debuted in March 1997 in the southeastern and southwestern United States with English and Spanish language television and radio advertising.[12] Citra was positioned as a light-hearted, youthful, and thirst-quenching soft drink. The brand's advertising emphasized the slogan "No Thirst Is Safe" and featured the adventures and misadventures of teenagers roaming the country in a recreational vehicle.[13]

---

[12]"Coca-Cola Rolling Out Citra in Two New Test Markets," *The Atlanta Journal and Constitution* (April 12, 1997), p. 2H.

[13]"Coca-Cola to Promote Citra on MTV's 'Road Rules' Show; Grapefruit Drink's Territory Expands," *The Atlanta Journal and Constitution* (March 4, 1999), p. 2G.

EXHIBIT 8   **Squirt Television Commercial**

(MUSIC BEGINS)

MALE VOCALIST: Everybody's a little wild, everybody's a little child.

Everybody's a little squirt. Be a squirt and squirt your thirst.

Everybody's a little cool, everybody breaks a little rule.

Everybody's a little squirt. Be a squirt and squirt your thirst.

Everybody's a little juvenile, everybody's a little infantile.

Everybody's a little squirt. Be a squirt and squirt your thirst.

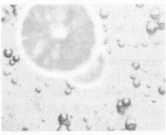

MALE ANNCR: Squirt, a cool citrus blend.

MALE VOCALIST: Everybody's a little squirt.

Be a squirt

and squirt your thirst.

Everybody's a little squirt. Be a squirt and squirt your thirst. (MUSIC ENDS)

EXHIBIT 9   **Ruby Red Squirt Television Commercial**

(MUSIC IN) MALE VOCALIST SINGS:
Everybody's a little wild.

Everybody's a little shy.

Everybody's a little squirt. Here, squirt,
squirt your thirst.

Everybody's a little cool. Everybody
breaks the little rules.

Everybody's a little squirt.

Here, squirt, squirt your thirst. Everybody's
a little juvenile.

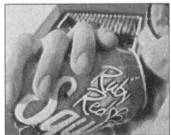

Everybody's a little infantile. Everybody's
a little squirt. Here,

Squirt, squirt your thirst.

MALE ANNCR: Ruby Red Squirt,

a citrus berry blast.

Everybody's a little Squirt. Here, squirt,
squirt your thirst.

Everybody's a little squirt. Here, squirt,
squirt— (MUSIC OUT)

By 1998, Citra was available in 50 percent of U.S. bottler markets. In February 1999, Coca-Cola announced that Citra would be available in 95 percent of U.S. bottler markets by 2000.[14]

DPSU consumer research indicated that few Squirt users considered Citra's positioning or advertising appealing to them. Additional DPSU consumer research and taste testing of Squirt and Citra indicated that Squirt scored higher on the thirst-quenching attribute. "Brand name, packaging, and Citra's newness supported by advertising appeared to drive [Citra's] initial sales," said an advertising agency executive. Subsequent consumer research uncovered potential opportunities for Squirt positioning and the creative execution in the brand's advertising. This research indicated that Squirt advertising effectively communicated the intended fun and thirst-quenching message, portrayed Squirt users in an interesting, unique, and involving manner, and engaged the target audience with music. However, a portion of both younger and older Squirt users considered aspects of the imagery in the commercials "juvenile." Furthermore, focus group interviews indicated that Citra users (mostly 18- to 24-year-olds) did not consider Squirt's positioning and creative execution in its advertising as speaking to their current lifestyle. Squirt's brand management requested a formal positioning review for Squirt in early 2001 by Foote, Cone & Belding and scheduled a presentation for June.

 SQUIRT POSITIONING REVIEW: JUNE 2001

The Squirt positioning review was presented to brand management on June 25, 2001. The review consisted of two parts: (1) a positioning analysis and (2) a recommendation.

Positioning Analysis

The Foot, Cone & Belding (FCB) presentation began by stating the purpose of the positioning review: "To develop a strategic platform to help grow volume and maintain Squirt's leadership as the number one grapefruit carbonated soft drink." After providing an historical review of Squirt advertising copy and creative strategy since 1994, attention turned to brand positioning.

Exhibit 10 shows FCB's analysis of the relative positioning of the seven major grapefruit and citrus brands in mid-June 2001. According to the FCB analysis, these seven brands were positioned along two prominent dimensions. Squirt was the most "thirst-quenching" beverage. Mountain Dew was the most "young, cool, and hip" beverage. Coca-Cola's Citra brand was the most closely positioned brand next to Squirt based on FCB's analysis. FCB personnel concluded, "A creative strategy needed to be developed to increase relevancy with a younger target [market] and focus on Squirt's thirst-quenching property."

Target Market and Positioning Recommendation

Following a review of U.S. Census 2000 statistics, Squirt consumption data, and its own and Dr Pepper/Seven Up research, FCB proposed a refinement in Squirt's target market and positioning. Citing research that featured Squirt's consumption by racial/ethnic group and age relative to carbonated soft drink users (Exhibit 11 on page 178), FCB recommended that Squirt be targeted at multicultural, 18- to 24-year-olds to tap into this heavy carbonated soft drink user segment.

---

[14]"Coke Takes Citra National," *Beverage Digest* (February 5, 1999), p. 22.

EXHIBIT 10   **Perceptual Map of Grapefruit and Citrus Brands: Mid-2001**

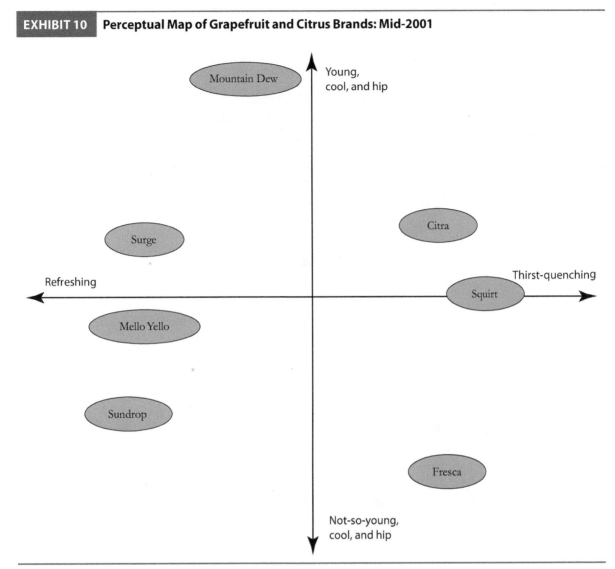

Source: Squirt Positioning Review, June 25, 2001.

Squirt positioning would continue to emphasize its "thirst-quenching" benefit. To increase the brand's relevancy to this segment, Squirt's positioning and advertising would speak to the unique 21- to 24-year-old life stage marked by the straddling of adult responsibilities and more carefree times. This recommendation was based on focus group interviews and other research suggesting that 21- to 24-year-old consumers experience a transition stage into adulthood bringing new challenges. These consumers also want to make the most out of life, work hard, and play even harder. The formal positioning statement for Squirt, upon which a creative advertising execution could be built, was stated as follows:

> For young multicultural adults who thrive on the excitement and spontaneity of living up to the max, Squirt citrus soda fuels your thirst for living life loud, with an exhilarating taste that's powerfully thirst-quenching!

This new positioning had five benefits, according to FCB personnel. First, it is appropriate for the carbonated soft drink category. Second, like carbonated soft drinks, it emphasizes instant gratification. Third, the positioning emphasizes the freedom that this demographic segment strives to maintain. Fourth, with proper

EXHIBIT 11   **Demographics of Squirt Consumption**

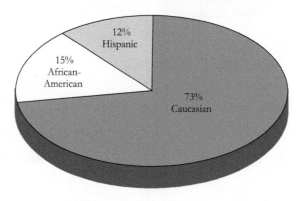

(A) Squirt Volume Breakdown by Racial/Ethnic Group:
Total U.S. Market

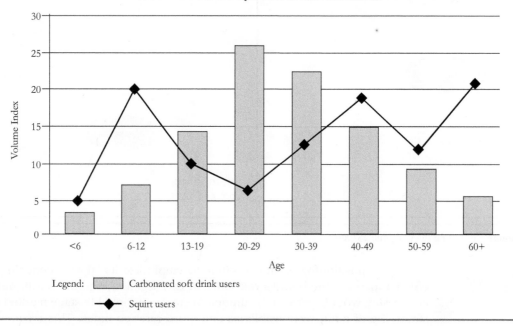

(B) Consumption Volume and Age Relationship Among Carbonated
Soft Drink Users and Squirt Users: Total U.S. Market

Legend: Carbonated soft drink users

    Squirt users

Source: Squirt Positioning Review, June 25, 2001.

creative execution, this positioning has the potential to break through the clutter of soft drink advertising. Finally, the new positioning is consistent with Squirt's product look and feel.

 # THE HISPANIC MARKET OPPORTUNITY

Kate Cox met briefly and informally with the Squirt brand management team the day following the FCB presentation. During the meeting, the popularity of fruit-flavored carbonated beverages among African American and Hispanic teens and young adults was discussed. Also, the reference to making Squirt relevant to multicultural, 18- to 24-year-olds initiated a discussion about simultaneously reaching current and potentially new Hispanic as well as African American Squirt customers. The meeting concluded with an assignment given to Jaxie Stollenwerck, the associate brand manager for Squirt, to prepare a profile of Hispanic and African American consumers in the United States from recently released U.S. Census 2000 data and any other relevant sources.

Hispanic Consumers in the United States

Kate Cox received an e-mail from Jaxie Stollenwerck the following week while on a visit with a Squirt bottler concerning a local promotion. A paraphrased summary of the report is reproduced here:

1. According to the U.S. Census 2000, the Hispanic population in the United States increased by 57.9 percent from 22.4 million in 1990 to 35.3 million in 2000, compared with an increase of 13.2 percent for the total U.S. population. In 2000, 58.5 percent of Hispanics in the United States were Mexican, 9.6 percent were Puerto Rican, 3.5 percent were Cuban, 8.6 percent were of Central or South American ancestry, and 19.7 percent were of other Hispanic ancestry or origins not classified. Hispanics accounted for 12.5 percent of the U.S. population in 2000. African Americans accounted for 12.3 percent of the U.S. population, or 34.7 million people.

2. More than 75 percent of Hispanics live in the western and southern United States (43.5 percent live in the West; 32.8 percent live in the South). Mexicans, Puerto Ricans, and Cubans are concentrated in different regions. Among Mexicans, 55.3 percent live in the West; 31.7 percent live in the South. Among Puerto Ricans, 60.4 percent live in the Northeast; 22.3 percent live in the South. Among Cubans, 74.2 percent live in the South; 13.6 percent live in the Northeast. For comparison, 54.8 percent of African Americans live in the South; just 8.4 percent live in the West.

3. More than half of all Hispanics live in just two states: California and Texas. There are 11 million Hispanics in California (77 percent of which are of Mexican ancestry) and 6.7 million Hispanics in Texas (76 percent of which are of Mexican ancestry).

4. The 10 largest "places" (defined by the U.S. Census Bureau) where Hispanics reside are shown here:

Rank	Place and State	Hispanic Population	Percent Hispanic of Total Population
1	New York, NY	2,160,554	27.0%
2	Los Angeles, CA	1,719,073	46.5
3	Chicago, IL	753,644	26.0
4	Houston, TX	730,865	37.4
5	San Antonio, TX	671,394	58.7
6	Phoenix, AZ	449,972	34.1
7	El Paso, TX	431,875	76.6
8	Dallas, TX	422,587	35.6
9	San Diego, CA	310,752	25.4
10	San Jose, CA	269,989	30.2

Among the 10 places with the largest Hispanic populations, Puerto Ricans represented the largest share (36.5 percent) of all Hispanics in New York, while Mexicans represented the largest share (varying from 63.5 percent in Los Angeles to 83.4 percent in San Diego) of all Hispanics in the nine other places. In Chicago, Mexicans represented 70.4 percent of all Hispanics. Of the 10 largest places where African Americans reside, just four overlap with Hispanic places: New York (first), Chicago (second), Houston (fifth), and Los Angeles (seventh). Detroit, one of our largest markets, ranks third in places where African Americans reside.

5. The relative youthfulness of the Hispanic population is reflected in its population under age 18 and its median age. While 25.7 percent of the U.S. population was under 18 in 2000, 35 percent of Hispanics were under 18. The median age for Hispanics was 25 years in 2000, while the median age for the entire U.S. population was 35.3 years. Mexicans had a median age of 24.2 years, Puerto Ricans 27.2 years, and Cubans 40.7 years. In high density Hispanic markets like Los Angeles, Hispanics under 20 represent 58 percent of all Los Angeles youth in that age group. This group will grow to capture 80 percent by 2003. The median age of African Americans was 30.2; 32.4 percent of African Americans were under 18, and 42.6 percent were under 25.

6. The diversity of nationalities that make up the U.S. Hispanic population is apparent in language and cultural differences. For example, research shows that, even though all nationalities speak Spanish, dialects differ. Also, since about 50 percent of Hispanics in the United States are immigrants, many prefer to converse in their native language. This seems relevant for advertising. According to Strategy Research Corp., 55.4 percent of Hispanics prefer to see and hear ads in Spanish, while 30.3 percent would choose English and 13.2 percent don't have a preference between the two languages. Young Hispanics aged 18 to 24 are about evenly split on language, with 44 percent preferring ads in English and 46 percent in Spanish. As an aside, I also ran across other interesting tidbits worth noting. It seems there is a strong brand link with heritage among Hispanics; authenticity is important as is an emotional connection with brands; Hispanics don't like "hard sell" approaches and prefer messages that are real and relevant to them.

7. Hispanics prefer shopping close to home and tend to patronize mom-and-pop grocery outlets, convenience stores, and bodegas (a small shop that sells food and other items, mostly to Spanish-speaking customers).

8. Finally, I came across some interesting statistics about the Mexican CSD (carbonated soft drink) market. Mexico is the second largest CSD market in the world and Squirt is the eighth largest CSD brand in Mexico. Squirt is the second most popular brand in the grapefruit category, which happens to be the second largest category (after cola) in Mexico, with a 41 percent share. Squirt is owned and marketed by Refremex AG in Mexico.

The information provided confirmed Kate Cox's suspicion about the size of the Hispanic community in major Squirt bottler markets. She also thought that the mention made to authenticity and the importance of an emotional link to brands coupled with being real and relevant in advertising paralleled the FCB analysis. Cox was particularly interested in the reference made to Squirt's prominence in Mexico. She knew Squirt was sold in Mexico, but not by Dr Pepper/Seven Up, and had heard the brand was popular there. However, this information, later confirmed, was particularly intriguing. She thought, "Could Squirt's popularity in Mexico be leveraged in the United States or had Squirt already benefited from its Mexican linkages?" She scheduled a meeting of the Squirt brand management team upon her return to discuss market targeting and positioning topics related to the annual advertising and promotion plan.

Squirt Advertising and Promotion Plan Development

Kate Cox assembled the Squirt brand management team in mid-summer 2001 to begin drafting the annual advertising and promotion plan for Squirt in the United States. Once drafted, the plan would be formally presented to senior management for review and approval prior to its implementation.

Kate Cox began the meeting by echoing FCB's purpose behind the recent Squirt positioning review. She emphasized that her strategic intent was to lay a solid foundation for Squirt's future growth with this year's advertising and promotion plan—her first as Squirt's brand manager. Market targeting and positioning for Squirt was the first agenda item. Three general options existed. First, the present market targeting and positioning strategy could be continued. Second, the market targeting and positioning recommendation made by FCB could be adopted. Third, another market targeting and positioning strategy could be developed, which might or might not include elements of the current and recommended strategy. She added that any examination of options should consider what role the multicultural market for carbonated soft drinks, the grapefruit/citrus category, and Squirt played in formulating a market targeting and positioning strategy and implementing the advertising and promotion plan.

More broadly, Cox asked the team members to consider how a "multicultural marketing mind-set" might guide the overall planning process itself. She said, "If we choose to focus on multicultural 18- to 24-year-olds, what might we need to do differently than if we simply focus on 18- to 24-year-olds or for that matter, 18- to 34-year-olds as we've done in the past?"

"Ultimately, our market targeting and positioning decision and recommendation will determine where and how we deploy our advertising and promotion dollars," Kate Cox continued. She reminded the brand management team that Squirt was roughly the ninth largest brand in the company brand portfolio and the objectives, strategy, and budget for advertising and promotion should consider this reality. "That certainly has implications for where and how we choose to spend the budget," injected an MBA student summer intern who recently joined the brand management team. He continued, "Suppose we choose to run a bilingual media advertising and bottler promotion campaign, or a Spanish-only program for selected markets that corresponds to FCB's estimate of Hispanic Squirt consumption. Don't we incur the risk of spreading the budget too thinly across the country, other things being equal?" Cox replied, "That's a possibility. But we may be getting ahead of ourselves by discussing spending. This may be a good time to discuss the topic of market targeting and positioning and see where it takes us."

Case

Sanger Automotive Companies

The Fisker Franchise Decision

In September 2011, Sanger Automotive Companies, Inc. (Sanger) executives were exploring the possibility of an exclusive franchise agreement with Fisker Automotive, Inc. (Fisker) for southwest Florida. Sanger is one of the most successful auto dealers in the United States, posting annual sales of $700 million through eight, mostly luxury, car dealerships in Florida and Georgia. Fisker is a California-based manufacturer for the Fisker Karma Sedan, one of the world's first truly luxury, plug-in hybrid electric vehicles, with a manufacturer's suggested list price from $96,000 to $109,000.

A decision whether or not to pursue a franchise for a plug-in hybrid electric vehicle was a complicated one. Plug-in hybrid electric vehicles were in the embryonic stage of the product life cycle. Consumer demand for these vehicles remained unclear due to acceptance of their value proposition. Production capacity of plug-in hybrid electric vehicle manufacturers was limited which affected their supply to automobile dealers. Finally, U.S. economic growth in 2011 was sluggish and the future demand for electric vehicles of all types was uncertain.

Nevertheless, the opportunity to sign an exclusive franchise agreement for a new generation of automobiles was attractive to Sanger for three reasons. First, Sanger would place itself at the forefront of marketing a luxury plug-in hybrid electric vehicle in southwest Florida. Second, Sanger was highly regarded in the U.S. automobile industry for its commitment to delivering world-class customer service in the purchase and ownership of luxury-class cars. The Fisker franchise agreement would add to this luxury-class car reputation. Third, Sanger had a vacant and up-to-date dealership location available to showcase and service the Fisker Automotive, Inc. product line. Therefore, no incremental cost for dealership land or construction was necessary.

THE U.S. ELECTRIC PASSENGER CAR MARKET

The U.S. electric passenger car market is divided into three major categories: hybrid electric vehicles (HEVs), battery-electric vehicles (BEVs), and plug-in hybrid electric vehicles (PHEVs). HEVs combine a conventional internal combustion engine propulsion system with an electric propulsion system. The most well-known HEV is the Toyota Prius. BEVs use chemical energy stored in rechargeable battery packs and use electric motors and motor controllers instead of, or in addition to, internal combustion engines for propulsion. The most well-known BEVs are the Tesla Roadster and the Nissan Leaf. PHEVs share the characteristics of HEVs, having an electric motor and an internal combustion engine; and of BEVs, having a plug to connect to the electrical grid. The Chevrolet Volt is the most well-known PHEV.

Market Size and Growth Projections

The U.S. market for electric passenger cars is in its infancy.[1] By year-end 2011, industry analysts projected volume for HEVs to be 300,000 units and BEVs and PHEVs, 30,000 units. The forecast for HEVs in 2015 is about 500,000 units, and for BEVs and PHEVs, from 45,000 to 200,000 units. Auto industry analysts attribute the unit volume growth differential from 2011 through 2015 for BEVs and PHEVs to different assumptions about gasoline prices, government purchase incentives, fuel economy standards, and BEV and PHEV availability. Still, electric (HEV, BEV, and PHEV) passenger car sales overall will represent about 2.6 percent of total new passenger car sales in the United States in 2011 and around 7 percent in 2015.

Competition

Competition in the electric passenger car market is projected to increase dramatically. No fewer than 20 new models by 12 different manufacturers are expected to be sold in the United States in 2012. Release dates, the manufacturer's suggested retail price, and the range (miles per electric charge) for representative models are shown in Exhibit 1 on page 184. (*Note*: The two-seat Tesla Roadster will be discontinued by year-end 2011 and replaced by the Tesla Model S Sedan in 2012.)

At the same time, manufacturers of passenger cars with internal combustion engines have promoted price, increases in fuel efficiency, and improved emission controls in the marketing of automobiles. Therefore, manufacturers of electric passenger cars find themselves competing for prospective buyers on two fronts: electric car buyers and conventional car buyers. Some industry analysts believe that prospective buyers will look to brands they trust when comparing different electric passenger cars. According to one analyst's study:

> Experience tells us that when it comes to automobile purchases, consumers are brand-driven; we believe they will buy EVs (electric vehicles) only from a brand they trust. Our study indicates that Toyota, Honda and Ford have "brand permission" in this space due in part to the "green equity" they have built with hybrid vehicles. We think that EVs from these three OEMs [original equipment manufacturers] will have the highest likelihood of success.[2]

---

[1]This discussion is based on the following sources: "Electric Vehicle Market Forecasts," Pike Research, October 2011; "U.S. Electric Vehicle Forecast," Baum and Associates Press Release, September 2011; and "Can Electric Cars Win Over the Mass Market?" DiscoveryNews.com, August 26, 2011.

[2]Deloitte Consulting, "Gaining Traction: A Customer View of Electric Vehicle Mass Adoption in the U.S. Automobile Marketing," April 20, 2010.

EXHIBIT 1 Electric Passenger Car Competition in the United States (Current and Projected)

All Electric Cars

	Release Date	Price*	Range (miles per charge)
Nissan Leaf	2010	$32,780	100
Ford Focus	Late 2011(e)	TBA	60–100
Toyota FT-EV II	2012(e)	TBA	50
Toyota RAV4 (Tesla battery pack)	2012(e)	TBA	100
Volkswagen	2012(e)	TBA	TBA
Honda Fit	2012(e)	TBA	100
Tesla Roadster	2008	$109,000	244
Tesla Model S Sedan	2012(e)	$58,000, $67,500, $80,000	160, 230, 300
Mitsubishi iMiEV	2012(e)	$30,000(e)	50–80(e)
Daimler Smartcar	U.S. 2010	For lease only $600/month	72

Plug-In Hybrids

	Release Date	Price*	Range (miles per charge)
GM Chevy Volt	2010	$41,000	50 all-electric miles
Ford C-MAX Energy PHEV	2012(e)	TBA	TBA
Ford Escape PHEV	2012(e)	$38,000	30–35 all-electric miles
Volvo V70 PHEV	2012(e)	TBA	30 all-electric miles
BYD F6DM	2009	$22,000	40–60 all-electric miles
Toyota Prius PHEV	2012(e)	$28,000	14 all-electric miles
Fisker Karma Sedan PHEV	2011	$96,000–$109,000	50 all-electric miles
Honda plug-in hybrid	2012(e)	TBA	TBA

(e) = expected.

*Prices do not factor in government subsidies.

TBA = To Be Announced

Sources: Nissan, Renault, Ford, *Los Angeles Business Journal*, Plug-In cars, *Wall Street Journal*, Tesla Motors, Fast Company, China Autoweb, Motornature, Greentech Media, Green Car Congress, CNet, CNN, Plug-in America, Toyota, Clean Fleet Report, Road and Track, Green Cars.

Buyer Behavior

Buyer behavior in the U.S. electric passenger car market is similar to buyer behavior for gasoline-powered cars. Vehicle purchase price, reliability, styling, appearance, features, performance (including fuel efficiency and safety), and resale or trade-in value are typically listed among the top purchasing criteria, although their relative importance will differ across consumer segments—for example, female versus male purchasers. Prospective electric passenger car purchasers also highlight environmental issues (e.g., carbon dioxide emissions) as an overriding consideration in the choice between electric versus gasoline-powered cars. Industry research also indicates that prospective buyers of electric passenger cars tend to come from households that live in urban or suburban locations in warmer climates, own two or more cars, and have an annual household income exceeding $100,000, with the head of household's age being over 40.

The principal reasons given by consumers for not considering an electric passenger car are the vehicle price, concerns about travel range (miles traveled per charge), and the size of cars. Vehicle price is a consideration for two reasons. First is consumers' lack of familiarity with electric vehicle technology as it relates to economic and environmental benefits of ownership relative to purchase price and operating cost. Second is that the purchase price consumers are willing to pay remains lower than current sticker prices for most BEVs and PHEVs, as shown below:[3]

Car Price Range	% Willing to Pay
Less than $24,000	32%
$25,000 to $34,000	41%
$35,000 to $44,000	16%
$45,000 to $54,000	6%
$55,000 or more	5%

However, a $7,500 consumer tax credit for the purchase of an all-electric or plug-in hybrid vehicle is available through the American Recovery and Reinvestment Act of 2009.

Consumer concerns about travel range (miles traveled per charge) is referred to as "range anxiety." According to a recent Consumer Electronics Association survey, 71 percent of U.S. consumers feared running out of a charge on the road.[4] Advocates of BEVs and PHEVs consider this concern to be exaggerated. Technically, a 50- to 100-mile electric range would meet the daily requirements of two-thirds of drivers on weekdays and over 70 percent of drivers on weekends.[5]

Car size is a concern for two reasons. First, BEVs and PHEVs are typically smaller in terms of cabin cubic feet and truck space. Second, safety concerns arise due to the weight of these cars compared with gasoline-powered vehicles.

There are three secondary reasons for not considering electric passenger cars. These include concerns about the need to charge batteries, safety (due to potential problems with battery and electrical systems), and perceived operating and maintenance performance relative to gasoline-powered passenger vehicles.

---

[3]Deloitte Consulting, "Gaining Traction."

[4]Josie Garthwaite, "Range Anxiety: Fact or Fiction?" nationalgeographic.com, March 10, 2011.

[5]National Household Travel Survey, http://cta.ornl.gov/data/chapter8.shtml.

FISKER AUTOMOTIVE, INC.

Fisker Automotive, Inc. is a U.S.-based car company founded in 2007. Company headquarters are located in Anaheim, California.

Background

Fisker Automotive's cofounder, CEO, and executive design director is Henrik Fisker. Prior to forming Fisker Automotive, Fisker held a variety of automobile design positions. He designed the Aston Martin V8 Vantage and was responsible for the production launch design of the Aston Martin DB9, variants of which were James Bond's preferred vehicles. He also designed the BMW 207 concept car (1997) and the Z8 roadster (1999), another Bond car. A native of Denmark, Fisker began his career in Germany at BMW's advanced design studio, BMW Technik GmbH, upon graduating from the Art Center of Design in Switzerland in 1989.

Bernhard "Barry" Koehler is cofounder and COO at Fisker Automotive. Koehler was formerly the director of Business and Operations for Ford Motor Company's Global Advanced Design Studio in Southern California. His responsibilities included meeting revenue targets, as well as Aston Martin's modeling and operations for design and concept. Prior to that Koehler served as director of Operations for 22 years at BMW's industrial design subsidiary Designworks USA in Southern California.

Fisker Automotive has raised more than $600 million in private equity and financing to fund the company's operations. In addition, the U.S. Department of Energy approved Fisker Automotive for a conditional loan of $528.7 million in 2009 under the Advanced Technology Vehicle Manufacturing loan program.

The Fisker Product Line

The first car produced by Fisker Automotive was the 2012 Fisker Karma Sedan, which Henrik Fisker defines as "Uncompromised Responsible Luxury."[6] The Fisker Karma Sedan runs on electric power, supplied by an advanced rechargeable lithium-ion battery for up to 50 miles. After that, a 175-kilowatt generator, driven by a 2.0-liter direct-injection turbocharged gasoline engine provides an additional 250 miles of electric range. The Fisker Karma Sedan can accelerate from zero-to-60 miles per hour in 5.9 seconds, yet can achieve the equivalent of more than 100 miles per gallon and 83 grams per kilometer carbon dioxide emissions in real-world driving on an annual basis. The Fisker Karma Sedan is also equipped with the world's largest seamless solar panel to convert radiated power from the sun into stored electric energy. Photos of the Fisker Karma Sedan appear in Exhibit 2.

The Fisker Karma four-passenger, four-door sedan, with its styling and features, is intended to compete with conventional luxury sedans such as the BMW 750Li ($81,000 to $137,000 MSRP), Mercedes-Benz S550 ($88,000 to $95,000 MSRP), Lexus LS 600h L ($112,750 MSRP), and Porsche Panamera ($75,000 + MSRP).[7] According to Fisker Automotive, the Karma Sedan will be the only environmentally responsible alternative for luxury car buyers. The MSRP for the Fisker Karma Sedan will range from roughly $96,000 to $109,000, depending

---

[6]"Fisker Karma Sedan: World's First True Electric Vehicle with Extended Range (EVer)," Fisker Automotive Press Release, undated.

[7]MSRP figures for 2012 models supplied by Edmunds.com.

EXHIBIT 2	Fisker Karma Sedan Photos

Source: Tony Cenicola/The New York Times/Redux. Used with permission.

on trim and options. The Karma Sedan is manufactured in Finland at the Valmet Automotive facility which also builds the Cayman and Boxster for Porsche. According to automotive industry analysts, this facility has the capacity to produce 15,000 vehicles annually, of which 40 percent are targeted for U.S. buyers. However, these same analysts speculate that it is more likely that only 7,000 vehicles will be built in 2012.[8]

Going forward, Fisker Automotive intends to produce a convertible version of its Karma Sedan. In addition, the company plans to launch three midsized luxury sedans using its Project Nina platform beginning in late 2012. These cars are expected to be priced in the $50,000-plus range and will be produced at a converted former General Motors plant in Wilmington, Delaware.[9]

Dealerships

By mid-2011, Fisker Automotive had 47 dealerships throughout the United States and Canada. Many of these dealerships are multisite, multibrand operations with a history of successfully selling and servicing luxury cars. Dealerships are expected to provide a dedicated showroom and service bay for the Fisker Karma Sedan. The typical financial investment required for a Fisker dealership is about $200,000.

---

[8]"Fisker Says Karma Will Meet 15,000 Production Target for 2012," autobloggreen.com, November 26, 2011.

[9]Nate Martinez, "Fisker Says Three Project Nina Cars by 2014; BMW Possible," motortrend.com, September 6, 2011.

THE MARKET AREA

Sanger Automotive Companies, Inc. was considering the possibility of seeking an exclusive franchise from Fisker Automotive, Inc. for essentially two counties located on the southeastern coast of Florida, namely Lee County and Collier County. Exhibit 3 shows the location of these counties in Florida. Each county has a Metropolitan Statistical Area (MSA) designated by the U.S. government for statistical purposes. Naples–Marco Island is the designated MSA for Collier County. Fort Myers–Cape Coral is the designated MSA for Lee County. The Gulf of Mexico coastline for Lee and Collier counties is often called the Paradise Coast.

Market Profile

The Naples–Marco Island MSA is considered to be one of the wealthiest in the United States. This MSA is home to about 12,500 households with $1 million in investible assets (cash, stocks, and bonds, excluding home value) and 1,800 households with $5 million or more in investible assets. The median household income for this MSA is $81,250, compared with the median income of $49,445 for all U.S. households.

The Naples–Marco Island MSA has an older population and a higher median household income than the surrounding Collier County. The MSA accounts for about 15 percent of households with incomes $100,000 or more in Collier County.

EXHIBIT 3   **Geographic Location for Fisker Automotive, Inc. Franchise**

Lee County

Cape Coral
Fort Myers
Fort myers Villas
Lehigh Acres
San Carlos Park
Sanbel
Bonita Beach

Immokalee
Naples park
Naples
East naples
Maxco
Goodland
Jerome

Collier County

EXHIBIT 4	Market Profiles for Naples–Marco Island MSA, Collier County, Fort Myers–Cape Coral MSA, and Lee County, Florida					

	Naples	*Marco Island*	*Collier County*	*Fort Myers*	*Cape Coral*	*Lee County*
Total population	22,188	17,977	331,006	62,615	169,335	631,900
Total households	11,180	8,601	133,640	25,323	67,898	270,485
Median household income ($)	85,795	72,588	62,811	35,550	55,586	53,145
Households with income of $100,000 or more (%)	43.2	34.7	20.2	10.2	15.3	18.3
Households with income of $250,000 or more (%)	18.7	12.8	8.5	2.2	2.4	4.4
Median Age	64.2	61.4	45.1	32.3	39.3	42.4
Best green cities rank[1]	#88	#88	#88	#105	#105	#105
Average commute time to work (minutes)	17.1	19.3	25.8	25.6	28.3	28.0

[1] The best green cities ranking is based on an assessment of 25 measures that focus on how "green" the city or county ranks among 379 areas studied.

Source: Bestplaces.net and U.S. census.

The Fort Myers–Cape Coral MSA is almost six times larger than the Naples–Marco Island MSA based on population. The MSA household median income is $50,120. The median age is noticeably lower than the Naples–Marco Island MSA. The Fort Myers–Cape Coral MSA accounts for about 26 percent of households with incomes $100,000 or more in Lee County. Exhibit 4 provides a socioeconomic and driving behavior profile for the market area.

About 1 in 100 households (1.2 percent) in the market area purchase a new passenger vehicle each year and 5 percent of new car registrations are for hybrid cars. These figures are slightly higher than the state of Florida registration statistics.

Dealer Competition

At the present time, the closest Fisker dealer franchise is located in Tampa, Florida, which is 130 miles north of Fort Myers. The next closest competition is in Miami, Florida, with two Fisker dealer franchises. The two Miami franchises are 132 miles southeast of Naples, Florida. The socioeconomic and travel behavior profile of these two markets is shown in Exhibit 5 on page 190.

Competition in Sanger's luxury-brand car market area consists of 16 automobile dealers. The following luxury brands are represented: Cadillac, BMW, Porsche, Land Rover, Jaguar, Mercedes-Benz, Maserati, Lexus, Bentley, and Rolls-Royce.

SANGER AUTOMOTIVE COMPANIES, INC.

Sanger Automotive Companies, Inc., a privately held company, is made up of eight, mostly luxury, car dealerships, in Florida and Georgia. The company operates Cadillac, Lexus, and BMW dealerships. Founded as a Cadillac dealership in Fort Myers, Florida, in 1950, Sanger has an established reputation for delivering

EXHIBIT 5 **Market Profiles for Tampa–St. Petersburg–Clearwater MSA and Miami–Fort Lauderdale–Miami Beach MSA, Florida**

	Tampa-St. Petersburg-Clearwater MSA	Miami-Fort Lauderdale-Miami Beach MSA
Total population	2,769,483	5,520,037
Total households	1,159,831	2,061,159
Median household income ($)	$47,840	$50,350
Households with income of $100,000 or more (%)	16.0%	20.2%
Households with income of $250,000 or more (%)	3.4%	5.0%
Median Age	41.4	40.4
Best green cities rank[1]	#204	#241
Average commute time to work (minutes)	28.3	31.0

[1]The best green cities ranking is based on an assessment of 25 measures that focus on how "green" the city or county ranks among 379 areas studied.

Source: Bestplaces.net and U.S. census.

exceptional customer service in the purchase and ownership of luxury-class cars and its loyal customer following. Robert Sanger, the son of the company's founder, currently serves as the company's president.

Sanger is largely responsible for increasing the number of luxury-car dealerships owned by the company. He notes:

Florida is a great place for luxury-car dealerships. The state is second only to California in the percent of cars sold that are luxury brands. About 14 percent of all new cars sold in Florida are luxury cars, just behind California with about 16 percent. We have benefitted from this. I think we at Sanger have also contributed based on our solid reputation for meeting the needs and desires of luxury-car buyers, regardless of brand we represent. In fact, 15 percent of new cars sold in our market are luxury brands.

Sanger thought that a Fisker Automotive franchise for southeastern Florida warranted attention for a variety of reasons. First, he believed that luxury plug-in hybrid cars, in general, had a future. Still, he acknowledged: "The expectations of one million electric-powered cars on the road by the Obama administration by 2014 is a stretch. Chevy Volt sales were below forecast (10,000 vehicles) with unit sales of 3,895 by September of this calendar year (2011)." Second, he believed the market area could support only one Fisker dealership. If Sanger passed on the opportunity, then it was highly likely that his company would be prohibited from opening a dealership, at least in the short run. Third, Sanger Automotive owned a vacant dealership location. The company had moved one of its luxury car dealerships to a more spacious location in 2010. The vacant dealership had a showroom and service area, a portion of which had been converted to a body shop. Therefore, no incremental investment in showroom display space and service facilities was necessary.

On the other hand, Sanger Automotive would incur incremental operating costs for the franchise. The company's vice president of dealership operations prepared a cost schedule for Robert Sanger's review. An annualized itemized schedule is shown as follows:

1. Overhead costs for showroom and service bay: $85,000.

2. Two full-time sales associates' salary and benefits: $79,500.

3. Sales associate sales commission, as a percentage of retail sales: 1 percent.

4. One service manager and one service bay technician salary and benefits: $90,250.

5. Incremental and targeted advertising, promotion, and public relations expense in the first year: $66,000.

6. Delivered cost of a vehicle to the dealership: 90 percent of the MSRp.

In addition, Robert Sanger was concerned about the possible "rationing" of vehicles per dealership. He said, "There is a real possibility that we [will] be limited in the number of cars we will be allotted." I think we will have on the showroom one of each trim size ready for sale each month. After that, we'll have to take orders with a down payment and tell buyers to expect 14 weeks for delivery. I'm not sure what the back-out rate will be given a three-month wait period."

"I'm prepared to self-fund the up-front franchise investment of about $200,000 out of company cash flow if the numbers work," said Sanger. "I'd like to see a complete payout rate (amortization) of the franchise investment in five years," he added. Sanger asked his vice president of dealer operations to analyze the Fisker Automotive franchise opportunity and make a "go–no go" recommendation in two weeks.

Case

Frito-Lay, Inc.

Sun Chips Multigrain Snacks

In mid-1990, Dr. Dwight R. Riskey, vice president of marketing research and new business at Frito-Lay, Inc., assembled the product management team responsible for Sun Chips Multigrain Snacks. The purpose of the all-day meeting was to prepare a presentation to senior Frito-Lay executives on future action pertaining to the brand.

Sun Chips Multigrain Snacks is a crispy, textured snack chip consisting of a special blend of whole wheat, corn, rice, and oat flours with a lightly salty multigrain taste and a slightly sweet aftertaste. The product contains less sodium than most snack chips and is made with canola or sunflower oil. The chip is approximately 50 percent lower in saturated fats than chips made with other cooking oils and is cholesterol-free. According to a Frito-Lay executive, it is "a thoughtful, upscale classy chip."

The product had been in test market for 10 months in the Minneapolis–St. Paul, Minnesota, metropolitan area. Even though it appeared consumer response was extremely favorable, Riskey and his associates knew their presentation to senior Frito-Lay executives would have to be persuasive. In addition to presenting a thorough assessment of test-market data, Riskey added:

> We will have to do heavy-duty selling [to top executives] because Sun Chips Multigrain Snacks required a new manufacturing process, carried a new brand name, and pioneered a new snack chip category. There is a huge capital investment and a huge marketing investment that could be financially justified only with a product that could be sustainable for an extended time period.

 FRITO-LAY, INC.

Frito-Lay, Inc. is a division of PepsiCo, Inc., a New York–based diversified consumer goods and services firm. Other PepsiCo, Inc. divisions include Pizza Hut, Inc., Taco Bell Corporation, Pepsi-Cola Company, Kentucky Fried Chicken, and

The cooperation of Frito-Lay, Inc. in the preparation of this case is gratefully acknowledged. This case was prepared by Professor Roger A. Kerin, of the Edwin L. Cox School of Business, Southern Methodist University, and Kenneth R. Lukaska, Product Manager, Frito-Lay, Inc., as a basis for class discussion and is not designed to illustrate effective or ineffective handling of an administrative situation. Certain company information is disguised and not useful for research purposes. Copyright © 1995 by Roger A. Kerin. No part of this case may be reproduced without written permission of the copyright holder.

PepsiCo Foods International. PepsiCo, Inc. recorded net income of $1.077 billion on net sales of $17.8 billion in 1990.

Company Background

Frito-Lay, Inc. is a worldwide leader in the manufacturing and marketing of snack chips. Well-known brands include Lay's brand and Ruffles brand potato chips, Fritos brand corn chips, Doritos brand, Tostitos brand, and Santitas brand tortilla chips, Cheetos brand cheese-flavored snacks, and Rold Gold brand pretzels. The company's major brands are shown in Exhibit 1 along with estimated worldwide retail sales. Other well-known Frito-Lay products include Baken-Ets brand fried pork skins, Munchos brand potato crisps, and Funyuns brand onion-flavored snacks. In addition, the company markets a line of dips, nuts, peanut butter crackers, processed beef sticks, Smartfood brand ready-to-eat popcorn, and Grandma's brand cookies.

Frito-Lay, Inc. accounts for 13 percent of sales in the United States snack-food industry, which includes candy, cookies, crackers, nuts, snack chips, and assorted other items. The company is the leading manufacturer of snack chips in the United States, capturing nearly one-half of the retail sales in this category. Eight of Frito-Lay's snack chips are among the top-10 best-selling snack

---

EXHIBIT 1   **Frito-Lay, Inc.: Major Brands**

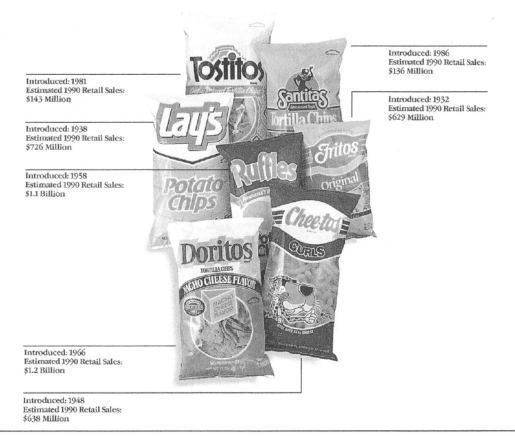

Introduced: 1981
Estimated 1990 Retail Sales:
$143 Million

Introduced: 1938
Estimated 1990 Retail Sales:
$726 Million

Introduced: 1958
Estimated 1990 Retail Sales:
$1.1 Billion

Introduced: 1986
Estimated 1990 Retail Sales:
$136 Million

Introduced: 1932
Estimated 1990 Retail Sales:
$629 Million

Introduced: 1966
Estimated 1990 Retail Sales:
$1.2 Billion

Introduced: 1948
Estimated 1990 Retail Sales:
$638 Million

Source: 1990 PepsiCo, Inc. Annual Report.

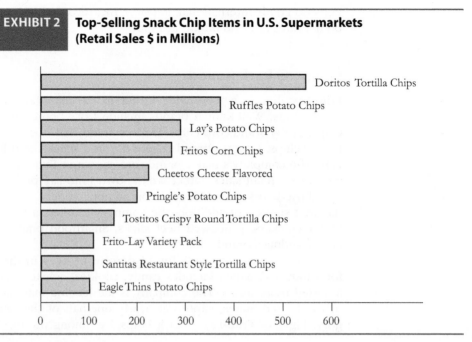

EXHIBIT 2   Top-Selling Snack Chip Items in U.S. Supermarkets (Retail Sales $ in Millions)

Source: 1990 PepsiCo, Inc. Annual Report.

chip items in U.S. supermarkets (see Exhibit 2). Doritos brand tortilla chips and Ruffles brand potato chips have the distinction of being the only snack chips with $1 billion in retail sales in the world.

Frito-Lay's snack-food business spans every aspect of snack-food production, from agriculture to stocking supermarket shelves. During 1990 in the United States alone, Frito-Lay used 1.6 billion pounds of potatoes, 600 million pounds of corn, and 55 million pounds of seasonings. The company has 39 manufacturing plants, more than 1,600 distribution facilities, and a 10,000-person route-sales team that calls on more than 400,000 retail store customers each week in the United States. Frito-Lay, Inc. recorded U.S. sales of $3.5 billion in 1990.

Product-Marketing Strategies

Frito-Lay pursues growth opportunities through four product-marketing strategies.

1. *Grow established Frito-Lay brands through line extension.* Recognizing that consumers seek variety in snack tastes and sizes without compromising quality, Frito-Lay marketing executives use line extensions to satisfy these wants. Recent examples of line extension include Tostitos brand bite-sized tortilla chips and Cheetos brand Flamin' Hot Cheese Flavored Snacks.

2. *Create new products to meet changing consumer preferences and needs.* Continuous marketing research at Frito-Lay is designed to uncover changing snacking needs of customers. A recent result of these efforts is evident in the launch of a low-oil light line of snack chips.

3. *Develop products for fast-growing snack-food categories.* Recognizing that snack-food categories experience different growth rates, Frito-Lay marketing executives continually monitor consumption patterns to identify new opportunities. For example, Frito-Lay acquired Smartfood brand popcorn in 1989. In 1990, this brand became the number one ready-to-eat popcorn brand in the United States.

4. *Reproduce Frito-Lay successes in the international market.* Initiatives pursued in the United States often produce opportunities in the international arena. Primary emphasis has been placed in large, well-developed snack markets such as Mexico, Canada, Spain, and the United Kingdom. Innovative marketing coupled with product development efforts produced $1.6 billion in international snack-food sales in 1990.

 ## THE SNACK CHIP CATEGORY

The United States snack-food industry recorded retail sales of $37 billion in 1990, representing a 5 percent increase over 1989. Dollar retail sales of snack chips consisting of potato, corn, and tortilla chips, pretzels, and ready-to-eat popcorn were estimated to be $9.8 billion—a 5 percent increase over 1989. A major source of growth in the snack chip category results from increased per capita consumption. In 1990, consumers in the United States bought 3.5 billion pounds of snack chips, or nearly 14 pounds per person; in 1986, snack chip per capita consumption was slightly less than 12 pounds.

Competitors

Three types of competitors serve the snack chip category: (1) national brand firms, (2) regional brand firms, and (3) private brand firms. National brand firms, which distribute products nationwide, include Frito-Lay, Borden (Guys brand potato and corn chips, and Wise brand potato chips, cheese puffs, and pretzels), Procter & Gamble (Pringles brand potato chips), RJR Nabisco (several products sold under the Nabisco name as well as Planter's brand pretzels, cheese puffs, and corn and tortilla chips), Keebler Company (O'Boisies brand potato chips), and Eagle Snacks (a division of Anheuser-Busch Companies, Inc., which sells Eagle brand pretzels and potato and corn chips). A second category of competitors consists of regional brand firms, which distribute products in only certain parts of the United States. Representative firms include Snyder's, Mike Sells, and Charles Chips. Private brands are produced by regional or local manufacturers on a contractual basis for major supermarket chains (for example, Kroger and Safeway).

Competition

The snack chip category is very competitive. As many as 650 snack chip products are introduced each year by national and regional brand companies. Most of the products are new flavors for existing snack chips. The new-product failure rate for snack chips is high, and industry sources report that fewer than 1 percent of new products generate more than $25 million in first-year sales.

Snack chip competitors rely heavily on electronic and print media advertising, consumer promotions, and trade allowances to stimulate sales and retain shelf space in supermarkets. Pricing is very competitive, and snack chip manufacturers often rely on price deals to attract customers. The nature of the technology used to produce snack chips allows snack chip manufacturers to react swiftly to new product (flavor) introductions by competitors. Extensive sales and distribution systems employed by national brand competitors, in particular, allow them to monitor new product and promotion activities and place competing products quickly in supermarkets.

DEVELOPMENT OF SUN CHIPS MULTIGRAIN SNACKS

Sun Chips Multigrain Snacks resulted from Frito-Lay's ongoing marketing research and product development program. However, its taste and name heritage can be traced to the early 1970s.

Product Heritage

Frito-Lay product development personnel first explored the possibility of a multigrain product in the early 1970s when corporate marketing research studies indicated consumers were looking for nutritious snacks. A multigrain snack chip called Prontos was introduced in 1974 with the following positioning statement: "The different, delicious new snack made from nature's own corn, oats, and whole grain wheat all rolled into one special recipe, together in a snack for the first time from Frito-Lay." The product was only mildly successful despite advertising and merchandising support. The product was subsequently withdrawn from national distribution in 1978 due to declining sales and manufacturing difficulties. According to Frito-Lay executives, the demise of Prontos in 1978 was driven by "noncommittal" copy, a confusing name, and a product that generated appeal among too narrow a target market. Reflecting on this experience, Riskey added, "I'm not sure there were dramatic things wrong with the product design so much as difficulty with the manufacturing process. It may have been invented and introduced before its time."

The brand name for the product had an equally arduous past. The Sun Chips name was originally assigned to a line of corn chips, potato chips, and puffed corn snacks in the early 1970s. In 1976, the brand name was given to a line of corn chips, but by 1985, this line was also withdrawn from distribution due to poor sales performance.

Product Development: The "Harvest" Project

Early 1980s   Interest in a multigrain snack was revisited in the early 1980s when Frito-Lay marketing executives began to worry whether the aging baby boomers (people born between 1946 and 1964) would continue to eat salty snacks such as potato, corn, and tortilla chips. According to Riskey:

> The aging baby boomers were a significant factor [in our thinking]. We were looking for new products that would allow them to snack. But we were looking for "better-for-you" aspects in products and pushing against that demographic shift.

In 1981, Frito-Lay marketing research and product development personnel instituted the "Harvest" project with an objective of coming up with a multigrain snack that would have consumer appeal. After several product concept tests and in-home product use tests failed to generate any consumer excitement, it was concluded that the market for wholesome snacks was not yet fully developed to accept such products. Other evidence seemed to support this view. In 1983, Frito-Lay test marketed O'Grady's brand potato chips. The results had been phenomenal. Projections based on test market performance indicated the brand would produce $100 million in annual sales, which it did in 1984 and 1985.

Mid-1980s The "Harvest" project continued in the mid-1980s, albeit at a slower pace due to staff changes and other responsibilities of project team members. At about this time, a change in top management and corporate objectives focused product development efforts on traditional snacks with an emphasis on flavor line extensions for established Frito-Lay brands (for example, Cool Ranch Doritos brand tortilla chips) and low-fat versions of its potato, corn, and tortilla chips. In addition, attention was placed on cost-containment measures coupled with continuous quality-improvement initiatives using existing manufacturing facilities and existing product and process snack chip technology.

Late 1980s Development efforts on a multigrain product were renewed in early 1988. Over the following 13 months, different product formulations (for example, low oil vs. regular oil; salt content; chip shape), alternative positionings, and branding options (extension of an existing Frito-Lay brand vs. a new brand name) were extensively studied using consumer taste tests and product concept tests. The combined results of these tests yielded a multigrain rectangular chip with ridges and an exceptional taste. Further testing of brand names and flavors revealed consumer preferences for two names (one of which was Sun Chips) and three flavors (original/natural, French onion, and mild cheddar).

Further consumer research revealed that the multigrain product concept and assorted flavors were perceived as a "healthier product." This research also indicated that consumer expectations prior to use (that is, before initial trial of the product) were that the product would not be an "everyday snack" item. Consumers who tried the product, however, perceived the multigrain product to be an "everyday snack," at least for the natural and French onion flavors. Exhibit 3 on page 198 shows a plot of pretrial consumer expectations and postuse perceptions of different flavors and representative snack chip brands and crackers. Concurrent research on brand names indicated a decided preference for the Sun Chips name. The name evoked positive consumer imagery and attributes of "wholesomeness, great taste, light and distinctive, and fun," according to a Frito-Lay executive.

Premarket Test

Positive consumer response to the product concept and brand name prompted an initial assessment of the commercial potential of Sun Chips Multigrain Snacks. A simulated test market or premarket test (PMT) was commissioned in April 1989 and conducted by an independent marketing research firm.

A PMT involves interviewing consumers about attitudes and usage behavior concerning a product category (for example, snack chips). Consumers would be exposed to a product concept using product descriptions or mock-ups of advertisements, and their responses would be assessed (see Exhibit 4 on page 199). These consumers would then be given an opportunity to receive the product if interested. After an in-home usage period of several weeks, they would be contacted by telephone and asked about their attitude toward the product, use of the product, and intention to repurchase. These data would be incorporated into computer models that would include elements of the product's marketing plan (price, advertising, distribution coverage). The output provided by the PMT would include estimates of household trial rates, repeat rates, average number of

EXHIBIT 3   **Consumer Expectations and Perceptions of Snack Chips and Multigrain Snacks**

PRETRIAL PRODUCT EXPECTATIONS

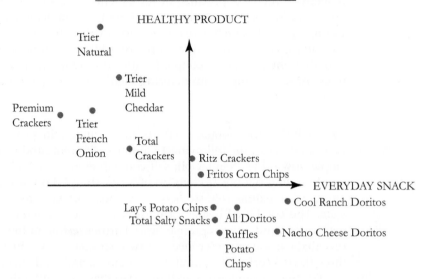

POSTUSE PERCEPTIONS: TRIER REPEATERS VS. TRIER NONREPEATERS

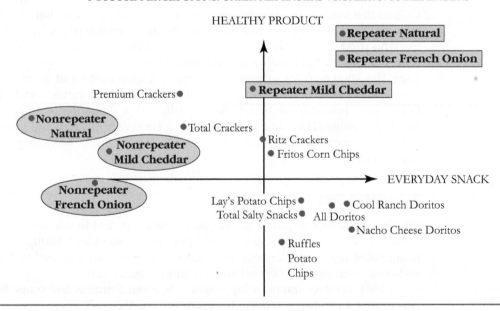

units purchased on the initial trial and subsequent repeats in the first year, product cannibalism, and first-year sales volume.[1]

The product concept tested in the PMT was priced at parity with Doritos brand tortilla chips. Planned distribution coverage was set at levels comparable for Frito-Lay potato, corn, and tortilla chips. Two-flavor combinations (natural and French onion and natural and mild cheddar) and three advertising

---

[1]Published validation data on premarket test models indicate that 75 percent of the time they are plus or minus 10 percent of actual performance when a product was introduced (see, for example, A. Shocker and W. Hall, "Pretest Market Models: A Critical Evaluation," *Journal of Product Innovation Management* 3, (1986), pp. 86–107.

| EXHIBIT 4 | Concept Board for the Premarket Test |

The great tasting snack chip for people who care about what they eat.

More and more people care about what they eat because they know that eating habits affect overall health and fitness. SUN CHIPS™ are a special blend of whole wheat, golden corn and other natural great tasting grains. These wholesome grains combined make a uniquely delicious chip with the golden goodness of corn and the nut-like flavor of wheat. They're cooked 'till lightly crisp and crunchy. Then they're lightly salted to let all that naturally good flavor come through. SUN CHIPS™ are a unique combination of great taste, great crunch, and natural goodness, all rolled into one remarkable chip.

So, try new SUN CHIPS™, the chip with the uniquely delicious taste for people who care about what they eat.

Available in these two delicious flavors:
● Natural ● French Onion

and merchandising expenditure levels ($11 million, $17 million, and $22 million) were tested.[2]

Results from the PMT indicated that Sun Chips Multigrain Snacks would produce a most likely first-year sales volume of $113 million at manufacturer's prices given the marketing plan set for the product, including a $22 million advertising and merchandising expenditure. The estimated first-year sales volume exceeded the $100 million Frito-Lay sales goal for new products. The natural and French

_____

[2]Advertising and merchandising expenditures included electronic and print media advertising, consumer promotions, and trade allowances.

EXHIBIT 5 **Simulated Test-Market Results (Selected Statistics)**

	Product and Promotion Strategy[a]			
	Natural & Mild Cheddar Combination		Natural & French Onion Combination	
	A&M Budget $17 million	A&M Budget $22 million	A&M Budget $17 million	A&M Budget $22 million
Purchase Dynamics				
Brand awareness (% of households)	40	48	40	48
Cumulative first-year trial rate (%)[b]	23	27	21	25
Cumulative first year repeat rate (%)[c]	61		57	
Number of purchases in first-year per repeating household	5.9		6.2	
Volume Projections ($ millions)				
Pessimistic	87	102	86	102
Most likely	96	113	95	113
Optimistic	106	125	106	125
Incremental annual volume (%)	50		58	
Cannibalized pound volume (%) (from Frito-Lay products)	50		42	

[a]The $11 million advertising and merchandising (A&M) budget for the two flavor combinations produced lower figures than those shown. For example, brand awareness was 35 percent and the cumulative first-year trial rate was 19 percent regardless of flavor combination.

[b]*Cumulative first-year trial* refers to the percentage of households that would try the product.

[c]*Cumulative first-year repeat* refers to the percentage of trier households that repurchased the product.

onion flavor combination produced the lowest cannibalization (42 percent) of other Frito-Lay brands. Summary statistics for the simulated test market are shown in Exhibit 5.

 TEST MARKET

Positive results from consumer research and the simulated test market led to a recommendation to proceed with Sun Chips Multigrain Snacks and implement a test market under Dwight Riskey's direction. The Minneapolis–St. Paul, Minnesota metropolitan area was chosen as the test site because Frito-Lay executives were confident it had a social and economic profile representative of the United States. Furthermore, Minneapolis–St. Paul, in general, represented a typical competitive environment in which to test consumer acceptance and competitive behavior. The Minneapolis–St. Paul metropolitan area contained 1.98 million households that were identified as users of snack chips, or 2.2 percent of the 90 million snack chip user households in the United States. Discussion among Frito-Lay marketing, sales, distribution, and manufacturing executives and the company's advertising agency indicated that the test market could begin October 9, 1989. Accordingly, a test-market plan and budget were finalized. The test market was scheduled to run for 12 months, with periodic reviews scheduled throughout the test.

Snack-food industry analysts became aware of Frito-Lay's development efforts on a multigrain snack chip soon after the company began preparation for the test market. According to one industry analyst:

> This is a departure from corn or potatoes. Wheat is different. Remember they departed from corn and potatoes a few years ago with Rumbles, Stuffers, and Toppels, and it was a distasteful business. I'm sure they will take their time and really test it. It's not like they don't have other products, so there's no hurry.[3]

Test-Market Plan

Product Strategy   Frito-Lay executives decided to introduce both the natural and French onion flavors given consumer research and simulated test-market results. Sun Chips Multigrain Snacks would be packaged in two sizes: a 7-ounce package and an 11-ounce package. These package sizes were identical to Doritos brand tortilla chips. A 2¼ -ounce trial package would be used as well.

Package design was considered to be extremely important. According to a Frito-Lay executive, "We wanted distinctive, contemporary graphics which would communicate new, different, and fun amidst positive images—sun and a sprig of wheat." This view materialized in a metalized flex bag with primary colors of black (natural flavor) and green (French onion flavor). Exhibit 6 on pages 202 and 203 shows the packages used in the test market.

Pricing Strategy   Sun Chips Multigrain Snacks would have the same suggested retail prices as Doritos brand tortilla chips. Research indicated these price points were consistent with consumer reference prices for snack chips and represented a good value. Suggested retail prices and Frito-Lay's selling prices to retailers are shown in Exhibit 7 on page 204.

Advertising and Merchandising Strategy   The primary audience for Sun Chips Multigrain Snacks television advertising was adults between the ages of 18 and 34, since they are the principal purchasers and heavy users of snack chips. A secondary audience expanded the age bracket to 49 years of age, since 34- to 49-year-olds appeared to be receptive to healthier snacks. Household members under 18 years of age would be exposed to the product through in-home usage. The advertising message would convey subtle messages, including wholesomeness, fun, and simplicity. One of the television commercials to be shown in the test market is reproduced in Exhibit 8 on page 204. In addition to television advertising, the brand would be supported by in-store displays and free-standing inserts (FSIs) in newspapers (see Exhibit 9 on page 205).

Coupons placed in newspaper FSIs were to be used during the test market to stimulate trial and repeat sales. In addition, free samples would be distributed in supermarkets. Trade allowances were provided to retailers as well.

Distribution and Sales Strategy   Distribution and sales of Sun Chips Multigrain Snacks would be handled through Frito-Lay's store-door delivery system, in which the duties of a delivery person and a salesperson are combined. Under this system, a delivery/salesperson solicits orders, stocks shelves, and introduces merchandising programs to retail store personnel. Sun Chips Multigrain Snacks

---

[3]"New Multigrain Chip Being Readied for Test," *Advertising Age* (June 26, 1989), p. 4. The products referred to were Stuffers cheese-filled snacks, Rumbles granola nuggets, and Toppels cheese-topped crackers. These products were introduced in the mid-1980s, failed to meet sales expectations, and were subsequently withdrawn from the market.

EXHIBIT 6 Sun Chips Multigrain Snacks Packaging: Original Flavor

EXHIBIT 6 (*Continued*)

EXHIBIT 7 — Sun Chips Multigrain Snacks Price List

Package Size	Suggested Retail Price	Frito-Lay Selling Price to Retailer
2$\frac{1}{4}$ ounce	$0.69	$0.385
7 ounce	$1.69	$1.240
11 ounce	$2.39	$1.732

EXHIBIT 8 — Sun Chips Multigrain Snacks Television Commercial

LEVINE, HUNTLEY, SCHMIDT
& BEAVER, INC.
CLIENT: FRITO-LAY, INC.
PRODUCT: SUNCHIPS

TITLE: "POLLY"
LENGTH: 30 Seconds
COMM'L NO.: PESU–9013

(Music under) GUY: Polly want one?

AVO: It seems everyone who tries new SUNCHIPS feels smarter eating them.

POLLY: Polly wants another one.

AVO: Smarter because they're multigrain.

POLLY: Polly wants you to fill her water cup.

AVO: Smarter because of the taste.

POLLY: Polly thinks you should paint this room and this time pick a better color.

AVO: Smarter because they're naturally delicious.

POLLY: Polly wants to know why one species feels it's OK to imprison another

purely for its own entertainment.

AVO: New SUNCHIPS.

You'll feel smarter eating them.

EXHIBIT 9   Sun Chips Multigrain Snacks Free-Standing Insert (FSI)

would be sold through supermarkets, grocery stores, convenience stores, and other retail accounts that already stocked Frito-Lay's snack products.

Manufacturing Considerations Frito-Lay manufacturing personnel worked concurrently with marketing personnel on matters related to mass production of a multigrain product. While prototypes were easily developed in limited quantities, large-scale manufacturing would require a production line capable of delivering an adequate product for a market test. Since a multigrain product required different product and process technology than corn or potato products, an investment in one new production line would be necessary. Approval was granted to create a production line to produce and package 1 million pounds of the multigrain snack per year at full theoretical capacity. The production line could be in operation to ship the product in two flavors and three package sizes for the test market in September 1989.

Test-Market Budget

The advertising and merchandising budget for the test market was equivalent to a $22 million expenditure on a nationwide distribution basis. Approximately 70 percent of the budget would be spent during the first six months of the test market.

Test-Market Results

Consumer response was monitored by an independent research firm from the beginning of the test market. Data gathered by the research firm were submitted to Frito-Lay monthly and consisted of the types of purchases, the incidence of trial and repeat-purchase behavior, and product cannibalization in the test market.

Type of Purchase Data supplied by the research firm indicated that the coupon program had a major impact on trial activity and approximately 90 percent of purchases were made in supermarkets and convenience stores. After 10 months in the test market, the 2¼-ounce package accounted for 15 percent of purchases, the 7-ounce package accounted for 47 percent of purchases, and the 11-ounce package accounted for 38 percent of purchases. Fifty-five percent of purchases were for the French onion flavor; 45 percent of purchases were for the natural flavor.

Trial and Repeat Rates Of critical concern to Frito-Lay executives were the incidences of household trial and repeat-purchase behavior for Sun Chips Multigrain Snacks. Exhibit 10 shows the cumulative trial and repeat rates for both flavors combined during the first 10 months of the test market. Almost one in five

---

EXHIBIT 10   Household Trial and Repeat Rates for Sun Chips Multigrain Snacks

	Tracking (4-Week Period)									
	1	2	3	4	5	6	7	8	9	10
Cumulative trial[a] (%)	4.7	8.2	9.8	11.3	14.1	15.7	16.5	17.4	19.5	19.9
Cumulative repeat[b] (%)	8.0	22.5	27.1	31.0	32.7	36.5	39.0	39.7	41.8	41.8

[a]*Trial* refers to the percentage of households that tried the product.

[b]*Repeat* refers to the percentage of trier households that repurchased the product.

households in the test market had tried the product, and 41.8 percent of these trier households had repurchased the product at least once over the 10-month period.

Equally important to Frito-Lay executives were the "depth of repeat" data supplied by the research firm. *Depth of repeat* is the number of times a repeat purchaser buys a product after an initial repeat purchase. Repeater purchasers of Sun Chips Multigrain Snacks purchased the product an average of 2.9 times. An estimated average purchase amount for triers was 6 ounces. Initial repeat and repeater households purchased an average of 13 ounces per purchase occasion.

Product Cannibalization   The independent research firm also identified the incidence of product cannibalization. The research firm's tracking data indicated that 30 percent of Sun Chips Multigrain Snack pound volume resulted from consumers switching from Frito-Lay's potato, tortilla, and corn snack chips. About one-third of the cannibalized volume from Frito-Lay's products came from Doritos brand tortilla chips.

The 30 percent cannibalism rate was not uncommon in new product introductions in the snack food industry. For example, when Frito-Lay introduced O'Grady's brand potato chips, one-third of its pound volume came from its Ruffles brand and Lay's brand potato chips. Even though cannibalization was an issue to be considered in evaluating test-market performance, Frito-Lay executives noted that the gross profit for Sun Chips Multigrain Snacks was higher than that for its other snack chips.[4] (*Case writer note*: Footnote 4 contains important information for case analysis purposes.)

 TEST-MARKET REVIEW

Riskey's presentation to senior Frito-Lay executives would conclude with his recommendation for the future marketing of Sun Chips Multigrain Snacks. He could recommend that the test be continued for another six months, or be expanded to other geographic areas with the same introductory strategy or some modification. Alternatively, he could recommend that Sun Chips Multigrain Snacks be readied for a national introduction with the strategy used in the test market or some modification in the strategy.

Planning Considerations

Numerous topics were raised in his meeting with the product management team responsible for Sun Chips Multigrain Snacks. Timing and competitive reaction were important issues. Riskey believed that national and regional competitors were monitoring Frito-Lay's test market. There was also a high probability that these competitors were examining the chip with the intention of developing their own version. Timing was a concern for a variety of reasons. First, if Riskey continued testing the product, a competitor might launch a similar product nationally or regionally and upstage Frito-Lay. The opportunity to be first-to-market would be lost. Second, if an expanded test market or a national introduction was

---

[4]Frito-Lay, Inc. does not divulge profitability data on individual products and product lines. However, for case analysis and class discussion purposes, a multigrain snack chip can be assumed to have a gross profit of $1.30 per pound, while other snack chips (potato, tortilla, and corn) can be assumed to have a gross profit of $1.05 per pound. Gross profit is the difference between selling price and the cost of materials and manufacturing (ingredients, packaging/cartons, direct labor, other assignable manufacturing expenses, and equipment depreciation).

considered, a decision would be needed quickly to assure adequate manufacturing capacity was in place and operating efficiently. Manufacturing capacity expansion would require a significant capital investment. Although preliminary figures represented rough estimates, manufacturing capacity capable of serving 25 percent and 50 percent of snack chip households in the United States would involve a capital expenditure recommendation of $5 million and $10 million, respectively. A full-scale national introduction would require a capital expenditure of $20 million.

Recommendations related to manufacturing capacity expansion would require a justification of the magnitude and sustainability of Sun Chips Multigrain Snacks sales over time. Accordingly, Riskey requested marketing research personnel to supply him with comparative brand awareness and cumulative household trial and repeat rate data for O'Grady's brand potato chips, since this brand was the most recent Frito-Lay product introduction to achieve $100 million in first-year sales.

Brand-awareness studies on the two brands indicated that O'Grady's brand potato chips achieved brand awareness among 28 percent of snack chip households during its market test compared with 33 percent for Sun Chips Multigrain Snacks. Exhibit 11 charts trial and repeat data for comparable test-market periods for Sun Chips Multigrain Snacks and O'Grady's brand potato chips. His interest in the sustainability of sales over time prompted a request for additional data on depth of repeat statistics for the two brands. The depth of repeat, or "repeats per repeater" for O'Grady's brand potato chips was 1.9 times, or about twice on an annual basis, compared with 2.9 times for Sun Chips Multigrain Snacks, or about three times on an annual basis.

EXHIBIT 11	Cumulative Trial and Repeat Rates for O'Grady's Potato Chips and Sun Chips Multigrain Snacks: 40-Week Test Market

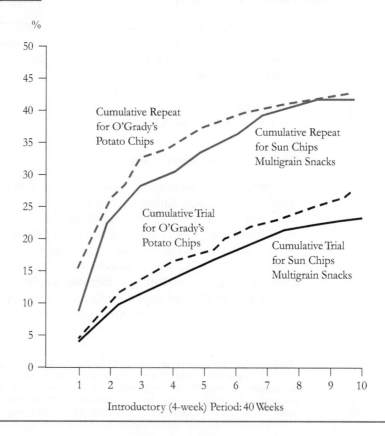

Strategy Considerations

Several strategy options were also discussed. Some product management team members advocated increased advertising and merchandising spending if the brand was tested further or launched nationally. They believed that brand awareness would increase with additional spending and felt that spending the national introduction equivalent of $30 million could stimulate brand trial as well. Others interpreted the purchase data to mean that additional volume was possible by introducing a larger package size (for example, a 15-ounce package). They believed that a fourth, larger package could add about ½ ounce to the average annual purchase amount per repeat (and repeater) purchase occasion. Priced at the same price per ounce as the 11-ounce size, this action would not have a material effect on the brand's gross profit per pound. Others believed that another package size made more sense after the brand was established in the marketplace. Furthermore, the manufacturing and marketing of four sizes could stretch the production capacity, increase inventory, and challenge Frito-Lay sales personnel to get retailer shelf and display space.

Some discussion was also directed toward building the household repeat and depth of repeat business. For example, a flavor extension (for example, mild cheddar) was proposed. An advocate of this approach suggested that a flavor extension could increase the "repeats per repeater" to an average of 3½ times per year given greater variety for consumers. However, the addition of another flavor could increase the cannibalization rate to 35 percent, some thought. Also, the mild cheddar flavor still needed to be perfected in large-scale production. Others noted that if a larger package and a flavor extension were simultaneously pursued, the number of stock-keeping units would double from six (2 flavors × 3 sizes) to twelve (3 flavors × 4 sizes). It was agreed by everyone that this action would cause severe manufacturing difficulties, since the multigrain snack process technology was still untested.

Case

Dermavescent
Laboratories, Inc.

On Friday, January 5, 2006, Phoebe Masters, the newly appointed product manager for hand and body lotions at Dermavescent Laboratories, Inc., was faced with her first decision one day after her promotion. She had to decide whether to introduce a new package design for the company's Soft and Silky Shaving Gel. The major questions were whether a 5½ ounce or a 10-ounce aerosol container should be introduced and whether she should approve additional funds for a market test. Timing was critical because the incidence of women's shaving would increase during the spring months and reach its peak during the summer months.

 ## THE COMPANY AND THE PRODUCT

Soft and Silky Shaving Gel is marketed by Dermavescent Laboratories, Inc., a manufacturer of women's personal-care products with sales of $258 million in 2005. The company's line of products includes facial creams, hand and body lotions, and a full line of women's toiletries sold under different brand names. Products are sold by drug and food-and-drug stores through rack jobbers. Rack jobbers are actually wholesalers that set up and merchandise retail displays. They receive a margin of 20 percent off the sales price to retailers.

Soft and Silky Shaving Gel was introduced in the spring of 1991. The product was viewed as a logical extension of the company's Soft and Silky brand of hand and body lotions and required few changes in packaging and manufacturing. The unique dimension of the introduction was that Soft and Silky Shaving Gel was positioned as a high-quality women's shaving gel. The positioning strategy was successful in differentiating Soft and Silky Shaving Gel from existing men's and women's shaving creams and gels at the time. Moreover, rack jobbers were able to obtain product placement in the women's personal-care section of drug and food-and-drug stores, thus emphasizing the product's positioning statement. Furthermore, placement apart from men's shaving products minimized direct price comparisons with men's shaving creams, since Soft and Silky Shaving Gel

EXHIBIT 1	Soft and Silky Shaving Gel Income Statement for the Year Ending December 31, 2005		
Sales			$3,724,000
Cost of goods sold (incl. freight)[a]			784,000
Gross profit			$2,940,000
Assignable costs:			
Advertising and promotion costs		$1,154,540	
Overhead and administrative costs		421,560	$1,576,100
Brand contribution			$1,363,900

[a]For analysis purposes, treat the cost of goods sold and freight cost as the only variable cost.

was premium-priced—with a suggested retail price of $3.95 per 5½ ounce tube. Retailers received a 40 percent margin on the suggested retail selling price.

Soft and Silky Shaving Gel has been sold in a tube since its introduction. This packaging was adopted because the company did not have the technology to produce aerosol containers. Furthermore, the company's manufacturing policy was and continues to be to utilize existing production capacity whenever possible. As of early 2006, all products sold by the company were packaged in tubes, bottles, or jars.

Soft and Silky Shaving Gel had been profitable from the time of its introduction. Although the market for women's shaving cream and gels was small compared to men's shaving cream and gels, Soft and Silky's unique positioning had created a "customer franchise," in the words of Heather Courtwright, the Soft and Silky brand assistant. "We have a unique product for the feminine woman who considers herself special." Soft and Silky Shaving Gel sales were $3,724,000 in 2005 with a 1,960,000 unit volume (see Exhibit 1).

WOMEN'S SHAVING IN THE UNITED STATES

Research on women's shaving in the United States commissioned by Masters' predecessors over the past decade had produced a number of findings useful in preparing annual marketing plans for Soft and Silky Shaving Gel. The major findings and selected marketing actions prompted by these findings are described below.

Methods of Hair Removal and Shaving Frequency

Women use a variety of methods for hair removal. The most popular method is simply shaving with razors and soap and water. Shaving with razors and shaving cream and gels is the next most used method, followed by shaving with electric razors. Women typically have their own razors and purchase their own supplies of blades. Approximately 90 million women (aged 13 and over) shave with a blade and razor; 5 million women use electric shavers.

Over 80 percent of women shave at least once per week. Women who work outside the home shave more frequently than those who do not. On average, women shave 11 times per month and shave 9 times more skin than men per shaving occasion (men shave 24 times per month on average). Shaving frequency varies by season, with the summer months producing the greatest shaving activity (see Exhibit 2 on page 212). Accordingly, in-store promotions and multipack deals were scheduled during the summer.

EXHIBIT 2 **Seasonality of Women's Shaving and Shaving Area (Percentage of U.S. Women)**

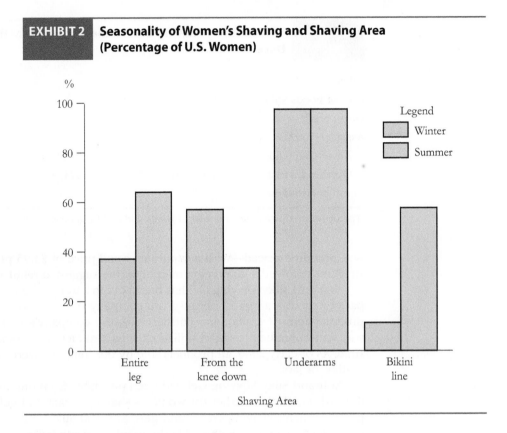

Attitudes Toward Shaving

Women view shaving as a necessary evil. When queried about their ideal shaving cream or gel, women typically respond that they want a product that contains a moisturizer, reduces irritation, and makes shaving easier. Four out of five women use a moisturizer after shaving.

These specific findings resulted in a change in the Soft and Silky Shaving Gel ingredient formulation in 1995. Prior to 1995, the product contained only aloe. In 1995, three additional moisturizers were added to the product, including lanolin and vitamin E. These ingredients were emphasized on the package and in-store promotions and media advertising.

Market Size and Competitive Products

Industry sources estimate the U.S. dollar value of women's "wet shaving" products (female-positioned blades, razors, and shaving creams and gels) to be about $550 million in 2005, at manufacturer's prices. Sales growth has been in the range of 3 to 5 percent per year since 2000. Razors and blades account for 77 percent of women's "wet shaving" products. Shaving creams and gels account for 23 percent of annual sales. Women spend, on average, $12.50 for razors, blades, and shaving preparations per year.

Historically, women who used shaving cream or gels had few "women's-only" products to choose from. However, since 1999, a vibrant women's shaving cream and gel category has emerged due to new-product activity, increased advertising and promotion, and improved shaving technology. Some industry analysts pointed toward the introduction of Gillette's Sensor Razor for Women and the Gillette Venus Razor for Women as important growth stimulants. Other analysts cited improvements in the quality of shaving creams and gels for women and increased

EXHIBIT 3	Representative Women's Shaving Products		
Brand (Manufacturer)	**Size[a]**	**Form**	**Price/Price per Oz.**
Skintimate (S. C. Johnson)	7 oz.	Gel	$2.79/$.40
Skintimate (S. C. Johnson)	10 oz.	Cream	$2.99/$.30
Satin Care (Gillette)	7 oz.	Gel	$2.99/$.43
Soft Shave (White Labs)	9 oz.	Lotion	$1.82/$.20
Aveeno Therapeutic Shaving Gel (S. C. Johnson)	7 oz.	Gel	$3.99/$.57
Inverness Ultra-Lubricating Shaving Gel (Inverness Corp.)	6 oz.	Gel	$6.95/$1.16
Soft and Silky Shaving Gel (Dermavescent Laboratories)	5.5 oz.	Gel	$3.95/$.72

[a]Several manufacturers also sold smaller 2-ounce sizes designed for travel purposes.

advertising. Until late 1993, only two competitive products were normally available in the drug and food-and-drug stores served by Dermavescent Laboratories, Inc. rack jobbers. These products were S. C. Johnson's Skintimate (formerly called Soft Sense) and Soft Shave, a lotion sold by White Laboratories. By late 2005, several competing brands existed in the women's shaving cream or gel category, even though all were not stocked by stores that carried Soft and Silky Shaving Gel. Exhibit 3 shows representative brands, sizes, forms (cream, gel, lotion), and typical retail prices. Advertising and promotion for Soft and Silky Shaving Gel had responded to the increase in competition. Expenditures had increased each year since 1995, reaching 31 percent of sales in 2005.

By 2005, the dominant packaging for women's shaving cream or gels had become the aerosol container. Only a few shaving gels and brands were sold in tubes or plastic bottles, including Soft and Silky Shaving Gel, Soft Shave lotion, and Inverness Ultra-Lubricating Shaving Gel.

NEW PACKAGE DESIGN

The idea for a new package design was provided by Masters' brand assistant, Heather Courtwright. She originally proposed the new package to Masters' predecessor in July 2005. Her recommendation was based on four developments. First, unit sales volume for Soft and Silky Shaving Gel had slowed and then plateaued in recent years (see Exhibit 4 on page 214). Second, the growth of Soft and Silky Shaving Gel had strained manufacturing capacity. In the past, production of Soft and Silky Shaving Gel had been easily integrated into the firm's production schedules. However, growth in the entire line of hand and body lotions, coupled with Soft and Silky Shaving Gel sales, had overburdened production capacity and scheduling. Moreover, inspection of shipping records indicated that the product's fill rate (that is, the company's ability to supply quantities requested by retailers) had dropped, leading to out-of-stock situations and lost sales. Third, the company had no manufacturing capacity expansion plans for the next three years. And finally, the aerosol packaging had become the dominant design for women's shaving creams and gels.

Courtwright's observations prompted a preliminary study of outsourcing opportunities for a new package design. Her study included visits to several firms

EXHIBIT 4   **Soft and Silky Shaving Gel Unit Sales Volume, 1991–2005**

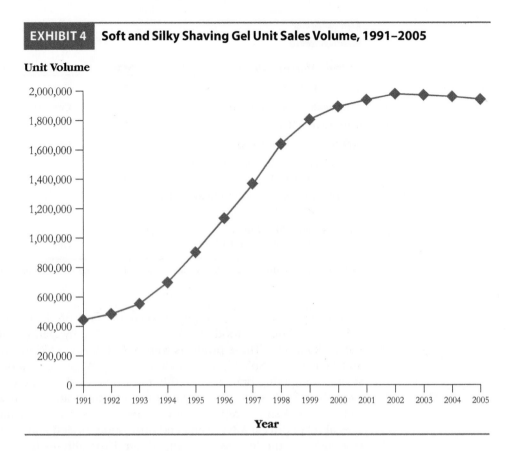

specializing in "contract filling" and requests for production proposals. A contract filler purchases cans, propellants, caps, and valves from a variety of sources and then assembles these components, including the product fill (that is, shaving gel), into the final container. The production method is called pressure filling. In this method, the cap and valve are inserted in the can and then sealed. At the same time, a vacuum is created in the container. The product fill and propellant are then injected under high pressure through the valve into the can.

Her review of supplier proposals led her to choose one that was capable of meeting production requirements and providing certain "value-added" features. For example, the chosen supplier could deliver a propellant with no chlorofluorocarbons (CFCs), which are harmful to the earth's ozone layer. Also, the container's bottom would be rustproof and leave no rust ring when wet. This feature was desired because most women shave in the bathtub or shower and tend to leave a wet can on the tub's porcelain, which can leave a rust stain. In addition, the supplier could produce and ship product directly from its manufacturing facility at a lower per unit cost than the tube container and was prepared to maintain an adequate safety stock of inventory. The only drawback in the supplier's proposal was that only 5½- and 10-ounce containers could be produced without making significant and expensive changes in its equipment. The typical sizes for women's shaving creams and gels ranged from 6-ounce to 10-ounce containers.

The estimated total cost of producing and delivering to jobbers a 10-ounce aerosol can of shaving gel was $0.29. A minimum order of 100,000 10-ounce cans would be required. Courtwright believed the suggested retail price would be set at $4.25 per 10-ounce can, reflecting Soft and Silky's premium-price strategy. The estimated total cost of producing and delivering to jobbers a 5½-ounce aerosol can of shaving gel was $0.24, and the suggested retail price would be $3.50. A 100,000-unit minimum order would be required. Courtwright recognized that the price per ounce for the aerosol containers was lower than the equivalent price per ounce for the tube package. She said the lower price reflected competitive realities in the category: "The dominant players (S. C. Johnson and Gillette) are very price competitive. We can retain our relative premium image even at the lower prices. I fully expect some cannibalization of the tube will take place just as I am confident the incremental volume will more than offset it." A one-time setup charge for the Soft and Silky Shaving Gel production line and package graphics was $10,000, due and payable by Dermavescent Laboratories, Inc. upon the signing of the supply agreement. This charge would be the same whether one or both sizes were produced.

 ## PRELIMINARY TESTS

In November 2005, Courtwright received authorization from Masters' predecessor to spend $35,000 to assess consumer response to the proposed container. Her proposal was approved on the basis of the cost data provided and the recognition that use of a contract filler would require no incremental investment in company manufacturing capacity.

Courtwright commissioned a large marketing research firm to conduct four focus-group studies. Two focus groups would involve current users of Soft and Silky Shaving Gel, and two focus groups would involve users of shaving creams and gels other than Soft and Silky Shaving Gel and soap and water users. The principal information sought from these focus group studies was as follows:

1. Are present customers and noncustomers receptive to the new package?
2. At what rate would present customers convert to the aerosol can, and would noncustomers switch over to Soft and Silky Shaving Gel?
3. Where, in drug and food-and-drug stores, would customers and noncustomers expect to find the aerosol can?
4. Is the suggested retail price acceptable?

In addition, the marketing research firm was asked to examine analogous situations of package changes and report its findings.

In late December 2005, the marketing research firm presented its findings to Courtwright, two days after Masters' predecessor resigned to take a position with another company. There were six principal findings from the focus groups:

1. Customers and noncustomers were unanimously in favor of the aerosol can. The 10-ounce can was the favorite, since it would require fewer purchases.
2. Twenty percent of Soft and Silky Shaving Gel customers said they would convert to the 10-ounce can; 25 percent said they would convert to the 5½-ounce can.
3. One-fourth of the noncustomers said they would switch over to the aerosol can irrespective of can size. These consumers' preference for the aerosol over the tube package was their principal reason (in addition to price) for not buying Soft and Silky Shaving Gel previously.
4. Customers expected to find the aerosol can next to the tube container. Noncustomers expected to find the aerosol container stocked with women's toiletries.
5. The pricing was acceptable and actually favored by current customers. Noncustomers thought the suggested retail price was somewhat high, but liked the value-added features and would try the product.

6. Current Soft and Silky Shaving Gel customers are extremely loyal to the brand. None of the brand's current customers had used a competing brand in the past two years. There was no evidence of such loyalty among noncustomers.

In addition to these findings, the marketing research firm presented ten case histories in which marketers of men's shaving cream had introduced a new package. (There was no distinction made with respect to size of package, whether the package change was from aerosol to nonaerosol, or vice versa, or previous sales performance.) Two statistics were highlighted: first-year sales with the combined packages and the cannibalization rate for the existing package. According to the report,

> It is difficult to draw one-to-one comparisons between the experience of other shaving creams and gels and that of Soft and Silky Shaving Gel, given its unique market position. We have tried to do so after examining ten product-design changes. Our estimates [Exhibit 5] are broken down into a "high" and a "low" forecast for each package size. Seven out of the ten products studied experienced the "high" situation presented; three experienced the "low" situation. We see the

---

EXHIBIT 5   **Soft and Silky Shaving Gel Sales Forecasts by Size and Type of Container**

Forecast A: Low estimate for 5½-ounce aerosol package addition

5½-ounce tube package volume			8,600,000 ounces
5½-ounce aerosol package volume:			
Cannibalized volume	2,145,174		
Net new volume	300,000		2,445,174
		Total	11,044,174 ounces

Forecast B: High estimate for 5½-ounce aerosol package addition

5½-ounce tube package volume			8,400,000 ounces
5½-ounce aerosol package volume:			
Cannibalized volume	2,345,174		
Net new volume	500,000		2,845,174
		Total	11,245,174 ounces

Forecast C: Low estimate for 10-ounce aerosol package addition

5½-ounce tube package volume			9,000,000 ounces
10-ounce aerosol package volume:			
Cannibalized volume	1,745,174		
Net new volume	800,000		2,545,174
		Total	11,545,174 ounces

Forecast D: High estimate for 10-ounce aerosol package addition

5½-ounce tube package volume			9,600,000 ounces
10-ounce aerosol package volume:			
Cannibalized volume	1,145,174		
Net new volume	1,500,000		2,645,174
		Total	12,245,174 ounces

10-ounce package as producing the largest increase in ounces sold. Even with the cannibalism effect operating, we believe that an additional package will produce higher sales, in ounces, than the Soft and Silky Shaving Gel forecasted volume of 10,745,174 ounces (1,953,668 5½-ounce tubes) for 2006. Only a market test can indicate what will actually occur.

THE PACKAGING AND TEST MARKET DECISION

Courtwright presented the research firm's findings to Phoebe Masters on January 5, 2006, one day after Masters became product manager for hand and body lotions. Masters listened attentively as Courtwright summarized the research findings and recommended that a market test be conducted to determine the best package size.

Courtwright's test-market recommendation included a proposal to introduce the new package design in a limited cross-section of drug and food-and-drug stores, including heavy-volume and low-volume stores, that presently carried Soft and Silky Shaving Gel. Test stores would be isolated geographically from nontest stores. The new package would be placed among women's toiletries, and the test would run for three months, beginning April 1, 2006. The April 1 start date was necessary to assure that adequate supply of the new package was available. One-half of the stores would carry the 5½-ounce container, and the other half would carry the 10-ounce container. The test would include a full complement of promotional aids, including newspaper ads and point-of-purchase displays, and would approximate a full-scale introduction.

Courtwright's estimated cost for the test market was $30,000, which included the cost of gathering marketing research data on the cannibalization rate and incremental sales growth. In addition, the $10,000 supplier setup charge would have to be paid. However, Courtwright negotiated a 20,000 unit minimum order for each package size for the test market. No other incremental costs would be charged against the products. Sales and marketing efforts for the existing tube package would remain unchanged during the course of the test.

Late in the evening of Friday, January 5, 2006, Masters found herself considering whether the 5½-ounce or the 10-ounce container should be introduced. She believed it unwise to introduce both sizes, given the uncertainty of market acceptance and packaging practices of most competitors. She also wondered whether Courtwright's test-market proposal should be adopted. Masters was confident that, given the product's sales history, the existing Soft and Silky Shaving Gel tube package would produce sales of 1,953,668 units (a 0.32 percent decrease from 2005) in 2006 if no new package was introduced. She was also confident that a new package would simultaneously cannibalize the existing package and generate incremental unit volume. Therefore, she knew that her decision on the package sizes and test market would have to focus on what was best for the Soft and Silky Shaving Gel product line, assuming an aerosol container would be marketed alongside the original tube container.

Masters also sensed that the new package had become a pet project for Courtwright. Courtwright had championed the idea for six months in addition to working on a variety of other assignments. Furthermore, she had heard that Courtwright felt that she, not Masters, should have been promoted to product manager for hand and body lotions given her association with the product line for five years. Given the situation, Masters believed that her handling of this decision would affect her working relationship with Courtwright.

Case

Oráteme, Inc.

"What should be our next move?" mused Drew Graves as he sat down at his desk. "The economy is in the tank and our clients are struggling to survive." Facing him was a file containing summary financial information for the year that had just ended. After 10 months at the helm of Oráteme, Inc., Graves thought he was ready to begin the company's long-range planning process.

After quickly reviewing the financial information, Graves asked his secretary to schedule a meeting with his senior leadership team. "Please tell David, Karolynn, Ram, and John to analyze the financials before the meeting as we will need to take a serious look at our marketing strategy and new revenue generators. And tell them to come with some big marketing ideas and to be prepared to make some decisions," he said as looked out his office window. "This is very interesting," he remarked to no one in particular. "We have a stable base of satisfied customers as reflected by a year-to-year customer retention rate that exceeds 93 percent and we now have the right people in the right places; it is time to look to the future."

THE COMPANY

Oráteme, Inc. was founded by five diverse if not somewhat naïve entrepreneurs in May 2000. Their desire was to create a company that would serve as a "virtual staff" for small professional and trade associations. The term Oráteme comes from the Greek words *oráda*, which means "group" and *episteme*, which means "knowledge" (thus "group knowledge"). Three of the founders had been on the staff of a private college. Two of them were computer programmers with extensive experience—one specialized in Web design whereas the other specialized in database management. The third founder was a college professor (hence the Greek company name), whereas the fourth was a retired executive. The fifth founder, David Flowers, had recently started, then shut down, an Internet service company. By mutual agreement of the founders, Flowers was named chief executive officer (CEO) of Oráteme. He also was the company's only salesperson the first two years of its existence.

Oráteme, Inc. is located about one-half mile off Route 128 in Boston, Massachusetts, in a high-tech area second only to Silicon Valley with respect to company start-ups. It was one of the last companies to receive venture capital funding when the dot-com economy was crashing. Two venture capital firms contributed the seed money to get the company started. Although the initial funding was slightly less than $1 million, the founders believed that the funds would be sufficient until the firm started generating revenues. Because of their investment, the venture firms received three of the five seats on the board of directors and 25 percent nondilutable equity in the company. Flowers held a fourth seat and an independent director held the fifth.

At the beginning of 2005, the venture capital firms brought in Jon Warren to be CEO and run the company. Previously Warren had been a partner at Runny & Ware, a large consulting firm headquartered in Chicago, where he had specialized in acquisitions and mergers involving Internet-based companies. In October 2004 he had been approached by a member of the board of directors of Oráteme about the possibility of becoming CEO. Although Warren was not even aware of Oráteme at that time, after a brief period of negotiation he accepted the job as CEO, replaced Flowers on the board of directors, and assumed full responsibility for managing the company. Flowers became president and decided to concentrate on the sales force.

Warren, watching the performance of early movers in the social media space such as Facebook and LinkedIn, raised a mezzanine round of $2 million to bring the capabilities of social media to the association industry. Unfortunately, his social media bet turned out to be wrong, and in mid-2007 he was ousted by the board and replaced by Flowers. Flowers regained his board seat and again assumed day-to-day control of company operations. To conserve cash, he stopped investing in new services, cut staff, and reduced marketing expenditures, focusing on maintaining the company's current client base.

In early 2011, in an example of déjà vu, Flowers once again turned over the reins of Oráteme to another outsider. This time it was Drew Graves. Graves, like Warren before him, was brought in by the board of directors to help Oráteme grow into the potential everyone in the company knew it had. Unlike Warren, Graves had a history of proven accomplishments in creating business winners. His resume was a testament to his success: He had started and sold two Web-based software companies, turned another around before selling it to a large European software conglomerate, and, most recently, managed the Internet businesses of a *Fortune* 500 high-tech firm. Graves spent most of 2011 delving into company problems, meeting clients, and continuing to build the company's cash position. Flowers again became president and returned to managing the sales force.

Strategic Goal

From the beginning, the strategic goal of Oráteme was to serve small (state, regional, and local) trade and professional associations by offering an inexpensive yet highly functional Web site and collective buying power for the associations and their members. When the company was created, research conducted by the founders, together with their personal experiences, convinced them that because small associations had limited financial resources and few technical skills to manage a Web site, they would be an ideal market for an easy-to-use site that could lead to more effective and efficient management. Moreover, given their limited resources and relatively small numbers of members, these associations did not possess either the time or expertise to search out and obtain the best prices of the products and services that they or their members needed.

By combining the associations into a single buying group and identifying the most value-producing products and services, Oráteme could provide major financial benefits to its client associations and their members. As Flowers continually reminded company employees and potential client associations, "by partnering with us, client associations can save money while creating value for their members. They only need to have someone manage their Web site, either a volunteer or staff member with minimal computer-related capabilities. We do the rest."

What attracted the venture capital funding was the company's business model. The model mandates that the company focus on annuity-type services. Thus, rather than focus on one-time transactions, the business model emphasizes long-term client relationships based on repeat purchases and an extensive service commitment. Given its strategic goal and business model, when the company was founded Flowers believed that it could realistically acquire 500 client associations by the end of its second year of operation and 2,000 client associations by the end of its fourth year of operation.

Product and Service Offerings

The first year of the company's existence was spent constructing its core Web site product—a branded, leading-edge, template-driven site that could be customized for an association—and creating a portfolio of value-based products and services. The site was designed such that, with minimal effort, the "look and feel" could be unique to an association. Simultaneously, the "back end" of the Web site was designed so that an association could easily make changes to administrative functions and databases and add or delete Web site content. Functions and databases included an online membership directory, an association-based e-mail capability, online newsletter tools, event calendar, job board, and conference registration and dues payment capabilities.

Whereas its competitors market fixed-price Web site products at prices ranging from $20,000 to more than $100,000, Oráteme licenses its site product to client associations at an annual targeted fee averaging about $5,000 the last two years (up from an annual targeted fee of $2,000 when the company started). For this fee, the company provides a branded Web site (i.e., the site has only the client association's name on it; Oráteme is not listed on it) and instructs the client association's staff on how to add and manage content as well as use other features and tools. Although Oráteme hosts the Web sites on its servers in Boston and Denver, until 2005 a client association was responsible for transferring content from its server to a company server and day-to-day upkeep after a training session conducted by an Oráteme customer support representative. In 2005, however, Oráteme began charging a setup fee for helping client associations migrate content from their server to an Oráteme server. On average it takes four hours of Oráteme customer support time to establish a new client Web site, even though many of the tasks are automated. In addition, Oráteme offers site design assistance and miscellaneous services for which it charges an hourly fee of $75 (a markup of $25 over the hourly cost of a customer support representative). In 2011 about 5 percent of company revenues were derived from Web site design- and transferal-related services.

Through a series of vendor-partners, Oráteme also offers client associations a portfolio of products and services that includes discounted long-distance conference calling, selected software packages, discounted rental car services, and co-branded credit cards. By combining client associations and their members into a single buying group, Oráteme increased their collective purchasing power. For example, Oráteme negotiated "bulk" prices on a variety of products and services so that client associations and their members could purchase at prices much less than they could if they attempted to purchase the products and services on their own. The company shares in the savings that accrue from such an arrangement and generates revenue each time a client association or its members make a purchase through the association's Web site. Presently the company receives 1 percent of the price of all products and services purchased by client associations or their members through the Oráteme vendor-partner program.

In 2007 the company created a job board offering for its client associations. Job boards are Web pages on a client association's site where organizations wanting to hire employees could place job advertisements and individuals looking for jobs could post their resumes. Thus, for example, a hospital attempting to hire nurses could place job advertisements on the Web sites of one or more nursing, hospital, and/or medically related client associations. Each job advertisement had a fee associated with it, and "packages" of postings could be placed on one or more association Web sites. Likewise, nurses looking for a new job could post their resumes on their association's site. There was no fee for members posting a resume on their association's site. Recently Oráteme, in concert with its client associations, began sending e-mails ("job flashes") containing job offers directly to association members. Fees from job boards and job flashes were shared by Oráteme and the client association, with 80 percent going to the company and 20 percent going to the association. For the association this was non-dues revenue that could be used to offset its annual fee.

Marketing Approach

Marketing to professional and trade associations is at times both straightforward and challenging. It is straightforward because Oráteme can easily identify potential client associations. There are numerous directories of associations, and most associations are listed on Web sites or have their own site. Thus, unlike much consumer marketing, it is possible to target specific, individual associations. At the same time, though, because many associations already have a Web site and oftentimes purchase decisions involve an association's board of directors due to limited financial resources and what might be termed political concerns, marketing to them can be quite time-consuming and challenging.

Oráteme employs a variety of marketing approaches to reach potential client associations. Using e-mail addresses supplied by contract labor or purchased from third-party suppliers, company sales representatives contact more than one thousand association executives each week. The e-mails invite recipients to call the company and direct them to the Oráteme Web site. Approximately 1 percent of the e-mails results in a response; in turn, about 20 percent of the responses lead to a Web site licensing agreement. Company sales representatives attend some four dozen association conferences and trade shows every year, where they interact both formally and informally with association executives and present the company's service offerings. Almost every conference attended by an Oráteme sales representative results in seven or eight new leads, oftentimes because of the face-to-face referrals that occur. Nearly half of the leads generated in this fashion result in licensing agreements.

Oráteme does relatively little advertising. However, it does provide complimentary (free) Web sites, especially to those associations whose members are association directors. Approximately 6 percent of the active Web sites powered by Oráteme at any one point in time are complimentary. By far the best way to acquire new client associations is to obtain referrals from existing client associations. Because association executives, especially in a particular industry, know each other and work together on common issues, referrals tend to be powerful marketing levers. Indeed, association referral fees are a notable component of selling expenses.

Once an association appears to be interested in the Oráteme Web site offering, association executives are given a 90 minute Web-based tour of a demonstration site and several active client association sites by an Oráteme sales representative. More than half of the association executives touring the Oráteme demonstration Web site purchase a license for their association. Oráteme sales representatives believe that once an association executive has toured the company's Web site offering, the site "sells itself." Indeed, company sales representatives believe that the marketing process is more akin to an education process than a selling process. As might be expected, sales representatives spend most of their 40 to 46 working hours per week on the telephone talking to potential client associations.

Company Performance

The company licensed its first client association in early 2001. By the end of 2001, 93 associations were licensed to use the Oráteme Web site template. The growth in client associations was dramatic over the next few years. There were, respectively, a total of 408 client associations at the close of 2002; 840 by the close of 2003; 1,410 by the close of 2004; 1,750 by the close of 2008; and 1,905 at the end of 2011. Client associations are disproportionately represented in the Northeast (principally Massachusetts, New Hampshire, and Vermont), Texas, and California. Moreover, client associations are scattered across more than 100 different industries and are more likely to be local-level (metropolitan) associations than state- or regional-level associations.

Company revenues were less than $200,000 in 2001. In 2002, revenues were nearly $655,000. In general, the revenue figures are consistent with the growth in number of client associations. The largest source of revenue has always been Web site licensing. The smallest source consists of commissions from the collective buying arrangements that Oráteme established with vendor-partners.

At the beginning of 2012, the company had 127 employees, up from 105 the year before. There were nine sales representatives, with six (an increase of two) being dedicated to selling job boards. The technical staff had increased to nearly four dozen individuals, and there were three dozen customer service representatives or account representatives who were responsible for managing particular categories of client associations. The remaining employees worked in standard functional areas such as accounting, finance, marketing, and secretarial support. Even so, according to Diane Pierson, the human resources director of the company, Oráteme was woefully understaffed. She noted that customer service representatives in particular were not able to spend the recommended one hour every week communicating with a client association in order to properly manage the company–client relationship.

The largest expense category consists of employee compensation. Not including Flowers, the nine sales representatives are each paid a base salary of $36,000 and a commission that averages 15 percent of the price of a first-time Web site license and 20 percent of a job board sale. The second-largest expense category consists of the direct (nonsalary) cost of sales (sales commissions, fees shared with associations, and so forth). Technology costs include hardware, software, and expenses associated with the company's server farms in Boston and Denver. Rent has decreased as the company consolidated its office locations. Technology expenses, rent, and general corporate expenses are allocated across product lines proportionally to revenues (see Exhibit 1 for 2009–2011 abbreviated profit and loss statements).

EXHIBIT 1	Orǻteme, Inc. 2009–2011 Abbreviated Profit and Loss Statements		
Revenue	*2009*	*2010*	*2011*
Website-related	$5,041,971	$ 6,112,836	$ 8,366,431
Job boards	3,414,950	4,638,039	6,439,396
Other	115,067	166,361	166,340
Total	$8,571,988	$10,917,236	$14,972,167
Expenses			
Payroll	$5,592,971	$ 7,045,795	$ 8,231,791
Cost of sales	1,482,752	2,113,848	3,682,616
Rent	528,655	475,587	394,224
Technology	566,833	611,177	840,160
Marketing	59,944	69,643	83,945
Other	210,862	270,445	388,678
General corporate	451,321	534,998	741,947
Total	$8,893,338	$11,121,493	$14,363,631
Profit (loss)	($321,350)	($204,257)	$ 608,806

Source: Company records (data are disguised).

THE ASSOCIATION MARKET

There are an estimated 1.2 million philanthropic, charitable, or not-for-profit organizations in the United States, ranging from college fraternities and sororities to elementary school parent–teacher associations to associations of dentists and banks and junkyards. Orǻteme believes that there are well in excess of 300,000 formal associations in the United States, where an association is a group of entities, such as people or firms, that voluntarily come together to accomplish a common purpose. These associations represent nearly every industry, profession, hobby, cause, and for-profit and not-for-profit interest group imaginable. There are more than 155,000 professional and trade local, state, and regional associations; 33,000 national associations; and 1,300 international associations headquartered in the United States. Approximately 8 out of 10 adult Americans belong to at least one association, and 1 out of 4 adults belong to four or more associations. As many as 1,000 new associations form each year. Two of the largest associations in the United States are the American Automobile Association (AAA; 52 million estimated members) and AARP (formerly the American Association of Retired Persons; over 40 million estimated members). Association budgets range from a few hundred dollars annually to several hundred million dollars annually.

With more than 2,500 associations, the Washington, DC, area has more associations than any other metropolitan area in the United States. In fact, associations constitute the third-largest industry in the Washington, DC, area, behind only government and tourism. New York City, with 2,000 associations, and Chicago, with 1,500 associations, are the second and third most popular locations for association headquarters.

Although some associations have millions of members, such as those that have consumers as members, a majority of associations, especially those that serve occupations or industries and are state, regional, or local associations, have less than 1,000 members. These smaller associations are in general the primary target markets of Oráteme. In 2011, the median number of members of the company's client associations was 730 (people or firms).

Associations are a major market for many products and services, either directly as end users or as intermediaries for their members. For example, it is estimated that more than $4 billion is spent annually on technology and communications by associations, and another $3 billion is spent annually by associations on printing magazines, newsletters, and so forth for their members. Almost by definition, associations dominate the convention industry; association members spend in excess of $85 billion each year traveling to and attending conventions, expositions, and meetings. Nearly $150 billion in insurance premiums annually pass through associations from members to insurance providers.

All formal professional and trade associations have some type of executive director and staff, and they usually have a board of trustees or directors. Frequently both the director and the staff members are volunteers or part-time employees, and association Websites are managed on an ad hoc basis. Recently there has been a growing tendency for private companies to professionally manage several associations simultaneously to control costs and increase efficiencies. In fact, it is not unusual for a private company to manage as many as 20 small (noncompeting) associations. There are even associations designed for association directors, with perhaps the most well known being the American Society of Association Executives (ASAE). ASAE has more than 22,000 association executives as members and represents more than 10,000 organizations in 50 countries; it is an important gateway for reaching the professional and trade association community.

Target Markets

Initially Oráteme's target markets consisted of small professional and trade associations at the state, regional, or local level whose staffs and members were likely to be at least somewhat computer literate. The founders strongly believed that this niche was greatly underserved and overlooked by possible competitors. Professional associations are designed to serve individuals, usually in particular occupational categories, such as psychologists, certified public accountants, teachers, and the like. Trade associations are designed to serve organizations, such as businesses, and are found in virtually all industries.

Nearly every professional occupation or industry has numerous associations ranging from national associations to regional, state, and even local associations. It is not unusual for a national association to have 6 regional chapters, 50 state chapters, and 300 local (metropolitan) chapters. Analogous to businesses, there are competing associations in almost every professional occupation or industry. Individuals join associations for a variety of reasons, including access to information, education, certification programs, reduced insurance premiums, representation before legislative and regulatory bodies, and networking opportunities.

 COMPETITION

Oráteme's competitive environment changed quickly over time. When it was first founded, the company had a few reasonably funded dot-com competitors such as Wego, IBelong Networks, and MyAssociation that focused on large national associations. However, many of the early competitors have fallen by the wayside or changed their business models significantly in the down economy. Unfortunately, previous competitors have been replaced by stronger ones. Among its current

competitors, Affiniscape, Avectra, Boxwood, and JobTarget are the most prominent and offer a variety of Web site packages for small associations.

Whereas Affiniscape and Avectra offer full-service solutions for associations,
JobTarget and Boxwood are specialists. JobTarget claims to be the largest third-
party operator of niche job boards in the world and the first company to offer
an integrated cross-posting/job distribution and strategy optimization technology
solution. It is very aggressive and has grown rapidly in the last few years. Boxwood has nearly 1,000 online career center association customers. By offering a
flat fee pricing option and flexible revenue-sharing plans (including convenient
pay-for-performance models) for its association customers, it claims to have generated more than $200 million in non-dues revenues for its association custom-
ers. It also claims to be the only job board provider endorsed by ASAE and the
Center for Association Leadership.

Of more concern is the tendency of large national professional associations to
require standardized Web sites for their state and local chapters. Presently many
state and local chapters of a national association are free to create their own site,
but to the extent that a common Web site design and functions are mandated and
even provided by the national association, a significant proportion of Orâteme's
target market of associations may be affected. In an attempt to counter the tendency of national associations to offer standardized Web sites to their chapters,
Drew Graves initially contemplated pursuing partnerships with national associations in which Orâteme would provide and even manage all of a national association's Web sites, from the national Web site down to chapter sites.

While Graves believed Orâteme could continue to compete successfully
against existing firms offering Web sites for associations, he was aware that a
large firm such as Google or even Facebook or LinkedIn might decide to swoop
into the association market and dominate it. In his mind, the ability to contact
millions of people through associations for marketing purposes made companies
such as Orâteme vulnerable to large firms seeking direct access to individuals
and organizations, in part because the cost per contact is much lower than, say,
direct mail, and in part because of the information available about each member
of an association. A large firm with "deep pockets," such as Google or Facebook,
or even Microsoft or Oracle, could enter the association market through an acquisition or a well-funded start-up and quickly change the competitive environment.
As David Flowers has often reminded employees, "The only significant barriers
to entry we have are satisfied client associations and outstanding value-added
services. Given the nature of our business, a rival could spring up overnight virtually any place on the globe. We are living on the edge."

 ## THE OPPORTUNITIES

While the company's early investment in social media missed the mark, the marketplace was finally warming to the benefits of them. Association members want
to easily communicate and even collaborate with other members and, much to
the chagrin of the associations, they are increasingly turning directly to social
media giants like Facebook, LinkedIn, and Twitter for solutions. Because smaller
associations are not able to meet their members' communication and interactivity
needs, they are not in a position to benefit from satisfying those needs.

Similarly, increased competition from numerous, for-profit privately held
companies has eaten away at the once-dominant associations. Competitors have
gained mind and market share in numerous services the associations had once
offered exclusively. For example, associations offering continuing education (CE)

for their members, such as lawyers, teachers, and accountants, are facing competition on what seems to be all fronts. Increasingly, the company's client associations and their members are turning to the Oráteme team to help in the areas of social media, continuing education, managing content on their Web sites, managing their underfunded yet profitable job boards, developing advertising strategies, and supporting products to help them capitalize on advertising.

Graves and his management team must decide where to invest the company's precious financial resources. Their client associations are clamoring for assistance, but Oráteme can afford to develop only one or at most two products or services to address its clients' needs. The question is: which one or two?

The Meeting

At precisely 10 A.M. on Friday, January 13, 2012, Drew Graves strode into the company's conference room. Seated at the table were David Flowers; Ramesh ("Ram") Visnaramathan, vice president of engineering; Karolynn Matheson, vice president of operations; and John Bushel, comptroller. On the table were three foot-high stacks of documents consisting of mainly financial statements and prior marketing plans. "Well," said Graves, "where should we begin on this Friday the 13th? Although our financials look OK, and we did all right last year, I think they are deceiving. I think we need to be 'cautiously optimistic.' Our sales pipeline is at a four-year low, and given the current economic climate, we need to be prepared for a possible slowdown in revenue. On top of this, our VCs are beginning to pressure us; they want some semblance of an exit strategy. Thus, while we need something to energize sales, and quickly, our purpose here today is to come up with a long-term strategic direction. Because you are among the brightest and most creative company employees, I have asked you here today to brainstorm. David, why don't you start off?" Graves sat down and began thumbing through the documents in front of him.

David Flowers leaned back in his chair and then began to speak slowly, "Let's begin by talking about our job boards. The job board offerings are targeted at employers and recruiters looking to get their job openings in front of qualified job seekers. By leveraging our job flashes [job e-mails] to appropriate client associations, we provide access to our network of associations and, by extension, their respective members. Currently, our biweekly job flashes are received by more than 1.5 million association members each month. We also have our dedicated 'career network' job boards that are dedicated to different industry verticals [e.g., the Nursing Career Network that reaches nurses, physicians, and hospitals] that are viewed by more than one million association members monthly as well."

Flowers continued, "We have worked hard on job boards the last five years. The Association Career Network [the company's career center] now drives more than $6 million in annual revenues, and the repeat-purchase rate is now up to 55 percent. With a back-of-the-envelope projected growth rate of 40 percent +, it is a core offering, both for the short and long term. Why not just focus on job boards?"

Karolynn Matheson spoke next. She began by saying that it is time for the company to get serious about continuing education. She reminded the executives that during the extended length of time that Oráteme team members had discussed and argued about the benefits of continuing education, traditional continuing education (CE) had become a fairly mature, $4 billion market that presently delivers nearly 1 percent of all content online. She said her research indicated that "the online CE marketplace is highly segmented with numerous third-party players offering numerous solutions. Each has claimed one or two vertical industries and most are competing with trade and professional associations such as legal and accounting rather than working with them. We have an opportunity to develop a series of CE offerings that would mutually benefit both Oråteme *and* our client associations where CE is required. However, I estimate that to develop a fully mature CE product offering will require several years and $3 to $5 million to bring one to market. This suggests that we should consider partnering with or acquiring a small player in the space that could be brought to our 1,900+ client associations. If we are lucky, we could grab 1 percent of the CE market, even if we have to share it 50–50 with a partner."

Matheson stopped to take a drink of water. "I know the choices for new product offerings can be difficult," she said. "I also know our associations are desperately looking for help with social media. While I agree that they really need help, the only way to monetize social media is through advertising. I am approached almost daily by firms that want to advertise a dizzying array of products and services to the members of our client associations. For us, the costs associated with developing any meaningful social media functionality may run as high as $900,000 and could take more than 18 to 24 months of development time before bringing sufficiently mature offerings to market. While our associations are pushing for this offering, given the existence of companies like Facebook and the uncertainty of an advertising-based revenue model in which we would share revenues with associations like we do for the job boards, I just don't know how viable this option is. Assuming we were successful with this initiative, it might be as profitable as our job boards."

"There is yet another strategic option," said Ramesh Visnaramathan. He noted that "managing content is a burgeoning market opportunity that has virtually no market penetration in the association market. Content providers like WebMD, which had $600 million in revenues last year, currently provide content through numerous channels but not yet in the association space. My team has monitored this space informally and believes we could generate $91 in revenue per client association member annually within five years based on 12 to 18 months of development. We could do this for less than $2 million if we could establish partnerships with content providers like WebMD and develop an advertising-based revenue sharing model."

John Bushel responded by saying, "Karolynn, you may be too pessimistic, and Ram, you may be too optimistic. Ram, do we want to go head-to-head with companies such as SmartBrief . . . or should we try to partner with or even purchase such a company? Remember our conversation last year. SmartBrief selects news globally, summarizes it, links to the original sources, and delivers it free of charge via online newsletters to some 3 million business decision makers in more than 100 associations every day. Many of these associations are probably in our space. The company could follow an advertising strategy along the lines that Karolynn is considering. Think about it."

Bushel continued, "From the year-end financials that we all received this week you can see that the company is in the black for the first time ever. Moreover, our cash position is good at $1.6 million and growing at 2 percent per month, and our sales expense ratio for Web site–related services is down to 5 percent. Although I agree that we need to do something, I recommend that we wait a year until there is more marketplace stability. Look, the credit ratings of France, Portugal, Italy, Spain, Austria, Malta, Slovakia, Slovenia, and Cypress were all downgraded this week by Standard & Poor. There is too much economic uncertainty right now to commit to anything long term. Let's continue to build cash this year."

"Guys, I'm not sure many of your ideas will fly." David Flowers grew impatient. "I have been here, in the trenches, from the beginning, from day one. We have tried many things, most of which were not well thought out and subsequently didn't work. We need some more in-depth thinking and analysis. For example, we could easily add more client-friendly features to our present job board offering that client associations could market to their members and organizations who want to hire their members, or work with the associations to get corporate sponsors for their Web sites. Adding such features would allow us to raise the base price of our product at least 5 to 10 percent and probably get us five or six new client associations a month."

Drew Graves closed the meeting by saying, "I personally have not been able to study our new financials in detail. Let's not get carried away with grandiose ideas until we have a better understanding of where we are. At the risk of being perceived as obstructive, I would like to sleep on these ideas and look at the financials more closely over the weekend. I'm not ready to take any action until I've mulled over and digested these documents. Can we reconvene next Monday at the same time? Please do your homework and refine your ideas. We need to make some decisions sooner rather than later."

Case

Pate Memorial Hospital

In mid-April 2000, Sherri Worth, assistant administrator at Pate Memorial Hospital (PMH) in charge of the hospital's Pate Health Clinic (PHC), uncovered an unsettling parcel of news. During a call on the employee benefits director at a downtown department store, she was told that a firm was conducting a study to determine whether sufficient demand existed to establish a clinic five blocks north of PMH's Pate Health Clinic. The description of the clinic's services sounded similar to those offered by the PHC, and the planned opening date was May 2001.

As Worth walked back to her office, she could not help but think about the possible competition. Upon arriving at her office, Worth called Dr. Roger Mahon, PMH's administrator, to tell him what she had learned. He asked her to contact other employee benefits directors and query patients to see whether they had been surveyed. He expressed concern for two reasons. First, a competitive clinic would attract existing and potential patients of the Pate Health Clinic. Second, a clinic that provided similar services could hamper the PHC's progress toward achieving its service and profitability objectives. Mahon requested that Worth summarize the Clinic's performance to date so that he could speak to members of the board of trustees' executive committee on what action, if any, the DHC should take to compete for patients.

THE HOSPITAL INDUSTRY AND AMBULATORY HEALTH CARE SERVICES

Health care, and specifically the hospital industry, has undergone a dramatic transformation in the past four decades. Until the 1960s, hospitals were largely charitable institutions that prided themselves on their not-for-profit orientation. Hospitals functioned primarily as workshops for physicians and were guided by civic-minded boards of trustees.

Federal legislation introduced in the 1960s created boom times for the hospital industry. The Hill-Burton Act provided billions of dollars for hospital construction, to be repaid by fulfilling quotas for charity care. Additional funds were poured into expansion and construction of medical schools. Medicare and

---

Medicaid subsidized health care for the indigent, disabled, and elderly. These programs reimbursed hospitals for their incurred costs plus an additional return on investment. This period also saw dramatic increases in commercial insurance coverage, offered as employee fringe benefits and purchased in additional quantities by a more affluent public. Accordingly, health care became accessible to an overwhelming majority of U.S. citizens, regardless of where they lived or their ability to pay. Federal intervention had changed the concept of health care services from privilege to entitlement.

By the 1980s, however, skyrocketing health care costs had forced the federal government to reassess its role in health care. Stringent controls were placed on hospital construction and expansion, and utilization and physician-review programs were implemented to ensure against too-lengthy inpatient stays. By the end of the decade, hospitals were initiating voluntary cost-cutting programs to stave off additional government intervention. Despite all efforts, however, health care expenditures continued to outpace the Consumer Price Index into the 1990s.

The late 1980s and early 1990s ushered in a very different health care environment, and hospitals particularly were hard hit by the changes. On the one hand, the federal government sought to reduce health care costs through cutbacks in subsidy programs and cost-control regulations, such as the Balanced Budget Act of 1997. On the other hand, innovations in health care delivery severely reduced the number of patients serviced by hospitals.

One innovation was preventive health care programs. These fall into two categories: health maintenance organizations (HMOs) and preferred provider organizations (PPOs). An HMO encourages preventive health care by providing medical services as needed for a fixed monthly fee. HMOs typically enter into contractual relationships with designated physicians and hospitals and have been successful in reducing hospital inpatient days and health care expenditures. PPOs establish contractual arrangements between health care providers (physicians and/or hospitals) and large employer groups. Unlike HMOs, PPOs generally offer incentives for using preferred providers rather than restricting individuals to specific hospitals or physicians. PPOs have the same effect on inpatient days and health care expenditures that HMOs have, and Mahon planned to expand the PPO for Pate Memorial Hospital using the Pate Health Clinic as a link to large employers in the downtown area.

A second innovation has been ambulatory health care services and facilities. Ambulatory health care services consist of treatments and practices that consumers use on an episodic or emergency basis. Examples include physical examinations, treatment of minor emergencies (such as cuts, bruises, and minor surgery), and treatment of common illnesses (such as colds and flu).

Ambulatory health care facilities are split into two categories: (1) minor emergency centers, known by acronyms such as FEC (Free-Standing Emergency Clinic) and MEC (Medical Emergency Clinic) and (2) clinics that focus on primary or episodic care.[1] Although regulation is nominal, if a clinic positions itself as an emergency care center, expressing this focus in its name, it generally is required (or pressured by area physicians) to be staffed 24 hours a day by a licensed physician and to have certain basic life support equipment.

Three factors account for the growth of ambulatory health care services. First, advances in medical technology, miniaturization, and portable medical equipment have made more diagnostic and surgical procedures possible outside the traditional

---

[1]*Primary care* is the point of entry into the health care system. It consists of a continuous relationship with a personal physician who takes care of a broad range of medical needs. Primary care physicians include general practitioners, internal medicine and family practice specialists, gynecologists, and pediatricians.

hospital setting. Second, consumers have adopted a more proactive stance on where they will receive their health and medical care. Consumers often choose the hospital at which they wish to be treated, and the incidence of "doctor shopping" is common. Third, the mystique of medical and health care has been altered with the growth of paramedical professionals and standardized treatment practices.

Most of the early centers emphasized quick, convenient, minor emergency care. Many new centers have positioned themselves as convenient, personalized alternatives to primary care physicians' practices. These operations typically employ aggressive, sophisticated marketing techniques, including branding, consistent logos and atmospherics, promotional incentives, and mass-media advertising (giving rise to vernacular designations such as "Doc-in-the-Box" and "McMedical"). Although ambulatory care facilities vary considerably among communities and owners, the following characteristics appear to be universal: (1) branding, (2) extended hours, (3) lower fees than emergency rooms, (4) no appointments necessary, (5) minor emergencies treated, (6) easy access and parking, (7) short waiting times, and (8) credit cards accepted.

PATE MEMORIAL HOSPITAL

Pate Memorial Hospital is a 600-bed, independent, not-for-profit, general hospital located on the southern periphery of a major western city. It is one of six general hospitals in the city and twenty in the county. It is financially stronger than most of the metropolitan-based hospitals in the United States. It is debt-free and has the highest overall occupancy rate among the city's six general hospitals. Nevertheless, the hospital's administration and board of trustees have serious concerns about its patient mix, which reflects unfavorable demographic shifts. Most of the population growth in recent years occurred in the suburban areas to the north, east, and west. These suburban areas attracted young, upwardly mobile families from the city. They also attracted thousands of families from other states—families drawn to the area's dynamic, robust business climate.

As hospitals sprang up to serve the high-growth suburban areas, PMH found itself becoming increasingly dependent on inner-city residents, who have a higher median age and higher incidence of Medicare coverage. Without a stronger stable inflow of short-stay, privately insured patients, the financial health of the hospital would be jeopardized. Accordingly, in the summer of 1998, the board of trustees authorized a study to determine whether to open an ambulatory facility in the downtown area about ten blocks north of the hospital.

PATE HEALTH CLINIC

The charter for the Pate Health Clinic contained four objectives:

1. To expand the hospital's referral base
2. To increase referrals of privately insured patients
3. To establish a liaison with the business community by addressing employers' specific health needs
4. To become self-supporting three years after opening

The specific services to be offered by the PHC would include (1) preventive health care (for example, physical examinations and immunizations), (2) minor-emergency care, (3) referral for acute and chronic health care problems,

(4) specialized employer services (for example, preemployment examinations and treatment of worker's compensation injuries), (5) primary health care services (for example, treatment of common illnesses), and (6) basic X-ray and laboratory tests. The PHC would be open 260 days a year (Monday–Friday) from 8:00 A.M. to 5:00 P.M.

The location for the PHC would be in the Greater West Office and Shopping Complex, situated on the corner of Main and West Streets (see Exhibit 1). This location was chosen because a member of the board of trustees owned the Greater West Complex and was willing to share construction, design, and equipment expenses with the hospital.

During the fall of 1998, construction plans for erecting the PHC were well under way, and the expense budget was developed (see Exhibit 2). During the winter months, PMH commissioned a study to determine the service radius of the PHC, estimate the number of potential users of the PHC, assess responsiveness to the services to be offered by the PHC, and review the operations of suburban ambulatory care clinics. The results indicated that the service area would have a five-block radius, since this was the longest distance office workers would walk.

EXHIBIT 1   Present and Planned Locations of Health Clinics and Service Areas

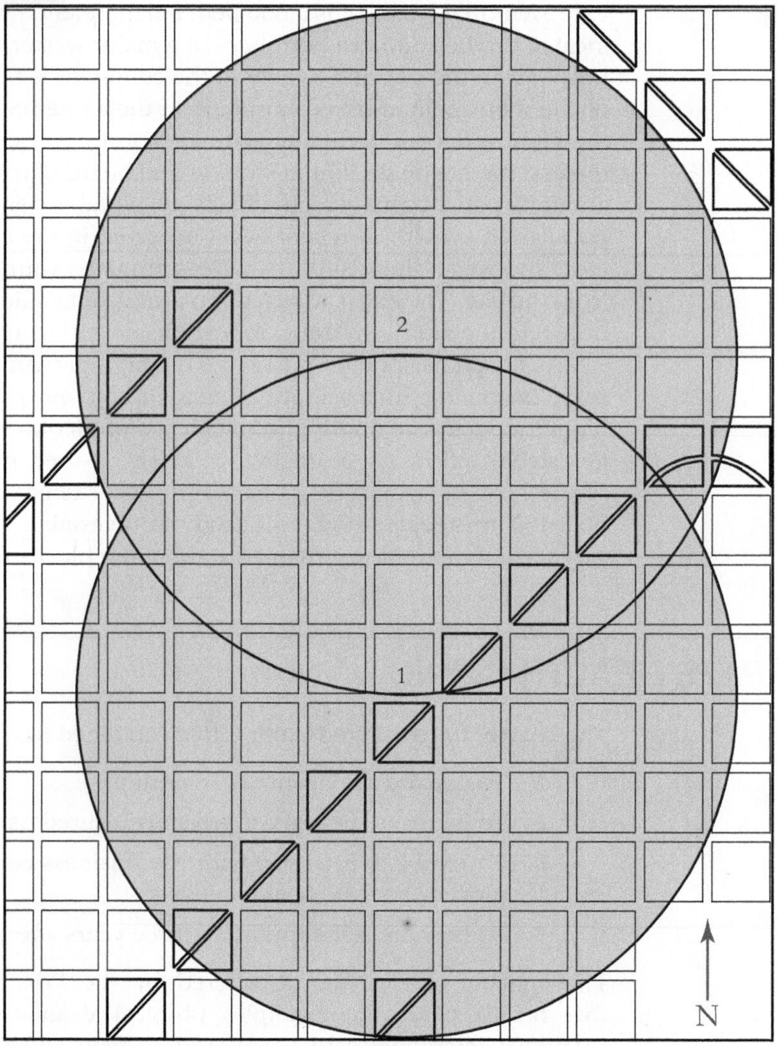

| EXHIBIT 2 | Pate Health Clinic: Preliminary 12-Month Expense Budget |

Item	*Expenditure*
Physician coverage: 260 days times 8 hr/day at $66/hr	$137,280
Professional fees	43,720
Lease	76,500
Supplies	46,894
Utilities	6,630
Personnel, including fringe benefits (director, nurse, laboratory assistant, X-ray technician, receptionist)	168,376
Amortization	30,648
Annual expenditure	$510,048

Note: Expenditures were based on the assumption that the DHC would have 4 visits per hour, or 32 visits per day, when operating at full capacity.

Discussions with city planners indicated the service area contained 11,663 office workers during the 9:00–5:00 Monday–Friday work week. The population in the area was expected to grow 6 percent per year, given new building and renovation activity. Personal interviews with 400 office workers, selected randomly, indicated that 50 percent would use or try the PHC if necessary and that 40 percent of these prospective users would visit the PHC at least once per year (see Exhibit 3 on page 234 for additional findings). Finally, the study of suburban ambulatory care facilities revealed the data shown in Exhibit 4 on page 235. Given their locations in suburban areas, these facilities were not considered direct competition, but their existence indicated that "the city's populace was attuned to ambulatory health care facilities," remarked Worth.

These results were viewed favorably by the board of trustees and "confirmed our belief that an ambulatory facility was needed downtown," noted Worth. The PHC was formally opened May 1, 1999. Except for the publicity surrounding the opening, however, no advertising or other types of promotion were planned. "Several members of the hospital staff shied away from advertising or solicitation, since it hinted at crass commercialism," said Worth.

Performance: May 1999–March 2000

A financial summary of PHC performance through March 2000 is shown in Exhibit 5 on page 236. According to Mahon:

> We are pleased with the performance to date and hope the PHC will be self-supporting by April 2001. We are getting favorable word of mouth from satisfied patients that will generate both new and repeat patients. We expect 410 patient visits in April [2000]. In addition, we have taken steps to improve our financial standing. For example, our bad debts have been costing us 4 percent of gross revenue. With a better credit and collection procedure established just last month, we will reduce this figure to 2 percent. We plan to initiate an 8 percent across-the-board increase in charges on May 1 and will experience only a 5 percent increase in personnel and professional services expenses next year.

Records kept by PMH revealed that the Clinic was realizing its objectives. For example, the referral objective was being met, since the Clinic had made 105 referrals to PMH and produced slightly over $378,000 in revenue and an estimated $30,000 in net profit. Almost all of these patients were privately insured. The service mix, though dominated by treatment of common illnesses and examinations,

EXHIBIT 3	Profile of PHC Service Area, Based on City and Survey Data

1999 Population Estimate (Source: City Planning Department)

Total office worker population in five-block radius	11,663
Expected annual growth, 1998–2003	6.0% yr
Sex breakdown in five-block radius:	
Male	40%
Female	60%

Results from Personal Interviews (January 1998)

Would use/try PHC if necessary for personal illness/exams	50%
Expected frequency of PHC use for personal illness/exams among those saying would use/try if necessary:[a]	
Once every other year	60%
Once per year	25%
Twice per year	10%
Three or more times per year	5%

Selected Cross-Tabulations

	Sex		
	Male	Female	Total
Would you use or try PHC if necessary?			
Yes	88[b]	168	256
No	72	72	144
Total	160	240	400

	Have Regular Physician (Excluding Gynecologist)		
	Yes	No	Total
Would you use or try PHC if necessary?			
Yes	58	198	256
No	130	14	144
Total	188	212	400

[a]No difference between males and females on frequency of use.

[b]Of the 160 males interviewed, 88 (55 percent) said they would use the PHC; 88 of the 256 interviewees (34 percent) who said they would use the DHC were male.

did indicate that the PHC was being used for a variety of purposes. A breakdown of the reasons for patient visits for the first 11 months of operations is as follows:

Personal illness exams	53%
Workers' compensation exam/treatment	25
Employment/insurance physical exams	19
Emergency	3
Total	100%

Patient records indicated that 97 percent of all visits were by first-time users of the PHC and 113 visits were by repeat patients. Approximately 5 percent of the visits in each month from October 1999 through March 2000 were repeat visits. "We are pleased that we are already getting repeat business because it shows we are doing our job," Worth commented. The average revenue per patient visit during

EXHIBIT 4   **Suburban Ambulatory Care Clinics: Operations Profile**

Operations	EmerCenter #1	EmerCenter #2	Adams Industrial Clinic	Health First	Medcenter
Opening	March 1990	November 1992	June 1992	May 1991	June 1997
Patients/year	9,030	6,000	8,400	5,700	8,661
Hours of operation	10:00 A.M.–10:00 P.M. Monday–Friday	10:00 A.M.–10:00 P.M. Monday–Sunday	8:00 A.M.–5:00 P.M. Monday–Friday	5:00 P.M.–11:00 P.M. Monday–Friday 10:00 A.M.–10:00 P.M Saturday–Sunday	8:00 A.M.–8:00 P.M. Monday–Sunday
Physicians/8-hr shift	2	2	2	2	2
Estimated patient visits/hour	3.8/hr	3.4/hr	5.0/hr	3.0/hr	3.0/hr
Estimated average charge per visit	$60.00	$62.00	$76.00	$62.00	$64.00
Services provided:					
Preventive health care			✓	✓	✓
Minor emergencies	✓	✓	✓	✓	✓
Employer services			✓		✓
X-ray/lab tests	✓	✓	✓	✓	✓
Miscellaneous	✓	✓	✓	✓	✓
Use direct-mail advertising	✓	✓		✓	✓

EXHIBIT 5 Pate Health Clinic Financial Summary

	1999								2000			Total Year to Date
	May	June	July	Aug.	Sept.	Oct.	Nov.	Dec.	Jan.	Feb.	Mar.	
Gross revenue	$8,150	$16,774	$17,688	$19,394	$22,412	$22,812	$23,344	$23,516	$25,692	$27,758	$29,430	$236,970
Variable expenses:												
Bad debt	326	710	708	776	896	912	934	940	1,026	1,110	1,176	9,514
Medical/surgical supplies	13,182	1,596	1,870	1,286	2,126	2,426	3,322	1,224	1,052	3,106	2,156	33,346
Drugs	318	108	130	104	610	186	0	112	372	506	152	2,598
Office supplies	1,294	444	1,192	1,436	630	(380)	48	562	934	0	128	6,288
Total variable expense	$15,120	$2,858	$3,900	$3,602	$4,262	$3,144	$4,304	$2,838	$3,384	$4,722	$3,612	$51,746
Contribution	$(6,970)	$13,916	$13,788	$15,792	$18,150	$19,668	$19,040	$20,678	$22,308	$23,036	$25,818	$185,224
Fixed expenses:												
Personnel	15,632	14,918	13,340	11,800	13,632	22,980	14,640	12,498	13,410	17,990	15,288	166,128
Professional services[a]	20,018	13,890	15,564	14,316	14,770	13,600	14,400	14,900	14,484	14,156	14,374	164,472
Facility[b]	6,444	5,074	5,780	5,810	5,244	5,310	5,240	5,226	5,672	5,244	5,438	60,482
Miscellaneous	1,410	214	266	280	476	90	222	152	212	246	114	3,682
Amortization	2,554	2,554	2,554	2,554	2,554	2,554	2,554	2,554	2,554	2,554	2,544	28,074
Total fixed expense	$46,058	$36,650	$37,504	$34,760	$36,676	$44,534	$37,056	$35,330	$36,332	$40,180	$37,758	$422,838
Net gain (loss)	$(53,028)	$(22,734)	$(23,716)	$(18,968)	$(18,526)	$(24,866)	$(18,016)	$(14,652)	$(14,024)	$(17,144)	$(11,940)	$(237,614)
Number of patient visits	109	231	275	277	322	320	321	366	383	463	423	3,490
Number of working days	22	21	21	22	20	23	22	20	22	21	23	237

[a]Includes professional fees paid (see Exhibit 2).

[b]Includes lease payments, utilities, and maintenance.

the first 11 months was $67.90.[2] A breakdown of the average charge by type of visit follows. The average charge was to increase 8 percent on May 1, 2000.

Personal illness/exam	$50 per visit
Workers' compensation exam/treatment	$78 per visit
Employment/insurance physical examination	$94 per visit
Emergency	$134 per visit

In an effort to monitor the performance of the PHC, patients were asked to provide selected health care information as well as demographic information. This information was summarized monthly, and Exhibit 6 on page 238 shows the profile of patients visiting the PHC for the first 11 months of operation. In addition to this information, patients were asked for suggestions on how the PHC could serve the downtown area. Suggestions typically fell into three categories: service hours, services offered, and waiting time. Thirty percent of the patients suggested expanded service hours, with an opening time of 7:00 A.M. and a closing time of 7:00 P.M. One-half of the female patients requested that gynecological services be added.[3] A majority of the patients expressed concern about the waiting time, particularly during the lunch hours (11:00 A.M.–2:00 P.M.). A check of PHC records indicated that 70 percent of patient visits occurred during the 11:00 A.M.–2:00 P.M. period and that one-half of the visits were for personal illnesses.

Worth believed all three suggestions had merit, and she had already explored ways to expand the clinic's hours and reduce waiting time. For example, the reason for her call on the employee benefits director at a local department store was to schedule employee physical examinations in the morning or late afternoon hours to minimize crowding during the lunch hour. Nevertheless, she believed a second licensed physician might be necessary, with one physician working the hours from 7:00 A.M. to 3:00 P.M. and the other working between 11:00 A.M. and 7:00 P.M. The overlap during the lunch period would alleviate waiting times, she thought. Expanding from 9- to 12-hour days would entail a 33 percent increase in personnel costs, however, as well as the cost of another physician.[4]

Worth believed that scheduling was more of a problem than she or the Clinic staff had expected. "You just can't schedule the walk-ins," she said, "and pardon me for saying it, but the people coming in with personal care needs have really caused the congestion." She added that the problem would get worse because the mix of patient needs was moving toward personal illnesses and examinations. "If the trend continues, we should have 20 percent more personal illness visits next year than last year."

Worth believed that gynecological services would be a plus, since 70 percent of the visits were made by women and almost all were under 35 years of age. She said:

> Women should see a gynecologist regularly at least once a year and often twice a year. We could add an additional 2,000 visits per year by having a hospital gynecologist work at the PHC two eight-hour days a week by appointment. An average charge per visit would be about $104 including lab work, and the physician cost would be $70 per hour.

Worth had also given some thought to how the PHC could improve its relations with the business community. Currently, business-initiated visits (workers' compensation examinations and treatments and employment/insurance physical examinations) accounted for 44 percent of the visits to the Clinic. Construction in the downtown area had stimulated worker's compensation activity, and growth

---

[2]The average charge per patient visit excluded the charge for basic x-ray and laboratory tests.
[3]*Gynecology* is that branch of medicine dealing with the female reproductive tract.
[4]Expanded hours would be staffed by part-time personnel, who would receive the same wages as full-time personnel.

EXHIBIT 6   **Profile of Pate Health Clinic Patients: Personal Illness/ Exam Visits Only**

Occupation

Clerical	48%
Professional/technical/managerial	23
Operator	19
Other	10
	100%

Sex

Male	30%
Female	70
	100%

Referral Source

Friend/colleague	35%
Employer	60
Other	5
	100%

Patient Origin

Distance:

One block	25%
Two blocks	28
Three blocks	22
Four blocks	15
Five blocks	8
More than five blocks	2
	100%

Direction:

North of PHC	10%
South of PHC	25
Northeast of PHC	5
Southwest of PHC	15
East of PHC	20
West of PHC	10
Southeast of PHC	10
Northwest of PHC	5
	100%

Have Regular Physician

Yes	18%
No	82
	100%

---

in employment in the five-block service radius had contributed to employment physicals. Worth believed worker's compensation visits would stabilize at about 81 per month and then decline with slowed building activity. Employment physicals accounted for 50 visits per month and were expected to remain at this level with the current operating hours. Insurance physicals were not expected to increase beyond current levels, nor were emergency visits.

Commenting on her calls on businesses, Worth remarked:

> I have actively called on businesses under the guise of community relations because the PMH staff has not sanctioned solicitation. My guess, after talking with business people, is that we could get virtually every new employment physical if we didn't interfere with employment hours and scheduled them before 8:00 A.M. or after 5:00 P.M. Given net new employment in the area and new employees due to turnover, I'd guess we could schedule an additional 65 employment physicals every month—that is, a total of 115 a month.

Worth added that she had also received approval to run an "informational advertisement" in the downtown weekly newspaper each week next year provided that the advertisement did not feature prices or appear to be commercial in its presentation. The weekly advertisement would cost $10,400 per year.

The Possibility of Competition

Worth's calls on local businesses and patient interviews indicated that someone was conducting a survey. She believed that Medcenter, a privately owned suburban ambulatory facility, was the sponsor. Medcenter appeared to be successful in its suburban location (see Exhibit 4) and had a reputation for being an aggressive, marketing-oriented operation. Even though Medcenter did not provide employer services at its suburban location, Worth thought the fact that an employee benefits director had been interviewed suggested that such services might be offered.

The proposed location for the new clinic was five blocks directly north of the PHC. Based on the research for the PHC, Worth estimated that the number of office workers within a five-block radius of the competitive clinic would be 11,652 in 2001 and 13,590 in 2002, and would grow at an annual rate of 7 percent through 2005 because of new construction and building renovation. Worth believed the competitor's service area had the same socioeconomic profile and the same usage and employment characteristics as the PHC's service area.

The overlap in service areas was due to the layout of the downtown area and the availability of high-quality street-level space. According to Worth, "It is possible that a third of our current personal illness/exam patients from the northern portion of our service area will switch to the new clinic and about 40 percent of potential personal illness/exam patients in this area will go to the new location." Worth went on to say that the overlap in service areas would cover 3,424 office workers in 2000.

The effect of the competing clinic on the volume of emergency, workers' compensation, and employment/insurance exam work was more difficult to assess. Worth felt that worker's compensation visits would not be materially affected because most construction was being undertaken in areas south, east, and west of the DHC. Emergency visits were so random that it was not possible to assess what effect the competing clinic would have. The projected volume of employment and insurance physicals could change with the addition of a competing clinic, however. Worth guessed, "At worst, we would see no increase in these types of visits over last year since we have not gotten many visits from this area."

A week after she first heard about the possibility of competition, Worth and Mahon met to review the information on the PHC. Just before Worth finished giving her overview, Mahon's administrative assistant interrupted to tell him he had to leave to catch a plane for a three-day hospital administration conference. As he left the room, Mahon asked Worth to draft a concise analysis of the PHC's position. He also asked her to specify and evaluate the alternatives for the PHC, assuming Medcenter either did or did not open a facility. "Remember," Mahon said, "we have a lot riding on the PHC. Making it work involves not only dollars and cents, but our image in the community as well."

Case

Procter & Gamble, Inc.

Scope

As Gwen Hearst looked at the year-end report, she was pleased to see that Scope held a 32 percent share of the Canadian mouthwash market for 1990. She had been concerned about the inroads that Plax, a prebrushing rinse, had made in the market. Since its introduction in 1988, Plax had gained a 10 percent share of the product category and posed a threat to Scope. As brand manager, Hearst planned, developed, and directed the total marketing effort for Scope, Procter & Gamble's (P&G) brand in the mouthwash market. She was responsible for maximizing the market share, volume, and profitability of the brand.

Until the entry of Plax, brands in the mouthwash market were positioned around two major benefits: fresh breath and killing germs. Plax was positioned around a new benefit—as a "plaque fighter"—and indications were that other brands, such as Listerine, were going to promote this benefit. The challenge for Hearst was to develop a strategy that would ensure the continued profitability of Scope in the face of these competitive threats. Her specific task was to prepare a marketing plan for P&G's mouthwash business for the next three years. It was early February 1991, and she would be presenting the plan to senior management in March.

 COMPANY BACKGROUND

Based on a philosophy of providing products of superior quality and value that best fill the needs of consumers, Procter & Gamble is one of the most successful consumer goods companies in the world. The company markets its brands in more than 140 countries and had net earnings of $1.6 billion in 1990. The Canadian subsidiary contributed $1.4 billion in sales and $100 million in net earnings in 1990. It was recognized as a leader in the Canadian packaged-goods industry, and its consumer brands led in most of the categories in which the company competed.

Between 1987 and 1990, worldwide sales of P&G had increased by $8 billion and net earnings by $1.3 billion. P&G executives attributed the company's success to a variety of factors, including the ability to develop truly innovative products to meet consumers' needs. Exhibit 1 contains the statement of purpose and strategy of the Canadian subsidiary.

This case was prepared by Professors Gordon H. G. McDougall and Franklin Ramsoomair, of the Wilfrid Laurier University, as a basis for class discussion and is not designed to illustrate effective or ineffective handling of an administrative situation. Used with permission.

| EXHIBIT 1 | A Statement of Purpose and Strategy: Procter & Gamble, Canada |

We will provide products of superior quality and value that best fill the needs of consumers.

We will achieve that purpose through an organization and a working environment which attracts the finest people; fully develops and challenges our individual talents; encourages our free and spirited collaboration to drive the business ahead; and maintains the Company's historic principles of integrity and doing the right thing.

We will build a profitable business in Canada. We will apply P&G worldwide learning and resources to maximize our success rate. We will concentrate our resources on the most profitable categories and on unique, important Canadian market opportunities. We will also contribute to the development of outstanding people and innovative business ideas for worldwide company use.

We will reach our business goals and achieve optimum cost efficiencies through continuing innovation, strategic planning, and the continuous pursuit of excellence in everything we do.

We will continuously stay ahead of competition while aggressively defending our established profitable businesses against major competitive challenges despite short-term profit consequences.

Through the successful pursuit of our commitment, we expect our brands to achieve leadership share and profit positions and that, as a result, our business, our people, our shareholders, and the communities in which we live and work, will prosper.

Source: Company records.

P&G Canada has five operating divisions, organized by product category. The divisions, and some of the major brands, are:

1. *Paper products:* Royale, Pampers, Luvs, Attends, Always
2. *Food and beverage:* Duncan Hines, Crisco, Pringles, Sunny Delight
3. *Beauty care:* Head & Shoulders, Pantene, Pert, Vidal Sassoon, Clearasil, Clarion, Cover Girl, Max Factor, Oil of Olay, Noxzema, Secret
4. *Health care:* Crest, Scope, Vicks, Pepto-Bismol, Metamucil
5. *Laundry and cleaning:* Tide, Cheer, Bounce, Bold, Oxydol, Joy, Cascade, Comet, Mr. Clean

Each division had its own brand management, sales, finance, product development and operations line management groups and was evaluated as a profit center. Typically, within each division a brand manager was assigned to each brand (for example, Scope). Hearst was in the health care division and reported to the associate advertising manager for oral care, who, in turn, reported to the general manager of the division. After completing her business degree (BBA) at a well-known Ontario business school in 1986, Hearst had joined P&G as a brand assistant. In 1987 she became the assistant brand manager for Scope, and in 1988 she was promoted to brand manager. Hearst's rapid advancement at P&G reflected the confidence that her managers had in her abilities.

 ## THE CANADIAN MOUTHWASH MARKET

Until 1987, on a unit basis the mouthwash market had grown an average of 3 percent per year for the previous 12 years. In 1987, it experienced a 26 percent increase with the introduction of new flavors such as peppermint. Since then, the growth rate had declined to a level of 5 percent in 1990 (Exhibit 2 on page 242).

EXHIBIT 2	Canadian Mouthwash Market				
	1986	*1987*	*1988*	*1989*	*1990*
Total retail sales (millions)	$43.4	$54.6	$60.2	$65.4	$68.6
Total factory sales (millions)	$34.8	$43.5	$48.1	$52.2	$54.4
Total unit sales (thousands)[a]	863	1,088	1,197	1,294	1,358
(% change)	3	26	10	8	5
(% change—"breath only")[b]	3	26	0	3	5
Penetration (%)[c]	65	70	75	73	75
Usage (number of times per week)[d]	2.0	2.2	2.3	2.4	3.0

[a]One unit or statistical case equals 10 liters or 352 fluid ounces of mouthwash.

[b]Excludes Plax and other prebrushing rinses.

[c]Percentage of households having at least one brand in home.

[d]For each adult household member.

Source: Company records.

The mouthwash market was initially developed by Warner-Lambert with its pioneer brand Listerine. Positioned as a therapeutic germ-killing mouthwash that eliminated bad breath, it dominated the market until the entry of Scope in 1967. Scope, a green, mint-tasting mouthwash, was positioned as a great-tasting, mouth-refreshing brand that provided bad-breath protection. It was the first brand that offered both effective protection against bad breath and a better taste than other mouthwashes. Its advertising focused, in part, on a perceived weakness of Listerine—medicine breath (for example, "Scope fights bad breath. Don't let the good taste fool you")—and in 1976, Scope became the market leader in Canada.

In 1977, Warner-Lambert launched Listermint mouthwash as a direct competitor to Scope. Like Scope, it was a green, mint-tasting mouthwash and positioned as a "good tasting mouthwash that fights bad breath." Within a year it had achieved a 12 percent market share, primarily at the expense of Listerine and smaller brands in the market.

In the 1970s, Merrell Dow, a large pharmaceutical firm, launched Cepacol, which was positioned very close to Listerine. It achieved and held approximately 14 percent of the market in the early 1980s.

During the 1980s, the major competitive changes in the Canadian mouthwash market were:

- Listerine, which had been marketed primarily on a "bad breath" strategy, began shifting its position and in 1988 introduced the claim "Fights plaque and helps prevent inflamed gums caused by plaque." In the United States, Listerine gained the American Dental Association seal for plaque but, as yet, did not have the seal in Canada.

- Listermint added fluoride during the early 1980s and added the Canadian Dental Association seal for preventing cavities in 1983. More recently, Listermint had downplayed fluoride and removed the seal.

- In early 1987, flavors were introduced by a number of brands including Scope, Listermint, and various store brands. This greatly expanded the market in 1987 but did not significantly change the market shares held by the major brands.

- Colgate Fluoride Rinse was launched in 1988. With the seal from the Canadian Dental Association for cavities, it claimed that "Colgate's new fluoride rinse fights cavities. And, it has a mild taste that encourages children to rinse longer and more often." Colgate's share peaked at 2 percent and then declined. There were rumors that Colgate was planning to discontinue the brand.

- In 1988, Merrell Dow entered a licensing agreement with Strategic Brands to market Cepacol in Canada. Strategic Brands, a Canadian firm that markets a variety of consumer household products, had focused its efforts on gaining greater distribution for Cepacol and promoting it on the basis of price.

- In 1988, Plax was launched on a new and different platform. Its launch and immediate success caught many in the industry by surprise.

 ## THE INTRODUCTION OF PLAX

Plax was launched in Canada in late 1988 on a platform quite different from the traditional mouthwashes. First, instead of the usual use occasion of "after brushing," it called itself a "prebrushing" rinse. The user rinses before brushing, and Plax's detergents are supposed to help loosen plaque to make brushing especially effective. Second, the product benefits were not breath-focused. Instead, it claimed that "Rinsing with Plax, then brushing normally, removes up to three times more plaque than just brushing alone."

Pfizer Inc., a pharmaceutical firm, launched Plax in Canada with a promotion campaign that was estimated to be close to $4 million. The campaign, which covered the last three months of 1988 and all of 1989, consisted of advertising estimated at $3 million and extensive sales promotions, including (1) trial-size display in three drugstore chains ($60,000), (2) co-op mail couponing to 2.5 million households ($160,000), (3) an instantly redeemable coupon offer ($110,000), (4) a professional mailer to drug and supermarket chains ($30,000), and (5) a number of price reductions ($640,000). Plax continued to support the brand with advertising expenditures of approximately $1.2 million in 1990. In 1990, Plax held a 10 percent share of the total market.

When Plax was launched in the United States, it claimed that using Plax "removed up to 300 percent more plaque than just brushing." This claim was challenged by mouthwash competitors and led to an investigation by the Better Business Bureau. The investigation found that the study on which Plax based its claim had panelists limit their toothbrushing to just 15 seconds—and didn't let them use toothpaste. A further study, where people were allowed to brush in their "usual manner" and with toothpaste, showed no overall difference in the level of plaque buildup between those using Plax and a control group that did not use Plax. Plax then revised its claim to "three times more plaque than just brushing alone." Information on plaque is contained in this case's Appendix.

 ## THE CURRENT SITUATION

In preparing for the strategic plan, Gwen Hearst reviewed the available information for the mouthwash market and Scope. As shown in Exhibit 2, in 1990, 75 percent of Canadian households used one or more mouthwash brands, and, on average, usage was three times per week for each adult household member. Company market research revealed that users could be segmented on frequency of use; "heavy" users (once per day or more) comprised 40 percent of all users, "medium" users (two to six times a week) comprised 45 percent, and "light" users (less than once a week) comprised 15 percent. No information was available on the usage habits of prebrushing rinse users. Nonusers currently don't buy mouthwash because they either (1) don't believe they get bad breath, (2) believe that brushing their teeth is adequate, and/or (3) find alternatives like gums and mints more convenient. The most important reasons why consumers use mouthwash are:

Most Important Reason for Using a Mouthwash	%
It is part of my basic oral hygiene	40*
It gets rid of bad breath	40
It kills germs	30
It makes me feel more confident	20
To avoid offending others	25

*Multiple reasons allowed.

During 1990, a survey was conducted of mouthwash users' images of the major brands in the market. Respondents were asked to rate the brands on a number of attributes, and the results show that Plax had achieved a strong image on the "removes plaque/healthier teeth and gums" attributes (Exhibit 3).

EXHIBIT 3 Consumer Perceptions of Brand Images

	All Users[a]					
Attributes	Cepacol	Colgate	Listerine	Listermint	Plax	Scope
Reduces bad breath	. . .	. . .	. . .	. . .	—	. . .
Kills germs	+	. . .	+	. . .	. . .	—
Removes plaque	. . .	. . .	. . .	. . .	+	—
Healthier teeth and gums	. . .	. . .	. . .	. . .	+	—
Good for preventing colds	. . .	. . .	+	. . .	. . .	. . .
Recommended by doctors/dentists	. . .	—	. . .	. . .	+	. . .
Cleans your mouth well	. . .	. . .	. . .	. . .	. . .	. . .

	Brand Users[b]					
Attributes	Cepacol	Colgate	Listerine	Listermint	Plax	Scope
Reduces bad breath	+	—	+	+	—	+
Kills germs	+	. . .	+	—	—	. . .
Removes plaque	—	+	+	—	+	—
Healthier teeth and gums	. . .	+	+	—	+	—
Good for preventing colds	+	—	+	—	—	—
Recommended by doctors/dentists	+	+	+	—	+	—

[a]Includes anyone who uses mouthwash. Respondents asked to rate all brands (even those they haven't used) on the attributes. A "+" means this brand scores *higher than average*. A ". . ." means this brand scored *about average*. A "—" means this brand scored *below average*. For example, Cepacol is perceived by those who use mouthwash as a brand that is good/better than most at "preventing germs."

[b]Includes only the users of that brand. For example, Cepacol is perceived by those whose "usual brand" is Cepacol as a brand that is good/better than most at "reducing bad breath."

Source: Company records.

| EXHIBIT 4 | Canadian Mouthwash Market Shares |

| | Units | | | 1990 Average | |
	1988	1989	1990	Food	Drug
Scope	33.0%	33.0%	32.3%	42.0%	27.0%
Listerine	15.2	16.1	16.6	12.0	19.0
Listermint	15.2	9.8	10.6	8.0	12.0
Cepacol	13.6	10.6	10.3	9.0	11.0
Colgate oral rinse	1.4	1.2	0.5	0.4	0.5
Plax	1.0	10.0	10.0	8.0	11.0
Store brands	16.0	15.4	16.0	18.0	15.0
Miscellaneous other	4.6	3.9	3.7	2.6	4.5
Total	100.0%	100.0%	100.0%	100.0%	100.0%
Retail sales (000,000)	$60.2	$65.4	$68.6	$24.0	$44.6

Source: Company records.

Market share data revealed there was a substantial difference in the share held by Scope in food stores, 42 percent (for example, supermarkets) versus drugstores, 27 percent (Exhibit 4). Approximately 65 percent of all mouthwash sales went through drugstores, while 35 percent went through food stores. Recently, wholesale clubs, such as Price Club and Costco, were accounting for a greater share of mouthwash sales.[1] Typically, these clubs carried Cepacol, Scope, Listerine, and Plax.

Competitive data were also collected for advertising expenditures and retail prices. As shown in Exhibit 5, total media spending of all brands in 1990 was $5 million, with Scope, Listerine, and Plax accounting for 90 percent of all advertising. Retail prices were calculated based on a 750-milliliter bottle, both Listerine

| EXHIBIT 5 | Competitive Market Data, 1990 |

Advertising Expenditures ($000s)

Scope	$1,700
Listerine	1,600
Plax	1,200
Listermint	330
Cepacol	170

Media Plans

	Number of Weeks on Air	GRPs[a]
Scope	35	325
Listerine	25	450
Plax	20	325

[1]Wholesale clubs were included in food store sales.

(continued)

EXHIBIT 5 **(Continued)**

	Food Stores	*Drugstores*
Scope	98	84
Listerine	129	97
Listermint	103	84
Colgate	123	119
Plax	170	141
Store brand	58	58
Cepacol	84	81
Total Market[b]	100	100

[a]GRP (Gross Rating Points) is a measurement of advertising impact derived by multiplying the number of persons exposed to an advertisement by the average number of exposures per person. The GRPs reported are monthly.

[b]An average weighted index of the retail prices of all mouthwash brands is calculated and indexed at 100 for both food stores and drugstores. Scope is priced slightly below this index in food stores and about 16 percent below in drugstores.

Source: Company records.

and Plax were priced at a higher level in food stores, and Plax was priced at a premium in drugstores.

Information on the U.S. market for 1989 was also available (see Exhibit 6). In contrast to Canada, Listerine held the dominant share in the U.S. market. Since early 1989, Listerine had been advertised heavily in the United States as "the only nonprescription mouthwash accepted by the American Dental Association for its significant help in preventing and reducing plaque and gingivitis." In clinical tests in the United States, Listerine significantly reduced plaque scores by roughly 20 to 35 percent, with a similar reduction in gingivitis. In Canada, the 1990 advertising campaign included the claim that Listerine has been clinically proven to "help prevent inflamed and irritated gums caused by plaque build-up." Listerine's formula relied on four essential oils—menthol, eucalyptol, thymol, and methyl salicylate—all derivatives of phenol, a powerful antiseptic.

Listerine had not received the consumer product seal given by the Canadian Dental Association (CDA) because the association was not convinced a mouthrinse could be of therapeutic value. The CDA was currently reviewing American tests for several products sold in Canada. In fact, any proposed changes to the formulation of mouthwashes or advertising claims could require approval from various regulatory agencies.

EXHIBIT 6 **Canada–U.S. Market Share Comparison, 1989 (% Units)**

Brands	*Canada*	*United States*
Scope	33.0	21.6
Listerine	16.1	28.7
Listermint	9.8	4.5
Cepacol	10.6	3.6
Plax	10.0	9.6

Source: Company records.

THE REGULATORY ENVIRONMENT

1. *Health Protection Branch:* This government body classifies products into "drug status" or "cosmetic status" based on both the product's action on bodily functions and its advertising claims. Drug products are those that affect a bodily function (for example, prevent cavities or prevent plaque buildup). For "drug status" products, all product formulations, packaging, copy, and advertising must be pre-cleared by the Health Protection Branch (HPB), with guidelines that are very stringent. Mouthwashes like Scope that claim to only prevent bad breath are considered as "cosmetic status." However, if any claims regarding inhibition of plaque formation are made the product reverts to "drug status," and all advertising is scrutinized.

2. *The Canadian Dental Association:* Will, upon request of the manufacturer, place its seal of recognition on products that have demonstrated efficacy against cavities or against plaque/gingivitis. However, those products with the seal of recognition must submit their packaging and advertising to the CDA for approval. The CDA and the American Dental Association (ADA) are two separate bodies and are independent of each other and don't always agree on issues. The CDA, for example, would not provide a "plaque/gingivitis" seal unless clinical studies demonstrating actual gum health improvements were done.

3. *Saccharin/Cyclamate sweeteners:* All mouthwashes contain an artificial sweetener. In Canada, cyclamate is used as the sweetener, as saccharin is considered a banned substance. In contrast, the United States uses saccharin because cyclamate is prohibited. Thus, despite the fact that many of the same brands compete in both Canada and the United States, the formula in each country is different.

 ## THE THREE-YEAR PLAN

In preparing the three-year plan for Scope, a team had been formed within P&G to examine various options. The team included individuals from product development (PDD), manufacturing, sales, market research, finance, advertising, and operations. Over the past year, the team had completed a variety of activities relating to Scope.

The key issue, in Hearst's mind, was how P&G should capitalize on the emerging market segment within the rinse category that focused more on "health-related benefits" than the traditional breath strategy of Scope. Specifically with the launch of Plax, the mouthwash market had segmented itself along the "breath-only" brands (like Scope) and those promising other benefits. Plax, in positioning itself as a prebrushing rinse, was not seen as, nor did it taste like, a "breath refreshment" mouthwash like Scope.

Gwen Hearst believed that a line extension positioned against Plax, a recent entry into the market, made the most sense. If the mouthwash market became more segmented, and if these other brands grew, her fear was that P&G would be left with a large share of a segment that focused only on "breath" and hence might decline. However, she also knew that there were questions regarding both the strategic and financial implications of such a proposal. In recent meetings, other ideas had been proposed, including "doing nothing" and looking at claims other than "breath" that might be used by Scope instead of adding a new product. Several team members questioned whether there was any real threat, as Plax was positioned very differently from Scope. As she considered the alternatives, Hearst reviewed the activities of the team and the issues that had been raised by various team members.

Product Development

In product tests on Scope, PDD had demonstrated that Scope reduced plaque better than brushing alone because of antibacterial ingredients contained in Scope. However, as yet P&G did not have a clinical database to convince the HPB to allow Scope to extend these claims into the prevention of inflamed gums (as Listerine does).

PDD had recently developed a new prebrushing rinse product that performed as well as Plax but did not work any better than Plax against plaque reduction. In fact, in its testing of Plax itself, PDD was actually unable to replicate the plaque reduction claim made by Pfizer that "rinsing with Plax, then brushing normally removes up to three times more plaque than brushing alone." The key benefit of P&G's prebrushing rinse was that it did taste better than Plax. Other than that, it had similar aesthetic qualities to Plax—qualities that made its "in-mouth" experience quite different from that of Scope.

The product development people in particular were concerned about Hearst's idea of launching a line extension because it was a product that was only equal in efficacy to Plax and to placebo rinses for plaque reduction. Traditionally, P&G had only launched products that focused on unmet consumer needs—typically superior performing products. However, Gwen had pointed out, because the new product offered similar efficacy at a better taste, this was similar to the situation when Scope was originally launched. Some PDD members were also concerned that if they couldn't replicate Plax's clinical results with P&G's stringent test methodology, and if the product possibly didn't provide any greater benefit than rinsing with any liquid, then P&G's image and credibility with dental professionals might be impacted. There was debate on this issue, as others felt that as long as the product did encourage better oral hygiene, it did provide a benefit. As further support they noted that many professionals did recommend Plax. Overall, PDD's preference was to not launch a new product but, instead, to add plaque-reduction claims to Scope. The basic argument was that it was better to protect the business that P&G was already in than to launch a completely new entity. If a line extension was pursued, a product test costing $20,000 would be required.

Sales

The sales people had seen the inroads Plax had been making in the marketplace and believed that Scope should respond quickly. They had one key concern. As stockkeeping units (SKUs) had begun to proliferate in many categories, the retail industry had become much more stringent regarding what it would accept. Now, to be carried on store shelves, a brand must be seen as different enough (or unique) from the competition to build incremental purchases—otherwise retailers argued that category sales volume would simply be spread over more units. When this happened, a retail outlet's profitability was reduced because inventory costs were higher, but no additional sales revenue was generated. When a new brand was viewed as not generating more sales, retailers might still carry the brand by replacing units within the existing line (for example, drop shelf facings of Scope), or the manufacturer could pay approximately $50,000 per stock-keeping unit in carrying fees to add the new brand.

Market Research

Market research (MR) had worked extensively with Hearst to test the options with consumers. Its work to date had shown:

1. A plaque reassurance on current Scope (that is, "Now Scope fights plaque") did not seem to increase competitive users' desire to purchase Scope. This meant that it was unlikely to generate additional volume, but it could prevent current users from switching.

   MR also cautioned that adding "reassurances" to a product often takes time before the consumer accepts the idea and then acts on it. The issue in Hearst's mind was whether the reassurance would ever be enough. At best it might stabilize the business, she thought, but would it grow behind such a claim?

2. A "Better-Tasting Prebrushing Dental Rinse" product did research well among Plax users, but did not increase purchase intent among people not currently using a dental rinse. MR's estimate was that a brand launched on this positioning would likely result in approximately a 6.5 percent share of the total mouthwash and "rinse" market on an ongoing basis. Historically, it had taken approximately two years to get to the ongoing level. However, there was no way for them to accurately assess potential Scope cannibalization. "Use your judgment," they had said. However, they cautioned that although it was a product for a different usage occasion, it was unlikely to be 100 percent incremental business. Hearst's best rough guess was that this product might cannibalize somewhere between 2 and 9 percent of Scope's sales. An unresolved issue was the product's name—if it were launched, should it be under the Scope name or not? One fear was that if the Scope name was used it would either "turn off" loyal users who saw Scope as a breath refreshment product or confuse them.

   MR had questioned Hearst as to whether she had really looked at all angles to meet her objective. Because much of this work had been done quickly, they wondered whether there weren't some other benefits Scope could talk about that would interest consumers and hence achieve the same objective. They suggested that Hearst look at other alternatives beyond just "a plaque reassurance on Scope" or a "line extension positioned as a 'Better-Tasting Prebrushing Rinse.'"

Finance

The point of view from finance was mixed. On the one hand, Plax commanded a higher dollar price per liter and so it made sense that a new rinse might be a profitable option. On the other hand, they were concerned about the capital costs and the marketing costs that might be involved to launch a line extension. One option would be to source the product from a U.S. plant where the necessary equipment already existed. If the product was obtained from the United States delivery costs would increase by $1 per unit. Scope's current marketing and financial picture is shown in Exhibits 7 and 8 on page 250 and an estimate of Plax's financial picture is provided in Exhibit 9 on page 251.

EXHIBIT 7 **Scope Historical Financials**

Year	1988		1989		1990	
Total market size (Units) (000)	1,197		1,294		1,358	
Scope market share	33.0%		33.0%		32.4%	
Scope volume (Units) (000)	395		427		440	
	$(000)	**$/Unit**	**$(000)**	**$/Unit**	**$(000)**	**$/Unit**
Sales	16,767	42.45	17,847	41.80	18,150	41.25
COGS	10,738	27.18	11,316	26.50	11,409	25.93
Gross margin	6,029	15.27	7,299	15.30	6,741	15.32

Scope Marketing Plan Inputs

Scope "Going" Marketing Spending

Year	1990	1989	1988
Advertising (000)	$1,700	—	—
Promotion (000)	1,460	—	—
Total (000)	$3,160	$3,733	$2,697

Marketing Input Costs

Advertising:		(See Exhibit 5)
Promotion:	Samples	(Including Distribution): $0.45/piece
	Mailed couponing	$10.00 per 1,000 for printing distribution
		$0.17 handling per redeemed coupon (beyond face value) redemption rates: 10% to 15%
	In-store promotion	$200/store (fixed)
		$0.17 handling per redeemed coupon (beyond face value) redemption rates: 85% +

Source: Company records.

EXHIBIT 8 **Scope 1990 Financials**

	$(000)	$/Unit
Net sales[a]	18,150	41.25
Ingredients	3,590	8.16
Packaging	2,244	5.10
Manufacturing[b]	3,080	7.00
Delivery	1,373	3.12
Miscellaneous[c]	1,122	2.55
Cost of goods sold	11,409	25.93
Gross margin	6,741	15.32

[a]Net sales = P&G revenues.

[b]Manufacturing: 50 percent of manufacturing cost is fixed of which $200,000 is depreciation; 20 percent of manufacturing cost is labor.

[c]Miscellaneous: 75 percent of miscellaneous cost is fixed. General office overhead is $1,366,000. Taxes are 40 percent. Currently the plant operates on a five-day one-shift operation. P&G's weighted average cost of capital is 12 percent. Total units sold in 1990 were 440,000.

Source: Company records.

EXHIBIT 9	Plax Financial Estimates ($/Unit)	
Net Sales		65.09
COGS		
Ingredients		6.50
Packaging		8.30
Manufacturing		6.50
Delivery		3.00
Miscellaneous		1.06
Total		25.36

Notes: General overhead costs estimated at $5.88/unit.

Source: P&G estimates.

Purchasing

The purchasing manager had reviewed the formula for the line extension and had estimated that the ingredients cost would increase by $2.55 per unit due to the addition of new ingredients. But, because one of the ingredients was very new, finance felt that the actual ingredient change might vary by ± 50 percent. Packaging costs would be $0.30 per unit higher owing to the fact that the setup charges would be spread over a smaller base.

Advertising Agency

The advertising agency felt that making any new claims for Scope was a huge strategic shift for the brand. They favored a line extension. Scope's strategy had always been "breath refreshment and good tasting" focused, and they saw the plaque claims as very different, with potentially significant strategic implications. The one time they had focused advertising only on taste and didn't reinforce breath efficacy, share fell. They were concerned that the current Scope consumer could be confused if plaque or any "nonbreath" claims were added and that Scope could actually lose market share if this occurred. They also pointed out that trying to communicate two different ideas in one commercial was very difficult. They believed the line extension was a completely different product from Scope with a different benefit and use occasion. In their minds, a line extension would need to be supported on a going basis separately from Scope.

 ## WHAT TO RECOMMEND?

Hearst knew the business team had thought long and hard about the issue. She knew that management was depending on the Scope business team to come up with the right long-term plan for P&G—even if that meant not introducing the new product. However, she felt there was too much risk associated with P&G's long-term position in oral rinses if nothing was done. There was no easy answer—and compounding the exigencies of the situation was the fact that the business team had differing points of view. She was faced with the dilemma of providing recommendations about Scope, but also needed to ensure that there was alignment and commitment from the business team, or senior management would be unlikely to agree to the proposal.

APPENDIX

Plaque

Plaque is a soft, sticky film that coats teeth within hours of brushing and may eventually harden into tartar. To curb gum disease—which over 90 percent of Canadians suffer at some time—plaque must be curbed. Research has shown that, without brushing, within 24 hours a film (plaque) starts to spread over teeth and gums and, over days, becomes a sticky, gelatinous mat, which the plaque bacteria spin from sugars and starches. As the plaque grows it becomes home to yet more bacteria—dozens of strains. A mature plaque is about 75 percent bacteria; the remainder consists of organic solids from saliva, water, and other cells shed from soft oral tissues.

As plaque bacteria digest food, they also manufacture irritating malodorous by-products, all of which can harm a tooth's supporting tissues as they seep into the crevice below the gum line. Within 10 to 21 days, depending on the person, signs of gingivitis—the mildest gum disease—first appear, gums deepen in color, swell, and lose their normally tight, arching contour around teeth. Such gingivitis is entirely reversible. It can disappear within a week after regular brushing and flossing are resumed. But when plaque isn't kept under control, gingivitis can be the first step down toward periodontitis, the more advanced gum disease in which bone and other structures that support the teeth become damaged. Teeth can loosen and fall out—or require extraction.

The traditional and still best approach to plaque control is careful and thorough brushing and flossing to scrub teeth clean of plaque. Indeed, the antiplaque claims that toothpastes carry are usually based on the product's ability to clean teeth mechanically, with brushing. Toothpastes contain abrasives, detergent, and foaming agents, all of which help the brush do its work.

Case

Frito-Lay Company

Cracker Jack

In mid-July 1997, Lynne Peissig, vice president and general manager for New Ventures at the Frito-Lay Company, a division of PepsiCo, Inc., assembled the business team responsible for studying the possible acquisition of Cracker Jack from Borden Foods Corporation. Cracker Jack had been owned by Borden since 1964 and was one of the oldest and best-known trademarks in the United States. Borden's intention to sell the Cracker Jack brand and related assets had become public in June 1997. Peissig and the New Ventures Division initiated a study of the Cracker Jack business potential within days of the announcement.

The purpose of the all-day meeting was to (1) consolidate the findings of the business team, (2) outline a plan for how Cracker Jack might be marketed as a Frito-Lay brand, and (3) estimate the "fair market value" of the Cracker Jack business. The valuation would assist senior PepsiCo executives in determining an acquisition price should they decide to submit a bid on the Cracker Jack brand and related assets.

The effort of the business team benefited from the involvement of Frito-Lay brand marketing, sales, distribution, manufacturing, finance, legal, and research and development personnel and PepsiCo merger and acquisition staff working with the New Ventures Division. Peissig was scheduled to deliver a formal presentation and recommendation to senior PepsiCo executives within two weeks. She knew that the marketing issues identified, the plan outline, and the financial valuation by the business team would carry considerable weight in her recommendation to pursue or pass on the business opportunity made possible by the acquisition of the Cracker Jack brand and related assets.

The cooperation of Frito-Lay, Inc. in the preparation of this case is gratefully acknowledged. BAKED LAY'S, BAKED TOSTITOS, CHEETOS, DORITOS, FRITOS, FUNYUNS, LAY'S, ROLD GOLD, RUFFLES, SANTITAS, SUN CHIPS, TOSTITOS, SMARTFOOD, and GRANDMA'S are trademarks used by the Frito-Lay Company. After the acquisition, CRACKER JACK, SAILOR JACK, and BINGO would be trademarks used by the Frito-Lay Company. This case was prepared by Professor Roger A. Kerin, of the Edwin L. Cox School of Business, Southern Methodist University, with the assistance of Daniel Goe and Rebecca Kaufman, graduate students, as a basis for class discussion and is not designed to illustrate effective or ineffective handling of an administrative situation. Certain company information, including names of Frito-Lay executives, are disguised and not useful for research purposes. Copyright © 1999 by Roger A. Kerin. No part of this case may be reproduced without written permission of the copyright holder.

FRITO-LAY COMPANY

Frito-Lay Company is a division of PepsiCo, Inc. Frito-Lay recorded an operating profit of $1.63 billion on net sales of $9.68 billion in 1996, which represented 31 percent of PepsiCo's net sales and 60 percent of PepsiCo's operating profit. The sales and operating profit compounded annual growth rate for Frito-Lay was 13 percent for the five-year period, 1991 to 1996. Frito-Lay Company is composed of Frito-Lay North America and Frito-Lay International. Frito-Lay North America, consisting of operations in the United States and Canada, recorded 68 percent of company sales and 79 percent of company operating profit in 1996.

Company Background

Frito-Lay is a worldwide leader in the manufacturing and marketing of snacks. Well-known company brands include Lay's and Ruffles potato chips, Fritos corn chips, Doritos, Tostitos, and Santitas tortilla chips, Cheetos cheese-flavored snacks, and Rold Gold pretzels. Other well-known Frito-Lay brands include Sun Chips Multigrain Snacks and Funyuns onion-flavored snacks. In addition, the company markets a line of dips, salsas, nuts, peanut butter and cheese-filled sandwich crackers, processed beef sticks, Smartfood brand ready-to-eat popcorn, and Grandma's brand cookies.

The company is the leading manufacturer of snack chips in the United States, capturing 54 percent of the retail sales in this category in 1996. Nine of Frito-Lay's snack chips are among the top 10 best-selling snack brands in U.S. supermarkets (see Exhibit 1). Doritos tortilla chips and Lay's and Ruffles potato chips each have the distinction of being the only snack chips with over $1 billion in retail sales in the world.

| **EXHIBIT 1** | **Top-Selling Snack Chip Items in U.S. Supermarkets (Retail Sales $ in Millions)** |

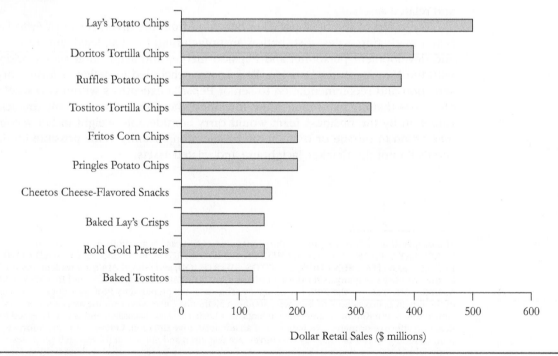

Source: 1996 PepsiCo, Inc Annual Report.

A major source of volume growth for Frito-Lay in the 1990s was due to the introduction of "better-for-you" low-fat and no-fat snacks. These snacks, including Baked Lay's potato crisps, Baked Tostitos tortilla chips, and Rold Gold pretzels, accounted for 47 percent of Frito-Lay's total pound volume growth in 1995 and 1996, and 40 percent of pound volume growth in 1994. Better-for-you products represented 15 percent of Frito-Lay's total snack volume in 1996, up from 5 percent in 1993.

Frito-Lay's U.S. snack food business spans every aspect of snack food production and distribution, from agriculture to stocking retailer shelves. During 1996 in the United States alone, Frito-Lay used 2.7 billion pounds of potatoes, one billion pounds of corn, and over 15 million pounds of cheese to produce its products. The company has 45 manufacturing plants in 26 states, including the world's largest snack food plant in Frankfort, Indiana, and operates more than 1,800 warehouses and distribution facilities. Frito-Lay employs 17,500 salespeople—the largest store-door-delivery sales force in the world—who make 750,000 sales and delivery calls on approximately 350,000 retail store customers each week. Frito-Lay's products receive constant attention from the company's sales force, which ensures constant replenishment of fresh product and proper facings of products on store shelves. Supermarkets and grocery stores accounted for more than 50 percent of Frito-Lay's total U.S. retail sales in 1996, followed by convenience stores (15 percent), mass merchandise/warehouse/club stores (11 percent), vending and food service operators (8 percent), and other retailers and institutions (10 percent).

Frito-Lay consistently ranks among the leading national advertisers in the United States, both in terms of dollars spent and creative execution. The company also uses trade and consumer promotions and sponsors special events, such as the Tostitos Fiesta Bowl postseason collegiate football game.

New Ventures Division

The New Ventures Division at Frito-Lay originated in December 1996 with a well-defined mission:

> To drive significant Frito-Lay growth by seeking and creating new business platforms and products which combine the best of Frito-Lay advantages with high-impact consumer food solutions.

According to Casey Joseph, Frito-Lay's senior vice president–worldwide marketing, the primary purpose of the New Ventures Division was to create meaningful growth outside of Frito-Lay's already successful existing snack businesses, and secondarily augment ongoing internal product development activities.

During the winter of 1997, the New Ventures mission manifested itself as a deliberate approach for identifying and developing sales and profit growth opportunities for Frito-Lay. After considerable discussion, three broad opportunity avenues emerged as possible routes for achieving meaningful future growth. One growth avenue consisted of opportunities for building Frito-Lay's existing snack business by expanding into new eating occasions for current or new products. Ongoing internal research and development efforts to identify "better-for-you" products for morning and all-day consumption fell into this category. A second growth avenue was the opportunity to successfully enter new product categories by capitalizing on Frito-Lay's store-door-delivery sales force strengths, broad distribution coverage, and brand marketing skills. This opportunity could be realized through internal research and development or through targeted distribution alliances and acquisitions. Possible new product categories for Frito-Lay included confectioneries (e.g., candies) and baked sweet pastries, single-serve cakes, or snack bars. A third growth avenue was labeled "opportunistic acquisitions" made possible by related food companies offering products or entire businesses for sale as a result of corporate restructuring. These acquisitions would be screened by the New Ventures Division on the basis of their strategic and operating fit with Frito-Lay's sales, distribution, manufacturing, and brand marketing capabilities and meaningful sales and profit growth potential.

The announcement by Borden of its intention to divest the Cracker Jack brand and related assets represented a potential fit with all three growth avenues. According to Lynne Peissig:

> Early in our discussions, the New Ventures Division came to believe that sweet snacks represented a potential incremental growth opportunity for Frito-Lay. Cracker Jack appeared to be a logical "step out" versus a "leap" into sweet snacks from a strategic perspective. It could provide the foundation for a sweet snack platform to build a successful business on and complement Frito-Lay's salty snack business. Cracker Jack, with its strong brand equities, was certainly worth the time and effort to explore as an acquisition.

THE READY-TO-EAT CARAMEL POPCORN PRODUCT CATEGORY

The ready-to-eat (RTE) caramel popcorn product category recorded U.S. retail sales of $192 million in 1996 and $205 million in 1995. Manufacturer sales of RTE caramel popcorn were $167.3 million in 1996, down 6.2 percent from 1995. The decline in 1996 category dollar sales followed a steady annual sales increase since 1993. Pound volume in the RTE caramel popcorn category declined from 59.3 million pounds in 1995 to 57 million pounds in 1996, following a steady annual volume growth since 1993. Category sales and volume growth in the 1990s was due primarily to the introduction of new flavors (i.e., butter toffee) and low-fat and no-fat varieties of established brands.

Competitors

Several different types of competitors serve the RTE caramel popcorn category: (1) national brand firms, (2) seasonal/specialty firms, (3) regional firms, and (4) private label firms. National brand firms, which distribute products throughout the United States, include Borden Foods (Cracker Jack brand), International Home Foods, Inc. (Crunch 'n Munch brand), Lincoln Foods (Fiddle Faddle brand), and SIM-GT Licensing Corporation, which markets the Richard Simmons brand. A second category of competitors consists of seasonal/specialty firms that produce and market their caramel popcorn on a seasonal basis (often around December and the Christmas holiday season) or as a specialty item frequently sold in collectible tins. Seasonal/specialty firms include Houstons Foods and Harry and David. A large number of small, regional firms produce and distribute RTE caramel popcorn in only certain parts of the United States. Private brands are produced by regional or local manufacturers on a contractual basis for major U.S. supermarket chains. Estimated 1996 sales and pound volume market shares for individual national brands, seasonal/specialty/regional brands, and private labels are shown in Exhibit 2.

International Home Foods, Inc. (Crunch 'n Munch) and Borden Foods (Cracker Jack) are the RTE caramel popcorn category dollar and volume market share leaders in the United States. Prior to 1996, International Home Foods was the consumer foods unit of American Home Products Corporation (AHP). AHP is a multinational human and animal health care and agricultural products company with net sales exceeding $14 billion in 1996. In November 1996, AHP sold a majority interest (80 percent) in the food unit for approximately $1.2 billion to

EXHIBIT 2 **Caramel Corn Category Dollar and Volume Share at Retail: 1996**

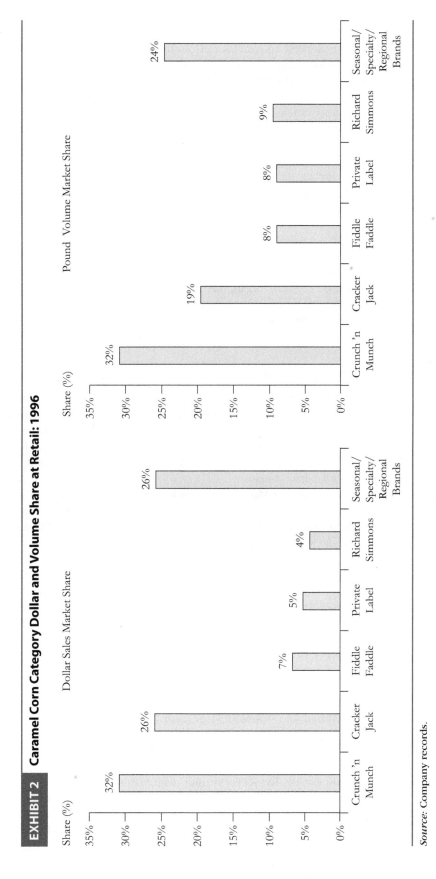

Source: Company records.

a limited partnership, of which the investment firm of Hicks, Muse, Tate & Furst is the general partner. International Home Foods produces and markets name-brand preserved foods. Its nationally known products include Chef Boyardee pastas (which represents nearly 30 percent of sales), Bumble Bee tuna, Polaner fruit spread, and PAM cooking spray. The company also sells southwestern cuisine foods (Ro*Tel canned tomatoes, Dennison's canned chili, and Ranch Style beans) and snack foods (Crunch 'n Munch caramel popcorn and Jiffy Pop popcorn). International Home Foods recorded net sales of $942.8 million in 1996.

Borden, Inc. is owned by the investment firm of Kohlberg Kravis Roberts & Co., which purchased the company for $1.9 billion in 1994. Although widely known for its dairy products, Borden divested its dairy business in 1997. Today, the company makes pasta, soup mixes, and bouillon (Borden Foods), snack foods (Wise Foods and Cracker Jack), consumer adhesives (Elmer's products), and industrial adhesives, coatings, and resins (Borden Chemical). Borden, Inc. recorded net sales of about $5.8 billion in 1996.

The decision by Borden to divest itself of Cracker Jack and related assets was prompted by a strategic assessment of the company's focus and resources. The company chose to focus on its pasta business and expand into grain-based meals that would require a significant resource investment. As a consequence of this assessment and growth plan, Borden Foods announced that Cracker Jack, along with Borden Brands North America and Borden Brands International, would be sold in 1997.

Marketing Practice

RTE caramel popcorn is generally viewed among snack food industry analysts as an "undermarketed" category, when compared with microwave popcorn and most other snack categories. Most brands in the category offer both caramel and butter toffee flavors and feature both regular and low-fat/fat-free varieties in different package sizes. An exception is the Richard Simmons brand, which is sold only as a fat-free product.

Only Crunch 'n Munch and Cracker Jack have been recently advertised in consumer media. Crunch 'n Munch leads the category in advertising expenditures, outspending Cracker Jack by a wide margin since 1993 (see Exhibit 3). The last time Cracker Jack spent significant funds for consumer advertising occurred in 1992, when $2.1 million was spent to launch the brand's butter toffee flavor. Consumer and trade promotions are often used by national and regional brands. Consumer promotions include in-store and newspaper couponing and product sampling; trade promotions include sales aids and off-invoice allowances for retailers.

Supermarkets and grocery stores and mass merchandise/warehouse/club stores are the principal retail outlets for RTE caramel popcorn. Supermarkets and grocery stores account for an estimated 44.7 percent of category dollar sales. About 42 percent of sales occur in mass merchandise/warehouse/club stores (Target, Kmart, Walmart). Drugstores account for 13 percent of sales. Remaining sales arise from a variety of other retail and food service outlets. In 1996, Crunch 'n Munch had an estimated 31 percent volume share in supermarkets and grocery stores, an 18 percent share in mass merchandise/warehouse/club stores, and a 13 percent share in drugstores. Cracker Jack's market share in these channels was 23 percent, 8 percent, and 11 percent, respectively, according to industry sources.

Retail outlets for RTE caramel popcorn are typically serviced via warehouse delivery systems. With a warehouse system, product is delivered from a manufacturer's plant or distribution center to a retailer's warehouse. The retailer assumes responsibility for distributing the product to its stores and stocking shelves.

Cracker Jack is the premium-priced brand in the RTE caramel popcorn category. Its total brand average price premium relative to Crunch 'n Munch has averaged about 28 percent over the past three years. Private (store) labels are

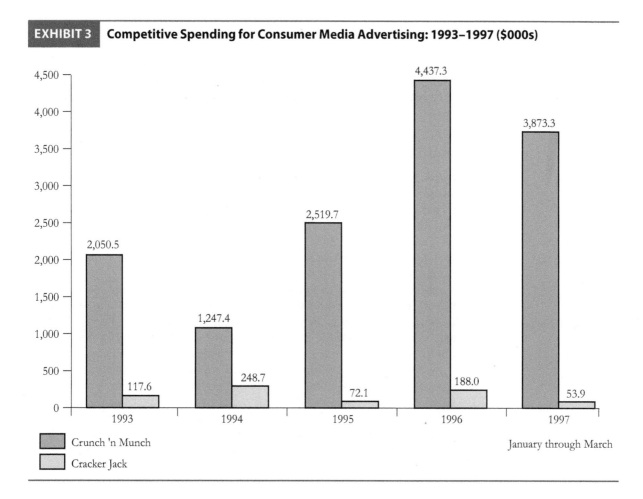

EXHIBIT 3 Competitive Spending for Consumer Media Advertising: 1993–1997 ($000s)

typically the lowest-priced brands. Regional brands are often priced between national brands and private labels. In some areas, regional "gourmet" brands and seasonal/specialty brands are priced at or near national brands.

Caramel Popcorn Consumer

Industry research shows that RTE caramel popcorn is a snack primarily eaten at home in the afternoon and evening as a treat or reward. Four of five users eat RTE caramel popcorn at home, and 80 percent of eating occasions are in the afternoon or evening hours. Only about 12 percent of U.S. households consume RTE caramel popcorn. Average consumption frequency is also low relative to other snack categories at less than two purchases per year. Whereas 2 percent of U.S. households consume RTE caramel popcorn at least once in a typical two-week period, 70 percent consume a salty snack (e.g., potato chips) and 31 percent consume candy (excluding gum and mints).

Industry research also shows that U.S. households with a female household head between the ages of 25 and 44, with children aged 4 to 17, are the heavy users of RTE caramel popcorn and Cracker Jack. This research further documents that:

1. Adult females consume 44 percent of caramel popcorn sold, adult males consume 29 percent, and children under age 18 consume 27 percent.

2. Fifty-four percent of heavy caramel popcorn users and 60 percent of heavy Cracker Jack purchasers reside in households with more than two members.

3. Fifty percent of heavy Cracker Jack purchasers and 42 percent of heavy caramel popcorn users are in households with children under age 18.

CRACKER JACK BRAND

Cracker Jack is one of the most recognized consumer food brands in the United States. The brand name enjoys a 97 percent awareness among persons between the ages of 15 and 60. Cracker Jack has a 95 percent brand name awareness among heavy users of caramel popcorn.

Brand Heritage

Cracker Jack is the original caramel popcorn. Invented by F. W. Ruekheim, the confection of popcorn, peanuts, and molasses was first made and sold in 1893 at the World's Fair Columbian Exhibition in Chicago, Illinois. The Cracker Jack name was coined in 1896 when a visiting salesman tasted the product and exclaimed, "That's a cracker jack!"—a 19-century slang phrase meaning, "That's great." In 1899, Cracker Jack was packaged in moisture-proof boxes making possible broadened distribution of the product.

Three developments in the early 1900s had lasting effects on the image of Cracker Jack. In 1908, the brand was immortalized in the song, "Take Me Out to the Ball Game," with its lyric "Buy me some peanuts and Cracker Jack." In 1912, F. W. Ruekheim introduced the prize-in-every-box novelty, featuring magnifying glasses, little books, beads, metal trains and whistles, and baseball cards, among other items. More than 17 billion Cracker Jack toys have been distributed since 1912. A patriotic flair was added to the Cracker Jack box during World War I (1914–1918) with the inclusion of red, white, and blue stripes. A saluting Sailor Jack and his dog, Bingo, were also added to the box and soon became the national Cracker Jack logo. Sailor Jack and Bingo have appeared on Cracker Jack packages with only slight variations since 1918.

Cracker Jack Product Line and Positioning

For 100 years, the Cracker Jack product line consisted only of caramel-coated popcorn and peanuts, using the original recipe developed by F. W. Ruekheim. In 1992, a Butter Toffee flavor was introduced, followed by Nutty Deluxe in 1994, and Cracker Jack Fat Free (in Original and Butter Toffee flavors) in 1995. Approximately 23 percent of Cracker Jack dollar and pound volume sales growth between 1993 and 1995 could be attributed to these product introductions. The breakdown of Cracker Jack 1996 net dollar sales by formulation is shown below:

Product Formulation	Net Dollar Sales (%)
Original/Butter Toffee	63.0%
Original/Butter Toffee Fat Free	26.0
Nutty Deluxe	6.7
Other*	4.3
Total	100.0%

*The other category consists primarily of inventory with limited shelf-life sold to a number of prequalified off-price retailers.

Cracker Jack is sold in a variety of packages. The product is packaged in 1.05-ounce and 1.25-ounce single-serve boxes and bags (introduced in December 1996) and 7-ounce and 8-ounce family-size bags and bags-in-boxes (introduced in 1992). The combinations of flavors, package sizes, and package forms (boxes, bags, and bags-in-boxes) resulted in a product line with 32 separate items or

EXHIBIT 4   **Cracker Jack Product Line**

stock-keeping units (SKUs) in 1996. Family-size bags-in-boxes accounted for 75 percent of net dollar sales; single-serve boxes accounted for 25 percent of net dollar sales in 1996. Single-serve and family-size bags represented an insignificant percentage of net dollar sales in 1996. Representative items in the Cracker Jack product line are shown in Exhibit 4.

Cracker Jack positioning over the past 30 years focused on its brand heritage as a traditional fun treat. This positioning manifested itself in the primary message for Cracker Jack advertising as illustrated below:

1. "What do you want when you've gotta have something . . . candy coated popcorn, peanuts and a prize" (1960s)

2. "When you're really good they call you Cracker Jack," featuring contemporary children excelling in athletics (1970s and early 1980s)

3. "Delicious then, delicious now," featuring a dual child–adult appeal reminding mothers how much they enjoyed Cracker Jack when growing up (mid-1980s)

4. "Only one snack says Cracker Jack," featuring its unique brand heritage (early 1990s). In 1992, the Butter Toffee flavor was introduced and positioned as a unique, all-family, all-occasion snack that provided a delicious-tasting, fun experience.

Cracker Jack's positioning was broadened in mid-1997 to emphasize the "better-for-you" qualities of Cracker Jack Fat Free in both Original and Butter Toffee flavors: "Cracker Jack, the sweet and crunchy fun snack you remember, has surprisingly less fat than you thought." The new positioning was being applied to all forms of brand communication, including packaging, consumer promotion, public relations, and consumer advertising.

Advertising and Promotion

Annual advertising and promotion spending for the Cracker Jack brand, as a percentage of sales, has ranged between 28 and 40 percent since 1993. Trade promotion, including incentives given retailers to reduce their cost or gain merchandising performance (off-invoice allowances, slotting fees, and market-development funds), represented the principal expense since 1993. Consumer promotion, including in-store and Sunday newspaper coupon insertions and redemption cost, and "other" promotions such as sales aids and samples accounted for the second largest expense item. Consumer advertising represented the smallest expense category. Cracker Jack has not been advertised nationally since 1993. However, as recently as 1980, Cracker Jack was the most advertised sweet snack in the United States, with a $6 million spending level.

The Cracker Jack toy surprise is another element of the advertising and promotion program. The choice of prizes is based on research among mothers and children to determine appeal. All toys must also pass rigorous safety testing to be considered as Cracker Jack prizes. In addition to long-time favorites, such as miniature baseball cards, Cracker Jack has licensed high-profile children's properties (e.g., Animaniacs, Looney Tunes, Wishbone, Scooby Doo) since 1995 to add value to the toy surprise. This effort has focused on promoting impulse purchases, particularly for Cracker Jack's highest gross margin items—the 1.05-ounce and 1.25-ounce single-serve box and bag.

Sales and Distribution

Cracker Jack sales volume is concentrated in the United States, where 98.9 percent of sales occur. Sales in Canada and a small export business represent the remaining 1.1 percent of volume. In 1996, 52 percent of Cracker Jack sales arose from supermarkets and grocery stores, 31 percent from mass merchandisers, 7 percent from drugstores, 4 percent from warehouse and club stores, and 6 percent from other outlets.

Cracker Jack is sold through a shared Borden sales force that also sells cheese and other Borden grocery brands such as Eagle Brand, Cremora, and ReaLemon. The retail grocery sales force includes 47 people who sell product to supermarkets and grocery stores through 65 independent food brokers. An independent broker organization of 20 people sells product directly to mass merchandise, military, drugstore, and club store customers.

Cracker Jack is shipped from 13 company distribution centers to retail store distribution centers or warehouses and subsequently delivered to retail outlets for stocking on store shelves by retail store personnel. Accordingly, Cracker Jack is typically placed in what is called the "warehouse-delivered snack aisles" of supermarkets and grocery stores versus the "direct-store delivery aisles," which are stocked and merchandised by a manufacturer's sales force and not retail store personnel.

Pricing

Borden Foods has employed a premium pricing strategy for Cracker Jack relative to competing national brands (e.g., Crunch 'n Munch). Cracker Jack prices have risen by an average of 5 to 6 percent per year since 1993. As a consequence,

Cracker Jack's average retail price premium relative to Crunch 'n Munch was about 28 percent on a per-ounce basis since 1993. The price premium was expanded in January 1997, when the price for Cracker Jack was increased by 6 percent. However, this price premium margin quickly eroded when the 10- and 5-ounce Crunch 'n Munch packages were downsized to 8- and 4-ounce packages, respectively, without a change in price. The effect of this move was to reduce the Cracker Jack price premium for the 7- and 8-ounce family-size packages to 14 percent.

Manufacturing

Borden Foods manufactures Cracker Jack at its Northbrook, Illinois, facility along with selected Borden Foods soup products. Cracker Jack equipment occupies about 32 percent of the facility's manufacturing space. This space houses 15 production lines, 11 box lines, and 4 bag lines. The production lines operate at approximately 33 percent capacity, and the box and bag lines operate at 85 percent capacity based on a five-day week and two eight-hour shifts per day. Approximately 450,000 to 500,000 packages are produced per day, warehoused at the site, and subsequently shipped to company distribution centers.

A unique feature of the production and packaging process is the Cracker Jack prize insertion activity. Prizes are collated on custom-made equipment designed by the company, and electric eyes are placed within the production lines to ensure that these prizes are inserted in boxes. In 1994, about 85 percent of the company's total capital expenditures was spent to automate the family-size bag-in-box packaging line and change the filling operation from a volumetric cup filler to a more accurate scale system.

Cracker Jack Strategy and Financial Performance: 1993–1996

Exhibit 5 on page 264 contains Cracker Jack Direct Product Contribution Income Statements for the period 1993 to 1996.[1] Cracker Jack recorded a negative Direct Product Contribution in each of the three previous years (1994 to 1996). Borden's current management attributed this performance to a variety of sources. Beginning in 1992, prior management pursued a volume-based strategy that focused on introducing family-size packages (7- and 8-ounce bags and bags-in-boxes) while reducing emphasis on the smaller box packages (e.g., 1.25-ounce box). This strategy achieved its intended effect. Cracker Jack pound volume in supermarkets and grocery stores, mass merchandisers, warehouse clubs, and drugstores combined increased to 12.4 million pounds in 1993, 13.5 million pounds in 1994, and 16.3 million pounds in 1995. However, the Cracker Jack gross margin percentage suffered due to a smaller margin contribution on large packages, which cannibalized higher margin small packages. In addition, rising material prices in 1994 and 1995 reduced margins since the added costs were not passed on with comparable price increases. Also, the introduction of Nutty Deluxe and Fat Free varieties in 1994 and 1995 was supported by a heavy financial investment in trade promotions. Even though these varieties accounted for almost one-fourth of Cracker Jack dollar and volume sales growth between 1993

---

[1]Direct Product Contribution Income Statements exclude certain direct and indirect expenses that customarily are allocated to products in accordance with Borden Foods' internal policies. These allocated expense categories, which change from time to time, represent the costs associated with the functional infrastructure of Borden Foods and include certain fixed sales and administrative expenses. In addition, costs related to certain systems, legal expenses, finance/accounting, and human resource/benefit services provided by Borden Foods Corporate headquarters have also been excluded in determining Direct Product Contribution. All financial information contained in these exhibits has been disguised and is not useful for external research purposes.

EXHIBIT 5 **Cracker Jack Direct Product Contribution Income Statement: 1993–1996 ($ in Millions)**

	1993	1994	1995	1996
Net trade sales	**$51.4**	**$ 51.7**	**$ 53.2**	**$48.4**
Cost of goods sold	26.0	33.8	32.2	27.1
Gross margin	**$ 25.4**	**$ 17.9**	**$ 21.0**	**$21.3**
Distribution expense	$ 4.6	$ 6.1	$ 5.5	$ 4.4
Trade promotion	11.4	16.0	15.6	8.6
Advertising, consumer, & other promotion	5.9	4.8	5.2	5.0
Variable sales	1.1	1.4	1.3	1.2
A & P management	0.3	0.4	0.8	0.8
Market research	0.3	1.0	2.3	2.5
Technical research	0.1	0.2	0.4	0.6
Direct product contribution[a]	**$ 1.7**	**($12.0)**	**($10.1)**	**($ 1.8)**
Other financial information:				
Depreciation expense	$ 1.5	$ 1.6	$ 1.4	$ 1.4
Capital expenditures	$ 1.4	$ 5.3	$ 0.8	$ 0.3
Working capital[b]	$ 16.4	$ 12.8	$ 6.3	$ 2.3

[a]Excludes effects of allocated selling costs, overhead, and other income and expense.

[b]Current assets (other than cash) minus current liabilities.

Explanatory Notes for Revenue and Expense Items:

Revenue recognition. Net trade sales are generally recognized when products are shipped. Liabilities are established for estimated returns, allowances, and consumer and trade discounts when revenues are recognized.

Cost of goods sold. Includes all variable costs associated with producing the product, including raw materials, packaging supplies, direct and indirect labor, and plant fixed overhead expenses including a BFC allocation for quality assurance and engineering.

Distribution expense. Expenses associated with moving finished goods from distribution centers to customers and all handling and storage charges of moving goods into, within, and out of third-party warehouses.

Variable sales. Commission or other payments to brokers associated with volume.

A & P management. Costs associated with business unit marketing personnel.

Market research. Syndicated consumer information, taste tests, package tests, focus groups, and other market research.

Advertising costs. Production costs of future media advertising are expensed on the first airdate or print-release date of the advertising. All other advertising is expensed as incurred.

Trade promotion. All incentives to the trade related to tactics to reduce price or gain merchandising performance. Included are off-invoice allowances, slotting, and market development funds.

Consumer promotion. Promotion expenses targeted at consumers including coupon insertion and redemption and consumer refunds/premiums in return for certain purchase level requirements.

Other promotion. Includes sales aids, samples, packaging development, and racks.

Technical research. Costs associated with product or process research and development.

Note: All financial information in this exhibit has been disguised and is not useful for external research purposes.

and 1995, this growth was not large enough to offset the incremental trade promotion costs.

Direct Product Contribution improved in 1996 due to a number of changes made by current Borden management. For example, trade promotion spending was reduced. The number of Cracker Jack SKUs was reduced from 47 in 1995 to 32 in 1996, which reduced inventory levels and improved the sales mix gross margin. However, Cracker Jack dollar sales declined by 9 percent and unit volume fell to 11.2 million pounds in 1996.

EXHIBIT 6	Cracker Jack Balance Sheet: December 31, 1996 ($ in Millions)

Assets

Cash and marketable securities	—
Net trade receivables*	$2.0
Inventories	4.2
Other current assets	0.2
Other long-term assets and intangibles	12.2
Net property, plant, and equipment	15.4
Total assets	$34.0

Liabilities and equity

Trade and drafts payable*	$3.1
Other current liabilities	1.1
General insurance	2.2
Pension liability	0.3
Nonpension postemployment benefits	2.5
Total liabilities	$9.2
Owner's investment	$24.8

*Net trade receivables, trade and drafts payable, and certain other current liabilities are not being sold and are presented for informational purposes only.

Note: All financial information in this exhibit has been disguised and is not useful for external research purposes.

Exhibit 6 shows the Cracker Jack balance sheet for the year ended December 31, 1996. In addition to the physical assets shown, other Cracker Jack assets include the trademarks Cracker Jack, the Sailor Jack and Bingo representation, Nutty Deluxe, and "When you're really good they call you Cracker Jack," and certain patents related to the manufacturing of Cracker Jack.

Cracker Jack Strategy and Financial Projections: 1997–2001

The financial performance of Cracker Jack through 1995 prompted a change in strategy in 1996. The new Cracker Jack strategy arose from a general strategic review of the entire Borden Foods Corporation begun in 1995. The strategy, adopted in 1996, had three objectives: (1) revitalize the base business, (2) improve operating efficiencies, and (3) extend the Cracker Jack trademark. These objectives would be realized by (1) expanded distribution within retail snack and food service marketing channels, (2) developing new packaging and flavors, (3) impactful product positioning, (4) enhanced gross margins via sustained price leadership, and (5) additional resources being allotted to consumer advertising.

Initial efforts in 1996 were designed to arrest the losses incurred in 1994 and 1995. The elimination of unprofitable trade promotions, the pruning of Cracker Jack SKUs from 47 to 32, and a higher gross margin resulted in a sizable improvement in the 1996 Direct Product Contribution. In late 1996 and early 1997, other actions were taken consistent with the new Cracker Jack strategy:

1. In December 1996, a single-serve (1.05- and 1.25-ounce) bag was introduced, primarily for distribution through vending machines and to Sam's Warehouse Clubs.

2. A 6 percent price increase was implemented in January 1997.

3. A new positioning that emphasized the low-fat content of Cracker Jack was initiated in mid-1997. This positioning—"Cracker Jack, the sweet and crunchy fun snack you remember, has surprisingly less fat than you thought"—highlighted the low-fat content of Original Cracker Jack (2.5 grams of fat per 1.25-ounce serving) and Cracker Jack Fat Free (0 grams of fat per serving).

Cracker Jack management believed that broadened distribution was the most important element of the new strategy. In December 1996, efforts were made to develop the vending machine business with the new single-serve bag using specialty distributors. Vending sales were projected to be almost $2 million in 1997. However, Cracker Jack management was of the view that the brand needed a totally new sales and delivery infrastructure to grow sales and product profitability. Specifically, the shared Borden sales force and broker/distributor network currently in use should be replaced by a direct-store-delivery (DSD) sales force. It was believed that a DSD sales force could provide product placement in grocery DSD snack aisles, which is the highest-velocity snack aisle in supermarkets. Limited, controlled store tests commissioned by Cracker Jack management indicated that placement in DSD snack aisles could initially boost dollar retail sales by as much as 38 percent. However, a DSD sales force is more resource intensive than Borden's present sales and distribution network. Borden Foods management was neither prepared to make the investments required nor equipped to handle a DSD sales force for Cracker Jack given the resource demands of other business opportunities.

Exhibit 7 details projected Direct Product Contribution Income Statements prepared by Cracker Jack management for the period 1997 to 2001. The projections

EXHIBIT 7	Cracker Jack Projected Direct Product Contribution Income Statements: 1997–2001 ($ in Millions)				
	1997	*1998*	*1999*	*2000*	*2001*
Net trade sales	**$50.5**	**$78.5**	**$191.4**	**$209.1**	**$258.9**
Cost of goods sold	27.3	37.4	97.5	108.3	127.8
Gross margin	**$23.2**	**$41.1**	**$93.9**	**$100.8**	**$131.1**
Distribution expense	$4.4	$4.6	$9.7	$11.0	$13.0
Trade promotion	6.2	10.2	23.8	22.3	23.9
Advertising, consumer, & other promotion	5.3	11.3	19.9	20.1	24.8
Variable sales	1.4	2.4	3.6	3.9	4.6
A & P management	0.9	0.4	0.4	0.4	0.6
Market research	1.0	1.6	2.6	3.0	3.4
Technical research	0.7	0.8	1.8	2.1	2.6
Direct product contribution[a]	**$3.3**	**$9.8**	**$32.1**	**$38.0**	**$58.2**
Other financial information:					
Depreciation expense	$1.4	$1.9	$3.7	$4.2	$4.7
Capital expenditures	$0.4	$4.0	$19.3	$4.3	$6.4
Working capital[b]	$3.0	$5.0	$13.2	$14.4	$18.0

[a]Excludes effects of allocated selling costs, overhead, and other income and expense.

[b]Current assets (other than cash) minus current liabilities.

Note: All financial information in this exhibit has been disguised and is not useful for external research purposes.

reflect the new strategy initiatives adopted by Borden's management and the integration of Cracker Jack into a national manufacturing, distribution, and sales infrastructure of a potential acquirer with an existing snack-related business.

The projection assumes significant revenue increases resulting from distribution expansion, primarily into grocery DSD, vending, and food service sales. It is also assumed that the acquirer would be willing and able to (1) fund trade promotions and consumer advertising to bolster sales of existing products and extend the product line and (2) raise prices. The projections also include capital expenditures, notably in 1999, that will be required to support the volume projections.

The Direct Product Contribution Income Statement projected for 1997 reflects Cracker Jack management's estimate of year-end results without a DSD sales force. Projected 1998 revenues demonstrate the estimated impact of a fully operational DSD sales force. These estimates focus exclusively on domestic opportunities for Cracker Jack and do not include potential export sales growth.

PROJECT BINGO

The New Ventures team met in June 1997 to decide whether or not to explore the Cracker Jack acquisition. Following a review of financial and operating data supplied by Borden in its Offering Memorandum, the decision was made to examine Cracker Jack as an acquisition. The effort was code-named "Project Bingo."

Project Bingo consisted of commissioned studies, internal company reviews, and cross-functional team analyses and evaluations orchestrated by Lynne Peissig. The target completion date was July 15, 1997, with a presentation and recommendation to Frito-Lay senior management scheduled for August 1, 1997. A nonbinding open bid for Cracker Jack and its related assets from prospective buyers was due August 6, 1997. The top bidders would be invited to Northbrook, Illinois, for a plant visit and a Borden management presentation. A binding letter of intent and bid would be submitted by interested parties toward the end of September 1997. Peissig believed that bids for Cracker Jack would be submitted by a number of investment firms and consumer foods companies, including General Mills, Nabisco, and Procter & Gamble.

The data-gathering effort was substantially complete by mid-July 1997. Preliminary analyses had been conducted in four areas: (1) brand management, (2) sales and distribution, (3) manufacturing and product assurance, and (4) finance and administration.

Brand Management

The consensus opinion among the New Ventures team was that brand management considerations would drive Project Bingo. Two studies were commissioned, including (1) a brand awareness, image, equity, and usage study; and (2) a simulated test market.

Brand Awareness, Image, Equity, and Usage Study An independent research firm that specialized in ongoing brand-tracking studies for consumer goods companies submitted its report to Project Bingo's brand marketing team in late June 1997. The principal findings are summarized below:

1. The Cracker Jack name registers virtually universal awareness. However, Cracker Jack Fat Free, Butter Toffee, and Nutty Deluxe exhibit consumer awareness levels below 50 percent.

2. The Cracker Jack name evokes distinct imagery and icons in consumers' minds. These include the product form itself (caramel, popcorn, peanuts), the prize/toy in the box, the boy/sailor and dog on the box, and taste/flavor. Overall, Cracker Jack was perceived to be:

- Traditional and old-fashioned in a way that evokes fond memories of growing up (but not very contemporary, and less contemporary than Crunch 'n Munch).
- Popular with kids more than teens, adults, or the family.
- More of a personal snack than a snack for sharing.
- A good treat, but not necessarily extendible across eating occasions.
- Fairly unique, particularly compared to other RTE caramel popcorn.
- Not at all "better for you" compared to many other snacks.
- Not as available for purchase, nor as easy to find in the stores as other RTE caramel popcorn.
- Lacking a good variety of flavors/types.

3. Cracker Jack has a respectable brand equity due largely to its heritage and generally favorable image foundation. It is a recognized brand with a positive reputation that appears to have lost momentum (popularity) in recent years.

4. Only 7.1 percent of U.S. households consume Cracker Jack. These households consume less than one pound of Cracker Jack annually. Exhibit 8 shows the major reasons why consumers do not buy Cracker Jack more often.

The study results were viewed favorably by the brand marketing team. According to one team member, "Cracker Jack is a trademark living off residual heritage with untapped opportunity."

Simulated Test Market Preliminary results from the simulated test market (STM) also proved "encouraging," according to a brand marketing team member. Unlike the brand awareness, image, equity, and usage study, the STM was commissioned to obtain an initial assessment of Cracker Jack's commercial potential.

The STM, conducted by another marketing research firm, consisted of four steps. First, consumers between the ages of 12 and 64, who had purchased a sweet or salty snack during the past three months, were recruited at shopping malls in 16 U.S. cities and escorted to a nearby research facility. These consumers were then exposed to an advertisement for Cracker Jack (see Exhibit 9 on page 270). Following this exposure, consumers proceeded to a mock store setup where Cracker Jack was available for sale along with competing RTE caramel popcorn brands. Consumers were given money and could purchase whatever brands they wished, keeping any money left over. Finally, consumers who bought Cracker Jack were given two complimentary packages of Cracker Jack to take home. These consumers were called after a two- to three-week time period, asked a series of questions about the product, and offered a chance to repeat purchase the brand.

Diagnostic information was also gathered as part of the Cracker Jack STM. Consumer attitudes toward the brand (likes and dislikes) and usage intentions were obtained. These data were incorporated into computer simulation models that also included elements of the brand's intended marketing plan. The STM output included estimates of household brand trial and repeat rates, purchase

EXHIBIT 8 Most Important Reasons for Not Buying Cracker Jack More Often

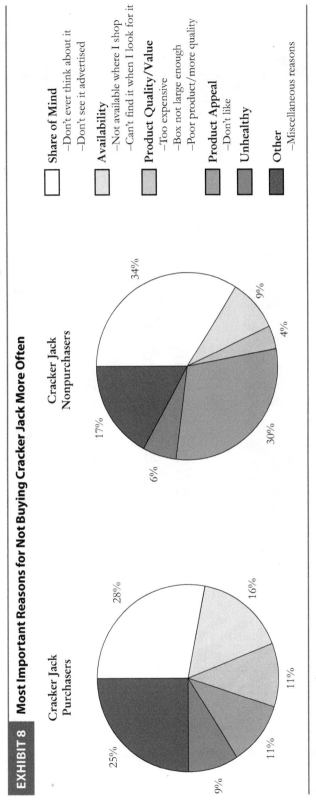

Cracker Jack
Purchasers

Cracker Jack
Nonpurchasers

Share of Mind
–Don't ever think about it
–Don't see it advertised

Availability
–Not available where I shop
–Can't find it when I look for it

Product Quality/Value
–Too expensive
–Box not large enough
–Poor product/more quality

Product Appeal
–Don't like

Unhealthy

Other
–Miscellaneous reasons

Source: Company records.

269

EXHIBIT 9 Cracker Jack Simulated Test Market Advertisement

amounts and frequency, product cannibalism, and first-year sales volume estimates.[2]

Fifteen different marketing plan options were tested in the Cracker Jack STM. Planned distribution coverage was set at levels comparable for Frito-Lay potato, corn, and tortilla chips. Two different store locations were tested: placement in the salty snack aisle versus the alternative snack aisle of stores. The present retail price of $1.69 for an 8-ounce box was tested, but the package type was varied to compare the 8-ounce box with a 7-ounce flex bag. Also, a $1.99 retail price was tested with an 8-ounce flex bag. Finally, three advertising and promotion expenditure levels ($15 million, $22 million, and $32 million) were simulated.

Diagnostic information gathered during the STM indicated that consumers had more "likes" than "dislikes" about Cracker Jack. Consumers gave favorable ratings to Cracker Jack's taste/flavor and texture/consistency. However, most consumers said there were not enough peanuts. Cracker Jack scored highly as an afternoon, early evening, and late evening snack, but low as a morning treat. Almost one-half (46 percent) of consumers said that the nuts, popcorn, and snack mix aisle was the preferred store location for buying Cracker Jack. The next most preferred store aisle was with salty snacks (24 percent), followed by the candy and cookie aisles and the checkout counter.

Exhibit 10 on page 272 shows preliminary first-year pound and net sales dollar volume estimates for each of the marketing plan options. First-year net sales estimates ranged from $46.6 million to $124.4 million at manufacturer prices. Estimates of product cannibalism indicated that 22 percent of Cracker Jack pound volume would come from other Frito-Lay snack chip brands when the advertising and promotion expenditure was $32 million.[3] (*Case writer note*: Footnote 3 contains important information for case analysis purposes.) This percentage was 7 percent at the $15 million expenditure level. No estimates were made for the $22 million expenditure level. The incidence of product cannibalism did not vary by store location (salty snack versus alternative snack aisle). According to a New Ventures team member, "These preliminary results indicate that Cracker Jack has considerable upside potential given broadened availability through our extensive sales and distribution network and advertising and promotion support."

Cracker Jack Extensions In subsequent meetings with the brand marketing team, discussions focused on Cracker Jack extension possibilities beyond the first year. Brand marketing personnel believed that attention in the first year should focus on establishing the Cracker Jack base business given a new sales and distribution infrastructure. However, brand and flavor extensions should be pursued in the second and third year of Cracker Jack marketing as a Frito-Lay brand.

Several brand marketing team members advocated a brand extension in the second year. Specifically, they proposed that a Cracker Jack snack bar be introduced. Cereal marketers had experienced considerable success with these bars following the trend toward "grab-and-go" eating. For example, Kellogg's Rice Krispies Treats snack bar recorded over $100 million in supermarket retail sales over the past two years. Quaker Oats recently extended its oatmeal cereal with the launch of Fruit & Oatmeal Cereal bars supported by $20 million in trade promotion and consumer advertising. Brand marketing team members speculated that a Cracker Jack snack bar could generate $50 to $100 million in incremental

---

[2]For an extended description of STMs, see K. Clancy, R. Shulman, and M. Wolf, *Simulated Test Marketing: Technology for Launching Successful New Products* (New York: Lexington Books, 1994).

[3]Frito-Lay does not divulge profitability data on individual products and product lines. However, for case analysis and class discussion purposes, Frito-Lay snack chip brands can be assumed to have a gross profit of $1.05 per pound.

EXHIBIT 10   Cracker Jack Simulated Test Market First-Year Volume Projections

Marketing Plan Elements

Preliminary Marketing Plan Options

Distribution/Product Placement	Salty Snack Aisle									Alternative Snack Aisle					
Package form and retail (consumer) price	8-oz. Bag-in-Box @ $1.69			7-oz. Flex Bag @ $1.69			8-oz. Flex Bag @ $1.99			8-oz Bag-in-Box @ $1.69			7-oz. Flex Bag @ $1.69		
Advertising and promotion ($ million)[a]	$15	$22	$32	$15	$22	$32	$15	$22	$32	$15	$22	$32	$15	$22	$32
First-Year Volume Projections[b]															
Pound volume (millions)	24.3	34.0	40.7	22.6	31.6	37.8	26.0	36.4	43.8	20.5	32.2	38.9	19.0	29.9	36.2
Dollar sales volume (millions) @ manufacturer price to retailer (mfr. net sales)	$59.6	$83.4	$99.0	$55.1	$77.1	$92.5	$73.9	$103.7	$124.4	$50.4	$79.1	$95.7	$46.6	$72.6	$88.6

[a]Advertising and Promotion Breakdown:

	At $15 million	At $22 million	At $32 million
Consumer Advertising	$0	$10	$15
Consumer Promotion	8	5	10
Trade Promotion	7	7	7

[b]Volume forecasts are subject to a ± 15% accuracy range.

Note: All financial information in this exhibit has been disguised and is not useful for external research purposes.

manufacturer net sales in the second year if supported by a $10 million trade and consumer advertising and promotion program. It was believed that incremental snack bar sales would be somewhat dependent on first-year sales; that is, higher first-year sales would result in higher incremental snack bar sales.

A flavor extension, added to the current caramel and butter toffee flavors, might be introduced in the third year, according to brand marketing team members. A specific flavor had not been proposed, but likely candidates were chocolate and peanut butter. The snack bar and flavor extension might produce an incremental dollar sales boost of 5 to 10 percent over the second-year sales volume if supported by a $5 to $10 million trade and consumer advertising and promotion program.

Sales and Distribution

Frito-Lay sales and distribution personnel were consulted soon after the Cracker Jack acquisition opportunity became public. Their initial reaction was positive, noting that Cracker Jack would fit the existing Frito-Lay sales and distribution infrastructure.

Sales and distribution personnel raised two issues related to the acquisition. First, the number of Cracker Jack SKUs (32) seemed large. The typical Frito-Lay brand had five to ten SKUs and the number of Cracker Jack SKUs could present a challenge in getting retailer shelf and display space. Second, the estimated cost of a direct-store-delivery (DSD) like that employed by Frito-Lay appeared to be understated. According to industry analysts, the selling and distribution cost of a DSD sales force selling comparable products was understated by a factor of one-half when stated as a percent of net sales.

Manufacturing and Product Assurance

Frito-Lay manufacturing and product assurance personnel were also favorably disposed toward the Cracker Jack acquisition. Like sales and distribution personnel, they expressed concerns about the number of Cracker Jack SKUs and the added complexity caused by this large number from a production perspective.

Without actually inspecting the Cracker Jack plant, manufacturing and product assurance personnel could not assess the condition of the facility and Cracker Jack production, box, and bag lines. However, they believed that it was highly unlikely that Frito-Lay would buy the Northbrook, Illinois, facility. The production, box, and bag lines might be purchased depending on their condition and relocated to an existing Frito-Lay manufacturing plant along with peanut and prize-insertion equipment. The ongoing capital expenditures projected by Borden management seemed appropriate if this were done.

Manufacturing personnel also said it was unlikely that Frito-Lay would need to make the substantial new plant and equipment capital expenditures indicated in Borden management's projection for 1999 (see Exhibit 7 on page 266). Rather, Frito-Lay had a long-standing and successful relationship with an independent supplier that produced caramel popcorn, among other savory and salty snack products, and also had the manufacturing capacity to produce the equivalent of $100 million in sales. Space was available at existing Frito-Lay manufacturing facilities to install additional production, box, and bag lines if Cracker Jack sales exceeded $100 million. These lines could be added incrementally for a minimal capital investment. Each $10 million capital investment for production and lines was estimated to provide capacity to manufacture the equivalent of $50 million in sales. The equipment itself would be most likely depreciated over 15 years using the straight-line method.

A senior Frito-Lay manufacturing executive also believed that the Cracker Jack cost of goods sold could be 10 percent less than Borden management's projections. This cost reduction could be realized by simplifying the Cracker Jack product line and building the flex bag volume relative to Cracker Jack sold in boxes and bags-in-boxes.

Finance and Administration

Lynne Peissig engaged Frito-Lay planning personnel and PepsiCo merger and acquisition specialists to begin a valuation analysis of the Cracker Jack business in June 1997. By mid-July, a variety of data had been gathered pertaining to recent acquisitions in the consumer foods industry. According to Diane Tousley, the New Ventures division finance director, the transaction prices for these types of acquisitions represented one to three times net revenues and 10 to 12 times after-tax earnings of the acquired companies. The higher multiples were associated with businesses that had strong brand names or trademarks, established distribution channels and trade relations, and a positive earnings history.

Tousley acknowledged that these data needed to be supplemented with a more rigorous financial appraisal, including a discounted cash flow valuation for Cracker Jack (see the Appendix for this case). She noted that Frito-Lay commonly applied a risk-adjusted discount rate to calculate the present value of after-tax future cash flows when performing a discounted cash flow analysis for new investments. (*Note*: According to the PepsiCo, Inc. annual report, 1997, p. 29, the effective 1997 PepsiCo, Inc. corporate income tax rate for continuing operations was 35.4 percent.) Depending on the level of the risk, the discount rate ranged from 12 to 18 percent with an average risk-adjusted discount rate of 15 percent. New Ventures team members agreed that an investment in Cracker Jack represented an "average risk" for Frito-Lay.

Revenue forecasts associated with marketing Cracker Jack as a Frito-Lay brand had not been finalized as of July 15, 1997. However, Peissig believed that the preliminary first-year sales projections provided by the STM and incremental dollar sales estimates resulting from brand and flavor extensions in the second and third year offered a starting point for making revenue forecasts. She also thought Cracker Jack dollar sales growth would likely stabilize at a rate of 2 or 3 percent in the fourth and fifth year following modest price and pound volume increases. Peissig added: "I suspect that considerable discussion will focus on Cracker Jack revenue projections when the business team is assembled."

Peissig also expected an animated discussion related to the Cracker Jack trade promotion and consumer advertising budget. She believed three years of focused brand development efforts supported by promotion and advertising spending would be necessary to rebuild and grow the business. After that, the Cracker Jack business might be sustained with an annual promotion and advertising budget representing about 4 to 8 percent of manufacturer net sales. Other costs would also be incurred by Cracker Jack. For example, Tousley estimated that initial and ongoing general and administrative costs associated with the marketing of Cracker Jack as a Frito-Lay brand would range from 4 to 7 percent of manufacturer net sales. These costs included product and process research and development, marketing research, and brand management and administrative salaries and fringe benefits.

Finally, Peissig believed that her presentation to senior PepsiCo executives should include consideration of the Cracker Jack acquisition relative to the internal development and commercialization of a new consumer food brand. According to industry sources, the financial investment to internally develop and launch a new brand (trademark) in a consumer food category was $75 to $100 million, including the cost of product research and development, test marketing, and a national introduction. The time interval from concept development to full-scale commercialization ranged from two to three years. The likelihood of a new product success was roughly one in ten.

 ## APPENDIX: NOTE ON VALUING A BUSINESS

Estimating a company's fair market value is a necessary first step in determining the purchase price for an acquisition. Fair market value is the cash, or cash-equivalent, price at which an asset would trade between a willing buyer and seller, with each in command of all information necessary to value the asset and neither under any pressure to trade.

Valuation experts have developed a variety of valuation techniques to assist in establishing a company's fair market value, although this value often may not represent the final transaction price. In practice, a transaction price involves consideration of a variety of factors that may vary depending on the characteristics of the company to be acquired and the objectives of the buyer and seller. For example, obtaining valuable trade names, taking control of another entity, or acquiring an increased market share for a particular product may affect the final purchase price. Still, determination of a transaction or purchase price or a reasonable price range generally involves quantitative techniques. This appendix briefly describes the discounted cash flow (DCF) technique that is used by investment bankers, research analysts, and valuation experts to estimate a company's fair market value. It is assumed that the reader is familiar with the vocabulary and mechanics of present value and discounted cash flow analysis.[4]

The Discounted Cash Flow Technique

The DCF valuation approach is the most frequently used fair market valuation technique. It provides a "going concern" value, which is the value indicated by the future commercial possibilities of a business. Using this technique, fair market value is calculated by the summation of the present value of projected cash flows for a determined period plus the present value of the residual or terminal value at the end of the projection period for a business. Typically, a 5- to 10-year projection period of after-tax operating cash flows, with various terminal or residual value estimates, will be discounted back to the present by the risk-adjusted, weighted-average cost of capital for the acquiring company. The cash flows are derived from the projected income statements and working and fixed capital expenditure plans. This calculation produces a result that represents the fair market value to both debt and equity holders. To arrive at the (owner's) equity value, the outstanding debt at the time of the acquisition is subtracted from the total capital value.

Four key areas must be assessed for accuracy and appropriateness when using the DCF technique. These include the (1) assumptions underlying the projection of cash flows, (2) length of the projection period, (3) residual or terminal value at the end of the projection period, and (4) appropriate discount rate.

---

[4]For background reading on the time value of money, present value analysis, and discounted cash flow, see the most recent edition of S. Ross, R. Westerfield, and B. Jordan, *Fundamentals of Corporate Finance* (Burr Ridge, IL: Irwin McGraw-Hill); or see R. Higgins, *Analysis for Financial Management* (Burr Ridge, IL: Irwin McGraw-Hill).

Financial Projection Assumptions and Projection Period   Five factors form the basis for basic financial projections: (1) historical sales growth; (2) business plans of the company to be acquired; (3) prevailing relevant business conditions including growth expectations and trends in light of competitive positioning, general market growth, and price pressure; (4) anticipated needs for working capital and fixed asset expenditures; and (5) historical and expected levels and trends of operating profitability. Each factor affects the estimation of projected cash flows for the business to be acquired.

Determining the length of the projection period is a matter of judgment. As a general rule, it is expected that at the end of the projection period, the operations of a business should be at a normal and sustainable operating level in order to more easily estimate a terminal or residual value (discussed next). Unusual circumstances, such as an excessive sales growth factor, an increase or decrease in operating profit margins, or an improvement in the accounts receivable or inventory levels, should no longer exist by the end of the projection period. For companies projecting normal sales growth rates and profitability margins, a 5- to 10-year projection period is usually employed.

Estimating the Terminal or Residual Value   The value of a business at the end of the projection period is often the least analyzed element of a valuation. However, it can represent a significant portion of the company's entire fair market value. The proper method for estimating the terminal or residual value depends on the financial projection factors described earlier and the length of the projection period in addition to the specifics of the business. A trade-off exists between the degree of reliability inherent within the two factors (DCFs during the projection period and the terminal value) used to calculate an ultimate fair market value. A shorter projection period places greater importance on the ability to develop a meaningful terminal or residual value estimate. A longer projection period places less reliance on the estimated terminal value but makes the annual cash flow assumptions more important.

The two most frequently used approaches for estimating a terminal value are the income capitalization and the multiple techniques. Both techniques estimate the future value of the business at the end of the projection period. This future value is then discounted back to determine the present value.

The income capitalization technique method adjusts either after-tax earnings or cash flow from the final year of the projection period by the discount rate. This technique assumes that after-tax earnings will either be constant or increasing at a constant rate from the last year of the projection period and that the proper risk-adjusted weighted-average cost of capital is the discount rate. The multiple approach applies some multiplier to either after-tax earnings or cash flow from the last year of the projection period. The resulting terminal value is then discounted to its present value using the discount rate from the final year of the projection period. The multiples are developed from publicly traded comparable companies or recent merger and acquisition transactions. A point to remember about the income capitalization and multiple approaches is that the calculated terminal value is dependent on the assumptions underlying the projection period. For example, aggressive sales growth rates will overstate after-tax earnings or cash flow for the last year of the projection period, which will in turn overstate the terminal value. Similarly, multiples may be distorted because of extrinsic influences on recent merger and acquisitions transactions and the fact that two companies are rarely alike.

Discount Rate   The proper discount rate is one of the most significant elements in a DCF. Because the present value changes inversely with changes in the discount rate, it is critical to the valuation to properly assess the inherent risk and thus the required yield of the business to be acquired.

The Capital Asset Pricing Model (CAPM) is generally accepted by the financial community as a means for estimating an investor's yield requirement and hence a company's cost of equity capital. Essentially, the CAPM states that the required cost of equity is equal to the cost of risk-free debt plus some additional risk premium relating to the company. A detailed discussion of CAPM can be found in most finance textbooks. The required rates of return on equity and debt are then weighted in order to arrive at the weighted-average cost of capital. The weighted-average cost of capital for *Fortune* 500 consumer goods companies averages around 10 to 12 percent.

DISCOUNTED CASH FLOW TECHNIQUE ILLUSTRATION

Exhibit A-1 on page 278 provides a simple illustration of the DCF computation for valuing a business. The upper portion of the illustration contains a five-year *pro forma* income statement, including projected business revenues, cost of goods sold, operating expenses, and earnings (net income) before interest and taxes. Also indicated is the provision for corporate income tax and after-tax earnings.

Cash Flow Calculation   The bottom portion of Exhibit A-1 details the cash flow calculation. The projected cash flows are obtained by adjusting the *pro forma* income statement for noncash items and changes in balance sheet items affecting cash.[5] This is shown by first adding depreciation expense (a noncash cost) for each year to after-tax earnings. After-tax earnings plus depreciation represents the annual cash flow from operations for a business.

The cash flow from operations then needs to be adjusted to reflect cash outflows. This is done by subtracting the estimated year-to-year *increase* in working capital (current assets minus current liabilities) and planned capital expenditures for each year from the estimated cash flow from operations. Increases to working capital in this illustration suggest that current assets, such as inventories and accounts receivables, net of current liabilities (e.g., accounts payable), increase each year at a constant amount of $100,000 given the constant (10 percent) annual revenue growth rate over the projection period shown in Exhibit A-1. The dollar amount for capital expenditures reflects annual cash investments in plant and equipment. In summary, after-tax earnings plus noncash expenses (e.g., depreciation) minus projected increases to working capital and annual capital expenditures result in a projected total annual cash flow for a business.

Present Value of Projected Cash Flows and Residual or Terminal Value

As described earlier, the fair market value of a business is calculated by the summation of the present value of projected cash flows for a determined period plus the present value of the residual or terminal value at the end of the projection period. Exhibit A-1 shows the present value calculation using a 15 percent discount rate (other discount rates are shown in Exhibit A-2 on page 279). The discount rate reflects the acquiring company's weighted-average cost of capital, plus any amount to be added for special risks entailed in the acquisition; hence, the frequently used term *risk-adjusted discount rate*. The summed, or cumulative, present value of projected cash flows over the 5-year projection period is $9,592,000, shown in Exhibit A-1.

---

[5]For simplicity, deferred taxes and amortization of goodwill are omitted from this example.

EXHIBIT A-1	Business Valuation Discounted Cash Flow Illustration ($ in Thousands)

	Year 1	Year 2	Year 3	Year 4	Year 5	Residual Value	Fair Market Value
Revenues (10% growth)	$10,000	$11,000	$12,100	$13,310	$14,641		
Cost of goods sold (40% of revenues)	4,000	4,400	4,840	5,324	5,856		
Gross profit (60% of revenues)	6,000	6,600	7,260	7,986	8,785		
Operating expenses (20% of revenues)	2,000	2,200	2,420	2,662	2,928		
Earnings before interest and taxes (EBIT) (40% of revenues)	4,000	4,400	4,840	5,324	5,856		
Income tax provision on EBIT (40% of EBIT)	1,600	1,760	1,936	2,130	2,343		
After-tax earnings before interest and taxes on interest (24% of revenues)	$2,400	$2,640	$2,904	$3,194	$3,514		
Add noncash items, including depreciation expense	700	850	1,050	1,300	1,600		
Funds provided	$3,100	$3,490	$3,954	$4,494	$5,114		
Subtract:							
Increases to working capital	(100)	(100)	(100)	(100)	(100)		
Capital expenditures	(500)	(750)	(1,000)	(1,250)	(1,500)		
Total cash flows exclusive of interest (net of tax)	$2,500	$2,640	$2,854	$3,144	$3,514	$45,682[a]	
Present value factor at 15%	0.87	0.756	0.658	0.572	0.497	0.497	
Present value	$2,174	$1,996	$1,877	$1,798	$1,747	$22,704	
Total present value of cash flows							$9,592
Present value of residual							22,704
Fair market capital value for the firm							$32,296

[a]Residual value using an after-tax earnings (cash flow) multiple. After-tax earnings (cash flow) from Year 5 times the multiple selected of twelve ($3,514 × 12).

As mentioned earlier, the residual or terminal value at the end of a projection period often represents a significant portion of the fair market value of a business. This is apparent in Exhibit A-1, which illustrates the multiple approach for estimating the residual or terminal value. In this illustration, an after-tax earnings (cash flow) multiple (12) is used, which is then discounted to its present value using the discount rate from the final year of the projection period. This results in a residual value of $22,704,000. The sum of the cumulative present value of projected cash flows ($9,592,000) and the present value of the residual or terminal value is the estimated fair market value shown as $32,296,000 in Exhibit A-1.

Alternatively, the income capitalization approach can be used. This approach adjusts either after-tax earnings or cash flow from the final year of the projection period by the discount rate. It can be assumed that after-tax earnings or cash flow

EXHIBIT A-2	Present Value of $1.00 Discounted at Discount Rate *K*, for *N* Years						

	Discount Rate (K)						
Period (N)	*12%*	*13%*	*14%*	*15%*	*16%*	*17%*	*18%*
1	0.893	0.885	0.877	0.870	0.862	0.855	0.847
2	0.797	0.783	0.769	0.756	0.743	0.731	0.718
3	0.712	0.693	0.675	0.658	0.641	0.624	0.609
4	0.636	0.613	0.592	0.572	0.552	0.534	0.515
5	0.567	0.543	0.519	0.497	0.476	0.456	0.437

will be either constant or increasing at a constant rate from the last year of the projection period.

The income capitalization approach for estimating a residual or terminal value can be applied given information contained in Exhibit A-1. Assuming that after-tax earnings (or cash flow) in Year 5 remain constant at $3,514,000 and a 15 percent discount rate applies, then the present worth of the residual value is $11,643,053 ([$3,514,000/0.15] × 0.497). When added to the present value of projected cash flows, the estimated fair market value is $21,235,053 ($9,592,000 + $11,643,053). Alternatively, if a 10 percent annual growth in after-tax earnings (or cash flow) is expected in the future as was apparent in Exhibit A-1 projections, then the present value of a perpetually growing after-tax earnings (cash flow) stream can be estimated. This is done using the formula, $E/(K - g)$, where E represents after-tax earnings (cash flow) in the last year of the projection period, K is the discount rate, and g is the growth rate in perpetuity. Applying this formula, the estimated residual value is $70,280,000 ($3,514,000/[0.15 − 0.10]). The present value of this amount is $34,929,160 (0.497 × $70,280,000). By adding the present value of the terminal value to the present value of projected cash flows, the estimated fair market value is $44,521,160.

Summary

The estimation of fair market value requires both a qualitative and quantitative appraisal of the future commercial possibilities of a business as a going concern. As demonstrated in this note, the determination of fair market value is by no means a simple matter and will often yield different dollar figures given different assumptions. The DCF valuation approach featured in this note, while conceptually correct, often requires a heavy dose of judgment in its application. Fair market value of a business lies in the eyes of the beholder, whether he or she is the buyer or the seller.

Chapter 6

Integrated Marketing Communication Strategy and Management

Marketing communication is the process by which information about an organization and its offerings is disseminated to selected markets. Given the role communication plays in facilitating mutually beneficial exchange relationships between an organization and prospective buyers, its importance cannot be overstated. The goal of communication is not just to induce initial purchases; it is also to achieve postpurchase satisfaction, thus increasing the probability of repeat sales. Even if prospective buyers possessed a pressing need and an organization possessed an offering that precisely met that need, no exchange would occur without communication. At a minimum, communication is necessary to inform buyers of the following:

- The availability of an offering
- The unique benefits of the offering
- The where and how of obtaining and using the offering

Exactly how potential buyers are to be informed—the actual message communicated—is one of the most subjective communication decisions. Although message development can be somewhat aided by research, there are no guaranteed message strategies available for all offerings, markets, or organizations. Each individual situation must determine whether the message is to be hard-sell, humorous, or informational. Whatever message format is chosen, the message communicated should be desirable to those to whom it is directed, exclusive or unique to the offering being described, and believable in terms of the benefit claims made for the offering.

It is the task of the marketing manager to manage the communication process most effectively. Marketing managers have at their disposal specific communication activities, often called *elements, functions, tools,* or *tasks.* These include electronic or print advertising, personal selling, and sales promotion. Collectively, the activities are termed the *marketing communication mix.*[1] Elements of the communication mix range from very flexible (for example, personal selling) to very inflexible (for example, mass advertising), and each has a unique set of characteristics and capabilities. To a certain extent, however, they are interchangeable and substitutable. It is the responsibility of the marketing manager to find the most effective communication mix at the least possible cost.

Marketing managers should not limit their thinking to which communication activity to use when designing communication strategies. Rare is the organization

281

that employs only one form of communication. Rather, managers should broaden their perspective to think of *integrated marketing communications*—the practice of blending different elements of the communication mix in mutually reinforcing ways to inform, persuade, and induce consumer action. In this context, attention is directed to which activity should be emphasized, how intensely it should be applied, and how communication activities can be most effectively combined and coordinated. For instance, advertising might be employed to develop offering awareness and consideration; sales promotion might be used to increase purchase intention; and personal selling might be utilized to obtain final conviction and purchase.

Increasingly, marketers are using the Internet as a platform for integrated marketing communications. This technology has the capability to take consumers and industrial users through the entire purchase process, from creating awareness to providing information in an interactive manner, to placing an order, to customer service after the sale. The role of the Internet in marketing communications is covered in this chapter. The Internet's role as a marketing channel is featured in Chapter 7.

INTEGRATED MARKETING COMMUNICATION STRATEGY FRAMEWORK

From a managerial perspective, the formulation of an integrated marketing communication strategy requires six major decisions. Once the offering and target markets have been defined, the manager must consider the following decisions:

1. What are the information requirements of target markets as they proceed through the purchase process?

2. What objectives must the communication strategy achieve?

3. How might the mix of communication activities be combined to convey information to target markets?

4. How much should be budgeted for communicating with target markets, and in what manner should resources be allocated among various communication activities?

5. How should the communication be timed and scheduled?

6. How should the communication process be evaluated as to its effectiveness, and how should it be controlled?

Theoretically, these questions are distinct and thus can be approached in a sequential manner. In practice, however, they are likely to be approached simultaneously.

INFORMATION REQUIREMENTS IN PURCHASE DECISIONS

The first step in designing an integrated marketing communication strategy is to determine how buyers purchase a particular offering and to define the role of information in the purchase process. This often requires use of a purchase-process (or purchase-funnel) model. Usually, such a model treats buyers as though they move through sequential stages in their purchase processes, such as

$$\text{Awareness} \rightarrow \text{Consideration} \rightarrow \text{Preference} \rightarrow \text{Purchase}$$

At any point in time, different buyers are in different stages of the model, and each stage requires a different communication strategy.

Most purchase-process models allow the marketing manager to distinguish between solitary and joint decision making. In any purchase decision, the person or persons involved can play several possible roles—purchaser, influencer, decision maker, and/or consumer. In certain purchase situations, one individual may play more than one role. In other purchase situations, such as a joint purchase decision, the roles may be played by different individuals. Consider the purchase of a breakfast cereal. Whereas a mother may be the family member who purchases breakfast cereal, her children may influence the brand purchase, and the father may consume the product. A similar situation could exist in an industrial setting. A purchasing agent may be the buyer, an engineer the influencer and decision maker, and a technician the user. Understanding who is playing the roles is a prerequisite for successfully determining what the communication message should be, as well as to whom it should be directed and how it should be communicated.

Similarly, the process used by buyers to purchase an offering influences the role of information, and hence the most effective communication strategy. For example, in industrial settings purchasing procedures are often prescribed. Therefore, understanding when, where, how, and what information is employed in the purchase decision will enable an organization to direct the proper communication to the proper individual at the proper time. These remarks also apply to communication directed toward consumers. Consider the case of consumers making a decision to buy a house. To communicate effectively, an organization must know *what* information these consumers think is necessary (price, location, size), *where* they will seek it (newspapers, the Internet, brokers, friends), *when* they will seek it (how far in advance, on what days), and *how* they will apply the information once obtained.

Finally, the way in which buyers perceive an organization and its offering is closely related to their information needs. The perceived importance of the offering and the perceived risk in making an incorrect purchase decision influence the extent to which buyers seek information, as well as their choice of information source(s). The more important or the riskier an offering is perceived to be (because of large dollar outlays, ego involvement, or health and safety reasons), the more likely it is that buyers will seek information from sources other than the organization providing the offering. For example, prospective new car and used buyers spend 11 to 12 hours researching brands, models, features, and prices online before physically shopping for a car.[2]

 # SETTING REASONABLE COMMUNICATION OBJECTIVES

The objectives set for communication programs will depend on the overall offering-market strategies of the organization and the stage of a product or service life cycle. Communication objectives will differ according to whether the strategy being employed is market penetration, market development, or product development. For instance, a market penetration strategy will suggest communication objectives that emphasize more frequent offering usage or that build preference for or loyalty to the offering. On the other hand, a market development strategy will encourage communication that will stimulate awareness and initial trial of the offering.

Life-cycle stage plays a role in determining whether communication objectives should stimulate primary demand or selective demand. Early in the life cycle, communication efforts focus on stimulating *primary demand*—demand for the product or service class, such as dairy products, personal computers, or financial planning. Typically, the message conveyed focuses on introducing the benefits of a product or service or overcoming objections to the product or service. Later in the life cycle, when substitute products or services exist, communication efforts focus on stimulating *selective demand*—demand for a particular brand, product, or service such as Borden milk, Hewlett-Packard personal computers, or Merrill Lynch financial planning. Typically, the message conveyed extols the benefits of a particular competitive offering and seeks to differentiate that offering from others.

Objectives must be articulated for the overall integrated marketing communications program as well as for individual communication tools. Consider the overall integrated marketing communication objectives for the introduction of the Apple iPod:

1. To define and communicate the concept of a comprehensive "digital lifestyle" and explain the value this brings to Apple's core creative consumer

2. To establish Apple as the premier provider of value-added digital components and deliver reliable, secure, and platform-neutral extensibility and integration

Specific objectives for advertising, in-store promotion, and store personnel were also stated. Both overall and specific communication objectives were tied directly to the tasks that the tools had to accomplish. In addition, the communication objectives and tasks had to meet three criteria common to any integrated marketing communications initiative. That is, they had to be *consistent* both among themselves and with other marketing mix elements, *quantifiable* for measurement and control purposes, and *attainable* with an appropriate amount of effort and expenditure and within a specific time frame. For the Apple iPod, the objectives were to be achieved in 24 months following its introduction.[3]

DEVELOPING AN INTEGRATED MARKETING COMMUNICATION MIX

Development of an integrated marketing communication mix requires the assignment of relative weights to particular communication activities based on communication objectives. Although no established guidelines exist for designing an optimal communication mix, several factors that influence the mix need to be considered. These factors are:

- The information requirements of potential buyers
- The nature of the offering
- The nature of the target markets
- The capacity of the organization

Information Requirements of Buyers

Identification of the relative value of communication tools at various stages in the purchase-decision process is the starting point in crafting an integrated communication mix. Marketers often use the term *consumer touch points* to designate where, when, and how a customer or prospective buyer comes in contact with a product, service, organization, or brand message or impression.

Consider a simple purchase-decision process for a new automobile. Through advertising and Web sites, such as GMBuyPower.com, manufacturers seek to stimulate awareness of the new models and to indicate where they can be purchased. Sales personnel provide information on specific options available, financing, and delivery. Sales promotion brochures provide descriptions of performance characteristics and other salient features. Which communication tool and consumer touch point has the greatest impact on prospective buyers? The answer to this question, while difficult to arrive at, will lead to a weighing of the importance of the communication tools. The manager will achieve an effective communication mix only by understanding the information requirements of potential buyers and by meeting those requirements with the appropriate communication mix elements.

Nature of the Offering

A major consideration in developing the communication mix is the organization's offering. A highly technical offering, one with benefits not readily apparent (such as performance or quality), or one that is relatively expensive is likely to require personal selling. On the one hand, advertising is a potent communication tool when the offering is not complex, is frequently purchased, is relatively inexpensive, or has benefits that readily differentiate it from competing offerings. Sales promotion lends itself to nearly every offering type because of the wide variety of forms it can assume. Its main use is to induce immediate action on frequently purchased products.

Target-Market Characteristics

The nature of the target market is another consideration. A target market consisting of a small number of potential buyers, existing in close proximity to one another and each purchasing in large quantities, might suggest a personal selling strategy. In contrast, a mass market that is geographically scattered generally calls for an emphasis on advertising. However, firms are finding that direct marketing also can be used to reach a geographically dispersed target market. This realization has led many firms to substitute mail and telephone solicitations for mass media (radio, print, and television) advertising and use the Internet as a communication medium to complement advertising for consumer products and services and a supplement to personal selling for industrial goods and services.

Organizational Capacity

A fourth consideration is the ability or willingness of the organization to undertake certain communication activities. The organization is continually faced with *make-or-buy decisions*. If an organization decides to employ a particular communication activity, should it perform the activity internally (that is, make it) or contract it out (in other words, outsource it or buy it)?

One such make-or-buy decision is the choice between a company sales force and independent sales representatives.[4] The decision has both economic and behavioral dimensions. The economic dimension relates to the issue of fixed versus variable costs. The cost of independent representatives is variable; they are paid on sales commission only. A company sales force, on the other hand, typically includes a variable-cost component *and* a fixed-cost component. If independent representatives fail to sell, no costs are incurred; however, if a company sales force fails to sell, the fixed costs still have to be paid. These concepts are useful in determining whether independent representatives or company sales representatives are more cost-effective at different sales levels.

Suppose independent representatives received a 5 percent commission on sales and company sales personnel received a 3 percent commission in addition to incurring a salary and administration cost of $500,000. At what sales level would company representatives become more or less costly than independent representatives? This question can be resolved by setting the cost equations for both types of representatives equal to each other and solving for the sales level amount, as follows:

$$\frac{\text{Cost of company reps}}{0.03\,(x) + \$500,000} = \frac{\text{Cost of independent reps}}{0.05\,(x)}$$

where x = sales volume. Solving for x, we get $25 million as the sales volume at which the costs of company and independent representatives are equal. This relationship is shown in Exhibit 6.1.

The calculation indicates that if the sales volume were below $25 million, the independent representative would be cheaper; above that amount, the company sales force would be cheaper. Of course, a fundamental issue is the likelihood of achieving a $25 million sales level.

Behavioral dimensions of this decision focus on issues of control, flexibility, effort, and availability of independent and company sales representatives. There is considerable difference of opinion as to the relative advantages and disadvantages of company and independent representatives with respect to each factor. Proponents of a company sales force argue that this strategy offers greater control, since the company selects, trains, and supervises sales personnel. The sales effort is enhanced because sales personnel are representing only one company's product line. Flexibility exists because the firm can change sales-call patterns and customers and can transfer personnel. Finally, availability of sales personnel is superior, because an independent representative might not exist in a geographic area, whereas a company representative can be relocated. Proponents of independent sales representatives argue that selection, training, and supervision of sales personnel can be done equally well by sales agencies and at no cost to the firm. Flexibility is improved, since fixed investment in a sales force is minimal. Effort is increased,

EXHIBIT 6.1 **Break-Even Chart for Comparing Independent Sales Representatives and a Company Sales Force**

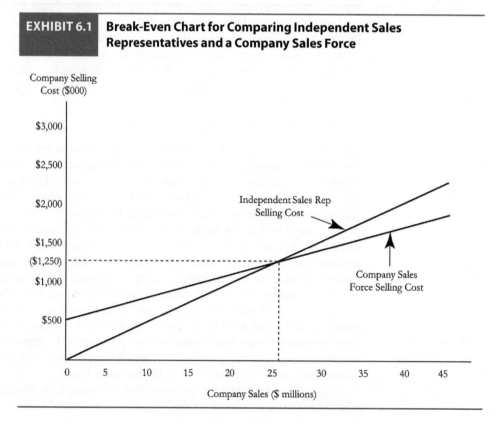

since independent representatives live on their commissions. Finally, availability is no problem, because the entrepreneurial spirit of these individuals will take them wherever effective demand exists. About 50 percent of all companies operating in North America use independent sales representatives in some capacity, whether for a piece of their product line or for a certain geographic region.[5]

Another make-or-buy decision relates to advertising. Often, it is advantageous to have intermediaries (such as wholesalers, retailers, and dealers) assume advertising costs and placement responsibilities. Cooperative advertising, in which a manufacturer and intermediaries share the costs of advertising or sales promotion, is an example of this type of communication strategy.

Push Versus Pull Communication Strategies

Two approaches that incorporate the topics just discussed are termed *push* and *pull communication strategies*. A *push communication strategy* is one in which the offering is pushed through a marketing channel in a sequential fashion, with each channel level representing a distinct target market. A push strategy concentrates on channel intermediaries, building relationships that can have long-term benefits. With such a strategy, advertisements are likely to appear in trade journals and magazines, and sales aids and contests are likely to be used as incentives to gain shelf space and distribution. A principal emphasis, however, is on personal selling to wholesalers and retailers. This strategy is typically used when (1) an organization has easily identifiable buyers, (2) the offering is complex, (3) buyers view the purchase as being risky, (4) a product or service is early in its life cycle, and/or (5) the organization has limited funds for direct-to-consumer advertising.

A *pull communication strategy* seeks to create initial interest among potential buyers, who in turn demand the offering from intermediaries, ultimately pulling the offering through a marketing channel. A pull strategy normally employs heavy end-user (consumer) advertising, free samples, and coupons to stimulate end-user awareness and interest. Consumers might be encouraged to ask their favorite retailer for the offering to pressure retailers into carrying it. Pennzoil Motor Oil's "Ask for Pennzoil" and Claritin's "Talk to your doctor . . ." advertising campaigns are prime examples of a pull communication strategy in practice.

The conditions favoring a pull strategy are opposite to those favoring a push strategy. A central issue in choosing a push strategy is the ability and willingness of wholesalers and retailers to implement selling and sales promotion programs advocated by manufacturers. An important consideration in using a pull strategy is whether an *advertising opportunity* exists for an offering. An advertising opportunity exists when (1) there is a favorable primary demand for a product or service category; (2) the product or service to be advertised can be significantly differentiated from its competitors; (3) the product or service has hidden qualities or benefits that can be portrayed effectively through advertising; and (4) there are strong emotional buying motives involved, such as buyers' concern for health, beauty, status, or safety. An advertising opportunity decreases if one or more of these conditions is not met. Nonprescription drugs and cosmetics satisfy most of these conditions and are frequently advertised. Commodities such as unprocessed grains (for example, corn, oats, and wheat) are rarely advertised; however, when they are processed and dietary supplements and flavors are added to produce cereals, they are advertised effectively.

Nevertheless, push and pull communication strategies are often used together. Investment in end-user advertising stimulates consumer demand, hence product or service sales volume. Investment in efforts to gain display space for products, promote specific services, and educate retail salespeople builds marketing channel relationships that have long-term benefits.

MARKETING WEB SITES AND INTEGRATED MARKETING COMMUNICATIONS

A continuing challenge for companies is the development and execution of an integrated marketing communication strategy that capitalizes on the evolving capabilities of Internet-enabled technology and marketing Web sites. Simply stated, a *Web site* is a place where information is made available to users of the Internet by the provider. Marketing Web sites engage buyers and potential buyers in interactive communication for the purpose of selling an organization's products or services or moving potential buyers closer to a purchase. They come in two general forms: (1) transactional sites and (2) promotional sites.

Purpose of Marketing Web Sites

Transactional Web sites are essentially electronic storefronts such as those operated by L.L.Bean, the catalog marketer, and Ethan Allen, a furniture manufacturer. They focus principally on converting an online browser into an online buyer. Successful transactional Web sites feature well-known, branded products and services and a technological infrastructure designed to create a favorable shopping and buying experience. L.L.Bean clothes, for example, have sold well via its Web site because most consumers know the brand and the merchandise and its site is easy to navigate. Transactional Web sites, which represent a form of direct distribution, are discussed further in Chapter 7 in the context of electronic marketing channels and multichannel marketing.

Promotional Web sites have a very different purpose than transactional sites. They promote a company's products and services and provide information on how items can be used and where they can be purchased. These sites often engage the visitor in an interactive experience involving games, contests, and quizzes with electronic coupons and other gifts as prizes. Procter & Gamble maintains separate promotional Web sites for 24 of its leading brands, including, Scope mouthwash, Folgers coffee, and Pampers diapers. Promotional sites can be effective in generating awareness of, interest in, and trial of a company's products and services. By doing so, promotional sites can support a company's advertising program and traditional marketing channel.[6] For example, Hyundai Motors reports that 80 percent of the people visiting a Hyundai store first visited the brand's Web site (hyundai .com). The Metropolitan Life Insurance Web site (metlife.com) is a proven vehicle for qualifying prospective buyers of its insurance and financial services for its agents. These sites also can be used for customer research and feedback.

Promotional Web sites also can be used to create *buzz*, a popular term for word-of-mouth behavior. Marketers have long known that word of mouth is the most powerful information source for consumers because it involves brand, product, and service recommendations from friends. Some marketers have capitalized on this phenomenon by creating buzz through viral marketing. *Viral marketing* is an Internet-enabled promotional strategy that encourages individuals to forward marketer-initiated messages to others via e-mail. A popular application of viral marketing is to offer consumers incentives (discounts, sweepstakes, or free merchandise) for referrals.

Leveraging Advertising and Personal Selling with Promotional Web Sites

Promotional Web sites can assume a unique role in leveraging different elements of the communication mix. Most companies employ a mix of communication tools to achieve various objectives in the marketing communication process, judiciously combining personal selling, advertising, and sales promotion in mutually reinforcing ways. Promotional Web sites and the Internet-enabled technology that supports them can leverage personal selling and advertising efforts, as described here:

> Personal selling is usually the largest single item in the industrial marketing communications mix. On the other hand, broadcast advertising is typically the dominant way used to reach consumers by marketers. Where do Web sites fit? The Web site is something of a mix between direct selling (it can engage the visitor in a dialogue) and advertising (it can be designed to generate awareness, explain/ demonstrate the product, and provide information—without interactive involvement). It can play a cost-effective role in the communication mix, in the early stages of the process-need recognition, development of product specifications, and supplier search, but can also be useful as the buying process progresses toward evaluation and selection. Finally, the site is also cost-effective in providing feedback on product/service performance. Web sites might typically be viewed as complementary to the direct selling activity by industrial marketers, and as supplementary to advertising by consumer marketers.[7]

 ## COMMUNICATION MIX BUDGETING

As one might expect, the question of how much to spend on communication is difficult to answer. Many factors, including those previously mentioned, must be considered in communication budget determination. In general, the greater the geographic dispersion of a target market, the greater the communication expenditure required; the earlier an offering is in its life cycle, the greater the necessary expenditure; and so forth.

The primary rule in determining a communication budget is to *make the budget commensurate with the tasks required of the communication activities*. The more important communication is in a marketing strategy, the larger the amount of funds that should be allocated to it. Conceptually, budget determination is straightforward—set the budget so that the marginal costs of communication equal the marginal revenues resulting from it. This, however, requires an assessment of the effectiveness of communication.

Because it is difficult to evaluate communication effectiveness, attempts to establish a relationship between budget size and communication effectiveness have proven unproductive. For this reason, there is no widely agreed-on approach for establishing the size of a communication budget. Instead, numerous approaches have been suggested.

The most widely used approach is the *percentage-of-sales approach*. Most frequently, past sales are employed, but anticipated sales are also occasionally used. Hence, when sales increase, communication expenditures increase. Although it creates certain conceptual problems (for example, which should come first— sales or communication?), this approach is commonly used as a starting point because of its simplicity. A related approach is to allocate a fixed dollar amount per offering unit for communication, and then to calculate the communication budget by multiplying this per-unit allocation by the number of units expected to be sold. This method is most often used by durable-goods manufacturers such as appliance and automobile companies.

The percentage-of-sales approach tends to be inflexible and not market-oriented, so it is often supplemented by other approaches. Management may use the *competitive-parity approach*, whereby an organization attempts to maintain a balance between its communication expenditures and those of its competitors. *Advertising share of voice* is commonly used for determining this balance and is defined as an organization's advertising expenditure expressed as a percentage of total advertising by all competitors in a market at a point in time. As an example, if total advertising expenditures for athletic shoes in North America is $100 million and Nike's expenditure is $30 million, Nike would have a 30 percent share of advertising, or a 30 percent share of voice. Companies seeking to improve their competitive position often seek to increase their share of voice.

Another approach is to budget *all available funds* for communication. This approach might be employed in introducing a new offering for which maximum exposure is desired. It is also sometimes used by nonprofit organizations that are stretched for funds to invest in marketing communications.

A final approach is termed the *objective-task approach*. Here an organization budgets communication as a function of the objectives set for a communication program and the costs of the tasks to be performed to accomplish the objectives. The approach involves three steps: (1) define the communication objectives, (2) identify the tasks needed to attain the objectives, and (3) estimate the costs associated with the performance of these tasks. Of the different approaches for communication mix budgeting, it is the closest to the primary rule in determining a communications budget: Make the budget commensurate with the tasks required of the communications activities.

Although all of these approaches are useful, each has limitations. Most managers would say that the objective-task approach is the best approach but the most difficult to apply in practice.[8] More often than not, managers use these approaches in conjunction with one another.

Communication Budget Allocation

Once a communication budget has been settled on, it must be allocated across the communication activities. This can be accomplished by using guidelines similar to those discussed previously for general communication budget determinations. Advertising and personal selling will be used to illustrate necessary budgetary allocation decisions. As a general rule, marketers of consumer products and services spend more for advertising as a percentage of their communication budget; marketers of industrial products and services spend more for personal selling as a percentage of their communication budget.

Advertising Budget Allocation   Decisions about advertising budget allocation revolve around media selection and scheduling considerations. Basically, there are six mass media—television, radio, magazine, newspaper, outdoor (billboard), and the Internet—that an organization can use in transmitting its advertising messages to target markets. Each of these media, or *channels*, consists of *vehicles*—specific entities in which advertisements can appear. In magazines, the vehicles include *Newsweek* and *Mechanics Illustrated*. *Newsweek* can be thought of as a mass-appeal vehicle, whereas *Mechanics Illustrated* might be considered a selective-appeal vehicle. Moreover, media can be *vertical* (reaching more than one level of a marketing channel) or *horizontal* (reaching only one level of a channel). For example, *Bon Appétit* is a vertical magazine while *Gourmet Retailer* is a horizontal magazine.

Media selection is based on numerous factors, the most important of which are cost, reach, frequency, and audience characteristics. Cost frequently acts as a constraint—for example, a 30-second national television commercial (spot) during the Super Bowl costs over $3 million, not including associated production costs. *Cost* is usually expressed as cost per thousand (CPM) readers or viewers to facilitate cross-vehicle comparisons. *Reach* is the number of buyers potentially exposed to an advertisement in a particular vehicle. *Frequency* is the number of times buyers are exposed to an advertisement in a given time period; total exposure equals reach multiplied by frequency. The more closely the characteristics of the target market match those of a vehicle's audience, the more appropriate the vehicle.

Other considerations include the purpose of the advertisement (image building, price, and so on), product needs, and the editorial climate of the vehicle. Whereas price advertisements (those emphasizing an immediate purchase) are more likely to be found in newspapers than in magazines, the opposite is true for advertisements of products requiring color illustration and detailed explanation. Finally, audience characteristics determine which advertisements are acceptable, as well as which are appropriate. For example, 89 percent of wives either influence or make outright purchases of men's clothing. Knowing this, Haggar Clothing, a menswear marketer, advertises in women's magazines such as *Vanity Fair* and *Redbook*.[9]

The timing, or scheduling, of advertisements is critical to their success. Purchases of many offerings (such as skis and swimsuits) are seasonal or may be limited to certain geographic areas. Thus, the advertising budgeting must take into account purchasing patterns. Advertising snowblowers in Ohio during the month of July is probably not a worthwhile endeavor.

There are numerous timing strategies that a marketing manager can employ when undertaking an advertising campaign. One alternative is to concentrate advertising dollars in a relatively short time period—a *blitz strategy*. This strategy is often used when new products or services are introduced. For example, movie studios spend 75 percent of an average new film's advertising budget of $22 million in the four to five days preceding the film's opening weekend.[10] Another alternative is to spend advertising dollars over the long term to maintain continuity. A *pulse strategy* might be employed, whereby an organization periodically concentrates its advertising but also attempts to maintain some semblance of continuity.

Sales-Force Budget Allocation   The sales-force budgeting problem is two-faceted: How many sales representatives are needed, and how should they be allocated? A commonly used formula is

$$NS = \frac{NC \times FC \times LC}{TA}$$

where

NS = number of sales representatives

NC = number of customers (actual or potential)

FC = necessary frequency of customer calls

LC = length of average customer call, including travel time

TA = average available selling time per sales representative (less time spent on administrative duties)

In most instances, the time period is one business year. Although this formula can be used for nearly all types of sales reps, from retail clerks to highly creative reps, it is more likely used with the latter.

Assume that the number of potential customers is 2,500 and four calls should be made per customer per year. If the length of the average call and travel time is two hours and there are 1,340 working hours per year available for selling (50 weeks × 40 hours × 67 percent available selling time per week), then

$$NS = \frac{2,500 \times 4 \times 2}{1,340} = 15 \text{ sales reps needed}$$

The formula is flexible. It is possible to create several different strategies simply by varying (1) how the various elements in this formula are defined and (2) the elements themselves; such as the frequency of calls with actual customers and potential customers.

A related decision concerns the allocation of sales representatives. Each one must have a territory, whether defined as square feet of selling space, a geographic area, or a delivery route. In determining how large the sales territory should be, decision makers should attempt to equate selling opportunities with the workload associated with each sales territory.

The question of how the sales force should be organized is perhaps more difficult to answer, as it directly relates to organization and marketing objectives, offering characteristics, competitor and industry practices, and the like. The alternatives include having sales reps specialize in certain offerings or in customer types or in a combination of offerings and customer types.[11] For instance, Procter & Gamble and Black & Decker organize their sales forces by customer size, with large customers (Walmart and Home Depot) having "customer specialists" who focus on delivering superior customer service. Firestone Tire and Rubber has a sales force that calls on its own dealers and another that calls on independent dealers, such as gasoline stations.

EVALUATION AND CONTROL
OF THE COMMUNICATION PROCESS

As part of every communication strategy, there must be mechanisms for evaluation and control. Without them, a marketing manager would be hard-pressed to manage the communication process effectively. There would be no way to determine whether a strategy had achieved its objectives, nor would there be a way to make changes in a strategy in response to competitive activities or environmental occurrences, whether fortuitous or not.

Implicit in both mechanisms is the concept of *continuousness*. The marketing manager must continuously monitor the execution of any communication plan or strategy to ensure that the communication objectives are being attained.

Ideally, evaluation and control should incorporate some measure of sales or profits. Although this is possible for certain communication tools (the sales effectiveness of a direct-mail program can be judged in a relatively straightforward way), for others, it is not. It is nearly impossible to isolate the contribution of institutional advertising to any individual sales transaction.

Budgeting is the ultimate form of control because slashing or adding to the budget of a communication activity effectively eliminates or accentuates the activity itself. The budgeting element is illustrated by the decision to add an additional sales representative with a yearly salary and fringe benefits of $75,000 or to allocate the same amount to a direct-mail sales promotion program, when the product mix contribution margin is 25 percent. A simple break-even calculation ($75,000 ÷ 0.25) reveals that $300,000 in additional sales must be generated to cover the incremental cost. The issue is therefore whether the new sales representative or the sales promotion is more likely to achieve this break-even sales volume. Incremental analysis of this type is increasingly being viewed as the appropriate approach for evaluating and controlling expenditures for sales promotion, advertising, and personal selling.

NOTES

1. Publicity is a fourth element often included in the communication mix, but it is not considered here for two reasons. First, publicity is often uncontrollable except through the broader public relations function of an organization; hence, it is not typically the responsibility of the marketing manager. Second, even if publicity is the responsibility of the marketing manager, it is often managed as a mixture of advertising and personal selling and, thus, does not require separate treatment.

2. "Online Vehicle Shopping Influences Choice, According to Study from polk, Autotrader.com," Polk.com, February 4, 2011.

3. Peter T. Graber, "IMC Objectives for Apple iPod," Grabers Modern Marketing Communications at grabers.com, November 2, 2004.

4. Independent representatives are individuals or firms paid commissions for selling a manufacturer's product. These individuals or companies represent several noncompeting products that are sold to one or several categories of customers. They do not carry product inventories or take legal title to goods. Their functions vary from selling only a firm's products to broader activities including applications engineering, in-store merchandising support (point-of-purchase displays, stocking), and product maintenance. Independent representatives go by a variety of names, including broker, manufacturer's representative, and sales agent. For an extended discussion on the decision to use a company sales force or independent representatives, see William T. Ross, Frederic Delsace, and Erin Anderson, "Should You Set Up Your Own Sales Force or Should You Outsource It?" *Business Horizons*, Vol. 48 (2005): 23–36.

5. William L. Cron and David W. Cravens, "Sales Force Strategy," in Robert A. Peterson and Roger A. Kerin, eds., *Marketing Strategy, Vol. 1. Wiley International Encyclopedia of Marketing* (Chichester, UK: Wiley, 2011): 197–208.

6. Tom Duncan, *Principles of Advertising and IMC*, 2nd ed. (Burr Ridge, IL: McGraw-Hill, 2009).

7. Richard T. Watson, Pierre Berthon, Leyland F. Pitt, and George Zinkhan, *Electronic Commerce: The Strategic Perspective* (Ft. Worth, TX: Dryden Press, 2000): 79.

8. George E. Belch and Michael A. Belch, *Introduction to Advertising and Promotion: An Integrated Marketing Communications Perspective*, 9th ed. (Chicago: McGraw-Hill, 2012).

9. "Men Buy, Women Shop: The Sexes Have Different Priorities When Walking Down the Aisles," Knowledge@Wharton, November 28, 2007.

10. Robert G. Friedman, "Motion Picture Marketing," in Jason E. Squire, ed., *The Movie Business Book*, 3rd ed. (New York: Simon & Schuster, 2004): 291–306.

11. William L. Cron and Thomas E. DeCarlo, *Dalrymple's Sales Management: Concepts and Cases*, 10th ed. (New York: John Wiley, 2009).

Case

Haverwood Furniture, Inc. (A)

Late in the evening of January 9, 2008, Charlton Bates, president of Haverwood Furniture, Inc., called Dr. Thomas Berry, a marketing professor at a private university in the Northeast and a consultant to the company. The conversation went as follows:

BATES: Hello, Tom. This is Chuck Bates. I'm sorry to call you this late, but I wanted to get your thoughts on the tentative 2008 advertising program proposed by Mike Hervey of Hervey and Bernham, our ad agency.

BERRY: No problem, Chuck. What did they propose?

BATES: The crux of their proposal is that we should increase our advertising expenditures by $225,000. They suggested that we put the entire amount into our consumer advertising program for ads in several shelter magazines.[1] Hervey noted that the National Home Furnishings Collaborative has recommended that wood furniture manufacturers spend 1 percent of their sales exclusively on consumer advertising.

BERRY: That increase appears to be slightly out of line with your policy of budgeting 5 percent of expected sales for total promotion expenditures, doesn't it? Hasn't John Bott [vice president of sales] emphasized the need for more sales representatives?

BATES: Yes, John has requested additional funds. You're right about the 5 percent figure too, and I'm not sure if our sales forecast isn't too optimistic. Your research has shown that our sales historically follow industry sales almost perfectly, and trade economists are predicting about a 4 percent increase for 2008. Yet, I'm not too sure. The stock market collapse last fall is worrisome.

BERRY: Well, Chuck, you can't expect forecasts to be always on the button. The money is one thing, but what else can you tell me about Hervey's rationale for putting more dollars into consumer advertising?

---

[1]Shelter magazines feature home improvement ideas, new ideas in home decorating, and so on. *Better Homes and Gardens* is an example of a shelter magazine.

BATES: He contends that we can increase our exposure and tell our quality and styling story to the buying public—increase brand awareness, enhance our image, that sort of thing. He also cited industry research data that showed that as baby boomers [consumers born between 1946 and 1964] age they become more home oriented and replace older, cheaper furniture with more expensive, longer-lasting pieces. Baby boomers make up 47 percent of all U.S. households. All I know is that my contribution margin will fall to 20 percent next year due to rising material costs.

BERRY: I appreciate your concern. Give me a few days to think about the proposal. I'll get back to you soon.

After hanging up, Berry began to think about Bates' summary of the proposal, Haverwood's present position, and the furniture industry in general. He knew that Bates expected a well-thought-out recommendation on such issues and a step-by-step description of the logic used to arrive at that recommendation.

EXHIBIT 1   Haverwood Furniture, Inc. Bedroom Furniture

Source: Courtesy of Haverwood Furniture, Inc.

THE COMPANY

Haverwood Furniture, Inc. is a manufacturer of medium- to high-priced wood bedroom, living room, and dining room furniture. (Exhibit 1 on page 295 shows an example of the company's bedroom furniture.) The company was formed in the early 1900s by Charlton Bates' great-grandfather. Bates assumed the presidency of the company upon his father's retirement. Year-end net sales in 2007 were $75 million with a before-tax profit of $3.7 million.

Haverwood sells its furniture through 1,000 high-quality department stores and independent furniture specialty stores nationwide, but all stores do not carry the company's entire line. The company is very selective in choosing retail outlets. According to Bates, "Our distribution policy, hence our retailers, should mirror the high quality of our products." As a matter of policy, Haverwood does not sell to furniture chain stores, such as Rooms To Go, or discount outlets.

The company employs 10 full-time salespeople and two regional sales managers. Sales personnel receive a base salary and a small commission on sales. A company sales force is atypical in the furniture industry; most furniture manufacturers use sales agents or representatives who carry a wide assortment of noncompeting furniture lines and receive a commission on sales. "Having our own sales group is a policy my father established years ago," noted Bates, "and we've been quite successful in having people who are committed to our company. Our people don't just take furniture orders. They are expected to motivate retail salespeople to sell our line, assist in setting up displays in stores, and give advice on a variety of matters to our retailers and their salespeople." He added, "It seems that my father was ahead of his time. I was just reading in the *Standard & Poor's Industry Surveys* for household furniture that the competition for retail floor space will require even more support, including store personnel sales training, innovative merchandising, inventory management, and advertising."

In early 2007, Haverwood allocated $3,675,000 for total promotional expenditures for the 2007 operating year, excluding the salary of the vice president of sales. Promotion expenditures were categorized into four groups: (1) sales expense and administration, (2) cooperative advertising programs with retailers, (3) trade promotion, and (4) consumer advertising (see Exhibit 2). Sales costs included salaries for sales personnel and sales managers, selling-expense reimbursements, fringe benefits, and clerical/office assistance, but did not include salespersons' commissions. Commissions were deducted from sales in the calculation of gross profit. The cooperative advertising budget is usually spent on newspaper advertising in a retailer's city. Cooperative advertising allowances are matched by funds provided by retailers on a dollar-for-dollar basis. Trade promotion is directed toward retailers and takes the form of catalogs, trade magazine

---

EXHIBIT 2 **Allocation of Haverwood Furniture Industries, Inc. Promotion Dollars, 2007**

Sales expense and administration	$ 995,500
Cooperative advertising allowance	1,650,000
Trade advertising	467,000
Consumer advertising	562,500
	$3,675,000

Source: Company records.

advertisements, booklets for consumers, and point-of-purchase materials, such as displays, for use in retail stores. Also included in this category is the expense of participating in trade shows. Haverwood is represented at two shows per year. Consumer advertising is directed at potential consumers through shelter magazines. The typical format used in consumer advertising is to highlight new furniture and different bedroom, living room, and dining room arrangements.

THE HOUSEHOLD FURNITURE INDUSTRY

The household furniture industry is divided into three general categories: upholstered, wood, and other (ready-to-assemble furniture and casual furniture). Total furniture industry sales in 2007 were estimated to be $31 billion at manufacturers' prices.

Household upholstered furniture sales represent 50 percent of total household furniture sales, followed by wood furniture (40 percent) and other forms (10 percent). The principal types of wood furniture are dressers, tables, and dining room suites. Bedroom and dining room furniture accounts for the majority of wood furniture sales.

In recent years, wood furniture manufacturers have increased their emphasis on quality by monitoring the entire production process from the raw materials used, to construction, finishes, and packaging. In addition to improving quality controls, companies also stress price points and basic styling features, and are trying to improve shipping schedules. Wood furniture manufacturers' dollar sales grew by 2.5 percent in 2007. Dollar sales were forecasted to increase by 4 percent in 2008.

About 1,000 furniture manufacturers operate in the United States. Ten manufacturers represent about one-third of furniture industry dollar sales. Furniture Brands International, Inc. (owner of the Drexel Heritage, Maitland-Smith, Hendredon, Broyhill, Lane, and Thomasville brands), La-Z-Boy, Inc., Ashley Furniture Industries, Inc., Klaussner Home Furnishings, Inc., Sauder Woodworking Company, Dorel Industries, Inc., and Ethan Allen Interiors, Inc. account for about 28 percent of industry sales (see Exhibit 3). Other well-known manufacturers/brands include Bassett Furniture Industries and Sherrill Furniture. The top 25 manufacturers account for over half of U.S. furniture sales.

EXHIBIT 3   **Top 10 U.S. Furniture Manufacturers**

Company	*Estimated 2006 Revenues ($ million)*
Ashley Furniture Industries, Inc.	$2,964
Furniture Brands International, Inc.	$2,321
La-Z-Boy, Inc.	$1,527
Klaussner Home Furnishings, Inc.	$ 804
Sauder Woodworking Company	$ 635
Ethan Allen Interiors, Inc.	$ 571
Dorel Industries, Inc.	$ 528
BerklineBenchCraft, LLC	$ 466
Lacquer Craft, Inc.	$ 451
Flexsteel Industries, Inc.	$ 369

Source: Company records.

Exports are not a major factor in the U.S. household wood furniture industry. However, imports, notably bedroom furniture from Asia, represent about 30 percent of industry sales. Also, many U.S. furniture manufacturers now outsource their furniture manufacturing. Imports have driven down furniture prices by as much as 30 percent in some furniture categories. U.S. furniture manufacturers have downsized significantly, closing more than 100 domestic furniture manufacturing plants between 2000 and 2007.

Consumer Expenditures for Furniture

Consumer spending for wood furniture is highly cyclical and closely linked to the incidence of new housing starts, consumer confidence, and disposable personal income. Because wood furniture is expensive and often sold in sets, such as a dining room table and chairs, consumers consider these purchases deferrable.

Expenditures for furniture of all kinds have fluctuated as a percentage of consumer disposable personal income. The most recent estimate is that about 1 percent of a U.S. household's disposable income is spent for household furniture and home furnishings. Furniture sales also vary by age. Exhibit 4 shows the average annual furniture expenditures by consumer age.

Furniture-Buying Behavior

Even though industry research indicates many consumers consider the furniture shopping process to be enjoyable, consumers acknowledge that they lack the confidence to assess furniture construction, make judgments about quality, and accurately evaluate the price of furniture. Consumers also find it difficult to choose among the many styles available, fearing they will not like their choice several years later or that their selection will not be appropriate for their home and they will be unable to return it. According to a recent summary of furniture-buying behavior published in *Standard & Poor's Industry Surveys*:

> Consumers are quite finicky when it comes to buying furniture—a procedure fraught with concerns that are often not associated with buying other consumer

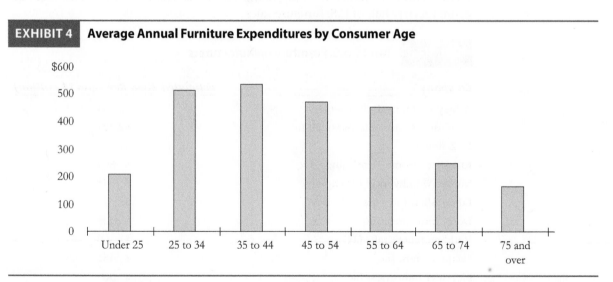

EXHIBIT 4   **Average Annual Furniture Expenditures by Consumer Age**

Source: U.S. Bureau of Labor Statistics.

durables, such as appliances and cars. With appliances and cars, consumers may have a more limited selection, they can do their own research, and they know what they are buying and what to expect.

On the other hand, most consumers know little about evaluating the price or quality of furniture. It is also difficult for consumers to imagine how furniture will look in their homes, or whether they will still like their purchase in several years. Furthermore, there are questions about delivery—as in whether the item will arrive on time and in good condition and whether it can be returned for a full refund.

The furniture industry's efforts to educate consumers over the past years have failed for the most part. These efforts have included in-depth market studies to learn what consumers look for when they buy furniture, improved distribution, and new programs for training sales personnel. Despite these efforts, consumers still find the quality of furniture difficult to discern, and tend to base their furniture choice on price.

Results of a consumer panel sponsored by *Better Homes and Gardens* and composed of its subscribers provide the most comprehensive information available on furniture-buying behavior. Selected findings from the *Better Homes and Gardens* survey are reproduced in the appendix following this case. Other findings arising from this research are as follows:

- 94 percent of the subscribers enjoy buying furniture somewhat or very much.
- 84 percent of the subscribers believe "the higher the price, the higher the quality" when buying home furnishings.
- 72 percent of the subscribers browse or window-shop furniture stores even if they don't need furniture.
- 85 percent read furniture ads before they actually need furniture.
- 99 percent of the subscribers agree with the statement "When shopping for furniture and home furnishings, I like the salesperson to show me what alternatives are available, answer my questions, and let me alone so I can think about it and maybe browse around."
- 95 percent of the subscribers say they get redecorating ideas or guidance from magazines.
- 41 percent of the subscribers have requested a manufacturer's booklet.
- 63 percent of the subscribers say they need decorating advice to "put it all together."

Consumer research data have prompted both furniture retailers and manufacturers to stress the need for well-informed retail sales personnel to work with customers. For example, many manufacturers have established education centers where they train retail salespersons in the qualitative and construction details of the furniture they sell. Some manufacturers also distribute product literature to customers via retailers.

Distribution

Furniture is sold through over 100,000 specialty furniture and home furnishing stores, department stores, and mass-merchandise stores in the United States. Specialty furniture and home furnishing stores account for 68 percent of retail sales. Industry trends indicate that the number of independently owned furniture stores has declined while furniture store chains have grown. The top 10 furniture retailers in the United States captured approximately 26 percent of total U.S. furniture retail sales. Ashley Furniture HomeStores is the largest furniture retailer in terms of retail sales, followed by Rooms To Go, and Ikea.

Furniture manufacturers have eschewed the Internet as a sales channel for the most part. Smaller manufacturers consider the up-front cost to build a Web site coupled with the ongoing cost to maintain a furniture Web site to be prohibitive. Also the costs of delivering and returning heavy items are a concern. These costs, plus the limited success of Internet furniture retailers, have led some larger manufacturers to instead build and operate promotional Web sites at roughly half the cost. These Web sites feature new styles and list retailer locations that sell their products. Examples of these Web sites are drexelheritage.com and thomasville .com. Ethan Allen is an exception. As a vertically integrated furniture manufacturer that sells exclusively through company-owned and franchised stores, Ethan Allen sells selected furniture and accessories at its ethanallen.com Web site.

A significant trend among furniture retailers is the movement toward the "gallery concept"—the practice of dedicating an amount of space in a store and sometimes an entire freestanding retail outlet to one furniture manufacturer. Freestanding retail outlets that carry one manufacturer's products are called single-vendor stores. An example is Bassett Furniture Direct. There are currently 11,000 galleries, and it is estimated this number will reach 12,500 by 2007. Commenting on the gallery concept, Charlton Bates said:

> The gallery concept has great appeal for a furniture manufacturer, since product is displayed in a unique and comfortable setting without the lure of competitive brands. We have galleries in a small number of our furniture stores. The fact that we are not getting our full line in all of our retailers galls me because the opportunity to even discuss the gallery concept with many of our retailers doesn't exist.

Bates added: "Galleries and upscale furniture and department stores attract and serve our target customer, the 40- to 59-year-old homeowner with an annual household income over $100,000. That's where our customers get ideas and buy the quality furniture we sell" (see Exhibit 5).

The selling of furniture to retail outlets is centered on manufacturers' expositions held at selected times and places around the country. The major expositions occur in High Point, North Carolina, in October and April. Regional expositions are also scheduled during the June–August period in locations such as Los Angeles, New York, and Boston. At these *marts*, as they are called in the

---

EXHIBIT 5   **Furniture Retailers That Upscale Shoppers (Household Income $100,000 and Up) Have Used for Ideas and Where They Buy**

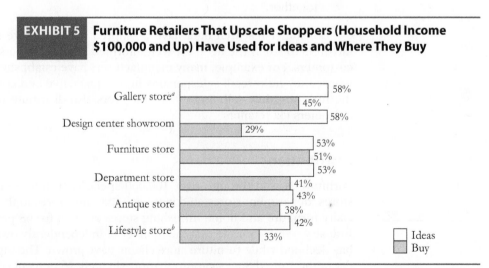

[a]Furniture from single company.
[b]Crate & Barrel, Pottery Barn, Ikea, etc.

furniture industry, retail buyers view manufacturers' lines and often make buying commitments for their stores. However, Haverwood's experience has shown that sales efforts in the retail store by company representatives account for as much as one-half of the company's sales in any given year.

Advertising Practices

Manufacturers of household furniture spend approximately 3.5 percent of annual net sales for advertising of all types (consumer, trade, and cooperative advertising). This percentage has remained constant for many years. The typical vehicles used for consumer advertising are shelter magazines such as *Better Homes and Gardens, Martha Stewart Living House Beautiful*, and *Southern Living*. Trade advertising directed primarily toward retailers includes brochures, point-of-purchase materials to be displayed on a retailer's sales floor, and technical booklets describing methods of construction and materials. Cooperative advertising, shared with retailers, usually appears in newspapers, but there are also some television and radio spots featuring the brands carried by retailers.

 # THE BUDGET MEETING

At the January 9 meeting attended by Hervey and Bernham executives and Haverwood executives, Michael Hervey proposed that the expenditure for consumer advertising be increased by $225,000 in 2008. Cooperative advertising and trade advertising allowances would remain at 2007 levels. Hervey further recommended that shelter magazines account for the bulk of the incremental expenditure for consumer advertising.

John Bott, Haverwood's vice president of sales, disagreed with the budget allocation and noted that sales expenses and administration costs were expected to rise by $65,000 in 2008. Moreover, Bott believed that an additional sales representative was needed to service company accounts because 50 new accounts were being added. He estimated that the cost of the additional representative, including salary and expenses, would be at least $70,000 in 2008. "That's about $135,000 in additional sales expenses that have to be added into our promotional budget for 2008," Bott noted. He continued:

> We recorded sales of $75 million in 2007. If we assume a 4 percent increase in sales in 2008, that means our total budget will be $3,975,000, if my figures are right—a $147,000 increase over our previous budget. And I need $135,000 of that. In other words, $12,000 is available for trade promotion, to assist our salespeople servicing new accounts.

Hervey's reply to Bott noted that the company planned to introduce several new styles of living room and dining room furniture in 2008 and that these new items would require consumer advertising in shelter magazines to be launched successfully. He agreed with Bott that increased funding of the sales effort might be necessary and thought that Haverwood might draw funds from cooperative advertising allowances and trade promotion.

Bates interrupted the dialogue between Bott and Hervey to mention that the $225,000 increase in promotion brought the budget up to the 5 percent percentage-of-sales policy limit. He pointed out, however, that higher material costs, pricing pressure, and a recent wage increase were forecasted to squeeze Haverwood's gross profit margin and threaten the company objective of achieving a 5 percent net profit margin before taxes. "Perhaps some juggling of the figures is necessary," he concluded. "Both of you have good points. Let me think about what's been said and then let's schedule a meeting for a week from today."

As Bates reviewed his notes from the meeting, he realized that the funds allocated to promotion were only part of the question. How the funds would be allocated within the budget was also crucial. A call to Tom Berry might be helpful in this regard, too.

APPENDIX: SELECTED FINDINGS FROM THE *BETTER HOMES AND GARDENS* CONSUMER PANEL REPORT—HOME FURNISHINGS[2]

Question: If you were going to buy furniture in the near future, how important would the following factors be in selecting the store to buy furniture? (Respondents: 449)

Factor	Very Important	Somewhat Important	Not Too Important	Not at All Important	No Answer
Sells high-quality furnishings	62.6%	31.0%	3.8%	1.1%	1.5%
Has a wide range of different furniture styles	58.8	29.2	8.2	2.9	0.9
Gives you personal service	60.1	29.9	7.8	0.9	1.3
Is a highly dependable store	85.1	12.7	1.1	–	1.1
Offers decorating help from experienced home planners	26.5	35.9	25.4	10.9	1.3
Lets you "browse" all you want	77.1	17.8	3.3	0.7	1.1
Sells merchandise that's a good value for the money	82.0	15.6	0.9	0.2	1.3
Displays furniture in individual room settings	36.3	41.2	18.7	2.4	1.3
Has a relaxed, no-pressure atmosphere	80.0	17.1	1.6	–	1.3
Has well-informed salespeople	77.5	19.8	1.6	–	1.1
Has a very friendly atmosphere	68.2	28.1	2.4	–	1.3
Carries the style of furniture you like	88.0	10.0	0.9	–	1.1

---

[2]Reprinted courtesy of the *Better Homes and Gardens* Consumer Panel.

Question: Please rate the following factors as to their importance to you when you purchase or shop for case-goods furniture, such as a dining room or living room suite, *1* being the most important factor, *2* being second most important, and so on, until all factors have been rated. (Respondents: 449)

Factor	*1*	*2*	*3*	*4*	*5*	*6*	*7*	*8*	*9*	*10*	*No Answer*
Construction of item	24.1%	16.0%	18.5%	13.1%	10.5%	6.9%	4.9%	1.6%	0.2%	1.1%	3.1%
Comfort	13.6	14.7	12.9	12.3	12.7	10.9	8.2	4.5	4.0	2.4	3.8
Styling and design	33.6	19.8	11.1	9.6	4.7	7.3	4.5	1.6	2.9	1.6	3.3
Durability of fabric	2.2	7.6	9.8	14.5	15.1	14.7	12.9	5.6	5.8	7.8	4.0
Type and quality of wood	10.9	17.8	16.3	15.8	14.7	5.8	5.3	3.1	4.9	2.0	3.4
Guarantee or warranty	1.6	3.8	1.6	5.3	8.7	10.0	13.8	25.2	14.5	11.1	4.4
Price	9.4	6.2	8.7	8.5	10.0	12.5	14.2	11.8	6.9	8.0	3.8
Reputation of manufacturer or brand name	6.2	3.6	4.7	5.6	6.2	6.2	12.7	17.1	22.7	11.6	3.4
Reputation of retailer	1.6	1.8	1.6	2.4	4.0	7.3	7.4	13.6	22.0	34.5	3.8
Finish, color of wood	4.7	7.6	10.2	8.0	8.9	13.4	10.7	10.0	10.2	12.7	3.6

Question: Below is a list of 15 criteria that may influence what furniture you buy. Please rate them from *1* as most important to *5* as least important. (Respondents: 449)

Criterion	*1*	*2*	*3*	*4*	*5*	*No Answer*
Guarantee or warranty	11.4%	11.1%	26.3%	16.9%	5.3%	29.0%
Brand name	9.1	6.5	14.3	25.6	11.6	32.9
Comfort	34.7	27.8	14.5	8.5	4.7	9.8
Decorator suggestion	4.0	2.4	2.7	8.2	44.8	37.9
Material used	14.9	24.1	14.9	13.4	6.2	26.5
Delivery time	0.7	0.5	1.3	2.9	55.2	39.4
Size	7.6	10.7	13.6	30.9	4.0	33.2
Styling and design	33.4	17.8	21.8	13.6	2.2	11.2
Construction	34.3	23.6	13.1	11.4	2.9	14.7
Fabric	4.0	25.6	24.9	14.0	4.5	27.0
Durability	37.0	19.4	13.6	6.9	4.9	18.2
Finish on wooden parts	5.8	14.7	16.7	10.7	16.7	35.4
Price	19.4	21.8	16.0	10.9	15.4	16.5
Manufacturer's reputation	4.2	9.1	15.4	22.9	14.3	34.1
Retailer's reputation	2.2	4.7	10.5	21.2	26.5	34.9

Question: Listed below are some statements others have made about shopping for furniture. Please indicate how much you agree or disagree with each one. (Respondents: 449)

Statement	Agree Completely	Agree Somewhat	Neither Agree nor Disagree	Disagree Somewhat	Disagree Completely	No Answer
I wish there were some way to be really sure of getting good quality in furniture	61.9%	24.7%	4.7%	4.2%	3.6%	0.9%
I really enjoy shopping for furniture	49.2	28.3	7.6	9.8	4.2	0.9
I would never buy any furniture without my husband's/wife's approval	47.0	23.0	10.9	9.8	7.1	2.2
I like all pieces in the master bedroom to be exactly the same style	35.9	30.7	12.7	11.1	7.6	2.0
Once I find something I like in furniture, I wish it would last forever so I'd never have to buy again	36.8	24.3	10.0	18.9	9.1	0.9
I wish I had more confidence in my ability to decorate my home attractively	23.1	32.3	12.5	11.6	18.7	1.8
I wish I knew more about furniture styles and what looks good	20.0	31.0	17.1	13.4	16.7	1.8
My husband/wife doesn't take much interest in the furniture we buy	6.5	18.0	12.3	17.8	41.4	4.0
I like to collect a number of different styles in the dining room	3.3	10.5	15.2	29.8	38.3	2.9
Shopping for furniture is very distressing to me	2.4	11.6	14.3	18.0	51.9	1.8

Question: Listed below are some factors that may influence your choice of furnishings. Please rate them with *1* being most important, *2* being second most important, and so on, until all factors have been rated. (Respondents: 449)

Factor	1	2	3	4	5	No Answer
Friends and/or neighbors	1.3%	16.9%	15.8%	22.1%	41.7%	2.2%
Family or spouse	62.8	9.4	14.3	9.8	2.0	1.7
Magazine advertising	16.3	30.3	29.6	17.6	4.2	2.0
Television advertising	1.1	6.7	14.7	32.5	42.3	2.7
Store displays	18.9	37.2	22.1	14.0	5.6	2.2

Question: When you go shopping for a *major piece* of furniture or smaller pieces of furniture, who, if anyone, do you usually go with? (Respondents: 449—multiple responses)

Person	Major Pieces	Other Pieces
Husband	82.4%	59.5%
Mother or mother-in-law	6.2	9.1
Friend	12.0	18.9
Decorator	4.2	1.6
Other relative	15.6	15.4
Other person	2.9	3.3
No one else	5.1	22.3
No answer	0.9	3.1

Question: When the time comes to purchase a *major* item of furniture or other smaller pieces of furniture, who, if anyone, helps you make the final decision about which piece to buy? (Respondents: 449—multiple responses)

Person	Major Pieces	Other Pieces
Husband	86.0%	63.5%
Mother or mother-in-law	2.4	4.5
Friend	3.6	8.0
Decorator	3.1	2.7
Other relative	10.0	12.9
Other person	1.6	1.8
No one else	7.1	24.3
No answer	0.9	2.2

Case

Haverwood Furniture, Inc. (B)

In April 2008, Haverwood Furniture, Inc. merged with Lea-Meadows, Inc., a manufacturer of upholstered furniture for living and family rooms. The merger was not planned in a conventional sense. Charlton Bates' father-in-law died suddenly in early February 2008, leaving his daughter with controlling interest in Lea-Meadows. The merger proceeded smoothly, since the two firms were located on adjacent properties and the general consensus was that the two firms would maintain as much autonomy as was economically justified. Moreover, the upholstery line filled a gap in the Haverwood product mix, even though it would retain its own identity and brand names.

The only real issue that continued to plague Bates was merging the selling effort. Haverwood had its own sales force, but Lea-Meadows relied on sales agents to represent it. The question was straightforward, in his opinion: "Do we give the upholstery line of chairs and sofas to our sales force, or do we continue using the sales agents?" John Bott, Haverwood's vice-president of sales, said the line should be given to his sales group; Martin Moorman, national sales manager at Lea-Meadows, said the upholstery line should remain with sales agents.

 ## LEA-MEADOWS, INC.

Lea-Meadows, Inc. is a small, privately owned manufacturer of upholstered furniture for use in living and family rooms. The firm is more than 75 years old. The company uses some of the finest fabrics and frame construction in the industry, according to trade sources. Net sales in 2007 were $5 million. Total industry sales of upholstered furniture manufacturers in 2007 were $15.5 billion. Forecasted 2008 industry sales for upholstered furniture were $16.1 billion. Company sales had increased 3 percent annually over the past five years, and company executives believed this growth rate would continue for the foreseeable future.

Lea-Meadows employed 15 sales agents to represent its products. These sales agents also represented several manufacturers of noncompeting furniture and home furnishings. Often, a sales agent found it necessary to deal with several buyers in a store in order to represent all the lines carried. On a typical sales call,

This case was prepared by Professor Roger A. Kerin, of the Edwin L. Cox School of Business, Southern Methodist University, as a basis for class discussion and is not designed to illustrate appropriate or inappropriate handling of administrative situations. All names and data are disguised. Copyright © 2008 by Roger A. Kerin. No part of this case may be reproduced without permission from the copyright holder.

a sales agent first visited buyers to discuss new lines, in addition to any promotions being offered by manufacturers. New orders were sought where and when it was appropriate. The sales agent then visited the selling floor to check displays, inspect furniture, and inform salespeople about furniture styles and construction. Lea-Meadows paid an agent commission of 5 percent of net company sales for these services. Moorman thought sales agents spent 10 to 15 percent of their in-store time on Lea-Meadows products.

The company did not attempt to influence the type of retailers that agents contacted, although it was implicit in the agency agreement that agents would not sell to discount houses. Sales records indicated that agents were calling on specialty furniture and department stores. An estimated 1,000 retail accounts were called on in 2006 and 2007. All agents had established relationships with their retail accounts and worked closely with them.

 ## HAVERWOOD FURNITURE, INC.

Haverwood Furniture, Inc. is a manufacturer of medium- to high-priced wood bedroom, living room, and dining room furniture.[1] Net sales in 2007 were $75 million; before-tax profit was $3.7 million. Industry sales of wood furniture in 2007 were $12.4 billion at manufacturers' prices. Projected wood furniture industry sales for 2008 were $12.9 billion.

The company employed 10 full-time sales representatives, who called on 1,000 retail accounts. These individuals performed the same function as sales agents but were paid a salary plus a small commission. In 2007, the average sales representative received an annual salary of $70,000 (plus expenses) and a commission of 0.5 percent on net company sales. Total sales administration costs were $130,000.

Haverwood Furniture's salespeople were highly regarded in the industry. They were known particularly for their knowledge of wood furniture and willingness to work with buyers and retail sales personnel. Despite these advantages, Bates knew that all retail accounts did not carry the complete Haverwood furniture line. He had therefore instructed Bott to "push the group a little harder." At present, sales representatives were making 10 sales calls per week, with the average sales call running three hours. Salespersons' remaining time was accounted for by administrative activities and travel. Bates recommended that the call frequency be increased to seven calls per account per year, which was consistent with what he thought was the industry norm.

 ## MERGING THE SALES EFFORTS

Through separate meetings with Bott and Moorman, Bates was able to piece together a variety of data and perspectives on the question of merging the sales efforts. These meetings also made it clear that Bott and Moorman differed dramatically in their views.

John Bott had no doubts about assigning the line to the Haverwood sales force. Among the reasons he gave for this view were the following. First, Haverwood had developed one of the most well respected, professional sales forces in the industry.

---

[1]Additional background information on the company and industry can be found in the case titled "Haverwood Furniture, Inc. (A)," on page 294.

The representatives could easily learn the fabric jargon, and they already knew personally many of the buyers who were responsible for upholstered furniture. Second, selling the Lea-Meadows line would require only about 15 percent of present sales call time. Thus, he thought that the new line would not be a major burden. Third, more control over sales efforts was possible. Bott noted that Charlton Bates' father had created the sales group 30 years earlier because of the commitment it engendered and the service "only our own people are able and willing to give." Moreover, the company salespeople have the Haverwood "look" and presentation style, which is instilled in every one of them. Fourth, Bott said that it wouldn't look right if both representatives and agents called on the same stores and buyers. He noted that Haverwood and Lea-Meadows overlapped on all their accounts. He said, "We'd be paying a commission on sales to these accounts when we would have gotten them anyway. The difference in commission percentages would not be good for morale."

Martin Moorman advocated keeping sales agents for the Lea-Meadows line. His arguments were as follows. First, all sales agents had established contacts and were highly regarded by store buyers, and most had represented the line in a professional manner for many years. He, too, had a good working relationship with all 15 agents. Second, sales agents represented little, if any, cost beyond commissions. Moorman noted, "Agents get paid when we get paid." Third, sales agents were committed to the Lea-Meadows line: "The agents earn a part of their living representing us. They have to service retail accounts to get the repeat business." Fourth, sales agents were calling on buyers not contacted by the Haverwood sales force. Moorman noted, "If we let Haverwood people handle the line, we might lose these accounts, have to hire more sales personnel, or take away 25 percent of the present time given to Haverwood product lines." Finally, Moorman took issue with Bott's view that Haverwood salespeople could easily learn about upholstered furniture. He said, "Lea-Meadows has some 1,000 different frames for sofas and upholstered chairs. If all combinations of fabric, skirts, pillows, springs, and fringes are considered, a Haverwood sales rep would need to be conversant in no fewer than 1 billion possibilities. I tremble just thinking about teaching Haverwood's salespeople the finer points of our prints, velvets, jacquards, and textures, such as chenille, and that's just our upholstery fabrics!"

As Bates reflected on the meetings, he felt that a broader perspective was necessary beyond the views expressed by Bott and Moorman. One factor was profitability. Existing Haverwood furniture lines typically had gross margins that were 5 percent higher than those for Lea-Meadows upholstered lines. Another factor was the "us and them" references apparent in the meetings with Bott and Moorman. Would merging the sales effort overcome this, or would it cause more problems? The idea of increasing the sales force to incorporate the Lea-Meadows line did not sit well with him. Adding new salespeople would require restructuring of sales territories, involve potential loss of commissions by existing salespeople, and be "a big headache." Still, it had been Haverwood's policy for many years to have its own sales force and not use sales agents. In addition, there was the subtle issue of Moorman's future. Moorman, who was 58 years old, had worked for Lea-Meadows for 30 years and was a family friend and godfather to Bates's youngest child. If the Lea-Meadows line was represented by the Haverwood sales force, Moorman's position would be eliminated. Given these circumstances, Bates also thought his wife's views had to be considered. He could bring up the topic on their way to the High Point, North Carolina, furniture exposition early next week.

Case

Cadbury Beverages, Inc.

Crush Brand

In January 1990, marketing executives at Cadbury Beverages, Inc. began the challenging task of relaunching the Crush, Hires, and Sundrop soft drink brands. These brands had been acquired from Procter & Gamble in October 1989.

After considerable discussion, senior marketing executives at Cadbury Beverages, Inc. decided to focus initial attention on the Crush brand of fruit-flavored carbonated beverages. Three issues were prominent. First, immediate efforts were needed to rejuvenate the bottling network for the Crush soft drink brand. Second, according to one executive, "[we had] to sort through and figure out what the Crush brand equity is, how the brand was built . . . and develop a base positioning."[1] Third, a new advertising and promotion program for Crush had to be developed, including setting objectives, developing strategies, and preparing preliminary budgets.

Kim Feil was assigned responsibility for managing the relaunch of the Crush soft drink brand. She had joined Cadbury Beverages, Inc. on December 12, 1989, as a senior product manager, after working in various product management positions at a large consumer goods company for five years. Recounting her first day on the job, Feil said, "I arrived early Wednesday morning to find 70 boxes of research reports, print ads, sales and trade promotions, and videotapes stacked neatly from the floor to the ceiling." Undaunted, she began to sift through the mountains of material systematically, knowing that her assessment and recommendations would soon be sought.

 ## CADBURY BEVERAGES, INC.

Cadbury Beverages, Inc. is the beverage division of Cadbury Schweppes PLC, a major global soft drink and confectionery marketer. In 1989, Cadbury Schweppes PLC had worldwide sales of $4.6 billion, which were produced by product sales

[1] Patricia Winters, "Fresh Start for Crush," *Advertising Age* (January 6, 1990): 47.

The cooperation of Cadbury Beverages, Inc. in the preparation of this case is gratefully acknowledged. This case was prepared by Professor Roger A. Kerin, of the Edwin L. Cox School of Business, Southern Methodist University, as a basis for class discussion and is not designed to illustrate effective or ineffective handling of an administrative situation. Certain information has been disguised and is not useful for research purposes. Crush is a registered trademark used by permission from Cadbury Beverages, Inc. Copyright © 1995 by Roger A. Kerin. No part of this case may be reproduced without written permission of the copyright holder.

in more than 110 countries. Cadbury Schweppes PLC headquarters are located in London, England; Cadbury Beverages, Inc., worldwide headquarters are in Stamford, Connecticut. Exhibit 1 shows the product list sold worldwide by Cadbury Beverages, Inc. Exhibit 2 details the product list for the United States.

History

Cadbury Schweppes PLC has the distinction of being the world's first soft drink maker. The company can trace its beginnings to 1783 in London, where Swiss national Jacob Schweppe first sold his artificial mineral water. Schweppe returned to Switzerland in 1789, but the company continued its British operations, introducing a lemonade in 1835 and tonic water and ginger ale in the 1870s. Beginning in the 1880s, Schweppes expanded worldwide, particularly in countries that would later form the British Commonwealth. In the 1960s, the company diversified into food products.

In 1969, Schweppes merged with Cadbury. Cadbury was a major British candy maker that traced its origins to John Cadbury, who began his business making cocoa in Birmingham, England, in the 1830s. By the middle of this century, Cadbury had achieved market presence throughout the British Commonwealth, as well as other countries.

In 1989, Cadbury Schweppes PLC was one of the world's largest multinational firms and was ranked 457th in *BusinessWeek*'s Global 1000. Beverages accounted for 60 percent of company worldwide sales and 53 percent of operating income in 1989. Confectionery items accounted for 40 percent of worldwide sales and produced 47 percent of operating income.

EXHIBIT 1 **Worldwide Product List for Cadbury Beverages, Inc.**

Carbonates	Waters	Still Drinks/Juices
Canada Dry	Schweppes	Oasis
Schweppes	Canada Dry	Atoll
Pure Spring	Pure Spring	Bali
Sunkist	Malvern	TriNaranjus
Crush		Vida
'C' Plus		Trina
Hires		Trina Colada
Sussex		Red Cheek
Old Colony		Allen's
Sundrop		Mitchell's
Gini		Mott's
		Clamato
		E. D. Smith
		Rose's
		Mr & Mrs "T"
		Holland House

EXHIBIT 2 **U.S. Product List for Cadbury Beverages, Inc.**

Schweppes	Canada Dry	Sunkist	Crush, Hires, Sundrop	Mott's, Red Cheek, Holland House, Mr & Mrs "T," Rose's
Tonic Water	Tonic Water	Sunkist Pineapple Soda	Crush Orange	Mott's 100% Pure Apple Juices
Diet Tonic Water	Sugar-Free Tonic Water	Sunkist Grape Soda	Crush Diet Orange	Mott's 100% Pure Juice Blends
Club Soda	Club Soda	Sunkist Fruit Punch	Hires Root Beer	Mott's Juice Drinks
Seltzer Water	Seltzer Waters	Sunkist Strawberry Soda	Hires Diet Root Beer	Mott's Apple Sauce
Sparkling Waters	Sparkling Mineral Waters	Sunkist Orange Soda	Hires Cream Soda	Mott's Apple Sauce Fruit Snacks
Grapefruit Soda	Barrelhead Root Beer	Sunkist Diet Orange Soda	Hires Diet Cream Soda	Mott's Prune Juice
Collins Mix	Barrelhead Sugar-Free	Sunkist Sparkling	Crush Strawberry	Clamato
Grape Soda	Root Beer	Lemonade	Crush Grape	Beefamato
Ginger Ale	Wink	Sunkist Diet Sparkling	Crush Cherry	Grandma's Molasses
Diet Ginger Ale	Ginger Ale	Lemonade	Crush Pineapple	Rose's Lime Juice
Raspberry Ginger Ale	Diet Ginger Ale		Crush Cream Soda	Rose's Grenadine
Diet Raspberry Ginger Ale	Cherry Ginger Ale		Sundrop Cherry Citrus	Red Cheek Apple Juice
Bitter Lemon	Diet Cherry Ginger Ale		Sundrop Diet Citrus	Red Cheek Juice Blends
Lemon Sour	Bitter Lemon			Mr & Mrs "T" Margarita Salt
Lemon Lime	No-Cal Brand Soft Drinks			Mr & Mrs "T" Bloody Mary Mix
	Cott Brand Soft Drinks			Mr & Mrs "T" Liquid Cocktail Mixers
	Lemon Ginger Ale			Mr & Mrs "T" Rich & Spicy
	Diet Lemon Ginger Ale			Holland House Cooking Wines
				Holland House Dry Mixers
				Holland House Wine Marinades
				Holland House Smooth & Spicy
				Holland House Coca Casa
				Cream of Coconut
				Holland House Liquid Mixers

Soft Drinks

Cadbury Schweppes PLC is the world's third largest soft drink marketer behind Coca-Cola and PepsiCo. The company has achieved this status through consistent marketing investment in the Schweppes brand name and extensions to different beverage products such as tonic, ginger ale, club soda, and seltzer in various flavors. In addition, the company has acquired numerous other brands throughout the world, each with an established customer franchise. For example, Cadbury Schweppes PLC acquired the Canada Dry soft drink brands and certain rights to Sunkist soft drinks in 1986. In 1989 the company acquired certain soft drink brands and associated assets (for TriNaranjus, Vida, Trina, and Trina Colada) in Spain and Portugal and purchased the Gini brand, which is the leading bitter lemon brand in France and Belgium. Also, in October 1989 the company acquired all the Crush brand worldwide trademarks from Procter & Gamble for $220 million.

Cadbury Schweppes PLC (Cadbury Beverages, Inc.) was the fourth largest soft drink marketer in the United States in 1989, with a carbonated soft drink market share of 3.4 percent. (The three leading U.S. soft drink companies, in order, were Coca-Cola, PepsiCo, and Dr Pepper/Seven Up.) Nonetheless, the company's brands were often the market leader in their specific categories. For example, Canada Dry is the top-selling ginger ale in the United States, Schweppes is the leading tonic water, and Canada Dry seltzers top the club soda/seltzer category. The combined sales of Sunkist and Crush brand orange drinks lead the orange-flavored carbonated soft drink category.

According to industry analysts, the 1989 acquisition of Crush meant that Canada Dry would account for 39 percent of Cadbury Beverages soft drink sales in the United States. Sunkist, Crush, and Schweppes would account for 22 percent, 20 percent, and 17 percent of U.S. sales, respectively. The remaining 2 percent of U.S. sales would come from other soft drink brands.[2]

 ## CARBONATED SOFT DRINK INDUSTRY

American consumers drink more soft drinks than tap water. In 1989, the average American consumed 46.7 gallons of carbonated soft drinks, or twice the 23 gallons consumed in 1969. Population growth compounded by rising per capita consumption produced an estimated $43 billion in retail sales in 1989.

Industry Structure

There are three major participants in the production and distribution of carbonated soft drinks in the United States. They are concentrate producers, bottlers, and retail outlets. For regular soft drinks, concentrate producers manufacture the basic flavors (for example, lemon-lime and cola) for sale to bottlers, which add a sweetener to carbonated water and package the beverage in bottles and cans. For diet soft drinks, concentrate producers include an artificial sweetener, such as aspartame, with their flavors.

There are over 40 concentrate producers in the United States. However, about 82 percent of industry sales are accounted for by three producers: Coca-Cola, PepsiCo, and Dr Pepper/Seven Up.

---

[2]Patricia Winters, "Cadbury Schweppes' Plan: Skirt Cola Giants," *Advertising Age* (August 13, 1990): 22–23.

Approximately 1,000 bottling plants in the United States convert flavor concentrate into carbonated soft drinks. Bottlers are either owned by concentrate producers or franchised to sell the brands of concentrate producers. For example, roughly one-half of Pepsi-Cola's sales are through company-owned bottlers; the remaining volume is sold through franchised bottlers. Franchised bottlers are typically granted a right to package and distribute a concentrate producer's branded line of soft drinks in a defined territory and not allowed to market a directly competitive major brand. However, franchised bottlers can represent noncompetitive brands and decline to bottle a concentrate producer's secondary lines. These arrangements mean that a franchised bottler of Pepsi-Cola cannot sell Royal Crown (RC) Cola but can bottle and market Orange Crush rather than PepsiCo's Mandarin Orange Slice.

Concentrate producer pricing to bottlers was similar across competitors within flavor categories. Exhibit 3 shows the approximate price and cost structure for orange concentrate producers and bottlers.

The principal retail channels for carbonated soft drinks are supermarkets, convenience stores, vending machines, fountain service, and thousands of small retail outlets. Soft drinks are typically sold in bottles and cans, except for fountain service. In fountain service, syrup is sold to a retail outlet (such as McDonald's), which mixes the syrup with carbonated water for immediate consumption by customers. Supermarkets account for about 40 percent of carbonated soft drink industry sales. Industry analysts consider supermarket sales the key to a successful soft drink marketing effort.

EXHIBIT 3   Approximate Price and Cost Structure for Orange Concentrate Producers and Bottlers

| | Concentrate Producers | | | |
| | Regular (Sugar) | | Diet (Aspartame) | |
	$/Case	Percentage	$/Case	Percentage
Net selling price	$0.76	100%	$0.92	100%
Cost of goods sold	0.11	14	0.12	13
Gross profit	$0.65	86%	$0.80	87%
Selling and delivery	0.02	3	0.02	2
Advertising and promotion	0.38	50	0.38	41
General and administrative expense	0.13	17	0.13	14
Pretax cash profit/case	$0.12	16%	$0.27	30%

| | Bottlers | | | |
| | Regular (Sugar) | | Diet (Aspartame) | |
	$/Case	Percentage	$/Case	Percentage
Net selling price	$5.85	100%	$5.85	100%
Cost of goods sold	3.16	54	3.35	57
Gross profit	$2.69	46%	$2.50	43%
Selling and delivery	1.35	23	1.35	23
Advertising and promotion	0.40	7	0.40	7
General and administrative expense	0.05	1	0.05	1
Pretax cash profit/case	$0.89	15%	$0.71	12%

Soft Drink Marketing

Soft drink marketing is characterized by heavy investment in advertising, selling, and promotion to and through bottlers to retail outlets, and consumer price discounting. Concentrate producers usually assume responsibility for developing national consumer advertising and promotion programs, product development and planning, and marketing research. Bottlers usually take the lead in developing trade promotions to retail outlets and local consumer promotions. Bottlers are also responsible for selling and servicing retail accounts, including the placement and maintenance of in-store displays and the restocking of supermarket and convenience store shelves with their brands.

Flavor and Brand Competition   Colas account for slightly less than two-thirds of total carbonated soft drink sales. Other flavors, such as orange, lemon-lime, cherry, grape, and root beer account for the remaining sales. Estimates of market shares for flavors in 1989 were as follows:

Flavor	*Market Share*
Cola	65.7%
Lemon-lime	12.9
Orange	3.9
Root beer	3.6
Ginger ale	2.8
Grape	1.1
Others	10.0
	100.0%

Diet soft drinks represented 31 percent of industry sales in 1989. Industry trend data indicate that sales of diet drinks accounted for a large portion of the overall growth of carbonated soft drink sales in the 1980s.

There are more than 900 registered brand names for soft drinks in the United States. Most of these brands are sold only regionally. Exhibit 4 shows the top 10 soft drink brands in 1989. Six of these brands were colas, and all 10 brands were marketed by Coca-Cola, PepsiCo, or Dr Pepper/Seven Up.

Soft Drink Purchase and Consumption Behavior   Industry research suggests that the purchase of soft drinks in supermarkets is often unplanned. Accordingly, soft drink purchasers respond favorably to price (coupon) promotions, in-store (particularly end-of-aisle) displays, and other forms of point-of-sale promotions (such as shelf tags). The importance of display is evidenced in the view held by an industry analyst who estimated that a brand is "locked out of 60 percent of the [supermarket soft drink] volume if it can't get end-aisle displays."[3] The typical supermarket purchaser of soft drinks is a married woman with children under 18 years of age living at home.

Soft drink buying is somewhat seasonal, with consumption slightly higher during summer months than winter months. Consumption also varies by region of the country. Per capita consumption in the East South Central states of Kentucky, Tennessee, Alabama, and Mississippi was highest in the United States in 1989, with 54.9 gallons compared with the national per capita average of 46.7 gallons.

---

[3]Patricia Winters, "Crush Fails to Fit on P&G Shelf," *Advertising Age* (July 10, 1989): 1, 42–43.

| EXHIBIT 4 | Market Share of Top 10 Soft Drink Brands in the United States, 1989 |

Brand	Market Share
1. Coca-Cola Classic	19.8%
2. Pepsi-Cola	17.9
3. Diet Coke	8.9
4. Diet Pepsi	5.7
5. Dr Pepper	4.5
6. Sprite	3.7
7. Mountain Dew	3.6
8. 7Up	3.2
9. Caffeine-free Diet Coke	2.5
10. Caffeine-free Diet Pepsi	1.6
Top 10 brands	71.4
Other brands	28.6
Total industry	100.0%

In the Mountain states of Montana, Idaho, Wyoming, Colorado, New Mexico, Arizona, Utah, and Nevada, per capita consumption was 37.1 gallons—the lowest in the nation.

Consumption of diet beverages was more pronounced among consumers over 25 years of age. Teenagers, and younger consumers generally, were heavier consumers of regular soft drinks.

ORANGE CATEGORY

Orange-flavored carbonated soft drinks recorded sales of 126 million cases in 1989, or 3.9 percent of total industry sales sold through supermarkets.[4] Prior to 1986, annual case volume had hovered in the range of 100 to 102 million cases. In the mid-1980s, PepsiCo introduced Mandarin Orange Slice, and Coca-Cola introduced Minute Maid Orange. Entry of these two brands, supported by widespread distribution and heavy advertising and promotion, revitalized the category and increased supermarket sales to 126 million cases. Annual supermarket case volume for the period 1984–1989 was as follows:

Year	Annual Supermarket Case Volume of Orange-Flavored Soft Drinks
1984	102,000,000
1985	100,000,000
1986	126,000,000
1987	131,000,000
1988	131,000,000
1989	126,000,000

---

[4] *Case author's note*: The soft drink industry uses supermarket sales and market shares as a gauge to assess the competitive position of different brands and flavors, since supermarket volumes affect sales through other retail outlets and fountain service. As an approximation and for analysis purposes, *total case* volume for a brand or flavor can be estimated as 2.5 times supermarket case volume. Therefore, total sales of orange-flavored soft drinks are 2.5 × 126,000,000 = 315 million cases.

EXHIBIT 5 | **Orange Carbonated Soft Drink Brand Market Shares, 1985–1989 (Rounded)**

Brand	Year				
	1985	1986	1987	1988	1989
Sunkist	32%	20%	13%	13%	14%
Mandarin Orange Slice	NA	16	22	21	21
Minute Maid Orange	NA	8	14	13	14
Crush	22	18	14	11	8
Total top four brands	54	62	63	58	57
Others	46	38	37	42	43

Major Competitors

Four brands captured the majority of orange-flavored soft drink sales in 1989. Mandarin Orange Slice marketed by PepsiCo was the category leader with a market share of 20.8 percent. Sunkist, sold by Cadbury Beverages, Inc., and Coca-Cola's Minute Maid Orange had market shares of 14.4 percent and 14 percent, respectively. Orange Crush had a market share of 7.5 percent. Other brands accounted for the remaining 43.3 percent of sales of orange-flavored soft drinks. Exhibit 5 shows the market shares for the major competitors for the period 1985–1989.

The major competitors sold both regular and diet varieties of orange-flavored drink. As shown in Exhibit 6, slightly over 70 percent of sales in this category were regular soft drinks. Orange Crush sales mirrored this pattern. Sunkist, however, exceeded the category average, with 82 percent of its case volume sales being the regular form. For Mandarin Orange Slice and Minute Maid Orange, case volume was almost evenly split between regular and diet drinks.

Major competitors also differed in terms of market coverage in 1989. Sunkist was available in markets that represented 91 percent of total orange category sales. By comparison, Orange Crush was available in markets that represented only 62 percent of orange category sales. Mandarin Orange Slice and Minute Maid Orange were available in markets that represented 88 percent of orange category sales. Exhibit 7 shows the market coverage by the four major competitors for the period 1985–1989.

Competitor Positioning and Advertising

Each of the four major competitors attempted to stake out a unique position within the orange category. For example, Minute Maid Orange appeared to emphasize its orange flavor, while Sunkist focused on the teen lifestyle. Mandarin

EXHIBIT 6 | **Case Volume in 1989 by Type of Drink: Regular Versus Diet**

Type	Total Soft Drinks	Total Orange	Crush	Sunkist	Mandarin Orange Slice	Minute Maid Orange
Regular	68.9%	73.2%	71.3%	82.1%	49.0%	53.1%
Diet	31.1	26.8	28.7	17.9	51.0	46.9
	100.0%	100.0%	100.0%	100.0%	100.0%	100.0%

EXHIBIT 7	Market Coverage of Orange Category by Major Competitors, 1985–1989

	Year				
Brand	*1985*	*1986*	*1987*	*1988*	*1989*
Crush	81%	81%	78%	78%	62%
Sunkist	95	83	79	86	91
Mandarin Orange Slice	10	68	87	88	88
Minute Maid Orange	10	60	87	88	88

Orange Slice and Minute Maid Orange appeared to be targeted at young adults and households without children. These brands also appeared to be emphasizing the "better for you" idea. Crush and Sunkist targeted teens and households with children at home. Exhibit 8 summarizes the apparent brand positionings of the major competitors and selected performance data compiled by the Crush marketing research staff.

Slightly over $26 million was spent on advertising by the four major brands in 1989. Mandarin Orange Slice and Minute Maid Orange accounted for 84 percent of all advertising expenditures in the orange category. Although both brands were advertised on network and cable television and both used spot television commercials in local markets, their advertising differed in other respects. Minute Maid Orange used outdoor billboards and network radio for advertising, but Mandarin Orange Slice did not. In comparison, Mandarin Orange Slice was advertised in magazines and newspapers, but Minute Maid Orange was not.

Crush and Sunkist spent less on advertising and used fewer advertising vehicles than did Minute Maid Orange and Mandarin Orange Slice. Crush was promoted most frequently on spot television, in newspapers, and on outdoor

EXHIBIT 8	Competitive Positioning and Performance, 1989

	Sunkist	*Mandarin Orange Slice*	*Minute Maid Orange*	*Crush*
Positioning	"Teens on the Beach"; "Drink in the Sun"	"Who's Got the Juice?" Contemporary youth culture	"The orange, orange" orange flavor, taste of real orange	"Don't just quench it, CRUSH it"; bold user imagery with thirst-quenching benefit
Target	Teens, 12–24	Young adults, 18–24	Young adults, 18–34	Teens, 13–29
Household size of purchaser	3–4 (children at home)	1–2 (no children)	1–2 (no children)	3–5 (children at home)
Package sales mix	Two-liter 51% Cans 42% Other 7%	Two-liter 54% Cans 42% Other 4%	Two-liter 54% Cans 41% Other 5%	Two-liter 64% Cans 31% Other 5%
Loyalty (percentage of brand buyer's orange volume)	36%	55%	48%	46%

Source: Crush Marketing Research Staff Report. Based on trade publications and industry sources.

| EXHIBIT 9 | Concentrate Producers' Advertising Expenditures for Broadcast and Print Media for Major Orange Soft Drink Brands, 1985–1989 ($ in Thousands) |

Brand	1985	1986	1987	1988	1989
Mandarin Orange Slice (total)	$17,809.4	$32,079.9	$29,555.8	$15,001.3	$11,388.1
Regular	12,739.4	27,704.2	20,123.2	10,247.9	11,199.5
Diet	5,070.0	4,375.7	2,676.4	1,881.9	
Regular and Diet			6,756.2	2,872.5	188.6
Sunkist (total)	$ 7,176.2	$ 4,013.0	$ 910.7	$ 1,719.3	$ 2,301.9
Regular	4,816.5	1,340.6	887.2	309.4	281.5
Diet	2,316.0	1,269.5	1.3		
Regular and Diet	43.7	1,402.9	22.2	1,409.9	2,020.4
Crush (total)	$ 4,371.2	$ 7,154.9	$ 4,296.7	$ 6,841.1	$ 1,853.6
Regular	3,282.7	4,712.9	2,729.8	2,561.6	1,382.2
Diet	1,004.6	2,413.1	959.4	1.2	127.7
Regular and Diet	83.9	28.9	607.5	4,278.3	343.7
Minute Maid Orange (total)	$ 174.4	$ 7,952.3	$ 9,027.2	$12,811.3	$10,463.1
Regular	174.4	7,508.2	7,211.6	9,252.5	10,191.9
Diet			1,745.1	3,450.2	
Regular and Diet		444.1	70.5	108.6	271.2

signage. Sunkist used newspapers, spot television, outdoor billboards, and some syndicated television.

Two advertising trends were evident in the orange category since 1986. First, total expenditures for measured print and broadcast media declined each year since 1986, when $52.2 million was spent for advertising. In that year, Mandarin Orange Slice and Minute Maid Orange were introduced nationally. Second, competitors increased the variety of media used for advertising. In 1986, spot television and outdoor billboards were used almost exclusively. By 1989, a broader spectrum of vehicles was used, including broadcast media (network, spot, syndicated, and cable television and network radio) and print media (outdoor, magazines, and newspapers). Exhibit 9 shows advertising expenditures for the four major brands for the period 1985–1989.

Competitor Pricing and Promotion

Concentrate pricing among the four major competitors differed very little. Typically, no more than a one-cent difference existed. The price differential between regular (with sugar) and diet (with aspartame) concentrate was virtually the same across competitors. The similarity in pricing as well as in raw material costs resulted in similar gross profit margins across competitors in the orange category. However, as noted in Exhibit 3, the gross profit margin differs between regular and diet soft drink concentrate.

Advertising and promotion programs were jointly implemented and financed by concentrate producers and bottlers. Concentrate producers and bottlers split advertising costs 50–50. For example, if $1 million were spent for television brand advertising, $500,000 would be paid by the brand's bottlers and $500,000 would be paid by the concentrate producer. Bottlers and concentrate producers split the cost of retail-oriented merchandise promotions and consumer promotions 50–50.

A variety of merchandising promotions are used in the soft drink industry. One kind of promotion, called a "dealer loader," is a premium given to retailers. A common form is a "display loader" such as ice chests, insulated can coolers, T-shirts, or sweatshirts, which are part of an in-store or point-of-purchase display. After the display is taken down, the premium is given to the retailer. End-of-aisle displays and other types of special free-standing displays are also provided, as are shelf banners. Concentrate producers will often allocate 10 cents (for shirts) to 20 cents (for displays) per case sold to bottlers who implement these merchandising promotions. Consumer promotions include sponsorship of local sports and entertainment events, plastic cups and napkins with the brand logo, and stylish baseball caps, T-shirts, or sunglasses featuring the brand name. Assorted other promotions are also used, including coupons, on-package promotions, and sweepstakes. Concentrate producers will offer anywhere from 5 cents (for cups, caps, or glasses) to 25 cents (for local event marketing including cups, caps, or glasses) per case sold to bottlers who use these promotions. Examples of trade and consumer promotions are shown in Exhibits 10 and 11 on pages 320 and 321.

Concentrate producers occasionally offer bottlers price promotions in the form of distribution incentives. These incentives are typically based on case sales and are frequently used to stimulate bottler sales and merchandising activity. These incentives are often in the range of 15 to 25 cents per case depending on the amount of effort desired or needed.

 # CRUSH MARKETING PROGRAM

In January 1990, several strategic marketing decisions were made concerning the Crush brand. Most notably, a decision was made to focus initial attention on the orange flavor. Even though the Crush line featured several flavors, orange (regular and diet) accounted for almost two-thirds of total Crush case volume. (Exhibit 12 on page 322 shows the Crush product line.) Second, marketing executives at Cadbury Beverages, Inc. decided to focus immediate attention and effort on re-establishing the bottling network for the Crush line, particularly Orange Crush. Third, it was decided that careful consideration of Crush positioning was necessary to build on the existing customer franchise and provide opportunities for further development of the Crush brand and its assorted flavors. Finally, the executives agreed to the development of an advertising and promotion program, including the determination of objectives, strategies, and expenditures.

Bottler Network Development

Recognizing the traditional and central role that bottlers play in the soft drink industry, company marketing and sales executives immediately embarked on an aggressive effort to recruit bottlers for the Crush line. The Crush bottling network had gradually eroded in the 1980s due in part to Procter & Gamble's decision to test a distribution system for selling Crush through warehouses rather than through bottlers. This action, which centralized bottling in the hands of a limited number of bottlers that shipped product to warehouses for subsequent delivery to supermarkets and other retail outlets, had led many in the Crush bottler network to question their future role with Crush. An outgrowth of this action was that Crush had the lowest market coverage of orange category sales potential among major competitors.

Recruitment efforts in early 1990 broadened the bottler network. By mid-1990, new bottling agreements had been arranged, and trade relations with 136 bottlers

EXHIBIT 10 **Example of Crush Trade Promotion**

HAVE A CRUSH ON US!
DEALER LOADERS

Item

A Crush Adventure Back Pack
B Beach Bag/Blanket
C Neon Cap
D Sony® Walkman
E Dirty Dunk®

were established. The revitalized bottler network meant that Crush would be available in markets that represented 75 percent of total orange category sales in time for the Crush relaunch. The broadened bottler network would also require promotional support. According to Kim Feil, "We knew that reestablishing trade relations was an important first step. However, we also knew that new and existing bottlers would be gauging the kind and amount of advertising and promotional support we would provide when we relaunched Crush."

EXHIBIT 11 **Example of Crush Consumer Promotion**

Positioning Issues

Numerous issues related to positioning were being addressed while the bottler recruitment effort was under way. First, since the company already marketed Sunkist, questions arose concerning the likely cannibalization of Sunkist sales if a clearly differentiated position for Orange Crush in the marketplace was not developed and successfully executed. A second issue concerned the relative emphasis on regular and diet Crush with respect to Mandarin Orange Slice and Minute Maid Orange. These two competitors had outpaced Crush and Sunkist in

EXHIBIT 12 **Crush Product Line**

attracting the diet segment of orange drinkers. Third, viable positions had to be considered that did not run contrary to previous positionings and would build on the customer franchise currently held by Orange Crush. In this regard, a historical review of Crush positioning was conducted. The results of this effort are reproduced in Exhibit 13.

Company executives recognized that issues relating to positioning needed to be addressed in a timely manner. Without a clear positioning statement, the creative process underlying the advertising program could not be initiated.

Advertising and Promotion

Crush marketing executives were pleasantly surprised to learn that the Crush brand had high name awareness in the markets served by existing and new bottlers. According to the company's consumer awareness tracking research, of the four major brands, Crush had the highest orange-brand awareness in Seattle, San Francisco, New York, Miami, Los Angeles, Chicago, and Boston. Nevertheless, numerous issues had to be addressed concerning the Crush advertising and promotion program.

In particular, objectives for the advertising and promotion had to be established and communicated to the advertising agency that would represent Crush. Next, the relative emphasis on consumer advertising and on types of trade and consumer promotion had to be determined. Specifically, this meant setting the budget for advertising expenditures and the amounts to be spent on a per case basis for promotions. Ultimately, a pro forma statement of projected revenues and expenses would be necessary for presentation to senior management at Cadbury Beverages, Inc. Implicitly, this required a case volume forecast for Orange Crush that realistically portrayed market and competitive conditions and "the quality of my marketing program," said Feil.

EXHIBIT 13   Positioning of Crush, 1954–1989

Year	Positioning	Target	Campaign
1954	Natural flavor from Valencia oranges	All-family	"Naturally—it tastes better, Orange Crush"
1957–Late 1960s (est.)	Good for you; fresh juice from specially selected oranges	All-family	"Tastes so good . . . so good for you!"
1963–1964 (est.)	Introduced full line of flavors: grape, strawberry, grapefruit, root beer, cherry	All-family	No clear introduction effort: • "Thirsty? Crush that thirst with Orange Crush" • "Delicious, refreshing, satisfying—Grape Crush" • "Clean fruit taste—Grapefruit Crush" • "Mellow Crush Root Beer"
Early 1970s (est.)	Unique taste, the "change of pace" drink	All-family directed toward purchaser who is female 18–35, promotions targeted children/young adults	"Ask for Crush, the taste that's all its own"
1979–1980	Competitive taste superiority	Maintained early 1970s TV but focused on young males with sports	Added "There is no orange like Orange Crush . . ." to "Ask for Crush, the taste that's all its own"
1980	Competitive taste superiority in fruit flavors	Added new radio for 10–19 target	Same as above
1981	100% natural flavors, contemporary wholesome brand	13–39 Teens and young adults	"Orange lovers have a Crush on us"
1980–1985	Great, irresistible taste	13–39	"Orange lovers have a Crush on us"
1981–1982	Great taste	13–39	Test: "First Crush"
1983	More orangey taste	13–39	"Orange lovers"
1984	Sugar-free Crush, great taste of Nutrasweet	13–49	"Celebrate"
1986–1987	Taste with 10% real juice	Teens, 12–17	"Peel Me a Crush"
1987	The drink that breaks monotony	Teens, 12–17	Test: "Color Me Crush"
1987–1989	Bold user imagery with thirst-quenching benefit	Teens, 13–29	"Don't just quench it, Crush it"

Case

Astor Lodge & Suites, Inc.

Late in the afternoon on April 4, 2005, Kelly Elizabeth, senior vice president of sales and marketing at Astor Lodge & Suites, Inc., met with Catherine Grace, vice president of advertising. The impromptu meeting followed a day-long senior vice president conference with Joseph James, the company's new president and chief executive officer. James, a seasoned hotel financial executive with 40 years of hotel management experience, was appointed the previous week following the sudden resignation of his predecessor. The charge given each of the company's four senior vice presidents was to prepare a one-hour presentation that described (1) his or her initiatives, expenditures, and outcomes for each of the past two fiscal years, and (2) planned initiatives and budgetary needs for fiscal 2006, beginning June 1, 2005. James also requested that each presentation provide the motivation for initiatives and expenditures so he could familiarize himself with company operations. Presentations would be made on April 11 to the chair of the board, president and CEO, and chief financial officer following a tour of company properties by James.

Fiscal 2005 was projected to be the fifth consecutive unprofitable year for Astor Lodge & Suites, Inc. James announced that his goal for the company was to achieve profitability within two years. Toward this end, he stated that the company would use growth in earnings before interest, taxes, depreciation, and amortization (EBITDA) as a corporate performance measure and a basis for determining senior management and executive incentive compensation. The use of EBITDA for these purposes had been endorsed by the company's board of directors. His overall corporate objective was a 7 percent annual increase in EBITDA over the next two fiscal years. Each senior vice president (lodging operations, corporate administration, information technology services, and sales and marketing) would be expected to address this objective when presenting their planned initiatives and budgetary needs. In addition, James requested that each senior vice president restate the effect of prior years' initiatives and expenditures from an EBITDA perspective as well as performance measures used previously. The company's vice president and chief accounting officer would supply available financial and operating data to prepare this analysis.

The charge given the four senior vice presidents represented a significant departure from past practice. Previously the annual planning and budgeting process had been more "top-down" than "bottom-up," and revenue focused rather than earnings driven; that is, budgets were initially prepared by the chief financial officer and the vice president and chief accounting officer in consultation with the president and CEO who met with the senior vice presidents to establish spending priorities within the budget. Budget amounts would be adjusted depending on the initiatives proposed and "a little negotiation," said Elizabeth. According to Elizabeth:

> The process seemed to work well during my tenure here. Sales and marketing was always generously funded. Brad [the previous president and CEO] was a veteran hospitality marketer who recognized the importance of sales and marketing initiatives and spending following the hotel industry's downturn in 2002 and 2003 with the 9/11 tragedy and a soft business and pleasure travel environment. Brad was of the view that successful companies grow sales not prune expenses. Since 2003, when Brad and I joined the company, our media advertising budget has grown 55 percent and our sales budget increased 15 percent. Revenue growth has exceeded industry averages even with a decline in the number of operating properties and guest rooms and suites since fiscal 2003.

She went on to say:

> The process outlined by Mr. James reflects a growing practice today. I was not surprised by the charge given us. Companies in the hotel industry are looking for and expecting a documented favorable financial return on their expenditures. Admittedly, sales and marketing has lagged behind other functions, such as lodging operations, in showing measurable profit results from its efforts. The new planning and budgeting process will be a challenge because it is "bottom-up" and profit driven rather than "top-down" and revenue driven. But it is a worthwhile undertaking to achieve profitability within two years. I hope the planning and budgeting process doesn't turn into a cost-cutting exercise.

THE U.S. HOTEL INDUSTRY

The U.S. hotel industry recorded revenue of $113.7 billion and grossed $16.7 billion in pretax profit in 2004. As of December 31, 2004, there were 4.4 million hotel rooms in the United States. Approximately two-thirds of all U.S. hotel rooms were affiliated with a brand; the remaining one-third were independently owned and not brand-affiliated. The U.S. hotel industry is highly fragmented, with no one company or brand controlling a majority of hotel rooms. Exhibit 1 on page 326 lists the ten largest hotel companies (and brands) in the United States based on the number of hotel rooms.

Hotel Segmentation

Hotels compete on the basis of amenities, price, and service. Smith Travel Research, a major U.S. lodging industry research firm, segments hotels by price and service levels. Price is often a function of service level and amenities offered. Full-service hotels offer food and beverage outlets such as restaurants and lounges; meeting, banquet, and convention facilities; and concierge, luggage service, and room service. Full-service hotel brands range from luxury hotels (such as Ritz-Carlton and Four Seasons) to upper upscale hotels (such as Hilton and Marriott) to upscale hotels (such as Courtyard by Marriott and Radisson) to midscale with food and beverage hotels (such as Holiday Inn and Ramada Inn). These full-service branded hotels accounted for about 1.6 million hotel rooms

EXHIBIT 1 **Ten Largest Hotel Companies in the United States: 2004**

Company	Rooms (U.S.)	Properties (U.S.)	Brands
1. Cendant Corporation	439,279	5,622	Amerihost Inn, Days Inn, Days Serviced Apartments, Howard Johnson, Howard Johnson Express, Knights Inn, Ramada, Ramada Limited, Super 8, Thriftlodge, Travelodge, and Wingate Inn
2. Marriott International, Inc.	380,218	2,236	Courtyard by Marriott, Fairfield Inn by Marriott, Marriott Conference Centers, Marriott Executive Apartments, Marriott Hotels and Resorts, Ramada Int'l Plaza, Ramada International Hotels & Resorts, Renaissance Hotels & Resorts, and Residence Inn
3. Hilton Hotels Corporation	357,332	2,184	Conrad, Doubletree, Doubletree Club, Embassy Suites, Embassy Vacation Resort, Hampton Inn, Hampton Inn & Suites, Hilton, Hilton Gaming, Hilton Garden Inn, and Homewood Suites
4. Inter-Continental Hotel Group	337,643	2,523	Candlewood, Centra, Crowne Plaza, Forum Hotel, Holiday Inn, Holiday Inn Express, Holiday Inn Garden Court, Holiday Inn Select, Inter Continental, Parkroyal, Posthouse, Staybridge Suites by Holiday Inn, and Sunspree Resorts
5. Choice Hotels International, Inc.	313,982	3,891	Clarion, Comfort Inn, Hotel & Suites, Econo Lodge, MainStay Suites, Quality Inn, Hotel & Suites, Rodeway Inn and Sleep Inn
6. Best Western International	186,422	2,181	Best Western
7. Accor North America	134,803	1,252	Coralia, Hotel Novotel, Hotel Sofitel, Mercure Hotel, Motel 6, Red Roof Inn, and Studio 6
8. Starwood Hotels & Resorts Worldwide, Inc.	123,747	355	Four Points Hotel by Sheraton, Sheraton, St. Regis/Luxury Collection, W Hotels, and Westin
9. Carlson Hospitality Worldwide	82,739	566	Country Inns & Suites by Carlson, Park Inns & Suites, Park Plaza Suites, Radisson and Regent Hotels
10. La Quinta	65,384	592	La Quinta Inns, La Quinta Inn & Suites, Baymount Inn & Suites, and Woodfield Suites

Source: Company Annual Reports and news releases.

in 2004. Limited-service hotels do not offer many of the full-service hotel facilities, such as restaurants, lounges, and banquet rooms. They focus primarily on renting hotel rooms. Limited-service hotel brands range from midscale without food and beverage hotels (such as Hampton Inn and Fairfield Inn) to economy hotels (such as Red Roof Inn and Motel 6). These limited-service branded hotels accounted for about 1.4 million hotel rooms in 2004. The breakdown of hotel

| EXHIBIT 2 | U.S. Hotel Properties and Rooms by Location, Room Rate, and Size: 2004 |

	By Location			*By Rate*			*By Size*	
	Properties	*Rooms*		*Properties*	*Rooms*		*Properties*	*Rooms*
Airport	1,914	273,839	Under $30	924	55,692	Under 75 rooms	27,464	1,163,668
Suburban	15,792	1,563,986	$30–44.99	7,995	508,785	75–149 rooms	14,326	1,524,099
Urban	4,648	706,235	$45–$59.99	16,054	1,044,610	150–299 rooms	4,235	847,089
Highway	6,666	446,122	$60–$85	14,280	1,367,826	300–500 rooms	1,070	398,491
Resort	4,055	595,272	Over $85	8,345	1,433,995	Over 500 rooms	503	478,561
Small Metro/Town	14,523	826,456						

Source: Company records.

properties and rooms by location, by room rate, and by size of property in the United States is shown in Exhibit 2.

Hotel Segment Performance and Projections

All hotel segments have evidenced improved performance since 2003 on the three most tracked operating statistics:[1] (1) occupancy, (2) average daily rate (ADR), and (3) revenue per available room (RevPAR). This improvement followed significant declines on all three measures in 2001 and 2002 after a peak year in 2000. In 2004, the average occupancy across all hotel segments was 61.3 percent, the average daily rate was $86, and the revenue per available room was $53. However, the five major hotel segments varied greatly on these performance measures. Exhibit 3 on page 328 shows the 2003 and 2004 occupancy, average daily rate, and revenue per available room for each hotel segment as well as projections for the 2005 calendar year.

Hotel Guest Profile

According to the American Hotel and Lodging Association, one-half of all guests stayed at hotels for business purposes and one-half stayed for leisure or vacation purposes.[2] In 2004, the typical business room night was generated by one adult male (67 percent), ages 35–54 (52 percent), employed in a professional or managerial position (50 percent), earning an average yearly household income of $81,100. Typically, these guests made reservations (89 percent), and paid $96 per room night. The typical leisure room night was generated by two adults

---

[1] Occupancy, average daily rate, and revenue per available room are defined as follows:

Occupancy = [Number of room-nights sold ÷ Total available rooms available] × 100

Average daily rate = Total lodging revenue ÷ Number of room-nights sold

Revenue per available room = Occupancy × Average daily rate

Note that the average daily rate is not the same as the posted, or "rack," rate for a room or suite. The average daily rate includes price discounts, free night stays from frequent guest programs, and various convention or group rates, exclusive of state and local taxes.

[2] American Hotel and Lodging Association at ahla.com, downloaded April 6, 2005.

EXHIBIT 3	U.S. Hotel Operating Statistics by Hotel Segment: Historical Data and Projection

Hotel Segment	Calendar Year	Occupancy (Percent)	Calendar Year	Average Daily Rate (ADR)	Calendar Year	Revenue per Available Room (RevPAR)
Luxury	2003	64.6%	2003	$221	2003	$113
	2004	68.1%	2004	$232	2004	$158
	2005 (proj.)	69.9%	2005 (proj.)	$246	2005 (proj.)	$172
Upper Scale	2003	66.3%	2003	$127	2003	$84
	2004	69.1%	2004	$132	2004	$91
	2005 (proj.)	70.9%	2005 (proj.)	$139	2005 (proj.)	$98
Upscale	2003	66.1%	2003	$93	2003	$62
	2004	69.2%	2004	$96	2004	$67
	2005 (proj.)	70.5%	2005 (proj.)	$101	2005 (proj.)	$71
Midscale with Food and Beverage	2003	55.2%	2003	$72	2003	$40
	2004	57.3%	2004	$74	2004	$42
	2005 (proj.)	58.4%	2005 (proj.)	$76	2005 (proj.)	$44
Midscale without Food and Beverage	2003	61.9%	2003	$69	2003	$42
	2004	64.1%	2004	$71	2004	$45
	2005 (proj.)	65.4%	2005 (proj.)	$73	2005 (proj.)	$48
Economy	2003	53.1%	2003	$48	2003	$25
	2004	54.5%	2004	$49	2004	$26
	2005 (proj.)	55.3%	2005 (proj.)	$50	2005 (proj.)	$27

Source: Table prepared based on information provided in *2005 National Lodging Report*, Ernst & Young Retail Advisory Services, 2005.

(51 percent), ages 35–54 (45 percent), earning an average yearly household income of $72,600. The typical leisure traveler traveled by auto (74 percent), made a reservation (90 percent), and paid $89 per room night.

For a hotel stay in 2004, 39 percent of all business travelers spent one night, 24 percent spent two nights, 27 percent spent three nights, and 10 percent spent four or more nights. Of leisure travelers staying in a hotel, 45 percent spent one night, 28 percent spent two nights, 20 percent spent three nights, and 7 percent spent four or more nights.

ASTOR LODGE & SUITES, INC.

Astor Lodge & Suites, Inc. is a 250-property hotel chain with locations in 10 western and Rocky Mountain states. Formed in 1979, the company operates 200 Astor Lodge properties and 50 Astor Lodge & Suites properties, each with an average of 120 individual guest room or suite units. The company projected lodging revenues of $422.6 million for fiscal 2005 and a net loss of $15.7 million.

Service Mission

The corporate service mission of Astor Lodge & Suites, Inc. is to provide principally business travelers with clean and comfortable guest accommodations in convenient locations at reasonable prices. Astor Lodge guest rooms feature a double or king-size bed; a cable television; a dataport telephone with voice mail and free local calls; a well-lit desk and wooden chair with an upholstered seat;

a large upholstered recliner chair; and a coffee maker, hair dryer, and iron and ironing board. Each Lodge offers a daily complimentary continental breakfast in the lobby and a soft drink vending machine and ice maker on each floor.

By comparison, Astor Lodge & Suites properties contain individual guest rooms plus two-room suites. Individual guest rooms have the same amenities as an Astor Lodge. Two-room suites provide separate sitting and sleeping areas, a sleeper sofa, two televisions, and a small refrigerator. Additional amenities in Astor Lodge & Suites properties include a self-service guest laundry room, an outdoor swimming pool with spa (in warmer southern climates) and an indoor sauna (in cooler northern climates).

Positioning

According to Astor Lodge & Suites, Inc. executives, the company is positioned as a limited-service hotel between economy hotels and full-service hotels. As such, neither Astor Lodge nor Astor Lodge & Suites include a restaurant, lounge, meeting rooms and concierge, luggage, or room service on the property. This positioning places Astor Lodge & Suites, Inc. between midscale hotels with food and beverage, such as Holiday Inn and Ramada Inn, and economy hotels such as Red Roof Inn and Motel 6. Company executives see Astor Lodge & Suites, Inc. positioned against Fairfield Inn by Marriott, Hampton Inn and Hampton Inn & Suites by Hilton, and La Quinta Inn & Suites, even though Astor Lodge & Suites, Inc. properties do not necessarily compete with these hotels in all markets.

The company's service mission and positioning directs Astor Lodge & Suites, Inc. site selection decisions. The company locates its properties on premium sites on major highways close to suburban industrial and office complexes, airports, and large regional shopping centers for the most part. Urban, downtown locations have been avoided.

Operations

As Astor Lodge & Suites, Inc. fiscal 2005 year (year-end, May 31) was drawing to a close, its senior executives recognized that the company was on course to record its third consecutive fiscal year of rising revenue following revenue declines in fiscal 2001 and fiscal 2002. The company's projected annual lodging revenue growth of 7.4 percent for fiscal 2005 was slightly below the overall hotel industry average of 7.6 percent, but higher than the limited-service segment growth rate of 5.8 percent. However, Astor Lodge & Suites, Inc. posted its third consecutive annual net loss while the hotel industry as a whole and the limited-service segment reported profitable operations over the past three years following improved economic conditions. Exhibit 4 on page 330 shows the company's consolidated statement of operations for fiscal 2003 and 2004, and projected results for fiscal 2005.

During fiscal 2005, Astor Lodge & Suites, Inc. closed two underperforming Astor Lodge properties and opened one Astor Lodge & Suites property. Since 2003, the company closed 12 underperforming Astor Lodge properties, and opened two Astor Lodge properties and three Astor Lodge & Suites properties.

Lodging Statistics

Astor Lodge & Suites, Inc. projected consolidated company occupancy to be 67.1 percent, with an average daily rate of $57.52. The projected revenue per available room would be $38.60. Astor Lodge and Astor Lodge & Suites properties each showed improvement in occupancy and revenue per available room over fiscal 2004. However, the average daily rate for each was projected to be lower in fiscal 2005 than fiscal 2004. This decline was partially attributed to a

| EXHIBIT 4 | Astor Lodge & Suites, Inc. Consolidated Statement of Operations: Fiscal 2003–2005 ($ in Thousands) |

	Year Ended May 31		
	2005 (proj.)	2004	2003
Lodging Revenue	$422,625	$397,980	$386,429
Expenses			
Direct Lodging Expense	$211,239	$194,887	$192,069
Other Lodging Expense	62,482	54,672	52,271
Sales, General & Administrative Expense	44,941	39,029	36,201
Depreciation & Amortization	70,135	78,044	69,190
Interest Expense	49,520	49,786	50,535
Total	$438,317	$416,419	$400,266
Net Income (Loss)	($ 15,692)	($ 18,439)	($ 13,737)

Source: Company records.

"free-night stay" discount promotion implemented during the summer of 2005, according to the senior vice president of Lodging Operations.

Lodging Expenses   Fiscal 2005 direct lodging expenses were projected to be $211 million. These expenses included variable costs directly associated with the operation of the hotel properties, such as direct labor, utilities, and hotel/room supplies (including breakfast food and beverage service). The direct cost per rented room/suite was projected to be $28.75 in fiscal 2005, due mostly to higher labor and utility expense. Direct lodging expenses were the responsibility of the Lodging Operations Department. Exhibit 5 details Astor Lodge and Suites, Inc. three-year operating statistics.

Other lodging expenses for fiscal 2005 were projected to be $62.5 million. These expenses included property taxes, general property maintenance and re-modeling, insurance, and corporate cost allocations charged to hotel operations, including the company's frequent customer loyalty program, reservation system, and Web site. The company's loyalty program, reservation systems, and Web site were managed by the Information Technology Services Department. Other lodging expenses (e.g., taxes, insurance) were the responsibility of the Corporate Administration Department. General property maintenance and remodeling was managed by the Lodging Operations Department.

Corporate Expenses   Sales, general, and administrative (S, G, & A) expense for fiscal 2005 was projected to be $44.9 million. S, G, & A expense included the cost of information technology services, legal, finance, accounting, human resources, sales, and marketing. The $5.9 million increase over fiscal 2004 expenses was due mostly to increases in corporate employee compensation, health care premiums, expenditures for information technology, and sales and marketing costs.

The company added two additional "national" sales representatives in early fiscal 2005. National sales representatives call on companies that have individuals traveling in markets served by Astor Lodge and Astor Lodge & Suites properties. Eleven national sales representatives focus on increasing guest room sales through the inclusion of the company's hotels on approved lodging lists of corporate travel managers and travel agencies as well as travel organizations such as the American Automobile Association. The remaining 54 sales representatives call on local businesses,

EXHIBIT 5	Astor Lodge Inn & Suites, Inc. Operating Statistics: Fiscal 2003–2005 (Projected)		
	Year Ended May 31		
	2005 (proj.)	2004	2003
Number of Lodge and Lodge & Suites Properties			
Astor Lodge Properties	200	202	210
Astor Lodge & Suites Properties	50	49	47
Total Properties	250	251	257
Number of Lodge Rooms and Suites			
Room Units	26,500	26,690	27,550
Suite Units	3,500	3,430	3,290
Total Units	30,000	30,120	30,840
Occupancy Rate			
Astor Lodge Properties	65.0%	61.5%	58.5%
Astor Lodge & Suites Properties	72.5%	64.0%	60.5%
Total Properties	67.1%	62.2%	59.0%
Average Daily Rate (ADR)			
Astor Lodge Properties	$55.40	$55.75	$57.05
Astor Lodge & Suites Properties	$66.00	$68.00	$64.00
Total Properties	$57.52	$58.20	$58.20
Revenue Per Available Room (RevPAR)			
Astor Lodge Properties	$36.01	$34.29	$33.37
Astor Lodge & Suites Properties	$47.85	$43.52	$38.72
Total Properties	$38.60	$36.20	$34.34
Direct Cost Per Rented Room/Suite			
Total Properties	$28.75	$28.50	$28.92

Source: Company records.

government agencies, universities, and other organizations that might require hotel accommodations for visitors in the markets served by the company's hotels.

Marketing costs rose due to added marketing research and media advertising. In mid-2004, the company commissioned a large-scale study to identify the Astor Lodge & Suite guest. This study replicated a study commissioned in mid-2002. The results of these two studies are provided in Exhibit 6 on pages 332–333. The media advertising expenditure for Astor Lodge & Suites, Inc. increased by $1.14 million to $12.5 million in fiscal 2005.

SALES AND MARKETING PLANNING AND BUDGETING

Kelly Elizabeth joined Astor Lodge & Suites, Inc. in January 2003 to lead the newly formed sales and marketing department. Previously, the sales function was managed by the senior vice president of Lodging Operations. She had 17 years of sales and marketing experience in the hotel/hospitality industry prior to assuming her position. As senior vice president of sales and marketing, she was responsible for sales, advertising, promotions, and marketing research. Catherine Grace was hired as vice president of advertising in February 2004. She was previously media director with the advertising and public relations firm that handled the Astor Lodge & Suites, Inc. advertising account.

	July–October 2004	July–October 2002
1. Average number of different occasions a guest stayed at Astor Lodge & Suites during the past twelve months:	10.8	9.9
2. Average number of nights stayed on most recent visit	2.6 nights	2.4 nights
3. Purpose of trip (percentages exceed 100% due to multiple answers)		
Personal	9.5%	10.0%
Business	79.8	81.8
Pleasure/Vacation	14.2	13.2
Convention	3.5	2.0
4. Frequency of staying at motels or hotels:		
Once a week or more	39.0%	37.0%
Once every few weeks	21.7	22.7
About once a month	13.1	19.0
Less often than every few months	21.2	21.3
5. Type of trip and payment on most recent visit:		
Business trip paid for by the company	65.7%	67.7%
Business trip paid for by self	16.3	16.3
Pleasure trip paid for by self	18.0	16.0
6. Rented a car on most recent trip:		
Yes	23.1%	25.5%
No	75.9	74.5
7. Mode of travel on most recent trip:		
Airline	34.0%	33.8%
Car	64.8	66.2
8. Reason for choice of a particular Astor Lodge & Suite on most recent visit (percentages exceed 100% due to multiple responses):		
Close to next day's activities	47.5%	47.0%
Saw hotel or sign when ready to stop	5.7	7.0
Recommended by friend, relative, etc.	15.4	15.0
Saw or heard advertising	9.7	8.5
Specified by the company	7.3	6.9
Personal preference based on previous experience	48.1	49.1
Price	36.6	35.4
Stayed here before	40.9	41.2
Friendly and courteous staff	27.9	28.0
Other lodging accommodations full	3.1	2.9
9. Source of reservations:		
Self	66.7%	68.5%
Company	11.2	12.1
Travel agency	2.7	2.2
Association or convention	2.2	2.3
Relative, friend, etc.	4.7	3.4
No reservations	12.5	11.5
10. Reservation booked prior to stay:		
No reservation	12.5%	11.5%
1 to 3 days	25.8	26.0
4 to 7 days	20.9	22.5
8 to 14 days	18.7	18.3
15 to 21 days	10.8	10.5
22 to 28 days	7.2	7.2
29 or more days	4.1	4.0

EXHIBIT 6   Astor Lodge & Suite Guest Profile: July–October 2004 Versus July–October 2002 (Astor Lodge and Astor Lodge & Suites, Inc. Properties Combined)

332

EXHIBIT 6 *(Continued)*

	July–October 2004	July–October 2002
11. Person(s) sharing room on most recent visit (percentages exceed 100% due to multiple responses):		
Spouse	21.6%	20.8%
Children	5.2	5.5
Friends	3.4	2.9
Business associates	4.1	4.2
None, stayed alone	68.9	69.0
12. Likelihood of staying at an Astor Lodge & Suites on return visit to the area:		
Extremely likely	54.2%	53.1%
Very likely	30.3	28.5
Somewhat likely	11.9	14.2
Not very likely	2.6	2.2
Not at all likely	1.0	2.0
13. Likelihood of staying at an Astor Lodge & Suites if one were available in another area visited:		
Extremely likely	45.5%	42.7%
Very likely	35.4	33.5
Somewhat likely	16.1	18.5
Not very likely	2.3	3.4
Not at all likely	.7	2.0
14. First stay in an Astor Lodge & Suites		
Yes	27.0%	25.5%
No	73.0	74.5

Source: Astor Lodge & Suites Guest Profile Analysis. November 2004 and November 2002. Company records.

The fiscal 2006 plan and budget for sales and marketing would be Elizabeth's third since joining Astor Lodge & Suites, Inc. A description of the previous two plans and budgets follows.

Fiscal 2004 Plan and Budget

The fiscal 2004 plan prepared by Kelly Elizabeth was a departure from previous Astor Lodge & Suites, Inc. sales and marketing plans. The primary objective was to increase overall occupancy for Astor Lodge & Suites, Inc. properties. Her plan included a modest emphasis on suite properties to attract the pleasure/vacation traveler. This new emphasis on the pleasure traveler was a response to sluggishness in the travel industry overall, and business travel in particular. The creative execution featured the tagline—"The Place to Stay on the Way"—with ads showing couples or families enjoying the amenities of suite properties as they traveled through western and Rocky Mountain states. This plan was supported by a substantial increase in the media advertising budget. Whereas Astor Lodge & Suites, Inc. had followed industry practice and budgeted about 2 percent of its total lodging revenue for media advertising prior to fiscal 2004, the fiscal 2004 budget was $11,360,000, or 2.7 percent of the company's total lodging revenue for fiscal 2004. About 28 percent of this expenditure was targeted at the pleasure/vacation traveler segment. The remaining 72 percent of media expenditures targeted the business traveler and featured the service, price, and location message consistent with the company's previous media advertising. All media advertising placement focused on western and Rocky Mountain states. Another unique aspect of the fiscal 2004 plan was the inclusion of Internet communications. "With one in five travelers today using the Internet to plan their trips and make reservations, this addition to the media mix was critical," said Catherine Grace.

The fiscal 2004 sales budget increased to $4.4 million with the addition of two national sales representatives plus added compensation and travel costs.[3] Each was given primary responsibility for contacting and working with both offline and online travel agencies and travel organizations to build the pleasure/vacation travel business.

Elizabeth summarized the results of the fiscal 2004 effort:

> We achieved our objective of increasing overall occupancy in fiscal 2004. This was important because our overall average daily rate was unchanged. Our properties with suites attracted the pleasure/vacation traveler as evidenced by a rise in weekend occupancy for both Astor Lodge and Astor Lodge & Suite properties. Total lodging revenue increased even with fewer properties and guest rooms as did our revenue per available room.

Fiscal 2005 Plan and Budget

The fiscal 2005 plan had three objectives: (1) to increase overall occupancy in both guest rooms and suites, (2) to attract first-time guests, and (3) to increase the length of stay per visit. The plan to increase overall occupancy would carry forward the creative and media initiatives from the prior year to maintain continuity. To attract first time guests, the scope of ad media placement would broaden to include midwestern states, including Texas and Oklahoma. This effort was called the "frontier strategy" and emphasized brand awareness and acceptance. To increase the length of stay, a summer promotion was implemented. This promotion was equivalent to a 50 percent discount on a third night stay in guest suite accommodations and a 25 percent discount on a third night stay in guest room accommodations. The promotion appeared in electronic and print ads run in April and May along with a direct-mail campaign, and required a reservation for June, July, or August.

The fiscal 2005 budget for media advertising was $12,500,000, or almost three percent of the company's total lodging revenue for fiscal 2005. The 10 percent increase in media expenditures was due exclusively to the added cost of "frontier" advertising. Approximately 35 percent of the media budget was targeted at the pleasure/vacation traveler; 65 percent was targeted at the business traveler.

Two additional national sales representatives were added in fiscal 2005. The additional $135,500 cost of these representatives, including travel and other additional costs, increased the sales budget to $4.7 million. The primary responsibility of national sales representatives was to develop working relationships with companies and organizations in midwestern states (including Texas and Oklahoma) that had individuals traveling in markets served by Astor Lodge & Suites, Inc. properties. The intention was to increase Astor Lodge & Suites, Inc. brand acceptance with companies.

Commenting on the fiscal 2005 plan, Elizabeth said:

> Our occupancy rates for all properties will be 7.9 percent higher than fiscal 2004 occupancy rates based on our year-end projections. We are now about where the company was in fiscal 2000 prior to the occupancy decline in the industry. The greatest lift came from Astor Lodge & Suites properties. Astor Lodge occupancy increased as well. We increased the percentage of new guests as a percentage

---

[3]The sales budget consists of salaries, fringe benefits, travel allowances, and sales administration for national and local salespeople, district managers, sales support and clerical staff, and the vice president of sales. It also includes sales material expenses. For budgeting purposes, salaries, fringe benefits, and travel allowances for the senior vice president of sales and marketing and the vice president of advertising were included in the sales budget.

| EXHIBIT 7 | Astor Lodge & Suites, Inc. Sales and Marketing Budget: Fiscal 2003–Fiscal 2005 |

A. Advertising Media Budget

Media	Fiscal 2005	Fiscal 2004	Fiscal 2003
Magazine	$ 3,236,240	$ 2,780,000	$1,659,800
Newspaper	4,096,965	3,975,000	3,020,000
Outdoor	519,700	558,500	651,750
Spot Television	2,340,266	1,875,500	1,488,420
Cable Networks	1,048,589	975,500	689,367
Radio	257,740	425,500	540,663
Internet	1,000,500	750,000	0
Total	$12,500,000	$11,360,000	$8,050,000

B. Sales Budget

Expense Category	Fiscal 2005	Fiscal 2004	Fiscal 2003
Sales Representatives (salary, bonus, fringe benefits)	$ 3,841,400	$ 3,634,255	$3,251,375
Sales and Marketing Administration (salary, bonus, fringe benefits)	500,200	479,960	354,450
Sales Materials	15,205	10,000	15,650
Travel	315,250	285,650	265,550
Sales and Marketing Research	60,000	0	50,000
Total	$ 4,732,100	$ 4,409,865	$4,117,025

Source: Company records.

of total guests. Our average stay increased slightly. The revenue growth of 6.2 percent outpaced our segment's growth of 5.8 percent even though we had one less property in fiscal 2005 than fiscal 2004. Our average daily rate per room/suite decreased slightly. However, our higher occupancy resulted in an increase in revenue per available room.

Exhibit 7 details the Astor Lodge & Suites, Inc. sales and marketing budget for fiscal 2003 through fiscal 2005.

Fiscal 2006 (June 1, 2005–May 31, 2006) Plan and Budget

Late in the afternoon on April 4, 2005, Kelly Elizabeth met with Catherine Grace to discuss what transpired at the day-long senior vice president conference with Joseph James, the company's new president and CEO. Both agreed that the idea of a formal presentation was in marked contrast to how planning and budgeting was conducted in the past. "It certainly is an efficient way to bring James up-to-speed," said Grace, "but it doesn't give us much time." "You're right about that!" Elizabeth replied. She added:

> Fortunately, we've already done a lot of thinking about next year's initiatives. Brad gave us a preliminary media budget range of $12.5 to $12.9 million and a

sales budget of \$4.85 to \$5 million to work with for fiscal 2006. But, we still have to make a number of decisions before the April 11 presentation. How we address EBITDA and incorporate it in our presentation will be a deciding factor on the success of our presentation . . . and approval of our plan and budget. Thomas [Thomas Klein, vice president of sales] is incommunicado in Nepal for another week climbing mountains, so we'll have to forge ahead without his direct input for the presentation.

In early March, Elizabeth and Grace agreed that the same media vehicles used in fiscal 2005 would be used again in fiscal 2006. Grace noted that media advertising cost would probably increase by 2 percent for fiscal 2006. No new sales representatives would be added in fiscal 2006 and the sales budget range of \$4.85 to \$5 million seemed reasonable and workable, according to Thomas Klein, based on previous conversations.

Elizabeth listed three issues that required immediate attention when preparing the April 11 presentation. At the top of her list was the allocation of media advertising dollars between the pleasure/vacation traveler and business traveler market. This issue had come up in previous executive committee meetings and during the meeting with James. The senior vice president of Lodging Operations thought that too much emphasis was being placed on the pleasure/vacation traveler market. He said: "Astor Lodge & Suites, Inc. built its business and reputation on providing a clean, comfortable, and convenient place for business travelers. The family business, in particular, detracts from this business concept. We have received complaints from our frequent business guests." The CFO expressed concerns as well. She noted that the pleasure/vacation traveler is more price sensitive than the business traveler. This, in turn, led to more "shopping" of hotels in planning trips for nonbusiness purposes. She added, "A dollar or so increase in our room rate is probably equivalent to a 5 to 10 percent increase in occupancy rates in terms of profitability at no out-of-pocket cost to us." Elizabeth believed her presentation would need to address these stated concerns head-on. "Similar concerns had been raised previously, but Brad dismissed them," recalled Elizabeth.

A second issue was the "frontier" strategy initiated in the fiscal 2005 plan. Elizabeth wondered whether this initiative should be carried forward into the fiscal 2006 plan. While she believed the results of the "frontier" strategy were positive, though mixed, it was too early to render a final judgment on its effectiveness. "Brand awareness and brand acceptance does not happen overnight." Brad understood this, but it remains to be seen if James is of a like mind," Elizabeth said.

A third issue related to promotions. Grace had recommended "weekend specials" as a replacement for the "free-night stay" promotion used in fiscal 2005. While still in the formative state, her idea was to run once-a-month "weekend specials" featuring a 25 percent discount off the posted room/suite rate for Saturday and Sunday night stays. (The average posted "rack" rate across all properties was \$62 for guest rooms and \$75 for suites.) These specials would appear on the company's Web site and in e-mail notifications to guests. According to Grace, "There would be virtually no additional advertising cost associated with this promotion. Also, this promotion has a high likelihood of boosting the weekend occupancy rate at company properties which is hovering at 60 percent." Elizabeth had not yet decided on whether or not this idea would be part of the fiscal 2006 plan. She did know that the direct cost per rented room/suite was projected to rise by 2 percent in fiscal 2006 and a price promotion recommendation might meet some resistance, particularly from the senior vice president of Lodging Operations. The various issues would need to be addressed over the next week and decisions would have to be made. In addition, the objectives that motivated the fiscal 2006 initiatives and budget needed to be identified in order to provide a coherent presentation at the April 11 meeting.

Case

Drypers Corporation

National Television Advertising Campaign

In late 1997, senior executives at Drypers Corporation were discussing the merits of spending upward of $10 million on national television advertising in 1998 for its Drypers brand of disposable diapers. The matter was significant for two reasons. First, the company had not used television advertising in its 10-year history. Second, a $10 million expenditure represented a 33 percent increase in the company's combined advertising and promotion budget, which was budgeted at about $30 million in 1997.[1]

The reasoning behind the national television advertising campaign was explained as follows:

> In the United States, diapers are highly promoted since many retailers rely on their diaper products to attract customers to their stores. In addition, Procter & Gamble and Kimberly-Clark spend a significant amount on mass media advertising to create demand for their products. In contrast, Drypers has relied more heavily on promotional spending and cooperative merchandising arrangements with retailers. Promotional activity, such as couponing, is geared toward initiating consumer trial and has been especially effective at targeting spending when less than full distribution has yet to be achieved.[2]
>
> [Television] advertising will build consumer awareness for Drypers as a national brand that stands for quality and innovation. Awareness will boost demand, and increased demand will yield three important results. One, we will increase our penetration of grocery outlets. Two, increased grocery penetration will help mass merchants see us in a new light and help us break into this all-important

---

[1] Laurie Freeman, "Flanking Maneuver," *Marketing News* (October 27, 1997): 1, 16.

[2] Drypers Corporation, *U.S. Securities and Exchange Commission Form 10-K*, for the fiscal year ended December 31, 1997, at p. 9.

This case was prepared by Professor Roger A. Kerin, of the Edwin L. Cox School of Business, Southern Methodist University, as a basis for class discussion and is not designed to illustrate effective or ineffective handling of an administrative situation. This case is based on published sources, including the Drypers Corporation annual reports, U.S. Securities and Exchange Commission Form 10-K and 10-Q reports, company news releases, published articles, and information provided by individuals knowledgeable about the industry. The information presented in the case does not necessarily depict the explicit situation faced by Drypers Corporation, but is introduced only for class discussion purposes. Where appropriate, quotes, statistics, and published information are footnoted for reference purposes. Copyright © 1999 Roger A. Kerin. No part of this case may be reproduced without written permission of the copyright holder.

retail channel. And three, we will move away from higher-cost, promotion-driven sales to brand-driven sales.[3]

The marketing rationale for television advertising was clear. However, discussions related to the national advertising campaign, including its short- and long-term sales and brand-building effect and profit impact, continued as part of the business planning process for 1998.

U.S. DISPOSABLE DIAPER AND TRAINING PANTS MARKET

The market for disposable diapers and training pants is often described as infants and children, primarily below age four, who use diapers and training pants, and their mothers, primarily between the ages of 18 and 49, who decide on the brand of diapers and training pants and usually make the purchase. A baby, on average, uses five diapers per day for 30 months, for a total of 4,500 diapers. At an average retail price in the range of 18 to 27 cents per diaper, each baby represents about $1,012.50 in retail sales.

The retail dollar value of unit volume of the U.S. disposable diaper market has recorded modest growth in recent years due to the trend in fewer infants under 30 months of age and diaper improvements in absorbency and leakage control. The retail dollar value of the U.S. disposable diaper market was estimated to be $3.93 billion in 1997. The retail dollar value of the training and youth pants market was estimated to be $595 million in 1997. Trends in U.S. retail sales, diaper and training pants unit volume, and population are shown in Exhibit 1.

Distribution Channels

Disposable diapers and training pants are distributed principally through grocery stores, drugstores, and mass merchants. Grocery stores accounted for approximately $2 billion in diaper and training pants retail sales in 1997. Grocery store distribution of diapers and training pants has been decreasing as a percentage of total retail sales since 1994. Grocery stores accounted for 51.2 percent of retail sales in 1997, compared with 60 percent in 1994.

Mass merchants and drugstores recorded diaper and training pants retail sales of about $1.9 billion in 1997. Mass merchants have increased their share of total diaper and training pants retail sales from 30 percent in 1994 to 39.4 percent in 1997. The drugstore share of diaper and training pants retail sales has declined from 10 percent in 1994 to 9.2 percent in 1997.

EXHIBIT 1	Trends in the U.S. Disposable Diaper and Training Pants Market			
	1994	*1995*	*1996*	*1997*
Infants (millions): birth to 30 months	10.0	9.8	9.7	9.7
Diapers sold (billions of units)	17.2	17.2	17.3	17.5
Diaper retail dollar sales (millions)	$3,880.0	$3,825.0	$3,855.0	$3,930.0
Children (millions): 18 months to 8 years	26.1	26.3	26.3	26.2
Training and youth pants sold (millions of units)	970.0	1,070.0	1,250.0	1,410.0
Training and youth pants retail dollar sales (millions)	$ 485.0	$ 510.0	$ 540.0	$ 595.0

[3] Drypers Corporation, *1997 Annual Report*, p. 11.

Competitors

Manufacturers of disposable diapers and training pants are typically grouped into three general categories: (1) premium-priced branded manufacturers, (2) value-priced branded manufacturers, and (3) private-label manufacturers. Procter & Gamble and Kimberly-Clark are the leading premium-priced branded manufacturers with their well-known Pampers and Huggies premium brands, respectively. They compete on the basis of product quality, product features and benefits, and price. Both manufacturers invest heavily in research and development. For example, Kimberly-Clark pioneered the first premium training pants for children and presently captures 77 percent of this market on a unit volume basis. Procter & Gamble and Kimberly-Clark also invest heavily in consumer advertising and marketing support for their brands. In 1997, Procter & Gamble spent an estimated $69.6 million in measured media advertising for its Pampers brand; Kimberly-Clark spent $75.6 million in measured media advertising for its Huggies brand. The following is a breakdown of their media expenditures:

		1997 Media Advertising ($ in Millions)		
Manufacturer	*Brand*	*Television*	*Print*	*Total*
Kimberly-Clark	Huggies	$57.2	$18.5	$75.6
Procter & Gamble	Pampers	52.8	16.8	69.6

Kimberly-Clark and Procter & Gamble brands commanded an estimated 78.9 percent of total U.S. retail dollar sales of disposable diapers and training pants in 1997. The combined share of these two companies has increased since 1994 (see Exhibit 2), due in part to their extensive distribution coverage in grocery, mass-merchant, and drugstore markets. For example, both companies sell their products in stores that account for over 90 percent of U.S. diaper and training pants sales. However, Kimberly-Clark and Procter & Gamble market shares differ by distribution channel. For example, Kimberly-Clark's 1997 market share

| EXHIBIT 2 | Combined Dollar Market Share for Disposable Diapers and Training Pants for Kimberly-Clark, Procter & Gamble, and Others: 1994–1997 |

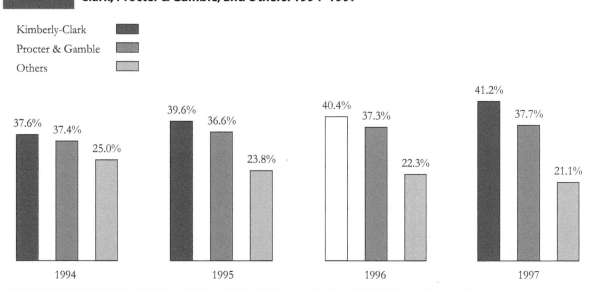

	Private Label	
EXHIBIT 3 Dollar and Unit Market Share of Private-Label Diapers and Training Pants by Distribution Channel		
Distribution Channel	Unit Share	Dollar Share
Grocery stores	23.0%	15.9%
Drugstores	31.3	21.7
Mass merchandisers	21.5	15.3
U.S. market share for private-label diapers and training pants	23.2%	16.1%

in U.S. grocery stores is an estimated 40.6 percent whereas Procter & Gamble's market share is 34.1 percent. Kimberly-Clark has an estimated 41.8 percent share of the mass merchant and drugstore channel; Procter & Gamble's share is 39.4 percent.

Value-priced branded manufacturers, such as Drypers Corporation, typically market their products through grocery stores due to their general lack of national brand-name recognition and less extensive national production and distribution capabilities necessary to supply large mass-merchant and drugstore chains. Value-priced branded manufacturers' strategies vary widely, ranging from an emphasis on quality and "good value for the money" to simply low prices. Products vary from premium-quality to low-quality diapers. Few of these manufacturers engage in extensive research and development or invest in national advertising. Instead, they rely on instore promotions and couponing, often using local or regional print advertising, and cooperative advertising and promotion programs with retailers.

Private-label manufacturers, such as Paragon Trade Brands, Inc. and Arquest, Inc. (the two largest U.S. private-label manufacturers), market their diapers and training pants under retailer-affiliated labels. These manufacturers typically emphasize lower price over quality and product features. Private-label manufacturers spend little on consumer advertising and marketing; however, retailers often promote their individual private-label brands. Private labels account for approximately 16 percent of 1997 retail dollar sales and 23 percent of unit sales for diapers and training pants. Private labels are the most prominent in the drugstore channel. The breakdown of private-label sales by channel is shown in Exhibit 3.

DRYPERS CORPORATION

Drypers Corporation (www.drypers.com) is a producer and marketer of premium-quality, value-priced disposable baby diapers and training pants sold under the Drypers brand name in the United States and under the Drypers name and other brand names internationally. The company also manufactures and sells lower-priced disposable diapers under other brand names (Comfees) in the United States and internationally, in addition to private-label diapers, training pants, and premoistened baby wipes. In 1997, branded products represent 88.9 percent of company net sales in the United States; sales of private-label and other products account for remaining sales. The company's Drypers premium-brand diapers and training pants account for 52.3 percent of total company and domestic net sales in 1997, down from 62.3 percent in 1996 and 61.3 percent in 1995. The company leases manufacturing, distribution, and administrative space in nine locations in the United States, Brazil, Puerto Rico, Argentina, and Mexico. Corporate headquarters are in Houston, Texas.

The company is the world's sixth largest producer of disposable baby diapers and the third largest marketer of brand-name disposable diapers in the United States. In 1997, the company's Drypers brand was the fourth largest selling diaper brand in the United States and the second largest selling training pants brand in U.S. grocery stores.

Company Sales and Profit History

Drypers Corporation has recorded double-digit sales growth since 1995. A 10-fold increase in international sales accounted for much of the sales increase, as shown below:

	1995		*1996*		*1997*	
	($ in Millions)					
Domestic[a]	$154.5	94.3%	$179.2	86.6%	$191.3	66.7%
International	9.4	5.7	27.8	13.4	95.7	33.3
Total net sales	$163.9	100.0%	$207.0	100.0%	$287.0	100.0%

[a]Domestic sales include the United States, Puerto Rico, and exports from these manufacturing operations.

The company's foreign-produced and exported products are sold in over 28 countries, but international marketing efforts have focused principally in Latin America. For example, in February 1997 the company acquired the Brazilian Puppet brand name and formed a joint venture to market this brand in Brazil. In addition, Drypers Corporation is the exclusive private-label supplier to Walmart stores in Latin America and also supplies Drypers premium-branded products to Walmart stores in Latin America.

The company has recorded a significant improvement in sales and profitability since 1995. In 1995, the company's financial performance was adversely affected by events outside its control.[4] Devaluation of the Mexican peso in December 1994, followed by economic uncertainty in Brazil, had a severe impact on sales and profitability. In addition, aggressive diaper promotional spending and pricing by Kimberly-Clark and Procter & Gamble in the United States and a rise in raw-material costs dampened the company's gross profit margin. These events occurred just as the company was converting its four regional U.S. brands (Drypers in the South, Baby's Choice in the West, Wee-Fits in the Midwest, and Cozies in the Northeast) into one common package design and brand name, Drypers. The lack of Drypers brand awareness in the markets previously served by regional brands materially affected sales.

Exhibit 4 on page 342 shows abbreviated income statements for Drypers Corporation for the years ended December 31, 1995, 1996, and 1997. The company generated earnings before interest, taxes, depreciation, and amortization (EBITDA) of $28.8 million for 1997. This strong cash flow, along with sales growth, enabled the company to raise $115 million in capital through a bond offering. Proceeds from the issuance of bonds were used to refinance debt and finance additional production capacity in the United States and Latin America. The company's working capital stood at $48.7 million at the end of 1997.

---

[4] Alexandra M. Biesada, "The Poop on Drypers," *Texas Monthly* (July 1996): 50ff.

EXHIBIT 4	Drypers Corporation Abbreviated Income Statements: 1995–1997 (Expressed as a Percentage of Net Sales)		

| | Year Ended December 31 | | |
	1995	1996	1997
Net sales	100.0%	100.0%	100.0%
Cost of goods sold	69.6	60.9	61.2
Gross profit	30.4	39.1	38.8
Selling, general, and administrative expenses	32.8	34.0	31.3
Unusual expenses	1.9	–	–
Restructuring charge	2.6	–	–
Operating income (loss)	(6.9)	5.1	7.5
Interest expense, net	4.9	4.3	3.5
Other income	–	–	0.1
Income (loss) before income tax provision (benefit) and extraordinary item	(11.8)	0.8	4.1
Income tax provision (benefit)	(2.4)	0.2	0.8
Extraordinary item	–	–	(2.7)
Net income (loss)	(9.4)%	0.6%	0.6%

Source: Drypers Corporation, U.S. Securities and Exchange Commission, Form 10-K, 1997, at p. 17.

Market Position

Drypers Corporation distributes its products principally through grocery stores in the United States. In 1997, the company estimated that its products were sold through 635 grocery retailers with an estimated 20,000 retail outlets. The sales of these retailers represented 66 percent of the total U.S. grocery store market for disposable diapers and training pants. In 1995, the company's distribution coverage in the grocery store channel represented 54 percent of the total U.S. grocery store market for these products. The company estimates that its brands captured 6.4 percent of the total dollar volume and 6.6 percent of the total unit volume for disposable diapers and training pants in the U.S. grocery store channel in 1997. However, in some grocery store markets, including Minneapolis, Minnesota, where Drypers are sold in grocery stores such as Super Valu and Cub Foods, the company estimates that its market share is as high as 20 percent, a figure comparable to Procter & Gamble's Pampers brand.

The company had less widespread distribution in mass-merchant and drug-store chain channels. As a consequence, Drypers' dollar market share in the total U.S. disposable diaper and training pants market is about 3.1 percent.[5] However, the company has recently obtained distribution through selected mass-merchant and drugstore chains, including Super Kmart stores of Kmart, Meijer, and Caldor. "We're trying to break into mass [merchants], to get on the shelf in Walmart and Target," said Dave Olsen, vice president of marketing. "We're doing that by showing retailers that we really do have product differentiation in Drypers

[5] Laurie Freeman, "Flanking Maneuver," *Marketing News* (October, 27, 1997): 16.

while maintaining our value position."[6] Terry Tognietti, co-CEO and president of Drypers North America, added, "What mass merchandisers want to see is that your product will move off the shelf on its own merit with little promotion, versus having them move it off the shelf for you."[7]

Marketing at Drypers Corporation

As the third largest marketer of brand-name disposable diapers in the United States, Drypers Corporation has found it necessary to compete against Kimberly-Clark and Procter & Gamble in novel ways. According to Terry Tognietti:

> We've always tried to compete with Kimberly-Clark and P&G in areas where they can't beat us by throwing money at us. When it comes to money, they beat us every time. So we need, and we try, to put ourselves in competitive situations where we are competing on ideas and quickness, not just who has the deeper pockets.[8]

Product Innovation and Pricing Drypers Corporation has demonstrated an ability to shift the ground rules in diaper marketing through product innovation. For example, in 1996 and 1997, the company was the first to introduce diapers that focused on skin care, in addition to diaper fit, absorbency, and leakage control. "We felt it was time for Drypers as a brand to begin to differentiate itself from the other brands," said Terry Tognietti. He added:

> We do not want to be just a high-quality, low-price, me-too diaper. We want consumers to buy Drypers because they're Drypers, and to do that, we've made significant strides in rolling out diapers that have different features—like the baking soda to address odor control, and the aloe vera as a skin-smoothing treatment.[9]

Drypers with Natural Baking Soda and Drypers with Aloe Vera, introduced in 1996 and 1997, respectively, were believed to be responsible for the increased penetration of the U.S. grocery store channel between 1995 and 1997. In addition, Drypers Corporation was presented the American Marketing Association's prestigious "Gold Edison" award in 1997 for the most innovative children's product on the basis of its Drypers with Aloe Vera product. The company also has provided value-added features to training pants, including a one-piece design and fit to make them look more like real underwear. These innovations, coupled with the addition of baking soda and aloe vera, have contributed to the company's market share in training pants. Drypers Corporation is second only to Kimberly-Clark in training pants sales, with a U.S. market share of 7.8 percent on a unit volume basis.

In 1997, Drypers Corporation entered into a licensing agreement to use the Sesame Street trademark and characters on the company's products, packaging, and advertising materials. This agreement was viewed as a validation of the company's product innovation efforts for children's products. "Children's Television Workshop is very careful who they license the Sesame Street characters to," according to Dave Olsen. "Sesame Street characters are seen as high end. That's the sizzle part."[10]

Drypers Corporation delivers on its value proposition with retail prices that are often 40 percent lower than premium-priced brands for comparable items.

---

[6]Ibid.

[7]Ibid.

[8]Ibid.

[9]Ibid.

[10]Ibid.

"Once consumers understand that our diapers are equal to the other national brands—and offered at a better price—we feel confident that we'll get our share of the diaper business," Tognietti said.

Advertising, Promotion, and Sales   Drypers Corporation has historically relied on print advertising in parent-oriented magazines and regularly places coupons in daily newspapers' food sections and Sunday newspaper free-standing inserts (FSIs). The company also does large volumes of direct mail, in-store promotions, and sampling in pediatricians' offices. For example, the company ships 8,000 to 10,000 diaper samples to pediatricians annually, along with several million coupons and/or diapers to day-care centers. Drypers Corporation's combined advertising and promotion budget was about $30 million in 1997. Of this amount, $3,219,000 was spent for advertising. Advertising expense in 1996 was $1,854,000.

The company does not have a dedicated sales force in the United States. Rather, the company uses in-house managers to coordinate brokerage companies that facilitate the distribution of products through grocery stores on a nonexclusive basis. This approach has expedited the company's entry into grocery store chains and independent grocers because of the favorable long-term relationships that many of these brokers have with these retailers. The use of brokers also minimized corporate overhead expense.

BUSINESS PLANNING FOR 1998

Senior executives at Drypers Corporation outlined an ambitious business plan for 1998. The company was registering its strongest year ever in 1997 in terms of sales and profitability, which was reflected in the upward trend in its common stock price (Exhibit 5). The time seemed right to continue existing efforts that had yielded favorable results and pursue new initiatives. The business plan focused on six key elements:

1. Continue product innovation to differentiate the Drypers brand.
2. Offer "Everyday Value" branded products to consumers.
3. Continue to pursue international expansion opportunities.

EXHIBIT 5 **Drypers Corporation High and Low Quarterly Common Stock Price: 1996–1997**

	1996		1997	
	High	*Low*	*High*	*Low*
Quarter:				
First	$4.13	$2.75	$4.75	$3.63
Second	4.00	2.75	7.75	3.88
Third	4.25	2.63	7.94	6.13
Fourth	5.63	3.50	9.00	5.13

The Company's common stock, $.001 par value, was listed on the NASDAQ National Market under the symbol "DYPR" from March 11, 1994, through January 28, 1996. Effective January 29, 1996, the Company's stock began trading on the NASDAQ SmallCap Market. The table sets forth, for the periods indicated, the high and low sales prices of the common stock as reported by the NASDAQ National Market and the NASDAQ SmallCap Market.

Source: Drypers Corporation, U.S. Securities and Exchange Commission, Form 10-K, 1997, at p. 12.

4. Expand product lines to include additional consumer products.

5. Provide higher-margin products for retailers.

6. Increase brand awareness and retail penetration.

Each element is described below.

Continue product innovation to differentiate the Drypers brand. Drypers Corporation has built its business on meaningful product differentiation that creates value for its customers. The 1998 business plan continued this focus with the scheduled introduction of Drypers Supreme with Germ Guard Liner in September 1998. The product would position Drypers as the only diaper in the industry to include an antibacterial treatment.

Offer "Everyday Value" branded products to consumers. Drypers Corporation's value position emphasizes premium-quality, value-priced diapers and training pants that offer consumers the recognition and reliability of a national brand coupled with product quality and features comparable to premium-priced diapers at generally lower prices. The 1998 business plan reaffirmed this value position and ongoing efforts for continuous improvement.

Continue to pursue international expansion opportunities. The international disposable diaper market is estimated to be $12 billion in annual manufacturers' sales. Growth opportunities exist in regions of the world with low consumer penetration of disposable diapers, including Latin America, the Pacific Rim, and Eastern Europe. Drypers Corporation will continue to expand its operations in Argentina, Mexico, and Brazil and seek further expansion opportunities through acquisition, joint venture, or other arrangements in the Pacific Rim and Latin America.

Expand product lines to include additional consumer products. Drypers Corporation will seek to produce and market additional high-quality consumer products that occupy specialty niches in large and fragmented consumer product categories and can be sold primarily through grocery stores, drugstores, and mass merchants. In October 1997, Drypers Corporation acquired an option to purchase NewLund Laboratories, Inc., a start-up company with a breakthrough laundry detergent technology. The technology provides a detergent, fabric softener, and static-control product in a single-sheet form. The 1998 business plan included a scheduled roll-out of this product by year-end 1998.

Provide higher-margin products for retailers. Drypers Corporation will continue to sell its products to retailers at a generally lower price than leading premium-priced national brands, which allows retailers to offer a lower price to consumers while achieving substantially higher margins. The ability to maintain attractive profit margins for retailers and a favorable price–value relationship for consumers will continue as a result of the company's ongoing emphasis in four areas: (1) delivering innovative product features that differentiate its products; (2) producing high-quality products at substantially the same cost as leading national brand manufacturers; (3) significantly lower advertising, promotion, and research and development expenditures; and (4) maintaining a low corporate overhead structure.

Increase brand awareness and retail penetration. Drypers Corporation has been building its brand equity in a deliberate manner since 1992 with consolidation of the three largest U.S.-branded regional disposable diaper producers. By 1995, the different operations, technology, and the brands themselves had been converted to Drypers. Through distinctive product innovations in 1996 and 1997, the Drypers brand had differentiated itself in the marketplace. All of these efforts have been aimed at achieving a single, clear corporate objective: full U.S. distribution of Drypers diapers and training pants. The decision to invest in a national television media campaign in 1998 by senior Drypers Corporation executives was considered a logical step toward realizing this objective: "We strongly believe that this investment in a national television campaign to build brand awareness is key to achieving full product distribution and higher overall sales."[11]

The 1998 business plan included an expenditure budget for upward of $10 million for a national television advertising campaign in the United States. The campaign would run during the first two quarters or six months of 1998, in combination with the company's existing promotional programs. In the second half of 1998, total advertising and promotion costs, as a percentage of sales, would be reduced to preadvertising levels. It was believed that building brand recognition through advertising should allow the company to gradually reduce its dependence on direct promotional spending and should increase the distribution of Drypers brand diapers and, in turn, increase sales in the second half of 1998.

Although it was clear why an investment in a national television advertising campaign should be made and what this investment should do, discussions continued as to what a national television advertising campaign would do. Discussions related to this initiative, including its short- and long-term sales and brand-building effect and profit impact, continued as the 1998 business plan took shape.

---

[11]Drypers Corporation, *1997 Annual Report*, p. 3.

Case

BBVA Compass

Marketing Resource Allocation

In December 2010, Frank Sottosanti, chief marketing officer of BBVA Compass, was discussing the allocation of the bank's marketing budget with Sheiludis Moyett, director of brand and corporate advertising and Chris Armstrong, advertising manager, along with Sharon Bernstein, director of insights, and Robert Galietti, group account director, both from the bank's media agency Media Contacts, the interactive arm of Havas, a global advertising and communications services group.

BBVA Compass was the 15th largest bank in the United States with a predominant presence in the Sunbelt region, stretching from California to Florida. It was part of the BBVA Group from Spain, a financial service provider with $755 billion in assets and operations in more than 30 countries. "The current economy and the recent financial crisis has put a lot of stress on every bank," said Sottosanti after welcoming everyone. "We are fortunate to have BBVA as a profitable and stable parent company. However, in each of our markets we compete with large U.S. banks such as Bank of America (BoA) and JPMorgan Chase, so we need to ensure that our marketing dollars are being used effectively. The goal of this meeting is to review our current performance and allocate our next year's marketing budget across various offline and online channels."

U.S. BANKING INDUSTRY[1]

In 2010, the U.S. banking market remained fragmented with more than 15,000 banks and credit unions vying for $10 trillion in deposits. The financial crisis had fueled growth in consumer savings rates as consumers reined in spending

---

[1] This section draws heavily from "Mintel Report on US Retail Banking," October 2010.

Professor Sunil Gupta and doctoral student Joseph Davies-Gavin prepared this case. Data in the case have been disguised to protect the confidentiality of the company. HBS cases are developed solely as the basis for class discussion. Cases are not intended to serve as endorsements, sources of primary data, or illustrations of effective or ineffective management.

and banks fought fiercely for deposits to meet funding needs and increase wallet share. In 2009, the 10 largest banks accounted for 46.4% of total deposits, with BoA as the largest bank followed by JPMorgan Chase, Citigroup, and Wells Fargo.

Revenues in retail banking were expected to remain weak due to limited growth in loans. Regulatory changes put a further strain on margins by restricting overdraft fees and debit card charges. The overdraft regulation alone was estimated to reduce fee revenues in the banking industry by $6 to $15 billion.

 ## COMPANY BACKGROUND

In 2010, Banco Bilbao Vizcaya Argentaria, S.A. (BBVA) was the second largest bank in Spain with 48 million customers and 104,000 employees in over 30 countries.[2] It had a large international presence and generated 49 percent of its income in the Americas, split across Central America, South America, and the United States. It operated the fifth largest financial services company in Puerto Rico, the largest bank in Mexico, and handled over 45 percent of money transfers between the United States and Mexico.[3]

BBVA entered the U.S. market in 2004 through the acquisition of Valley Bank, with banking services targeted at Mexican immigrants. Through a series of acquisitions, including Compass Bank in 2007 and the FDIC-assisted acquisition of Guaranty Bank in 2009, BBVA's U.S. operation under the trade name of BBVA Compass established itself as the 15th largest commercial U.S. bank by deposit market share and a significant regional player in the Sunbelt region of the United States (see Exhibit 1).[4] With over 700 branches and $49 billion in deposits across seven states, BBVA Compass was small compared to BoA, which had over 5,900 branches and $916 billion in assets.[5]

Sottosanti explained the bank's goal and its position in the banking market:

> Our goal is to become one of the top 10 banks in the U.S. We plan to stay within our current geographical footprint in the Sunbelt area where we see significant population growth. We are positioned as a regional bank between large banks like BoA and Wells Fargo, and local credit unions. We can offer personal banking like a credit union while maintaining economies of scale. In essence, we are small enough to offer customized solutions while big enough to offer breakthrough innovations.

BBVA Compass had three primary lines of business units: retail banking for individual consumers and small–medium businesses with less than $5 million revenue; corporate and commercial banking for businesses with more than $5 million revenue; and wealth management for individuals with more than $1 million in investable assets. For retail consumers, the bank offered deposit

---

[2]"BBVA, Facing the Future with Strength," company presentation, Barcelona, September 2010, http://inversores.bbva.com/TLBB/fbin/20092010_AHORRO_CORP_Conf_tcm240-233146.pdf#tcm:240-76670-64, downloaded December 2010.

[3]"BBVA Concludes the Acquisition of Laredo National Bancshares," press release, April 28, 2005, www.bbva.com/TLBB/tlbb/jsp/ing/relinver/noticias/RILa4447.jsp, downloaded December 2010.

[4]"BBVA Compass FDIC Assisted Acquisition of Guaranty Bank," BBVA company presentation, August 21, 2009, http://inversores.bbva.com/TLBB/fbin/200809_Guaranty_adquisition_tcm240-200524 .pdf#tcm:240-76670-64, download December 2010.

[5]Company reports; FDIC, "Top 50 Commercial Banks and Savings Institutions by Total Domestic Deposits as of June 2010," www2.fdic.gov/sod/sodSummary.asp?barItem=3, downloaded December 2010.

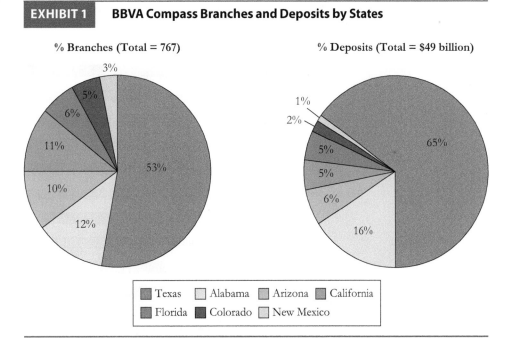

EXHIBIT 1   **BBVA Compass Branches and Deposits by States**

% Branches (Total = 767)   % Deposits (Total = $49 billion)

Texas | Alabama | Arizona | California
Florida | Colorado | New Mexico

Source: "BBVA Compass FDIC Assisted Acquisition of Guaranty Bank," BBVA company presentation, August 21, 2009.

(e.g., checking and savings), lending (e.g., loans, mortgages, credit cards), and third-party insurance products.

 # BBVA COMPASS CUSTOMERS

Target

In its early days the bank focused on Mexican immigrants, but the target demographics grew more mainstream with the acquisitions of Compass Bank and Guaranty Bank. Armstrong described the customer target:

> We aim for consumers identified as "Strivers" who are both aggressive and anxious when it comes to their money. These consumers want a partner who thinks about them and their needs as individuals. While checking accounts are a mass-market product, our ideal targets are consumers 25 to 54 years old, with annual household income of more than $75,000, and financial needs that extend to other products like loans and investments.

Customer Acquisition

According to a study conducted in September 2010, the top three criteria used by U.S. consumers for choosing their bank were free checking services, convenient branch locations, and easy online banking services (Exhibit 2 on page 350).[6]

BBVA Compass acquired customers through its branches, Web site, telephone, and direct mail. "About 5 percent of our new checking accounts come from the online channel, 80 percent through our branches, and the remaining

---

[6]"Reasons U.S. Consumers Chose Their Primary Bank," *eMarketer* (September 9, 2010).

EXHIBIT 2   **Reasons for Choice of Primary Bank, August 2010 (n = 2,800)**

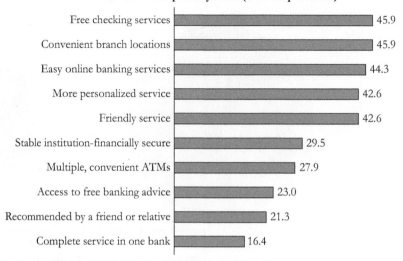

Reasons for choice of primary bank (% of respondents)

Free checking services	45.9
Convenient branch locations	45.9
Easy online banking services	44.3
More personalized service	42.6
Friendly service	42.6
Stable institution-financially secure	29.5
Multiple, convenient ATMs	27.9
Access to free banking advice	23.0
Recommended by a friend or relative	21.3
Complete service in one bank	16.4

Source: "Reasons US Consumers Chose Their Primary Bank," *eMarketer* (September 9, 2010).

through telephone and direct mail," said Sottosanti. "In the banking industry, the lifetime value of a new checking account over its five-year expected life is about $800. We aim to keep our customer acquisition cost below $200 per new account. Acquisition cost between $100 to $150 is good, and below $100 is great."

To understand its customer acquisition efforts and the types of customers acquired through bank branches versus those acquired online, the bank tracked new accounts opened during July 2007 to September 2010. Armstrong highlighted the key results from this study:

> There are significant differences in customers who open new accounts in our branches compared to those who apply online. Average annual retention rate of our customers acquired online is about 55 percent compared to 65 percent retention rate for those acquired through branches. Online customers have lower balances and end up paying higher fees. The net annual income from online customers is therefore slightly higher than that from branch customers. However, new regulations imposed by the government after the recent financial crisis may change our fee income significantly.

MARKETING RESOURCE ALLOCATION

Goals

Sottosanti explained how marketing had to achieve multiple objectives:

> We have multiple goals and our biggest challenge is to allocate our limited resources in such a way that we can balance these different objectives. First and foremost, we need to build awareness and trust in our brand. This is especially important in the current economic environment when consumers have lost faith in the financial system. At the same time we need to support various lines of business such as checking, savings, mortgage, commercial banking, etc. Marketing is also responsible for bringing in new customers and increasing the total

number of accounts at the bank. Finally, we want to improve satisfaction and retention of our current customers and cross-sell to them.

The bank's strategy of growing by acquiring other banks made the marketing task even more challenging since it required merging different cultures and practices, aligning various customer databases, and supporting new geographic regions covered by acquired banks.

Budget Allocation Process

"Budget allocation is a combination of art and science," noted Sottosanti. "We look at our overall sales goals and corporate objectives, assess the growth potential of various channels and markets and review our past performance. For example, only 5 percent of our overall sales come from the Internet, but we allocate more than 5 percent of our budget to this channel since we view it as a growth opportunity."

Moyett elaborated, "Our allocation also varies by market. We spend more resources in our biggest and most important markets where we have significant number of bank branches. Birmingham, Dallas, and Houston continue to be our most important markets."

Armstrong highlighted the trade-off between online and offline advertising, "We can accurately track online activity and, therefore, have a good sense of return on investment (ROI) on our online advertising. In contrast, it is difficult to measure the effectiveness of offline advertising. As a result offline channels can lose budget even though they are critical to our overall success."

Marketing Budget

BBVA Compass' marketing budget was significantly smaller than the budget of large national banks such as BoA and JPMorgan Chase (Table 1). Banks typically spent about 25 percent to 30 percent of their budget on *measured* media (i.e., media spend tracked by third parties) such as television, print, and Internet ads, and the remaining budget on *unmeasured* media that included direct marketing and promotions.

"Our marketing budget has decreased over the years," said Moyett. "Our total budget in 2009 was about $50 million, and in 2010 it is significantly lower. So we have to do more with less." Armstrong elaborated, "Major part of our budget goes for supporting branches, direct mail and other promotional activities. Our discretionary budget for advertising and creative development is a relatively small part of our total budget." Table 2 on page 352 shows the 2010 advertising budget allocation by media. About 50 percent of the offline advertising budget was spent on brand building and the remaining was used for various product lines (e.g., savings and mortgage) and for regional initiatives.

Table 1 U.S. Marketing Spending by Major Banks ($ Million)

Year	BoA	Chase	Wells Fargo	Citi	BBVA Compass	Industry
2008	2,111	1,852	525	971	56	6,930
2009	1,588	1,341	572	560	50	8,067

Note: Industry includes banks and credit cards.

Source: Adapted from *Advertising Age* data center and company documents.

Table 2 BBVA Compass Bank's Advertising Budget by Media, 2010

	Newspaper	Magazine	Outdoor	Online	TV	Radio	Total
Budget (%)	4%	1%	7%	21%	53%	14%	100%

Source: Company documents.

OFFLINE MARKETING

Brand Building

The major goal of offline advertising was to build brand awareness and improve consideration among potential bank customers (see Exhibits 3A and 3B). Moyett explained:

> In 2007 and 2008, aided awareness for the Compass Bank brand was over 80 percent. In 2009, to maximize the global awareness of the BBVA brand we adopted the trade name BBVA Compass. Awareness for this new name dropped to 48 percent in 2009. Our goal in 2010 is to raise our brand awareness to 53 percent and we are very close to achieving this goal.

The marketing group used brand-tracking studies to monitor brand health metrics including awareness, consideration, and brand positioning.

Sponsorships

In September 2010, BBVA Group signed a multiyear sponsorship deal with the National Basketball Association (NBA) that would make it the official bank for the NBA, Women's National Basketball association (WNBA), and the NBA Development League in the United States, Spain, and Puerto Rico.[7] In a press release it stated, "This partnership enhances BBVA's overall commitment to sports—which includes its existing title sponsorship of La Liga BBVA, Spain's top professional soccer league—and fully identifies the bank with the values of passion, teamwork, and fair play inherent in both sports."[8]

In November 2010, BBVA Compass and ESPN Regional Television, Inc. (ERT), a subsidiary of ESPN, announced a multiyear marketing agreement to become the title sponsor of the former Papajohns.com Bowl, a major college football event. The 2010 BBVA Compass Bowl scheduled to take place in Birmingham's Historic Legion Field on January 8, 2011, would feature bowl eligible teams from the Southeastern Conference (SEC) and the Big EAST Conference. The agreement with ESPN also included Associate Sponsorship of the Texas Bowl in Houston, the Bell Helicopter Armed Forces Bowl in Fort Worth, and the New Mexico Bowl in Albuquerque.

"The agreement with ESPN will allow us a channel where we can connect with our customers' passion," said Manolo Sanchez, president and CEO of BBVA Compass.[9] Sottosanti added, "These bowl games help supplement the NBA sponsorship, particularly in markets that do not have NBA team affiliations."

---

[7]Ken Belson, "N.B.A. Has Sponsorship Deal with Global Bank," *New York Times,* September 12, 2010, www.nytimes.com/2010/09/13/sports/basketball/13nba.html, downloaded December 2010.

[8]"BBVA Signs Multiyear Marketing Partnership with the NBA," company press release, September 13, 2010, http://investors.compassbank.com/phoenix.zhtml?c=77589&p=irol-newsArticle&ID=1470455&highlight=, downloaded December 2010.

[9]"ESPN and BBVA Compass Announce Title Sponsorship of Major College Football Bowl Game," company press release, November 4, 2010, http://investors.compassbank.com/phoenix.zhtml?c=77589&p=irol-newsArticle&ID=1492219&highlight=, downloaded December 2010.

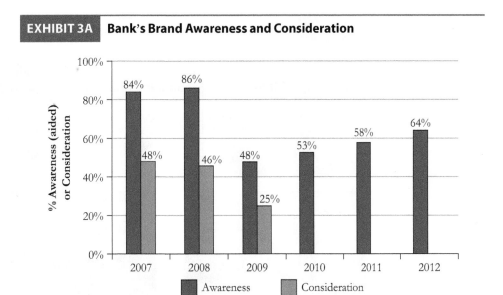

EXHIBIT 3A Bank's Brand Awareness and Consideration

Note: Awareness numbers for 2010–2012 reflect the company goals.

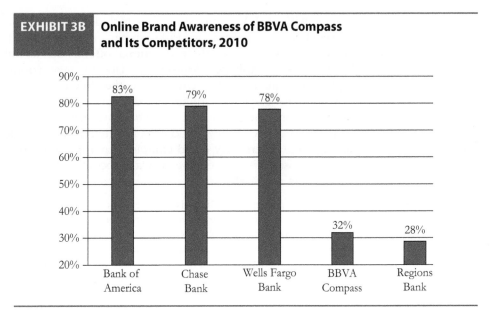

EXHIBIT 3B Online Brand Awareness of BBVA Compass and Its Competitors, 2010

Source: Company documents.

ONLINE MARKETING

The goals of online marketing were to build online brand awareness and acquire new customers for various lines of businesses (see Exhibit 4A on page 354 for online brand creative). In 2010, almost half of the online budget was allocated for acquiring new checking account customers.

Both search and display advertising were used and were generally accompanied by a promotional offer to encourage customers to open a new checking

| EXHIBIT 4A | Examples of Online Brand Campaigns |

account with BBVA Compass. Offers included an iPod Nano or iPod Touch, 5 percent cash back, $100 or $150 cash back (see Exhibit 4B for examples). "We put certain conditions on the promotional offers, such as online bill payment or direct deposit," explained Armstrong. "Due to these conditions, not all newly acquired customers qualify. On average, the effective cost of these promotions is about $100 for each new online checking customer."

When consumers searched for a checking account on Google or encountered a display ad on AOL, they could click on the ad, which took them to the bank's landing page where they could complete an application for a new checking account. Sottosanti explained the typical process of how a new online checking account was acquired:

> About 10 percent of online visitors who click on our paid search or display ads start an application, the others are probably curious about our offers but may find our branch locations inconvenient for them. Less than 50 percent of the people who start an application actually complete it. Those who abandon the application may simply be browsing to see what is required to open an account, or they may be unwilling to provide the necessary information. Once a consumer completes an application, it has to be approved by the bank to ensure that s/he meets a minimum credit score and therefore able to pay any potential overdrafts and account service charges. About 80 percent of online applications are approved, compared to 95 percent to 100 percent approval rate for applications that come from our branches. Once the bank approves an account, the consumer needs to fund this account by depositing money within a certain time period to avoid it from being canceled. Only about two-thirds of the online accounts approved actually fund it within the required time frame.

BBVA Compass Bank's media-buying agency, Media Contacts, was responsible for online budget allocation across search and display advertising as well as for monitoring the results of these campaigns. Sharon Bernstein explained the process of allocating and optimizing the online budget:

> Our primary goal for the checking account is to get as many new customers as we can with our budget. We allocate roughly equal amount to paid search and display ads since they serve different purposes and reach different audiences. We

EXHIBIT 4B **Examples of Paid Search and Display Ads for Checking Account**

$150 Cash - Limited Time
Open a BBVA Compass Checking
Account Online. Apply Now.
BBVACompass.com

Earn $150 Cash When You
Open A BBVA Compass Bank Checking
Account. Apply Online Now.
BBVACompass.com

Source: Company documents.

evaluate the performance of these campaigns based on a variety of factors such as cost per application, the volume of applications, and the efficiency or speed of conversion.

Paid Search

Paid search advertising involved buying keywords on the three main search engines: Google, Yahoo, and Bing. Bernstein described the process:

> Google has the largest share of search queries, so not surprisingly, we spend the largest portion of our paid search budget on Google. We buy generic keywords such as *consumer checking*, *checking account*, and *free checking account*, as well as branded keywords such as *BBVA Compass* and *BBVA brand*. Our bid management tool helps us manage the buys for these keywords based on competitive prices, search volume and share of voice for each keyword. We track how many clicks we get on the different engines, click-through rates, cost per click, and cost per application.

Media Contacts sent weekly performance reports with analysis and recommendations for campaign optimization to Armstrong and Moyett (see Exhibit 5 on page 356 for the performance of paid search marketing and Exhibit 6 on page 356 for the performance of sample paid search campaigns).

Display

Display advertising entailed buying advertising space on Web sites where the bank's prospects were likely to visit. Bernstein explained the process of planning the display campaign:

> For BBVA Compass, we look for high reach placements within relevant content areas in the targeted geography. We typically work with advertising networks as

EXHIBIT 5   Paid Search Marketing Metrics for Checking Campaign (January 2010 – November 2010)

Site	Media Spend	Impressions	Clicks	Applications Started	Applications Completed	Cost per Application
Google	$288,000	5,575,637	234,963	19,571	3,717	$77
MSN	$ 37,000	897,406	50,242	3,101	663	$56
SuperPages	$ 70	116,922	1,410	103	16	$ 4
Yahoo	$177,000	4,435,709	165,166	16,246	2,419	$73
Unified Marketplace	$ 14,000	503,563	20,652	1,632	292	$48
Total	$516,000	11,529,237	472,433	40,653	7,107	$73

Source: Company estimates (budgets are approximate and may not add up due to rounding).

EXHIBIT 6   Performance of Sample Paid Search Campaigns (January 2010 – February 2010)

Campaign	Impressions	Clicks	CTR	CPC	Position	Share of Voice
Consumer Checking	306,043	9,586	3.13%	$7.39	2.7	39.57%
Free Checking	30,911	721	2.33%	$9.11	2.9	66.78%
Free Checking KWs	43,969	1,776	4.04%	$9.02	2.9	77.22%
Checking Account	150,623	2,123	1.41%	$6.45	3.7	22.75%
Free Checking Account	4,757	120	2.52%	$9.67	5.5	63.21%
BBVA Brand Geo	52,617	3,142	5.97%	$0.77	1.2	62.83%
BBVA Brand	609,245	60,696	9.96%	$0.20	1.1	74.37%
BBVA Compass Brand	355,574	29,408	8.27%	$0.46	1.1	18.43%
BBVA Compass Brand Geo	115,854	6,978	6.02%	$0.82	1.2	22.38%

Source: Company documents.

Note: CTR or click-through rate is equal to the number of clicks divided by the number of impressions. CPC or cost per click is the total cost of a campaign divided by the number of clicks. Position is the average position of the search engine sponsored ad link. Share of voice of an ad shows how often that ad appears as compared to the total impressions available for the specific keyword groups (only available from Google).

they can provide reach across multiple publishers and domains, sophisticated targeting, and efficient pricing. Currently, there are hundreds of ad networks, each with a different strength and optimization approach. We also work directly with publishers and portals, like AOL and Yahoo, as Media Contacts also purchases local content placements.

We provide a budget to the partners along with our goals and the profile of target customers. The networks use their algorithms, and in some cases their proprietary data, to identify sites where our ads are displayed. With networks, we typically do not know the exact sites where our ads appear (cheaper pricing in exchange for transparency) but we get performance reports from them that help us ascertain the effectiveness of our ads.

Display ads generated fewer clicks than paid search ads but delivered a much higher number of impressions (Table 3). In general, display ads could be bought either on the basis of cost per thousand (CPM) impressions or cost per acquisition (CPA). However, for the online checking account almost all display placements were bought based on CPM and CPA.

Table 3 Online Marketing for Checking Accounts (January 2010 – November 2010)

	Display	*Search*	*Total Online*
Annual budget for 2010	$ 677,000	$ 545,000	$ 1,222,000
Amount spent Jan.–Nov. 2010	$ 637,000	$ 516,000	$ 1,153,000
Impressions	309,274,438	11,529,237	320,803,675
Clicks	139,474	472,433	611,907
Completed applications	7,209	7,107	14,316
Cost per application (CPA)	$ 88	$ 73	$ 81

Source: Company documents (budgets are approximate and disguised).

EXHIBIT 7 Display Marketing Metrics for Checking Campaign (January 2010 – November 2010)

Ad Network	*Media Spend*	*Impressions*	*Clicks*	*Applications Started*	*Applications Completed*	*Cost per Application*
AOL	$176,000	97,466,342	34,777	7,350	2,934	$ 60
Tribal Fusion	$107,000	38,780,477	21,861	2,730	1,002	$107
Casale	$ 90,000	64,222,377	38,450	2,283	881	$102
Revenue Science	$ 74,000	30,949,214	11,572	2,244	862	$ 86
24/7 Real Media	$ 62,000	13,979,255	4,635	1,366	577	$107
InterClick	$ 38,000	12,678,327	9,643	1,090	411	$ 92
Yahoo	$ 30,000	9,878,699	3,875	457	174	$172
Traffic Marketplace	$ 29,000	28,285,629	8,730	563	207	$140
Datran Media	$ 15,000	5,672,167	3,394	167	63	$238
ValueClick	$ 10,000	3,753,083	1,151	158	64	$156
AdBrite	$ 3,000	3,113,646	1,088	56	15	$200
Total	$637,000	309,274,438	139,474	18,520	7,209	$ 88

Source: Company estimates (budgets are approximate and may not add up due to rounding).

Ad networks differed in their performance (Exhibit 7) and their reach (Exhibit 8 on page 358). Networks also had substantial duplication since many of them partnered with the same content Web sites and reached the same set of consumers (see Exhibit 9 on page 359). Bernstein highlighted additional complexity involved in assessing the performance of display ads:

> In the first 11 months of this year, we generated 7,209 applications when consumers clicked on a display ad. However, the consumer decision-making process is quite complex and consumers go through multiple exposures before opening an account. For example, a consumer may see a display ad on site A, another display ad on site B, do a search on Google, see more display ads on several sites and finally click on a paid search term in Yahoo to open an account. In such a case, we just give credit to the last click on Yahoo without taking into account the journey that may have led this consumer to the final click.

To get a better understanding of consumers' journey and the indirect effects of display, Bernstein used consumers' cookie data to chart out typical consumer paths from exposure to conversion and summarized this information by ad networks (Exhibit 10 on page 360).

EXHIBIT 8 **Reach of Display Sites and Ad Networks (January–February, 2010)**

Site/Ad Network	Reach[a]	% Reach[b]	Exclusive Reach[c]	% Exclusive Reach[d]	Duplicate Reach[e]	% Duplicate Reach[f]
24/7 Real Media	1,767,393	4%	786,307	3%	981,086	56%
AdBrite	1,217,595	3%	675,568	3%	542,027	45%
AOL	9,165,496	21%	5,811,658	23%	3,353,838	37%
Casale	5,152,497	12%	2,946,104	11%	2,206,393	43%
Datran Media	1,772,829	4%	1,204,341	4%	748,488	42%
InterClick	3,568,891	8%	1,847,802	7%	1,721,089	48%
Revenue Science	4,992,957	11%	2,765,169	11%	2,227,788	45%
Yahoo	3,017,113	7%	1,774,526	7%	1,242,587	41%
Traffic Marketplace	6,637,292	15%	4,444,214	17%	2,193,078	33%
Tribal Fusion	5,051,966	12%	2,980,939	12%	2,071,027	41%
ValueClick	1,398,327	3%	644,979	2%	753,348	54%
Yellow Pages	156,771	0.4%	102,265	0.4%	54,506	35%
Total Campaign	43,899,127	100%	25,803,872	100%	18,095,255	41%

Source: Company documents.

[a]Reach of a site is the total number of unique users exposed to the campaign on that site.
[b]Percent reach of a site is the reach of that site divided by the total reach of the entire campaign.
[c]Exclusive reach of a site is the number of unique users exposed on that site only.
[d]Percent exclusive reach of a site is exclusive reach of that site divided by the total exclusive reach of the entire campaign.
[e]Duplicate reach of a site is the number of unique users exposed on that site and any of the other sites in the campaign.
[f]Percent duplicate reach of a site is its duplicate reach divided by its total campaign reach.

LOOKING AHEAD

After reviewing the performance of the bank's offline and online marketing efforts, Sottosanti said, "Next year will bring a new set of challenges. Although we will benefit from the NBA and the BBVA Compass Bowl sponsorships, our next year's marketing budget is likely to be the same or less than the budget for 2010. What is the best way for us to allocate this limited budget most effectively?"

EXHIBIT 9 **Display Site Overlap, Percentage (January–February 2010)**

Site	%Reach	24/7 Real Media	AdBrite	AOL	Casale	Datran Media	Inter Click	Revenue Science	Yahoo	Traffic Market	Tribal Fusion	Value Click	Yellow Pages
24/7 Real Media	4%		4%	34%	21%	4%	17%	19%	10%	14%	17%	9%	0.3%
AdBrite	3%	6%		15%	13%	4%	10%	13%	4%	15%	12%	7%	0.2%
AOL	21%	7%	2%		10%	2%	8%	10%	7%	11%	10%	3%	0.2%
Casale	12%	7%	3%	17%		3%	11%	13%	5%	13%	13%	6%	0.3%
Datran Media	4%	4%	3%	13%	10%		8%	18%	8%	8%	10%	4%	0.5%
Inter Click	8%	9%	3%	21%	16%	4%		16%	9%	15%	12%	9%	0.2%
Revenue-Science	11%	7%	3%	18%	13%	6%	12%		8%	12%	11%	5%	0.4%
Yahoo	7%	6%	2%	21%	9%	5%	10%	13%		9%	9%	3%	0.2%
Traffic Marketplace	15%	4%	3%	15%	10%	2%	8%	9%	4%		8%	3%	0.2%
Tribal Fusion	12%	6%	3%	18%	13%	4%	9%	11%	5%	10%		5%	0.3%
Value Click	3%	11%	6%	23%	21%	5%	17%	19%	7%	14%	17%		0.4%
Yellow Pages	0.4%	3%	2%	12%	9%	5%	5%	14%	5%	7%	9%	4%	

Source: Company documents.

Note: To be read as: Of the total users reached by the display checking campaign in Jan–Feb 2010, 7 Real Media reaches 4% of unique consumers. However, 4% of its users overlap with users of AdBrite, 34% of its users overlap with AOL, and so on.

EXHIBIT 10 · Display Advertising's Effect on Paid Search Clicks and Conversions (January–February 2010)

Display Site	Paid Search Clicks	Conversions	Conversion Rate
Not Exposed[a]	87,152	1,095	1.26%
Datran Media[b]	2,870	95	3.31%
Yellow Pages	734	18	2.45%
Tribal Fusion	12,024	261	2.17%
Yahoo	10,441	165	1.58%
Real Media	15,489	208	1.34%
AOL	25,513	337	1.32%
AdBrite	2,379	31	1.30%
Revenue Science	21,071	227	1.08%
Traffic Marketplace	12,187	131	1.07%
Casale	16,001	162	1.01%
ValueClick	7,111	67	0.94%
InterClick	17,291	160	0.93%
Total Exposed[c]	49,504	734	1.48%

Source: Company documents.

[a]During Jan-Feb 2010, users who were not exposed to any display ads clicked on a paid search ad 87,152 times; 1,095 of those users converted by completing a checking account application, resulting in a conversion rate of 1,095/87,152 or 1.26%.

[b]During Jan-Feb 2010, users who were exposed to a display ad through the ad network Datran Media clicked on a paid search ad 2,870 times within 14 days of display ad exposure, which resulted in 95 completed applications and a conversion rate of 3.31%.

[c]During Jan-Feb 2010, users who were exposed to a display ad through any one of the ad networks clicked on a paid search ad 49,504 times within 14 days, which resulted in 734 completed applications and a conversion rate of 1.48%. The number of paid search clicks and conversions for "total exposed" is not equal to the sum of clicks and conversions of individual ad networks due to duplication among networks.

Chapter 7

Marketing Channel and Supply Chain Strategy and Management

Marketing channels and supply chains play an integral role in an organization's marketing strategy. A *marketing channel* consists of individuals and organizations involved in the process of making a product or service available for consumption or use by consumers and industrial users.

Channels not only link a producer of goods to the goods' buyers through intermediaries such as agents, wholesalers, and retailers, but also provide the means through which an organization implements its marketing strategy. Marketing channels determine whether the target markets sought by an organization are reached. The effectiveness of a communications strategy is determined, in part, by the ability and willingness of channel intermediaries to perform sales, advertising, and promotion activities. An organization's price strategy is influenced by the markup and discount policies of intermediaries. Finally, product strategy is affected by intermediaries' branding policies, willingness to stock and customize offerings, and ability to augment offerings through installation or maintenance services, the extension of credit, and so forth. For these reasons, marketers often use the term *go-to-market strategy* to describe how their organizations select and employ marketing channels to cost-effectively deliver a value proposition to each of its chosen target markets.

A *supply chain* consists of individuals and organizations that perform logistical activities required to create or source and deliver a product or service to consumers and industrial users. Logistical activities involve the movement and storage of raw materials, in-process inventory, and finished goods and related information, such as order processing and transportation scheduling. In short, logistical activities focus on getting the right amount of the right products and services to the right place at the right time in the right condition at the right price for final consumption or use.

Whereas marketing channels link a producer of goods to the goods' buyer, a supply chain includes suppliers to a producer as well as intermediaries between the producer and its final customers. In this regard, a supply chain is essentially a series of linked suppliers and customers in which every customer is, in turn, a supplier to another customer until a finished product reaches the ultimate consumer or industrial user. Exhibit 7.1 on page 362 shows the relation among marketing channels, logistics, and supply chains.

Like marketing channels, a supply chain should be aligned with an organization's marketing strategy. Just as companies have different marketing strategies, they also design and manage supply chains differently to achieve a competitive

361

EXHIBIT 7.1   The Relation Among Marketing Channels, Logistics, and Supply Chains

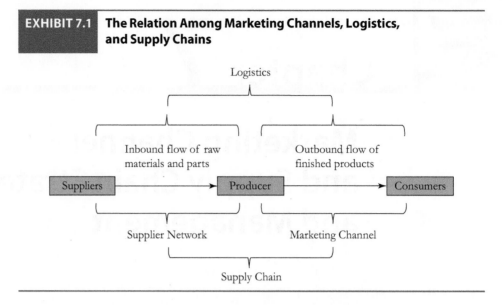

advantage and create customer value, often expressed in terms of quickness to market and lower delivered cost. Supply chain management focuses on the integration of logistics activities and information communication across organizations in a supply chain.

Marketing channel and supply chain strategy and management has assumed greater significance with the onset of electronic commerce. The Internet has challenged marketers to innovatively employ this technology in marketing channel and supply chain strategy and management in a manner that creates customer value at a profit.

 # THE CHANNEL-SELECTION DECISION

Making the channel-selection decision is not so much a single act as it is a process of making various component decisions. The process of channel selection involves specifying the type, location, density, and functions of intermediaries, if any, in a marketing channel. However, before addressing these decisions, the marketing manager must conduct a thorough market analysis in order to identify the target markets that will be served by a prospective marketing channel. The target markets sought and their buying requirements form the basis for all channel decisions. In other words, the marketing manager needs answers to fundamental questions such as these: Who are potential customers? Where do they buy? When do they buy? How do they buy? What do they buy? By working backward from the ultimate buyer or user of an offering, the manager can develop a framework for specific channel decisions and can identify alternative channel designs.[1]

Consider Avon Products, Inc., the world's leading direct seller of beauty and related items to women in over 100 countries.[2] For more than 115 years, the company had successfully marketed its products through an extensive network of independent representatives, which numbered 6.5 million worldwide. However, Avon's marketing research indicated that 59 percent of women who don't buy Avon products would if they were more accessible. The message to Avon's senior management was clear: Give busy women a choice in how, where, and when they do their buying—through an Avon representative, in a retail setting, or online.

According to Avon's chief executive officer, "While direct selling will always be our principal sales channel, expanding access to new customers will help accelerate top-line [sales] growth." Today, Avon products are sold by independent representatives, at kiosks in shopping malls, and on its Web site (avon.com).

The Design of Marketing Channels

Exhibit 7.2 illustrates traditional channel designs for consumer and industrial offerings. Also indicated is the number of levels in a marketing channel, which is determined by the number of intermediaries between the producer and the ultimate buyers or users. As the number of intermediaries between the producer and the ultimate buyer increases, the marketing channel increases in length.

Direct Versus Indirect Distribution   The first decision facing a manager is whether the organization should (1) use intermediaries to reach target markets or (2) contact ultimate buyers directly using its own sales force or distribution outlets, or the Internet through a marketing Web site or electronic storefront. If the manager elects to use intermediaries, then the type, location, density, and number of channel levels must be determined.

Organizations usually elect to contact ultimate buyers directly rather than through intermediaries when the following conditions exist. Direct distribution is usually employed when target markets are composed of easily identifiable buyers, when personal selling is a major component of the organization's communication program, when the organization has a wide variety of offerings for the target market, and when sufficient resources are available to satisfy target market requirements that would normally be handled by intermediaries (such as credit, technical assistance, delivery, and postsale service). Direct distribution must be considered when intermediaries are not available for reaching target markets, or when intermediaries do not possess the capacity to service the requirements of target markets. For example, Procter & Gamble sells its soap and

EXHIBIT 7.2 **Traditional Marketing Channel Designs**

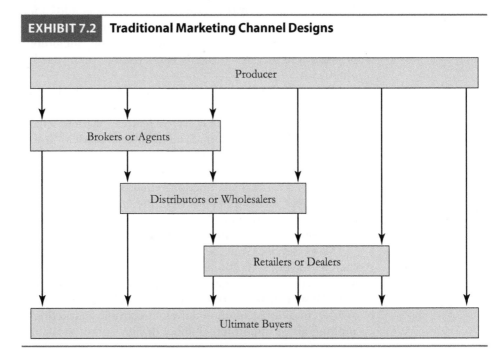

laundry detergents door to door (direct) in the Philippines because there are no other alternatives in many parts of the country. When Ingersoll-Rand first introduced pneumatic tools, a direct channel was used because considerable buyer education and service were necessary. As buyers became more familiar with these products, the company switched to using industrial distributors. Certain characteristics of offerings also favor direct distribution. Typically, highly technical offerings such as mainframe computers, unstandardized offerings such as custom-built machinery, and offerings of high unit value are distributed directly to buyers. Finally, the overall marketing strategy might favor direct distribution. An organization might seek a certain aura of exclusivity not generated by using intermediaries, or an organization might want to emphasize the appeal of "buying direct," presumably important to certain market segments. Direct distribution may also be appropriate if the organization seeks to differentiate its offering from others distributed through intermediaries. A part of the successful value proposition delivered by Zappos.com is its exclusive focus on Internet purchases of shoes and related apparel for consumers who prefer to buy online.[3]

Even though a variety of conditions favor direct distribution, an important caveat must be noted. The decision to market directly to ultimate buyers involves the absorption of all functions (contacting buyers, storage, delivery, and credit) typically performed by intermediaries. The marketing principle "You can eliminate intermediaries but not their functions" is particularly relevant to the manager considering direct distribution. This point is occasionally overlooked by marketing managers when they elect to distribute directly. The costs of performing these functions can be prohibitive, depending on the organization's financial resources and the opportunity cost of diverting financial resources from other endeavors. Therefore, even though all signs favor direct distribution, the capacity of the organization to perform tasks normally assigned to intermediaries may eliminate this alternative from final consideration. A similar caveat must be noted with respect to intermediaries that consider acquiring functions typically performed by channel members above or below them in the channel (for example, a retailer who wishes to perform wholesaling functions).

Electronic Marketing Channels   The Internet adds a technological twist to the analysis of direct versus indirect distribution. *Electronic marketing channels* employ some form of electronic communication, including the Internet, to make products and services available for consumption or use by consumers and industrial users.

Exhibit 7.3 shows the electronic marketing channels for books (Amazon.com), automobiles (Autobytel.com), reservations services (Travelocity.com), and personal computers (Dell.com). A feature of these channels is that they often combine electronic and traditional intermediaries. The inclusion of traditional intermediaries for product marketing (distributors for books and dealers for cars) is due to the logistics function they perform—namely, handling, storage, shipping, and so forth. This function remains with traditional intermediaries or with the producer, as evident with Dell, Inc. and its Dell.com direct channel. It is also noteworthy that two-thirds of the sales through Dell.com involve human sales representatives—a common practice with direct distribution as described earlier.

Many services can be distributed through electronic marketing channels, such as travel reservations marketed by Travelocity.com, financial securities by Schwab.com, and insurance by MetLife.com. Software also can be marketed this way. However, many other services such as health care and auto repair still involve traditional intermediaries. Electronic marketing channels represent yet another, albeit important, channel design option available for marketers. Like all

EXHIBIT 7.3 **Representative Electronic Marketing Channels**

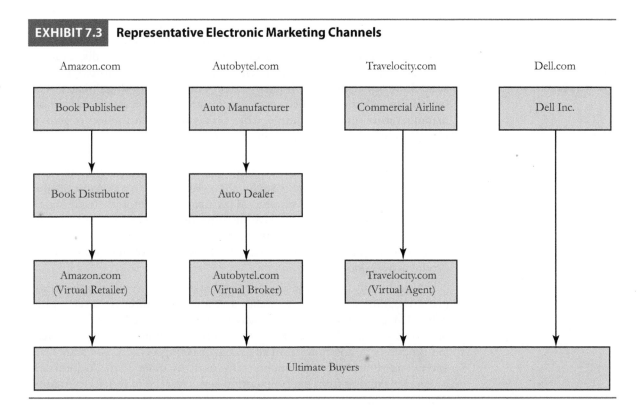

options, it too must be assessed on its revenue-producing capability relative to the costs of achieving market coverage and satisfying buyer requirements.

Channel Selection at the Retail Level

In the event that traditional intermediaries are chosen as the means for reaching target markets, the channel-selection decision then focuses on the type and location of intermediaries at each level of the marketing channel, beginning with the retail level.

Consider the case of a manufacturer of sporting goods. If retail outlets are chosen, the question becomes, What type of retail outlet? Should hardware stores, department stores, sporting goods stores, or some combination be selected to carry the line of sporting goods? Also, where should these retail outlets be located? Should they be in urban, suburban, or rural areas, and in what parts of the country?

Recognizing that numerous routes to buyers exist, three questions need to be addressed when choosing a marketing channel and intermediaries:

1. Which channel and intermediaries will provide the best coverage of the target market?

2. Which channel and intermediaries will best satisfy the buying requirements of the target market?

3. Which channel and intermediaries will be the most profitable?

Target Market Coverage Achieving the best coverage of the target market requires attention to the density and type of intermediaries to be used at the retail level of distribution. Three degrees of distribution density exist: intensive, exclusive, and selective.

1. *Intensive distribution* at the retail level means that a manager attempts to distribute the organization's offerings through as many retail outlets as possible. More specifically, a manager may seek to gain distribution through as many outlets of a specific type (such as drugstores) as possible. In its extreme form, intensive distribution refers to gaining distribution through almost all types of retail outlets, as soft drink and candy manufacturers do. For example, Coca-Cola's retail distribution objective is to place its products "within an arm's reach of desire."

2. *Exclusive distribution* is the opposite of intensive distribution in that typically *one* retail outlet in a geographic area or *one* retail chain carries the manufacturer's line. Usually, the geographic area constitutes the defined trade area of the retailer. Mark Cross wallets and Regal shoes are distributed under an exclusive distribution arrangement. Sometimes retailers sign exclusive distribution agreements with manufacturers. For many years, Radio Shack sold only the RCA brand of audio and video products in its stores.

   Occasionally, the exclusive-distribution strategy involves a contractual arrangement between a retailer and a manufacturer or service provider that gives the retailer exclusive rights to sell a line of products or services in a defined area in return for performing specific marketing functions. A common form of an exclusive agreement is a franchise agreement. Franchise agreements now exist in more than 70 industry categories ranging from tax preparation services (H & R Block) to donuts (Dunkin' Donuts).

3. *Selective distribution* is between these two extremes. This strategy calls for a manufacturer to select a few retail outlets in a geographic area or authorize a few retail chains to carry its offering. Selective distribution weds some of the market coverage benefits of intensive distribution to influence over resale practices evident with exclusive distribution. Dell, Inc. chose selective distribution when it began selling its personal computers through retail chain stores in 2007. According to the company's chair and CEO, "There were plenty of retailers who said 'sell through us,' but we looked for significant relationships. We didn't want to show up everywhere."[4]

The popularity of selective distribution has come about also because of a phenomenon called effective distribution. *Effective distribution* means that a limited number of outlets at the retail level account for a significant fraction of the market potential. An example of effective distribution is a situation in which a marketer of expensive men's wristwatches distributes through only 40 percent of available outlets, but these outlets account for 80 percent of the volume of the wristwatch market. Increasing the density of retail outlets to perhaps 50 percent would probably increase the percentage of potential volume to 85 percent; however, the costs of this action might lead to only a marginal profit contribution at best.

The decision as to which of the three degrees of density to select rests on how buyers purchase the manufacturer's offering, the amount of control over resale desired by the manufacturer, the degree of exclusivity sought by intermediaries, and the contribution of intermediaries to the manufacturer's marketing effort. Intensive distribution is often chosen when the offering is purchased frequently and when buyers wish to expend minimum effort in its acquisition. Convenience goods such as confectionery products, personal care products, and gasoline fall into this category. Limited-distribution strategies (exclusive and selective) are chosen when the offering requires personal selling at the point of purchase. Major household appliances and industrial goods are typically distributed exclusively or selectively.

The density of retail distribution varies inversely with the amount of control over resale and aura of exclusivity desired by manufacturers and retailers. That is, retail density decreases as control over resale practices and desired exclusivity increases. Gucci, one of the world's leading luxury goods producers with its Yves Saint Laurent, Sergio Rossi, Boucheron, Opium, and Gucci brands, has systematically dropped retail outlets for its brands that have not met its stringent sales, service, and display standards. Large toy retailers routinely obtain proprietary rights to market specific toys sold by Mattel, Hasbro, and other producers. Such exclusivity gives these retailers a competitive advantage and higher profit margins.[5]

Satisfying Buyer Requirements   A second consideration in channel selection is the identification of channels and intermediaries that satisfy at least some of the interests buyers want fulfilled when purchasing a firm's products or services. These interests fall into four broad categories: (1) information, (2) convenience, (3) variety, and (4) attendant services.

Information is an important requirement when buyers have limited knowledge or desire specific data about a product or service. Properly chosen intermediaries communicate with buyers through in-store displays, demonstrations, and personal selling. Consumer electronics manufacturers such as Sony and Apple have opened their own retail outlets staffed with highly trained personnel to inform buyers how their products can better meet each customer's needs.

Convenience has multiple meanings for buyers, such as proximity or driving time to a retail outlet. For example, 7-Eleven stores with more than 40,000 outlets worldwide satisfy this interest for buyers, and candy and snack food firms benefit by gaining display space in these stores. For other consumers, convenience means a minimum of time and hassle. Jiffy Lube promises to change engine oil and filters quickly, appealing to this aspect of convenience. For those who shop on the Internet, convenience means that Web sites are easy to locate and navigate, and image downloads are fast. A common view among Web site developers is the "8-second rule": Consumers will abandon their efforts to enter or navigate a Web site if download time exceeds 8 seconds.[6]

Variety reflects buyers' interest in having numerous competing and complementary items from which to choose. Variety is evident in both the breadth and depth of products and brands carried by intermediaries, which enhances their attraction to buyers. Thus, manufacturers of pet food and supplies seek distribution through pet superstores such as Petco and PetSmart, which offer a wide array of pet products.

Attendant services provided by intermediaries are an important buying requirement for products such as large household appliances that require delivery, installation, and credit. Therefore, Whirlpool seeks dealers that provide such services.

Profitability   The third consideration is channel profitability, which is determined by the margins earned (revenues minus cost) for each channel member and for the channel as a whole. Channel cost is the critical dimension of profitability. These costs include distribution, advertising, and selling expenses associated with different types of marketing channels. The extent to which channel members share these costs determines the margins received by each member and by the channel as a whole.

Channel Selection at Other Levels of Distribution

After having determined the nature of retail distribution, the marketing manager must then specify the type, location, and density (if any) of intermediaries that will be used to reach retail outlets. These specific selection decisions closely parallel the retail network decisions made earlier.

If a second-level intermediary (wholesaler, broker, or industrial distributor) is decided on, the question becomes, What type of wholesaler? Should the manager select a specialty wholesaler, which carries a limited line of items within a product line; a general-merchandise wholesaler, which carries a wide assortment of products; a general-line wholesaler, which carries a complete assortment of items in a single retailing field; or a combination of wholesalers? Obviously, an important consideration is what types of wholesalers sell to the retail outlets desired. When Mr. Coffee decided to use supermarkets to sell its replacement coffee filters, it had to recruit food brokers to call on these retailers. Often the decision is based on what is available. If the available wholesalers do not meet the requirements of the manufacturer in terms of satisfying retailers' requirements for delivery, inventory assortment and volume, credit, and so forth, then direct distribution to retailers becomes the only viable alternative. However, careful study of a wholesaler's role in distribution should precede any decision to bypass it, particularly in countries outside the United States. The Gillette Company's experience in Japan is a classic case in point.[7] Gillette attempted to sell its razors and blades through company salespeople in Japan as it does in the United States, thus eliminating wholesalers traditionally involved in marketing toiletries. Warner-Lambert Company sold its Schick razors and blades through the traditional Japanese channel involving wholesalers. The result? Gillette captured 10 percent of the Japanese razor and blade market and Schick captured 62 percent.

The location of wholesalers is determined by the location of retail outlets to the extent that geographic proximity affects logistical considerations such as transportation costs and fast delivery service. The density of wholesalers is influenced by the density of the retail network and wholesaler service capabilities. Generally, as the density of retail outlets increases, the density of wholesalers necessary to service them also increases. Retail bookseller Barnes & Noble, Inc. faced this issue. It attempted to acquire the Ingram Book Group, the largest U.S. book wholesaler with 11 strategically placed distribution locations. The addition of these wholesalers could have cut transportation costs to its more than 1,000 stores and reduced delivery time for its growing number of online customers reached through barnesandnoble.com. The acquisition did not materialize, and Barnes & Noble found it necessary to expand its own wholesale distribution network.[8]

Similar kinds of decisions are required for each level of distribution in a particular marketing channel; their determination will depend on the extent of market coverage sought and the availability of intermediaries. Suffice it to say that the number of levels in a marketing channel generally varies directly with the breadth of the market sought.

DUAL DISTRIBUTION AND MULTI-CHANNEL MARKETING

The discussion thus far has focused on the selection of a single marketing channel. However, many organizations use multiple channels simultaneously. Two common approaches are dual distribution and multi-channel marketing.

Dual Distribution

Dual distribution occurs when an organization distributes its offering through two or more different marketing channels that may or may not compete for similar buyers. For example, General Electric sells its appliances directly to house and apartment builders but uses retailers, including Lowe's home centers, to reach consumers.

Dual distribution is adopted for a variety of reasons. If a manufacturer produces its own brand as well as a private store brand, the store brand might be distributed directly to that particular retailer, whereas the manufacturer's brand might be handled by wholesalers. Or a manufacturer may distribute directly to major large-volume retailers, whose service and volume requirements set them apart from other retailers, and may use wholesalers to reach smaller retailer outlets. Finally, geography itself may affect whether direct or indirect methods of distribution are used. The organization might use its own sales group in high-volume and geographically concentrated markets but use intermediaries elsewhere. In some instances, companies use multiple channels when a multibrand strategy is used (see Chapter 5). Hallmark sells its Hallmark brand greeting cards through its franchised Hallmark stores and select department stores, and its Ambassador brand of cards through discount and drugstore chains.

The viability of the dual-distribution approach is highly situational and will depend on the relative strengths of the manufacturer and retailers. If a manufacturer decides to distribute directly to ultimate buyers in a retailer's territory, the retailer may drop the manufacturer's line. The likelihood of this depends on the importance of the manufacturer's line to the retailer and the availability of competitive offerings. If a retailer accounts for a sufficiently large portion of the manufacturer's volume, elimination of the line could have a negative effect on the manufacturer's sales volume. This happened to Shaw Industries, the world's largest carpet and rug manufacturer. When Shaw Industries announced it would begin operating its own retail stores and commercial dealer network, Home Depot dropped Shaw Industries as a carpet and rug supplier and switched to Mohawk Industries' products.[9]

Multi-Channel Marketing

Like dual distribution, multi-channel marketing involves the use of two or more marketing channels that may or may not compete for similar buyers. *Multi-channel marketing* involves the blending of an electronic marketing channel (electronic storefront or Web site) and a traditional channel in ways that are mutually reinforcing in attracting, retaining, and building relationships with customers.

Multi-channel marketing is pursued for a number of reasons.[10] First, the addition of an electronic marketing channel can provide incremental revenue. Consider Victoria's Secret, the well-known specialty retailer of intimate apparel for women ages 18 to 45. It reports that almost 60 percent of the buyers at its Web site are men, most of whom generate new sales for the company. Second, an electronic marketing channel can leverage the presence of a traditional channel. Ethan Allen, Inc., the furniture manufacturer, markets its products through ethanallen.com and also through its 300 Ethan Allen retail stores in the United States. Customers can browse and buy at its electronic storefront or in its retail furniture stores. Ethan Allen's Web site prominently lists retail store locations, and customers who buy online can have their furniture shipped from a nearby store, reducing delivery charges. Finally, multi-channel marketing can satisfy buyer requirements. The Clinique Division of Estée Lauder Companies, which markets cosmetics through department stores and through clinique.com, provides information about its products, skin care, and cosmetic applications through its Web site. Clinique reports that 80 percent of current customers who visit its Web site later purchase a Clinique product at a department store; 37 percent of browsers make a Clinique purchase after visiting the company's Web site.

The viability of multi-channel marketing depends on a variety of considerations.[11] A major consideration is the extent to which an electronic marketing channel generates incremental revenue or cannibalizes sales from traditional channel intermediaries. In general, incremental revenue is likely if (1) an electronic channel reaches a different segment of customers than the traditional channel or (2) traditional and electronic channels are mutually reinforcing in attracting, retaining, and building customer relationships.

Relationships between a manufacturer or service supplier and traditional channel intermediaries also must be considered. This consideration was prominent when Callaway Golf Company decided to launch its Web site, callaway .com, where consumers can browse and buy the company's golf equipment and merchandise. Orders are filled by and credited to the retailer closest to the buyer. According Callaway's CEO: "This arrangement allows us to satisfy the consumer but to do so in a way that didn't violate our relationship with our loyal trade partners—those 15,000 outlets that sell Callaway products."

Intermediaries, and particularly retailers, are concerned with *disintermediation*— the practice whereby a traditional intermediary member is dropped from a marketing channel and replaced by an electronic storefront. Disintermediation is considered more serious than cannibalization by intermediaries. Whereas cannibalism affects only a portion of an intermediary's sales, disintermediation affects their survival. Companies have avoided multi-channel marketing because of complaints by intermediaries and threats to discontinue carrying their products and delivering their services. For example, Levi Strauss and Norwegian Cruise Line discontinued their electronic storefronts for jeans and online booking reservations, respectively, following retailer and travel agent complaints.

SATISFYING INTERMEDIARY REQUIREMENTS AND TRADE RELATIONS

The role of intermediaries in channel selection has been cited several times; however, a number of specific points require elaboration. The impression given so far may be that intermediaries are relatively docile elements in a marketing channel. Nothing could be further from the truth!

Even though reference has been made to "selecting" intermediaries, selection in actual practice is a two-way street. Intermediaries often choose those suppliers with whom they wish to deal. The previously described decisions by Radio Shack to sell only RCA audio and video products and Home Depot to replace carpeting from Shaw Industries with Mohawk Industries' products vividly illustrate this point.

Intermediary Requirements

Experienced marketing managers know that they must be sensitive to possible requirements of intermediaries that must be met in order to establish profitable exchange relationships. Intermediaries are concerned with the adequacy of the manufacturer's offering in improving its product assortment for its own target markets. If the product line or individual offering is inadequate, then the intermediary must look elsewhere. Intermediaries also seek marketing support from manufacturers. For wholesalers, support often involves promotional assistance; for industrial distributors, it includes technical assistance. As noted earlier, intermediaries concerned with competition usually seek a degree of exclusivity in handling the manufacturer's offering. The ability of the intermediary to provide adequate market coverage, given an exclusive agreement, will determine whether this interest can be satisfied by the manufacturer. Finally, intermediaries expect a profit margin on sales consistent with the functions they are expected to perform. In short, trade discounts, fill-rate standards (that is, the ability of the manufacturer to supply quantities requested by intermediaries), cooperative advertising and other promotional support, lead-time requirements (that is, the length of time from order placement to receipt), and product-service exclusivity agreements each contribute to long-term exchange relationships. A manager who fails to recognize these facts of life often finds that the functions necessary to satisfy buyer requirements, such as sales contacts, display, adequate inventory, service, and delivery, are not being performed.

Trade Relations

Trade relations also are an important consideration in marketing channel management and strategy. Marketing managers recognize that conflicts often arise in trade relations.

Channel Conflict *Channel conflict* arises when one channel member (such as a manufacturer or an intermediary) believes another channel member is engaged in behavior that is preventing it from achieving its goals. Four sources of conflict are common.[12] First, conflict arises when a channel member bypasses another member and sells or buys direct. When Walmart elected to purchase products directly from manufacturers rather than through manufacturers' agents, these agents picketed Walmart stores and placed ads in the *Wall Street Journal* critical of the company. Second, there can be conflict over how profit margins are distributed among channel members. For example, when General Motors and Fiat demanded lower prices for original equipment tires supplied by Michelin, the tire maker refused and canceled the supply contract when its term ended. The lower prices prohibited Michelin from achieving its targeted profit margin goals. A third source of conflict arises when manufacturers believe wholesalers or retailers are not giving their products adequate attention. For example, Nike stopped shipping popular sneakers such as Nike Shox NZ to Foot Locker in retaliation for the retailer's decision to give more shelf space to shoes costing under $120. The fourth source of conflict occurs when a manufacturer engages in dual distribution and particularly when different retailers or dealers carry the same brands. For example, Tupperware's decision to sell its merchandise in Target stores alienated many independent dealers who built their businesses hosting Tupperware parties in homes. Tupperware's U.S. sales plummeted and the company pulled its merchandise from Target.

Channel Power Conflict can have destructive effects on the workings of a marketing channel. To reduce the likelihood of conflict, one member of the channel sometimes seeks to coordinate, direct, and support other channel members. This channel member assumes the role of a *channel captain* because of its power to influence the behavior of other channel members.

Channel power can take four forms. First, economic power arises from the ability of a firm to reward or coerce other members, given its strong financial position or consumer franchise. Microsoft Corporation and Walmart have economic power. Expertness is a second source of power. For example, American Hospital Supply helps its customers—hospitals—manage order processing for hundreds of medical supplies. Identification with a particular channel member may also bestow power on a firm. For instance retailers may compete to carry Ralph Lauren, or clothing manufacturers may compete to be displayed by Neiman-Marcus or Nordstrom. Finally, power can arise from the legitimate right of one channel member to dictate the behavior of other members. This would occur under contractual arrangements (such as franchising) that allow one channel member to legally direct how another behaves.

 ## CHANNEL-MODIFICATION DECISIONS

An organization's marketing channels are subject to modification but less so than other marketing mix elements. A change in marketing strategy often initiates a channel-modification program. Consider Fila, a higher-end active-wear apparel manufacturer. The company sold its line through mostly specialty athletic stores and pro shops and recently decided to broaden its market coverage. It signed a distribution agreement with Kohl's department stores for a line of moderately priced active-wear bearing the Fila brand. According to a company spokesperson, "The [Fila] label sells mainly to 14- to 24-year-olds. [Kohl's] gives us a chance to reach women between 25 and late 40s, the family consumer."[13]

Whatever the reason for modifying an organization's marketing channels, at the base of the channel-modification decision should lie the marketing manager's intent to (1) provide the best coverage of the target market sought, (2) satisfy the buying requirements of the target market, and (3) maximize revenue and minimize cost. Channel-modification decisions involve an assessment of both the benefits and costs of making a change.

Qualitative Factors in Modification Decisions

The qualitative assessment of a modification decision rests on a series of questions. These questions imply that the modification decision involves a comparative analysis of the existing and new channels.

1. Will the change improve the effective coverage of the target markets sought?
2. Will the change improve the satisfaction of buyer needs? How?
3. Which marketing functions must be absorbed in order to make the change?
4. Does the organization have the resources to perform the new functions?
5. What effect will the change have on other channel participants?
6. What will be the effect of the change on the achievement of long-range organizational objectives?

Quantitative Assessment of Modification Decisions

A quantitative assessment of the modification decision considers the financial impact of the change in terms of revenues and expenses. Suppose an organization is considering replacing its wholesalers with its own distribution centers. Wholesalers receive $5 million annually from the margin on sales of the organization's offering. The organization's cost of servicing the wholesalers is $500,000 annually. Therefore, the cost of using wholesalers in this instance is the margin received by wholesalers plus the $500,000 devoted to servicing them, for a total of $5.5 million. Stated differently, the organization would save this amount if the wholesalers were eliminated.

If it eliminated the wholesalers, however, the organization would have to assume their functions, including the costs of sales to retail accounts formerly assumed by the wholesalers. Sales administration costs would be incurred also. In addition, since the wholesalers carry inventories to service retail accounts, the cost of carrying the inventory would have to be assumed, as well as the expenses of delivery and storage. Finally, since wholesalers extend credit to retailers, the cost of carrying the accounts receivable must be included.

Once the costs incurred by eliminating the wholesaler have been estimated, an evaluation of the modification decision from a financial perspective is possible. Such an evaluation follows with illustrative dollar values.

Cost of Wholesalers		*Cost of Distribution Centers*	
Margin to wholesalers	$5,000,000	Sales to retailers	$1,500,000
Service expense	500,000	Sales administration	250,000
Total cost	$5,500,000	Inventory cost	935,000
		Delivery and storage	1,877,000
		Accounts receivable	438,000
		Total cost	$5,000,000

Since using wholesalers costs $5.5 million and the cost of distribution centers would be $5 million, a cost perspective suggests selection of the latter option. However, the effect on revenues must be considered. This effect can be determined by first addressing the questions noted earlier and then translating market coverage, the satisfaction of buyer needs, and channel-participant response into dollar values.

SUPPLY CHAINS AND MARKETING STRATEGY

All companies are members of one or more supply chains. Consider the automotive supply chain.[14] A carmaker's supplier network includes thousands of firms that provide 2,000 functional components, 30,000 parts, and 10 million lines of software code in a typical automobile. In addition, supplier networks provide items ranging from raw materials such as steel and rubber, to transmissions, tires, brakes, windshields, and seats, to complex subassemblies and assemblies, like those found in a chassis and suspension systems. The automotive supply chain also includes the car dealer network. Here attention is focused on (1) getting the right mix of models delivered to each dealer for sale, and (2) supplying spare and service parts to satisfy car maintenance and repair needs of car owners.

Aligning a Supply Chain with Marketing Strategy

What's missing from this automotive supply chain illustration is the linkage between a specific company's supply chain and its marketing strategy. The specific firm's marketing strategy determines whether its supply chain needs to be more responsive or efficient in meeting buyer needs.

There are a variety of supply chain configurations, each of which is designated to perform different tasks well.[15] Marketers today recognize that the choice of a supply chain follows from a clearly defined marketing strategy and involves three steps:

1. *Understand the customer.* To understand the customer, a company must identify the needs of the customer segment being served. These needs, such as a desire for a low price or convenience of purchase, help a company define the relative importance of efficiency and responsiveness in meeting customer requirements.

2. *Understand the supply chain.* A company must understand what a supply chain is designed to do well. Supply chains range from those that emphasize being responsive to buyer needs and demand to those that emphasize efficiency with a goal of supplying products at the lowest possible delivered cost.

3. *Harmonize the supply chain with the marketing strategy.* A company needs to ensure that what the supply chain is capable of doing well is consistent with the targeted customer's needs and its marketing strategy. If a mismatch exists between what the supply chain does particularly well and a company's marketing strategy, the company will either need to redesign the supply chain to support the marketing strategy or change the marketing strategy.

Supply Chain Responsiveness and Efficiency

How are these steps applied and how are efficiency and responsive considerations built into a supply chain? Two well-known companies—Dell and Walmart—provide examples of harmonizing a supply chain and marketing strategy.[16]

Dell: A Responsive Supply Chain
The Dell marketing strategy primarily targets customers who desire having the most up-to-date computer systems customized to their needs. These customers are also willing to (1) wait to have their customized computer system delivered in a few days, rather than picking up a model at a retail store; and (2) pay a reasonable, though not the lowest, price in the marketplace. Given Dell's customer segment, the company has the option of adopting an efficient or responsive supply chain.

An efficient supply chain may use inexpensive, but slower modes of transportation emphasize economies of scale in its production process by reducing the variety of system configurations offered, and limit its assembly and inventory storage facilities to a single location, say Austin, Texas, where the company is headquartered. If Dell opted only for efficiency in its supply chain, it would be difficult to satisfy its target customers' desire for rapid delivery and a wide variety of customizable products.

Dell instead opted for a responsive supply chain. It relies on more expensive express transportation for receipt of components from suppliers and delivery of finished products to customers. The company achieves product variety and manufacturing efficiency by designing common platforms across several products and using common components. Also, Dell has invested heavily in information technology to link itself with suppliers and customers.

Walmart: An Efficient Supply Chain
Walmart's marketing strategy is to be a reliable, lower-price retailer for a wide variety of mass-consumption consumer goods. This strategy favors an efficient supply chain designed to deliver products to 300 million consumers each year at the lowest possible cost. Efficiency is achieved in a variety of ways. For instance, Walmart keeps relatively low inventory levels, and most is stocked in stores available for sale, not in warehouses

gathering dust. The low inventory arises from Walmart's use of *cross-docking*—a practice that involves unloading products from suppliers, sorting products for individual stores, and quickly reloading products onto its trucks for a particular store. No warehousing or storing of products occurs, except for a few hours or, at most, a day. Cross-docking allows Walmart to operate only a small number of distribution centers to service its vast network of Walmart stores, Supercenters, Neighborhood Markets, Marketside stores, and Sam's Clubs, which contributes to efficiency. On the other hand, the company runs its own fleet of trucks to service its stores. This does increase cost and investment, but the benefits in terms of responsiveness justify the cost in Walmart's case.

Walmart has invested much more than its competitors in information technology to operate its supply chain. The company feeds information about customer preferences and demand from its stores back to its suppliers, which manufacture only what is being demanded. This large investment has improved the efficiency of Walmart's supply chain and made it responsive to customer needs.

Three lessons can be learned from these two examples. First, there is no one best supply chain for every company. Second, the best supply chain is the one that is consistent with the needs of the customer segment being served and complements a company's marketing strategy. And finally, marketing managers are often called on to make trade-offs between efficiency and responsiveness on various elements of a company's supply chain.

NOTES

1. Anne T. Couglan, Erin Anderson, Lois W. Stern, and Adel I. El-Ansary, *Marketing Channels*, 7th ed. (Upper Saddle River, NJ: Prentice Hall, 2006): Chapter 2.

2. Avoncompany.com, downloaded January 5, 2012; "Calling Avon's Lady," *Newsweek* (December 2004): 28–30; and Tim Parry, "Live from E-Tail: Avon Embracing Social Networking," Multichannelmerchant.com, August 5, 2008.

3. Roger A. Kerin, Steven Hartley, and William Rudelius, *Marketing*, 10th ed. (Burr Ridge, IL: McGraw-Hill, 2011): 225–226.

4. Christopher Lawton, "Dell Trends Carefully into Selling PCs in Stores," *Wall Street Journal* (January 3, 2008): B1, B2.

5. Joshua Levine and Matthew Swibel, "Dr. No," *Forbes* (May 28, 2001): 72–76; "Retailers Won't Share Their Toys," *Wall Street Journal* (December 4, 2001): B1, B4.

6. Ward A. Hanson and Kirthi Kalyanam, *Internet Marketing & Electronic Commerce* (Mason, OH: Thompson Higher Education, 2007).

7. "Gillette Tries to Nick Schick in Japan," *Wall Street Journal* (February 4, 1991): B3, B4.

8. "Barnes & Noble Likely to Build Centers for Distribution If Ingram Deal Fails," *Wall Street Journal* (June 2, 1999): B8.

9. "Carpet Firm's Dynamic Chief Must Weave Succession," *Wall Street Journal* (August 19, 1998): B4.

10. This discussion is based on Mary Lou Roberts, *Internet Marketing: Online and Offline Strategies*, 2nd ed. (Mason, OH: Thomson, 2008): Chapter 12; Darrell Rigby, "The Future of Shopping," *Harvard Business Review* (December 2011): 64–76; and "Retailers' Panty Raid on Victoria's Secret," *Wall Street Journal* (June 20, 2007): B1, B2.

11. This discussion is based on Stephanie Kang, "Callaway Will Use Retailers to Sell Goods Directly to Consumers Online," *Wall Street Journal* (November 6, 2006): B5; and Jeffrey F. Rayport and Bernard J. Jaworski, *e-Commerce*, 2nd ed. (Burr Ridge, IL: McGraw-Hill, 2004).

12. Anne T. Coughlan, "Marketing Channel Strategy," in Robert A. Peterson and Roger A. Kerin, eds., *Wiley International Encyclopedia of Marketing: Vol. 1. Marketing Strategy* (Chichester, UK: Wiley, 2011): 133–142. "Feud with Seller Hurts Nike Sales, Shares,"

Dallas Morning News (June 28, 2003): 30; Rick Brooks, "A Deal with Target Put Lid on Revival at Tupperware," *Wall Street Journal* (February 18, 2004): A1, A9; "Michelin Cancels Supply Contract with GM Europe," *Wall Street Journal* (May 30, 2002): D6.

13. "Kohl's Seeks Cachet in Exclusive Fila Pact," *Wall Street Journal* (November 13, 2007): B4.

14. This discussion is based on *The Smarter Supply Chain of the Future: Industry Edition* (Somers, NY: IBM Corporation, 2009); and John Paul MacDuffie and Takahiro Fujimoto, "Why Dinosaurs Will Keep Ruling the Automobile Industry," *Harvard Business Review* (June 2010); 23–25.

15. Major portions of this discussion are based on Sunil Chopra and Peter Meindl, *Supply Chain Management: Strategy, Planning, and Operations*, 4th ed. (Upper Saddle River, NJ: Prentice Hall, 2010): Chapters 1–3.

16. This discussion is based on Brett Booen, "Wal-Mart's Supply Chain Acts as If Every Day Is Black Friday," Supply Chain Digital (November 19, 2010); Kathryn Jones, "The Dell Way," *Business 2.0* (February 2003): 61–66; Charles Fishman, "The Wal-Mart You Don't Know," *Fast Company* (December 2003): 68–80; "Michael Dell: Still Betting on the Future of Online Commerce and Supply Chain Efficiencies," Knowledge@Wharton (September 7, 2006); and Chopra and Meindl, *Supply Chain Management*.

Case

Hawaiian Punch

Go-to-Market Strategy

In July 2004, Kate Hoedebeck was promoted to director of marketing—Hawaiian Punch at Cadbury Schweppes Americas Beverages. Hawaiian Punch is the number one fruit punch drink sold in the United States. It is also the company's fourth largest brand, measured by volume, behind Dr Pepper, Snapple, and 7Up. Hoedebeck held several brand management and strategic planning positions with Dr Pepper/Seven Up, Inc. prior to assuming her new responsibility.

Hoedebeck's appointment followed a consolidation of three autonomous U.S. business units of London-based Cadbury Schweppes, PLC—Dr Pepper/Seven Up; Snapple Beverage Group; and Mott's—into one integrated company named Cadbury Schweppes Americas Beverages.[1] Commenting on the consolidation, the president and chief executive officer announced:

> Our goal is to create a premier beverage marketing and sales organization that capitalizes on the terrific brand portfolios managed by the Dr Pepper/Seven Up, Snapple and Mott's organizations. We are designing an organization that will continue to be competitive, grow our beverage business and develop new products that meet the desires of our bottlers, distributors, retailers and consumers. We are committed to building an organization that makes it easy for consumers to prefer our brands, and makes it convenient and profitable for retailers to stock and sell them.

The newly named president of sales of Cadbury Schweppes Americas Beverages echoed these sentiments, saying:

> I am truly excited about the opportunity to put our great stable of brands together in a unified sales organization. Retailers and foodservice customers have been asking for this and it is something we must do to remain competitive.

The integration of the three Cadbury Schweppes, PLC business units had special significance for the Hawaiian Punch business and brand marketing given

---

[1]"Cadbury Schweppes Americas Beverages Restructures for Growth, Changing Marketplace," company press release, September 18, 2003.

The cooperation of Cadbury Schweppes Americas Beverages in the preparation of this case is gratefully acknowledged. This case was prepared by Professor Roger A. Kerin of the Edwin L. Cox School of Business, Southern Methodist University, as a basis for class discussion and is not designed to illustrate effective or ineffective handling of an administrative situation. Certain company information has been disguised and is not useful for research purposes. All financial information pertaining to Hawaiian Punch is disguised and is not useful for research purposes. Hawaiian Punch is a registered trademark of Dr Pepper/Seven Up, Inc. © 2006 Dr Pepper/Seven Up, Inc. Used with permission. Case copyright © 2006 Roger A. Kerin. No part of this case may be reproduced without written permission of the case copyright holder.

its history. Cadbury Schweppes, PLC acquired all rights to Hawaiian Punch from Procter & Gamble in 1999. Since the acquisition, Dr Pepper/Seven Up, Inc., the third largest soft drink manufacturer in the United States, distributed the brand through its bottler network in the carbonated soft drink aisle or location in supermarkets and other retail outlets. At the same time, Mott's, a major U.S. supplier of noncarbonated beverages, juices, mixers, and apple sauce in the United States, distributed the brand through an independent food broker and warehouse network in the juice aisle or location in supermarkets and other retail outlets. Hawaiian Punch was the only brand marketed by Cadbury Schweppes Americas Beverages that employed two distinct and separate manufacturing, sales, and distribution networks to stock and serve an identical beverage for the same retail customer.

As Hoedebeck began to prepare the 2005 Hawaiian Punch business marketing plan, one of the top items on her agenda was a review of the two manufacturing, sales, and distribution networks. The role each played in the future sales, profitability, and equity of the Hawaiian Punch brand franchise was foremost on her mind since she had profit-and-loss responsibility for the business.

 ## THE U.S. FRUIT JUICE AND JUICE DRINK CATEGORY

The average U.S. consumer drinks 182.5 gallons of beverages annually, including tap water. The composition of the beverages consumed, however, has changed over the past decade as shown in Exhibit 1. Whereas carbonated soft drinks remain the most popular consumer beverage, bottled water and sports drinks evidenced the highest rate of consumption growth. Powdered drinks recorded the largest per capita consumption decline.

EXHIBIT 1   U.S. Per Capita Beverage Consumption

Beverage Category	Gallons			Market Share (%)		
	1994	2003	2004 (est.)	1994	2003	2004 (est.)
Carbonated soft drinks	50.0	52.3	52.3	27.4	28.7	28.7
Beer	22.4	21.7	21.6	12.3	11.9	11.8
Milk	23.0	20.4	20.1	12.6	11.2	11.0
Bottled water	9.6	16.6	17.7	5.3	9.1	9.7
Coffee	23.3	16.7	16.6	12.8	9.2	9.1
Juice and juice drinks	9.0	8.5	8.6	4.9	4.7	4.7
Tea	7.1	7.0	7.0	3.9	3.8	3.8
Sports drinks	1.2	3.0	3.5	0.7	1.6	1.9
Powdered drinks	4.8	2.5	2.6	2.6	1.4	1.4
Wine	1.7	2.1	2.1	0.9	1.2	1.2
Distilled spirits	1.3	1.3	1.3	0.7	0.7	0.7
All other (incl. tap water)	29.2	30.4	29.1	16.0	16.7	15.0
Total	182.6	182.5	182.5	100.0	100.0	100.0
U.S. Population (millions)	260.3	290.9	293.7			

Note: Per capita beverage consumption is calculated by dividing total gallons consumed by the total population in a given year. Numbers may not add due to rounding.

Source: Company records based on various industry trade sources and the U.S. Census Bureau.

Fruit Juice and Juice Drinks Varieties

Fruit juice and juice drinks account for 4.7 percent of the total beverage consumption in the United States. This percentage has fluctuated little over the past decade. Fruit juice and juice drinks come in four varieties based on the amount of fruit content in the beverage:

- *100 percent juice*: Reconstituted and frozen 100 percent juice, as well as 100 percent juice not made from concentrate. Example: Mott's Apple Juice.
- *Nectars (25–99 percent juice)*: Manufactured drinks using a base of concentrated juice or a pasteurized purée of the fruit pulp, to which a sweetener and water are or can be added. Example: Nantucket Nectars.
- *Juice drinks (up to 25 percent juice)*: Manufactured drinks made of fresh juice or concentrate, not exceeding 24 percent, to which a sweetener and water are or can be added. Example: Hawaiian Punch.
- *Fruit-flavored drinks (no juice content)*: Manufactured fruit-flavored drinks that have no juice, fruit, or pulp content. Example: Kool-Aid Soft Drink Mix.

The largest-selling variety is 100 percent juice, which commands a 54.9 percent share of the fruit juice and juice drink category, based on volume sold. Juice drinks are second with a 33.7 percent share of the category. Nectars and fruit-flavored drinks account for 6.1 percent and 5.3 percent of the category, respectively.

Fruit juice and juice drinks are packaged in multiple ways. The 100 percent juice variety is often refrigerated and sometimes sold as a frozen concentrate. Nectars, juice drinks, and fruit-flavored drinks require no refrigeration and are called "shelf-stable." Shelf-stable drinks are packaged as a powdered mix, in bottles and cans, and in aseptic containers (notably boxes and pouches). Shelf-stable beverages account for about 60 percent of category volume. Package sizes also differ greatly, ranging from gallon containers to single-serve packages that typically contain 20 ounces or less of a beverage. Single-serve packages account for 20 percent of fruit juice and juice drink category volume. They are most prominent in the soft drink aisle or location in retail stores where they account for 75 percent of sales, measured by volume. About 15 percent of the volume in the juice aisle is attributed to single-serve packages.

Retail Distribution

Fruit juices and juice drinks are sold through many types of outlets. Supermarkets sell over half (53.5 percent) of the fruit juices and juice drinks in the United States, based on volume. Trade sales, including sales to restaurants, foodservice companies, and institutional buyers (e.g., schools, hospitals), represent 18.5 percent of sales. Convenience stores and discounters account for 10.6 percent and 9.5 percent of sales, respectively. The retail sales distribution for fruit juices and juice drinks is shown below:

Outlet	Percentage of Sales (Volume)
Supermarkets	53.5%
Trade	18.5
Convenience stores	10.6
Discounters	9.5
Independent food retailers	5.8
Vending machines	0.2
Other	1.9
	100.0%

EXHIBIT 2	Representative Advertising Expenditures by Brand and Primary Media		

Brand (Company)	Primary Media	Expenditure by Primary Media ($000)	Total All Media Expenditure ($000)
Capri Sun (Kraft Food, Inc.)	Television Magazine	$24,358.3 4,994.6	$30,830.1
Ocean Spray (Ocean Spray Cranberries, Inc.)	Television Magazine	$28,677.0 2,942.5	$32,255.3
Juicy Juice (Nestlé USA)	Television	$ 1,503.3	$ 1,503.3
SunnyD (Sunny Delight Beverage Co.)	Television	$44,178.9	$44,178.9
Kool-Aid (Kraft Food, Inc.)	Television Magazine	$ 6,991.0 3,681.5	$10,677.7
Minute Maid (Coca-Cola Co.)	Television Magazine	$18,459.0 7,179.5	$25,770.9
Hi-C (Coca-Cola Co.)	Television Magazine	$ 2,471.2 184.6	$ 2,842.7
Welch's (Welch's, Inc.)	Television Radio	$ 9,838.6 5,877.6	$15,729.6
Tropicana (PepsiCo, Inc.)	Television Magazine	$36,921.9 14,011.0	$52,581.5

Source: Company records.

Competitors and Brands

Eight companies distribute the most well-known brands in the U.S. fruit juice and juice drink category. They are the Coca-Cola Co.; PepsiCo, Inc.; Kraft Food, Inc.; Ocean Spray Cranberries, Inc.; Sunny Delight Beverage Company; Cadbury Schweppes Americas Beverages; Welch's, Inc.; and Nestlé USA. The brands marketed by these companies represent about 55 percent of category sales. Private brands or store labels account for approximately 20 percent of category sales.

Competitors seek to differentiate their brands through flavor and package innovation, product (re)positioning, and advertising. Increasingly, companies are adding new flavors that appeal to Hispanic households and expanding their lines of single-service packages since both represent growth opportunities. Some companies, notably those that market 100 percent orange juice, have repositioned their brands to focus more on the health benefits of consumption for adults as well as children. The primary media employed by competitors are television and magazines. Exhibit 2 shows the primary media and total expenditures for major brands. On average, competitors spend the equivalent of 24 cents per case sold on consumer media advertising.

HAWAIIAN PUNCH

Hawaiian Punch is the top-selling fruit punch drink in the United States. The 70-year-old brand has a 94 percent brand awareness among U.S. consumers.

Hawaiian Punch History

Hawaiian Punch origins can be traced to a converted garage in Fullerton, California. It was there in 1934 that A. W. Leo, Tom Yates, and Ralph Harrison developed the first Hawaiian Punch recipe—a blend of natural fruits including pineapple, passion fruit, papaya, and guava. They wanted a tropical-tasting syrup to add to their line of ice cream toppings sold under the trade name Pacific Citrus Products Company. "Leo's Hawaiian Punch," as the brand was called at the time, was sold to area restaurants, soda fountains, and ice cream manufacturers. "Leo's" was dropped from the name several years later.

A group of investors purchased the company in 1946 and renamed it the Pacific Hawaiian Products Company. Although consumers had discovered that Leo's Hawaiian Punch concentrate was a delicious drink when mixed with water, they could not purchase it directly. Pacific Hawaiian Products remedied the situation by introducing quart bottles of the concentrate for sale in retail grocery stores in the western United States, and later offered a ready-to-serve red Hawaiian Punch in a 46-ounce can in 1950. During the 1950s, skyrocketing sales for the Hawaiian Punch brand and other fruit juice products catapulted Pacific Hawaiian Products to the middle ranks of U.S. beverage corporations. In 1955, the company introduced frozen concentrate in 6-ounce cans to grocery stores. Later in the year, Hawaiian Punch became a national brand due to its widespread distribution.

To take advantage of the fun tropical image of the brand, the company's advertising agency created the familiar "Punchy" mascot in December 1961 (see Exhibit 3). Punchy made his television debut in 1962 and became an instant advertising success and brand identifier. Punchy's "How about a nice Hawaiian

---

EXHIBIT 3   **Hawaiian Punch "Punchy" Mascot**

Source: Courtesy of Cadbury Schweppes Americas Beverages.

Punch?" tagline personified the brand's image and advertising. The Punchy mascot and tagline remained in use through the 1990s.

In 1963, RJ Reynolds (RJR) Company acquired Hawaiian Punch for approximately $40 million. In 1981, the business was transferred to Del Monte, a wholly owned subsidiary of RJR. Del Monte grew the Hawaiian Punch business and introduced several new products, such as a powder version, plus soft drinks and other flavors for the brand. Del Monte also expanded Hawaiian Punch to new distribution channels.

Procter & Gamble Co. (P&G) bought Hawaiian Punch from Del Monte in 1990 for $150 million. P&G subsequently doubled the size of the concentrate business and established the gallon bottle as a leading juice drink package. P&G also created several convenient packages for food and convenience store delivery and invested in brand advertising featuring the Punchy mascot. In May 1999, Cadbury Schweppes, PLC purchased all rights to Hawaiian Punch from P&G for $203 million.[2] Hawaiian Punch had annual revenues of $133.3 million based on a volume of 54 million cases at the time (1 case = 288 fluid ounces, or 2.25 gallons).

Hawaiian Punch Product Line and Pricing

The Hawaiian Punch product line in 2004 consisted of 11 flavors. They are: (1) Fruit Juicy Red (the original flavor); (2) Green Berry Rush; (3) Mazin' Melon Mix; (4) Bodacious Berry; (5) Tropical Vibe; (6) Wild Purple Smash; (7) Orange Ocean; (8) Grape Geyser; (9) Berry Blue Typhoon; (10) Strawberry Surfin'; and (11) Lemonade. The most popular flavor, by a wide margin, is the original: Fruit Juicy Red. A Hawaiian Punch Light version of Fruit Juicy Red was recently introduced with 60 percent less sugar.

Hawaiian Punch is a shelf-stable juice drink packaged in a 1-gallon bottle, a half-gallon bottle, a 2-liter (67.6 ounce) bottle, a 20-ounce bottle, a 6.75-ounce single-serve standup pouch, and 12-ounce cans. Representative Hawaiian Punch packaging for the Fruit Juicy Red flavor is shown in Exhibit 4. The brand is competitively priced at both the retail and wholesale level.

EXHIBIT 4	Representative Hawaiian Punch Packaging

Source: Courtesy of Cadbury Schweppes Americas Beverages.

---

[2]"Cadbury Agrees to Buy Hawaiian Punch From P&G. Brock Says Deal Shows US Commitment," *Beverage Digest* (May 30, 1999): 28.

Hawaiian Punch Advertising and Promotion

Media advertising for Hawaiian Punch totaled approximately $2.2 million. This expenditure was split equally between radio and magazine print advertising. Exhibit 5 on page 384 shows two print advertisements for Hawaiian Punch. Promotion expenditures include the cost of an interactive Web site (hawaiian-punch .com), coupons, shelf banners, and in-store/end-of-aisle displays. A portion of the Hawaiian Punch advertising and promotion budget is earmarked for bottlers to support local marketing initiatives. Another portion of the budget is for product placement allowances paid to retail customers for shelf space in the juice and juice drink aisle.

Hawaiian Punch Manufacturing, Sales, and Distribution

Cadbury Schweppes Americas Beverages relied on two distinct and separate manufacturing, sales, and distribution networks for Hawaiian Punch to serve supermarkets and other retail customers. One is called "finished goods"; the other, "direct-store delivery."

Finished Goods   The finished goods manufacturing, sales, and distribution network for Hawaiian Punch operates as follows. Cadbury Schweppes Americas Beverages manufactures the Hawaiian Punch juice drink, which is then packaged in ready-to-serve containers at one of three company-owned facilities located in Aspers, Pennsylvania; Williamson, New York; and Tecate, Mexico. The packaged drink (or finished good) is then shipped to warehouses or distribution centers for delivery to retail outlets, or to other institutional customers. The sales responsibility resides with independent food brokers and company sales representatives who represent Hawaiian Punch to retail customers. Their primary contact is with the juice or juice drink retail buyer who, among other tasks, is involved in merchandising the juice and juice drink aisle or location in supermarkets and other retail outlets.

Hawaiian Punch flavors sold through the finished goods network include: (1) Fruit Juicy Red; (2) Orange Ocean; (3) Grape Geyser; (4) Berry Blue Typhoon; (5) Green Berry Rush; (6) Strawberry Surfin'; and (7) Lemonade. The packages sold exclusively through the finished goods network include the 1-gallon bottle, half-gallon bottle, and the 6.75-ounce single-serve standup pouch. The recently introduced Hawaiian Punch Light Fruit Juicy Red was sold only in the gallon bottle in the finished goods network.

Direct-Store Delivery   The direct-store delivery (DSD) manufacturing, sales, and distribution network for Hawaiian Punch operates as follows. Cadbury Schweppes Americas Beverages manufactures and sells Hawaiian Punch concentrate to licensed bottlers in exclusive territories. A bottler purchases the concentrate, which it combines with sweeteners and water, packages it in bottles and/ or cans, and sells to retailers. Hawaiian Punch is licensed to various Coca-Cola bottlers, Pepsi-Cola bottlers, Dr Pepper/Seven Up bottlers, and independent bottlers in the United States. The bottler's primary sales contact is with a retailer's soft drink buyer. Contrary to the finished goods network, bottlers in a DSD network typically deliver and shelve drinks in the soft drink aisle or location in supermarkets and other retail outlets in their exclusive territory, rather than using warehouses or distribution centers. Bottlers do not service the juice or juice drink aisle. (Similarly, the soft drink aisle is not serviced by the finished goods network.) Bottlers also stock vending machines and combine the concentrate with a sweetener to yield a syrup that they deliver to fountain customers, such

Source: Courtesy of Cadbury Schweppes Americas Beverages.

| EXHIBIT 6 | Hawaiian Punch Income Statement for the 12-Month Period Ending June 30, 2004 |

| | | Manufacturing, Sales, and Distribution Network | |
	Total Hawaiian Punch Trademark	Broker/ Warehouse (Finished Goods)	Direct-Store Delivery (Concentrate)
Case volume (1 case = 288 fluid ounces)	77,291,366	49,267,000	28,024,366
Gross sales volume	$292,460,214	$241,086,000	$51,374,214
Less: Discounts and allowances[1]	69,761,800	56,890,000	12,871,800
Net sales volume	$222,698,414	$184,196,000	$38,502,414
Cost of goods sold	151,185,544	144,021,000	7,164,544
Gross contribution before marketing	$ 71,512,870	$ 40,175,000	$31,337,870
Less: Sales controlled marketing[2]	756,021	—	756,021
Marketing controlled marketing[3]	4,494,439	977,000	3,517,439
Gross contribution after marketing	$ 66,262,410	$ 39,198,000	$27,064,410

[1]*Discounts and allowances* include coupons, price promotions, and product placement allowances paid to retailers for juice aisle shelf space.

[2]*Sales controlled marketing* includes local market funds for bottlers.

[3]*Marketing controlled marketing* includes media advertising, nonprice promotions, in-store merchandising, consumer research, and product research and development.

Source: Company records. All figures are disguised and are not useful for research purposes.

as restaurants, which then add water for noncarbonated drinks and carbonated water for soft drinks.

Hawaiian Punch flavors sold through the DSD network include: (1) Fruit Juicy Red (including the Light version); (2) Green Berry Rush; (3) Bodacious Berry; (4) Mazin' Melon Mix; (5) Tropical Vibe; and (6) Wild Purple Smash. The principal packages sold exclusively through the DSD network are the 2-liter bottle, 20-ounce bottle, and 12-ounce can.

Economics of the Hawaiian Punch Manufacturing, Sales, and Distribution Networks   Exhibit 6 illustrates the economics of the two Hawaiian Punch manufacturing, sales, and distribution networks in the form of the brand's 12-month income statement, ended June 30, 2004. Of special note are the differences in the cost of goods sold expense between the two networks. With finished goods, the Hawaiian Punch cost of goods sold expense represents about 78 percent of net dollar sales volume. The DSD cost of goods sold expense is about 19 percent of net dollar sales volume. The expense difference is due to the bottling and distribution costs associated with producing finished goods. These costs do not exist in the DSD network because Hawaiian Punch concentrate only is sold to licensed bottlers. Bottlers incur the cost of bottling and distribution.

HAWAIIAN PUNCH 2005 BRAND MARKETING

As director of marketing—Hawaiian Punch, Kate Hoedebeck was responsible for developing national marketing, promotion, and advertising programs as well as consumer research and product development for the brand. In addition, she was involved in bottler, broker, and retailer trade relations related to the brand. "Getting to know the Hawaiian Punch consumer, trade customer, and brand equity as quickly as possible was the first order of business," said Hoedebeck. Shortly after assuming her new position, she commissioned a consumer purchasing study using ACNielsen Homescan panel data.

Consumer Insights

Four major consumer insights emerged from the ACNielsen Homescan study. Prominent among the findings was that 14 percent of Hawaiian Punch buyers purchased the brand from both aisles (juice aisle and soft drink aisle) of a supermarket. These buyers purchased 25 percent of Hawaiian Punch case volume. The breakdown of Hawaiian Punch buyers and volume by supermarket aisle is shown in Exhibit 7. Twenty percent of Hawaiian Punch juice aisle buyers and 34 percent of Hawaiian Punch soft drink aisle buyers shop both supermarket aisles. Second, both supermarket aisles attract Hawaiian Punch buyers from households with children under 18 years old. The juice aisle was shopped more by households with children in the "under 6" to 12-year-old age group. The soft drink aisle was more popular among households with children in the 6- to 17-year-old age range and skewed toward households with teens. Third, regional differences existed in supermarket aisle shopping. Shopping for Hawaiian Punch in the soft drink aisle was more pronounced in western and central states. Shopping in the juice aisle was more pronounced in eastern and southern states. Finally, 77 percent of Hawaiian Punch buyers purchased only one package size. Gallon and half-gallon package size Hawaiian Punch buyers exhibited the greatest exclusivity. About 68 percent of buyers purchasing the gallon size and 53 percent of buyers purchasing the half-gallon size did not purchase another size. The 2-liter bottle and 20-ounce bottle size buyers were the least exclusive in their purchasing. About 35 percent of Hawaiian Punch buyers purchasing the 2-liter bottle and 38 percent of buyers purchasing the 20-ounce bottle did not purchase another size.

Trade Customer Insights

Following her appointment as director of marketing—Hawaiian Punch, Hoedebeck visited with Hawaiian Punch bottlers, food brokers, company sales representatives, and retailers, which included all major U.S. supermarket chains and Walmart. All were satisfied with the performance of the brand and trade relations. Hawaiian Punch had a 7 percent average annual increase in case sales since being purchased by Cadbury Schweppes, PLC. However, Hawaiian Punch case sales growth slowed in the past year following slower growth in the overall juice drink category.

EXHIBIT 7	Hawaiian Punch Buyer Shopping Practices in Supermarkets	
Supermarket Buyer Shopping Practice	*Percent of Hawaiian Punch Buyers*	*Percent of Hawaiian Punch Volume*
Shop juice aisle exclusively	58.1%	56.7%
Shop soft drink aisle exclusively	27.7	18.1
Shop both aisles	14.2	25.2
	100.0%	100.0%

Source: Company records.

The brand's category share was unchanged. "Everyone believed the category and brand would benefit from more marketing spending," said Hoedebeck. "And everyone was curious about new marketing initiatives."

Bottlers, food brokers, and retailers alike believed the juice drink category had growth potential. Innovation in the category was considered critical and typically took the form of new flavors and new packaging supported by consumer media advertising and trade promotion. The introduction of Hawaiian Punch Light was welcomed by trade customers given consumer health concerns related to calorie intake. However, conversations with trade customers revealed that innovation in the Hawaiian Punch manufacturing, sales, and distribution networks came with subtleties. Hoedebeck learned that flavor and packaging innovation in the DSD network was more economical than in the finished goods network because bottlers assumed the costs of packaging. But Hawaiian Punch bottlers often faced capacity and distribution constraints in producing and shelving a greater variety of flavors and package sizes. Bottlers also expected new flavors and package sizes to be supported with media advertising and local marketing funds. Flavor and packaging innovation in the finished goods network did not face capacity constraints since Hawaiian Punch was bottled at company-owned facilities. However, the sale of new flavors and package sizes through the finished goods network involved product placement allowances paid to retailers for shelf space. Although the dollar amounts varied, it was common for a new flavor or package size to incur a $2.8 million allowance cost per SKU (stock-keeping unit) for juice and juice drink aisle shelf space for national supermarket distribution.[3] The allowance ranged from $15,000 to $250,000 per SKU for a supermarket account. Such allowances did not apply to the soft drink aisle supplied by bottlers in a DSD network.

Brand Equity Insights

From company research, Hoedebeck learned that Hawaiian Punch benefited from strong brand equity. Its significant brand name awareness and authenticity coupled with favorable brand associations linked with fun childhood consumption experiences, unique and refreshing taste, vitamin C content, and Punchy mascot made it a popular and preferred beverage among households with children under 18 years of age. Single-serve pouches, 20-ounce bottles, and 12-ounce cans expanded the usage occasion away from home. For many U.S. consumers, Hawaiian Punch is synonymous with ready-to-serve fruit punch. Nevertheless, Hoedebeck also learned from company research that recent flavor extensions (e.g., Bodacious Berry, Tropical Vibe, etc.) lacked the consumer awareness of the original Fruit Juicy Red flavor.

Go-to-Market Strategy

In mid-September 2004, Kate Hoedebeck assembled the Hawaiian Punch brand team, none of whom had previously worked on the brand. The purpose of the gathering was to alert the team to issues that required attention and decisions that had to be made prior to preparing the 2005 Hawaiian Punch marketing

---

[3]A stock-keeping unit (SKU) is a specific unit of inventory that is carried as a separate identifiable unit. A 2-liter bottle and a gallon bottle of the same product would be separate SKUs for inventory purposes. Similarly, different flavors for a single brand would each represent a separate SKU. Therefore, two new flavors packaged in two different size packages would be counted as four SKUs for inventory purposes.

plan. She began the meeting by drawing a triangle on the conference room white board and labeling each of the vertices:

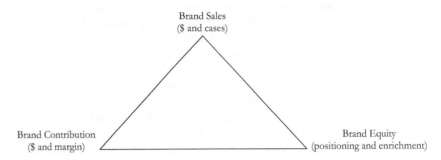

Hoedebeck's opening remarks focused the discussion on the two manufacturing, sales, and distribution networks used by Hawaiian Punch. She emphasized that these networks were central to the 2005 Hawaiian Punch "go-to-market" strategy. Hoedebeck concluded her introduction by referring to the triangle on the board. She noted that issues to be addressed and decisions to be made would need to be examined with regard to Hawaiian Punch brand sales, brand contribution, and brand equity. "A price change is not an option," she said.

Positioning   First, Hoedebeck wanted the brand team to clarify the positioning of Hawaiian Punch. Following the acquisition of Hawaiian Punch from P&G, aspects of its traditional child-centered focus had been played down. For example, the Punchy mascot no longer occupied a prominent role in media advertising as it did with P&G, even though the Punchy mascot remained on the packaging. Also, Cadbury Schweppes Americas Beverages had a policy of not advertising to children under 8 years old.

Based on prior strategy presentations, Hoedebeck learned that Hawaiian Punch positioning differed between the finished goods and DSD networks. Positioning in the finished goods network focused on "Mom," with Mom being the purchaser (gatekeeper) for the family. This positioning skewed slightly more toward African American and Hispanic mothers in its execution. Hawaiian Punch positioning in the DSD network focused on urban, multicultural teens and featured flavor variety and action-oriented appeals. Its execution is reflected in the advertisements shown in Exhibit 5.

As a first item for discussion, Hoedebeck wanted the brand team to prepare a positioning statement for Hawaiian Punch that would guide the 2005 brand marketing plan. In her view, positioning would influence the relative emphasis given the finished goods and DSD networks.

Innovation   A second matter for consideration was innovation. Hoedebeck believed that the Hawaiian Punch brand would benefit from Hispanic-inspired flavors, which would also appeal to non-Hispanic households (e.g., mango). Beginning in 2002, Hawaiian Punch added five flavors for the purpose of expanding the trademark beyond fruit punch. According to prior Hawaiian Punch strategy presentations, this was done to satisfy the need for variety and innovation among tweens (children ages 8 to 12 years) and teens. The new flavors were sold principally through the finished goods network, although many but not all bottlers sold the new flavors. By mid-2004, company research indicated that the new flavors registered little awareness among households with children under 18 years of age. New flavor case sales were modest compared to the original Fruit Juicy Red flavor. Hoedebeck wanted the brand team to consider flavor innovation in the context of the finished goods and DSD networks.

Allowances and Advertising   A third topic for consideration dealt with product placement allowances in the finished goods network. She wanted the team to address allowances relative (1) to innovation in Hawaiian Punch finished goods and DSD networks and (2) to media advertising. Hoedebeck asked the team: "Are product placement allowances and media advertising substitutes or complements for each other? Which will give us the biggest 'bang for the buck' in terms of incremental sales, incremental contribution, and equity enrichment?"

Following a brief discussion, including distribution of category, consumer, and competitive data, the meeting adjourned with a charge given the brand team. "Give the information careful study over the next few days. I'd like everyone to be prepared to engage in lively give-and-take on the issues and decisions."

Case

CUTCO Corporation

Jim Stitt, CEO and board of directors chair of CUTCO Corporation, closed the door to his office, walked through the empty building and across the parking lot, and got into his car. It was the first of January, and he noticed that the initial snow of 2012 was beginning to dust the pavement and his car. Stitt had spent the day alone in his office, relishing the fact that because of the holiday there were no interruptions for the first time in many weeks. As he started his car he began to think about the year ahead. "This should be an interesting year," he thought. "Vector revenues were strong last year, and total revenues are almost back to where they were in 2009. Now we can concentrate on finding ways to grow revenues to at least $500 million annually in the next five years . . . so that we ultimately get to $1 billion in annual revenues. The key is going to be synergy."

Company executives were scheduled to meet in three weeks, and Stitt had been pressing them to agree on a strategic focus for the decade ahead. When he arrived at his office that morning, Stitt opened the "issues file" that he had been compiling since last fall. Each of the issues was important, but identifying the major growth driver to focus on in the upcoming decade and laying the groundwork for its implementation was considered the most important strategic issue facing the company, and the one that needed the most effort to develop thoroughly.

 ## CUTCO CORPORATION

Although CUTCO Corporation celebrated its 60th year of operation in 2009, its roots go back yet another half-century. In 1902, ALCOA, Aluminum Company of America, created the WearEver subsidiary to market aluminum cookware using in-home (non-store) demonstrations. In 1948, ALCOA and W. R. Case & Sons, then the leading cutlery producer in the United States, formed a joint venture to manufacture high-quality kitchen cutlery that would be marketed through ALCOA's WearEver subsidiary. The joint venture was incorporated as Alcas Cutlery Corporation (*Al* for ALCOA and *cas* for Case), and a manufacturing facility was established in Olean, now a city of 17,000 people on the western edge of

EXHIBIT 1   **CUTCO Headquarters in Olean**

New York about 75 miles south of Buffalo. In 1949, the first CUTCO cutlery was produced. See Exhibit 1 for a picture of corporate headquarters.

Case sold its 49 percent interest in Alcas Cutlery Corporation to ALCOA in 1972. Ten years later, in September 1982, ALCOA sold Alcas Cutlery Corporation through a leveraged buyout to a management team led by Erick Laine, then the president of Alcas Cutlery Corporation. Since 1982 the company has been a closely held private company. Annual company revenues at the time of the leveraged buyout were slightly less than $5 million.

After a period of aggressive growth and a series of reorganizations and acquisitions, Alcas Cutlery Corporation changed its name to ALCAS Corporation in 1990 and eventually morphed into a "family" consisting of seven interrelated companies. ALCAS Corporation became the parent holding company of CUTCO Cutlery Corporation, KA-BAR Knives, CUTCO International, Vector Marketing Corporation, Schilling Forge, and CUTCO Stores Inc., all of which are administratively headquartered in Olean, and all of which are profit centers. CUTCO Cutlery Corporation manufactures the cutlery that Vector Marketing Corporation markets in North America (the United States and Canada), and CUTCO International markets CUTCO products outside North America.

KA-BAR Knives, a marketer of sport and utility knives established in 1898 under the name of Union Razor Company, was acquired by ALCAS in 1996. KA-BAR knives are marketed domestically through independent sales representatives and internationally by an in-house staff to wholesalers and retailers. CUTCO Cutlery Corporation manufactures nearly 80 percent of the KA-BAR knife products. The rest is manufactured by several suppliers located in Asia. Although KA-BAR knives vary widely in price, the best-selling ones are priced between $40 and $70. Schilling Forge is a small manufacturer of precision forgings for scissors and the like; it was purchased so that CUTCO could maintain an American manufacturer of forgings. CUTCO Stores Inc. was created in 2005 to test multi-channel marketing from a single location—a retail store in the front of a commercial facility and a direct-sales operation in the back of the facility.

The ALCAS corporate vision was to "become the largest, most respected and widely recognized cutlery company in the world." By the end of 2002, ALCAS was the only manufacturer of high-quality kitchen cutlery and accessories in the United States. All U.S. competitors had moved their manufacturing operations offshore. In 2009 ALCAS officially changed its corporate name to CUTCO Corporation. This was done to take advantage of the outstanding reputation of CUTCO cutlery and create a more consistent corporate brand umbrella. Presently the company employs more than 800 people at its Olean headquarters and has revenues in excess of $250 million.

 ## THE CUTCO PRODUCT LINE

The original CUTCO product line consisted of 10 basic items, including a table knife, paring knife, trimmer, French chef knife, large fork, carving knife, small fork, butcher knife, slicer, and spatula. (The CUTCO name was derived from a company once owned by ALCOA, *C*ooking *UT*ensil *CO*mpany.) On April 29, 1949, the first order of CUTCO cutlery—six knives, two forks, a spatula, and two storage trays—was shipped by automobile from Olean to New Kensington, Pennsylvania. The CUTCO product line has since grown to include more than 500 SKUs (stock-keeping units), nearly double that of a decade ago. Even so, the core of the product line still consists of 10 basic knives that can be purchased individually or in various sets ranging from a two-item gift pack to the Signature Set, which consists of the 10 basic knives, hardy slicer, santuko-style knife, cheese knife, shears, and 10 table knives displayed in a wooden block. Exhibit 2 shows the Signature Set displayed in the wooden block. Retail prices in 2011 ranged from $30 for a vegetable peeler to $1,599 for the Signature Set (prices include shipping and handling).

The company also offers a five-piece set of flatware (teaspoon, dinner fork, table knife, soup spoon, salad fork) and a set of six serving pieces as well as a complementary line of accessory kitchen products, including various types of shears, potato masher, pizza cutter, cleaver, pocket and hunting knives, and garden tools. Recently the company added several santuko-styled knives to the line and a joint CUTCO–KA-BAR explorer knife. Despite these non-knife additions, "cutting edge" cutlery items still account for about 90 percent of sales.

From the first product produced, CUTCO cutlery was designed to be the finest cutlery in the world. Prices of CUTCO products are increased by an average of 5 percent every other year (e.g., 2007, 2009, 2011), primarily to offset one-half of rising labor and material costs. (The other half of rising labor and material costs are to be covered with improved manufacturing efficiencies.)

In addition to being known for its outstanding quality, CUTCO cutlery is instantly recognizable because of its exclusive and unique wedge-lock handle and the Double-D knife blade grind. First introduced in 1952 and improved considerably in 1972, the (universal) wedge-lock handle is an ergonomically designed and scientifically contoured handle that creates a firm, yet comfortable and safe grip. Handles are made from thermo-resin material that will not chip, crack, fade, or absorb moisture and come in two colors—classic brown and pearl white.

EXHIBIT 2 **Signature Set**

Every CUTCO product has a full lifetime ("forever") guarantee that includes free factory sharpening. If any product is found to be defective, it will be replaced at no cost to the customer.

The Double-D grind, which was added to certain knife blades in 1960, consists of three razor-sharp edges angled and recessed in such a fashion that a blade can cut forward, backward, and straight down without the cutting edges becoming worn through contact with plates, cutting boards, or countertops. Unlike the typical serrated knife blade, the Double-D knife blade does not rip or tear what is being cut and can be resharpened (at the factory).

Over time CUTCO cutlery has become an American icon. It has been featured in television programs such as *Saturday Night Live* and *The Simpsons*, and showcased in *Made in America* and *Modern Marvels*. The cutlery has been used in the Betty Crocker national bake-offs and countless food-related events such as the Epcot International Food & Wine Festival and the National Pork Board Taste of Elegance.

Exhibit 3 on page 394 contains consolidated revenues for the most recent five years of the CUTCO Corporation.

EXHIBIT 3	CUTCO Corporation Revenues ($ 000)				
	2007	*2008*	*2009*	*2010*	*2011 Est.*
Vector (Direct Sales)	$157,000	$170,000	$218,000	$217,000	$219,000
Vector (Catalog)	19,000	16,000	17,000	18,000	18,000
Cutco International	11,000	12,000	13,000	6,000	4,000
Ka-Bar/Schilling/Internet	10,000	11,000	11,000	13,000	19,000
TOTAL	$197,000	$209,000	$259,000	$254,000	$260,000

ª Some numbers are disguised.

VECTOR MARKETING CORPORATION

CUTCO cutlery was marketed from 1949 through 1970 by a segment of the WearEver sales force. In 1970 the CUTCO sales force was merged with the rest of the WearEver cookware sales force and the two product lines marketed together for the next decade. In 1981, WearEver decided to convert its sales force into approximately 100 small, independent distributorships that would market the CUTCO product line. On January 1, 1982, Alcas Cutlery Corporation assumed responsibility for all CUTCO marketing activities.

During the next three years, several multi-state independent distributorships evolved through mergers and buyouts. In 1985, the company realized the need to have greater control over its sales efforts and took steps to create a nationwide in-house CUTCO sales and marketing infrastructure. It did so by first acquiring the largest independent distributor, Vector Marketing Corporation, which operated in the eastern part of the United States. Vector Marketing Corporation became a wholly owned subsidiary of ALCAS. Shortly thereafter, ALCAS acquired a second independent distributorship, CWE Industries, which operated in the western part of the United States. The acquisition of BrekMar Corporation, which operated in the Midwest, and three southern-based distributorships followed, all of which were merged into Vector Marketing Corporation.

During the 50th anniversary of ALCAS Corporation, Erick Laine, then chair of the company's board of directors, reflected back on the time when Vector Marketing Corporation was acquired in 1985. He remarked:

> The addition of Vector Marketing was the most significant organizational move we made since we purchased Alcas Cutlery Corporation from ALCOA in 1982. Acquiring an in-house CUTCO marketing capability—Vector—gave us complete control over our major market. With that capability, marketing decisions relating to new office locations, expansion plans, rate of growth, and distribution methods were under the control of the company.

CUTCO cutlery has always been marketed through direct selling. This is viewed as a distinct advantage by the company because it allows the quality and performance features of the product to be explained and demonstrated directly to potential customers. Direct selling sets the company apart from its major competitors, J. A. Henckels Zwillingswerk, Inc. ("Henckels"), Wusthof-Trident, and Shun Cutlery. These competitors have traditionally used department stores and mass merchandisers to market their products. Of the three major competitors, Henckels, a German company, is the largest, with U.S. retail sales approximating those of Vector. Although the "street price" of Henckels cutlery is typically 25 percent less than its list price, Vector and Henckels list prices are very similar for comparable items.

Vector Marketing Corporation Structure

Vector Marketing Corporation sales efforts are organized by geographic location. The United States consists of six geographic sales regions: Central, Midwest, Northeast, Eastern, Southwest, and Western. These six regions are respectively combined into two "companies"—Vector East (Midwest, Northeast, and Eastern regions) and Vector West (Central, Southwest, and Western regions). Each of these two companies is headed by a president and CEO of sales. These two presidents, plus the president and COO of Vector Marketing Corporation, are referred to in CUTCO as the "triad." The triad reports directly to Jim Stitt. Canada is treated as a separate region and is headed by a sales manager who reports to the CEO of sales of Vector East.

Each of the six regions is headed by a regional sales manager, which in one region is an executive vice president. Within each region are five to seven divisions, and within these divisions are a total of approximately 300 district or permanent offices and another 325 "branch offices." Branch offices are summer offices that operate for about 17 weeks every summer. A district office operates throughout the year and typically is located in an area with a population base of at least 200,000 people.

The individuals actually selling CUTCO cutlery are independent contractors who, in essence, operate their own business. As such, these sales representatives are paid a commission on the products they sell. Although they are eligible for demonstration-based compensation, sales representatives usually move to a full sales commission compensation system that exceeds demonstration-based compensation soon after they start selling. None of the sales representatives receives a salary from the company.

What makes the sales representatives unique is that, for the most part, they are college students who sell CUTCO products during their summer vacations. As a consequence of this "summer selling season," a majority of Vector Marketing Corporation's sales occur in the May–August time period each year. Fifty-five percent of the sales representatives are males. Every year tens of thousands of college students are recruited to sell CUTCO products. In the past, recruiting was traditionally done through a variety of methods, including newspaper advertisements, direct mailings, fliers posted around campuses, personalized letters to potential recruits, on-campus recruiting through booths, and personal one-on-one recruiting. Recently, though, traditional recruiting vehicles—such as newspapers, campus flyers, and letters to potential recruits—are being rethought and even discontinued because of cost and ineffectiveness. Vector Marketing Corporation is structured to facilitate recruiting, training, and motivating college students to sell CUTCO products, and it does so very well. Indeed, the very top sales representatives can earn more than $20,000 for a summer of selling.

Sales are made through in-home presentations in which sales representatives demonstrate the superiority of CUTCO cutlery by cutting food items as well as rope and leather. These presentations are prearranged through referrals and appointments and are considered key to company selling success. As Marty Domitrovich, a former Vector executive with more than 30 years of experience, frequently stated,

> Selling yourself is paramount in any sales situation. I firmly believe that people buy from individuals they like, and there is no better way to make a solid first impression than face to face. There is no substitute for the personal touch that comes from sitting across from someone in his or her home and allowing them to actually try your product. Personal, professional demonstrations sell CUTCO cutlery, period.

Oftentimes a sales representative's first sale is made to his or her parents, relatives, or neighbors. Interestingly enough, about one-in-six sales are made each year to previous purchasers of CUTCO products. Because CUTCO products tend to "sell themselves" after people have seen a demonstration, there is relatively little need for a "hard sell" on the part of sales representatives. Training emphasizes appointment setting, demonstrations, order writing, and referrals. There is no "cold calling" or door-to-door selling.

Sales representatives typically meet with their Vector managers Monday evenings to discuss the prior week's activities and plan the current week's activities. During these meetings, the sales representatives turn in their sales orders and any money collected from the prior week. (More than 80 percent of orders are pre-entered by the sales representatives by means of a company Web site.) Managers overnight the orders and money to Olean, where orders are approved and filled.

In 2011, the company filled more than 750,000 separate orders in the United States, up from 580,000 orders in 1999, with each order representing one direct-sales customer. Products are shipped directly to customers within two to three weeks during the summer selling season, and within one to two weeks at other times. Both UPS and the U.S. Postal Service are used to deliver products. The operating margin of Vector Marketing Corporation on direct sales is approximately 7 percent.[1]

To motivate sales representatives, Vector Marketing Corporation employs a variety of promotional activities, events, and competitions. Not only are the sales representatives rewarded directly for the sales they make (through commissions that range from 10 to 50 percent depending on the level of sales), they are also eligible to receive trophies, bonuses, trips, and even scholarships for achieving certain sales levels. Those sales representatives who are particularly successful have the additional opportunity to establish and manage one of the Vector branch offices. Managing a branch office requires a dedicated and active program of recruiting and training throughout the preceding school year as well as an entrepreneurial mindset at all times.

The particular direct-selling model that Vector Marketing Corporation uses differs from the direct-selling models used by virtually all other direct-selling firms. Only one other direct-selling company, the Southwestern Company in Nashville, Tennessee, uses college students as its primary sales force to market a variety of books and related educational materials during summer vacations. Even so, Vector and Southwestern possess very different marketing strategies. For example, whereas Vector trains small groups of sales representatives at district or branch offices, Southwestern simultaneously trains hundreds of sales representatives at its Nashville headquarters. Moreover, whereas Vector sales representatives use a referral system for sales leads, Southwestern sales representatives focus on door-to-door presentations. Finally, whereas Vector sales representatives typically sell in their home cities, Southwestern sales representatives typically are assigned to sell in a city away from their home.

Vector Catalog Sales

Because over 90 percent of Vector Marketing Corporation sales representatives sell only for one summer, the customers they create often lose contact with CUTCO products and the company. To maintain a continuing relationship with, and service to, these customers, Vector initiated a small catalog mailing in 1985.

---

[1]All operating margins are disguised, although the relationships among them are representative.

This catalog has since been expanded such that there are now multiple mailings of a variety of catalogs to more than 4.6 million CUTCO customers throughout the year. Most mailings are timed to occur in September through December so as not to conflict with the summer selling season. In 2011, catalog mailings generated more than 120,000 orders and approximately $18 million in sales, with a corresponding operating margin of about 9 percent. If the customer of a current Vector Marketing Corporation sales representative makes a catalog purchase, the sales representative and the sales representative's manager receive a reduced commission. The sales representative will continue to receive commissions on catalog sales for as long as he or she maintains a very modest level of sales activity. If a sales representative is no longer actively selling for Vector, only the sales representative's manager receives a commission on a catalog purchase.

Vector Internet Activities

Vector Marketing Corporation personnel spent several years developing a strategy using the Internet to recruit college students to be sales representatives and promote cutlery. One result was a recruiting Web site (www.workforstudents .com). The number of applications received through this site has been very encouraging, and the Internet recruiting strategy as a whole is very successful.

A second result was a customer-oriented Web site (www.cutco.com) focusing on customer service and product information. No sales were permitted. Simultaneous with the introduction of the Web site, Vector service representatives began frequently reporting that they had received numerous requests from consumers who are not currently CUTCO product owners but who want to order CUTCO products online. These consumers initially were advised that they could order only from a sales representative. However, this changed because the triad strongly believed that Vector had to serve its customers:

> We have a very important responsibility to make sure that we are meeting the needs of our customers. With a 60-year reputation for product quality and service, it is imperative that Vector meet customer expectations. One of these expectations is the ability to order CUTCO products online. However, while it is important that we meet the expectations of our customers, it is critically important that we protect the interest of our field sales organization.

This change resulted in a "closed customer site" such that, beginning in 2000, only existing customers were allowed to view prices and place orders. As part of direct marketing efforts, sales on this closed site have grown every year. In 2011, approximately 56,000 purchases of CUTCO products were made online, with corresponding revenues of $8.7 million and an operating margin of 9 percent.

While catalog and Internet sales to existing customers have been significant, corporate executives are adamant that the company will not do anything with catalogs or the Internet that would harm the field sales organization. They believe that selling CUTCO products to first-time buyers requires a personal demonstration and a hands-on opportunity to "test drive" that only the Vector field sales organization can provide.

In early 2010 CUTCO conducted an extensive e-commerce test in two Canadian provinces in which existing and new customers were permitted to purchase CUTCO products at full retail price through an open e-commerce site. To avoid adversely impacting the summer selling season, the e-commerce site was pulled down over the summer months but then reestablished in September. The test allowed the company to track such metrics as click-throughs, key words, and meta-tags as well as advertising effectiveness. The results indicated that neither recruiting nor direct sales was influenced by the e-commerce site. Simultaneously, though, the incremental online revenue produced was inconsequential. This testing is continuing today.

Other Marketing Initiatives

In addition to venturing into catalogs and the Internet, Vector Marketing Corporation has pursued other sales channels in attempts to broaden its offering portfolio beyond direct selling. One avenue has been booths at county fairs and shows. Sales representatives have had considerable success displaying and selling CUTCO cutlery at such events. In 2011, nearly 1,800 fairs and shows were booked, and revenue exceeded $9.0 million. Another avenue has been a realtor program wherein real estate agents purchase CUTCO cutlery for gifts to home buyers or potential customers. Nearly $4 million in revenue was generated through this program in 2011. Because revenue from other marketing initiatives reflects direct-sales efforts, it is recorded under direct sales. The estimated operating margin was about 5 percent for both initiatives.

The Vector Customer

The most recent estimate is that more than 16 million customers have purchased CUTCO products since its inception in 1949. Many of the early customers' names were not captured, but since 1989, when Vector Marketing Corporation began systematically capturing and retaining customers' names and addresses, a database of more than 10.5 million customers has been created. The "typical" Vector customer is a married homeowner with one or more older children, relatively affluent, and holds a managerial or professional employment position. The average annual income of a typical customer is more than $50,000, and in certain geographic areas the average customer's annual income is in excess of $100,000. Most Vector customers have at least a bachelor's degree. Sixty percent are between 40 and 59 years of age. There is no discernible difference between Vector's direct-sales customers and customers who purchase from its catalogs, on the Internet, or through other initiatives. The typical customer enjoys reading, traveling, cooking, and gardening.

CUTCO Stores Inc.

The CUTCO Stores Inc. subsidiary was created in 2005, and in April 2006 a small retail store was established in Erie, Pennsylvania, a city with a population of about 102,000 located within driving distance of Olean. Erie had previously been serviced by a branch office, but a decision was made to make it a district office managed out of Olean. Its primary purpose was to carefully study the efficacy of a retail outlet. Because there was a conscious effort to not negatively influence the field-sales organization, the store was branded as, and managed by, CUTCO, not Vector Marketing Corporation. An attempt was made to have the store do "double duty" as a retail outlet (front-door enterprise) and a training location for the direct-sales force (back-door entity). CUTCO products were priced the same in the store as through direct selling. The cost of getting the store presentable for the public was about $150,000. It was expected that the store would have annual revenues of $250,000 to $300,000, with an operating margin of 6 percent.

After five years of operations, company executives learned that the store had a "neutral" effect on direct sales in the area and that operating a retail store required a different set of skills and competencies than managing a Vector district or branch office. Indeed, company executives quickly realized that, analogous to a direct-selling district or branch office, the success of a retail outlet depends on the quality and dedication of the person managing it. Other issues, such as could enough volume be generated through customer acquisition events to make the store profitable at an operational level, remained unresolved.

Subsequent to the Erie pilot store, two other pilot retail stores were opened in, respectively, Okemos, Michigan (a suburb of Lansing), and Indianapolis, Indiana, to test the retail store concept under different geographic and population conditions. The Okemos retail store, a converted district office that previously had a good direct-sales-revenue record, was opened in the fall of 2009. It was designed to explore whether one person could manage both the retail store and the field-sales operation. The Indianapolis retail store was brought on line in the spring of 2011 to test the effect of separate people managing the retail store and the field-sales organization. Exhibit 4 contains a picture of the Indianapolis storefront.

Use of Social Media

Both Vector Marketing Corporation and CUTCO Corporation use social media to reach customers and recruit sales representatives. For example, CUTCO Corporation maintains an active fan page on Facebook, where customers and potential customers can connect to trade recipes, share excitement about their purchases, and discuss techniques for using CUTCO cutlery in the kitchen. Keeping fans engaged on CUTCO's Facebook page reinforces Vector Marketing sales efforts. Vector Marketing uses social media in the recruiting process, primarily through Vector's Facebook fan page. Links to the page are posted on the company's Web sites and in selected advertising. A first-time visitor to the page will see a

EXHIBIT 4 **CUTCO Retail Storefront**

welcome message that includes an easy link to Vector's job application Web site. Once a person joins the fan page, he or she can ask questions about the selling opportunity and become familiar with the company.

Vector sales representatives are encouraged to use Facebook and Twitter to connect with both potential and existing customers. They can post product specials and information about cooking and entertaining, and announce special sales on their pages. By providing customers with relevant, timely, and interesting tips, sales representatives offer a value-added service through social media that keeps customers connected and more likely to think of CUTCO products when they are looking for a gift or want additional cutlery or utensils for their kitchen.

Building a social community is perhaps the most effective use of social media in direct selling. This is because direct selling is inherently dependent on a strong community. With the advent of social media, Vector Marketing is able to "meet" its representatives and managers where they are—online. Facebook and Twitter give the company platforms for recognition, promotion, and communication with the field sales organization. A page for a particular division can announce contests, acknowledge top sellers, provide event information, and offer sales tips. Other pages specifically for sales representatives and managers give the field a chance to share sales strategies, discuss customer objections and responses, and ask questions and get help with challenges. An exciting trend noticed within Vector is representatives helping one another through social media channels, providing encouragement, and building long-lasting friendships.

INTERNATIONAL EXPANSION

International expansion began in 1990, with the establishment of Vector Marketing Canada, Ltd. By the end of 2010, Canadian sales accounted for about 5.8 percent of corporate revenues. CUTCO Korea began as a corporate subsidiary in 1992. For cultural reasons the standard Vector marketing approach was not very successful in South Korea. Several different marketing approaches have been tried in subsequent years but have not been successful. Consequently, the company spun off the Korea organization; it had about $1.8 million in revenue in 2011.

CUTCO International was created in 1994 to manage marketing efforts beyond North America, and CUTCO Korea was placed under its control that year. Australian and German sales organizations were established in 1996 under the direction of CUTCO International. The German operation was converted to an independently owned distributorship in 1999 due to accumulating losses. In 2001 the decision was made to discontinue the Australian operation because of losses experienced there. Other international entries included those in the United Kingdom and Costa Rica. The CUTCO International operating margin is about 2.5 percent.

A NOTE ON DIRECT SELLING

Direct selling is face-to-face selling away from a fixed business location. Therefore, it is a form of non-store retailing. The direct-selling industry consists of numerous well-known firms such as Amway, Avon, Mary Kay Cosmetics, and Tupperware. At the same time, however, the industry itself is not well known, principally because it is "invisible." By definition, there are no physical stores and, because direct selling is essentially a push marketing strategy, direct-selling firms do very little advertising. Hence, there is less public awareness of most direct-selling firms than of major retailers. In addition, the majority of direct-selling firms are relatively small, privately owned firms created and operated by entrepreneurs, many of whom often want a low public profile.

According to the Direct Selling Association, the direct-selling industry trade association, direct sales in the United States are currently about $29 billion; globally, direct sales are estimated to be about $117 billion. Virtually all direct sellers are independent contractors. Of the estimated 15.9 million direct sellers in the United States in 2011, 88 percent were women, and 77 percent were married. Seventy-nine percent were 35 years of age or older. Only 12 percent work more than 20 hours per week in direct selling, and one source estimated that nearly half earn less than $500 annually. A survey of direct sellers conducted for the Direct Selling Association revealed that substantial numbers worked only to earn money for a particular purchase (such as a vacation), worked only because they liked and used a product or service themselves, or worked because they enjoyed the social aspect of direct selling.

Seventy percent of direct selling takes place in a residence, and nearly two-thirds takes place on a one-to-one basis. The other major form of direct selling is the "party plan." Party plan selling represents a combination of group selling and entertainment; approximately one-quarter of direct selling takes place through group sales or party plans. The Longaberger basket party or the Tupperware party, in which six to eight women get together at the home of a host, are quintessential examples of party plan selling.

The most popular form of one-to-one direct selling is network or multilevel marketing. About 95 percent of all independent contractors sell through a multilevel marketing program. Direct sellers in a multilevel marketing program are rewarded not only for the sales that they personally make, but also for the sales that people they recruit make, and the sales of people in turn recruited by the individuals they recruited, and so on (i.e., their "downline" in multilevel marketing terms, hence the notion of multi or many levels).

The Typical Direct-Selling Customer

Of the products and services marketed through direct selling, personal care and home-related products and services are among the most popular. Cosmetics, vitamins and dietary supplements, kitchenware, and cleaning products are currently among the best-selling products in the direct-selling industry. Even so, virtually any product or service seems to be amendable to this mode of marketing. In Japan, for example, a large percentage of new automobiles are sold door-to-door.

Although estimates differ, about three-quarters of the adults in the United States have purchased a product or service from a direct-selling firm. This suggests that the typical direct-selling customer should have characteristics similar to people in general or at least people who shop retail stores. More specifically, direct-selling customers tend to be affluent females 35 to 54 years of age. Relative to the overall population in the United States, the typical direct-selling customer has somewhat more education and a larger household income.

 # CUTCO GROWTH DRIVERS

Beginning in 1982, when Alcas Cutlery Corporation was purchased from ALCOA, the company has sequentially focused on selected "growth drivers" to move it forward. Initially the CUTCO product, by virtue of its high performance, high quality, and exceptional demonstrability, constituted the major driver of the business. Company executives termed the years when products were the focus of attention "phase one."

The second phase consisted of consolidating ("rolling up") the various independent entities selling CUTCO products and creating a nationally distributed sales force through Vector Marketing Corporation. This led to the third phase, the introduction of the Vector College Recruiting Program. This recruiting program brought in college students who, by virtue of their intelligence, trainability, and ability to present themselves well, made outstanding sales representatives. The approaches used to recruit these college students generated many more recruits than any prior recruiting approach. Moreover, the fact that the recruits tend to be college students results in a large number of candidates for management opportunities after graduation. The large number of managerial candidates in turn provides management talent to open substantial numbers of new offices. New offices in turn fuel a high rate of geographic growth.

Based on the success of the recruiting program, the triad decided to make major investments in money and energy to increase the effectiveness of key elements of the program. These investments went into activities such as enhancing the effectiveness of recruiting and training activities, including instituting a very solid and effective program for "field training"—an enhancement over the "classroom" training given every sales representative as he or she begins selling CUTCO products. This phase was followed by the present phase, investing in people/investing in structure. Significant investments in new leadership and building sales management structures in the mid-2000s spurred one of the strongest growth periods in the history of the company and resulted in the development of what is clearly the strongest, most effective sales management organization the company has ever had.

At the same time, though, since history has shown that growth drivers change over time, the triad believes that there would most likely need to be a new growth driver if the revenue goals of $500 million and $1 billion are to be met. Consequently, the triad met repeatedly with Jim Stitt and other corporate executives in 2011 to craft a long-range growth strategy. Interestingly enough, one individual in the meetings continually argued—in August, October, and December—that a "status quo strategy" should be seriously considered:

> After all, manufacturing can barely keep up with demand as it is, and the growth that we are naturally experiencing at the present time will be enough to carry the company to its goals. There are about 113 million households in the United States; the median household income is above $50,000; and there are more than 14 million college students. Thus, both our potential market and our sales representative pool are sufficiently large to carry us without doing anything different. The risks associated with doing anything new or different are simply too great at this point in time. The economy is in a slump—the credit ratings of half of the countries in the European Union have been recently downgraded—consumers are hoarding what little money they have left, and the economic outlook in general is bleak. We need to ride out the coming storm.

 STRATEGIC OPTIONS

By the end of 2011 executives had narrowed down strategic options to five:

- Investment in recruiting approaches and recruiting structures
- Investment in expanding CUTCO brand recognition/preference
- Expansion into international markets

- Supplemental sales channels
- Full entry into the retail sales channel

Each of these options had its advocates and detractors.

Recruiting Approaches

Since the number of recruits is such an obvious driver of Vector's revenue growth, there was widespread agreement that additional investment and intensive efforts to improve the recruiting approaches could be a major growth driver. Vector is already very proactive in Internet recruiting, but it is conceivable there could be a substantial expansion of that activity and/or the application of new Internet technologies. It was also agreed that an investment of at least $5 to $10 million in technology and recruiting management infrastructure would be necessary to produce any measurable results.

Vector executives expressed considerable enthusiasm for the prospect of gaining additional growth through intensive energy and investment devoted to improving recruiting approaches and strategies. They reminded everyone that significant sales gains were previously made by implementing a variety of improved recruiting procedures and that with new Web-based technologies available at a much more sophisticated level, there could be additional gains made by investing in recruiting procedures.

There is no question that experienced district managers are needed to fuel direct-selling growth; the issue is how best to train and retain the best and brightest district managers. Perhaps, some thought, there is a way to harness Vector's social media efforts to better exploit them. As one executive quipped, "our sales representatives and district managers are media savvy; we in this room are media dinosaurs."

CUTCO Brand Recognition

Marketing staff members present at the meetings pointed out that brand recognition is always a positive and, indeed, a necessary, marketing component to generate consumer product sales. Over the last 20 years, and the last 15 years in particular, the CUTCO product line had grown substantially, not only in its brand recognition, but also in brand preference, with virtually no formal mass-market advertising. One staff member offered the opinion that because brand preference was presently so high, it might be possible to dramatically increase current "word-of-mouth" brand recognition with relatively little additional expenditures and subsequently create significant revenue increases. For example, the staff member noted, annual public relations expenditures in the neighborhood of $1 to $2 million might ultimately increase annual revenues by as much as $10 to $20 million.

Vector's director of marketing spoke enthusiastically of the long-term sales benefits that could be gained through investments in creating more consumer exposure to the CUTCO brand. He reinforced the marketing staff member's opinion that because CUTCO already had significant brand recognition and preference, dramatic increases in brand recognition could likely be gained without a great deal of extra investment.

International Expansion

Beginning with the entry into Canada in 1990 and then into Korea in 1992, the company has periodically attempted to expand internationally. However, only Canada (which is part of Vector Marketing Corporation) has been considered successful. Because North American revenue growth has been strong recently, company executives have pulled back somewhat from international activities but still recognize that there is a huge potential in international markets.

However, given the state of the present global economy, the potential of reenergizing major international marketing efforts to capture a share of the consumer product market in Asian countries is equivocal at best. Although company executives realize that reengagement of aggressive international entries would take substantial financial resources (it is estimated that an expenditure of $10 to $15 million per entry would apply), and that it would require substantial investment of management personnel as well, a few executives suggested the possibility of a strategic partner to take the CUTCO product line into China and Japan. "The Chinese in particular are crazy about high-quality American products," enthused the director of marketing. "We really need to think about some way of reaching into that market."

Supplemental Sales Channels

Vector Marketing Corporation is presently utilizing both catalogs and the Internet as supplementary channels to the direct-selling channel. The prospect that catalog and online revenues could be increased significantly is clearly evident given their recent history, but not without the risk of some negative consequences for the conventional (direct-selling) college student program. All of the executives present in the planning meetings were clearly aware of the potential of catalogs and the Internet to generate higher profit margins than the direct-selling channel, and a wide-ranging discussion took place among the executives in which everyone participated. One fact discussed at length during the December meeting was that 50 percent of catalog purchases originated on the Internet. A key point of the discussion was the relatively minimal cost of expanding the two supplementary channels; an expenditure of $3 million was considered more than adequate to significantly increase both catalog and online revenues. However, as Stitt noted, "The cash expenditures required to obtain expanded catalog and Internet sales are only a small portion of the total cost. If we don't do this right, the negative impact on our Vector sales force could be dramatic and result in lost sales far greater than any gains we could project from these two channels."

Retail Sales Channel

Of the strategic options being considered, one stood out because it represented a radical departure from past marketing practice. This option was the retail (indirect) sales channel, and it posed the greatest risk and reward of any of the strategic options. The risk was that it could devastate the sales force. The reward was that it could potentially increase revenues multifold. At issue was whether the retail channel should be approached on a large scale and, if so, whether it would be approached using outlets that are company-owned, whether outlets would be franchised entities, or whether the cutlery would be sold through traditional retailers such as department stores or specialty stores.

CUTCO Corporation is posed to open a fourth pilot retail store in St. Louis, Missouri, in the spring of 2012. Whereas the marketing activities in other pilot retail stores could be considered low-key and conservative, actually downplaying the role of the store, one of the goals of the St. Louis pilot is to determine the effect of aggressive advertising on the field-sales organization in the Missouri area and whether Vector's existing direct-sales customers could be attracted to a retail environment. The extent to which advertising for the retail store created actual or perceived conflict would be instrumental in the decision to be made about retail stores.

Of enormous interest to the triad was the possibility of marketing CUTCO products in conjunction with high-end vacuum cleaners. Thomas Oreck, whose father David Oreck established the vacuum cleaner and air purifier company that bears his name, serves on the board of CUTCO and has been in discussions with Stitt about marketing CUTCO products in 400 Oreck retail stores. Simultaneously, thought has been given to marketing CUTCO products through department stores and specialty merchandisers.

As Stitt drove out of the employees' parking lot, he realized that the company would soon need to make a decision as to whether to continue the pilot program, halt it, or expand it. This decision, apart from trying to select a growth driver strategy, would need to be made soon, but in the context of the larger strategic decision.

Case

Yorktown Technologies

Alan Blake was pacing his office. Blake, CEO and co-founder of Yorktown Technologies, was concerned about what marketing strategy to recommend to the company's board of directors at its next meeting. On November 21, 2003, Yorktown Technologies had announced that it would be marketing GloFish genetically modified tropical zebra fish. Almost immediately Yorktown Technologies became the most highly publicized new company in the United States; more than 1,000 newspaper and magazine articles were published about it, and television and radio coverage was universal.

To fund Yorktown Technologies, Blake had raised $500,000 from local investors in 2002 and 2003, based largely on pro forma sales projections that indicated the company would generate $4,000,000 in profit in 2004. However, company revenues in 2004 were a disappointing $500,000 and expenses were $620,000, producing an operating loss of more than $120,000. Nearly a quarter of the 2004 revenue occurred in January. Fast-forward to the present. Blake knew that if Yorktown Technologies were to be successful, the board of directors would need to approve key changes in the firm's marketing strategy, and soon.

 ## ZEBRA DANIO FISH

Zebra danios are freshwater fish that are in the minnow family and indigenous to India and surrounding countries. Traditional zebra fish are about 1½ inches long, translucent, and light gray with black stripes (hence the name "zebra fish"). Zebra danios tend to be community or "shoaling" fish in that they do best in groups of 6 to 10, with 3 being the minimum number that should be in an aquarium. They are very active but not aggressive in terms of being predators or fighting fish.

Not only are they popular ornamental fish—more than 200 million have been sold in the United States alone in the past half-century—they are also used extensively in research on genetics to better understand important issues in cellular development, molecular biology, and vertebrate development, in part because

This case was previously prepared as GloFish LLC by Professors William H. Cunningham and John Sibley Butler of the McCombs School of Business, The University of Texas at Austin. It has been updated with publicly available information by Robert A. Peterson as a basis for class discussion and is not designed to illustrate effective or ineffective handling of an administrative decision. Because certain information and names in the case have been disguised or modified, case information is not useful for research purposes. © 2012 Robert A. Peterson.

they can be produced inexpensively (a female zebra fish can produce more than 2,000 offspring per year). They have been particularly helpful in understanding cellular disease and development, as well as cancer and gene therapy.

Fluorescent zebra fish can be produced by injecting natural fluorescent protein genes into recently fertilized zebra fish embryos. A gene from sea coral can be used to produce fluorescent red zebra fish, whereas a gene from jellyfish can be used to produce fluorescent green zebra fish. Once initial fluorescent zebra fish are produced, subsequent offspring can be bred from the existing fluorescent zebra fish. Depending on the gene "promoter" that is linked to the injected gene, the fluorescent protein can be expressed in virtually any tissue or organ that may be desired. Fluorescent fish absorb light and then re-emit it (that is, they do not generate their own light; they simply reflect it). This creates the perception that they are glowing, particularly when shining an ultraviolet or black light on the fish in a completely dark room. As Blake has often noted, "The GloFish fluorescent fish provide marine colors at freshwater prices."

The scientists who created GloFish fluorescent fish hoped to one day use the fish to quickly and easily determine when waterways are contaminated. The first step in developing these pollution-detecting fish was to create fish that would be fluorescent all of the time; these were the fish that Blake was interested in marketing. The next step, which is still in progress, is the addition of a "switch" that will cause the always fluorescing zebra fish to selectively fluoresce in the presence of environmental toxins. A non-fluorescing fish will signal that the water is safe, while a fluorescing fish will signal trouble. Although these switching fish are not currently available, scientists hope to complete this work soon.

 ## COMPANY HISTORY

Yorktown Technologies was founded by Alan Blake and Richard Crockett in November 2001. Blake and Crockett had previously co-founded a company that provided Web sites for university professors. In the process, they were involved in raising over $4 million and oversaw the hiring and daily operations of more than 50 employees. Although the company ultimately ceased operations due to a shortfall in funding, Blake and Crockett learned a great deal from the experience that they were able to apply to Yorktown Technologies.

The idea for GloFish originated when Crockett was studying a category of fluorescent protein genes. Crockett believed that he could patent the concept of producing ornamental fish that expressed fluorescence throughout their bodies. However, in August 2001, after doing a significant amount of intellectual property research, Crockett and Blake concluded that it would not be possible to obtain a patent on this idea because these fish had already been developed for research purposes. Consequently, Crockett and Blake changed their business strategy to one of licensing existing technology in hopes of packaging and reselling it to a large industry player.

In September 2001, Crockett and Blake met with Dr. Ivan Pruchansky, a university geneticist. Dr. Pruchansky had developed fluorescent zebra fish in his university laboratory and expressed an interest in working with Yorktown Technologies to market his creation. However, Dr. Pruchansky was concerned that his university would not allow him to commercialize the technology since he anticipated there would be substantial resistance from the environmental community. Nonetheless, Crockett and Blake began to actively research how they could commercialize Dr. Pruchansky's fish. They determined that, in addition to acquiring a license from Dr. Pruchansky's university, they would need a license from

Cellflash, a company that had patented the genetic components Dr. Pruchansky used to create his fish. With a good-faith agreement from Dr. Pruchansky to move forward, they could secure the appropriate licenses. Blake and Crockett formally incorporated Yorktown Technologies in November 2001.

By January 2002, the company had verbal commitments from Dr. Pruchansky and Cellflash to license their technologies to Yorktown Technologies. Unfortunately, what seemed to be a "done deal" in January began to unravel in the spring, and had completely fallen apart by the summer. Dr. Pruchansky decided that he did not want to recommend to his university that it license his fish to Yorktown Technologies. Not only was he worried that he would be attacked by the environmentalist community, he was also concerned that he would be criticized by his academic colleagues. Moreover, the president of Cellflash determined that for "personal, ethical concerns" he would not allow his company to sign the license agreement.

After a year of intensive efforts to license the technology to create fluorescent zebra fish, Yorktown Technologies was seemingly in no better position than it was on the day that Blake and Crockett founded the company. In a final attempt to salvage the company, Blake contacted the National University of Singapore (NUS) because scientists there had developed their own fluorescent zebra fish in 1999. Blake had avoided NUS previously because he expected it to be a likely competitor of Yorktown Technologies. To Blake's surprise, the NUS scientists had given up hope of commercializing their fish due to the enormously complicated fluorescent protein gene intellectual property landscape. They immediately committed to licensing the NUS technology to Yorktown Technologies for a 16 percent royalty fee with an annual minimum royalty of $150,000.

A formal agreement was reached in September 2002 that gave Yorktown Technologies exclusive rights to lines of red, green, yellow, and orange fluorescent zebra fish. Most importantly, the license agreement gave the company exclusive rights to a patent that covered all fluorescent ornamental fish (the filing of which predated the fish developed for research). These rights would provide the company with an effective barrier to entry against potential competitors.

While the genes in the green, yellow, and orange fluorescent zebra fish that Yorktown Technologies had licensed from NUS incorporated technology from Cellflash, the gene in the line of red fluorescent zebra fish was covered by patents that were owned by Farsighted Fish Genetics (FSG). Unlike Cellflash, FSG was willing to exclusively license its red fluorescent protein gene to Yorktown Technologies (at a royalty rate of 20 percent). Simultaneously, Blake confirmed that there were no federal or state regulatory prohibitions that would preclude the sale of GloFish fluorescent zebra fish. It finally appeared that Yorktown Technologies had the exclusive rights required to market its first line of fish, the GloFish Red Zebra Danio.

Investors

The company's fundraising strategy was to raise only as much capital as it needed to complete each specific business activity milestone. This strategy would allow the founders and early investors to retain as much ownership as possible while simultaneously reducing risk for later investors.

Initially, Blake and Crockett used their savings and borrowed against their personal credit cards when they founded the company. Yorktown Technologies accepted its first outside investment in January 2002 from Dr. John Rosemary. Rosemary, a renowned professor of management at a major business school, also agreed to become the company's first board member. The company then raised additional seed capital from family and close friends, for a total of $17,500 on a valuation of $100,000. Shortly thereafter, Dr. Will Hughes, a colleague of

Dr. Rosemary, became an investor in and advisor to the company. He was followed by Parker Davis, an attorney, who agreed to work for the firm and defer compensation for his legal advice until the company was financially sound.

In January 2003, after obtaining the rights to market red fluorescent zebra fish from NUS, Blake and Hughes met with four ornamental fish distributors in Florida. All were interested in producing and marketing the fish. After reporting this information to prospective investors in early February 2003, Yorktown Technologies raised the additional capital needed to fund its operations through mid-2003 from angel investors, at a firm valuation of $600,000. By March, the company closed co-exclusive distribution contracts with two of the largest Florida freshwater ornamental fish producers and distributors in the United States, 5-D Tropical and Segrest Farms, and raised additional capital to fund its business operations at a valuation of $2.5 million. The company completed an additional round of fundraising in early November 2003, just two months ahead of its anticipated January 5, 2004, launch date, at a valuation of $5 million. By then there were more than three dozen different investors.

REGULATORY OBSTACLES AND MARKETING ACTIVITIES

Blake and Crockett were initially told that there were no federal or state agencies that would prohibit marketing of their biotech fish. However, this changed in February 2003, when the California Fish and Game Commission passed a blanket regulation that prohibited the possession of any genetically modified fish in California. Although the regulation was aimed at biotech food fish, Yorktown Technologies was notified that it would need to prove "beyond any doubt" that its fish were safe for the environment if it wanted to sell them in California.

Blake recognized that the Yorktown Technologies product was being asked by the California Fish and Game Commission to pass a much higher standard than faced by many existing products. However, he also understood that, with a population exceeding 33 million that had a reputation for purchasing innovative products as well as being extremely cautious with regard to environmental concerns, California was a very important market for Yorktown Technologies. As a result, he decided to consult with two of the world's leading scientists on ecological risk assessment for genetically modified fish. The scientists' report was unambiguous: fluorescent zebra fish were no more of a risk to the environment than were normal zebra fish. Unfortunately, Blake soon learned that the opinion of these scientists would not be sufficient to stop the anti-biotechnology groups in California from opposing Yorktown Technologies. Therefore, in September 2003, Blake decided to hire a lobbyist to help deal with the opposition activities in California. The question of whether Yorktown Technologies could market its fish in California was scheduled to be heard by the California Fish and Game Commission in early December 2003, only weeks before the company's anticipated January 5, 2004, nationwide launch date.

Public Relations

Blake was concerned that anti-biotechnology activists would try to disrupt the launch of Yorktown Technologies product by spreading misinformation concerning the safety of its fish. Yorktown Technologies did not have enough money to support a national advertising campaign to announce the availability of its new genetically modified tropical fish. Therefore, Blake began working with Phil Croswell, an experienced principal at a major public relations firm, on a public relations initiative. Croswell believed that his firm could successfully defend the product against false accusations as well as create a great deal of "buzz" around the GloFish launch, since it would be the first commercially available biotech animal in the United States.

Blake approved Croswell's recommendations to initiate a modest national public relations campaign only days ahead of the product launch. The primary goal of the campaign would be to educate the public about the fish and help it understand that the GloFish Red Zebra Danio was safe; a secondary goal was to build market demand for the fish. If all went well, there would be little information about the availability of the fish until just days before their launch, and the fish would be in stores before biotechnology activist groups would be able to organize a misinformation campaign. Blake also decided to advertise in two ornamental fish trade magazines that had a combined circulation of 100,000 aquarium fish aficionados. The advertisement was slated to run in the first issues of the magazines in early 2004. (See Exhibit 1 for a copy of one of the first GloFish advertisements.)

Product Launch

In mid-November 2003, the Associated Press and *Los Angeles Times* discovered that Yorktown Technologies had made a request to the California Fish and Game Commission to market its fish in California. Both news organizations planned stories on the GloFish product and asked Yorktown Technologies to comment on the request. Based on advice from Croswell, Blake determined that he had no choice but to advance the launch date of the public relations campaign, since maintaining the planned campaign launch date would have allowed anti-biotechnology activists to distort the debate by using the same scare tactics that they had used in the past to attack other products. Croswell drafted a press release that described Yorktown Technologies' genetically modified tropical fish, and the company unveiled its Web site at www.glofish.com. Within 24 hours, news of the upcoming GloFish launch was on the front page of the *New York Times, Los Angeles Times*, and most other major daily newspapers in the United States. Fox News, CNN, and MSNBC carried multiple news stories about the GloFish Red Zebra Danio.

Over the next 72 hours, media reports built to a crescendo, with hundreds of articles worldwide, television interviews on all the major networks, and heated discussions on local radio networks about ethical and environmental questions surrounding the sale of genetically modified tropical fish. Blake was overwhelmed by all of the media attention that he and Yorktown Technologies received. Even so, he was able to always remain on message: with the exception of color, the GloFish Red Zebra Danio was just like any other zebra fish. Given the overwhelming publicity and subsequent demand for the fish, Yorktown Technologies' distributors decided to immediately begin marketing a limited number of fish. After months of careful planning and consideration, the product launch date had jumped ahead by several weeks.

Ten days later, staff scientists at the California Department of Fish and Game released their report, concluding that fluorescent zebra fish were universally believed by the scientific community to be safe, and the news cycle began anew. Unfortunately, a few days later, on December 3, 2004, the Fish and Game Commission rejected the staff scientists' advice to allow the sale of the fish in California because several of the commissioners thought that marketing them was ethically "wrong."

With all of the media attention focused on Yorktown Technologies, the U.S. Food and Drug Administration (FDA) was asked to formally weigh in on the issue. The FDA's judgment was critical because it has jurisdiction over all

EXHIBIT 1

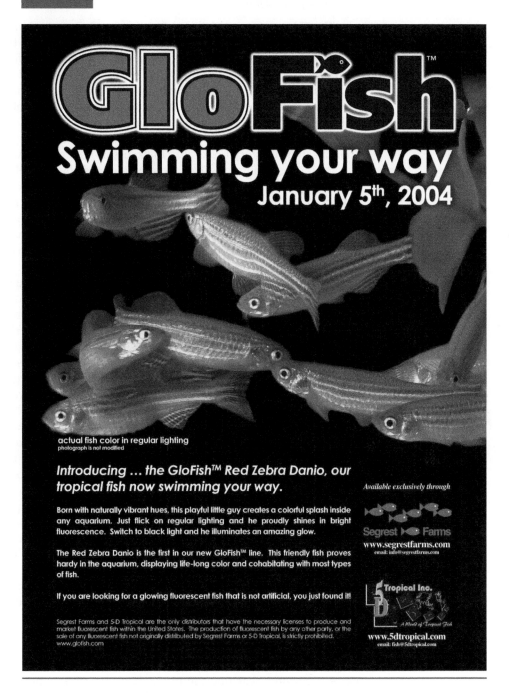

genetically modified animals since it considered a modified gene to be an animal drug. Yorktown Technologies provided considerable information to the FDA about its fish, and on December 9, 2003, the FDA issued the following statement:

> Because tropical aquarium fish are not used for food purposes, they pose no threat to the food supply. There is no evidence that these genetically engineered zebra danio fish pose any more threat to the environment than their unmodified counterparts which have long been widely sold in the United Stated. In the

absence of a clear risk to the public health, the FDA finds no reason to regulate these particular fish.[1]

The FDA statement definitively addressed the question regarding the safety of the fish and was soon followed by a similar conclusion from a newly created State of Florida task force assigned regulatory oversight for biotech fish. Even so, the news media continued to run wild with the story. Ultimately, there were more than 1,000 stories written worldwide about Yorktown Technologies and an equal number of stories appearing on television and radio about the new biotech fish. Croswell stated that he had never experienced so much free publicity for a new product. He estimated that the number of media impressions in the first two months after the story broke was in excess of 500 million worldwide.

By the beginning of 2004, the media uproar had largely subsided, although several regulatory challenges persisted. A strident anti-biotechnology group filed a lawsuit against the FDA, asserting that it had failed to properly regulate the new biotech fish. This group recruited Dr. Pruchansky, the same scientist who had refused to work with the company because of concerns that there would be an environmentalist backlash against him, to substantiate its claims that the Glo-Fish Red Zebra Danio fish were not safe.

Dr. Pruchansky had been working tirelessly to convince regulators that Yorktown Technologies' products were a threat to the environment. At the same time, he insisted that his own fluorescent zebra fish were unequivocally safe. Because the anti-biotechnology group had a history of filing frivolous lawsuits, and Dr. Pruchansky's motives were questionable, Blake fully expected the lawsuit to be dismissed.[2] However, the company was nonetheless forced to devote resources to address the concerns that had been raised, particularly where opponents attempted to use the pending lawsuit to discourage retailers from carrying the GloFish Red Zebra Danio.

In April 2004, the California Fish and Game Commission recognized that the public had overwhelmingly accepted the GloFish product and agreed to begin the regulatory process that would ultimately allow the fish to be sold in California. However, the process was fraught with bureaucratic and procedural obstacles and would take a great deal of time and money to complete. To date Yorktown Technologies has not invested the time, money, and effort required to produce the comprehensive report necessary to satisfy the government and enter California.

Consumer acceptance of the company's products was quite positive. The company received only a few negative comments in 2004 through its Web site, and there were no reports of a protest or any other tangible sign of public concern from the retailers that carried its fluorescent zebra fish. However, the larger retail chains still had not agreed to carry the fish, leaving the company only able to sell into a fraction of its potential market.

Product Enhancements

Once it became clear that the public had accepted its product, the company realized that the greatest issue it faced was the fact that its fluorescent zebra fish were not nearly attractive enough to sell in the numbers that it had hoped. While the GloFish Red Zebra Danio was dramatically different in color from traditional

---

[1] www.fda.gov/bbs/topics/NEWS/2003/NEW00994.html. While GloFish did not obtain formal FDA "approval," as would a new pharmaceutical drug or food, the response of the FDA is common for products deemed of little or no concern and has long been used for a variety of aquaculture products, including everyday substances such as hydrogen peroxide.

[2] In fact, the lawsuit was dismissed on March 30, 2005.

zebra fish, it was still not as bright as the market wanted, and the fish lost some of its color as it matured and its natural pigment thickened. Moreover, Blake realized that the company would need more than a single product offering if it were to be successful long term. As more than one retailer noted, "Fish lovers are finicky. They are always looking for new and different fish for their aquariums. Variety drives purchases."

Fortunately, Blake learned that scientists at the National University of Singapore had developed a new generation of genetically modified zebra fish that would be significantly more colorful than the original product and would maintain their color as they matured. After successfully completing federal and state regulatory reviews, the company introduced a new fluorescent red zebra fish trademarked "Starfire Red" in June 2005. This was followed by a green fluorescent zebra fish (trademarked "Electric Green"), an orange fluorescent zebra fish (trademarked "Sunburst Orange") in mid-2006, and, subsequently, a blue fluorescent zebra fish (trademarked "Cosmic Blue") and a purple fluorescent zebra fish (trademarked "Galactic Purple").

 ## MARKETING FRESHWATER ORNAMENTAL FISH

Freshwater ornamental fish can be farm-raised or caught in the wild. The vast majority, however, about 90 percent, are farm-raised. Generally speaking, there are four steps in the physical production and distribution of farm-raised freshwater ornamental fish. Freshwater ornamental fish are typically raised in outdoor earthen ponds that average 2,000 square feet in surface area at an aquaculture facility under very controlled conditions. About 95 percent of all aquaculture facilities in the United States are located in Florida, which has an ideal aquaculture climate.

Before being shipped, the fish are removed from the ponds and held for several days to ensure health and marketability. After this quarantine period, they are packed into large plastic shipping bags (with water and pure oxygen), placed in polystyrene containers, and sent out for truck delivery if the destination is local, or shipped by commercial passenger airlines for nonlocal destinations. In the case of nonlocal shipments, the fish are retrieved from destination airports and loaded onto trucks for delivery to retail establishments.

There are only a couple of hundred freshwater ornamental fish producers in the United States. Each producer typically produces millions of fish each year, with about 25 percent of these being shipped to domestic wholesalers or retailers; the rest are either exported or not deemed marketable. Approximately 200 million freshwater ornamental fish are produced and sold annually in the United States. Some two dozen regional wholesalers located throughout the country distribute freshwater ornamental fish to an estimated 5,000 retail establishments for sale to consumers. However, some freshwater ornamental fish producers bypass wholesalers and sell directly to retailers. For example, one of Yorktown Technologies' suppliers, 5-D Tropical, produces and distributes freshwater ornamental fish both to local retailers and regional wholesalers, whereas the other, Segrest Farms, ships directly to retailers, circumventing wholesalers completely. It is widely believed that the prices of freshwater ornamental fish are controlled at the retail end of the distribution channel. Partly because a significant number of freshwater ornamental fish are imported into the United States, especially from China, Indonesia, Singapore, Taiwan, and Thailand, competition is found at all distribution channel levels.

The majority of the retailers in the United States that sell freshwater ornamental fish are small, independent establishments; many sell a variety of pets and pet-related products in addition to fish. These stores serve both true freshwater ornamental fish lovers and people who find it convenient to purchase freshwater ornamental fish from them. According to data from the United States Census Bureau, the number of pet stores is declining at an annual rate of 2 percent. At the same time, though, total sales of pet stores are increasing at an annual rate of 7 percent. The average pet store in the United States has total sales of about $1.7 million; however, this number is probably a bit inflated because of the sales of very large chain pet stores.

The consumer market for freshwater ornamental fish and related products in the United States exceeds $700 million annually and is growing at a rate of nearly 9 percent per year, whereas the worldwide market is approaching $2 billion per year. Of the $700 million, Blake estimated that about $4 million was spent on Yorktown Technologies products by consumers in 2008. At any one point in time, one out of every eight households in the United States, 14.4 million, has a freshwater fish aquarium, with each aquarium holding approximately 14 fish whose collective cost was $27.

Traditional zebra fish are sold to wholesalers for 5 cents each, who then sell them to retailers for 25 cents each (shipping included). Retailers in turn sell them to consumers for between 75 cents and one dollar each. In contrast, 5-D Tropical and Segrest Farms were selling GloFish Red Zebra Danios to retailers for $1.50 with a suggested retail price of $5.00.[3]

A majority of the freshwater ornamental fish sold in the United States are purchased from three major retail chains: Walmart, PetSmart, and PETCO. Walmart, with 2011 sales well in excess of $300 billion in the United States, is not only the largest retailer in the world; it is also the leading retailer of freshwater ornamental fish in the United States. These three large chains sell freshwater ornamental fish primarily to price-sensitive customers who are not tropical fish enthusiasts. They also sell large numbers of aquamarine kits to people who are purchasing freshwater ornamental fish for the first time. Yorktown Technologies' suppliers and distributors of its fluorescent red zebra fish, 5-D Tropical and Segrest, have been regular suppliers of tropical fish to Walmart, PetSmart, and PETCO for several years.

None of the three major chains agreed to carry the Yorktown Technologies GloFish product when it was introduced. Walmart executives did not make any public comments about why their stores would not carry the fluorescent zebra fish. PetSmart executives stated they were considering carrying the fish, although one of PetSmart's executives said there simply was no demand for the fish by its customers at the present time. PETCO executives said they were opposed to selling genetically modified pets. Subsequently, however, PETCO and Walmart began carrying the GloFish product line in many of their stores.

Shopping mall kiosks have enjoyed explosive growth, both in terms of numbers and revenue. Collectively, sales at these stores-without-walls were running about $10 billion annually, with 40 percent of the revenues occurring in November and December. These outlets sell a variety of products ranging from cell phones to perfumes to live animals, such as hermit crabs that come in containers along with food for them. Kiosks have also sold colorful beta "fighting" fish. Blake thought that it might be possible to sell his firm's fish through kiosks, which would provide the added benefit of being able to offer GloFish-branded tanks and supplies, fish food, and water conditioner. However, he was aware that the cost of leased space in a shopping mall for a single Yorktown Technologies kiosk could range from $12,000 to $36,000 per year.

---

[3] Some retailers price the fish at $9.95 each, whereas a few price them as high as $12.00.

Blake was also considering the possibility of marketing the GloFish product line through the Internet directly to consumers. He was aware of numerous dot-com firms that marketed tropical fish to consumers over the Internet. Although the prices of these fish were competitive, delivery costs typically were several times higher than the price of the fish. Some dot-com firms even offered overnight delivery, but Blake thought the delivery cost was excessive except for fish that retailed for $40 or more. He noted that tropical fish were even being marketed on eBay. One Internet company that caught his eye was petsolutions.com. This company offered a Starfire Red fish for $7.99 and a Sunburst Orange fish for $5.99; next-day delivery of a fish (including the cost of the fish) was about $43, when shipping and taxes were considered.

Finally, Blake thought that international markets also represented a huge opportunity for Yorktown Technologies, particularly if the company could sterilize its fish to prevent illegal breeding in areas where it could not otherwise control its intellectual property. In addition to sterilization, Yorktown Technologies would have to consider foreign regulations that would apply to its genetically modified fish. Because of such considerations, Yorktown Technologies could market only in countries that did not prohibit its product. The most lucrative foreign market appeared to be in Asia, whereas Australia, Canada, and the European Union were essentially closed.

However, Blake was aware that the company would likely face strong competition in Asia, especially in Taiwan. In 2000 researchers at the National University of Taiwan were able to create a fluorescent green medaka fish (Japanese killifish), a fish similar to a zebra danio. The researchers were able to work with Taikong, the largest producer of aquarium fish in Taiwan, to mass-produce and market the fish in 2003. It was reported that 100,000 fluorescent green medaka fish were sold (at a price of US$18.60 each) the first month they were on the market. Blake was also aware of rumors that some of the genetically altered medaka fish were being introduced in the United States and sold at prices considerably below those of GloFish.

 ## BLAKE'S RECOMMENDATION

Blake believed that a large market existed for biotech, freshwater ornamental fish. Although Yorktown Technologies sales had increased every year, he believed the company had not yet reached its potential. He felt very lucky that his investors seemed to be patient, but he knew their patience would not last forever. Blake, along with most of his investors, also knew that distribution was the key to market success. He listed four distribution alternatives he thought should be on the board of directors' agenda—independent pet stores, chain stores, kiosks, and Internet—and began writing down the pros and cons of each. As he began to put pencil to paper, he realized that his recommendation would have to be consistent with the resources that Yorktown Technologies presently had available as well as fit other elements of the company's marketing strategy. He also anticipated that the board of directors would question him about a possible international strategy.

Irrespective of the distribution decision, Blake knew that Yorktown Technologies had to quickly address what he believed to be a crucial marketing weakness. Despite the company's efforts to educate its retailers, most of them refused to display the fish under optimal lighting and aquarium conditions that would showcase the fish. It was clear to Blake that the company would never reach its revenue goals unless it could solve this problem.

Case

SaskTel

It was January 2007. Pat Tulloch, senior director of marketing at SaskTel, was in her Regina, Saskatchewan, office reviewing product information for the LifeStat™ health monitoring system. SaskTel's executive committee had recently approved a proposal to launch this system into the Canadian marketplace. In preparation for the proposed July 1, 2007, product launch, Tulloch had been given the task of developing a marketing plan, which she would have to present to the executive committee in two weeks' time. To create this plan, Tulloch would need to quickly make some distribution and promotion decisions and conduct a financial analysis of the product's potential profitability.

 ## CANADA'S HEALTH-CARE SYSTEM

History

Canada's health-care system, introduced more than 40 years ago, provided universal, comprehensive coverage for medically necessary hospital and physician services. These services were provided on the basis of need rather than on the patients' ability to pay. This health insurance program, known to Canadians as "Medicare," was best described as an interlocking set of 10 provincial and three territorial health insurance plans, all of which shared certain common features and basic standards of coverage.[1] This universal health-care system was funded primarily through personal and corporate taxation, with private donations accounting for about a quarter of the funding. Roles and responsibilities for Canada's health-care system were shared between the federal and provincial-territorial governments. Under the Canada Health Act (CHA), federal health insurance

---

[1] Health Canada, www.hc-sc.gc.ca/hcs-sss/medi-assur/index-eng.php, accessed August 18, 2008.

Marsha Watson prepared this case under the supervision of Elizabeth M. A. Grasby solely to provide material for class discussion. The authors do not intend to illustrate either effective or ineffective handling of a managerial situation. The authors may have disguised certain names and other identifying information to protect confidentiality. Ivey Management Services prohibits any form of reproduction, storage or transmittal without its written permission. This material is not covered under authorization from CanCopy or any reproduction rights organization. To order copies or request permission to reproduce materials, contact Ivey Publishing, Ivey Management Services, c/o Richard Ivey School of Business, The University of Western Ontario, London, Ontario, Canada, N6A 3K7; phone (519) 661-3208; fax (519) 661-3882; e-mail cases@ivey.uwo.ca. Copyright © 2009, Ivey Management Services Version: (A) 2009-04-22. Used with permission.

legislation, criteria and conditions had to be satisfied by the provincial and territorial health-care insurance plans in order for them to qualify for funding. Health Canada was the federal department responsible for helping Canadians maintain and improve their health, while respecting individual choices and circumstances. Provincial and territorial governments were responsible for the management, organization and delivery of health services for their residents.[2]

2000–2007

The costs of illness in Canada were expected to exceed $140 billion due to an aging population. To control costs, the number of hospital beds had been decreased by over 11.5 percent from 1999 to 2004. As well, Health Canada had adopted a preventive vision and an active role in health-care across the country,[3] subscribing to the belief that an active role in prevention by all Canadians could help lower the costs of health care, increase quality of life and reduce wait times. With wait times and overcrowded emergency rooms, many Canadians began to look at other options for faster treatment. One of these options was private clinics where services were paid for by the patient.

With chronic diseases among the costliest to the health-care system, Health Canada had been forced to consider alternatives to acute care and had begun funding programs that provided patients with the ability to manage their own condition. In 2006, 3 percent of Canada's health-care spending (approximately $3.9 billion) was spent on information technology. This market was expected to grow by approximately 15 percent for the next five years,[4] with software and services growing the most rapidly, followed by mobile health care.

 ## SASKATCHEWAN

With a population of 968,157,[5] Saskatchewan was Canada's sixth largest province and the birthplace of Medicare.[6] Because of its large landmass, many of Saskatchewan's population lived in rural communities that focused on agriculture, forestry, and mining. Almost 95 percent of the goods produced in the province were dependent on natural resources. With China's need for potash and commodity prices on the rise, Saskatchewan's economy had been booming, and the province had become one of the world's top producers of uranium. Oil and natural gas production were also important industries, attracting Canadians from across Canada to the province. Saskatchewan had the highest proportion of citizens over the age of 65 in Canada, and 14.88 percent of the population was of aboriginal descent.

---

[2] Health Canada, www.hc-sc.gc.ca/hcs-sss/medi-assur/index-eng.php, accessed August 18, 2008.

[3] Health Canada, www.hc-sc.gc.ca, accessed August 18, 2008.

[4] Among developed nations, Canadians were the highest users of the Internet and computer technology.

[5] Government of Saskatchewan, www.gov.sk.ca, accessed August 19, 2008.

[6] The Canadian universal health-care system was modeled on Saskatchewan's public hospital insurance program and Medicare program. The program, enacting hospital coverage in 1947 and medical coverage in 1962, was the first of its kind in Canada. Envisioned and promoted by Thomas C. Douglas (1904–1986) a politician from Saskatchewan. (Source: www.mta.ca/about_canada/study_guide/doctors/delivery.html)

SASKTEL

Company Background

SaskTel, in operation for nearly 100 years, was a provincial Crown corporation[7] that specialized in full-service communication to the province of Saskatchewan. Its service offerings ranged from voice, data and dial-up high-speed Internet, entertainment, Web hosting, text messaging, cellular, wireless, home phone, business solutions, and multimedia data services. Through its subsidiaries, SaskTel offered security monitoring, directory assistance, hospital-room communications to the health-care sector, and international telecommunications consulting.[8]

SaskTel had posted a consolidated net income of $64.4 million in 2005, and the company had exceeded $1 billion in operating revenue in 2006, resulting in a consolidated net income of $72.2 million. SaskTel and its subsidiaries employed 5,200 people, had been ranked by *Maclean's* magazine as one of Canada's top 100 employers six years in a row, had won the human resources award from the International Association for Native Employment and had been deemed by J.D.Power and Associates[9] to have the highest customer satisfaction levels for contracted wireless providers of any service provider in Canada.

Robert Watson

In late 2004, Robert Watson, a telecommunications veteran, assumed the position of president and chief executive officer at SaskTel. Watson had held executive positions in many telecommunications companies across Canada, was the recipient of the Saskatchewan Centennial Medal, and had served on the boards for the Information Technology Association of Canada and the Canadian Prostate Cancer Network.

Pat Tulloch

Upon graduating from the University of Regina's marketing program, Pat Tulloch was immediately hired by SaskTel as a marketing associate. She progressed within the company where she had worked on many projects for various products, including the launch of Max Entertainment Service, merchandising programs for the SaskTel stores, and promotional activities for the 2006 Juno Awards[10] in Saskatoon. Tulloch was promoted to senior director of marketing in 2005.

 ## LIFESTAT™

Product Description

The LifeStat™ service was a monitoring device that enabled the communication of a client's health information and could be used by the client, a direct relative (or a loved one), or a professional caregiver. Clients used tools such as blood

---

[7] A Crown corporation was a government-owned business that did not pay income tax. Most Crown corporations operated at arm's length from the government, with control exercised on budgeting and appointments only.

[8] SaskTel, www.sasktel.ca/about-us/company-information/corporate-profile.html, accessed August 16, 2008.

[9] J.D.Power and Associates is a global marketing service company known for its customer satisfaction research.

[10] The Juno Awards are presented annually to Canadian music artists acknowledged for their achievements in aspects of music.

EXHIBIT 1   Hardware Cost to Retailer

Hardware Needed	Purchase Price
Glucometer BT* accessory	$ 48
Landline BT access point	$120
Blood pressure monitor	$120
Cell phone	$150
Glucometer	$ 51

Source: Company files.

pressure monitors, scales, glucose meters, and heart rate monitors (see Exhibit 1) to collect information, which was then transmitted to SaskTel's secure data center. Thus, the service linked the communication gap between patients and their caregivers to ensure personal health and well-being were maintained. Life-Stat™ also provided a means for the patient to be monitored around the clock by health-care professionals who would contact the client in the event of an emergency (see Exhibit 2).

SaskTel had trademarked LifeStat™ with the Canadian Intellectual Properties Office and had a patent on the technology for Canada. To date, the system has undergone three successful trials (seven First Nations reserves with the Battleford, Saskatchewan, Tribal Council, St. Paul's Hospital in Saskatoon, and the Diabetes Education Centre at the Royal University Hospital in Saskatoon) and was showing promising results for its public launch.

EXHIBIT 2   LifeStat™ Service Breakdown

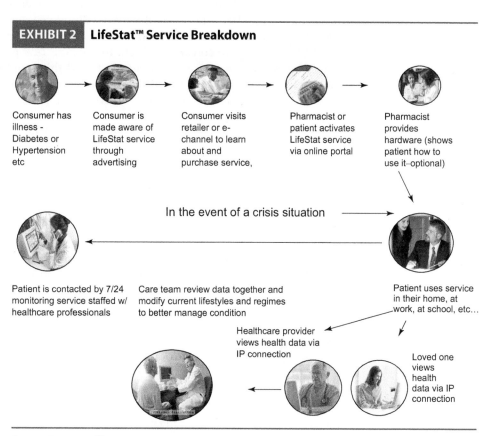

Consumer has illness - Diabetes or Hypertension etc → Consumer is made aware of LifeStat service through advertising → Consumer visits retailer or e-channel to learn about and purchase service, → Pharmacist or patient activates LifeStat service via online portal → Pharmacist provides hardware (shows patient how to use it–optional)

In the event of a crisis situation

Patient is contacted by 7/24 monitoring service staffed w/ healthcare professionals   Care team review data together and modify current lifestyles and regimes to better manage condition

Patient uses service in their home, at work, at school, etc...

Healthcare provider views health data via IP connection

Loved one views health data via IP connection

Source: Company files.

Potential Customers

Tulloch had identified two potential customer segments that would benefit from the LifeStat™ technology: individuals with diabetes and individuals with hypertension.

Diabetes Customers The LifeStat™ system had recently gained attention from the Diabetes Association of Canada and was being promoted as a resource to aid in the self-management of blood sugar levels. There are two main types of diabetes. Type 1 diabetes occurs when the pancreas is unable to produce insulin, and Type 2 diabetes occurs when the pancreas does not produce enough insulin or the body does not use the insulin it produces. If blood sugar levels are not properly controlled through monitoring and regulation, complications could lead to long-term health problems ranging from vascular disease, coronary artery disease, stroke, gangrene, and dementia. Typically, monitoring was performed by the individual at home or at work through a small monitoring device; however, no data were transferred to the patient's caregiver, so it was left to the individual to ensure that his or her own glucose levels were within the normal range and to administer self-treatment when needed.

Approximately 8.3 percent of the Canadian population[11] had been diagnosed with diabetes,[12] and, in an independent survey, 8 percent of individuals diagnosed with diabetes indicated they would purchase LifeStat™ at a monthly cost of between $50 and $65 to help monitor their blood glucose levels. In Saskatchewan, 8.1 percent of the population had reported being diagnosed with diabetes, with a high prevalence in aboriginals.

Hypertension Customers Hypertension is the persistence of high blood pressure and is the number one cause of strokes. Blood pressure measures the force of blood against the walls of the blood vessels, and readings consistently higher than 140/90 mm Hg are considered high. In Canada, 14.9 percent of the population had been diagnosed with hypertension, and this number was expected to grow to close to 20 percent by 2011. Self-monitoring was the primary doctor-recommended preventive action for hypertension patients. In Saskatchewan, 15.9 percent of the population has been diagnosed with hypertension and, in an independent survey, 2 percent of those diagnosed said they would purchase LifeStat™ at a monthly cost of between $50 and $65.

When managing their health, both hypertension and diabetes patients searched for products that were reasonably priced, convenient, easy to use, and that added to their independence.

Competition

Three major technology and communications companies—CyberNet Medical, Philips Medical Systems, and AMD Telemedicine—posed potential competition for LifeStat™.

CyberNet Medical CyberNet Medical Corporation was a division of CyberNet Systems Corporation, which was located in Ann Arbor, Michigan. Founded in 1988, CyberNet Systems focused on robotics technology with developments in

---

[11] Canada's population in 2006 was 31,612,897.

[12] *2005: Statistics Canada, Canadian Community Health Survey*, 2005.

commercial Web devices and national defense robotics. CyberNet's medical monitoring system offered to the public was called MedStar. Users collected physiological information from in-home devices and sent the information, via the Internet, to a data management system where medical reports could be compiled to individual specifications. The MedStar unit retailed in the United States for $975 to $2,946, depending on the specific devices needed for the unit. There was also a $37.50 monthly account monitoring fee.

Philips Medical Systems Philips Medical Systems, a division of Philips Electronics, operated in 63 countries, including Canada, with over 6,000 sales professionals and service technicians. As of 2004, Philips Electronics had yearly revenues of US$30 billion and assets exceeding US$4.4 billion. In 2006, Philips purchased LifeLine Inc., a medical alarm company that serviced over 500,000 Canadians. This service included telephone reminders, personal help buttons, and speaker phone devices. Philips' medical monitoring device was called the Motiva Interactive, which used broadband television, along with home vital sign measurement devices, to connect individuals to a health-care provider and monitoring system. The monitoring service cost $140 per month. This fee did not include a one-time cost for the specific devices needed to take physiological measurements.

AMD Telemedicine, Inc. AMD Telemedicine, Inc. (AMD) had over 4,000 installations in 58 countries and was considered to be the leader in the telemedicine industry. In 2006, AMD signed a contract with the Visiting Nurses Association, the oldest home care agency in the United States. U.S. home care nurses cared for over 24,000 patients and made more than 400,000 home visits a year. AMD's health monitoring system, the CareCompanion, provided event reminders and medication prompts and measured vital signs through the user's peripheral monitoring equipment. This information was then transmitted over the Internet to the patient's health-care professional for monitoring. This service was currently available only in the United States and retailed for US$125 per month plus a one-time cost for the specific devices needed to take physiological measurements.

Distribution Options

Market research indicated that 70 percent of respondents would prefer to purchase LifeStat™ through their local pharmacy, while the majority of the remainder of the respondents preferred to be able to purchase the product online. After discussions with a number of pharmaceutical representatives, Tulloch narrowed her distribution options to three possible retail chains: Shoppers Drug Mart, London Drugs, and Safeway Pharmacy. She would have to choose which of the retailers should be offered the product to ensure its success.

Shoppers Drug Mart Shoppers Drug Mart (Shoppers) represented a large portion of the pharmaceutical retail market. A well-known brand with more than 1,055 stores across Canada, Shoppers presented a significant opportunity to LifeStat™ for national sales. Although Shoppers was the best option for national distribution, Tulloch wondered whether a nationwide launch would be too aggressive so early in the product's life cycle. Shoppers maintained margins of 45 percent on all hardware and expected a $75 commission on all one-year contracts sold.

London Drugs A leader in western Canada, London Drugs had not yet entered the eastern Canada market. With more than 45 million customers across British Columbia, Alberta, Saskatchewan, and Manitoba, London Drug's pharmacy was still the center of the business, despite the company's having diversified into small appliances, furniture, computers, and cosmetics. London Drugs maintained a 48 percent margin on all hardware sold in-store and expected a $75 commission on all one-year contracts sold.

Safeway Pharmacy Safeway Pharmacy was a division within the Safeway grocery stores that were prevalent across western Canada and the United States. With over 1,775 locations, this option had the greatest potential for diversification into the United States. Within Canada, Safeway had 182 stores west of Thunder Bay, Ontario. Safeway Pharmacy offered a focus on diabetes health and wellness through education and preventive education. On all hardware, Safeway expected margins of 40 percent and a $75 commission on each one-year contract signed.

Promotion

Tulloch needed to determine LifeStat's™ promotional plan for fiscal 2007. The 2007 marketing budget was set at $300,000 for a Saskatchewan-only launch and at $1.2 million for a national launch, and she would have to effectively allocate these resources to various promotional activities. After the first year, the promotional budget would be 8 percent of sales. It was critical that the promotional campaign should create awareness and interest to foster sales and profitability. See Exhibit 3 for a breakdown of prices for various promotional alternatives.

Projected Costs

SaskTel's goal to achieve profits in the first year was an aggressive one. Upfront costs for the project's development were $2,200,000. Annual research and development was projected at $47,000, and technical support per subscriber was projected at $25 per month. Due to the risk involved with medical monitoring,

---

EXHIBIT 3 **Sample Costs for Promotional Alternatives**

Promotional Channel	Cost
Television	
Discovery Health Channel	$420 per 30-second spot
Diva/Showcase	$100 per 30-second spot
Radio	$350 per 30-second spot
In-store Demonstration	$5,000 for 10 in-store demos
Direct Mail	$10,000 per 50,000 pieces
Trade Show	
Canadian Diabetes Association	$4,500
E-Health conference	$2,500
Newspaper	
The Globe and Mail (1/8 of page)	$300 per weekday
	$500 Saturday
Canadian Health magazine	$6,200 per issue
Direct Sales Team	$10 per hour per employee

Source: Company files.

insurance would need to be purchased for $71,000 annually, and Internet security would cost $3,500 every two months. Other additional annual costs included hiring of five more employees at a cost of $200,000 (including benefits), server costs of $53,000, a $167,000 licensing fee, and $150,000 for general and administration expenses.

 ## CONCLUSION

Although LifeStat™ had shown promising results in clinical trials, Tulloch knew she faced a challenging task to get this product "off the ground" in six months. Tulloch wondered what the campaign should entail, which distribution and pricing strategy would be best, how to maximize the current marketing budget, and how many units would need to be sold in order to recoup the costs. Tulloch knew the success of LifeStat™ would rely on an effective marketing campaign, and she would have to decide quickly on an appropriate marketing mix to meet the expectations.

Case

Pyramid Door, Inc.

In November 2005, the company planning process for Pyramid Door, Inc. had just concluded, and Richard Hawly, director of sales and marketing, was reviewing the corporate sales goal for 2006. The plan established a sales goal of $12.5 million for 2006, which represented a 36 percent increase in sales over projected 2005 year-end sales.

During the planning process, a number of fellow executives had voiced concern over whether the distribution approach used by Pyramid Door was appropriate for the expanded sales goal. Hawly felt that their concerns had merit and should be given careful consideration. Though he had considerable latitude in devising the distribution strategy, the final choice would have to be consistent with achieving the 2006 sales goal. His approach and action plan had to be prepared in a relatively short time to permit implementation in January 2006.

 ## THE COMPANY

Pyramid Door, Inc. is a privately owned regional manufacturer of residential and commercial garage doors. Projected year-end company sales were $9.2 million in 2005 with a net income of $460,000 (see Exhibit 1). The company manufactures both insulated and noninsulated steel residential and commercial garage doors and supplies springs, cables, rollers, and side roller tracks for its products. Surveys of its dealers indicate that the majority of its doors are replacement purchases in the home remodeling segment of the residential housing market, with the balance of sales going to the new residential housing market and the commercial replacement garage door market.

The company distributes its garage doors through 300 independent dealers that typically offer three different garage door manufacturer brands and 50 exclusive dealers that stock and sell only Pyramid doors. (Exclusive dealers often service competing brands of garage doors in their market area.) Combined, these 350 dealers service 150 markets in 11 western and Rocky Mountain states

This case was prepared by Professor Roger A. Kerin, of the Edwin L. Cox School of Business, Southern Methodist University, as a basis for class discussion and is not designed to illustrate effective or ineffective handling of an administrative situation. Certain names and data have been disguised. Copyright © 2010 by Roger A. Kerin. No part of this case may be reproduced without written permission of the copyright holder.

EXHIBIT 1	Pyramid Door, Inc. Income Statement Projection: For the Period Ending December 31, 2005

Net Sales	$9,200,000
Cost of Goods Sold	6,900,000
Gross Profit	$2,300,000
Selling, General & Administrative Expenses	1,840,000
Net Profit Before Income Tax	$ 460,000

and parts of north and west Texas.[1] The exclusive dealers, however, are the sole Pyramid Door dealers in 50 markets. According to Hawly, this disparity in distribution policy and market coverage occurred as a result of the company's early history in gaining distribution. Hawly added, "Pyramid does not have a policy on exclusive versus nonexclusive dealers. As it so happens, the 50 exclusive dealers have been consistent performers for us. We have chosen not to distribute through other dealers in their markets given the mutually beneficial relationship we have enjoyed."

The 350 dealers that sell Pyramid doors engage in garage door sales, installation, and service. Most dealers operate from a single location. All stock and sell garage door openers and hardware. The two major garage door opener suppliers are Overhead Door, which also sells the Destiny, Odyssey, and Legacy brands, and Chamberlain, which makes openers under its own label, as well as Craftsman and LiftMaster brands. All 350 Pyramid Door dealers are located in markets with populations of approximately 250,000 or less. All 150 markets are roughly equivalent in terms of population and housing units according to U.S. Census 2000 figures.

Pyramid Door operates two distribution centers. These distribution centers allow the company to maintain an inventory of garage doors and hardware near dealer for quick delivery. A distribution facility also operates at the company's manufacturing plant. The company employs 10 technical sales representatives. Eight representatives call on each independent (nonexclusive) dealer twice a month on average. Two representatives call on the 50 exclusive dealers.

 ## THE RESIDENTIAL GARAGE DOOR INDUSTRY

The residential garage door industry in the United States was expected to post sales of $2.2 billion at manufacturer's prices in 2005. Steel garage doors account for 90 percent of industry sales. The home remodeling (replacement) market accounted for the bulk of steel garage door sales. Demand for replacement steel garage doors was driven by the continued aging of the housing stock in the United States and the conversion by homeowners from wood doors to lighter weight, easier-to-maintain steel doors. Also, product innovations such as insulated steel

---

[1] A "market" is defined by Pyramid Door as roughly equivalent to a U.S. Census–designated metropolitan statistical area (MSA). An MSA consists of (1) a city having a population of at least 50,000 or (2) an urbanized area with a population in excess of 50,000, with a total metropolitan population of at least 100,000. An MSA may include counties that have close economic and social ties to the central county. Examples of metropolitan statistical areas include the Modesto, California MSA; Pueblo, Colorado MSA; and the Cheyenne, Wyoming MSA.

EXHIBIT 2   Residential Garage Door Survey Results Summary: 2005

1. Residential garage door name awareness was very low. Just 10 percent of prospective buyers could provide a brand name when asked.

2. When asked what criteria they would use in buying a new residential garage door, price, quality, reliability of the installer, and aesthetic appeal of the door were mentioned most frequently in that order.

3. Friends, relatives, and neighbors were the principal sources identified when asked where they would look for information about residential garage doors. The Yellow Pages and newspaper advertisements were the next most frequently mentioned information sources. A company that may have installed or serviced a garage door opener or repaired an existing door also was considered an information source.

4. Thirty percent of prospective buyers expected to get at least two bids on a residential garage door installation. Virtually all expected to receive and review product literature, including warranty information, prior to installing a new door.

5. Fifteen percent of prospective buyers said they would install their own residential garage door when a replacement was needed.

6. Steel garage doors were preferred to wood garage doors by a nine to one margin.

---

doors, new springing systems, and residential garage doors with improved safety features have made steel doors popular. Projected 2006 sales of residential garage doors to the home remodeling market were $2.25 billion, representing a 2.4 percent increase.

There are several large national manufacturers and many regional and local manufacturers in the U.S. residential garage door industry. The largest garage door manufacturer in the United States is the Clopay Corporation. Clopay Corporation markets its garage doors through a network of some 2,000 independent dealers and large home center chains, including Home Depot, Menards, and Lowe's Companies. Other large, well-known garage door manufacturers are Overhead Door Corporation, Wayne-Dalton Corporation, Amarr Garage Doors, and Raynor Garage Doors. Pyramid Door, Inc. is considered to be one of the smaller regional garage door manufacturers in the industry.

In early 2005, Richard Hawly commissioned two studies of the residential garage door industry in the markets served by Pyramid Door. One study was a survey of 3,000 prospective residential garage door buyers in 25 cities that represented a cross section of the company's markets. A summary of the survey results is shown in Exhibit 2. A second study was commissioned to identify the number of dealers that installed residential and commercial steel garage doors in the 150 markets served by Pyramid Door and estimate their approximate sales volume. Telephone directories listing independent garage door sellers and installers were the primary data source for identifying the companies. Using industry data to adjust for sales of garage door openers, labor installation charges, garage door and opener maintenance and repair revenue, and the like, this study identified 3,002 independent garage door dealers with estimated 2005 steel garage door sales (at manufacturer prices after adjusting for markups) of $316.8 million. Replacement parts sold to dealers added another $31.7 million to the estimated garage door sales, bringing the total market size to $348.5 million in 2005. This research also reported that independent garage door dealers did not sell all brands of garage doors carried at an equal rate. As a rule, for dealers that sold three different manufacturer brands, the dominant brand accounted for 60 percent of their sales, the second brand, 30 percent of sales, and the third brand, 10 percent of sales. Commenting on the research, Hawly said, "These numbers indicate that our market share is about 2.6 percent. I know we can do better than that. In fact, the ambitious sales goal of $12.5 million in 2006 is achievable given the potential existing in our present markets."

THE DISTRIBUTION STRATEGY ISSUE

The strategic planning process had affirmed the overall direction and performance of Pyramid Door's sales and marketing initiatives with good reason. The company recorded sales gains in each of the past 10 years that exceeded the industry growth rate and had added 50 dealers in the past decade. The $12.5 million sales goal for 2006 was driven principally by supply considerations. Senior executives were of the firm belief that the company had to attain a larger critical mass of sales volume to preserve its buying position with suppliers, particularly with respect to raw materials for its garage doors, namely, galvanized steel and insulated foam.

During the planning process, company executives agreed that additional investment in advertising and promotion dollars was necessary to achieve the ambitious sales goal. Accordingly, Hawly was able to increase his marketing budget by 20 percent for 2006. It was decided that this incremental expenditure should be directed at the 100 highest-potential markets currently served by Pyramid Door. These included the 50 markets served by exclusive dealers and 50 markets served by independent dealers, which had yet to be finalized. The remaining 50 markets and independent dealers would continue to receive the level of advertising and promotion support provided in 2005. This support was typically in the form of cooperative advertising allowances for Yellow Pages advertising, with additional incentives for featuring the Pyramid Door name, and product literature (see Exhibit 3).

EXHIBIT 3	Dealer Cooperative Advertising Ad Slick

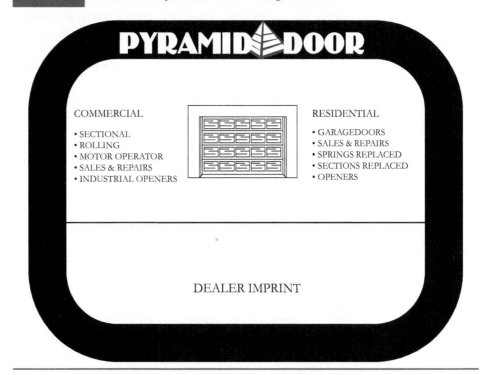

Hawly saw his charge as determining the characteristics, the number, and the locations of the dealers Pyramid Door would need to meet its sales goal of $12.5 million in 2006. Initially this would involve identifying the types of dealers that would work closely with Pyramid Door in meeting company objectives.

A number of different viewpoints had been voiced by Hawly's fellow executives. One viewpoint favored increasing the number of dealers in the markets currently served by the company. The reasoning behind this position was that it would be difficult for existing dealers to attain the sales goal specified in the corporate plan. Executives expressing this view noted that even with a 2.4 percent increase in sales following the industry trend, it would be necessary to add at least another 100 dealers. They said these dealers would likely be independent (nonexclusive) dealers located in the 100 markets not served by exclusive dealerships. Hawly believed that adding another 100 dealers in its present markets over the next year would not be easy and would require increasing the sales force that serviced nonexclusive dealers. Executives acknowledged that this plan had more merit in the long run of, say, three to four years. However, their idea had merit as a long-term distribution policy, they thought. The incremental direct cost of adding a sales representative was $80,000 per year.

A second viewpoint favored the development of a formal exclusive franchise program, since 27 nonexclusive dealers had posed such a possibility in the last year. Each of these dealers represented a different market, and each of these markets was considered to have high potential and be a candidate for the new advertising and promotion program. These dealers were prepared to sell off competing lines, most of which were supplied by regional and local garage door manufacturers. They would sell Pyramid doors exclusively in their market for a specified franchise fee. In exchange for the dealer's contractual obligation to stock, install, and service the company's products in a specified manner consistent with Pyramid Door's policies, the company would drop present dealers in their markets and not add new dealers. Furthermore, these executives noted, the company's current contractual arrangements with its independent dealers allowed for cancellation by either party, without cause, with 90 days' advance notification. Thus, the program could be implemented during the traditionally slow first quarter of the upcoming year. If adopted, company executives believed the franchise program in these 27 markets could be served by the advertising and promotion program. The other 50 markets served by exclusive dealers would be unaffected, since the advertising and promotion program was already budgeted for these dealers. The remaining 73 markets would also be unaffected, except for increased advertising in 23 high-potential markets.

A third viewpoint called for a general reduction in the number of dealerships without granting any formal exclusive franchises. Executives supporting this approach cited a number of factors favoring it. First, analysis of dealers' sales indicated that 50 of Pyramid Door's dealers (all exclusive dealers) produced 70 percent of company sales. This success was achieved without a formal franchise program. Second, these executives believed that committing the company to an exclusive franchise program could limit its flexibility in the future. And, third, an improvement in sales-force effort and possibly increased sales might result if more time were given to fewer dealers. Although a number had not been set, some consideration had been given to the idea of reducing the number of dealers in the 150 markets served by the company from 350 to 250. This would mean that the 50 exclusive dealers would be retained and 200 nonexclusive dealers would operate in the remaining 100 markets of which the top 50 would benefit from the additional marketing spending.

A fourth viewpoint voiced by several executives was not to change either the distribution strategy or the dealers. Rather, they believed that the company should do a better job with the current distribution policy and network.

Case

Crafton Industries, Inc.

In early July 2010, Suzanne Goldman was scheduled to meet with Robert Meadows, president of Crafton Industries, Inc. Goldman expected the meeting would relate to the recent board of directors meeting. In her position as special assistant to the president, or "troubleshooter," as she called herself, Goldman had noticed that such meetings often led to a project of some type. Her expectations were met, as Meadows began to describe what had happened at the board meeting.

> The directors were generally pleased with our performance last year. Despite a slowdown, we recorded a profitable sales growth of 3.6 percent. Our net profit margin of 4 percent is respectable and our cash flow is more than sufficient to fund our present initiatives. Board members were quite complimentary in their comments about senior management and the recommended bonuses and raises were approved. You deserve the credit for pulling together a really professional packet of materials for the meeting.
>
> The possibility of establishing our own distribution centers or wholesale operation was raised, given the recent developments in the industry and our competitive position. We looked at this issue 10 years ago and concluded it wasn't strategically in our interest to do so. Besides we were too small and couldn't afford it. Would you examine such a program for me for fiscal 2011 and prepare a position paper for the October board meeting? Focus only on residential business, since we handle contract sales on a direct basis already, assume the same sales level as in fiscal 2010 to be conservative, and address both the strategic and economic aspects of a change in distribution practices. Remember that our policy is to finance programs from internal funds except for capital expansion. I know you'll do the same comprehensive job that you did on the advertising and sales program last year.

THE U.S. CARPET AND RUG INDUSTRY

U.S. consumers and businesses spent about $17 billion for floorcoverings in 2009, based on manufacturer sales. The single largest floorcovering product category is carpet and rugs, followed by vinyl, ceramic tile, hardwood, stone, laminate, and rubber. Floorcovering industry sales are divided between "contract," or commercial, sales and residential sales. Residential sales account for two-thirds of floorcovering industry sales.

EXHIBIT 1	U.S. Floorcovering Market Shares and Dollar Sales at Manufacturer Prices

| | 2007 | | 2009 | |
	Dollar Sales	Market Share	Dollar Sales	Market Share
Floorcovering Type	($ millions)	(Percent)	($ millions)	(Percent)
Carpet and rug	$ 13,173	56.7%	$ 9,335	54.5%
Ceramic tile	2,704	11.6	1852	10.8
Hardwood	2,190	9.4	1,848	10.8
Vinyl	2,042	8.8	1,944	11.4
Stone	1,689	7.3	1,079	6.3
Laminate	1,276	5.5	912	5.3
Rubber	153	0.7	152	0.9
Total*	$ 23,227	100.0%	$ 17,122	100.0%

*Data may not equal total due to rounding.

The U.S. floorcovering industry was dealt a severe blow with the onset of a recession in 2007. Industry sales tumbled 29 percent at current prices and 27 percent after adjusting for inflation. The sales decline in carpet and rug category was the second largest (after stone) among the different floorcovering categories. Vinyl flooring was the least affected category, due in part to its lower cost.

Carpet and Rug Sales and Trends

The U.S. carpet and rug manufacturers posted sales of $9.36 billion at manufacturer's prices in 2009. Carpet and rugs commanded 54.5 percent of total U.S. floorcovering sales in 2009, down from 56.7 percent in 2007, and 68.1 percent in 1999 (see Exhibit 1).

Some industry analysts claim that the carpet and rug industry itself is partially to blame for the present situation. Lack of marketing, particularly in the residential carpet and rug replacement segment, is an often-cited problem area. Even though manufacturers continue to improve the quality of their products and develop new patterns, critics say the industry has not communicated these value-added dimensions to consumers and differentiated carpet and rugs from other floorcoverings. They note that the industry as a whole spends 0.9 percent of its sales on consumer advertising. For comparison, other manufacturers of consumer durable products, such as household furniture and household appliances, spend 2.7 percent and 1.7 percent of sales, respectively, for advertising. Instead, price had become the dominant marketing tool for much of the past decade and manufacturers focused attention on cost reduction and achieving economies of scale. A result of these efforts was an erratic upward trend in dollar sales over the past decade but marginal profitability for the industry as a whole.

Competitors

The U.S. carpet and rug segment has undergone consolidation since the mid-1980s. Mergers, acquisitions, and bankruptcies among manufacturers brought about by declining demand for carpet and rugs, excess manufacturing capacity, and dwindling profit margins reduced the number of carpet and rug manufacturers from more than 300 in the mid-1980s to fewer than 100 companies today. Mergers and acquisitions since 1995 reflected a push to build further economies of scale in the production and distribution of carpet and rugs.

By 2009, five companies produced about 75 percent of carpet and rug sales in the United States. The sales distribution in the residential segment was even more skewed. Three companies—Shaw Industries, Mohawk Industries, and Beaulieu of America—accounted for about 85 percent of U.S. residential carpet and rug sales.

The U.S. industry sales leader is Shaw Industries, with 2009 sales of $3.0 billion. The company also has the distinction of being the largest carpet and rug manufacturer in the world. Exhibit 2 lists the top five carpet and rug manufacturers based on annual sales in 2009.

Wholesale and Retail Distribution

Wholesale and retail distribution in the U.S. carpet and rug industry has undergone three distinct changes since the 1980s.

Direct Distribution In the 1980s, the largest carpet and rug manufacturers began to bypass floorcovering wholesalers (distributors) and sell directly to retailers in greater numbers. In many instances, direct distribution involved establishing sales offices located in manufacturer-operated distribution centers. The intent was to capture the margins paid to floorcovering wholesalers and offset declining and often negative manufacturer profit margins at the time. Lacking the capital to invest in distribution centers, smaller manufacturers continued to rely on floorcovering wholesalers that were increasingly expanding their product line to include ceramic, hardwood, and resilient floorcoverings. Although no statistics were available, it was believed that the majority of carpet and rug sales for residential use were distributed through company distribution centers to retailers by 1990. However, the majority of carpet and rug manufacturers still used floorcovering wholesalers.

Distribution through floorcovering wholesalers remained popular with the majority of carpet and rug manufacturers because of the retail distribution of residential carpet and rugs. In the 1980s, independent (and often small) floorcovering specialty stores were responsible for 58 percent of residential carpet and rug sales volume. Department stores and furniture stores accounted for 21 percent and 19 percent, respectively, of residential sales volume. Mass merchandisers, chain stores, and discount stores were relatively minor retail outlets for carpet and rugs until the early 1990s.

EXHIBIT 2	Top U.S. Carpet and Rug Manufacturers: 2009	
Manufacturer	*Dollars in Sales ($ million)*	*Percent Total*
Shaw Industries	$3,025	32.4%
Mohawk Industries	2,479	26.6
Beaulieu of America	857	9.2
Interface Flooring	423	4.5
The Dixie Group	199	2.1
Others	2,352	25.2
Total	$9,335	100.0%

Wholesale and Retail Consolidation   The 1990s was marked by a second significant change in wholesale and retail distribution for residential carpet and rugs in the United States. Department stores, furniture outlets, and independent retail stores were being replaced by large mass-merchandise and discount stores (Kmart and Walmart) and later by home centers such as Home Depot. The growing number of large retailers that were capturing an increasing share of residential carpet and rug sales spawned a new phenomenon in the retail floorcovering industry among specialty outlets: the buying group.

A retail buying group is an organization of similar retailers that combine their purchases to obtain price (quantity) discounts from manufacturers. These pooled purchases allowed independent specialty floorcovering retailers to buy less inventory per order while still getting a lower price, which reduced their costs and pressure for markdowns caused by overordering. Lower carpet and rug cost plus an emphasis on service gave independent specialty floorcovering retailers a basis with which they could compete against their larger competitors. Logistical aspects of shipping and storing inventory varied from group to group. Some buying groups took physical custody of goods through a central warehouse which often replaced floorcovering wholesalers. Others simply requested manufacturers to deliver the goods directly to buying-group members from the manufacturer's mill or distribution center.

By 1995, three retail buying groups—CarpetMax, Carpet One, and Abbey Carpets—registered $3 billion in floorcovering purchases. Another 10 smaller buying groups made another $1 billion in purchases. According to one industry observer, almost one-half of all U.S. residential carpet and rug sales volume was accounted for when buying group purchases were combined with those of large to medium-size carpet store chains (e.g., Carpet Exchange), mass merchandisers and discount stores, and home centers (e.g., Home Depot). Although estimates varied, about 40 percent of the roughly 23,000 retail outlets that carried carpet and rugs were members of buying groups, large mass-merchandise, discount, or home center chains. By 1999, CarpetMax, Carpet One, and Home Depot would account for 45 percent of total U.S. floorcovering sales.

Increased consolidation of retail purchasing evident in buying groups, chain stores, and large mass-merchandise, discount, and home center stores had either a positive or negative effect on manufacturers. Even with price discounting, and assuming the retail buying organization operated a central warehouse, it was easier and less expensive for a manufacturer to supply one location with large orders than to supply several separate retailers with smaller orders. On the other hand, if a buying organization flexed its buying power and persuaded manufacturers to take lower-than-normal margins (prices) and ship to diverse locations, a manufacturer risked seeing a lower dollar volume and profit.

Direct distribution by manufacturers in the 1980s followed by consolidated purchasing and warehousing by retailers in the 1990s put many floorcovering wholesalers in a precarious position in the residential segment of the carpet and rug industry. Wholesalers that typically served small and medium-sized independent floorcovering specialty stores were particularly vulnerable to the ascension of retail buying groups that operated their own warehouse facility. These wholesalers advocated their role in distribution to both manufacturers and retailers. They argued that working with a buying group was worthwhile to a manufacturer only if the functions performed by the buying group were not only better than those offered by floorcovering wholesalers but also significant enough to justify the price discounts demanded by a buying group. Similarly, they argued that retailers benefited from wholesaling functions above and beyond the warehousing function. Nevertheless, the absolute number of floorcovering wholesalers had declined in recent years and was expected to decline further.

Forward Integration into Retailing   In late 1995, the carpet and rug industry watched as yet another change in distribution practices unfolded. On December 12, 1995, Shaw Industries, the largest carpet and rug manufacturer and sales leader, announced plans to engage itself directly in the residential and contract segments of the floorcovering industry. It would do this by operating its own retail stores and commercial dealer network. In announcing this initiative, Robert E. Shaw, the president and CEO of Shaw Industries, said:

> We have realized for some time that the manufacturer must become significantly involved in the retail environment to enhance the viability of our industry. Today, our industry offers products of exceptional quality and unsurpassed value, yet we continue to lose consumer dollars to other product groups. Moreover, because consumers have traditionally price-shopped our products, profits have stagnated for years, from fiber producer to manufacturer to retailer.
>
> Although our industry has matured considerably in recent years, the current structure cannot address many fundamental problems the industry is facing. A manufacturer-dealer affiliation was inevitable, since the only practical way to improve these adverse conditions is by consolidating the combined resources of the two.[1]

Shortly afterward, Shaw Industries announced that it had purchased a number of commercial carpet dealers and contractors and Carpetland USA, a retail chain of 55 stores.

In response to this initiative, Home Depot dropped Shaw Industries as a carpet and rug supplier and switched to Mohawk Industries. Carpet One and Abbey Carpets, two buying groups, asked their members not to do business with Shaw. Other carpet manufacturers courted floorcovering specialty stores with promises to support them with product and not to enter the retail market as competitors. Shaw Industries countered these actions by creating its own retail buying group—the Shaw Alignment Incentive Program—which operated 275 retail stores in 26 states with annual sales of $575 million by mid-1998. Then, in June 1998, Shaw Industries announced it would sell off its retail stores to the Maxim Group, the owner of CarpetMax floorcovering stores, for about $93 million.[2] In 1999, Home Depot was again stocking Shaw carpet.

Movement toward direct distribution and wholesale and retail consolidation continued from 2000 to 2009. Recessionary pressures in the United States from 2001 to 2003 and again from 2007 to 2010 prompted this activity. However, no carpet and rug manufacturer ventured into retail distribution following the experience of Shaw Industries.

 ## THE COMPANY

Crafton Industries, Inc. is a privately held manufacturer of a full line of medium- to high-priced carpet primarily for the residential segment. The company markets its products under the Masterton and Chesterton brand names. Contract sales to institutions and businesses are also made but account for only 28 percent of company sales and occur principally in the southeastern United States. The company had no export sales. Total company sales in fiscal 2010 were $75 million, with a

---

[1] Quoted in "The North American Top 50 Carpet & Rug Manufacturers," *Carpet & Rug Industry* (April 1996), pp. 12–13.

[2] "Shaw Industries to Sell Retail Arm to Maxim Group," *Wall Street Journal* (June 24, 1998), p. B11.

| EXHIBIT 3 | Crafton Industries, Inc. Financial Statements (For the Fiscal Year Ending June 30, 2010) |

Income Statement

Net sales	$75,000,000
Less cost of goods sold	56,250,000
Gross margin	$18,750,000
Distribution expenses	$ 2,250,000
Selling and administrative expenses	11,250,000
Other expenses	2,250,000
Net income before tax	$ 3,000,000

Balance Sheet

Current assets	$26,937,500
Fixed assets	24,000,000
Total assets	$50,937,500
Current liabilities	$10,312,500
Long-term debt and net worth	40,625,000
Total liabilities and net worth	$50,937,500

Source: Company records.

net profit before tax of $3 million. Exhibit 3 shows abbreviated company financial statements.

The company currently distributes its line through seven floorcovering wholesalers located throughout the United States. These wholesalers, in turn, supplied 4,000 retail accounts, including department stores, furniture stores, and floorcovering specialty stores. Inspection of distribution records revealed that 80 percent of residential segment sales were made through 50 percent of its retail accounts. This relationship exists within all market areas served by the company. Meadows believed these sales-per-account percentages indicated that at the retail level the company was gaining adequate coverage, if not overcoverage. The review of distribution records also indicated that it cost Crafton Industries 6 percent of its residential segment sales to service the seven floorcovering wholesalers.

Advertising by the company appeared primarily in shelter magazines and newspapers. The emphasis in advertisements was on fiber type, colors, durability, and soil resistance. A cooperative advertising program with retailers had been expanded on the basis of Goldman's recommendation. According to Goldman, "The co-op program is being well received and has brought us into closer contact with retail accounts." The company employed two regional sales coordinators who acted as a liaison with wholesalers, assisted in managing the cooperative advertising program, and made periodic visits to large retail accounts. In addition, they were responsible for handling contract sales for institutions and businesses.

Floorcovering wholesalers played a major role in the company's marketing strategy. Its seven wholesalers had long-term relationships with the company. Two had represented the company's products for over 30 years, four had been with the company for 20 to 25 years, and one had been with the company for 10 years. The company's wholesalers maintained extensive sales organizations, with the average wholesaler employing 10 salespeople. On average, retail accounts received at least one sales call per month. Goldman's earlier evaluation of the sales program revealed that wholesaler sales representatives performed a variety of tasks, including checking inventory and carpet samples, arranging point-of-purchase displays, handling retailer questions and complaints, and taking orders. About 25 percent of an average salesperson's time was spent on non-selling activities (preparing call reports, acting as a liaison with manufacturers, traveling, and so forth). About 40 percent of each one-hour sales call was devoted to selling Crafton Industries carpeting; 60 percent was devoted to selling noncompeting products. This finding disturbed company management, which felt that a full hour was necessary to represent the product line. In addition to making sales, wholesalers also stocked carpet inventory. Crafton Industries wholesalers typically carried sufficient stock to keep the number of their inventory turnovers at five per year. Crafton Industries executives felt that inventory levels sufficient for four turns per year were necessary to service retailers properly, however. Finally, wholesalers extended credit to retail accounts. In return for these services, wholesalers received a 20 percent margin on sales billed, at the price to retailers. Wholesalers typically applied a mark-up on cost of 125 percent for carpeting sold to retailers.

At a June 2010 meeting with its wholesalers, Crafton Industries executives were informed that several wholesalers were feeling increased pressure to shave their profit margins to accommodate retailer pricing demands. It seemed that an increasing number of their retail accounts had joined regional retail buying groups and were seeking price breaks comparable to those made possible through their group purchases. Subsequent probing on this topic led Crafton Industries executives to conclude that about 1,200 of the company's current retailers were members of buying groups; they represented about a third of the company's residential segment sales. The meeting concluded with Crafton Industries executives agreeing to consider a reduction in its price to wholesalers that could be passed on to retailers. At the same time, wholesalers agreed to consider a modest reduction in their margins as well. The "Margin Sharing" proposal, so named by a wholesaler, would be given top billing at the next meeting in January 2011. In the meantime, price accommodations would be made where and when it was necessary to meet the competition.

 ## DIRECT DISTRIBUTION EXPERIENCE OF COMPETITORS

Following her meeting with Meadows, Goldman sought out information on competitors' experience with direct distribution. Despite conflicting information from trade publications and knowledgeable industry observers, she was able to arrive at several important conclusions.

First, competitors with their own warehousing or direct distribution operations located them in or near seven metropolitan areas: Atlanta, Chicago, Dallas–Fort Worth, Denver, Los Angeles, New York City, and Philadelphia. Crafton Industries had wholesalers already operating in these metropolitan areas, except for Dallas–Fort Worth and Atlanta. The company serviced these two areas from wholesalers located in Houston, Texas, and Richmond, Virginia, respectively. Second, a minimum volume of approximately $7 million in wholesale sales was necessary to operate a warehouse operation economically. The average warehouse operation could be operated at an annual fixed cost (including rent, personnel, operations) of $700,000. Goldman was informed that suitable warehouse space was available in the metropolitan areas under consideration; therefore, the company would not have to embark on a building program. Third, salaries and expenses of highly qualified sales representatives would be about $70,000 each annually. One field sales manager would be needed to manage eight sales representatives. Salary and expenses would be approximately $80,000 per field sales manager per year. Sales administration costs (including fringe benefits) were typically 40 percent of the total sales force and management costs per year. Delivery and related transportation costs to retail accounts were estimated to be about 4 percent of sales, and inventory and accounts receivable carrying costs were each 10 percent. Retail accounts receivable take about 90 days to collect, on average. Though these figures represented rough approximations, in Goldman's opinion and in the opinion of others with whom she conferred, they were the best estimates available.

In late September 2010, just as Goldman was about to draft her position paper for Robert Meadows, she received a disturbing telephone call from a long-time successful wholesaler of the company's products. The wholesaler told her that he and others were disappointed to hear of her inquiries about direct distribution possibilities given what transpired at the June meeting. Through innuendo, the wholesaler threatened a mass exodus from Crafton Industries once the first company warehouse operation was opened. He implied that plans were already under way to establish a trade agreement with a competitor. This conversation would have significant impact on her recommendation if direct distribution was deemed feasible. In short, a rollout by market area looked less likely. A rapid transition would be necessary, which would require sizable cash outlays and an aggressive sales-force recruiting program.

Case

VF Brands

Global Supply Chain Strategy

It was August 2009. Chris Fraser, president, Supply Chain International for VF Brands, was driving to his office just outside Milan near Lake Como. On this sunny morning, the sparkling lake was a picture of tranquility, a striking contrast to the turbulence of the global apparel industry. In the shorter term, the economic crisis of 2008–2009 was taking its toll on the entire business from the largest marketing companies to the smallest subcontractors. But beyond the crisis, Fraser also foresaw long-term structural changes in the apparel business that could call for profound changes in the way VF, the world's largest publicly owned apparel company, managed its supply chain. Fraser noted, "For the past few decades, supply chain strategy in apparel was focused on chasing low cost labor from one country to the next. Today, apparel is produced just about everywhere on Earth, and we have basically run out of new "low cost" places to source production—until, of course, penguins learn to sew. We have to start finding cost saving by how we manage our supply chain."

For some time, Fraser had been advocating that VF shift its supply chain strategy. VF currently procured apparel both from its own plants and from a large network of suppliers. Like its competitors, VF's outsourcing strategy emphasized flexibility. Most suppliers in the garment industry received short-term contracts (typically a few months) to produce a specific garment in specific volumes. This strategy allowed garment marketers like VF to shift production among suppliers in different locations in order to optimize costs and to respond to changes in exchange rates, tariffs, and other cost factors. Many believed that this approach also provided strong incentives for suppliers to reduce costs in order to compete for future contracts. Fraser admitted that while this approach had worked well for many years, it had its drawbacks. The lack of coordination and trust between suppliers and apparel companies led to higher inventory and long lead times. In addition, Fraser felt that a company like VF, with its strong internal manufacturing capabilities, had expertise that it could share with suppliers in order to improve

Professors Gary Pisano (Harvard Business School) and Pamela Adams (Franklin College) prepared this case. HBS cases are developed solely as the basis for class discussion. Cases are not intended to serve as endorsements, sources of primary data, or illustrations of effective or ineffective management.

processes and reduce costs. He noted, "For products coming from our own manufacturing plants, we can move things through the supply chain in days instead of weeks. That allows us to respond very quickly to the market. That's the value of having our own plants. But from a capital point of view, it may not make sense for VF to continue to build its own plants. What I would like to see is that we create supplier relationships that work as closely with us as our internal plants do."

Fraser called this approach the Third Way sourcing strategy because it represented an alternative to both in-house manufacturing and traditional sourcing. Fraser had first pitched the Third Way strategy five years ago, but encountered skepticism from some groups within the organization. To date, VF had experimented with a limited number of Third Way supplier relationships. Fraser now felt VF had the data and the experience to reflect on this experiment and to decide, once and for all, whether the Third Way should be implemented more extensively.

 # VF BRANDS AND THE APPAREL INDUSTRY

In 2008, VF Corporation had total revenues of just over $7.6 billion (see Exhibit 1 on page 439 and Exhibit 2 on page 440). The company's roots could be traced back to 1899 as the Reading Glove and Mitten Company based in Pennsylvania. In 1914, the company expanded into lingerie and in 1917 changed its name to Vanity Fair. In 1969, Vanity Fair entered the jeans business through the acquisition of the Lee Company. By 1983, jeans accounted for 75 percent of the company's $1 billion in sales. In 1984, the company embarked on a series of acquisitions aimed at expanding the jeans product line and diversifying into new areas. It acquired Blue Bell (owner of the Wrangler, Rustler, and Girbaud jeans brands), Jantzen (sportswear and backpacks), and RedKap (occupational apparel and uniforms). Through much of its history, Vanity Fair pursued a vertically integrated manufacturing strategy in jeans, with many of its factories located in the United States.

In 2004, the company made a significant shift in strategy. Its new "Growth Plan" called for the transformation of Vanity Fair (now VF) from a company focused on basic apparel (like jeans) into a global lifestyle apparel company with strong brands. Fraser noted, "We used to be a company that sold what we could manufacture. With the Growth Plan, we decided to focus on marketing, and source products from the outside." While continuing to invest in growing "heritage brands" like Wrangler and Lee, the company acquired new brands with global appeal through a series of acquisitions. These included The North Face, Vans, Nautica, Reef, Kipling, Eastpak, Majestic, Napapijri, Eagle Creek, John Varvatos, 7 For All Mankind, and lucy. In 2000, heritage brands accounted for 90 percent of sales. By 2008, heritage brands represented only 56 percent of sales revenue with lifestyle brands making up the remaining 44 percent. The company's goal was to have 40 percent of sales from heritage brands and 60 percent from lifestyle brands.

There were two other critical elements of the company's strategic growth plan. One was to expand sales outside the United States, particularly in rapidly developing countries like Russian, India, and China. In 2001, international sales constituted only 19 percent of revenues. By 2008, this figure had grown to 30 percent. Further growth in international sales was targeted. The final element of the company's strategic growth plan was to expand its direct to consumer business. VF, like other apparel companies, historically had sold its products through independent stores. However, following a recent trend in the apparel business, VF was creating its own, single-brand stores as well as expanding its Web-based retailing. By 2009, the company had over 700 single-brand stores (mostly The North Face, Napapirji, lucy, John Varvatos, and 7 For All Mankind).

EXHIBIT 1 VF Consolidated Statements of Income (In Thousands, Except per Share Amounts)

In thousands, except per share amounts	2008	2007	2006
Net Sales	$ 7,561,621	$ 7,140,811	$ 6,138,087
Royalty Income	80,979	78,548	77,707
Total Revenue	7,642,600	7,219,359	6,215,794
Costs and Operating Expenses			
Cost of goods sold	4,283,680	4,080,022	3,515,624
Marketing, administrative and general expenses	2,419,925	2,173,896	1,874,026
	6,703,605	6,253,918	5,389,650
Operating Income	938,995	965,441	826,144
Other Income (Expense)			
Interest Income	6,115	9,310	5,994
Interest Expense	(94,050)	(72,122)	(57,259)
Miscellaneous, net	(3,103)	2,941	2,359
	(91,038)	(59,871)	(48,906)
Income from Continuing Operations Before Income Taxes	847,957	905,570	777,238
Income Taxes	245,209	292,324	242,187
Income from Continuing Operations	602,748	613,246	535,051
Discontinued Operations	----	(21,625)	(1,535)
Net Income	602,748	591,621	533,516
Earnings Per Common Share- Basic			
Income from continuing operations	$ 5.52	$ 5.55	$ 4.83
Discontinued Operations	----	(0.20)	(0.01)
Net Income	5.52	5.36	4.82
Earnings Per Common Share- Diluted			
Income from continuing operations	$ 5.42	$ 5.41	$ 4.73
Discontinued operations	----	(0.19)	(0.01)
Net Income	5.42	5.22	4.72
Cash Dividends Per Common Share	$ 2.33	$ 2.23	$ 1.94

Source: Company documents.

These stores acted as showcases for the brand, but also drove significant revenue growth. VF planned on opening 75 to 100 single-brand stores annually, with a target of 1,300 stores globally by 2012. In keeping with its international expansion strategy, the company was emphasizing the Asian markets for the location of new stores. The company's distribution strategy balanced different types of channels: specialty stores (16 percent), domestic and international retailers (16 percent), department stores (2 percent), chains (7 percent), upscale department stores (3 percent), mass retailers (15 percent), royalty income (13 percent), and international wholesale (28 percent).

VF organized its businesses into five major "coalitions." Each coalition was responsible for the product lines, marketing, and sales of a set of related brands globally. Two of these coalitions were heritage businesses: jeanswear and imagewear. *Jeanswear*, consisting of the Lee, Wrangler, and Rustler brands, was the

---

EXHIBIT 2 **Consolidated Balance Sheets (In Thousands)**

In thousands	2008	2007
Assets		
Current Assets		
Cash and equivalents	$ 381,844	$ 321,863
Accounts receivable, net	851,282	970,951
Inventories	1,151,895	1,138,752
Deferred income taxes	96,339	104,489
Other current assets	171,650	109,074
Total current assets	2,653,010	2,645,129
Property, Plant and Equipment	1,557,634	1,529,015
Less accumulated depreciation	914,907	877,157
	642,727	651,858
Intangible Assets	1,366,222	1,435,269
Goodwill	1,313,798	1,278,163
Other Assets	458,111	436,266
	$6,433,868	$6,446,685
Liabilities and Stockholders' Equity		
Current Liabilities		
Short-term borrowings	$ 53,580	$ 131,545
Current portion of long-term debt	3,322	3,803
Accounts payable	435,381	509,879
Accrued liabilities	519,899	489,160
Total current liabilities	1,012,182	1,134,387
Long Term Debt	1,141,546	1,144,810
Other Liabilities	724,248	590,659
Commitments and Contingencies	----	----
Common Stockholders' Equity		
Common Stock	109,848	109,798
Additional paid-in capital	1,749,464	1,619,320
Accumulated other comprehensive income (loss)	(276,294)	61,495
Retained earnings	1,972,874	1,786,216
Total common stockholders' equity	3,555,892	3,576,829
	$6,433,868	$6,446,685

Source: Company documents.

largest coalition with $2.8 billion in revenue (2008). On its own, the VF Jeanswear coalition sold more pairs of jeans than any other company in the world. The *Imagewear* coalition provided uniforms for commercial or industrial use (e.g., Federal Express employee uniforms) as well as for sports franchises (the NBA, the NFL, and collegiate sports). The Imagewear coalition had sales of $1 billion. Three additional coalitions were associated with the lifestyle brands. The *Outdoor and Action Sports* coalition contained the Eastpak, Vans, Reef, The North

EXHIBIT 3 2008 Sales Revenue by Coalition

Coalition	Name Brands	Sales Revenue (in Millions)
Jeanswear	Wrangler, Lee, Rustler	2,751
Outdoor and Action Sports	JanSport, Eastpak, The North Face, Vans, Reef, Napapijri, Eagle Creek	2,751
Imagewear	Red Kap, Bulwark, The Force, NFL, CSA, Chase Authentics, Majestic, Harley-Davidson	994
Sportswear	Nautica, John Varvatos, Kipling	611
Contemporary Brands	7 For All Mankind, lucy	383
Other		153
Total Sales Revenue		**7,643**

Source: Company documents.

Face, Napapirji, and Eagle Creek brands and had $2.8 billion in 2008 revenues. The *Sportswear* coalition housed the Nautica, Kipling, and John Varvatos brands, and had 2008 revenues of $625 million. *Contemporary Brands*, the newest coalition (established in 2007), included 7 For All Mankind and lucy and had 2008 sales of approximately $350 million. Exhibit 3 provides an overview of the financial performance of each coalition.

VF took great pains to preserve the organizational cultures and unique brand identities of the companies it acquired. A critical part of this strategy was to allow acquired companies to keep their design groups intact and in their original locations. As a result, design at VF was highly decentralized. For instance, Vans' (clothing and shoes for skating, surfing, and snowboarding) design was done at the organization's southern California home. Napapirji design continued to be based near Milan. The North Face had design studios in the United States (San Francisco Bay Area) and Italy (Treviso). Chris Fraser noted, "We try not to monkey around with brand heritage. We keep the design and culture the way it was."

The Apparel Industry

The apparel industry encompassed the design, manufacture, and marketing of clothing, accessories, and personal luxury goods. Global sales in 2008 (at retail prices) of apparel were approximately $1.3 trillion.[1] The sector included an extremely broad range of products and price points, from basic garments likes socks and underwear to casual clothing and sportswear to super-premium "haute couture" suits and dresses. Most garment companies were associated with a product segment that represented their traditional "base." VF, for instance, was known for many years as a "jeans" company. Van Heusen was a "shirts" company. But over time, the larger companies (like VF, Liz Claiborne, Phillips-Van Heusen, and Sara Lee) had branched out into a growing number of product lines. In addition, companies which had traditionally competed in shoes and footwear, like Nike and adidas, had entered the apparel business and had become major players in certain segments (such as sportswear). Similarly, many apparel companies (including VF) had acquired shoe lines. Given the sheer size and breadth

[1] Datamonitor, Global Apparel and Textiles: Industry Profile, March 2009.

of the industry, competition was highly fragmented and even the largest players typically had only single digit market shares. Even within specific segments of the market, rivalry was generally intense, with dozens of brands competing directly. Jeanswear was a good example. While VF was the largest seller of jeans globally, its $2.8 billion in annual jeans sales constituted only about 5 percent of the total market (approximately $50 billion in sales). In such competitive environments, substantial and continuous investments in brand building were essential to maintaining margins. Most major apparel companies (VF, Christian Dior, Nike, adidas, Ralph Lauren, Liz Claiborne) invested 7 to 12 percent of their revenues in advertising.

Another major trend in the apparel industry was the growing power of large mass-retailing chains in the distribution of clothing. Walmart, for instance, had become the largest jeans retailer in the United States. Volume gave merchants like Walmart significant bargaining leverage with respect to raw materials and logistics costs along with supplier contracts. In addition, large retailers were developing and marketing their own "private-label" store brands. Walmart had introduced its own brand of jeans (Faded Glory) that it sold for $9 per pair (compared to its $16 price for Wranglers). It had also recently launched a line of jeans made exclusively for them by Jones Apparel, called *L.e.i.*, specifically targeted at teenage girls.

Most apparel companies typically concentrated on design and marketing, and generally performed little or none of their own production, much of which had been transferred to low cost countries around the world. In fact, while 49 percent of retail apparel sold in the United States was made domestically in 1992, by 1999 this figure had dropped to only 12 percent. Extensive outsourcing had become the norm for a number of reasons. The production of garments was generally a labor intensive process offering few scale advantages. Barriers to entry into production were relatively low. As a result, there were *hundreds of thousands* of small contract garment manufacturers scattered around the globe. Moreover, the skills required to produce garments (cutting and stitching fabric) were relatively generic. This enabled garment companies to source production of their design on highly competitive terms. In addition, garment production was subject to complex and ever changing tariffs and quotas. Bilateral trade deals generally dictated from which countries garments were imported. Further complicating matters was the fact that there were separately negotiated duties and quotas for fabrics and textiles. These could dramatically change the economics of production in one country versus another. Historically, garment companies "chased quota"; that is, they sought out low-cost producers from countries that had not yet hit their quotas for importing into a certain country. While tariffs and quotas on textiles and garments were being reduced under the auspices of the 2005 World Trade Organization accord, it was still far from an open market. The largest apparel companies that sold products in all major global markets thus found it advantageous and less risky to have an extremely broad geographic base of suppliers so that they could shift production in response to changes in tariffs and quotas.

Fraser noted that while tariffs and quotas had come down over the past two decades, those barriers had left the industry with a highly fragmented and often illogical supply chain. For instance, for a sweater sold in the U.S. market, the raw wool might be sourced in Australia. That wool would then be sent to China for spinning into yarn. The yarn might then be sent back to Australia for dying and knitting into fabric panels. Those panels would then be sent to China again where the sweater would be assembled. From there, it would be shipped to the United States. Fraser noted, "Ideally, we are trying to line up all the vertical steps in a region or a country. Thailand, for instance, is an ideal place to assemble backpacks. We can shorten lead times significantly if we can procure fabric, components, and other raw materials there as well. If we do a similar thing with other products in China where our stores are located, and we can move the goods right out of the packing area directly into the stores, all the better!"

As supply chains globalized, the challenges of finding suppliers, managing sourcing relationships, and coordinating product flows had been steadily increasing. In the 1990s, many American- and European-based apparel companies found that they lacked both the skills and relationships for effective sourcing in Asia. To fill this need, some Asian manufacturers shifted their business models to provide fully integrated supply chain services to apparel companies. Hong Kong–based Li & Fung was a good example of this breed of supply chain service company. Founded in 1906 as a trading company, Li & Fung now managed the supply chains and sourcing for many of the world's largest brands (in apparel, footwear, and other consumer products). In essence, Li & Fung acted as an intermediary between the brand companies and a network of sub-contractors scattered around the globe. In recent years, Li & Fung, like other supply chain intermediaries, had begun to integrate forward into its own brands and retail chains.

Over the past 10 years, the upstream segment of the supply chain—garment production—had been undergoing dramatic changes. Since 2001 (the first year garment quotas were eliminated), fabric producers in the CAFTA region (which included Central America, the United States, and the Dominican Republic) had been steadily losing market share to imports from China (which had increased their share of the U.S. market from 7 percent in 2001 to 45 percent in 2009). In the past decade alone, the United States had lost 50 percent of its fabric production capacity. Fraser reflected, "It is getting harder to maintain apparel production in places where we cannot get cheap and speedy supply of fabric."

In 2008–2009, the world economy was gripped with the worst recession since the Great Depression of the 1930s. Falling gross domestic products and plummeting consumer demand in the United States, Europe, and many developing economies did not spare the global apparel industry. Total industry revenues fell by 10 percent. VF was weathering the storm relatively well compared to its competitors. While it had seen sales decline by 9 percent (and significantly less when exchange rates were taken into account) in the first half of 2009 (compared to first half of 2008) and earnings decline by 30 percent over the same period, the company's financial position was strong. It had a cash position, relatively low debt, an A-bond rating, and ample untapped lines of credit. The bigger concern among some senior managers was the long-term effect of the crisis on the supply base. Many garment contractors were small shops, operating on razor-thin margins, and with virtually no financial cushion. As volumes fell, many were forced to shut down. In China alone, it was reported that over 60,000 small production shops had closed their doors in 2008–2009. Sudden closures of suppliers could be very disruptive. For instance, one of VF's suppliers of jeans (supplying over 15 million pairs of jeans per year to VF) had given VF less than three months' notice that it was closing down its plants in Nicaragua and moving production to Vietnam, a location much less favorable to VF due to quota, tariffs, and logistics. VF had to scramble to find an alternative supplier.

 ## VF OPERATIONS STRATEGY

VF used a mixture of both internal manufacturing and outsourcing, a relatively unique operations strategy in the apparel industry. Beginning in the 1980s, many major apparel companies began to sell off their internal manufacturing operations and source their products from specialized suppliers. Many of VF's major competitors, like Liz Claiborne, Ralph Lauren, Levi Strauss, and Sara Lee, no longer had any internal manufacturing and relied completely on outsourcing. At the other extreme, companies like Benetton and Zara were completely vertically integrated from garment production through retail, and did limited outsourcing.

As noted earlier, VF had historically been an apparel manufacturer. At one point, it owned approximately 100 factories. With the acquisition of The North Face, in the late 1990s, this began to change. The North Face, like many of the organizations VF would subsequently acquire, had no internal manufacturing. VF's existing manufacturing infrastructure was not well suited to these lifestyle brands for two reasons. First, VF's plants were largely focused on jeans and denim products, while many of the lifestyle brand products were not. Second, VF plants were located in Mexico and the Caribbean in order to optimize the logistic costs and tariffs to serve the U.S. market, VF's traditional focus. With the strategy of expanding into lifestyle brands and international markets, the company needed to expand its outsourcing in Asia. This was a significant shift in the company's philosophy. A painful part of this new strategy included the closing of many of VF's internal manufacturing plants. By 2009, VF produced about 30 percent of its products in-house (in its 40 remaining plants), and sourced the rest from independent suppliers. Of course, there was significant variance across product lines in sourcing. For instance, VF produced about 60 percent of its jeans in-house. Imagewear, which was largely targeted at the U.S. market, and which required very quick response times, also sourced the vast majority of its products internally. On the other hand, VF used outsourcing for 100 percent of its lifestyle apparel, footwear, and backpacks.

Still, VF was proud of the internal manufacturing capabilities the company had accumulated over 125 years, and believed those capabilities provided it a significant competitive advantage. A recent benchmarking study by a consulting firm indicated that VF's internal manufacturing plants were among the very best in the world in terms of quality, efficiency, and reliability. The time needed to produce a garment in VF-owned factories was much shorter than the industry average. VF's factories also had defect rates well below industry averages. On production lead times, VF-owned factories required 10 days from "cut to ship" compared to 30 to 50 days for external suppliers. VF also believed it had built up technical and engineering capabilities for apparel manufacturing that few companies could match. For instance, its Mexican and Nicaraguan plants employed about 50 engineers focused on improving processes. The company had developed novel techniques and even proprietary equipment for manufacturing jeans. Mike Green, managing director of VF Asia, a member of Fraser's international sourcing team, had spent 26 years at VF in engineering, plant management, and sourcing roles. He commented, "There is no doubt that VF plants set the standard in the industry."

On the sourcing side, building up a reliable and high-quality supplier network required an enormous investment in time. Prospective suppliers needed to be visited and their manufacturing capabilities carefully assessed. In addition, VF had a strict policy of doing business only with suppliers who followed internationally established standards for worker safety and protection. It also took time to establish good working relationships with suppliers, and only experience could really tell which ones were reliable. By 2009, VF had relationships with more than 1,600 contractors and 30 distribution centers around the world. The top 20 suppliers accounted for about 45 percent of the outsourced volume procured by VF on an annual basis. To manage this, the company hired Chris Fraser in 2000. He came from another sourcing position in a large apparel company located in Asia. When he arrived, sourcing represented only a small portion of total sales. Between 2000 and 2009, with the acquisition of many new lifestyle brands, the company's sourcing volume in Asia alone increased 15-fold to reach a total value of $1.8 billion. As VF gained experience with sourcing, the management team also began to understand that its supply chain network provided a significant platform for growth. Fraser provided an example: "When we acquired Napapirji, they had a very strong brand, but they would have had to invest years and millions of dollars to grow to $300 million in sales. By being part of VF, they now had access to our supply chain network. We could just plug them in to our system."

One of biggest challenges of running such a large apparel supply chain was the sheer complexity of the product line. VF, for instance, currently had over 600,000 SKUs (stock-keepin units), where an SKU was defined by only style and color (and not article size). Jeanswear alone had approximately 100,000 SKUs. Moreover, while some "classic" product lines change little from year to year, the lifestyle brand product typically had very short product life cycles, and required nearly constant replenishment of new designs. On average, about half of VF's SKUs were essentially new product designs every year.

A second complexity was the widely differing needs and priorities of the brand coalitions. For instance, in more fashion-oriented products where VF competed with companies like Liz Claiborne and Tommy Hilfiger, product design was considered "king." Product designers in those lines focused almost solely on creating an exciting menu of products that would hit the fashion "sweet spot" in the coming season. In these product lines, cost was not such a critical issue. Products sold in VF's brands stores typically fit into this category. In other products lines, the name of the game was low cost and rapid replenishment. For instance, large retailers in the United States demanded that VF be able to replenish store inventories within eight days in order to minimize inventory costs. For product lines competing with Zara, a chain well known for being able replenish inventories continuously throughout a season, the supply chain had to be extremely responsive. There were also significant differences in product requirements across regions, even for seemingly very similar products. Consider jeans. In the American market, jeans were by and large a nonfashion clothing item (Fraser, an American, pointed out, "Americans wear jeans as an 'anti-fashion' statement"). A good-quality pair of Wranglers could be bought for $16 to $30 depending on the retailer. But in Europe, jeans were worn as a fashion item. They had different cuts, design, and fit, and were often made of different denim than jeans sold in the U.S. market. They also sold at smaller retailers and at much higher prices than in the United States (e.g., a pair of Wranglers could sell for $60 to $80 a pair).

Floyd Perkins, a 26-year VF veteran, was corporate vice president for supply chain which included all aspects of procurement, manufacturing, sourcing, and distribution. Procurement, manufacturing, and distribution were managed from the United States, while international sourcing was based in Europe and Asia (Hong Kong), with local offices in China, Pakistan, India, and Bangladesh. Perkins' organization supported all of the coalitions. While the coalitions were responsible for the designs, volume decisions, pricing, and margin goals for their product lines, the supply chain organization planned capacity (internally or externally), managed inventory, and coordinated all the processes required to go from fabric to a finished product on the store shelf.

THE APPAREL SUPPLY CHAIN: FROM DESIGN TO STORE SHELF

It is August 2009 and The North Face store on Newbury Street in Boston is bustling. The summer heat grips Boston, but the shoppers are browsing the autumn collection, contemplating the cool days ahead. Few are aware that the fleece vests, rain jackets, t-shirts, pants, shirts, and backpacks they see on the store shelves are the culmination of a process that began a slightly more than a year ago. It all began in June 2008 when VF designers began to sketch their preliminary ideas for the fall 2009 collection, and made commitments to broad design themes and colors. Over the next few months, designers would create literally hundreds of preliminary designs encompassing the entire product line. It was a highly iterative process. Design concepts were dropped and others were added, hues and shades were tweaked, new patterns created (and discarded), pockets moved a centimeter higher (or lower), and trims adjusted. Ultimately, the design and marketing teams would have to make judgments about what would appeal to customers more than a year hence.

At some point, even the most detailed drawing was not enough to judge a design, and physical prototypes had to be sewn. These would be used internally by management to evaluate the design as well as to show to prospective customers (e.g., large retailers). For the sake of speed and secrecy, VF made prototypes in their own or partnered development centers. This process typically took four weeks. More iterations might follow, and in some cases, additional prototypes might be fabricated. While the designs were taking shape, the marketing groups were forecasting prices, volumes, and margins for each item. These forecasts would have a critical impact on the supply chain strategy. By September of 2008, the design and marketing management would have to make a final decision on the entire 2009 autumn collection. Design decisions were reviewed at both the brand and coalition levels.

Once design commitments had been made and volume orders placed, Perkins' operations took over (prior to this point, operations was often consulted informally on product manufacturing or supply chain issues that might affect design choices, volumes, or prices). The first step for operations was to develop a sourcing strategy for each product (internal vs. external supplier, location of suppliers, etc.). Sourcing had to be done at multiple levels of the supply chain, not just for final garment assembly. Sources for raw materials, fabrics, and accessories had to be identified and lined up. Several criteria went into the choice of supplier. Location choices were influenced by both economic factors (cost of production and transportation) and trade quota or tariff considerations. Suppliers were then chosen according to their managerial as well as technical skills and expertise in specific garments. Sourcing offices located throughout the world were responsible for identifying and managing the procurement process with suppliers in the local region.

From September through December, the sourcing organization was focused on identifying suppliers, obtaining price quotes, and producing samples. Sample production was critical for the supplier to really know what was involved in production of a particular garment (e.g., how much labor time would be required) and thus critical for cost estimation. Sample production was used by VF to evaluate a supplier's capability to produce a product to its specifications. It was not unusual at this stage to discuss technical challenges in the production process that required design modifications (for instance, the angle of a seam specified by the designer might be hard to sew in high volumes). While typically minor, each potential design change required a discussion between the supplier, VF sourcing offices, and VF designers. Designers typically did not like to make changes in the design for the sake of manufacturing. Perkins explained, "We don't just make what we can make and that's it. The product really rules. If the designer says the jean needs three legs, then we'll put three legs on it. But if we have a better way of doing it than what's been handed to us, and it's OK with them, then we try to improve the design." Samples were used by VF sales and marketing personnel to show to retailers and wholesalers in the sales process during October and November.

By January 2009, contracts would be signed for all products in the fall 2009 collection, and suppliers (or VF) would begin placing their orders for raw materials and fabrics. The long lead times made forecasting particularly critical. For some seasonal products (like backpacks where 90 percent of all products were sold in the "back to school" shopping season), inaccurate forecasts could be particularly costly. Depending on the fabric, the procurement lead time could be anywhere from 4 weeks to 12 weeks. Once suppliers had all the necessary raw materials and fabrics, they would begin production of garments. Contracts generally specified a target volume. Virtually all suppliers performed work for multiple garment companies. A critical factor affecting their economic viability was running factories at full capacity, and thus they typically scheduled production in batches in order to optimize utilization. VF could expect that its fall 2009 products were being cut, sewn, and assembled in the March to June time frame. During this time period, VF could make some adjustments to its orders as it updated its demand forecasts. The products would then be shipped to regional distribution centers where they were sorted and packed for bulk shipping to target markets. Transportation (via ship) from a distribution center in Asia to a U.S. port could add another 2 weeks of lead time. From the port, products would clear customs and be shipped to a VF distribution center in the United States, where they would then be sent (via truck) to a store. Retailers could expect the fall collection to begin arriving during the early part of July.

Historically, apparel supply chains were very inflexible. Retailers and wholesalers placed their orders 8 to 10 months prior to a particular season. Product would usually arrive at the beginning of the selling season. After this point, the retailer had limited ability to adjust stocks in response to actual customer demand. If a particular shoe line was proving to be exceptionally "hot," the retailer probably could not restock midseason. They would simply run out of product and lose prospective sales. Conversely, if a highly anticipated new line of jackets was experiencing disappointing sales, the retailer would likely be stuck with excess inventory and be forced to discount this item substantially. Thus, retailers suffered the costs of both excess inventory and stock-outs.

Over the past decade, both retailers and garment manufacturers had been trying different strategies to build in more flexibility. Zara, for instance, used a combination of vertically integrated manufacturing, small lot production, and information technology to adjust inventories on a weekly basis. Zara stores stocking out of a hot item could expect a replenishment shipment in two weeks. Companies that relied solely on outsourced production had less scope to change production schedules, as they often had to commit to production volumes well in advance of the selling season. However, even in these cases, companies were trying to make the supply chain more responsive through better information exchange and through inventory management. VF had found that it could be highly responsive for jeans products manufactured in its own Mexican plants and destined for the U.S. market. Fraser explained, "For jeans sourced out of our factories in Mexico, we might cut fabric on a Monday. By Thursday, those jeans have been sewn and washed. Friday, they are packed and probably put on a truck heading to the United States. By the next Monday, those jeans are in our U.S. distribution center. By that Thursday, those jeans could be on a store shelf."

 ## THIRD WAY SUPPLY CHAIN STRATEGY

In 2004, Chris Fraser felt that VF had created a highly efficient, globally diversified supply chain. There were a few basic types of sourcing relationships VF could establish with a supplier. One type was known as "cut and make" (CM) contracts. Under this approach, VF would strike separate contracts for suppliers at each stage of the production process (fabric, components, cutting, sewing, washing, finishing, etc.). VF owned the inventory and suppliers were paid for the value added of their particular step. VF was also responsible for coordinating the flow of product from one supplier to the next. The advantage of this approach is that it allowed VF to maintain very tight control over costs at each stage. CM contracts were used mostly for heritage lines out of Central American and Caribbean suppliers and were managed in conjunction with internal manufacturing operations. A second approach was known as "package sourcing." Under package sourcing, a single supplier took responsibility for the entire process from raw materials to finished goods and shipping into the market. They were paid on a piece basis and are responsible for paying subcontractors, raw material suppliers, and logistic costs. In this case, VF did not have ownership of the materials along the process. Full-package sourcing was used mostly for the lifestyle brands throughout Asia, Europe, and northern Africa.

VF's coalitions were very pleased with the quality and reliability of the service they received from sourcing. In addition, VF had driven down costs by continually expanding the supplier base to ever lower-cost locations. An aggressive focus on low-cost sourcing had enabled VF to hit its overall corporate margin targets of 10 to 15 percent. It was at that point, however, that Fraser and Green began to think about next steps. Fraser believed that VF needed to shift its focus from finding even lower-cost suppliers to doing a better job managing the supplier base it had. Fraser continued, "The supply chain could be made more efficient."

Some of the inefficiency was due to lack of coordination and, more precisely, lack of trust between apparel companies and their suppliers. Historically, apparel companies and apparel suppliers showed little loyalty to one another. Contracts were short-term (typically one season). In their aggressive pursuit of low costs, apparel companies drove hard bargains on pricing and freely shifted production from one supplier to another. There were no guarantees in either direction. Every year, suppliers had to bid to get new business from a company and never guaranteed production capacity beyond a very short time horizon (covered by the contract). They also took on products for as many companies as possible (often competitors) in order to diversify their risks. In addition, suppliers never shared production information (capacity, inventory, costs) with apparel companies, for fear such information would be used against them in the bidding process.

One manifestation of this lack of trust was excess inventory. Perkins provided an example: "When you own the factory there is no question of trust or commitment. Therefore we are able to operate on incredibly lean inventory levels. We have 3 days of work in process in our factories and maybe half a day's work ahead of the line. By contrast, our external suppliers often require that we provide them 30 days of raw materials. Why? Because they don't trust us to come through. The inventory gives them security."

The process was also very time-consuming. Because there was no pre-set menu of prices for different design features (e.g., a pocket or a stone wash), the price of each garment had to be negotiated from scratch with each supplier. For instance, if VF wanted to add a pocket to a pair of pants, a supplier having a good year might ask for a 27 cent price increase while another who needed to fill capacity might ask for only 21 cents. Fraser commented, "There is a lot of transaction time and gamesmanship in the negotiations with suppliers."

Another problem with current sourcing was the lack of process improvement. Because garment contractors operated on razor-thin margins, they invested little, if anything, in process technology. Engineering skills were not only hard to come by, they were not highly valued or sought after by contractors. In fact, because they were generally born in very low-wage environments, productivity improvements were never a high priority. If problems arose, the answer was generally to add more workers or overtime.

Fraser and Green believed that VF's technical capabilities represented a "trump card" that no other competitor had. Perkins agreed:

> You go to places today to source where labor in incredibly cheap. That is not going to be the differentiator anymore. We need to look for other benefits like speed to market, material utilization, lower inventories, less work in process, and lower cost to quality. Competitive advantage no longer comes from reducing the amount of needle time that goes into the garment, but from managing the whole supply chain. And that is where we might be able to beat another brand that does not know how to manage the supply chain.

Fraser explained that the biggest barrier to growing internal manufacturing was VF's desire to minimize investments in fixed plant and equipment. He noted, "One could argue that we should be buying more factories and leveraging our expertise in production that way. But even if it only costs $10 to $15 million to build a good factory, such a strategy would not be consistent with VF's corporate capital deployment strategy. That money is better invested in our brands and our retail operations."

Was there a way for VF to leverage its internal technical expertise and gain a greater degree of control over the supply chain without actually owning suppliers? Fraser believed that if VF could put its "hard technical skills" into the supply chain, it would have an advantage over apparel companies that lacked internal manufacturing competences. Perkins commented:

> We have an abundance of engineering skills dedicated to our own factories. If we could take our engineers in Mexico who are shaving pennies off the cost of garments that have been engineered for 100 years now, and transfer them to places where 60 percent of our products are made now, that could have a big impact. We had one recent example that just blew me away. We sent this one young engineer from Mexico to one of our Asian suppliers. He came back and said they don't load the containers as efficiently as we do in Mexico. So we had him develop some guidelines for them for container utilization. The result was a $2 million annual savings.

Fraser thought he had a strategy for making the supply chain much more efficient. He called it Third Way sourcing. Third Way sourcing was designed to be a halfway point between full integration and traditional outsourcing. The idea was to create a true partnership between VF and the supplier. While the details might differ across specific suppliers, Fraser saw the key elements of a Third Way sourcing relationship as follows:

- VF would strike an agreement with a supplier for a specific product line (e.g., backpacks) and commit to a volume forecast over a number of years (instead of one season). The supplier would not produce the same category of product (e.g., backpacks) for competitors, and would agree not to do so in the future.

- The supplier would set up production lines dedicated to VF's products, investing in the building, machinery, equipment, labor supervision, logistics services, and administrative infrastructure to manage the operations.

- VF and the supplier would develop production schedules jointly to meet each partner's needs. Information on order forecasts and production capacity were to be shared between the partners.

- VF and the supplier would work together on process improvements. VF would make available (without charge) its engineering resources to improve production processes. A portion of the savings realized by these improvements would be passed through to VF.

- The supplier would own the factory and the equipment and be responsible for managing the work force. VF would make certain investments in specialized equipment and capital when necessary.
- VF would utilize its purchasing capacity to help the suppliers procure fabric and other raw materials at discounted prices. VF would agree to buy back any unused fabric or raw material from the supplier.
- The supplier would be paid on a cost plus basis with a margin to meet its ROA requirements.

Fraser recalled his first presentation of the idea back in 2005 to a group of senior managers. Concerns about the idea came from all directions. Some within the marketing organization were worried about the loss of flexibility the new approach might entail. Fraser commented, "Sourcing was viewed as a big 'candy shop' where you could get just about anything you wanted. The marketing folks were concerned that if we went away from our sourcing strategy, we could lose flexibility to serve them." The manufacturing organization, on the other hand, was frustrated by the continued closing of internal plants despite their strong performance. At another level, they were also not happy about handing over their engineering resources to be managed by the sourcing team.

But the real concern of internal manufacturing revolved around the sharing of its proprietary expertise with outside suppliers. They raised serious concerns about the leakage of VF's hard-earned process expertise that could eventually be used to produce for competitors. Fraser and Green, however, did not share these concerns. They had no plans to transfer VF's proprietary equipment to Third Way partners. Rather, their focus was on using the skill sets of internal manufacturing to improve supplier performance in terms of cost, quality, and speed. As Green explained, "There is a philosophy of how we train our engineers and the training programs from a junior engineer all the way through a division engineer. It's about what we teach them and how we teach them, and copying that is not as easy as just flipping on a light switch or reading some manual."

Despite the objections of these internal groups, Fraser and Green persisted. By 2009, they had formed five Third Way partnerships. One was for the production of backpacks in Thailand; a second was for jeans production in Bangladesh; a third was for jeans production in Morocco; a fourth was for jeans production in China for the Chinese market; and a fifth was for outerwear production in China. One of the interesting things Fraser and Green learned was that it was much easier to convince new suppliers than existing suppliers to sign up for a Third Way partnership. When they broached the concept to some of VF's best existing suppliers, they got a cold reception. Green recalled, "It's hard to convince suppliers this is a good idea for them. The experienced ones can be pretty set in their ways about how they run their plants and their operations. They were really not that interested in us coming in there and changing their processes. We also had a hard time to get partners to share information about costs and processes within their factories."

Another challenge of implementing Third Way partnerships was staffing. In fact, Green noted that he found it difficult to move forward on the plans more quickly. He either had to find experienced engineers from VF's own factories that would be willing to move across the world, or hire locals and then send them through a rigorous training program within VF's manufacturing division. Green provided an example from the Bangladesh partnership: "We hired some top graduates out of a Bangladesh university. We then put them into a mentoring program with two of our engineers with 10 and 20 years' experience that we brought over to Hong Kong to work with these guys. The next phase for us will be to create a routine for this training process. Tom and Floyd are constantly saying move faster, but you can only do so much so fast."

EXHIBIT 4 **Comparative Results for Alternative Sourcing Solutions: VF Jeanswear Five-Pocket Jeans**

Alternative Sourcing Solutions	VF - Owned & Operated	Packaged Sourced	Packaged Sourced	Packaged Sourced	Third Way	Third Way
Fabric Source	Mexico	China	India	India	India	India
Cut, Sew, Finish	Mexico	China	Bangladesh	Morocco	Bangladesh	Morocco
Days Leadtime						
Leadtime	17	60	71	75	48	52
Finished goods inventory	24	83	99	104	68	85
Total days forward	41	143	170	179	116	137
Cost per unit ($)						
Cost fabric/yard (incl. freight)	2.64	2.23	2.25	2.37	2.25	2.37
Fabric/unit	3.03	2.72	2.76	2.90	2.76	2.90
Cut, Sew, Finish (incl. Transport)	2.62	1.93	1.90	2.36	1.90	2.36
Total COGS ($)	5.65	4.65	4.66	5.26	4.66	5.26
Local manufacturing and margin	0.38	0.38	0.39	0.50	0.39	0.50
FOB price ($)	6.03	5.03	5.05	5.76	5.05	5.76
VF overhead	0.14	0.32	0.32	0.34	0.22	0.24
Finished product freight	0.16	0.35	0.35	0.28	0.35	0.28
Duties		0.73	0.73		0.73	
Landed cost ($)	6.33	6.43	6.45	6.38	6.35	6.28
Inventory carrying costs	0.19	0.52	0.52	0.49	0.43	0.42
Markdown provision	0.03	0.19	0.19	0.18	0.16	0.14
Net cost ($)	6.55	7.14	7.16	7.05	6.94	6.84
Charge for capital per unit ($)	0.93				0.12	0.12
Total Costs ($)	7.48	7.14	7.16	7.05	7.06	6.96

Source: Company documents.

Note: Data and locations have been disguised for purposes of confidentiality.

All $ figures calculated at exchange rates prevailing on August 1, 2009.

All duties and freight rates as of August 1, 2009.

The experience to date, while limited, gave VF management a glimpse into the potential cost benefits of Third Way sourcing. Exhibit 4 provides an overview of the lead times, inventory, and costs of producing a standard "five-pocket jean" in different locations and under different sourcing arrangements (internal manufacturing, traditional packaged source, and Third Way partnerships).

Not all partnerships ended as planned, as illustrated by VF's experience with its Moroccan partner. Despite VF's volume guarantees and technical help to improve operations, the Moroccan jeans plant was not able to dig itself out of debt (largely due to drastic declines in its business with other companies). By early 2009, its financial position had deteriorated to the point that the owner considered halting operations. To protect its supply base, and in the face of a highly favorable price due to exchange rates, VF decided to buy out the partner, and the Moroccan plant is now a wholly owned VF operation. VF transferred a manager from one of its Mexican plants to Morocco to run the operations.

Perkins felt the real benefits of the Third Way strategy had not even been seen yet, because they lay in the design process. He commented, "If you think about speed to market, which is always one of the challenges of the supply chain, about two-thirds of the time is spent in the product development process. Only one-third is the time it takes to go from the order to the delivery to the store shelf. I think we also need to focus on those first stages to see how we can shorten leadtimes."

Fraser felt that the Third Way strategy had reached a critical cross-road. VF's ambitious international expansion goals, particularly for Asia, meant that they would need to bring on significant new capacity over the next several years. They could do that by expanding Third Way sourcing, expanding internal manufacturing, or by simply doing more traditional sourcing. The decision, Fraser felt, would have a profound impact on VF's competitive capabilities for years to come.

Chapter 8

Pricing Strategy and Management

Whether or not it is so recognized, pricing is one of the most crucial decision functions of a marketing manager. According to one marketing authority: "Pricing is an art, a game played for high stakes; for marketing strategists, it is the moment of truth. All of marketing comes to focus in the pricing decision."[1] To a large extent, pricing decisions determine the types of customers and competitors an organization will attract. Likewise, a single pricing error can effectively nullify all other marketing-mix activities. Despite its importance, price rarely serves as the focus of marketing strategy, in part because it is the easiest marketing-mix activity for the competition to imitate.

It can be easily demonstrated that price is a direct determinant of profits (or losses). This fact is apparent from the fundamental relationship:

$$\text{Profit} = \text{total revenue} - \text{total cost}$$

Revenue is a direct result of unit price times quantity sold, and costs are indirectly influenced by quantity sold, which in turn is partially dependent on unit price. Hence, price simultaneously influences both revenues and costs.

Despite its importance, pricing remains one of the least understood and most challenging marketing-mix activities. Price effects on buying behavior and price determination continue to be the focus of intensive study and discussion.

 ## PRICING CONSIDERATIONS

Although the respective structures of demand and cost obviously cannot be neglected, other factors must be considered in determining pricing objectives and strategies. Most important, the pricing objectives have to be consistent with an organization's overall marketing objectives. Treating profit maximization as the sole pricing objective not only is a gross oversimplification but also may undermine the broader objectives of an organization. Other pricing objectives include enhancing brand image, improving customer value, obtaining an adequate return on investment or cash flow, and maintaining price stability in an industry or market. It is common for companies to state more than one pricing objective and prioritize the objectives.

EXHIBIT 8.1   **Conceptual Orientation to Pricing**

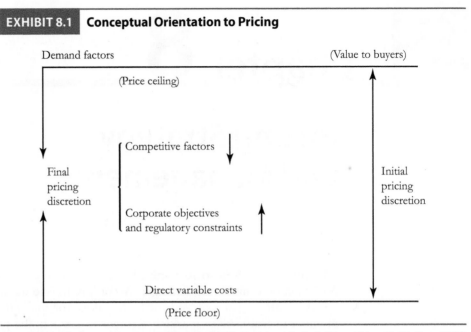

Source: Kent B. Monroe, *Pricing: Making Profitable Decisions,* 3rd ed. (Burr Ridge, IL: McGraw-Hill/
Irwin, 2003). Reproduced with permission of McGraw-Hill/Irwin.

Exhibit 8.1 shows how numerous factors affect a marketing manager's pricing discretion. Demand for a product or service sets the price ceiling. Costs, particularly direct (variable) costs, determine the price floor. More broadly, consumer value perceptions and buyer price sensitivity will determine the maximum price(s) that can be charged. Campbell Soup Company executives can attest to this view.[2] The company spent seven years and $55 million developing a line of Intelligent Quisine (IQ) food products. The 41 breakfasts, lunches, dinners, and snacks would be the first foods "scientifically proven to lower high levels of cholesterol, blood sugar, and blood pressure." After 15 months in test market, Campbell Soup yanked the entire IQ line. Consumers found the products too expensive and lacking in variety. On the other hand, the price(s) chosen must at least cover unit variable costs; otherwise, for each product sold or service provided, a loss will result. Some companies that sell products via the Internet have come to recognize that unit variable costs of a transaction (including order fulfillment and distribution expenses) often can exceed the price of the products sold. The result? Increasing dollar sales and sizable financial losses.[3]

Although demand and cost structures set the upper and lower limit of prices, government regulations, the price of competitive offerings, and organizational objectives and policies narrow a manager's pricing discretion. Regulations prohibiting predatory pricing, the level of differentiation among competitive offerings, and the financial goals set by the organization are all factors that may affect the price range within broad demand and cost boundaries.

There are still other factors that must be considered in pricing a product or service. The life-cycle stage of the product or service is one factor—greater price discretion exists earlier in the life cycle than later. The effect of pricing decisions on profit margins of marketing channel members must be assessed. The prices of other products and services provided by the organization must be considered as well; that is, price differentials should exist among offerings such that buyers perceive meaningful value differences.

Price as an Indicator of Value

In determining value, consumers often pair price with the perceived benefits derived from a product or service. Specifically, *value* can be defined as the ratio of perceived benefits to price:[4]

$$\text{Value} = \frac{\text{perceived benefits}}{\text{price}}$$

This relationship shows that for a given price, value increases as perceived benefits increase. Also, for a given price, value decreases as perceived benefits decrease. Seasoned marketers know that value is more than a low price. According to a Procter & Gamble executive, "Value is not just price, but is linked to the performance and meeting expectations of consumers."[5]

For some products, price alone influences consumers' perception of quality—and ultimately value. For example, in a *Better Homes and Gardens* survey of home furnishing buyers, 84 percent agreed with the statement "The higher the price, the higher the quality."

Price also affects consumer perceptions of prestige so that as price increases, consumer demand for the item may actually rise.[6] Rolls-Royce automobiles, Cartier jewelry, Chanel perfumes, fine china, Swiss watches, and Lalique crystal may sell worse at lower prices than at higher ones. The success of Swiss watchmaker TAG Heuer is an example. The company raised the average price of its watches from $250 to $1,000, and its sales volume increased sevenfold. TAG Heuer is now the number two luxury watch brand behind Rolex.

Consumer value assessments are often comparative. In such cases, determining value involves a judgment by a consumer as to the worth and desirability of a product or service relative to substitutes that satisfy the same need. A consumer's comparison of the costs and benefits of substitute items gives rise to a "reference value." Although Splenda, a sugar substitute, might be more expensive than sugar, some consumers value it more highly than sugar because it has no calories. Retailers have found that they should not price their store brands more than 20 to 25 percent below manufacturers' brands. When they do, consumers often view the lower price as signaling lower quality.[7]

Price Elasticity of Demand

An important concept used to characterize the nature of the price–quantity relationship is that of *price elasticity of demand*. The coefficient of price elasticity, *E*, is a measure of the relative responsiveness of the *quantity* of a product or service demanded to a change in the *price* of that product or service. In other words, the coefficient of price elasticity measures the ratio of the percentage change in the quantity purchased of a product or service to the underlying percentage change in the price of the product or service. This relationship can be expressed as follows:

$$E = \frac{\text{percentage change in quantity demanded}}{\text{percentage change in price}}$$

If the percentage change in quantity demanded is greater than the percentage change in price, demand is said to be *elastic*. In such cases, a small reduction in price will result in a large increase in the quantity purchased; thus, total revenue will rise. Conversely, if the percentage change in quantity demanded is less than the percentage change in price, demand is *inelastic*, and a price reduction will have less of an impact on revenues. Price elasticity of demand is an important factor, for example, in the setting of airline prices for business and leisure fares.[8] Business fares are less price elastic than leisure fares.

A number of factors influence the price elasticity of demand for a product or service. In general,

- The more *substitutes* a product or service has, the greater its price elasticity.
- The more *uses* a product or service has, the greater its price elasticity.
- The higher the *ratio* of the price of the product or service to the income of the buyer, the greater the price elasticity.

Product-Line Pricing

In practice, it is common to apply the concept of price elasticity simultaneously to more than one product or service. By computing the *cross-elasticity of demand* for product A and product B, it is possible to measure the responsiveness of the quantity demanded of product A to a price change in product B. Products are considered complements (substitutes) if lowering (raising) the price of one product leads to an increase in the unit sales of the other product.[9] An understanding of the implications of cross-elasticity is especially important for successful implementation of product-line pricing, in which product demand is interrelated and the organization's objective is to increase revenue and profit for the entire line and not just for individual products or services.

Consider a marketer of shaving razors and blades (or video game players and video games). Should the marketer price razors very low, perhaps close to or even below cost, in order to promote blade sales? Blades could then be marketed at relatively high prices. Or should an opposite strategy be used—selling high-priced razors but low-priced blades? Examples of these pricing strategies abound. For instance, Nintendo, a market leader in video game players and games, traditionally prices its players at or near cost and makes its profit on video game sales.[10] The important point is that in most organizations products are not priced in isolation. In certain instances, individual products may be sold at a loss to entice buyers or to ensure that the organization can offer potential buyers complete product lines. In such situations, the price may bear little relationship to the actual cost of a product.

In addition, **product-line pricing** involves determining (1) the lowest-priced product price, (2) the highest-priced product and price, and (3) price differentials for all other products in the line. The lowest- and highest-priced items in the product line play important roles. The highest-priced item is typically positioned as the premium item in quality and features. The lowest-priced item is the traffic builder designed to capture the attention of the hesitant or first-time buyer. Price differentials between items in the line should make sense to customers and reflect differences in their perceived value of the products offered. Behavioral research also suggests that the price differentials should get larger as one moves up the product line from less expensive to more expensive items.[11]

Estimating the Profit Impact from Price Changes

In Chapter 2, the basic principles of break-even analysis and leverage were described. These same principles can be applied when assessing the effect of price changes on volume.[12]

The impact of price changes on profit can be determined by looking at cost, price, and volume data for individual products and services. Consider the data shown in the top half of Exhibit 8.2 for two products, alpha and beta. These products have identical prices ($10), unit volumes (1,000 units), and net profits ($2,000), but their cost structures differ. Product alpha has a unit variable cost of $7 and assignable fixed costs of $1,000. Product beta has a unit variable

EXHIBIT 8.2 **Estimating the Effect of Price Changes**

	Product Alpha	*Product Beta*
Cost, Volume, and Profit Data		
Unit sales volume	1,000	1,000
Unit selling price	$10	$10
Unit variable cost	$7	$2
Unit contribution (margin)	$3 (30%)	$8 (80%)
Fixed costs	$1,000	$6,000
Net profit	$2,000	$2,000
Break-Even Sales Change		
For a 5% price reduction	+20.0%	+6.7%
For a 10% price reduction	+50.0%	+14.3%
For a 5% price increase	−14.3%	−5.9%
For a 10% price increase	−25.0%	−11.1%

cost of $2 and assignable fixed costs of $6,000. The unit break-even volume for product alpha is 333.3 units ($1,000/$3). Product beta's unit break-even volume is 750 units ($6,000/$8).

The calculation for determining the unit volume necessary to break even on a price change is as follows (percentages expressed in whole numbers):

$$\text{Percentage change in unit volume to break even on a price change} = \frac{-(\text{percentage price change})}{\left(\frac{\text{original contribution}}{\text{margin}}\right) + \left(\frac{\text{percentage}}{\text{price change}}\right)}$$

For example, if a product has a 20 percent contribution margin, a 5 percent price decrease will require a 33 percent increase in unit volume to break even:

$$+33 = \frac{-(-5)}{[20] + [-5]}$$

Alternatively, a product with the same contribution margin can absorb a 20 percent decline in unit volume if its price increases 5 percent without incurring a loss in profit:

$$-20 = \frac{-(+5)}{[20] + [+5]}$$

The lower half of Exhibit 8.2 illustrates the potential profit impact of price changes for products alpha and beta. For product alpha to profit from a 10 percent price cut, its unit volume would have to increase by 50 percent. In contrast, unit sales of product beta, with its larger contribution, would only have to increase by slightly more than 14 percent for a profit to be realized.

The same analysis can be applied to price increases. If product alpha's price were increased 10 percent, its unit volume could decrease by 25 percent before profits would decline. On the other hand, product beta, with its higher contribution, could absorb only an 11 percent unit volume decline with a 10 percent price increase.

PRICING STRATEGIES

Because of the difficulty of estimating demand, most pricing strategies have a decided reliance on cost as a basic foundation. To a great extent, price strategies can be termed either full-cost or variable-cost strategies. *Full-cost price strategies* are those that consider both variable and fixed costs (sometimes termed *direct* and *indirect costs*). *Variable-cost price strategies* take into account only the direct variable costs associated with offering a product or service.

Full-Cost Pricing

Full-cost pricing strategies generally take one of three forms: markup pricing, break-even pricing, and rate-of-return pricing. *Markup pricing* is a strategy in which the selling price of a product or service is determined simply by adding a fixed amount to the cost of a product, which is usually expressed as a percentage of the total product cost. If the total unit product cost is $16 and a manager desires to earn a 20 percent markup, the unit selling price is $20 as shown below:

$$\text{Markup price} = \frac{\text{total unit cost}}{(1-\text{desired markup})} = \frac{\$16}{(1-0.20)} = \$20$$

Markup pricing is frequently used in routine pricing situations, such as with grocery or clothing items, but it is also sometimes employed in pricing unique products or services—for example, military equipment or construction projects. Although it possesses decided drawbacks (especially if a single percentage is applied across products without regard to their elasticities or competition), its simplicity, flexibility, and controllability make it highly popular.

As noted in Chapter 2 when discussing the financial aspects of marketing management, break-even analysis is a useful tool for determining how many units of a product or service must be sold at a specific price for an organization to cover its total costs (fixed plus variable costs). Through judicious use of break-even analysis, it is also possible to calculate the break-even price for a product or service. Specifically, the break-even price of a product or service equals the per-unit fixed costs plus the per-unit variable costs.

Rate-of-return pricing is slightly more sophisticated than either markup or break-even pricing. Still, it contains the basic ingredients of both of these strategies and can be viewed as an extension of them. In *rate-of-return pricing*, price is set so as to obtain a prespecified rate of return on investment (capital) for the organization. Since rate of return on investment (ROI) equals profit (Pr) divided by investment (I),

$$\text{ROI} = \text{Pr}/I = \frac{\text{revenues} - \text{cost}}{\text{investment}} = \frac{P.Q - C.Q}{I}$$

where P and C are, respectively, unit selling price and unit cost, and Q represents the quantity sold.

By working backward from a predetermined rate of return, it is possible to derive a selling price that will obtain that return rate. If an organization desires an ROI of 15 percent on an investment of $80,000, total costs per unit are estimated to be $0.175, and a demand of 20,000 units is forecast, then the necessary price will be

$$\frac{(\text{ROI}) \times I + CQ}{Q} = P = \frac{(0.15)\$80,000 + \$0.175 \times 20,000}{20,000} = \$0.775$$

This pricing strategy is most commonly used by large firms and public utilities whose return rates are closely watched or are regulated by government agencies or commissions. Like other types of full-cost pricing strategies, rate-of-return pricing assumes a standard (linear) demand function and insensitivity of buyers to price. This assumption often holds true only for certain price ranges, however.

Variable-Cost Pricing

An alternative to full-cost pricing strategies is a variable-cost, or contribution, pricing strategy. This type of strategy is sometimes used when an organization is operating at less than full capacity and fixed costs constitute a great proportion of total unit costs. The basic idea underlying *variable-cost pricing* is that, in certain short-run pricing situations, the relevant costs to consider are the variable costs, not the total costs. Specifically, in this strategy, variable unit cost represents the minimum selling price at which the product or service can be marketed. Any price above this minimum represents a contribution to fixed costs and profit.

Variable-cost pricing is a form of demand-oriented pricing. As such, it can serve two different purposes: (1) stimulate demand and (2) shift demand. Since variable-cost prices are lower than full-cost prices, the assumption is that they will *stimulate demand* and increase revenues and, hence, will lead to economies of scale, lower unit costs, and greater profits. This is why airlines offer different classes of fares, hotels offer special weekend rates, and movie theaters have discounts for senior citizens. Variable-cost pricing also makes sense because fixed costs must be met no matter whether a product or service is sold—the airline must maintain its flight schedule whether or not there are any passengers; the hotel or movie theater has to remain open even if it is only partially filled—and the incremental (variable) costs of serving one more customer are minimal.

Consider a bus line making a daily departure from Chicago, Illinois, to Miami, Florida. The standard price of a one-way ticket is $119, and on an average trip the bus is 60 percent full. If the unit variable cost per seat is $15, should the bus line offer a half-price fare for children under five years of age? Ignoring price elasticity and the like for the moment, the answer is yes, the reduced fare should be offered. The reduced fare ($59) covers the variable cost ($15) and makes a contribution of $44 to fixed costs. Since the bus line will make the trip regardless of how many passengers there are, in the short run every reduced-fare ticket sold contributes $44 to fixed expenses. Such a pricing approach always assumes that no more profitable use may be made of the revenue-generating activity.

In addition to stimulating demand, variable-cost pricing can be used to *shift demand* from one time period to another. Movie theaters sometimes have lower matinee ticket prices to encourage customers to switch from evening to afternoon attendance. Likewise, certain electrical and natural gas utilities have different price schedules to shift demand away from peak load times and smooth it out over extended time periods.

New-Offering Pricing Strategies

Full- and variable-cost pricing strategies are *technical strategies* that can be used when an organization initially sets its prices or when it changes them. When pricing a new product or service, however, a manager also has to consider other, more *conceptual* strategies.

When introducing a new product or service to the marketplace, an organization can employ one of three alternative pricing strategies.[13] With a *skimming pricing strategy*, the price is set very high initially and is typically reduced over time. A skimming strategy may be appropriate for a new product or service if any of the following conditions hold:

1. Demand is likely to be price inelastic.
2. There are different price-market segments, thereby appealing first to buyers who have a higher range of acceptable prices.
3. The offering is unique enough to be protected from competition by patent, copyright, or trade secret.
4. Production or marketing costs are unknown.
5. A capacity constraint in producing the product or providing the service exists.
6. An organization wants to generate funds quickly to recover its investment or finance other developmental efforts.
7. There is a realistic perceived value in the product or service.

Many of these conditions were present when Gillette decided to price its innovative Fusion shaving system 30 percent higher than its hugely successful Mach3 shaving system. Gillette Fusion posted $1 billion in annual worldwide sales within three years of its introduction.[14]

At the other extreme, an organization may use a *penetration pricing strategy*, whereby a product or service is introduced at a low price. This strategy may be appropriate if any of the following conditions exist:

1. Demand is likely to be price elastic in the target market segments at which the product or service is aimed.
2. The offering is not unique or protected by patents, copyrights, or trade secrets.
3. Competitors are expected to enter the market quickly.
4. There are no distinct and separate price-market segments.
5. There is a possibility of large savings in production and marketing costs if a large sales volume can be generated.
6. The organization's major objective is to obtain a large market share.

Amazon considered these factors and consciously chose a penetration strategy when it introduced its Amazon Fire tablet computer at $199 when competitive models were priced at $499. This price catapulted Amazon's market share.[15]

Between these two extremes is an *intermediate pricing strategy*. As might be expected, this type of strategy is the most prevalent in practice. The other two types of introductory pricing strategies are, so to speak, more flamboyant; given the vagaries of the marketplace, however, intermediate pricing is more likely to be used in the vast majority of initial pricing decisions.

Pricing and Competitive Interaction

No discussion of pricing strategy and management is complete without mention of competitive interaction.[16] Because price is the one element of the marketing mix that can be changed quickly and easily, competitive interaction is common. Competitive interaction in a pricing context refers to the sequential action and reaction of rival companies in setting and changing prices for their offering(s) and assessing likely outcomes, such as sales, unit volume, and profit for each company and an entire market. Competitive interaction is like playing chess. Those players who make moves one at a time, seeking to minimize immediate losses or to exploit immediate opportunities, invariably are beaten by those who can envision the game a few moves ahead.

Somewhat surprisingly, research and practice suggest that marketing managers infrequently look beyond an initial pricing decision to consider competitor counter-moves, their own subsequent moves, and outcomes. Two remedies are often proposed to overcome this nearsightedness. First, managers are advised to focus less on short-term outcomes and attend more to longer-term consequences of actions. Competitive interactions are rarely confined to one period, that is, an action followed by a reaction. Also, the consequences of actions and reactions are not always immediately observable. Therefore, managers are advised to "look forward and reason backward" by envisioning patterns of future pricing moves, competitor countermoves, and likely outcomes. Second, managers are advised to step into the shoes of rival managers or companies and answer a number of questions:

1. What are competitors' goals and objectives? How are they different from our goals and objectives?

2. What assumptions has the competitor made about itself, our company and offerings, and the marketplace? Are these assumptions different from ours?

3. What strengths does the competitor believe it has and what are its weaknesses? What might the competitor believe our strengths and weaknesses to be?

Failure to answer these questions can lead to misjudgments about the price(s) set or changed by competitors and misguide subsequent pricing moves and countermoves among competitors. Misreading the situation can result in price wars.

A *price war* involves successive price cutting by competitors to increase or maintain their unit sales or market share.[17] Over the past decade, price wars have broken out in a variety of industries: from personal computers to disposable diapers, from soft drinks to airlines, and from grocery retailing to cellular telephone services. Price wars do not just happen. Managers expecting that a lower price will result in a larger market share, higher unit sales, and greater profit for their offering(s) often initiate them. This may indeed occur. However, if competitors match the lower price, other things being equal, the expected share, sales, and profit gain are lost. More importantly, the overall price level resulting from the lower price benefits none of the competitors. Marketing managers are advised to consider price cutting only when one or more conditions exist: (1) The company has a cost or technological advantage over its competitors, (2) primary demand for a product class will grow if prices are lowered, and (3) the price cut is confined to specific products or customers (as with airline tickets) and not across-the-board.

Certain industry settings are prone to price wars. Exhibit 8.3 shows that the risk of price wars is higher or lower when an industry exhibits certain

EXHIBIT 8.3 | **Industry Characteristics and the Risk of Price Wars**

Industry Characteristics	Risk Level	
	Higher	*Lower*
Product/Service type	Undifferentiated	Differentiated
Market growth rate	Stable/Decreasing	Increasing
Price visibility to competitors	High	Low
Buyer price sensitivity	High	Low
Overall industry cost trend	Declining	Stable
Industry capacity utilization	Low	High
Number of competitors	Many	Few

characteristics. For example, if a product or service supplied by the industry is undifferentiated, price tends to be an important buying factor. This situation increases the likelihood of price competition and price wars. A stable or declining market growth rate coupled with low-capacity utilization by companies tends to result in corporate unit volume growth objectives, often promoted through price cutting. Clearly visible competitor prices, highly price sensitive buyers, and declining costs in an industry also increase the risk of price wars.

NOTES

1. E. Raymond Corey, *Industrial Marketing: Cases and Concepts*, 4th ed. (Upper Saddle River, NJ: Prentice Hall, 1991): 256.

2. Vannessa O'Connell, "How Campbell Saw a Breakthrough Menu Turn into Leftovers," *Wall Street Journal* (October 6, 1998): A1, A12.

3. "Lessons of Cyber Survivors," *BusinessWeek* (April 22, 2002): 42.

4. For a seminal overview of the price-quality-value relationship, see Valerie A. Zeithaml, "Consumer Perceptions of Price, Quality, and Value," *Journal of Marketing* (July 1988): 2–22. Also see Ronald J. Baker, *Pricing on Purpose: Creating and Capturing Value* (New York: John Wiley & Sons, 2006).

5. "Laundry Soap Marketers See the Value of 'Value'!" *Advertising Age* (September 21, 1992): 3, 56.

6. Jean-Noel Kapferer, *The New Strategic Brand Management*. 5th ed. (London: Kogan Page, 2012); and Stacy Meichtry, "What Your Time Is Really Worth," *Wall Street Journal* (April 7–8, 2007): P1, P4.

7. Jagmohan S. Raju, Raj Sethuraman, and Sanjay Dhar, "National Brand-Store Brand Price Differential and Store Brand Market Share," *Pricing Strategy and Practice*, Vol. 3, No. 2 (1995): 17–24.

8. H. Yang, "Airlines' Futures," *Journal of Revenue and Pricing Management* (December 2007): 309–311.

9. For an extensive discussion on product complements and substitutes and marketing implications, see Allan D. Shocker, Barry Boyus, and Namwoon Kim, "Product Complements and Substitutes in the Real World: The Relevance of Other Products," *Journal of Marketing* (January 2004): 28–40.

10. "Video Games: Everything to Play For," *The Economist* (May 13, 2006):75.

11. Kent B. Monroe, *Pricing: Making Profitable Decisions*, 3rd ed. (Burr Ridge, IL: McGraw-Hill/Irwin, 2003): Chapter 15.

12. This discussion is based on Thomas T. Nagle, John E. Hogan, and Joseph Zale, *The Strategy and Tactics of Pricing*, 5th ed. (Upper Saddle River, NJ: Prentice Hall, 2011): Chapter 3.

13. The conditions favoring skimming versus penetration pricing are described in Monroe, *Pricing: Making Profitable Decisions*, 380–383.

14. "Gillette Fusion Case Study" (New York: Datamonitor, June 6, 2008).

15. Amazon's Kindle Fire to Surpass iPad Rivals in 4Q, Will.com (December 2, 2011).

16. This discussion is based on Kevin P. Coyne and John Horn, "Predicting Your Competitor's Reaction," *Harvard Business Review* (April 2009): 90–97; "How Companies Respond to Competitors: A McKinsey Global Survey," *The McKinsey Quarterly* (May 2008); David B. Montgomery, Marian Chapman Moore, and Joel E. Urbany, "Reasoning About Competitive Reactions: Evidence from Executives," *Marketing Science* (Winter 2005): 138–149; and John Czepiel and Roger A. Kerin, "Competitor Analysis, in Venkatesh Shanker and Gregory Carpenter, eds., *Handbook of Marketing Strategy* (Cheltenham, UK: Edward Elgar Publishers, 2010): Chapter 4.

17. The remaining discussion is based on Michael R. Baye, *Managerial Economics and Business Strategy*, 7th ed. (Burr Ridge, IL: McGraw-Hill, 2010): Chapters 9–10; and Akshay R. Rao, Mark E. Burgen, and Scott Davis, "How to Fight a Price War," *Harvard Business Review* (March–April 2000): 107–116.

Case

EMI Group, PLC

CD Pricing in the Recorded Music Industry

On September 3, 2003, Doug Morris, chair and CEO of Universal Music Group (UMG), stunned the music industry with a surprising announcement. As the worldwide sales leader in the recorded music industry, UMG announced its intention to reduce the suggested retail prices in North America on nearly all its CDs to $12.98 beginning in early October. According to Morris:

> We're going to reinvigorate the record business in North America. Our new pricing policy will allow us to take the initiative in making music the best entertainment value and most compelling option for consumers. UMG is responsible for almost 30 percent of album sales in the U.S. so we are uniquely positioned to try this new strategy . . . . We strongly believe that when prices are dramatically reduced on so many titles, we will drive consumers back to stores and significantly bolster music sales.[1]

On September 4, 2003, senior executives at EMI Group, PLC, the world's third largest music company, witnessed a 10 percent drop in the company's stock price. Industry analysts speculated that EMI and other music companies would be forced into a potentially damaging price war in the United States. According to one industry analyst, "Universal already has so much market share in the U.S., and the price cuts mean that they will probably take even more retail shelf space."[2]

---

[1] Ethan Smith, "Universal Slashes CD Prices in Bid to Revive Music Industry," *Wall Street Journal* (September 4, 2003): B1, B8; "Universal Music Group Dramatically Reduces CD Prices," TheWeb-Newsroom@azreporter, September 3, 2003.

[2] Annie Lawson, "EMI Feels the Squeeze Over CD Price Cuts," URL media.guardian.co.uk, (September 5, 2003); "EMI Group PLC: Universal Music's Price Cuts, Merger Talks Hit Share Price," *Wall Street Journal* (September 5, 2003): B4.

This case was prepared by Professor Roger A. Kerin of the Edwin L. Cox School of Business, Southern Methodist University, as a basis for class discussion and is not designed to illustrate effective or ineffective handling of an administrative situation. This case is based on published sources including company annual reports, SEC filings, company and industry news releases, published articles, and information provided by individuals knowledgeable about the industry. Consequently, the interpretation and perspectives presented in the case are not necessarily those of Universal Music Group or EMI Group, PLC or any of their employees. Where appropriate, quotes, statistics, and published information are footnoted for reference purposes. Copyright © 2004 Roger A. Kerin. No part of this case may be reproduced without the written permission of the copyright holder.

Alain Levy, chair and CEO—EMI Recorded Music, declined to say what action, if any, EMI would pursue in response to UMG's announced price cut in North America, and particularly the United States. He and other EMI senior executives thought that UMG's pricing action would have to be examined carefully given the size of the North American recorded music market and EMI's competitive position in the United States. North America is the world's largest market for recorded music and the source for almost one-third of EMI's total revenue and about 27 percent of the company's operating profit in fiscal 2003 (year-end March 31, 2003).[3]

 # THE RECORDED MUSIC INDUSTRY

The recorded music industry consists of companies engaged in releasing, promoting, and distributing musical recordings. These companies manufacture or arrange for the manufacture of CDs, audio cassettes, vinyl records, music videos, and audio and video DVDs and promote and distribute these products to retailers or directly to the public. Companies in this industry produce master recordings themselves, or obtain reproduction and distribution rights to master recordings produced by other record companies. The industry employs singers, musicians, sound engineers, music promoters, CD manufacturing and warehouse workers, record store management and clerks, and music company administrative staff, including marketing, public relations, and sales personnel.

Industry Size and Developments

The worldwide recorded music industry posted sales of $32 billion in 2002.[4] This figure represented a 7 percent decline in dollar sales and an 8 percent decrease in unit volume from 2001. Compared to 2001, sales of CD albums fell globally by 6 percent, and there were continued declines in sales of CD singles (down 16 percent) and cassettes (down 36 percent). Sales of music videos and DVDs grew 9 percent in 2002.

The United States is the largest market for recorded music, followed by Western Europe. In 2002, recorded music dollar sales in the United States were $12.6 billion, or 39.4 percent of worldwide sales. However, recorded music dollar sales and unit volume in the United States has been declining since 2000. Exhibit 1 shows the unit shipment trend of CD albums in the United States for the period 1993 through 2002 and estimated unit sales for 2003. Unit volume peaked at 942.5 million units in 2000. Estimated volume for 2003 was 729 million units.

Western Europe (including the United Kingdom) accounts for about 36 percent of industry sales and unit volume and has registered only modest growth in the past two years. Recorded music sales in Asia have declined 10 percent in the past year. Sales in Latin America also have declined. Mexico—the largest Latin American market for recorded music—experienced two consecutive years of declining sales, with sales down 19 percent in 2002.

Mass downloading from unauthorized file sharing on the Internet, the proliferation of CD burning, competition from other entertainment formats (such as

---

[3] EMI Group, PLC, *2003 Annual Report*, p. 66.

[4] This discussion is based on "Global Sales of Recorded Music Down 7% in 2002," International Federation of Phonographic Industry press release, April 9, 2003; "2002 Yearend Statistics," Recording Industry Association of America press release, February 28, 2003.

EXHIBIT 1 **Unit Sales Trend for CD Albums in the United States: 1993–2003 est.**

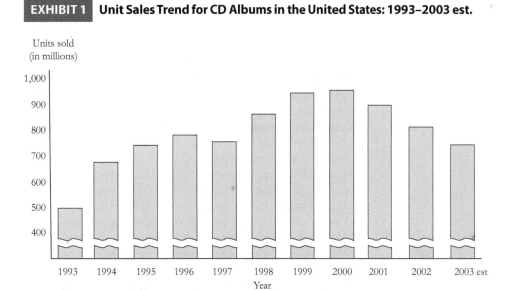

Units sold
(in millions)

Source: 1993–2002 data are provided by Recording Industry Association of America's 2002 Yearend Statistics. Used with permission. The 2003 estimate is based on "RIAA Releases 2003 Mid-Year Shipments," RIAA press release, August 29, 2003.

DVD films and new video game consoles), and poor economic conditions worldwide have all contributed to the recent downward sales trend in the recorded music industry. Industry analysts estimate that unauthorized file sharing alone has accounted for $700 million in lost sales to the industry in 2002. CD burning is also widespread. In Japan, an estimated 236 million CDs were burned in 2002, while legitimate CD sales were 229 million units. As a consequence, major music companies have shut down CD manufacturing facilities and laid off thousands of employees due to the downturn in worldwide industry sales. Still, major music companies had considerable unused manufacturing capacity and high operating leverage. Industry forecasters predict that CD album unit sales in the United States and globally will drop almost 30 percent from their 2000 peak by 2007 if the present pace of unauthorized downloading continued.[5]

Music industry executives acknowledge that CD downloading and burning represents a popular trend that will grow with the use of broadband Internet connections. Music companies now authorize online stores to sell digital songs. These authorized stores include iTunes Music Store owned by Apple Computer, Rhapsody, MP3.com, Buymusic.com, and Musicnet.com. The cost per individual song ranges from $0.79 to $0.99. However, file sharing Web sites such as KaZaA, Grokster, and Morpheus are not authorized by music companies to download songs.

The Recording Industry Association of America (RIAA), which represents music companies, has initiated numerous programs designed to educate consumers and government officials in the United States and European Union on the legal and economic implications of unauthorized CD downloading and CD burning. In early September 2003, RIAA filed 261 separate lawsuits in the United States against individuals engaged in unauthorized file sharing. Industry analysts expected that litigation would have a short-run dampening effect on unauthorized CD downloading and burning. However, litigation was viewed as having a minimal long-run effect on these practices.

---

[5] "Study: CDs May Soon Go the Way of Vinyl," CNN.com, September 8, 2003.

Competition in the Recorded Music Industry

The recorded music industry is very competitive. A music company's competitive position depends on its ability to attract, develop, and promote recording artists, the public acceptance of those artists, and the number and popularity of a company's recordings released in a particular period. A company's revenues and profits are driven by hit recordings, with a relatively small proportion of new releases in a given year commanding the majority of sales. Industry sources estimate that superstar artist recordings account for 50 percent of a major music company's unit sales in a typical year.

Advertising, promotion, and publicity for artists and recordings are central elements in a music company's marketing program. Marketing and promotion expenses (including media advertising) represent a sizable percentage of a music company's costs. Public appearances and performances are also important in the marketing of artists and recordings. Music companies arrange for television and radio appearances and provide financing for concert tours.

Five music companies dominate the global recorded music industry and the recorded music market in the United States. They are Universal Music Group, Sony Music Entertainment, EMI Group, Warner Music Group, and BMG Entertainment. These five companies commanded 75.6 percent of the global recorded music market for CDs and audio DVDs in 2002. Exhibit 2 shows the worldwide market shares of the five major music companies for the period 1999 through 2002.

Universal Music Group   Universal Music Group (UMG) is a unit of Vivendi Universal, S.A., based in Paris, France. Vivendi Universal is one of the world's largest media and telecommunications companies in the world with interests in telecommunications, recorded music, film, television, theme parks and resorts, and interactive entertainment and educational software. In early September 2003, Vivendi Universal and General Electric were finalizing negotiations whereby Vivendi's film, television, theme parks, and resorts would be merged into General Electric's NBC entertainment unit.

UMG is the world's largest music company and was not part of the merger negotiations with General Electric. Its major recording labels include Island/Def Jam, Interscope/Geffen/A&M, MCA Records, Mercury Records, Universal Motown Records, Decca, and Mercury Nashville. Representative artists under contract with UMG, directly or through third parties, include Ashanti, Cecilia Bartoli, Mary J. Blige, blink 182, Andrea Bocelli, Bon Jovi, Vanessa Carlton, Jacky Cheung, Sheryl Crow, Dr. Dre, Eminem, Mylène Farmer, 50 Cent, Johnny Hallyday, Enrique Iglesias, India.Arie, Ja Rule, Elton John, Ronan Keating, t.A.T.u, Limp Bizkit,

---

| **EXHIBIT 2** | **Worldwide Market Shares of the Top Five Music Companies: 1999–2002** | | | |

| | *Year* | | | |
Company	*1999*	*2000*	*2001*	*2002*
Universal Music Group	21.7%	22.9%	23.5%	25.9%
Sony Music Entertainment	17.0	14.4	14.7	14.1
EMI Group, PLC	11.8	13.5	13.4	12.6
Warner Music Group	11.4	12.0	11.9	11.9
BMG Entertainment	10.1	8.4	8.2	11.1
Total	72.0%	71.2%	71.7%	75.6%

Source: Company annual reports.

Nelly, Nickelback, No Doubt, Florent Pagny, Luciano Pavarotti, Puddle of Mudd, André Rieu, Paulina Rubio, Texas, The Who, Shania Twain, and Stevie Wonder.

In addition to recently released recordings, UMG owns one of the largest catalogs of recorded music in the world which it markets, licenses, and sells. The catalog includes artists such as ABBA, Louis Armstrong, James Brown, Eric Clapton, John Coltrane, Ella Fitzgerald, Jimi Hendrix, Billie Holiday, Bob Marley, The Police, Rod Stewart, and the Motown catalog, which includes The Four Tops, Marvin Gaye, The Supremes, and The Jackson Five. Through Universal Music Publishing Group, UMG is one of the leading global music publishing companies with over one million owned or administered titles including some of the world's greatest songs, such as "Strangers in the Night;" "Respect;" "I Want to Hold Your Hand;" "Candle in the Wind;" and "I Will Survive". Among the significant artists and songwriters represented are U2, Prince, Chuck Berry, The Beach Boys, Leonard Bernstein, Anastacia, Björk, and Emilio and Gloria Estefan.

UMG markets its recorded music in 71 countries. The company derives 44.2 percent of its revenue from North America and 41.2 percent from Europe. According to the 2002 Vivendi Universal *Annual Report* (year-end December 31, 2002), UMG revenues decreased by 4 percent in 2002 and operating income was 556 million euros, down 22.7 percent from 2001. UMG recorded a loss of 42 million euros in the first six months of 2003 (1 euro = US$1.15).

Sony Music Entertainment   Sony Music Entertainment is a unit of Sony Corporation, the world's leading consumer electronics company. Sony Music Entertainment itself has three divisions: Sony Music (U.S. music operations), Sony Music International (music operations outside the United States and Japan), and Sony Classical. The company markets its recorded music in 60 countries.

Sony Music Entertainment is the world's second largest music company. Its major recording labels include Columbia, Epic, Sony Classical, Legacy Records, Sony Nashville, and Sony Music Soundtrax. Artists who record for Sony Music Entertainment include AC/DC, Aerosmith, Marc Anthony, Tony Bennet, Black Sabbath, Miles Davis, Destiny's Child, Dixie Chicks, Celine Dion, Bob Dylan, Beyonce Knowles, Jennifer Lopez, Wynton Marsalis, Ricky Martin, John Mayer, Pearl Jam, Shakira, Will Smith, Bruce Springsteen, and Barbra Streisand.

A joint venture operated by Sony Music Entertainment, Sony Music Entertainment Japan, and Michael Jackson, called Sony/ATV Music Publishing, owns or administers copyrights for music artists, including Hank Williams, Roy Orbison, and The Everly Brothers. In addition, the company has a large catalog of recordings it markets, licenses, and sells. Industry analysts estimate that about one-third of Sony Music Entertainment's sales are derived from North America. According to the 2003 Sony Corporation *Annual Report* (year-end March 31, 2003), the company registered a 5 percent decline in fiscal 2003 music sales with an operating loss of $72 million.

Warner Music Group   Warner Music Group is a unit of AOL Time Warner. AOL Time Warner is the world's leading media and entertainment company whose businesses include interactive services, cable TV systems, filmed entertainment, television networks, music, and publishing.

Warner Music Group is the world's fourth largest music company. Its major recording labels include Warner Brothers, Atlantic, Elektra, and Word. Its artist roster includes Josh Groban, Enya, Kid Rock, Faith Hill, Red Hot Chili Peppers, Linkin Park, Missy Elliott, P.O.D., Michelle Branch, and Nappy Roots. The Warner Music International division of the Warner Music Group operates through various subsidiaries and affiliates and their nonaffiliated licensees in over 70 countries around the world. Warner/Chappell, the music publishing division of the Warner

Music Group, owns or controls the rights to more than one million musical compositions. Its catalog includes works from Madonna, Staind, Barry Gibb, George and Ira Gershwin, and Cole Porter. Warner/Chappell also administers the music of several television and motion picture companies, including Lucasfilm, Ltd. and Hallmark Entertainment. Industry analysts estimate that over half of Warner Music Group's sales are derived from North America.

According to the 2002 AOL Time Warner *Annual Report* (year-end December 31, 2002), Warner Music Group recorded a 4 percent increase in sales in 2002 and posted an operating loss of $1.3 billion.[6] Warner Music Group reported an $8 million loss in the first half of 2003.

BMG Entertainment   BMG Entertainment is a unit of Bertelsmann AG, a German corporation. Bertelsmann is one of the world's largest media firms with interests in book and magazine publishing, recorded music, and broadcasting.

BMG Entertainment is the world's fifth largest music company with operations in 41 countries. Its major recording labels include Ariola, Arista Records, Jive Records, RCA, and Zomba Records. Artists who record for BMG Entertainment include Backstreet Boys, Christina Aguilera, Clint Black, Dave Mathews Band, Foo Fighters, Kenny G, Whitney Houston, Alicia Keys, Sarah McLachlan, Britney Spears, Santana, TLC, and George Winston. In addition, BMG Music Publishing owns the rights to more than 700,000 popular and classical titles by artists such as Elvis Costello, Eurythmics, Aretha Franklin, Puccini, and Verdi.

BMG Entertainment derives 44.1 percent of its revenue from the United States and 37 percent from Europe. According to the 2002 Bertelsmann AG *Annual Report* (year-end December 31, 2002), the company reported a 9 percent drop in recorded music revenue and an operating income of 226 million euros. However, BMG Entertainment posted a loss of 117 million euros in the first half of 2003. In early September 2003, the parent companies of BMG Entertainment and the Warner Music Group engaged in discussions to merge their respective music companies. The discussions ended without an agreement in mid-September 2003.

Economics of Recorded Music: CD Prices and Costs

Profitability in the recorded music industry is determined, in large measure, by the costs of CD manufacturing, distribution and marketing, consumer demand for CDs, competition among music companies, and the prices for alternative forms of recorded music and entertainment. The importance of CDs to the recorded music industry lies in the fact that over 90 percent of industry sales revenue is generated by CD sales.

CD Prices   Between 1983 (when CDs were first introduced) and 1996, the average manufacturer's suggested retail list price (MSRP) of a CD fell by more than 40 percent. However, the average MSRP of a CD album increased by 17.6 percent between 1996 and 2002. Between 2000 (when CD album unit volume peaked in the United States and worldwide) and 2002, the average CD album MSRP increased 4 percent per year; annual unit volume declined by an average of 8 percent per year. Industry analysts speculated that the rising CD price, coupled with cheaper prices for movie DVDs, increased file-sharing, and frequent CD burning, contributed to declining CD unit sales since 2000. They also believed

---

[6] The operating loss was due primarily to a $1.499 billion goodwill and other intangible asset impairment charge in 2002. Without this charge, Warner Music Group would have recorded a $482 million profit as measured by EBITDA (earnings before interest, taxes, depreciation, and amortization).

that recorded music buyers have become more price sensitive in recent years. Music companies argue that even at higher suggested retail list prices, CD albums, which are played often over many years, remain a good value compared with other forms of entertainment, such as movies, sporting events, and concert tickets.[7]

A music company's suggested MSRP for a CD album is typically set at or near one of three price points. Superstar artist recordings are priced at $18.98 and represent one-half of industry unit sales. Other artist recordings are priced at $16.98 or $17.98. The remaining 50 percent of industry unit sales are split between these latter two price points in a typical year (35 percent of unit sales are at $17.98; 15 percent of unit sales are at $16.98). A short-term promotional "developing artist" list price of $12.98 is sometimes used. In addition, music companies provide discounts off the MSRP to retailers that are occasionally passed on to recorded music buyers in the form of lower prices. The typical retailer gross profit margin is 36.7 percent on the MSRP for a CD album. However, mass merchandise stores often sell CD albums below the MSRP and thus at a lower retailer margin.

CD Costs The unit cost of CD manufacturing, distribution, shipping, artist and songwriter royalties, and retailer incentives is reflected in CD album prices. A music company's unit variable cost for CD manufacturing, distribution, and shipping is $1.92. Cooperative advertising allowances and discounts given to retailers, both variable costs, total $0.85 per unit. These variable cost categories and dollar amounts are the same across music companies and the three CD album price points in the industry. Artist and songwriter dollar royalty amounts will vary according to the price at which music companies sell their CD albums to retailers. These royalties are a fixed percentage of the price at which music companies sell CD albums to retailers. This figure averages 18.5 percent. For example, a CD album with a $16.98 MSRP would be sold to a retailer for $10.75 (a 36.7 percent retail gross profit margin); the artist and songwriter royalty per unit would be $1.99 (18.5 percent of $10.75). Sales and marketing expense and music production are typically fixed overhead expenditures and considered part of a music company's selling, general, and administrative cost.

The U.S. Recorded Music Market

The United States is the largest single country market for recorded music. Therefore, music companies pay particular attention to consumer buying trends and their respective competitive positions in the United States.

Profile of Recorded Music Buyers Research conducted on behalf of the Recording Industry Association of America details the profile of recorded music buyers in the United States. Results from this research are shown in Exhibit 3 on page 470.

Rock is, and has been for the past decade, the single most popular musical genre when buyers are asked to classify their music preference. Rap and hip-hop replaced country music as the second most popular musical genre in 2000. Full-length CDs (albums) represent 90.5 percent of all recorded music purchases.

There is no material difference between men and women in the incidence of purchasing recorded music. Slightly over 25 percent of recorded music buyers are 45 years old or older. Another 25 percent are between the ages of 15 and 24. The 15–24 age group represented about 32 percent of recorded music buyers

---

[7] Jennifer Odronez, "CDs on the Discount Rack," wsjclassroomedition.com, September 2, 2003.

EXHIBIT 3 **Profile of Recorded Music Buyers in the United States: 1993–2002**

Music Genre	1993	1994	1995	1996	1997	1998	1999	2000	2001	2002
Rock	30.2%	35.1%	33.5%	32.6%	32.5%	25.7%	25.2%	24.8%	24.4%	24.7%
Rap/Hip-Hop[1]	9.2	7.9	6.7	8.9	10.1	9.7	10.8	12.9	11.4	13.8
R&B/Urban[2]	10.6	9.6	11.3	12.1	11.2	12.8	10.5	9.7	10.6	11.2
Country	18.7	16.3	16.7	14.7	14.4	14.1	10.8	10.7	10.5	10.7
Pop	11.9	10.3	10.1	9.3	9.4	10.0	10.3	11.0	12.1	9.0
Religious[3]	3.2	3.3	3.1	4.3	4.5	6.3	5.1	4.8	6.7	6.7
Jazz	3.1	3.0	3.0	3.3	2.8	1.9	3.0	2.9	3.4	3.2
Classical	3.3	3.7	2.9	3.4	2.8	3.3	3.5	2.7	3.2	3.1
Soundtracks	0.7	1.0	0.9	0.8	1.2	1.7	0.8	0.7	1.4	1.1
Oldies	1.0	0.8	1.0	0.8	0.8	0.7	0.7	0.9	0.8	0.9
New Age	1.0	1.0	0.7	0.7	0.8	0.6	0.5	0.5	1.0	0.5
Children's	0.4	0.4	0.5	0.7	0.9	0.4	0.4	0.6	0.5	0.4
Other[4]	4.6	5.3	7.0	5.2	5.7	7.9	9.1	8.3	7.9	8.1
Product Form										
Full-Length CDs	51.1	58.4	65.0	68.4	70.2	74.8	83.2	89.3	89.2	90.5
Full-Length Cassettes	38.0	32.1	25.1	19.3	18.2	14.8	8.0	4.9	3.4	2.4
Singles (All Types)	9.2	7.4	7.5	9.3	9.3	6.8	5.4	2.5	2.4	1.9
Music Videos/Video DVDs[5]	1.3	0.8	0.9	1.0	0.6	1.0	0.9	0.8	1.1	0.7
DVD Audio[6]	NA	NA	NA	NA	NA	NA	NA	NA	1.1	1.3
Digital Download[6]	NA	NA	NA	NA	NA	NA	NA	NA	0.2	0.5
Vinyl LPs	0.3	0.8	0.5	0.6	0.7	0.7	0.5	0.5	0.6	0.7
Age										
10–14 Years	8.6	7.9	8.0	7.9	8.9	9.1	8.5	8.9	8.5	8.9
15–19 Years	16.7	16.8	17.1	17.2	16.8	15.8	12.6	12.9	13.0	13.3
20–24 Years	15.1	15.4	15.3	15.0	13.8	12.2	12.6	12.5	12.2	11.5
25–29 Years	13.2	12.6	12.3	12.5	11.7	11.4	10.5	10.6	10.9	9.4
30–34 Years	11.9	11.8	12.1	11.4	11.0	11.4	10.1	9.8	10.3	10.8
35–39 Years	11.1	11.5	10.8	11.1	11.6	12.6	10.4	10.6	10.2	9.8
40–44 Years	8.5	7.9	7.5	9.1	8.8	8.3	9.3	9.6	10.3	9.9
45+ Years	14.1	15.4	16.1	15.1	16.5	18.1	24.7	23.8	23.7	25.5
Purchase Source										
Record Store	56.2	53.3	52.0	49.9	51.8	50.8	44.5	42.4	42.5	36.8
Other Store	26.1	26.7	28.2	31.5	31.9	34.4	38.3	40.8	42.4	50.7
Tape/Record Club	12.9	15.1	14.3	14.3	11.6	9.0	7.9	7.6	6.1	4.9
TV, Newspaper, Magazine Ad or 800 Number	3.8	3.4	4.0	2.9	2.7	2.9	2.5	2.4	3.0	2.5
Internet[7]	NA	NA	NA	NA	0.3	1.1	2.4	3.2	2.9	3.4
Gender										
Female	49.3	47.3	47.0	49.1	51.4	51.3	49.7	49.4	51.2	50.6
Male	50.7	52.7	53.0	50.9	48.6	48.7	50.3	50.6	48.8	49.4

[1] "Rap": Includes rap (10.5%) and hip-hop (3.3%).

[2] "R&B": Includes R&B, blues, dance, disco, funk, fusion, Motown, reggae, soul.

[3] "Religious": Includes Christian, gospel, inspirational, religious, and spiritual.

[4] "Other": Includes ethnic, standards, big band, swing, Latin, electronic, instrumental, comedy, humor, spoken word, exercise, language, folk, and holiday music.

[5] 2001 is the first year that music video DVD was recorded separately.

[6] 2001 is the first year that data was collected on DVD audio and digital download purchases.

[7] "Internet": Does not include record club purchases made over the Internet.

Source: Recording Industry Association of America. Used with permission. Columns may not total 100%.

from 1993 to 1996. However, this age group has been identified as the most active downloaders and CD burners in the United States today. According to Edison Media Research, 56 percent of 12- to 17-year-olds and 44 percent of 18- to 24-year-olds are downloading music files off the Internet. Half of all Americans between the ages of 12 and 24 are burning their own music CDs. Nearly 3 out of 4 teens and 60 percent of 18- to 24-year-olds do not believe there is anything morally wrong about downloading music without paying for it even though this practice is illegal. Four in 10 teens and one-fourth of 18- to 24-year-olds believe paying for music is a "thing of the past."[8]

More than 87 percent of recorded music buyers purchase their music at retail stores. Major chain record stores (e.g., Tower Records, Wherehouse Entertainment) have lost their status as the primary buyer source for recorded music. In 2002, "other" stores (notably mass merchants; e.g., Best Buy, Kmart, Target, and Walmart) accounted for 50.7 percent of recorded music purchases. These stores often treat recorded music as a "loss leader" featuring lower than manufacturers' suggested retail list prices to increase store traffic. For example, retail analysts estimate that CDs account for between 5 and 20 percent of Best Buy's sales. However, CDs draw as many as 50 percent of the store's customers.[9] Related research indicates that recorded music buyers perceive greater value for the money spent at mass merchandise stores than chain record stores and are attuned to price differentials across retailers.[10]

Competitors   The same five music companies that dominate the global recorded music industry also command a dominant share of recorded music sales in the United States. These five companies account for slightly more than 85 percent of U.S. recorded music sales. Music company market shares in the United States as of August 2003, are shown below:[11]

Music Company	*U.S. Market Share*
Universal Music Group	29.4%
Warner Music Group	16.6
BMG Entertainment	16.3
Sony Music Entertainment	13.0
EMI Group, PLC	9.8
Others	14.9
	100.0%

EMI GROUP, PLC

EMI Group, PLC is the world's third largest music company. It is the world's largest independent music company, not being a unit, subsidiary, or division of a larger corporation. EMI's headquarters are located in London, England.

---

[8] "Study Links Burning and Downloading to Falling Music Sales," writenews.com, June 20, 2003.

[9] Ethan Smith, "Universal's CD Price Cuts Will Squeeze Music Retailers," *Wall Street Journal* (September 18, 2003):B1, B4.

[10] "Cracking the Value Code: An Early View," NARM Research Briefs, National Association of Recording Merchandisers, June 2002.

[11] Market share data are reported in Ethan Smith, "Universal Slashes CD Prices in Bid to Revive Music Industry," *Wall Street Journal* (September 4, 2003):B1, B8.

Company Background

Electric & Musical Industries (EMI) was established in 1931. In 1955, the company bought Los Angeles–based Capitol Records, which featured artists such as Frank Sinatra and Nat "King" Cole. In 1962, The Beatles signed their first contract with Parlophone, an EMI record label, and their hit single, "Love Me Do," was released. In 1979, EMI merged with Thorn Electrical Industries, a large British appliance and electronics company. The company was renamed Thorn EMI. Thorn EMI acquired a 50 percent interest in Chrysalis Records in 1989. The following year the company purchased Filmtrax music publishing. In 1992, the company bought the Virgin Music Group from Richard Branson. This purchase boosted the company's share of the U.S. recorded music market and made it one of the world's major music companies.

In 1996, Thorn EMI split into separate companies and EMI Group, PLC was formed. The purchase of half interest in Berry Gordy's Jobete companies (subsequently increased to 80 percent) and its 15,000-song Motown catalog soon followed. In the late 1990's, EMI continued to purchase additional record labels. In 2000, merger talks with Time Warner's Warner Music Group were conducted, but stopped with the merger of AOL and Time Warner. EMI subsequently engaged in merger talks with Bertelsmann AG and BMG Entertainment in 2001. However, negotiations ended due to pressure from European Union regulators.

On September 22, 2003, EMI reported that it began nonexclusive discussions with AOL Time Warner with regard to a possible transaction involving the recorded music division of the Warner Music Group. EMI's press release indicated the discussions were preliminary. Any potential transaction would be subject to shareholder and regulatory approval.[12]

EMI's Music Business

EMI's music business is comprised of two main groups: (1) EMI Recorded Music and (2) EMI Music Publishing. EMI Recorded Music accounted for 81.6 percent of EMI Group PLC's sales and 59.3 percent of the company's operating profit in fiscal 2003 (year-end March 31, 2003).

EMI Recorded Music   EMI has over 100 recording labels featuring some of the greatest rock and pop artists in recorded music history. Its major recording labels include Capitol Records and Capitol Records Nashville, Chrysalis, EMI Classics, Java Records, Mosaic Records, Mute, Parlophone, and Virgin Records America, Nashville, and UK. Its artists, with major albums in 2002 and 2003, include David Bowie, The Beatles, Blue, Coldplay, Utada Hikaru, Norah Jones, Atomic Kitten, Paul McCartney, Kylie Minogue, Massive Attack, Queen, Rolling Stones, Snoop Dogg, and Robbie Williams. Other artists on its roster include Garth Brooks, Ice Cube, Janet Jackson, Pink Floyd, Radiohead, and Smashing Pumpkins. Norah Jones, and her debut album *Come Away with Me*, was the recipient of eight Grammy Awards in February 2003. Over 13 million copies of this album have been sold worldwide.

Looking forward toward the 2004 fiscal year (beginning April 1, 2003), Alain Levy, chair and CEO—EMI Recorded Music, said:

Looking ahead to the current financial year, the markets are likely to remain challenging. However, we are confident of being able to face the issues, both in

---

[12] "EMI Group PLC Entering into Non-exclusive Discussions with AOL Time Warner, Inc.," EMI Group PLC, September 22, 2003.

terms of supplying high-quality music, for which there is growing demand, and in maximizing the revenue EMI Recorded Music generates from this music. On this basis, we expect to improve market share.[13]

EMI Music Publishing   EMI Music Publishing owns the rights to more than one million musical compositions, which it markets, licenses, and sells. For example, the company has licensed songs to Philips Electronics (for a television commercial featuring The Beatles' "Getting Better") and Sony (for a PlayStation game featuring "The James Bond Theme"). Royalties derived from EMI-owned compositions for the sale of music in the CD format comprised 53 percent of EMI Music Publishing revenue in fiscal 2003. Performance income, derived from the public performance of songs in EMI's catalog, accounted for 25 percent of EMI Music Publishing revenue. Songs from EMI Music Publishing's catalogs are also included in a variety of musicals. Current shows include *We Will Rock You*, based on the Queen catalog; *Mamma Mia*, using the songs of ABBA; and *Our House*, featuring the songs of Madness. Representative artists and songwriters in EMI Music Publishing's catalogs include Nirvana, Pink, Cliff Magness, Sean Paul, Queen, Sting, Norah Jones, Alan Jackson, and White Stripes.

EMI Operating Performance

Market Performance   EMI Group, PLC markets its music worldwide in nearly 50 countries. North America accounted for 32.4 percent of company sales and 26.9 percent of the company's operating profit in fiscal 2003. Continental Europe produced 30.4 percent of company sales and 34.9 percent of operating profit. The United Kingdom and Ireland represented 15.2 percent of company sales and 27.2 percent of operating profit. About 22 percent of EMI's sales and 11 percent of its operating profit came from other regions.

EMI's highest market share was in the United Kingdom and Ireland where the company had a 20.5 percent share, followed by Australasia (17 percent share) and Continental Europe (15.2 percent share). Except for Japan and Asia, EMI's market share declined in each of its regional markets during fiscal 2003. The company's worldwide market share dipped from 13.4 percent in fiscal 2002 to 12.6 percent in fiscal 2003. Exhibit 4 on page 474 shows EMI's market shares by region for 2002 and 2003.

Financial Performance   EMI Group, PLC recorded worldwide sales of £2,175.4 million in fiscal 2003 (one British pound £ = approximately US $1.50). Fiscal 2003 sales were 11.1 percent below fiscal 2002 sales, due mostly to a drop in recorded music sales. Operating profit for the company increased 33.1 percent between 2002 and 2003 (see Exhibit 5 on page 475).

The sales decline in recorded music reflected the worldwide slump in CD unit sales volume. The improvement in operating profit was due to a comprehensive reorganization of the EMI Recorded Music division, including a 1,900 employee reduction and ongoing efforts to reduce overhead costs and improve operating efficiency. This effort yielded positive results, particularly in the North American market for recorded music. Even though EMI's North American sales decreased 1.5 percent in fiscal 2003, operating income jumped from a loss of £2.1 million in fiscal 2002 to a £68.3 million profit in fiscal 2003. A profitable North American business in fiscal 2003 followed five consecutive years of losses for EMI in this market.

---

[13] EMI Group, PLC, *2003 Annual Report*, p. 14.

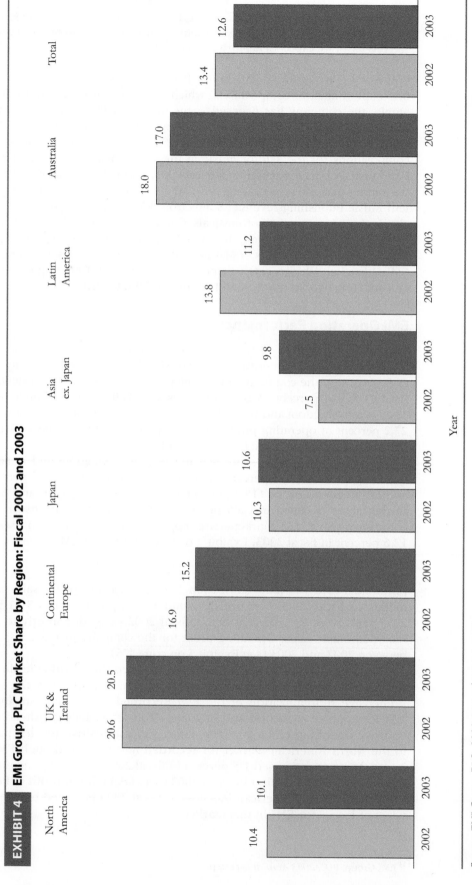

EXHIBIT 4 EMI Group, PLC Market Share by Region: Fiscal 2002 and 2003

Source: EMI Group, PLC, *2003 Annual Report*, p. 12

474

| EXHIBIT 5 | EMI Group, PLC Sales and Operating Profit: Fiscal 2002 and Fiscal 2003 (Year-end March 31) | | | | | |

	Turnover (Sales) in Millions			Operating Profit in Millions*		
	2003 £m	2002 £m	Change %	2003 £m	2002 £m	Change %
Recorded music	1,774.2	2,029.4	(12.6)	150.5	83.1	81.1
Music publishing	401.2	416.4	(3.7)	103.5	107.8	(4.0)
Group total	2,175.4	2,445.8	(11.1)	254.0	190.9	33.1

* Before exceptional items and amortization of goodwill and music copyrights.

Source: EMI Group, PLC, *2003 Annual Report*, p. 27.

During the first half of the fiscal 2004 operating year (April 1 through September 30, 2003), EMI reported sales of £960.3 million and an operating profit of £79.7 million. Sales were unchanged from the same period the previous year. Operating profit increased 0.9 percent.

UNIVERSAL MUSIC GROUP'S PRICING INITIATIVE

On September 3, 2003, the Universal Music Group (UMG) announced a pricing initiative designed "to reinvigorate the record business in North America." The announcement was followed by a 29-page document detailing for its retailers how the initiative would be implemented. UMG's competitors did not have access to this document. However, published interviews with retailers, UMG officials, and music industry analysts provided a general description of its contents.[14]

Outline of UMG's Pricing Initiative

UMG's pricing initiative included a suggested retail price reduction, retailer display space requirements, and abolishment of retailer cooperative allowances and discounts. Each major element of UMG's initiative is described below.

Price Reduction   The most publicized element of UMG's pricing initiative was the announcement that nearly all of the company's CD albums sold in North America would feature a $12.98 manufacturer's suggested retail price. Doug Morris, UMG's chair and CEO said, "We are making a very bold, strategic move to bring people back to music stores." The CDs affected by the price cut currently carry suggested retail prices of $16.98 to $18.98. Only classical and Latin-music titles and multi-CD boxed sets, which represented a small percentage of unit volume, were excluded from the price cut. According to UMG officials, the new suggested retail price was based on extensive company research indicating that a $12.98 suggested retail price was the "sweet spot" for recorded music buyers.

---

[14] This discussion is based on information from the following sources: Ethan Smith, "Universal Slashes CD Prices in Bid to Revive Music Industry," *Wall Street Journal* (September 4, 2003):B1, B8; Jon Fine, "Universal Move Upends Music Biz," *Advertising Age* (September 8, 2003):3, 91; Ed Christman, "Retail Pays for UMG's Price Cut," *Billboard Magazine* (September 13, 2003):1, 68; "Selling CDs for a Song," *Newsweek* (September 15, 2003):58; Ethan Smith, "Universal's CD Price Cuts Will Squeeze Music Retailers," *Wall Street Journal* (September 18, 2003):B1, B4; and "Sticker Price Scrapped for Universal CDs," BizReport.com, September 24, 2003.

UMG also would reduce its CD prices to retailers. Except for superstar artist titles, UMG would lower the wholesale CD price it charges retailers to $9.09, according to *Billboard Magazine*. UMG's price reduction would allow retailers to price these CDs at $9.99 to consumers and make a $0.90 gross profit on each CD sold. Superstar artist titles would be priced at $10.10 to retailers, but still carry a $12.98 suggested retail price. With the new pricing policy applying only to North America, UMG intended to limit retailers from exporting CDs to other countries by imposing penalties on accounts that engaged in this practice.

Jump Start Sales Plan   UMG's $9.09 and $10.10 prices would be available only to retailers that adopted display space policies outlined in the company's "Jump Start" sales plan. According to industry sources, this plan required retailers to guarantee that UMG titles would be given about 27 percent of a store's display space, or 33 percent of the display space retailers used to promote the major music company's releases. UMG would also retain the right to determine which of its CDs were promoted. If some retailers elected not to guarantee display space under UMG's terms, they did not have to participate in the Jump Start program. For these retailers, CD album prices would be between $0.50 and $0.55 lower than UMG's current prices to retailers. Retailers were expected to notify UMG whether or not they intended to participate in the Jump Start sales program by September 19, 2003.

Soon after UMG announced its Jump Start plan, UMG conceded to retailer concerns about putting the $12.98 manufacturer suggested retail price sticker on CD album packages. The original plan introduced to retailers stated that the $12.98 price would be placed on CD packages by UMG. Retailers opposed this practice for three reasons. First, on principle, retailers objected to having CDs delivered to them with price tags. Second, if retailers put a higher sticker price on a CD that already had a $12.98 MSRP on it, a retailer could suffer from consumer enmity. Third, larger retailers wanted the flexibility to set CD prices below the $12.98 suggested retail price. In a September 17 letter to retailers, UMG changed its position on price stickers, stating, "While delivering a great value to the consumer is the primary goal behind Jump Start, we believe that, at this time, the goal can be reached without the MSRP."[15] Instead, UMG would consider alternative CD package labeling such as "Great Music, Great Price," or "Revolutionary New Price." Following this change, UMG announced that almost all of the company's top 30 retailers in the United States agreed to provisions in the Jump Start plan by September 19, 2003. These retailers included several major chain record stores and most mass merchants.

Advertising Allowances and Discounts   Whether or not retailers participated in UMG's Jump Start program, the company stated that it would eliminate all retailer cooperative advertising allowances and discounts. Cooperative advertising allowances and discounts, as a cost item, average about $0.85 per CD. According to Jim Urie, president of Universal Music & Video Distribution, "Co-op advertising was a misnomer. It was money that went to the retailers, they didn't cooperate in any way." Instead, UMG officials said they intended to triple the company's media advertising expenditure with an emphasis on "artist-driven" advertising. UMG spent $4.7 million for U.S. media advertising in 2002. Sony Music Entertainment spent $8.3 million, Warner Music Group, $242,000, BMG Entertainment, $8.8 million, and EMI, $734,000.[16]

---

[15] "Sticker Price Scrapped for Universal CDs," BizReport.com, September 24, 2003.

[16] "AD $ Summary: Multi-Media Service, January–December 2002." CMR/Taylor Nelson Sofres U.S.

Initial Reaction to UMG's Pricing Initiative

By late September 2003, none of the major music companies had publicly responded to UMG's pricing initiative with a pricing initiative of their own.[17] However, executives at some of these companies did comment, provided they were not identified in press reports. A few executives characterized UMG's action as "too radical." They predicted it would require an impossibly large increase in sales volume to offset the squeeze on already declining music company profit margins. UMG's chief operating officer, Zach Horowitz, responded, saying, "We need an increase in sales to make it [the price reduction] permanent." Other music company executives believed UMG's pricing was less aggressive than it initially appeared. A senior financial executive at a large competing music company said, "Since UMG plans to keep a $10.10 price point for about a dozen superstar titles a year and those albums account for 50 percent of UMG's sales, the company isn't taking as big a hit as the price reduction suggests. We are seriously evaluating their initiative." Some music company executives expressed concern that the lower prices would also lower artist royalties. However, a talent agency executive noted, "It's going to lessen money going to artists and into the production company pockets. But it's worth it if we can sell a lot of records."

Mass merchant retailers generally welcomed UMG's retail pricing initiative. Many were already pricing superstar artist CDs at $9.99 to consumers. Music specialty store merchants were more guarded in their reaction. They noted that the suggested retail price would reduce their CD gross profit and store net profit margin. They also voiced concern about the elimination of cooperative advertising allowances and discounts. Many specialty store merchants had relied on cooperative advertising allowances to remain profitable instead of buying advertising. Also, music company discounts were not always passed on to consumers in the form of lower retail prices for the same reason. According to an industry analyst, "The elimination of [these allowances and discounts], if it turns into an industry-wide trend, would turn barely profitable [music specialty] stores into money losers and could bury those already in trouble." In fact, some large music store chains such as Musicland, Tower Records, and Wherehouse Entertainment were already experiencing serious financial difficulties.

Some industry analysts speculated that UMG's actions could be construed as being "a grab for share in a declining market" as much as an effort "to reinvigorate the record business in North America." Industry analysts also speculated on what the implications might be for other regions in the world if UMG's price reduction initiative in the United States was successful. Price reductions in Continental Europe and the United Kingdom could follow given UMG's market share prominence in these markets. UMG had a leading European market share of 27.3 percent in 2002 according to the Vivendi Universal 2002 *Annual Report*.

 ## FORMULATING EMI'S RESPONSE TO UMG'S INITIATIVES

EMI officials needed to assess the likely impact of UMG's actions on the recorded music industry in general and how EMI's response would influence its own competitive position in the United States.[18] Numerous issues had to be considered.

---

[17] The following text is based on material contained in Steve Knopper, "Artists Question Cheaper CDs," RollingStone.com, September 29, 2003, and Ethan Smith, "Universal Slashes CD Prices in Bid to Revive Music Industry," *Wall Street Journal* (September 4, 2003):B1, B8.

[18] This discussion is based on "Universal Slashing CD Prices," Hoover's.com, September 4, 2003; and Annie Lawson, "EMI Feels the Squeeze over CD Price Cuts," media.guardian.co.uk, September 5, 2003.

Doug Morris, UMG's chair and CEO, said he was hopeful that other major music companies would drop their suggested retail price as well. Industry analysts believed that all major music companies were giving this option serious consideration. At issue was the question of what EMI and other music companies would gain or lose by dropping or not dropping their suggested retail price for CDs and the price charged to retailers. UMG's retailer display requirements and decision to eliminate cooperative advertising allowances and retailer discounts warranted consideration. UMG also announced it would triple its media advertising in the United States. What was to be gained or lost by EMI and other music companies by matching these UMG initiatives in addition to the price cut? Ultimately, EMI's senior executives would need to determine the sales and profit impact and competitive consequences of whatever response they decided on.

Case

Southwest Airlines

In late January 1995, Dave Ridley, vice president—marketing and sales at South-west Airlines, was preparing to join Joyce Rogge, vice president—advertising and promotion, Keith Taylor, vice president—revenue management, and Pete McGlade, vice president—schedule planning, for their weekly "Tuesday meeting." The purpose of this regularly scheduled meeting was to exchange ideas, keep one another informed about external and internal developments pertaining to their areas of responsibility, and coordinate pricing and marketing activities. This informal gathering promoted communication among functional areas and fostered the team spirit that is an integral part of the Southwest corporate culture.

A recurrent "Tuesday meeting" topic during the past six months had been the changing competitive landscape for Southwest evident in the "Continental Lite" and "Shuttle By United" initiatives undertaken by Continental Airlines and United Airlines, respectively. Both initiatives represented targeted efforts by major carriers to match Southwest's price *and* service offering—a strategy that no major carrier had successfully implemented in the past. In early January 1995, Continental's effort was being scaled back due to operational difficulties and resulting financial losses.[1] However, United's initiative remained in effect. Launched on October 1, 1994, "Shuttle By United" was serving 14 routes in California and adjacent states by mid-January 1995, nine of which were in direct competition with Southwest. When "Shuttle By United" was announced, United's CEO predicted: "We're going to match them (Southwest) on price and exceed them on service."[2] In response to United's initiative, Southwest's chair Herb Kelleher said, the "United Shuttle is like an intercontinental ballistic missile targeted directly at Southwest."

Just as the meeting began, a staff member rushed in to tell the group that United had just made two changes in its "Shuttle By United" service and pricing. First, its service for the Oakland–Ontario, California, market would be discontinued effective April 2, 1995. This market had been among the most hotly contested routes among the nine where United and Southwest competed head-to-head and

[1] Bridget O'Brian, "Continental's CALite Hits Some Turbulence in Battling Southwest," *Wall Street Journal* (January 10, 1995): A1, A5.

[2] Quoted in Jon Proctor, "Everyone Versus Southwest," *AIRWAYS Magazine* (November/December 1994): 6–13.

The cooperation of Southwest Airlines in the preparation of this case is gratefully acknowledged. This case was prepared by Professor Roger A. Kerin, of the Edwin L. Cox School of Business, Southern Methodist University, as a basis for class discussion and is not designed to illustrate effective or ineffective handling of an administrative situation. Certain information is disguised and not useful for research purposes. Copyright © 1996 by Roger A. Kerin. No part of this case may be reproduced without written permission of the copyright holder.

Southwest had lost market share on this route since October 1994. Second, the one-way walk-up first class and coach fare on all 14 "Shuttle By United" routes had just been increased by $10. "Shuttle By United" had previously matched Southwest's fare on the nine competitive routes and, as of mid-January 1995, had been increasing the number of flights on these routes and the five routes where they did not compete.

Changes in United's pricing and service for its shuttle operation caught Southwest executives by surprise. The original agenda for the "Tuesday meeting" was immediately set aside. Attention focused on (1) what to make of these unexpected developments and (2) how Southwest might respond, if at all, to the new "Shuttle By United" initiatives.

THE U.S. PASSENGER AIRLINE INDUSTRY

The U.S. Department of Transportation classified U.S. passenger airlines into three categories on the basis of annual revenue.[3] A "major carrier" was an airline with more than $1 billion in annual revenue. A "national carrier" had annual revenues between $100 million and $1 billion, and a "regional and commuter airline" had annual revenues less than $100 million. Major carriers accounted for more than 95 percent of domestic passengers carried in 1994. Five carriers—American Airlines, Continental Airlines, Delta Airlines, Northwest Airlines, and United Airlines—accounted for over 80 percent of all major carrier domestic passenger traffic. Exhibit 1 shows major air carrier estimated market shares for 1994 in the United States.

Industry Background

The status of the U.S. passenger airline industry in early 1995 could be traced to 1978. Prior to 1978, and for 40 years, the U.S. airline industry was regulated by the federal government through the Civil Aeronautics Board (CAB). The CAB regulated airline fares, routes, and company mergers, and CAB approval was required before any changes in fares or route systems could be made. In this

---

EXHIBIT 1 **Estimated Market Shares for Major U.S. Carriers in 1994 Based on Revenue Passenger Miles Flown**

Carrier	Market Share (%)	Carrier	Market Share (%)
1. United Airlines	22.1	6. USAir	7.8
2. American Airlines	20.2	7. Trans World Airlines	5.1
3. Delta Airlines	17.6	8. Southwest Airlines	4.4
4. Northwest Airlines	11.8	9. America West Airlines	2.5
5. Continental Airlines	8.5		

Source: Southwest Airlines company records. Figures rounded.

---

[3] This section is based on information provided in *FAA Aviation Forecasts* (Washington, D.C.: U.S. Department of Transportation, March 1995): *Standard & Poor's Industry Surveys* (New York: Standard & Poor's, January 1995); *U.S. Industrial Outlook* 1995 (Washington, D.C.: U.S. Department of Commerce, January 1995); Timothy K. Smith, "Why Air Travel Doesn't Work," *Fortune* (April 3, 1995):42–56; and Jon Proctor, "Everyone Versus Southwest," *AIRWAYS Magazine* (November/December 1994):6–13.

capacity, the CAB assured that individual airlines were awarded highly profitable and semi-exclusive routes necessary to subsidize less profitable routes, which they were also assigned in the public interest. Price competition was suppressed, airline cost increases were routinely passed along to passengers, and the CAB allowed airlines to earn a reasonable rate of return on their investments. In 1978, the Airline Deregulation Act was passed. This act allowed airlines to set their own fares and enter or exit routes without CAB approvals. Jurisdiction for mergers was first transferred to the U.S. Department of Transportation and subsequently assigned to the U.S. Justice Department in 1988. The CAB was dissolved in 1985.

Deregulation and a Decade of Transition   Public policy makers and industry analysts expected that deregulation would proceed in an orderly manner with multiple existing major carriers serving previously semi-exclusive routes, bringing about healthy price competition. However, the carriers responded to deregulation with unexpected changes in their operations that would have long-term effects on the industry.

Two changes in particular were noteworthy. First, major carriers turned their attention to serving nonstop "long-haul" routes anchored by densely populated metropolitan areas or city-pairs which had been highly profitable in a regulated environment. This meant that longer routes such as New York to Los Angeles and Chicago to Dallas were favored over "short-haul" routes between smaller city pairs such as Baltimore and Newark, New Jersey. As major carriers pruned or reduced service on these short-haul routes, existing regional carriers and new airlines filled the void. In 1978, the United States had 36 domestic carriers; by 1985 the number had grown to 100. Second, major carriers almost uniformly abandoned point-to-point route systems and adopted the hub-and-spoke route system. Point-to-point systems involved nonstop flights between city-pairs and often "shuttle" flights back and forth between city-pairs. The hub-and-spoke system featured "feeder flights" from outlying cities to a central hub city, where passengers would either continue their trip on the same plane or transfer to another plane operated by the same carrier to continue to their final destination. The key to this route system was to schedule numerous feeder flights into the hub airport to coincide with the more profitable long hauls, with each spoke adding passengers to the larger aircraft flying these longer distances. Potential increased revenue and some cost economies from flying more passengers longer distances, however, were offset by increased costs resulting from reduced utilization of aircraft as they waited to collect passengers, the capital investment in hub facilities, and the need for a larger ground staff.

Competition to survive and succeed intensified in the airline industry immediately following deregulation. Newly formed airlines and regional carriers, which had been permitted to serve only regional markets in a regulated environment, expanded both the number and length of their routes. These carriers typically retained the point-to-point route system, which was more economical to operate than hubs. Absent the higher costs associated with the hub-and-spoke system, and with lower debt than older major carriers had assumed during the regulation era, these carriers had an immediate cost advantage. This advantage resulted in lower fares on both short- and long-haul routes. Price competition quickly erupted as all airlines scrambled to fill their seats. Price competition lowered the average fares paid on the formerly profitable long-haul routes serviced by major carriers while their operating costs remained high. The profit squeeze caused major carriers to cut their schedules and further reduce the number of short-haul routes.

Within five years after deregulation, the major carriers found themselves in a price-cost predicament best described by a senior airline executive: "Either we don't match (fares) and we lose customers, or we match and then because our costs are so high, we lose buckets of money."[4] This situation continued through the remainder of the 1980s as a price war of attrition was waged, ultimately resulting in a flurry of acquisitions by major carriers. Noteworthy acquisitions included Ozark Airlines by Trans World Airlines (TWA), Western Airlines by Delta, and Republic Airlines by Northwest in 1986. In 1987, AMR (American Airlines' parent company), acquired Air California and USAir acquired Pacific Southwest Airlines.

Financial Calamity in the Early 1990s Acquisition activity in the mid-1980s led industry analysts to believe the U.S. airline industry would soon evolve into an oligopoly with a few carriers capturing a disproportionate share of domestic traffic. By the late 1980s, eight airlines controlled 91 percent of U.S. traffic, but their financial condition was fragile due to a decade of marginal profitability.

Carrier bankruptcy and collapse marked the early 1990s due to a recession, a doubling of fuel prices during the Gulf War in 1991, and excess capacity in the industry. The U.S. airline industry recorded a cumulative deficit of $12 billion from 1990 through 1993. (See Exhibit 2, which plots U.S. air carrier operating revenues and expenses for fiscal years 1979 to 1994.) Between 1989 and 1992, Pan American Airlines (Pan Am), Continental Airlines, America West Airlines, Midway Airlines (a national carrier), Eastern Airlines, and TWA all filed for protection under Chapter 11 of the U.S. Bankruptcy Code. Eastern, Pan Am, and Midway ceased operations in 1991. Continental and TWA emerged from bankruptcy in 1993 as did America West in late 1994, and the industry as a whole recorded a modest operating profit in the 1994 fiscal year. Exhibit 3 shows 1994 financial and operating statistics for major U.S. carriers.

EXHIBIT 2 **U.S. Air Carrier Operating Revenues and Expenses, 1979–1994**

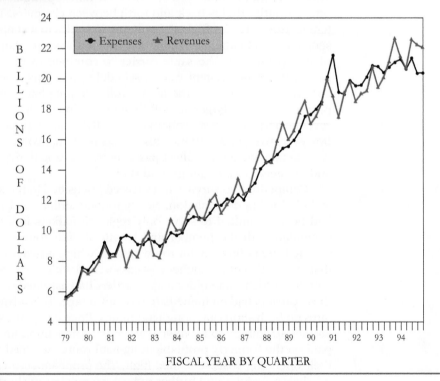

FISCAL YEAR BY QUARTER

Source: U.S. Department of Transportation.

---

[4] William M. Carley, "Rough Flying: Some Major Airlines Are Being Threatened by Low-Cost Carriers," *Wall Street Journal* (October 12, 1983):23.

EXHIBIT 3 1994 Financial and Operating Statistics for Major Carriers in the United States

	American Airlines (AMR)	America West Airlines	Continental Airlines	Delta Airlines	Northwest Airlines	Southwest Airlines	Trans World Airlines	United Airlines (UAL)	USAir
Financial Data ($ millions)									
Operating revenue	$14,895	$1,409	$5,670	$12,062	$8,343	$2,592	$3,408	$13,950	$6,997
Passenger	13,616	1,320	5,036	11,197	7,028	2,498	2,876	12,295	6,358
Freight/other	1,279	89	634	865	1,315	94	532	1,655	639
Operating expenses[a]	$14,309	$1,319	$5,921	$12,151	$7,879	$2,275	$3,883	$13,801	$7,773
Operating income	$586	$90	$(251)	$(89)	$464	$317	$(475)	$149	$(776)
Other income (expense)	$(593)	$2	$(399)	$(325)	$52	$(17)	$39	$22	$91
Net income before tax	$(7)	$92	$(650)	$(414)	$516	$300	$(436)	$171	$(685)
Operating Statistics									
Available seat miles (millions)	157,047[e]	18,060	65,861[f]	130,198	85,016	32,124	39,191	152,193	61,540
Revenue passenger miles (millions)	101,382	12,233	31,588	86,296	57,872	21,611	24,906	108,299	37,941
Load factor (%)	64.6	67.7	63.1	66.3	68.1	67.3	63.5	71.2	61.3
Yield (¢)[b]	13.40	10.79	11.44	12.97	12.14	11.56	11.31	11.35	16.76
Cost per available seat mile (¢)[c]	9.11	7.30	7.86	9.33	9.26	7.08	9.91	9.06	12.63
Labor productivity[d]	1,739	1,695	1,668	1,915	1,968	2,019	1,502	2,125	1,451

[a] Operating expenses include interest expense.

[b] Passenger revenue per revenue passenger mile.

[c] Operating expenses including interest expense per available seat mile.

[d] Thousands of available seat miles per employee.

[e] Includes the American Eagle commuter airline and transportation business only.

[f] Continental Airlines operating statistics are for jet operations only.

Source: Company annual reports. Data and calculations (all rounded) are useful for case analysis but not for research purposes. Revenue, expense, and operating statistics also include international operations.

As existing airlines collapsed, new airlines were formed. The majority of new carriers, such as ValuJet, Reno Air, and Kiwi International Airlines, positioned themselves as "low-fare, low-frill" airlines. Benefiting from a cheap supply of aircraft grounded by major carriers from 1989 to 1993, the availability of furloughed airline personnel, and cost economies of point-to-point route systems, these new entrants had cost structures that were again significantly below most major carriers. For example, Kiwi was started by former Eastern and Pan Am personnel and was largely funded by its employees (pilots paid $50,000 each to get jobs; other employees paid $5,000). These new "low-fare, low-frill" carriers reported combined revenues of about $1.4 billion in 1994 compared with $450 million in 1992. Although accounting for a small percentage of industry revenue, their pricing practices depressed fares on a growing number of routes also served by major carriers. In 1994, 92 percent of airline passengers bought their tickets at a discount, paying on average just 35 percent of the posted full fare.

Industry Economics and Carrier Performance

The financial performance of individual carriers and the U.S. airline industry as a whole could be attributed, in part, to the underlying economics of air travel. The majority of a carrier's costs (e.g., labor, fuel, facilities, planes) were fixed, regardless of the numbers of passengers served. The largest single cost to a carrier was people (salaries, wages, and benefits) followed by fuel. These two cost sources represented almost one-half of an airline's costs and were relatively fixed at a particular level of operating capacity. Fuel costs were uncontrollable and the industry had been periodically buffeted with skyrocketing fuel prices, most recently during the Gulf War in 1991. Fuel cost was expected to increase by 4.3 cents per gallon in late 1995 based on a tax imposed by the Revenue Reconciliation Act of 1993. Industry observers estimated that this tax would cost the U.S. airline industry an additional $500 million annually in fuel expense.

Labor cost, by comparison, was a controllable expense within limits, and more than 100,000 airline workers lost their jobs between 1989 and 1994. Recent efforts by major carriers to reduce labor cost included United Airlines, which completed an employee buyout of 55 percent of the company in exchange for $4.9 billion in labor concessions in the summer of 1994. In the spring of 1994, Delta Airlines announced a three-year plan to reduce operating expenses by $2 billion, which would involve 12,000 to 15,000 jobs being eliminated.

Carrier Operating Performance Whereas the majority of a carrier's costs were fixed at a particular capacity level regardless of the number of passengers carried, a carrier's passenger revenues were linked to the number of passengers carried and the fare paid for a seat at a particular passenger capacity level. A carrier's passenger capacity is measured by the available seat miles (ASMs) it can transport given its airplane fleet, flight scheduling, and route length. An ASM is defined as one seat flown one mile whether the seat is occupied by a passenger or is empty. Carrier productivity is typically tracked by dividing a carrier's total operating cost by available seat miles. Carrier utilization is measured by what is termed a load factor. Load factor is computed by dividing a carrier's revenue passenger miles (RPMs) by its available seat miles. An RPM is defined as one seat flown one mile with a passenger in it and is a measure of a carrier's traffic. Yield is the measure of a carrier's passenger revenue-producing ability and is expressed as an average dollar amount received for flying one passenger one mile. Yield is calculated by dividing passenger revenue by revenue passenger miles.

The following expression shows how yield, load factor, and cost combine to determine the profitability of passenger operations for individual carriers, routes, and the industry:

$$\text{Operating income} = (\text{yield} \times \text{load factor}) - \text{cost, or}$$

$$\frac{\text{Operating income}}{\text{ASM}} = \left(\frac{\text{passenger revenue}}{\text{RPM}} \times \frac{\text{RPM}}{\text{ASM}} \right) - \frac{\text{operating cost}}{\text{ASM}}$$

By setting operating income to zero and monitoring yield and cost, individual carriers frequently computed a break-even load factor for passenger operations which was continually compared with actual load factors. Actual load factors higher than the break-even load factor produced an operating income for passenger operations; actual load factors below a break-even load factor resulted in an operating loss.

Industry Trends   Exhibit 4 charts available seat miles, revenue passenger miles, and load factors for all FAA certified airlines for the 1974 fiscal year through the 1994 fiscal year. While revenue passenger miles and available seat miles for the industry have shown an upward trend, load factor fluctuated due to periodic imbalances between industry capacity and passenger demand. For example, domestic airline capacity (ASMs) increased by only 1.6 percent in fiscal year 1994 while revenue passenger miles increased 6.5 percent, producing a load factor of 64.3 percent. This figure represented the highest industry load factor ever achieved on domestic routes. Domestic passenger yields evidenced a long-term downward trend for 25 years in real (adjusted for inflation) dollars. In terms of real yield (discounting fares for inflation), fares in the years 1969 to 1971 produced an average yield of 21.4 cents in 1994 dollars. By 1994, the average industry yield was 12.73 cents.

EXHIBIT 4   **Available Seat Miles, Revenue Passenger Miles, and Load Factors for All Certified U.S. Airlines, 1974–1994 Fiscal Years**

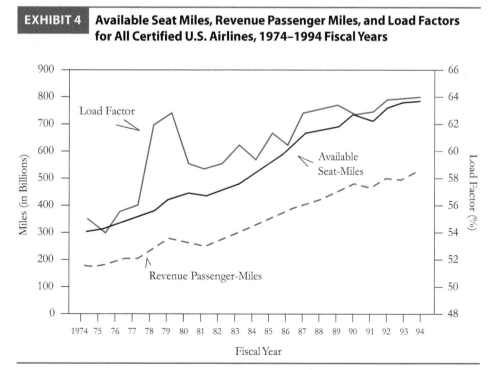

Source: U.S. Department of Transportation.

Cost per available seat mile also exhibited a downward trend since 1978 despite periodic fluctuations in fuel prices. Nevertheless, labor cost reduction and productivity improvements coupled with the gradual addition of more fuel-efficient and lower cost maintenance planes by major carriers had not kept pace with the declining yields in the industry. Efforts by major carriers to reduce labor cost, described earlier, reflected the continuing attention to reducing the cost per available seat mile.

The Airline-Within-an-Airline Concept

Only Southwest Airlines, among the major carriers, appeared able to effectively navigate the economics of air travel and avoid the financial calamity that had befallen the airline industry in the early 1990s. Operating primarily short-haul, point-to-point routes, with minimal amenities, and able to make a fast turn-around of its aircraft between flights, Southwest had much lower operating costs than other major carriers. Lower operating costs were passed on to customers in the form of consistently low fares. From 1990 through 1994, Southwest more than doubled its operating revenues and almost quadrupled its operating income. Its operating practices and financial performance prompted a 1993 U.S. Department of Transportation study to conclude: "The dramatic growth of Southwest has become the principal driving force in changes occurring in the airline industry . . . . As Southwest continues to expand, other airlines will be forced to develop low-cost service in short-haul markets."[5]

With Southwest's operating practices as a blueprint, several major carriers had already explored ways to implement a low-cost airline service in short-haul markets and produce a "clone" of Southwest. An outcome of this effort was the "airline-within-an-airline" concept. This concept involved operating a point-to-point, low-fare, short-haul, route system alongside a major carrier's hub-and-spoke route system.

Continental Lite   Continental was the first major carrier to implement this concept. Having just emerged from bankruptcy with lower operating costs and armed with a preponderance of consumer research showing that 75 percent of customers choose an airline on the basis of flight schedule and price, Continental unveiled what came to be known as "Continental Lite" on October 1, 1993. This service initially focused on Continental routes in the eastern and southeastern United States. By December 1994, Continental had converted about one-half of its 2,000 daily flights into low-fare, short-haul, point-to-point service, but was experiencing operating difficulties. In early January 1995, with operating difficulties resulting in a sizable financial loss, the "Continental Lite" initiative began folding back into Continental's hub-and-spoke system.

Shuttle By United   United, the world's largest airline in 1994, inaugurated its "airline-within-an-airline" on October 1, 1994. Branded "Shuttle By United," this initiative followed the United employee buyout in the summer of 1994 when employee wage cuts and more flexible work rules made possible a lower-cost shuttle operation alongside the United hub-and-spoke route system. "Shuttle By United" was designed to be a high-frequency, low-fare, minimal amenity, short-haul flight operation initially serving destinations in California and adjacent states. If successful, United executives noted that the initiative could be expanded to 20 percent of United's domestic operations, and particularly to areas where the

---

[5] U.S. Department of Transportation press release, May 11, 1993.

airline had a significant presence. One such area was the Midwest, where United operated a large hub-and-spoke system out of Chicago's O'Hare Airport.

Beginning with 8 routes, 6 of which involved United's San Francisco hub, "Shuttle By United" expanded to 14 routes by January 1995. Eight of the 14 routes involved point-to-point routes separate and apart from United's San Francisco hub. Nine of the routes competed directly with Southwest. In early December 1994, United executives reported that the initiative was exceeding expectations and some routes were profitable. "The Shuttle is working well," said its president, A. B. "Sky" Magary.[6]

SOUTHWEST AIRLINES

Southwest Airlines was the eighth largest airline in the United States in 1994 based on the number of revenue passenger miles flown. Southwest recorded net income of $179.3 million on total operating revenue of $2.6 billion in 1994, thus marking 22 consecutive years of profitable operations—a feat unmatched in the U.S. airline industry over the past two decades. According to Southwest's chair, president, CEO, and cofounder, Herb Kelleher, Southwest's success formula could be succinctly described as, "Better quality plus lesser price equals value, plus spiritual attitude of our employees equals unbeatable."

The Southwest Model

Southwest began scheduled service on June 18, 1971, as a short-haul, point-to-point, low-fare, high-frequency airline committed to exceptional customer service. Beginning with three Boeing 737 aircraft serving three Texas cities—Dallas, Houston, and San Antonio—Southwest presently operates 199 Boeing 737 aircraft and provides service to 44 cities primarily in the midwestern, southwestern, and western regions of the United States. Fifty-nine percent of Southwest's capacity, measured in available seat miles flown, was deployed in the western United States, 22 percent in the Southwest (Texas, Oklahoma, Arkansas, and Louisiana), and 19 percent in the Midwest. Exhibit 5 on page 488 shows the Southwest route map in early 1995.

Except for the acquisitions of Muse Air in 1985 and Morris Air in 1993, Southwest's management has steadfastly insisted on growing internally and refining and replicating what came to be known as the "Southwest Model" in the airline industry. This model was a mixture of a relentless attention to customer service and operations, creative marketing, and Southwest's commitment to its people. A healthy dose of fun was added for good measure.

Customer Service   Southwest's attention to customer service was embodied in the attitudes of its people. According to Kelleher:

> What we are looking for, first and foremost, is a sense of humor. Then we are looking for people who have to excel to satisfy themselves and who work well in a collegial environment. We don't care that much about education and expertise, because we can train people to do whatever they have to do. We hire attitudes.[7]

A sense of humor, compassion for passengers and fellow workers, a desire to work, and a positive outlook manifested themselves in customer service at

---

[6] Quoted in Michael J. McCarty, "New Shuttle Incites a War Between Old Rivals," *Wall Street Journal* (December 1, 1994):B1, B5.

[7] Quoted in Kenneth Labich, "Is Herb Kelleher America's Best CEO?" *Fortune* (May 2, 1994):28–35.

EXHIBIT 5   Southwest Airlines Route Map in Early 1995

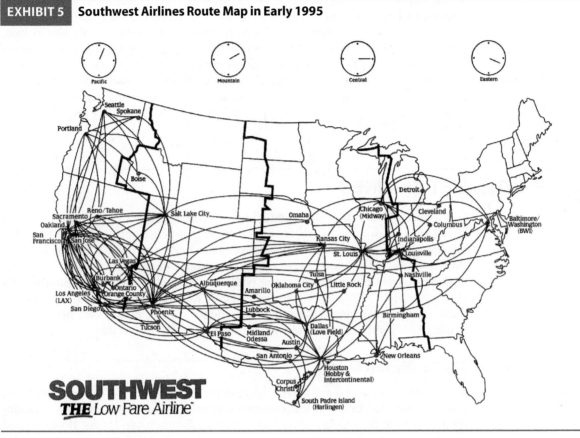

Source: Courtesy of Southwest Airlines.

Southwest. Pilots could be found assisting at a boarding gate; ticket agents could be seen handling baggage. So important was the attention to customer service that Southwest chronicled legendary achievements in an internal publication titled *The BOOK on Service: What Positively Outrageous Service Looks Like at Southwest Airlines.*

The Southwest focus on customer service also produced tangible results. In 1994, Southwest won the annual unofficial "triple crown" of the airline industry for the third consecutive year by ranking first among major carriers in the areas of on-time performance, baggage handling, and overall customer satisfaction (see Exhibit 6). No other airline had ever won the "triple crown" for even a single month.

Operations   Southwest dedicated its efforts to delivering a short-haul, low-fare, point-to-point, high-frequency service to airline passengers. As a short-haul carrier with a point-to-point route system, it focused on local, not through or connecting, traffic that was common among carriers using a hub-and-spoke system. As a result, approximately 80 percent of its passengers flew nonstop. In 1994, the average passenger trip length was 506 miles and the average flight time was slightly over one hour. From its inception, Southwest executives recognized that flight schedules and frequency were important considerations for the short-haul traveler. This meant that Southwest aircraft had to "turn" quickly to maximize time in the air and minimize time on the ground. Turn referred to the elapsed time from the moment a plane arrived at the gate to the moment

EXHIBIT 6 | U.S. Department of Transportation Rankings of Major Air Carriers for 1994 by On-Time Performance, Baggage Handling, and Customer Satisfaction

On-Time Performance		Baggage Handling		Customer Satisfaction	
Southwest	1	Southwest	1	Southwest	1
Northwest	2	America West	2	Delta	2
Alaska	3	American	3	Alaska	3
United	4	Delta	4	Northwest	4
American	5	Alaska	5	American	5
America West	6	United	6	United	6
Delta	7	TWA	7	USAir	7
TWA	8	USAir	8	America West	8
USAir	9	Northwest	9	TWA	9
Continental	10	Continental	10	Continental	10

Source: U.S. Department of Transportation.

when it was "pushed back," indicating the beginning of another flight.[8] More than half of Southwest's planes were turned in 15 minutes or less while the remainder were scheduled to turn in 20 minutes. The U.S. airline industry turn time averaged around 55 minutes. A result of this difference was that Southwest planes made about 10 flights per day, which was more than twice the industry average.

Southwest's operations differed from major carriers in other important ways. First, Southwest generally avoided major airline hubs in large cities. Instead, airports in smaller cities or less congested airports in larger cities were served. Midway Airport in Chicago, Illinois, and Love Field in Dallas, Texas, were examples of less congested airports in larger cities from which Southwest operated. Less congestion meant Southwest flights experienced less aircraft taxi time and less airport circling while awaiting landing permission. The practice of using secondary rather than hub airports also meant that Southwest did not transfer passenger baggage to other major airlines. In fact, Southwest did not coordinate baggage transfers with other airlines even in the few hub airports it served, such as Los Angeles International Airport (LAX).

Second, Southwest stood apart from other major carriers in terms of booking reservations and providing seat assignments. Rather than making reservations through computerized reservations systems, passengers and travel agents alike had to call Southwest. As a result, fewer than one-half of Southwest's seats were booked by travel agents. (Most airlines rely on travel agents to write up to 90 percent of their tickets.) Savings on travel agent commissions to Southwest amounted to about $30 million per year. Also, contrary to other major airlines, Southwest did not offer seat assignments. As Kelleher said, "We still reserve your seat. We just don't tell you whether it's 2C or 38B!" Instead, reusable, numbered boarding passes identified passengers and determined boarding priority. The

---

[8] Numerous activities occurred during a turn's elapsed time. Passengers got on and off the plane and baggage was loaded and unloaded. The cabin and lavatories were tidied and the plane was refueled, inspected, and provisioned with snacks and beverages.

first 30 passengers checked in at the gate board first, then a second group of 30 (31–60) boarded, and so forth.

Third, only beverages and snacks were served on Southwest flights. The principal snack was peanuts, and 64 million bags of peanuts were served in 1994. Cookies were offered on longer flights.

Finally, Southwest flew only Boeing 737 jets in an all-coach configuration since no fare classes (first class, economy, business, etc.) existed. This practice differed from other major carriers, which flew a variety of jet aircraft made by Airbus Industries, Boeing, and McDonnell Douglas, and reduced aircraft maintenance costs. Southwest's fleet was among the youngest of the major airlines at 7.6 years and had 25 new Boeing 737 aircraft scheduled for delivery in 1995. In 1994, less than 1 percent of Southwest flights were canceled or delayed due to mechanical incidents and Southwest was consistently ranked among the world's safest air carriers.

The combined effect of Southwest's operations was apparent in its cost structure. In 1994, Southwest's 7.08-cent cost per available seat mile was the lowest among major U.S. carriers.

Marketing   Creative marketing was used to differentiate Southwest from other airlines since its beginning. As Kelleher put it, "We defined a personality as well as a market niche. [We seek to] amuse, surprise and entertain."

Southwest's marketing orientation was intertwined with its customer and operations orientation. In this regard, service, convenience, and price represented three pillars of Southwest's marketing effort. As with customer service and operations, Southwest's unique twist on marketing set it apart from other airlines. In the domain of pricing, for example, Southwest had always viewed the automobile as its primary competitor, not other airlines. According to Colleen Barrett, Southwest's executive vice president with responsibility for customers: "We've always seen our competition as the car. We've got to offer better, more convenient service at a price that makes it worthwhile to leave your car at home and fly with us instead." In 1994, Southwest's average passenger fare was $58.44. Marketing communications continually conveyed the benefits to customers of flying Southwest. Advertising campaigns over the past 24 years featured Southwest service in "The Love Airline" campaign, convenience in "The Company Plane" campaign, and most recently, low price in "*The* Low Fare Airline" campaign (see Exhibit 7).

Southwest offered a frequent flyer program called "The Company Club," but again with a difference. Consistent with its focus on flight frequency and short-hauls, passengers received a free ticket to any city Southwest served with 8 round-trips completed within 12 months. For 50 round-trips in a 12-month period, Southwest provided a companion pass valid for one year. Having no mileage or other qualifying airlines to track, the costs of "The Company Club" were minimal compared with other frequent flyer programs and rewarded the truly frequent traveler.

Southwest also flew uniquely painted planes that signified places on its route structure. Planes were painted to look like Shamu the Killer Whale to highlight Southwest's relationship with both Sea World of California and Texas. Other planes were painted to look like the Texas state flag and called "The Lone Star Over Texas," while others, such as "Arizona One," featured the Arizona state flag (see Exhibit 8 on page 492).

People Commitment   The bond between Southwest and its workers was generally regarded by the company as the most important element in the Southwest

EXHIBIT 7 **Representative Southwest Airlines Print Advertising Campaign**

WHEN YOU WANT A LOW FARE, LOOK TO THE AIRLINE THAT OTHER AIRLINES LOOK TO.

SOUTHWEST
THE Low Fare Airline

Call your travel agent or 1-800-I-FLY-SWA

Source: Courtesy of Southwest Airlines.

model. Herb Kelleher referred to this bond as "a patina of spirituality." He added:

> I feel that you have to be with your employees through all their difficulties, that you have to be interested in them personally. They may be disappointed in their country. Even their family might not be working out the way they wish it would. But I want them to know that Southwest will always be there for them.[9]

_____

[9] Quoted in Kenneth Labich, "Is Herb Kelleher America's Best CEO?" *Fortune* (May 2, 1994):28–35.

EXHIBIT 8   **Southwest Airlines Aircraft**

Source: Courtesy of Southwest Airlines.

The close relationship among all Southwest employees contributed to Southwest's recent listing as one of the top 10 best companies to work for in a recent study of U.S. firms. The study noted that the biggest plus at Southwest was that "it's a blast to work here"; the biggest minus was that "you may work your tail off."[10]

Southwest's commitment to its people was evident in a variety of forms. The company had little employee turnover compared with other major airlines and was the first U.S. airline to offer an employee profit-sharing plan. Through this

---

[10] Robert Levering and Milton Mosckowitz, *The 100 Best Companies to Work for in America* (New York: Doubleday/Currency, 1993).

plan, employees owned about 10 percent of Southwest stock. Eighty percent of promotions were internal and cross-training in different areas as well as team building were emphasized at Southwest's "People University."

Competitive and Financial Performance

Southwest's attention to customer service and efficient operations, creative marketing, and people commitment produced extraordinary competitive and financial results.

Competitive Performance According to the U.S. Department of Transportation, Southwest carried more passengers than any other airline in the top 100 city-pair markets with the most passengers in the 48 contiguous United States.[11] These 100 markets represented about one-third of all domestic passengers. In its own top 100 city-pair markets, Southwest had an average 65 percent market share compared with about a 40 percent market share for other airlines in their own top 100 city-pair markets. Southwest consistently ranked first or second in market share in more than 90 percent of its top 50 city-pair markets. In Texas, where Southwest began operations in 1971, it ranked first in passenger boardings at 10 of the 11 Texas airports served and had an intra-Texas market share of 70.8 percent in mid-1994. Southwest recorded a market share of 56.4 percent in the intra-California market in mid-1994, compared with a market share of less than 3 percent in 1989.

Financial Performance Southwest's average revenue and income growth rate and return on total assets and stockholders' equity were the highest of any U.S. air carrier during the 1990s. Exhibit 9 on page 494 provides a five-year consolidated financial and operating summary for Southwest Airlines.

Even though Southwest achieved record revenue and income levels in 1994, net income in the fourth quarter 1994 (October 1–December 31, 1994) fell 47 percent compared to the fourth quarter 1993. The last time Southwest reported quarterly earnings that were less than the same quarter a year earlier was in the third quarter of 1991. Fourth quarter 1994 operating revenues were up only three percent compared to the same period in 1993. This result was considerably less than the double-digit gains in operating revenues recorded in each of the preceding three quarters compared to 1993. Southwest's fourth quarter financial report sent the company's stock price reeling to close at a 52-week low of $15.75 in December 1994 in New York Stock Exchange composite trading, down from a record $39.00 in February 1994.

Southwest's fourth quarter 1994 earnings performance reflected the cumulative effect of numerous factors. These included the conversion of recently acquired Morris Air Corporation to Southwest's operations, competitors' persistent use of fare sales, which Southwest often matched, and the airline-within-an-airline initiatives launched by Continental and United. Commenting on the fourth quarter financial and operating performance, Kelleher said:

> While these short-term results will be disappointing to our shareholders, the recent investments made to strengthen Southwest Airlines are vitally important to our long-term success. We are prepared emotionally, spiritually and financially to meet our increased competition head-on with even lower costs and even better customer service.[12]

[11] U.S. Department of Transportation press release, May 11, 1993.

[12] Quoted in Terry Maxon, "Southwest Forecasts Dip in Earnings," *The Dallas Morning News* (December 8, 1994):D1, D3.

EXHIBIT 9   Southwest Airlines Five-Year Financial and Operating Summary (Abridged)

Selected Consolidated Financial Data[a]

(In Thousands Except Per-Share Amounts)	1994	1993	1992	1991	1990
Operating revenues:					
Passenger	$2,497,765	$2,216,342	$1,623,828	$1,267,897	$1,144,421
Freight	54,419	42,897	33,088	26,428	22,196
Charter and other	39,749	37,434	146,063	84,961	70,659
Total operating revenues	2,591,933	2,296,673	1,802,979	1,379,286	1,237,276
Operating expenses	2,275,224	2,004,700	1,609,175	1,306,675	1,150,015
Operating income	316,709	291,973	193,804	72,611	87,261
Other expenses (income), net	17,186	32,336	36,361	18,725	(6,827)[f]
Income before income taxes	299,523	259,637	157,443	53,886	80,434
Provision for income taxes[c]	120,192	105,353	60,058	20,738	29,829
Net income[c]	$179,331	$154,284[d]	$97,385[e]	$33,148	$50,605
Total assets	$2,823,071	$2,576,037	$2,368,856	$1,854,331	$1,480,813
Long-term debt	$583,071	$639,136	$735,754	$617,434	$327,553
Stockholders' equity	$1,238,706	$1,054,019	$879,536	$635,793	$607,294

Consolidated Financial Ratios[a]

Return on average total assets	6.6%	6.2%[b]	4.6%[e]	2.0%	3.5%
Return on average stockholders' equity	15.6%	16.0%[b]	12.9%[e]	5.3%	8.4%
Debt as a percentage of invested capital	32.0%	37.7%	45.5%	49.3%	35.0%

Consolidated Operating Statistics[b]

Revenue passengers carried	42,742,602[g]	36,955,221[g]	27,839,284	22,669,942	19,830,941
RPMs (thousands)	21,611,266	18,827,288	13,787,005	11,296,183	9,958,940
ASMs (thousands)	32,123,974	27,511,000	21,366,642	18,491,003	16,411,115
Load factor	67.3%	68.4%	64.5%	61.1%	60.7%
Average length of passenger haul	506	509	495	498	502
Trips flown	624,476	546,297	438,184	382,752	338,108
Average passenger fare	$58.44	$59.97	$58.33	$55.93	$57.71
Passenger revenue per RPM	11.56¢	11.77¢	11.78¢	11.22¢	11.49¢
Operating revenue per ASM	8.07¢	8.35¢	7.89¢	7.10¢	7.23¢
Operating expenses per ASM	7.08¢	7.25¢[b]	7.03¢	6.76¢	6.73¢
Number of employees at year-end	16,818	15,175	11,397	9,778	8,620
Size of fleet at year-end[i]	199	178	141	124	106

[a]The Selected Consolidated Financial Data and Consolidated Financial Ratios for 1992 through 1989 have been restated to include the financial results of Morris.

[b]Prior to 1993, Morris operated as a charter carrier; therefore, no Morris statistics are included for these years.

[c]Pro forma assuming Morris, an S Corporation prior to 1993, was taxed at statutory rates.

[d]Excludes cumulative effect of accounting changes of $15.3 million ($.10 per share).

[e]Excludes cumulative effect of accounting change of $12.5 million ($.09 per share).

[f]Includes $2.6 million gains on sales of aircraft and $3.1 million from the sale of certain financial assets.

[g]Includes certain estimates for Morris.

[b]Excludes merger expenses of $10.8 million.

[i]Includes leased aircraft.

Source: Southwest Airlines *1994 Annual Report*.

SOUTHWEST VERSUS SHUTTLE BY UNITED

The maiden flight for "Shuttle By United" departed Oakland International Airport for Los Angeles International Airport at 6:25 A.M. on Saturday, October 1, 1994. Later that morning, United's executive vice president of operations, who flew in from United's world headquarters near Chicago to mark the occasion, spoke to the media. He said:

> What we're doing is getting back into the market and getting our passengers back. We used to own Oakland and LA, and then Herb (Kelleher) came in. What we have to do is protect what's ours.[13]

At the time, Dave Ridley believed that the Oakland flight had "symbolic significance" for two reasons. First, until the late 1980s, United was the dominant carrier at the Oakland airport, but left in the early 1990s following head-to-head competition with Southwest. Second, Oakland had become the main base of Southwest's Northern California operation and was the fastest growing of California's 10 major airports in terms of air traffic.

Shuttle by United[14]

Created by a team of United Airlines managers and workers over the course of a year and code-named "U2" internally, "Shuttle By United" was designed to replicate many operational features of Southwest: point-to-point service, low fares, frequent flights, and minimal amenities. Lowering operating cost was a high priority since United's cost for shorter domestic routes (under 750 miles) was 10.5 cents per available seat mile. United's targeted cost per seat mile was 7.5 cents for its shuttle operation.

Like Southwest, "Shuttle By United" featured Boeing 737 jets with a seating capacity of 137 passengers, focused on achieving 20-minute aircraft turns, and offered only beverage and snack (peanuts and pretzels) service. Management and ground crews alike had attended "enculturalization" and motivational classes that emphasized team-work and customer service. Unlike Southwest, "Shuttle By United" provided first-class (12 seats) and coach seating. Rather than boarding passengers in groups of 30 like Southwest, a boarding process—known as WILMA for windows, middle, and aisle seat—was used for seat assignments. Passengers assigned window seats boarded first, followed by middle seat travelers, and then aisle customers. United's "Mileage Plus" frequent flyer program was available to passengers, with an option that matched Southwest's offer of one free ticket for each eight shuttle round trips.

"Shuttle By United" was inaugurated with eight routes. Six of these were converted United routes involving the airline's San Francisco hub. Only three of the original eight routes competed directly with Southwest: San Francisco–San Diego, Oakland–Los Angeles, and Los Angeles–Sacramento. On these three routes, the "Shuttle By United" one-way, walk-up coach fare was identical to Southwest's $69 "California State Fare," which was Southwest's highest fare on

---

[13] Quoted in Catherine A. Chriss, "United Shuttle Takes Wing," *The Dallas Morning News* (October 3, 1994):1D, 4D.

[14] Portions of this discussion are based on Jesus Sanchez, "Shuttle Launch," *Los Angeles Times* (September 29, 1994):D1, D3; Randy Drummer, "The Not-So-Friendly Skies," *Daily Bulletin* (September 30, 1994):C1, C10; "United Brings Guns to Bear," *Airline Business* (November 1994): 10; Michael J. McCarthy, "New Shuttle Incites a War Between Old Rivals," *Wall Street Journal* (December 1, 1994):B1, B5.

all seats and flights within California.[15] One-way walk-up coach fares varied on the five noncompeting routes. Service from San Francisco to Burbank and to Ontario was priced at $104. Fares for the remaining San Francisco routes were $89 to Los Angeles, $99 to Las Vegas, and $139 to Seattle. The "Shuttle By United" first-class fare was typically $20 higher than its coach fare. "Shuttle By United" was advertised heavily using print and electronic media.

"Shuttle By United" soon expanded its route system to include six additional routes. All six routes competed directly with Southwest. Service out of Oakland included Oakland–Burbank, Oakland–Ontario, and Oakland–Seattle. Los Angeles to Phoenix and to Las Vegas and San Diego–Sacramento rounded out the new service. Except for the Oakland–Seattle route, all one-way walk-up coach fares were $69 for Southwest and "Shuttle By United." A one-way walk-up coach fare of $99 was charged on the Oakland–Seattle route by the two airlines. "Shuttle By United" also increased its flight frequency in 12 of 14 city-pair markets, primarily out of its San Francisco hub. Cities served by "Shuttle By United" appear in the map shown in Exhibit 10.

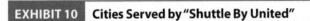

EXHIBIT 10   **Cities Served by "Shuttle By United"**

---

[15] Walk-up fares refer to the fare available at any time, with no restrictions, no penalties, and no advance purchase requirements.

In early December 1994, United reported that the cost per available seat mile of its shuttle operation had not yet achieved its targeted 7.5 cents. In an interview, "Sky" Magary said, "We're vaguely better than halfway there."[16]

Southwest Airlines

Southwest's planning for United's initiative began months before the "Shuttle By United" scheduled October 1 launch. In June 1994, a Southwest spokesperson said the airline would "vigorously fight to maintain our stronghold in California."

Prior to the launch of "Shuttle By United," Southwest committed additional aircraft to the California market to boost flight frequencies on competitive routes. By mid-January 1995, Southwest had deployed 16 percent of its total capacity (in terms of available seat miles flown) to the intra-California market. Thirteen percent of Southwest's total available seat mile capacity overlapped with "Shuttle By United" by late January 1995.

Southwest also boosted its advertising and promotion budget for the intra-California market, with particular emphasis in city-pairs where "Shuttle By United" competed directly with Southwest. Southwest's *The* Low Fare Airline" advertising campaign spearheaded this effort. Southwest's walk-up fare remained at $69 during the fourth quarter of 1994, unchanged from the fourth quarter of 1993. However, Southwest's 21-day advance fares and other discount fares were being heavily promoted. The effect of this pricing was that Southwest's average passenger fare in the markets also served by "Shuttle By United" (excluding Oakland–Seattle) was $44 during the fourth quarter of 1994 and into early January 1995, compared with $45 in the third quarter of 1994. The average 1994 fourth-quarter fare for the Oakland–Seattle route was $51, down from $60 in the third quarter of 1994. Dave Ridley estimated that the average passenger fare for "Shuttle By United" was 5 to 10 percent higher than the average Southwest fare in the nine markets where it competed directly with Southwest, and about $20 higher than the average Southwest fare in the five markets served out of San Francisco where it did not compete directly with Southwest. The difference in average passenger fares between the airlines was due to first-class seating offered by "Shuttle By United" in competitive markets and generally higher fares in noncompetitive markets.

 ## THE TUESDAY MEETING

The original agenda for the "Tuesday meeting" in late January 1995 focused mostly on operational issues. For example, Southwest would begin scheduled service to Omaha, Nebraska, in March 1995, and advertising, sales, promotion, and scheduling matters still required attention. Southwest's "ticketless" travel system, or "electronic ticketing" was also on the agenda. This system, whereby travelers make reservations by telephone, give their credit card number and receive a confirmation number, but receive no ticket in the mail, was scheduled to go nationwide on January 31, 1995, after a successful regional test. Final details were to be discussed.

Dave Ridley also intended to apprise his colleagues of the competitive situation in California. A staff member had prepared a report showing fourth quarter load factors by route for Southwest and estimated load factors for "Shuttle By

---

[16] Michael J. McCarthy, "New Shuttle Incites a War Between Old Rivals," *Wall Street Journal* (December 1, 1994):B1, B5.

EXHIBIT 11 Daily Scheduled City-Pair Round Trips by Southwest Airlines and "Shuttle By United" and Quarterly Load Factor Estimates

Market (City-Pair)	Air Miles	Southwest Airlines Daily Round-Trip Flights		Shuttle By United Daily Round-Trip Flights		1994 4th-Quarter Load Factor		1994 3rd-Quarter Load Factor		1993 4th-Quarter Load Factor	
		October–December 1994	Mid–January 1995	October–December 1994	Mid–January 1995	United	Southwest	United	Southwest	United	Southwest
San Francisco–Los Angeles	338	No Service →		31	40	66%	–	77%	–	68%	–
San Francisco–Burbank	359	No Service →		11	12	60%	–	70%	–	64%	–
San Francisco–Ontario	364	No Service →		11	12	47%	–	63%	–	64%	–
San Francisco–Las Vegas	417	No Service →		9	10	73%	–	85%	–	74%	–
San Francisco–Seattle	678	No Service →		13	16	74%	–	89%	–	77%	–
San Francisco–San Diego	417	12	12	10	12	77%	61%	87%	68%	84%	70%
Oakland–Los Angeles	338	19	25	10	15	62%	59%	–	74%	–	63%
Oakland–Burbank	326	13	16	7	11	40%	63%	–	80%	–	70%
Oakland–Ontario	362	12	14	7	7	32%	57%	–	68%	–	65%
Oakland–Seattle	671	4	7	4	5	52%	66%	–	77%	–	–
Los Angeles–Sacramento	374	5	6	5	6	81%	65%	73%	53%	67%	–
Los Angeles–Phoenix	366	25	23	9	10	48%	61%	–	60%	–	56%
Los Angeles–Las Vegas	241	13	19	10	12	61%	65%	–	73%	–	61%
San Diego–Sacramento	481	9	9	5	5	50%	68%	–	78%	–	67%

Source: Southwest Airlines company records. For analysis purpose, load factors can be applied to daily round-trip flights for both airlines on both legs of a round trip.

United." He wanted to share this information with the group (see Exhibit 11), along with other recent developments. For example, a few days earlier, "Shuttle By United" had reduced its one-way walk-up coach fare on the San Francisco–Burbank route to $69. This fare was identical to the one charged on the Oakland–Burbank route by both airlines. In addition, Southwest's consolidated yield and load factor for January 1995 were tracking lower than the consolidated yield and load factor for January 1994. If present traffic patterns continued, Southwest's consolidated load factor would be about five points lower in January 1995 as compared to January 1994.

Unexpected news that "Shuttle By United" intended to discontinue some service and raise fares altered the original meeting agenda and posed a number of questions for Southwest executives. For instance, did the fare increase signify a major modification in United's "We're going to match Southwest" strategy? If so, what were the implications for Southwest? How might Southwest react to these changes, if at all? Should Southwest follow with a $10 fare increase of its own or continue with its present price and service strategy? What might be the profit impact of United's action and Southwest's reaction, if any, for each airline? And how, if at all, was United's pricing action linked to the announced withdrawal from the Oakland–Ontario market?

Case

Hi-Value Supermarkets

Everyday Low Pricing

In early April 2006, James Ellis was reviewing the first-quarter financial results for Hi-Value Supermarkets. As senior vice president at Hall Consolidated and president of Hi-value Supermarkets, he was about to meet with the district manager responsible for three Superior stores in Centralia, Missouri. Others in attendance would be Hall Consolidated's vice president of retail operations and the controller for Hi-Value Supermarkets. The agenda for the first of four quarterly meetings scheduled for 2006 was to discuss the district's progress toward achieving planned goals and address any issues related to the district manager's supermarkets.

In anticipation of the quarterly review, Randall Johnson, District III manager for Hi-value Supermarkets, had proposed that everyday low pricing be reconsidered for his three stores in Centralia.[1] He cited company research documenting Hi-Value's relatively higher prices in Centralia and the growing price consciousness among Centralia shoppers. He also noted that Hi-value Supermarkets could lose market share in Centralia since store sales were below budgeted levels in this first quarter of 2006. He added that 2005 fourth-quarter sales revenue, which was normally a heavy sales period due to the Thanksgiving and Christmas holidays, was also lower than sales for the same period in 2004.

The everyday low pricing strategy option for Centralia had been discussed briefly in August 2005 as part of the annual planning process. However, a decision was made to continue Hi-Value's current pricing strategy pending further study. James Ellis believed that the time had come to formally address the question in detail.

 ## THE COMPANY

Hi-Value Supermarkets is a division of Hall Consolidated, a privately owned wholesale and retail food distributor. Hall Consolidated was formed in 1959 and initially included a number of wholesale food operations and produce companies. The company's first retail grocery store chain was purchased in 1970. The Hi-Value

---

[1] With an everyday low price policy, a retailer charges a constant, lower everyday price for merchandise with few, if any, price discounts. This practice differs from a "Hi-Lo" price policy whereby a retailer charges higher prices on an everyday basis but then runs frequent promotions, sales, or specials in which selected merchandise prices are deeply discounted.

Supermarket chain was acquired in 1975. By 2002, Hall Consolidated distributed food and related products to some 150 company-owned supermarket units operating under three supermarket chain names through 12 wholesale distribution centers. These distribution centers also supplied about 1,100 independent grocery stores in the United States. Hall Consolidated sales in 2002 were $2.3 billion.

Hi-Value is the smallest of the three supermarket chains owned by Hall Consolidated with sales of $192.2 million in 2002. Hi-Value operates conventional supermarkets in trade areas that served small cities and towns in the South Central United States. The median size of a Hi-Value Supermarket was 20,730 square feet, which is considered small by industry standards (the median size of a supermarket in the United States is about 44,000 square feet). Nevertheless, Hi-Value was the number one or number two ranked supermarket chain in each of its trade markets as measured by market share.

COMPETITIVE ENVIRONMENT IN CENTRALIA, MISSOURI

Centralia is the primary trade area in Scott County, which is located in central Missouri. The Centralia trade area had total retail sales of $725 million in 2002. Food and beverage retail store sales were $62.3 million in 2002, which represented a 4.6 percent increase over 2001. There are 20 establishments in Centralia that sell food and beverages.

According to the U.S. Census 2000, Centralia has a total population of 41,000, including 13,500 households. The median age of the Centralia population was 35 years; the median household income was $36,000; and 80 percent of residents had a high school education or more. Slightly over one-half (51.5 percent) of Centralia's residents were employed by manufacturing, retail trade, and education, health, and social services establishments. Exhibit 1 shows the age and household income distribution of Centralia residents.

EXHIBIT 1	Centralia Population Profile: Age and Household Income Distribution

Age Distribution		Household Income Distribution	
Category	*Percent*	*Category*	*Percent*
19 years and under	29.6	Less than $10,000	10.4
20 to 24 years	6.8	$10,000 to $14,999	7.5
25 to 34 years	13.8	$15,000 to $24,999	16.1
35 to 44 years	14.9	$25,000 to $34,999	14.5
45 to 54 years	12.9	$35,000 to $49,999	19.8
55 to 59 years	4.4	$50,000 to $74,999	19.8
60 to 64 years	3.5	$75,000 to $99,999	6.3
65 to 74 years	6.9	$100,000 to $149,999	3.8
75 years and over	7.3	$150,000 or more	1.9
	100.0		100.0

Source: U.S. Census 2000.

Major Competitors

Four grocery chain stores accounted for 85 percent of all food sales in Centralia in 2002 (see Exhibit 2). The remainder of the retail food business was shared primarily by two small independent grocery stores, several convenience stores, specialty food stores (bakeries, butcher shops) and a seasonal Farmers' Market. Three of the chains—Harrison's, Grand American, and Missouri Mart—operated one store in Centralia. Hall operated three Hi-Value Supermarkets in Centralia. Each of the three Hi-Value stores was smaller than the other chains' stores. Grand American, Harrison's, and Missouri Mart drew their customers from larger geographic areas than did Hi-Value, including business from outside Centralia. Missouri Mart, in particular, enjoyed a sizable trade from outside Centralia. Store locations are shown in Exhibit 3.

Harrison's   Harrison's supermarket on West Main Street was built in 1976, expanded in 1990, and remodeled in 1999. About 15 percent of the store's 50,000 square feet is devoted to an extensive assortment of general merchandise and a small pharmacy. Hall officials believe that Harrison's has captured most of the business of the middle and upper-income groups in Centralia with annual household incomes in excess of $40,000. Harrison's supermarket has the second highest sales of all the major chain stores. Its store in Centralia is one of the company's 65 supermarkets located throughout Missouri and Illinois.

Harrison's is well managed, clean, orderly, and attractive. The decor is warm, the staff friendly, and the physical layout easy to shop. Its merchandising strength is a balanced variety of groceries, quality meats, and produce. The store is conveniently located, with excellent parking facilities. The store's principal promotion theme is everyday low prices, as evidenced by its advertising slogan, "Save on the Total." According to Hall executives, Harrison's has an extremely favorable customer image.

Grand American   The Grand American store, measuring 39,800 square feet, opened in mid-2001 and is located at the corner of Fairview and West Main. This store replaced an older, smaller facility located several blocks northeast of the new site. The Centralia store is one of 148 supermarkets operated by Grand American, a large regional food distributor and retailer. The Grand American store is the most modern store in Centralia and has the finest fixtures and decor. It has wide aisles and is relatively easy to shop.

Hall officials consider the Grand American store a secondary competitor. According to Hall executives, the store is highly regimented and lacks any

---

EXHIBIT 2	Estimated Share of Market for Supermarkets in Centralia							
	1995	*1996*	*1997*	*1998*	*1999*	*2000*	*2001*	*2002*
Hi-Value	24%	29%	27%	30%	31%	22%	23%	23%
Grand American	22	11	7	6	6	6	6	13
Missouri Mart	25	25	26	28	30	34	34	27
Harrison's	9	14	19	16	14	20	20	22
Others	20	21	21	20	19	18	17	15

Note: Share-of-market estimates were made by Hall Consolidated executives on the basis of information they considered reliable. The total market (100%) represents all food sales made in Centralia.

Source: Company records.

| **EXHIBIT 3** | **Location of Stores, Major Traffic Arteries, and Principal In-City Trade Areas of Major Supermarket Chain Stores in Centralia** |

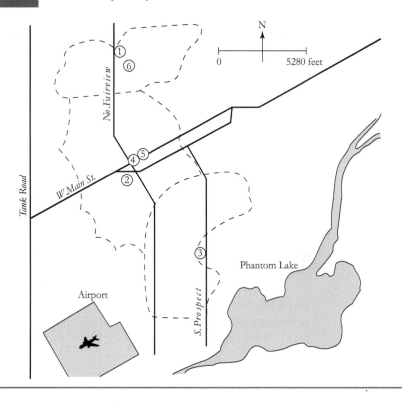

Key:

1. Hi-value (N. Faireview)   4. Grand American

2. Hi-value (W. Main St.)   5. Harrison's

3. Hi-value (S. Prospect)   6. Missouri Mart

Note: Trade area boundaries were drawn on the basis of personal interviews with customers in each Hi-value store. The address of each interviewee was then plotted on the map and boundaries drawn.

---

innovative merchandising appeal. It has modest variety in meats, produce, and groceries, but its dairy department is highly regarded by Centralia shoppers. The store carries a skeleton variety of general merchandise and houses a small pharmacy. Grand American's weekly advertising emphasizes high-volume items and also attempts to create a low-price image by highlighting competitive prices on items listed in each ad. The store also offers double coupons and in-store "Manager's Specials." The store's customers come from residential areas similar to those of Harrison's customers; however, the annual household income of Grand American customers ranges from $20,000 to $35,000.

Missouri Mart   According to Hall officials, Missouri Mart is the food sales volume leader in Centralia and is the principal competitor of Superior supermarkets. Approximately 32 percent of Hi-Value customers shop Missouri Mart regularly. Most of Missouri Mart's customers are middle-aged and older families whose annual household incomes exceed $30,000. Sixty percent of the store's 120,000 square feet is allotted to general merchandise; 40 percent is devoted to food items. The store was remodeled in 2001. Managers of the three Hi-Value stores maintain that "Missouri Mart's primary merchandising strength is in groceries and special purchase displays." One manager stated that "orderliness and

EXHIBIT 4   Hi-Value Supermarket Sales in Centralia: 2000–2002

Store	2000	2001	2002
North Fairview	$4,050,277	$4,287,686	$4,437,632
West Main	5,194,972	5,174,051	5,374,517
South Prospect	4,098,898	4,227,304	4,514,551
Total	$13,345,147	$13,689,041	$14,326,700

Source: Company records.

cleanliness are sacrificed for production, and the store lacks the quality and freshness present in the other supermarkets in Centralia." Ads feature very low prices on particular items, which are displayed in large quantities at the ends of aisles in the grocery section of the store. Unlike Harrison's and Grand American, which are free-standing, the Missouri Mart store is part of a complex of other types of stores, including several service shops, a bakery, a drug store, and a furniture store. Missouri Mart, Inc., the regional chain that built the Centralia store and operated it for many years, recently franchised it to an independent businessperson who continues to operate the store under the Missouri Mart banner.

Hi-Value Supermarkets   The three Hi-Value Supermarkets in Centralia were generally older than those of its major competitors. Each of the stores anchored a strip shopping center (owned by Hall Consolidated) consisting of a Hi-Value supermarket and a drugstore, plus two or three shops (e.g., a dry cleaner, a shoe repair shop, a barber shop, or a florist). Sales for the three stores had increased over the past three years reaching $14,326,700 in 2002 (see Exhibit 4). The overall gross profit margin for the three stores was 28.8 percent in 2002. By comparison, the median U.S. supermarket industry gross profit margin was 26.4 percent.

Sales of the three Hi-Value stores were divided as follows: grocery (including dairy), 50 percent; fresh meat, poultry and seafood, 20 percent; produce, 18 percent; seasonal and general merchandise (including health and beauty care items), 7 percent; and bakery (including bread and baked goods) and deli (including self-serve and service deli), 5 percent. Gross profit margins in each of these departments were grocery (including dairy), 30 percent; fresh meat, poultry, and seafood, 18 percent; produce, 30 percent; general merchandise (including health and beauty items), 33 percent; and bakery and deli, 50 percent.

Company officials believed that Hi-Value stores offered a more limited variety of merchandise than the major competitors but that Superior carried high-quality merchandise, particularly in grocery items and fresh produce. Officials recognized that the fresh meat, poultry, and seafood departments of the three stores varied in consumer acceptance.

Hi-Value follows both Missouri Mart and Harrison's in terms of overall advertising exposure, measured in terms of newspaper advertising space, circulars, and newspaper inserts, radio spots, and outdoor. Grand American's advertising exposure is considerably less than Hi-Value in these media. Hi-Value features a value positioning in its advertising: Hi-Value Supermarkets = Superior Value. In 2002, Superior spent $127,500 for advertising or .89 percent of its sales. Missouri Mart and Harrison's were spending the equivalent of about 1 percent of their sales on advertising, Hall officials believed. None of the food stores in Centralia advertise on television.

Hi-Value supermarkets are the highest-priced food stores in the Centralia area, based on comparison market-basket studies of supermarket competitors. (Exhibit 5 shows the dollar breakdown of products sold in Centralia

EXHIBIT 5	How $100 Is Spent in a Typical Centralia Supermarket		
Perishables			$49.67
Fresh meat, poultry, and seafood	$14.32		
Produce	9.70		
Dairy	9.08		
Frozen foods	6.95		
Service deli	3.38		
Bread and baked goods	3.15		
In-store bakery	2.14		
Self-serve deli	0.77		
Floral	0.18		
Food grocery			$30.95
Beverages	10.71		
Main meal items	8.44		
Snack food	6.39		
Miscellaneous	5.41		
Non-food grocery			$8.77
Health and beauty care			3.72
General merchandise			3.45
Pharmacy			2.49
Unclassified			0.95
			$100.00

Source: Company records.

supermarkets.) Nevertheless, it advertises high-volume items at deeply discounted prices and features "loss leaders"—items sold to the customer at or near
their cost to the seller. Soft drinks, bread, eggs, and flour are popular loss leaders in the Centralia market.

North Fairview   Built in 1975, the North Fairview store is the oldest of the
three Hi-Value stores in Centralia. Improvements were made to the store in 1990
and 1995, including new checkstands and new freezers. The store is located less
than two blocks from the shopping complex that houses Missouri Mart. About
20 percent of the North Fairview store's customers come from outside Centralia.
Most of these customers live approximately three to four miles from the store.

West Main Street   The Hi-Value store on West Main Street was opened in 1977.
Substantial improvements to the store were made in 1992, including an expansion
of the frozen food and dairy departments and the addition of new checkstands. A
"mini-deli" was added in 2000 as part of a modest renovation. The deli prepares
items for sale on the premises and for delivery to and sale at the North Fairview
and South Prospect stores.

   Two competitors, Harrison's and Grand American, are situated across the
street. Although both are strong competitors, Hall executives believe that the West
Main Street store draws most of its customers from the area south of the store, and
that Harrison's and Grand American draw fewer customers than Hi-Value does
from that area. Approximately 22 percent of the West Main store's sales come
from people living beyond the city limits.

South Prospect The South Prospect store was built in 1982 and substantially remodeled in 2000. No major competitors presently exist in the immediate vicinity of the store. The South Prospect store has the only on-premise "scratch" bakery among the three Hi-Value stores. Deliveries are made to the other stores daily. Company executives believe that the bakery offers high-quality items but less variety than the typical retail bakery shop in Centralia. About 23 percent of the store's sales are to people who live outside Centralia.

CONSUMER RESEARCH INITIATIVES

In mid-2002, Hall commissioned an independent marketing research firm to conduct a series of studies for the three Hi-Value stores in Centralia. Two objectives were outlined for these studies. First, Hall executives sought (1) to develop an updated profile of Hi-Value shoppers and (2) to determine the shopping behavior of these customers. This information was to be used in making store merchandising and renovation decisions. Second, executives hoped that questioning shoppers about what they liked and disliked about the Hi-Value stores would reveal what kind of retail image the stores projected. The question of store image had been a subject of discussion among corporate officials since 2000, when a retailing consultant to the company had concluded that the stores in Centralia failed to reach their full sales and profit potential because of the lack of a strong consumer image.

The first study consisted of a telephone survey of 400 Centralia residents, who were asked to comment on the principal strengths of the Hi-Value stores, Missouri Mart, Grand American, and Harrison's. More than 30 percent of the interviewees considered Hi-Value's prices "above average." In contrast, some 20 percent of the respondents thought the prices at Missouri Mart and at Grand American were below average. Harrison's was thought to have the lowest everyday prices. Additional results from this study appear in Exhibit 6.

EXHIBIT 6 **Association of Store Characteristics with Major Food Stores in Centralia**

Characteristic	Grand American	Harrison's	Hi-Value	Missouri Mart	Don't Know	Total
Most reasonable prices	11%	36%	7%	34%	12%	100%
Most convenient	18	21	35	25	1	100
Best-quality meat	20	27	18	11	24	100
Widest variety of meats	22	25	20	18	15	100
Best-quality produce	24	35	21	11	9	100
Widest variety of produce	24	30	14	18	14	100
Best store service	12	30	28	13	17	100
Quality of canned goods	12	24	14	14	26	100
Best overall variety	6	8	2	74	10	100
Best store layout	27	24	14	9	26	100
Best bakery	5	20	25	5	45	100
Best deli	5	9	9	2	75	100

Source: Company records.

A second study consisted of two focus groups recruited to discuss various aspects of food store choice and patronage in Centralia. A summary of their comments follows:

Price. Price is the most important store choice determinant. Focus group participants believe that for grocery items, in particular, Centralia stores carry the same national brands and the stores' private labels have similar quality. Harrison's is perceived as having the best overall prices.

Meat. Twenty of the 24 focus group participants stated that the quality of meat is the second-most important determinant of store choice and patronage. They like to see cleanliness in the meat department and bargains that are not simply poor cuts of meat. Meat display is also an important consideration. Harrison's was judged to have the best quality and variety of meat. Missouri Mart received the lowest marks on meat.

Produce. Produce quality, variety, and display follows meat as a major store choice and patronage determinant. Focus group participants tended to equate produce quality (and meat quality) with a quality store image. Harrison's is the "produce store" in Centralia. Missouri Mart rates lowest in produce quality, variety, and display.

Shopping Convenience. Focus group participants tended to lump together a host of factors that seem to represent a fourth major consideration in store choice and patronage. These factors tend to represent shopping convenience. Convenience includes ease of getting into and out of store parking lots, quick checkout, carry-out service, well-stocked and orderly shelves, and helpful store personnel. Closeness to home or work also seems important, particularly for last-minute shopping trips.

Stores in General. Focus group participants are generally pleased with their food shopping options. They shop for food twice a week on average. One trip is for major food purchases; the second trip is for fill-in items. They usually shop more than one store on a regular basis.

Missouri Mart. The typical comment made by focus group participants in reference to Missouri Mart was that "you can't stick to your budget if you shop at Missouri Mart because there are so many things to buy." However, they don't like the service at Missouri Mart, nor do they care for the quality of meat.

Grand American. Most remarks about Grand American were in a neutral or negative vein. Focus group participants stated that the store is often out of stock and that it usually overadvertises. Grand American-advertised specials are not in fact specials at all, according to some focus group participants.

Harrison's. Harrison's is winning the price competition with Missouri Mart in Centralia. Harrison's is recognized as having the best in price, courtesy, quality of merchandise, and service. Focus group participants believe Harrison's "Save on the Total" advertising.

Hi-Value (combined stores). Hi-Value appears to be the winner on shopping convenience. Focus group participants from all parts of Centralia considered Hi-Value to be a good neighborhood store. The "Hi-Value Supermarkets 5 Hi-Value Value" advertising was questioned given the perceived higher grocery, meat, and produce prices.

A third study involved personal interviews with 587 Hi-Value customers at the three store sites. Customers were asked to respond to questions asked by the interviewer and to comment on the store. Responses to questions are tabulated in Exhibit 7 on page 508 for each store and for all three stores combined.

In commenting on Hi-Value stores, shoppers emphasized that lower prices and greater variety were needed. Shoppers suggested that the dairy section be cleaner, the prices of meats be lower, the variety of goods in the bakery be greater, the out-of-stock situation in private labels be improved, and the quality and freshness of produce be enhanced. Questions concerning features of the Hi-Value stores liked by shoppers generated a variety of responses. Appearance and cleanliness, friendliness, service, and convenient to home or work were liked most by shoppers.

EXHIBIT 7   Hi-Value Supermarket Shopper Interview Results

	S. Prospect	W. Main	N. Fairview	Hi-Value, Combined
Age of customer (years):				
Over 65	7.5%	16.8%	9.7%	10.7%
64–50	13.7	25.5	28.0	21.6
49–35	33.0	35.8	33.1	33.8
34–25	18.9	15.3	24.0	19.7
24–18	21.2	6.6	4.0	11.6
Under 18 and no response	5.7	0	1.2	2.6
Average persons per household	2.6	1.9	1.9	2.1
Frequency of store visits:				
4 times a week	18.1%	11.7%	9.7%	13.4%
3 times a week	19.9	21.2	22.7	21.2
2 times a week	28.2	38.0	40.0	35.0
Once a week	10.6	11.2	9.2	10.3
3 times a month	0.9	1.7	5.4	2.6
2 times a month	6.0	4.5	7.0	5.9
Once a month	9.7	8.9	5.4	8.1
Other	6.5	2.8	0.5	3.5
Length of patronage:				
Less than 1 year	11.4%	10.0%	7.1%	7.6%
1–3 years	19.3	8.8	8.0	12.5
3 or more years	69.3	81.2	84.9	77.9
Proportion of total food needs purchased:				
Almost all	13.0%	12.4%	24.4%	17.0%
About ¾	18.8	14.1	13.3	15.0
About ½	50.0	58.2	47.2	51.7
About ¼ to ½	6.7	7.9	7.2	7.1
Less than ¼	11.5	7.3	7.8	9.2
Departments shopped:				
Grocery, meat, produce	22.5%	17.4%	30.2%	23.4%
Grocery, meat	10.7	10.4	13.6	11.5
Grocery, produce	11.2	7.3	5.4	8.2
Meat, produce	6.5	3.7	2.2	4.3
Grocery only	33.5	45.1	32.2	36.9
Meat only	1.4	2.4	4.3	2.7
Produce only	0.9	3.7	2.7	2.3
General Merchandise, including:				
Health/beauty items	15.2	9.2	7.5	10.9
Frozen foods	22.4	20.8	28.5	23.9
Dairy	39.6	37.6	49.7	42.3
Bakery and/or Deli	23.3	22.4	29.1	24.9

EXHIBIT 7 *(Continued)*

	S. Prospect	W. Main	N. Fairview	Hi-Value, Combined
Other stores shopped most regularly:				
Grand American	7.6%	7.8%	4.9%	6.8%
Harrison's	30.8	40.8	16.8	29.5
Missouri Mart	29.0	22.1	43.8	31.6
Superior	0.6	0.6	–	0.4
Independent 1	5.8	–	0.6	2.2
Independent 2	4.7	0.6	3.7	1.8
Other	3.5	3.0	0.1	3.4
None	18.0	15.0	30.1	14.3
Liked best about other regular store:				
Prices	33.8%	29.5%	19.5%	27.0%
Meat	8.8	22.7	7.8	11.6
Produce	10.3	9.1	6.5	8.5
Location	10.3	9.1	5.2	7.9
Other responses	36.8	29.6	61.0	45.0

(No one category accounted for more than 7% of the total.)

Source: Company records.

THE QUARTERLY REVIEW MEETING

James Ellis convened the quarterly review meeting soon after pleasantries were exchanged among the participants. The performance of the 15 stores in Randall Johnson's District III were reviewed. Except for the three Hi-Value Supermarkets in Centralia, Missouri, all met planned quarterly sales, gross profit margin, expense, and profit goals. The three stores in Centralia had posted a 1 percent negative variance on sales. Inspection of the stores' sales mix, which evidenced an increase in the percentage sales among higher gross margin categories (grocery, general merchandise, and bakery/deli), had boosted the stores' gross profit margin percent. The slightly higher gross margin percent, coupled with lower operating expenses, resulted in the stores' net profit margin being slightly under 1 percent—just shy of the budgeted 1 percent net profit margin for the first quarter of 2003. In addition, customer counts at all three stores were higher than the first quarter of 2002. Over all, District III was performing according to plan.

Everyday Low Pricing Discussion

Following the District III quarterly performance review, the discussion turned to Randall Johnson's proposal to implement everyday low pricing in Centralia, Missouri. He reiterated the points made in an earlier memo to James Ellis: (1) Superior's prices were higher than the competition at a time of growing price consciousness among Centralia shoppers and (2) Hi-Value could lose market share in Centralia due to the price differential. Sales in Centralia were already down 3 percent in the first quarter of 2003 compared with budgeted sales goals. This decline, following a slower than expected fourth quarter of 2002, "could indicate the beginning of a trend," Johnson said. He added, "We are running the risk of losing our hold as the second largest supermarket (based on market share) in Centralia."

Hall Consolidated had selectively employed everyday low pricing in well-defined market areas served by each of its three supermarket chains. According to Hall's vice president of retail operations,

> Our success with everyday low pricing has been a mixed bag. We've learned that this pricing strategy tends to work better when it is part of a broader store positioning strategy and supported with advertising. We've also learned that for everyday low pricing to work, we don't have to be the lowest priced supermarket in the trade area.

Ellis agreed with these observations and added:

> Everyday low pricing has to be used by all stores in a trade area, otherwise we'll only confuse our store image or positioning. In short, I think we need to take a hard look at our recent consumer research to see how we are positioned in Centralia and how everyday low pricing will change our image.

The controller for Hi-Value Supermarkets pointed out that everyday low pricing had the potential to reduce operating costs. He said:

> Everyday low pricing can lower our operating costs in two ways. It can reduce our inventory and handling costs due to more steady and predictable demand. It can also reduce our labor costs related to less frequent temporary price reductions. Our experience indicates that we can get an additional 50 basis points (.5 percent of sales) due to lower inventory and handling costs. The need to remark merchandise and shelf tags, including labor expense, costs us 60 basis points (0.6 percent of sales), which could be eliminated with everyday low pricing. Both savings could be added to our gross profit margin.

Johnson injected, "Or we use the savings to bolster our advertising budget featuring our new everyday low pricing strategy." Everyone agreed that such an option existed.

Everyday Low Pricing Implementation Considerations

"Let's not rush to a conclusion on everyday low pricing yet," said James Ellis. "We still have a few things to consider, not the least of which are the knotty implementation questions."

All of the Hall executives acknowledged that Hi-Value Supermarkets were "rightly perceived by supermarket shoppers as having the highest prices in Centralia." However, everyone agreed that few shoppers had specific product or brand price knowledge upon which to compare stores. To the extent that price knowledge existed, it tended to be category dependent. Prior company consumer research indicated that shoppers tended to have a relatively good idea of prices for products they purchased frequently. For example, new parents have a better price knowledge of baby foods and diapers. These price-knowledgeable shoppers also tended to recognize attractive (lower) and unattractive (higher) prices and were proficient at detecting a "good deal" when they saw it either in an ad or in the store.

"When we consider everyday low pricing, we have to consider whether or not we adopt this pricing strategy across-the-board for all our products or just certain categories," Ellis said. Randall Johnson was in favor of the across-the-board approach, noting that the impact on shopper perceptions would be greater. The vice president of retail operations favored limiting everyday low pricing to grocery (including dairy items) and seasonal and general merchandise (including health and beauty care items) from an operational standpoint. The controller agreed: "We are more likely to see cost savings due to everyday low pricing in these categories than in the others. These categories represent 57 percent of Hi-Value's sales in Centralia and everyday low pricing there should convey the image we want to project."

Ellis continued, "Another consideration is the pricing itself. How much should we lower our prices?" The market-basket studies of supermarket competitors consistently showed that Hi-Value's everyday (nonpromotional) prices were about 10 percent higher than Harrison's prices and about 7 percent higher than Grand American and Missouri Mart. "That is, if there is such a thing as an everyday price at Grand American or Missouri Mart given their frantic discounting," said Johnson. All of the Hall executives agreed that Hi-Value could not "outprice" Harrison's and any suggestion that Hi-Value intended to do that in Centralia would be unwise. "We are not about to start a price war in a market that has been profitable for us," said Ellis. "Besides," said the vice president for retail operations, "we offer greater convenience of shopping with our three stores and that is worth something."

At that moment, the telephone rang and James Ellis was told his scheduled meeting with the District II manager was running late. "Randy, I promised you that we would get closure on the everyday low pricing proposal while you are in town," said Ellis. He concluded the meeting saying, "We've made some progress this morning, but I think the matter requires further attention. Let's all meet again tomorrow morning. In the meantime, all of us need to look hard at the Centralia situation, consider our present competitive position in the market, and agree on how we might proceed."

Case

Burroughs Wellcome Company

Retrovir

"I think that Burroughs Wellcome is very interested in getting all their money back as soon as possible, because the sun won't shine forever."[1]

> Cofounder of Project Inform,
> an AIDS treatment information agency
> (1987)

"Once the drug is out on the marketplace, the company controls the pricing."[2]

> Dr. George Stanley,
> Food and Drug Administration (1987)

"To make AZT accessible to everyone who should be on it, Burroughs Wellcome has an obligation to give up a significant amount of money to allow people to get access."[3]

> Executive director,
> National Gay and Lesbian Task Force
> (1989)

"There's no plan to make another price cut."[4]

> Sir Alfred Sheppard,
> chair of the board,
> Wellcome PLC
> (1989)

---

[1] "The Unhealthy Profits of AZT," *The Nation* (October 17, 1987):407.

[2] Ibid.

[3] "AZT Maker Expected to Reap Big Gain," *New York Times* (August 29, 1989):8.

[4] "Wellcome Seeks Approval to Sell AZT to All Those Inflicted with AIDS Virus," *Wall Street Journal* (November 17, 1989):B4.

This case was prepared by Professor Roger A. Kerin, of the Edwin L. Cox School of Business, Southern Methodist University, with the assistance of Angela Bullard, graduate student, as a basis for class discussion and is not designed to illustrate effective or ineffective handling of an administrative situation. The case was prepared from published sources. Quotes, statistics, and published operating information are footnoted for reference purposes. Copyright © 1995 by Roger A. Kerin. No part of this case may be reproduced without the written permission of the copyright holder.

In January 1990, Burroughs Wellcome executives were under continued pressure to reduce the price of Retrovir. Retrovir brand zidovudine is the trade name for a drug called azidothymidine (AZT), which had been found to be effective in the treatment of acquired immune deficiency syndrome (AIDS) and AIDS-related complex (ARC). AIDS is a disease caused by a virus that attacks the body's immune system and damages the system's ability to fight off other infections. Without a functioning immune system, a person becomes vulnerable to infection by bacteria, protozoa, fungi, viruses, and other malignant agents, which may cause life-threatening illnesses, such as pneumonia, meningitis, and cancer. AIDS is caused by HIV (human immunodeficiency virus), a human virus first discovered in 1983. AZT is classified as an antiviral drug that interferes with the replication of HIV. As such, AZT is a treatment, not a cure, for AIDS.

In 1987, Burroughs Wellcome obtained approval from the U.S. Food and Drug Administration to market Retrovir, the first and, as of 1990, the only drug authorized for the treatment of AIDS. Soon after Burroughs Wellcome made Retrovir available for prescription sales on March 19, 1987, the company became embroiled in controversy related to the price of the drug. Critics charged that Burroughs Wellcome, which sold the drug to wholesalers at a price of $188 for a hundred 100-milligram capsules, engaged in price gouging of a "highly vulnerable market." The company's president, T. E. Haigler, responded that the high price was due to the "uncertain market for the drug, the possible advent of new therapies, and profit margins customarily generated by significant new medicines."[5]

Nevertheless, the company reduced its price by 20 percent in December 1987, and again by 20 percent in September 1989. Prior to the 1989 price reduction, the Subcommittee on Health and the Environment of the U.S. House of Representatives had launched an investigation into possible "inappropriate" pricing of Retrovir. Soon after the announced price reduction in 1989, the chair of the House subcommittee said that this was "a good first step. But I think the company can do better."[6] In November 1989, the chair of Wellcome PLC, the parent company of Burroughs Wellcome, was quoted as saying, "There's no plan to make another price cut."[7] However, pressure to again reduce the price continued.

 ## ACQUIRED IMMUNE DEFICIENCY SYNDROME

Acquired immune deficiency syndrome can be traced to a blood sample taken and stored in the Central African nation of Zaire in 1959 (see Exhibit 1 on page 514 for a chronology of important events). It was not until 1982, however, that the Centers for Disease Control and Prevention in Atlanta, Georgia, labeled the disease and warned that it might be spread by a virus in bodily fluids such as blood and semen. In 1983 and 1984, French and American scientists isolated a suspected AIDS-causing virus that was subsequently named human immunodeficiency virus, or HIV, in 1988. HIV is a retrovirus that can become an extra link in the genetic code, or DNA, of a cell. HIV inhibits and eventually destroys the T-4 cell, which is a key part of a person's immune

---

[5] "The High-Cost AIDS Drug: Who Will Pay for It?" *Drug Topics* (April 6, 1987):52.

[6] "How Much for a Reprieve from AIDS?" *Time* (October 2, 1989):81.

[7] "Wellcome Seeks Approval to Sell AZT," *Wall Street Journal* (November 17, 1989):B4.

EXHIBIT 1	AIDS Chronology, 1959–1990

1959	Blood sample taken and stored in the Central African nation of Zaire. Retesting the sample in 1986, physicians discover it to be HIV-infected.
1978	Doctors determine that a child in New York died as a direct result of immune system breakdown.
1981	The Centers for Disease Control (CDC) reports breakdowns of the immune systems of several male homosexuals with the resulting occurrence of infectious diseases and cancers.
1982	CDC names the "mystery disease" acquired immune deficiency syndrome (AIDS) and warns that it may be spread by a virus in bodily fluids such as blood and semen.
1983	Scientists at the Pasteur Institute in Paris, France, isolate a suspected AIDS-causing virus.
1984	U.S. researchers identify an AIDS-causing virus as the same one isolated by the French scientists.
1985	A test is licensed to detect an AIDS-causing virus in blood.
1986	The AIDS-causing virus is named human immunodeficiency virus, or HIV.
1987	U.S. Food and Drug Administration permits sale of azidothymidine (AZT), which eases some of the symptoms of AIDS and AIDS-related complex (ARC).
1988–1990	AIDS fatalities continue to increase while the pharmaceutical industry searches for a cure.

system that attacks foreign germs. Without T-4 cells, people succumb to all manner of infections. The identification of HIV was a major breakthrough, especially since, prior to 1984, it was not established in the scientific community that retroviruses like HIV caused human diseases.

Incidence and Cost of HIV and AIDS

Efforts to track and forecast the incidence and cost of HIV and AIDS began in earnest in 1986. Research focused on identifying high-risk individuals, determining the geographic concentration of the disease, and arriving at estimates of the number of in people afflicted with HIV and AIDS.[8] This research found that almost 90 percent of AIDS victims were gay men or intravenous drug users. One-half of all reported AIDS cases were in the San Francisco, Miami, New York City, Los Angeles, and Houston metropolitan areas.

Tracking and forecasting the incidence of AIDS cases and HIV infections proved to be more difficult. The CDCP reported 5,992 AIDS cases in 1984 and 35,198 cases in 1989. Estimates of HIV infections in 1990 ranged between 800,000 and 1,300,000 Americans, depending on the estimation procedure employed. The incidence of AIDS cases in the period 1981–1989 is charted in Exhibit 2. The

---

[8] Portions of this material are based on statistics reported in Brad Edmundson, "AIDS and Aging," *American Demographics* (March 1990):28–34; Fred J. Hellinger, "Forecasting the Personal Medical Care Costs of AIDS from 1988 through 1991," *Public Health Reports* (May–June 1988): 309–319; William L. Roper and William Winkenwerder, "Making Fair Decisions about Financing Care for Persons with AIDS," *Public Health Reports* (May–June 1988):305–308; Centers for Disease Control and Prevention, "Human Immunodeficiency Virus Infection in the United States: A Review of Current Knowledge," *Morbidity and Mortality Weekly Report* (December 18, 1987):2–3, 18–19; "Now That AIDS Is Treatable, Who'll Pay the Crushing Cost?" *BusinessWeek* (September 11, 1989):115–116; Centers for Disease Control and Prevention, "HIV/AIDS Surveillance Report" (U.S. Department of Health and Human Services, Public Health Services: December 1990).

EXHIBIT 2 **AIDS Cases, 1981–1989**

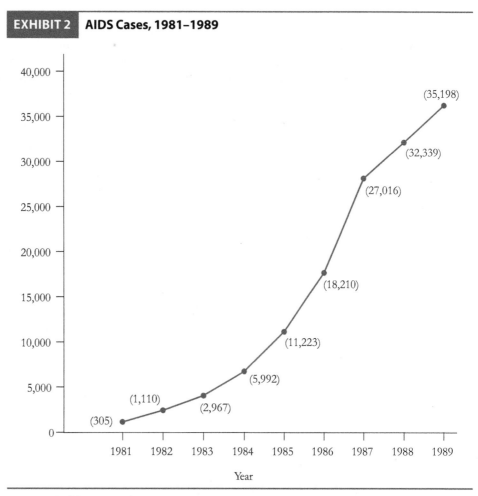

Source: Based on Centers for Disease Control and Prevention, "HIV/AIDS Surveillance Report" (U.S. Department of Health and Human Services, Public Health Services: December 1990).

fatality rate for persons infected with AIDS was about 91 percent in 1981 and 46 percent in 1989.

Treating AIDS patients has proved to be extremely expensive. According to a 1987 study by the RAND Corporation, an internationally recognized research organization, the lifetime medical costs of an AIDS patient in his thirties were estimated to be between $70,000 and $141,000. For comparison, the lifetime cost of treating a person in his thirties with digestive tract cancer was $47,000; leukemia, $29,000; and a heart attack, $67,000.

An estimated 40 percent of persons with AIDS have received care under the Medicaid Program, which is administered by the Health Care Financing Administration and funded jointly by the federal government (55 percent) and individual states (45 percent). Estimated annual costs for AIDS care and treatment funded by Medicaid ranged between $700 and $750 million in 1988. Medicaid spending for AIDS was estimated to reach $2.4 billion in 1992. In addition, private insurers paid $250 million annually in AIDS-related medical payments.

Anti-HIV Drug Treatment

The identification of HIV in the mid-1980s prompted numerous pharmaceutical companies to search for antiviral drugs. Burroughs Wellcome led the research effort in part because of its prior development of drugs that combat viral diseases.

In addition to AZT supplied by Burroughs Wellcome, other compounds were in various stages of development and commercialization.[9] One antiviral drug has been given limited approval by the FDA and is available to patients who have a negative reaction to AZT. This drug, produced by Bristol Myers and called DDI, is an antiviral drug that appears to inhibit reproduction of HIV and slow the damage it causes. DDI was initially studied for AIDS use by the National Cancer Institute. Like AZT, it interferes with the ability of HIV-infected cells to produce new viruses and slows the progression of HIV infection, but does not eradicate or eliminate the infection. The principal advantage of DDI over AZT is that it appears to be less toxic. DDC, developed by Hoffman-LaRoche, was in clinical trials in 1989. Other drugs produced by Glaxo and Triton Biosciences, Inc. were being tested as well. Industry analysts believed that one or more of these drugs would obtain FDA approval for prescription sales by 1991.

 # BURROUGHS WELLCOME COMPANY

Burroughs Wellcome is the American subsidiary of Wellcome PLC, an English public limited company with headquarters in London.[10] Wellcome PLC is a multinational firm with manufacturing operations in 18 countries and employs 20,000 people. Approximately 18 percent of the company's employees are

EXHIBIT 3	Selected Financial and Operating Ratios of Wellcome PLC		
	*Fiscal Year**		
	1989	*1988*	*1987*
Financial Ratios			
Gross profit margin (gross profit/sales)	70.6%	68.1%	67.5%
Return on sales (net income before tax/sales)	20.0	17.7	14.9
Return on assets (net income before tax/total assets)	20.0	18.0	15.0
Return on equity (net income before tax/common equity)	35.0	36.0	32.0
Operating Ratios			
R&D expenditures/sales	13.4	13.1	12.6
Selling, general, and administration costs/sales	36.9	36.5	39.2

*Fiscal year ends August 31.

Source: Wellcome PLC annual reports.

---

[9] Portions of this material are based on "A Quiet Drug Maker Takes a Big Swing at AIDS," *BusinessWeek* (October 6, 1986):32; "There's No Magic Bullet, but a Shotgun Approach May Work," *BusinessWeek* (September 11, 1989):118.

[10] Much of this material is described in Wellcome PLC's 1989 and 1990 annual reports; "Burroughs Wellcome Company," Burroughs Wellcome news release, December 13, 1990; Brian O'Reilly, "The Inside Story of the AIDS Drug," *Fortune* (November 5, 1990):112–29. Financial figures and percentages represent approximations, since information is reported in U.S. dollars and the British pound sterling. These figures are not useful for research purposes.

EXHIBIT 4	Selected Financial and Operating Ratios for Pharmaceutical Firms in the United States, 1989

	Pharmaceutical Firm					
	Schering-Merck & Co.	**Pfizer, Inc.**	**Abbott Labs**	**Upjohn**	**Plough**	**Eli Lilly**
Financial Ratios*						
Gross profit margin	76.3%	63.6%	52.5%	69.8%	73.8%	69.9%
Return on sales	34.8	16.2	22.2	15.8	20.4	31.9
Return on assets	33.8	11.0	24.6	14.2	17.9	22.7
Return on equity	64.9	20.2	43.8	26.5	33.0	35.4
Operating Ratios						
R&D/sales	11.5	9.4	9.3	14.0	10.3	14.5
SG&A/sales	30.7	37.2	20.5	40.3	42.3	27.5

*See Exhibit 3 for definitions of ratios.

Source: Company annual reports.

engaged in research and development efforts. The company's primary business, which accounts for 89 percent of its fiscal 1989 revenue, is human health care products, both ethical (prescription) and over the counter (nonprescription). Two ethical products account for 34 percent of its human health care revenue: Zovirax and Retrovir. Zovirax, which is used in the treatment of herpes infection, is the company's single largest-selling product with annual sales of $492 million in 1989. Retrovir is its second largest-selling product with sales of $225 million in fiscal 1989. In addition, the company markets Actifed and Sudafed, cough and cold preparations, as over-the-counter products. These two products combined account for annual sales of $253 million. Wellcome PLC had an animal health care business that accounted for about 11 percent of company revenue. This business was divested in late 1989.

North America represents the largest market for the products sold by Wellcome PLC, with annual sales of $997 million. Sales in the United States are roughly equivalent to 42 percent of Wellcome PLC's worldwide sales. The United Kingdom is the company's second largest market and accounts for about 10 percent of worldwide sales.

Wellcome PLC recorded total revenues of $1.75 billion and net profit before tax of $262.1 million in fiscal 1987. Total revenues for fiscal 1989 (fiscal year ended August 31, 1989) were $2.1 billion with net profit before taxes of $475 million.[11] Selected financial and operating ratios for Wellcome PLC for the fiscal years 1987–1989 are shown in Exhibit 3. Exhibit 4 presents comparative statistics for other major firms in the U.S. pharmaceutical industry. Percentage sales and the net income growth since fiscal 1985 for Wellcome PLC are shown below:

Fiscal Year	Sales Growth	Net Income Growth
1985–1986	0.2%	7.2%
1986–1987	12.6	47.3
1987–1988	10.4	35.1
1988–1989	12.6	42.9

[11] These figures are based on the average exchange rate of $1.55 = £1 in 1987, and $1.68 = £1 in 1989 (*Wellcome PLC 1990 Annual Report*).

DEVELOPMENT OF RETROVIR

Burroughs Wellcome's AIDS research program began in June 1984 with an extensive search for likely drug candidates. According to Philip Furman, head of virus research, "We looked at all our known antivirals on the off chance that one would work against retroviruses."[12]

Laboratory Testing

Burroughs Wellcome scientists examined hundreds of compounds over a period of five months, but none proved acceptable. In November 1984, AZT was found to inhibit animal viruses in a laboratory setting. AZT had been synthesized in 1964 by a researcher at the Michigan Cancer Foundation. It was hoped then that the drug would be useful in the treatment of cancer, but when investigated, it was found to have no potential as an anticancer agent. In the early 1980s, Burroughs Wellcome scientists resynthesized AZT in their exploration of compounds with possible effectiveness against bacterial infection. This research provided information about the spectrum of the drug's antibacterial activity and its toxicity and metabolism in laboratory animals, but intensive development was not pursued. The drug was not examined again until late 1984 when it showed promise as an AIDS treatment. (Exhibit 5 details significant events in the development of Retrovir.)

Following *in vitro* demonstration of its potential by Burroughs Wellcome's scientists, 50 coded compounds including AZT were sent to Duke University, the National Cancer Institute (NCI), and the FDA for independent testing to assess their *in vitro* activity against the human retrovirus.[13] Early in 1985 these tests showed that AZT was, in fact, active against HIV in the test tube. The company then began extensive preclinical toxicologic and pharmacologic testing in the spring of 1985. At the same time, work began on scaling up synthesis of the drug in preparation for clinical testing in patients with HIV. On June 14, 1985, Burroughs Wellcome submitted an application to the FDA to obtain Investigational New Drug (IND) status for the compound, which would allow its use in a limited number of severely ill AIDS and ARC patients. A week later, the FDA notified Burroughs Wellcome that the submitted data were sufficient to allow clinical studies in humans to be initiated.

Human Testing

Retrovir was administered to patients for the first time on July 3, 1985, at the Clinical Center of the National Institutes of Health (NIH) in Bethesda, Maryland. This initial (Phase I) study, conducted under a protocol developed by Burroughs Wellcome in collaboration with scientists at the NCI, Duke University, the University of Miami, and UCLA, involved 40 patients infected with HIV. The purpose of Phase I testing was to determine how Retrovir acted in the body, the appropriate dosage, and potential adverse reactions or side effects. Initial results were encouraging. Some of the patients showed evidence of improvement, including

---

[12] This material is based on "The Development of Retrovir," Burroughs Wellcome news release, June 1990; L. Wastila and L. Lasagna, "The History of Zidovudine (AZT)," *Journal of Clinical Research and Pharmacoepidemiology*, Vol. 4 (1990): 25–29; "The Inside Story of the AIDS Drug," *Fortune* (November 5, 1990):112–129; "AIDS Research Stirs Bitter Fight over Use of Experimental Drugs," *Wall Street Journal* (June 18, 1986):26.

[13] *In vitro*, a Latin phrase meaning "in glass," is used medically to mean to isolate from a living organism and artificially maintain in a test tube.

EXHIBIT 5	Retrovir Milestones, 1984–1990
June 1984	Burroughs Wellcome begins an AIDS research program to search for chemical compounds that might be effective against HIV.
November 1984	Burroughs Wellcome scientists identify AZT as potentially useful against AIDS.
Spring 1985	*In vitro* activity of AZT against HIV is confirmed by laboratories at Duke University, FDA, and NCI. This confirmatory work, requested by Burroughs Wellcome, is done on coded samples whose chemical identity is not revealed to the outside laboratories.
Spring 1985	Burroughs Wellcome continues toxicologic and pharmacologic testing of AZT. Work begins on scaling up synthesis of the drug, as the compound has never been produced beyond the few grams used for research purposes.
June 1985	FDA permits Burroughs Wellcome to begin clinical trials of AZT in humans.
July 1985	AZT is designated an "orphan drug" for the treatment of AIDS (a designation made when the affected population is less than 200,000).
July 1985	Burroughs Wellcome begins a collaborative Phase I study with NCI and Duke University to assess AZT's safety and tolerance in humans.
December 1985	Enrollment in the Phase I study, eventually involving 40 patients and investigators from NCI, Duke University, University of Miami, and UCLA, continues. Patient responses are encouraging.
February 1986	Burroughs Wellcome initiates and is the sole sponsor of a Phase II study at 12 academic centers, eventually involving 281 patients.
September 1986	The Phase II study is halted when an interim analysis by an independent data safety and monitoring board shows a significantly lower mortality rate in patients receiving AZT compared to those randomized to receive a placebo.
October 1986	Burroughs Wellcome, National Institutes of Health, and FDA establish a Treatment IND (Investigational New Drug) program as a means of providing wider access to AZT prior to FDA clearance.
December 1986	Burroughs Wellcome completes submission of a New Drug Application to FDA.
March 1987	The FDA clears Retrovir brand zidovudine (AZT) as a treatment for advanced ARC and AIDS.
February 1988	Burroughs Wellcome is issued a U.S. patent for the use of Retrovir as a treatment for AIDS and ARC based on the innovative work done by company scientists.
August 1989	Controlled clinical trials indicate that certain HIV-infected early symptomatic and asymptomatic persons can benefit from Retrovir with fewer or less severe side effects.
October 1989	Burroughs Wellcome establishes a Pediatric Treatment IND program, providing wider access to Retrovir for medically eligible children prior to FDA clearance.
January 1990	The FDA clears modified dosage guidelines for therapy with Retrovir patients with severe HIV infection.

Source: Abridged from a Burroughs Wellcome news release. "Retrovir Milestones," dated December 13, 1990.

an increased sense of well-being, weight gain, and positive changes in various measures of the immune system function. Extended treatment, however, lowered production of red blood cells and certain white blood cells in some patients who had taken high doses.

By early 1986, sufficient data on Retrovir were available to proceed with more extensive human testing. The need now was to prove that the drug could provide useful therapy for AIDS and ARC patients. More volunteers and an objective basis for comparison were essential to the conduct of the Phase II trial. A double-blind, placebo-controlled trial, conducted and financed by Burroughs Wellcome, began on February 18, 1986. A total of 281 patients participated. Safeguards built into the study provided for data to be reviewed periodically by a board of impartial experts convened under the auspices of the National Institute of Allergy and Infectious Diseases (NIAID). If either the placebo or the drug-treated group did either so poorly or so well that it would be unethical to continue the trial, the study would be stopped.

About this time, both the medical community and the general public had heard of the Phase II trial. As publicity about the trial gained momentum, AIDS patient-advocacy groups became impatient with what they perceived as an overly tedious and unnecessary process. They began accusing Burroughs Wellcome and the FDA of delaying the drug's availability. These critics argued that withholding potentially effective therapy from AIDS patients was inhumane and unethical, as was the use of a placebo. David Barry, vice president and head of the research, medical, and development divisions, defended the trial process, asserting that, if placebo controls were removed, "it could destroy the most modern and rapid clinical research plans ever devised."[14]

In September 1986, the review board recommended that the administration of the placebo be terminated. Analysis of the data had shown a significantly lower mortality rate among those patients who had received Retrovir for an average period of six months. When the trial stopped, there had been 19 deaths among the 137 patients receiving the placebo and 1 death among those patients taking Retrovir. The group receiving Retrovir also had a decreased number of infections. In addition, the weight gain, improvements in the immune system, and ability to perform daily activities noted in the Phase I trial were confirmed. However, patients involved in the Phase II trial also experienced adverse reactions similar to those reported in the earlier trial. Since it was no longer appropriate to withhold drug treatment from placebo-treated patients, all patients who had formerly received the placebo were offered Retrovir treatment with the agreement of the FDA.

Expanded distribution of the drug meant that the company would have to obtain a larger supply of thymidine, a biological chemical first harvested from herring sperm and a key raw material in AZT. In 1986, the world's supply of thymidine was 25 pounds. Recognizing that this supply would be exhausted quickly, the head of technical development at Burroughs Wellcome began a worldwide search for a thymidine supplier, recognizing that it took months and 20 chemical reactions to produce this material. This search uncovered a small German subsidiary of Pfizer, Inc., a New York–based pharmaceutical firm, which had produced thymidine in the 1960s. This company was persuaded to produce thymidine by the ton.

In March 1987, the FDA released Retrovir for treatment for adult patients with symptomatic HIV infection, those patients for whom the drug had been

---

[14] David Barry, testimony before the House Committee on Government Operations Subcommittee on Intergovernmental Relations and Human Resources, July 1, 1987.

shown to be beneficial in clinical trials. Although no hard figures were available, it was believed that about 50,000 individuals in the United States had symptomatic HIV infection. The recommended dosage for symptomatic HIV patients was 1,200 milligrams every day, administered in twelve 100-milligram capsules.

Research and Development Costs

The direct research and development costs associated with Retrovir were estimated to be about $50 million, according to industry analysts.[15] This cost was considered low, since the typical cost of developing a new drug in the United States is $125 million. Indeed, Wellcome PLC had spent $726 million for research and development on dozens of drugs in the five years preceding approval of Retrovir without producing a major commercial success. However, when the costs of new plant and equipment to produce Retrovir were also considered, total research and development cost estimates ranged from $80 to $100 million. Furthermore, the company provided the equivalent of $10 million of the drug free to 4,500 AIDS patients and supplied free of charge a metric ton of AZT to the National Institutes of Health's AIDS Clinical Trials Group.

Burroughs Wellcome's research and development effort did benefit from AZT being designated as an "orphan drug" in 1985 under provisions of the Orphan Drug Act of 1983. This act, which applies to drugs useful in treating 200,000 or fewer people in the United States, confers special consideration to suppliers of these drugs. For example, the orphan drug designation for Retrovir provided a seven-year marketing exclusivity after its commercial introduction, tax credits, and government subsidization of clinical trials.

 ## MARKETING OF RETROVIR

Initial distribution of Retrovir was limited because of its short supply in March 1987. A special distribution system was set up to ensure availability of the drug to those patients who had been shown to benefit from its use. This system remained in place until September 1987, when supplies were adequate and broader distribution was possible.

The initial price set for Retrovir to drug wholesalers in March 1987 was $188 for a hundred 100-milligram capsules. This price represented an annual cost to AIDS patients ranging from $8,528 to $9,745 depending upon wholesaler and pharmacy margins, which combined ranged from 5 to 20 percent. An immediate controversy was created, with the public, media, and AIDS patient-advocacy groups seeking justification of the price for Retrovir, a decrease in its price, or federal subsidization. Critics pointed out that, for comparison, the annual cost of interferon, a cancer-fighting drug, was only $5,000. The cofounder of Project Inform, an AIDS treatment information agency, said, "I think that Burroughs Wellcome is very interested in getting all their money back as soon as possible, because the sun won't shine forever."[16] Congressional hearings resulted in the chair of the House Subcommittee on Health and the Environment charging that Burroughs Wellcome's "expectation was that those people who want to buy the drug will come up with the money" and that the government would "step in" to

---

[15] Cost estimates have been made by industry analysts and have not been confirmed or denied by Burroughs Wellcome.

[16] "'The Unhealthy Profits of AZT,'" *The Nation* (October 17, 1987):407.

subsidize those who could not.[17] Congress subsequently created a $30 million emergency fund for AIDS patients who were unable to afford the cost of AZT.[18]

Company officials acknowledged that the pricing decision was difficult to make. According to one official, "We didn't know the demand, how to produce it in large quantities, or what competing drugs would come out in the market. There was no way to find out." Another company official said, "I guess we assumed that the drug . . . would be paid in some manner by the patient himself out of his own pocket or by third-party payers. We really didn't get into a lot of calculation along those lines."[19]

On December 15, 1987, the capsule price of Retrovir was reduced by 20 percent. The company announced that the price reduction was made possible because of cost savings achieved in the production process and an improved supply of synthetically manufactured thymidine. The company continued its research on AZT throughout 1988 into 1989, including treatments for children with HIV infection. In August 1989, this research program indicated that Retrovir produced positive results in postponing the appearance of AIDS in HIV-infected people. This development expanded the potential users of the drug to between 600,000 and 1 million people. (However, industry sources believe that fewer than one-half of the people with HIV have been tested and told of their condition and would thus be seeking treatment.) FDA approval for marketing to this larger population was expected by March 1990.

Recognizing the expanded potential patient population and anticipated production economies, the capsule price of Retrovir was again reduced by 20 percent in September 1989. In reference to this price reduction, Burroughs Wellcome's *1989 Annual Report* noted:

> In arriving at our decision to reduce the price, we carefully weighed a number of factors. These included our responsibility to patients and shareholders, the very real remaining uncertainties in the marketplace, and the vital need to fund our continuing research and development programmes.[20]

The new price to drug wholesalers was set at $120 for a hundred 100-milligram capsules. The retail price to users was about $150 for a hundred 100-milligram capsules. Industry analysts estimated that the direct cost of manufacturing and marketing Retrovir was 30 to 50 cents per capsule.[21]

Sales of Retrovir since its introduction are shown in Exhibit 6. Unit volume for Retrovir in fiscal 1990 was forecasted to be 53 percent higher than fiscal 1989 unit volume.

Patient-advocacy groups continued to criticize the pricing of Retrovir. AIDS activists chanted such slogans as "Be the first on your block to sell your Burroughs Wellcome stock" while picketing stock exchanges in London, New York, and San Francisco. The executive director of the National Gay and Lesbian Task Force said, "To make AZT accessible to everyone who should be on it, Burroughs Wellcome has an obligation to give up a significant amount of money to allow people to get access."[22] Members of Senator Edward Kennedy's staff began researching possible ways to nationalize the drug by invoking a law that allows the U.S. government to revoke exclusive licenses in the interest of national security. In addition, there were published reports that the American Civil Liberties Union was considering a

---

[17] 1987 FDC Reports—the Pink Sheet 49 (11):5.

[18] "Find the Cash or Die Sooner," *Time* (September 5, 1988):27.

[19] "The Inside Story of the AIDS Drug," *Fortune* (November 5, 1990):124–125.

[20] Wellcome PLC, *1989 Annual Report*, p. 13.

[21] "How Much for a Reprieve from AIDS?" *Time* (October 2, 1989):81.

[22] "AZT Maker to Reap Big Gain," *New York Times* (August 19, 1989):8.

| EXHIBIT 6 | Retrovir Sales Volume, Fiscal 1987–1989 |

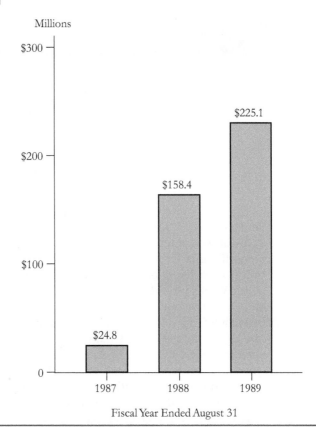

Note: U.S. dollar sales volume computed using average exchange rates £1 = $1.55 (1987), £1 = $1.76 (1988), and £1 = $1.68 (1989).

Source: Wellcome PLC, *1990 Annual Report.*

suit against Burroughs Wellcome. The suit would challenge the 17-year-use patent awarded Burroughs Wellcome for Retrovir, arguing that government scientists discovered AZT's efficacy against HIV.[23] The Subcommittee on Health and the Environment of the U.S. House of Representatives, which had already launched an investigation into possible "inappropriate" pricing of the drug, continued its hearings. However, Sir Alfred Sheppard, the company's chair, remained firm, saying "There's no plan to make another price cut." Later in 1990, he added, "If we wrapped the drug in a £10 note and gave it away, people would say it cost too much."[24]

In January 1990, the FDA approved modified dosage guidelines for Retrovir. These guidelines reduced the recommended adult dosage to 500 milligrams per day for some symptomatic AIDS patients from the original recommended dosage of 1,200 milligrams per day established in 1987. However, some clinicians warned that lower dosages should be prescribed cautiously. Also in January, congressional lobbyists began a campaign to curb "excessive profits earned by the drug industry as a whole." Industry observers were speculating that the price of Retrovir might have to be cut again sometime in 1990 because of continued pressure from the U.S. Congress, the media, and AIDS patient-advocacy groups.[25]

[23] "A Stitch in Time," *The Economist* (August 18, 1990):21–22.

[24] "The Inside Story of the AIDS Drug," *Fortune* (November 5, 1990):124–125.

[25] "Profiting from Disease," *The Economist* (January 27, 1990):17–18.

Case

Circle Corporation

January 1, 2012, found Yong Soo Kang, CEO of Circle Corporation, sitting alone in his office contemplating a decision weighing heavily on the future of his company. Kang is frequently mistaken for being older, often by a factor of two decades, most likely because of his many six-to seven-day workweeks at Hyundai Motor Works plus countless hours managing his own company, and today he felt old. Dr. David Sorell, head of noise suppression at Quiet Climate Control (QCC), had just left his office. Quiet Climate Control is a division of AutoAC Corporation, one of the largest Tier 1 suppliers of air-conditioning systems for automobile manufacturers. Kang had recently returned from visiting one of its factories in Ontario, Canada, and today Dr. Sorell had asked Kang to submit a bid to supply air-conditioning mufflers to QCC. At hand is a major opportunity for Circle Corporation to dramatically expand its business beyond the borders of South Korea, but meeting QCC's price target could put the company in jeopardy. Kang has until March 15, 2012, to obtain answers to a number of questions, develop a strategic plan, and determine if he should submit a bid at QCC's targeted price— or simply pass on the opportunity. Production of 2013 model automobiles is expected to begin in June. If Circle's bid is accepted, QCC will need to complete its redesign of the Circle-enhanced noise suppression components for insertion into new automobiles by the end of May.

 THE COMPANY

Using his personal savings of US $350,000, Yong Soo Kang established Circle Corporation as a small machine shop in 2001. Kang had spent the previous 21 years working for the Hyundai Motor Group in South Korea, starting as a machinist but eventually managing the sheet-metal-forming manufacturing processes for the Elantra (Avante in Korea) automobile line launched in October 1990. Kang had received a bachelor's degree in mechanical engineering in 1980 from the Korea Advanced Institute of Science & Technology (KAIST), considered South Korea's best engineering school, where he was voted the most creative student in his class.

Circle Corporation is headquartered on the southeastern tip of the Korean peninsula in Busan, South Korea's second-largest city, about 280 miles southeast of

Seoul. With a population of 3.6 million inhabitants, Busan is the fifth-largest seaport in the world. Circle manufactures various machine parts but specializes in mufflers and ferrules for automotive air-conditioning (A/C) systems to reduce noise and increase system reliability.[1] Currently Circle employs 23 people, including Kang. Among these employees is a very talented R&D team consisting of Jeong Oh Kwon, a specialist in material engineering; Sang Rhee, a specialist in stamping machinery responsible for design and drawing; David Park, a process management system specialist responsible for quality assurance; Tae Su Kang, an expert in manufacturing machinery, precision processes, and electronic diagrams; and Nancy Kim, an expert in electronic measurement. The team has created and patented several technologies for extruding, stamping, and manipulating aluminum. Kang himself holds four design patents and a patented process for manufacturing a seamless muffler.

By the end of 2010, Circle was producing approximately 3.5 million ferrules and 120,000 A/C mufflers every month, roughly 5.5 percent and 3.0 percent, respectively, of the worldwide market for ferrules and A/C mufflers, even though it marketed its products only in South Korea. One of Circle's largest customers is the Hyundai Kia Automotive Group. Although company revenues increased from US $2.7 million in 2007 to $6.2 million in 2010, in 2011 they increased by only $400,000, to $6.6 million. Consequently, the company is looking for new sources of revenue, especially outside South Korea.

In December 2011, Kang visited the Quiet Climate Control (QCC) Division of AutoAC Corporation in Ontario, Canada. AutoAC is a leading global automotive supplier that designs, engineers, and manufactures climate control systems and interior electronic and lighting products for automobile manufacturers, and provides a range of products and services to aftermarket customers. AutoAC conducts business with all of the world's major automotive manufacturers. It has manufacturing facilities in 26 countries and corporate offices in the United States, China, and the United Kingdom, and employs approximately 30,000 people.

During Kang's visit to the QCC, AutoAC engineers were enthusiastic about the technology that Circle had developed and agreed to evaluate Circle's A/C muffler in one of their vehicle platforms. A successful evaluation may lead to standardization of the Circle Corporation design across all vehicle platforms. AutoAC and its subsidiaries produce approximately 2.6 million automotive air-conditioning systems per year. Capturing AutoAC's business would be a major step toward gaining a significant portion of the annual global demand for automotive A/C mufflers. AutoAC's production may represent only a relatively small percentage of total automobile A/C demand, but the company is highly respected by automotive original equipment manufacturers (OEMs), and obtaining its business would help reduce the stigma of Circle Corporation being thought of as just one of Hyundai's "captive" in-country suppliers. Although QCC has provided Kang with a price target that Circle's muffler would need to meet if AutoAC is to consider switching, he does not know whether Circle should, or even could, meet the price target.

 ## AUTOMOTIVE AIR-CONDITIONING MUFFLERS

Automotive air-conditioning mufflers dampen the offending pressure pulsation sound generated by A/C compressor pulses and the expansion and contraction of refrigerant as it cycles between liquid and gas states. Most automobile owners

---

[1] A ferrule is a circular ring of metal or plastic used to hold wires, fibers, or posts together. Examples include the metal sleeve that is crimped to hold an eraser in place on a pencil or a plastic band that binds the bristles of a brush to its handle.

EXHIBIT 1	Common Automotive Air-Conditioning Muffler Assembly

are not aware that their vehicle's A/C system has or needs a muffler—a testament to these mufflers' effectiveness. (See Exhibit 1 for pictures of a common automotive air-conditioner muffler assembly.)

Circle Corporation has developed an improved automotive A/C muffler whose unique design seamlessly integrates a muffler with the flow tubes that carry the refrigerant. The design includes a patented process for manufacturing A/C muffler components. The process in turn permits the fabrication of a one-piece muffler and flow tube that takes the place of an equivalent assembly made up of three to four separate fabricated components that must be assembled and welded or brazed together. Whereas the traditional design requires multiple-process streams and alloys, the Circle A/C muffler is formed from a single aluminum tube blank in a single-process stream, thereby eliminating likely points of failure, including leaks where the tube and muffler are welded or brazed together. This process also has the potential to reduce the cost of production, provided economies of scale can be met to offset the significant fixed cost of equipment required. Circle's patented process also enables a baffle to be integrated inside the muffler that extends the muffler's range of performance. Exhibit 2 contains various automotive A/C mufflers and ferrules and the Circle seamless muffler. Exhibit 3 illustrates steps in the standard automotive air-conditioner muffler stamping process and the steps in Circle's stamping process.

EXHIBIT 2	Varieties of A/C Mufflers, Ferrules, and the Circle Seamless Muffler

Variety of A/C mufflers

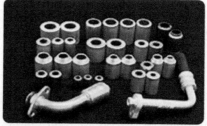

Variety of ferrules

Circle seamless muffler with integrated hose

| EXHIBIT 3 | Standard Stamping Process Versus Circle's Three-Step Process |

Standard 11-to 14-step stamping process

Circle's three-step process

Benefits of the Circle muffler to automotive A/C manufacturers include eliminating steps in the manufacturing process to improve efficiency, eliminating potential leak sites in the finished product, and reducing tooling costs and complexity by creating a standard muffler component that can be used across all vehicle platforms for all OEM customers.

 ## AUTOMOTIVE INDUSTRY

To gain entry into the hypercompetitive automobile industry, Circle Corporation needs to understand the interdependencies of the various parties and how these interdependencies shape the buying decisions of each party. Only by understanding these interdependencies will Circle be able to make an informed decision as to whether it should try to gain an international foothold.

At the top of the automobile manufacturing food chain are the original equipment manufacturers (OEMs), who are the name-brand automobile manufacturers, like Ford Motor Company, General Motors, Honda, Hyundai, Toyota, Volkswagen, and so forth. A Tier 1 supplier is a company that makes products specifically for one or more of the OEMs. Tier 1 suppliers include companies like Delphi, Johnson Controls, Visteon, and, of course, AutoAC. A Tier 2 supplier sells products to a Tier 1 supplier. Tier 2 companies supply parts that are a component of a system that a Tier 1 company supplies to OEMs. Circle Corporation is a Tier 2 supplier.

Both OEMs and Tier 1 suppliers tend to have primary and secondary suppliers to manage costs and ensure availability of critical components. An OEM will have a primary Tier 1 supplier that it relies on for designs and assistance and to which it may give 60 percent of its business for a particular component, and two or more secondary or "backup" Tier 1 suppliers that share the remainder of its business for the component. Similarly, Tier 1 suppliers follow the OEMs' strategy of using primary and secondary Tier 2 suppliers to foster competition and be assured of on-time delivery of parts and components.

Automotive Suppliers

The increasing and unrelenting pressure for shorter lead times in the automotive industry has led to shorter delivery cycles, lean manufacturing, slashed costs, exemplary quality, and generally just-in-time manufacturing, forcing many companies to take a nontraditional look at their supply chains. In the past, OEMs and their suppliers exploited one another as much as possible to either increase revenue or reduce costs. However, as competition among automobile brands increased, both groups began to realize that they were actually losing their competitive edge as a result. This led to a wave of downsizing, primarily to reduce labor costs. Unfortunately, downsizing had negative consequences because the employees who remained had more work than they could effectively handle, which in turn led to poor quality, production, and delivery problems.

One result of downsizing was that automobile manufacturers or OEMs shifted away from internal component design and manufacturing by contracting with Tier 1 suppliers to provide modular segments. The bulk of the responsibility for both design concepts and manufacturing of modules now lies with the Tier 1 suppliers chosen by the OEMs. Modules include systems such as the interior lighting package, fuel system storage, braking system, and air-conditioning system. OEMs typically provide the basic automobile design, engine, and drive train, whereas related accessories are left to Tier 1 suppliers for development and production.

To be considered a Tier 1 supplier, an automotive supplier must typically comply with the standards published by the International Organization for Standardization or ISO. These standards are designed to help organizations ensure they meet the needs of customers and other stakeholders. The basic concept is to ensure that zero defects, 100 percent on-time delivery, and continuous improvement are the key factors of supply chains. ISO 9000 deals with the fundamentals of quality management systems, including management principles on which the family of standards is based. ISO 9001 deals with the requirements that organizations wishing to meet the standard have to fulfill. More than one million organizations worldwide are independently certified ISO 9001, making it one of the most widely used management tools in the world today.

Contracts between OEMs and their Tier 1 suppliers frequently include a provision that the supplier reduce its price by a specified amount at predetermined intervals throughout the term of a contract. Thus, one objective of a supplier is to lower costs sufficiently to meet or exceed an OEM's price targets, otherwise profit margins will decline and the supplier may even lose money. When a Tier 1 supplier examines a new part or component from a Tier 2 supplier for possible replacement of a part or component presently in use, even if the part or component is better, quieter, more efficient, more reliable, lighter, smaller, or faster, there may not be enough of an advantage for the Tier 2 supplier to obtain a sale. Usually the possible replacement part or component must also be less costly or at least at cost parity with the current part or component.

Due to the complex nature of automobiles, each consisting of thousands of parts, OEMs literally scrutinize costs down to the penny. A four-cent increase in the cost of an A/C muffler may represent only 3 percent of a muffler's total cost and only 0.009 percent of an entire A/C system cost, but for the OEM that is purchasing 3 million A/C mufflers per year, it could represent $120,000 in lost profit that could have been avoided. Although the $120,000 represents only a minute fraction of the OEM's multibillion-dollar revenue stream, given the volume of fixed expenditures that OEMs are saddled with, the intense competition they face, and lower-cost competitors in South Korea and, in the near future, China, lopping $120,000 off profits, even with a better product, will not necessarily result in OEM sales. However, if an OEM could lower the cost of 250 parts by an average of just four cents each, it could add $30 million to the company's annual profit.

To remain a preferred Tier 1 or Tier 2 supplier, companies rely on their ability to drive down the cost of production through economies of scale. For the machine parts industry, economies of scale are critical toward reducing per-unit cost:

- Most machine parts are commodity items.

- Investment in expensive automated fabrication equipment translates into high fixed costs.

- Because of this, competitors attempt to gain competitive advantage by reducing unit costs through economies of scale.

Financial Stability

The business and financial stability of Tier 2 suppliers is important to Tier 1 suppliers. Tier 1 suppliers in the automotive industry typically supply only a few to a handful of OEMs. Losing any one of these business relationships could result in financial disaster. If a small, but critical component no longer becomes available to a Tier 1 supplier because of financial issues faced by a Tier 2 supplier, it can take months for the Tier 1 and new (replacement) Tier 2 suppliers to develop the needed component, sufficiently test it, then gear-up manufacturing to produce it in large-enough quantities to meet an OEM's needs. As a consequence, Tier 1 suppliers typically insist that their Tier 2 suppliers pass certain financial thresholds to minimize the possibility of financial instability. For example, AutoAC requires candidate suppliers to complete a Financial Health Assessment (FHA). The FHA consists of U.S. standard financial documents including an audited balance sheet setting forth income, cash flow, debt structure, and working capital.

Competition

Although Circle Corporation would face competition from firms such as Yam Corporation in South Korea and Jiangtong Mechanical Group in China if it tries to break into the international market, its main competition for the AutoAC business would be PowerPress Corporation in Tennessee. PowerPress presently supplies QCC with most of its mufflers and ferrules. Almost 25 percent of PowerPress's revenue comes from AutoAC. The relationship between AutoAC and PowerPress has been a close one for many years. Should PowerPress lose AutoAC's muffler or ferrule business, it is likely that PowerPress would have to lay off part of its workforce. Besides mufflers and ferrules, PowerPress manufactures other components for AutoAC. Should it fall into financial difficulty, PowerPress may find its survival in jeopardy. In a head-to-head competition with PowerPress, Circle must consider the roles and costs of parts other than A/C mufflers and ferrules that PowerPress supplies to AutoAC.

Yam Corporation is Hyundai's other major supplier of A/C mufflers and ferrules. Recently Yam made its first sale outside South Korea and is now supplying GM's Daewoo division. Jiangtong Mechanical Group provides machine parts to many Chinese automobile manufacturers, including Chery Automotive, Geely Automobile, and Changfeng Motors. All three manufacturers export some models outside China and are expected to enter the U.S. market by 2014. On several occasions Circle has competed with Jiangtong, but in all but one instance has lost the bid due to Jiangtong's aggressive pricing strategy.

All of Circle's competitors use the conventional IMPACT production technology. Although more wasteful of material and energy than Circle's production technology, IMPACT equipment is standardized, readily available, and investments in equipment by the competitors have already taken place and may only need to be supplemented.

 ## THE DECISION

Kang knew that Circle's A/C seamless muffler was neither less costly nor even at cost parity with the current AutoAC muffler. He therefore hired a consultant to meet with David Sorell. Kang asked the consultant if she would contact Sorell to gain some perspective as to whether QCC might have some flexibility in its pricing, especially in light of the benefits that it would receive with the Circle seamless muffler. Following her discussion with Sorell, the consultant told Kang that Dr. Sorell was indeed very pleased with Circle's seamless muffler, saw a lot of promise in the design, and was looking forward to the evaluation. She mentioned, however, that the ultimate buyer of the muffler would be OEMs, and OEMs almost never pay more for something they did not specify in their contract. Although Circle's muffler possessed attractive advantages, the primary beneficiary would be AutoAC. Dr. Sorell commented to the consultant, "Ford will not spend more money so their suppliers have fewer headaches assembling systems. In the past, when we've shown them a quality improvement that increased the price just eighteen cents a unit, unless they had specifically asked for it or they will realize a profitable return on it within two years or less, they will not even consider it."

Kang and his R&D team, although optimistic, know they need to go "outside the box" if they are to have a chance of winning AutoAC's business. One alternative is to make a weighty financial gamble by submitting a bid at or under AutoAC's price target. AutoAC's acceptance of the bid would entail a significant capital expenditure for Circle that could quickly drive the company into unprofitability if it did not obtain a significant slice of AutoAC's business. At Kang's request, Chris Kim, Circle's comptroller, compiled a table (see the following table) setting forth the specific QCC requested bid in terms of desired muffler sizes, number of units it would purchase in 2012, and price targets. Kim also included Circle's unit break-even price and "normal" price for comparison.

Part Number	Muffler Description	2012 Volume	Unit Price (USD)		
			QCC Target	Circle's Break-Even	21% Profit Target
F8DH-19E920-EA	9.25" w/3" muffler	53,000	$0.88	$0.91	$1.10
F8DH-19E920-FA	9.75" w/3" muffler	65,000	0.96	0.99	1.20
F8DH-19E920-GA	10.5" w/3.5" muffler	74,000	1.05	1.10	1.33
F8DH-19E920-HA	11" w/3.5" muffler	52,000	1.14	1.18	1.43

After reviewing the QCC bid parameters, Kang asked Kim to explain the numbers. Kim replied that Kang should "look at the first row for muffler part F8DH-19E920-EA. QCC wants a bid for 53,000 units for which it is willing to pay $0.88 per unit. Unfortunately, our break-even price is $0.91, so we would actually lose $0.03 on every unit sold. Moreover, our normal unit price for this part, including our standard profit margin of 21 percent, is $1.10. Neither the desired quantity nor price target makes sense for us." Kim continued, "I have created a similar table [see the following table], but this time based it on hypothetical demand estimates that would permit our company to capitalize on economies of scale. What do you think of these numbers?"

Dr. Sorell had told Kang when they met in Busan that even if all goes well with the evaluation, AutoAC is most likely to roll out the Circle A/C muffler when existing automobile models undergo a significant update (models are typically updated every four to five years). AutoAC, like other component suppliers to automobile manufacturers, will normally wait until production of a new model or redesign of an existing model to begin integration of a new part—it is reluctant to restructure current manufacturing, assembly, and testing procedures on a line currently in operation unless a breakdown occurs that requires the new part. Completely new models, though, could be designed with the new muffler from day one, but such introductions occur rarely. Given the QCC bid parameters, Circle is faced with producing as few as 20,000 A/C mufflers a month during the first year of the contract, or less than 15 percent of a new stamping machine's capacity.

Part Number	Muffler Description	Annual Volume	Unit Price (USD)		
			QCC Target	Circle's Break Even	21% Profit Target
F8DH-19E920-EA	9.25" w/3" muffler	212,000	$0.88	$0.81	$0.98
F8DH-19E920-FA	9.75" w/3" muffler	260,000	0.96	0.84	1.01
F8DH-19E920-GA	10.5" w/3.5" muffler	296,000	1.05	0.88	1.06
F8DH-19E920-HA	11" w/3.5" muffler	208,000	1.14	0.92	1.11

Kang speculated that Circle may have a chance with a bid slightly above QCC's price target. Following a successful evaluation and pilot program, AutoAC may at least standardize on Circle's muffler for systems supplied to its premium brands such as Mercedes, BMW, and Jaguar. Kang was unsure whether AutoAC would switch to the new muffler for its U.S. luxury brands, Cadillac and Lincoln, because many of the models share the same platform with their corresponding mainstream brands (i.e., Chevrolet and Ford). Since reducing parts proliferation was a major objective of all OEMs, it would not make sense to change one air-conditioning system but not the other.

For an outsider attempting to gain entry as a Tier 2 supplier, obtaining economies of scale becomes a catch-22. As Nancy Kim put it, "If we're selected as the new supplier and the customer gives us all or most of its business, we can obtain economies of scale. However, to get most or all of the business, we need to already be scaled up with new capital equipment in place."

One possible solution to the problem is for Circle to win AutoAC's considerable ferrule business. Because Circle's patented manufacturing process reduces raw material loss by 20 to 40 percent when producing ferrules, and because there is excess capacity on Circle's ferrule manufacturing machines, it may be possible to meet any AutoAC ferrule price target and "get a foot in the door," regardless of the outcome of the QCC A/C muffler bid. This would provide Circle needed income for the required muffler capital expenditure, and may help Circle obtain a grant from the South Korean government. The government offers grants to Korean SMEs (small and medium-size enterprises) that attempt to market their products internationally. Although a grant would not lower the variable cost of producing Circle's mufflers, it would lower Circle's capital expense and allow it to accelerate production readiness.

Because of the capital expenditure required, Kang began to contemplate whether the company could get by with just its current stamping machine in the first year if it is able to contract with QCC. The numbers that Kim had reported were based on the assumption that a second stamping machine was needed. A second custom-designed, patented stamping machine would require an upfront investment of approximately $700,000. Moreover, the high fixed cost of such a machine would be the same whether it's producing 1,000 or 100,000 mufflers per month. Circle's operations director, Kaycee Sung, cautioned that current production is at 90 percent of capacity, that Hyundai's sales were picking up, and that the company surely should not risk falling short of its number one customer's needs. Based on his prior analysis, Kim estimated that Circle could profitably meet QCC's price target once a second machine is producing at least 50,000 to 60,000 seamless mufflers per month. Sung again cautioned the management team, stating that "mass production of the integrated muffler and connecting pipe design is untested—all samples have been 'one-offs' so far. Current production has been just the muffler made from aluminum tube blanks rather than the proposed practice of stamping solid blanks of metal. If AutoAC is going to take the leap with Circle, it will only be interested in going with the most advanced and potentially trouble-free design, the seamless muffler and hose."

The FHA Issue

In preparation for submitting a bid to AutoAC, Circle's accountant submitted its Financial Health Assessment documents to AutoAC. A week after submitting the documents, Circle received a financial assessment grade of "D." Kang was informed that AutoAC requires at least a "C" grade from its candidate suppliers. Circle's FHA assessment disqualified it from being a supplier to AutoAC.

When Kang reviewed the FHA documents, he realized that there was some misunderstanding due to language translation difficulties. In particular, there were a number of responses to the financial items that did not accurately reflect the respective accounting item's definition in the United States. These included:

- Accounts Receivable: Circle provides its major customers 60-day payment invoices. In AutoAC's FHA, only accounts receivable 30 days or less qualify for "current" status. Most of Circle's customers are large corporations with good payment records. Sixty-day payment invoices are a common practice in Korea.

- Other Assets: Circle recorded practically no value under Plant, Property & Equipment, but a very high figure under Other Assets—normally reserved for such "soft" assets as intellectual property. Due to different asset classification practices, almost the entire dollar amount that Circle placed under Other Assets represented its Plant, Property & Equipment.

- Income Statement: Circle's 2008 total revenue was 3,500,072,609 Korean won. The initial FHA reported 2008 total revenue as $2,672,000, whereas the corrected FHA reported $3,174,000. The Circle accountant mistakenly used the average exchange rate for the first half of FY '09 rather than the average for 2008.

- Total Revenue: The KRW/USD exchange rate during Q1 averaged $1 = 1,377 KRW. Because the US dollar was 25 percent stronger than last year's average, Circle's revenue converted to dollars also appeared 25 percent lower than it was in fact.

- Debt Structure: Korea Industrial Bank showed the amount Circle borrowed as of 3/31/10 as $1,022,000. Three months later it showed $0. Circle restructured its debts. Circle is acknowledged as an "innovation corporation" in Korea—thus most debts are guaranteed by the Korean government through what is called a Technology Warranty. Banks typically treat these companies as having less than average risk. This treatment provides Circle with latitude to retire or extend debts in accordance with company objectives, opportunities, and interest rates.

Once corrections were made and the FHA resubmitted to AutoAC, Circle received a financial assessment grade of "B."

Customs and Shipping

With PowerPress's Tennessee plant just two days by truck to Ontario, Canada, plus the advantage of very small import duties because of NAFTA, Kang had assumed that PowerPress had an insurmountable advantage in transportation costs and import fees to QCC's plants. To confirm his assumption, Kang contacted an import specialist who put him in touch with the U.S. Customs & Border Protection, Department of Homeland Security's national import specialist overseeing aluminum pipes and tubes. After seeing photos and diagrams of the A/C mufflers, the specialist stated they could be classified as HS#760900. (The Harmonized Commodity Description and Coding System [HS] determines the tariff nomenclature of an item. Each HS number is subject to the specific duties that an importing country chooses to impose on the item.) To his surprise, Kang discovered that even with NAFTA, parts entering Canada from South Korea and classified under HS#760900 carry less import duty than parts from the United States. This surprising circumstance is due to a general preferential tariff (GPT) that Canada grants South Korea on certain HS classifications.

The QCC division of AutoAC has plants around the world, including Mexico, Czech Republic, Argentina, China, and India. If QCC is willing to receive shipments of Circle's A/C mufflers intended for its Mexico plant at its El Paso, Texas, facility, then under Mexico's Program of Sectoral Promotion (PROSEC), South Korean goods would not have any import duties imposed. The remaining countries where QCC operates impose identical import duties regardless of whether the A/C mufflers are produced in the United States or South Korea.

Closer review of the locations of QCC's global plants revealed that Circle actually holds a shipping advantage over PowerPress. For example, the QCC manufacturing plant in Nanchang City, China, is just south of Busan. Being located in Busan means that shipping to any city in the world does not require inland transportation to get Circle's products to a port of embarkation. Using standardized shipping containers, ocean freight can be very economical, even for heavy metal items. Thus, while Kang initially believed that Circle's importation and transportation costs would be considerably higher than those of PowerPress, after identifying several nuances in parts classifications and preferential tariffs, he calculated that annual company shipping and delivery expenses would be approximately $140,000 less than Kim initially calculated when estimating tariffs, customs broker charges and customs fees, shipping expenses, merchandise processing fees, and harbor maintenance fees.

Case

Augustine Medical, Inc.

The Bair Hugger Patient Warming System

Augustine Medical, Inc. was incorporated as a Minnesota corporation to develop and market products for hospital operating rooms and postoperative recovery rooms. The first two products the company planned to produce and sell were a patented patient warming system designed to treat postoperative hypothermia in the recovery room and a tracheal intubation guide for use in the operating room and in emergency medicine.

Company executives were now actively engaged in finalizing the marketing program for the patient warming system, named Bair Hugger Patient Warming System. The principal question yet to be resolved was how to price this system.

 ## THE BAIR HUGGER PATIENT WARMING SYSTEM

The Bair Hugger Patient Warming System is a device designed to control the body temperature of postoperative patients. Specifically, the device is designed to treat hypothermia (a condition defined as a body temperature of less than 36 degrees Centigrade or 96 degrees Fahrenheit) experienced by patients after operations.

Medical research indicates that 60 to 80 percent of all postoperative recovery room patients are clinically hypothermic. Several factors contribute to postoperative hypothermia. They are (1) a patient's exposure to cold operating room temperatures (which are maintained for the surgeons' comfort and for infection control), (2) heat loss due to evaporation of the fluids used to scrub patients, (3) evaporation from the exposed bowel, and (4) breathing of dry anesthetic gases.

The Bair Hugger system consists of a heater/blower unit and a separate inflatable plastic/paper cover, or blanket. A photo of the system is shown in Exhibit 1. The heater/blower unit is a large, square, boxlike structure that heats, filters, and blows air through a plastic cover. An electric cord wraps around the

This case was prepared by Professor Roger A. Kerin, of the Edwin L. Cox School of Business, Southern Methodist University; Michael Gilbertson, of Augustine Medical, Inc.; and Professor William Rudelius, of University of Minnesota, as a basis for class discussion and is not designed to illustrate effective or ineffective handling of administrative situations. Certain names and data have been disguised. The assistance of graduate students Anne Christensen, Joanne Perty, and Laurel Wichman of the University of Minnesota is appreciated. The cooperation of Augustine Medical, Inc. in the preparation of the case is gratefully acknowledged. Copyright © 2000 by Roger A. Kerin. No part of this case may be reproduced without the written permission of the copyright holder.

EXHIBIT 1 **Bair Hugger Patient Warming System**

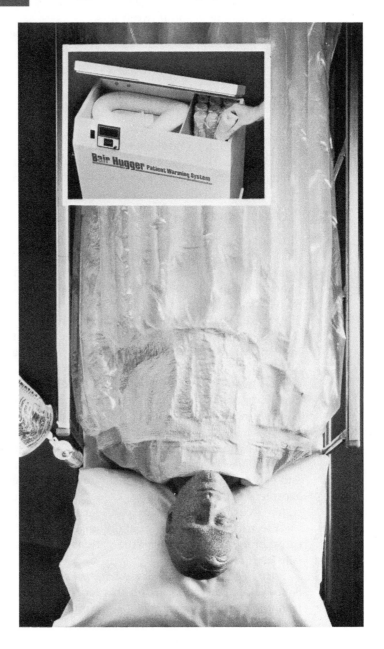

back of the unit for storage, and the unit is mounted on wheels for easy transport. The blower tubing attaches to the warming cover through a simple cardboard connector strap and can be retracted into the top of the unit for storage. Temperature is set by a dial with four settings on the top of the unit. A top lid opens to a storage bin that holds 12 warming covers for easy access. The disposable warming covers come packaged in 18-inch-long tubes. When unrolled, the plastic/paper cover is flat and covers an average-sized patient from shoulders to ankles. The blanket consists of a layer of thin plastic and a layer of plastic/paper material laminated into full-length channels. Small holes punctuate the inner surface of the cover. When inflated through a connection at the feet of the patient, the tubular structure arcs over the patient's body, creating an individual patient environment. The warm air exits through the slits on the inner surface of the blanket, creating a gentle flow of warm air over the patient. The warming time per patient is about two hours.

The plastic cover was patented. There is no patent protection for the heater/blower unit.

COMPETING TECHNOLOGIES

Many competing technologies are available for the prevention and treatment of hypothermia. These technologies generally fall into one of two broad types of patient warming: surface warming or internal warming.

Surface-Warming Technologies

Warmed hospital blankets are the most commonly used treatment for hypothermia in recovery rooms and elsewhere. An application of warmed hospital blankets consists of placing six to eight warmed blankets in succession on top of a patient. Almost all patients receive at least one application; it is estimated that 50 percent of the postoperative patients require more than one application. The advantages of warmed hospital blankets are that they are simple, safe, and relatively inexpensive. The main disadvantage is that they cool quickly, provide only insulation, and require the patient's own body heat for regenerating warmth.

Water-circulating blankets are the second most popular postoperative hypothermic treatment. Water-circulating blankets can be placed under a patient, over a patient, or both. If a blanket is placed just under the patient, only 15 percent of the body's surface area is affected. However, hospitals typically place water-circulating blankets either just over the patient or over and under the patient, forming an insulated environment that encloses 85 to 90 percent of the body's surface area. The disadvantages of water-circulating blankets are that they are heavy and expensive and can cause burns on pressure points. Moreover, although a widely used and accepted method of warming, especially for more severe cases of hypothermia, water-circulating blankets are considered only slightly to moderately effective.

Electric blankets are generally unacceptable as a hypothermic treatment because of the risk of burns to the patient and of explosion in areas where oxygen is in use.

Air-circulating blankets and mattresses are not in common use in the United States, although variations on this technology have been used in the past. This technology relies on warmed air flowing over the body to transfer heat to the patient. The advantages of warmed-air technology are that it is safe, lightweight, and theoretically more effective than warmed hospital blankets or water-circulating blankets. Products using this technology are not widely found in the U.S. market, however.

Thermal drapes, also known as reflective blankets, have recently been introduced and are gaining acceptance as a preventive measure used in the operating room. They consist of head covers, blankets, and leggings placed on the uninvolved portions of the patient's body. Their use is recommended when 60 percent of a patient's body surface can be covered. The advantages of this technology are that it is simple, safe, and inexpensive and has been shown to reduce heat loss. The disadvantage is that it merely insulates the patient and does not transfer heat to someone who is already hypothermic.

Infrared heating lamps are popular for infant use. When placed a safe distance from the body and shone on the skin, they radiate warmth to the patient. The advantages of heat lamps are that they are effective and illuminate the patient for observation or therapy. A disadvantage is that since the skin needs to be exposed, modesty prevents widespread use among adults. (They are, however, used in adult skin-graft operations.) Nurses dislike radiant heat lamps and panels because they tend to heat the entire recovery room and are uncomfortable to work under.

Partial warm-water immersion has been used in the past, especially in cases where a patient was deliberately cooled to slow down metabolism. With this method, the patient is placed in a bath of warm water and watched carefully. The advantages of this technology are that it transfers heat very effectively and it is simple. The disadvantages are that the system is inconvenient to set up and requires close monitoring of the patient, which increases labor costs. In addition, water baths must be carefully watched for bacterial growth, and they are very expensive to purchase and use.

Increasing room temperature is the most obvious way to prevent and treat hypothermia, but it is seldom used. The advantages of this method are that it is simple and relatively inexpensive and has been proven effective at temperatures of over 70 degrees Fahrenheit. The disadvantage is that warm room temperatures are not acceptable to the nurses and surgeons who must work in the environment. Furthermore, warm temperatures increase the risk of infection.

Internal-Warming Technologies

Inspiring *heated and humidified air* is a fairly effective internal-warming technique currently being used with intubated patients (those having a breathing tube in the trachea). However, delivery of heated and humidified air by mask or tent to nonintubated patients is not acceptable in postoperative situations, because mask or tent delivery would interfere with observation and communication and, in the case of a tent, might increase the chance of infection. The fact that the patient must be intubated is a disadvantage, since the vast majority of postoperative patients are not intubated.

Warmed intravenous (IV) fluids are used in more severe hypothermic cases to directly transfer heat to the circulatory system. Warmed IV fluids are very effective because they introduce warmth directly into the circulatory system. The disadvantages of this technology are that it requires very close monitoring of the patient's core temperature and high physician involvement.

Drug therapy diminishes the sensation of cold and reduces shivering but does not actually increase body temperature. Although drug therapy is convenient and makes patients feel more comfortable, it does not warm them and in fact slows their recovery from anesthesia and surgery.

COMPETITIVE PRODUCTS

A variety of competitive products that use the above-mentioned technologies are available (see Exhibit 2 on page 538). A review of competitors' sales materials and interviews with hospital personnel provided the following breakdown of competitive products.

Warmed Hospital Blankets

For treating adult hypothermia, hospitals use their own blankets, which they warm in large heating units. Many manufacturers produce heating units for hospital use. The cost of laundering six to eight two-pound hospital blankets averages $0.13 per pound. Laundering and heating costs are absorbed in hospital overhead.

EXHIBIT 2	Representative Competitive Products and Prices		

Product	List Price	Company	Comments
Blanketrol 200	$2,995/manual unit; $4,895/automatic unit; $165–$305/reusable blanket; $20/disposable blanket	Cincinnati Sub-Zero	Hypothermia equipment is a small part of its overall business.
MTA 4700	$4,735/unit; $139/reusable blanket; $24/disposable blanket	Gaymar Industries	Hypothermia equipment seems to be a major part of its business.
Aquamatic	$4,479/unit	American Hamilton (division of American Hospital Supply)	Hypothermia equipment is a very minor part of American Hospital Supply's business.
Climator	$4,000/unit	Hosworth Air Engineering Ltd.	The company could begin distribution of hypothermia equipment in the United States soon.

Water-Circulating Blankets

Several manufacturers produce water-circulating mattresses and blankets, but Cincinnati Sub-Zero, Gaymar Industries, and Pharmaseal are the major suppliers. Prices of automatic control units that measure both blanket and patient temperatures range from $4,850 to $5,295. Manual control units are priced at about $3,000, although they appear to be discounted by as much as 40 percent in actual practice.

The average life of water-circulating control units is 15 years. Reusable blankets list at from $168 to $375, depending on quality. Disposable blankets list at from $20 to $26. Volume discounts for blankets can reduce the list price by almost 50 percent.

Water-circulating blanket technology has changed little over the past 20 years except for the addition of solid state controls. There is little differentiation among the products of different firms.

Reflective Thermal Drapes

O. R. Concepts sells a product named the Thermadrape, which comes in both adult and pediatric sizes. Adult head covers list for $0.49 each; adult drapes list for $2.50 to $3.98, depending on size; leggings are priced at $1.50 each.

Air-Circulating Blankets and Mattresses

Two competitors are known to provide an air-circulating product like the Bair Hugger Patient Warming System; however, neither is currently sold in the United States. The Sweetland Bed Warmer and Cast Dryer was in use 25 years ago but is no longer manufactured. This product consisted of a heater/blower unit that directed warm air through a hose placed under a patient's blanket. The Hosworth-Climator is an English-made product that provides a controlled-temperature microclimate by means of air flow from a mattress. The Climator comes in a variety of models for use in recovery rooms, intensive care units, burn units, general wards, and patients' homes. The model most suitable for postoperative recovery rooms is priced at $4,000. This product could be distributed in the United States within the next year. A summary of representative competitor products and list prices is shown in Exhibit 2.

THE HOSPITAL MARKET

Approximately 21 million surgical operations are performed annually in the United States, or 84,000 operations per average eight-hour work day. Approximately 5,500 hospitals have operating rooms and postoperative recovery rooms.

Research commissioned by Augustine Medical, Inc. indicated that there are 31,365 postoperative recovery beds and 28,514 operating rooms in hospitals in the United States. An estimated breakdown of the number of postoperative hospital beds and the percentage of surgical operations is shown below:

Number of Postoperative Beds	Number of Hospitals	Estimated Percentage of Surgical Operations
0	1,608	0%
1–6	3,602	20
7–11	1,281	40
12–17	391	20
18–22	135	10
23–28	47	6
29–33	17	2
>33	17	2

Given the demand for postoperative recovery room beds, the research firm estimated that hospitals with fewer than seven beds would not be highly receptive to the Bair Hugger Patient Warming System. The firm also projected that one system would be sold for every eight postoperative recovery room beds.

Interviews with physicians and nurses, followed by a demonstration of the system, yielded a variety of responses:

1. Respondents believed that the humanitarian ethic "to make the patient feel more comfortable" is important.

2. Respondents felt that the Bair Hugger Patient Warming System would speed recovery for postop patients.

3. Respondents wanted to test the units under actual conditions in postoperative recovery rooms. They were reluctant to make any purchase commitments without testing. A typical comment was "No one today, in this market, ever buys a pig in a poke."

4. Respondents felt that the product was price-sensitive to alternative methods. Respondents were very receptive to the notion of using the heater/blower free of charge and paying for only the disposable blankets. Physicians wanted to confer with others who would be responsible for using the product to administer the warming treatment, however, such as the head nurse in postoperative recovery rooms and the chief anesthesiologist.

5. Respondents believed that the pressure to move patients through the operating room and out of postop is greater than in the past. *Efficiency* is the byword.

6. Capital expenditures in hospitals were subject to budget committee approval. Although the amounts varied, expenditures for equipment over $1,500 were typically subject to a formal review and decision process.

 AUGUSTINE MEDICAL, INC.

Augustine Medical, Inc. was founded by Dr. Scott Augustine, an anesthesiologist. His experience had convinced him that hospitals needed and desired a new approach to warming patients after surgery. His medical knowledge, coupled with

---

EXHIBIT 3 **Sales Literature for the Bair Hugger Patient Warming System**

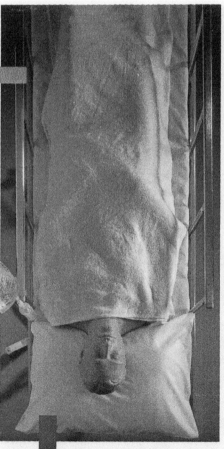

EXHIBIT 3 *(Continued)*

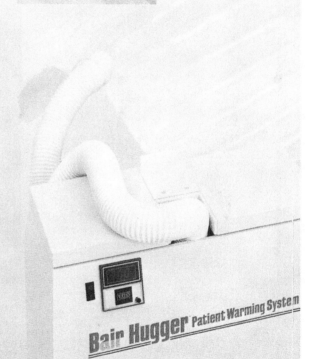

A Warm Welcome for Your Recovery Room Patients

Augustine Medical, Inc.'s new Bair Hugger™ Patient Warming System is the most practical and comforting solution for post-operative hypothermia available today.

Every year more than 10,000,000 hospital patients experience the severe discomfort and vital signs instability associated with post-operative hypothermia. Years later, patients can still vividly recall this discomfort. Augustine Medical's new Patient Warming System is a warm and reliable solution to post-operative hypothermia.

A Practical Solution to Post-Operative Hypothermia

The Bair Hugger™ Patient Warming System consists of a Heat Source and a separate disposable Warming Cover that directs a gentle flow of warm air across the body and provides for safe and comfortable rewarming.

The Bair Hugger Heat Source uses a reliable, high efficiency blower, a sealed 400W heating element, and a microprocessor-based temperature control to create a continuous flow of warm air. There are no pumps, valves or compressors to maintain. Special features include built-in storage space for the air hose, power cord and a convenient supply of disposable Warming Covers. The Heat Source complies with all safety requirements for hospital equipment.

1. PATENTED SELF SUPPORTING DESIGN
   As the tubes fill with air, the Warming Cover naturally arches over the patient's body.
2. TISSUE PAPER UNDERLAYER
   The tissue paper underlayer of the Warming Cover is soft and comfortable against the patient's skin.
3. AIR SLITS
   Tiny slits in the underlayer allow warm air from the Heat Source to gently fill the space around the patient.
4. SHOULDER DRAPE
   The shoulder drape is designed to tuck under the chin and shoulders, trapping warm air under the cover and preventing air flow by the patient's face.
5. DISPOSABLE COVERS
   The disposable Covers prevent cross contamination and reduce laundry requirements.

(continued)

a technical flair, prompted the development of the Bair Hugger Patient Warming System.

The Bair Hugger Patient Warming System has several advantages over water-circulating blankets. First, warm air makes patients feel warm and stop shivering. Second, the system cannot cause burns, and water leaks around electrical equipment are not a problem, as they are with water-circulating blankets. Third, the disposable blankets eliminate the potential for cross-contamination among patients. Finally, the system does not require that the patient be lifted or rolled. Augustine's personal experience indicated that all of these features would be welcomed by nurses and patients alike. Features and benefits of the Bair Hugger Patient Warming System are detailed in the company's sales literature, shown in Exhibit 3.

Investor interest in Augustine Medical and the medical technology it provided produced an initial capitalization of $500,000. These funds were to be used for further research and development, staff support, facilities, and marketing. It

EXHIBIT 3 *(Continued)*

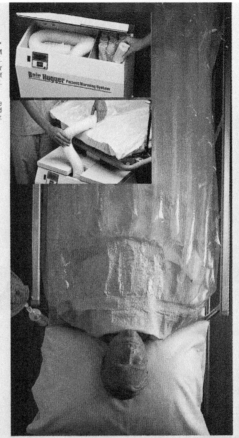

THE BAIR HUGGER™
PATIENT WARMING SYSTEM
IS SO EASY TO USE.
Remove a new Warming Cover
from the storage compartment
and unroll over the patient.

Connect the heater hose to the
inlet of the Warming Cover and
turn on the heater.

6. SIMPLE CONTROLS
A preprogrammed temperature range
and a preset high temperature limit of
110°F. make the Bair Hugger safe and
simple to use.

7. INTERNAL WARMING COVER STORAGE
The storage compartment provides a
convenient supply of Warming Covers
ready for immediate use.

8. INTERNAL HOSE STORAGE
The hose retracts into its own
compartment for ready access.

9. LIGHTWEIGHT, COMPACT DESIGN
The Heat Source is designed for
convenience and portability. While in
use, it tucks under the foot of the gurney.
The unit's light weight and small size
make it simple to move and store.

10. BUILT-IN POWER CORD STORAGE
The power cord storage holds up to 12
feet of cord, making the Heat Source
portable and easy to store.

11. 5μ AIR FILTER
The air filter assures dust-free air
circulation through the Bair Hugger
Warming Cover. The filter is simple to
change when necessary.

The Bair Hugger™ Warming Cover:

The Warming Cover consists of a layer of plastic and a layer of tissue paper laminate bonded together into long tubular channels. The self-supporting Warming Cover is designed to arch over the patient's body creating a warm, comfortable environment.

The Warming Cover is convenient to use because no straps, tapes or other fasteners are required to stabilize the cover and the patient does not have to be disturbed or moved.

When the Warming Cover is completely inflated, warm air from the Heat Source exits the tubular channels through slits in the Cover's soft underlayer, surrounding the patient with a gentle flow of warm air.

was believed that this initial investment would cover the fixed costs (including salaries, leased space, and promotional literature) of the company during its first year of operation. The company would subcontract the production of the heater/blower unit and would manufacture warming covers in-house using a proprietary machine. Only minor assembly would be performed by the company.

The Bair Hugger Patient Warming System would be sold by and through medical products distributor organizations in various regions around the country. These distributor organizations would call on hospitals, demonstrate the system, and maintain an inventory of blankets. The margin paid to the distributors would be competitively set at 30 percent of the delivered (that is, less discounts) selling price on the heater/blower unit and 40 percent of the delivered (discounted if necessary) price on the blankets.

EXHIBIT 3 *(Continued)*

A Warm and Practical Discovery:
Bair Hugger™ Patient Warming System

Post-Operative Hypothermia–
A Common Problem

As a practicing anesthesiologist, Dr. Scott D. Augustine observed that there was no practical treatment for the common problem of post-operative hypothermia. An extensive review of post-operative hypothermia revealed several important facts:

- Post-operative hypothermia ($T < 36°C$ or $<96.7°F$) occurs in 60-80% of all post-operative patients (1). This extremely common problem affects more than 10,000,000 surgical patients every year.

- Several factors contribute to post-operative hypothermia including the patient's exposure to cold operating room temperatures, heat loss due to evaporation of fluids used to scrub the patient, evaporation of moisture from exposed bowels, and the breathing of dry anesthetic gases.

- Unlike environmental hypothermia, post-operative hypothermia is not usually life threatening. However, it can have serious side effects for older or unstable patients. Negative effects include a decrease in cardiovascular stability and an increase in oxygen consumption of up to 400% during unaided rewarming, as well as severe shivering and significant patient discomfort (2).

- Patients with unstable body temperatures require intensive nursing care, which means higher costs. Recovery room time may also be prolonged due to the instability caused by post-operative hypothermia.

Variety of Treatments–Only One
Practical Solution

Many methods have been used to try to warm patients after surgery including warmed hospital blankets, water mattresses and heat lamps (3). Studies have shown, though, that these methods are ineffective.

The most common method of treating hypothermia–heated hospital blankets–does not actively heat the patient. The small amount of heat retained by a cotton blanket quickly dissipates, thereby requiring patients to rewarm themselves. Because multiple blankets are typically used, this method is both inconvenient and time-consuming for nursing staff and produces large amounts of laundry.

Another common method used to try to rewarm post-operative hypothermia patients is the use of a water circulating mattress. Water circulating equipment is heavy, complex, expensive and prone to leakage. While water mattresses have been used for many years, there is no clinical evidence that documents their effectiveness (4, 5). This lack of effectiveness can be explained by the minimal body surface area in contact with the mattress, (only 15%) and the lack of blood flow to this area. The weight of the patient creates a pressure which prevents normal cutaneous blood flow. The heat in the mattress cannot be transported away from the skin and the contact surface becomes an insulator effectively minimizing potential heat transfer to the patient.

New Approach Needed

As Dr. Augustine discussed the problem of post-operative hypothermia with doctors, nurses, and industry experts he became convinced that a new approach to warming patients was needed. A survey of anesthesiologists showed that most were dissatisfied with the current technology available for treating hypothermia. A new technology was definitely needed.

As a result of his research, Dr. Augustine developed the Bair Hugger™ Patient Warming System. Numerous studies and reports have shown that increased ambient room temperatures will prevent hypothermia (6-10). Indeed, before the advent of air conditioning, the average ambient temperature of the OR was higher and hyperthermia in the peri-operative period was not uncommon. Surgical patients will predictably lose or gain heat depending on the ambient temperature of the surrounding environment. The Bair Hugger™ System simulates a warm room by surrounding the patient in a gentle flow of warm air–A Focused Thermal Environment™.

The Bair Hugger™ Patient Warming System combines the convenience and effectiveness of warm air to safely rewarm hypothermic patients. The Warming System's minimal cost is rapidly recovered in saved nursing time, reduced linen expenses and lower overall recovery room costs. There is now a practical and cost-effective solution to post-operative hypothermia.

Two-week Free Trial

To arrange for a free two-week trial of the Bair Hugger™ Patient Warming System, fill out the enclosed reply card or call us collect at (612) 941-8866.

SPECIFICATIONS HEATER/BLOWER UNIT	
Size	26" high x 14" deep x 22" wide
Weight	65 lbs.
Power Requirements	110VAC
Temperature Range	Ambient to 110°F Max
Enclosure	Enameled steel
Displayed Variables	Temperature °F
Power Cable	12 Feet long
Display	.5 inch (1.2 cm) Character LCD
COVERS	
Size	54" x 36"
Weight	8 ounces
Material	Polyethylene and tissue paper laminate.

AUGUSTINE MEDICAL INC.

PRACTICAL SOLUTIONS TO COMMON PROBLEMS IN ACUTE CARE™

10393 West 70th St., Suite 100 Eden Prairie, Minnesota 55344

References: (1) Vaughan MS, Vaughan RW, Cork RC. Anesthesia and Analgesia 60 746-751, 1981. (2) Bay J, Nunn JG, Prys-Roberts C. British Journal of Anaesthesia 40, 398-406, 1968. (3) Kucha DH, Nichols GH, Christ NM, Bynum JW. Military Medicine 139 388-390, 1974. (4) Morris RH, Kumar A. Anesthesiology 36 408-411, 1972. (5) Goundsouzian NG, Morris RH, Ryan JF. Anesthesiology 39 351-353, 1973. (6) Morris, RH. Annals of Surgery 173 230-233, 1971. (7) Morris RH, Wilkey BR. Anesthesiology 32 102-107, 1970. (8) Clark RE, Orkin LR, Rovenstine EA. JAMA 154 311-319, 1954. (9) Bigler JA, McQuistow WO. JAMA 146 551, 1951. (10) Harrison GG, Bull AB, Schmidt HJ. British Journal of Anaesthesia 40 398-406, 1960.

Preliminary estimates from subcontractors and a time-and-motion study on assembly indicated that the direct cost of the heater/blower unit would be $380. The cost of materials, manufacturing, and packaging of the plastic disposable blankets was estimated to be $0.85 per blanket.

The central issue at this time was the determination of the list price to hospitals for the heater/blower unit and the plastic blankets, given the widespread incidence of price discounting. Immediate attention to the price question was important for at least three reasons. First, it was felt that the price set for the Bair Hugger Patient Warming System would influence the rate at which prospective buyers would purchase the system. Second, price and volume together would influence the cash flow position of the company. Third, the company would soon have to prepare price literature for its distributor organizations and for a scheduled medical trade show, where the system would be shown for the first time.

Case

Metabical

Pricing, Packaging, and Demand Forecasting for a New Weight-Loss Drug

In April 2008, after 10 years of testing and $400 million in research and development costs, Cambridge Sciences Pharmaceuticals' (CSP) newest prescription drug, Metabical (pronounced Meh-tuh-*bye*-cal), was about to receive its coveted Food and Drug Administration (FDA) approval. CSP was an international health care company with over $25 billion in sales in 2007. The company, based in Cambridge, Massachusetts, focused on developing, manufacturing, and marketing products that treated metabolic disorders, gastrointestinal diseases, and immune deficiencies, as well as other chronic and acute medical conditions. Metabical was part of a strategic initiative that would allow CSP to enter the $3.74 billion market for weight-control products in the United States.[1]

CSP's chief marketing officer, Bernard Long, said of the new product:

> Metabical is revolutionary. It will be the first and only prescription drug to receive FDA approval to meet the needs of the millions of individuals struggling with moderate weight-loss goals. Previous prescription weight-loss drugs had negative side effects that, in the agency's judgment, outweighed the benefits provided to individuals who were not considered obese. Metabical will be approved for use by those looking to shed between 10 to 30 pounds. Initial reviews from the medical community indicate a strong endorsement of Metabical. Our product will offer moderately overweight adults a medically proven, effective method to reach a desirable weight and improve their overall health.

---

[1] According to Mintel International Group's *Weight Control Products—US—March 2007* Report, total U.S. retail sales of weight control products in 2007 were estimated at $3.717 billion.

HBS Professor John A. Quelch and writer Heather Beckham prepared this case solely as a basis for class discussion and not as an endorsement, a source of primary data, or an illustration of effective or ineffective management. The authors thank the following for their valuable contributions to the development of this case: Cynthia Banditrat of Pfizer, Inc. (HBS MBA 2009), E. B. Brakewood of Merck & Co. (HBS MBA 1994), and Shanaya Deboo of Pfizer, Inc. (HBS MBA 2002).

This case, though based on real events, is fictionalized, and any resemblance to actual persons or entities is coincidental. There are occasional references to actual companies in the narration.

Barbara Printup, senior director of marketing for CSP, was in charge of managing the upcoming January 2009 launch of Metabical in the United States. Printup had spent over 20 years in the pharmaceutical industry and specialized in developing marketing strategies for new drugs. She had just concluded work on her sixth new-drug campaign, Zimistat, which was CSP's most successful product launch to date. It was now nine months from launch, and Printup was eager to finalize her launch plan in anticipation of the FDA's formal announcement of approval. In addition to developing initial demand forecasts for the product, she still had to determine the optimal packaging and pricing strategy for the drug.

OBESITY EPIDEMIC IN THE UNITED STATES

The alarming rise in overweight Americans was of grave concern to those in the government and medical communities. According to the Centers for Disease Control and Prevention (CDC), heart disease, high blood pressure, type 2 diabetes, cancer, gallbladder disease, osteoarthritis, sleep apnea, and respiratory problems were just a few of the negative health risks that were directly linked to excess weight. The surgeon general issued a warning that "even moderate weight excess (10 to 20 pounds for a person of average height) increases the risk of death, particularly among adults aged 30 to 64 years."[2]

In 1998, the National Institutes of Health (NIH) abandoned traditional height/weight charts to determine healthy weight and adopted the body mass index (BMI) scale. The BMI scale[3] calculated the relationship between weight and height associated with body fat and health risk, and was appropriate for both men and women. Three categories of excess weight were established for this scale. Those adults with BMIs over 25 were considered "overweight"; adults with BMIs over 30 were categorized as "obese"; and those with BMIs over 40 were categorized as "severely (or morbidly) obese."

That excess weight was a growing problem in the United States could be seen in almost every demographic. By 2008, over 65 percent of the 230 million adults in the United States were considered overweight, obese, or severely obese. Excess weight affected both men and women, young and old, rich and poor, educated and noneducated. Exhibit 1 on page 546 presents statistics on the pervasiveness of overweight and obese individuals in the United States.

COMPETITIVE LANDSCAPE: WEIGHT-LOSS OPTIONS

Weight-loss options ranged from prescription drugs to over-the-counter (OTC) remedies to various diet and exercise plans.

Prescription weight-loss drugs were approved for use in both obese (BMI ≥ 30) and severely obese (BMI ≥ 40) individuals. There were two categories of prescription diet drugs: appetite suppressants and fat-absorbing blockers. Sibutramine hydrochloride monohydrate (marketed as Meridia) worked to suppress appetite through increasing levels of serotonin and catecholamine in the body. However, serious potential side effects of this drug included hypertension, tachycardia,

---

[2] Office of the Surgeon General, U.S. Department of Health and Human Services, *Overweight and Obesity Health Concerns* (January 11, 2007), www.surgeongeneral.gov/topics/obesity/calltoaction/fact_consequences.htm, downloaded March 18, 2010.

[3] BMI = body weight in kilograms divided by height in meters squared.

EXHIBIT 1 **Trends: Percentage of Overweight, Obese, and Severely Obese Adults in the United States, 1976–2001[a]**

	% Of Overweight (25 ? BMI < 30)	% Of Obese (30 ? BMI < 40)	% Of Severely Obese (BMI ? 40)	U.S. Adult Population (millions)[b]
1999 to 2000	34.0	25.8	4.7	209 in 2000
1988 to 1994	33.0	20.1	2.9	185 in 1990
1976 to 1980	31.6	14.4	No Data	163 in 1980

	1999-2000 Men (BMI > 25) Prevalence (%)	Women (BMI > 25) Prevalence (%)
Overall	67.0	62.0
Age (Years)		
20 to 34	58.0	51.5
35 to 44	67.6	63.6
45 to 54	71.3	64.7
55 to 64	72.5	73.1
65 to 74	77.2	70.1
75 and older	66.4	59.6

Education Level	2001 Obesity (%)	Income Level	2001 Obesity (%)
Less than High School	27.4	Less than $25,000	32.5
High School	23.2	$25,000-$40,000	31.3
Some College	21.0	$40,000-$60,000	30.3
College	15.7	More than $60,000	26.8

[a] *American Obesity Association Fact Sheet* (May 2, 2005). http://obesity1.tempdomainname.com/subs/fastfacts/obesity_US.shtml, downloaded March 18, 2010.

Miranda Hitti, (May 2, 2005). *Rich-Poor Gap Narrowing in Obesity;* http://www.webmd.com/diet/news/20050502/rich-poor-gap-narrowing-in-obesity, downloaded March 18, 2010.

Statistical Abstract of the United States: 2006, http://www.census.gov/prod/2005pubs/06statab/pop.pdf, downloaded March 18, 2010.

[b] U.S. Adult population was approximately 230 million in 2008.

heart palpitations, seizures, and serotonin syndrome (a potentially life-threatening condition caused by elevated serotonin levels in the body). Orlistat (marketed as Xenical) blocked the body's absorption of fat. Potential side effects included liver damage, kidney stones, severe stomach pain, and gallbladder disease. Due to the serious side effects associated with both types of drugs, they were prescribed for use only by obese and severely obese individuals (BMI ≥ 30).

There were no prescription-drug options available specifically for the overweight segment (BMI between 25 and 30) in 2008. While a plethora of over-the-counter weight-loss solutions existed, only the OTC drug Alli was approved by the FDA for weight-loss use. Alli users took one pill with each meal. Alli was a reduced-strength version of the prescription drug *orlistat* and shared many of its negative side effects. Printup learned FDA regulators were reviewing over 30 reports of liver damage in patients taking Alli and Xenical between 1999 and 2008, including six cases of liver failure.[4] All other OTC weight-loss solutions (e.g., hoodia, chromium, green tea extract, conjugated linoleic acid, chitosan, bitter orange, etc.) were categorized as herbal or dietary supplements by the FDA and were therefore unregulated by the agency. Various entities in the weight-loss industry had faced safety concerns, and over the years, some had been accused of deceptive marketing claims that dampened enthusiasm for the products. Since herbal remedies and dietary supplements did not require stringent FDA testing and approval, health complications from their use might not be discovered until after the product was widely in use. In one high-profile example, the dietary supplement *ephedra* was linked to several cases of sudden cardiac death and other serious health risks. Consequently, the FDA instituted an outright ban on the purchase or sale of ephedra. Such events hurt industry credibility. In early 2007, the Federal Trade Commission required manufacturers of popular OTC weight-loss drugs TrimSpa, Xenadrine EFX, CortiSlim, and One-A-Day WeightSmart to pay $25 million to settle allegations that the products' weight-loss claims were unsubstantiated.

Due to the lack of regulation and safety concerns associated with OTC weight-loss drugs, many overweight individuals gravitated to other options such as diet plans (e.g., Atkins Nutritional Approach, The Zone Diet), exercise plans (e.g., fitness trainers at local gyms), meal replacement products (e.g., Slimfast), weight management support programs/meetings (e.g., Weight Watchers), and pre-portioned packaged food delivery services (e.g., Jenny Craig Direct, Nutrisystem).

All of these conditions resulted in an attractive business opportunity for CSP. Long felt Metabical was well positioned to capture share from those overweight individuals who were dissatisfied with current offerings.

 METABICAL

CSP's Metabical would be the first prescription drug approved specifically for overweight individuals (i.e., those with a BMI between 25 and 30). Individuals in this category had weight-loss goals of approximately 10 to 30 pounds. Metabical's formulation was not very effective in helping obese individuals lose weight and was therefore not recommended for their use.

Metabical was a dual-layer, controlled-release formulation. The first layer contained an appetite suppressant, calosera, while the second layer contained a fat blocker and calorie absorption agent, meditonan. CSP's research and development team created these two ingredients and felt they were far superior to the current obesity drugs orlistat and sibutramine. Calosera and meditonan worked in low-dose levels and therefore were shown to have less adverse impact on heart, liver, or gallbladder functions than orlistat and sibutramine. The main negative side effects of Metabical were experienced when users consumed high levels of fat and calories. These side effects were similar to the

---

[4] On August 24, 2009, the FDA announced it was reviewing adverse event reports of liver injury in patients taking the weight-loss drug *orlistat*, marketed as the prescription drug Xenical and OTC medication Alli. At press time of the case, the FDA's analysis of these data was still ongoing, and no definite association between liver injury and orlistat had been established. *Early Communication about an Ongoing Safety Review Orlistat* (August 24, 2009). www.fda.gov/Drugs/DrugSafety/PostmarketDrugSafetyInformationforPatientsandProviders/DrugSafetyInformationforHeathcare-Professionals/ucm179166.htm, downloaded March 18, 2010.

gastrointestinal discomfort of orlistat, only less severe. The FDA would only approve Metabical as a prescription medication (vs. OTC drug) due to the therapeutic strength of the ingredients calosera and meditonan. CSP researchers felt this formulation was essential to provide an aggressive treatment for weight loss.

Clinical trials showed Metabical to be effective in helping overweight individuals lose weight. These studies found that overweight individuals with BMIs of 28 to 30 lost an average of 26 pounds when taking Metabical compared with an average loss of 6 pounds for those in a control group who took a placebo. For subjects with BMIs of 25 to 28, weight loss averaged 15 pounds for Metabical users versus an average of 2 pounds for those in the control group. Because Metabical had some negative side effects from excess fat and calories in the diet, it also helped with behavior modification and healthier eating habits. On average, individuals who took Metabical maintained weight loss levels within 10 percent of the clinical trials results for at least three years.

Results from an extensive marketing survey of overweight individuals commissioned by CSP in 2007[5] revealed considerable interest in a prescription drug for moderate weight-loss goals. Highlights from the survey included the fact that 70 percent of the respondents were not satisfied with their current weight, 35 percent were actively trying to lose weight, and 15 percent of that number were comfortable using drugs to help reach their weight-loss goals. When respondents were asked specifically about a prescription weight-loss drug for overweight individuals, 12 percent said they would immediately make an appointment with their health care provider and request a prescription.

In principle, Metabical would be attractive to all overweight individuals, but Printup established a primary target audience for the purpose of developing a communications strategy. Although there was a higher prevalence of overweight men (67 percent) than women (62 percent), and although obesity was more prevalent for those with less education, the ideal Metabical consumer was found to be overweight females, age 35 to 65, who were college-educated. Through comprehensive analysis of market data and CSP consumer studies, Printup concluded this target consumer was more health-conscious and visited the doctor more often. Moreover, the best consumers for Metabical were people who did not chase every new fad diet, and this target group was found to be most interested in protecting their health and raising self-esteem. Printup's research suggested approximately 4.3 million women fell into this target population.

 ## PACKAGING AND PRICING

Packaging and pricing Metabical were two critical launch-strategy decisions. Unlike other drugs in CSP's portfolio, most health insurance carriers were not expected to reimburse patients for Metabical costs. Initial reports found that few prescription drug plans would cover them. Printup was aware of the current standard in which many health insurance plans excluded anti-obesity drugs from coverage. As a result, Printup put a lot of thought into how many pills should be included in a package and how that package should be priced.

---

[5] Survey included 1,000 men and 1,000 women, ages 18 to 70 with BMIs between 25 and 30, from varying socioeconomic levels.

Packaging

In the FDA trials, the majority of individuals reached their weight-loss goals by week 12 and realized only minimal weight loss after that, so CSP expected the drug to be approved as a 12-week treatment plan. Because of its low-dose formulation, individuals needed to take Metabical at the same time every day. To be fully effective, the drug had to be a constant presence in the blood stream; if individuals skipped a day, effectiveness was significantly reduced. Therefore, CSP determined the optimal package would be a days-of-the-week, "blister"-style package similar to birth-control packages. This package design allowed individuals to easily keep track of dosing by seeing each pill and its corresponding day of the week. The question that remained was how many pills should be included in the blister pack. CSP needed to provide the FDA with its final packaging policy prior to formal approval, so a decision would need to be made immediately.

Ideally, CSP would have liked to package a 12-week supply in one dosing because individuals who completed the entire program would have an increased likelihood of experiencing positive, long-lasting results. The 12-week supply in one package would limit the number of individuals who dropped off because they forgot or were too busy to get their prescription refilled. As Printup pointed out:

> Standards for prescription drug dosing in the industry range from a one-week supply to a three-month supply. Depending on the pricing, I think a 12-week price tag may be out of reach for many individuals to pay at the outset. We just needed to find the right balance between the individuals' ability to pay and maximizing the likelihood that they complete the entire 12-week regimen.

Pricing

Printup first looked to the options in the current weight-loss marketplace to find pricing benchmarks. The closest comparable was Alli, the nonprescription form of orlistat that had to be taken three times per day (one pill with each meal). Retail pricing for a 50-day starter pack (which included 150 pills, portable pill container, reference books, and access to online resources) was approximately $120. A 40-day "refill" supply of 120 pills retailed for approximately $70. Printup also researched the cost of other weight-control programs such as Weight Watchers meetings (approximately $40 for a monthly meeting pass) and prepackaged meal delivery service such as Jenny Craig (average price of $11–$20 per day for food, plus $20–$50 per month for membership fee). A summary of Printup's pricing comparison research is provided in Exhibit 2 on page 550.

Printup developed three initial pricing models to consider (Exhibit 3 on page 550). The first model was to use Alli as a benchmark and price Metabical at a premium to it. Printup reasoned that individuals should be willing to pay considerably more for a prescription-strength medication that limited harmful side effects and needed to be taken only once per day. Under this scenario, she determined a four-week supply of the drug would retail for $75. The second model was based on a comparison of other CSP drug margins. The average CSP gross margin for a new prescription drug was approximately 70 percent. Using this logic, the retail price would be $125 for a four-week supply.[6]

A third pricing option concentrated on the value to consumers of successfully completing the program. From a cost-savings perspective, CSPs

---

[6] A retailer would normally receive a 33 percent gross margin and the variable cost to produce a four-week supply was $25.20.

EXHIBIT 2   **Weight-Loss Options: Price Comparison Summary**

Option	Description	Approximate Retail Price[a]
Alli	Non-prescription, FDA-approved weight loss drug for overweight individuals	$190 for three-month supply
OTC drugs	Herbal remedy, no FDA approval	$300 for three-month supply
Weight Watchers	Weight-control program and meetings	$120 for three months
Jenny Craig	Diet and weight-control program that included prepackaged, delivered meals and support	$1,000–$1,600 for three months of program (includes food)
Gym Membership	Access to workout facilities	$245 for three month membership and initiation fee

[a] Alli price comparison included initial starter pack and 90-day supply of pills.

OTC drug pricing based off MSRP; however deep discounts were usually available.

Weight Watchers price included monthly meeting pass and access to internet tools.

Jenny Craig price included membership fees and prepackaged food (replaced ~50% - 75% of the client's normal food purchases).

Average gym membership price included one-time initiation fee of approximately $125.

Outcomes Research Group established that overweight individuals spent roughly $450 out-of-pocket more each year on health care versus a person who did not carry excess weight. Keeping this in mind, Printup determined a third pricing option which resulted in a $150 retail price for a four-week supply. A pricing study conducted with respondents from the ideal target market found this retail price acceptable. However, when tested with the general overweight market, the price was above what consumers indicated they would be willing to pay.

In the process of evaluating different pricing options, Printup had gathered cost information associated with Metabical. Annual fixed costs associated with manufacturing the drug and other overhead came to approximately $1.2 million, and the preliminary marketing budget was approximately $23 million. Printup was also acutely aware that CSP needed to recoup its $400 million research and development costs for Metabical, and CMO Bernard Long informed her that CSP wanted to achieve a minimum 5 percent ROI within five years of the new product's launch.

EXHIBIT 3   **Pricing Options: Four-Week Supply**

	Option 1	Option 2	Option 3
Retail price	$75.00	$125.00	$150.00
Retail gross margin	$25.00	$41.67	$50.00
Manufacturer price	$50.00	$83.33	$100.00
Variable cost	$25.20	$25.20	$25.20
Manufacturer gross margin	$24.80	$58.13	$74.80
	50%	70%	75%

DEMAND FORECASTING

Both Long and Printup were confident that sales of Metabical would quickly take off once health care providers and overweight individuals understood the value proposition of the new drug. Long expected Printup to use her experiences with past drug launches, together with the marketing research CSP had commissioned, to provide guidance on the expected unit volumes for Metabical in its first five years.

Printup decided to project demand using three different approaches that were based on varying assumptions about how potential customers would respond to Metabical. Her first approach forecasted demand by looking at the number of overweight individuals in the United States (BMI between 25 and 30) and narrowing down that population to those who were actively trying to lose weight (35 percent, according to the CSP study). She felt this pool of potential users should again be narrowed to the 15 percent of those who were comfortable with weight-loss drugs. Printup's experiences taught her that Metabical was likely to capture 10 percent of those individuals in the first year, and in subsequent years she could expect an additional 5 percent, up to 30 percent by the fifth year. In addition, test trials suggested that 60 percent of the first-time users would repurchase a second supply and 20 percent of these would finish out the entire Metabical program by repurchasing the remaining supply.

Printup also developed a more aggressive forecast using the results from the CSP survey that specifically addressed consumer interest in a prescription weight-loss drug for the overweight. Again, her starting point would be the number of overweight individuals in the United States, but this time she concentrated on the data point that 12 percent of the respondents were ready to immediately go to their health care provider to request a prescription. She believed the previously developed penetration guidelines (10 percent increasing by 5 percent per year) and the 60 percent/20 percent model for repeat purchases would also apply to this forecast scenario.

In a third approach to forecasting, Printup focused on the ideal target consumer: educated females, 35 to 65 years of age with BMIs between 25 and 30. Metabical was expected to capture a higher penetration of this ideal target (4.3 million potential users) than that of the general overweight population. Printup estimated Metabical would capture 30 percent of the ideal target market in the first year, with a 5 percent increase in share each year (up to 50 percent by year five). She felt the 60 percent/20 percent model for repeat purchases would hold true for this group of users as well.

Printup knew that her pricing and packaging decisions would have a direct impact on sales forecasts. All the pieces of the puzzle were starting to come together, and she was eager to analyze the potential demand and subsequent profitability to help her provide the best recommendations to Long.

CONCLUSION

Printup sat down with her reports and notes stacked neatly around the perimeter of her desk. She had several critical decisions to make regarding Metabical's product launch. First, she wanted to determine the optimal package size for the drug. Next, she needed to put more thought into her pricing recommendation. She had developed three initial models for pricing, but felt she needed to explore how each of these would impact profitability before making her recommendation. To do this, she would have to establish initial demand forecasts for the product in its first five years and ensure that her pricing recommendation met the company's desired ROI.

Chapter 9

Marketing Strategy Reformulation: The Control Process

Marketing strategies are rarely, if ever, timeless. As the environment changes, so must product-market and marketing-mix plans. Moreover, as organizations strive for gains in productivity, constant attention must be given to improving the efficiency of marketing efforts.

The marketing control process serves as the mechanism for achieving strategic adaptation to environmental change and operational adaptation to productivity needs. Marketing control consists of two complementary activities: strategic control, which is concerned with "doing the right things," and operations control, which focuses on "doing things right." *Strategic control* assesses the direction of the organization as evidenced by its implicit or explicit goals, objectives, strategies, and capacity to perform in the context of changing environments and competitive actions. The ever-present issue of defining the fit between an organization's capabilities and objectives and environmental threats and opportunities is at the core of strategic control. *Operations control* assesses how well the organization performs marketing activities as it seeks to achieve planned outcomes. It is implicitly assumed that the direction of the organization is correct and that only the organization's ability to perform specific tasks needs to be improved.

The distinction between strategic and operations control is important to grasp. It has been noted that a "poorly executed plan can produce undesirable results just as easily as a poorly conceived plan."[1] Though undesirable results (declining sales, eroding market share, or sagging profits) may be identical, remedial actions under the two types of control will differ. Remedial efforts drawn from an operations-control perspective focus on heightening the marketing effort or identifying ways to improve *efficiency*. Alternatively, remedial efforts based on a strategic-control orientation focus on improving the *effectiveness* of the organization in seeking opportunities and mitigating threats in its environment. Improper assessment of the need for strategic versus operations control can lead to a disastrous response in which an organization pours additional funds into an ill-conceived strategy, only to realize further declines in sales, market share, and profit.

 ## STRATEGIC CHANGE

Strategic change is defined here as change in the environment that will affect the long-run well-being of the organization. Strategic change may represent opportunities or threats to an organization, depending on the organization's competitive posture. For example, the gradual aging of the U.S. population represents a potential threat to organizations catering to children, whereas this change represents an opportunity to organizations providing products for and services to elderly persons.

Sources of Strategic Change

Strategic change can arise from several sources.[2] One source is *market evolution*, which results from changes in primary demand for a product class. For example, increased primary demand for calcium in the diets of children and adults prompted marketers of Tums antacid, Total Cereal, Nutri-Grain bars, and Minute Maid orange juice to promote the presence of calcium in their products. Similarly, consumer concerns about Internet privacy and security have created primary demand for software and computer systems that keep a consumer's personal data safe from abuse.

Technological innovation creates strategic change as newer technologies replace older technologies. The word-processing capabilities of personal computers pushed typewriters into decline. Internet downloads did the same to compact discs in the prerecorded music industry. DVDs have largely replaced videocassettes. Technological innovation also affects marketing practice, as evident by the impact of the Internet on marketing communications and marketing channels as described in Chapters 6 and 7.

Market redefinition is another source of strategic change. *Market redefinition* results from changes in the offering demanded by buyers or promoted by competitors. Apple redefined the mobile phone market with the launch of its iPhone, which included wireless Internet technology and a host of new features that changed the definition of a mobile phone to a smartphone.

Change in marketing channels is a fourth source of strategic change. The increasing role of Internet technology, the continuing focus on reducing distribution costs, and power shifts within marketing channels represent three opportunities or threats, depending on a marketer's relative position in a market. Strategic change, along these dimensions, is apparent in the distribution of automobiles in the United States.[3] Consumers today can price-comparison shop on the Internet without visiting dealers. The erosion in industry profit margins has caused manufacturers and dealers alike to look for cost-cutting opportunities, particularly in distribution costs, which represent 25 to 30 percent of the retail price of a new car.

Strategic Change: Threat or Opportunity?

Threat severity or opportunity potential is determined by the organization's business definition. In other words, does the threat or opportunity relate to the types of customers served by the organization, the needs of the customers, the means by which the organization satisfies these needs, or some combination of these factors?

The effects of strategic change are apparent in the transformation of the world-wide watchmaking industry.[4] Although Swiss watchmakers had dominated this industry for a century, market evolution, technological innovation, market redefinition, and marketing channel changes combined to spell disaster for the Swiss. While a technologically motivated market evolution changed the offering from jeweled watches to quartz and electronic watches, the primary marketing channel changed from select jewelry stores to mass merchandisers and supermarkets. Moreover, a redefinition of the term *watch* occurred. No longer was a watch defined solely in terms of craftsmanship or elegance as jewelry.

Many people began to think of a watch as an economical and disposable time-piece. These changes, brought about by Timex and such Japanese firms as Seiko and Citizen, severely affected the Swiss watchmakers. Today, Swiss watchmakers have, for the most part, pursued a highly specialized market niche, which can be identified as the prestige, luxury, artistry watch segment. For example, Swiss watches "tell you something about yourself" (Patek) and are "the most expensive in the world" (Piaget).

This example highlights how strategic change can affect an entire industry and its individual participants. Several options exist for dealing with strategic change:

1. An organization can attempt to marshal the resources necessary to alter its technical and marketing capabilities to fit market-success requirements. (Swiss watchmakers did not do this but, rather, devoted modest research funds to perfecting the design of mechanical watches, in which they had a distinctive competency. Only Ebauches S.A. invested in electronic technology and pursued the marketing opportunity available for an inexpensive fashion watch—the Swatch. The Swatch Group is today the world's largest watchmaker, accounting for roughly one-quarter of global watch sales.)

2. An organization can shift its emphasis to product markets where the match between success requirements and the firm's distinctive competency is clear and can cut back efforts in those product markets where it has been out-flanked. (Many Swiss watchmakers chose this option.)

3. An organization can leave the industry. (Over 1,000 Swiss watchmakers selected this option, thereby eliminating more than 45,000 Swiss jobs.)

 # OPERATIONS CONTROL

The goal of operations control is to improve the productivity of marketing efforts. Because cost identification and allocation are central to the appraisal of marketing efforts and profitability, marketing-cost analysis is a fundamental aspect of operations control. This section provides an overview of marketing-cost analysis and selected examples of product-service mix analysis, sales analysis, marketing-channel analysis, and customer analysis.

Nature of Marketing-Cost Analysis

The purpose of *marketing-cost analysis* is to trace, assign, or allocate costs to a specified marketing activity or entity (hereafter referred to as a *segment*) in a manner that accurately displays the financial contribution of activities or entities to the organization. Marketing segments are typically defined on the basis of (1) elements of the product-service offering, (2) sales divisions, districts, or territories, (3) marketing channels, and/or (4) type or size of customers. Cost allocation is based on the principle that certain costs are directly or indirectly traceable or assignable to every marketing segment.[5]

Several issues arise in regard to the cost-allocation question:

1. *How should costs be allocated to separate marketing segments?* As a general rule, the manager should attempt to assign costs in accordance with an identifiable measure of application to an entity.

2. *What costs should be allocated?* Again, as a general rule, costs arising from the performance of a marketing activity or charged to that activity according to administrative policy are the costs that should be allocated.

3. *Should all costs be allocated to marketing segments?* The answer to this question will depend on whether the manager opts for a "whole equals the sum of parts" income statement. If so, then all costs should be fully allocated. If it appears that certain costs have no identifiable measure of application to a segment or do not arise from one particular segment, however, these costs should not be allocated.

The manager should follow two guidelines in considering the cost-allocation question. First, when costs are allocated, fundamental distinctions between cost behavior (fixed and variable cost) patterns should be maintained. Second, the more joint costs there are (costs that have no identifiable basis for allocation or that arise from a variety of marketing segments), the less exact cost allocations will be. In general, greater detail in cost allocation or traceability will provide more useful information for remedial action.[6]

Product–Service Mix Analysis

Proper analysis of the product–service mix involves two interrelated tasks. First, the manager must assess the performance of offerings in the relevant markets. Second, the manager must appraise the financial worth of product–service offerings.

Sales volume, as an index of performance, can be approached from two directions. Growth or decline in unit sales volume provides a quantitative indicator of the acceptance of offerings in their relevant markets. Equally important is the proportion of sales coming from individual offerings in the product–service mix and how this sales distribution affects profitability. Many firms experience the "80–20 rule"—80 percent of sales or profits come from 20 percent of the firm's offerings. For example, in the early 1990s, 20 percent of Kodak's products contributed more than 80 percent to the firm's sales. Such an imbalance in the mix can have a disastrous effect on overall profitability if sudden changes in competitive or market behavior threaten the viability of this 20 percent. This happened to Kodak when technological innovations such as digital imaging cameras began to redefine the photographic market. Also, Fuji proved to be an aggressive competitor in Kodak's traditional film and photographic markets.[7]

Market share complements sales volume as an indicator of performance. Market share offers a means for determining whether an organization is gaining or losing ground in comparison with competitors, provided it is used properly. Several questions must be considered when market share is used for control purposes. First, what is the market on which the market-share percentage is based, and has the market definition changed? Market share can be computed by geographic area, product type or model, customer or channel type, and so forth. In the Goodyear Tire and Rubber Company case in this chapter, the market share for tires was reported by geography (U.S. versus worldwide), product type (passenger car and truck), type of retail outlet (company-owned stores, discount tire stores, etc.), as well as by manufacturers' total sales. Second, is the market itself changing? For example, high market share by itself may be misleading, since overall sales in the market may be declining or growing. Finally, the unit of analysis—dollar sales or unit sales—must be considered. Because of price differentials, it is better to use unit rather than dollar volume in examining market share.

A second aspect of product–service control consists of appraising the financial contribution of market offerings. An important step in this process is to assign or trace costs to offerings in a manner that reflects their profitability. However, this step is difficult and often requires astute managerial judgment. Moreover, the definition of an offering is itself illusive. For example, a "red-eye" flight (early morning or late evening) scheduled by an airline might be viewed as

| EXHIBIT 9.1 | Disaggregating Service Station Costs for Product–Service Mix Analysis (Thousands of Dollars) | | | |

| | | Department | | |
| | | | General | |
	Total	Gasoline	Merchandise	Automobile
Sales	$4,000	$2,000	$1,700	$300
Cost of goods sold and variable expenses	3,000	1,600	1,220	180
Contribution margin	1,000	400	480	120
Fixed expenses	900	500	310	90
Net income	$100	$(100)	$170	$30

an offering. The decision by McDonald's and Taco Bell to open for the breakfast trade can be viewed as a market offering, the costs of which include not only the cost of producing the menu items but also the cost of being open.

From an analysis perspective, the manager should examine the financial worth of market offerings using a *contribution-margin approach*, in which the relevant costs charged against an offering include direct costs and assignable overhead. The units by which these costs are broken down should be those that contribute most meaningfully to the analysis.

Consider the situation in which the owner of a chain of gasoline service stations is examining operating performance. Exhibit 9.1 shows the operating performance before and after cost allocation by department. Examination of the total yields little managerially relevant information. When costs are disaggregated and measured by department, however, it becomes apparent that gasoline operates at a net loss, whereas general merchandise and automobile service operate profitably. Fortunately, each department "contributes" to overhead; that is, each department's revenue exceeds its allocated variable costs.

This analysis serves a useful purpose in identifying potential trouble spots. Several alternatives exist for taking corrective action. If the owner decided to drop the unprofitable line and leave the selling space empty, then general merchandise and automobile service would have to cover the total fixed costs, which will continue. It is doubtful that this would occur. (Note that gasoline does contribute to the payment of fixed costs.) Another possibility is that the manager might expand the other departments to use the empty space. Estimates of market demand and forecasts of revenue would be needed for further consideration of this action. Moreover, a commitment of resources would have to occur that would in effect significantly alter the nature of the business.

Sales Analysis

Sales analysis directs a manager's attention to both the behavioral and the cost aspects of sales activity. The behavioral element consists of sales effort and allocation of selling time. The cost aspect consists of expenses arising from the performance and administration of the sales function.

Sales analysis is usually based on a performance assessment by sales territories or districts, size and type of customers or accounts, products, or some combination of these variables. Various measures used to assess sales performance include sales revenue, gross profit, sales call frequency, penetration of accounts in a sales territory, and selling and sales administration expenditures.

EXHIBIT 9.2 | **Performance Summary for Two Sales Representatives**

	(1)	*(2)*	*(3)*	*(4)*	*(5)*	*(6)*	*(7)*
Account Category	*Potential Accounts in Sales District[a]*	*Active Accounts[b]*	*Sales Volume[c]*	*Gross Profit[d]*	*Total Calls[e]*	*Selling Expenses[f]*	*Sales Administration[g]*
A	80	60	$48,000	$14,000	195	$18,400	
B	60	40	44,000	15,400	200	17,900	
C	40	10	25,000	12,250	50	11,250	
D	20	6	33,000	16,500	42	9,000	
Totals	200	116	$150,000	$58,550	487	$56,550	$10,000

[a] Based on marketing research data identifying potential users of company products.

[b] Current accounts.

[c] Based on invoices.

[d] Based on invoice price for full mix of products sold.

[e] Based on sales call reports cross-referenced by customer name.

[f] Direct costs of sales including allocated salaries of two sales representatives.

[g] Costs not assignable on a meaningful basis; includes office expense.

Consider a situation in which a district sales manager has requested a quarterly performance review of two sales personnel in a territory within the district. These individuals have failed to achieve their sales, gross profit, and profit quotas. Exhibit 9.2 displays the representatives' performance according to customer-volume account categories. These categories were established by the national sales manager on the basis of industry norms, as were the following expected quarterly call frequencies:

Account Definition	*Expected Frequency of Quarterly Calls*
A: $1,000 or less in sales	2
B: $1,000–$1,999 in sales	4
C: $2,000–$4,999 in sales	6
D: $5,000 or more in sales	8

Both representatives had an equal number of A, B, C, and D accounts.

Exhibit 9.3 shows various indices prepared by the district sales manager from the performance summary shown in Exhibit 9.2. Among the principal findings evident from Exhibit 9.3 are the following:

1. The representatives' account penetration varied inversely with the size of the account. Whereas representatives had penetrated 75 percent of the smaller A accounts, only 30 percent of the potentially large D accounts were listed as active buyers.

2. Part of the reason for this performance appears to lie in the call frequency of the representatives. The representatives exceeded the call norm on the A and B accounts, but fell short on call frequency on the C and D accounts. Moreover, their "effort" level appears questionable (487 calls [div] 90 days [div] 2 representatives [equals] 2.7 calls per day).

3. The gross profit percentage derived from sales to smaller accounts was considerably lower than that derived from sales to the larger accounts, which in turn affected profitability.

EXHIBIT 9.3 Selected Operating Indices of Sales Performance

Sales Volume/ Active Account (Col. 3 ÷ Col. 4)	Gross Profit/ Active Account (Col. 4 ÷ Col. 2)	Selling Expenses/ Active Account (Col. 6 ÷ Col. 2)	Contribution to Sales Administration (Gross Profit − Selling Expenses)
A: $800	$240	$307	−$67
B: $1,100	$385	$448	−$63
C: $2,500	$1,225	$1,125	$100
D: $5,500	$2,750	$1,500	$1,250

Account Penetration (Col. 2 ÷ Col. 3)	Call Frequency/ Active Account (Col. 5 ÷ Col. 2)	Selling Expense per Call (Col. 6 ÷ Col. 5)	Gross Profit %/ Active Account (Col. 4 ÷ Col. 3)
A: 75%	3.25	$94.36	30%
B: 67%	5.0	$89.50	35%
C: 25%	5.0	$225.00	49%
D: 30%	7.0	$214.29	50%

4. When account sales volume is matched with gross profit and selling expenses, it becomes apparent that the smaller accounts actually produced a net contribution dollar loss.

The sales analysis in this instance revealed that the two representatives were not actively calling on accounts (only 2.7 calls per day) and that their allocation of call activity focused on smaller-volume, less profitable accounts that were in fact contributing a *loss* to overhead. Redirection of effort is clearly called for in this situation.

Marketing Channel Analysis

Marketing channel analysis consists of two complementary processes. The manager must first assess environmental and organizational factors that may alter the structure, conduct, and performance of marketing channels. These considerations were highlighted in Chapter 7. Second, the manager must evaluate the profitability of marketing channels.

Profitability analysis for marketing channels follows the general format outlined for product–service mix analysis. Cost identification and allocation differ, however. Two types of costs—order-getting and order-servicing costs—must be identified and traced to different marketing channels. *Order-getting costs* include sales expenses and advertising allowances. *Order-servicing costs* include packing and delivery costs, warehousing expenses, and billing costs.[8]

Consider a hypothetical marketer of furniture polishes, cleaners, and assorted furniture improvement products. This firm uses its own sales force to sell its products through three marketing channels: furniture stores, hardware stores, and home improvement stores. Exhibit 9.4 on page 560 shows income statements for all three channels combined, as well as individually (general and administration costs are not allocated or included). It is apparent that when costs and revenues are traced by channel, furniture store and hardware store channels generate equal sales revenue; however, furniture stores incur a sizable loss and hardware stores account for almost all of net income. Why are the returns so different?

| EXHIBIT 9.4 | Disaggregated Costs of Furniture Improvement Products for Marketing Channel Analysis (Thousands of Dollars) |

| | | *Marketing Channel* | | |
	Total	*Furniture Stores*	*Hardware Stores*	*Home Improvement Stores*
Sales	$12,000	$5,000	$5,000	$2,000
Cost of goods sold	8,000	3,500	3,100	1,400
Gross margin	4,000	1,500	1,900	600
Expenses				
Selling	1,000	617	216	167
Advertising	750	450	150	150
Packing and delivery	800	370	300	130
Warehousing	400	200	150	50
Billing	600	300	250	50
Total expenses	3,550	1,937	1,066	547
Net channel income (loss)	$450	$(437)	$834	$53

Inspection of disaggregated costs suggests the following:

1. The gross margin percentage on the mix of products sold to hardware stores is 38 percent, whereas the gross margin percentage on products sold to furniture stores and home improvement stores is 30 percent. Thus, lower-margin products are being sold through furniture and home improvement stores on the average.

2. Order-getting costs (selling and advertising) run about 21 percent of sales for furniture stores, but only 7 percent for hardware stores and 16 percent for home improvement stores.

3. Order-servicing costs are 17 percent of sales for furniture stores, 14 percent for hardware stores, and about 12 percent for home improvement stores.

In short, a manager can conclude that the effort (reflected in costs) necessary to generate sales and service in the furniture store channel is much greater than that needed for hardware and home improvement stores. Moreover, furniture stores purchase products with a lower gross margin. Once these problems have been identified, efforts to remedy the situation can be explored in a more systematic fashion.

Customer Profitability Analysis

Advances in information technology and database management techniques have made it possible to identify an individual customer's contribution to an organization's profitability. A profitable customer is a person, household, or company that, over time, yields a revenue stream that exceeds, by an acceptable amount, the organization's cost of attracting, selling, and servicing that customer.[9] Note the emphasis is on a continuing stream of revenue and cost traced to a customer, not on the profit from a particular customer sales transaction.

Customer profitability analysis yields insights consistent with those obtained from the types of analysis previously discussed. For example, variations of the

"80–20 rule" have been observed. Consider the case of LSI Logic.[10] This high-tech semiconductor manufacturer discovered that 90 percent of its profit arose from 10 percent of its customers. Moreover, the company was losing money on half of its customers! The implication from this observation is the company could improve its profit picture by "firing" its worst customers by not soliciting their future business. Recall from the marketing channel analysis discussion that two types of cost are considered when assessing the profitability of marketing channels: (1) order-getting costs, and (2) order-servicing costs. Both costs also apply when performing a customer profitability analysis, but different terms are used. Order-getting costs are called "customer acquisition" costs; order-servicing costs are called "customer retention" costs. The subtraction of these costs from a customer's dollar gross margin stream results in customer profitability. When this is done for each customer, it is possible to classify customers into different profit tiers. One such classification scheme is to label customers as platinum customers (highly profitable), gold customers (profitable), iron customers (low profitability, but desirable), and lead customers (unprofitable and undesirable).[11] Once done, a manager's task is to move iron customers to the gold tier and gold customers to the platinum tier by cross-selling the company's offerings or up-selling offerings; that is, introducing customers to a company's more profitable offerings. Marketers are advised to drop lead customers, or charge them higher prices, or reduce the cost of serving them to make them more profitable. The financial-services industry has done this for years, lavishing attention on its profitable customers and charging fees to its unprofitable customers for using ATMs or tellers or obtaining bank records. These practices, while common, can have undesirable customer-relations consequences and need to be considered carefully.

CONSIDERATIONS IN MARKETING CONTROL

Proper implementation of strategic and operations control requires that the manager be aware of several pertinent considerations. Three of these considerations follow.

Problems Versus Symptoms

Effective control, whether at the strategic or the operations level, requires that the manager recognize the difference between root problems and surface symptoms. This means that the manager must develop causal relationships between occurrences. For example, if there is evidence of a sales decline or poor profit margins, the manager must "look behind" the numbers to identify the underlying causes of such performance and then attempt to remedy them. This diagnostic role is similar to that of a physician, who must first establish patient symptoms in order to identify the ailment.

Effectiveness Versus Efficiency

A second consideration is the dynamic tension that exists between effectiveness and efficiency. Effectiveness addresses the question of whether the organization is achieving its intended goals, given environmental opportunities and constraints and organizational capabilities. Efficiency relates to productivity—the levels of output, given a specified unit of input. Suppose a sales representative has a high call frequency per day and a low cost-per-call expense ratio. The individual might be viewed favorably from an efficiency perspective. If the emphasis of the organization is on customer service and problem solving, however, this person might be viewed as ineffective.

Data Versus Information

A third consideration is the qualitative difference between data and information. Data are essentially *reports* of activities, events, or performance. Information, on the other hand, may be viewed as a *classification* of activities, events, or performance designed to be interpretable and useful for decision making. The distinction between data and information was illustrated in the discussion of the various types of analyses described in this chapter, where data were organized into meaningful classifications and operating ratios.

NOTES

1. Thomas Bonoma, "Making Your Marketing Strategy Work," *Harvard Business Review* (March–April 1984): 68–76.

2. These concepts were drawn from Derek Abell, "Strategic Windows," *Journal of Marketing* (July 1978): 21–26.

3. Evan R. Hirsh et al., "Changing Channels in the Automotive Industry: The Future of Automotive Marketing and Distribution," *Strategy & Business* (First Quarter 1999): 42–50; and "Click Here for a New Sedan! (Not Yet, Alas)," *Newsweek* (November 11, 2002): E10–E12.

4. Amy Glasmeier, "Technological Discontinuities and Flexible Production Networks: The Case of Switzerland and the World Watch Industry," in Michael Tushman and Philip Anderson, eds., *Managing Strategic Innovation and Change*, 2nd ed. (Cambridge, UK: Oxford University Press, 2004): 42–58; David S. Landes, *Revolution in Time*, rev. ed. (Cambridge, MA: Harvard University Press, 2000); and Anthony Young, "Markets in Time: The Rise, Fall, and Revival of Swiss Watchmaking" (New York: The Foundation for Economic Education, September 9, 2005).

5. B. Ames and J. Hlavacek, "Vital Truths about Managing Your Costs," *Harvard Business Review* (January–February 1990): 140–47; and S. L. Mintz, "Two Steps Forward, One Step Back," *CFO* (December 1998): 21–25.

6. Ronald W. Hilton, *Managerial Accounting*, 9th ed. (Burr Ridge, IL: McGraw-Hill/Irwin, 2011): Chapter 12.

7. "Kodak Tries to Bring Its Digital Revival into Focus," *Bloomberg Businessweek* (September 5–September 11, 2011): 21–22.

8. For an example of cost identification in marketing channels, see Robin Cooper and Robert S. Kaplan, "Profit Priorities from Activity-Based Costing," *Harvard Business Review* (May–June 1991): 130–137.

9. V. Kumar, *Managing Customers for Profit* (Upper Saddle River, NJ: Pearson Education, 2008).

10. Bob Donath, "Fire Your Big Customers? Maybe You Should," *Marketing News* (June 21, 1999): 9.

11. Valerie Zeithaml, Roland Rust, and K. Lemon, "The Customer Pyramid: Creating and Serving Profitable Customers," *California Management Review* (Summer 2001): 118–142.

Case

Sonance at a Turning Point

INTRODUCTION

In 2004, Scott Struthers and Geoff Spencer returned to Sonance, the high-end audio company they founded in 1982, to wrestle with a number of important decisions. After several years under the leadership of an outside CEO, Chip Brown, the loudspeaker maker seemed to have lost its strategic focus. Sonance had grown rapidly through the early and mid-1990s, positioning itself as an innovative designer of in-wall speakers sold exclusively through custom installation dealers. In the early 2000s, struggling to adjust to new, lower-priced competition, Brown pursued a strategy of diversification that reaccelerated growth but began to erode the company's brand equity with its core customer base. Struthers and Spencer, together with a new CEO, Shawn Sugarman, set out to plot a new course of action for their ailing company.

To help formulate and execute new strategy, Sugarman brought in a number of new executives, including chief sales officer Ari Supran, a 2004 graduate of Columbia Business School. Supran came to Sonance from Lutron Electronics Inc., the high-end lighting controls company. As residential marketing director at Lutron, Supran worked with the architect and interior design communities and had valuable experience marketing high-end lighting products to the luxury home market. One of Supran's first tasks at Sonance was to help develop strategy for the company to regain its leadership position in the industry. Supran joined in late 2005 and had less than a year to plan Sonance's relaunch at the CEDIA (Custom Electronic Design and Installation Association) EXPO, the industry's most prominent trade show. CEDIA EXPO was organized by a trade association of companies specializing in planning and installing home electronics systems and typically attracted over 25,000 custom installation dealers. Sonance wanted to unveil its revised mission and product lineup to its key constituency at this event. But before Supran and Sonance's management could focus on the CEDIA EXPO, they had to decide what the new mission and product lineup should be.

This case was written Natalie Mizik, Gantcher Associate Professor of Business, Columbia Business School. This case was prepared as a basis for class discussion rather than to illustrate either effective or ineffective or handling of a business situation. All proprietary company data are disguised to protect the confidentiality of parties involved. The author is grateful for the time and effort donated by Shawn Sugarman (CEO, Sonance) and Ari Supran (COO, Sonance) in the development of this case. Danielle Fox provided research and writing support. This case was originally published by Columbia Caseworks of Columbia University as case number 080515. Used with permission.

ISSUES DEFINED

Slow Growth

The greatest challenge Supran and Sugarman faced going into 2006 was concern about the slow growth in Sonance's core product line of in-wall speakers. Some of Sonance's competitors began to focus more on sound-system integration, offering fancy touch-screen control systems, and used speakers as a loss leader. The control and video segments of the market were booming, but Sonance was not participating in this growth because speakers were its core offering and its main revenue source. In light of these trends, Sonance's management was deliberating whether to expand its product offering to tap the integration and controls segments or to revamp its existing line of speakers to make it more appealing.

Distribution Channels

From its inception, Sonance had focused on custom installation dealers who specialized in planning and installing electronic systems for luxury homes. The hard-earned credibility that the company had built with these professionals was now at risk: From 2000 through 2004, in an attempt to take advantage of the residential construction boom and strong retail sales growth, Chip Brown took the Sonance brand directly to new production home developers (builders of large-scale housing developments), as well as to the mass-market consumer through big-box retailers like Best Buy and Lowe's. This incensed the custom installers, who marketed their services to custom homebuilders, architects, and interior designers based on exclusivity of their product lines. Was this a problem, or was this a natural transition to a new channel structure in the changing industry? wondered the founders.

Consolidation Considerations

The consumer electronics industry had undergone a lot of changes since Sonance's founding. By 2005, audio equipment manufacturing had moved from the United States to China and the industry began to consolidate. The basic question of whether Sonance could and should proceed as an independent entity was at the top of everyone's mind. Shortly after joining Sonance, Sugarman surveyed the landscape and recommended that the founders sell the company. Its profitable niche seemed to be disappearing, the market share was shrinking under the assault of cheaper competition, and Sugarman worried that the founders were nostalgic for a past that was gone forever.

SONANCE'S FOUNDING AND DEVELOPMENT: BREAKING THE BARRIERS

Struthers and Spencer, two friends, hi-fi enthusiasts, and professional custom installers, founded Sonance in 1982 in San Juan Capistrano, California. They did something that was revolutionary in the audio industry at the time: they moved speakers off the floor and bookshelf and into the wall and ceiling. For the first time, consumers were able to enjoy music throughout their homes without compromising interior design and architectural considerations to accommodate bulky cabinet speakers. The focus on aesthetics allowed Sonance to develop cachet with high-end custom installation dealers. Exhibit 1 provides a timeline of major company events.

| **EXHIBIT 1** | **Timeline of Major Company Events** |

1982	Designs the first in-wall speaker for home customer installation
1983	Develops and markets Sonance 1 in-wall speaker model
1986	Invents the first in-wall subwoofer—unique dual driver speaker using vent technology
1988	Develops the first three-channel amplifier—bass, left, and right
1989	Introduced the first in-wall speaker with adjustable high-frequency control
1991	Develops Sonamp 260, the first amplifier for multiroom use
1994	Creates the first in-wall home theater speaker with pivoting tweeter
1997	Patents Amplified Volume Control technology for multiroom audio
1998	Launches the first THX Ultra in-wall speaker system
2000	Chip Brown becomes CEO upon the retirement of the founders
2001	Patents the SonicEye, a coaxially mounted, pivoting midrange and tweeter mechanism
2002	Invents the Ellipse, the world's first speaker designed specifically for in-ceiling home theater
	Introduces the world's first customizable multiroom amplifier—Sonamp SAT275 with SmartAmp bay for install module
2003	Develops the industry's first in-wall and in-ceiling high-fidelity speakers for extreme temperatures moisture, and marine environments—Symphony Extreme
2004	The founders become actively engaged in company management again and bring in Shawn Sugarman as CEO to replace Chip Brown
	Introduces the iPort, the first in-wall music system for the Apple iPod

---

Over the next several years, Sonance continued to introduce a number of innovative audio products and developed a reputation for selling sleek, technically sophisticated products. By the end of 1999, it grew to over $46 million in sales and 60 employees. At that point, the founders hired an outside CEO to run the company and took time away from the business.

Initially, when Struthers and Spencer just started the company, Sonance manufactured its speakers locally, partnering with a nearby cabinet-speaker maker in California to make its products. At the time, Sonance's Original Series in-wall speakers cost about $75 per pair to manufacture and sold for about $195 to its dealers, who sold and installed the speakers for a total price of $550 per pair to the consumer. The in-wall speaker category offered the dealers 65 percent gross margin on the hardware, the highest among the product categories they sold.

This local manufacturing arrangement lasted for about 10 years, at which point Sonance's manufacturing partner decided to enter the in-wall speaker market and began to sell speakers virtually identical to Sonance's, but at lower prices, under the SpeakerCraft brand name. Sonance moved its manufacturing to Asia, which reduced its manufacturing costs.

SpeakerCraft quickly emerged as a serious threat to Sonance's growth and profitability. After a protracted legal battle over copyrights, Sonance lost its case against SpeakerCraft, in part, due to poor legal advice. Sonance and SpeakerCraft battled for market share through the 1990s, and Chip Brown was recruited as CEO in 2000 to help stem Sonance's declining sales. By 1999, the competition drove Sonance's speaker price to consumers down to $400 per pair, while a pair had COGS (Cost of goods sold) of about $50 and sold to dealers at $140. Brown immediately refocused Sonance's strategy on two rapidly growing customer segments—mass-market

EXHIBIT 2 **Sonance's Key Revenue Sources**

Business line	Year 1999	. . .	Year 2003	Year 2004
Dealers:				
Number of dealer accounts	1,000		600	500
Average selling price per pair	140		140	140
Dealer revenue ($)	42,000,000		25,200,000	21,000,000
Mass Merchandisers:				
Average selling price per pair			120	120
Best Buy revenue ($)			10,000,000	10,000,000
Lowe's revenue ($)			6,000,000	withdrawn
Other Retail (hi-fi Boutiques):				
Number of outlets	127		221	289
Average selling price per pair	140		140	140
Revenues for the small retail ($)	3,000,000		4,500,000	5,500,000
Production Housing Builders:				
Number of production builder accounts	8		85	125
Price per pair of speakers	140		90	90
Builder revenue ($)	1,075,200		7,344,000	10,800,000
Total Revenue all Categories ($)	**46,075,200**		**53,044,000**	**47,300,000**

Source: Company data.

consumer electronics retailers and production home builders. At the time, Best Buy was growing annually at over 20 percent in sales and nearly 15 percent in square footage. Although new home sales were choppy in early 2000 amid rising interest rates, they were showing signs of recovery and ended the year up 13 percent. Brown responded to these trends by directing Sonance to sell its products directly through mass merchandisers and large production builders.

The retail and production builder strategy helped reinvigorate sales, bringing Sonance's revenues to $53 million by 2003, but it disenfranchised Sonance's traditional customer, the custom installer. SpeakerCraft's sales reps eagerly snapped photos of Sonance's products sitting on Best Buy's shelves and shared these photos with Sonance's high-end audio dealers. By 2004 Sonance had only half the 1,000 dealer accounts it had in 1999, as high-end installers dropped Sonance's products from their portfolios. Revenue was still high thanks to Best Buy, Lowe's, and builders, and the founders were content with earnings. But in 2004, after Lowe's decided to exit the in-wall speaker category, Sonance's sales dropped to just above $47 million. It was time to reassess the company's position and strategy. Exhibit 2 shows the change in revenue by distribution channel.

 # INDUSTRY: HIGH-END AUDIO

High-performance audio, also known as "hi-fi" or "high end," falls within the audio segment of consumer electronics. It includes preamplifiers, sound processors, power amplifiers, speakers, turntables, disc players, radio tuners, cabling, and accessories. The heyday of hi-fi was in the 1970s, when Vietnam veterans brought components back from Asia and introduced high-quality sound systems to the mainstream consumer.

Consumer Electronics Association (CEA) defines high-performance audio as "the premier category of home audio products that reproduce music so realistic that it sounds like a live performance."[1] For a long time, mass-market audio products lacked the musical accuracy of high-performance systems; but eventually performance differentials narrowed. The marginal benefits of technical improvements began to diminish, leading some high-end audio companies to focus more on other product attributes, including integration, controls, and aesthetics.

According to the U.S. Census Bureau, there were $101 billion in consumer electronics retail sales in 2004, up 7.7 percent from 2003, and the forecasts predicted continuous growth for the next few years. Between 1990 and 2004, the industry's annual growth rate averaged 6.7 percent. A combination of product life cycle and economic factors drives the overall demand for consumer electronics: The drop in average selling prices for personal computers helped drive explosive industry growth in the mid-1990s, while sagging consumer confidence and job losses were blamed for slow industry growth in 2000 and 2001.

When Sugarman and Supran teamed up to redirect Sonance, the audio segment of the consumer electronics industry had about $5.6 billion in factory sales and had been teetering on decline for several years (Exhibit 3 on page 568). Industry observers attributed the slump to the lack of product innovation, difficulty conveying product features to consumers in most retail settings, and greater interest in video-related categories. However, there was hope that the shift from analog, tube TVs to digital, flat-panel TVs would spur overall category demand in the near future.

 ## TRADITIONAL CHANNEL: CUSTOM INSTALLATION DEALERS

Most high-end audio purchases were made through specialty retailers and custom installers. The need to tailor the product to accommodate environmental issues like room features made for a highly consultative sale. As a result, the CEA recommended consumers to work with a specialty audio dealer to design and install an audio system. Unlike mass-market sales, high-end sales usually required installation by a custom installer.

Few large custom installation companies with satellite locations throughout the country operated in this space. Some, like Modia and HiFi House, were hybrid retailers, a mix of retail outlets and consulting services. Others, like Audio Command and Audio Video Systems, were custom-only installers. In 2005 the largest 100 custom installation companies logged gross revenues of $703.8 million, and the whole custom installation industry revenues were over $10 billion.[2] The median revenues for a custom installation dealer, however, were around $737,900 in 2005[3] as the majority of custom installation dealers were small businesses with five full-time employees, two or three of whom were master installers and one or two of whom were sales/design personnel. In busy times, dealers typically hired independent contractors to help with installation, but with the housing boom, by 2005, it became virtually impossible to find qualified independent professionals willing to take on ad-hoc projects. Housing growth attracted new entrants, with nearly one-third of custom installation companies surveyed in 2004 operating for less than five years. The custom-only installers tended to have strong ties to the architectural community. Many belonged to CEDIA, the trade group that provided certification and held annual trade shows.

---

[1] "What Is High-Performance Audio?" CEA.com, downloaded September 2008.

[2] Jason Knott, "CE Pro 100 Reports 104% Jump in Install Price," *CE Pro Newsletter* (May 1, 2007).

[3] "State of the Industry Special Report," *CE Pro Magazine* (January 2007).

EXHIBIT 3   Total Factory Sales of Consumer Electronics (Millions of Dollars)

	2000	2001	2002	2003	2004	2005E
TV, Video Players	17,927	16,607	18,505	19,267	21,654	26,095
Home & Portable Audio Products	6,323	5,726	5,111	4,779	5,531	5,650
Mobile Electronics	17,071	16,799	16,188	17,184	19,007	20,150
Home Information Products	36,855	34,923	33,504	38,282	41,433	44,238
Blank Media	2,169	2,679	3,210	3,750	5,255	7,947
Accessories & Batteries	6,299	5,968	6,460	7,041	7,545	8,275
Electronic Gaming	8,550	9,689	10,848	10,253	10,970	11,122
Home Security	1,750	1,820	1,965	2,055	2,150	2,250
Grand Total	**96,944**	**94,211**	**95,791**	**102,611**	**113,545**	**125,727**

Select Detail on Total Factory Sales of CE (millions of dollars)

	2000	2001	2002	2003	2004	2005E
TV, Video Players						
Analog Direct-View Color TV	6,503	5,130	5,782	4,756	3,505	1,311
Analog Projection TV	1,481	1,060	733	293	85	18
Monochrome TV	15	15	12	9	5	4
Digital Direct-view and Projection TV	1,355	2,485	3,574	4,351	6,099	11,046
LCD TV	107	101	246	664	2,022	3,074
Plasma TV	-	116	515	1,590	2,518	3,558
TV/VCR Combinations	968	790	733	778	665	349
Videocassette Players	14	5	4	2	2	1
VCR Decks	1,869	1,058	826	407	134	75
Camcorders	2,838	2,236	2,361	2,002	1,701	1,649
Direct to Home Satellite Systems	790	1,175	1,116	1,476	1,886	1,776
Personal Video Recorders	77	144	57	178	541	682
Separate Component DVD Players	1,717	2,097	2,427	2,698	2,460	2,538
Set-Top Internet Access Devices	193	195	119	63	31	14
Total	**17,927**	**16,607**	**18,505**	**19,267**	**21,654**	**26,095**
Home & Portable Audio Products						
Rack Audio Systems	84	42	17	9	2	1
Compact Audio Systems	1,776	1,357	965	731	900	769
Separate Audio Components*	1,545	1,261	1,202	981	1,140	1,064
Home Theater-in-a-Box	331	794	896	961	971	983
Portable Equipment	2,156	1,846	1,526	1,355	980	889
Portable MP3 Players	80	100	205	424	1,204	1,653
Home Radios	351	326	300	318	334	291
Total	**6,323**	**5,726**	**5,111**	**4,779**	**5,531**	**5,650**

*Includes speakers

Source: Consumer Electronics Association, January 2005 CE Sales and Forecasts

EXHIBIT 4 Custom Installation Dealer Sales by Product Category in 2005

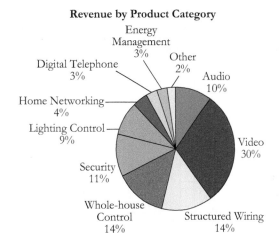

Revenue by Product Category

Source: Company estimates based on CEDIA Member Survey 2005.

The 2004 CEDIA Member Survey revealed a high degree of optimism among dealers and installers. Over half the respondents, more than double the percentage in the prior year, said business improved greatly from 2003. CEDIA members typically managed comprehensive installation projects that included audio, video, lighting control, home networking, structured wiring, digital telephone, whole-house control, security, and energy management systems (Exhibit 4). Each such project typically took about three weeks to complete. CEDIA members reported in 2004 sales increases in distributed audio and video categories and Sonance's management estimated that a total of almost 100,000 homeowners had used dealer's services to install in-wall speakers. But looking ahead, the dealers were most bullish on home networking and security.

Most custom installation dealers were given a budget by their client and asked to provide a complete home theater and multiroom audio and video distribution system for the home with an extended warranty on labor and hardware within that budget. It was typically a part of a much larger new building or renovation project coordinated by an architect or interior designer, who sought out a custom installer to handle the audio and video portion. The budget could vary anywhere from $25,000 up to $1 million plus. A custom installer's average budget was about $100,000 with about 8 percent going to the speakers.

It was typically up to the dealer to decide how to distribute a client's budget across home control systems, speakers, amplifiers, televisions, and video projectors, and to plan for the installation. In-wall and in-ceiling speakers typically offered dealers the highest profit margin of any category with gross margins of 60 percent plus (Exhibit 5 on page 570). Margins on video, which typically took a large share of the project's budget, were lower and dropping to below the 30 percent range. Control systems averaged 50 percent but required a lot of after-sales support because they often needed to be reprogrammed as consumer needs changed over time. In-wall and in-ceiling speakers were one of the few products dealers could install and forget about as they rarely broke and did not need to be serviced or programmed.

Until 2000, Sonance maintained relationships with about 1,000 dealers. These relationships were nonexclusive as dealers carried several competing brands to accommodate designers' wishes and clients' budgets. Each of Sonance's dealers used Sonance speakers in about 15 major projects per year with an average job

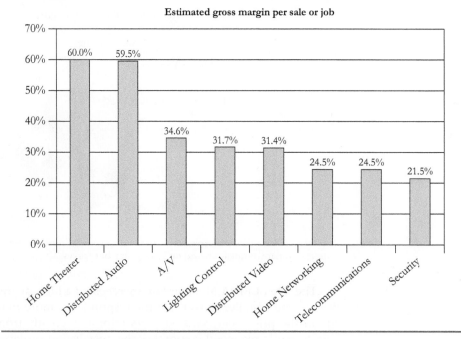

EXHIBIT 5 | **Custom Installation Dealer Profitability by Product Segment in 2005**

Source: Company estimates based on CEDIA Member Survey 2005.

requiring 20 pairs of speakers. In 2000, about 150 of Sonance's 1,000 dealers operated primarily at the highest end of the luxury housing market and undertook only $500,000 plus projects, which typically involved larger properties and required over 30 to 40 pairs of speakers.

Before 2000, Sonance acquired dealer relationships through in-house training programs and networking events and had a 95 percent account retention rate. But the dealers began to defect once Sonance moved into the production builder and retail markets, and acquiring new dealer accounts became increasingly difficult. In 2004, Sonance had only 500 dealer accounts as more and more resentful installers turned elsewhere for high-end speakers. Sugarman noted, "We go into some of the most expensive homes in the world. We were one of the first luxury custom installers in the world." And Supran added, "We depend on word-of-mouth among dealers, and reputation is the greatest asset. Custom installers don't have store fronts; they have high-end appointment-only showrooms. With the move to the mass-market and the production housing segments, we lost both great customers and great employees."[4]

SONANCE'S CUSTOMERS

Mass Market: The Retail Consumer

According to CEA research, the vast majority of the home audio sales fell into three categories: home theater in a box (HTIB), A/V receiver (AVR), and A/V receiver plus speakers. Altogether, they accounted for an estimated $9 billion in annual retail sales in 2004. There were some key differences among the categories,

---

[4] Interview with Sonance management team, San Clemente, California, August 2008.

but to buyers in all three categories, price and sound quality were very important and buyers often went online to research products. The average amount spent in 2004 was about $650 for HTIB, $450 for AVR, and $600 for AVR plus speakers. The spending, however, varied significantly. It was typically well above average in specialized retail outlets, above average at the general electronics stores (which were the top retail destination for home audio purchases), and below average at mass merchants (the next most popular outlet). The retail customers typically installed the products themselves.

Chip Brown put Sonance's sales force to task in 2000 to acquire new retail accounts and place the company's in-wall speakers at all three retail categories, from the discount mass-merchandisers to high-end audio-video boutiques. Best Buy and Lowe's were the largest retail accounts, bringing in $9 million and $6 million, respectively, in 2003. Sonance speakers sold particularly well at Lowe's as most of Lowe's consumers were not intimidated by the idea of cutting out a hole in the drywall to set up their speaker system. The additional revenues from the mass market, however, came at a cost to Sonance's profitability as the average selling price per pair of the Original Series speakers, Sonance's main product, was reduced to $120 to acquire these accounts.

Brown had also expanded the R&D department and funding and directed 50 percent of the $3 million annual R&D budget toward the development of new nonspeaker product ideas. The hope was to refocus the pipeline and eventually develop products that could be suitable for retail consumer. This R&D effort had germinated by 2004, most notably, with the development of iPort, an in-wall docking station for Apple's iPod.

Production Housing: New Home Owners

Sonance successfully tapped the new construction market under Chip Brown. While this segment was dominated by SpeakerCraft and Bose, the housing boom and high growth in new production housing starts provided opportunities for Sonance to carve a share of this market. A typical production housing project consisted of 80 to over 150 semicustom housing units. The builder allowed the homeowner to customize some of the house features and provided a menu of options. To develop a menu, the builder signed exclusive deals with vendors to deliver the upgrades if requested by the homeowner. The homeowner had a choice whether to request an upgrade option or not. If requested, the installation was performed by the builder at the time the house was built. About half the homeowners selected the distributed audio option when it was offered and, on average, each of Sonance's production development accounts provided 80 installation jobs, each requiring 10 to 14 pairs of speakers. Developers liked the partnership because they could advertise the "fully wired for distributed audio" option to prospective home buyers.

Before Brown, Sonance did not actively pursue production housing and, in 1999, sold its speakers to only eight production housing projects. These were higher-end production developments, and the dealers purchased speakers from Sonance at $140 a pair. Most developers, however, wanted to offer distributed audio option at a very low cost to the homeowner to make the overall home value appear attractive. To make its products more suitable to production property developers, Sonance had to provide "quantity discounts" for large development projects and soon came to accept a $90 sales price per pair of speakers, matching the sale price of its main competitor, SpeakerCraft..

Production housing segment was growing the fastest in the Sonance portfolio. By the end of Brown's tenure in 2004 Sonance had 125 production developer accounts, a 47 percent growth over the prior year. Sales in 2005 were headed for another record with 180 deals with developers, and the sign-ups with developers for 2006 delivery were already up almost 40 percent over the 2005 numbers.

There were some clear economies of scale for Sonance to work with production builders because one salesperson could manage and pursue multiple large accounts. However, builder relationships were not as stable as those with custom installation dealers. While each builder account provided a large one-time sale, there was little repeat business as each new development project was courted by multiple audio vendors, who bid on the right to serve the entire development.

Custom Designer Homes: High End of the High End

Working as professional custom installers in the 1980s, Struthers and Spencer noticed that affluent home buyers wanted advanced sound systems, but they objected to the clunky look of tower speakers. At the time, the hi-fi audio segment of the consumer electronics industry was dominated by technology enthusiasts rather than design experts. From its inception, Sonance focused exclusively on a niche within high-end audio and emphasized superior design rather than acoustic superiority in order to fill this gap in the market. Sugarman summed up Sonance's mantra: "What Sonance did, changed the relationship between audio and architecture. We put a hole in the wall with a hammer and the customer loved it! We built a brand around the aesthetics of the product."[5]

Sonance invented the category that scored the highest marks on what was known in the industry as the WAF (Wife's Approval Factor) scale. Supran explained:

> Typically the man demands high-end audio equipment. If you ask our consumers what they want in their home audio system, they always say best sound quality. And there is no question that high-end tower and ribbon speakers provide the best sound quality. But when it comes down to placing tower speakers in the design-oriented luxury homes, the lady of the house, who often has spent countless hours working with the architect and interior designer to match the layout, furniture, the color scheme, and accessories, is not too pleased with such prospect. When it comes down to selecting the speaker system, the look and style come to the forefront.[6]

The typical custom homeowners were usually wealthy couples in their fifties. Many were technology entrepreneurs, hedge fund managers, or investment bankers. Sonance's products found their way into the homes of the rich and famous. This clientele wanted everything top-notch and took superior technical specifications as a given.

Whether sales were to custom installers or to production builders, it took some time to translate contracts into dollars. With individual homeowners, buyers first had to engage an architect to draw up plans for their new structure or major renovation. Sometimes the architect would include the sound system, but sometimes that came later, when an interior decorator got involved. Months later, as construction began, the architect or design professional would seek out a custom installer. Then the custom installer would place an order with Sonance or one of its competitors five to six months in advance of needed delivery date. Working directly with builders cut out the custom installer as the builder's employees or subcontractors performed the installation. But builders often took much longer to get projects under way after signing the deal because they needed to secure zoning and financing. Once Sonance delivered the product, it usually took three to four months to receive payment.

---

[5] Interview with Sonance management team, San Clemente, California, August 2008.
[6] Ibid.

COMPETITION: FACING LARGER PLAYERS

Competition in consumer electronics was intense with large Asian manufacturers dominating the industry. In the mass-market retail in-wall speaker category, key competitors included Yamaha, Bose, Polk, Klipsch, and Boston Acoustics. In the production developer segment, Bose, Niles, SpeakerCraft, and Sonance were the key players. The custom installation segment was dominated by B&W, Niles, Meridian, Linn, Elan, SpeakerCraft, and Sonance.

Some of Sonance's competitors were large, with more diversified revenue bases and significant research and development budgets. Sonance's archrival, SpeakerCraft, seemed to be growing larger and more powerful. In 2003, SpeakerCraft was acquired and became a subsidiary of Nortek, a diversified manufacturer of residential and commercial building products with about $1.5 billion in annual sales. Nortek used a portion of the $625 million it raised through a private placement with Thomas H. Lee Partners L.P. in the early 2000s to acquire three of Sonance's competitors (Niles, Elan, and SpeakerCraft), making its residential audio products division four times as big as Sonance's. It was this changing competitive landscape and intensifying price competition that led Sugarman to question whether Sonance could continue as an independent company.

"Once again we are the industry leader in the In-wall, In-ceiling speaker category at almost twice the percentage of our closest competitor," boasted SpeakerCraft on its Web site in 2005. It highlighted its manufacturing role in the advent of in-wall speakers and characterized its break from Sonance as a quest for quality. SpeakerCraft actively promoted its bracketless in-wall speakers, which were easier and faster to mount. It had also just introduced flush tweeters and speakers that could pivot, which significantly alleviated placement concerns.

While for a long time SpeakerCraft's speakers were virtually identical to Sonance's, in the late 1990s, SpeakerCraft streamlined its speaker design eliminating the mounting brackets. This redesign reduced SpeakerCraft's manufacturing cost for a pair of speakers to $40. SpeakerCraft sold a pair of speakers to the dealers at $90, who in turn installed the speakers for a total price of $365 to the consumer. SpeakerCraft promoted its product to the dealers emphasizing the 75 percent gross margin the dealer received on hardware sale and the easier and faster installation. While it took on average one hour and $60 in labor cost to install a pair of Sonance's speakers, SpeakerCraft's speakers could be installed in half that time, allowing the dealer to save $30 in installation costs.

With SpeakerCraft shifting its focus from pricing to design features, competition at the high end was becoming increasingly intense. Supran and Sugarman realized that SpeakerCraft's latest generation of speakers would be very appealing to installers because it offered higher margins and cheaper installation than Sonance's products.

CONTEXT: TIED TO THE BROADER ECONOMY

Consumer electronics sales are closely tied to consumer confidence and the housing and labor markets. The housing market and its luxury segment were experiencing strong growth and Coldwell Banker, one of the nation's leading real estate brokerage firms, reported a 47 percent increase in $1 million plus home sales in 2004. According to CE Pro, custom installers derived about 60 percent of customer installation revenues from new construction in 2004. The remaining 40 percent came from remodeling and retrofitting. Remodeling segment tended to be particularly sensitive to greater economic trends. The luxury designer new housing ($7 million plus properties), on the other hand, seemed less affected by economic fluctuations. Of the new construction, Sonance estimated that each year about 2,500 houses falling into the luxury designer home category installed in-wall speaker products, and Sonance had about 25 percent of this market with its Original Series.

 NEW PRODUCTS

Sonance's R&D department had a few new product ideas in the works and two projects, a modified iPort and the new in-wall "Architectural Series" speakers, were close to completion. Supran and Sugarman knew they had to prioritize development effort as time was running out and Sonance did not have resources to bring both products to the market by September 2006.

 IPORT

In 2004, Sonance introduced the iPort, an in-wall docking station for the Apple iPod (Exhibit 6). It had a list price of $598 and was sold exclusively through custom installation dealers, who paid Sonance $300 per unit. It cost on average $150 to install. *PC Magazine* described the iPort as follows:

> If you have to ask how much yacht fuel costs, you probably can't afford to put that big a boat in the harbor. The same holds true, on a smaller scale, for the Sonance iPort, a gorgeous in-wall cradle and stereo connector for Apple iPods that costs two or three times what you pay for an iPod in the first place. But it's a beautiful device for moving iPod-resident audio to your stereo system.[7]

Sugarman wondered if maybe there was a way to adapt the iPort for the mass market and tap into the explosive demand for iPods. Target, in particular, was rumored to be making a bigger push into consumer electronics. With the discount store's emphasis on style, it seemed like a good fit with Sonance's design expertise. Having access to Target's nearly 1,400 stores could potentially quickly recoup the $6 million in lost revenues after Lowe's dropped the in-wall speaker category. But would the Target shopper accept iPort's price tag? Another challenge was making the iPort installation easier so that a consumer could handle it without the help of a professional installer.

Sugarman and Supran met with the iPort design team. The engineers confirmed that they could redesign the in-wall iPort to be detached from the wall so that the unit could be integrated with the consumer's home audio system. They could also eliminate the remote control and power surge features, which would lower manufacturing cost per unit from $150 to $125. This would allow Sonance to sell a consumer version of the iPort to the retailer at $240 to $250, which with the 33 to 40 percent retail margins, would keep the retail price at around $330 to $350. This was definitely an improvement, but the iPort, technically an accessory, would still be more expensive than most iPod models. In 2005 Apple has taken off $50 from the prices of existing iPod models: a four-gigabyte iPod was selling at $199 and the new six-gigabyte version went down to $249.[8]

---

[7] *PC Magazine* online, March 9, 2004.

[8] "Apple Lowers iPod Prices," *WebProNews* (February 24, 2005).

EXHIBIT 6 iPort

How it works

1. The iPort In-Wall is installed into a wall and permanently affixed. Similar to a wall switch it is integrated into an environment.

2. Power, music and video sources are all routed to an iPort Wallplate.

3. The iPort Audio Wallplate provides power to the iPort from an off-board DC power supply. RCA, RS-232, RJ-45 connections provide connectivity, and a Video Wallplate provides video to a display device.

4. An audio or video system controls the iPort output to loudspeakers or video monitors.

5. Optional items include an iPort Remote Control and other system connectivity kits to make your iPort powerfully convenient.

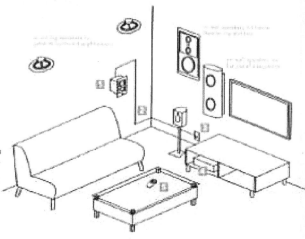

Simplifying installation of the iPort was another challenging task. Sonance's engineers estimated that they would need an additional $1,225,000 to undertake the cost reduction and redesign of iPort to make it compatible with non-Sonance audio systems and an additional $400,000 to complete all compatibility and consumer safety tests. But even then, the installation and integration would still require about an hour and a half of time for a "technically adept" consumer. The plug-and-play design was simply not feasible because the entire home audio system would likely need to be reconfigured to incorporate the iPort device.

Sonance's tiny marketing group was very enthusiastic about the iPort and strongly supported its development. In 2004, Apple's iPod accounted for about half of all MP3 sales and 2005 iPod sales were clearly headed through the roof. In its just released 10-K statement, Apple announced that it sold 22.5 million iPods in fiscal year 2005, an increase of 409 percent from the 4.4 million iPods sold in 2004.[9] About 47 percent of iPod unit sales were in the United States. It had now shipped more than 30 million iPods since the first member in its MP3 player family launched in November 2001. While iPort's pricing and installation were of concern, if Sonance did not enter the booming market in 2006 it might never have such an opportunity again. The iPort R&D group guaranteed that if it were fully funded, the iPort could be ready to go into production by September 2006, just in time for the CEDIA EXPO and the holiday shopping season.

The question that concerned Supran was how to estimate potential demand for the consumer version of the iPort. The in-wall iPort sales through dealers could, at best, be described as sluggish, but marketing argued that dealer orders were no indication of the consumer acceptance of the new detached iPort version. The other concern Supran had was that several electronics manufacturers and most of Sonance's competitors already had iPod docking stations on the market. Some models were sold with speakers attached but others, like Sonance's in-wall iPort, sold as an add-on to be integrated with a specific brand of the audio system. SoundDock from Bose, for example, was a single dock-and-play unit integrated with two speakers and was on the market for over a year. It was priced at $199 to $399 and seemed to be sold everywhere, but there were no data on how large the sale numbers were. Altec Lansing's portable docking station for iPod was selling for $150 at CompUSA. It came with four speakers and a remote control and was getting surprisingly good reviews from the users.

Sonance's marketing group was bullish on the iPort and asked for a $3.5 million budget to take the iPort to mass market for the holiday shopping season and to present it with a splash at the Consumer Electronics show in Las Vegas in January 2007. The key benefit of Sonance's detached iPort, marketing argued, was that while labor intensive, it could be integrated with most brands of home audio systems. What bothered Supran was that his marketing colleagues did not have hard numbers, beyond pointing to iPod's explosive growth, to justify their enthusiasm for the iPort. He also wondered whether the investment in the iPort was the right strategic direction for the company. This would be the first true consumer product and the first ever mass-market marketing campaign for Sonance.

Architectural Series

Sonance's R&D department was also working on a radical redesign of its core product, the in-wall speakers. By late 2005, the design team had the prototype for the first truly flush-mount trimless speaker that completely eliminated

---

[9] Apple Computer Inc. 2005 10-K report.

sightlines. The new advanced bracket held the speaker perfectly flush with the wall surface, and the speakers were literally invisible and could be painted or wallpapered over. Sonance called this model the Architectural Series, and some in the company believed that Sonance was on the brink of a breakthrough innovation.

Supran and Sugarman met with their speakers R&D team and designers in late December 2005. The engineers estimated that it would cost additional $2 million to finish the development of the Architectural Series and be another half a year before the Architectural Series can go into production. They estimated that a pair would cost about $200 to manufacture and warned that installation would be more involved and more expensive than for the Original Series. Installing new speakers would require two full hours of a master installer's time and cost about $200, as master installers charged $90 to $110 per hour.

The initial focus groups with architects and designers indicated that the owners of high-end custom homes simply wanted the best and, within reason, cost was not a concern for their clients. The designers indicated that they would expect to pay at least $2,000 per pair for totally flush speakers. Supran was excited about this finding. He suggested offering the dealers a 65 percent margin and setting the price to the consumer at $2,500. Supran thought he could use the custom installation dealers to move the product to the right clients.

Supran's enthusiasm was not shared by some in the top management team. The marketing team, in particular, argued that the high-end luxury market was too small, and that dealers would not accept a $2,500 ticket price after SpeakerCraft had driven consumer prices for in-wall speakers to the mid-$300 level and was offering 75 percent gross margins and easy installation to the dealers. Marketing guesstimated that the best Sonance could hope for was a $740 to $750 price to consumers, which would allow the dealers to cover their installation cost of $200 and to make the $245 profit they were used to getting on a pair of SpeakerCraft's speakers. This would leave Sonance about $100 margin on a pair of Architectural Series speakers. But there were some in the top management team who thought that Sonance would not be able to recoup the additional development costs even at the $750 price, and that there was no hope for a wide market acceptance—this was clearly a niche product. They argued that Sonance should cut its losses and scrap the Architectural Series project before it burned through even more cash. The simple reality was that the high-end dealers had turned away from Sonance.

Supran knew that if Sonance were to launch the Architectural Series, his sales team would need to gain back the high-end custom installers who discontinued Sonance's speaker line during the Chip Brown years. He pondered the challenge. He knew he had to run through the numbers to evaluate the options. It had been three years since he took the final exam in his Marketing Strategy core course at Columbia Business School, but the basic concepts of break-even, economic value to the customer, and the lifetime value of a customer were suddenly more useful than ever. Was his enthusiasm about the Architectural Series unjustified and the $2,500 price unreasonable? Was he too cautious about the consumer iPort simply because he did not have expertise in mass marketing? How large was the iPort's potential? How much was a production developer versus a custom installation dealer worth to Sonance in the long run? What was the right long-term strategy for Sonance? Supran knew that some of these questions can be easily answered with the back-of-the-envelope calculations. For others, however, he did not have enough reliable data and had to make assumptions. He had to propose and justify a profitable growth strategy for Sonance or, he knew, Sonance's future as an independent company was in jeopardy.

THE OPTIONS: ANALYZING ALTERNATIVES

As 2005 drew to a close, Sugarman and Supran had to prepare their plans for 2006 and the CEDIA EXPO. They were facing some tough decisions. Sonance began with a narrow focus on custom installers, but now it was also selling speakers to production builders and through mass merchants. Diversification had led to fast overall growth, but resentment among custom installers had eroded sales and market share in the high-end custom installation business.

Time was running out for Sugarman and Supran: they had to make an executive decision. Should Sonance try to mend its relationships with and recommit to its historical base of high-end custom installers? Should it introduce the Architectural Series and at what price point, $750 or $2,500? Should it more aggressively pursue the large-scale new production construction with the Original Series? Or should the company focus on the retail consumer markets and put full support behind the iPort redesign and marketing?

Whatever strategy Sonance pursued, it had to have all product development completed and marketing plans finalized to be ready for launch at the CEDIA EXPO, less than a year away.

Case

Nundies

Panty lines are the ultimate fashion faux pas!

Jan Strimple, international model
and fashion event producer

In January 2008, Will Mortensen, president and chief financial officer of Advanced Materials, Inc., assembled the company's sales and marketing team to consider future marketing initiatives for Nundies. Nundies is a single-use, disposable panty that sticks to the inseam of women's pants, leggings, athletic wear, shorts, and jeans. Nundies—a contraction of *no undies*—is an ultra-thin nylon-and-Lycra liner for women who dislike visible panty lines and don't like to wear underwear or thongs.

Nundies were introduced to the fashion media and retail trade in the fall of 2006. By December 2007, the product was available in 232 women's boutique and specialty shops and 10 Neiman Marcus department stores in 40 states, online at www.nundies.com, and on numerous store Web sites. According to David Pokorski, national sales manager for Advanced Materials, Inc., "We have had success in getting Nundies into stores, now we have to get Nundies off the display rack." Advanced Materials, Inc. had shipped 11,383 units of Nundies to stores through December 2007 and sold 285 units online. A unit consisted of a package containing five liners. However, the store repurchase rate had not met expectations. About 6 percent of stores had placed orders for additional units beyond the initial purchase. Reorders represented about 10 percent of total units sold to retailers through December 2007.

Mortensen believed that the launch program for Nundies had yielded considerable publicity, stimulated store buyer interest, and prompted store decisions to stock and display the product. But he believed new initiatives were necessary to bolster unit volume and specifically reorders. He asked that the sales and marketing team revisit the market and sales potential for Nundies and propose strategy initiatives necessary to realize this potential, including the expected sales and profit impact of these initiatives in 2008 for budgeting purposes.

The cooperation of Advanced Materials, Inc. in the preparation of this case is gratefully acknowledged. This case was prepared by Professor Roger A. Kerin, of the Edwin L. Cox School of Business, Southern Methodist University, as a basis for class discussion and is not designed to illustrate effective or ineffective handling of an administrative situation. Nundies is a registered trademark of Advanced Materials Group, Inc. All cost information is disguised and not useful for research purposes. Copyright © 2008 Roger A. Kerin. No part of this case may be reproduced without written permission of the copyright holder.

ADVANCED MATERIALS, INC.

Advanced Materials, Inc. (AMI) is the principal subsidiary of Advanced Materials Group, Inc., a Dallas, Texas–based company. The company manufactures a variety of products made from specialty flexible materials, including foams, foils, fabrics, nonwoven paper products, needle felts, films, and adhesive products. These products consist primarily of components and finished products for the medical, consumer, aerospace, technology, and automotive markets. In addition, the company manufactures private label products for medical accounts including electrosurgical grounding pads, sponges, neck braces, knee pads, and other specialty products. Most of these private label products were designed and produced to meet the specifications of each customer.

Most of the company's sales are to large industrial customers. Sales to the company's three largest customers account for about 60 percent of sales. In fiscal year 2007 (ending November 30, 2007), the company posted sales of $10.7 million with a net profit of $850,000.

In 2003, AMI's senior management set the company's strategic focus on branding its own products and converting its product development capabilities into consumer-based solutions, primarily for the medical and consumer market. According to Mortensen: "We take flexible material—foams, fabrics, films, various materials—and we laminate those with medical-grade adhesives for one-time use products that are cut into special shapes. That's our core capability." Successful medical products arising from this strategic focus included single-use ice packs, diet patches, mammography pads, and wound-care items.

NUNDIES DEVELOPMENT AND INITIAL LAUNCH

The development and launch of Nundies was "a huge departure for us, absolutely huge," said Mortensen. He added, "[Nundies] is one of the most innovative things we've ever come up with and a true testament to thinking outside the box."

Product Development

In late 2003, interest in a panty liner emerged as part of the company's strategic focus on branded consumer-based solutions. Then, in the spring of 2006, the idea for a single-use, disposable panty that sticks to the inseam of women's pants surfaced. Consumer research indicated that most women hated panty lines, but wanted to maintain a degree of protection while "going commando." (Going commando is an expression that means "wearing no underwear." The expression was popularized on the *Friends* television series.)

The development process resulted in an ultra-thin, flexible, tulip-shaped nylon and Lycra liner that featured a proprietary medical-grade adhesive tape to avoid allergic reactions or skin rashes. In addition, "Nundies are easy to peel, place, wear once, and then toss," said Mortensen.

AMI manufacturing executives estimated that the labor and material cost to produce a single liner would be $0.60. Three colors/package options would be produced including black, buff, and assorted. The decision was made to package the liners in a colorful 5-count plastic pillow package. The plastic pillow package itself cost about $0.45 per unit to produce.[1] Exhibit 1 shows a Nundies package and liners.

---

[1] Product cost information in the case is disguised and not useful for research purposes.

EXHIBIT 1   **Nundies Pillow Package and Liners**

Nundies Marketing Research

Women 18 years of age and older in the United States spend about $16 billion annually for underwear. Among women who wear underwear, 52 percent prefer panties, 30 percent prefer thongs, 14 percent prefer boyshorts, and 4 percent prefer other styles. These products account for about a quarter of total women's underwear retail sales in the United States. A small percentage of women prefer to wear no underwear at any time. According to a 2005 poll conducted by freshpair.com, a leading Internet retailer of women's and men's intimate apparel, 6 percent of women 18 years of age and older fall into this category. By comparison, 7 percent of men 18 years of age or older prefer to wear no underwear.

Women's boutique and specialty shops account for the largest percentage of women's underwear sales (30.9 percent), followed by department stores (30.7 percent), and the combined category of discount, mass merchandise, and warehouse club stores (29.1 percent). Other retail outlets, such as Internet retailers, off-price retailers, and factory outlet stores, account for 9.1 percent of retail sales.

Survey Research   A nationwide Internet survey commissioned by AMI among 1,042 women 18 to 49 years old revealed that:

1. Eighty-four percent of women "would be interested in a product that would eliminate panty lines when they wore pants, shorts, workout, or maternity clothes."

2. When asked, "Have you tried any of the following solutions to eliminate panty lines or other visible underwear issues," the breakdown by solution was as follows (multiple responses accepted):

No-seam panties	58%
Thongs	48
Panty smoothers	12
No panties	22

3. Eighty-one percent of women said "yes" to the question: "Would you be interested in a product that provides the hygiene and comfort benefits of panties between them and their clothing, but is not underwear."

4. When women were asked, "Would you be interested in a garment-safe disposable product that adheres to the inseam of your pants/shorts to provide comfort, hygiene, and protection, but no panty lines," 36 percent of women said "yes"; 41 percent said "maybe."

5. Women who said "yes" to question 4 were asked, "Would you actively seek out this product if you knew it was for sale at your favorite store," 28 percent of women said "yes"; 49 percent said "maybe."

6. Among women who answered "yes" to question 5, 29 percent would have an occasion to use such a product 1 to 2 times per week, 35 percent said 3 to 5 times per week, and 19 percent said 6 or more times per week. Seventeen percent of women would wear the product only on special occasions (about once per month on average).

7. When women were asked, "Where would you expect to shop for a product like this," the breakdown by store type was as follows (multiple responses accepted):

Upscale department stores (Neiman Marcus, Bloomingdale's)	38%
Midlevel department stores (JCPenney)	49
Mass-merchandise stores (Target, Walmart)	64
Women's boutique/specialty stores	28
Online/Internet	41

Exhibit 2 provides cross-tabulations detailing the relationship among selected survey responses.

Focus Group Research   A focus group emphasized product packaging concepts, display concepts and location in stores, user impressions, and purchase practices. Focus group participants included women between the ages of 21 and 60 with annual household incomes of $25,000 or more. All participants held college degrees and half were single.

Focus group participants liked the packaging graphics and plastic pillow packages as well as the free-standing Nundies display. Participants expected to find Nundies in the lingerie and "contemporary concepts" location in stores. Several participants had difficulty determining how Nundies were actually placed on the inseam of pants and jeans. Once placement was demonstrated, participant reaction to Nundies was favorable. Some participants believed that in-store samples and a knowledgeable sales associate would be helpful in making a use and purchase decision. They also thought that having unpackaged liners available to see and handle prior to purchase would be welcome. Others had no difficulty

---

EXHIBIT 2 **Selected Cross-Tabulations of Survey Responses**

A. Incidence of Possible Usage by Age Category

	Age Category				
	18–24	25–29	30–35	36–40	41–49
How many times per week would you have an occasion to use a no-panty-line product?					
1–2 times/week	41.7%*	31.1%	31.0%	31.6%	20.4%
3–5 times/week	33.3%	31.9%	39.8%	29.6%	37.1%
6+ times/week	8.3%	19.3%	14.6%	20.3%	25.7%
Only on special occasion	16.7%	17.6%	14.6%	19.3%	16.8%
	100%	100%	100%	100%	100%

* *Read*: 41.7% of respondents 18–24 years old said they would have occasion to use a no-panty-line product 1–2 times per week.

B. Intention to Seek Out This Product by Age Category

	Age Category				
	18–24	25–29	30–35	36–40	41–49
Would you actively seek out this product if you knew it was for sale at your favorite store?					
Yes	29.4%*	31.1%	28.4%	25.2%	28.5%
No	29.4%	21.6%	22.3%	24.8%	20.5%
Maybe	41.2%	47.3%	49.2%	50.0%	51.0%
	100%	100%	100%	100%	100%

* *Read*: 29.4% of respondents 18–24 years old said "yes" to the question: "Would you actively seek out this product if you knew it was for sale online or at your favorite store?"

C. Expectations of Places to Shop for This Product by Age Category

	Age Category				
	18–24	25–29	30–35	36–40	41–49
Expect to shop at _____ for a product like this:					
Upscale department store	21.2%*	18.1%	16.3%	16.3%	18.2%
Mid-level department store	21.2%	21.1%	21.7%	23.9%	22.5%
Mass-merchandise store	33.3%	31.9%	29.1%	29.3%	26.5%
Women's boutique store	9.1%	12.8%	12.7%	12.5%	12.9%
Online/Internet	15.2%	16.1%	20.2%	17.9%	19.9%
	100%	100%	100%	100%	100%

* *Read*: 21.2% of respondents 18–24 years old would shop for a product like this at an upscale department store.

(continued)

EXHIBIT 2 *(Continued)*

D. Intention to Seek Out This Product by Incidence of Possible Usage

Would you actively seek out this product if you knew it was for sale at your favorite store?	How many times per week would you have an occasion to use a no-panty-line product?			
	1–2 times	*3–5 times*	*6+ times*	*Only on Special Occasions*
Yes	23.9%*	41.2%	58.6%	11.2%
No	7.4%	4.4%	5.9%	20.9%
Maybe	68.7%	54.4%	35.5%	67.9%
	100%	100%	100%	100%

* *Read*: 23.9% of respondents who would have an occasion to use a no-panty-line product 1 to 2 times per week replied "yes" to the question: "Would you actively seek out this product if you knew it was for sale at your favorite store?"

E. Intention to Seek Out This Product by Expectation of Places to Shop for This Product

Would you actively seek out this product if you knew it was for sale at your favorite store?	Expect to shop at _____ for a product like this.				
	Upscale Dept. Store	*Mid-Level Dept. Store*	*Mass Merch. Store*	*Women's Boutique Store*	*Online/ Internet*
Yes	38.4%*	32.0%	27.5%	38.1%	28.4%
No	13.9%	15.4%	20.2%	27.0%	18.5%
Maybe	47.7%	52.7%	52.3%	34.9%	53.1%
	100%	100%	100%	100%	100%

* *Read*: 38.4% of respondents who expect to shop for this product at an upscale department store replied "yes" to the question: "Would you actively seek out this product if you knew it was for sale at your favorite store?"

understanding the product or its purpose. According to one participant, "With the name 'Nundies,' I got it right away."

All participants expected to find and purchase Nundies in department stores. Online purchasing was positively viewed only for reorders and then only infrequently.

Participants believed the Nundies $15 price for a 5-count package to be on the high side of reasonable. However, since Nundies was not viewed as a product for everyday use by participants, the price point was not a major issue in the focus group discussion. A participant mentioned that she could easily afford Nundies, "but I would think about the purchase less if there were 10 liners in a $15 package."

Nundies Launch

AMI engaged a well-known Dallas-based public relations agency to launch Nundies in October 2006. The agency successfully introduced Nundies to New York City–based retail buyers for women's boutiques and specialty shops as well as lingerie editors at fashion and retail trade magazines. Complimentary feature articles about Nundies subsequently appeared in *Women's Wear Daily*, *Southern Vanity*, and *Fashion*, among other magazines. In addition, a Nundies sample package was placed in gift bags for women at major celebrity events such as the 2007 Academy Awards, the Grammys, and the Women in Film fete.

The market for Nundies was seen as the 36.7 million women between the ages of 15 and 60 in households with an annual income of $25,000 or more.

EXHIBIT 3	Population Distribution of Women and Percentage of Households with an Annual Income of $25,000 or More		
Women's Age Category	*Population (millions)*	*Percent of Households with Annual Income of $25,000 or More*
15 to 24	13,267	13.5%*
25 to 34	17,151	48.8%
35 to 44	19,199	52.8%
45 to 54	20,135	55.4%
55 to 60	9,575	54.7%

* *Read*: 13.5 percent of 13,267,000 women ages 15 to 24 reside in households with an annual income of $25,000 or more.

Commenting on the higher age range, Katie Cole, marketing assistant for Nundies, said, "With respect to women's fashion and lifestyle, 60 is the new 40." Exhibit 3 shows the distribution of women aged 15 to 60 with a household annual income of $25,000 or more based on the U.S. Census.

The manufacturer's suggested retail price (MSRP) for a 5-count Nundies package was $15. Nundies sold online direct to consumers were also priced at $15. This retail price point was chosen to reflect normal retail trade margins, competition from substitutes (such as no-seam panties and panty smoothers), manufacturing cost, and company profit goals. According to James Goodman, Nundies representative, "The product and price point dictated to us that higher-end women's boutique and specialty shops and upscale department stores would be mainly interested in carrying Nundies. I'd say that represents about 6,000 out of the 34,000 or so women's boutique and specialty shops and about 1,000 out of 5,500 or so department stores in the U.S." The wholesale price to retail stores was $7 for each 5-count package.

Five regional manufacturer's agent organizations that specialized in women's apparel and accessories were enlisted in January and February of 2007 to build the distribution coverage among women's boutique and specialty shops for Nundies. Each manufacturer's agent organization operated a showroom at an apparel market in their region. The five apparel markets were located in Atlanta, Georgia; Chicago, Illinois; Dallas, Texas; Los Angeles, California; and New York City. Buyers for women's boutique and specialty shops visit these showrooms and make decisions about which apparel and accessory lines to carry. Nundies were also exhibited at the Lingerie Americas Trade Show in New York City and Las Vegas, Nevada, in 2007.

AMI supplied each manufacturer's agent organization with product information and sales materials, such as that shown in Exhibit 4 on pages 586 and 587. Agents were paid a 12 percent commission on the wholesale price for each 5-count package sold. The minimum store purchase order consisted of 36 packages at a price of $252. As a rule, the manufacturer's agent's sales responsibility ended with the purchase order. Agents did not typically call on individual stores or store buying offices and did not engage in merchandising products at stores.

Media advertising supporting the Nundies launch was limited. A print advertisement for Nundies focused on retail trade buyers and appeared in *Women's Wear Daily*. Exhibit 5 on page 588 shows the Nundies print advertisement. There was no consumer-oriented media advertising. The total out-of-pocket cost for product and process development, marketing research, and the launch program was about $800,000. No new or additional production facilities were required to manufacture Nundies. Advanced Materials, Inc. had manufacturing

| EXHIBIT 4 | Example of Nundies Sales Material Used by Manufacturer's Agents |

Product Options

Naughty Black →

← Blushing Buff

Sassy Assorted* →

*Actual colors may vary

← Counter Display

Optional Hanging Tabs →

Nundies® are a product of Advanced Materials, Inc. · patents pending · ©2007 Advanced Materials, Inc.

capacity in place to produce 100,000 liners annually without further investment in plant and equipment.

Nundies Results to Date

By the end of December 2007, Nundies were available in 232 women's boutique and specialty shops and 10 Neiman Marcus department stores in 40 states. Advanced Materials, Inc. had shipped 11,383 units of Nundies to these stores.

EXHIBIT 4 *(Continued)*

Pricing Guide

Suggested Retail Price: $15.00/pkg

Starter Case*

36 Packages   **$7.00/package**

Each starter case contains 1 box Naughty Black, 1 box Blushing Buff, and 1 box Sassy Assorted Nundies, unless otherwise requested.

Each box contains 12 *Nundies* packages.

*Starter cases are still available after the first order!

Standard Case

72 Packages   **$7.00/package**

Each standard case contains 6 boxes at 12 packages per box. Each box contains one color of your choice; color choice may not be mixed within each box.

Add-On Options

Counter Display
$20.00/unit

Optional Hanging Tabs
(one tab per package)

$10.00/order of 72 packages or less

Nundies® are a product of Advanced Materials, Inc. · patents pending · ©2007 Advanced Materials, Inc.

This figure included reorders from 15 stores for 1,177 units. Online sales sold through nundies.com totaled 285 units. Exhibit 6 on page 589 details the number of new store accounts added, new units sold, and unit reorders by month. Almost all store purchases were for the $252 minimum order.

According to Goodman, "We have seen that Nundies is a low-risk item for store buyers. The minimum order of $252 is small when compared to buying apparel

EXHIBIT 5   Nundies Print Advertisement in *Women's Wear Daily*

and accessories where the minimum purchase order can run in the thousands of dollars. At the same time, there appears to be a disconnect between the buying of Nundies at market and the selling of Nundies at stores. It seems like store managers and sales associates are unclear as to how they should merchandise Nundies once they arrive at the store."

| **EXHIBIT 6** | **Monthly Department Store and Women's Boutique and Specialty Store Sales Counts for 2007** |

	*Number of New Store Accounts**	*Number of Nundies New Units Ordered*	*Number of Nundies Units Reordered*
First Quarter			
January	6	240	0
February	1	108	168
March	4	144	0
Total	11	492	168
Second Quarter			
April	46	2,052	36
May	36	1,590	73
June	21	864	236
Total	103	4,506	345
Third Quarter			
July	14	630	36
August	44	1,896	72
September	25	1,188	108
Total	83	3,552	216
Fourth Quarter			
October	20	720	0
November	23	864	432
December	2	72	16
Total	45	1,656	468
Grand Total	242	10,206	1,177

* The total number of store locations was 275 since some store accounts were multi-site operators.

Note: E-commerce sales through the Nundies Web site totaled 285 units.

Goodman's impressions were confirmed by Nicki Wilk, Nundies account manager. Her observations, based on visits to 25 stores in the Dallas–Fort Worth metropolitan area that carried Nundies, led her to conclude that:

1. Store personnel seem to assume that Nundies will sell itself.

2. Store customers who are already going panty-free at times "get" Nundies. Those who don't are either intimidated or embarrassed by Nundies.

3. The Nundies display tends to get lost in many stores. Our 36-package display is attractive, but on the small side. If the sales staff does not talk about it and give suggestions for use, then customers tend to not inquire about Nundies or know what Nundies are all about.

She said: "We really need to get the word out to the average consumer so they will start coming into stores on their own and asking for Nundies."

 ## FUTURE SALES AND MARKETING INITIATIVES

In January 2008, Will Mortensen assembled the sales and marketing team responsible for Nundies. The purpose of the meeting was to review the performance of Nundies to date and discuss various proposals for new sales and marketing initiatives. An overriding concern expressed by Mortensen was the need to assess these initiatives and their cost and profit impact in light of the market and sales potential for Nundies. Ideally, a course of action for 2008 would arise from the meeting.

Marketing Channel Proposals

Three marketing channel proposals were raised for consideration. They were (1) continued development of the women's and specialty store channel; (2) pursue upscale department store accounts; and (3) pursue midlevel department store accounts. A combination of channels was also possible. Discount, mass merchandise, and warehouse club store channel proposals were dismissed early due to profit margin considerations.

Continued Development of the Women's Boutique and Specialty Store Channel This proposal meant continued reliance on manufacturer's agent organizations to recruit stores through showrooms at apparel markets and exhibiting at the Lingerie Americas Trade Show twice per year. The annual out-of-pocket expense to attend these events was roughly $14,400 for Advanced Materials' personnel travel, lodging, and meals, market registration fees, exhibit setup costs, and sales materials.

Pursue the Upscale Department Store Channel This proposal meant pursuing upscale department store accounts such as Bloomingdale's, Nordstrom, Saks Fifth Avenue, and Lord & Taylor. Upscale department stores vary in terms of their merchandise buying practices. For example, Bloomingdale's uses "centralized buying" for its 36 stores. Purchase decisions are made at its headquarters in New York City. By comparison, Nordstrom uses "decentralized buying." Each of the company's 157 stores makes individual buying decisions. Neiman Marcus uses decentralized buying. Ten out of its 39 stores have chosen to stock Nundies.

This initiative would require the identification of and an agreement with an apparel manufacturer's agent organization that specializes in selling to upscale department stores. Alternatively, Advanced Materials could treat upscale department stores that engage in centralized buying as "house accounts." For example, Neiman Marcus is a "house account." These upscale department store accounts would be contacted by Applied Materials executives directly with the assistance of a retail sales consultant with expertise in developing formal sale presentations for department store buyers and buying offices. The sales presentation would include elements of a typical marketing plan. For example, the target market, including its estimated size, and positioning statement would be described. Identification of competitive products and points of difference or superiority would be required as well as a recommended retail price point. These elements of the sales presentation would be supported by marketing research. Point-of-sales displays and advertising plans (media as well as advertisements) would be presented. Finally, the company's ability to produce and deliver product in a timely manner in the right quantities would be documented.

Upscale department store chains were split about equally in terms of centralized and decentralized buying practices. The top five upscale department stores with centralized buying offices had a combined total of about 300 stores in their chains. The top five upscale department stores with decentralized buying had a combined total of about 350 stores in their chains. If manufacturer's agents were used, they would be paid a 12 percent commission on wholesale sales. It was estimated that the cost to make presentations to the top five upscale department store chains with centralized buying offices would be in the range of $20,000 to $30,000 in 2008, including retail consultant fees.

Pursue Midlevel Department Store Accounts   This proposal involved pursuing department store chains other than those considered to be upscale department stores, discount stores, or mass-merchandise stores. For the most part, these department store chains, such as JCPenney with about 1,000 stores and Kohl's with about 930 stores, use centralized buying. Macy's, with 863 stores, centralizes buying in each of its seven regional buying offices. Midlevel department stores could be handled as "house accounts" and approached directly by Advanced Materials' executives with the involvement of a retail sales consultant.

As envisioned, this proposal would require a different brand name. Different package graphics and a paper, not plastic, package would be used. This proposal also recommended more liners per package—a 7-count package—with an MSRP of $8 to $10. The target retail margin percentage would be the same as that for current store accounts.

The 2008 out-of-pocket expense for new package design graphics and the sales material would be in the range of $25,000 to $35,000. It was believed that the direct (variable) cost to produce a single liner would be $0.43 with this proposal, assuming longer production runs and modifications in the material composition for liners. Also, the less expensive paper package would cost about $0.25 per unit. It was estimated that the cost to prepare and deliver formal sale presentations to the top five midlevel department store chains with a combined 3,400 store count would be the same as that for the top five upscale department stores with centralized buying practices.

Department Store Fees, Discounts, and Allowances   The department store channel often included additional fees, particularly for new items. These included line fees (to have the product listed), warehouse fees (to cover the cost of distribution to branches), settlement fees (a discount for prompt payment by the retailer; typically 2 percent of the wholesale price), catalog fees (to have the product included in print or electronic catalog), and cooperative advertising allowances (to cover store advertising; typically 3 percent of the wholesale price).

In most cases, fees are based on a percentage of annual sales, but some are levied as one-time costs. Fees and charges are negotiable as well. Informal discussions with industry sources suggested that it was highly likely that Nundies would pay line, warehouse, and catalog fees up front at a cost of ranging from $35,000 to $55,000 for a large department store chain with centralized buying practices.

Advertising and Promotion Proposals

The sales and marketing team acknowledged that broadened distribution did not address the issue of "getting Nundies off the display rack" in stores already stocking the product. During the past year, e-mail messages were sent to managers of women's boutique and specialty stores that stocked Nundies. As an example, "Tips for Getting to Know Your Nundies!" described product features, benefits, and usage situations, plus suggestions for introducing Nundies to store customers (see Exhibit 7 on page 592). No reorders could be specifically attributed to this effort.

Three advertising and promotion proposals were raised for consideration. Each proposal could be viewed as a complement for one or more of the marketing channel proposals.

Fashion Magazine Advertising   This proposal involved a national fashion magazine advertising program. For example, a print advertisement program featuring Nundies could include either *Cosmo Girl* or *Cosmopolitan* magazines. *Cosmo Girl* focused on fashion and trends for teens and women under 23 years

---

EXHIBIT 7 **Trade Promotion**

Tips for Getting to know your Nundies®!

1) Great for all of your low-rise denim and expensive loungewear. Nundies® allows you to wash your favorite pants a little less, keeping them in pristine condition MUCH longer!

2) They are a one-time use, disposable, tulip-shaped 'panty' that is used as an alternative to traditional underwear

3) Made out of a nylon/Lycra blend – Extremely Soft

4) NO Visible-Panty-Lines (or VPL for the "posh")

5) Great for working out - no tight thongs or bunching panties while exercising.

6) Sexy for "nights out" and your favorite low hip-hugging jeans! Nundies® offer comfortable protection in the most discreet fashion!

7) Comforting for health fanatics- Nundies® protect what they need to, and nothing more. Made by a company that produces medical products, Nundies® are a hygienic option for even the most timid health fanatic. It's like cutting out the gusset of your underwear and tossing the rest.

8) Trendy for traveling- with all the restrictions these days, it's much less space in your luggage- Nundies® fit in your purse. They're with you whether or not your luggage stays in the same city.

9) If you're pregnant, Nundies® is a less expensive and much more comfortable alternative to purchasing maternity panties.

10) Nundies® can be found in some of the top-tier retailers such as: Neiman Marcus, Henri Bendel and Bliss spas.

11) Wonderful for add-on sales on all loungewear, denim, dress pants and shorts.

Nundies® are a product of Advanced Materials, Inc
Patents Pending
©2007 Advanced Materials, Inc.

---

of age; *Cosmopolitan* focused on fashion and trends for women 23 years of age and older. A 4-color, full-page advertisement placed over three consecutive issues would cost about $115,000 for *Cosmo Girl* and $200,000 for *Cosmopolitan*. A similar advertising program for *Marie Claire* would cost about $119,000 and target "20-something" women, while *Vogue* would cost about $125,000 and reach "30-something" women, on average. According to apparel industry research, fashion magazines were "a source of fashion inspiration" for 56 percent of females aged 13 years old or older.

Metropolitan-Area Advertising   A second proposal was to advertise in the major newspapers and outdoor venues in the six metropolitan areas where stores carrying Nundies were most numerous (such as Dallas, Texas; Los Angeles, California; and New York City). Print advertisements would be placed in the weekly Style or Fashion section of these newspapers over four consecutive weeks. The cost would range from $27,000 to $33,000 for these six metropolitan areas for a half-page, 4-color print advertisement. Apparel industry research indicated that newspapers were "a source of fashion inspiration" for 26 percent of females aged 13 years old or older.

Alternatively, or in addition to newspapers, outdoor billboards or kiosks placed in high automobile traffic or pedestrian locales in the six metropolitan areas was possible. An outdoor billboard in a high traffic site in each of the six metropolitan markets would cost from $24,000 to $50,000 per year. Similarly, advertising placed on kiosks in high pedestrian walk areas (e.g., shopping malls) was a possibility. As a rough estimate, space on five kiosks in each of the six metropolitan areas could be purchased for $1,000 to $1,400 per month. This advertising would run for two months.

A related proposal was to contact newspaper editors and columnists in these metropolitan areas to arrange for interviews about Nundies. The genesis for this proposal was an interview with Will Mortensen and a Nundies photo that appeared in the *Dallas Morning News* on April 15, 2007. Although short-lived, the article about Nundies did stimulate sales at several Neiman Marcus stores in Dallas, Texas. This proposal was virtually cost-free and paid out of the ongoing fees to the public relations agency for Nundies.

Search Engine Marketing   A third proposal was to engage in search engine marketing. Specifically, Advanced Materials, Inc. would pay for keyword search items on a search engine such as Google. The keywords might be panty, Nundies, lingerie, thongs, or other words related to intimate apparel. When online visitors entered the keyword during a search, they would be offered a link to nundies.com, which included product information and store locations. A rough estimate for the search engine marketing cost was $20,000 per month in each of six major metropolitan markets, or $120,000 per month.

Budget Considerations

After the Nundies sales and marketing team previewed the various proposals, Mortensen again emphasized the importance of linking market and sales potential with the sales and profit impact of the different initiatives. He also noted that it was unlikely that all initiatives could be funded for budgetary reasons. He added, "Now that we have the proposals on the table, let's think creatively about how we might proceed assuming a cash budget for Nundies marketing of $300,000 in 2008."

Case

Coleman Art Museum

In early 2005, Ashley Mercer, director of development and community affairs, and Donald Smith, director of finance and administration of the Coleman Art Museum, met to discuss what had transpired at a meeting the previous afternoon. The meeting, attended by the senior staff of the museum and several members of the Board of Trustees, had focused on the financial status of the museum. The Coleman Art Museum recorded its third consecutive annual loss in 2004, and Mercer and Smith were assigned responsibility for making recommendations that would reverse the situation.

 ## COLEMAN ART MUSEUM

The Coleman Art Museum (CAM) is a not-for-profit corporation located in Universal City, a large metropolitan area in the western United States. Founded in 1925, the museum was originally chartered as the Fannel County Museum of Fine Arts and funded by an annual appropriation from Fannel County. In 2000, the name was changed to the Jonathon A. Coleman Art Museum to recognize the museum's major benefactor, Jonathon A. Coleman. Coleman, a wealthy local landowner and philanthropist, had provided the museum with a sizable endowment. According to the terms of a $25 million gift given to the museum upon his death, the museum's charter was revised and its name changed. The charter of the museum stated that its purpose was

> To provide an inviting setting for the appreciation of art in its historical and cultural contexts for the benefit of this and successive generations of Fannel County citizens and visitors.

Randall Brent III, the museum director, noted that this charter differentiated CAM from other art museums. He said:

> Our charter gives us both an opportunity and a challenge. By spanning both art and history, the museum offers a unique perspective on both. On the other hand, a person can only truly appreciate what we have here if they are willing to become historically literate—that is our challenge.

In 1997, CAM benefited from a $28 million county bond election, which led to the construction of a new and expanded facility in the central business district of Universal City, the county seat of Fannel County. The location, six blocks from the museum's previous site, had extensive parking availability and access through public transportation. The site was made available for $1.00 from Jonathon Coleman's real estate holdings. At the dedication of CAM in January 2000, Brent said:

> I will always believe that the greatest strength of our new museum is that it was publicly mandated. The citizens of Fannel County and the vision and generosity of Jonathon Coleman have provided the setting for the appreciation of art and its historical and cultural contexts. As stewards of this public trust, the Coleman Art Museum can now focus on collecting significant works of art, encouraging scholarship and education, and decoding the history and culture of art.

MUSEUM COLLECTION AND DISPLAY

CAM has over 15,000 works of art in its permanent collection. However, as with most museums, CAM does not display all of its collection at the same time because of space limitations. Artworks in the collection are rotated, with some periodically loaned to other museums.

The CAM collection includes pre-Columbian, African, and Depression-era art, as well as European and American decorative arts. The art is displayed in different portions of the museum, where the building architecture accents the display. For example, Depression-era art is displayed in an Art Deco setting of the 1920s and 1930s; decorative and architectural art of the late nineteenth century is displayed in the Art Nouveau wing. In addition, museum docents provide a historical context for the artworks during tours.

The CAM collection is open for viewing Monday through Saturday from 10:00 A.M. to 6:00 P.M. and Thursday evenings until 8:00 P.M. Sunday hours are from 12:00 noon to 6:00 P.M. There is no charge for viewing the permanent collection; however, a modest fee of $5.00 to $7.50 is charged for special exhibitions. CAM is also available for private showings and is often used for corporate, foundation, and various fund-raising events during weekday and weekend evenings. Exhibit 1 shows museum attendance for the period 1996–2004.

EXHIBIT 1   **Museum Attendance**

Year	Total Museum Attendance	Special Exhibitions[a] Attendance	Proportion of Total Attendance
1996	269,786	N/A	N/A
1997	247,799	N/A	N/A
1998	303,456	N/A	N/A
1999	247,379	N/A	N/A
2000	667,949	220,867	0.33
2001	486,009	140,425	0.29
2002	527,091	227,770	0.43
2003	468,100	203,800	0.44
2004	628,472	284,865	0.45

[a]Special exhibitions attendance includes attendance at private corporation, foundation, and fund-raising events held at the museum.

Museum Organization

The museum is organized by function: (1) Collections and Exhibitions, (2) Development and Community Affairs, and (3) Finance and Administration. Each function is headed by a director who reports to the museum director, Randall Brent III. The museum has a staff of 185 employees. In addition, 475 volunteers work at the museum in a variety of capacities.

The Collections and Exhibitions staff, headed by Thomas Crane, oversees the museum's art collections, arranges special exhibits, is responsible for educational programming, and provides personnel and administrative support for museum operations that directly involve the artwork. The Finance and Administration staff, headed by Donald Smith, is responsible for the daily operation of the museum. The museum's profit centers (the Skyline Buffet restaurant, parking, gift shop, and special exhibitions events) are also managed by this function. The Development and Community Affairs staff, under the direction of Ashley Mercer, is responsible for marketing, public relations, membership, and grants. This function engages in fund-raising for the museum, which provides supplemental funds for general operating support, endowment, and acquisitions. This function also handles all applications for foundation, federal, state, and local grants.

Museum Finances

Exhibit 2 shows the financial condition of CAM for the period 2002–2004. Total revenues and expenses during this period are shown below:

	2004	2003	2002
Total revenue	$10,794,110	$7,783,712	$8,694,121
Total expenses	11,177,825	7,967,530	8,920,674
Net income (loss)	($ 383,715)	($ 183,818)	($ 226,533)

The three consecutive years of losses followed seven consecutive years of either break-even or profitable status. The cumulative loss of $794,066 had depleted the museum's financial reserves.

During a recent Board of Trustees meeting, several observations and projections were made that indicated that the museum's financial condition needed attention:

1. The appropriation from Fannel County would decline. Whereas the county appropriated about $2 million annually to CAM, the museum could expect no more than $1.6 million in county appropriations in 2005 and for the foreseeable future.

2. Low interest rates in 2003 and 2004 indicated that earnings from CAM endowment and investments would probably remain flat or decline.

3. Income from grants and other contributions in 2004 were extraordinary, and it was unlikely that the same amounts would be forthcoming in 2005.

4. Membership revenues were down for the fifth consecutive year. Membership represented the single largest source of revenue for the museum.

5. Income from auxiliary activities—those that were intended to produce a profit—continued to show a positive contribution to museum operations.

Special exhibitions and events were very profitable. Nevertheless, limited availability of special exhibitions in 2005, a declining number of scheduled events, and rising costs (for insurance as an example) indicated that the revenues from such activities would probably decline and costs increase in 2005. The Skyline

EXHIBIT 2 Summary of Income and Expenses, 2002–2004

Operations	Year Ending December 31		
	2004	*2003*	*2002*
Income			
Appropriations by Fannel County	$1,786,929	$1,699,882	$1,971,999
Memberships	2,917,325	2,956,746	3,134,082
Contributions	338,664	221,282	42,244
Grants	763,581	281,164	645,853
Investment income	27,878	28,537	32,205
Earnings from endowment	673,805	693,625	583,612
Other	149,462	128,628	196,195
Total revenue	$6,657,644	$6,009,864	$6,606,190
Expenses			
Personnel	$1,973,218	$1,086,177	$1,681,653
Memberships	854,461	869,043	906,314
Publications/public information	594,067	404,364	441,710
Education	616,828	519,805	542,076
Administration*	3,777,042	3,345,153	3,389,124
Total expenses	$7,815,616	$6,224,542	$6,960,877
Operating income	($1,157,972)	($214,678)	($354,687)
Auxiliary Activities			
Revenue from auxiliary			
Special exhibitions	$1,655,200	$510,415	$451,347
Museum gift shop	1,596,775	606,503	810,123
Skyline Buffet	515,843	305,952	418,960
Museum parking	131,512	45,068	64,651
Museum Association	337,136	305,910	342,850
Revenue from auxiliary	4,236,466	1,773,848	2,087,931
Expenses from auxiliary			
Special exhibitions	814,741	313,057	137,680
Museum gift shop	1,679,294	662,685	990,090
Skyline Buffet	592,051	457,841	462,475
Museum parking	31,168	16,528	16,536
Museum Association	344,955	292,877	353,016
Expenses from auxiliary	3,462,209	1,742,988	1,959,797
Profit from auxiliary activities	$774,257	$30,860	$128,134
Net income	($383,715)	($183,818)	($226,553)

*Administration expenses included mostly overhead costs, such as insurance, maintenance, utilities, equipment lease agreements, and so forth.

Buffet restaurant, gift shop and parking, and the Museum Association were operating at about break-even.

MUSEUM MARKETING

As director of development and community affairs, Ashley Mercer was responsible for marketing at CAM. Her specific responsibilities related to enhancing the image of the museum, increasing museum visitation, and building museum memberships. Reflecting on her responsibilities, she said:

> In reality, museum image, visitation, and membership are intermingled. Image influences visitation and membership. Visitation is driven somewhat by membership, but membership seems to also drive visitation and, in a subtle way, affects the image of the museum.

Museum Image

Interest in the public image of CAM began soon after the new facility was dedicated. The new four-story building, situated downtown adjacent to skyscrapers, was occasionally referred to as the "marble box" by its critics, since the building facade contained Italian marble. When asked about CAM's image, Brent commented:

> It is basically correct to say that, in the mind of the public, CAM has no image. There is nothing about this [building] that says, "I'm a museum," or "Come in." There are a lot of people that are not interested in high culture and think this is a drive-in bank or an office building.
>
> Most art museums in America have a problem with image. One of the things that makes me mad is that people think there is something wrong with the museum. CAM is one of the most public in the country, and more heavily dependent on the membership contribution than any other [museum]. Like most, it is under-endowed and underfunded from reliable public funds. In fact, the American Association of Museums reports that only about 60 percent of America's 2000-plus art museums have enough income from their endowment to cover their operating costs. Nevertheless, this institution has chosen to be public, with free access, and this is very noble. It is wonderful that the museum has decided not to belong to an agglomeration of very rich people.
>
> This museum has more character than it thinks it has. It has the best balanced collection between Western and non-Western art of any museum in the country. We have not chosen to sell or promote the unique aspects of this collection or the museum's emphasis on historical context. What we have are the makings of an institution that is very different from other museums, and we ought to be able to make that into an advantage rather than apologize for it.

Other staff members believed either that an image existed but was different for the various publics the museum served or that CAM had not made a sufficient effort to create an image for itself. According to Mercer:

> Based on our marketing research, I think there are two distinctly different images. One is a non-image. People don't know what the museum is. They also don't know what we have to offer in the way of lunch, dinner, brunch, shopping, movies, etc. They are not familiar with our collections. They are probably proud, however, that their community has a beautiful art museum.
>
> The other image is that we are only for specific people. This image is probably based on our membership. About 85 percent of members are college-educated (compared to 70 percent of the county population of 2.5 million), 60 percent have household incomes in excess of $70,000 (compared to 20 percent

of the county population), half are over 40 years old (compared to 25 percent of the county population), and 98 percent are white (compared to 75 percent of the county population).

Janet Blake, staff assistant in charge of membership, noted:

> Among our membership, CAM is viewed as a community organization that has a cachet of class. It is exciting, educational, convenient, and inviting. It is a great place to bring visitors to our city for an afternoon of lunch and browsing.

A critic of the museum said:

> The Coleman Art Museum has a definite image in my opinion. It's a great place to have lunch or brunch, buy an art or history book for the coffee table, and see a few things if time permits. Its parking facility is strategically located to allow its members to park conveniently for downtown shopping, particularly during the Christmas holidays.

Museum Visitation

Because there is a general belief that increased numbers of visitors lead to increased membership, Mercer's staff has historically focused its efforts on increasing the traffic through the museum. "Social, cultural, and educational activity in the museum is a major goal, and is not exclusive to the viewing of art," said Mercer. These efforts can be separated into general and outreach programs and programs involving special exhibitions and events.

Press Relations   CAM continually promotes its special exhibitions and activities by sending out press releases, and it maintains a close relationship with the local media. Stories about art and history, public programs, and human interest issues are often featured in the local media. A five-year anniversary party was held at the museum in January 2005, designed as a free special event aimed to involve the general public with the museum.

Education and Outreach   CAM has many programs directed toward educating the public. Among these are public programs such as adult tours, school tours, lectures, art films, and feature films. The museum engages in programming to create community involvement and lends performing space to local performing arts organizations.

Special Exhibitions   Public service announcements written by the museum are aired on local radio stations to promote special exhibitions. Advertisements are run in local newspapers in a five-county area for special exhibitions. For major special exhibitions, advertising is usually sponsored by a local corporation.

Mercer believed that these efforts increased museum attendance. For example, periodic visitor surveys indicate that on a typical day when only the permanent collection was available for viewing, 85 percent of visitors were non-CAM members. She added that even though less than 1 percent of nonmembers actually applied for membership during a visit, this exposure helped in the annual membership solicitation.

Museum Membership

According to Mercer:

> Museum membership and the revenue earned from membership play significant roles in the success and daily operations of CAM. The museum and its members have a symbiotic relationship. Members provide the museum with a volunteer

base, without which our cost of operation would be astronomical. Member volunteers provide tours, assist at the information desk, help in the gift shop and the Skyline Buffet, and are invaluable in recruiting new members and renewing existing members.

The Museum Association was created to encourage membership involvement in CAM. The association, with some 1,000 members, makes our volunteer effort possible—95 percent of our 475 volunteers are Association members. The association's assistance in fund-raising is critical, and we appreciate what its members have done for CAM. Last year alone, the association was directly responsible for raising almost $350,000. In return, CAM sponsors social events for association members, offers them lectures by authorities on art and history, and provides various other privileges not available to the general membership.

Member Categories, Benefits, and Costs   CAM has two distinct memberships: (1) personal and (2) corporate. These two memberships are further divided into categories based on dollar contributions and benefits received. There are six categories of personal membership ranging from $50 per year to $5,000 per year. Corporate memberships are divided into four categories ranging from $1,000 per year to $10,000 per year. These categories and participation levels were created with the move to the new building. In 2004, there were 17,429 personal memberships and 205 corporate memberships.

Exhibit 3 shows the benefits received by each personal membership category. Exhibit 4 provides a breakdown of personal memberships by category and the revenue generated by each category over the past five years. In 2004, personal memberships accounted for almost 80 percent of membership revenue.

Corporate memberships provide many of the same benefits as the $500 or higher personal memberships. In addition, corporate members are given "Employee Memberships" depending on their category. For example, corporate

EXHIBIT 3   Membership Benefits by Membership Categories

Benefits	$50	$100	$250	$500	$1,500	$5,000
Invitations to special previews/events	*	*	*	*	*	*
Free limited parking	*	*	*	*	*	*
Free admission to special exhibits	*	*	*	*	*	*
15% discount at Skyline Buffet and gift shop	*	*	*	*	*	*
Monthly calendar	*	*	*	*	*	*
Discounts on films/lectures	*	*	*	*	*	*
Reciprocal membership in other museums		*	*	*	*	*
Invitations to distinguished lectures			*	*	*	*
Listing in annual report			*	*	*	*
Personal tours of exhibition areas				*	*	*
Invitations to exclusive previews/events					*	*
Free unlimited parking					*	*
Unique travel opportunities					*	*
Recognition on plaques in the museum					*	*
First views of new acquisitions					*	*
Priority on all museum trips						*
Dinner with the director						*

EXHIBIT 4	Personal Membership Categories and Revenues by Year, 2000–2004

		Number of Members				
Membership Category	Amount	2004	2003	2002	2001	2000
Regular	$50	13,672	12,248	13,483	16,353	17,758
Associate	$100	2,596	2,433	2,548	2,576	2,465
Collector	$250	364	325	397	461	454
Patron	$500	102	85	65	0	0
Partner	$1,500	604	638	679	741	882
Director's Club	$5,000	91	86	98	0	0
Total membership		17,429	15,815	17,370	20,131	21,559

		Membership Revenue[a]				
		2004	2003	2002	2001	2000
Regular	$50	$639,664	$556,120	$611,864	$600,188	$662,631
Associate	$100	234,871	232,398	249,317	244,961	242,981
Collector	$250	81,415	76,987	97,474	108,432	105,840
Patron	$500	48,100	44,293	35,500	0	0
Partner	$1,500	815,666	958,419	968,239	1,187,728	1,041,898
Director's Club	$5,000	406,673	405,016	458,938	282,219	0
Total membership revenue[b]		$2,298,449	$2,334,583	$2,485,352	$2,451,638	$2,079,330

[a]The number of memberships times the dollar value does not equal the amounts given as the membership revenue, since some memberships are given gratis.

[b]The inconsistency between these figures and the figures shown on the income and expense statement is due to memberships given gratis.

members that fall into the $1,000 category are given 25 employee memberships; those in the $10,000 category are given 250 such memberships.

The direct cost of benefits provided by CAM to personal and corporate members was estimated by the museum's accounting firm. CAM was required to do this because of income tax laws that limited the deductibility of membership to the difference between the direct cost of membership and the value of the benefits received. The estimated total cost of member benefits provided exceeded $1 million each year since 2000.[1] An itemized summary of benefit costs by category in 2004 follows.

Category	Benefit Cost
Regular ($50)	$631,016
Associate ($100)	81,903
Collector ($250)	64,135
Patron ($500)	39,628
Partner ($1,500)	99,567
Director's Club ($5,000)	15,975
Corporate (all categories)	125,576
Total cost	$1,057,800

[1] The estimated cost of benefits exceeds the membership expense shown in Exhibit 2 because the cost of publications and other items is included in this estimate. These costs are allocated across several different items in Exhibit 2.

The principal cost items in each category were (1) free admissions to exhibits; (2) parking; (3) the monthly calendar of museum activities, exhibits, and events; and (4) discounts at the Skyline Buffet restaurant and gift shop.

Member Recruiting and Renewals   "Recruiting new members and renewing existing members is a major undertaking," said Mercer. While some recruiting and renewals occur at the museum during visitation, the recruitment effort mostly revolves around mail, telephone, and personal solicitations. Mail and telephone solicitations focus primarily on recruiting and renewing personal memberships in the $50 to $250 categories. Personal solicitations by the Museum Association are used to recruit and renew personal memberships in the $500 to $5,000 categories and corporate memberships.

CAM uses mailing and telephone lists obtained from other cultural organizations and list agencies. These lists are culled to target zip codes and telephone prefix numbers. Mail solicitations include a letter from the museum director, a brochure describing the museum, and a membership application form. Telephone solicitations include a follow-up brochure and application form.

The economics of direct-mail solicitation are illustrated below, based on an August 2004 mailing considered typical by Mercer.

Total mail solicitations	148,530
Total memberships obtained	1,532
Response rate	1.03%
Total membership revenue	$84,280.00
Total direct-mail costs	$66,488.80

Two direct-mail solicitations of this magnitude are conducted each year.

The solicitation process for personal memberships in larger dollar categories and corporate memberships relies on personal contact by CAM volunteers and corporate member executives. Prospective members are identified on the basis of personal contacts and from the lapsed membership roster, the society page, other organizations' membership lists, and lower-membership-level lists. Once identified, these prospects are approached on a one-to-one basis. An initial letter is sent introducing the prospect to the museum. This first letter is followed by a personal telephone call or another letter inviting the prospect to an informal gathering at the museum. At the gathering, the prospect is introduced to other members and is asked directly to become a member.

Renewal efforts include mail, telephone, and Internet solicitation. In addition, membership parties, special previews, and special inserts in the monthly calendar of CAM activities are used.

Museum records indicate that 70 percent of the $50 members do not renew their membership after the first year. Among those that do, 50 percent renew in each successive year. Members in the $100 to $500 categories have a renewal rate of 60 percent, and members in the $1,500 and $5,000 categories have a renewal rate of 85 percent. Mercer believed that less than 10 percent of personal members who do renew their membership increase the dollar value of their membership. Renewal rates among corporate members is about 75 percent, regardless of category.

CONSIDERATIONS FOR 2005

Ashley Mercer and Donald Smith met to discuss measures they might recommend to the Board of Trustees to reverse the deteriorating financial condition of CAM. Smith noted that at an earlier meeting with his staff, personnel reductions were discussed. Specifically, he felt that a 10 percent reduction in personnel and administration costs was possible. Furthermore, his staff estimated that the appropriation from Fannel County, contributions, grants, investment income, endowment earnings, and other income would be 15 percent below 2004 levels. A "best guess" estimate from the director of collections and exhibitions indicated that special exhibitions and events would generate revenues of $1.2 million and cost $675,000 in 2005. Parking revenues and expenses resulting from nonmember visitors would remain unchanged from 2004. Rough budgets for education programs indicated that an expenditure of $500,000 for 2005 was realistic, given planned efforts. Smith said that changes in other auxiliary activities for which he was responsible, namely the Skyline Buffet restaurant and gift shop, were not planned.

Mercer was impressed with the attention Smith had already given to the museum's situation. She too had given consideration to matters of museum image, visitation, and membership prior to the meeting. Unfortunately, an earlier meeting with her staff had raised more issues than hard-and-fast recommendations. Staff suggestions ranged from implementing a modest admission fee of $2 per adult (with no charge for children under 12 years old) to instituting student (ages 13 to 22) and senior citizen (60 and older) memberships at $30. The need for institutional advertising was raised, since CAM had been promoting only special exhibitions and events. Other staff members said that the benefits given to members needed to be enhanced. For example, raising discounts at the Skyline Buffet and gift shop to 20 percent was suggested. Another possibility raised was commissioning a "coffee table" book featuring major artwork at CAM to be given with personal memberships of $500 or more.

Mercer listened to these suggestions, knowing that some were unlikely to receive Board of Trustee approval. These included any proposal to increase expenses for publications/public information (for example, new books and paid institutional advertising). She had already been informed that expenses for such activities could not exceed the 2004 expenditure. Improving the member benefit package seemed like a good idea. Increasing restaurant and gift shop discounts, even though 65 percent of the business for both was already on discount, seemed like a good idea, at least at the margin. Smith said that he would give this suggestion consideration, but asked that Mercer think further about it in the context of the overall member-benefit package. Charging a nominal admission fee for nonmembers also seemed reasonable. Visitor surveys had shown that 50 percent of nonmember visitors said that they would be willing to pay a $2 admission fee for viewing the permanent collection (access to special exhibitions would continue to have admission fees). Furthermore, members could then be given an additional benefit, that is, free admission. However, Smith noted that CAM had always prided itself on free access, and he wondered how the Board of Trustees would view this suggestion. Additional membership categories below $50 and for students and senior citizens also seemed to provide new opportunities to attract segments of the population that had not typically yielded members.

Mercer and Smith believed that their initial meeting had produced some good ideas, but both thought that they had to give these matters further thought. They agreed to meet again and begin to prepare an integrated plan of action and a pro forma income statement for 2005.

Case

Goodyear Tire and Rubber Company

In early 1992, Goodyear Tire and Rubber Company executives were reconsidering a proposal made by Sears, Roebuck and Company. Sears management had approached Goodyear about selling the company's popular Eagle brand tire in 1989. The proposal was declined. At the time, Goodyear's top management believed that such an action would undermine the tire sales of company-owned Goodyear Auto Service Centers and franchised Goodyear Tire Dealers, which were the principal retail sources for Goodyear brand tires. However, following a $38 million loss in 1990 and a change in Goodyear top management in 1991, the Sears proposal resurfaced for consideration.

Two factors contributed to the renewed interest in the Sears proposal.[1] First, between 1987 and 1991, Goodyear brand tires recorded a 3.2 percent decline in market share for passenger car replacement tires in the United States. This share decline represented a loss of about 4.9 million tire units. It was believed that the growth of warehouse membership club stores and discount tire retail claims coupled with multibranding among mass merchandisers contributed to the market share erosion (see Exhibit 1). Second, it was believed that nearly 2 million worn-out Goodyear brand tires were being replaced annually at some 850 Sears Auto Centers in the United States. According to a Goodyear executive, the failure to repurchase Goodyear brand tires happened by default "because the remarkable loyalty of Sears customers led them to buy the best tire available from those offered by Sears," which did not include Goodyear brand tires.

The Sears proposal raised several strategic considerations for Goodyear. First, as a matter of distribution policy, Goodyear had not sold the Goodyear tire brand through a mass merchandiser since the 1920s, when it sold tires through Sears. A decision to sell Goodyear brand passenger car tires again through Sears would represent a significant change in distribution policy and could create

---

[1] "Newsfocus," *Modern Tire Dealer* (March 1992):13.

This case was prepared by Professor Roger A. Kerin, of the Edwin L. Cox School of Business, Southern Methodist University, as a basis for class discussion and is not designed to illustrate effective or ineffective handling of an administrative situation. The case is based on published sources. The author wishes to thank Professor Arthur A. Thompson Jr. of the University of Alabama for kindly granting permission to extract information from his industry note, "Competition in the World Tire Industry, 1992," for use in this case, the Goodyear Tire and Rubber Company for comments on a previous draft of the case and permission to reproduce its advertising copy, and Michelin Tire Corporation for permission to reproduce its advertising copy. Copyright © 2005 by Roger A. Kerin. No part of this case may be reproduced without written permission of the copyright holder.

| EXHIBIT 1 | U.S. Market Share of Replacement Tire Sales by Type of Retail Outlet, 1982 and 1992 |

Type of Retail Outlet	1982	1992*
Traditional multibrand independent dealers	44%	44%
Discount multibrand independent dealers	7	15
Chain stores, department stores	20	14
Tire company stores	10	9
Service stations	11	8
Warehouse clubs	–	6
Other	8	4
	100%	100%

*Estimate.

Source: Goodyear Tire and Rubber Company.

conflict with its franchised dealers. Second, if the Sears proposal was accepted, several product policy questions loomed. Specifically, should the arrangement with Sears include (1) only the Goodyear Eagle brand or (2) all of its Goodyear brands? Relatedly, should Goodyear allow Sears to carry one or more brands exclusively and have its own dealers carry certain brands on an exclusive basis? Goodyear presently has 12 brands of passenger and light-truck tires sold under the Goodyear name, ranging from lower-priced tire brands to a very expensive special high-speed tire for a Corvette that bears the Goodyear name.

THE TIRE INDUSTRY

The tire industry is global in scope, and competitors originate, produce, and market their products worldwide.[2] World tire production in 1991 was approximately 850 million tires, of which 29 percent were produced in North America, 28 percent in Asia, and 23 percent in Western Europe. Ten tire manufacturers account for 75 percent of world wide production. Groupe Michelin, with headquarters in France, is the world's largest producer and markets the Michelin, Uniroyal, and BF Goodrich brands. Goodyear is the second-largest producer, with Goodyear, Kelly-Springfield, Lee, and Douglas being its most well-known brands. Bridgestone Corporation, a Japanese firm, is the third-largest tire producer. Its major brands are Bridgestone and Firestone. These three firms account for almost 60 percent of all tires sold worldwide.

The Original Equipment Tire Market

The tire industry divides into two end-use markets: (1) the original equipment tire market and (2) the replacement tire market. Original equipment tires are sold by tire manufacturers directly to automobile and truck manufacturers. Original equipment tires represent 25 to 30 percent of tire unit production volume each

---

[2] Portions of the tire industry overview are based on "Competition in the World Tire Industry, 1992," in Arthur A. Thompson Jr. and A. J. Strickland III, *Strategic Management: Concepts & Cases*, 7th ed. (Homewood, IL, 1993):581–614.

EXHIBIT 2	Manufacturer Brand U.S. Market Share for Original Equipment Passenger Car Tires

Original Equipment (OE) Buyer	Tire Manufacturer (Brand)						
	Goodyear	Firestone	Michelin	Uniroyal Goodrich	General Tire	Dunlop	Bridgestone
General Motors	33.5%	1.5%	14.5%	32.5%	18.0%	0.0%	0.0%
Ford	26.0	39.0	23.5	0.0	11.5	0.0	0.0
Chrysler	83.0	0.0	0.0	0.0	17.0	0.0	0.0
Mazda	15.0	50.0	0.0	0.0	0.0	0.0	35.0
Honda of U.S.	30.0	0.0	47.0	0.0	0.0	16.0	7.0
Toyota	15.0	40.0	0.0	0.0	3.0	42.0	0.0
Diamond Star	100.0	0.0	0.0	0.0	0.0	0.0	0.0
Nissan	0.0	35.0	22.0	0.0	35.0	8.0	0.0
Nummi (GM-Toyota)	50.0	50.0	0.0	0.0	0.0	0.0	0.0
Volvo	0.0	0.0	100.0	0.0	0.0	0.0	0.0
Saturn	0.0	100.0	0.0	0.0	0.0	0.0	0.0
Isuzu	15.0	35.0	0.0	50.0	0.0	0.0	0.0
Subaru	0.0	0.0	100.0	0.0	0.0	0.0	0.0
Hyundai	35.0	0.0	65.0	0.0	0.0	0.0	0.0
Overall OE market share	38.0%	16.0%	16.0%	14.0%	11.5%	2.75%	1.25%

Source: Modern Tire Dealer, January 1991, p. 27.

year. Goodyear is the perennial market share leader for original equipment tires, capturing 38 percent of this segment in 1991. Exhibit 2 shows the original equipment tire market shares for major tire suppliers.

Demand for original equipment tires is derived; that is, tire volume is directly related to automobile and truck production. Overall original equipment tire demand is highly price inelastic given the derived demand situation. However, the price elasticity of demand for individual tire manufacturers (brands) was considered highly price elastic, since car and truck manufacturers could easily switch to a competitor's brands. Accordingly, price competition among tire manufacturers was fierce and motor vehicle manufacturers commonly relied upon two sources of tires. For example, General Motors split its tire purchases among Goodyear, Uniroyal/Goodrich, General Tire, Michelin, and Firestone brands in the early 1990s. Even though the original equipment market was less profitable than the replacement tire market, tire manufacturers considered this market strategically important. Tire manufacturers benefited from volume-related scale economics in manufacturing for this market. Furthermore, it was believed that car and truck owners who were satisfied with their original equipment tires would buy the same brand when they replaced them.

The Replacement Tire Market

The replacement tire market accounts for 70 to 75 percent of tires sold annually. Passenger car tires account for 75 percent of annual sales. Primary demand in this market is affected by the average mileage driven per vehicle. Every 100-mile change in the average number of miles traveled per vehicle produces a 1-million-unit change in the unit sales of the replacement market, assuming an average

EXHIBIT 3   **Unit Tire Sales in the United States, 1987–1991**

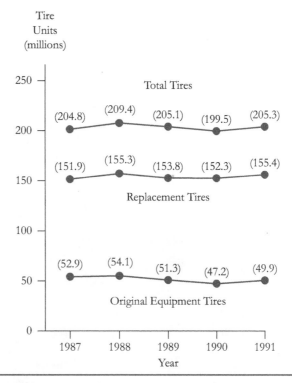

Source: *Modern Tire Dealer,* 1993 Facts/Directory.

treadwear life of 25,000 to 30,000 miles per tire.[3] Worldwide unit shipments in this segment have been "flat" due in part to the longer treadlife of new tires. Exhibit 3 shows original equipment and replacement unit sales in the United States for the period 1987 to 1991.

Tire manufacturers produce a large variety of grades and lines of tires for the replacement tire market under both manufacturers' brand names and private labels. Branded replacement tires are made to the tiremaker's own specifications. Some private-label tires supplied to wholesale distributors and large chain retailers are made to the buyer's specifications rather than to the manufacturer's standards.

The major tire producers often used network TV campaigns to promote their brands, introduce new types of tires, and pull customers to their retail dealer outlets. Their network TV ad budgets commonly ran from $10 to $30 million, and their budgets for cooperative ads with dealers were from $20 to $100 million. Print media were also used extensively. As an illustration, a Michelin print ad featuring the slogan "Michelin. Because So Much Is Riding on Your Tires" is shown in Exhibit 4 on page 608. Several tire companies also sponsored auto racing events to promote the performance capabilities of their tires.

Goodyear is the perennial market-share leader in the U.S. replacement tire market. The company holds a leadership position in the passenger car, light-truck, and highway truck product categories (see Exhibit 5 on page 608).

---

[3] "Competition in the World Tire Industry, 1992," 587.

EXHIBIT 4   Michelin Print Advertisement

MICHELIN. BECAUSE SO MUCH IS RIDING ON YOUR TIRES.

MICHELIN

EXHIBIT 5   Estimated U.S. Market Shares of the Top 10 Brands in the Replacement Tire Market, 1991

Passenger Car Tires		Light-Truck Tires		Highway-Truck Tires	
Brand	*Share*	*Brand*	*Share*	*Brand*	*Share*
Goodyear	15.0%	Goodyear	11.0%	Goodyear	23.0%
Michelin	8.5	BF Goodrich	10.0	Michelin	15.0
Firestone	7.5	Firestone	5.0	Bridgestone	11.0
Sears	5.5	Michelin	6.0	General Tire	7.0
General	4.5	Cooper/Falls	5.0	Firestone	6.0
BF Goodrich	3.5	Kelly-Springfield	5.0	Kelly-Springfield	6.0
Bridgestone	3.5	Armstrong	4.0	Dunlop	6.0
Cooper	3.5	General Tire	4.0	Yokohama	5.0
Kelly-Springfield	3.0	Bridgestone	3.0	Cooper	4.0
Multi-Mile	3.0	Dunlop	2.0	Toyo	3.0
Others	42.5%	Others	44.0	Others	14.0
	100.0%		100.0%		100.0%

Source: *Modern Tire Dealer*, January 1991, p. 27; *Market Data Book*, 1991; *Tire Business*, January 1992, p. 13.

| EXHIBIT 6 | Estimated Number of Retail Points of Sale for Major Tire Brands in the United States, 1991 |

Tire Brand (Parent Company)	Number of Retail Points of Sale
Armstrong (Pirelli)	978
Bridgestone (Bridgestone Corp.)	5,960
Cooper (Cooper Tire and Rubber)	1,518
Dunlop (Sumitomo)	2,046
Firestone (Bridgestone Corp.)	4,208
General (Continental A.G.)	2,107
Goodrich (Groupe Michelin)	4,215
Goodyear (Goodyear Tire and Rubber)	7,964
Kelly-Springfield (Goodyear Tire and Rubber)	2,421
Michelin (Groupe Michelin)	7,159
Pirelli (Pirelli Group)	2,133
Uniroyal (Groupe Michelin)	2,321

Source: *Market Data Book*, 1991; *Tire Business*, January 1992, p. 14.

Retail Distribution Major brand-name tire manufacturers capitalized on their reputation and experience as producers of original equipment tires by building strong wholesale and retail dealer relationships and networks through which to sell their brand-name replacement tires to vehicle owners. The tire industry uses "retail points of sale" to gauge the retail coverage of tire manufacturers and their brands. Goodyear brand tires have the broadest retail coverage with almost 8,000 "retail points of sale," most of which are company-owned Goodyear Auto Service Centers or franchised Goodyear Tire Store dealers with multiple locations. Groupe Michelin is estimated to have almost 14,000 "points of sale" for its three major brands—Michelin, Goodrich, and Uniroyal. The number of "retail points of sale" for major tire brands is shown in Exhibit 6.

Retail Marketing[4] Independent tire dealers usually carried the brands of several different major manufacturers and a discount-priced private-label brand so as to give replacement buyers a full assortment of qualities, brands, and price ranges to choose from. Service stations affiliated with Exxon, Chevron, and Amoco marketed Atlas brand tires produced by Firestone (Bridgestone). Other service stations, especially those that emphasized tire sales, stocked one or two manufacturers' brand tires and a private-label brand. Retail tire outlets that were owned or franchised by the manufacturers (that is, Goodyear Tire Stores and Firestone Auto Master Care Centers) carried only the manufacturer's name brands and perhaps a private-label or lesser-known, discount-priced line made by the manufacturer. Department stores and the major retail chains such as Montgomery Ward and Sears, Roebuck and Company occasionally carried manufacturers' brand tires but usually marketed only their own private-label brands.

Manufacturers found it advantageous to have a broad product line to appeal to most buyer segments to provide tires suitable for many different types of vehicles driven under a variety of road and weather conditions. When vehicle

---

[4] This material is extracted from "Competition in the World Tire Industry, 1992," 588–591.

owners went to a tire dealer to shop for replacement tires, they had a variety of tread designs, tread widths, tread durabilities, performance characteristics, and price categories to choose from. Car and light-truck owners were often confused by the number of choices they had; few buyers were really knowledgeable about tires. Many buyers ended up choosing a tire on the basis of price, while others followed the recommendation of the local dealer whom they regularly patronized. The retail prices of replacement tires ranged from retreaded (or recapped) tires selling for under $20 to $35 each to top-of-the-line tires going for $125 to $175 each. Tire dealers ran frequent price promotion ads in the local newspapers, making it easy for price-sensitive buyers to watch for sales and buy at off-list prices. In recent years, consumers had become more price conscious and less brand loyal (thus eroding the importance of securing replacement sales through original equipment sales to vehicle manufacturers). However, it was often difficult for car owners to comparison shop on the basis of tire quality and tread durability because of the proliferation of brands, lines, grades, and performance features. Manufacturers had resisted the development of standardized specifications for replacement tires, and there was a general lack of common terminology in describing tire grades and construction features.

In most communities, the retail tire market was intensely competitive. Retailers advertised extensively in newspapers, on outdoor billboards, and occasionally on local TV to establish and maintain their market shares. Price was the dominant competitive appeal. Many dealers featured and pushed their private-label "off-brand" tires because they could obtain higher margins on them than they could selling the name-brand tires of major manufacturers. Dealer-sponsored private-label tires accounted for 15 to 20 percent of total replacement tire sales in the United States in 1991. Surveys showed dealers were able to influence a car owner's choice of replacement tires, both as to brand and type of tire. Most replacement car tire buyers did not have strong tire brand preferences, making it fairly easy for tire salespeople to switch customers to tire brands and grades with the highest dealer margins. Normal dealer margins on replacement tires were in the 35 to 40 percent range, but many dealers shaved margins to win incremental sales.

Retailer Profitability   Since the mid-1970s, tire retailers' profit margins had been under competitive pressure, partly because of stagnant growth in tire sales and partly because of declining retail prices since 1980. To bolster profitability, tire dealers had expanded into auto repair services (engine tune-ups, shock-absorber and muffler replacement, and brake repair), retreading, and automobile accessories. Some tire retailers were experimenting with becoming "total car care centers." Auto service work was very attractive because gross profit margins were bigger than the margins earned on replacement tire sales. A recent survey of independent tire dealers indicated that 38.2 percent of their sales and 45.8 percent of their earnings came from automobile service.[5]

 ## GOODYEAR TIRE AND RUBBER COMPANY

Goodyear Tire and Rubber Company, headquartered in Akron, Ohio, was founded in 1898 by Frank and Charles Seiberling. The company began as a supplier of bicycle and carriage tires, but soon targeted the fledgling automotive industry. The introduction of the Quick Detachable tire and the Universal Rim

[5] "Dealer Attitude Survey Concerning Automotive Service," *Modern Tire Dealer* (Spring 1992):1.

(1903) helped make Goodyear the world's largest tire manufacturer by 1916, the same year the company introduced the pneumatic truck tire. Goodyear held the distinction as the world leader in tire production until November 1990, when Groupe Michelin acquired the Uniroyal Goodrich Tire Company (then the second largest U.S. tire manufacturer) for a purchase price of $1.5 billion.

Goodyear's principal business is the development, manufacture, distribution, and sale of tires throughout the world. Tires and tire tubes represented 83 percent of Goodyear's corporate sales of $10.9 billion in 1991. Corporate-wide earnings in 1991 were $96.6 million. In addition to Goodyear brand tires, the company owns the Kelly-Springfield Tire Company, Lee Tire and Rubber Company, and Delta Tire. The company also manufactures private-label tires.

Goodyear controls 20 to 25 percent of the world's tire manufacturing capacity and about 37 percent of U.S. tire-making capacity. Sales outside the United States accounted for about 42 percent of company revenues.

Market Presence

Approximately 60 percent of Goodyear worldwide sales were in the tire replacement market and 40 percent were to the original equipment market. The Goodyear brand is the market share leader in North America and in Latin America and number two throughout Asia outside Japan (behind Bridgestone). The Goodyear brand is third in market share in Europe behind Michelin and Pirelli. Goodyear is second to Groupe Michelin (Michelin, Uniroyal-Goodrich) in terms of worldwide market share for auto, truck, and farm tires (see Exhibit 7). The company operates 44 tire products plants in 28 countries and seven rubber plantations.

Tire Product Line and Pricing

Goodyear produces tires for virtually every type of vehicle. It has the broadest line of tire products of any tire manufacturer. The broad market brand names sold under the Goodyear umbrella include the Arriva, Corsa, Eagle, Invicta, Tiempo, Decathlon, Regatta, S4S, T-Metric, Wrangler (light-truck tire), and Aquatred. The Aquatred brand was the most recent introduction and featured a new tread design that prevented hydroplaning (see Exhibit 8 on page 612). Sales of this brand were expected to reach 1 million units in 1992 based on initial sales figures.

The Goodyear name is one of the best known brand names in the world. Goodyear brand tires have been traditionally positioned and priced as premium

| EXHIBIT 7 | Worldwide Market Shares of Tire Makers, 1990 |

Tire Manufacturer (Brands)	*Market Share*
Michelin/Uniroyal-Goodrich	21.5%
Goodyear	20.0
Bridgestone/Firestone	17.0
Continental/General	7.5
Pirelli/Armstong	7.0
Sumitomo/Dunlop	7.0
Others	20.0
	100.0%

Source: Goodyear Tire and Rubber Company, 1991 annual report, p. 5.

EXHIBIT 8 **Aquatred Print Advertisement**

ONE GALLON PER SECOND.

POURING BUCKETS? GOODYEAR AQUATRED® PUMPS UP TO A GALLON OF WATER AWAY AS YOU DRIVE.

 The award-winning* Aquatred, with its deep-groove AquaChannel™ moves up to one gallon of water away per second at highway speeds. This keeps more of the tire's tread area in contact with the road for superb wet traction. **ONLY FROM GOODYEAR.** For your nearest Goodyear retailer call 1-800-GOODYEAR.

Aquatred features a 60,000-mile treadlife limited warranty. Ask your retailer for details.

*Which awards? *Popular Science*, 1991 Best of What's New. *Popular Mechanics*, 1992 Design & Engineering Award. *Fortune*, a 1992 "Product of the Year." Industrial Designers Society of America, Gold Industrial Design Excellence IDEA Award. *Discover*, Discover Award for Technological Innovation.

THE BEST TIRES IN THE WORLD HAVE GOODYEAR WRITTEN ALL OVER THEM.

Experience Goodyear traction for your high-performance, passenger and multi-purpose vehicles.

EAGLE GS-C.®
Dual tread zone for high-performance traction.

AQUATRED.®
Deep-groove design for outstanding wet traction.

WRANGLER GS-A.®
"Triple Traction" tread for all-surface traction.

Source: Courtesy of the Goodyear Tire and Rubber Company.

EXHIBIT 9 **Goodyear Brand Passenger Car Tires (Including Minimum Assigned Grades for Treadwear, Traction, and Temperature)**

| | Treadwear[a] | | | |
Brand	Rim Diameter 13"	All Others	Traction[b]	Temperature[c]
Aquatred	320	340	A	B
Arriva	260	310	A	B
Corsa GT	280	280	A	B
Decathlon	220	240	B	C
Eagle GA	280	300	A	B
Eagle GA (HNIZ)	280	300	A	A
Eagle GS-C	–	220	A	A
Eagle GS-D	–	180	A	A
Eagle GT (H)	–	200	A	A
Eagle GT II	–	320	A	B
Eagle GT + 4	–	240	A	B
Eagle GT + 4 (HNIZ)	–	240	A	A
Eagle ST IV	280	300	A	B
Eagle VL	–	220	A	A
Eagle VR	–	220	A	A
Eagle ZR	–	220	A	A
Invicta	–	280	A	B
Invicta GA	–	280	A	B
Invicta GA (HN)	–	280	A	A
Invicta GA (L)	–	300	A	B
Invicta GA (L) (HN)	–	220	A	A
Invicta GFE	280	300	A	B
Invicta GL	260	280	A	B
Invicta GL (H)	–	280	A	A
Invicta GLR	260	280	A	B
Invicta GS	320	340	A	B
Regatta	300	320	A	B
S4S	240	280	A	B
Tiempo	240	280	A	B
T-Metric	240	240	B	C

Note: The U.S. Department of Transportation (DOT) requires tire manufacturers to state the size, load and pressure, treadwear, traction, and temperature on their tires. This information is provided by manufacturers based on their own tests and not provided by the DOT. Treadwear, traction, and temperature are all useful quality indicators and appear on the tire sidewall.

[a]Treadwear. This is an index based on how quickly the tire tread wears under conditions specified by the U.S. government, relative to a "standard tire." The index does not specify how long a tire tread will last on a car because driving conditions vary. However, a tire with a treadwear index of 200 should wear about twice as long as a tire with an index of 100 under similar conditions.

[b]Traction. This is a measure of a tire's ability to stop on wet pavement under specific conditions. Grades range from A (highest) to C (lowest).

[c]Temperature. This is a measure of a tire's resistance to heat buildup under simulated high-speed driving. Grades range from A (highest) to C (lowest).

Source: "How to 'Read' a Tire," *Consumer Reports* (February 1992): 78.

quality brands. Nevertheless, the company has recently introduced mid-priced tire brands. These include the Decathlon and T-Metric brands with lower tread-wear and traction performance characteristics than its other brands (see Exhibit 9 on page 613).

Kelly-Springfield Tire Company and Lee Tire and Rubber Company, two Goodyear subsidiaries, also sell some 16 tire brands and engage in private-label manufacturing. For example, Walmart sells the Douglas brand made by the Kelly-Springfield unit.

Goodyear Advertising and Distribution

Goodyear is one of the leading national advertisers in the United States. The company also has maintained a high profile in auto racing to emphasize the high-performance capabilities of its tires and the company's commitment to product innovation. The Goodyear name is prominently featured on the company's well-known blimps frequently seen at special events in communities throughout the United States. The company's advertising slogan, "The best tires in the world have Goodyear written all over them," communicates the Goodyear positioning as a high-quality, worldwide tire manufacturer and marketer.

Goodyear distributes its tire products through almost 8,000 retail points of sale in the United States and some 25,000 retail outlets worldwide. The company operates about 1,000 company-owned Goodyear Auto Service Centers and sells through 2,500 franchised Goodyear Tire Dealers in the United States, many of which are multisite operators. These retail outlets account for a major portion of Goodyear brand annual tire sales. In addition, the company sells its tires through some multibrand dealers. As of early 1992, the company did not typically sell Goodyear brand tires through discount multibrand dealers, mass-merchandise chain stores, or warehouse clubs.[6]

STRATEGIC CONSIDERATIONS IN BROADENING DISTRIBUTION

Interest in reconsidering Sears Auto Centers for selling Goodyear brand tires meant that Goodyear executives would have to revisit the company's long-standing distribution policy. Furthermore, a product policy question relating to which brands might be sold through Sears had to be considered. Decisions on these policy issues were further complicated by Goodyear Tire dealer franchisee reaction to broadened distribution and estimates of incremental sales possible through expanded distribution.

An immediate reaction was forthcoming from franchised Goodyear tire deal-ers who heard about the Sears proposal. According to comments appearing in the *Wall Street Journal*, one dealer said, "We went with them through thick and thin, and now they're going to drown us."[7] Other dealers indicated they would add private-label brands to their product line. One dealer said: "We [will] sell what we think will give the customer the best value, and that's not necessar-ily Goodyear." While it was clear that some franchise dealers were critical of

---

[6] Goodyear brand tires could sometimes be purchased at discount multibrand dealers because of "diverting." Diverting is the practice whereby a manufacturer's authorized distributors/dealers sell the manufacturer's products to unauthorized distributors/dealers who, in turn, distribute the manufacturer's products to customers. This practice is common for many consumer products. See W. Bishop Jr., "Trade Buying Squeezes Marketers," *Marketing Communications* (May 1988):52–53.

[7] "Independent Goodyear Dealers Rebel," *Wall Street Journal* (July 8, 1992):B2.

broadened distribution of any kind, the pervasiveness of this view was unknown. Furthermore, it was not readily apparent how many dealers would actually carry competitive brands.

Tire industry analysts expected Sears to benefit from carrying Goodyear brand tires. According to market share estimates made by *Modern Tire Dealer*, an industry trade publication, Sears' share of the U.S. replacement passenger car tire market had declined from 6.5 percent in 1989 to 5.5 percent in 1991.[8] Goodyear brand tires would certainly enhance the company's product mix and draw tire buyers who were already Sears customers. The extent of the draw, however, would depend on how many or which Goodyear brands were sold through Sears Auto Centers.

Cannibalization of company-owned Goodyear Auto Service Center and franchised Goodyear Tire Dealers tire sales also meant that Goodyear executives had to consider the incremental replacement passenger car tire sales from broadened distribution. In other words, even though distribution through Sears could increase sales of Goodyear brand tires from the manufacturer's perspective, the danger would be that company-owned and franchised Goodyear Tire Dealers might incur a loss in unit sales. This could be particularly evident in communities where Sears had a strong market presence.

---

[8] Statistics reported in *Modern Tire Dealer* (January 1991): 27; "Tire Makers Are Traveling Bumpy Road as Car Sales Fall, Foreign Firms Expand," *Wall Street Journal* (October 19, 1990):B1.

Chapter 10

Global Marketing Strategy and Management

World trade is driven largely by global competition among global companies for global consumers. Today, many companies originate, produce, and market their offerings worldwide, which has given rise to a set of unique issues, decisions, and practices that collectively fall into the domain of global marketing.

Global marketing involves the performance of activities designed to plan, price, promote, and direct the flow of an organization's offerings in more than one country for a profit.[1] The strategic aspect of global marketing comes into play in the managerial choice of *where* an organization wishes to compete and *how* it chooses to compete in a global setting. Where to compete begs the primary question of whether global marketing is appropriate for an organization, followed by the question of which countries and markets to pursue. How to compete includes the mode and means by which an organization markets its offerings outside its home country and to whom. *Mode* refers to different options for entering and competing outside an organization's home country, such as exporting, licensing, joint ventures, and direct investment. *Means* refers to market targeting and marketing mix choices within and between countries.

This chapter focuses on why, where, and how organizations compete in a global environment. Special attention is placed on the considerations and choices confronting a marketing manager. A recurrent theme in this chapter is that successful global marketers standardize marketing strategies whenever possible and customize them whenever necessary.

THE DECISION TO GO GLOBAL

Organizations choose to market their products and services outside their own country for four major reasons:[2]

1. *To gain access to new buyers.* Expanding into foreign markets offers potential for increased revenues, profits, and long-term growth and becomes an especially attractive option when a company's home country markets are mature. For example, 80 percent of new Burger King restaurants opening from 2008 through 2013 were outside North America.

2. *To spread business risk across a wider market base.* A company spreads business risk by marketing in a number of different foreign countries rather than depending entirely on operations in its own country. Thus,

617

if sales in Asia turn down for a period of time, a company's business in North America or Europe may offset the decline.

3. *To capitalize on an organization's distinctive competencies and capabilities.* A company may be able to leverage its distinctive competencies and capabilities into a competitive advantage in foreign markets as well as its domestic market. Nokia's competencies and capabilities in mobile phones propelled it to global market leadership in the wireless telecommunications business.

4. *To achieve lower costs and enhance an organization's competitiveness.* Many companies are driven to market their offerings in more than one country because domestic sales volume is not sufficient to fully capture operating efficiencies and thereby improve the firm's cost-competitiveness. The relatively small size of country markets in Europe explains why companies like Unilever (Netherlands) and Nestlé (Switzerland) began selling their products across Europe long ago and then entered markets in North America, Asia, Latin America, and Africa.

Translating the reasons for "going global" into a profitable marketing opportunity in another country is demanding and detailed work. A necessary first step for marketers is to identify where profitable marketing opportunities may exist outside their own country.

IDENTIFYING GLOBAL MARKETING OPPORTUNITIES

The process of identifying global marketing opportunities varies little between companies that are considering entry into a foreign country for the first time and companies that are already marketing in several countries. The process begins by establishing and prioritizing criteria for screening countries. Information pertaining to these criteria is then gathered, summarized, and interpreted for each country. Countries are subsequently classified on the basis of their marketing attractiveness based on the screening criteria, compared with the marketing competences and practices of the company considering a move into a foreign country.

Country Screening Criteria

Numerous quantitative and qualitative screening criteria are used to evaluate prospective countries. The most prominent quantitative criteria are market and profit potential. The chain ratio approach described in Chapter 4, or some variation, is often used to determine market potential. As an example, consider the determination of market potential for coffee in China and India for Starbucks. Exhibit 10.1 offers a simple illustration using population characteristics. Even though the population of China is slightly larger than that of India, India's market potential for coffee is about twice that of China. This illustration shows how demographic variables such as age and urbanization and usage variables such as per capita coffee consumption combine to yield one estimate of market potential.

Seasoned executives recognize that other qualitative variables need to be included as screening criteria. A sampling of these criteria include: (1) sociocultural nuances that underlie business and consumer behavior; (2) country economic and technological infrastructure differences that affect marketing practices; (3) trade regulations that govern marketing practices within countries, or free-trade zones such as the European Union; and (4) the marketing prowess and

EXHIBIT 10.1	Estimating Coffee Consumption in China and India	
	China	*India*
Total population	1,328,340,000	1,143,080,000
Population percent: 15–64	× 68%	× 63%
Urban population percent	× 44%	× 26%
Per capita coffee consumption (kilograms)[1]	× 0.02	× 0.09
Total coffee consumption (kilograms)	7,948,786.56	16,851,285.36

[1] One kilogram = 2.2 pounds.

strength of local and foreign competitors within countries or free-trade zones. Information pertaining to these criteria will influence market, sales, and profit potential and often the success or failure of the venture.[3] Indeed, Campbell Soup exited Russia four years after introducing its condensed soup to that country due to these factors.[4]

Marketing Attractiveness

The attractiveness of a global marketing opportunity will also depend on the characteristics of the organization itself. An organization's strengths and weaknesses, offerings, marketing policies and practices, financial resources, and the like need to be aligned with the requirements necessary to compete effectively in a foreign country. More often than not, adaptation of an organization's offerings and marketing policies and practices increases as the differences between an organization's own country and a foreign country increase. Not surprisingly, organizations typically begin their global expansion "close to home" where sociocultural, legal, economic, and technological infrastructure differences are modest.

ENTERING AND COMPETING IN FOREIGN MARKETS

Once an organization decides to market its offering in another country, it must select a mode of market entry. Four general options exist: (1) exporting, (2) licensing, (3) joint venture, and (4) direct investment.[5] As Exhibit 10.2 demonstrates, the amount of financial commitment, risk, marketing control, and profit potential increases as an organization moves from exporting to direct investment.

EXHIBIT 10.2	Four General Modes of Entry into Foreign Markets

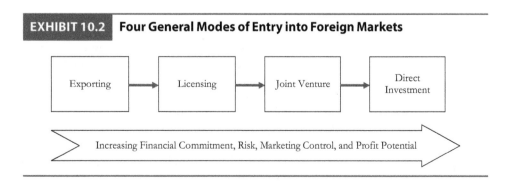

Exporting

Exporting involves producing offerings in one country and selling them in another country. This entry option allows a company to make the least number of changes in terms of its offering, its organization, or its marketing practices.

Exporting can be either indirect or direct. With indirect exporting, a firm sells its domestically produced goods in a foreign country through an intermediary. This practice has the least amount of financial commitment and risk but will probably return the least profit. Indirect exporting is ideal for a company that has no foreign business contacts. The intermediary is often a distributor that has the marketing know-how and resources necessary for the effort to succeed. Often, indirect exporting means that the organization sells to another organization in its home country, which in turn exports the product. These organizations include large retailers such as Walmart, wholesale supply houses, trading companies, and others that buy an organization's offerings to supply buyers outside its home country.

Direct exporting exists when a firm sells its domestically produced goods in a foreign country without intermediaries. Most companies become involved in direct exporting when they believe their volume of sales will be sufficiently large and easy to obtain so that they do not require intermediaries. For example, the exporter may be approached by foreign buyers that are willing to contract for a large volume of purchases. Direct exporting involves more risk than indirect exporting for the company but also opens the door to increased profits. The Boeing Company applies a direct exporting approach and is the largest U.S. exporter.

Licensing

With licensing, a company (licensor) offers the right to a trademark, patent, trade secret, or other similarly valued items of intellectual property to another (licensee) in return for a royalty or a fee. The advantages to the company granting the license are low risk and a capital-free entry into a foreign country. The licensee gains information that allows it to start with a competitive advantage. Yoplait yogurt is licensed from Sodima, a French cooperative, by General Mills for sale in the United States.

There are drawbacks to this mode of entry, however. The licensor forgoes control of its offering and reduces the potential profits gained from it. In addition, while the relationship lasts, the licensor may be creating its own competition. A licensee might modify the product and serve the market with an offering and marketing knowledge gained at the expense of the company that got it started. To offset this disadvantage, a licensor strives to stay innovative so that the licensee remains dependent on it for improvements and a successful operation. Finally, should the licensee prove to be a poor choice, the name or reputation of the licensor may be harmed.

Two variations of licensing, contract manufacturing and contract assembly, represent alternative ways to produce a product within the foreign country. With contract manufacturing, a U.S. company may contract with a foreign firm to manufacture products according to stated specifications. The product is then sold in the foreign country or exported back to the United States. With contract assembly, the U.S. company may contract with a foreign firm to assemble (not manufacture) parts and components that have been shipped to that country. This practice has been an economic boon to Taiwan where the majority of the world's notebook computers are made.

A third variation of licensing is franchising. Franchises include soft drink, motel, retailing, fast-food, and car rental operations and a variety of business services.

McDonald's is a premier global franchiser. With some 32,000 locations outside the United States, about 66 percent of McDonald's sales come from non-U.S. operations.

Joint Venture

When a foreign company and a local firm invest together to create a local business, it is called a joint venture. These two companies share ownership, control, and profits of the new company. For example, Starbucks entered India in 2007 through a joint venture with New Horizons, an India-based company.

Joint ventures occur for two primary reasons. First, one company may not have the necessary financial, physical, managerial, or marketing resources to enter a foreign country or market alone. Cereal Partners Worldwide, a joint venture between General Mills and Nestlé to market breakfast cereals, is a case in point.[6] In 1990, General Mills had a limited presence in Europe. Nestlé was a major consumer package goods marketer in Europe. General Mills provided the knowledge in cereal technology, including some of its proprietary manufacturing equipment, its portfolio of proven brands, and its know-how for marketing these products to consumers. Nestlé provided its name on the box, access to retailers, and production capacity that could be converted to making General Mills' cereals in Europe. Today, Cereal Partners Worldwide markets breakfast cereals in more than 130 international markets that span the globe. Second, a government may strongly encourage a joint venture before it allows a foreign company to enter its country. This was the case in China. More than 50,000 Chinese–foreign joint ventures operate in China.

A challenge with joint ventures is that they are often difficult to manage. The choice of partners and the qualities of the relationships between the executives are important factors leading to success or failure. Several other factors contribute to their success or failure as well: how control is shared, relations with partners, institutional (legal) environments, and the extent that knowledge is shared across partners. Despite this complexity, nearly all companies active in world trade participate in at least one international joint venture somewhere.

Direct Investment

The biggest commitment a company can make when entering the global market is direct investment, which entails a domestic firm actually investing in and owning a foreign subsidiary or division. Examples of direct investment are Nissan's Smyrna, Tennessee, plant that produces Nissan, Altima, Xterra, and Pathfinder brands that makes the M-Class, R-Class, and the GL-Class sports utility vehicles. Many U.S.-based companies also use this mode of entry. Reebok entered Russia by creating a subsidiary known as Reebok Russia.

For many companies, direct investment often follows one of the other three market-entry strategies. For example, both FedEx and UPS entered China through joint ventures with Chinese companies. Each subsequently purchased the interests of its partner and converted the Chinese operations into a division. Following on the success of its European and Asian exporting strategy, Harley-Davidson now operates wholly owned marketing and sales subsidiaries in Germany, Italy, the United Kingdom, and Japan, among other countries. Acquisition is also a means of direct investment. Kyocera Corporation, a Japanese high-tech company, is an example. It acquired Qualcomm's wireless consumer phone business as a means for quick entry into the United States.

The advantages to direct investment include some cost savings, better understanding of local market conditions, and fewer local restrictions. Firms entering foreign markets using direct investment believe that these advantages outweigh the financial commitment and risks involved.

CRAFTING A GLOBAL MARKETING STRATEGY

The choice of a market-entry strategy is a necessary first step for an organization when joining the community of global marketers. The next step involves the challenging task of designing and implementing a marketing strategy. Successful global marketers standardize marketing strategies whenever possible and customize them wherever necessary. This is the art of global marketing.

Global Market Segmentation and Targeting

Global market segmentation involves dividing the globe or large regions of the world into distinct subsets of customers that behave in the same way or have similar needs and preferences. Evidence exists of a global middle-income class, a youth market, and an elite segment, each consuming or using a common assortment of products or services, regardless of geographic location. A variety of companies capitalize on global market segmentation. Whirlpool, Sony, and IKEA have benefited from the growing global middle-income class desire for kitchen appliances, consumer electronics, and home furnishings, respectively. Levi's, Nike, Coca-Cola, and Apple have tapped the global youth market. DeBeers, Chanel, Gucci, Rolls-Royce, and Sotheby's and Christie's, the world's largest fine art and antique auction houses, cater to the elite segment for luxury goods worldwide.

As highlighted in Chapter 4, two broad types of variables are commonly used for market segmentation. Socioeconomic characteristics of consumers, such as gender, age, occupation, income, family life cycle, education, and geographic location make up one type. The other type consists of behavioral variables, including benefits sought from products and services, usage behavior, lifestyle, and attitudes. For industrial buyers, socioeconomic characteristics may include company size and location, and industry or customers served. Behavioral variables may include purchasing objectives and practices as well as product and service benefits.

The appropriateness of any one or combination of segmentation variables in a specific situation will depend on whether or not a variable relates to consumer purchasing, use, or consumption behavior and responsiveness to marketing programs. For example, automobile manufacturers use two variables to segment the passenger car market in Europe: (1) car owner social status, and (2) value orientation. As described in the Chevrolet Europe case study in this chapter, these two variables permit automakers to identify and target consumers across national boundaries and create Pan-European marketing programs.

Offering and Communication Strategies

Organizations have five strategies for matching offerings and their communication efforts to global markets. As Exhibit 10.3 shows, the strategies focus on whether a company extends or adapts its offering and communication messages for consumers in different countries and cultures.[7]

An offering may be sold globally in one of three ways: (1) the same as in its home country market, (2) with some adaptations, or (3) as a totally new offering.

1. *Offering extension.* Selling virtually the same offering in other countries is an offering extension strategy. It works well for products such as Coca-Cola, Gillette razors, Wrigley's gum, Levi's jeans, Sony consumer electronics, Harley-Davidson motorcycles, and Nike apparel and shoes. As a general rule, this strategy seems to work best when the consumer

EXHIBIT 10.3   Five Global Offering and Communication Strategies

market target for the offering is alike across countries and cultures—that is, consumers share the same desires, needs, and uses for the offering.

2.   *Offering adaptation.* Changing an offering in some way to make it more appropriate for a country's climate or consumer preferences is an offering adaptation strategy. Maybelline's makeup is formulaically adapted to local skin types and weather across the globe, including an Asia-specific mascara that doesn't run during the rainy season. Frito-Lay produces and markets its potato chips in Russia, but the flavors are unlike the chips eaten in North America. Russians prefer dairy, meat, and seafood-flavored potato chips.

3.   *Offering invention.* Alternatively, organizations can invent totally new offerings designed to satisfy common needs across countries. Black & Decker did this with its Snake Light Flexible Flashlight. Created to address a global need for portable lighting, the product became a best-seller in North America, Europe, Latin America, and Australia. Similarly, Whirlpool developed a compact, automatic clothes washer specifically for households in developing countries with annual household incomes of $2,000. The washer features bright colors because washers are often placed in home living areas, not hidden in laundry rooms (which do not exist in many homes in developing countries).

An identical communication message is used for the product extension and product adaptation strategies around the world. Gillette uses the same global message for its men's toiletries: "Gillette, the Best a Man Can Get." Even though ExxonMobil adapts its gasoline blends for different countries based on climate, the communication message is unchanged: "Put a Tiger in Your Tank."

Global marketers may also adapt their communication message. For instance, the same product may be sold in many countries but advertised differently. As an example, L'Oréal, a French health and beauty products marketer, introduced its Golden Beauty brand of sun care products through its Helena Rubenstein subsidiary in Western Europe with a communication adaptation strategy. Recognizing that cultural and buying motive differences related to skin care and tanning exist, Golden Beauty advertising featured dark tanning for northern Europeans, skin protection to avoid wrinkles among Latin Europeans, and beautiful skin for Europeans living along the Mediterranean Sea, even though the products were identical.

Marketing Channel and Pricing Strategies

Recall that successful global marketers standardize marketing programs whenever possible and customize them whenever necessary. Compared with offering and communication strategies, standardization presents a unique challenge for marketing channel and pricing strategies due to country trade regulations and consumer buying preferences and practices.

Consider the case of Dell, Inc. when it recently decided to enter the market for personal computers in Asia, notably China and India.[8] The company's vaunted online direct marketing channel that worked well in North America and Europe had to be replaced with a marketing channel featuring retail stores in China and India. Why? First-time personal computer buyers in these countries, especially, want face-to-face help from store clerks when making purchase decisions. Dell subsequently signed distribution agreements with Chinese and Indian retail chains to sell its desktop and notebook models.

Competitive, political, tax and exchange rates, and legal constraints affect the pricing latitude and strategy of global marketers. Walmart's experience in Germany is an example. Antitrust authorities in Germany limited Walmart from selling some items below cost to lure shoppers. Without this practice, which is considered acceptable in most countries, Walmart was unable to compete against German discount stores. This, along with other factors, prompted Walmart to leave Germany in 2006 following eight years without posting a profit.[9] Today, global marketers of expensive consumer goods sell their products within a narrow price range to discourage "gray markets" whereby individuals buy items in a lower-priced country from a manufacturer's authorized retailer, ship them to higher-priced countries, and then sell below the manufacturer's suggested retail price through unauthorized retailers.

Global Brands and Positioning

Recall from Chapter 5 that a *global brand* is a brand marketed under the same name in multiple countries with similar and centrally coordinated marketing programs, including positioning. Kevin Lane Keller, an authority on brand management, has identified six product or service characteristics that underlie successful global brands:[10]

1. *High-technology products with strong functional images:* Examples are televisions (Sony), watches (Rolex), computers (Hewlett-Packard), cameras (Olympus), and automobiles (Porsche). Such products tend to be universally understood and are not typically part of the cultural heritage.

2. *High-image products with strong associations to fashionability, sensuality, wealth, or status:* Examples are cosmetics (L'Oreal), designer apparel (Giorgio Armani), and jewelry (Tiffany). Such products appeal to the same type of market worldwide; namely, the global elite.

3. *Services and business-to-business products that emphasize corporate images in their global marketing campaigns:* Examples are airlines and financial services such as American Express, MasterCard, and Visa.

4. *Retailers that sell to upper-class individuals or that specialize in a salient but unfulfilled need:* Examples include Gucci with over 200 retail stores worldwide and IKEA with more than 315 locations in 36 countries.

5. *Brands positioned primarily on the basis of their country of origin:* An example is Australia's Foster's beer.

6. *Products that do not need customization or other special products to be able to function properly:* Examples include medical products such as heart pacemakers by Medtronic and heavy equipment sold by Caterpillar.

Global brands have the same product formulation or service concept, deliver the same benefits to consumers, and use consistent positioning and communications across multiple countries and cultures. This is not to say that global brands are not sometimes tailored to specific cultures or countries. However, adaptation is used only when necessary to better connect the brand to consumers in different markets. Consider McDonald's.[11] This global marketer has adapted its proven formula of "food, fun, and families" across some 120 countries. Although the Golden Arches and Ronald McDonald appear worldwide, McDonald's tailors other aspects of its marketing program. It serves beer in Germany, wine in France, and coconut, mango, and tropical fruit milk shakes in Hong Kong. Sandwiches are made with different meats and spices in Japan, Thailand, India, and the Philippines. But the McDonald's world-famous French fry is standardized.

NOTES

1. Philip R. Cateora, Mary Gilly, and John L. Graham, *International Marketing*, 15th ed. (Burr Ridge, IL: McGraw-Hill/Irwin, 2011): 9.

2. Arthur A. Thompson Jr., A. J. Strickland III, and John E. Gamble, *Crafting and Executing Strategy*, 15th ed. (Burr Ridge, IL: McGraw-Hill/Irwin, 2007): 196; "Here Comes a Whopper," *The Economist* (October 25, 2008): 78; Gordon Walker, *Modern Competitive Strategy*, 3rd ed. (Burr Ridge, IL: McGraw-Hill/Irwin, 2009): Chapter 9.

3. Pankaj Ghemawat, "Distance Still Matters: The Hard Reality of Global Expansion," *Harvard Business Review* (September 2001): 137–147.

4. Julie Jargon, "Campbell Soup to Exit Russia," *Wall Street Journal* (June 29, 2011): B9.

5. For an extensive description and examination of these market-entry modes, see, for example, Johnny K. Johansson, *Global Marketing: Foreign Entry, Local Marketing, and Global Management*, 5th ed. (Burr Ridge, IL: McGraw-Hill/Irwin, 2009); Michael R. Czinkota and Ilkka A. Ronkainen, *International Marketing*, 8th ed. (Mason, OH: South-Western, 2007); and Cateora et al., *International Marketing*.

6. "Second-Largest Cereal Producer Turns 20, with Style," General Mills press release, September 13, 2010.

7. This classification is based on Walter J. Keegan and Mark C. Green, *Global Marketing*, 4th ed. (Upper Saddle River, NJ: Prentice Hall, 2005). The examples that appear in this discussion are found in Roger A. Kerin, Steven W. Hartley, and William Rudelius, *Marketing*, 10th ed. (Burr Ridge, IL: McGraw-Hill/Irwin, 2012): Chapter 7.

8. Benjamin Sutherland, "Shifting Gears at Dell," *Newsweek* (November 3, 2008): E6; "Dell to Sell PCs Through China Retail Titan," *Wall Street Journal* (September 24, 2007): A4; "How Dell Conquered India," CNNMoney.com, February 10, 2011.

9. "With Profits Elusive, Wal-Mart to Exit Germany," *Wall Street Journal* (July 29, 2006): A1, A6.

10. Kevin Lane Keller, *Strategic Brand Management*, 3rd ed. (Upper Saddle River, NJ: Pearson/Prentice Hall, 2008): 619.

11. Keller, *Strategic Brand Management*: 602; and Michael Fielding, "Global Brands Need Balance of Identity, Cultural Respect," *Marketing News* (September 1, 2006): 8, 10.

Case

Jolson Automotive Hoist:
The Market-Entry Decision

In September 2000, Mark Jolson, president of Jolson Automotive Hoist, Inc., had just finished reading a feasibility report on entering the European market in 2001. The company manufactured surface automotive hoists, a product used by garages, service stations, and other repair shops to lift cars for servicing (Exhibit 1). The report, prepared by the company's marketing manager, Pierre Gagnon, outlined the opportunities in the European Union and the entry options available.

Mark Jolson was not sure if his company was ready for this move. While the company had been successful in expanding sales into the U.S. market, he wondered if this success could be repeated in Europe. He thought that, with more effort, sales could be increased in the United States. On the other hand, there were some positive aspects to the European idea. He began reviewing the information in preparation for the meeting the following day with Gagnon.

 ## JOLSON AUTOMOTIVE HOIST, INC.

Mark Jolson, a design engineer, had worked for eight years for the Canadian subsidiary of a U.S. automotive hoist manufacturer. During those years, he had spent considerable time designing an above-ground (or surface) automotive hoist. Although he was very enthusiastic about the unique aspects of the hoist, including a scissor lift and wheel alignment pads, senior management expressed no interest in the idea. In 1990, Mark left the company to start his own business with the express purpose of designing and manufacturing the hoist. He left with the good wishes of his previous employer, who had no objections to Mark's plans to start a new business.

Over the next three years, Jolson obtained financing from a venture capital firm, opened a plant in Lachine, Quebec, and began manufacturing and marketing the hoist, called the Jolson Lift (Exhibit 1).

From the beginning, Mark had taken considerable pride in the development and marketing of the Jolson Lift. The original design included a scissor lift and a safety locking mechanism that allowed the hoist to be raised to any level and

This case was prepared by Professor Gordon H. G. McDougall, Wilfrid Laurier University, as the basis for class discussion rather than to illustrate either effective or ineffective handling of an administrative situation. Certain names and data have been disguised and are not useful for research purposes. Used by permission.

| EXHIBIT 1 | Examples of Automotive Hoists |

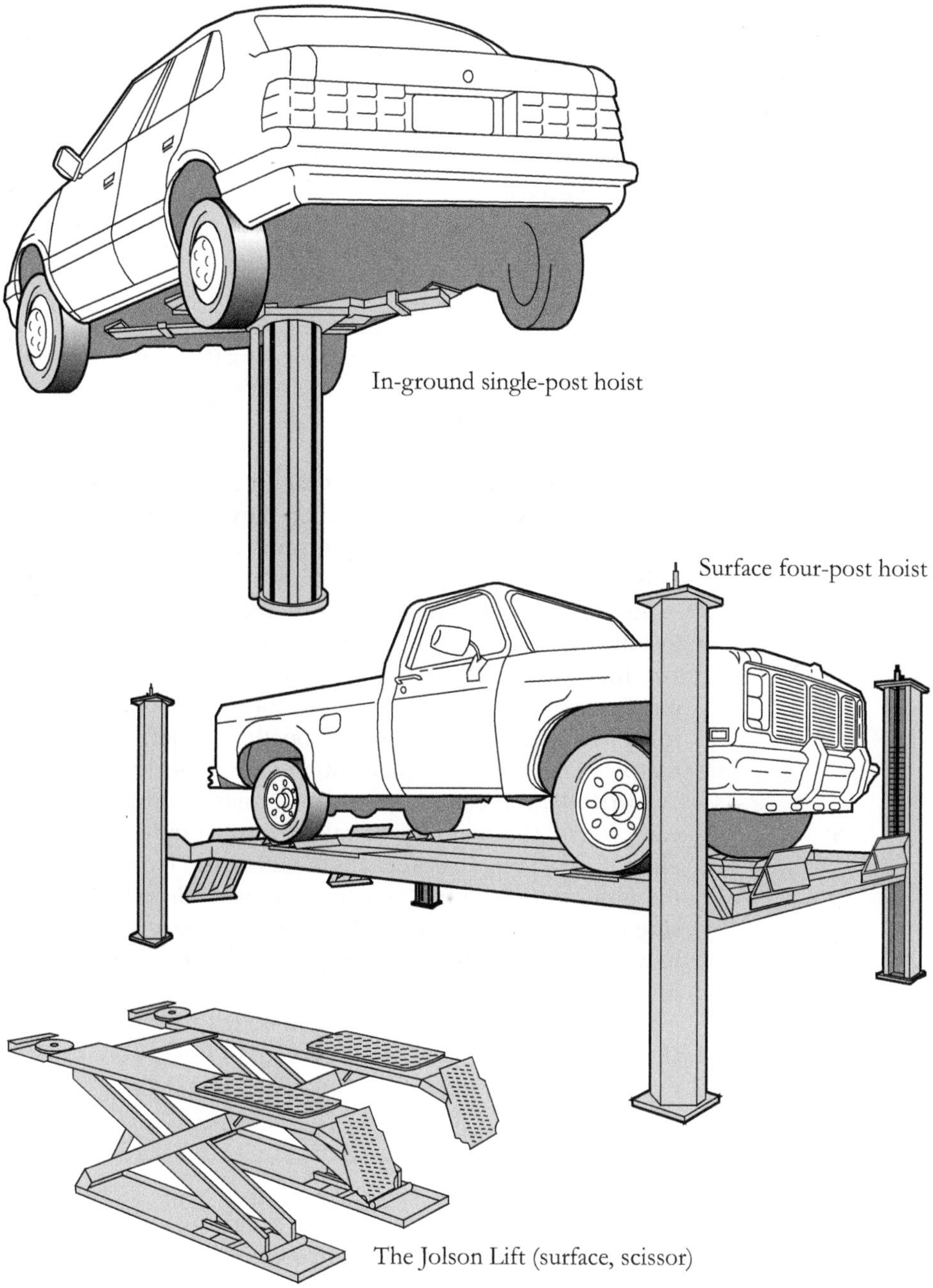

In-ground single-post hoist

Surface four-post hoist

The Jolson Lift (surface, scissor)

---

locked in place. As well, the scissor lift offered easy access for the mechanic to work on the raised vehicle. Because the hoist was fully hydraulic and had no chains or pulleys, it required little maintenance. Another key feature was the alignment turn plates that were an integral part of the lift. The turn plates meant that mechanics could accurately and easily perform wheel alignment jobs. Because it was a surface lift, it could be installed in a garage in less than a day.

Mark continually made improvements to the product, including adding more safety features. In fact, the Jolson Lift was considered a leader in automotive lift

EXHIBIT 2	Jolson Automotive Hoist, Inc.—Selected Financial Statistics (1997–1999)		
	1997	*1998*	*1999*
Sales	$6,218,000	$7,454,000	$9,708,000
Cost of sales	4,540,000	5,541,000	6,990,000
Contribution	1,678,000	1,913,000	2,718,000
Marketing expenses*	507,000	510,000	530,000
Administrative expenses	810,000	820,000	840,000
Earnings before tax	361,000	583,000	1,348,000
Units sold	723	847	1,054

* Marketing expenses in 1999 included advertising ($70,000), four salespeople ($240,000), marketing manager, and three sales support staff ($220,000).

Source: Company records.

safety. Safety was an important factor in the automotive hoist market. Although hoists seldom malfunctioned, when they did it often resulted in a serious accident.

The Jolson Lift developed a reputation in the industry as the "Mercedes" of hoists; the unit was judged by many as superior to competitive offerings because of its design, the quality of the workmanship, the safety features, the ease of installation, and the five-year warranty. Mark held four patents on the Jolson Lift, including the lifting mechanism on the scissor design and the safety locking mechanism. A number of versions of the product were designed that made the Jolson Lift suitable (depending on the model) for a variety of tasks, including rustproofing, muffler repairs, and general mechanical repairs.

In 1991, the company sold 23 hoists and had sales of $172,500. During the early years, the majority of sales were to independent service stations and garages specializing in wheel alignment in the Quebec and Ontario market. Most of the units were sold by Gagnon, who was hired in 1992 to handle the marketing side of the operation. In 1994, Gagnon began using distributors to sell the hoist to a wider geographic market in Canada. In 1996, he signed an agreement with a large automotive wholesaler to represent Jolson Automotive Hoist in the U.S. market. By 1999, the company had sold 1,054 hoists and had sales of $9,708,000 (Exhibit 2). In 1999, about 60 percent of sales were to the United States with the remaining 40 percent to the Canadian market.

 INDUSTRY

Approximately 49,000 hoists were sold each year in North America. Hoists were typically purchased by any automotive outlet that serviced or repaired cars, including new-car dealers, used-car dealers, specialty shops (e.g., muffler repair, transmission repair, wheel alignment), chains (e.g., Firestone, Goodyear, Canadian Tire), and independent garages. It was estimated that new-car dealers purchased 30 percent of all units sold in a given year. In general, the specialty shops focused on one type of repair, such as mufflers or rust proofing, while "nonspecialty" outlets handled a variety of repairs. Although there was some crossover, in general Jolson Automotive Hoist competed in the specialty shop segment and, in particular, those shops that dealt with wheel alignment. This included chains such as Firestone and Canadian Tire as well as new-car dealers (e.g., Ford) that devoted a certain percentage of their lifts to the wheel alignment business and independent garages that specialized in wheel alignment.

The purpose of a hoist was to lift an automobile into a position where a mechanic or service person could easily work on the car. Because different repairs required different positions, a wide variety of hoists had been developed to meet specific needs. For example, a muffler repair shop required a hoist where the mechanic could gain easy access to the underside of the car. Similarly, a wheel alignment job required a hoist that offered a level platform where the wheels could be adjusted as well, providing easy access for the mechanic. Gagnon estimated that 85 percent of company sales were to the wheel alignment market in service centers like Firestone, Goodyear, and Canadian Tire, and independent garages that specialized in wheel alignment. About 15 percent of sales were made to customers who used the hoist for general mechanical repairs.

Firms purchasing hoists were part of an industry called the *automobile aftermarket*. This industry was involved in supplying parts and service for new and used cars and was worth more than $54 billion at retail in 1999 while servicing the approximately 14 million cars on the road in Canada. The industry was large and diverse; there were more than 4,000 new-car dealers in Canada, more than 400 Canadian Tire stores, more than 100 stores in each of the Firestone and Goodyear chains, and more than 220 stores in the Rust Check chain.

The purchase of an automotive hoist was often an important decision for the service station owner or dealer. Because the price of hoists ranged from $3,000 to $15,000, it was a capital expense for most businesses.

For the owner/operator of a new service center or car dealership, the decision involved determining what type of hoist was required and then what brand would best suit the company. Most new service centers or car dealerships had multiple bays for servicing cars. In these cases, the decision would involve what types of hoists were required (for example, inground, surface). Often more than one type of hoist was purchased, depending on the service center/dealership needs.

Experienced garage owners seeking a replacement hoist (the typical hoist had a useful life of 10 to 13 years) would usually determine what products were available and then make a decision. If the garage owners were also mechanics, they would probably be aware of two or three types of hoists but not very knowledgeable about the brands or products currently available. Garage owners or dealers who were not mechanics probably knew very little about hoists. The owners of car or service dealerships often bought the product that was recommended and/or approved by the parent company.

 ## COMPETITION

Sixteen companies competed in the automotive lift market in North America: 4 Canadian and 12 U.S. firms. With the advent of the Free Trade Agreement in 1989, the duties on hoists between the two countries were phased out over a 10-year period; by 1999 exports and imports of hoists were duty-free. For Mark Jolson, the import duties had never played a part in any decisions—the fluctuating exchange rates between the two countries had a far greater impact on selling prices. In the past three years the Canadian dollar had fluctuated between $0.65 and $0.70 versus the U.S. dollar (i.e., CDN$1.00 buys US$0.65) and forecast rates were expected to stay within this range.

A wide variety of hoists were manufactured in the industry. The two basic types of hoists were in-ground and surface. As the names imply, in-ground hoists required a pit to be dug "in-ground," where the piston that raised the hoist was installed. In-ground hoists were either single post or multiple post, were permanent, and obviously could not be moved. In-ground lifts constituted approximately 21 percent of

EXHIBIT 3	North American Automotive Lift Unit Sales, by Type (1997–1999)		
	1997	*1998*	*1999*
In-ground			
Single post	5,885	5,772	5,518
Multiple post	4,812	6,625	5,075
Surface			
Two-post	27,019	28,757	28,923
Four-post	3,862	3,162	3,745
Scissor	2,170	2,258	2,316
Other	4,486	3,613	3,695
Total	48,234	50,187	49,272

Source: Company records.

total lift sales in 1999 (Exhibit 3). Surface lifts were installed on a flat surface, usually concrete. Surface lifts came in two basic types, post lift hoists and scissor hoists. Surface lifts, compared to in-ground lifts, were easier to install and could be moved if necessary. Surface lifts constituted 79 percent of total lift sales in 1999. Within each type of hoist (e.g., post lift surface hoists), there were numerous variations in terms of size, shape, and lifting capacity.

The industry was dominated by two large U.S. firms, AHV Lifts and Berne Manufacturing, that together held approximately 60 percent of the market. AHV Lifts, the largest firm with approximately 40 percent of the market and annual sales of about $60 million, offered a complete line of hoists (that is, in-ground, surface) but focused primarily on the in-ground market and the two-post surface market. AHV Lifts was the only company that had its own direct salesforce; all other companies used (1) only wholesalers or (2) a combination of wholesalers and company salesforce. AHV Lifts offered standard hoists with few extra features and competed primarily on price. Berne Manufacturing, with a market share of approximately 20 percent, also competed in the in-ground and two-post surface markets. It used a combination of wholesalers and company salespeople and, like AHV Lifts, competed primarily on price.

Most of the remaining firms in the industry were companies that operated in a regional market (e.g., California, British Columbia) and/or that offered a limited product line (e.g., four-post surface hoist).

Jolson Automotive Hoist had two competitors that manufactured scissor lifts. AHV Lift marketed a scissor hoist that had a different lifting mechanism and did not include the safety locking features of the Jolson Lift. On average, the AHV scissor lift was sold for about 20 percent less than the Jolson Lift. The second competitor, Mete Lift, was a small regional company with sales in California and Oregon. It had a design that was very similar to the Jolson Lift but lacked some of its safety features. The Mete Lift, regarded as a well-manufactured product, sold for about 5 percent less than the Jolson Lift.

MARKETING STRATEGY

As of early 2000, Jolson Automotive Hoist had developed a reputation for a quality product backed by good service in the hoist lift market, primarily in the wheel alignment segment.

The distribution system employed by the company reflected the need to engage in extensive personal selling. Three types of distributors were used: a company sales force, Canadian distributors, and a U.S. automotive wholesaler. The company sales force consisted of four salespeople and Gagnon. Their main task was to service large "direct" accounts. The initial step was to get the Jolson Lift approved by large chains and manufacturers, and then, having received the approval, to sell to individual dealers or operators. For example, if General Motors approved the hoist, then Jolson Automotive Hoist could sell it to individual General Motors dealers. Jolson Automotive Hoist sold directly to the individual dealers of a number of large accounts including General Motors, Ford, Petro-Canada, Firestone, and Goodyear. Jolson Automotive Hoist had been successful in obtaining manufacturer approval from the big three automobile manufacturers in both Canada and the United States. Jolson Automotive Hoist had also received approval from service companies such as Canadian Tire and Goodyear. To date, Jolson Automotive Hoist had not been rejected by any major account; however, in some cases, the approval process had taken more than four years.

In total, the company sales force generated about 25 percent of the unit sales each year. Sales to the large "direct" accounts in the United States went through Jolson Automotive Hoist's U.S. wholesaler.

The Canadian distributors sold, installed, and serviced units across Canada. These distributors handled the Jolson Lift and carried a line of noncompetitive automotive equipment products (for example, engine diagnostic equipment, wheel balancing equipment) and noncompetitive lifts. These distributors focused on the smaller chains and the independent service stations and garages.

The U.S. wholesaler sold a complete product line to service stations as well as manufacturing some equipment. The Jolson Lift was one of five different types of lifts that the wholesaler sold. Although the wholesaler provided Jolson Automotive Hoist with extensive distribution in the United States, the Jolson Lift was a minor product within the wholesaler's total line. While Gagnon did not have any actual figures, he thought that the Jolson Lift probably accounted for less than 20 percent of the total lift sales of the U.S. wholesaler.

Both Mark Jolson and Pierre Gagnon felt that the U.S. market had unrealized potential. With a population of 264 million people and more than 146 million registered vehicles, the U.S. market was almost 10 times the size of the Canadian market (population of 30 million, approximately 14 million vehicles). Gagnon noted that the six New England states (population over 13 million); the three largest mid-Atlantic states (population over 38 million), and the three largest mid-Eastern states (population over 32 million) were all within a day's drive of the factory in Lachine. Jolson and Gagnon had considered setting up a sales office in New York to service these states, but they were concerned that the U.S. wholesaler would not be willing to relinquish any of its territory. They had also considered working more closely with the wholesaler to encourage it to "push" the Jolson Lift. It appeared that the wholesaler's major objective was to sell a hoist, not necessarily the Jolson Lift.

Jolson Automotive Hoist distributed a catalog-type package with products, uses, prices, and other required information for both distributors and users. In addition, the company advertised in trade publications (for example, *AutoInc.*), and Gagnon traveled to trade shows in Canada and the United States to promote the Jolson Lift.

In 1999, Jolson Lifts sold for an average retail price of $10,990 and the company received, on average, $9,210 for each unit sold. This average reflected the mix of sales through the three distribution channels: (1) direct (where Jolson Automotive Hoist received 100 percent of the selling price), (2) Canadian distributors (where Jolson Automotive Hoist received 80 percent of the selling price), and (3) the U.S. wholesaler (where Jolson Automotive Hoist received 78 percent of the selling price).

Both Jolson and Gagnon believed that the company's success to date was based on a strategy of offering a superior product that was primarily targeted to the needs of specific customers. The strategy stressed continual product improvements, quality workmanship, and service. Personal selling was a key aspect of the strategy; salespeople could show customers the benefits of the Jolson Lift over competing products.

 ## THE EUROPEAN MARKET

Against this background, Mark Jolson had been thinking of ways to continue the rapid growth of the company. One possibility that kept coming up was the promise and potential of the European market. The fact that Europe became a single market in 1993 suggested that it was an opportunity that should at least be explored. With this in mind, he asked Gagnon to prepare a report on the possibility of the company entering the European market. The highlights of Gagnon's report follow.

History of the European Union

The European Union (EU) had its basis formed from the 1957 Treaty of Rome, in which five countries decided it would be in their best interests to form an internal market. These countries were France, Spain, Italy, Germany, and Luxembourg. By 1990, the EU consisted of 15 countries (the additional 10 were Austria, Belgium, Denmark, Finland, Greece, Ireland, the Netherlands, Portugal, Sweden, and the United Kingdom) with a population of more than 376 million people. Virtually all barriers (physical, technical, and fiscal) in the European Community were scheduled to be removed for companies located within the EU. This allowed the free movement of goods, persons, services, and capital.

In the last 15 years, many North American and Japanese firms had established themselves in the EU. The reasoning for this was twofold. First, these companies regarded the community as an opportunity to increase global market share and profits. The market was attractive because of its sheer size and lack of internal barriers. Second, there was continuing concern that companies not established within the EU would have difficulty exporting to the EU due to changing standards and tariffs. To date, this concern has not materialized.

Market Potential

The key indicator of the potential market for the Jolson Lift hoist was the number of passenger cars and commercial vehicles in use in a particular country. Four countries in Europe had more than 20 million vehicles in use, with Germany having the largest domestic fleet of 44 million vehicles followed in order by Italy, France, and the United Kingdom (Exhibit 4). The number of vehicles was an important indicator, since the more vehicles in use meant a greater number of service and repair facilities that needed vehicle hoists—potentially the Jolson Lift.

An indicator of the future vehicle repair and service market was the number of new-vehicle registrations. The registration of new vehicles was important as this maintained the number of vehicles in use by replacing cars that had been retired. Again, Germany had the most new cars registered in 1997 and was followed in order by France, the United Kingdom, and Italy.

EXHIBIT 4	Number of Vehicles (1997) and Population (000s)			
	Vehicles in Use (000s)			
Country	*Passenger*	*Small Commercial*	*New Vehicle Registrations (000s)*	*Population (000s)*
Germany	41,400	2,800	3,500	82,100
France	28,000	4,900	2,200	59,000
Italy	33,200	2,700	1,800	56,700
United Kingdom	23,500	4,000	2,200	59,100
Spain	15,300	2,800	1,000	39,200

Based primarily on the fact that a large domestic market was important for initial growth, the selection of a European country should be limited to the "Big Four" industrialized nations: Germany, France, the United Kingdom, or Italy. In an international survey, companies from North America and Europe ranked European countries on a scale of 1 to 100 on market potential and investment-site potential. The results showed that Germany was favored for both market potential and investment site opportunities, while France, the United Kingdom, and Spain placed second, third, and fourth respectively. Italy did not place in the top four in either market or investment-site potential. However, Italy had a large number of vehicles in use, had the fourth largest population in Europe, and was an acknowledged leader in car technology and production.

Little information was available on the competition within Europe. There was, as yet, no dominant manufacturer as was the case in North America. At this time, there was one firm in Germany that manufactured a scissor-type lift. The firm sold most of its units within the German market. The only other available information was that 22 firms in Italy manufactured vehicle lifts.

Investment Options

Pierre Gagnon felt that Jolson Automotive Hoist had three options for expansion into the European market: licensing, joint venture, or direct investment. The licensing option was a real possibility, as a French firm had expressed an interest in manufacturing the Jolson Lift.

In June 2000, Gagnon had attended a trade show in Detroit to promote the Jolson Lift. At the show he met Phillipe Beaupre, the marketing manager for Bar Maisse, a French manufacturer of wheel alignment equipment. The firm, located in Chelles, France, sold a range of wheel alignment equipment throughout Europe. The best-selling product was an electronic modular aligner that enabled a mechanic to use a sophisticated computer system to align the wheels of a car. Beaupre was seeking a North American distributor for the modular aligner and other products manufactured by Bar Maisse.

At the show, Gagnon and Beaupre had a casual conversation where both explained what their respective companies manufactured; they exchanged company brochures and business cards, and both went on to other exhibits. The next day, Beaupre sought out Gagnon and asked if he might be interested in having Bar Maisse manufacture and market the Jolson Lift in Europe. Beaupre felt the lift would complement Bar Maisse's product line and the licensing would be of mutual benefit to both parties. They agreed to pursue the idea. Upon his return to Lachine, Gagnon told Mark Jolson about these discussions and they agreed to explore this possibility.

Gagnon called a number of colleagues in the industry and asked them what they knew about Bar Maisse. About half had not heard of the company but those who had commented favorably on the quality of its products. One colleague with European experience knew the company well and said that Bar Maisse's management had integrity and would make a good partner. In July, Gagnon sent a letter to Beaupre stating that Jolson Automotive Hoist was interested in further discussions; he enclosed various company brochures including price lists and technical information on the Jolson Lift. In late August, Beaupre responded, stating that Bar Maisse would like to enter a three-year licensing agreement with Jolson Automotive Hoist to manufacture the Jolson Lift in Europe. In exchange for the manufacturing rights, Bar Maisse was prepared to pay a royalty rate of 5 percent of gross sales. Gagnon had not yet responded to this proposal.

A second possibility was a joint venture. Gagnon had wondered if it might not be better for Jolson Automotive Hoist to offer a counterproposal to Bar Maisse for a joint venture. He had not worked out any details, but he felt that Jolson Automotive Hoist would learn more about the European market and probably make more money if they were an active partner in Europe. Gagnon's idea was a 50–50 proposal where the two parties shared the investment and the profits. He envisaged a situation where Bar Maisse would manufacture the Jolson Lift in its plant with technical assistance from Jolson Automotive Hoist. Gagnon also thought that Jolson Automotive Hoist could get involved in the marketing of the lift through the Bar Maisse distribution system. Further, he thought that the Jolson Lift, with proper marketing, could gain a reasonable share of the European market. If that happened, Gagnon felt that Jolson Automotive Hoist was likely to make greater returns with a joint venture.

The third option was direct investment, where Jolson Automotive Hoist would establish a manufacturing facility and set up a management group to market the lift. Gagnon had contacted a business acquaintance who had recently been involved in manufacturing fabricated steel sheds in Germany. On the basis of discussions with his acquaintance, he estimated the costs involved in setting up a plant in Europe at (1) $250,000 for capital equipment (welding machines, cranes, other equipment); (2) $200,000 in incremental costs to set up the plant; and (3) carrying costs to cover $1,000,000 in inventory and accounts receivable. While the actual costs of renting a building for the factory would depend on the site location, he estimated that annual building rent including heat, light, and insurance would be about $80,000. Gagnon recognized that these estimates were guidelines, but he felt that the estimates were probably within 20 percent of actual costs.

 ## THE DECISION

As Mark Jolson considered the contents of the report, a number of thoughts crossed his mind. He began making notes concerning the European possibility and the future of the company:

- If the company decided to enter Europe, Gagnon would be the obvious choice to head up the "direct investment" option or the "joint venture" option. Jolson felt that Gagnon had been instrumental in the success of the company to date.

- While the company had the financial resources to go ahead with the direct investment option, the joint venture would spread the risk (and the returns) over the two companies.

- The company had built its reputation on designing and manufacturing a quality product. Regardless of the option, Mark wanted the firm's reputation to be maintained.

- Either the licensing agreement or the joint venture appeared to build on the two companies' strengths; Bar Maisse had knowledge of the market, and Jolson Automotive Hoist had the product. What troubled Mark was whether this apparent synergy would work or whether Bar Maisse would seek to control the operation.

- It was difficult to estimate sales under any of the options. With the first two (licensing and joint venture), it would depend on the effort and expertise of Bar Maisse; with the third, it would depend on Gagnon.

- The company's sales in the U.S. market could be increased if the U.S. wholesaler would "push" the Jolson Lift. Alternatively, the establishment of a sales office in New York to cover the eastern states could also increase sales.

As Mark reflected on the situation, he knew he should probably get additional information—but it wasn't obvious exactly what information would help him make a yes or no decision. He knew one thing for sure—he was going to keep this company on a fast growth track, and at tomorrow's meeting he and Gagnon would decide how to do it.

Case

Fairchild Water Technologies, Inc.

"A pity I couldn't have stayed for Diwali," thought Rahul Chatterjee. "But anyway it was great to be back home in Calcutta." The Diwali holiday and its festivities would begin in early November 2000, some two weeks after Chatterjee had returned to the United States. Chatterjee worked as an international market liaison for Fairchild Water Technologies, Inc. This was his eighth year with Fairchild Water Technologies, Inc. and easily his favorite. "Your challenge will be in moving us from just dabbling in developing countries to our thriving in them," his boss had said when Chatterjee was promoted to the job last January. Chatterjee had agreed and was thrilled when asked to visit Bombay and New Delhi in April. His purpose on that trip was to gather background data on the possibility of Fairchild Water Technologies, Inc. entering the Indian market for home water purification devices. Initial results were encouraging and prompted the second trip.

Chatterjee had used his second trip primarily to study Indian consumers in Calcutta and Bangalore and to gather information on possible competitors. The two cities represented quite different metropolitan areas in terms of location, size, language, and infrastructure—yet both suffered from similar problems in terms of water supplied to their residents. These problems could be found in many developing countries and were favorable to home water purification.

Information gathered on both visits would be used to make a recommendation on market entry and on elements of an entry strategy. Executives at Fairchild would compare Chatterjee's recommendation to those from two other liaisons that were focusing their efforts on Argentina, Brazil, and Indonesia.

 ## INDIAN MARKET FOR HOME WATER FILTRATION AND PURIFICATION

Like most aspects of India, the market for home water filtration and purification took a good deal of effort to understand. Yet despite expending this effort, Chatterjee realized that much remained either unknown or in conflict. For example,

This case was written by Professor James E. Nelson, University of Colorado at Boulder. He thanks students at the Indian Institute of Management, Calcutta, for their invaluable help in collecting all data needed to write this case. He also thanks Professor Roger Kerin, Southern Methodist University, for his helpful comments in writing this case. The case is intended for educational purposes rather than to illustrate either effective or ineffective decision making. Some data as well as the identity of the company are disguised. Copyright by James E. Nelson. Used with permission.

the market seemed clearly a mature one, with four or five established Indian competitors fighting for market share. Or was it? Another view portrayed the market as a fragmented one, with no large competitor having a national presence and perhaps 100 small, regional manufacturers, each competing in just one or two of India's 25 states. Indeed, the market could be in its early growth stages, as reflected by the large number of product designs, materials, and performances. Perhaps with a next generation product and a world-class marketing effort, Fairchild could consolidate the market and stimulate tremendous growth—much like the situation in the Indian market for automobiles.

Such uncertainty made it difficult to estimate market potential. However, Chatterjee had collected unit sales estimates for a 10-year period for three similar product categories—vacuum cleaners, sewing machines, and color televisions. In addition, a Delhi-based research firm had provided him with estimates of unit sales for Aquaguard, the largest selling water purifier in several Indian states. Chatterjee had used the data in two forecasting models available at Fairchild along with three subjective scenarios—realistic, optimistic, and pessimistic—to arrive at the estimates and forecasts for water purifiers shown in Exhibit 1. "If anything," Chatterjee had explained to his boss, "my forecasts are conservative because they describe only first-time sales, not any replacement sales over the 10-year forecast horizon." He also pointed out that his forecasts applied only to industry sales in larger urban areas, which was the present industry focus.

One thing that seemed certain was that many Indians felt the need for improved water quality. Folklore, newspapers, consumer activists, and government officials regularly reinforced this need by describing the poor quality of Indian water. Quality suffered particularly during the monsoons because of highly polluted water entering treatment plants and because of numerous leaks and unauthorized withdrawals from water systems. Such leaks and withdrawals

EXHIBIT 1 Industry Sales Estimates and Forecasts for Water Purifiers in India, 1995–2010 (Thousands of Units)

| Year | Unit Sales Estimates | Unit Sales Forecast Under . . . | | |
		Realistic Scenario	Optimistic Scenario	Pessimistic Scenario
1995	60			
1996	90			
1997	150			
1998	200			
1999	220			
2000	240			
2001		250	250	250
2002		320	370	300
2003		430	540	400
2004		570	800	550
2005		800	1,200	750
2006		1,000	1,500	850
2007		1,300	1,900	900
2008		1,500	2,100	750
2009		1,600	2,100	580
2010		1,500	1,900	420

often polluted clean water after it had left the plants. Politicians running for national, state, and local government offices also reinforced the need for improved water quality through election campaign promises. Governments at these levels set standards for water quality, took measurements at thousands of locations throughout the nation, and advised consumers when water became unsafe.

During periods of poor water quality, many Indian consumers had little choice but to consume the water as they found it. However, better educated, wealthier, and more health-conscious consumers took steps to safeguard their family's health and often continued these steps year around. A good estimate of the number of such households, Chatterjee thought, would be around 40 million. These consumers were similar in many respects to consumers in middle- and upper-middle-class households in the United States and the European Union. They valued comfort and product choice. They saw consumption of material goods as a means to a higher quality of life. They liked foreign brands and would pay a higher price for such brands, as long as purchased products outperformed competing Indian products. Chatterjee had identified as his target market these 40 million households plus those in another four million households who had similar values and lifestyles, but as yet took little effort to improve water quality in their homes.

Traditional Method for Home Water Purification

The traditional method of water purification in the target market relied not on any commercially supplied product but instead on boiling. Each day or several times a day, a cook, maid, or family member would boil two to five liters of water for 10 minutes, allow it to cool, and then transfer it to containers for storage (often in a refrigerator). Chatterjee estimated that about 50 percent of the target market used this procedure. Boiling was seen by consumers as inexpensive, effective in terms of eliminating dangerous bacteria, and entrenched in a traditional sense. Many consumers who used this method considered it more effective than any product on the market. However, boiling affected the palatability of water, leaving the purified product somewhat "flat" to the taste. Boiling also was cumbersome, time-consuming, and ineffective in removing physical impurities and unpleasant odors. Consequently, about 10 percent of the target market took a second step by filtering their boiled water through "candle filters" before storage. Many consumers who took this action did so despite knowing that water could become recontaminated during handling and storage.

Mechanical Methods for Home Water Filtration and Purification

About 40 percent of the target market used a mechanical device to improve their water quality. Half of this group used candle filters, primarily because of their low price and ease of use. The typical candle filter comprised two containers, one resting on top of the other. The upper container held one or more porous ceramic cylinders (candles) that strained the water as gravity drew it into the lower container. Containers were made of either plastic, porcelain, or stainless steel and typically stored between 15 and 25 liters of filtered water. Purchase costs depended on materials and capacities, ranging from Rs.350 for a small plastic model to Rs.1,100 for a large stainless-steel model.[1] Candle filters were slow, producing 15 liters (one candle) to 45 liters (3 candles) of filtered water each 24 hours. To maintain this productivity, candles regularly needed to be removed,

---

[1] In 2000, 35 Indian Rupees (Rs.) were equivalent to US$1.00.

cleaned, and boiled for 20 minutes. Most manufacturers recommended that consumers replace candles (Rs.40 each) either once a year or more frequently, depending on sediment levels.

The other half of this group used "water purifiers," devices that were considerably more sophisticated than candle filters. Water purifiers typically employed three water processing stages. The first removed sediments, the second objectionable odors and colors, and the third harmful bacteria and viruses. Engineers at Fairchild Water Technologies, Inc. were skeptical that most purifiers claiming the latter benefit actually could deliver on their promise. However, all purifiers did a better job here than candle filters. Candle filters were totally ineffective in eliminating bacteria and viruses (and might even increase this type of contamination), despite advertising claims to the contrary. Water purifiers generally used stainless steel containers and sold at prices ranging from Rs.2,000 to Rs.7,000, depending on manufacturers, features, and capacities. Common flow rates were one to two liters of purified water per minute. Simple service activities could be performed on water purifiers by consumers as needed. However, more complicated service required units to be taken to a nearby dealer or an in-home visit from a skilled technician.

The remaining 10 percent of the target market owned neither a filter nor a purifier and seldom boiled their water. Many consumers in this group were unaware of water problems and thought their water quality acceptable. However, a few consumers in this group refused to pay for products that they believed were mostly ineffective. Overall, Chatterjee believed that only a few consumers in this group could be induced to change their habits and become customers. The most attractive segments consisted of the 90 percent of households in the target market who either boiled, boiled and filtered, only filtered, or purified their water.

All segments in the target market showed a good deal of similarity in terms of what they thought important in the purchase of a water purifier. According to Chatterjee's research, the most important factor was product performance in terms of sediment removal, bacteria and virus removal, capacity (either in the form of storage or flow rate), safety, and "footprint" space. Purchase price also was an important concern among consumers who boiled, boiled and filtered, or only filtered their water. The next most important factor was ease of installation and service, with style and appearance rated almost as important. The least important factor was warranty and availability of financing for purchase. Finally, all segments expected a water purifier to be warranted against defective operation for 18 to 24 months and to perform trouble free for 5 to 10 years.

 ## FOREIGN INVESTMENT IN INDIA

India appeared attractive to many foreign investors because of government actions begun in the 1980s. The broad label applied to these actions was "liberalization." Liberalization had opened the Indian economy to foreign investors, stemming from recognition that protectionist policies had not worked very well and that Western economies and technologies—seen against the collapse of the Soviet Union—did. Liberalization had meant major changes in approval requirements for new commercial projects, investment policies, taxation procedures, and, most important, attitudes of government officials.

If Fairchild Water Technologies, Inc. entered the Indian market, it would do so in one of three ways: (1) joint working arrangement, (2) joint venture company, or (3) acquisition. In a joint working arrangement, it would supply key purifier components to an Indian company which would manufacture and market the assembled product. License fees would be remitted to Fairchild on a per unit basis over the term of the agreement (typically five years, with an option to renew for three more). A joint venture agreement would have Fairchild partnering with an existing Indian company expressly for the purpose of manufacturing and marketing water purifiers. Profits from the joint venture operation would be split between the two parties per the agreement, which usually contained a clause describing buy/sell procedures available to the two parties after a minimum time period. An acquisition entry would have Fairchild Water Technologies, Inc. purchasing an existing Indian company whose operations then would be expanded to include the water purifier. Profits from the acquisition would belong to Fairchild.

Beyond understanding these basic entry possibilities, Chatterjee acknowledged that he was no expert in legal aspects attending the project. However, two days spent with a Calcutta consulting firm had produced the following information. Fairchild Water Technologies, Inc. must apply for market entry to the Foreign Investment Promotion Board, Secretariat for Industrial Approvals, Ministry of Industries. The proposal would go before the board for an assessment of the relevant technology and India's need for the technology. If approved by the board, the proposal then would go to the Reserve Bank of India, Ministry of Finance, for approvals of any royalties and fees, remittances of dividends and interest (if any), repatriations of profits and invested capital, and repayment of foreign loans. While the process sounded cumbersome and time consuming, the consultant assured Chatterjee that the government usually would complete its deliberations in less than six months and that his consulting firm could "virtually guarantee" final approval.

Trademarks and patents were protected by law in India. Trademarks were protected for 7 years and could be renewed on payment of a prescribed fee. Patents lasted for 14 years. On balance, Chatterjee had told his boss that Fairchild would have "no more problem protecting its intellectual property rights in India than in the United States—as long as we stay out of court." Chatterjee went on to explain that litigation in India was expensive and protracted. Litigation problems were compounded by an appeal process that could extend a case for easily a generation. Consequently, many foreign companies preferred arbitration, as India was a party to the Geneva Convention covering Foreign Arbitral Awards.

Foreign companies were taxed on income arising from Indian operations. They also paid taxes on any interest, dividends, and royalties received, and on any capital gains received from a sale of assets. The government offered a wide range of tax concessions to foreign investors, including liberal depreciation allowances and generous deductions. The government offered even more favorable tax treatment if foreign investors would locate in one of India's six Free Trade Zones. Overall, Chatterjee thought that corporate tax rates in India probably were somewhat higher than in the United States. However, so were profits—the average return on assets for all Indian corporations in recent years was almost 18 percent, compared to about 11 percent for United States corporations.

Approval by the Reserve Bank of India was needed for repatriation of ordinary profits. However, approval should be obtained easily if Fairchild could show that repatriated profits were being paid out of export earnings of hard currencies. Chatterjee thought that export earnings would not be difficult to realize, given India's extremely low wage rates and its central location to wealthier South Asian countries. "Profit repatriation is really not much of an issue, anyway," he thought. Three years might pass before profits of any magnitude could be realized; at least five years would pass before substantial profits would be available for repatriation. Approval of repatriation by the Reserve Bank might not be required at this time, given liberalization trends. Finally, if repatriation remained difficult, Fairchild could undertake crosstrading or other actions to unblock profits.

Overall, investment and trade regulations in India in 2000 meant that business could be conducted much easier than ever before. Hundreds of companies from the European Union, Japan, Korea, and the United States were entering India in all sectors of the country's economy. In the home appliance market, Chatterjee could identify 11 such firms—Carrier, Electrolux, General Electric, Goldstar, Matsushita, Singer, Samsung, Sanyo, Sharp, Toshiba, and Whirlpool. Many of these firms had yet to realize substantial profits, but all saw the promise of a huge market developing over the next few years.

 # FAIRCHILD WATER TECHNOLOGIES, INC.

Fairchild Water Technologies, Inc. was founded in 1980 by Eugene Fairchild, after he left his position in research and development at Culligan International Company. The company's first product was a desalinator used by mobile home parks in Florida to remove salts from brackish well water supplied to residents. The product was a huge success, and markets quickly expanded to include nearby municipalities, smaller businesses, hospitals, and bottlers of water for sale to consumers. Geographic markets also expanded, first to other coastal regions near the company's headquarters in Tampa, Florida, and then to desert areas in the southwestern United States. New products were added rapidly as well and, by 2000, the product line included desalinators, particle filters, ozonators, ion exchange resins, and purifiers. Industry experts generally regarded the product line as superior in terms of performance and quality, with prices higher than those of many competitors.

Company sales revenues for 2000 would be almost $400 million, with an expected profit close to $50 million. Annual growth in sales revenues averaged 12 percent for the past five years. Fairchild Water Technologies, Inc. employed over 4,000 people, with 380 having technical backgrounds and responsibilities.

Export sales of desalinators and related products began at Fairchild in 1985. Units were sold first to resorts in Mexico and Belize and later to water bottlers in Germany. Export sales grew rapidly, and the company found it necessary to organize its International Division in 1990. Sales in the International Division also grew rapidly and would reach almost $140 million in 2000. About $70 million would come from countries in Latin and South America, $30 million from Europe (including shipments to Africa), and $40 million from South Asia and Australia. The International Division had sales offices, small assembly areas, and distribution facilities in Frankfurt, Germany; Tokyo, Japan; and Singapore.

The Frankfurt office had been the impetus in 1995 for development and marketing of the company's first product targeted exclusively to consumer households—a home water filter. Sales engineers at the Frankfurt office began receiving consumer and distributor requests for a home water filter in 1994. By late 1995, two models had been designed in the United States and introduced in Germany (particularly to the eastern regions), Poland, Hungary, Romania, the Czech Republic, and Slovakia.

Company executives watched the success of the two water filters with great interest. The market for clean water in developing countries was huge, profitable, and attractive in a socially responsible sense. However, the quality of water in many developing countries was such that a water filter usually would not be satisfactory. Consequently, in late 1999, executives had directed the development of a water purifier that could be added to the product line. Engineers had given the final design in the project the brand name "Delight." For the time being, Chatterjee and the other market analysts had accepted the name, not knowing if it might infringe on any existing brand in India or in the other countries under study.

 ## DELIGHT PURIFIER

The Delight purifier used a combination of technologies to remove four types of contaminants found in potable water—sediments, organic and inorganic chemicals, microbials, or cysts, and objectionable tastes and odors. The technologies were effective as long as contaminants in the water were present at "reasonable" levels. Engineers at Fairchild Water Technologies, Inc. had interpreted "reasonable" as levels described in several World Health Organization (WHO) reports on potable water and had combined the technologies to purify water to a level beyond WHO standards. Engineers had repeatedly assured Chatterjee that Delight's design in terms of technologies should not be a concern. Ten units operating in the company's testing laboratory showed no signs of failure or performance deterioration after some 5,000 hours of continuous use. "Still," Chatterjee thought, "we will undertake a good bit of field testing in India before entering. The risks of failure are too large to ignore. And, besides, results of our testing would be useful in convincing consumers and retailers to buy."

Chatterjee and the other market analysts still faced major design issues in configuring technologies into physical products. For example, a "point of entry" design would place the product immediately after water entry to the home, treating all water before it flowed to all water outlets. In contrast, a "point of use" design would place the product on a countertop, wall, or at the end of a faucet and treat only water arriving at that location. Based on cost estimates, designs of competing products, and his understanding of Indian consumers, Chatterjee would direct engineers to proceed only with "point of use" designs for the market.

Other technical details were yet to be worked out. For example, Chatterjee had to provide engineers with suggestions for filter flow rates, storage capacities (if any), unit layout and overall dimensions, plus a number of special features. One such feature was the possibility of a small battery to operate the filter for several hours in case of a power failure (a common occurrence in India and many other developing countries). Another might be one or two "bells or whistles" to tell cooks, maids, and family members that the unit indeed was working properly. Yet another might be an "additive" feature, permitting users to add fluoride, vitamins, or even flavorings to their water.

Chatterjee knew that the Indian market would eventually require a number of models. However, at the outset of market entry, he probably could get by with just two—one with a larger capacity for houses and bungalows and the other a smaller capacity model for flats. He thought that model styling and specific appearances should reflect a Western, high-technology school of design in order to distinguish the Delight purifier from competitors' products. To that end, he had instructed a graphics artist to develop two ideas that he had used to gauge consumer reactions on his last visit (see Exhibit 2). Consumers liked both models but preferred the countertop design over the wallmount design.

FAIRCHILD WATER TECHNOLOGIES, INC.

EXHIBIT 2 Delight Water Purifier Wallmount and Countertop Designs

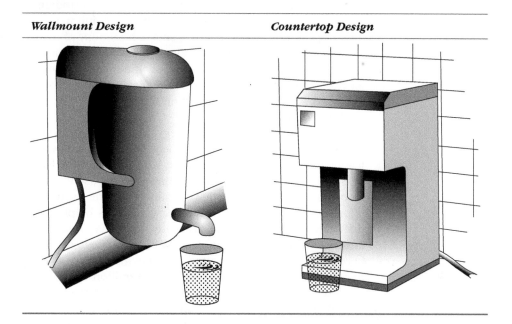

Wallmount Design — *Countertop Design*

COMPETITORS

Upward of 100 companies competed in the Indian market for home water filters and purifiers. While information on most of these companies was difficult to obtain, Chatterjee and the Indian research agencies were able to develop descriptions of three major competitors and brief profiles of several others.

Eureka Forbes

The most established competitor in the water purifier market was Eureka Forbes, a joint venture company established in 1982 between Electrolux (Sweden) and Forbes Campbell (India). The company marketed a broad line of "modern lifestyle products" including water purifiers, vacuum cleaners, and mixers/grinders. The brand name used for its water purifiers was "Aquaguard," a name so well established that many consumers mistakenly used it to refer to other water purifiers or to the entire product category. Aquaguard, with its market history, was clearly the market leader and came close to being India's only national brand. However, Eureka Forbes had recently introduced a second brand of water purifier called "PureSip." The PureSip model was similar to Aquaguard except for its third stage process, which used a polyiodide resin instead of ultraviolet rays to kill bacteria and viruses. This meant that water from a PureSip purifier could be stored safely for later usage. Also in contrast to Aquaguard, the PureSip model needed no electricity for its operation.

However, the biggest difference between the two products was how they were sold. Aquaguard was sold exclusively by a 2,500-person salesforce that called directly on households. In contrast, PureSip was sold by independent dealers of smaller home appliances. Unit prices to consumers for Aquaguard and PureSip were approximately Rs.5,500 and Rs.2,000, respectively. Chatterjee believed that unit sales of PureSip were much smaller than unit sales for Aquaguard but growing at a much faster rate.

An Aquaguard unit typically was mounted on a kitchen wall, with plumbing required to bring water to the purifier's inlet. A two-meter-long power cord was connected to a 230-volt AC electrical outlet—the Indian standard. If the power supply were to drop to 190 volts or lower, the unit would stop functioning. Other limits of the product included a smallish amount of activated carbon that could eliminate only weak organic odors. It could not remove strong odors or inorganic solutes like nitrates and iron compounds. The unit had no storage capacity and its flow rate of one liter per minute seemed slow to some consumers. Removing water for storage or connecting the unit to a reservoir tank could affect water quality, like a candle filter.

Aquaguard's promotion strategy emphasized personal selling. Each salesperson was assigned to a specific neighborhood and was monitored by a group leader who, in turn, was monitored by a supervisor. Each was expected to canvass the neighborhood, select prospective households (e.g., those with annual incomes exceeding Rs.70,000), demonstrate the product, and make an intensive effort to sell the product. Repeated sales calls helped educate consumers about their water quality and to reassure them that Aquaguard service was readily available. Television commercials and advertisements in magazines and newspapers (see Exhibit 3) supported the personal selling efforts. Chatterjee estimated that Eureka Forbes spent about Rs.120 million on all sales activities or roughly 11 percent of its sales revenues. He estimated that about Rs.100 million of the Rs.120 million would be spent in the form of sales commissions. Chatterjee thought the company's total advertising expenditures for the year would be only about Rs.1 million.

Eureka Forbes was a formidable competitor. The salesforce was huge, highly motivated, and well managed. Moreover, Aquaguard was the first product to enter the water purifier market and the name had tremendous brand equity. The product itself was probably the weakest strategic component—but it would take much to convince consumers of this. And, while the salesforce offered a huge competitive advantage, it represented an enormous fixed cost and essentially limited sales efforts to large urban areas. More than 80 percent of India's population lived in rural areas, where water quality was even lower.

Ion Exchange

Ion Exchange was the premier water treatment company in India, specializing in treatments of water, processed liquids, and wastewater in industrial markets. The company began operations in 1964 as a wholly owned subsidiary of British Permutit. Permutit divested its holdings in 1985 and Ion Exchange became a wholly owned Indian company. The company presently served customers in a diverse group of industries, including nuclear and thermal power stations, fertilizers, petrochemical refineries, textiles, automobiles, and home water purifiers. Its home water purifiers carried the family brand name, ZERO-B (Zero-Bacteria).

ZERO-B purifiers used a halogenated resin technology as part of a three-stage purification process. The first stage removed suspended impurities via filter pads, the second eliminated bad odors and taste with activated carbon, and the third killed bacteria using trace quantities of polyiodide (iodine). The latter feature was attractive because it helped prevent iodine deficiency diseases and permitted purified water to be stored up to eight hours without fear of recontamination.

The basic purifier product for the home carried the name "Puristore." A Puristore unit typically sat on a kitchen counter near the tap, with no electricity or plumbing hookup needed for its operation. The unit stored 20 liters of purified water. It sold to consumers for Rs.2,000. Each year the user must replace the halogenated resin at a cost of Rs.200.

EXHIBIT 3 **Aquaguard Newspaper Advertisement**

DON'T JUST
GUARD YOUR
FAMILY THIS
MONSOON.
AQUAGUARD IT.

The monsoons bring a welcome relief from the long hot summer. But they also bring along some of the most dangerous water-borne diseases. Like cholera, dysentry, gastro-enteritis and jaundice. Which is why you need an Aquaguard Water Purifier, to safeguard your family.

Today, Aquaguard is synonymous with clean, pure and safe drinking water.

Aquaguard is a 3 stage water purification system using the latest Ultra Violet technology, which destroys disease causing bacteria and virus in the water. It also has a unique

Electronic Monitoring System which stops water flow automatically if the purification level falls below pre-determined standards.

In addition, with Aquaguard you have the Eureka Forbes guarantee of After-Sales-Service at your doorstep.

So install on Aquaguard today. And help your family enjoy the monsoons better.

For a free demonstration at your home call the friendly man from Eureka Forbes or write to us at the addresses given below

Aquaguard
EUREKA FORBES LTD.

Calcutta: Mani Tower, Block Uttara, 1st Flr., 31/41 Vinoba Bhave Rd., Calcutta - 700 038. Tel: 4786645/5444. * 27 A, Lal Mohan Bhattacharjee Rd., 2nd Flr., Calcutta - 700 014. Tel: 245154B/2325. * 12 D, Chakraberia Rd. (North), Calcutta - 700 020. Tel: 746411/5326. * 177, Raja Dinendra Street, Opp. Desbandhu Park, Shyam Bazar, Calcutta - 700 004. Tel: 5545729/7248. * 21 G, Deodar Street, Calcutta - 700 019. * Guwahati: G.N.B.Rd., Silpukhuri, Above Jungle Travels, Near Goswami Service Station, Guwahati - 781 003. Tel: 31574. * Howrah: 105/106 A Panchsheel Apt., 1st Flr., 493, B.G.T. Road (South), Howrah - 711 102. Tel: 6606042. * Siliguri: 521 Swamiji Sarani, 1st Flr., Hakimpara P.O. Siliguri, Dist. Darjeeling, Tel: 26332.

Chatterjee estimated that ZERO-B captured about 7 percent of the Indian water purifier market. Probably the biggest reason for the small share was a lack of consumer awareness. ZERO-B purifiers had been on the market for a few years. They were not advertised heavily nor did they enjoy the sales effort intensity of Aquaguard. Distribution, too, was limited. During Chatterjee's visit, he could find only five dealers in Calcutta carrying ZERO-B products and none in Bangalore. Dealers that he contacted were of the opinion that ZERO-B's marketing efforts soon would intensify—two had heard rumors that a door-to-door salesforce was planned and that consumer advertising was about to begin.

Chatterjee had confirmed the latter point with a visit to a Calcutta advertising agency. A modest number of 10-second TV commercials soon would be aired on Zee TV and DD metro channels. The advertisements would focus on educating consumers with the position, "It is not a filter." Instead, ZERO-B is a water purifier and much more effective than a candle filter in preventing health problems. Apart from this advertising effort, the only other form of promotion used was a point of sale brochure that dealers could give to prospective customers (see Exhibit 4).

On balance, Chatterjee thought that Ion Exchange could be a major player in the market. The company had over 30 years' experience in the field of water purification and devoted upward of Rs.10 million each year to corporate research and development. "In fact," he thought, "all Ion Exchange really needs to do is to recognize the market's potential and to make it a priority within the company." However, this might be difficult to do, given the company's prominent emphasis on industrial markets. Chatterjee estimated that ZERO-B products would account for less than 2 percent of Ion Exchange's total sales, estimated at Rs.1,000 million. He thought the total marketing expenditures for ZERO-B would be around Rs.3 million.

Singer

The most recent competitor to enter the Indian water purifier market was Singer India Ltd. Originally, Singer India was a subsidiary of The Singer Company, located in the United States, but a minority share (49 percent) was sold to Indian investors

EXHIBIT 4 **ZERO-B Sales Brochure**

in 1982. The change in ownership had led to construction of manufacturing facilities in India for sewing machines in 1983. The facilities were expanded in 1993 to produce a broad line of home appliances. Sales revenues for the entire product line—sewing machines, food processors, irons, mixers, toasters, water heaters, ceiling fans, cooking ranges, and color televisions—would be about Rs.900 million.

During Chatterjee's time in Calcutta, he had visited a Singer Company showroom on Park Street. Initially he had hoped that Singer might be a suitable partner to manufacture and distribute the Delight purifier. However, much to his surprise, he was told that Singer now had its own brand on the market, "Aquarius." The product was not yet available in Calcutta but was being sold in Bombay and Delhi.

A marketing research agency in Delhi was able to gather some information on the Singer purifier. The product contained nine stages (!) and sold to consumers for Rs.4,000. It removed sediments, heavy metals, bad tastes, odors, and colors. It also killed bacteria and viruses, fungi, and nematodes. The purifier required water pressure (8 PSI minimum) to operate but needed no electricity. It came in a single countertop model that could be moved from one room to another. Life of the device at a flow rate of 3.8 liters per minute was listed as 40,000 liters—about four to six years of use in the typical Indian household. The product's life could be extended to 70,000 liters at a somewhat slower flow rate. However, at 70,000 liters, the product must be discarded. The agency reported a heavy advertising blitz accompanying the introduction in Delhi—emphasizing TV and newspaper advertising, plus outdoor and transit advertising as support. All 10 Singer showrooms in Delhi offered vivid demonstrations of the product's operation.

Chatterjee had to admit that photos of the Aquarius purifier shown in the Calcutta showroom looked appealing. And a trade article he found had described the product as "state of the art" in comparison to the "primitive" products now on the market. Chatterjee and Fairchild Water Technologies, Inc. engineers tended to agree—the disinfecting resin used in Aquarius had been developed by the U.S. government's National Aeronautics and Space Administration (NASA) and was proven to be 100 percent effective against bacteria and viruses. "If only I could have brought a unit back with me," he thought. "We could have some test results and see just how good it is." The trade article also mentioned that Singer hoped to sell 40,000 units over the next two years.

Chatterjee knew that Singer was a well-known and respected brand name in India. Further, Singer's distribution channels were superior to those of any competitor in the market, including those of Eureka Forbes. Most prominent of Singer's three distribution channels were the 210 company-owned showrooms located in major urban areas around the country. Each sold and serviced the entire line of Singer products. Each was very well kept and staffed by knowledgeable personnel. Singer products also were sold throughout India by over 3,000 independent dealers, who received inventory from an estimated 70 Singer-appointed distributors. According to the marketing research agency in Delhi, distributors earned margins of 12 percent of the retail price for Aquarius while dealers earned margins of 5 percent. Finally, Singer employed over 400 salespeople who sold sewing machines and food processors door-to-door. Like Eureka Forbes, the direct salesforce sold products primarily in large urban markets.

 ## OTHER COMPETITORS

Chatterjee was aware of several other water purifiers on the Indian market. The Delta brand from S & S Industries in Madras seemed a carbon copy of Aquaguard, except for a more eye-pleasing countertop design. According to promotion literature, Delta offered a line of water-related products—purifiers, water softeners, iron removers, desalinators, and ozonators. Another competitor was Alfa Water Purifiers, Bombay. The company offered four purifier models at prices from Rs.4,300 to Rs.6,500, depending on capacity. Symphony's Spectrum brand sold well around Bombay at Rs.4,000 each but removed only suspended sediments, not heavy metals or bacteria. The Sam Group in Coimbatore recently had launched its "Water Doctor" purifier at Rs.5,200. The device used a third stage ozonator to kill bacteria and viruses and came in two attractive countertop models, 6- and 12-liter storage. Batliboi was mentioned by the Delhi research agency as yet another competitor, although Chatterjee knew nothing else about the brand. Taken all together, unit sales of all purifiers at these companies plus ZERO-B and Singer probably would account for around 60,000 units in 2000. The remaining 190,000 units would be Aquaguards and PureSips.

At least 100 Indian companies made and marketed candle filters. The largest of these probably was Bajaj Electrical Division, whose product line also included water heaters, irons, electric light bulbs, toasters, mixers, and grillers. Bajaj's candle filters were sold by a large number of dealers who carried the entire product line. Candle filters produced by other manufacturers were sold mostly through dealers who specialized in small household appliances and general hardware. Probably no single manufacturer of candle filters had more than 5 percent of any regional market in the country. No manufacturer attempted to satisfy a national market. Still, the candle filters market deserved serious consideration—perhaps Delight's entry strategy would attempt to "trade-up" users of candle filters to a better, safer product.

Finally, Chatterjee knew that sales of almost all purifiers in 2000 in India came from large urban areas. No manufacturer targeted rural or smaller urban areas and at best, Chatterjee had calculated, existing manufacturers were reaching only 10 to 15 percent of the entire Indian population. An explosion in sales would come if the right product could be sold outside metropolitan areas.

RECOMMENDATIONS

Chatterjee decided that an Indian market entry for Fairchild Water Technologies, Inc. was subject to three "givens," as he called them. First, he thought that a strategic focus on rural or smaller urban areas would not be wise, at least at the start. The lack of adequate distribution and communication infrastructure in rural India meant that any market entry would begin with larger Indian cities, most likely on the west coast.

Second, market entry would require manufacturing units in India. Because the cost of skilled labor in India was around Rs.20 to Rs.25 per hour (compared to $20 to $25 per hour in the United States), importing complete units was out of the question. However, importing a few key components would be necessary at the start of operation.

Third, Fairchild should find an Indian partner. Chatterjee's visits had produced a number of promising partners: Polar Industries, Calcutta; Milton Plastics, Bombay; Videocon Appliances, Aurangabad; BPL Sanyo Utilities and Appliances, Bangalore; Onida Savak, Delhi; Hawkins India, Bombay; and Voltas, Bombay. All companies manufactured and marketed a line of high-quality household appliances, possessed one or more strong brand names, and had established dealer networks (minimum of 10,000 dealers). All were involved to greater or lesser degrees with international partners. All were medium-size firms—not too large that a partnership with Fairchild Water Technologies would be one-sided, not too small that they would lack managerial talent and other resources. Finally, all were profitable and looking to grow. However, Chatterjee had no idea if any company would find the Delight purifier and Fairchild attractive or if they might be persuaded to sell part or all of their operations as an acquisition.

Field Testing and Product Recommendations

The most immediate decision Chatterjee faced was whether or not he should recommend a field test. The test would cost about $25,000, placing 20 units in Indian homes in three cities and monitoring their performance for three to six months. The decision to test really was more than it seemed—Chatterjee's boss had explained that a decision to test was really a decision to enter. It made no sense to spend this kind of time and money if India were not an attractive opportunity. The testing period also would give Fairchild representatives time to identify a suitable Indian company as either a licensee, joint venture partner, or acquisition.

Fundamental to market entry was product design. Engineers at Fairchild had taken the position that purification technologies planned for Delight could be "packaged in almost any fashion as long as we have electricity." Electricity was needed to operate the product's ozonator as well as to indicate to users that the unit was functioning properly (or improperly, as the case might be). Beyond this requirement, anything was possible.

Chatterjee thought that a modular approach would be best. The basic module would be a countertop unit much like that shown in Exhibit 2. The module would outperform anything now on the market in terms of flow rate, palatability, durability, and reliability, and would store two liters of purified water. Two additional modules would remove iron, calcium, and other metallic contaminants that were peculiar to particular regions. For example, Calcutta and much of the surrounding area suffered from iron contamination, which no filter or purifier now on the Indian market could remove to a satisfactory level. Water supplies in other areas in the country were known to contain objectionable concentrations of calcium, salt, arsenic, lead, or sulfur. Most Indian consumers would need neither of the additional modules, some would need one or the other, but very few would need both.

Market Entry and Marketing Planning Recommendations

Assuming that Chatterjee recommended proceeding with the field test, he would need to make a recommendation concerning mode of market entry. In addition, his recommendation should include an outline of a marketing plan.

Licensee Considerations   If market entry were in the form of a joint working arrangement with a licensee, Fairchild Water Technologies Inc. financial investment would be minimal. Chatterjee thought that the company might risk as little as $30,000 in capital for production facilities and equipment, plus another $5,000 for office facilities and equipment. These investments would be completely offset by the licensee's payment to Fairchild for technology transfer and personnel training. Annual fixed costs to the company should not exceed $40,000 at the outset and would decrease to $15,000 as soon as an Indian national could be hired, trained, and left in charge. Duties of this individual would be to work with Fairchild personnel in the United States and with management at the licensee to see that units were produced per the company's specifications. Apart from this activity, Fairchild would have no control over the licensee's operations. Chatterjee expected that the licensee would pay royalties to the company of about

Rs.280 for each unit sold in the domestic market and Rs.450 for each unit that was exported. The average royalty probably would be around Rs.300.

Joint Venture/Acquisition Considerations   If entry were in the form of either a joint venture or an acquisition, financial investment and annual fixed costs would be much higher and depend greatly on the scope of operations. Chatterjee had roughed out some estimates for a joint venture entry, based on three levels of scope (see Exhibit 5). His estimates reflected what he thought were reasonable assumptions for all needed investments plus annual fixed expenses for sales activities, general administrative overhead, research and development, insurance, and depreciation. His estimates allowed for the Delight purifier to be sold either through dealers or through a direct, door-to-door salesforce. Chatterjee thought that estimates of annual fixed expenses for market entry via acquisition would be identical to those for a joint venture. However, estimates for the investment (purchase) might be considerably higher, the same, or lower. It depended on what was purchased.

Chatterjee's estimates of Delight's unit contribution margins reflected a number of assumptions—expected economies of scale, experience curve effects, costs of Indian labor and raw materials, and competitors' pricing strategies. However, the most important assumption was Delight's pricing strategy. If a skimming strategy were used and the product sold through a dealer channel, the basic module would be priced to dealers at Rs.5,500 and to consumers at Rs.5,900. "This would give us about a Rs.650 unit contribution, once we got production flowing smoothly," he thought. In contrast, if a penetration strategy were used and the product sold through a dealer channel, the basic module would be priced to dealers at Rs.4,100, to consumers at Rs.4,400, and yield a unit contribution of Rs.300. For simplicity's sake, Chatterjee assumed that the two additional modules would be priced to dealers at Rs.800, to consumers at Rs.1,000, and would yield a unit contribution of Rs.100. Finally, he assumed that all products sold to dealers would go directly from Fairchild Water Technologies, Inc. to the dealers (no distributors would be used).

If a direct salesforce were employed instead of dealers, Chatterjee thought that prices charged to consumers would not change from those listed above. However, sales commissions would have to be paid in addition to the fixed costs necessary to maintain and manage the salesforce. Under a skimming price strategy, the sales commission would be Rs.550 per unit and the unit contribution would be Rs.500. Under a penetration price strategy, the sales commission would be Rs.400 per unit and the unit contribution would be Rs.200. These financial estimates, he would explain in his report, would apply to the expected first year of operation.

EXHIBIT 5	**Investments and Fixed Costs for a Joint Venture Market Entry**		
	Operational Scope		
	Two Regions	*Four Regions*	*National Market*
2003 Market potential (units)	55,000	110,000	430,000
Initial investment (Rs.000)	4,000	8,000	30,000
Annual fixed overhead expenses (Rs.000)			
Using dealer channels	4,000	7,000	40,000
Using direct salesforce	7,200	14,000	88,000

Skimming versus penetration was more than just a pricing strategy. Product design for the skimming strategy would be noticeably superior, with higher performance and quality, a longer warranty period, more features, and a more attractive appearance than the design for the penetration strategy. Positioning, too, most likely would be different. Chatterjee recognized several positioning possibilities: performance and taste, value for the money/low price, safety, health, convenience, attractive styling, avoiding diseases and health-related bills, and superior American technology. The only position he considered "taken" in the market was that occupied by Aquaguard—protect family health and service at your doorstep. While other competitors had claimed certain positions for their products, none had devoted financial resources of a degree that Delight could not dislodge them. Chatterjee believed that considerable advertising and promotion expenditures would be necessary to communicate Delight's positioning. He would need estimates of these expenditures in his recommendation.

"If we go ahead with Delight, we'll have to move quickly," thought Chatterjee. "The window of opportunity is open but if Singer's product is as good as they claim, we'll be in for a fight. Still, Aquarius seems vulnerable on the water pressure requirement and on price. We'll need a product category 'killer' to win."

Case

Chevrolet Europe

In early 2004, Patricia Messar, the director for brand and marketing at Chevrolet Europe, assembled the Project Midas group. Project Midas was the name given to the strategy to introduce the General Motors Chevrolet brand of passenger cars to Europe in 2005.

Messar and the Project Midas team faced a unique challenge given the circumstances surrounding the Chevrolet brand launch. Specifically, the Chevrolet brand would replace the Daewoo brand in Europe. The Daewoo brand was introduced to Europe in the mid-1990s by Daewoo Motor Company of Seoul, Korea. In October 2002, General Motors took on part ownership and management control of the automobile business and began marketing the GM Daewoo brand in Europe through GM Daewoo Europe, a wholly owned subsidiary of GM Daewoo Auto & Technology, with headquarters in Zurich, Switzerland. Following General Motors' corporate strategy to market GM Daewoo vehicles under the Chevrolet brand in Asia (except South Korea), South America, and North America in 2003, the Project Midas team was assigned responsibility for making the brand conversion from GM Daewoo to Chevrolet in the European passenger car market. The conversion would further the transformation of Chevrolet into a global brand name. "The GM Daewoo products, quality, styling, and customer acceptance was considered an excellent starting point," said one senior General Motors executive.

Chevrolet brand positioning was the assignment for the assembled Project Midas marketing group. Brand positioning also had its unique circumstances and challenges. The Chevrolet brand launch had to be accomplished with the existing GM Daewoo product line, carry-over names for individual product models, and the same dealers and operating policies and practices. Based on industry, market, and consumer insights accumulated in the months prior to the meeting, the Project Midas workgroup set out to craft a Chevrolet positioning statement that would (1) resonate with European car buyers; (2) complement General Motors' multibrand portfolio in Europe; and (3) be consistent with the global perception of the Chevrolet brand.

The cooperation of Chevrolet Europe in the preparation of this case is gratefully acknowledged. This case was prepared by Professor Roger A. Kerin and Professor Raj Sethuraman, Edwin L. Cox School of Business, Southern Methodist University, as a basis for class discussion and is not designed to illustrate effective or ineffective handling of an administrative situation or for research purposes. Certain information in the case is disguised for proprietary reasons. All General Motors brand names are trademarks of General Motors Corporation and used with permission. Copyright © 2007 by Roger A. Kerin and Raj Sethuraman. No part of this case may be reproduced without written permission of the copyright holders.

In addition, the Project Midas marketing group was given a 2005 market share goal of 1 percent for the Chevrolet brand in the European passenger car market and a 75 million euro media budget (1 euro = US$1.13) to achieve this goal. This market share goal represented an increase over GM Daewoo brand sales of 132,200 units in 2003, which represented less than 0.85 percent market share.

 THE EUROPEAN PASSENGER CAR MARKET: EARLY 2004

Europe is the largest passenger car producer in the world. Of the 42 million passenger cars produced worldwide in 2003, 41 percent were produced in Europe. Western Europe alone accounted for 36 percent of worldwide passenger car production. Europe is also the global leader in new passenger car registrations, representing 43 percent of all new passenger car registrations worldwide. Exhibit 1 shows the number of new car registrations by country in 2003. Five Western European countries—Germany, the United Kingdom, Italy, France, and Spain—recorded about 74 percent of new European passenger car registrations in 2003. New passenger car registrations in 2003 increased 0.6 percent over 2002. This increase followed two consecutive years of declining new car registrations. Total new passenger car registrations in Europe in 2003 were 4.4 percent lower than 2000 registrations. Industry analysts in Europe were forecasting a 1 to 2 percent annual increase in new car registrations for 2004 and 2005.

Automakers and Brands

The European passenger car market is highly competitive. Some 20 automakers offer more than 50 brands in over 200 models. Eight automakers are prominent in Europe: the Volkswagen Group, the Peugeot Group, Renault, Ford, General

EXHIBIT 1 New Passenger Car Registrations by Country in 2003

Country	2003 Units	Percent of Total	Country	2003 Units	Percent of Total
Germany	3,236,938	20.86	Turkey	226,496	1.46
United Kingdom	2,579,050	16.62	Czech/Slovak Republic	212,723	1.37
Italy	2,247,019	14.48	Hungary	208,426	1.34
France	2,009,246	12.95	Portugal	189,792	1.22
Spain	1,382,109	8.90	Finland	147,222	0.95
Belgium & Luxembourg	502,416	3.24	Ireland	145,223	0.94
Netherlands	488,841	3.15	Denmark	96,078	0.62
Poland	358,432	2.31	Norway	89,921	0.58
Austria	300,121	1.93	Southeast Europe		
Switzerland	270,309	1.74	(e.g., Slovenia,		
Sweden	261,206	1.68	Croatia, Yugoslavia,		
Greece	257,293	1.66	Romania, Bulgaria)	494,310	3.18
			Total	15,520,755	100.00

Source: Company records.

Motors (Opel/Vauxhall/Saab), Fiat Group, DaimlerChrysler, and BMW. These automakers commanded 83.9 percent of new passenger car unit sales in 2003. Nine brands marketed by these eight automakers accounted for 69.2 percent of new passenger car unit sales in 2003. The Volkswagen Group has been the market share leader in the European passenger car market for many years with its Volkswagen, Audi, Seat, and Skoda brands. However, Renault has retained a brand share leadership position in Europe for many years. Opel/Vauxhall, GM's core brand in Europe, has evidenced a strong market presence as well.

Exhibit 2 shows the new car market share trends for automakers and brands over the period 1999 to 2003. Japanese automaker brands (Toyota, Nissan, Mitsubishi,

| EXHIBIT 2 | Manufacturer and Brand Market Shares in Europe: 1999–2003 (All Figures Rounded) |

A. Manufacturer Market Share (%)

Automaker*	1999	2000	2001	2002	2003
Volkswagen Group	17.7	17.6	17.9	17.4	17.0
Peugeot Group	11.8	12.8	14.3	14.9	14.8
Renault	11.5	11.3	11.5	11.6	11.5
Ford in Europe	11.0	10.2	10.6	10.7	10.7
General Motors in Europe	10.3	9.7	9.2	9.8	10.6
Fiat Group	10.5	10.9	10.4	9.2	8.4
DaimlerChrysler	5.6	6.2	6.4	6.6	6.5
BMW	3.2	3.4	3.7	4.3	4.4
Japanese Manufacturers	11.5	11.4	10.5	11.3	12.5
Other Manufacturers	6.9	6.5	5.0	4.2	3.6

B. Brand Market Share (%)

Brand	1999	2000	2001	2002	2003
Renault	11.5	11.3	11.5	11.6	11.5
Volkswagen	10.5	10.1	10.0	9.6	9.2
Opel/Vauxhall	9.8	9.2	9.3	8.8	9.1
Ford	8.9	8.2	8.5	8.5	8.6
Fiat	8.7	9.0	8.4	7.6	6.9
Peugeot	7.0	7.4	8.3	8.6	8.3
Citroën	4.8	5.4	6.0	6.3	6.5
Mercedes-Benz	4.6	4.8	5.0	5.1	5.1
BMW	3.2	3.4	3.7	4.3	4.4
Other Brands	31.0	31.3	29.3	29.6	30.5

*Automakers market a variety of brands. Representative manufacturer brands in 2003 are shown below:

GM in Europe:	Opel/Vauxhall, Saab, GM Daewoo
VW Group:	VW, Audi, Seat, Skoda
Peugeot Group:	Peugeot, Citroën
Ford in Europe:	Ford, Jaguar, Volvo, Land Rover
Fiat Group:	Fiat, Alfa Romeo, Lancia
Daimler Chrysler:	Mercedes-Benz, Jeep, Chrysler

Source: Company records.

Suzuki, Honda, and Mazda) captured 37 percent of "Other Brand" sales in 1999 and 40.6 percent of "Other Brand" sales in 2003. Korean nameplates (Daewoo, Kia, and Hyundai) captured 10.2 percent of "Other Brand" sales in 1999 and 9.8 percent of "Other Brand" sales in 2003.

In general, European passenger car buyers tend to perceive automakers and brands on the basis of national origin and manufacture. The largest European automakers have strong national identifications. The Volkswagen Group, BMW, and DaimlerChrysler are German-based companies. German brands stand for quality and technology. Opel is strongly perceived as a German brand even though it is owned by General Motors. The Peugeot Group and Renault are French-based companies. French brands stand for innovation and comfort. The Fiat Group is an Italian-based company. Italian brands stand for style, but suspect quality. As a further generalization, European automakers' brands evidence prominent market shares in the countries for which they are strongly identified.

European car buyers also have distinct perceptions of cars and service based on continent of origin; namely, Europe, America (United States), and Asia (Japan and Korea). Exhibit 3 on page 656 illustrates these perceptual differences.

Media Advertising

Passenger cars are among the most heavily advertised consumer products in Europe. An estimated 5 billion euros (US$5.6 billion) was spent by automakers in 2003 to advertise their brands. Six automakers (Peugeot, Volkswagen, Ford, Renault, General Motors, and Fiat) accounted for about 73 percent and 70 percent of estimated media advertising expenditures in 2002 and 2003, respectively.

Exhibit 4 on page 657 shows consumer media advertising expenditures by automakers for 2002 and 2003, based on estimates made by *Advertising Age*, the world's leading authoritative publication for the advertising profession. Also shown is "share of voice." Share of voice represents the media spending of a particular brand or company when compared to others in a product category or industry. Share of voice is typically expressed as a percentage of total media spending. European automakers have the highest collective share of voice in Europe, followed by U.S. automakers, and Asian (Japanese and Korean) automakers.

Passenger Car Size and Body Types

The European passenger car market is typically described by car size and body type. Small cars (including microvans and compacts) have an interior volume under 3.12 cubic meters (110 cubic feet) and are referred to as city cars or small family cars. Examples include the Fiat Panda and the Opel Corsa. Medium-size cars have an interior volume between 3.12 and 3.40 cubic meters (110 to 120 cubic feet) and are called large family cars. Examples include the Volkswagen Passat and Saab 9-3. Executive cars are defined as a passenger car larger than a large family car, but not an SUV. Examples include the Mercedes-Benz S-Class and Cadillac CTS. Small cars accounted for 34.2 percent and medium-size cars accounted for 46.1 percent of annual new passenger car registrations across Europe in 2003 with only modest differences between countries in Western and Central Europe.

Five body types are common in Europe. Saloons (or sedans in North America) are the dominant passenger car body type purchased in Europe. A saloon seats four or more passengers and has a fixed roof that is full-height up to the rear window with a separate trunk space as distinct from hatchbacks. Estates (or station wagons in North America) have historically represented the second most popular body type. However, mono-space vehicles (micro- and minivans, hatchbacks, and

EXHIBIT 3 European Passenger Car Buyer Perceptions of Cars and Service by Continent of Origin

Europe	*America*	*Asia*
Product	*Product*	*Product*
• Stylish/nice design	• Big/huge/large	• Well equipped (as standard)
• Attention to detail	• Bulky/big boxes	• Less expensive/economical
• Robust/solid	• Less appealing design	• Copies of European cars
• Safe	• Too showy/ostentatious	• Less refined interior
• Smaller size (vs. USA)	• Very comfortable	
• Smaller engines (vs. USA)	• Automatic transmission	*Japan* — *Korea*
• Better reputation/heritage	• High fuel consumption	• High tech — • Proven tech
• Higher status (vs. Asia)	• Big engines	• Sporty looks — • Distinctive
• More expensive (vs. Asia)	• Designed for the highway	• Performance — • Inexpensive
• Better resale value	• Not practical in cities	• Dependable — • Less reliable
Service	*Service*	*Service*
• Availability of spare parts	• Lack of parts	• Outstanding warranty
• Large dealer network	• Poor dealer network	• Friendly staff
• Standard across Europe	• Not tailored for Europe	• Lack of parts
• Consistency		• Less dealers (but better than USA)
• Improved customer care		• Expensive insurance
• Catching up on Japanese		• Expensive repairs
		Japan — *Korea*
		• Pioneers — • Followers
		• More dealers — • Fewer dealers

Source: Company records.

656

| EXHIBIT 4 | Measured Consumer Media Advertising in Europe for Major Automobile Manufacturers (U.S. Dollars) |

Manufacturer	2002 Advertising Expenditure ($ million)	2002 Share of Voice (%)	2003 Advertising Expenditure ($ million)	2003 Share of Voice (%)
Peugeot Group	859	15.45	791	14.11
Volkswagen Group	756	13.60	788	14.05
Ford Motor Company	746	13.42	738	13.16
Renault	712	12.81	656	11.70
General Motors Corp.	522	9.39	551	9.83
Fiat Group	456	8.20	412	7.35
Toyota Motor Corp.	347	6.24	398	7.10
DaimlerChrysler	356	6.40	350	6.24
BMW	225	4.05	209	3.73
Nissan Motor Co.	125	2.25	185	3.30
Honda Motor Co.	108	1.94	136	2.43
Mazda Motor Corp.	113	2.03	117	2.09
Hyundai Motor Co.	99	1.78	96	1.71
Suzuki Motor Co.	72	1.29	69	1.23
Mitsubishi Motors Corp.	20	.36	58	1.03
Total (includes others)	5,560	100.00	5,607	100.00

Source: Advertising expenditure data are provided courtesy of *Advertising Age*, "Top 100 Global Marketers." Used with permission.

SUVs) have grown in popularity in recent years. In 2003, saloons were the best seller with 62.2 percent of new passenger car registrations, followed by mono-space passenger cars (14.5 percent), and estates (13.2 percent). Coupes, convertibles, and "other" body types accounted for 10.1 percent of new passenger car registrations.

Market Segmentation

The European passenger car market is traditionally segmented on the basis of car owner social status and value orientation across national boundaries. A common form of segmentation used in Europe is the SIGMA Milieu Segmentation framework displayed in Exhibit 5 on page 658. A description of individual segments follows, including representative car brands typically identified with each segment.

Traditional Segments   Four traditional segments have been identified and represent 46 percent of European car owners. The *Upper Conservative Segment* is comprised of the upper class European elite who hold conservative, religious, and increasingly technocratic values. This segment represents 7 percent of car owners and is identified with Mercedes-Benz and Ford's Jaguar and Land Rover brands. The *Traditional Mainstream Segment*, representing 16 percent of car owners, seek status, performance, and enjoyment in moderation. Mercedes-Benz, Fiat's Lancia, and Ford's Land Rover are identified with the smaller upper middle

EXHIBIT 5   European Passenger Car Ownership Segmentation and Brand Identities (Numbers in Parentheses Represent the Percentage of Car Owners)

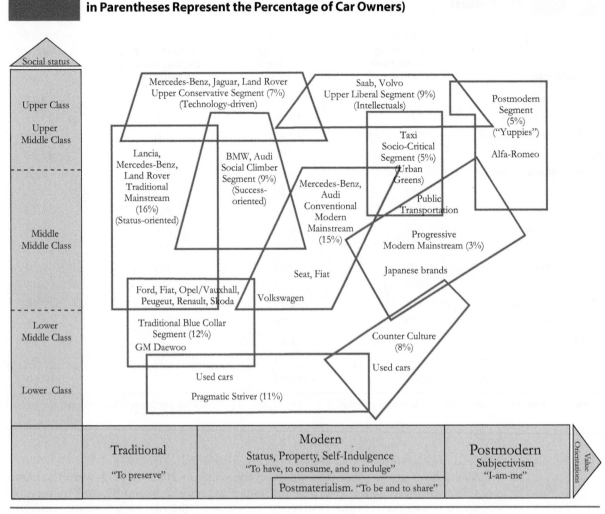

Source: SIGMA Milieus Euro5, copyright SIGMA GmbH, Mannheim, Germany, www.sigma-online.com. Used with permission.

class in this segment. Ford, Opel/Vauxhall, Fiat, Peugeot, and Volkswagen's Skoda are identified with the larger middle middle class in this segment.[1]

The *Traditional Blue Collar Segment* includes skilled blue-collar workers who are flexible in their brand selection and willing to spend money on cars. This segment represents 12 percent of car owners. Ford, Opel/Vauxhall, Fiat, Peugeot, Renault, and Volkswagen's Skoda are identified with the larger middle middle class in this segment. The GM Daewoo brand is identified with the smaller lower middle class in this segment. The *Pragmatic Striver Segment* consists of lower middle class and lower class car owners who are frustrated because they cannot afford their desired products. Used cars, mostly large and well-known European brand family cars, dominate in this segment. Eleven percent of car owners fall into this segment.

Mainstream Segments   Three mainstream segments represent 35 percent of European car owners. The *Social Climber Segment*, consisting of upper middle

---

[1] The middle middle class is considered to be the "traditional" middle class in terms of social status and considered distinct from upper and lower middle class.

class and middle class car owners, aims for the lifestyle of the European "elite," is consumption-oriented, and leans toward sporty cars. They represent 9 percent of car owners and are identified with BMW and Volkswagen's Audi. The *Conventional Modern/Progressive Modern Mainstream Segment* consists of younger, middle middle class car owners who are mostly well educated with above-average incomes, and bridges the modern and postmodern value orientation. They tend to spend more on cars and are open to considering new or "other brands," including major Japanese brands, notably Toyota and Nissan, and Hyundai and Kia, two major Korean brands. These combined segments represent 18 percent of car owners. The *Counter Culture Segment* prefers to escape routine and values a sense of community. This segment spans the lower class to middle middle class of car owners and buys larger European used, not new, cars. Eight percent of car owners fall into this segment.

Postmodern/Materialistic Segments   Three segments strive for a variety of lifestyles, evidence tolerance toward different lifestyles, and are attuned to cultural "openness." These segments combined represent 19 percent of car owners. The *Upper Liberal Segment* is part of the upper class European elite and combines post-material values of emancipation and individuality while striving for financial success and an epicurean philosophy of life. General Motors' Saab and Ford's Volvo are identified with this segment. This segment represents 9 percent of car owners. The *Socio-Critical Segment* consists of "60s-generation" consumers or believers in this generation's ideals, including postmaterialist convictions and philosophies. This segment, made up of upper middle class and middle middle class consumers, is sometimes referred to as "Urban Greens" and favors car sharing (taxi cabs) and public transportation over car usage. Five percent of car owners are in this segment. The *Postmodern Segment* consists of car owners who believe they control their own destiny, live in the European metropolis, and exude self-confidence. Fiat's Alfa-Romeo is identified with this segment. Five percent of car owners fall into this segment.

GENERAL MOTORS IN EUROPE

Europe is the second largest global regional market for General Motors Corporation after North America. About one-fifth of total company unit sales are derived from Europe. General Motors in Europe reported net sales and revenues of US$27.5 billion in 2003 compared to US$23.9 billion in 2002.

Background

General Motors' presence in Europe dates back to 1911, just three years after the corporation was formed. At the time, the General Motors Export Company was organized to sell cars and trucks worldwide. General Motors started building Chevrolet brand cars in Denmark in 1923 and Belgium in 1925 before acquiring Vauxhall Motors Ltd. in England (1925) and Opel AG in Germany (1929). Over the years, Opel/Vauxhall became GM's core volume brand in Europe, accounting for more than 80 percent of GM's euro sales—while the manufacture of Chevrolet passenger cars was subsequently discontinued in Europe, except for a small number of products imported from North America. The company acquired a 50 percent stake in Saab Automobile AB of Sweden in 1989, taking full ownership in 2000.

In October 2002, GM Daewoo Auto & Technology Company (GM DAT) was formed. The assets taken over from Daewoo Motor Company by GM DAT included research, design, and engineering facilities as well as manufacturing facilities in South Korea and Vietnam. GM Daewoo Europe was then established to coordinate

GM Daewoo sales subsidiaries and marketing in Europe. In 2003, General Motors operated 11 production and assembly facilities in eight European countries. The company employed about 63,000 people. Exhibit 6 shows the nature and geographic scope of General Motors European operations in 2003.

Car Brands and Models

Three passenger car brands were prominent in the General Motors Europe brand portfolio based on 2003 unit sales. They were Opel/Vauxhall, Saab, and GM Daewoo.

Opel/Vauxhall   Opel/Vauxhall accounted for 87.1 percent of General Motors Europe unit sales in 2003. Opel/Vauxhall was positioned as a fresh-thinking brand that surprises modern mainstream customers with vehicles that lead with bold, dynamic style, versatility, and driving excitement.

EXHIBIT 6   General Motors Europe Operations in 2003

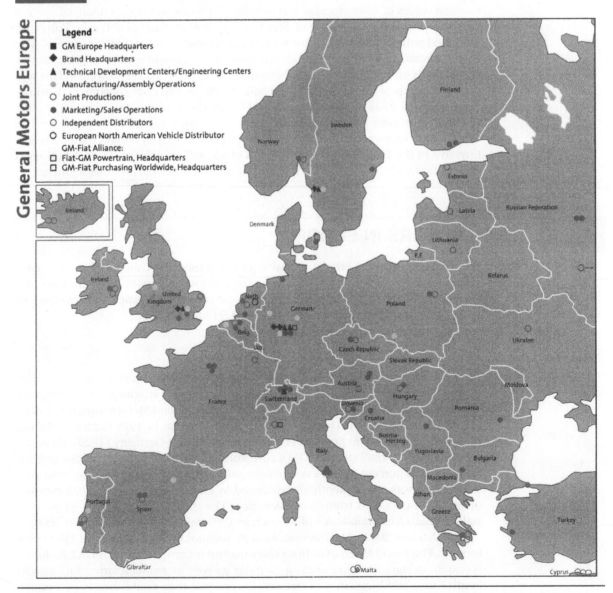

Source: Company records.

This brand is sold in 30 European countries (the Vauxhall brand is sold exclusively in the United Kingdom) and features 16 models in the small, compact, and medium-size car segments. The Opel/Vauxhall Corsa, Astra, and Zafira models, all small and compact cars, were the best-sellers in General Motors' model line in Europe. These models accounted for about two-thirds of Opel/ Vauxhall European sales in 2003. Opel 2003 unit sales were about equal to 2002 unit sales, but down 18 percent compared with 2000 unit sales. Vauxhall 2003 unit sales increased 2.4 percent over 2002 unit sales and were 10 percent higher than 2000 unit sales. Exhibit 7a shows a 2003 print advertisement for Opel.

EXHIBIT 7   **Opel and Saab Advertising**

A. Print Advertisement for Opel in 2003

B. Print Advertisement for Saab in 2003

Source: Company records.

Saab   Saab registered 4.5 percent of General Motors Europe unit sales in 2003. Saab was positioned as a brand that offers modern independent-minded customers an alternative premium experience, embodied in cars that are progressive, sporty, and surprisingly practical. The Saab brand is sold in 33 European countries and features two models in the medium-size car segment. Saab is popular in Sweden, given its Swedish origins, where it posts a consistent market share above 10 percent. Saab 2003 unit sales increased slightly over 2002 sales, but were 7.8 percent less than 2000 unit sales. Exhibit 7b show a 2003 print advertisement for Saab.

GM Daewoo Europe   GM Daewoo represented 8 percent of General Motors Europe unit sales in 2003. This brand is sold in 32 European countries and features six models, five in the small/compact car segment and one in the medium-size car segment. European unit sales increased 21.7 percent in 2003 following the assumption of sales and marketing responsibilities by GM Daewoo Europe.

Exhibit 8 shows the market share for General Motors in Europe by country and brand for the period 2001 to 2003. Other brands marketed by General Motors in Europe, such as Cadillac, Hummer, and the Chevrolet Corvette, are not shown given their small unit volume relative to the company's more prominent brands in Europe. Similarly, some European countries are not shown due to their small new passenger car unit volumes.

POSITIONING THE CHEVROLET BRAND IN EUROPE

Barbara Rübel, the manager for brand strategy, convened the Project Midas marketing group in early 2004. The purpose of the gathering was to craft a positioning statement for the Chevrolet brand in Europe. The Project Midas marketing team had to do this without changing the GM Daewoo product line, model characteristics, manufacturer's suggested retail prices, dealer sales practices, or distribution coverage already in place.

Daewoo in Europe

The Daewoo brand was introduced to Europe in 1994 by Daewoo Motor Company of Seoul, Korea. However, a material market presence did not emerge until 1997 with the launch of the Daewoo Matiz (Exhibit 9 on page 664 shows the Daewoo Matiz). In 1998, the Daewoo Matiz, a microvan or city car in the small car segment, was chosen as one of the top three car brands based on a consumer survey in 13 European countries by *Auto Motor und Sport*, the world's largest automobile publication. Matiz posted particularly high car buyer ratings in Italy, Portugal, the Czech Republic, and Poland. According to *Quattroruote*, an Italian automotive publication, "Those who drive a Daewoo know it as a good car, think it is reliable and, above all, very good value for the money." The Matiz was also the winner in the small car segment at "The World's Most Beautiful Automobile of 1998" awards held in Milan, Italy.

In 1999, the Daewoo Motor Company declared bankruptcy due to a heavy debt burden. Over the next two years, the company lost its momentum in Europe as well as other markets. Financial difficulties and an inconsistent marketing strategy across Europe eroded unit sales in 2001 and 2002, as shown in Exhibit 10 on page 664.

EXHIBIT 8 General Motors Europe Market Share by Country and Brand: 2001–2003 (Based on New Passenger Car Registrations)

Country	2001			2002			2003			
	Market Share GM Total (%)	Market Share (%) Opel	Market Share (%) Saab	Market Share GM Total (%)	Market Share (%) Opel	Market Share (%) Saab	Market Share GM Total (%)	Market Share (%) Opel	Market Share (%) Saab	Market Share (%) Daewoo
Austria	9.9	9.70	0.07	9.1	8.78	0.21	9.5	8.84	0.20	0.40
Belgium and Lux.	10.6	10.04	0.51	10.5	9.91	0.53	11.3	9.80	0.60	0.86
Denmark	7.5	6.97	0.42	5.5	4.88	0.62	6.3	4.40	0.60	1.30
Finland	12.5	10.68	1.64	7.5	5.97	1.36	6.8	4.71	1.21	0.74
France	6.3	6.11	0.16	5.9	5.71	0.17	6.4	6.02	0.14	0.22
Germany	12.2	11.88	0.24	10.6	10.34	0.21	10.9	10.30	0.16	0.39
Greece	10.5	10.32	0.14	7.9	7.71	0.15	10.4	7.66	0.31	2.40
Ireland	9.9	9.29	0.61	8.4	7.82	0.58	9.1	7.39	0.75	0.96
Italy	9.2	9.06	0.13	8.6	8.45	0.14	9.1	7.40	0.19	1.50
Netherlands	13.9	12.96	0.79	11.7	10.84	0.73	14.0	11.38	0.76	1.76
Norway	11.0	8.71	2.29	9.2	6.62	2.58	9.2	6.54	2.33	0.33
Portugal	12.9	12.78	0.12	10.7	10.57	0.13	10.1	9.36	0.21	0.53
Spain	11.7	11.36	0.31	10.9	10.61	0.26	11.6	9.74	0.22	1.63
Sweden	15.8	5.17	10.02	14.9	3.82	10.29	15.3	3.83	10.35	0.35
Switzerland	11.7	10.54	0.80	11.0	9.92	0.78	11.2	9.17	0.85	0.96
United Kingdom[a]	13.3	12.65[a]	0.63	13.0	12.46[a]	0.54	13.7	12.64[a]	0.57	0.50
Czech/Slovak Rep.	5.4	5.35	0.05	4.1	4.05	0.05	6.2	4.74	0.05	1.41
Poland	8.6	8.54	0.06	9.0	8.93	0.07	9.7	9.64	0.06	–
Turkey	11.1	11.03	0.07	11.2	11.10	0.10	11.7	11.66	0.04	–
Southeast Europe[b]	9.5	9.40	0.10	9.0	8.91	0.09	12.3	9.43	0.10	2.77

[a] Vauxhall in the United Kingdom.
[b] Southeast Europe in this table includes countries such as Slovenia, Croatia, Bosnia–Herzegovina, Albania, Macedonia, Bulgaria, Romania, Yugoslavia, and Moldova.
Source: Company records.

EXHIBIT 9   Daewoo Matiz

Source: Company records.

EXHIBIT 10   Daewoo Unit Sales in Europe: 1995–2003

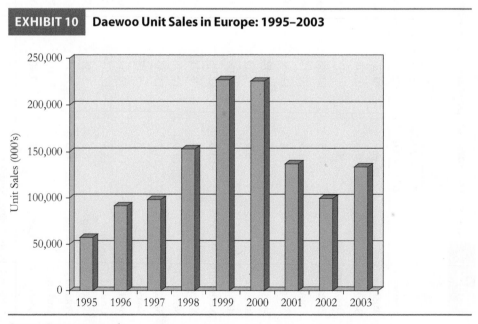

Source: Company records.

GM Daewoo Europe   Financial stability returned to the brand in late 2002 following the formation of GM Daewoo Auto & Technology and GM Daewoo Europe. Unit sales increased to 132,200 passenger cars in 2003. A sizable portion of this sales gain came from southeast European countries. Still, the brand had not reached the sales level that accompanied the Matiz launch in 1998. Product issues remained in the development and quality arena while its car prices had increased. No significant marketing initiatives had been undertaken and brand advertising was limited. According to one General Motors executive at the time, "GM Daewoo's image is still the seller of cheap imported products. We need to focus on the strengths of the brand and avoid selling on price."

In 2003, GM Daewoo Europe commissioned research to examine the perception of the product and brand among GM Daewoo dealers and owners. A summary of this research appears in the form of a SWOT framework shown in Exhibit 11.

GM Daewoo Customers   Qualitative research commissioned by GM Daewoo Europe in 2003 examined both the core and potential GM Daewoo customer. According to this research, core GM Daewoo customers were loyal to the brand. They tended to be traditional in their value orientation. Compared to other car buyers, they choose to spend less of their disposable income on a car purchase. GM Daewoo customers wanted a cost-effective, but expressive means of transportation. As such, they wanted something practical, but distinctive from a car. A car is not a status object for them.

EXHIBIT 11   **GM Daewoo SWOT Analysis in Current Markets: 2003 (Based on GM Daewoo Dealer and Consumer Feedback)**

Strengths	*Opportunities*
• Good design—distinctive, yet in line with European tastes • Great value for the money—good equipment at low price (at least until recently) • Very loyal customer base • Good brand awareness (16 percent) with little prejudice • Favorable image among those who know the brand	• Japanese brands trading up—leaving room on the lower price end of the market • Good reputation of Asian service established by Japanese brands • The GM umbrella (GM Daewoo Europe) • "Stealing" market share from European value brands—especially from Fiat (Italy)
Weaknesses	*Threats*
• A limited product range (especially compared to Hyundai) • No diesel engines • Relatively poor workmanship recently (though improved) • No 0% finance (vs. tough competition) • Lack of brand advertising • Low product awareness beyond Matiz • Lack of consistency (contracts, dealerships) • The lack of any significant marketing or product development initiatives since Nov. 2002	• Erosion of value for the money—e.g., recent decreasing equipment level and increasing price tag • High level of depreciation associated with all Korean brands • Bankruptcy weakening the image • Transition to GM creating confusion and poor satisfaction record among current customer base

Source: Company records.

This research also explored what potential GM Daewoo customers would want from a car brand. Potential GM Daewoo customers want a brand that goes out of its way for them and brings them something distinctive and of decent quality (reliability). They believe car buyers have the right to expect a lot for their hard-earned money. Potential GM Daewoo customers do not want a brand that will stereotype them. Rather, a brand should embrace their desire for individuality and personal expression.

GM Daewoo Positioning Research   An independent positioning study was commissioned after GM Daewoo Europe was formed. The primary objective of this study: to determine which positioning territory was most appealing, relevant, unique, important, and credible. The study consisted of 35 consumer focus groups conducted in five European countries. Six positioning concept terms were tested. The concept terms were *Smart, Honest, Easy, People's Car, Challenger,* and *Spontaneous.* For each concept term, the research identified a target insight, an emotional benefit, a functional benefit, and a brand attitude to be conveyed. The results of this research appear in Exhibit 12. The independent research firm noted that each concept had its strengths and weaknesses. However, the Challenger concept was recommended as the first choice. Smart was the second choice. Action was not taken on this research given the impending brand conversion from GM Daewoo to Chevrolet.

The Chevrolet Brand

The Chevrolet brand is named for Louis Chevrolet, the son of a clockmaker from La Chaux-de-Fonds in Switzerland. In 1901, Louis Chevrolet left his job in a French bicycle shop and migrated to the United States where he enjoyed a successful car racing career in the early 1900s. William Durant, who would create General Motors, approached Louis Chevrolet in 1909 to design a passenger car to compete against the Ford Motor Company. The two men joined forces to form the Chevrolet Motor Car Company on November 11, 1911. The Chevrolet "bowtie" logo appeared for the first time in 1914. According to legend, the bowtie

---

EXHIBIT 12   Results of GM Daewoo Positioning Research in Europe

Positioning Concept Term	Smart	Honest	Easy	People's Car	Challenger	Spontaneous
Target Insight	The savvy shopper	Car realists who want to be treated like humans	The "life comes first" consumer	People with other financial priorities	People up for change	The "anything goes" consumer
Emotional Benefit	Satisfaction (at being a step ahead)	Trust	Freedom	Pride	Breaking through	Instant gratification
Functional Benefit	Best price/value	Open, respectful relationship; agreed value	No-hassle ownership/ convenience	Making it possible by basic price & financial packages/ incentives	Convention overturned; style/value	No more waiting
Brand Attitude	Street smart	A blast of fresh air	Effortless	Democratic	Disruptive	Fleet of foot

Source: Company records.

shape of the logo was inspired by a wallpaper pattern in a Paris hotel room seen by William Durant in 1908 or based on the "shape" of Louis Chevrolet's home country of Switzerland. One in every 16 cars driven in the world today bears the Chevrolet brand name and bowtie logo.

Cross-national research conducted by General Motors identified "expressive value" as a common perception of the Chevrolet brand. Expressive value manifested itself across national boundaries in terms of both passenger car preferences and consumer characteristics.

Car Preferences Car preferences indicative of "expressive value" were uniform across national boundaries. These include:

- Peace of mind
- Cars that are as robust and reliable as possible
- Practical cars—no excessive "frills"
- Cars that perform well in urban settings, for short-distance driving
- Attractive styling
- Friendly dealership personnel

Customer Profile Likewise customers who exhibited these car preferences were common across national boundaries. These included:

- Down-to-earth, unpretentious
- Traditional meaning of life
- Broad age range, often middle-aged, older people
- Mainly married
- Modest formal education
- Blue-collar, working class
- Free time is essentially devoted to the family and improving the home (e.g., do-it-yourself projects, gardening, etc.)
- The family is a place for solidarity, mutual help
- No excessive consumer aspirations, no prestige consumption

Chevrolet Brand in Europe The Chevrolet brand was virtually unknown among European car buyers in early 2004. Research in Europe indicated that less than 1 percent of European car buyers were aware of the Chevrolet brand name and bowtie logo.

Some Project Midas group members considered the lack of Chevrolet brand awareness among European car buyers as a positive finding: The lack of awareness provided a clean slate upon which to position the Chevrolet brand in Europe. On the other hand, some members of the Project Midas group thought that European car buyers might believe Chevrolet brand cars "were not for them due to preconceptions of American cars as gas-guzzling yank tanks."

"What we saw was a potential huge disconnect between the consumer belief about the [Chevrolet] brand and realities of [the GM Daewoo] product portfolio in Europe," said Barbara Rübel, the manager for brand strategy. As an example, a comparison between Opel and GM Daewoo physical product characteristics by car size segment evidenced more similarities than differences. The most observable difference between Opel and GM Daewoo within each car segment was that Opel offered diesel-powered engine models whereas GM Daewoo did not (see Exhibit 13 on page 668). However, Opel was seen as a higher quality and higher priced brand than GM Daewoo: higher price with higher quality.

EXHIBIT 13 **Opel and GM Daewoo Model Product Characteristics and Price Range (Euros) by European Car Size Segment in 2003**

Segment: Microvan

Model	Product Characteristics	Model	Product Characteristics
Opel Agila	Front wheel drive	GM Daewoo Matiz	Front wheel drive
	5-door		5-door hatchback
Price Range:	5-speed manual	Price Range:	5-speed manual
10,000–14,300	2 petrol engines (60–75 hp)	8,000–10,300	2 petrol engines (52–64 hp)
	1 diesel engine (70 hp)		

Segment: Small Car

Model	Product Characteristics	Model	Product Characteristics
Opel Corsa	Front wheel drive	GM Daewoo Kalos	Front wheel drive
	3- and 5-door hatchback		4- and 5-door hatchback
Price Range:	5-speed manual/Easytronic	Price Range:	5-speed manual/
11,000–17,900	4 petrol engines (60–125 hp)	10,000–12,500	4-speed automatic
	2 diesel engines (70–100 hp)		3 petrol engines (72–94 hp)

Segment: Compact

Model	Product Characteristics	Model	Product Characteristics
Opel Astra	Front wheel drive	GM Daewoo Lacetti	Front wheel drive
	5-door hatchback		5-door hatchback
Price Range:	5-speed manual/6-speed manual/	Price Range:	5-speed manual/
15,200–20,100	Easytronic/4-speed automatic	13,500–17,600	4-speed automatic
	4 petrol engines (90–170 hp)		3 petrol engines (93–122 hp)
	2 diesel (turbo) engines (80–100 hp)		

Segment: Compact Van

Model	Product Characteristics	Model	Product Characteristics
Opel Zafira	Front wheel drive	GM Daewoo Rezzo	Front wheel drive
	5-door		5-door
Price Range:	5-speed manual/4-speed automatic	Price Range:	5-speed manual/
13,400–23,400	3 petrol engines (100–147 hp)	12,000–17,300	4-speed automatic
	2 diesel engines (100–125 hp)		2 petrol engines (105–121 hp)

Segment: Medium

Model	Product Characteristics	Model	Product Characteristics
Opel Signum	Front wheel drive	GM Daewoo Evanda	Front wheel drive
	5-door		4-door sedan
Price Range:	5-speed manual/6-speed manual/	Price Range:	5-speed manual/
23,000–28,500	CVT/5-speed automatic	21,000–22,400	4-speed automatic
	4 petrol engines (122–211 hp)		1 petrol engine (131 hp)
	5 diesel (turbo) engines (120–177 hp)		

Source: Company records.

Case

Qingdao Haier Ltd

Considering the Maytag Acquisition

We are paying great attention to events concerning the acquisition of Maytag, but have so far made no decisions yet.

> "Haier Undecided on Maytag Bid as Deadline Looms," Reuters.com, June 17, 2005

In early June 2005, senior executives at Qingdao Haier Ltd., China's largest home appliance maker, faced a major decision. They had to determine whether or not to bid on the purchase of Maytag Corporation, the third-largest U.S. home appliance manufacturer. In May, a private U.S.-based investment group made a $1.13 billion bid to acquire Maytag, which the company agreed to consider. Maytag's Board of Directors was willing to entertain competitive offers.

Acquiring a venerable company like Maytag would put Haier (pronounced HIGH-ER) on the same stage as Lenovo Group Ltd., China's largest computer manufacturer. Lenovo bought IBM's personal computer business for $1.75 billion in late 2004, and became the world's third-largest producer of PCs behind Dell and Hewlett-Packard. The Maytag acquisition would elevate Haier's major home appliance market position in the United States and worldwide.

A decision by Haier to purchase Maytag would be consistent with the Chinese government's encouragement of its large companies to consider overseas acquisitions for the purpose of turning these companies into transnational corporations featuring a single corporate global brand name. For example, IBM PCs would be marketed under the Lenovo name. The Chinese government had named Haier as one of six domestic companies it hoped to transform into one of the world's top 500 companies by 2010. According to Haier's vice president of marketing, "We really want [Haier] to become a first-class brand. It's our business strategy."[1]

---

[1] "'Made in China' Woos World," Chinadaily.com, October 10, 2003.

A decision to purchase Maytag would depend heavily on competitive issues and the marketing opportunity that the Maytag business and assets could provide Haier in the United States and worldwide. At the same time, the strengths and resources that Haier could bring to Maytag warranted consideration. Even though Maytag's market position and profitability in the United States had eroded in recent years, the company was likely to attract other suitors.

 QINGDAO HAIER LTD

Qingdao Haier Ltd., which started out as a nearly bankrupt refrigeration plant (Qingdao Refrigerator Plant), was founded in 1984 with imported refrigerator production technology from Germany's Liberhaier Company. Since then, the company has become one of the top 50 transnational corporations in developing countries. Haier manufactures a wide range of household appliances—15,000 varieties of items in some 90 product lines, including refrigerators, freezers, washing machines and dryers, dishwashers, microwave ovens, and air conditioners, among a number of other products such as television sets and mobile phones—all sold with the Haier brand name. When asked to explain why Haier offered such a diversified portfolio of products under a single brand name, the company's chair and CEO, Zhang Ruimin, said:[2]

> Diversification is still a controversial topic in China. Some people say companies shouldn't diversify, because some manufacturers that were very good in the past died after they diversified. But at Haier we offer a lot of products like refrigerators, air conditioners, washing machines, TVs, and cell phones. We feel that from the consumer's perspective it's not diversification but rather specialization. The target customer group for all these products is one and the same. For example, a consumer satisfied with a refrigerator from Haier is more likely to buy related products from us, too, such as washing machines or air conditioners.

Haier's sales revenue was $12.1 billion in 2004. Household appliances accounted for about 70 percent of the company's sales revenue which has grown rapidly since 2000 (see Exhibit 1).

With a 30 percent share of China's $13 billion household appliance market, Haier is China's dominant household appliance company. It enjoys leading domestic (China) market shares in washing machines, refrigerators, vacuum cleaners, and air conditioners. Haier has built a reputation in its domestic market for product quality, continuous innovation, and customer service and was recently recognized as China's most valuable brand name

| EXHIBIT 1 | Haier Operating Revenues ($ in Billions) |

	Year				
	2000	2001	2002	2003	2004
Operating Revenue	$4.9	$7.3	$8.6	$9.7	$12.1
Growth Rate (yr. over yr.)	–	48%	18%	13%	25%

Source: United States Information Technology Office, Beijing China, June 2005. Operating Revenue expressed in U.S. dollars: $1.00 = 8.27 yuan.

---

[2] Yibing Wu, "Interview: China's Refrigerator Magnate," *The McKinsey Quarterly* (Number 3, 2003).

by *Forbes* magazine. Haier is the world's fifth-largest household appliance company behind U.S.-based Whirlpool Corporation and General Electric, Sweden's Electrolux, and Germany's Bosch-Siemens based on sales revenue. "Our objective is . . . number three," said Zhang Ruimin.[3] Haier has the world's largest unit brand share for refrigerators and is the world's second-largest volume producer of household appliances.

Haier Worldwide

The company markets its Haier-branded products in 160 countries with global networks for design, production, distribution, and after-sales service. The company operates 18 design institutes (8 outside China), 10 industrial complexes (4 outside China), 12,000 after-sale service centers, and 22 factories (13 outside China) that produce mostly home appliances.

Global Markets
The consumer and competitive environment for Haier varies significantly across regions of the world.[4] North America (United States and Canada) is the largest market for large household appliances in the world based on dollar sales. It is also the most "mature" region in the world for these appliances based on household saturation levels (saturation level refers to the percentage of households that own a particular appliance). For instance, refrigerators and cooking equipment (excluding microwaves) are present in virtually 100 percent of North American households. Washing machines are found in 94 percent of households and clothes dryers are owned by 81 percent of households. Four manufacturers account for over 90 percent of large household appliance sales in North America. Whirlpool is the market share leader. The remaining three companies are General Electric, Maytag, and Electrolux, which markets the Frigidaire brand in the United States. Haier's market share in the North American market is about three percent.

The Western and Eastern European market has household saturation levels for most large household appliances that are roughly half of what they are in North America. Thirty-five companies manufacture home appliances for this market. No one company has a commanding market share. The largest competitors in Europe are Electrolux with a 16.2 percent market share, followed by Bosch-Siemens (15.2 percent share), Italy's Indesit Company (14.7 percent share), and Whirlpool (8.6 percent share). Haier's market share in the Western and Eastern European market is close to 2 percent.

Asia is the world's largest consumer market for large household appliances in terms of population and potential spending power. Industry analysts believe that consumers in Asia could purchase as many or more appliances as North American and Western European consumers by 2025 given the low saturation levels for home appliances, particularly in China and Southeast Asia. China is already the world's biggest unit volume market for refrigerators. The potential in China and Southeast Asia has attracted 50 appliance manufacturers to the region, sparked intense price competition, and eroded company profit margins. Matsushita Electric Industrial is the largest appliance supplier in Japan, Haier is China's leading producer, and Whirlpool captures nearly one-third of

---

[3] "Interview: China's Refrigerator Magnate."

[4] Portions of this discussion are based on "Comparative Regional Strengths of Major Players: Large Kitchen Appliances"; "Global Sector Shares: Large Kitchen Appliances—Manufacturer & Brand," Euromonitor.com, January and February, 2004; and "China's Home Appliances Industry: 2004," Asia Case Research Centre, The University of Hong Kong, 2005.

the appliance market in India. Haier is the leader in Asia with about 10 percent of the Asian market for household appliances.

Australasia (Australia and New Zealand) evidences household saturation levels for major appliances that are similar to Western Europe. About 15 appliance manufacturers compete in this market. Electrolux captures about 28 percent of this market, followed by South Korea's LG Electronics (10 percent), Maytag (6 percent), and Whirlpool (5 percent). Haier's market share is about 1 percent.

Latin America is considered to be a future growth market for large household appliances, according to industry analysts. There are 25 home appliance manufacturers in Latin America. Whirlpool and its majority-owned subsidiaries capture about 33 percent of the Latin American large household appliance market—far more than its nearest rivals with barely double-digit market shares. Some Chinese competitors, such as Wuxi Little Swan Company Ltd., have targeted Latin America as a growth opportunity. Haier's Latin American market share is under 2 percent.

Perspective on Global Marketing   The thinking behind Haier's strategy for expanding into global markets was recently described by Zhang Ruimin:[5]

> The objective of most Chinese enterprises is to export products and earn foreign currency. This is their only purpose. Our purpose in exporting is to establish a brand reputation overseas. We have created an important brand in China, and we are taking that brand to other markets. In other ways, too, our strategy is very different from that of other export-oriented Chinese enterprises. They will usually explore easier markets first and difficult markets later. Many Chinese enterprises will first export to Southeast Asia, for instance, which has competitive markets but where there are no strong, dominant competitors, as there often are in Western markets. But our strategy is the other way around: we go to easier markets after we first penetrate difficult markets such as the United States and Europe. These are much bigger markets. They are also the home markets of our largest global competitors, and we believe that if we can succeed there we can succeed in easier markets. Haier started exporting to the United States in 1990; it has been more than ten years now and the results have been good. We've established a brand reputation in the U.S. market and earn higher margins on sales, while many Chinese companies can do only OEM work for foreign brands and manufacturers, at lower margins.

He went on to say:

> All success relies on one thing in overseas markets—creating a localized brand name. We have to make Americans feel that Haier is a localized U.S. brand instead of an imported Chinese brand. The same goes for the European market. It's very difficult to set up a name brand. But if you don't take this road, you will always work for others.

The presence of Chinese brands in the global marketplace is a relatively recent phenomenon, compared with Japanese global corporate brands (e.g., Sony, Canon, Nintendo, and Honda) and South Korean global corporate brands (e.g., Samsung, LG Electronics, and Hyundai). Cross national research generally supports the view that Western consumers (North Americans and Western Europeans) are open to Chinese-brand products—if they offer something unique.[6] In the United States, 36 percent of consumers associate Chinese

---

[5] "Interview: China's Refrigerator Magnate."

[6] Geoffry A. Fowler, "Buying Spree by China Firms Is a Bet on Value of U.S. Brands," *Wall Street Journal* (June 23, 2005):A1, A6.

brands with low cost (price) products, 26 percent associate them with innovation, and 24 percent associate them with advanced features and good value for the money.

Haier America

Haier America is the U.S. sales and marketing division of Qingdao Haier Ltd.[7] Haier America's headquarters is located in New York City, which also houses a research and development laboratory, and product showrooms. Camden, South Carolina, is the site of the Haier America Industrial Park that includes a state-of-the-art refrigerator manufacturing facility capable of producing 400,000 refrigerators annually. Haier is the first Chinese company to open a factory in the United States. A U.S. factory also allows Haier to stick a "Made in the U.S.A." label on its refrigeration products.

Haier began exporting refrigerators to the United States under several brand names, including Welbilt. In 1999, it began marketing its appliances under the Haier brand name with the creation of Haier America, a joint venture involving a U.S. investor group and Haier, the majority partner. Since its formation, Haier America sales have grown rapidly and are expected to approach $1 billion in 2005. The company's success has been attributed to product feature innovation, quick product design and delivery in response to retailer needs, competitive prices, product quality, and the development of new product categories in the household appliance market that larger U.S. manufacturers overlooked. In the span of five years, Haier America has achieved commanding unit market shares in several niche appliance categories including compact refrigerators under 6.5 cubic feet (50 percent), compact chest freezers under 7 cubic feet (38 percent), and freestanding refrigerated wine cellars (50 percent). Haier America captures 10 percent of the U.S. refrigerator market and 9 percent of the freezer market. In addition, the company markets Haier-brand air conditioners, clothes washers and dryers, dishwashers, and microwave and convection ovens, among other appliances. Haier America expects to roll out 24 new washers and dryers and 15 new dishwashers in 2005, up from 12 washers and dryers and six dishwashers it sold in 2004. The company does not market conventional ovens or ranges in the United States.

Haier America distributes its household appliances primarily through national chain retailers in the United States. These include Walmart, Lowe's, Target, Sears, and Best Buy. Exhibit 2 on page 674 shows Haier-branded products sold through these retailers. Walmart carries the most complete line of Haier-brand products. Haier America also sells selected Haier-branded appliances through regional chains such as BrandsMart and Menards and some items at specialty chain stores, including Bed Bath & Beyond and Linens 'n Things.

Haier America generally prices its products below Whirlpool, General Electric, and Maytag brands. However, the products are not necessarily deeply discounted. The company also budgets limited funds for media advertising. About 80 percent of Haier America's advertising budget of roughly $7.5 million goes toward retailer-directed campaigns, such as print advertisements in appliance trade magazines.

---

[7] Portions of this discussion are based on HaierAmerica.com, downloaded June 17, 2005; Andy Raskin, "When Your Customer Says Jump . . ." *Business 2.0* (October 2003):78–80; Jonathan Sprague, "Haier Reaches Higher," *Fortune* (September 5, 2002):148–153; and Cheryl Lu-Lien Tan, "The New Asian Imports: Your Washer and Drier," WSJ.com, June 16, 2005.

EXHIBIT 2	Haier-Brand Products Sold by National Retail Chains (June 2005)
Retail Chain	*Products Sold*
Best Buy	Compact refrigerator; portable dishwasher; freestanding clothes washer and dryer; portable air conditioner; refrigerated beer dispenser, and wine cellar
Lowe's	Refrigerated wine cellar
Target	Built-in and portable dishwasher; compact and full-size refrigerator and freezer; refrigerated wine cellar and beer dispenser; microwave oven; freestanding clothes washer and dryer
Sears	Countertop portable dishwasher
Walmart	Compact and full-size refrigerator and freezer; portable air conditioner and dehumidifier; microwave oven; refrigerated wine cellar; beverage center; beer dispenser; compact dishwasher; freestanding clothes washer

Source: Retailer Web sites, downloaded June 5, 2005.

In interviews related to the Haier America marketing strategy in the United States, Michael Jemal, the company's CEO, is quoted as saying:[8]

> Our primary purpose and goal is to develop the Haier brand in the U.S. . . . We promote Haier as a global brand—not Chinese or American, but global. In fact, most people think it is a German brand. Our slogan is "What the World Comes Home To." . . . Right now we are displacing the derivative brands owned by the top three players—Amana owned by Maytag, Hotpoint owned by GE, and Roper owned by Whirlpool.

THE LARGE HOUSEHOLD APPLIANCE INDUSTRY IN THE UNITED STATES

The U.S. large household appliance industry consists of manufacturers, distributors (wholesalers and retailers), and consumers that produce, sell, and buy refrigeration and cooling appliances, home laundry appliances, dishwashers and trash compactors, and large cooking appliances, including microwave ovens.[9] In 2004, U.S. consumers spent $30.5 billion for these appliances, which represented an 8.9 percent increase over 2003. The Association of Home Appliance Manufacturers reports that total shipments for large household appliances increased 7.5 percent to 79.2 million units in 2004. Exhibit 3 shows U.S. appliance shipment data for the period 2000 to 2004 and year-end projections for 2005 and 2006.

---

[8] "Mainland Brands Think Globally," English.eastday.com, downloaded June 15, 2005; "Haier in America," Kotler Marketing Group, April 2002.

[9] Portions of this discussion are based on "Household Durables," *Standard & Poor's Industry Surveys*, March 17, 2005; *A New Deal for Durables*, (Boston: The Boston Consulting Group, 2005); "Large Kitchen Appliances in the USA," Euromonitor.com, June 2004; and "Where to Buy Appliances," *Consumer Reports* (September 2005):32–34.

EXHIBIT 3	Industry Shipments of Major Appliances: Trends and Forecasts—2000 to 2006 (Thousands of Units)						
Product Category	*2000*	*2001*	*2002*	*2003*	*2004*	*2005ᴱ*	*2006ᴱ*
Cooking—Total	**20,846**	**21,548**	**21,917**	**23,315**	**25,390**	**25,141**	**25,760**
Electric Ranges—Total	5,026	5,066	5,338	5,622	6,145	6,265	6,361
Free-Standing	3,826	3,842	4,030	4,238	4,612	4,690	4,757
Built-In	706	726	7780	841	963	996	1,016
Surface Cooking Units	494	498	528	543	570	579	588
Gas Ranges—Total	3,176	3,036	3,268	3,419	3,719	3,802	3,914
Free-Standing	2,729	2,580	2,781	2,897	3,124	3,185	3,280
Built-In	70	72	71	67	67	67	67
Surface Cooking Units	377	384	416	455	528	550	567
Microwave Ovens	12,644	13,446	13,311	14,274	15,526	15,074	15,485
Home Laundry—Total	**14,070**	**13,863**	**14,637**	**15,480**	**16,754**	**16,959**	**17,412**
Automatic Washers	7,495	7,362	7,745	8,146	8,832	8,932	9,111
Dryers—Total	6,575	6,501	6,892	7,334	7,922	8,027	8,301
Electric	5,095	5,117	5,402	5,718	6,262	6,350	6,603
Gas	1,480	1,384	1,490	1,616	1,660	1,677	1,698
Kitchen Clean-Up—Total	**11,430**	**11,291**	**12,137**	**12,831**	**13,884**	**14,203**	**14,413**
Disposers	5,485	5,547	5,815	6,277	6,649	6,700	6,775
Dishwashers	5,827	5,627	6,207	6,428	7,106	7,377	7,513
Built-In	5,663	5,478	6,049	6,280	6,953	7,231	7,367
Portable	164	149	158	148	153	146	146
Compactors	118	117	115	126	129	126	125
Food Preservation—Total	**11,180**	**11,520**	**12,279**	**12,544**	**13,429**	**13,458**	**13,760**
Refrigerators	9,217	9,305	9,744	10,021	10,913	11,019	11,246
Freezers—Total	1,863	2,215	2,535	2,523	2,516	2,439	2,514
Chest	1,075	1,285	1,492	1,518	1,529	1,463	1,510
Upright	888	930	1,043	1,005	987	976	1,004
Home Comfort—Total	**7,471**	**6,381**	**6,952**	**9,527**	**9,754**	**7,819**	**8,726**
Room Air Conditioners	6,496	5,575	6,153	8,216	8,082	6,500	7,400
Dehumidifiers	975	806	799	1,311	1,672	1,319	1,326
Total Shipments	**64,997**	**64,603**	**67,922**	**73,697**	**79,211**	**77,580**	**80,071**
AHAM 6***	**38,408**	**38,230**	**40,785**	**42,495**	**46,055**	**46,732**	**47,805**

ᴱ Includes shipments for the U.S. market whether imported or domestically produced. Export Shipments are *not* included. Forecasts as of April 30, 2005. Forecasts are a median of the participating companies' forecasts.

Includes units of 6.5 cu. ft. and over.

Total industry shipments may not add due to rounding.

*** The AHAM 6 includes: Washers, Dryers, Dishwashers, Refrigerators, Freezers, and Free-Standing and Built-In Ranges.

Source: Copyright © 2005 Association of Home Appliance Manufacturers. Used with permission.

Manufacturers and Manufacturing

Four manufacturers dominate the core U.S. household appliance market, which consists of clothes washers and dryers, refrigerators, freezers, dishwashers, and freestanding and built-in ranges. Whirlpool claimed 33.4 percent of the U.S. market in 2004, followed by General Electric, with a 25.7 percent market share. Electrolux's Frigidaire Home Products division posted a 19.0 percent market share. Maytag had a 15.1 percent market share. These four companies accounted for 93.2 percent of the U.S. core appliance market in 2004. However, manufacturer market share varied by product category. Measured by unit volume, the largest core appliance category is refrigerators. Here, General Electric was the market leader with a 29 percent market share, followed by Electrolux with its Frigidaire brand (25 percent), and Whirlpool (25 percent). The second largest category, washing machines, was led by Whirlpool, with 51 percent of the market, followed by Maytag (20 percent), and General Electric (17 percent).

Although not a core appliance, microwave ovens represented a sizable unit volume. In 2004, the U.S. market share leaders were Asian companies LG Electronics (with 38 percent of the microwave oven market), Sharp Electronics Corporation (23 percent), and Samsung Electronics (11 percent). Whirlpool was the top U.S. manufacturer with a market share of 4 percent. Exhibit 4 details the U.S. market shares of large household appliance manufacturers by product category.

Appliance production is capital intensive and there are significant initial and ongoing cash costs for manufacturing plants. For example, the capital investment necessary to build a new appliance manufacturing facility from scratch ranges between $200 and $800 million, depending on capacity and the appliance made. Accordingly, manufacturers often add to or retool existing manufacturing plants. The capital investment necessary to modify or upgrade an existing facility ranges between $55 and $75 million.

Appliance manufacturing facilities are highly mechanized, with assembly lines designed for long production runs. Manufacturing fixed cost of operations is high. Variable cost consists mostly of raw materials (steel, aluminum, packing materials, energy, etc.), shipping, and labor. Raw materials account for about 60 percent of a manufacturer's cost of goods sold; labor represents about 20 percent. Rising raw material costs since 2002 have depressed manufacturer gross profit margins worldwide, which historically fluctuated between 21 and 24 percent. Even lower labor cost manufacturers, such as Haier, have recorded smaller gross profit margins due to rising material cost. For example, Haier's gross profit margin in 2004 for air conditioners fell to 11.2 percent from 12.4 percent in 2003. Its gross profit margin for refrigerators declined to 16.5 percent from 19.2 percent.[10] At the same time, manufacturers have encountered competitive pressure and retailer demands to reduce home appliance prices. Prices for major household appliances in the United States declined 3 percent on average in 2004, following a 3.7 percent decline in 2003.

Distributors and Distribution Channels

Appliance manufacturers in the United States distribute their products to consumers through chain retailers, independent appliance retailers, and distributors/wholesalers. About 70 percent of appliance manufacturer sales in the United States are to chain retailers. Sears is the largest home appliance retailer, with a 38.6 percent retail market share, due to the wide range of brands and models it

---

[10] "News & Commentary: Haier," Bloomberg.com, June 21, 2005.

EXHIBIT 4 U.S. Market Shares of Major Household Appliance Manufacturers by Product: 2004 (Unit Sales)

Product Major Manufacturers	Market Share (%)	Product Major Manufacturers	Market Share (%)
Refrigerators		Dishwashers	
General Electric	29	Whirlpool	33
Whirlpool	25	General Electric	29
Electrolux	25	Electrolux	19
Maytag	11	Maytag	16
Haier	10	Washers	
Freezers		Whirlpool	51
Electrolux	68	Maytag	20
W. C. Wood	21	General Electric	17
Haier	9	Electric Dryers	
Microwave Ovens		Whirlpool	56
LG Electronics	28	Maytag	19
Sharp	23	General Electric	14
Samsung	11	Gas Dryers	
Daewoo	10	Whirlpool	55
Electric Ranges		Maytag	25
General Electric	49	General Electric	11
Whirlpool	23		
Maytag	12		
Gas Ranges			
General Electric	36		
Electrolux	27		
Maytag	18		

Source: Case author estimates based on "Household Durables," *Standard & Poors' Industry Surveys,* March 17, 2005, and interviews with appliance industry analysts.

carries, including its own Kenmore brand appliances, a large portion of which are made by Whirlpool. However, its retail share has declined from 42 percent in 2002. Lowe's is the second largest appliance retailer, with a 13.8 percent market share, followed by Home Depot (8.1 percent) and Best Buy (6 percent). Lowe's, Home Depot, and Best Buy increased their combined home appliance retail market share from 22 percent in 2002. Walmart Stores, the world's largest retailer, ranks seventh in major home appliance sales and its Sam's Club ranks ninth. Chain retailers purchase appliances directly from manufacturers and operate warehouses to stock inventories for truck delivery to stores.

Independent appliance retailers account for 25 percent of home appliance sales, down from 30 percent in 2002. These retailers, like Sears, typically sell appliances at the manufacturer's suggested retail price, drawing customers with well-stocked inventories and knowledgeable salespeople. In contrast, Home Depot and Walmart often sell appliances at a discount on the manufacturer's suggested retail price. About 85 percent of independent appliance retailers purchase their products through national buying groups. A buying group is organized by small- and medium-size appliance retailers to purchase products in higher volumes from producers, and achieve price discounts equivalent to larger national retail chains. A buying group also enhances efficiency by combining warehousing or distributor functions.

Distributors and wholesalers sell appliances to commercial buyers, such as builders and contractors, who install appliances in mostly homes and apartments. They account for about 5 percent of home appliance sales. Exhibit 5 displays the distribution channels for large household appliances in the United States along with the percentage of dollar sales sold through each.

Marketing Practices

Major U.S. appliance manufacturers offer a complete appliance product line in the United States. Each line (e.g., clothes dryers) contains multiple models with different features, sizes, colors, performance specifications (e.g., energy efficiency), and configurations (e.g., top-loaded vs. front-loaded dryers).

Manufacturers position their products along a "price–quality" continuum using sub-branding and multibranding strategies. For example, each major manufacturer has a flagship corporate brand (e.g., General Electric, Maytag, and

EXHIBIT 5 **Home Appliance Distribution Channels in the United States and Dollar Sales Breakdown**

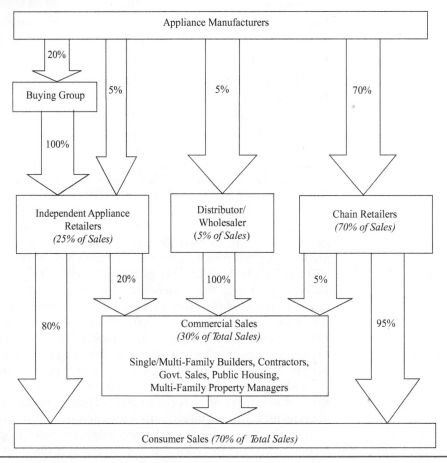

Sources: Case author estimates based on "Household Durables," *Standard & Poors' Industry Surveys*, March 17, 2005, and interviews with appliance industry analysts.

Whirlpool). These manufacturers use sub-branding to differentiate individual products within the corporate brand line. For example, General Electric uses sub-branding featuring the GE *Momentum* sub-brand targeted at the high-end market. The Maytag *Neptune* sub-branded clothes dryer with numerous value-added features is priced higher than Maytag's conventional dryer. Home Depot sells the Maytag *Neptune* for between $999 and $1,069, depending on model. In contrast, the retailer sells conventional Maytag dryers for between $799 and $869.

Manufacturers also employ multibrand strategies. Different brand names are used to further differentiate products along the price–quality continuum. For instance, Whirlpool markets the "higher-end" Kitchen Aid brand and a "lower-end" Roper brand, along with its corporate brand in the United States. General Electric and Maytag also market lower-end brands such as Hotpoint and Admiral, respectively. This multibrand strategy often parallels distribution strategies. As an example, Maytag mostly markets its high-end Jenn-Air brand products through independent appliance retailers and through wholesalers/distributors to builders and contractors. Maytag recently pulled its "midlevel" Amana brand out of Lowe's and Best Buy. The company now distributes the brand through independent appliance retailers to convey a more upscale market position. By and large, major U.S. household appliance manufacturers derive the bulk of their sales from products bearing the corporate brand. Non-U.S. manufacturers employ a corporate brand exclusively and avoid multibranding. The Frigidaire brand marketed by Electrolux in the United States is a notable exception.

South Korean electronics manufacturers, LG Electronics and Samsung, entered the U.S. household appliance market in the last three years. Both companies first introduced refrigerators, followed by clothes washers and dishwashers, positioned in the mid- to higher-end level on the price–quality continuum with an emphasis on styling and electronics. LG Electronics and Samsung intend to offer a full line of large household appliances for the U.S. market under their corporate brand name. According to industry sources, LG Electronics has its sights on becoming the number one or two appliance manufacturer in the United States by differentiating itself as a fashion and innovation brand.[11] For example, it offers a $3,000+ refrigerator that features a 13.1-inch flat-panel, cable-ready, LCD television with built-in radio and speakers. LG Electronics and Samsung branded household appliances are sold at Home Depot and Best Buy.

Large household appliance manufacturers spend, on average, about 1.4 percent of their dollar sales on consumer brand advertising in the United States.[12] Advertising focuses on introducing and positioning new models and building or sustaining overall corporate brand equity. Exhibit 6 shows the estimated U.S. advertising

EXHIBIT 6 | **U.S. Appliance Manufacturer Advertising Dollar Expenditures in the United States: 2001–2004 ($ in Millions)**

Manufacturer	Year			
	2004	2003	2002	2001
Whirlpool	$63.7	$44.3	$11.4	$59.6
General Electric	$36.0	$42.7	$22.8	$20.7
Maytag	$101.9	$105.7	$115.0	$88.2

Source: Case author estimates from company annual reports.

[11] Karl Greenberg, "Upmarket Tacks Avoid a Washout," *BRANDWEEK* (June 23, 2003):S18.

[12] "2004 Advertising to Sales Ratios for 200 Largest Ad Spending Industries," AdAge.com, June 5, 2005.

expenditures for U.S.-based appliance manufacturers for the period 2001 to 2004. Maytag is the largest home appliance advertiser in the United States.

Appliance Buying Behavior

Large household appliances in the United States are infrequently purchased due to their durability. Most purchases involve replacement of an existing appliance. Approximately 70 percent of large household appliance sales through retail chains are replacement purchases. The majority of these replacement purchases are due to appliance failure. Thirty percent of appliance sales are discretionary or first-time purchases. Buying behavior at independent appliance retailers is slightly different. About 47 percent of appliance purchases arise from appliance failure. The remaining 53 percent of purchases are due to remodeling (17 percent), first-time purchasers (15 percent), upgrading for additional features (11 percent), and moving (10 percent). Large household appliance brand selection also differs between retail chains and independent appliance retailers. According to *Consumer Reports*, about 10 percent of Sears shoppers choose a different brand than they planned after visiting the store. Just 1.5 percent of independent appliance store shoppers bought an unplanned brand.

Industry research on buying behavior indicates that appliance replacement buyers purchase the same brand more often than not. Interestingly, as the time interval between the original purchase and the replacement purchase increases, the incidence of buying the same brand increases. When shopping stores for large household appliances, U.S. consumers rank product selection as a store's most important attribute, which includes the size of a store's appliance display area and brand availability. "Getting the best price" is ranked second. Convenience, including store location and hours, ranks third. The fourth most important attribute is service and knowledge that a retailer will stand behind its products. Industry analysts attribute Sears' high retail market share for large household appliances to this factor, in addition to brand availability and display area, since Sears does not offer the lowest household appliance prices at its stores.

Appliance product preferences in the United States are also changing. According to a recent *Boston Consulting Group* study, household durable goods consumers are either "trading-up to affordable luxuries" or "trading-down to products that offer low-cost functional benefits." "Stuck in the middle" products that provide neither a price advantage nor a functional or emotional benefit are in grave danger of declining sales. This view is consistent with large household appliance industry data showing the market share growth of "high-end" and "low-end" appliances on the product price–quality continuum and the market share decline of midlevel appliances (see Exhibit 7). According to one retail appliance analyst, "The middle is thinning. [Consumers] buy the opening price point or just go to the high end."

 ## MAYTAG CORPORATION

Maytag Corporation is a *Fortune* 500 (#410) company headquartered in Newton, Iowa.[13] The company was formed in 1893 by F. L. Maytag and three associates to produce feeder attachments for grain threshing machines. In 1907, the company produced its first washing machine, a hand-cranked wooden tub model.

---

[13] This discussion is based on Maytag Corporation, Form 10-K, filed February 18, 2005, and Form 10-K filed April 22, 2005; "Maytag Corporation," Hoovers.com, downloaded June 17, 2005; *Standard & Poors' Industry Surveys*, March 17, 2005; and Lorie Grant, "Maytag Stores Let Shoppers Try Before They Buy," USAtoday.com, downloaded June 6, 2004.

| EXHIBIT 7 | Large Household Appliance Share by Price–Quality Segment |

| Price–Quality | Year | | |
Segment	1995	2000	2004
High-end	22%	30%	35%
Midrange	55	45	31
Low-end	23	25	34
Total	100%	100%	100%

Source: Case author estimates based on charts shown in "Stepping Up: Middle Market Shrinks as Americans Migrate Toward the High End," *Wall Street Journal* (March 29, 2002), pp. Alff; and "A New Deal for Durables," Boston: The Boston Consulting Group, 2005.

The Company: 2004

Maytag designs, manufactures, sells, and services home and commercial appliances in North America and in selected international markets. In 2004, 94 percent of consolidated Maytag sales were to the home appliance market; 6 percent were to the commercial market. Eighty-eight percent of consolidated company sales were in the United States; 12 percent of sales were in other countries.

Home Appliances Maytag brands are among the most recognizable and respected names in the U.S. large household appliance market. Over the years, the company positioned its flagship Maytag corporate brand as a premium midpriced market entry based on product quality (notably dependability) and innovative product features. The company's long-running "Lonely Maytag Repairman" advertising campaign, featuring a rarely called service person for Maytag appliances, effectively conveyed this positioning. In addition to the Maytag brand, the company markets the value-priced Admiral and Magic Chef brands, the midlevel Amana brand, and the high-end Jenn-Air brand. Maytag's vice president of marketing differentiated its non-value brands as follows:[14]

> For Amana, its characteristics include craftsmanship, convenience, and styling.
> For Maytag, it's dependability, product performance, and intelligent innovation.
> And for Jenn-Air, it's kitchen performance and product elegance.

The company also owns the Hoover brand, which is well known for vacuum cleaners. Hoover is the North American floor care products market leader.

Maytag sold its home appliances through large chain retailers (Sears, Home Depot, Best Buy, and Lowe's) and numerous independent appliance retailers and distributors in 2004. Among national chain retailers, Sears accounted for about 13 percent of consolidated Maytag sales in 2004 (down from 15 percent in 2003). Home Depot and Lowe's each account for about 10 percent of consolidated Maytag sales. Best Buy accounts for 1 percent of consolidated company sales. Maytag did not distribute its brands through Walmart or Target.

Maytag also has a retail presence with its Maytag stores. The stores are independently run, in some cases by owners of existing appliance stores who want to expand with a separate Maytag location. Appliance shoppers are encouraged to use Maytag products in the stores by baking cookies or washing and drying a load of clothes. "The environment lets us showcase the product," said a Maytag executive of the 50 stores opened since 2000.

---

[14] Joe Jancsurak, "Marketing Challenges," ammagazine.com, August 2002.

Commercial Products   Maytag also manufactures and sells commercial-grade cooking equipment under the Jade brand name and vending equipment under the Dixie-Narco brand name. These products are primarily sold to distributors, soft drink bottlers (Coca-Cola and PepsiCo), restaurant chains, and dealers in the United States.

Manufacturing   Maytag manufactures about 75 percent of its products in the United States (compared with about 50 percent for General Electric and Whirlpool). The company has offices and 13 manufacturing facilities in Arkansas, California, Illinois, Iowa, Ohio, South Carolina, Tennessee, and Texas. The company operates two manufacturing facilities in Mexico. In late 2004, Maytag manufacturing facilities were operating at roughly 60 percent of their productive capacity.

Maytag outsources some of its appliance manufacturing to South Korean companies. Since 2003, Daewoo Electronics has custom manufactured top-freezer refrigerators for Maytag. Samsung recently began producing front-loading washers. Both products carry the Maytag name and are sold through existing Maytag distribution channels. Maytag disposed of its 50.5 percent stake in Rongshida-Maytag, a Chinese producer of washing machines and refrigerators, in 2002 following lackluster performance of the joint venture.

Global Presence   Maytag has a modest global business with 12 percent of its total sales from non-U.S. markets. By comparison, about 35 percent of Whirlpool sales are from non-U.S. markets. Maytag embarked on a major globalization initiative in the late 1980s with an emphasis on Western European markets. However, following aggressive competition from Sweden's Electrolux and Germany's Bosch-Siemens, the company shut down its European operations in 1995. Today, Maytag is estimated to have modest market shares (less than 1 percent) in Western Europe and Latin America and a respectable market share (6 percent) in Australasia. It has no material market presence in China, Southeast Asia, or Eastern Europe.

Financial Performance   Maytag's consolidated net sales in 2004 totaled $4.7 billion—a 1.5 percent decline from 2003 sales. Home appliance sales were down $40 million, or 0.9 percent compared to 2003. Commercial product sales declined by $30.4 million, or 10.4 percent compared to 2003. Maytag's overall gross profit in 2004 was $660.2 million, or $799.3 million less than 2003. Consolidated operating income declined to $40.4 million, or 0.9 percent of net sales in 2004 from $228.3 million, or 4.8 percent of net sales in 2003. Ongoing restructuring efforts since 2001 were a major expense and reduced Maytag's operating income over the past three years. Home appliance operating income declined to $47.4 million, or 1.1 percent of net sales in 2004 and from $212.3 million, or 4.7 percent of net sales in 2003. Commercial products registered an operating loss of $7.1 million in 2004 compared to an operating income of $16 million in 2003. Maytag consolidated financial statements for 2002, 2003, and 2004 appear in Exhibit 8. The company also reported that "[unit] sales of major appliances increased slightly in 2004 compared to the prior year but market share declined in all categories in a strong industry."[15] In fact, Maytag's U.S. retail market share has eroded since 2001. Maytag's CEO also said that market share in home appliances suffered as a result of competitors offering better trade margins to retailers.[16]

---

[15] Maytag Corporation, Form 10-K, p. 8.

[16] Karl Greenberg, "Newbies Load Up, Put Squeeze on Big Four," *BRANDWEEK* (June 20, 2005):S23.

(A) Maytag Corporation Consolidated Balance Sheets ($ in Thousands)

	Year-End		
	January 1, 2005	January 3, 2004	December 28, 2003
ASSETS			
Current assets			
Cash and cash equivalents	$164,276	$6,756	$8,106
Accounts receivable, less allowance for doubtful accounts	629,901	596,832	586,447
Inventories	515,321	468,345	468,433
Other current assets	135,999	232,390	260,613
Total current assets	$1,445,497	$1,304,323	$1,323,599
Noncurrent Assets			
Deferred income taxes	$253,428	$183,685	$190,726
Goodwill	259,413	269,013	280,952
Other noncurrent assets	140,524	220,184	242,864
Total noncurrent assets	$653,365	$672,882	$714,542
Property, plant, and equipment			
Land	$15,489	$23,365	$24,532
Buildings and Equipment	2,229,680	2,605,620	2,470,376
	$2,245,169	$2,628,985	$2,492,908
Less accumulated depreciation	1,324,007	1,582,050	1,428,800
Total property, plant, and equipment	$921,162	$1,046,935	$1,066,108
Total assets	$3,020,024	$3,024,140	$3,104,249
LIABILITIES AND SHAREOWNERS' EQUITY (Deficit)			
Current liabilities			
Notes payable	$–	$71,491	$178,559
Accounts payable	545,901	466,734	363,639
Other current liabilities	364,162	445,565	621,542
Total current liabilities	$910,063	$983,790	$1,163,740
Noncurrent liabilities			
Long-term debt, less current portion	$972,568	$874,832	$738,767
Postretirement benefit liability	531,995	538,105	517,510
Accrued pension cost	496,480	398,495	488,751
Other noncurrent liabilities	183,942	163,107	153,342
Total noncurrent liabilities	$2,184,985	$1,974,539	$1,898,370
Shareowners' equity (deficit)	$(75,024)	$65,811	$42,139
Total liabilities and shareowners' equity (deficit)	$3,020,024	$3,024,140	$3,104,249

(continued)

EXHIBIT 8 *(Continued)*

(B) Maytag Corporation Consolidated Statements of Operations ($ in Thousands)

	Year-End		
	January 1, 2005	January 3, 2004	December 28, 2003
Net sales	$4,721,538	$4,791,866	$4,666,031
Cost of sales	4,061,319	3,932,335	3,661,429
Gross profit	660,219	859,531	1,004,602
Selling, general and administrative expenses	507,013	555,092	577,995
Restructuring and related charges	69,758	64,929	67,112
Asset impairment	–	11,217	–
Goodwill impairment—Commercial products	9,600	–	–
Front-load washer litigation	33,500	–	–
Operating income	40,348	228,293	359,495
Interest expense	(56,274)	(52,763)	(62,390)
Other income (loss)	(5,392)	4,415	(1,449)
Income (loss) from continuing operations before income taxes	(21,318)	172,760	295,656
Income tax expense (benefit)	(11,973)	58,382	100,523
Income (loss) from continuing operations	(9,345)	114,378	191,401
Gain (loss) from discontinued operations	339	5,755	(2,607)
Net income (loss)	$(9,006)	$ 120,133	$188,794
Earnings per common share	$(.11)	$ 1.53	$ 2.43

(C) Maytag Corporation Consolidated Statements of Cash Flows ($ in Thousands)

	Year-End		
	January 1, 2005	January 3, 2004	December 28, 2003
Operating activities			
Net income (loss)	$(9,006)	$120,133	$188,794
Depreciation and amortization	169,782	165,785	163,708
Accounts receivable	(29,207)	1,403	35,211
Other current liabilities	139,386	67,061	(22,996)
Net cash provided by continuing operating activities	$270,955	$354,382	$364,717
Investing activities			
Capital expenditures—continuing operations	$(94,420)	$(199,300)	$(229,764)
Settlement of Amana purchase contract	–	11,939	–
Proceeds from business and property disposition	25,495	16,168	–
Investing activities—continuing operations	$(68,921)	$(171,193)	$(229,764)
Financing activities			
Net proceeds (reduction) of notes payable	$(71,491)	$(107,068)	$30,312
Proceeds from issuance of long-term debt	100,000	200,000	–
Dividends on common stock	(56,899)	(56,524)	(56,010)
Other	(16,323)	(221,067)	(211,245)
Financing activities—continuing operations	$(44,713)	$(184,659)	$(236,943)
Effect of exchange rates on cash	199	120	726
Increase (decrease) in cash and cash equivalents	157,520	(1,350)	(101,264)
Cash and cash equivalents at beginning of year	6,756	8,106	109,370
Cash and cash equivalents at end of year	$164,276	$6,756	$8,106
Cash flows from discontinued operations	$(5,811)	$3,014	$(4,727)

Source: Maytag Corporation, Form 10-K reports.

The Company: First Quarter 2005

Maytag reported first quarter 2005 consolidated net sales of $1.17 billion. Consolidated net sales decreased 4.2 percent compared with first quarter 2004 results. Net sales declined 2.8 percent in Home Appliances and 26.3 percent in Commercial Products. Maytag's overall operating income was $24.1 million compared to $63.6 million in first quarter of 2004. Home Appliances operating income of $26.6 million offset a $2.5 million operating loss in Commercial Products.

In January 2005, Maytag announced that it would no longer sell its major home appliances to Best Buy. According to a Best Buy spokesperson:[17]

> [Best Buy has] decided to no longer sell Maytag's large appliances because customers were responding positively to products made by new foreign suppliers, such as LG Electronics, Samsung, and Bosch-Siemens. Customers liked the style and innovation of the new brands. . . . Maytag makes innovative products, too, but Best Buy has to respond to what customers want.

In addition, Maytag announced that Home Depot added LG Electronics and Samsung home appliances to its product line. Maytag executives acknowledged that the decisions made by Best Buy and Home Depot might adversely affect the company's home appliance sales in 2005. Also in January, Maytag raised the prices on its major appliances by 5 to 8 percent, citing higher raw material cost as the reason. In February, Maytag reported additional factory layoffs at its Newton, Iowa, washer and dryer production facility.[18] Maytag had laid off about 330 production workers at the Newton facility during the past year, trimming the factory work force to an estimated 1,430 people, compared with around 2,500 as recently as 2002.

 ## MAYTAG BID CONSIDERATIONS

Haier's decision to bid on Maytag would depend heavily on an assessment of competitive issues and the marketing opportunity that the Maytag business and assets could provide Haier in the United States and abroad. For example, a competitor might acquire Maytag, (re)build its business, and achieve a more advantageous competitive position in the United States in terms of brands owned and marketed and display space in retail outlets. In late 2002, industry analysts speculated that Electrolux considered Maytag to be an acquisition target.[19] On the other hand, a successful bid would establish Haier as a major home appliance manufacturer in the United States, broaden its U.S. appliance product lines, and give Haier brand recognition with the Maytag name. It could also provide Haier access to new retail channels given Maytag's long-standing trade relations with independent appliance retailers, national chain retailers, and appliance distributors/wholesalers.

Haier executives would also need to consider the Maytag purchase in light of Haier's long-term corporate initiatives, strengths and weaknesses, and the future marketing of Maytag and Haier-branded appliances in the United States and worldwide. A plan would need to be developed that described how Maytag could further Haier's initiatives, capitalize on its strengths, and overcome its weaknesses in

---

[17] "Maytag, Best Buy Decide It's Over," DesMoinesRegister.com, January 20, 2005.

[18] "Maytag to Cut More Jobs at Newton Plant," ApplianceMagazine.com, February 9, 2005.

[19] "Repairing Maytag," Forbes.com, November 11, 2002.

the United States and abroad. In addition, attention to the integration of Maytag's business into Haier's business (or vice versa) in the United States was necessary. In particular, decisions related to the offering and brand portfolio of the combined companies would have to be made. For example, should Haier continue with its multiproduct brand strategy or adopt Maytag's multibrand strategy?

The initial May bid for Maytag by a private U.S.-based investment group was $1.13 billion, or about $14.00 per share. The investment group would also assume Maytag's $969 million in debt. Haier had the capital to exceed this bid should company officials determine that the financial value of Maytag exceeded this figure. Furthermore, Haier's cost of capital was virtually zero given its preferred status according to the Chinese government's plans for global expansion. According to financial analysts, the average price-earnings ratio (P/E) multiple in the household appliance industry fluctuated in the 16 to 20 range in the prior five years (that is, corporate stock prices were trading at 16 to 20 times corporate earnings-per-share). Financial analysts also projected Maytag's earnings-per-share to be $0.54 in 2005, $0.75 in 2006, and $0.80 in 2007 following a successful completion of Maytag's restructuring effort. Maytag's stock price was trading at $15.31 per share on June 15. Exhibit 9 shows the Maytag stock price trend over the past 10 months.

On the other hand, Haier executives had to consider whether such a financial investment might be better directed at building the Haier brand and business in the United States following the corporate growth strategy of Japan's Sony Corporation and South Korea's Samsung Corporation. Both companies built their core businesses and corporate brands over an extended time period rather than through acquisitions.

EXHIBIT 9 **Maytag Corporation Common Stock Price Trend: September 2, 2004, to June 15, 2005**

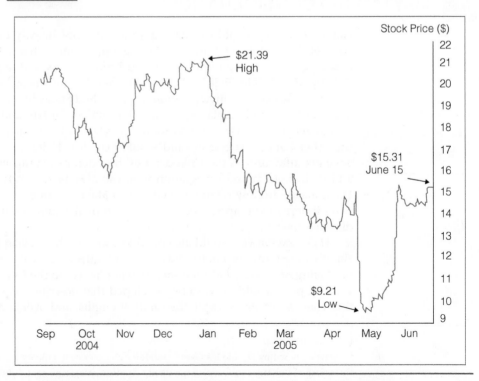

Source: Adapted from Maytag Corporation Web site, downloaded June 16, 2005.

APPENDIX

Preparing a Written Case Analysis

Chapter 3 outlined an approach to marketing decision making and case analysis. The purpose of this appendix is to provide a more detailed description of what is involved in a thorough written case analysis through the use of an example. The following case—Republic National Bank of Dallas: NOW Accounts—describes an actual problem encountered by bank executives. The case is accompanied by a student analysis in the format described in Chapter 3. The student analysis shows how to organize a written case and the nature and scope of the analysis, which includes both qualitative and quantitative analyses. You should read and analyze the case before examining the student analysis.

CASE

Republic National Bank of Dallas

NOW Accounts

 ## INTRODUCTION

In early 1977, Ruth Krusen, marketing officer for Republic National Bank of Dallas (RNB), was asked to assess the impact on Republic Bank of offering NOW (negotiable order of withdrawal) accounts if they became legal nationwide. Specifically, she was asked to:

1. Determine the impact on profits that Republic National Bank could anticipate from NOW accounts

2. Recommend a NOW account marketing strategy

The cooperation of Republic National Bank of Dallas in the preparation of this case is gratefully acknowledged. This case was prepared by Professor Roger A. Kerin, of the Edwin L. Cox School of Business, Southern Methodist University, as a basis for class discussion and is not designed to illustrate effective or ineffective handling of an administrative situation. Certain data have been disguised.

NOW accounts, which are effectively interest-bearing checking accounts, have been in use since 1972 in New England. In early 1977, however, a bill was introduced in Congress that would allow commercial banks and thrift institutions in all 50 states to provide this service.[1] Despite opposition in Congress, observers were of the opinion that legislation enabling NOW accounts would be passed by the first quarter of 1978 and would become effective January 1979.

 ## BANKING IN TEXAS

Texas is a "unit banking" state. This means that individual banks cannot operate branch banks. The regulation that limits a bank to a single location was specified in the state constitution of 1876. In 1971, however, amendments to the Bank Holding Act allowed individual banks to acquire smaller institutions if the identity of the acquired bank was maintained. Since 1971, large banks in Texas have formed holding companies to improve their lending capability in order to better serve large commercial accounts. By 1977, 33 bank holding companies were operating in Texas. Holding companies owned 250 of the state's 1,360 banks and held about 55 percent of the state's total bank deposits in 1977.

Three of the largest bank holding companies in Texas are based in Dallas. Each operates its largest bank in downtown Dallas. First International Bancshares, which operates First National Bank, is the largest bank holding company in Texas. Republic of Texas Corporation operates the Republic National Bank of Dallas and is the second-largest holding company. Mercantile Texas Corporation operates Mercantile National Bank and is the fifth-largest bank holding company in terms of total assets.

Banking activity in Texas generally corresponds to pockets of urban and commercial growth. Accordingly, banking activity is concentrated in the Dallas–Fort Worth and Houston metropolitan areas. The San Antonio metropolitan area has shown a dramatic increase in banking activity due in part to population growth and increased economic growth.

 ## COMPETITIVE SITUATION IN DALLAS

The Dallas banking market consists of 57 banks in the city of Dallas and an additional 43 banks in Dallas County. At the end of 1976, the 57 banks in the city of Dallas recorded total deposits of $13.27 billion. The 43 banks in Dallas County recorded deposits of about $1.25 billion.

Three large downtown banks dominate the Dallas banking market. At the end of 1976, Republic National Bank, First National Bank, and the Mercantile National Bank accounted for approximately 78 percent of total bank deposits in the city of Dallas and 71 percent of Dallas County bank deposits. Republic National Bank was the leader with approximately $4.6 billion in deposits, followed closely by First National Bank with $4.4 billion. Mercantile National Bank recorded total deposits of about $1.3 billion at the end of 1976. These three banks are located within walking distance of one another, as well as of some 12 other banks.

Competitive activities of Dallas banks have historically focused on retail (consumer) or wholesale (business) bank account development. Banks located

---

[1] Thrift institutions include mutual savings banks, cooperative banks, credit unions, and savings and loan associations. Thrift institutions differ from commercial banks in that only banks have the authority to accept demand deposits or checking accounts or offer commercial loans.

in suburban areas typically emphasized the retail business, whereas downtown banks emphasized the wholesale business. Nevertheless, the Dallas competitive environment in recent years has been characterized by aggressive bank marketing efforts on both fronts. According to one observer of the Dallas banking scene:

> The competitive marketing furor is fierce, and it's not just the catchy advertising themes. . . . There's a scramble going on to repackage consumer services, put forth new services, cross-sell services, and woo corporate customers. There's Saturday banking, extended hours banking, 24-hour tellers, foreign currency sales, cash machines, no-charge checking package deals, automatic payroll deposits, pension fund management services, computer billing services, specially arranged travel tours, traveler's checks to spend on travel tours, equipment leasing, credit card loans, loan syndications, lock boxes, and on and on. First National Bank in Dallas alone lists more than 400 different bank "products" in its inventory of services.[2]

Krusen confirmed the observation that the Dallas banking market was competitive. She noted that RNB continues to be competitive in banking services, but "the question of how aggressive we should be has not been resolved at least as regards retail account marketing." RNB has at least as many bank services for customers as competitors do, if not more services than are offered by the vast majority of commercial banks in Dallas.

In addition to commercial banks, savings and loan association (S&Ls) also compete for passbook savings accounts among Dallas County residents. At the end of 1976, deposits of the 22 Dallas County–based savings and loan associations were $2.85 billion. Dallas Federal Savings was the largest savings and loan association with about $909.6 million in deposits, or about 32 percent of total deposits. Texas Federal Savings and First Texas Savings combined accounted for approximately $992 million in deposits, or 35 percent of total deposits. Dallas-based savings and loan associations operated approximately 150 offices in Dallas County. Savings and loan associations based outside Dallas County also operated about 50 offices in the county.

Savings and loan associations have aggressively sought deposits in recent years. Dallas-based associations have historically outpaced the national average for savings and loan deposit volume growth. Savings associations have emphasized two competitive advantages in their passbook savings marketing programs. First, they could pay 5¼ percent on passbook savings, whereas commercial banks were limited by law to 5 percent on passbook savings. Second, they could develop branch operations with a common name, whereas commercial banks were limited to a single location in Texas.

Savings and loan associations have placed greater emphasis on consumer, or installment, loans in recent years. Texas is unique among states in that it allows savings associations to provide installment loans, and some associations have used this opportunity to attract deposit volume. According to an industry observer, "S&Ls have historically attracted older customers. Installment loans are a useful service to bring in younger customers, introduce them to S&Ls, and get them to open a passbook savings account."

Credit unions also represent a competitive force in the Dallas market. By the end of 1976, 218 credit unions were located in the city of Dallas and its immediate environs. These credit unions operated 232 offices. Combined, credit unions held over $666 million in assets and served almost one-half million members.

Credit unions compete effectively in the Dallas market in three ways. First, they offer consumer, or installment, loans to their members at competitive

---

[2] Dave Clark, "A Big Pitch for Bucks," *Dallas–Fort Worth Business Quarterly* 1, no. 2.

interest rates. They hold a significant share of the automobile loans in the Dallas market. Second, credit unions hold substantial funds in member savings accounts. Third, credit unions provide share drafts to their members. A *share draft* is a withdrawal document that permits credit union members to make payments from interest-bearing savings accounts. These drafts resemble checks but are actually drafts drawn on a credit union and payable through a bank.

REPUBLIC NATIONAL BANK

Republic National Bank was founded in 1920. At that time, the bank was called Guaranty Bank and Trust, and it held a state banking charter. After several name changes, the present name was adopted in 1937, and RNB obtained a national bank charter. Today, RNB is the largest member of the Republic of Texas Corporation bank holding-company system. By the end of 1977, RNB would be ranked twenty-first in the United States in total assets and deposits and would be the largest bank in Texas and the South in terms of total assets, deposits, loans, and equity capital. Also by the end of 1977, RNB would be ranked 150th among the 500 largest banks in the non-Communist world, according to *American Banker* magazine. RNB had total assets exceeding $6 billion and a net income of approximately $36.3 million by that time.

Retail Account Marketing

Although figures are not available for competing banks, RNB is considered to have one of the largest, if not the largest, retail account bases in the Dallas area. According to Krusen, this occurred as a result of RNB's historic position of "taking chances on the little guy and community service." It was estimated that about 55 percent of RNB's retail checking accounts in 1977 were under $500. Exhibit 1 shows the distribution of accounts by account size.

EXHIBIT 1 **Estimated Distribution of Personal Checking Account Balances in Early 1977**

Account Size	Percentage of Accounts	Percentage of Total Checking Account Deposits
Under $200	32%	3%
$200–$499	23	3
$500–$999	14	4
$1,000–$4,999	18	13
$5,000–$9,999	7	11
$10,000–$24,999	3	13
$25,000–$100,000	2	20
Over $100,000	1	33
	100%	100%

Number of personal checking accounts: 45,000

Personal checking account deposits: $150 million

Note: Figures reported in this exhibit reflect approximations drawn from 1977 *District Bank Averages: Functional Cost Analysis* (Dallas: Federal Reserve Bank of Dallas, 1977).

This philosophy is communicated in RNB advertising. Beginning in the late 1960s with its "Silver Star Service" campaign and continuing with the "Star Treatment" advertising campaign, RNB communicated to present and potential customers that they were special and that RNB had a number of special services to provide them. In early 1977 the "Republic National Bank *Is* Dallas" campaign was launched, with Orson Welles narrating television and radio advertising spots and the Dallas Symphony playing the theme music. This campaign was designed to reflect the mutual traditions of RNB and Dallas residents as progressive and growth-oriented, as well as emphasize the interdependence of banking leadership and service with the prosperity and quality of Dallas life. Marketing research has shown that RNB has had the highest "top-of-mind awareness" of any bank in the Dallas area since 1975.

Retail Account Services

RNB retail account marketing efforts have resulted in a variety of traditional as well as innovative bank services for its customers. For example, RNB provides its Teller 24 Service, which is an automatic bank teller/cash machine. This service operates 24 hours a day at 26 locations around the city of Dallas and in six other Texas cities. Another innovation, the *Starpak* Account, is a complete package of banking services provided to customers for a fixed monthly fee of $3. Exhibit 2 on page 692 gives a description of this service. RNB personal checking is highly competitive in the Dallas market, with no service charge for accounts that maintain a minimum monthly balance of $400. A $1 charge accrues to accounts with a minimum monthly balance of $300, a $2 charge with a minimum monthly balance of $200, and a $3 charge with no minimum balance requirement.

Retail Checking Account Revenue and Cost Estimates

In the course of preparing her report, Krusen contacted the RNB Controllers Division to obtain revenue and cost data on retail checking accounts. The Controllers Division report, based largely on Federal Reserve statistics, indicated that approximately 85 percent of retail checking account deposits were investable. In other words, about 15 percent of checking account deposits must be held in reserve. Ninety-six percent of savings accounts balances were investable.

The Controllers Division also indicated that RNB would realize an average yield on loans and securities of about 7.5 percent in 1977. Krusen noted that this figure was the lowest experienced by RNB in recent years. In 1974 RNB had realized an average yield of 10.59 percent. Other figures obtained directly from Federal Reserve statistical averages for commercial banks with total deposits of over $200 million were as follows:

Service and handling charge revenue per account per month:	$1.56
Account cost per month (including checks, deposits, and other assignable overhead):	$5.24

NOW ACCOUNTS

NOW accounts came into being as the result of the attempt of a Massachusetts mutual savings bank to circumvent the prohibition against thrift institutions' offering checking accounts. After a two-year regulatory and legal battle, Consumer Savings Bank of Worcester, Massachusetts, won its case and in June 1972 began to offer a savings account on which checklike instruments called negotiable orders of withdrawal could be written. Other mutuals in Massachusetts and New Hampshire soon followed suit.

EXHIBIT 2   **Components of Republic National Bank's Starpak Account**

1. *Unlimited Checking*—There's no minimum balance requirement, no per check charge, and no limit on the number of checks you write when you have a Starpak personal checking account.

2. *Free Personal Checks*—They're prenumbered and personalized with your name, address, and phone number, and you can order as many as you need any time you need them.

3. *Reduced Loan Rates*—With this feature alone, many people make Starpak pay for itself. At the end of the loan period, we'll refund 10 percent of the total interest you paid on installment loans of $1,000 or more, when the loan has been repaid as agreed. Of course, your loan is subject to normal credit approval.

4. *No Bank Charge for Traveler's Checks*—Or for money orders or cashier's checks when you show us your Starpak Account Card.

5. *Free Safe Deposit Box*—We'll give you the $5 size free. Or take $5 off the rent for a larger size.

6. *Combined Monthly Statement*—Your monthly statement can include status reports on any or all of the accounts you and your spouse have at Republic. You select the accounts you want the Combined Statement to cover. We can include your checking, savings, personal certificates of deposit, and even personal loans. Yes, you'll also receive separate regular statements on each of your Republic accounts you include in the Combined Statement.

7. *Numerical Check Listing*—Your monthly statement will report each check in the order written. That makes it much easier to reconcile your statement each month.

8. *Automatic Overdraft Protection*—This optional service gives you additional peace of mind and the opportunity to take advantage of an exceptional bargain. It works this way. If the checks you write exceed your balance, we'll cover the overdrafts up to the limit of your Republic Master Card or VISA Credit. Finance charges for deferred payment will apply at the normal rate. Repayment will be through your monthly Master Card or VISA account payment.

9. *Teller 24® Service*—You can get cash from your Starpak Checking Account, or your Republic Master Charge or VISA Card, at any of 26 Teller 24 machines located in Dallas and six other Texas cities, and at 12,000 banks nationwide. With Teller 24 your money is available 24 hours a day, 7 days a week.

10. *Automatic Loan Repayment*—If you have an installment loan at Republic, we will, at your request, withdraw your monthly loan payment from your Starpak Checking Account. It's a good way to make sure you can take advantage of the 10 percent interest refund.

11. *Automatic Savings Account Deposits*—If you've never been able to save before, this plan solves the problem. Just tell us how much and on what day of the month. On the date you specify, we'll automatically transfer the amount you select from your checking to your savings account. Then, to help your savings grow even faster, we'll pay the highest interest rates allowable.

12. *Starpak Account Card*—It identifies you as a preferred customer of Republic National Bank, entitled to the privileges and special savings available with your Starpak Account.

13. *No Separate Charges*—All these Starpak services are available for the flat monthly fee of $3. There's no separate charge.

Plus these other services available to all Republic National Bank customers—We pay postage both ways when you bank by mail. We'll validate your in-bank parking stub when you bank. And you'll have a personal banker assigned to your accounts so that you can call for advice or assistance with any banking need.

Source: Bank brochure.

Although regulatory authorities persist in regarding the NOW account as a savings account on which checks can be written, from a consumer point of view (and from an operational point of view) it is a checking account that pays interest. As consumers gradually became educated about NOWs, commercial banks began to lose customers to this attractive type of account, with which they were unable to compete. In response, federal and state laws were passed permitting commercial banks as well as mutuals and S&Ls in Massachusetts and New Hampshire to offer NOW accounts starting in January 1974. As of March 1976, financial institutions in the other New England states were granted the same powers. In two of the states (Connecticut and Maine), state-chartered thrifts had been empowered to offer checking accounts a few months earlier.

In New England, NOW accounts may be offered to individuals and to nonprofit organizations (except that in Connecticut, thrifts can offer NOWs only to individuals).[3] A uniform rate ceiling of 5 percent applies to all institutions. Excerpts from a report prepared by the RNB Marketing Division on the development of NOW accounts in New England are presented in the appendix at the end of this case.

NOW ACCOUNT MARKETING STRATEGY

The task facing Krusen was difficult for a number of reasons. First, the only NOW account information available pertained to the New England experience. Although this information would be useful in gauging the rate of adoption of NOW accounts, it was not entirely clear how the Dallas-area banks and thrift institutions would react. Second, several contingency plans would have to be charted. If NOW accounts were not deemed appropriate for RNB by top management, then Krusen would have to recommend a strategy to maintain the RNB customer base. This strategy would depend on whether a "free" NOW account program became popular in the Dallas area or a more conservative approach was adopted by competitors. If the NOW account was adopted by RNB, she realized, the NOW account package (separate account or part of an existing bank service) and the price (service charges, if any) would have to be defined. The package and price would be, in part, determined by the competitive environment that developed and the cost of NOW accounts.

Timing was a third consideration. Should RNB be a leader and set the competitive tenor in the market or take a "wait and see" stance? Finally, if RNB decided to adopt the NOW account, then a question of communications would arise. For example, should RNB quietly inform present customers of NOW account availability or actively communicate availability to the Dallas market as a whole via an advertising program?

APPENDIX: NOW ACCOUNTS IN NEW ENGLAND, A REPORT PREPARED BY THE MARKETING DIVISION OF REPUBLIC NATIONAL BANK OF DALLAS

The objectives of this investigation of NOW accounts in New England were

1. To learn the speed and magnitude of NOW account impact as a basis for estimating the impact on RNB

2. To identify and evaluate various marketing strategies and their possible relevance to our own market

---

[3] At the time of this case and for analysis purposes, only retail (personal and nonprofit) checking accounts were affected by NOW accounts in the Dallas area.

EXHIBIT A.1	NOW Account Adoption in New England as of August 1976

	Percentage of Institutions Offering		Commercial Bank's Share of NOW Market	
	Thrifts	Commercial Banks	Percentage of Accounts	Percentage of Balances
Massachusetts	94[a]	72	32	52
New Hampshire	81[a]	64	43	62
Connecticut	69	53	35	74
Maine	32	40	68	81
Vermont	23	29	89	93
Rhode Island[b]	25	75	83	85

[a] Mutual savings banks only; in each state two-thirds of the savings and loans also offer NOWs.

[b] Rhode Island has a unique situation of affiliated mutual savings banks and commercial banks. Figures in exhibit refer only to unaffiliated thrifts and commercial banks. NOWs are offered by 66 percent of the affiliated group.

Penetration of NOWS

Reaction of New England financial institutions given the power to offer NOWs is shown in Exhibit A.1. It indicates the percentages of thrifts and commercial banks that were offering NOWs by August 1976 and the market shares of commercial banks. By August 1976 mutual savings banks in Massachusetts and New Hampshire had been able to offer NOWs for 50 months, commercial banks for 30 months. In the other states, all institutions had been able to offer them for only 6 months.

Despite the resistance of commercial banks in Massachusetts and New Hampshire to offering NOWs, Exhibit A.1 shows that a substantial majority are now providing them. In the other New England states, commercial banks have moved more quickly to adopt NOW accounts. This is one of the reasons that they have a larger share of NOW accounts and balances than do commercial banks in Massachusetts and New Hampshire. Nevertheless, even in the latter states, commercial banks have captured more of the total NOW balances than have thrifts.

One conclusion supported by the data is that the competitiveness of financial institutions is directly related to the degree to which the state's population is concentrated in large urban markets.

The additional data on Massachusetts and New Hampshire shown in Exhibit A.2 indicate the substantial impact of NOWs in the personal payment account market. Exhibit A.2 shows that after four years, 72 percent of checking account balances in New Hampshire have been converted to NOWs and 44 percent have

EXHIBIT A.2	Personal Payment Accounts, August 1976

	Personal Payment Balances	
	Percentage in NOWs	Percentage in Thrifts
New Hampshire	72%	27%
Massachusetts	44	21

Note: Personal payment accounts consist of all checking balances plus 80 percent of NOW balances. The 20 percent of NOW balances estimated to have come from savings accounts have been deducted.

been converted in Massachusetts. Thrifts have captured 27 percent of this market in New Hampshire and 21 percent in Massachusetts.

Marketing Strategies

Massachusetts and New Hampshire As simple as the concept of an interest-bearing checking account appears to be, NOW account introduction in New England produced an initial confusion of positioning, pricing, and marketing strategies.

Positioning For a variety of reasons, thrifts initially positioned NOWs as savings accounts with a special convenience feature in getting access to funds. Consumers who opened them did not regard them as checking accounts and there was relatively low account activity. Adding to the confusion, when banks began to offer NOWs, some of them were very negative in their presentations. They told customers, in effect, "We have NOW accounts, but you don't really want to spend your savings, do you?"

In time, thrifts and then banks became more daring in presenting NOWs as accounts that were identical in function to checking accounts but paid interest. NOWs are by now recognized as a substitute for checking accounts, are opened instead of checking accounts (or an existing checking account is closed when it is realized that it is no longer needed), and have virtually the same level of activity as checking accounts.

Pricing Pricing was initially fairly conservative. In New Hampshire, NOWs were usually offered at a lower rate of interest than savings account, while in Massachusetts per-item charges were prevalent. Then a price war began and increasing numbers of institutions offered free NOWs—that is, maximum rate of interest, no service or item charges, and no minimum balance requirements.

The proportion of institutions offering free NOWs increased until mid-1975, but since then the trend has been reversed, largely because late entrants into the field have offered less generous terms. It has also been true that some institutions that previously offered free NOWs have imposed charges or minimum balance requirements.

The free NOW resulted from a variety of causes and motives:

1. At the time of introduction, money market rates were so high that the cost of NOW funds might still allow a margin of profit.

2. Thrifts were inexperienced in the costs involved in servicing checking accounts.

3. Some thrifts were determined to establish a good market share early, regardless of short-run lack of profitability.

4. In the major market areas, there was a free checking environment.

Price and Service Package Pricing structures on NOWs in New England are as varied as checking account charges have historically been. The possibility of competing through the interest rate paid is the only new element. When NOW accounts are not free, some variant of the following occurs:

1. *Interest rates.* Initially, some institutions paid less than the maximum rate on savings accounts. However, under competitive pressure, rates rose to the 5 percent ceiling in all major markets. However, some institutions do not pay on a day-of-deposit to day-of-withdrawal basis. While

very few now pay only on collected balances, several large banks are contemplating going in that direction. A few banks pay only on minimum balances.

2. *Balance requirements.* Balances above which the NOW account is "free" range from $200 to $1,000. In most cases, this is the minimum balance, although one large bank, Shawmut, has an average balance requirement. What happens when the balance that goes below the minimum varies? In some cases, no interest is paid; in others, a transaction or service fee is imposed; and in some cases, both. In some isolated markets, fees are imposed on all accounts, but in competitive major markets, NOWs become free at some balance level.

3. *Transaction charges.* Charges per check range from 10 to 25 cents. Usually, the charge is levied on all checks if the balance is below the required level. In some cases, a certain number of checks are free (5 to 15 per month), and in some other cases the number of free checks is related to balances (for example, 5 checks per $100 of average balance).

4. *Service charge.* Some banks charge flat fees rather than per-transaction charges. Fees generally are $1 or $2.

Other New England States   By the time NOW accounts were authorized in the other New England states, both thrifts and commercials had the opportunity to assess the cost and competitive impact of NOWs in the two original states, and money market conditions had changed. These facts are reflected in the response of financial institutions in offering NOWs. Commercial banks have moved more rapidly than they did in Massachusetts and New Hampshire. At the same time, both thrifts and commercial banks have been more conservative in pricing.

Connecticut. Thrifts have moved aggressively to offer both checking accounts and NOWs. Although free checking prevails in major Connecticut markets and although about one-third of the thrifts offer free NOWs, large Connecticut banks have offered NOWs on conservative terms (high minimum balances with transaction charges for lower-balance accounts). The effect of this strategy is reflected in the high average balances of commercial bank NOWs—over $4,000.

Rhode Island. The financial market is highly concentrated in a very few institutions. Six months after NOWs became legal, six of the nine commercial banks affiliated with thrift institutions, six of the eight unaffiliated banks, and one of the four unaffiliated thrifts were offering NOWs. None of them offered free NOWs. As in the checking account market in this state, relatively high minimum balances are required. It should be noted that because of the thrift-commercial bank affiliations, a majority of thrifts have in effect been able to offer checking accounts to their customers.

Maine. Thrifts have concentrated harder on selling checking accounts than on offering NOWs. Neither thrifts nor commercial banks have moved very fast to offer NOWs. Few offer them free.

Vermont. This state shows the slowest gain in institutions offering NOWs. None offers them free.

Republic National Bank of Dallas

NOW Accounts

STRATEGIC ISSUES AND PROBLEMS

Ruth Krusen, marketing officer for RNB, has been given responsibility for (1) determining the profit impact RNB could anticipate from NOW accounts, and (2) recommending a contingency plan for a NOW account marketing strategy. Her task involves a number of important factors. She must assess the likelihood that the Dallas competitive environment will be liberal or conservative in its marketing of NOW accounts. An important consideration is RNB's role in affecting this environment, given its dominant position in the Dallas market and its posture regarding aggressiveness in retail account marketing. Ultimately, she must make a "go–no go" decision. A "go" decision requires a recommendation in the form of the service, its target market, its price reflected in service charges, and promotion. A "no go" decision must take into consideration RNB's competitive position without NOW accounts and measures to minimize their impact. The problem facing RNB is how to retain its dominant competitive position given an environmental threat (NOW accounts) while at the same time preserving profitability and its customer base.

INSIGHTS FROM THE NEW ENGLAND EXPERIENCE

The NOW account experience, based on the data in the report of the marketing division, reveals the following:

1. The faster commercial banks move to adopt NOW accounts, the larger their share of NOW accounts and NOW account balances.

2. Cannibalization of checking accounts occurs when NOW accounts are available; 72 percent of checking account balances in New Hampshire have been converted to NOW accounts, and 44 percent of checking accounts in Massachusetts have been converted to NOWs. These figures developed over 50 months (four years) after the NOW introduction (see Case Exhibit A.2).

3. Exhibit 1 in the case provides some evidence that NOW account balances are high. This could mean that those individuals with high checking account balances are more likely to switch to NOWs. Alternatively, the Connecticut experience would indicate that minimum balance requirements increase NOW account balances. Data for Massachusetts and New Hampshire—both of which experienced "free NOWs"—would tend to support the point that individuals with high account balances convert to NOWs.

4. NOW account usage activity approaches checking account activity; hence checking account costs are merely transferred to managing NOW accounts.

5. Competitive activity, reflected in the NOW package provided, reveals that "free NOWs" were initially provided. Financial institutions subsequently offered less generous terms, however.

6. NOW account packages differ greatly with respect to minimum balances, service charges, and positioning against checking and savings accounts.

Results from the New England experience suggest that three scenarios are possible in the Dallas market.

Environment	*Environment Description*
No NOW adoption:	Financial institutions refrain from adoption.
Liberal NOW adoption:	NOWs are adopted with no minimum balance, service charges, 5 percent interest, an active promotion/communication program.
Conservative NOW adoption:	NOWs are adopted with some form of minimum service charges, less than 5 percent interest, little promotion or communication.

Numerous factors will affect the likelihood of each environment's developing in the Dallas market.

Factors in favor of a no-NOW environment:

1. The New England experience suggests that a no-win possibility exists for all financial institutions. For example, banks will have to pay interest on previously interest-free funds, and S&Ls and credit unions will incur costs not previously encountered.

2. Money market rates are quite low at present, suggesting little spread to make an adequate profit margin.

Factors in favor of a NOW environment:

1. The New England experience suggests that where NOWs are legalized, they are adopted in some form, by someone.

2. If the Dallas market is competitive *and* various financial institutions are vying for deposits, then NOWs offer a means to attract deposits. Moreover, the New England experience suggests that "getting in first" is crucial. "Followership" is not rewarded.

3. S&Ls are poised to take some advantage of NOWs in that their interest rate paid on deposits will fall from 5¼ percent to 5 percent, assuming a 5 percent ceiling level.

Factors in favor of a liberal NOW environment:

1. Thrifts might view NOWs as a way of gaining deposits quickly.

2. S&Ls will benefit from NOWs even if 5 percent interest is offered on NOW accounts, since they are currently paying 5¼ percent on savings.

3. Share drafts provided by credit unions have characteristics similar to those of NOWs; NOW accounts would seem like a logical extension.

Factors in favor of a conservative NOW environment:

1. This appears to be the trend in New England states.

2. Dallas banks do not generally offer free checking.

3. Money market rates are low.

It would seem that a potential determinant of how the NOW environment evolves will be the decision of RNB, given its dominance in the Dallas banking market. RNB's dominant position would seem to affect the environment *only* if RNB acts immediately with a well-thought-out NOW account program. NOWs are probably inevitable—that is, the no-NOW environment seems unlikely. The question, then, is whether a liberal or a conservative NOW environment will develop. The environment could be influenced by RNB.

REPUBLIC NATIONAL BANK

RNB dominates the Dallas financial market. Its assets alone ($6 billion) are almost 10 times *total* assets of all credit unions ($666 million). RNB's deposits ($4.6 billion) exceed the total for *all* S&Ls ($2.85 billion). RNB has the largest deposit base of all Dallas banks *and* the largest retail account deposit base in Dallas.

Nevertheless, RNB management apparently has not resolved how aggressive the bank should be in retail account marketing efforts. The aggressiveness issue would seem to be related to the bank's emphasis on the wholesale rather than the retail business.

Exhibit 1 in the case indicates that about 55 percent of RNB's checking accounts are under $500. However, 96 percent of total checking account balances are accounted for by accounts of $500 and up, and 53 percent of total deposits are accounted for by accounts of over $25,000. The average account size is $3,333 ($150 million in deposits divided by 45,000 accounts). A profitability analysis of checking account sizes reveals that RNB loses money on accounts that are less than $500 on an annual basis (see Exhibit 1 in this analysis). This profitability analysis indicates that accounts below $500 produce a *loss* of $519,210 annually:

Accounts under $200:	14,400 accounts × ($24.24) =	($349,056)
Accounts $200–$499:	10,350 accounts × ($16.44) =	($170,154)
Loss	=	($519,210)

EXHIBIT 1   RNB Retail Account Profit Analysis (Based on Exhibit 1 in the Case)

Account Size	Average Interest Revenue per Account[a]	+	Average Service/ Handling Revenue per Account[b]	=	Average Revenue per Account	−	Account Cost[b]	=	Profit/ (Loss)
Less than $200	$19.92		$18.72		$38.64		$62.88		$(24.24)
$200–$499	27.72		18.72		46.44		62.88		(16.44)
$500–$999	60.71		18.72		79.43		62.88		16.55
$1,000–$4,999	153.47		18.72		172.19		62.88		109.31
$5,000–$9,999	333.93		18.72		352.65		62.88		289.77
$10,000–$24,999	920.83		18.72		939.55		62.88		876.67
$25,000–$100,000	2,125.00		18.72		2,143.72		62.88		2,080.84
Greater than $100,000	7,083.00		18.72		7,101.72		62.88		7,038.84

[a] Computed as follows: $\dfrac{\text{Account size deposit volume}}{\text{Number of accounts in category}} \times 85\% \times 0.075$.

For an account size of $200, using Exhibit 1 data: $\dfrac{\$4.5 \text{ million}}{14,440} \times 0.85 \times 0.075 = \$19.92$.

[b] Annualized average account revenue and cost given in the case where service/handling charge revenue per account per month = $1.56; account cost per month = $5.24.

More important, this analysis provides important data on the pricing of NOW accounts and the form of the service, as will be discussed later.

 ## PLAN OF ACTION

There are two primary alternatives open to RNB: to offer NOWs or not to offer NOWs. If NOWs are considered, then the form, price, and promotion must be determined. The alternatives are:

1. Do not offer NOW accounts.

2. Offer NOW accounts with no conditions and promote them heavily or modestly.

3. Offer NOW accounts with conditions and promote them heavily or modestly.

The advantages and disadvantages of the options available to RNB can be outlined as follows:

1. Not offering NOW accounts:

Advantages

- RNB is dominant and has the resources to wait and see what will happen.

- The impact on revenue of offering NOWs would be too severe. Assuming that *all accounts* are cannibalized by NOWs and the interest yield drops from 7½ percent to 2½ percent because of 5 percent interest on NOWs, the interest revenue lost will be about $6.0 million.

Checking Deposits		*Percentage Investable*		*Investable Deposits*
$150 million	×	85%	=	$127.5 million
				Interest Revenue
$127.5 million	×	0.075	=	$9,562,500
$144 million	×	0.025	=	−3,600,000
Interest revenue lost				$5,962,500

Note that NOW accounts are viewed as savings accounts, and 96 percent of deposits are investable.

Disadvantages

- RNB will lose an opportunity to be an innovator or the "first to market," which has been shown in New England to be advantageous.

- Erosion of accounts may occur, as individuals switch to institutions offering NOW accounts. This factor is particularly important if *large* accounts switch, and they are most likely to do so, since they stand to benefit most from NOW accounts.

2. Offering NOW accounts with no conditions:

Advantages

- Nonconditional NOWs will have a dramatic impact on the Dallas banking market. Banks offering them will most likely attract deposits and accounts in great numbers, particularly since they are a better deal than checking accounts with minimum balances or service charges, *plus* they give interest!

- Nonconditional NOW accounts will set the competitive tenor of the market; retail banks not offering them may be unable to compete.

- By offering nonconditional NOWs, RNB will keep current accounts from being attracted to competitors (preemptive cannibalism).

Disadvantages

- This strategy could be very expensive. As noted earlier, in addition to the account costs, a loss of interest of $6 million is possible.

- This strategy will cannibalize checking accounts almost totally.

3. Offering NOW accounts with conditions:

Advantages

- A minimum-balance condition would allow RNB to accept only those accounts on which it can make money.

- A service/handling charge condition would also result in greater account selectivity.

- A break-even analysis shows how RNB can determine a minimum balance given current service charge and account costs per year. The break-even point is the point at which total (interest plus handling/service charges) minus total costs (account cost per month) equals zero. Since RNB will net 2.5 percent in account interest revenue, has an $18.72 handling and service revenue per account per year ($1.56 $\times$ 12 months), and has an annual account cost of $62.88 ($5.24 $\times$ 12 months), solving for the minimum account balance reveals the following:

$$\text{Profit} = \frac{\text{acct. interest}}{\text{revenue}} + \frac{\text{handling/}}{\text{service charge}} - \frac{\text{acct.}}{\text{cost}}$$

$$0 = 0.025X + \$18.72 - \$62.88$$
$$\$44.16 = 0.025X$$
$$\$1,766.40 = X$$

Thus, RNB breaks even at an account balance of $1,766.40, given existing handling/service revenue per account and account maintenance costs. This minimum balance level would be a condition that from 80 to 90 percent of RNB's accounts could meet (see Exhibit 1 in the case).

Disadvantages

- This strategy leaves RNB open to being undercut by competitors if conditions are too stringent.

- Overly complex conditions and the likelihood of customers' being unexpectedly hit with service charges could hurt goodwill, particularly among larger balance account holders.

 ## RECOMMENDED NOW ACCOUNT MARKETING STRATEGY

The previous analysis indicates that RNB can shape the NOW account environment in Dallas. The following NOW account marketing strategy will ensure that this will happen.

Goals and Objectives

1. RNB should pioneer NOW accounts in the Dallas market to set the competitive tone and create a "rational" NOW environment.
2. RNB should focus on achieving 85 percent customer retention.
3. RNB should break even on NOW accounts.

Target Market

The target market for NOW accounts should be current customers with large account balances. Specifically, current customers with a minimum account size of $1,800.00 is the primary target market. This market represents almost all of RNB's current accounts. There is little to gain from attracting new customers for NOW accounts.

Marketing Mix

Product Strategy NOW accounts will be included with an existing service bundle—the Starpak Account. It is expected that NOW accounts will cannibalize existing accounts. RNB's focus on current customers is a form of preemptive cannibalism necessary to retain existing customers.

Price Strategy NOW accounts should carry a service charge. The recommended charge is $18.75 per account. This service charge, given the account cost and an account interest revenue, will allow RNB to break even on an estimated annual minimum account balance of $1,766.40.

Distribution and Sales NOW accounts will be provided at all locations by the New Account staff. Training for the New Account RNB staff should begin immediately. Documentation for the Starpak Account should be immediately modified to incorporate NOW accounts.

Advertising and Promotion A modest advertising and promotion (A&P) program is recommended for NOW accounts. The A&P program should focus on current customers via a direct-mail program and specifically inserts in monthly statements. Starpak print and TV advertising should incorporate reference to NOW accounts.

Glossary of Selected Marketing Terms and Concepts

Advertising opportunity. Conditions suggesting that a product or service would benefit from advertising. They are (1) favorable primary demand for the product or service category, (2) the product or service to be advertised can be significantly differentiated from its competitors, (3) the product or service has hidden qualities or benefits that can be portrayed effectively through advertising, and (4) there are strong emotional buying motives for the product or service.

Advertising share of voice. An organization's advertising expenditure expressed as a percentage of total advertising expenditures by all competitors in a market at a point in time.

Brand equity. The added value a brand name bestows on a product or service beyond the functional benefits provided.

Brand extension strategy. The practice of using a current brand name to enter a completely different product class.

Break-even analysis. The unit or dollar sales volume at which an organization neither makes a profit nor incurs a loss. The formula for determining the number of units required to break even is: unit break-even = total dollar fixed costs ÷ (unit selling price − unit variable costs).

Bundling. The practice of marketing two or more product or service items in a singe "package" with one price.

Business mission. Describes the organization's purpose with reference to its customers, products or services, markets, philosophy, and technology.

Cannibalism. The process whereby the sales of a new product or service come at the expense of existing products (services) already marketed by the firm.

Chain ratio method. A technique for estimating market sales potential that involves multiplying a base number by several adjusting factors that are believed to influence market sales potential.

Channel captain. A member of a marketing channel with the power to influence the behavior of other channel members.

Channel conflict. A situation that arises when one channel member believes another channel member is engaged in behavior that is preventing it from achieving its goals.

Co-branding. The pairing of two brand names of two manufacturers on a single product.

Consumer touch points. Where, when, and how a customer or prospective buyer comes in contact with a product, service, organization, or brand message or impression.

Contribution. The difference between total sales revenue and total variable costs, or, on a per-unit basis, the difference between unit selling price and unit variable cost. Contribution can be expressed in percentage terms (contribution margin) or dollar terms (contribution per unit).

Cost of goods sold. Material, labor, and factory overhead applied directly to production.

Cross-elasticity of demand. The percentage responsiveness of the quantity demanded of one product or service to a percentage price change in another product or service.

Customer lifetime value. The present value of future cash flows arising from a customer relationship.

Customer value proposition. A cluster of benefits that an organization promises customers to satisfy their needs.

703

Discounted cash flows. Future cash flows expressed in terms of their present value.

Disintermediation. The elimination of traditional intermediaries and direct distribution, often through electronic marketing channels.

Distinctive competency. An organization's unique strengths or qualities, including skills, technologies, or resources that distinguish it from other organizations. These competencies are imperfectly imitable by competitors and provide superior customer value.

Diversification. A product-market strategy that involves the development or acquisition of offerings new to the organization and the introduction of those offerings to publics (markets) not previously served by the organization.

Dual distribution. The practice of distributing products or services through two or more different marketing channels that may or may not compete for similar buyers.

Effective demand. The situation when prospective buyers have both the willingness and ability to purchase an organization's offerings.

Electronic marketing channels. Marketing channels that employ some form of electronic communication, including the Internet, to make products and services available for consumption or use by consumers and industrial users.

Exclusive distribution. A distribution strategy whereby a producer sells its products or services in only one retail outlet in a specific geographic area.

Fighting brand strategy. The practice of adding a new brand whose sole purpose is to confront competitive brands in a product class being served by an organization.

Fixed cost. Expenses that do not fluctuate with output volume within a relevant time period (usually defined as a budget year), but become progressively smaller per unit of output as volume increases. Fixed costs divide into programmed costs, which result from attempts to generate sales volume, and committed costs, which are those required to maintain the organization.

Flanker brand strategy. The practice of adding new brands on the high or low end of a product line based on a price–quality continuum.

Full-cost price strategies. Those that consider both variable and fixed cost (total cost) in the pricing of a product or service.

Global brand. A brand marketed under the same name in multiple countries with similar and centrally coordinated marketing programs.

Global marketing. The performance of activities designed to plan, price, promote, and direct the flow of an organization's offerings in more than one country for a profit.

Go-to-market strategy. A description of how an organization selects and employs marketing channels to cost-effectively deliver a value proposition to each of its chosen target markets.

Gross margin (or gross profit). The difference between total sales revenue and total cost of goods sold, or, on a per-unit basis, the difference between unit selling price and unit cost of goods sold. Gross margin can be expressed in dollar or percentage terms.

Harvesting. The practice of reducing the investment in a business entity (division, product) to cut costs or improve cash flow.

Integrated marketing communications. The practice of blending different elements of the communication mix in mutually reinforcing ways to inform, persuade, and induce consumer action.

Intensive distribution. A distribution strategy whereby a producer sells its products or services in as many retail outlets as possible in a geographic area.

Life cycle. The plot of sales of a single product, brand, or service, or a class of products or services, over time.

Line extension strategy. The practice of adding offerings with the same brand name in a product or service class currently served by the organization. Line extensions include new flavors, package sizes and forms, and ingredients.

Market. Prospective buyers (individuals or organizations) who are willing and able to purchase the existing or potential offering (product or service) of an organization.

Market-development strategy. A product-market strategy whereby an organization introduces its offerings to markets other than those it is currently serving. In global marketing, this strategy can be implemented through exportation, licensing, joint ventures, or direct investment.

Market evolution. Changes in primary demand for a product class.

Market-penetration strategy. A product-market strategy whereby an organization seeks to gain greater dominance in a market in which it already has an offering. This strategy often means capturing a larger share of an existing market.

Market redefinition. Changes in the offering demanded by buyers or promoted by competitors.

Market sales potential. The maximum level of sales that might be available to all organizations serving a defined market in a specific time period given (1) the marketing-mix activities and effort of all organizations, and (2) a set of environmental conditions.

Market segmentation. The breaking down or building up of potential buyers into groups on the basis of some sort of homogeneous characteristic(s) (e.g., age, income, geography) relating to purchase or consumption behavior.

Market share. Sales of a firm, product, service, or brand divided by the sales of the served "market," expressed as a percentage.

Market targeting (or target marketing). The specification of the particular market segment(s) the organization wishes to pursue. Differentiated marketing means that an organization simultaneously pursues several different market segments, usually with a different strategy for each. Concentrated marketing means that only a single market segment is pursued.

Marketing audit. A comprehensive, systematic, independent, and periodic examination of a company's or business unit's marketing environment, objectives, strategies, and activities with a view of determining problem areas and opportunities and recommending a plan of action to improve the company's marketing performance.

Marketing channel. Individuals and organizations involved in the process of making a product or service available for consumption or use by consumers and industrial users.

Marketing-cost analysis. The practice of assigning or allocating costs to a specified marketing activity or entity in a manner that accurately displays the financial contribution of activities or entities to the organization.

Marketing mix. Those activities controllable by the organization that include the product, service, or idea offered, the manner in which the offering will be communicated to customers, the method for distributing or delivering the offering, and the price to be charged for the offering.

Mass customization. Tailoring products and services to the tastes and preferences of individual buyers in high volumes and at a relatively low cost.

Multibranding. The practice of giving a company's products or product lines a distinct name.

Multi-channel marketing. The blending of an electronic marketing channel and a traditional channel in ways that are mutually reinforcing in attracting, retaining, and building relationships with customers.

Multiproduct branding. The use of one name for all of a company's products in a product class. Sometimes called family branding or corporate branding.

Net profit margin (before taxes). The remainder after cost of goods sold, other variable costs, and fixed costs have been subtracted from sales revenue, or simply, total revenue minus total cost. Net profit margin can be expressed in dollar or percentage terms.

New brand strategy. The development of a new brand and often a new offering for a product class that has not been previously served by the organization.

Offering. The sum total of benefits or satisfaction provided to target markets by an organization. An offering consists of a tangible product or service plus related services, warranties or guarantees, packaging, and so on.

Offering mix or portfolio. The totality of an organization's offering (products and services).

Operating leverage. The extent to which fixed costs and variable costs are used in the production and marketing of products and services.

Operations control. The practice of assessing how well an organization performs marketing activities as it seeks to achieve planned outcomes.

Opportunity analysis. The process of identifying opportunities, matching the opportunity to the organization, and evaluating the opportunity.

Opportunity cost. Alternative uses of resources that are given up when pursuing one alternative rather than another. Sometimes referred to as the benefits not obtained from not choosing an alternative.

Payback period. The number of years required for an organization to recapture its initial investment in an offering.

Penetration pricing strategy. Setting a relatively low initial price for a new product or service.

Positioning. The act of designing an organization's offering and image so that it occupies a distinct and valued place in the target customer's mind relative to competitive offerings. A product or service can be positioned by (1) attribute or benefit, (2) use or application, (3) product or service user, (4) product or service class, (5) competitors, and (6) price and quality.

Price elasticity of demand. The percentage change in quantity demanded relative to a percentage change in price for a product or service.

Pro forma income statement. An income statement containing projected revenues, budgeted (variable and fixed) expenses, and estimated net profit for an organization, product, or service during a specific planning period, usually a year.

Product-development strategy. A product-market strategy whereby an organization creates new offerings for existing markets through product innovation, product augmentation, or product-line extensions.

Product-line pricing. The setting of prices for all items in a product line. It involves determining (1) the lowest-priced product price, (2) the highest-priced product, and (3) price differentials for all other products in the line.

Pull communication strategy. The practice of creating initial interest for an offering among potential buyers, who in turn demand the offering from marketing intermediaries, ultimately "pulling" the offering through the marketing channel. The principal emphasis is on consumer advertising and consumer promotions.

Push communication strategy. The practice of "pushing" an offering through a marketing channel in a sequential fashion, with each channel representing a distinct target market. The principal emphasis is on personal selling and trade promotions directed toward wholesalers and retailers.

Regional marketing. The practice of using different marketing mixes to accommodate unique preferences and competitive conditions in different geographic areas.

Relevant cost. Expenditures that (1) are expected to occur in the future as a result of some marketing action and (2) differ among marketing alternatives being considered.

Sales forecast. The level of sales a single organization expects to achieve based on a chosen marketing strategy and an assumed competitive environment.

Sales mix. The relative combination of products or services sold by a company.

Selective distribution. A distribution strategy whereby a producer sells its products or services in a few retail outlets in a specific geographic area.

Served market. The market in which a company, product, service, or brand competes for targeted customers.

Situation analysis. The appraisal of operations to determine the reasons for the gap between what was or is expected and what has happened or will happen.

Skimming pricing strategy. Setting a relatively high initial price for a new product or service.

Strategic change. Environmental change that will affect the long-term well-being of the organization.

Strategic control. The practice of assessing the direction of the organization as evidenced by its implicit or explicit goals, objectives, strategies, and capacity to perform in the context of changing environments and competitive actions.

Strategic marketing management. The analytical process of (1) defining the organization's business, mission, and goals; (2) identifying and framing organizational opportunities; (3) formulating product-market strategies; (4) budgeting marketing, financial, and production resources; and (5) developing reformulation and recovery strategies.

Sub-branding. The practice of combining a corporate or family brand with a new brand name.

Success requirements. The basic tasks that must be performed by an organization in a market or industry to compete successfully. These are sometimes "key success factors," or simply KSFs.

Sunk cost. Past expenditures for a given activity that are typically irrelevant in whole or in part to future decisions. The "sunk cost fallacy" is an attempt to recoup spent dollars by spending still more dollars in the future.

Supply chain. Individuals and organizations that perform logistical activities required to create or source and deliver a product or service to consumers and industrial users.

SWOT analysis. A formal framework for identifying and framing organizational growth opportunities. SWOT is an acronym for an organization's *Strengths* and *Weaknesses* and external *Opportunities* and *Threats*.

Trade margin. The difference between unit sales price and unit cost at each level of a marketing channel. Trade margin is usually expressed in percentage terms.

Trading down. The process of reducing the number of features or quality of an offering and lowering the purchase price.

Trading up. The practice of improving an offering by adding new features and higher quality materials or augmenting products with services and raising the purchase price.

Value. The ratio of perceived benefits to price for a product or service.

Variable cost. Expenses that are uniform per unit of output within a relevant time period (usually defined as a budget year); total variable costs fluctuate in direct proportion to the output volume of units produced. Variable costs include cost of goods sold and other variable costs such as sales commissions.

Variable-cost price strategies. Those that consider only direct (variable) costs associated with the offering in pricing a product or service.

Viral marketing. An Internet-enabled promotion strategy that encourages individuals to forward marketer-initiated messages to others via e-mail.

Working capital. The dollar value of an organization's current assets (such as cash, accounts receivable, prepaid expenses, inventory) *minus* the dollar value of current liabilities (such as short-term accounts payable for goods and services, income taxes).

Subject Index

Advertising opportunity, for offering, 287
Advertising/promotion
budget allocation for, 290–291
collateral, 121
in disposable diaper case study, 337–346
in disposable panty case study, 591–593
in energy beverages case study, 101–102, 104
in European passenger care case study, 655, 657
fruit juice/juice drink case study, 383
in health-care monitoring case study, 422
in marketing plan, 31–32
media selection factors for, 290–291
in mouthwash case study, 251
price, 291
promotional web sites, personal selling and, 288–289
in snack food case study, 262
in soft drink case study, 165–166, 170–172, 181, 316–318, 322, 323
timing strategies for, 291
in tire case study, 612, 614
Advertising share of voice, 289–290
Airline industry case study, 479–499. *See also* Southwest Airlines (Case Study)
All-available-funds budgeting approach, 290
Apparel industry case study, 437–452. *See also* VF Brands (Case Study)
Appliance market case study, 669–686. *See also* Qingdao Haier Ltd (Case Study)
Art museum case study, 594–603. *See also* Coleman Art Museum (Case study)
Astor Lodge & Suites, Inc. (Case Study), 324–336
background, 324–325
company information, 328–331
hotel industry, 325–328
sales and marketing planning and budgeting, 331–336
Attendant services, 367
Audio industry case study, 563–578. *See also* Sonance at a Turning Point (Case Study)
Augustine Medical, Inc. (Case Study), 534–543
background, 534
Bair Hugger patient warming system, 534–536

company information, 540–543
competing technologies, 536–537
competitive products, 537–539
hospital market, 539–540
Automobiles in Europe case study, 652–668. *See also* Chevrolet Europe (Case Study)
Automotive air-conditioning muffler case study, 524–533. *See also* Circle Corporation (Case Study)
Automotive hoist case study, 626–635. *See also* Jolson Automotive Hoist: The Market-Entry Decision (Case Study)

Backpay period, 136
Banking case study, 347–358. *See also* BBVA Compass (Case Study)
BBVA Compass (Case Study), 347–360
background, 347
banking industry, 347–348
company information, 348–349
customer information, 349–350
marketing resource allocation, 350–352
offline marketing, 352–353
online marketing, 353–358
Beer distributorship case study, 123–132. *See also* South Delaware Coors, Inc. (Case Study)
Billing, electronic. *See* Fiserve Takes on the E-Billing Market (Case Study)
Blitz strategy, 291
Brand equity
creation of, 142–143
explanation of, 141–142
in fruit juice/juice drink industry, 387
method to value, 143
Brand extension strategy, 146, 271–273
Brand growth strategy, 145–147
Brand recognition, in kitchen cutlery market, 403
Brands/branding
in banking case study, 352
in energy beverages case study, 103
in European passenger care case study, 652–655, 660–668
explanation of, 141–142
in fruit juice/juice drink case study, 380, 385–389
global, 143–144, 624–625
in hair care product case study, 152–153
multibranding, 144
multiproduct, 143–144

in soft drink industry case studies, 166, 314
strategic options to grow, 145–147
Break-even analysis
explanation of, 39–40, 292
multiple product, 42
new offerings and, 136
Breeder's Own Pet Foods, Inc. (Case Study), 113–122
company and product background, 113
company meeting, 114
packaging and distribution modifications, 114
proposal presentation, 114–122
Budgets/budgeting
in banking case study, 351–352
control through, 292
in disposable panty case study, 593
in hotel case study, 331–336
for integrated marketing communication mix, 289–292
sales force, 291–292
types of, 14
Bundling, 134
Burroughs Wellcome Company (Case Study), 512–523
acquired immune deficiency syndrome information, 513–516
background, 512–513
company information, 516–517
Retrovir development, 518–521
Retrovir marketing, 521–523
Business
defining your, 2
goals of, 3–4
mission of, 3
Business analysis, 136–137
Business risk, 617–618

Cadbury Beverages, Inc. (Case Study), 309–323
background, 309
carbonated soft drink industry, 312–315
company information, 309–312
Crush brand marketing program, 319–323
orange-flavored drinks, 315–319
Canada
health-care system in, 416–417
mouthwash market in, 241–243
Cannibalism
assessment of, 43–45
explanation of, 10, 43, 370
preemptive, 147
in tire case study, 615

Carbonated soft drink industry case
    studies, 162–181, 309–323. *See also*
    Cadbury Beverages, Inc. (Case
    Study); Dr Pepper/Seven Up, Inc. –
    Squirt Brand (Case Study)
Carpet and rug industry case study,
    429–436. *See also* Crafton Industries,
    Inc. (Case Study)
Case analysis
    approaches to, 61–62
    class discussion of, 64
    communication of, 64–65
    examples of, 687–702 (*See also*
        Republic National Bank of Dallas
        (Sample Case Analysis); Republic
        National Bank of Dallas (Sample
        Student Analysis))
    formulation of, 62–63
    function of, 56
    oral presentations of, 64–65
    team-based, 63
Case analysis worksheet, 62
Case studies
    Astor Lodge & Suites, Inc., 324–336
    Augustine Medical, Inc., 534–543
    BBVA Compass, 347–360
    Breeder's Own Pet Foods, Inc.,
        113–122
    Burroughs Wellcome Company,
        512–523
    Cadbury Beverages, Inc., 309–323
    Chevrolet Europe, 652–668
    Circle Corporation, 524–533
    Coleman Art Museum, 594–603
    Crafton Industries, Inc., 429–436
    CUTCO Corporation, 390–405
    Dermavescent Laboratories, Inc.,
        210–217
    Dr Pepper/Seven Up, Inc., 162–181
    Dr Pepper Snapple Group, Inc.,
        91–104
    Drypers Corporation, 337–346
    EMI Group, PLC, 463–478
    Fairchild Water Technologies, Inc.,
        636–651
    Fiserve Takes on the E-Billing
        Market, 83–90
    Frito-Lay, Inc. - Cracker Jack,
        253–279
    Frito-Lay, Inc. - Sun Chips Multigrain
        Snacks, 192–209
    Goodyear Tire and Rubber Company,
        604–615
    Haverwood Furniture, Inc. (A),
        294–305
    Haverwood Furniture, Inc. (B),
        306–308
    Hawaiian Punch, 377–389
    Hi-Value Supermarkets, 500–511
    Janmar Coatings, Inc., 105–112
    Jolson Automotive Hoist: The Market-
        Entry Decision, 626–635
    Lancer Gallery, 80–82
    Mary Kay India: The Hair Care
        Product Line Opportunity, 149–161
    Metabical, 544–551
    Nundies, 579–593
    Orâteme, Inc., 218–228
    Pate Memorial Hospital, 229–239

Procter & Gamble, Inc. - Scope,
    240–252
Pyramid Door, Inc., 424–428
Qingdao Haier Ltd, 669–686
Sander Automotive Companies,
    182–191
SaskTel, 416–423
Sonance at a Turning Point, 563–578
South Delaware Coors, Inc., 123–132
Southwest Airlines, 479–499
VF Brands, 437–452
Yorktown Technologies, 406–415
Cash flow. *See* Discounted cash flow
Catalog sales, in kitchen cutlery
    market, 396–397
Chain ratio method, 78
Channel captain, 371–372. *See also*
    Marketing channels
Channel conflict, 371. *See also*
    Marketing channels
Channels. *See* Marketing channels
Chevrolet Europe (Case Study),
    652–668
    background, 652–653
    brand positioning, 662–668
    European passenger car market,
        653–659
    General Motors in Europe, 659–662
Chief marketing officer (CMO), 1
Circle Corporation (Case Study),
    524–533
    automotive air-conditioning mufflers,
        525–527
    automotive industry, 527–530
    background, 524
    business decision making, 530–533
    company information, 524–525
Class discussions, of case analysis, 64
Co-branding, 146
Coleman Art Museum (Case Study),
    594–603
    background, 594–595
    considerations for 2005, 602–603
    museum collection and display,
        595–598
    museum marketing, 598–602
Collateral advertising, 121
Committed costs, 36
Communication strategies. *See*
    also Integrated marketing
    communications
    evaluation and control of, 292
    framework for, 282
    in global markets, 622–623
    objectives for, 283–284
Company analysis (marketing plan), 26
Competition/competitors
    in airline case study, 493, 495–499
    in audio industry case study, 573
    in automotive air-conditioning muffler
        case study, 529–530
    in automotive hoist case study,
        629–630
    in carpet and rug case study,
        430–431, 435–436
    in disposable diaper and training
        pants case study, 339–340
    in electric passenger car case
        study, 183, 184

in energy beverages case study,
    98–99
in fruit juice/juice drink case
    study, 380
in health care industry case
    study, 239
in health-care monitoring case study,
    420–421
in home water purification case
    study, 643–648
in hypothermia prevention products
    case study, 537–539
in mouthwash case study, 245–246
in paint coatings case study, 106–107
in recorded music case study,
    466–468, 471
in snack food case study, 195,
    256–258
in soft drink case study, 165
in supermarket chain case study,
    501–506
in weight-loss drug industry, 545–547
Competitive interaction, pricing and,
    460–462
Competitive-parity approach, 289
Competitor analysis (marketing plan),
    25–26
Concentrated marketing, 74–75
Concept test, in electronic billing case
    study, 87, 89
Consistency, in offering mix, 135
Consolidation, in consumer electronics
    industry, 564
Consumer electronics industry case
    study, 563–578. *See also* Sonance at
    a Turning Point (Case Study)
Consumer research, in supermarket
    case study, 506–509
Consumers
    attitude toward electronic billing,
        88–90
    in banking case study, 349–350
    brand equity and, 142–143
    channel selection and, 367, 374
    in electric passenger car case
        study, 185
    in fruit juice/juice drink case study,
        386–387
    in health-care monitoring case
        study, 420
    in large household appliance case
        study, 680
    requirements of, 367
Contingency plans, 15
Contract assembly, 620
Contract manufacturing, 620
Contribution, 39
Contribution analysis
    break-even analysis and, 39–40
    cannibalization and, 43–45
    explanation of, 39
    market size and, 43
    multiple product break-even analysis
        and, 42
    performance measurement
        and, 43
    profit impact and, 41–42
    sensitivity analysis and, 41
Contribution margin, 40

Contribution-margin approach, 557
Contribution per unit, 41, 42
Control. *See* Marketing control; Operations control
Convenience, as buyer requirement, 367
Core competencies (marketing plan), 22
Corporate branding, 143–144
Cost of capital, 46
Cost of goods sold, 35
Cost per thousand (CPM) readers/ viewers, 290
Costs
    allocation of, 555–556
    analysis of, 555–556
    disaggregated, 560
    fixed, 35–36
    in health-care monitoring system project, 422–423
    order-getting, 559
    order-servicing, 559
    variable, 335
Crafton Industries, Inc. (Case Study), 429–436
    background, 429
    carpet and run industry in United States, 429–433
    company information, 433–435
    direct distribution experience of competitors, 435–436
Cross-docking, 375
Cross-elasticity of demand, 456
Cumulative cash flow, 46
Customer analysis (marketing plan), 27–28
Customer lifetime value (CLV), 47–49
Customer profitability analysis, 560–561
Customer value proposition
    explanation of, 12
    in marketing plan, 29
CUTCO Corporation (Case Study), 390–405
    background, 390–392
    catalog sales, 396–397
    CUTCO stores, 398–399
    direct selling, 400–401
    global expansion, 400
    growth drivers, 401–402
    Internet activities, 397–398
    product line, 392–393
    social media, 399–400
    strategic options, 402–405
    Vector Marketing Corporation, 394–400

Data, information vs., 562
Decision analysis, 57, 59
Decision making, positioning, 141
Decision-making process
    best alternatives identification in, 57–59
    consideration of relevant information in, 57
    decision evaluation in, 60–61
    enumeration of decision factors in, 56
    implementation plan development in, 60
    problem definition in, 56
    steps in, 55

Decision tree
    example of, 58
    format for, 11–12
Demand
    cross-elasticity of, 456
    effective, 69
    price elasticity of, 455–456
    in weight-loss drug case study, 551
Demographics, of soft drink consumption, 166–167, 178
Deregulation, in airline industry case study, 481–482
Dermavescent Laboratories, Inc. (Case Study), 210–217
    company and product, 210–211
    package design, 213–215
    packaging and test market decision, 217
    preliminary tests, 215–217
    women's shaving in United States, 211–213
Differentiated marketing, 74, 75
Direct distribution
    in carpet and rug industry, 431, 432, 435–436
    explanation of, 363–364
Direct exporting, 620
Direct investment
    explanation of, 621
    function of, 9
Direct selling
    in hair care products case study, 150
    in kitchen cutlery case study, 400–401
Direct store delivery (DSD), 383, 385
Disaggregated costs, 560
Discounted cash flow
    explanation of, 45–46
    illustration of, 277–279
    for valuation, 275–277
Disintermediation, 370
Disposable panty case study, 579–593. *See also* Nundies (Case study)
Distinctive competencies, 4–5
Distribution
    in audio industry case study, 564
    in automotive hoist case study, 631
    in carpet and rug case study, 431–432
    channel selection and levels of, 368
    density of, 365–367
    direct, 363–364, 431, 432, 435–436
    in disposable diaper and training pants case study, 338
    dual, 369
    effective, 366
    exclusive, 366–367
    in fruit juice/juice drink case study, 379, 383, 385
    in health-care monitoring case study, 421
    indirect, 363–364
    intensive, 366
    in large household appliance case study, 676–678
    in marketing plan, 32
    in pet food case study, 114
    in residential garage door case study, 427–428
    retail, 365–367, 379
    selective, 366–367
    in tire industry case study, 609, 614–615

Diversification, 10, 11
Dr Pepper/Seven Up, Inc. - Squirt Brand (Case Study), 162–181
    carbonated soft drink industry in United States, 163–167
    company background, 162–181 162–163
    Hispanic market opportunity, 178–181
    Squirt brand heritage and marketing, 168–176
    Squirt positioning review: June 2001, 176–178
Dr Pepper Snapple Group, Inc. - Energy Beverages (Case Study), 91–104
    company background, 91, 92
    company business strategy, 94–96
    company operations, 92–93
    company strengths, 93–94
    energy beverage market in United States, 96–100
    marketing decisions, 103–104
    marketing plan considerations, 100–102
    pricing and profitability, 104
    sports drink market and accelerade RTD launch, 102
Drypers Corporation (Case Study), 337–346
    background, 337–338
    business plan, 344–346
    company information, 340–344
    disposable diaper and training pants market, 338–340
Dual distribution, 368, 369

E-billing case study. *See* Fiserve Takes on the E-Billing Market (Case Study)
Economy, consumer electronics sales and, 573–574
Effective demand, 69
Effective distribution, 366
Effectiveness, of organizations, 553, 561–562
Efficiency, in organizations, 553, 561–562
80-20 rule, 556, 561
Electric car case study, 182–191. *See also* Sanger Automotive Companies (Case Study)
Electronic billing case study, 83–90. *See also* Fiserve Takes on the E-Billing Market (Case Study)
Electronic marketing channels
    explanation of, 364–365
    multi-channel marketing and, 369–370
Elimination, offering, 138–139
EMI Group, PLC (Case Study), 463–478
    background, 463–464
    company information, 471–475
    economics of recorded music, 468–469
    global recorded music industry, 464–465
    industry competition, 466–468
    recorded music market in United States, 469–471
    Universal Music Group's pricing initiative, 475–478

Energy beverage case study, 91–104. *See also* Dr Pepper Snapple Group, Inc. - Energy Beverages (Case Study)

Energy beverage market (U.S.), 96–100, 102

Environmental forces, product-market strategy and, 11

Environmental opportunities, 4–5

Ethics. *See* Marketing ethics

European passenger car case study, 652–668. *See also* Chevrolet Europe (Case Study)

Evaluation
in marketing plan, 34
opportunity, 69

Exclusive distribution, 366–367

Expected monetary value (EMV), 59, 60

Expected monetary value of perfect information (EMVPI), 59, 60

Exporting
direct vs. indirect, 620
function of, 8–9

Fairchild Water Technologies, Inc. (Case Study), 636–651
background, 636
company information, 641–642
competition, 643–648
Delight purifier, 642, 643
foreign investment in India, 639–641
Indian market for home water filtration and purification, 636–639
recommendations, 648–651

Family branding, 143–144

Fighting brand strategy, 147

Financial budget, 14

Financial concepts. *See also specific financial concepts*
contribution analysis, 39–45
customer lifetime value, 47–49
discounted cash flow, 46–47
fixed costs, 35–36
liquidity, 45
margins, 36–39
operating leverage, 45–46
pro forma income statement, 49–50
relevant costs, 36
sunk costs, 36
variable costs, 35

Financial data
in art museum case study, 596–598
in large household appliance case study, 682–684
in marketing plan, 32–33
in mouthwash case study, 249–251
in snack food case study, 263–267

Financial goals, 3

Fiserve Takes on the E-Billing Market (Case Study), 83–90
background of, 83–84
e-billing market research, 87–89
e-billing opportunities and challenges, 86–87
e-billing revenue model and conversion costs, 89–90
electronic bill payment, 85
research results, 90

Five-year projections, in marketing plan, 33

Fixed costs, 35–36

Flanker brand strategy, 147

Focus groups
in disposable panty case study, 582–584
in electronic billing case study, 87
in women's shaving product case study, 215

Franchising, 620–621

Frequency, of media exposure, 290–291

Freshwater ornamental fish case study, 406–415. *See also* Yorktown Technologies (Case Study)

Frito-Lay, Inc. - Cracker Jack (Case Study), 253–279
background, 253
company information, 254–255
Cracker Jack, 260–267
discounted cash flow technique, 277–279
new venture division, 255–256
Project Bingo, 267–275
ready-to-eat caramel popcorn product category, 256–259
valuation, 275–277

Frito-Lay, Inc. - Sun Chips Multigrain Snacks (Case Study), 192–209
company background, 192–194
product-marketing strategies, 194–195
snack chip category, 195
sun chips multigrain snack development, 196–200
test market, 200–207
test market review, 207–209

Fruit juice/juice drink case study, 377–389. *See also* Hawaiian Punch (Case Study)

Full-cost pricing, 458–459

Furniture industry case studies, 294–308. *See also* Haverwood Furniture, Inc. (A) (Case Study); Haverwood Furniture, Inc. (B) (Case Study)

Garage door case study, 424–428. *See also* Pyramid Door, Inc. (Case Study)

Global brands, 143–144

Global markets/global marketing
apparel industry and, 438–443
attractiveness of, 619
in automotive hoist case study, 632–634
explanation of, 617
global brands and positioning and, 143–144, 624–625
growth opportunities in Asia-Pacific markets, 150–151
identifying opportunities in, 618–619
kitchen cutlery and, 400, 403–404
in large household appliance case study, 671–673
market-development strategy and, 8–9
marketing channels and pricing strategies and, 624
modes of entry into, 619–621
offering and communication strategies and, 622–623

reasons to engage in, 617–618
segmentation and targeting and, 622

Goals, business, 3–4

Goodyear Tire and Rubber Company (Case Study), 604–615
advertising and distribution, 614
background, 604–605
company information, 610–614
market presence, 611
product line and pricing, 611–614
strategic considerations to broaden distribution, 614–615
tire industry, 605–610

Go-to-market strategy
explanation of, 361
in fruit juice/juice drink industry, 387–388

Gross margin, 37

Gross profit. *See* Gross margin

Groupthink, 63

Growth drivers, in kitchen cutlery case study, 401–402

Hair care products case study, 149–161. *See also* Mary Kay India: The Hair Care Product Line Opportunity (Case Study)

Harvesting, 138

Haverwood Furniture, Inc. (A) (Case Study), 294–305
background, 294–295
budget meeting, 301–302
company information, 296–297
consumer panel report findings, 302–305
household furniture industry, 297–301

Haverwood Furniture, Inc. (B) (Case Study), 306–308
company information, 306, 308
Lea-Meadows, Inc., 306–307
merging sales efforts, 307–308

Hawaiian Punch (Case Study), 377–389
advertising and promotion, 383, 384
background, 377–378
brand marketing, 385–389
fruit juice and juice drinks in United States, 378–380
Hawaiian Punch drink, 380–382
manufacturing, sales and distribution, 383, 385
product line and pricing, 382

Health care monitoring system case study, 416–423. *See also* SaskTel (Case Study)

Health clinic case study, 229–239. *See also* Pate Memorial Hospital (Case Study)

High-end audio case study, 563–578. *See also* Sonance at a Turning Point (Case Study)

Hispanic consumers
soft drink case study and, 178–181
statistics related to, 179–181

Hi-Value Supermarkets (Case Study), 500–511
background, 500
company information, 500–501
competitive environment, 501–506
consumer research initiatives, 506–509
quarterly review meeting, 509–511

Home appliance market case study, 669–686. *See also* Qingdao Haier Ltd (Case Study)
Home water filtration and purification case study, 636–651. *See also* Fairchild Water Technologies, Inc. (Case Study)
Hospital ambulatory health services case study, 229–239. *See also* Pate Memorial Hospital (Case Study)
Hotel industry case study, 324–336. *See also* Astor Lodge & Suites, Inc. (Case Study)

Implementation plan, in marketing plan, 34
Income statements. *See* Pro forma income statement
Independent sales representatives, 285–287
India
  branded beauty and personal care market in, 153–156
  foreign investment in, 639–641
  home water filtration and purification market in, 636–639
  Mary Kay India, 151–153
Indirect distribution, 363–364
Indirect exporting, 620
Industry analysis (marketing plan), 24–25
Information
  data vs., 562
  in decision-making process, 57
  for purchase decisions, 282–285, 367
Innovation
  in fruit juice/juice drink case study, 388
  product, 9
Integrated marketing communications
  evaluation and control of, 292
  explanation of, 282
  marketing web sites and, 288–289
  objectives for, 283–284
  purchase decisions and, 282–283
  strategic framework for, 282
Integrated marketing communications mix
  budgeting for, 289–292
  information requirements of buyers and, 282–283
  nature of offering and, 285
  organizational capacity and, 285–287
  push vs. pull communication strategies and, 287
  target-market characteristics and, 285
Intensive distribution, 366
Intermediaries
  buyer requirements and, 367
  channel selection and, 361–363, 370
  electronic, 364
  in foreign trade, 620
  requirements of, 370–371
  retail level and, 365, 368
Intermediate pricing strategy, 460
Internet. *See also* Web sites
  banking industry marketing on, 353–358
  electronic marketing channels and, 364–365
  kitchen cutlery market and, 397–398

marketspace and, 13
price-comparison shopping on, 554
recruiting on, 397, 403
Investment
  in automotive hoist case study, 633–634
  in beer distributorship case study, 126–132
  in India, 639–641

Janmar Coatings, Inc. (Case Study), 105–112
  company background, 109–110
  paint coatings industry in United States, 105–108
  planning meeting, 111–112
  service area, 108–109
Joint ventures
  with foreign firms, 621
  function of, 9
  in home water purification case study, 650
Jolson Automotive Hoist: The Market-Entry Decision (Case Study), 626–635
  background, 626
  company information, 626–628
  competition, 629–630
  European market, 632–634
  industry information, 628–629
  marketing strategy, 630–632, 634–635

Key success factors (KSFs), 5
Kitchen cutlery case study, 390–405. *See also* CUTCO Corporation (Case Study)

Lancer Gallery (Case Study), 80–82
Leverage, operating, 45–46
Licensing
  function of, 9
  in home water purification case study, 649–650
  types of, 620–621
Life-cycle stage
  communication objectives and, 283–284
  explanation of, 137–138
  pricing and, 454
Line extension strategy, 146
Liquidity, 45
Logistics, 361, 362

Make-or-buy decisions, 285–287
Margins
  explanation of, 36
  gross, 37
  net profit, 38–39
  trade, 37–38
Market
  definition of, 69
  for new offering, 135
  served, 71
Market-development strategy, 8–9
Market evolution, 554
Marketing
  in art museum case study, 598–602
  to associations, 221–224

in banking case study, 350–358
concentrated, 74–75
differentiated, 74
in disposable diaper and training pants case study, 342–344
in disposable panty case study, 589–593
in freshwater ornamental fish case study, 413–415
goals for, 3
in hotel case study, 331–336
in large household appliance case study, 678–680
multi-channel, 369–370
purpose of, 1
in snack food case study, 258–259
in soft drink case study, 165–167, 169–176
Marketing audit, 14–15
Marketing channels
  analysis of, 559–560
  design of, 363–365
  direct vs., 363–364
  in disposable panty case study, 590–591
  dual distribution and, 368, 369
  effect of change in, 554
  electronic, 364–365, 369–370
  in energy beverages case, 101
  explanation of, 361, 362
  in global markets, 624
  intermediary requirements and, 370–371
  modification decisions related to, 372–373
  multi-channel marketing and, 369–370
  profitability and, 367, 559
  retail-level, 365–367
  selection decisions for, 362–363
  target market and, 361, 363–367
  trade relations and, 371–372
  at various levels of distribution, 368
Marketing communication mix, 281
Marketing communications, 281–282. *See also* Integrated marketing communications
Marketing control
  considerations in, 561–562
  customer profitability analysis and, 560–561
  marketing channel analysis and, 559–560
  marketing-cost analysis and, 555–556
  operations control and, 553
  product-service mix analysis and, 556–557
  sales analysis and, 557–559
  strategic change and, 553–555
  strategic control and, 553
Marketing-cost analysis, 555–556
Marketing decision making. *See* Decision making; Decision-making process
Marketing ethics, 15–16
Marketing management. *See* Strategic marketing management

Marketing managers, 1
Marketing mix
  explanation of, 12
  formulation of, 12–13
  implementation of, 13–14
Marketing objectives (marketing plan),
  28–29
Marketing plans
  components of, 21–34
  in energy beverages case study,
    100–102
  function of, 15
  long-run, 15
  short-run, 15
  writing and style considerations for,
    19–20
Marketing programs
  in marketing plan, 30–32
  market segmentation and, 72
Marketing research
  in disposable panty case study,
    581–584
  in mouthwash case study, 249
Marketing resources, allocation of, 72
Marketing Web sites, 288–289
Market-penetration strategy, 7–8
Market potential, screening for,
  618–619
Market redefinition, 554
Market sales potential
  estimation of, 76–77
  explanation of, 76
  sales and profit forecasting and,
    77–78
Market segmentation
  bases for, 72–73
  benefits of, 71–72
  in European passenger care case
    study, 657–659
  explanation of, 71
  global, 622
  requirements for, 73, 622
Market segments
  explanation of, 71
  requirements for, 73
Market share
  explanation of, 70–71, 556
  in tire case study, 607, 608, 611
Market size
  contribution analysis and, 43
  estimates of, 76
  product development and, 10
Marketspace, 13
Market structure, 69–70
Mark-on, 37
Markup, 37
Markup pricing, 458
Mary Kay India: The Hair Care Product
  Line Opportunity (Case Study),
  149–161
  branded beauty and personal care
    market in India, 153–156
  company background, 149–151
  hair care product opportunity,
    156–161
  India operations, 151–153
Media
  budget allocation for advertising,
    290–291

  in pet food industry case, 119–122
  selection of, 290
Media channels, 290
Media reach, 290
Metabical (Case Study), 544–551
  background, 544–545
  company information, 547–548
  competitive environment, 545–547
  demand forecasting, 551
  obesity epidemic in United
    States, 545
  packaging and pricing decisions,
    548–550
Mission, of organizations, 3
Mission statements, 3
Mouthwash market case, 240–252. *See
  also* Procter & Gamble, Inc. - Scope
  (Case Study)
Multibranding, 144
Multi-channel marketing, 369–370
Multiple product break-even
  analysis, 42
Multiproduct branding, 143–144
Museum case study, 594–603. *See also*
  Coleman Art Museum (Case study)

Net cash flow, 46
Net profit margin (before taxes),
  38–39
New brand strategy, 146–147
New products
  in audio industry case study, 574
  identifying opportunities to develop,
    71–72
  pricing strategy for, 459–460
Nundies (Case study), 579–593
  Advanced Materials, Inc., 580
  background, 579
  future sales and marketing initiatives,
    589–593
  market research, 581–584
  product development, 580
  product launch, 584–586
  results to date, 586–589

Objective-task budgeting approach, 290
Offering adaptation, 623
Offering extension, 623–624
Offering invention, 623
Offering mix, 134–135
Offerings
  advertising opportunity for, 287
  branding, 141–142
  communication mix and nature
    of, 285
  concept of, 133–134
  definition of, 133
  elimination of, 138–139
  in global markets, 622–623
  harvesting, 138
  life-cycle concept and, 137–138
  marketing positioning decision
    for, 141
  modification of, 138
  positioning approaches for,
    139–140
  positioning statement for, 140–141
  procedure to develop new, 136–137
  repositioning, 141

  seasonal, 291
  use of term, 69
Operating budget, 14
Operating leverage, 45–46
Operations control
  customer profitability analysis and,
    560–561
  explanation of, 553, 555
  marketing channel analysis and,
    559–560
  marketing-cost analysis and,
    555–556
  product-service mix analysis and,
    556–557
  sales analysis and, 557–559
Operations strategy, in apparel industry
  case study, 443–445
Opportunities. *See* SWOT analysis
Opportunity analysis, 67–68
Opportunity evaluation, 69
Opportunity evaluation matrix, 68
Opportunity identification, 67–68
Opportunity-organization matching,
  68–69
Oral presentations, of case analysis,
  64–65
Orâteme, Inc. (Case Study), 218–228
  association market, 223–224
  company background, 218–219
  company performance, 222, 223
  competition, 224–225
  marketing approach, 221–222
  opportunities, 225–228
  product and service offerings,
    220–221
  strategic goals, 219–220
Order-getting costs, 559
Order-servicing costs, 559
Organizational opportunities
  converting environmental
    opportunities to, 4–5
  SWOT analysis and, 5–7
Organizational resources, in offering
  mix, 135
Organizations
  communications mix and abilities of,
    285–286
  effectiveness of, 553, 561–562
  efficiency in, 553, 561–562
  identifying strengths of, 93–94

Packaging
  in weight-loss drug case study,
    548–549
  in women's shaving product case
    study, 213–315
Paint coatings industry case study,
  105–112. *See also* Janmar Coatings,
  Inc. (Case Study)
Paint coatings industry data, 105–108
Passenger automobiles in Europe case
  study, 652–668. *See also* Chevrolet
  Europe (Case Study)
Pate Memorial Hospital (Case Study),
  229–239
  background, 231
  hospital industry and ambulatory
    health care services, 229–231
  Pate Health Clinic, 231–239

Patient warming system case study,
    534–543. *See also* Augustine
    Medical, Inc. (Case Study)
Payoff table, 58–59
Penetration pricing strategy, 460
Percentage-of-sales approach, 289
Performance measurement,
    contribution analysis and, 43
Personal selling, marketing
    communication process and,
    288–289
Pet food industry case study, 113–122.
    See also Breeder's Own Pet Foods,
    Inc. (Case Study)
Pharmaceutical industry case study,
    512–523. *See also* Burroughs
    Wellcome Company (Case Study)
Point of difference
    in marketing plan, 29
    new products and, 10
Portfolio. *See* Offerings
Positioning
    decision making for, 141
    explanation of, 139
    in fruit juice/juice drink case
        study, 388
    in global markets, 624–625
    of offerings, 139–140
    in snack food case study,
        260–262
    in soft drink case study, 172–178
Positioning statement, 140–141
Preemptive cannibalism, 147
Premarket test (PMT), in snack chip
    case study, 197–200
Present value
    of money, 46
    of projected cash flows, 277–279
Present-value analysis, 46, 47
Price elasticity of demand,
    455–456
Price/pricing
    conceptual orientation to, 454
    considerations for, 453–454
    importance of, 453
    as indicator of value, 455
    markup, 458
    product-line, 456
    profit impact from changes in,
        456–457
    rate-of-return, 458, 459
Price wars, 461–462
Pricing strategies
    competitive interaction and,
        460–462
    in energy beverages case
        study, 104
    in fruit juice/juice drink case
        study, 382
    full-cost, 458–459, 4458
    in global markets, 624
    in home water purification case
        study, 650–651
    intermediate, 460
    in marketing plan, 31
    new-offering, 459–460
    penetration, 460
    in pharmaceutical case study,
        521–523

in recorded music case study,
    463–464, 475–478
    skimming, 459–460
    in snack food case study, 262–263
    in soft drink case study, 318–319
    in supermarket case study, 509–511
    in tire case study, 610
    trade margins and, 37–38
    variable-cost, 458, 459
    in weight-loss drug case study,
        548–550
Primary demand, 283–284
Private branding, 144–145
Procter & Gamble, Inc. - Scope (Case
    Study), 240–252
    company background, 240–241
    current state, 243–246
    mouthwash market in Canada,
        241–243
    plaque, 252
    Plax introduction, 243
    regulatory environment, 247
    three-year plan, 247–251
Product augmentation, 9
Product development
    in disposable panty case study, 580
    explanation of, 9–10
    identification of opportunities for,
        71–72
    in mouthwash case study, 248
    in snack chip case study, 196–200
Product innovation, 9
Production goals, 3
Product life cycle, 137, 138
Product line
    in energy beverage case study,
        100–101, 103
    fruit juice/juice drink case study, 382
    in kitchen cutlery case study,
        392–393
    in snack food case study, 260–262
    in tire case study, 611–614
Product-line pricing, 456
Product-market strategies
    diversification and, 10
    explanation of, 7
    Frito-Lay, 194–195
    market development and, 8–9
    marketing mix and, 12–14
    in marketing plan, 28–29
    market penetration and, 7–8
    product development and, 9–10
    selection of, 10–12
Product placement allowances, in fruit
    juice/juice drink case study, 389
Product proliferation, in energy
    beverages case study, 99–100
Product-service mix analysis,
    556–557
Profitability analysis, 559
Profit analysis, 136
Profit plans, 14
Profit/profitability
    contribution analysis and, 41–42
    in energy beverages case study, 104
    marketing channels and, 367, 559
    price changes and, 456–467
    in recorded music case study,
        468–469

Pro forma income statement
    explanation of, 14
    preparation of, 49–50
    sales and profit forecasting and, 78
Programmed costs, 36
Promotion. *See* Advertising/promotion
Promotional web sites, 288–289
Public relations, for genetically
    modified fish, 409–410
Pull communication strategy, 287
Purchase decisions
    information requirements for,
        282–285
    in paint coatings case study, 107–108
Purchase-process model, 282–283
Push communication strategy, 287
Pyramid Door, Inc. (Case Study),
    424–428
    background, 424
    company information, 424–425
    distribution strategy, 427–428
    residential garage door industry,
        425–427

Qingdao Haier Ltd (Case Study),
    669–686
    background, 669–670
    company information, 670–674
    large household appliance industry in
        United States, 674–680
    Maytag bid considerations, 685–686
    Maytag Corporation, 680–685

Rate-of-return pricing, 458, 459
Reach, media, 290
Recorded music industry case study,
    463–478. *See also* EMI Group, PLC
    (Case Study)
Recovery strategies, 14–15
Recruiting, Internet, 397, 403
Reformulation strategies, 14–15
Regulatory environment
    in Canada, 247
    for genetically modified fish,
        409–412
Relevant costs, 36
Relevant information, in decision-
    making process, 57
Repositioning, of offering, 141
Republic National Bank of Dallas
    (Sample Case Analysis)
    appendix: NOW accounts in New
        England, 693–696
    banking in Texas, 688
    company information, 690–691
    competitive situation in Dallas,
        688–690
    introduction, 687–688
    NOW account marketing strategy, 693
    NOW accounts, 691–693
Republic National Bank of Dallas
    (Sample Student Analysis)
    company information, 699–700
    insights from New England
        experience, 697–699
    plan of action, 700–701
    recommended NOW account
        marketing strategy, 701–702
    strategic issues and problems, 697

Research proposal, in South Delaware Coors case study, 124–126
Retail outlets/retail sales
  in audio industry case study, 570–571
  in carpet and rug case study, 432, 433
  distribution at, 365–367, 379
  in kitchen cutlery case study, 398–399, 404–405
  marketing channel selection and, 365–367
Return on investment (ROI), 136–137
Revenue, 453
Risk-adjusted discount rate, 277

Sales analysis
  explanation of, 136, 557
  findings of, 558–559
Sales force
  budget allocation for, 291–292
  independent sales representatives vs. company, 285–287
Sales forecasts
  explanation of, 77–78
  for new offering, 136
  for water purifiers in India, 637
Sales mix, 42
Sales revenue, in marketing plan, 32
Sanger Automotive Companies (Case Study), 182–191
  background, 182, 189–191
  electric passenger car market in United States, 183–185
  Fisker Automotive, Inc., 186–187
  market area, 188–189
SaskTel (Case Study), 416–423
  company background, 418–419
  distribution options, 421–422
  health-care system in Canada, 416–417
  potential customers, 420–421
  projected costs, 422–423
  promotion, 422
  Saskatchewan statistics, 417
Seasonal offerings, 291
Selective demand, 284
Selective distribution, 366–367
Sensitivity analysis, 41
Served market, 71
Simulated test market (STM), in snack food industry, 268–271
Situation analysis
  function of, 4
  marketing plan (sample), 22–28
Skimming pricing strategy
  explanation of, 459–460
  in home water purification case study, 650–651
Snack food industry, 192–209, 253–279. See also Frito-Lay, Inc. - Cracker Jack (Case Study); Frito-Lay, Inc. - Sun Chips Multigrain Snacks (Case Study)
Social media, in kitchen cutlery market, 399–400
Social responsibility, 15–16

Soft drink case study, 162–181. See also Dr Pepper/Seven Up, Inc. - Squirt Brand (Case Study)
Sonance at a Turning Point (Case Study), 563–578
  alternatives analysis, 578
  background, 563
  company background, 564–566
  company issues, 564
  competition, 573
  customers, 570–572
  custom installation dealers, 567–570
  economic conditions, 573–574
  high-end audio industry, 566–567
  iPort, 574–577
  new products, 574
South Delaware Coors, Inc. (Case Study), 123–132
  background of Coors, 124
  investing and operating data, 126–132
  Larry Brownlow, 123
  Manson research proposal, 124–126
Southwest Airlines (Case Study), 479–499
  airline industry in United States, 480–487
  background, 479–480
  company information, 487–493
  competitive and financial performance, 493, 494
  Shuttle By United and, 479–480, 495–499
Southwestern art gallery case study, 80–82. See also Lancer Gallery (Case Study)
Sponsorships, in banking industry case, 252–253
Strategic chance
  effects of, 554–555
  explanation of, 553–554
  methods to deal with, 555
  sources of, 554
Strategic control, 553
Strategic focus and plan (marketing plan), 21–22
Strategic marketing management
  budgeting and, 14
  business definition, mission, and goals and, 2–4
  marketing ethics and social responsibility and, 15–16
  marketing plan and, 15
  organizational growth opportunities and, 4–7
  processes of, 1
  product-market strategies and, 7–14
  reformulation and recovery strategies and, 14–15
  supply chains and, 373–375
Sub-branding, 144
Success requirements, 5
Sunk costs, 36

Supermarket case study, 500–511. See also Hi-Value Supermarkets (Case Study)
Supply chains
  apparel industry, 445–452
  example of efficient, 374–375
  explanation of, 361–362
  marketing strategy and, 373–374
  responsiveness and efficiency of, 374
Survey research, in disposable panty case study, 582–584
Sustainable competitive advantage (marketing plan), 22
SWOT analysis
  for case analysis, 63
  explanation of, 5–7
  in marketing plan, 23–24

Target market
  approaches to, 74
  associations as, 224
  communication mix and, 285
  in energy beverages case study, 100, 103
  how to compete in, 74
  issues related to, 74–76
  marketing channels and, 361, 363–367
  in marketing plan, 29
  media selection for, 290
  sales forecasting and, 77
  in soft drink case study, 176–178
Team-based case analysis, 63
Technological innovation. See also Internet
  e-billing case study, 83–90
  explanation of, 554
  in hypothermia prevention, 536–537
Test market
  explanation of, 137
  simulated, 268–271
  in snack chip case study, 200–209
  in women's shaving product case study, 217
Time value of money, 46–47
Tire industry case study, 604–615. See also Goodyear Tire and Rubber Company (Case Study)
Trade margin, 37–38
Trade relations, 371–372
Trading down, 138
Trading up, 138
Transactional web sites, 288

United States
  airline industry in, 480–487
  banking industry in, 347–348
  carbonated soft drink industry in, 163–167, 312–315
  carpet and rug industry in, 429–433
  disposable diaper and training pants market in, 338–340
  electric passenger car market in, 183–185
  energy beverage market in, 96–100

fruit juice/juice drink market in, 378–380
hospital market in, 229–231, 539–540
hotel industry in, 325–328
household furniture industry in, 297–301
large household appliance industry in, 674–680
obesity epidemic in, 545
paint coatings industry in, 105–108
recorded music market in, 469–471
residential garage door industry in, 425–427
snack-food industry in, 195
tire industry in, 605–610
women's shaving in, 211–213

Valuation techniques, 275
Value, price as indicator of, 455
Variable-cost pricing, 458, 459
Variable costs, 35
Variety, as buyer requirement, 367

VF Brands (Case Study), 437–452
apparel industry data, 438–443
apparel supply chain, 445–447
background, 437–438
operations strategy, 443–445
third way supply chain, 447–452
Virtual staff development case study, 218–228. *See also* Orâteme, Inc. (Case Study)

Water purification case study, 636–651. *See also* Fairchild Water Technologies, Inc. (Case Study)
Weaknesses. *See* SWOT analysis
Web sites. *See also* Internet
explanation of, 288
marketing, 288–289
promotional, 288
transactional, 288
Weight-loss drug case study, 544–551. *See also* Metabical (Case Study)

Wholesalers
in carpet and rug case study, 432, 433
location of, 368
quantitative assessment of use of, 372–373
Women's shaving product case study, 210–217. *See also* Dermavescent Laboratories, Inc. (Case Study)
Written reports, of case analysis, 65

Yorktown Technologies (Case Study), 406–415
background, 406
CEO recommendations, 415
company history, 407–409
freshwater ornamental fish marketing, 413–415
product enhancements, 412–413
product launch, 410–412
public relations, 409–410
regulatory obstacles, 409–412
zebra fish, 406–407

Brand, Company, and Name Index

A. T. Kearney, 11
AAA. *See* American Automobile Association
AARP (formerly the American Association of Retired Persons), 223
ABBA, 467, 473
Abbey Carpets, 432, 433
Abbott Labs, 517
Accelerade RTD, 91, 95, 102
Accor North America, 326
AC/DC, 467
Ace Hardware, 107
ACNielsen, 92, 93, 100
ACNielsen Homescan, 386
Actifed, 517
Adams, Lori, 83
Adams Industrial Clinic, 235
AdBrite, 357–360
adidas, 72, 441, 442
Adkins-Green, Sheryl, 149, 150, 153, 156, 160
Admiral brand, 679, 681
Advanced Materials, Inc. (AMI), 579, 580, 582, 584, 585–586, 590, 591, 593
Advanced Materials Group, Inc., 580
Advanced Technology Vehicle Manufacturing loan program, 186
Advertising Age, 655
Aerosmith, 467
Affiniscape, 225
African Collector (magazine), 82
Aguafiel, 93
Aguilera, Christina, 468
AHV Lifts, 630
Aim, 139
Airbus Industries, 490
Air California, 482
Alaska Airlines, 489
ALCAS Corporation, 391, 392
Alcas Cutlery Corporation, 390–391, 394, 401
ALCOA (Aluminum Company of America), 390–391, 401
Aleve, 147
Alfa Romeo, 654, 658
Alfa Water Purifiers, Bombay, 648
Allen's, 310
Alli, 546–547, 550
Allure (magazine), 73
Almay, 137
Alpo, 117, 122
Alpo Lite, 122
Alpo Prime Cuts, 118
Altec Lansing, 576
Altima, 621
Always, 241

Amana, 674
Amana brand, 679, 681
Amarr Garage Doors, 426
Amazon, 460
Amazon.com, 364, 365
Amazon Fire tablet, 460
Ambassador brand of cards, 369
AMD Telemedicine, Inc. (AMD), 420, 421
American Airlines, 146, 480, 482, 483, 489
American Association of Museums, 598
American Automobile Association (AAA), 223, 330
American Civil Liberties Union, 522–523
American Dental Association (ADA), 242, 246, 247
American Express, 143, 624
American Hamilton (division of American Hospital Supply), 538
American Home Products Corporation (AHP), 256–258
American Hospital Supply, 372, 538
American Hotel and Lodging Association, 327
American Marketing Association, 343
American Red Cross, 3
American Society of Association Executives (ASAE), 224, 225
American Veterinary Medical Association, 118
America West Airlines, 480, 482, 483, 489
Amoco, 609
AMP Energy, 98–100
AMR, 482, 483
Amway, 400
Amway India, 157
Amway India Enterprises, 154
Anastacia, 467
Anheuser-Busch Companies, Inc., 10, 16, 98–99, 126, 147, 195
Animaniacs, 262
Anthony, Marc, 467
AOL, 354, 356, 357–360, 472
AOL Time Warner, 467, 468
A&P, 13–14
Apple, 9, 143, 284, 367, 554, 622
Apple Computer, 465
Aquaguard, 643–645, 648
Aquamatic, 538
Aquarius, 647, 651
Aquatred tires, 611, 613
"Architectural Series," 574, 576–578
Ariola, 468
Arista Records, 468

Arm & Hammer, 140, 143
Armstrong, Chris, 347, 349, 350, 354, 355
Armstrong, Louis, 467
Armstrong tires, 608, 609, 611
Arquest, Inc., 340
Arriva tires, 611, 613
Arrow shirts, 56
Art Center of Design, 186
ASAE. *See* American Society of Association Executives
Ash, Mary Kay, 149–150
Ashanti, 466
Ashley Furniture HomeStores, 300
Ashley Furniture Industries, Inc., 297
Associated Press, 410
Association Career Network, 226
Association of Home Appliance Manufacturers, 674
Aston Martin, 186
Astor Lodge & Suites, Inc. case, 324–336
Astra, 661
Atkins Nutritional Approach, 547
Atlantic, 467
Atlantic Blend, 70–71
Atlas brand tires, 609
Atoll, 310
Atomic Kitten, 472
Attends, 241
Audi, 654, 658
Audio Command, 567
Audio Video Systems, 567
Augustine, Scott, 540
Augustine Medical, Inc. case, 534–543
AutoAC, 527, 529–533
AutoAC Corporation, 524, 525
Autobytel.com, 364, 365
Auto Motor and Sport, 662
Avante, 524
Avectra, 225
Aveeno Therapeutic Shaving Gel, 213
Avis, 140
Avon, 400
Avon Products, Inc., 4, 154, 362–363
A&W, 92
A&W All-American Food, 93
A&W Brands, 169
A&W Root Beer, 162–163
AZT (azidothymidine), 512–514, 516, 518–523

Baby's Choice, 341
Backstreet Boys, 468
Bair Hugger Patient Warming System, 534–543
Bajaj Consumer Care Ltd., 155

Bajaj Electrical Division, 648
Baked Lay's, 72, 254, 255
Baked Tostitos, 254, 255
Baken-Ets, 193
Bali, 310
Banco Bilbao Vizcaya Argentaria, S.A.
    (BBVA), 348
Bank of America (BoA), 347, 348,
    351, 353
Barbie, 147
Barker, Andrew, 91, 100, 102–104
Bar Maisse, 633–635
Barnes & Noble, 368
Barq's Root Beer, 164
Barrett, Colleen, 490
Barry, David, 520
Bartoli, Cecilia, 466
Bassett Furniture Direct, 300
Bassett Furniture Industries, 297
Bates, Charlton ("Chuck"), 294–295,
    300, 301–302, 307
Batliboi, 648
BBVA Compass case, 347–360
The Beach Boys, 467
The Beatles, 472, 473
Beaulieu of America, 431
Beaupre, Phillipe, 633, 634
Bed Bath & Beyond, 673
Beggin' Strips, 117, 118
Beneful, 117, 122
Benetton, 444
Benjamin Moore, 106
Bennet, Tony, 467
Bentley, 189
BerklineBenchCraft, LLC, 297
Berne Manufacturing, 630
Bernstein, Leonard, 467
Bernstein, Sharon, 354–357
Berry, Chuck, 467
Berry, Thomas, 294–295
Berry, Tom, 302
Bertelsmann AG, 468, 472
Best Buy, 471, 564, 566, 571, 673, 674,
    677, 679, 681, 685
Best Western International,
    Inc., 326
Better Business Bureau, 243
Better Homes and Gardens (magazine),
    299, 301, 302–305
Better Homes & Gardens, 455
Betty Crocker, 393
Beverage Digest, 94, 96, 167
BF Goodrich tires, 605, 608
Big EAST Conference, 352
Big G Milk 'n Cereal Bar, 10
Big Red, 164
Bil Jac, 117
Billboard Magazine, 476
Bing, 355
Bishop, Herb, 169
Björk, 467
Black, Clint, 468
Black, Jon, 83–87, 90
Black & Decker, 144, 292, 623
Black Sabbath, 467
Blake, Alan, 406–410, 413, 414–415
Blake, Janet, 599
Blanketrol 200, 538
Blige, Mary J., 466
blink 182, 466
Bloomingdale's, 582, 590
Blue, 472

Blue Bell, 438
BMG Entertainment, 466, 468, 471,
    472, 476
BMG Music Publishing, 468
BMW, 186, 189, 531, 654, 655,
    657–659
BMW brand, 653–654
BoA. See Bank of America
Bocelli, Andrea, 466
Boeing, 490
Boeing 737, 487, 490, 495
Boeing Company, 620
Bold, 241
Bon Appétit (magazine), 290
Bon Jovi, 466
Borden, Inc., 258
Borden Brands International, 258
Borden Brands North America, 258
Borden Chemical, 258
Borden Foods Corporation, 195, 253,
    256, 258, 262–267, 273–274
Borden milk, 284
Bosch-Siemens, 671, 682, 685
Bose, 571, 573, 576
Bose audio systems, 142
Boston Acoustics, 573
Boston Consulting Group, 680
Bott, John, 294, 301, 306, 307–308
Boucheron, 367
Bounce, 241
Bowie, David, 472
Boxwood, 225
BPL Sanyo Utilities and Appliances,
    Bangalore, 648
Branch, Michelle, 467
BrandsMart, 673
Branson, Richard, 472
BRATZ brand dolls, 147
Breeder's Mix, 113–122
Breeder's Own Pet Foods, Inc. case,
    113–122
BrekMar Corporation, 394
Brent, Randall III, 594, 596, 598
Bridgestone Corporation, 605, 609
Bridgestone tires, 605, 606, 608,
    609, 611
Bristol Myers, 516
Brooks, Garth, 472
Brooks Products, 169
Brown, Chip, 563–565, 571, 577
Brown, James, 467
Brownlow, Larry, 123–126, 132
Broyhill, 297
Brut, 140
Bud Light, 126, 131
Budweiser, 124, 126, 131
Bulwark, 441
Bumble Bee tuna, 258
Burger King, 93, 617
Burns, Ronald, 105, 107, 109, 111, 112
Burroughs Wellcome Company case,
    512–523
Busch, 126, 131
Bushel, John, 226, 227
BusinessWeek (magazines), 310
Busy Bone, 117
Buymusic.com, 465
B&W, 573
BYD F6DM, 184

CAB. See Civil Aeronautics Board
Cadbury, John, 310

Cadbury Beverages, Inc., 309–323
Cadbury PLC, 9, 242
Cadbury Schweppes, 143
Cadbury Schweppes Americas
    Beverages, 377–378, 380, 383, 388
Cadbury Schweppes PLC, 162, 168,
    169, 172, 173, 309–310, 312,
    377–378, 382, 386
Cadillac, 189–190, 531, 662
Cadillac CTS, 655
CAFTA, 443
Caldor, 342
California Department of Fish and
    Game, 410
California Fish and Game Commission,
    409, 410
Callaway Golf Company, 370
Calosera, 547
Cambridge Sciences Pharmaceuticals
    (CSP), 544, 545, 547, 549–551
Campbell Soup Company, 134, 143,
    146, 147, 454, 619
Camp Carnival, 141
Canada Dry, 92, 162–163, 310–312
Canadian Dental Association (CDA),
    242–243, 246, 247
Canadian Diabetes Association, 422
Canadian Health magazine, 422
Canadian Intellectual Properties
    Office, 419
Canadian Prostate Cancer Network, 418
Canadian Tire, 628, 629, 631
Canon, 672
Capitol Records, 472
Capitol Records Nashville, 472
Capri Sun, 380
CareCompanion, 421
Carlson Hospitality Worldwide, 326
Carlton, Vanessa, 466
Carnival Cruise Lines, 141
Carpet Exchange, 432
Carpetland USA, 433
CarpetMax, 432, 433
Carpet One, 432, 433
Carrier, 641
Cartier, 455
Casale, 357–360
Cascade, 241
Caterpillar, 624
CavinKare Pvt. Ltd., 154–156
CDA. See Canadian Dental Association
CEA. See Consumer Electronics
    Association
CEDIA (Custom Electronic Design and
    Installation Association), 563,
    567, 569
CEDIA EXPO, 563, 576, 578
Cellflash, 407–408
Cendant Corporation, 326
Center for Association Leadership, 225
Centers for Disease Control and
    Prevention (CDC), 513, 514, 545
Cepacol, 242–246
CE Pro, 573
Cereal Partners Worldwide, 621
Cesar Select, 117, 118
CF Diet Coke, 164
Chamberlain, 425
Chanel, 455, 622
Changfeng Motors, 529
Channel Average, 100
Charles Chips, 195

Charles of the Ritz, 140
Chase Authentics, 441
Chase Bank, 353
Chatterjee, Rahul, 636–651
CheckFree, 84, 85
Cheer, 144, 241
Cheetos, 193, 194, 254
Chef Boyardee, 258
Chery Automotive, 529
Chesterton, 433
Cheung, Jacky, 466
Chevrolet, 531
Chevrolet, Louis, 666–667
Chevrolet brand, 652–653, 659, 662, 666–667
Chevrolet Corvette, 662
Chevrolet Europe, 622
Chevrolet Europe case, 652–668
Chevrolet Volt, 14, 183, 190
Chevron, 609
Chik, 155
Children's Television Workshop, 343
Chips Ahoy, 146
Choice Hotels International, Inc., 326
Christian Dior, 442
Christie's, 622
Chrysalis, 472
Chrysalis Records, 472
Chrysler, 606
Chrysler brand, 654
Chua, KK, 150
Church & Dwight, 143
Cincinnati Sub-Zero, 538
Circle Corporation case, 524–533
Citibank, 85, 146
Citigroup, 348
Citizen, 555
Citra, 170, 172–177
Citroën brand, 654
Citrus Club, 169
Civil Aeronautics Board (CAB), 480–481
Clamato, 92, 93, 310
Clapton, Eric, 467
Clarion, 241
Claritin, 287
Clear, 155
Clearasil, 241
Cliff Magness, 473
Climator, 538–539
Clinic All Clear, 155
Clinic Plus, 154, 155, 158
Clinique Division of Estée Lauder Companies, 369–370
Clopay Corporation, 426
Cluett Peabody and Company, 56
CNN, 410
Coca-Cola, 10, 77, 93, 94, 98, 102, 103, 135, 142, 162, 164, 167, 170, 176, 312, 314, 316, 366, 622, 682
Coca-Cola bottlers, 383
Coca-Cola Bottling Company of Southern California, 167
Coca-Cola Classic, 164, 315
Coca-Cola Company, 99, 163–165, 167, 172–173, 380
Coca-Cola Enterprises, Inc. (CCE), 163, 169, 170
Coca-Cola North America, 167
Coldplay, 472
Coldwell Banker, 573
Cole, Katie, 585

Cole, Nat "King," 472
Coleman, Jonathon A., 594, 595
Coleman Art Museum (CAM) case, 594–603
Colgate, 139, 242–246
Colgate Fluoride Rinse, 242–243
Colgate-Palmolive Company, 116
Colgate-Palmolive (India) Ltd., 154
Coltrane, John, 467
Columbia, 467
Columbia Business School, 477
Comet, 241
Comfees, 340
Compass Bank, 348, 349
CompUSA, 576
Consumer Electronics Association (CEA), 185, 567, 570, 576
Consumer Reports, 680
Continental A.G., 609
Continental Airlines, 479, 480, 482, 483, 486, 489, 493
"Continental Lite," 479, 486
Continental tires, 611
Cooking Utensil Company, 392
Cool Ranch Doritos, 197, 198
Cooper/Falls tires, 608
Cooper Tire and Rubber, 609
Cooper tires, 608, 609
Coors, 123, 125–127, 130–132
Coors, Adolph, 124
Coors, Inc., 124
Corsa tires, 611, 613
CortiSlim, 547
Corvette, 605
"Cosmic Blue" fish, 413
Cosmo Girl (magazine), 591–592
Cosmopolitan (magazine), 591–592
Costco, 24, 245
Costello, Elvis, 468
Cott Corp., 164
Courtwright, Heather, 211, 213–216
Courtyard by Marriott, 325
Courtyard hotels, 144
Cover Girl Cosmetics, 12–13, 241
Cox, Kate, 162, 178–181
Cozies, 341
'C' Plus, 310
Cracker Jack, 143, 253–275
Crafton Industries, Inc. case, 429–436
Craftsman, 144, 425
Crane, Thomas, 596
Cremora, 262
Crest, 72, 139, 140, 241
Crisco, 241
Crockett, Richard, 407–409
Croswell, Phil, 409–410
Crow, Sheryl, 466
Crunch 'n Munch, 256–259, 262–263, 268
Crush Brand, 309–323
CSA, 441
CSP. See Cambridge Sciences Pharmaceuticals
Cub Foods, 342
Culligan International Company, 641
CUTCO Corporation, 390–405
CUTCO International, 391, 394, 400
CUTCO Korea, 400
CUTCO Stores, Inc., 391, 392, 398–399
CWE Industries, 394

CyberNet Medical Corporation, 420–421
CyberNet Systems, 420–421

Dabur India Ltd., 154, 155
Dabur Vatika, 155
Daewoo, 529, 652, 655, 663, 664
Daewoo brand, 662, 677
Daewoo Electronics, 682
Daewoo Matiz, 662, 664, 665
Daewoo Motor Company, 652, 659
Daewoo Motor Company of Seoul, Korea, 662
DaimlerChrysler, 653–655, 657
Daimler Smartcar, 184
Datran Media, 357–360
Dave Matthews Band, 468
Davis, Miles, 467
Davis, Parker, 409
DDI, 516
DD metro channels, 646
DeBeers, 622
Decathlon tires, 611, 613, 614
Decca, 466
Delaware Department of Revenue, 125
Delight Purifier, 642, 647–651
Dell, 143, 374, 669
Dell, Inc., 364, 366, 624
Dell.com, 364, 365
Del Monte, 116, 117, 143, 145, 382
Delphi, 527
Delta Airlines, 480, 482, 483, 489
Delta Tire, 611
Delta water purifiers, 647–648
Dennison's, 258
Department of Homeland Security, 533
Dermavescent Laboratories, Inc. case, 210–217
Designworks USA, 186
Destiny, 425
Destiny's Child, 467
DeWalt, 144
Dewey, John, 56
DHC, 229, 234
Diabetes Association of Canada, 420
Diabetes Education Centre, 419
Dial, 145
Diamond Star, 606
Diehard, 144
Diet Coke, 164, 315
Diet Pepsi, 164, 315
Diet Squirt, 169
Dion, Celine, 467
Direct Selling Association, 401
Discovery Health Channel, 422
Disney, 144
Diva/Showcase, 422
Dixie Chicks, 467
The Dixie Group, 431
Dixie-Narco brand, 682
Dr. Dre, 466
Dr. Pepper, 92, 93, 162–164, 315, 377
Dr. Pepper/Seven Up, Inc. Bottling Group, 169
Dr. Pepper/Seven Up, Inc. (Cadbury Schweppes), 164
Dr. Pepper/Seven Up, Inc. (DPSU), 162–181, 312, 314, 377, 378
Dr. Pepper/Seven Up bottlers, 383
Dr. Pepper Snapple Group, Inc. case, 91–104

Dr. Pepper Soda Fountain
    Classics, 93
Dog Chow, 117, 118
Dog Fancy, 121
Domitrovich, Marty, 395
Don Miguel, 28
Dorel Industries, Inc., 297
Doritos, 15, 72, 193, 194, 198, 201,
    207, 254
Douglas tires, 605, 614
Dove shampoo, 156
Drexel Heritage, 297, 300
Drucker, Peter, 55
Drypers Corporation case, 337–346
Drypers Supreme with Germ Guard
    Liner, 345
Drypers with Aloe Vera, 343
Drypers with Natural Baking Soda, 343
Dubar, 155
Duke University, 518, 519
Duncan Hines, 241
Dunkin's Donuts, 366
Dunkin's Donuts cereal, 146
Dunlop, 606
Dunlop tires, 608, 609, 611
Duracell batteries, 142
Durant, William, 666–667
Dylan, Bob, 467

E. D. Smith, 310
Eagle Brand, 262
Eagle brands, 147
Eagle brand tires, 604
Eagle Creek, 438, 440–441
Eagle Snacks, 10, 195
Eagle Thins Potato Chips, 194
Eagle tires, 611, 613
Eastern Airlines, 482, 484
Eastman Kodak, 135
Eastpak, 438, 440–441
Ebauches S.A., 555
eBay, 143
Edison Media Research, 471
Elan, 573
Elantra (Avante in Korea), 524
"Electric Green" fish, 413
Electric & Musical Industries (EMI),
    472, 476
Electrolux, 641, 671, 672, 677, 679, 685
Electrolux's Frigidaire Home
    Products, 676
Electrolux (Sweden), 643, 682
Elektra, 467
Eli Lilly, 517
Elizabeth, Kelly, 324, 325, 331, 333,
    334–336
Elizabeth Arden, 145
Elliott, Missy, 467
Ellipse, 565
Ellis, James, 500, 509–511
Elmer's, 258
El Nacho Foods, 56, 57–59
Elvive, 155
Emami Ltd., 155
EmerCenter #1, 235
EmerCenter #2, 235
EMI. *See* Electric & Musical
    Industries
EMI Classics, 472
EMI Group, PLC case, 463–478
EMI Music Publishing, 472, 473
Eminem, 466

EMI Recorded Music, 464, 472–473
Encyclopaedia Britannica, 2
Endurox, 102
Energy Brands, Inc., 94
Energy PHEV, 184
Environmental Protection Agency
    (EPA), 106
Enya, 467
Epic, 467
Era, 144
ESPN, 352
ESPN Regional Television, Inc.
    (ERT), 352
Estefan, Emilio and Gloria, 467
Ethan Allen, 288, 300, 369
Ethan Allen Interiors, Inc., 297
Eureka Forbes, 643–644, 647
Euromonitor International, 154
European Union (EU), 632, 638
Eurythmics, 468
The Everly Brothers, 467
Exxon, 609
ExxonMobil, 5, 623

Fabergé, 140
Facebook, 219, 225, 227,
    399, 400
Faded Glory, 442
Fairchild, Eugene, 641
Fairchild Water Technologies, Inc. case,
    636–651
Fairfield Inn, 144, 147, 326, 329
Fannel County Museum of Fine
    Arts, 594
Fanta, 167
Farmer, Mylène, 466
Farsighted Fish Genetics (FSG), 408
Fashion (magazine), 584
FCB. *See* Foote, Cone & Belding
FDA. *See* U.S. Food and Drug
    Administration
FEC (Free-Standing Emergency
    Clinic), 230
Federal Express, 440
Federal Trade Commission, 547
FedEx, 140, 621
Feil, Kim, 309, 320, 322
Fiat, 371, 655, 658, 665
Fiat brand, 654
Fiat Group, 653–654, 657
Fiat Panda, 655
Fiat's Alfa-Romeo, 659
Fiat's Lancia, 657–658
Fiddle Faddle, 256, 257
50 Cent, 466
Fila, 372
Filmtrax, 472
Firestone, 628, 629, 631
Firestone Auto Master Care
    Centers, 609
Firestone Tire and Rubber, 292,
    606, 608
Firestone tires, 605, 609, 611
First Data Processing of Milwaukee, 85
Fiserv case, 83–90
Fisker, Henrik, 186
Fisker Automotive, Inc. (Fisker),
    182–191
Fisker Automotive franchise, 182,
    190, 191
Fisker Karma Sedan, 182, 186–187
Fisker Karma Sedan PHEV, 184

Fitzgerald, Ella, 467
5-D Tropical and Segrest Farms, 414
Flamin' Hot Cheese Flavored Snacks,
    194
Flava brand, 147
Flexsteel Industries, Inc., 297
Florida Orange Growers Association, 8
Flowers, David, 218–220, 222, 225–228
FluMist, 135
Focus, 146
Folgers, 8, 69, 288
Foo Fighters, 468
Foote, Cone & Belding (FCB), 162, 172,
    176–178, 180, 181
Foot Locker, 371
Forbes Campbell (India), 643
Forbes (magazine), 670–671
The Force, 441
Ford, 183, 531, 606, 628, 631,
    653–655, 658
Ford, Henry, 71
Ford auto, 71
Ford brand, 654
Ford C-MAX, 184
Ford Escape PHEV, 184
Ford Focus, 184
Ford Fusion, 146
Ford in Europe, 654
Ford Motor Company, 59, 139, 527,
    657, 666
Ford Motor Company's Global
    Advanced Design Studio, 186
Ford's Land Rover, 657–658
Ford's Volvo, 659
Ford Taurus, 146
Foreign Investment Promotion
    Board, 640
Foster's, 624
Four Seasons, 325
The Four Tops, 467
Fox News, 410
Franklin, Aretha, 468
Fraser, Chris, 437–438, 441, 442, 444,
    445, 447–450, 452
Fresca, 164, 170, 172, 173, 177
Frigidaire, 671
Frigidaire brand, 676, 679
Frito-Lay, Inc., 9, 15, 71–72, 76, 143,
    147, 192–209, 253–279, 623
Frito-Lay International, 254
Frito-Lay North America, 254
Frito-Lay Variety Pack, 194
Fritos, 15, 194, 198, 254
Frosty Paws Frozen Treats for
    Dogs, 116
Fruit & Oatmeal Cereal bars, 271
Fuji, 556
Full Throttle, 98–101
Full Throttle Demon, 99
Funyuns, 193, 254
Furman, Philip, 518
Furniture Brands International,
    Inc., 297

Gagnon, Pierre, 626, 628, 631–635
"Galactic Purple" fish, 413
Galietti, Robert, 347
Garnier Fructis Shampoo + Oil,
    156, 158
Gatorade, 8, 9, 102, 142, 144
Gatorade Be Tough, 144
Gatorade Bring It, 144

Gatorade G2, 144
Gaye, Marvin, 467
Gaymar Industries, 538
GE, 674
Geely Automotive, 529
GE Momentum, 677
General Electric, 134, 369, 466, 641,
    671, 673, 676–679, 682
General Electric's NBC entertainment
    unit, 466
General Mills, 10, 146, 267,
    620, 621
General Motors, 14, 63, 187, 371, 527,
    606, 631, 652, 655, 657, 659–661,
    665–667
General Motors Europe, 660, 662
General Motors Export
    Company, 659
General Motors in Europe, 654
General Motors (Opel/Vauxhall/Saab),
    653–654
General Motor's Saab, 659
General Tire, 606
General tires, 608, 609, 611
Gerber, 74–75, 143
Gerber Products Company, 10
Gershwin, George and Ira, 468
Gibb, Barry, 468
Gillette Company, 4, 135, 143, 213,
    215, 368, 623
Gillette Fusion shaving system, 5, 10,
    135, 460
Gillette India Ltd., 154
Gillette Mach3 shaving system, 460
Gillette razors, 622
Gillette's Sensor Razor for Women, 212
Gillette Venus razor, 5
Gillette Venus Razor for Women, 212
Gini, 310, 312
Giorgio Armani, 624
Girbaud, 438
Glacéau, 94
Glamour (magazine), 73
Glaxo, 516
Glidden, 106
GloFish, 406–408, 410–412, 414, 415
GloFish Red Zebra Danio, 408,
    410–414
GM, 663
GMBuyPower.com, 284
GM Chevy Volt, 184
GM Daewoo, 654, 658, 659–660, 662,
    665–667
GM Daewoo Auto & Technology
    Company (GM DAT), 652, 659, 665
GM Daewoo brand, 652–653
GM Daewoo Europe, 652, 659–660,
    662, 665, 666
GM Daewoo Evanda, 668
GM Daewoo Kalos, 668
GM Daewoo Lacetti, 668
GM Daewoo Matiz, 668
GM Daewoo Rezzo, 668
Godrej, 155
Godrej Consumer Products Ltd.,
    154, 155
Golden Beauty, 623
Goldman, Suzanne, 429, 434–436
Goldstar, 641
Goodman, James, 585, 587, 589
Goodrich tires, 609
Goodyear, 628, 629, 631

Goodyear Auto Service Centers, 604,
    609, 614, 615
Goodyear Eagle brand, 605
Goodyear Tire and Rubber
    Company, 556
Goodyear Tire and Rubber Company
    case, 604–615
Goodyear Tire Dealers, 604, 614, 615
Goodyear tires, 609, 611, 614, 615
Goodyear Tires Stores, 609
Google, 225, 354–357, 593
Gordy, Berry, 472
Gourmet Retailer (magazine), 290
Grace, Catherine, 324, 331, 334,
    335–336
Grand American, 502–507, 509, 511
Grandma's, 193, 254
Graves, Drew, 218, 219, 225, 226, 228
Greater West Office and Shopping
    Complex, 232
Green, Mike, 444, 448–450
Groban, Josh, 467
Grokster, 465
Groupe Michelin, 605, 609, 611
Grow Group, 107
Guaranty Bank, 348, 349
Gucci, 143, 367, 622, 624
Guys brand, 195

Haggar Clothing, 291
Haier, 677
Haier America, 673–674
Haier America Industrial Park, 673
Haier brand, 669–674
Haigler, T. E., 513
Hall Consolidated, 500–506, 510, 511
Hallmark, 140, 369
Hallmark Entertainment, 468
Hallyday, Johnny, 466
Hampton Inn & Suites, 326, 329
Hansen Natural Corporation, 98,
    99, 101
Harley-Davidson, 8, 73, 143, 146, 441,
    621, 622
Harrison, Ralph, 381
Harrison's, 502, 504–507, 509, 511
Harry and David, 256
Hasbro, 367
Havas, 347
Haverwood Furniture, Inc. (A) case,
    294–305
Haverwood Furniture, Inc. (B) case,
    306–308
Hawaiian Punch, 92, 143, 162–163
Hawaiian Punch case, 377–389
Hawkins India, Bombay, 648
Hawly, Richard, 424–428
Head & Shoulders, 155, 157, 241
Health Canada, 417
Health Care Financing
    Administration, 515
Health First, 235
Health Protection Branch (HPB), 247
Hearst, Gwen, 240, 241, 243,
    247–249, 251
Helena Rubenstein, 623
Hendison Electronics Corporation, 3
Hendredon, 297
Hendrix, Jimi, 467
Hershey Foods, 9, 146
Hershey's chocolate morsels, 146
Hertz, 140

Hervey, Michael ("Mike"), 294, 301
Hervey and Bernham, 294, 301
Hewlett-Packard, 140, 284,
    624, 669
Hi-C, 380
Hicks, Muse, Tate & Furst, 258
Hi-Fi House, 567
Hikaru, Utada, 472
Hill, Faith, 467
Hill's Pet Nutrition, 116
Hilton, 325
Hilton Hotels Corporation, 326
Himani, 155
Hindustan Unilever, 153–158
Hires, 309–311
Hi-Value Supermarkets, 500–511
Hoedebeck, Kate, 377, 378, 385–389
Hoffman-LaRoche, 516
Holiday, Billie, 467
Holiday Inn, 325, 329
Holland House, 310, 311
Home Depot, 74, 107, 108, 292, 369,
    370, 426, 432, 433, 677, 679,
    681, 685
Home Improvement Research
    Institute, 107
Honda, 183, 527, 672
Honda brand, 644–655
Honda Fit, 184
Honda Motor Co., 657
Honda of U.S., 606
Honda plug-in hybrid, 184
Hooter's Airlines, 146
Hoover brand, 681
Hopi, 81
Horowitz, Zach, 477
Hosworth Air Engineering, Ltd., 538
Hosworth-Climator, 538–539
Hotpoint, 674, 679
Houston, Whitney, 468
Houstons Foods, 256
Howlin' Coyote, 21, 26–34
H & R Block, 366
Huggies, 146, 339
Hughes, Will, 408–409
Hummer, 662
Hygienic Research, 155
Hyundai, 527, 529, 532, 606, 655, 659,
    665, 672
Hyundai Kia Automotive
    Group, 525
Hyundai Motor Co., 288, 524, 657

Iams, 116–118
IBelong Networks, 224
IBM, 85, 669
Ice Cube, 472
Iglesias, Enrique, 466
IKEA, 300, 622, 624
Imperial Chemicals, 106
Indesit Company, 671
India.Arie, 466
Information Technology Association of
    Canada, 418
Ingersoll-Rand, 364
Ingram Book Group, Inc., 368
Intelligent Quisine (IQ), 454
InterClick, 357–360
Inter-Continental Hotel Group, 326
Interface Flooring, 431
International Association for Native
    Employment, 418

International Home Foods, Inc., 256, 258
International Organization for Standardization (ISO), 528
Interscope/Geffen/A&M, 466
Inverness Corp., 213
Inverness Ulta-Lubricating Shaving Gel, 213
Invicta tires, 611, 613
Ion Exchange, 644–646
iPad, 2
iPhone, 2
iPod, 9, 284, 565, 571, 574, 576
iPod Nano, 354
iPod Touch, 354
iPort, 565, 571, 574–578
Island/Def Jam, 466
Isuzu, 606
iTunes Music Store, 465

J. A. Henckels Zwillingswerk, Inc. ("Henckels"), 394
Jackson, Alan, 473
Jackson, Janet, 472
Jackson, Michael, 467
The Jackson Five, 467
Jade brand, 682
Jaguar, 139, 189, 654, 658
James, Joseph, 324, 325, 336
Janmar Coatings, Inc. case, 105–112
JanSport, 441
Jantzen, 438
Jaquar, 531
Ja Rule, 466
Java Records, 472
JCPenney, 582, 591
J.D.Power and Associates, 418
Jean Naté, 140
Jeep, 654
Jemal, Michael, 674
Jenn-Air, 679, 681
Jenny Craig Direct, 547, 550
Jiangtong Mechanical Group, 529
Jiffy Lube, 367
Jiffy Pop, 258
Jive Records, 468
Jobete companies, 472
JobTarget, 225
John, Elton, 466
Johnson, Randall, 500, 509–511
Johnson Controls, 527
Johnson & Johnson, 137, 141, 146
Johnston, Michelle, 83, 85, 87, 90
John Varvatos, 438, 441
Jolson, Mark, 626–629, 631–635
Jolson Automotive Hoist case, 626–635
Jolson Lift, 626–628, 630–634
Jonathon A. Coleman Art Museum, 594
Jones, Norah, 472, 473
Jones Apparel, 442
José Olé, 28
Joseph, Casey, 255
Joy, 241
J.P. Morgan Chase, 347
JPMorgan Chase, 348, 351
Juicy Juice, 380

KA-BAR Knives, 391, 394
Kang, Tae Su, 525, 530–533
Kang, Yong Soo, 524, 525

Kars, Inc., 116
KaZaA, 465
Keating, Ronan, 466
Keebler Company, 195
Kelleher, Herb, 479, 487, 489–491, 493, 495
Keller, Kevin Lane, 624
Kellogg's Rice Krispies Treats, 271
Kelly-Springfield Tire Company, 605, 608, 609, 611, 613, 614
Kenmore, 144, 676–677
Kennedy, Edward, 522
Kenny G, 468
Kentucky Fried Chicken, 192–193
Keys, Alicia, 468
KFC, 93
Kia, 655, 659
Kibbles 'N Bits, 117
Kid Rock, 467
Kight, Pete, 85
Kim, Chris, 530
Kim, Nancy, 525, 531, 532
Kimberly-Clark, 146, 337, 339–341, 343
Kipling, 438, 441
Kitchen Aid brand, 679
Kiwi International Airlines, 484
Klaussner Home Furnishings, Inc., 297
Kleenex facial tissues, 142
Klipsch, 573
Kmart, 108, 258, 342, 432, 471
Knowles, Beyonce, 467
Kodak, 556
Koehler, Bernhard "Barry," 186
Kohlberg Kravis Roberts & Co., 258
Kohl's, 372
Kool-Aid, 380
Kool-Aid Soft Drink Mix, 379
Korea Advanced Institute of Science & Technology (KAIST), 524
Korean Industrial Bank, 532
Kraft Foods, Inc., 8, 380
Kroger, 93, 145, 195
Kwon, Jeong Oh, 525
Kyocera Corporation, 621

Lacquer Craft, Inc., 297
Laine, Erick, 391, 394
La Liga BBVA, 352
Lalique, 455
Lancer Gallery case, 80–82
Lancia, 654, 658
Land Rover, 139, 189, 654
Lane, 297
La Quinta, 326
La Quinta Inn & Suites, 329
Lay's, 9, 15, 193, 194, 198, 254
La-Z-Boy, Inc., 297
Lea-Meadows, Inc., 306–307
Lee, 438, 439–440
Lee Company, 438
Lee Tire and Rubber Company, 611, 613, 614
Lee tires, 605
Legacy, 425
Legacy Records, 467
Legion Field, 352
L.e.i., 442
Lenovo Group Ltd., 669
Leo, A. W., 381
Leo's Hawaiian Punch, 381
Levi business attire, 146

Levi's, 622
Levi's jeans, 622
Levi Strauss, 370, 443–444
Levy, Alain, 464, 472–473
Lexus, 186, 189
LG Electronics, 672, 676, 677, 679, 685
Liberhaier Company, 670
LifeLine Inc., 420, 421
LifeStat, 416, 418–423
LiftMaster, 425
Li & Fung, 443
Limp Bizkit, 466
Lincoln, 531
Lincoln Foods, 256
Linens 'n Things, 673
Lingerie Americas Trade Show, 585, 590
LinkedIn, 219, 225
Linkin Park, 467
Linn, 573
Listerine, 59, 242, 244, 245–246, 248
Listermint, 242, 244–246
Liz Claiborne, 441–445
L.L.Bean, 288
London Drugs, 421–422
Long, Bernard, 544, 547, 550, 551
Longaberger, 401
Long John Silver's, 93
The Look: Mary Kay India Catalog, 160–161
Looney Tunes, 262
Lopez, Jennifer, 467
Lord & Taylor, 590
L'Oréal, 623, 624
L'Oréal Excellence, 155
L'Oréal India, 158
L'Oréal India Pvt. India, 154
L'Oréal India Pvt. Ltd., 154–156
L'Oréal Paris, 158
L'Oréal Professionnel, 155
Los Angeles International Airport (LAX), 489, 495
Los Angeles Times, 410
Lotus & Bamboo Indulgent Bath Bar, 149, 158–159
Louis Vuitton luggage, 142
Love Field, 489
Lowe's, 8, 74, 107, 370, 564, 566, 571, 574, 673, 674, 677, 679, 681
Lowe's Companies, 426
LSI Logic, 561
Lucasfilm, Ltd., 468
lucy, 438, 441
Lutron Electronics, Inc., 563
Luvs, 241

Maclean's (magazine), 418
Macy's, 591
Madness, 473
Madonna, 468
Magary, A. B. "Sky," 487, 497
Magic Chef brand, 681
Mahon, Roger, 229, 233, 239
Maitland-Smith, 297
Majestic, 438, 441
Malvern, 310
Mandarin Orange Slice, 313, 315–318, 321
Manson and Associates, 123–126, 132
Manzana Lift, 167
Manzana Mía, 167
Marico Ltd., 154, 155, 156, 157

Marie Claire (magazine), 592
Mark Cross wallets, 366
Marketing Momentum Unlimited, 113, 114
Marley, Bob, 467
Marriott, 325
Marriott Edition hotels, 144, 147
Marriott hotels, 144, 147
Marriott International, 144, 326
Mars, Inc., 9, 116
Marsalis, Wynton, 467
Martha Stewart Living House Beautiful, 301
Martin, Ricky, 467
Mary Kay, 160
Mary Kay, Inc., 149–152
Mary Kay Beauty Centers, 153, 160
Mary Kay beauty consultants, 156
Mary Kay brand, 150
Mary Kay Cosmetics, 149–150, 400
Mary Kay India case, 149–161
Mary Kay MelaCEP Whitening System, 152–153
Mary Kay Miss Beautiful Skin, 152
Maserati, 189
Massive Attack, 472
MasterCard, 146, 624
MasterFoods, 117
MasterFoods USA, 116
Masters, Phoebe, 210, 211, 213, 217
Masterton, 433
Matheson, Karolynn, 226–227
Matsushita, 75–76
Matsushita Electric Industrial, 671–672
Mattel, 147, 367
Matushita, 641
Max Entertainment Service, 418
Max Factor, 241
Maxim Group, 433
Maxwell House, 8, 69
Maybelline, 623
Mayer, John, 467
Maytag, 671–674, 676–680
Maytag, F. L., 680
Maytag brand, 681
Maytag Corporation, 669, 670, 680–686
Maytag Neptune, 679
Mazda, 606
Mazda brand, 644–655
Mazda Motor Co., 657
MCA Records, 466
McCartney, Paul, 472
McCleans, 139
McDonald's, 93, 134, 164, 313, 557, 621, 625
McDonnell Douglas, 490
McGlade, Pete, 479
McLachlan, Sarah, 468
Meadows, Robert, 429, 435, 436
Mechanics Illustrated (magazine), 290
MEC (Medical Emergency Clinic), 230
Medcenter, 235, 239
Media Contacts, 347, 354–356
Medicaid, 230
Medicaid Program, 515
Medicare, 229–230, 416, 417
meditonan, 547
MedStar, 421
Medtronics, 624
Meijer, 342
Mello Yello, 170, 172, 173, 177

Menards, 426, 673
Mercedes, 531
Mercedes-Benz, 186, 189, 654, 657–658
Mercedes-Benz S-Class, 655
Mercer, Ashley, 594, 596, 598, 599, 602, 603
Mercury Nashville, 466
Mercury Records, 466
Merida, 545
Meridian, 573
Merrell Dow, 242, 243
Merrill Lynch, 284
Messar, Patricia, 652
Metabical case, 544–551
Metamucil, 241
Mete Lift, 630
MetLife.com, 364
Metropolitan Life Insurance, 76, 135, 288
MGA Entertainment, 147
Michelin, 12, 143, 371, 605–609, 611
Michelob, 126, 131
Michigan Cancer Foundation, 518
Microsoft, 85, 142, 225
Microsoft Corporation, 371–372
Midway Airlines, 482
Midway Airport, 489
Mighty Dog, 117, 118
Mike Sells, 195
Milk Bone, 116, 117, 118
Miller, 124, 126, 131, 132
Miller Lite, 126, 131
Milton Plastics, Bombay, 648
Minogue, Kylie, 472
Minute Maid, 380
Minute Maid Orange, 315–318, 321
Minute Maid orange juice, 554
Miramax, 144
Mission Foods, 28
Missouri Mart, 502–507, 509, 511
Mr. Clean, 241
Mr. Coffee, 368
Mitchell's, 310
Mitsubishi, 654–655
Mitsubishi iMiEV, 184
Mitsubishi Motor Co., 657
M&Ms, 9
Modern Tire Dealer, 615
Modia, 567
Mohawk Industries, 369, 370, 431, 433
Monarch Co., 164
Monster Energy, 96, 98–101
Montgomery Ward, 609
Moorman, Martin, 306–308
Morpheus, 465
Morris, Doug, 463, 475, 478
Morris Air, 487
Morris Air Corporation, 493
Mortensen, Will, 579, 580, 589–590, 593
Mosaic Records, 472
Motel 6, 326, 329
Motiva Interactive, 421
Motown, 467, 472
Mott's, 92, 310, 311, 377, 378
Mott's Apple Juice, 379
Motts for Tots, 93
Mountain Dew, 164, 167, 170, 172, 173, 176, 177, 315
Mountain Dew Code Red, 170
Mountain Dew MDX, 99

Moyett, Sheiludis, 347, 351, 355
MP3.com, 465
Mr & Mrs "T," 310, 311
MSN, 356
MSNBC, 410
MTA 4700, 538
Multi-Mile tires, 608
Munchos, 193
Muse Air, 487
Musicland, 477
Musicnet.com, 465
Mustang, 146
Mute, 472
MyAssociation, 224

Nabisco, 146, 195, 267
Nacho Cheese Doritos, 198
NAFTA, 533
Nagarajan, Hina, 153
Nantucket Nectars, 379
Napapirji, 438, 440–441, 445
Nappy Roots, 467
National Aeronautics and Space Administration (NASA), 647
National Basketball Association (NBA), 352, 358
National Beverage, 164
National Business Hall of Fame, 150
National Cancer Institute (NCI), 516, 518, 519
National Gay and Lesbian Task Force, 512, 522
National Home Furnishings Collaborative, 294
National Institute of Allergy and Infectious Diseases (NIAID), 520
National Institutes of Health (NIH), 518, 519, 521, 545
National Pork Board, 393
National Pork Producers Council, 140
National University of Singapore (NUS), 408, 413
National University of Taiwan, 415
Nautica, 438, 441
Nautica Spa, 141
Navajo, 81
NBA, 440. *See* National Basketball Association
NBA Development League, 352
NCI. *See* National Cancer Institute
Neiman Marcus, 372, 579, 582, 586, 590, 593
Nelly, 467
Nestlé, 117, 618, 621
Nestlé Purina ONE, 116
Nestlé Purina PetCare, 116
Nestlé SA, 116
Nestlé USA, 380
Neutrogena, 137
New Balance, 72
New Horizons, 621
NewLund Laboratories, Inc., 345
Newman's Own Organics, 118
Newsweek (magazine), 290
New York Times, 410
NFL, 440, 441
Nickelback, 467
NIH. *See* National Institutes of Health
Nihar, 155
Nike, 72, 142, 143, 290, 441, 442, 622
Nike Shox NZ, 371
Niles, 573

Nintendo, 456, 672
Nirvana, 473
Nissan, 606, 621, 654–655, 659
Nissan Leaf, 183, 184
Nissan Motor Co., 657
No Doubt, 467
Nokia, 72, 74, 75, 618
Nordstrom, 372, 590
Nortek, 573
The North Face, 438, 440–441, 444, 445
Northwest Airlines, 480, 482, 483, 489
Norwegian Cruise Line, 370
Noxzema, 241
Nummi (GM-Toyota), 606
Nundies case, 579–593
Nursing Career Network, 226
NutraSweet, 169, 323
Nutri-Grain bars, 554
Nutrisystem, 547
Nyle, 155

Oakland International Airport, 495
Oasis, 310
Obama, Barack, 190
O'Boisies, 195
Ocean Spray, 380
Ocean Spray Cranberries, Inc., 380
Odyssey, 425
O'Grady's, 196, 207, 208
O'Hare Airport, 487
Oil of Olay, 241
Olay cosmetics, 137
Old Colony, 310
Old Milwaukee, 126, 131
Olsen, David, 81, 82, 342–343
Olympus, 624
One-A-Day WeightSmart, 547
Onida Savak, Delhi, 648
Opel, 655, 663, 667
Opel AG, 659
Opel Agila, 668
Opel Astra, 668
Opel Corsa, 655, 668
Opel Signum, 668
Opel/Vauxhall, 654, 658–661
Opel/Vauxhall Corsa, 661
Opel Zafira, 668
Opium, 367
O. R. Concepts, 538
Oracle, 225
Orange Crush, 313, 316, 317, 322–323
Orâteme, Inc. case, 218–228
Orbison, Roy, 467
Oreck, David, 405
Oreck, Thomas, 405
Original Series, 574
Orlistat, 546
Outcomes Research Group, 550
Overhead Door Corporation, 425, 426
Oxydol, 241
Ozark Airlines, 482

Pacific Citrus Products Company, 381
Pacific Hawaiian Products
    Company, 381
Pacific Health Laboratories, Inc., 102
Pacific Southwest Airlines, 482
Packaged Facts, 96
Pagny, Florent, 467
PAM cooking spray, 258
Pampers, 241, 288, 339

Pan American Airlines (Pan Am),
    482, 484
Pantene, 157, 241
Pantene Pro-V, 155
Papajohns.com, 352
Parachute, 155, 157
Paradise Kitchens, Inc., 15, 20–24,
    26–28, 32–34
Paragon Trade Brands, 144–145, 340
Park, David, 525
Parlaphone, 472
Pasteur Institute, 514
Pate Health Clinic (PHC), 229–239
Patek, 555
Pate Memorial Hospital (PMH) case,
    229–239
Pathfinder, 621
Paul, Sean, 473
Pavarotti, Luciano, 467
PC Magazine, 574
Pearl Jam, 467
Pedigree, 116
Pedigree Mealtime, 117
Peissig, Lynne, 253, 256, 267, 274
Peñafiel, 93
Pennzoil Motor Oil, 287
Pepsi Bottling Group, Inc., 163,
    169, 170
PepsiCo, 8, 93, 99, 102, 144, 274, 312,
    314, 682
PepsiCo, Inc., 192–193, 253, 254,
    274, 380
PepsiCo Canada, 99
PepsiCo Foods International, 192–193
Pepsi-Cola, 77, 98, 99, 102, 135, 162,
    164, 167, 313, 315, 316
Pepsi-Cola bottlers, 383
Pepsi-Cola Company, 163–165,
    172–173, 192–193
Pepto-Bismol, 241
Perkins, Floyd, 445, 446, 448,
    449, 452
Permutit, 644
Pert, 241
PETCO, 115, 414
Petco, 367
Peters, Leah E., 21
Peters, Randall F., 21
Petro-Canada, 631
PetSmart, 115, 367, 414
Peugeot, 655, 658
Peugot brand, 654
Peugot Group, 653–655, 657
Pfizer, Inc., 243, 248, 517
P&G. See Procter & Gamble
Pharmaseal, 538
PHC. See Pate Health Clinic
Philips Electronics, 421, 473
Philips Medical Systems, 420, 421
Phillips-Van Heusen, 441
Piaget, 555
Pillsbury, 59
Pink, 473
Pink Floyd, 472
Pirelli Group, 609
Pirelli tires, 609, 611
Pizza Hut, Inc., 93, 192–193
Planter's, 195
Plax, 240, 243–251
Plough, 517
PMH. See Pate Memorial Hospital
P.O.D., 467

Pokorski, David, 579
Polaner fruit spread, 258
Polar Industries, Calcutta, 648
The Police, 467
Polk, 573
Porsche, 144, 189, 624
Porsche Boxster, 144, 187
Porsche Carrera, 144
Porsche Cayman, 187
Porsche Panamera, 186
Porter, Cole, 468
Powerade, 102
PowerPress Corporation, 529, 533
PPG Industries, 106–107
Pratt & Lambert, 107
Prego, 147
Premium Crackers, 198
Price Club, 245
Prince, 467
Pringles, 194, 195, 241, 254
Printup, Barbara, 545, 547–551
Procter & Gamble, Canada, 241
Procter & Gamble, Inc. case,
    240–252
Procter & Gamble India Ltd., 154
Procter & Gamble (P&G), 8–10, 72,
    116, 137, 140, 143, 144, 155, 195,
    247, 248, 251, 267, 288, 292, 309,
    312, 319, 337, 339–343, 363–364,
    378, 382, 388, 455
Proctor & Gamble India, 157
Project Inform, 512, 521
Project Midas, 652–653, 662, 667
Project Nina, 187
Prontos, 76, 196
Pruchansky, Ivan, 407–408
Puccini, 468
Puddle of Mudd, 467
Pup-Peroni, 118
Puppet, 341
PureSip, 643, 648
Pure Spring, 310
Purina ONE, 118
Puristore, 644
Pyramid Door, Inc. case, 424–428

QCC. See Quiet Climate Control
Qingdao Haier Ltd. See also Haier
Qingdao Haier Ltd. case, 669–686
Qingdao Refrigerator Plant, 670
Quaker Oats, 8, 143, 271
Qualcomm, 621
Quattroruote, 662
Queen, 472, 473
Quick Detachable tire, 610–611
Quiet Climate Control (QCC), 524, 525,
    529–533

Radiohead, 472
Radio Shack, 145, 366, 370
Radisson, 325
Ralcorp, 144–145
Ralph Lauren, 372, 442, 443–444
Ramada Inn, 325, 329
Ranch Style beans, 258
RAND Corporation, 515
Rangard, Myron, 80–82
Rayovac, 144–145
Rbk Custom, 67–68
RCA, 366, 370, 468
RC Cola, 135, 162–163

Reading Glove and Mitten
 Company, 438
ReaLemon, 262
Real Media, 360
Reckitt Benckiser Ltd., 154
Recording Industry Association of
 America (RIAA), 465
Redbook (magazine), 291
Red Bull, 96, 98, 100–102, 104
Red Bull GMBH, 98
Red Bull North America, 98
Red Cheek, 310, 311
Red Hot Chili Peppers, 467
RedKap, 438, 441
Red Roof Inn, 326, 329
Reebok, 621
Reebok International, Ltd., 67–68
Reebok Russia, 621
Reef, 438, 440–441
Reese's Peanut Butter Puffs, 146
Regal shoes, 366
Regatta tires, 611, 613
Rembrandt, 139
Renaissance hotels, 144
Renault, 653–655, 657, 658
Reno Air, 484
Republic Airlines, 482
Reserve Bank of India, 640–641
Retrovir, 512–523
Revenue Science, 357–360
Revlon Cosmetics, 69, 137
Revson, Charles, 69
Rhapsody, 465
Rhee, Sang, 525
Richard Simmons brand, 256–258
Ridley, Dave, 479, 495, 497
Rieu, André, 467
Riskey, Dwight R., 192, 196, 200,
 207, 208
Ritz-Carlton, 325
Ritz Crackers, 198
RJ Reynolds Company, 382
RJR Nabisco, 195
Robert Morris Associates, 125
Roche Holding, Ltd., 147
Rockstar, 96, 98–100
Rockstar Energy, 99, 101
Rogers, Richard, 149–150
Rogge, Joyce, 479
Rold Gold, 193, 254, 255
Rolex, 455, 624
Rolling Stones, 472
Rolls-Royce, 189, 455, 622
Rome, John, 124, 126, 132
Rongshida-Maytag, 682
Rooms To Go, 296, 300
Roper, 674, 679
Rosemary, John, 408–409
Rose's, 310, 311
Ro*Tel canned tomatoes, 258
Royal Crown Company, 135, 164
Royal Crown (RC) Cola, 313
Royale, 241
Royal University Hospital, 419
Roynor Garage Coors, 426
Rübel, Barbara, 662, 667
Rubio, Paulina, 467
Ruby Red Squirt, 170, 172–173
Ruckheim, F. W., 260
Ruffles, 72, 193, 194, 198, 207, 254
Ruimin, Zhang, 670–672
Ruiz Foods, 28

Runny & Ware, 219
Rust Check, 629
Rustler, 438–440

S. C. Johnson, 213, 215
Saab, 654, 658, 660–663
Saab 9-3, 655
Saab Automobile AB, 659
Safeway, 93, 195
Safeway Pharmacy, 421, 422
St. Joseph Aspirin, 141
St. Paul's Hospital, 419
Saks Fifth Avenue, 590
Sam Group, 648
Sam's Club, 375, 677
Samsung, 143–144, 641, 672, 677, 679,
 682, 685, 686
Samsung Electronics, 676
Sam's Warehouse Clubs, 107, 265
Sanchez, Manolo, 352
Sanger, Robert, 190–191
Sanger Automotive Companies, Inc.
 (Sanger) case, 182–191
Santana, 468
Santinique, 157
Santitas, 193, 194, 254
Sanyo, 641
Sara Lee, 441, 443–444
SaskTel case, 416–423
SaskTel stores, 418
Satin Care, 213
Satinique, 154
Saturn, 606
Sauder Woodworking Company, 297
Schering-Merck & Co., 517
Schick, 368
Schilling Forge, 391, 394
Schultz, Howard, 68
Schwab.com, 364
Schweppe, Jacob, 310
Schweppes, 162–163, 310–312
Scooby Doo, 262
Scope, 240–252, 288
Seagram, 164
Sears, 107, 108, 144, 145, 604, 605,
 608, 609, 615, 673, 674, 676–677,
 680, 681
Sears Auto Center, 614
Seat, 654, 658
Sea World, 490
Secret, 241
Seiberling, Charles, 610
Seiberling, Frank, 610
Seiko, 555
Self (magazine), 73
Sergio Rossi, 367
Sesame Street, 343
7-Eleven, 93, 367
7 For All Mankind, 438, 441
7Up, 92, 94–95, 162–164, 315, 377
Shakira, 467
Sharp, 641
Sharp Electronics Corporation,
 676, 677
Shaw, Robert E., 433
Shaw Industries, 369, 370, 431, 433
Sheppard, Alfred, 512, 523
Sherrill Furniture, 297
Sherwin-Williams, 106–108
Shoppers Drug Mart (Shoppers), 421
Shun Cutlery, 394

"Shuttle By United," 479–480, 486–487,
 495–499
SIM-GT Licensing Corporation, 256
Simon, Herbert, 55
Sinatra, Frank, 472
Singer, 641, 646, 651
The Singer Company, 646–647
Singer India Ltd., 646–647
Skinsimple, 145
Skintimate, 213
Skin-Tique Corp., 213
Skoda, 654, 658
Sloan, Alfred, 63
SmartAmp, 565
SmartBrief, 227
Smartfood, 193, 194, 254
Smashing Pumpkins, 472
Smith, Donald, 594, 596, 602, 603
Smith, Will, 467
Smythe, Andrew, 82
Snake Light Flexible Flashlight, 623
Snapple, 92, 143, 377
Snapple Antioxidant Waters, 93, 94
Snapple Beverage Group, 377
Snickers, 9
Snoop Dogg, 472
Snyder's, 195
SoBe Adrenaline Rush, 98, 99
Sodima, 620
Soft and Silky Shaving Gel, 210–217
Soft Sense, 213
Soft Shave, 213
Sonamp, 565
Sonance case, 563–578
SonicEye, 565
Sony, 75, 143, 367, 622, 624, 672
Sony/ATV Music Publishing, 467
Sony Classical, 467
Sony Corporation, 467, 686
Sony Music, 467
Sony Music Entertainment, 466, 467,
 471, 476
Sony Music Entertainment Japan, 467
Sony Music International, 467
Sony Music Soundtrax, 467
Sony Nashville, 467
Sony PlayStation, 473
Sony Walkman, 320
Sorell, David, 524, 530, 531
Sotheby's, 622
Sottosanti, Frank, 347–351, 354, 358
SoundDock, 576
South Delaware Coors, Inc. case,
 123–132
Southern Living (magazine), 301
Southern Vanity (magazine), 584
Southwest Airlines case, 479–499
SpeakerCraft, 565, 571, 573, 577
Spears, Britney, 468
Spectrum water purifiers, 648
Spencer, Geoff, 563–565, 572
Splenda, 455
Springstein, Bruce, 467
Sprite, 164, 315
Squirt, 93, 162–181
Squirt/Ruby Red, 172–173, 175
S & S Industries, 647
S4S tires, 611, 613
Staind, 468
Standard & Poor, 227
Standard & Poor's Industry Surveys,
 296, 298

Stanley, George, 512
Starbucks, 68, 618, 621
"Starfire Red" fish, 413, 415
Starwood Hotels & Resorts Worldwide,
    Inc., 326
Stewart, Rod, 467
Sting, 473
Stitt, Jim, 390, 395, 402
Stollenwerck, Jaxie, 179
Strategic Brands, 243
Strategy Research Corp., 180
Streisand, Barbra, 467
Strimple, Jan, 579
Stripe, 139
Struthers, Scott, 563–565, 572
Subaru, 606
Sudafed, 517
Sugarman, Shawn, 563–565, 567, 570,
    573, 574, 577, 578
Sumitomo, 609, 611
"Sunburst Orange" fish, 413, 415
Sun Chips, 76, 196
Sun Chips Multigrain Snacks,
    192–208, 254
Sundrop, 163, 170, 172, 173, 177,
    309–311
Sung, Kaycee, 532
Sunkist, 92, 142, 310–312,
    316–318, 321
SunnyD, 380
Sunny Delight, 241
Sunny Delight Beverage Co., 380
Sunshine State Systems of Tampa, 85
Sunsilk, 155–158
Superior supermarket, 500, 503, 504, 509
Super Kmart, 342
SuperPages, 356
Super Valu, 342
Super Vasmol, 155
Supply Chain International for VF
    Brands, 437
Supran, Ari, 563, 564, 567, 570, 573,
    574, 576–578
The Supremes, 467
Surge, 170, 172, 173, 177
Sussex, 310
Suzuki brand, 644–655
Suzuki Motor Co., 657
Swatch Group, 555
Sweetland Bed Warmer and Cast
    Dryer, 538
Symphony, 648
Symphony Extreme, 565

Tab Energy, 98–101, 103
Taco Bell, 93, 192, 557
Taco Bell Corporation, 192
TAG Heuer, 455
Tantus, 144
Target, 24, 93, 258, 342, 371, 471, 574,
    582, 673, 674, 681
Tata Motors, 139
t.A.T.u., 466
Taylor, Keith, 479
Tesla Model S. Sedan, 183, 184
Tesla Roadster, 183, 184
Texas, 467
Thermadrape, 538
Thomas H. Lee Partners L.P., 573
Thomasville, 297, 300
Thorn Electrical Industries, 472
Thorn EMI, 472

3M Company, 3
Tide, 144, 241
Tiempo tires, 611, 613
Tiffany, 624
Time Warner, 472
Time Warner's Warner Music
    Group, 472
Timex, 555
TLC, 468
T-Metric tires, 611, 613, 614
Tognietti, Terry, 343, 344
Tommy Hilfiger, 445
Topol, 139
Toshiba, 641
Tostitos, 72, 193, 254
Tostitos Crispy Round Tortilla
    Chips, 194
Tostitos Fiesta Bowl, 255
Total Cereal, 554
Total Salty Snacks, 198
Touchstone Picture, 144
Tousley, Diane, 274
Tower Records, 471, 477
Town Place Suites, 144
Toyota, 183, 527, 606, 654–655, 659
Toyota FT-EV II, 184
Toyota Motor Corp., 657
Toyota Prius, 183
Toyota Prius PHEV, 184
Toyota RAV4, 184
Toyo tires, 608
Traffic Marketplace, 357–360
Trans World Airlines (TWA), 480, 482,
    483, 489
Travelocity.com, 364, 365
Triarc Companies, 143
Tribal Council, 419
Tribal Fusion, 357–360
Trier, 198
TrimSpa, 547
Trina, 310, 312
Trina Colada, 310, 312
TriNaranjus, 310, 312
Triton Biosciences, Inc., 516
Tropicana, 380
True Value, 107
Tulloch, Pat, 416, 418, 420–423
Tums antacid, 554
Tupperware, 371, 400, 401
TWA. *See* Trans World Airlines
Twain, Shania, 467
24/7 Real Media, 357–359
Twitter, 225, 400
Tylenol, 146
Tylenol Cold & Flu, 146
Tylenol PM, 146

U2, 467
UCLA, 518
Ultra Brite, 139
UMG. *See* Universal Music Group
Unified Marketplace, 356
Unilever, 144, 618
Union Razor Company, 391
Uniroyal Goodrich, 606, 611
Uniroyal tires, 605, 609
United Airlines (UAL), 479, 480, 483,
    484, 486, 489, 493, 495, 498
Universal Motown Records, 466
Universal Music Group (UMG), 463,
    464, 466–467, 471, 475–477
Universal Music Publishing Group, 467

Universal Music & Video
    Distribution, 476
Universal Rim, 610–611
University of Miami, 518, 519
University of Regina, 418
Upjohn, 517
UPS, 396, 621
Urie, Jim, 476
U.S. Census Bureau, 125, 176, 179,
    425, 567
U.S. Congress, 523
U.S. Customs & Border Protection, 533
U.S. Department of Energy, 186
U.S. Department of Transportation,
    480, 481, 486, 489, 493
U.S. Food and Drug Administration
    (FDA), 135, 410–412, 512–514, 516,
    518–520, 522, 544–550
U.S. House of Representatives, 513,
    521, 523
U.S. Justice Department, 481
U.S. Postal Service, 396
USAir, 480, 482, 483, 489

Vacation Clubs, 144
Valley Bank, 348
Valmet Automotive, 187
Valspar Corporation, 107
ValueClick, 357–360
ValuJet, 484
Van Heusen, 441
Vanity Fair (magazine), 73, 291, 438
Vans, 438, 440–441
Vauxhall Motors Ltd., 659
Vector College Recruiting Program, 402
Vector Marketing Canada, Ltd., 400,
    403–404
Vector Marketing Corporation, 390,
    391, 394, 395–400, 403–404
Verdi, 468
Vernors, 163
VF Brands, 437–452
VF Contemporary coalition, 441
VF Corporation, 437
VF Imagewear coalition, 439, 440–441
VF Jeanswear coalition, 439–441
VF Outdoor and Action Sports
    coalition, 440–441
VF Sportswear coalition, 441
Vicks, 241
Victoria's Secret, 369
Vida, 310, 312
Vidal Sassoon, 241
Videocon Appliances, Aurangabad,
    648
Virgin Music Group, 472
Virgin Records America, 472
Virgin Records Nashville, 472
Virgin Records UK, 472
Visa, 146, 624
Visnaramathan, Ramesh ("Ram"),
    226, 227
Visteon, 527
Vivendi Universal, S.A., 466, 467
Vogue (magazine), 592
Volkswagen, 144, 184, 527, 654,
    655, 658
Volkswagen Group, 653–655, 657
Volkswagen Passat, 655
Volkswagen Phaeton, 144
Volkswagen's Audi, 659

Volkswagen Touareg, 144
Voltas, Bombay, 648
Volvo, 140–141, 606, 654, 658
Volvo V70 PHEV, 184

W. C. Wood, 677
W. R. Case & Sons, 390–391
Wall Street Journal, 371, 614
Walmart, 12, 24, 74, 93, 98, 99, 107, 115, 145, 258, 292, 342, 371–372, 374–375, 386, 414, 432, 442, 471, 582, 614, 620, 624, 673, 674, 681
Walmart Marketside stores, 375
Walmart Neighborhood Markets, 375
Walmart Stores, 375, 677
Walmart Supercenters, 375
Warner Brothers, 467
Warner/Chappell, 467–468
Warner-Lambert Canada, Ltd., 59, 242
Warner-Lambert Company, 368
Warner Music Group, 466, 467–468, 471, 472, 476
Warner Music International, 467
Warren, Jon, 219
Water Doctor, 648
Watson, Robert, 418
Wayne-Dalton Corporation, 426
WearEver, 390, 394
WebMD, 227
Wee-Fits, 341
Wego, 224
Weight Watchers, 547, 550
Welbilt, 673
Welch's, 380

Wellcome PLC, 513, 516, 517, 521
Wells Fargo, 348, 353
Western Airlines, 482
Wherehouse Entertainment, 471, 477
Whirlpool, 145, 367, 622, 623, 641, 671–674, 676–679, 682
White Laboratories, 213
White Stripes, 473
The Who, 467
Wilk, Nicki, 589
Williams, Hank, 467
Williams, Robbie, 472
Winston, George, 468
Wipro Ltd., 154
Wise, 195
Wise Foods, 258
Wiseview, 144
Wishbone, 262
Women's National Basketball association (WNBA), 352
Women's Wear Daily (magazine), 584, 585
Wonder, Stevie, 467
Word, 467
workforstudents.com, 397
World Health Organization (WHO), 642
World's Fair Columbian Exhibition, 260
World Trade Organization, 442
Worth, Sherri, 229, 233, 234, 237–239
Wrangler, 438–441, 445
Wranglers, 442
Wrangler tires, 611
Wrigley's gum, 622
Wusthof-Trident, 394

Wuxi Little Swan Company Ltd., 672
www.nundies.com, 579
Wyeth Pharmaceuticals, 135

Xenadrine EFX, 547
Xenical, 546, 547
Xerox Corporation, 3
Xterra, 621

Yahoo, 355–360
Yamaha, 573
Yam Corporation, 529
Yates, Tom, 381
Yellow Pages, 358–360, 427
Yepp, 144
Yokohama tires, 608
Yoplait, 620
Yorktown Technologies case, 406–415
Yum! Brands, 93
Yves Saint Laurent, 367

Zafira, 661
Zappos.com, 364
Zara, 444, 445, 447
Zebra Danio Fish, 406–407
Zee TV, 646
ZERO-B (Zero-Bacteria), 644–646, 648
Zimistat, 545
Zomba Records, 468
The Zone Diet, 547
Zovirax, 517